LSAT® PREMIER
2016–2017

KAPLAN

PUBLISHING

New York

Special thanks to those who made this book possible:

Matthew Belinkie, Kim Bowers, Jack Chase, Chris Cosci, Lola Disparte, John Fritschie, Bobby Gautam, Beth Gebeloff, Joseph Gordon, Joanna Graham, Robert Gray, Craig Harman, Ged Helm, Gar Hong, Rebecca Houck, Samer Ismail, Brandon Jones, Greg Mitchell, Joseph Moulden, Rachel Reina, Larry Rudman, Glen Stohr, Jay Thomas, Bob Verini, Walker Williams, Dan Wittich

Published by Kaplan Publishing, a division of Kaplan, Inc.
750 Third Avenue
New York, NY 10017

Printed in the United States of America

10 9 8 7 6 5 4 3 2 1

ISBN: 978-1-62523-130-7

Kaplan Publishing print books are available at special quantity discounts to use for sales promotions, employee premiums, or educational purposes. For more information or to purchase books, please call the Simon & Schuster special sales department at 866-506-1949.

TABLE OF CONTENTS

PART THREE: LOGICAL REASONING

About Your Kaplan Resources

Welcome to Kaplan's *LSAT Premier* book! Your Kaplan LSAT resources will be all you need to prepare for the LSAT. Included with the book is your Online Center with recordings of lessons from The LSAT Channel, Kaplan's nightly live LSAT instruction platform. More on those in a bit. Let's start with how you should use this book.

HOW TO USE THIS BOOK

First—Get Acquainted with the LSAT

Start by reading the "About the LSAT" chapter. There, you'll find details about the LSAT's structure and scoring, how to register for the test, and how best to study.

Second—Start Becoming an LSAT Expert

In the subsequent chapters, you'll work on the skills needed for LSAT success. We've broken down each of the skills into discrete **Learning Objectives**. Each section of the book will inform you of the Learning Objectives you're about to master, and you'll be provided with an opportunity to practice them thoroughly. This may involve full LSAT questions, or it may involve drills that help to hone your fundamental skills. Each of the full questions presented in this book is from a real LSAT. Each year, the LSAT is administered four times, and three of those exams are released by the Law School Admission Council for use as study material.

Each released exam contains four scored sections and is called a **PrepTest**. This book contains more than 200 LSAT questions from PrepTests 24, 27, 28, 29, 71, B, and June 2007. Beneath each LSAT-released question in this book you'll see a Source ID (e.g., PrepTest27 Sec2 Q2, which means that question appeared originally as the second question of Section 2 of PrepTest 27). Every question with a Source ID is licensed from the LSAC and comes from an official, scored LSAT.

Throughout this book, you'll see how LSAT experts—Kaplan teachers who have scored in the 99th percentile—analyze questions, games, and passages from released LSAT exams. Study these "worked examples" carefully; they provide a chance for you to think along with an LSAT expert as he or she attacks the LSAT efficiently and accurately. Expert analysis is always laid out with the test material in the left-hand column and the expert's thinking immediately to the right or beneath. Where the LSAT expert demonstrates a multistep method, we've included the steps to help you train to take the most effective route through the question.

Here are a few things to be aware of whenever you study expert analyses:

This column contains test material; always read it first, so you know what the expert is analyzing.

In this column, you'll see the LSAT expert's analysis of each part of the test question—here's your coach "thinking out loud" for your benefit.

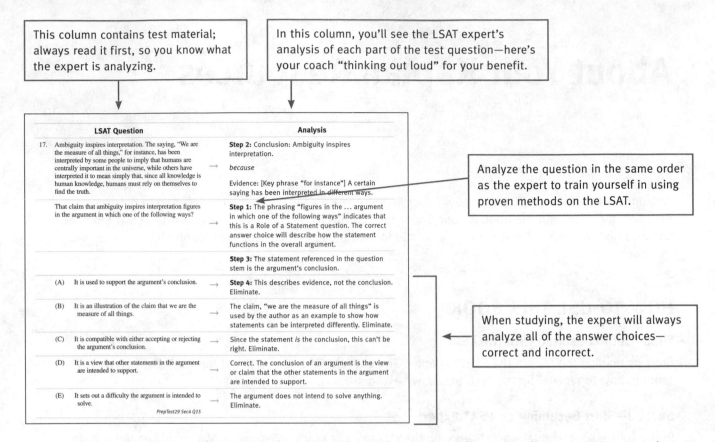

Analyze the question in the same order as the expert to train yourself in using proven methods on the LSAT.

When studying, the expert will always analyze all of the answer choices—correct and incorrect.

From time to time, you'll have practice exercises in which you'll have the chance to analyze a question. Use the spaces in the right-hand column to record your own analysis. On the following pages, we'll always provide expert analysis so that you can compare your thinking to that of an LSAT expert.

LSAT Question	My Analysis
25. Laura: Harold is obviously lonely. He should sell his cabin in the woods and move into town. In town he will be near other people all the time, so he will not be lonely anymore.	Step 2:
Ralph: Many very lonely people live in towns. What is needed to avoid loneliness is not only the proximity of other people but also genuine interaction with them.	
Ralph responds to Laura by pointing out that	Step 1:
	Step 3:
(A) something needed for a certain result does not necessarily guarantee that result.	Step 4:
(B) what is appropriate in one case is not necessarily appropriate in all cases.	
(C) what is logically certain is not always intuitively obvious.	
(D) various alternative solutions are possible for a single problem.	
(E) a proposed solution for a problem could actually worsen that problem.	

PrepTest28 Sec3 Q10

The format of our expert analyses is the result of work by leading academics in learning science. Merely answering LSAT questions and checking to see whether you got the right answer is good for you, but studies indicate that studying expert thinking alongside actual test material produces better results and is a more effective (and faster) way to master LSAT skills. As you complete the questions, don't just check to see if you got them right or wrong. Use each question as an opportunity to better understand the patterns of the test as well as your own strengths and weaknesses.

At the end of select chapters, we provide Question Pools—officially released LSAT questions not covered in the chapter text—so that you can assess your performance. Explanations for these questions follow each of the Question Pools. The easiest way to find them is to look at the top of any Question Pool page for a navigational direction on where to find the explanation for that question.

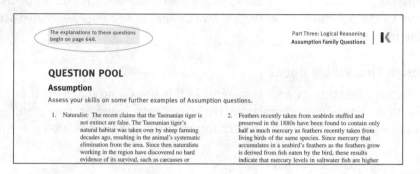

The explanations break each question down step-by-step and provide detailed reasons why the one credited answer is correct and each of the others is wrong. The explanations also include information about the difficulty of the question you just attempted. Each question is rated on a star system: One-star questions are the easiest, four-star questions are the hardest. These star rankings reflect the actual performance of thousands of Kaplan students who have used our products and studied for the LSAT just as you are about to do.

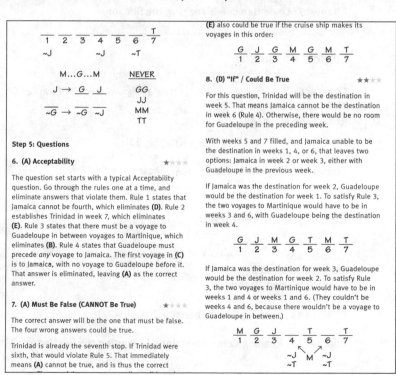

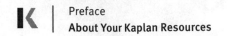

Third—Assess Your LSAT Skills

Every chapter of the book provides ample opportunity to practice the skills and question types associated with that chapter's learning objectives. Chapters 6, 9, 10, 11, and 15 contain the Question Pools mentioned earlier. Use these Question Pools to assess your strengths and weaknesses in specific areas of the test—which have you mastered, and which warrant further study?

When you are ready to assess your overall LSAT performance, there is a complete, officially released LSAT (PrepTest 54) in your Online Center. Download and print that test, and then take it under timed conditions. When you are finished, you can score the test using the webgrid in your Online Center. Scoring the test through the webgrid reveals your score, provides analysis of your results, and unlocks complete explanations for every question, and every correct and incorrect answer choice, on the test. Additional LSATs are available for purchase from the LSAC, which sells PrepTests individually and in books of ten (recommended). NOTE: Students who enroll in one of Kaplan's comprehensive LSAT Prep courses—*In Person*, *Live Online*, or *Self-Paced*—receive access to every official, released LSAT available from the LSAC.

Do I Have to Go through This Whole Book?

You may have already noticed that there's a lot of material in this book, and that's great for those who have the time and determination to maximize their preparation. Other students, however, may prefer to focus on targeted practice before the exam. Here's a quick rundown of chapters that may be considered prerequisites for others.

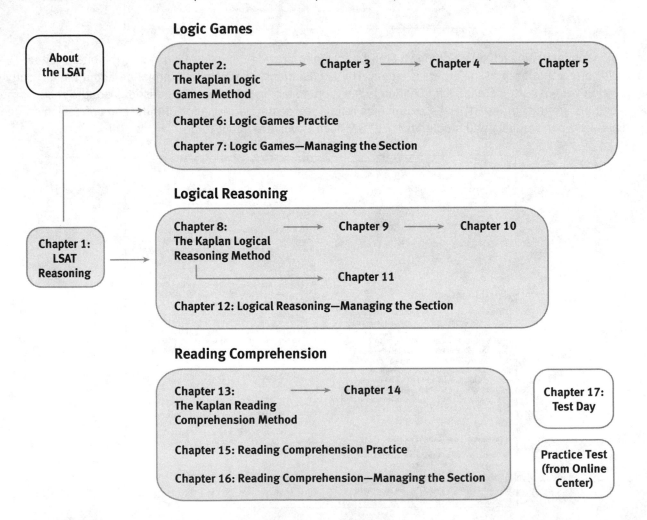

HOW TO USE THE ONLINE RESOURCES

First—Register for Your Online Center

The Online Center gives you access to even more prep, including the full PrepTest 54, ten recorded lessons from Kaplan's exclusive LSAT Channel, Smart Reports® (our data analysis of your performance), and more!

Register for your Online Center using these simple steps:

1. Go to kaptest.com/booksonline and find the appropriate book listed. Click the "Register" button next to it.

2. Enter the password as directed and click on "Next."

3. The Online Center will appear in your shopping cart free of charge. Click "Proceed to checkout" and complete your registration.

4. Once registered, click on the "personalized Student Homepage" link to access your online materials.

Please have your book with you because you will need information from the book to access your account.

Access to the Online Center is limited to the original owner of this book and is nontransferable. Kaplan is not responsible for providing access to the Online Center for customers who purchase or borrow used copies of this book. Access to the Online Center expires one year after you register.

Second—Study Plans

This is a big book, and you might not have the time to approach everything in it. That's where our online study plans come in. In your Online Center, you'll find study plans to review that provide guidance on how best to use the resources, depending on the hours/days/weeks/months you have available to study.

Third—LSAT Channel Lessons

Students in Kaplan's comprehensive LSAT courses enjoy nightly episodes of The LSAT Channel, live instruction from Kaplan's highest rated instructors. To supplement your work with this copy of *LSAT Premier*, we've included ten LSAT Channel episodes covering valuable topics from Logic Games, Formal Logic, Logical Reasoning, and Reading Comprehension, along with episodes dedicated to improving your law school application. In these LSAT Channel recordings, you'll hear from experts who have scored in the 99th percentile on the test, law school admissions officers, and professional admissions consultants. Don't miss out.

Fourth—Smart Reports®

From your Online Center, you'll be able to download and print a copy of LSAT PrepTest 54. After you take the exam, use the webgrid to score it and review your results in Smart Reports®, Kaplan's exclusive performance analysis system. Smart Reports® will provide your overall score, a breakdown of your performance by section and question type, and explanations for every question on the test.

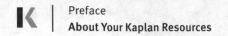
LOOKING FOR MORE?

At Kaplan, we're thrilled you've chosen us to help you on your journey to law school. Beyond this book, there's a wealth of additional resources that we invite you to check out to aid you with your LSAT preparation and your law school application.

- · —Our blog, featuring several articles a week on the nuances of LSAT preparation and applying to law school, authored by Kaplan instructors and admissions experts.

- · Free events—Take a real, previously released LSAT under proctored conditions, enroll in an LSAT Preview Class, experience what it's like being Inside the Classroom, and more. We host several free events each month, both in person and live online. Check out our full schedule of upcoming free events at kaplanlsat.com.

- · LSAT Courses—Of course, we'd be remiss if we did not mention the world's most popular LSAT preparation courses. Visit our website to learn about our comprehensive prep options. Choose from In Person, Live Online, Self-Paced, and Private Tutoring options depending on your needs and learning style. View course options and upcoming class schedules at kaplanlsat.com.

- · —The LSAT Channel—Kaplan's new course feature, The LSAT Channel, features over 100 unique episodes of live, online instruction on every facet of the LSAT by our best teachers. Learn more at kaplanlsat.com. You have access to recordings of select LSAT Channel episodes in the Online Center that accompanies this book.

- · —Facebook, Twitter, YouTube—Kaplan is wherever you are. Like us. Follow us. Subscribe to us. Get regular tips all throughout the course of your study.

You have a lot to do. Ready to get started? Let's do this!

List of LSAT Channel Episodes

The following is a list of all episodes and lessons presented on The LSAT Channel at the time that this book went to print. We update and expand the list of episodes every testing cycle. LSAT Channel episodes cover every LSAT question type, the Writing Sample, study skills, and the law school application process. They are taught by Kaplan's most highly rated instructors and, collectively, cover over 500 officially released LSAT questions from recent exams. **Recordings of the Channel sessions listed in bold type below are available in the Online Center that accompanies this book.**

Subject	Rating	Title	Content
FL	**Foundations**	**Black Tie Optional**	**Formal Logic Basics**
FL	**For Everyone**	**Points Lost in Translation**	**Turning Prose Into Formal Logic**
FL	For Everyone	Me and My Arrow	Formal Logic Drills
FL	Advanced	Black Tie Required	Advanced Topics in Formal Logic
LG	**Foundations**	**The A, B, C's**	**Strict Sequencing Basics**
LG	**Foundations**	**Twice the Fun**	**Hybrid Games Basics**
LG	Foundations	The Game of Games	Identifying Game Types
LG	For Everyone	Getting Sketchy	LG Method Steps 1 & 2—Overview & Sketch for Sequencing/Selection Games
LG	For Everyone	Rules Rush In	LG Method Step 3—The Rules for Sequencing/Selection Games
LG	For Everyone	Will It Blend?	LG Method Step 4—Deductions in Sequencing/Selection Games
LG	For Everyone	One More Thing	LG Method Step 5—New Ifs
LG	For Everyone	Curveballs	LG Method Step 5—Other Question Types
LG	For Everyone	Straight Up With a Twist	Unusual Strict Sequencing Games
LG	For Everyone	Pick and Choose	Selection Games
LG	For Everyone	Getting Sketchy	LG Method Steps 1 & 2—Overview & Sketch for Matching/Distribution/Hybrid Games
LG	For Everyone	Rules Rush In	LG Method Step 3—The Rules for Matching/Distribution/Hybrid Games
LG	For Everyone	Will It Blend?	LG Method Step 4—Deductions in Matching/Distribution/Hybrid Games
LG	For Everyone	Loose Fitting	Loose Sequencing Games
LG	For Everyone	The Match Game	Matching/Distribution Games
LG	**For Everyone**	**Keep Your Options Open**	**Spotting Limited Options in Logic Games**
LG	For Everyone	Warp Zones	Using Previous Work in Logic Games
LG	For Everyone	Master Sketches of the Damned	Incomplete Logic Game Sketches
LG	For Everyone	Be the Testmaker	Building a Logic Game
LG	For Everyone	Beat the Clock	Logic Games Section Management
LG	Advanced	The A, B, C, D, E, F's	Difficult Strict Sequencing Games
LG	Advanced	Double Trouble	Difficult Hybrid Games
LG	Advanced	The Dinosaur Game	A Study in Unusual Hybrid Games

Subject	Rating	Title	Content
LR	Foundations	Get to the Point	Identifying Conclusions
LR	Foundations	In Other Words	Paraphrasing in Logical Reasoning
LR	Foundations	Behind the LR Curtain	Creating Your Logical Reasoning Inner Monologue
LR	Foundations	Filler Up	Five Logical Reasoning Fillers
LR	Foundations	Don't Take This Family For Granted	Assumption Family Questions Basics
LR	Foundations	Putting Two and Two Together	Inference Basics
LR	**For Everyone**	**In Conclusion**	**Argument-Based Questions**
LR	For Everyone	Mind the Gap	Preview of Assumption Family Questions
LR	**For Everyone**	**Different Scopes**	**Arguments with Mismatched Concepts**
LR	**For Everyone**	**Consider the Alternative**	**Arguments with Overlooked Possibilities**
LR	For Everyone	Under Advisement	Arguments with Recommendations
LR	For Everyone	One Thing Leads to Another	Causal Arguments
LR	For Everyone	Heredity Now	Assumption Family Genetics
LR	For Everyone	Required Gaps	Necessary Assumptions
LR	For Everyone	Good Enough to Get There	Sufficient Assumptions
LR	For Everyone	Apples and Oranges	Mismatched Concepts Flaw Questions
LR	For Everyone	Don't You Forget About Me	Overlooked Possibilities Flaw Questions
LR	For Everyone	How to Annoy Your Friends	Pointing Out Flaws in Real Life
LR	For Everyone	Defend and Attack	Strengthen/Weaken Questions
LR	For Everyone	Parallel Universes	Parallel Reasoning and Parallel Flaw Questions
LR	For Everyone	Words to Live By	Principle Questions Asking for Strengtheners or Assumptions
LR	**For Everyone**	**The Truth Is Out There**	**Must Be True Inference Questions**
LR	For Everyone	Making the Connection	Strongly Supports Inference Questions
LR	For Everyone	Magical Mystery Tour	Paradox Questions
LR	For Everyone	Broadening and Narrowing Your Horizons	Principle Questions Asking for Inferences
LR	For Everyone	Beat the Clock	Logical Reasoning Section Management
LR	Advanced	The Harder They Fall	The Most Challenging Argument-Based Questions
LR	Advanced	The Harder They Fall	The Most Challenging Assumption Questions
LR	Advanced	The Harder They Fall	The Most Challenging Flaw Questions
LR	Advanced	The Harder They Fall	The Most Challenging Strengthen/Weaken Questions
LR	Advanced	The Harder They Fall	The Most Challenging Inference Questions
RC	Foundations	Behind the RC Curtain	Creating Your Reading Comp Inner Monologue
RC	**Foundations**	**Six Words More the Richer**	**Using Keywords in RC**

Subject	Rating	Title	Content
RC	Foundations	Attention Gumshoes	RC Questions with Content Clues
RC	**For Everyone**	**You've Got to Summarize Up**	**Effective Margin Notes and Big Picture Summaries**
RC	**For Everyone**	**Research and Destroy**	**Putting Your Roadmap and Big Picture Summaries to Work**
RC	For Everyone	I Know Your Type	Intro to RC Passage Types
RC	For Everyone	Here's a Thought	Focus on Theory/Perspective Passages
RC	For Everyone	Here's the Situation	Focus on Event/Phenomenon Passages
RC	For Everyone	Two for the Price of One	Comparative Reading
RC	For Everyone	The Roadmap Less Traveled	2-Minute Roadmaps
RC	For Everyone	The Man Who Knew Too Much	Overfamiliarity in RC
RC	For Everyone	Reading Rainbow	Identifying RC Question Types
RC	For Everyone	RC Crystal Ball	Using Passage Structure to Anticipate RC Question Set
RC	For Everyone	Roadmaps of the Damned	Incomplete Reading Comp Roadmaps
RC	For Everyone	Be the Testmaker	Building an RC Question Set
RC	For Everyone	Beat the Clock	Reading Comprehension Section Management
RC	Advanced	Dangerous Passage	Roadmapping Difficult RC Passages
RC	Advanced	Clue-less	Answering Difficult RC Questions
Test Review	For Everyone	The Morning After	Diagnostic Test LG Review
Test Review	For Everyone	The Morning After	Diagnostic Test LR Review
Test Review	For Everyone	Stargazing	Understanding LSAT Question Difficulty Levels
Test Review	For Everyone	The Morning After	Midpoint Test LG & RC Review
Test Review	For Everyone	The Morning After	Midpoint Test LR Review
Test Review	For Everyone	Back to the Future	The Diagnostic Test Revisited
Test Review	For Everyone	The Morning After	Final Test LG & RC Review
Test Review	For Everyone	The Morning After	Final Test LR Review
Test Review	For Everyone	The Morning After	PT 67 Review
Test Review	For Everyone	The Morning After	PT 70 Review
Test Review	For Everyone	The Morning After	PT 71 Review
Test Review	For Everyone	The Morning After	PT 72 Review
Test Review	For Everyone	The Morning After	PT 73 Review
Test Review	For Everyone	The Morning After	PT 74 Review
Test Review	For Everyone	The Morning After	PT 75 Review
Test Review	For Everyone	The Morning After	PT 76 Review
Test Review	Advanced	Star-stuck	Diagnostic Test Review—4-Star Questions
Test Review	Advanced	Star-stuck	Midpoint Test Review—4-Star Questions
Test Review	Advanced	Star-stuck	Final Test Review—4-Star Questions
Test Review	Advanced	Star-stuck	PT 67 Review—4-Star Questions

Subject	Rating	Title	Content
Test Review	Advanced	Star-stuck	PT 70—Challenging Questions
Test Review	Advanced	Star-stuck	PT 71—Challenging Questions
Test Review	Advanced	Star-stuck	PT 72—Challenging Questions
Test Review	Advanced	Star-stuck	PT 73—Challenging Questions
Test Review	Advanced	Star-stuck	PT 74—Challenging Questions
Test Review	Advanced	Star-stuck	PT 75—Challenging Questions
Test Review	Advanced	Star-stuck	PT 76—Challenging Questions
Study Skills	For Everyone	The Test Taker's Guide to the LSAT Galaxy	Study Planning & Walk-Through of Kaplan LSAT Resources
Study Skills	For Everyone	Don't Believe Everything You Read	LSAT Fact & Fiction
Study Skills	For Everyone	The Dirty Dozen	Revisiting LSAT Study Techniques
Study Skills	For Everyone	Breaking Out of Your Rut	Alternative Study Techniques
Study Skills	For Everyone	Keeping Your Cool	Stress Management and the LSAT Lifestyle
Study Skills	For Everyone	Coach	How to Best Use Your Tutoring Hours
Study Skills	For Everyone	Back to School	A Guide to Prepping for the Repeat LSAT Student
Study Skills	For Everyone	To Take Or Not to Take	Deciding Whether to Postpone
Study Skills	For Everyone	Anh-Chi's Prep Rally	Reading is FUNdamental
Study Skills	For Everyone	Bob's Prep Rally	You've Got This
Study Skills	For Everyone	Bobby's Prep Rally	LR Ninja
Study Skills	For Everyone	Ged's Prep Rally	LR is a Flat Circle
Study Skills	For Everyone	Gene's Prep Rally	The End is Near
Study Skills	For Everyone	Hannah's Prep Rally	To the Max
Study Skills	For Everyone	Jeff's Prep Rally	Office Hours
Study Skills	For Everyone	The 180	We Predict the LSAT
Beyond LSAT	For Everyone	The Write Answer	How the Writing Sample Relates to LR
Beyond LSAT	For Everyone	The Write Stuff	Brainstorming the Writing Sample
Beyond LSAT	For Everyone	The Write Way	Structuring the Writing Sample
Beyond LSAT	**For Everyone**	**Getting to 1L**	**Do's and Don'ts of Law School Admissions**
Beyond LSAT	For Everyone	Best. Selfie. Ever.	Creating Your Personal Statement Thesis
Beyond LSAT	For Everyone	Humblebragging	Your Personal Statement—Tone and Style
Beyond LSAT	For Everyone	Not Only But Also	Application Addenda and Supplementary Essays

About the LSAT

WHY THE LSAT?

You're reading this book because you want to be a law student. Well, your legal education starts now.

Every year, Kaplan surveys the admissions officers from law schools all around the country, and every year, the majority of them tell us that the LSAT is the most important factor in your law school application—more important than GPA, the personal statement, letters of recommendation, and other application requirements. Admissions officers routinely cite poor LSAT scores as the biggest "application killer," and they tell us it is the part of the application that they check first. You may already know how important the LSAT is, but what you may not know is why. The LSAT tests skills relevant to law school and to the practice of law. Moreover, the LSAT is the one factor common to all applications. It levels the playing field for candidates regardless of background. The LSAT doesn't care what you majored in or where you went to school.

The LSAT is probably unlike any other test you've taken in your academic career. Most tests you've encountered in high school and college have been content-based—that is, they required you to recall a certain body of facts, formulas, theorems, or other acquired knowledge. But the LSAT is a skills-based test. It doesn't ask you to repeat memorized facts or to apply learned formulas to specific problems. You will be rewarded for familiarity with patterns that make the LSAT predictable, and ultimately all you'll be asked to do on the LSAT is think—thoroughly, quickly, and strategically. There's no required content to study! Sound too good to be true? Well, before you get the idea that you can skate into the most important test of your life without preparing, let's clarify the skills that you'll need to build. Admissions officers care about your score because the LSAT tests the skills you'll use on a daily basis in law school. It's the best predictor law schools have of the likelihood of your success at their institution.

FOUR CORE SKILLS—WHAT THE LSAT TESTS

Now you may be thinking, "What does the Logic Games section have to do with torts? How can Logical Reasoning predict my success in Civil Procedure?" In this book, you are going to be taught a series of Learning Objectives, which are bundled around four key skills—key because they're what the LSAT rewards, key because they're what law school demands. We'll call them the Core Skills:

Reading Strategically

Reading for structure and staying ahead of the author (anticipating) is what Strategic Reading is all about. Both your law professors and the LSAT want you to cut through the jargon and explain what the case or passage says. Reading strategically helps you zero in on exactly what opinions are present and how that knowledge will be rewarded in the question set.

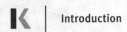

Analyzing Arguments

The essence of Logical Reasoning and the essence of lawyering is Analyzing Arguments. To analyze an argument in the LSAT sense, you must distinguish the argument's conclusion from its evidence. Then, determine what the person making the argument is taking for granted. The assumptions the author makes are what allow you to strengthen or challenge arguments on the LSAT. Likewise, in a courtroom, attorneys will need to understand, analyze, evaluate, manipulate, and draw conclusions from the arguments of their opponent, their own clients, and the judge.

Understanding Formal Logic

Conditional, or If/Then statements, are incredibly important in rules of law. "If/Thens" tell you what must, can, or can't be true in a given situation or when a particular rule is or isn't applicable. The very first chapter will train you to seek out the Formal Logic embedded in LSAT questions and logic games and to manage the implications flawlessly. For a lot of students, this is the most intimidating of the Core Skills, but facing up to it is incredibly valuable. It brings a rigor to your reasoning that will allow you to answer questions—on the LSAT and in law school—with precision.

Making Deductions

Making Deductions is rewarded in every section of the test, but it is key in Logic Games. In that section, you're given a set of conditions and rules and then asked to apply them to various hypothetical cases: "If J goes on Wednesday, what must be true . . ." "If the van has more miles than the sedan, and the sedan has more miles than the motorcycle, what could be false . . . ." That's just what law school exams demand. In law school, the rules and restrictions come from the dozens (potentially hundreds) of cases and statutes you will read during a semester. Just as you'll learn to do with Logic Games rules, judges synthesize rules in order to determine the outcome of a case.

STRUCTURE OF THE LSAT

The LSAT consists of five multiple-choice sections: two Logical Reasoning sections, one Logic Games section, one Reading Comprehension section, and one unscored "experimental" section that will look exactly like one of the other multiple-choice sections. These five multiple-choice sections can appear in any order on Test Day. A 15-minute break will come between the third and fourth sections of the test. The unscored, 35-minute Writing Sample essay section is always administered after the multiple-choice sections are concluded.

Section →	Number of Questions →	Minutes	
Logical Reasoning	24–26	35	
Logical Reasoning	24–26	35	
Reading Comprehension	26–28	35	May occur in any order
Logic Games	22–24	35	
"Experimental"	22–28	35	
Writing Sample	One essay	35	

Familiarize yourself with the structure of each section.

Logical Reasoning

Each of the two Logical Reasoning sections consists of 24–26 questions based on short passages, which we'll call *stimuli*, which are typically two to five sentences each. Each stimulus may be a short argument or a series of statements of fact. Each stimulus will also have one corresponding question that tests your ability to do such things as spot the structure of arguments, identify assumptions and flaws, strengthen or weaken arguments, or find inferences. Together, the two Logical Reasoning sections comprise the most important part of the test, counting for approximately half of your overall score.

Reading Comprehension

This section consists of three passages, typically made up of two to five paragraphs—about 55–65 lines of text (i.e., about 500 words apiece)—and one set of paired passages, together about the same length as each of the three longer passages. Each passage is accompanied by anywhere from five to eight questions. A Reading Comprehension section can have 26–28 questions but has had 27 questions on every released test since 2007. Reading Comprehension on the LSAT is an exercise in reading for structure and for multiple points of view. You'll learn to trace the outline of the passage as you read and to distinguish the author's viewpoint from the viewpoints of others mentioned in the passage, as well as to stay a step ahead of where the author is going by reading predictively.

Logic Games (Analytical Reasoning)

Analytical Reasoning, otherwise known popularly and in this book as Logic Games, consists of four game scenarios along with accompanying rules. Each game is accompanied by 5–7 questions. A Logic Games section can have 22–24 questions but has had 23 questions on every released test since 2007. With only 23 questions, it is the least valuable of the scored sections. Logic Games may nevertheless be the section you fear the most—many students do. Others, however, immediately take to the puzzle aspect of the section. Logic Games tests your ability to apply, combine, and manipulate rules and to deduce what can and cannot happen as a result. While the games may look daunting at first, they can be mastered with a systematic technique and proper use of scratchwork.

Experimental

The experimental section is an additional, unscored section of Logical Reasoning, Reading Comprehension, or Logic Games. You will not know what type of section you will get, and it can show up anywhere, including after the break. You'll have to bring your A-game for the entire test, as there is no reliable way to determine which section is experimental while you're taking the test. In case you're wondering, the LSAC includes an experimental section on the LSAT as a way to test questions for future administrations of the exam.

The Writing Sample

After you complete the five multiple-choice sections of the test, you'll write a short essay in which you choose between courses of action and explain your choice. While unscored, your Writing Sample is submitted to all law schools to which you apply, and law schools use it as part of the evaluation process.

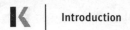

LSAT Scored Sections

Logic Games

One section with four games and 22–24 questions

Logic Games reward you for sequencing, matching, distributing, or selecting entities on the basis of rules that combine to limit the acceptable arrangements.

Logical Reasoning

Two sections with 24–26 questions each

Logical Reasoning rewards you for analyzing arguments to strengthen or weaken them or to identify their assumptions and flaws. Other LR questions require you to draw valid inferences from a set of facts.

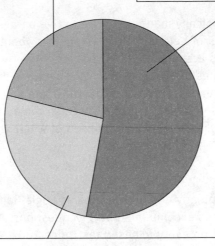

Reading Comprehension

One section with four passages and 26–28 questions

Reading Comp questions reward you for identifying the author's purpose and main idea, drawing valid inferences from the passage, and determining how and why the author uses certain details.

HOW THE LSAT IS SCORED

Here's how the LSAT is scored. Your performance is assessed on three scales: raw score (# correct), scaled score, and percentile.

Percentile (Scaled score)	10th (139)	20th (143)	30th (146)	40th (149)	50th (151)	60th (154)	70th (156)	80th (160)	90th (164)	95th (167)	99th (172)
# Correct	38	44	49	54	58	63	67	74	80	85	92

Source – PrepTest 74 (December 2014)

LSAT Score Breakdown

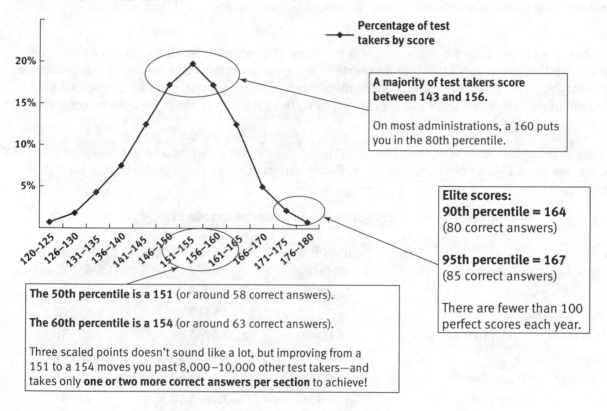

Percentage of test takers by score

A majority of test takers score between 143 and 156.

On most administrations, a 160 puts you in the 80th percentile.

Elite scores:
90th percentile = 164
(80 correct answers)

95th percentile = 167
(85 correct answers)

There are fewer than 100 perfect scores each year.

The 50th percentile is a 151 (or around 58 correct answers).

The 60th percentile is a 154 (or around 63 correct answers).

Three scaled points doesn't sound like a lot, but improving from a 151 to a 154 moves you past 8,000–10,000 other test takers—and takes only **one or two more correct answers per section** to achieve!

Raw score is simply the number of questions answered correctly.

Scaled score, the familiar 120–180 number, is a conversion of the raw score. Here, a raw score of 67—that is, 67 correct answers—converts to a scaled score of 156. A raw score of 58—meaning 58 correct answers—converts to a scaled score of 151. On a different test, a raw score of 58 might convert to a 150 or a 152. To account for differences in overall difficulty, each test has a slightly different raw score-to-scaled score conversion table.

Percentile score indicates how a test taker performed relative to other test takers over a three-year period. The conversion from scaled score to percentile score remains relatively stable, with only minor variations over the years. Test after test, a 151 scaled score is approximately a 50th percentile score.

The way in which the LSAT is scored has three important implications for your performance:

- First, the number of *right* answers determines your score. There is no guessing penalty. Never leave a question blank on the LSAT.
- Second, every question is worth the same, regardless of how hard it is. Learn to spot difficult questions and leave them for the end of each section. Find the easy questions and rack up points. If you're going to run out of time or need to guess, you want to do so on the tough stuff.
- Third, every additional correct answer can leapfrog you ahead of hundreds—or even thousands—of other test takers, your competition. How's that for inspiration?

What's a Good LSAT Score?

What you consider a good LSAT score depends on your own expectations and goals, but here are a few interesting statistics.

If you got about half of all of the scored questions right (a raw score of roughly 50), you'd earn a scaled score of roughly 146 or 147, putting you in about the 30th percentile—not a great performance. However, as you saw above, a little improvement goes a long way. Getting only 1 additional question right every 10 minutes (throughout the scored sections) would give you a raw score of 64, pushing you up to 154, which is about the 60th percentile—a huge improvement.

So, you don't have to be perfect to do well. On a typical LSAT, you can still get 25 wrong and end up in the 160s—or about 20 wrong and get a 164, a 90th percentile score. Even a perfect score of 180 often allows for a question or two to be missed.

Here is a chart detailing some top law schools and the scores of their admitted students.

Rank*	School	25th–75th %ile LSAT* (Scaled)	25th–75th %ile UGPA*	25th–75th %ile LSAT** (Raw)
1	Yale University	170–176	3.82–3.97	89–95
6	New York University	167–172	3.56–3.87	85–92
8	University of California—Berkeley	164–169	3.67–3.88	80–88
8	Duke University	166–170	3.66–3.85	84–89
15	University of Texas—Austin	163–168	3.43–3.82	79–86
22	George Washington University	159–166	3.42–3.80	72–84
26	Boston University	160–165	3.42–3.74	74–82
31	University of Wisconsin—Madison	157–163	3.30–3.76	68–79
42	University of Arizona	156–163	3.25–3.72	67–79
50	Tulane University	157–163	3.18–3.61	68–79
63	University of Miami (FL)	155–160	3.19–3.63	65–74
82	University of Oregon	154–159	2.97–3.56	63–72
87	St. Louis University	151–158	3.19–3.65	58–70

* *U.S. News & World Report*, 2016 Law School Rankings
** LSAT PrepTest 74, December 2014 Exam

REGISTRATION FOR AND ADMINISTRATION OF THE LSAT

The LSAT is administered by the Law School Admission Council (LSAC) (www.lsac.org) four times each year.

LSAT FACTS

Each year, the LSAT is administered on:

· A Saturday morning in February
· A Monday afternoon in June
· A Saturday morning in late September or early October
· A Saturday morning in December

There are some exceptions. For example, Saturday Sabbath observers have the option to take the test on a specified weekday following a typical Saturday administration. Dates and times may also be different for tests administered outside the United States, Canada, and the Caribbean.

How do I register for the LSAT? Register for the LSAT online at www.lsac.org. Check the LSAC website for details on the procedures, deadlines, and fee schedules.

When should I register? Register as soon as you have chosen your test date. Test sites may fill up quickly. Registration is typically due about five weeks before Test Day, with an additional week of registration allowed subject to a "Late Registration" fee.

Can I change my test date or location? You can change your test dates or locations (subject to an additional "change" fee) via the LSAC website. Timely changes of test date are not reported to schools; "no shows" are reported, however.

What is the CAS? Upon signing up for the LSAT, you also need to register with the Credential Assembly Service (CAS) as part of the application process required by every ABA-approved law school. CAS receives your undergraduate transcripts and distributes a summary of your undergraduate performance, along with your letters of recommendation, evaluations, and LSAT score report to each of the law schools to which you apply. www.lsac.org lists the fees and sign-up details for CAS.

When are law schools' application deadlines? All law schools provide their application deadlines on their websites. Some schools require the LSAT be taken by December for admission the following fall; others will accept a February LSAT score. Because most schools use a "rolling admissions" process, taking the test in June or September/October is preferable; also, taking the test earlier gives the test taker a chance to repeat the LSAT prior to most application deadlines.

Can I repeat the LSAT? The LSAT can be taken up to three times in a two-year period. This limit includes tests that have been canceled. More on that in the Test Day chapter. Any test taker who wishes to take the test a second time will need to reregister for the test.

How do law schools view multiple LSAT scores? This varies from school to school. Few schools now average multiple scores as was the policy in the past, but most consider *all scores from a five-year period* when evaluating applications. Applicants cannot choose which scores to report with their application. Find more information on repeating the test at www.lsac.org/jd/lsat/about-the-lsat.

Can I receive accommodations? The LSAC grants accommodation testing for physical, learning, and cognitive impairments, and there are a wide variety of accommodations available. A test taker must be registered for a test date before requesting accommodations. Full information about accommodated testing is available at www.lsac.org/jd/lsat/accommodated-testing.

Accommodations

If you have a disability, you may be able to receive testing accommodations for the LSAT. Accommodations are granted for physical, learning, and cognitive impairments severe enough to qualify as a disability relevant to test taking. A wide variety of accommodations are available. You must be registered for a test date before you can request accommodations, however, so register early. Your application for accommodations will require you to submit a full evaluation by a qualified professional who specializes in your particular disability as well as score reports from previous standardized admissions tests (SAT, GRE, etc.), any records of accommodations you received for those tests, and any records of accommodations you received from your undergraduate institution(s). All of these things can take time to prepare and must be submitted several weeks before your test date, so start your process as early as possible. If for any reason you move test dates, you will be required to resubmit your application, so be sure to hold on to copies of your records just in case.

Be aware that qualifying for accommodations on the LSAT is generally harder than it is for undergraduate accommodations, though recent policy changes by the LSAC now treat prior accommodations on other standardized admissions tests as sufficient evidence to grant you similar accommodations for the LSAT. Keep in mind that LSAC grants accommodations only when documentation clearly demonstrates disability in an area directly related to test taking. If you are denied accommodations and feel the denial was in error, you can submit an appeal with additional documentation provided that there is enough time for the LSAC to process the appeal before Test Day.

If you are granted accommodations from LSAC, your score will not be flagged as accommodated on your official score report. Law schools are now unable to distinguish an accommodated score from a score received under standard testing conditions. Given that the greatest difficulty many test takers face on Test Day is the timing demands of the LSAT, you should seek out accommodations as soon as possible if you feel you are qualified for them.

If you believe you have a disability that requires testing accommodations, start by reviewing the accommodations page on the LSAC website to get the most updated information on deadlines and required forms. Remember that this process is subject to change by LSAC at any time, so it is crucial that you get the most recent information directly from LSAC.

LSAT STUDY SKILLS

Imagine you want to lose a few pounds, so you get yourself a gym membership. Will the gym membership be sufficient for you to shed the weight? Of course not. You actually have to use the gym. And, once you get started, you'll need to use proper technique to maximize your results. If you're not sure how to get started, if you're overwhelmed by all the machines you find, or if you try to take shortcuts and don't put in the appropriate time and effort, you may not see the results you were hoping for.

You see where this is going. Kaplan is your gym. We're your mental workout. You've already committed to using our materials. But just as showing up at the gym is not enough for you to lose weight, picking up this book is not enough to raise your score either. You need to work out. You've been provided with a suite of assets, both print and online. But it's up to you to use them. And here's the best part: The work of dozens of Kaplan teachers, researchers, and testing experts has gone into creating not only the expert analysis in this book but also the Smart Reports® analytics, online material, and study plans that accompany it.

The LSAT is entirely a skills-based test. It is coachable. It is practicable. And there are lots of ways to practice. Some methods are great; others not so much. Expect us to show you the best ways to practice. Expect us to show you the patterns of the test and how to tackle every question type. Expect us to show you how to manage every section.

To reach your full potential on the LSAT, you're going to need to work hard. We will show you precisely what you need to do, but ultimately it's up to you to do it.

LSAT Strategy and the Three Levels of Practice

On Test Day, you'll be asked to deal with stringent testing policies and procedures, answer approximately 125 multiple-choice questions (of which typically 101 will count toward your score), and write a short essay. It's grueling and intense. And, depending on how efficient your test proctors are, the entire process may end up lasting five or more hours.

For those sections that count toward your score, taking control means increasing your speed only to the extent you can do so without sacrificing accuracy. Your goal is not to attempt as many questions as possible; your goal is to get as many questions correct as possible.

For many people, the single biggest challenge of the LSAT is time. If you had unlimited time to take this test, you'd likely perform quite well. But you don't. You have a strict 35 minutes to complete each section, and many students are not able to tackle every question in the time allotted. For you, this means three things:

- It's important that you learn not only how to answer the questions effectively but also how to answer them efficiently.
- It's important to approach each section strategically, knowing which questions to attack first and which questions to save for last.
- It's important that you prepare for the rigors of 3½ hours of testing. You'll want to maintain your focus in the final section as well as you did in the first.

Achieving these goals won't happen overnight. Obviously you need to put in the work to get better. Specifically, though, you need to work on your foundational knowledge first, then improve on moving through the test more quickly and efficiently. To achieve your goals, you'll want to incorporate three levels of practice: Mastery, Timing, and Endurance.

Mastery is about learning the patterns of the exam and how to identify them in new questions. You'll gain command of new efficient, effective techniques that you will repeatedly practice on specific drills as well as on individual question types. You'll study the answers and explanations to learn how the testmaker builds questions and answer choices. You'll identify why right answers are right and why wrong answers are wrong. What traps do you consistently fall into? How do you avoid them? That's precisely what Mastery practice is for.

Once you've learned the skills individually, it's time to try full-length section practice, or *Timing*. At 3½ hours, the LSAT can seem like a marathon, but it's really a series of sprints—five 35-minute tests, plus a writing sample. Section management—how to recognize and apply the patterns you've learned efficiently to maximize the number of questions you get correct—is what Timing practice teaches you to do.

And finally, there's *Endurance*. Can you maintain your ability to identify and apply these patterns efficiently throughout the whole exam? Some students discover that they are great at focusing for two hours, then struggle through the last two sections of the test. Taking practice tests will help you build your stamina. But a word of warning: the single biggest trap students fall into as they prepare for the LSAT is taking test after test after test. Think about it like learning a musical instrument. If you're trying to learn the piano, do you schedule a piano recital every other day? No, of course not. It's the piano *practice* that allows you to improve. While practice tests are important, they should be spaced out and taken only when you're sure you've made some improvement through your Mastery and Timing practice.

By approaching your preparation this way—starting with Mastery and then layering in Timing first and then Endurance—you'll be fully and properly prepared by Test Day.

Keeping Time on the LSAT

One of the most common concerns heard about the LSAT is "If I only had more time, I would be able to get through all the Games/Reading Comp passages/Logical Reasoning questions." Though it may seem unfortunate that you only have 35 minutes for each section, keep in mind that this timing constraint is deliberate. You are not alone in thinking that it's difficult to get through the sections in the given time. But the timing constraint isn't necessarily a hindrance to success; precisely *because* concerns about timing are so universal, you can get a big leg up on your competition by understanding how to maximize your performance in those 35 minutes.

Initially, your goal when working on Mastery questions is to understand and use Kaplan Methods while becoming more familiar with question types and gaining greater competency. Once a degree of mastery has been attained, it is time to turn your attention to completing a section within the 35-minute time period.

On Test Day, you cannot count on being able to see a clock in the testing room. The proctors may put the start and stop time of each section on the board and will occasionally note the time; a verbal five-minute warning will be given toward the end of the section. However, it is ultimately your responsibility to keep track of the time. While it is rare, proctors have been known to forget to give five-minute warnings, and in some facilities, clocks don't keep accurate time. As you begin your LSAT prep, invest in the purchase of a watch—one with a large face and easy-to-read numbers. Remember, LSAC does not allow the use of digital watches, stopwatches, or timers; you are allowed to use only a good, old-fashioned watch with hands, known as an analog watch.

Get used to using your watch. During timing practice, use your watch to read and Roadmap a passage or to set up a game in four minutes. Keep track of how long it is taking to work through Logical Reasoning questions.

Here is a quick tip for efficiency on Test Day: As you begin every section, set your watch back to 12:00. At a glance, you will be able to tell how much time you have used and how much time is left until 12:35, when the section will end. This way, you won't need to waste precious time calculating the minutes left.

LSAT Attitude

In the succeeding chapters, we will arm you with the tools you need—both content and strategy—to do well on the LSAT. But you must wield this LSAT arsenal with the right spirit. This involves taking a certain stance toward the entire test.

Those who approach the LSAT as an obstacle and rail against the necessity of taking it don't fare as well as those who see the LSAT as an opportunity. Think about it: this is your chance to show law schools your proficiency in the Core Skills. A great LSAT score will distinguish your application from those of your competition.

- Look at the LSAT as a challenge but try not to obsess over it; you certainly don't want to psych yourself out of the game.
- Remember that the LSAT is important, but this one test will not single-handedly determine the outcome of your life.
- Try to have fun with the test. Learning how to unlock the test's patterns and to approach its content in the way the testmaker rewards can be very satisfying, and the skills you'll acquire will benefit you in law school and your career.

Confidence

Confidence in your ability leads to quick, sure answers and a sense of well-being that translates into more points. Confidence feeds on itself; unfortunately, so does self-doubt. If you lack confidence you end up reading sentences and answer choices two, three, or four times, until you confuse yourself and get off track. This leads to timing difficulties that perpetuate a downward spiral of anxiety, rushing, and poor performance.

If you subscribe to the proper LSAT mindset, however, you'll gear all of your practice toward taking control of the test. When you've achieved that goal—armed with the principles, techniques, strategies, and methods Kaplan has to offer—you'll be ready to face the LSAT with confidence.

Stamina

The LSAT is a grueling experience, and some test takers simply run out of gas before it's over. To avoid this, take full-length practice tests in the weeks before the test. That way, five sections plus a writing sample will seem like a breeze (well, maybe not a breeze, but at least not a hurricane). On the other hand, don't just rush from one practice test right into another. Learn what you can from your review of each test, then work on your weaknesses and build your strengths before tackling another full-length test. You should plan on spending just as much time to review your practice tests as you did to take them.

Managing Stress

Take Control. Research shows that if you don't have a sense of control over what's happening in your life, you can easily end up feeling helpless and hopeless. Try to identify the sources of the stress you feel. Which of these can you do something about?

Set Realistic Goals. Facing your problem areas gives you some distinct advantages. What do you want to accomplish in the time remaining? Make a list of realistic goals. You can't help but feel more confident when you know you're actively improving your chances of earning a higher test score.

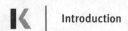

Acknowledge Your Strengths. Make a list of your strengths that will help you do well on the test. Many students are experts at listing which aspects of the test they struggle with. But a student who also has knowledge of her ever-expanding list of strengths will have more confidence and a better perspective on what to target to improve.

Get Exercise and Eat Well. Whether it is jogging, biking, yoga, or a pickup basketball game, physical exercise stimulates your mind and body and improves your ability to think and concentrate. Likewise, good nutrition helps you focus and think clearly. A surprising number of students fall out of good habits in these areas, ironically because they're spending so much time preparing for the test.

Keep Breathing. Conscious attention to breathing is an excellent way to manage stress. Most of the people who get into trouble during tests take shallow breaths. They breathe using only their upper chests and shoulder muscles and may even hold their breath for long periods of time. Breathe deeply in a slow, relaxed manner.

Stretch. If you find yourself getting spaced out or burned out as you're studying for or taking the test, stop for a brief moment and stretch. Stretching will help to refresh you and refocus your thoughts.

Imagine Yourself Succeeding. If you are continually filled with self-doubt about the test, it will be difficult to overcome those feelings and perform well on the test. Although preparing for the test can take many weeks or months of extensive practice, you must be able to visualize that you will gain confidence and take control of the test. Confidence gained through preparation will lead to better performance. Do not wait for it to occur the other way around.

The Dirty Dozen

This list highlights the most common mistakes students make when preparing for the LSAT. Read them now, but expect them to become even more meaningful as you progress through your practice and encounter more and more of the situations discussed here. If you want to spend your prep time wisely, avoid these pitfalls. Revisit this list as you prep to make sure you are not falling into any of these unfavorable practices.

#12 Doing the same thing as everybody else

While you may be an ace at logic games, your study buddy may struggle to make Formal Logic deductions. Each of you needs a distinct study plan; while your buddy should work on improving in logic games, you may need to spend more time working on arguments. Each LSAT test taker has his or her own unique strengths and weaknesses. Determine what yours are early on, then use that knowledge to help you study effectively.

#11 Letting stress get in the way

A little bit of stress can be a good thing; it's what propels you to study and work hard. But becoming consumed and overwhelmed by stress can lead to disastrous outcomes. One of the best ways to manage test anxiety is to become familiar with the LSAT and to develop action steps for each section and each question on the test. Focus on what you can control; anything that doesn't get you closer to correct answers should not be a consideration.

#10 Timing yourself in the beginning

Being able to work through problems *quickly* on the LSAT does you no good if you're not also able to work through them *correctly*. Success on the LSAT starts with Mastery. You must first learn how the test's arguments, games, and passages fundamentally operate. Once you have that knowledge, then you can begin to time yourself and push yourself to get through questions more quickly.

#9 Overly focusing on difficulty levels

Every correct answer on the LSAT is worth the same—unlike your eighth-grade history exam, no bonus points are awarded for difficulty level. That means there's no benefit to trying to find and correctly answer the most difficult questions on practice tests or during your studies. In fact, one particularly bad habit some students fall into is they immediately seek out the toughest problems to do in practice. This is because, they imagine, if they can do the hard ones, then they can also do the easy ones. This is a recipe for frustration and failure. If you were learning the piano, you wouldn't start with Rachmaninoff's Piano Sonata No. 2; you'd start with "Chopsticks." It's the same here. Start with the basics and develop your Mastery with one-star games/passages/arguments. Once you have that foundational understanding, move up to harder questions.

#8 Testing under non-test-like conditions

If you were trying to become certified to be a pilot, you wouldn't practice by driving a car. Instead, you'd find every opportunity to log actual practice hours in the air. The LSAT is the same. It doesn't do you much good to get really proficient at taking practice LSATs in your pajamas, late at night, in your bedroom because you're not going to take the LSAT in your pajamas, late at night, in your bedroom. Whenever you take a practice LSAT, try to replicate the experience of Test Day as much as possible. Find a library or academic building and take the test in the morning, starting around 8:30 A.M. (or 12:00 P.M. for June test takers). And, though this should go without saying, remember to always strictly time yourself when taking practice tests.

#7 Not committing to your study schedule

Lawyers are professionals who need to complete projects in a set amount of time. Imagine the LSAT as a case that you're working on. You wouldn't put it off and then roll into court unprepared. Give the LSAT the attention it requires by formulating a study schedule and sticking to it in the months prior to the test.

#6 Reading now/practicing later

As you prepare for the exam, be sure you are always putting into practice the various strategies, methods, and approaches that you are learning. It's not enough to say, "Okay, so in an Assumption question, you need to find the gap between the evidence and the conclusion. Got it. What next?" The LSAT is just not that easy. It's a test that evaluates skills, not content, and becoming proficient in those skills requires time, practice, and reflection.

#5 Only studying the right answers/only reviewing questions you got wrong

Because the LSAT is a test of repeatable patterns, it's invaluable to understand the underlying structure and logic of every question you face, as well as every answer choice you see. When you answer a question correctly, look at the explanations to see if your thinking lined up with the thinking of a Kaplan expert. Did you just get lucky, or did you approach the question methodically and with purpose? Additionally, check out the way the testmaker phrases incorrect answer choices and learn why those answer choices are incorrect. This is a skill that will help you tackle future questions.

#4 Ignoring your strengths

When law schools review your application, they'll see your LSAT score, but they won't see how well you did in each individual section. So if your target score is, say, a 165, and you're currently only scoring around 60 percent in Logic Games but 80% in Reading Comp and Logical Reasoning, you have a choice to make. Do you sink all of your efforts into bringing up that Logic Games score, or do you balance your time and continue to work to improve in Reading Comp and Logical Reasoning as well? The student who sinks all of his or her time into Logic Games is flirting with disaster: not only is there no guarantee that that section will increase, there's also no guarantee that the other sections won't see a score drop. If you are particularly strong in a section, keep devoting time to it to maintain that high level and possibly even push it higher. Don't forget about your strengths just to work on your weaknesses.

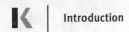

#3 Forgoing explanations and resenting mistakes

Making mistakes as you practice for the LSAT isn't a bad thing—it only becomes a bad thing if you end up making those same mistakes on Test Day. As you practice and review, embrace your mistakes. It's by tackling a question incorrectly that you are able to recognize an error in your thinking and then fix it. That's why it's so important to always read the explanations of every question you face in practice. Make sure you're approaching the questions correctly. Don't move on until you understand what you did wrong and how to avoid it in the future.

#2 Making it about the number, not the process

As we mentioned before, LSAT Mastery starts with the fundamentals. First, understand the structure and logic of the test; then worry about improving your score. If you are trying to adopt a new way of thinking, and if you are truly working on developing new skills, then it's entirely possible that the score on your second (or even third) practice test will stay the same or even go down a bit. But that's absolutely okay, because at the end of the day, nobody cares about what you got on an LSAT practice test. The only thing that matters is your score on Test Day. Always focus on continuing to develop your skills and use your test results to determine where your thinking was in error and how you can improve. Students who have this mindset early often see big gains later.

#1 Taking test after test after test after test

Because the LSAT is a skills-based test, you must develop your skills before you see score improvement. Taking practice tests will help you determine your present skill level, and it will help you build your endurance, but it won't help you figure out the test any better. Instead, always fully review your results and continue to practice for Mastery. A good standard is to never take another practice test until you have seen significant improvement in your Mastery and Timing practice.

APPLYING THE CORE SKILLS

Now that you've learned about the test, it's time to get better at it. As you turn to the chapter on LSAT Reasoning and the subsequent chapters on the various sections and question types, keep in mind the skills-based nature of the exam. While you're learning the specific methods and strategies that will help you master the test, reflect on how each of them is helping you to apply the Core Skills. The refinement and rigor you'll learn to bring to the LSAT is going to benefit you not only on Test Day, but even later, as you matriculate at law school.

PART ONE

LSAT
Reasoning

CHAPTER 1

LSAT Reasoning

Welcome to your LSAT studies! By the time you get to the end of this book, you'll have learned all of the skills and strategies necessary to master the LSAT. You'll begin that process, however, by building foundational skills. In this chapter, you'll build important critical thinking and reasoning skills and thereby lay the groundwork for all that is to come. In fact, it's likely that you'll want to come back to this chapter several times as you encounter the skills introduced here applied to LSAT questions in the various sections of the test.

By the way, if you haven't read the front section titled "How to Use This Book," you'll want to do that now, before proceeding. There, you'll learn how the chapters and sections are organized, what to study first, and the most efficient ways to practice with the material.

You need very little "content" knowledge for the LSAT. There's no math, science, or history you're supposed to know. The LSAT is largely a test of skills—skills you'll use in law school and in legal practice. By working with dozens of expert LSAT test takers, psychometricians (those who measure mental processes), and learning scientists, we've identified the most important of these skills and devised methods and strategies that you can apply successfully to the test. There is little doubt that you'll think, read, and analyze information differently (and more skillfully) when you've mastered the LSAT.

LEVELS OF TRUTH

Throughout the test, you'll be asked to assess the truth or validity of certain statements. You'll be asked to apply these analyses to the complex rules of logic games; the short, dense statements and arguments in Logical Reasoning questions; and the dry, academic prose of the Reading Comprehension passages. In each case, your ability to distinguish what could be true from what must be false in a given scenario will make the difference between right and wrong answers. This may sound somewhat complicated (and for many unprepared test takers, it turns out to be harder than it sounds), but LSAT experts recognize that it breaks down into a handful of patterns they'll use again and again.

LEARNING OBJECTIVES

In this section, you'll learn to:

- Characterize the levels of truth in statements (and thus of the correct and incorrect answers in various LSAT question stems).
- Determine what must be true, what could be true or false, and what must be false given a set of statements.

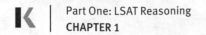
Characterizing Levels of Truth

As a first step, it's important to understand that LSAT thinking and deductions are deeply rooted in recognizing that every statement displays what we'll call a "level of truth." There are three such levels of truth in the universe: true, false, and possible. Statements that are true are true at all times without question. Statements that are false are false at all times without question. Statements that are possible could be true or could be false—we just don't know without being given more information. To complete our understanding of these, let's look at the opposites of "must be true" and "must be false":

> If a statement does not qualify as "must be true," then it is either false or possible.

> If a statement does not qualify as "must be false," then it is either true or possible.

Now, "possible" can be expressed as "could be true" and also as "could be false"—possible statements could be either true or false, so those two phrases describe the same thing. However, it's useful for us to get used to those two phrases because the LSAT often includes them in its question stems. Teasing out "possible" into those two alternatives gives us two more pairs of opposites:

> If a statement does not qualify as "could be true," then it must be false.

> If a statement does not qualify as "could be false," then it must be true.

Understanding all those pairs of opposites is very useful in thinking through what LSAT question stems are asking for. Consider how an LSAT expert views a very common LSAT question:

Question Stem		Analysis
Which one of the following must be true?	$\longrightarrow$	The right answer must be true.
		Therefore, the four wrong answers must be false, or are merely possible (i.e., could be false).

So you can think of your job on this question in two different ways: Identify the statement that must be true, or eliminate all of the statements that are false or merely possible. Notice that the test taker above took a moment to make clear not only which level of truth the correct answer would display but also which categories of truth she should eliminate as denoting wrong answers.

Consider another common LSAT question stem:

Question Stem		Analysis
Each of the following must be true EXCEPT:	$\longrightarrow$	We're looking for the one thing that is NOT a "must be true." In other words, the right answer will be a false statement or else a statement that's merely possible (could be false).
		All of the wrong answers must be true.

A couple of useful pointers here: First, as you may have already guessed, it's critical that you separate in your mind the concepts of "right answers" and "wrong answers" from the concepts of "true statements" and "false statements" and "could be true/could be false statements." The example we just saw demonstrates that sometimes on the LSAT, *false statements* are *right answers*. And *true statements* could be *wrong answers* while the *right answer* is a merely *possible statement*, and so forth.

Second, notice what the word EXCEPT (which the LSAT will put in all caps to help you notice it) does to the question stem: You are looking for the one statement that does not fit the description right before the "EXCEPT." Thus, you can remember that the phrase before the "EXCEPT" always describes the wrong answers. Suppose, to use a silly and unrealistic example, that an LSAT question said, "Each of the following is a purple spotted lizard EXCEPT": You'd know automatically to cross off all of the purple spotted lizards and circle the one thing that isn't a purple spotted lizard.

Let's establish one more thing before we go any further:

LSAT STRATEGY

The LSAT always gives you exactly one right answer, so there's only ever one answer that falls into the level of truth targeted by the question stem.

There will never be a correct answer and another somehow "more correct" answer to fool you. There's only *one* answer that does the job, and the other four will always be objectively, demonstrably wrong. "One right, four wrong" will become your mantra. Remember that throughout your LSAT studies.

Now, if you're wondering how you'll know which answer choices are true, which are false, and which are possible, that's what the rest of this book is about. But first you need to develop the mental habit of classifying all statements as being true, false, or possible. You also need to get very good at determining which level of truth you're being asked for.

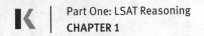
Practice

Now get some practice with this. For each of the following, make a note of which level or levels of truth the correct answer choice must display. Then make a note of which level or levels of truth the wrong answer choices will display. At any time, you can compare your analysis to the expert thinking immediately following these question stems.

Question Stem	My Analysis
1. Which of the following could be true?	
2. Which of the following could be false?	
3. Which of the following must be false?	
4. Each of the following must be false EXCEPT:	
5. If James chooses the peach, then Suzy can choose the	
6. Bob's schedule on Monday could include all of the following EXCEPT:	
7. Based on the statements above, it is possible that which of the following is true of honeybees?	

Question Stem	**My Analysis**
8. Which of the following is an acceptable assignment of players to seats?	
9. Each of the following could be true EXCEPT:	
10. Which of the following paddles can never be assigned?	
11. The schedule of performances CANNOT include:	
12. Each of the following could be false EXCEPT:	
13. If Larissa is assigned the second shift, then the third shift must go to	
14. The basketball player could wear the	
15. Entrée selections must include all of the following EXCEPT:	

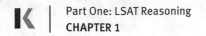

Expert Analyis

Here's how an LSAT expert analyzed each of those question stems.

Question Stem	Analysis
1. Which of the following could be true? →	The correct answer could be true. In this question, a "must be true" answer could also fill the bill.
	Wrong answer choices will all be "must be false" statements.
2. Which of the following could be false? →	The correct answer could be false. So a correct answer could be either false or merely possible.
	Wrong answer choices will all be "must be true" statements.
3. Which of the following must be false? →	The correct answer must be false.
	Wrong answer choices will be true or possible statements.
4. Each of the following must be false EXCEPT: →	The correct answer will be true or possible.
	Incorrect answer choices will all be "must be false" statements.
5. If James chooses the peach, then Suzy can choose the →	"Can" signals "possible." The correct answer will be what Suzy does choose or could choose. In other words, the correct answer will be true or possible.
	Wrong answer choices will all be things Suzy can't choose—that is, they all must be false.
6. Bob's schedule on Monday could include all of the following EXCEPT: →	The correct answer is one thing that isn't possible: correct answer must be false.
	Incorrect answers are things Bob's schedule could or does include. They'll be "must be true" or possible statements.
7. Based on the statements above, it is possible that which of the following is true of honeybees? →	"[P]ossible" is the key word here. The correct answer will be a statement that could be true.
	Incorrect choices will be "must be false" statements.
8. Which of the following is an acceptable assignment of players to seats? →	"An acceptable assignment" is one that can work, so this is equivalent to a "could be true." The correct answer is true or possible.
	Incorrect choices will all be impossible—that is, they must be false.

Question Stem		Analysis
9. Each of the following could be true EXCEPT:	$\longrightarrow$	The correct answer is a "must be false" statement.
		Incorrect answer choices all "could be true"—they'll be either true or possible statements.
10. Which of the following paddles can never be assigned?	$\longrightarrow$	"[C]an never" signals that the right answer must be false.
		Incorrect answer choices are possible or true.
11. The schedule of performances CANNOT include:	$\longrightarrow$	The correct answer must be false.
		Incorrect answer choices are things that are or could be included in the schedule—that is, they're true or possible statements.
12. Each of the following could be false EXCEPT:	$\longrightarrow$	The correct answer must be true.
		Incorrect answer choices all "could be false." A "must be false" statement would also qualify as an incorrect answer here.
13. If Larissa is assigned the second shift, then the third shift must go to	$\longrightarrow$	"Must go" signals that the correct answer must be true.
		Incorrect answer choices are possible or false.
14. The basketball player could wear the	$\longrightarrow$	"Could" indicates that the correct answer is something the ball player *could* wear or *does* wear: true or possible.
		Incorrect answers are all things she cannot wear—that is, they're all "must be false" statements.
15. Entrée selections must include all of the following EXCEPT:	$\longrightarrow$	The correct answer is an entrée that is definitely or possibly not included.
		Incorrect answer choices are entrées that must be included.

Reflection

Every time you do practice problems in this book, you'll be invited to pause afterward and look over your practice to learn more. Don't speed through this step. Carefully reviewing your practice can hugely enrich your understanding of:

- why a right answer is right—maybe you got a question right for the wrong reasons, and you need to clarify your understanding.
- why the wrong answers are wrong—maybe your intuition told you an answer was wrong, but you couldn't explain or replicate your thinking.
- which of your LSAT skills are already strong and which of them do you need to work on.
- what patterns LSAT questions display—the best thing you can do on the LSAT is to learn to spot its patterns, and frequently, it is in the review stage that students begin to do so.

In this case, look back at your practice and think about the following questions.

- Where was it easier for me to correctly identify the level of truth I was being asked for?
- Once I had identified the level of truth the correct answer would display, did I always take a moment to think about what level or levels of truth would be displayed by the wrong answers?
- What did I find challenging about this exercise?

Determining What Must Be True, What Must Be False, and What Could Be True or False from a Set of Statements

Gaining facility with levels of truth is the groundwork for thinking logically. Despite the fact that the LSAT has dozens of different types of questions, they really all test the same thing: your ability to think logically.

What is logical thinking? It's not synonymous with thinking in general because lots of mental activities can be described as thinking. Rather, logic is one type of thinking—specifically, a way of thinking in which you are given premises and you make deductions (that is, you conclude what else must be true) on the basis of them. A premise is a statement you can accept as true. Premises serve to provide support for deductions or conclusions. The LSAT is often said to involve "Formal Logic" because the test asks you to ignore whether given premises are true in real life and to focus instead on how to draw logical deductions (removed from real-world knowledge).

The ability to make valid deductions is at the heart of the LSAT because law schools understand how important this skill is to your success in the practice of law. The LSAT tests deductions in a number of ways. Sometimes, the test will give you premises and ask you to make a valid deduction. In other cases, the LSAT gives you somebody's premises and conclusion and asks you why his conclusion does not follow validly from his premises. In yet other question types (very important ones given the number of LSAT points they represent), the LSAT testmaker gives you a conclusion and a premise or premises purported to support it and asks you to supply a missing premise that would make the reasoning valid or complete. In all of these cases, the exam is really testing the same reasoning skill, just in different ways.

Let's start making deductions. For example, if you are given the premises . . .

> Navel oranges never have seeds.
> This orange is a navel orange.

. . . then you could make a correct deduction:

> This orange does not have seeds.

Given the first two statements, the third statement must be true. You just engaged in a piece of logical thinking.

If that example were an LSAT question, the correct deduction would be one of five answer choices. Your task in that case would be to sort out the correct deduction—the "must be true"—from among four other statements—each a false or "could be false" statement. For example:

> Navel oranges never have seeds.
> This orange is a navel orange.

Based on the statements above, which of the following must be true?

- This orange is delicious.
- This orange has seeds.
- This orange doesn't have seeds.
- There is not enough evidence to deduce whether this orange has seeds or not.
- The next orange will not have seeds.

How would an expert LSAT test taker look at a question like that? Take a look at the analysis on the following page.

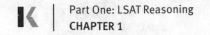

Here's the LSAT expert's analysis laid out piece-by-piece.

Logic Example		Analysis
Navel oranges never have seeds. This orange is a navel orange. Based on the statements above, which of the following must be true?	$\longrightarrow$	Determine which statement *must be true*; it will be helpful to classify the other statements as either false or possible (could be true/could be false).
This orange is delicious.	$\longrightarrow$	Could be true/could be false: We don't have any information about whether this orange is delicious or not.
This orange has seeds.	$\longrightarrow$	Must be false: Based on the premises, the orange can't have seeds.
This orange doesn't have seeds.	$\longrightarrow$	Must be true: This is correct.
There is not enough evidence to deduce whether this orange has seeds or not.	$\longrightarrow$	Must be false: We do have enough evidence to determine that this orange does not have seeds.
The next orange will not have seeds.	$\longrightarrow$	Could be true/could be false: We have no information about other oranges.

Notice that the first and fifth statements are merely possible—not *necessarily* false. An answer choice isn't false just because it isn't supported by the premises. Only if an answer choice *contradicts* the premises is it false. Given the same premises, other *possible* statements could be these:

Some oranges have seeds.

Many oranges don't have seeds.

Maria's orange has seeds.

Blood oranges have seeds.

Some Seville oranges are navel oranges.

There are no snakes in Ireland.

Joe will win the tennis tournament.

All of these statements could be true or could be false: None of them are supported by the premises, but none contradict the premises, either.

(By the way, have you ever eaten a freakish navel orange that had seeds? Maybe you have. It doesn't matter. As we mentioned earlier, the LSAT doesn't test your knowledge of the real world or ask you to apply it to the test questions. The LSAT uses carefully worded language—"Which one of the following, *if true*" or "*If* the above statements are *true*, then . . ."—to remind you to work with premises as though they were true. Don't argue with the rules in logic games or with the evidence used to support arguments in the Logical Reasoning or Reading Comprehension sections.)

Practice

Here are some opportunities for you to engage in logical thinking skills.

In the following exercise, you are given a set of premises and a set of statements that may or may not be valid deductions given those premises. Note whether each would-be deduction is true (that is, a valid deduction), false, or merely possible (could be true/could be false). After each, you can check the expert thinking on the next page.

Premises and Possible Deductions	My Analysis
April showers always bring May flowers. However, when it doesn't rain in April, then May flowers do not bloom. This year, there was no rain during the month of April. Based solely on the statements given, characterize each of the following statements as must be true, must be false, or merely possible.	
16. If it rained in April last year, then May flowers bloomed last year.	
17. A lack of April rain is the only reason May flowers do not bloom.	
18. It is unlikely that May flowers will bloom next year.	
19. No May flowers bloomed this year.	
20. May flowers are the most beautiful flowers of the year.	
21. Even if it rains next April, there may be no May flowers next year.	

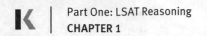
Expert Analysis

Here's how an LSAT expert would analyze the example you just worked with.

Premises and Possible Deductions		Analysis
April showers always bring May flowers. However, when it doesn't rain in April, then May flowers do not bloom. This year, there was no rain during the month of April. Based solely on the statements above, characterize each of the following statements as must be true, must be false, or merely possible.		
16. If it rained in April last year, then May flowers bloomed last year.	→	Must be true according to the first statement.
17. A lack of April rain is the only reason May flowers do not bloom.	→	Merely possible (could be true or false). Nothing in the statements indicates that a lack of rain is the *only* reason May flowers will not bloom, just that it is one reason.
18. It is unlikely that May flowers will bloom next year.	→	Merely possible (could be true or false). Nothing in the statements makes any prediction about next year.
19. No May flowers bloomed this year.	→	Must be true. The second and third premises, taken together, establish that no flowers bloomed in May of this year.
20. May flowers are the most beautiful flowers of the year.	→	Merely possible (could be true or false). None of the statements tell us how to rate the beauty of flowers.
21. Even if it rains next April, there may be no May flowers next year.	→	Must be false. This contradicts the first statement.

Reflection

Look back over your practice.

- Did you keep the task clearly in mind and stay focused on identifying what was true, false, and possible?
- Did you find yourself getting confused between true and possible statements or between false and possible statements?

This kind of analysis is something you can do all the time. You hear or read arguments that purport to draw conclusions from one or more premises every time you listen to a political commentator, read an editorial, or even watch a television commercial. Pay attention to the deductions you hear or see other people making and try to evaluate their validity based on the premises in those arguments.

FORMAL LOGIC: CONDITIONAL STATEMENTS

Now that you have some practice with logical thinking, you're ready to expand those skills. Frequently on the LSAT, the premises from which you make deductions are conditional statements—that is, they're statements that can be expressed in "if . . . then" form (though not all conditional statements contain those exact words). Before we address the statement in parentheses, take a closer look at what an "if . . . then" statement is and what it means.

LEARNING OBJECTIVES

In this section, you'll learn to:

- Identify what is and is not a conditional statement (that is, understand what it means for a statement to be a conditional statement).
- Understand conditional statements that include *and* or *or*.
- Translate a sentence that expresses a conditional relationship into If/Then format.
- Make deductions on the basis of conditional statements.

Identifying Conditional Statements

Consider this conditional statement:

> If you are in New York, then you are in the United States.

What does that statement mean? It expresses a relationship of *logical necessity:* Being in New York logically necessitates—that is, requires—that you be in the United States. On the other hand, "if . . . then" language does not necessarily express a causal relationship: Being in New York doesn't *cause* you to be in the United States. (Consider the case of someone who flies from Atlanta to New York: She was in the United States the whole time.) And the word "then" doesn't express a chronological relationship: You aren't in New York *before* you're in the United States.

Every conditional statement has two parts: the "sufficient term" and the "necessary term":

- The *sufficient term* is the part that immediately follows "if." "Sufficient" means "enough," and this part of a conditional statement is sufficient—it's enough—to require the other part. You don't need any additional information to know that the other part is true. Being in New York is enough to know that you are in the United States. In this book, we may also sometimes call this sufficient term the *trigger* because it precipitates the occurrence or truth of something else, logically speaking.

- The *necessary term* is the part that immediately follows the "then." "Necessary" means "required," and this part of a conditional statement is required whenever the sufficient term is present. Being in the United States is required—it's necessary—whenever you're in New York. If you're not in the United States, you simply cannot be in New York. We may also call this term the *result* because it's the logical consequence of the "trigger" in the sufficient term. Whenever you have the trigger, you've got to have the result.

Let's focus a little more on what a conditional statement does and doesn't mean. In the previous example, you absolutely cannot be in New York without being in the United States (because being in the United States is necessary to being in New York). But can you be in the United States without being in New York? Sure—you could be in California, South Dakota, or Texas. So, the necessary term doesn't serve as a logical trigger.

Let's look at another real-world example to clarify this further. Consider this statement: If you're driving your car, then your car has an engine.

You driving your car logically necessitates that it have an engine. And you driving it is sufficient—that is, it's all we need to know—to determine that your car has an engine. But can it have an engine without you driving it? Obviously! At times when your car is sitting in the garage, cold and unused, it still most likely has an engine.

Do you find yourself nevertheless tempted to tease out the logical possibilities by beginning a sentence like this?

"So if your car has an engine, then . . . "

. . . resist that temptation! There's no way, given only the original statement, to complete that sentence. There's no logical result of your car having an engine other than, well, your car having an engine.

The fact that the necessary term by itself doesn't logically trigger anything is a tremendously important concept to remember on the LSAT. Unless the LSAT argument or game explicitly tells you otherwise, always assume that it's possible to have the necessary term without having the sufficient term. Moreover, the LSAT uses many examples that involve fictional people or ambiguous terms, which means that you can't rely on real-world knowledge to sort out what triggers something else or what is necessary for the trigger as you could with the previous examples. Let's demonstrate how to think about this using a rule from a logic game. Here's how an expert test taker would understand a conditional statement in a logic game:

Conditional Statement		Analysis
If James volunteers, then so does Rebekkah.		If James volunteers, that's sufficient to know that Rebekkah must volunteer.
	$\rightarrow$	Or, to put that another way, if James volunteers, it is necessary that Rebekkah volunteers also. So James cannot be the only person who volunteers.
		But Rebekkah could volunteer without James volunteering. Given only this rule, Rebekkah could volunteer alone.

We identify and understand conditional statements all the time in the real world. Each of the following expresses a relationship of sufficiency and necessity:

> No shirt, no shoes, no service.
>
> You can't legally drink unless you're 21 or older.
>
> You must be over 48 inches tall to ride the roller coaster.

Most likely, you intuitively understand statements like this in real life. They're simply relationships in which one thing is needed for another to happen, and that's the essence of a conditional relationship. However, you'll notice that none of them contain the words *if* or *then*. And just as in real life, many conditional statements on the LSAT are phrased in ways that don't involve the specific words *if* and *then*. On the test, it's important for you to spot conditional relationships when they appear, regardless of how they're phrased.

Consider whether each of the following statements contains a trigger-and-result ("if" . . . "then") relationship. Keep in mind there are a couple of ways to think about spotting these: if one thing is sufficient—is enough—to make the other happen, then they have a trigger-and-result relationship. Similarly, if one thing is necessary—is required—whenever something else happens, that also signals a trigger-and-result relationship. In the Analysis here, the LSAT expert categorizes the statements "Yes, it contains a sufficient-necessary relationship" or "No, it does not."

Statement		Analysis
Drivers must pay a toll to cross the bridge.	→	Yes. Paying a toll is *necessary* for anyone wishing to cross the bridge.
The company ought to adopt the consultant's proposal.	→	No. This is a recommendation. It doesn't contain a condition necessary for another condition to occur.
How many tomatoes did you buy?	→	No. Like recommendations, questions do not express a Formal Logic relationship.
The state of California requires that all passengers wear a seatbelt when riding in a moving vehicle.	→	Yes. The word *requires* indicates wearing a seatbelt is *necessary* for passengers riding in a moving vehicle in California.
Any student in the halls after the bell rings will get a detention slip.	→	Yes. Regardless of the student's status or reason for being in the hallway, the fact that he is there after the bell rings is *sufficient* to tell us that he will receive a detention slip.
The LSAT is a prerequisite for getting into law school.	→	Yes. The word *prerequisite* indicates that the LSAT is *required* for getting into law school.
You can't make an omelet without breaking a few eggs.	→	Yes. *Without* is the word to pay attention to here. In order to make an omelet, it is *necessary* to break a few eggs.
Let them have cake.	→	No. This is simply a declarative statement with neither a necessary nor a sufficient condition.
Cheaters never prosper.	→	Yes. The knowledge that someone is a cheater is *sufficient* to know that she will never prosper.
Sara cannot go to the movies unless she cleans her room.	→	Yes. The word *unless* makes a clean room a *necessary* condition that must be met for Sara to go to the movies.

Each of the statements that received a "yes" answer—that is, every conditional statement—can be expressed in If/Then format. A bit later in this chapter, we'll devote a section to learning how to make those translations. For now, though, it's critical to hone your ability to spot trigger-and-result relationships in prose.

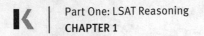
Practice

Here's your chance to practice this. Take a look at each of the following statements and note to yourself whether it expresses a relationship of sufficiency and necessity and how you know whether it does or not. After each one, you can look ahead to see the expert thinking.

Statement	My Analysis
22. There's a strong possibility the election will oust the incumbent senator.	
23. The car cannot run without gasoline.	
24. Each of the apples in the basket has been rinsed off.	
25. Make it so.	
26. It may be the case that germs cause your headaches.	
27. Everything on the menu is vegan-friendly.	
28. Mammals don't have gills.	

Statement	My Analysis
29. Only members of the book club receive that discount.	
30. Did you pick up milk on your way home?	
31. Unless they beat the Eagles, the Lions won't make it to the playoffs.	
32. The car needs an oil change before your trip.	
33. Some wildcats are striped.	

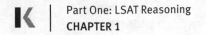
Expert Analysis

Here's how an LSAT expert would evaluate the statements on the basis of whether each is an example of a conditional Formal Logic statement.

Statement		Analysis
22. There's a strong possibility the election will oust the incumbent senator.	→	No. This is a possibility and contains no condition sufficient or necessary for another to occur. No Formal Logic here.
23. The car cannot run without gasoline.	→	Yes. Gasoline is *necessary* for the car to run. The car running is *sufficient* to tell you it has gas.
24. Each of the apples in the basket has been rinsed off.	→	Yes. Telling me an apple is in that basket is enough, or *sufficient*, for me to know that it has been rinsed off. If it's in the basket, it's required for it to have been rinsed off.
25. Make it so.	→	No. This is just a command.
26. It may be the case that germs cause your headaches.	→	No. Because it only "may" be the case, you can't say that either term is sufficient for or requires the other.
27. Everything on the menu is vegan-friendly.	→	Yes. Knowing that an item appears on this menu is *sufficient* to tell you that it's vegan-friendly. "Vegan-friendly" is a status *required* of any item that is on the menu.
28. Mammals don't have gills.	→	Yes. Knowledge that an animal is a mammal is *sufficient* to know that it does not have gills. Likewise, it is *necessary* for mammals to lack gills. (Having gills would be a sure sign that an animal is not a mammal.)
29. Only members of the book club receive that discount.	→	Yes. Being a member of the book club is *necessary* to receive this discount, and if a person is getting the discount, that's enough (*sufficient*) to guarantee that the person is in the book club.
30. Did you pick up milk on your way home?	→	No. Questions do not express conditional statements.
31. Unless they beat the Eagles, the Lions won't make it to the playoffs.	→	Yes. Beating the Eagles is a *necessary* condition for the Lions to make it to the playoffs. The Lions making the playoffs is *sufficient* to know that the Lions beat the Eagles.
32. The car needs an oil change before your trip.	→	Yes. An oil change is *necessary* if this car goes on a trip. If you're driving this car on your trip, that's enough to guarantee that this car had an oil change.*
33. Some wildcats are striped.	→	No. It is not necessary for a wildcat to be striped because only some of them are.

*Note that in day-to-day experience we often use *need* very loosely in place of *ought* or *should*. On the LSAT, you must treat a word such as *need* very strictly.

Again, each one of the exercises that is a conditional statement can be expressed in If/Then format, and later in this chapter, you'll get lots of practice with making those translations.

Reflection

Look back over your practice.

- Did you accurately identify which statements were conditional statements and which weren't?
- What words were helpful to you in identifying that relationship of logical necessity?
- Did you notice all of the different ways in which sufficient-and-necessary relationships can be phrased?

Practice identifying conditional, Formal Logic statements in everyday life. Even simple interactions often reveal our understanding of necessary-sufficient relationships. Have you ever responded to someone who told you some electrical device wasn't working by asking, "Are you sure it's plugged in?" Your response is based on the fact that you know that a power source is necessary for the electrical device to operate. In no time, you'll treat all sorts of statements—"I can't serve you unless I see an ID," "Registration required," and so on—as indicative of Formal Logic.

A Note About Cause-and-Effect Relationships

We're going to steadily build on our understanding of conditional statements because you're going to see multiple instances of them on every section of the LSAT. Before we proceed, however, take a moment for an important caveat about conditional statements and cause-and-effect relationships. In a causal relationship, one thing is the reason *why* another happens. Examples of statements indicating cause-and-effect relationships include these:

> Mike gets good grades because he studies every night.

> Low pressure systems can cause headaches.

> Many house fires are the result of faulty wiring.

The cause is the reason why the effect occurred, and the effect is what the cause brought about.

It's tempting to assume that causal relationships can be expressed in If/Then terms. Indeed, *sometimes* they can. For example, imagine a scientific experiment in which every time, without exception, pressing a button causes a bell to ring. In that case, you could say:

> If you press the button, then the bell will ring.

The cause here (pressing the button) becomes the sufficient term, and the effect (the bell ringing) becomes the necessary term.

At other times, however, it is inappropriate to express causal relationships using conditional If/Then terms. Consider another example:

> Colds are caused by exposure to germs.

Germs are the cause, and colds are the effect. Can we validly say the following?

> If someone is exposed to germs, then he gets a cold.

The If/Then terminology doesn't fit here because the statement isn't true in all cases. We're exposed to cold germs all the time without necessarily getting colds; we only get colds a small percentage of the time. However, it is the case that every single person who has a cold has been exposed to cold germs, so we can say:

> If you have a cold, then you have been exposed to germs.

Notice that in this case, the cause becomes the necessary term, and the effect becomes the sufficient term—very different from the example about the button and bell.

Take another example:

> Throwing a brick at the window may cause the window to break.

Can we put that into If/Then format, like this?

> If you throw a brick at the window, then the window will break.

No, because of that word *may*. It's possible that in some circumstances the window doesn't break when someone throws a brick at it. So it isn't always a true statement. (Now, it would be legitimate to say, "If you throw a brick at the window, then the window *may* break." But If/Then statements with *maybe* in them usually aren't terribly useful and, thus, are not very common on the LSAT.)

If you're confused at this point, don't worry about it. The takeaway here is merely that *you must not automatically conflate cause-and-effect relationships with sufficient-necessary relationships.* Remember that throughout your LSAT studies.

Understanding Conditional Statements with "And" or "Or"

Let's look at a variation some conditional statements can display. So far, we've seen conditional statements of the form "If *x*, then *y*," but sometimes a conditional statement can involve more than two items, linked with *and* or *or*. It's important to understand what those simple conjunctions mean in logical statements:

LSAT STRATEGY

In Formal Logic

- *And* means you need both terms for the conditional to be relevant or fulfilled.
- *Or* means you need at least one of the terms (the first or the second or both) for the conditional to be relevant or fulfilled. *Or* does not express a mutually exclusive relationship unless you're explicitly told otherwise.

Let's explain a little further about *and*. *And* might appear in the trigger:

> If X and Y, then Z.

In that case, both X and Y must be true to apply the conditional statement. X by itself doesn't ensure that Z will happen; neither does Y by itself. So the conditional statement simply isn't relevant unless we have *both* X and Y.

And could also appear in the result:

> If A, then B and C.

Here, whenever we have A, we have to have *both* B and C. Once we have A, it's just not possible that we could have B without C, or C without B. Given A, the statement can't be fulfilled without both B and C.

What about *or*? *Or* could appear in the trigger:

> If G or H, then J.

Either G or H by itself is sufficient to ensure that you've got to have J. And if you have both G and H, this conditional still applies: You still have to have J.

Or could also appear in the result:

> If M, then N or P.

Given M, then we have to have at least one of either N or P. If we have M, we don't *have* to have both N and P, but we do have to have one of them. And we *might* even have all three: M, N, and P all happening doesn't violate this rule.

Notice that in the last two examples, the word *or* doesn't preclude the possibility of having both of the terms linked by *or*. In other words, *or* doesn't express a relationship of mutual exclusivity. If the LSAT wants you to know that two items joined by *or* do have a relationship of mutual exclusivity, it will make this explicit as follows:

> If S, then T or V, *but not both*.

Here, if we have S, we have to have either T or V. But, given S, we *can't* have both T and V. Whenever you *do not* see language that explicitly expresses *but not both*, however, you should assume that the two things joined by *or* could go together.

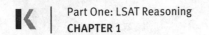
Let's see how an expert test taker would think through some conditional statements containing *and* or *or*.

Conditional Statement	Analysis
If Miranda goes to the store, then she will buy apples or bananas.	Miranda going to the store logically necessitates that she buy either apples, or bananas, or *both* apples and bananas. This statement allows her to buy both, but she doesn't have to.
	→ Say that Miranda went to the store and that she didn't buy apples. In that case, she definitely did buy bananas.
	No logical deductions stem from a statement beginning "If Miranda buys apples or bananas or both," because those are necessary but not sufficient conditions for Miranda's going to the store. Miranda might buy her fruit elsewhere.
If the league doesn't approve the new contract, then the players will go on strike and the city will lose valuable revenue.	The league's failure to approve the contract would necessitate both a strike by the players and the loss of revenue by the city.
	→ Suppose the players were on strike and the city had lost valuable revenue. No deduction about whether the league had approved or denied the new contract would follow from that. (And if the league actually did approve a new contract, the players could still strike or the city could still lose revenue for other reasons.)

Conditional Statement	**Analysis**
If Fatima does the grocery shopping and Pablo cleans the house, then the chores will be done before noon.	Fatima's grocery shopping and Pablo's house cleaning logically guarantee that the chores will be done before noon. If Fatima does the grocery shopping but Pablo doesn't clean the house, this statement simply doesn't apply. It's impossible to deduce whether the chores will get done before noon or not. (For example, someone else might clean the house.) Likewise, if the chores are finished before noon, it's not certain that Pablo cleaned the house or that Fatima went grocery shopping. Those two activities are sufficient to know that the chores are done before noon but not necessary to the completion of the chores by that time. (So, if the chores are done by noon, perhaps a third person pitched in to help or Pablo did everything himself. Who knows?)
If the chicken is soaked in buttermilk or brine, then it will stay moist while cooking.	A soak in either buttermilk or brine will ensure that the chicken stays moist while cooking. Do either one and the chicken will be moist. What would happen if the chicken was soaked in BOTH buttermilk and brine? Again, the chicken would be moist, guaranteed! (Although it might not taste that good.) The "or" here is not exclusive; it doesn't have to be just one or the other.

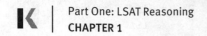
You'll notice, both on the LSAT and in life, that *and* and *or* relationships can be expressed in a variety of ways. In particular, when those terms are negated, you might see them joined by *neither . . . nor*. Just make a mental note now that *neither x nor y* means *not x and not y*. Like this:

Conditional Statement		Analysis
If it neither rains nor snows, then we'll go on our trip tomorrow.	→	If it does not rain and it does not snow, then we'll go on our trip tomorrow.
Neither Jane nor Thomas will go to the dinner if it starts later than 8 P.M.	→	If the dinner starts later than 8 P.M., then Jane will not go and Thomas will not go.

What if a conditional statement includes a phrase like *but not both*? We have to work that into our understanding of the statement, and the easiest way to do that is to think of it as being two statements.

Conditional Statement		Analysis
If the sous chef makes the soup, she will also make either the salad or the dessert but not both.	→	(1) The sous chef making the soup is sufficient to tell us that she must also make the salad or the dessert.
		(2) The sous chef making the soup also requires that she NOT make both salad and dessert.

Practice

Check your understanding of each of the following conditional statements.

Conditional Statement	My Analysis
34. If Meagan buys a juicer, then she buys kale or mangos.	

What do we know if Meagan buys a juicer?
What do we know if Meagan buys kale?
What do we know if Meagan buys mangos?
What do we know if Meagan buys neither
    mangos nor kale?

| 35. If Ian draws a spaceship, he gives it lasers or a tractor beam, but not both. | |

What do we know if we are told Ian is
    drawing a spaceship?
What do we know if Ian is drawing lasers?
What do we know if Ian is drawing a tractor
    beam?
What do we know if Ian is drawing both
    lasers and a tractor beam?

| 36. If Patricia makes nachos, then she'll also make salsa and bean dip. | |

What do we know if we are told that Patricia
    makes nachos?
What do we know if we are told that Patricia
    doesn't make salsa?
What do we know if we are told that Patricia
    makes salsa and bean dip?

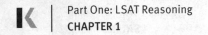

Expert Analysis

Here's how an LSAT expert would analyze the conditional statements you just analyzed.

Conditional Statement		Analysis
34. If Meagan buys a juicer, then she buys kale or mangos.		
What do we know if Meagan buys a juicer?	$\longrightarrow$	She buys kale or mangos or both.
What do we know if Meagan buys kale?	$\longrightarrow$	Nothing additional.
What do we know if Meagan buys mangos?	$\longrightarrow$	Nothing additional.
What do we know if Meagan buys neither mangos nor kale?	$\longrightarrow$	Then she can't have bought a juicer.
35. If Ian draws a spaceship, he gives it lasers or a tractor beam, but not both.		
What do we know if we are told Ian is drawing a spaceship?	$\longrightarrow$	He gives his spaceship either lasers or a tractor beam, but he absolutely won't give it both lasers and a tractor beam.
What do we know if Ian is drawing lasers?	$\longrightarrow$	Nothing additional. Indeed, he may not even be drawing them on a spaceship in this case.
What do we know if Ian is drawing a tractor beam?	$\longrightarrow$	Nothing additional. Indeed, he may not even be drawing them on a spaceship in this case.
What do we know if Ian is drawing both lasers and a tractor beam?	$\longrightarrow$	Then he can't have drawn a spaceship.
36. If Patricia makes nachos, then she'll also make salsa and bean dip.		
What do we know if we are told that Patricia makes nachos?	$\longrightarrow$	Then she'll make both salsa and bean dip. She can't make just one of those—she has to make both.
What do we know if we are told that Patricia doesn't make salsa?	$\longrightarrow$	Then she can't have made nachos.
What do we know if we are told that Patricia makes salsa and bean dip?	$\longrightarrow$	Nothing additional.

Translating Conditional Statements into If/Then Format

It's helpful at this point to develop a simple system of notation for conditional statements. (The value of a uniform notation will become very clear when you start working with real LSAT problems.) Whenever you see a conditional statement on the LSAT, translate it into something that looks like this:

> If Trigger (sufficient) → Result (necessary)

Write the sufficient term on the left, the necessary term on the right, and an arrow in the middle pointing from left to right (to indicate which direction the logical trigger-and-result relationship flows). If the statement includes a negative (*not* or *no*), there are a couple of ways to handle this. Some people write out the word *not*, others use a tilde symbol to mean *not*, and still others strike through a negated term. So you might write the statement "If A then not B," in shorthand in any of these ways:

> If A → NOT B
> If A → ~B
> If A → B̸

Symbolize negated terms however you like, but be consistent about it and make sure the entire term is legible. We'll alternate between using the word *not* and using the tilde in this book and in our online materials.

Armed with that simple notation, you're ready to learn how to distill conditional relationships from sometimes complicated prose into clear, brief shorthand notes. You've already learned that conditional statements can be phrased in lots of different ways; you'll see that some of those are more common than others on the LSAT, but they all appear from time to time. This section will give a library of ways that the testmaker phrases conditional statements so that you can quickly and easily translate them into If/Then form.

Think of If/Then statements as generalizations (or rules) that do not admit any exceptions. In the example we started with, every single time anybody is in New York, she has to be in the United States. The test could express this "rule" in a number of ways:

> All people in New York are in the United States.
>
> Everyone who is in New York is in the United States.
>
> When (or whenever) someone is in New York, he is in the United States.
>
> A person is in the United States every time he is in New York.

In these sentences, the word that tells you you're looking at a generalization (*all*, *any*, *every*, etc.) also serves to denote the sufficient term. Let's make a short catalog:

LSAT STRATEGY

Words that denote that one thing is sufficient for another to happen:

- *All*
- *Any* (*any time, any place, anybody*, etc.)
- *Every* (*every time, everybody,* etc.)
- *Whenever*
- *Each*

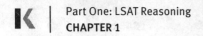
Negatives

The same is true for the opposites of those words: Words such as *none* or *no one* or *never* also signal a generalization without exceptions—that is, they also signal a sufficient-and-necessary relationship. These deserve special discussion, however, because sentences containing these negative words frequently employ a word order that can be confusing if you aren't familiar with how to parse it. Consider an example:

> No one who is in New York is in Europe.

It may be tempting, if you just glance at the word order, to start your If/Then translation with "If not New York . . . ." But think about the statement's subject: The sentence isn't about people who are not in New York. Rather, it's about people who *are* in New York, and it's saying that those people are *not* in Europe.

> If in New York → NOT in Europe

Be very careful about the way sentences are worded. A good practice is to always ask yourself: Who or what is this sentence *about*? That will point you to the sufficient term.

LSAT STRATEGY

Negative words that indicate a sufficient-necessary relationship include:

- None
- Never
- Not
- No one

Only

Just as there are words and phrases that signal that one thing is sufficient for another to happen, there are words and phrases that signal conditional relationships by denoting the necessary term, and a common one on the LSAT is the word *only*. To return to our original example:

Only people in the United States can be in New York.

Whom is this sentence about? It's about people in New York. Thus, "[o]nly" signals the necessary term. You can translate *only* to *then*:

If in New York → in United States

Consider a similar example:

A person can be in New York only if she is in the United States.

Who is the subject of this sentence? The sentence is about people in New York. Don't let the word "if" throw you off there; when "if" follows "only" to make "only if," it always signals a necessary term:

If in New York → in United States.

Treat this as another rule to memorize: "Only if" equals *only* equals *then*.

There is one use of the word *only*, however, that produces a different interpretation. When *only* is preceded by the definite article, the ensuing phrase—*the only*—signals the sufficient term in a conditional relationship:

The only people who are in New York are people who are in the United States.

Again, whom is this sentence about? People in New York, so that's the sufficient term. The translation now looks familiar:

If in New York → in United States.

Note: The meaning of the statement remains the same throughout all three examples. (Of course it does, as it is a statement we know to be true from real life in this case.) The part of the conditional logic signaled by the word *only*, however, was different: "Only" (by itself) and "only if" indicated necessity, whereas "the only" indicates sufficiency.

LSAT STRATEGY

The word *only* in Formal Logic

- *Only* signals the necessary term.
- *Only if* signals the necessary term.
- *The only* signals the sufficient term.

(By the way, notice that, in the prose previous examples, the sufficient and necessary terms appear in either order; the sufficient term doesn't always appear first in the plain-language English sentence. Nevertheless, in every Formal Logic "translation," the order was identical: If sufficient → necessary.)

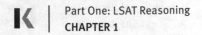

Unless/Without

Take a look at another way of expressing the same sufficient-necessary relationship we've been illustrating throughout this section:

> No one can be in New York unless he's in the United States.

Once again, this translates to our familiar If/Then statement:

> If in New York → in United States.

This one needs some unpacking, but close examination will show you that it conforms to the way you use *unless* all the time in day-to-day conversation. *Unless* signals a requirement—that is, it signals the necessary term—so you can think, "*unless* equals *then*." But notice what "unless" does to the phraseology in the sufficient clause—we've had to add the negation "no one." The original statement ("If a person is in New York, then he is in the United States") didn't have a *no* in it. Do you see why? The word "unless" indicates that were the necessary condition to be absent, the sufficient condition would have to be absent as well. That means that to fit the sufficient condition Into a sentence containing *unless*, you must negate the sufficient term.

If this seems tricky, just put it into an easily understandable real-life situation. Most people don't want to eat dry cereal without milk. For them, "I will not eat cereal unless I have milk," is an easy rule to articulate. Now, just think through what that means in Formal Logic terms. Because the person won't eat cereal unless she has milk, "milk" is *necessary* for her to eat cereal. Thus, the rule could just as easily be expressed in If/Then terms: If eat cereal → have milk.

What does a sentence containing *unless* mean if the sufficient term is not negated? Again, apply a real-world example and work it out. Imagine you hear a friend say, "I will go to the mall unless it rains." (Notice that this time, the term at the beginning of the sentence is positive—"I *will* go to the mall"—as opposed to the "I will *not* eat cereal" in the example above.) Treat your friend's statement as a rule; he means precisely what he says. His statement means "I will go to the mall in every case except one: rain." So, you can translate your friend's rule into "If I do *not* go to the mall, then it is raining."

As the following Strategy Box illustrates, you can translate any Formal Logic statement with *unless* by negating the sufficient statement and substituting *then* for the word *unless*.

LSAT STRATEGY

The word *unless* in Formal Logic

- "No X unless Y" translates to "If X then Y."
- "A unless B" translates to "If not A then B."

Note: The word *without* functions exactly the same way as *unless* in conditional Formal Logic statements. For example, "I will not eat cereal without having milk" has the same meaning as "I will not eat cereal unless I have milk."

If, But Only If

One other Formal Logic structure you'll occasionally see on the LSAT is *if, but only if.* Here's an example:

> Piper goes to the beach if, but only if, Kinsley goes to the beach.

This means that Piper's going to the beach is sufficient *and* necessary for Kinsley's going. (Notice that the term "Kinsley goes to the beach" is preceded in the sentence by "if" [sufficient] and by "only if" [necessary].) It can be broken down into two statements:

> If Piper goes to the beach → Kinsley goes to the beach

> If Kinsley goes to the beach → Piper goes to the beach

Ultimately, the impact is this: Either they both go or neither of them does.

LSAT STRATEGY

The phrases "if, but only if" and "if, and only if" indicate a biconditional relationship. Each term in the relationship is both sufficient AND necessary for the other term.

"X if, and only if Y" can be written:

> If X ⟶ Y

> If Y ⟶ X

> or, alternatively

> X ⟷ Y

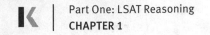
The expert LSAT test taker automatically (either mentally or in simple shorthand) translates all conditional statements into If/Then format. Follow the expert's lead by practicing these skills until they are second nature. Here are a number of conditional statements along with the expert's translations:

Conditional Statement		Analysis
All visitors must check in at the front desk.	→	"All" is modifying "visitors," which makes that term sufficient: *If visitor → check in at the front desk*
Each of the contestants has been given one hour to prepare a dish.	→	"Each" indicates that being a contestant is sufficient: *If contestant → one hour to prepare a dish*
Every building on this street was built before the turn of the century.	→	"Every" is a modifier for the entire phrase "building on this street" and indicates sufficiency: *If building on this street → built before the turn of the century*
Anyone not on the list will be asked to leave.	→	"Anyone" is categorical language pertaining to all people not on the list; it indicates sufficiency: *If NOT on the list → asked to leave*
In order to start the car, the key must be in the ignition.	→	The phrase "in order to" and the word "must" combine to indicate that the key is required (necessary) for the car to start: *If start the car → key in the ignition*
The children in Ms. Hatcher's class all speak French.	→	The word order of this sentence is a little tricky. Whom is this sentence about? It's about students who are in Ms. Hatcher's class. Accordingly, "all" (which indicates sufficiency) is modifying the children in Ms. Hatcher's class: *If in Ms. Hatcher's class → speaks French*

Conditional Statement		Analysis
No one in Ms. Hatcher's class speaks German.	→	Whom is this sentence about? The kids in Ms. Hatcher's class. "No one" indicates that being in that class is sufficient to know a student does not speak German: *If in Ms. Hatcher's class → NOT speak German*
The only people allowed on the field at this time are members of the press.	→	"The only," because it has the definite article, indicates sufficiency: *If allowed on the field → member of the press at this time*
Everyone in the audience will get a copy of my new book.	→	"Everyone" indicates that being a person in the audience is sufficient to receive a copy of the new book: *If in the audience → book*
In order for us to make a diagnosis, we need an accurate patient history.	→	The phrase "in order to" and the word "need" combine to indicate that an accurate patient history is necessary for a diagnosis: *If diagnosis → accurate patient history*
They will name the baby Maya if, but only if, it's a girl.	→	"If but only if" indicates that a statement is both sufficient and necessary for the other and vice versa. *If baby named Maya → girl* *If girl → baby named Maya*

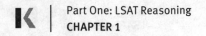

Practice

Using the previous pages as a glossary, translate each of the following statements, each of which expresses a sufficient-and-necessary relationship, into If/Then format. Note them down in simple shorthand relationships using arrows.

Conditional Statement	My Analysis
37. All employees are required to attend the meeting.	
38. I'll skip the party only if I'm sick.	
39. Malinda will not win the race unless she trains hard and avoids injuries.	
40. All of those in the path of the tornado are being evacuated.	
41. Everyone in the cinema must turn their cell phones off now.	
42. Only if you have proper identification and a ticket will you be allowed to board the plane.	
43. All of those in attendance this evening are asked to give generously to the scholarship fund.	

Conditional Statement	**My Analysis**
44. Anyone over the age of fifty can remember disco music.	
45. Every city in the tristate region is currently suffering through the worst flu epidemic in twenty years.	
46. Candace will sign up for softball this year only if Jarvis or Tempest signs up as well.	
47. School is not canceled for bad weather unless there is snow accumulation in excess of three feet.	
48. A lake has experienced an infestation of Frankenfish if, but only if, it's in Travis County.	
49. Any fruit we received in the last shipment is bound to be spoiled by now.	
50. The only rooms big enough to accommodate the wedding party are booked for that weekend.	
51. Only when spring arrives and warmer weather returns do the swallows return to Capistrano.	

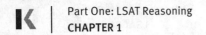
Expert Analysis

Here's how an LSAT expert would notate each of the examples you just worked on. In every case, the shorthand employs the format "If [sufficient] → [necessary]."

	Conditional Statement		Analysis
37.	All employees are required to attend the meeting.	→	If employee → attend
38.	I'll skip the party only if I'm sick.	→	If skip party → sick
39.	Malinda will not win the race unless she trains hard and avoids injuries.	→	If Malinda wins → trained hard AND avoided injuries
40.	All of those in the path of the tornado are being evacuated.	→	If path of tornado → evacuated
41.	Everyone in the cinema must turn their cell phones off now.	→	If in cinema → turn cell phone off
42.	Only if you have proper identification and a ticket will you be allowed to board the plane.	→	If allowed to board the plane → proper ID AND a ticket
43.	All of those in attendance this evening are asked to give generously to the scholarship fund.	→	If in attendance → asked to give to scholarship
44.	Anyone over the age of fifty can remember disco music.	→	If over 50 → remember disco
45.	Every city in the tristate region is currently suffering through the worst flu epidemic in twenty years.	→	If city in tristate region → suffering flu epidemic
46.	Candace will sign up for softball this year only if Jarvis or Tempest signs up as well.	→	If Candace signs up → Jarvis signs up OR Tempest signs up
47.	School is not canceled for bad weather unless there is snow accumulation in excess of three feet.	→	If school canceled for bad weather → more than 3 feet of snow
48.	A lake has experienced an infestation of Frankenfish if, but only if, it's in Travis County.	→	If lake in Travis County → infested with Frankenfish If infested with Frankenfish → lake in Travis County
49.	Any fruit we received in the last shipment is bound to be spoiled by now.	→	If fruit from last shipment → spoiled
50.	The only rooms big enough to accommodate the wedding party are booked for that weekend.	→	If big enough to hold the party → booked
51.	Only when spring arrives and warmer weather returns do the swallows return to Capistrano.	→	If swallows return → spring arrives AND warmer weather returns

Reflection

Review your practice. Consider these questions:

- How well did you spot the sufficient and necessary terms? What words or phrases tended to mislead you?
- When noting the statements down in shorthand, did you always keep the sufficient term on the left and the necessary term on the right, with an arrow pointing to the necessary term?
- If you were able to spot which thing is needed for another in some of the examples, did you remember what that means about which one is necessary and which one is sufficient?

Translating conditional, Formal Logic statements is something you can practice every day. When you hear friends, coworkers, or others use words like *all*, *every*, *none*, *never*, *if*, *only if*, *unless*, and so on, treat their statements as rules and determine how the statements they've made would translate into If/Then statements.

Making Valid Deductions from Conditional Statements

Now that you understand conditional relationships and know how to spot them when you come across them in prose, you're ready to think about how to combine them to make deductions. You saw a small example of this in our demonstration about navel oranges above, and you'll see a great deal of it in the course of learning how to do Logic Games and Logical Reasoning questions on the LSAT.

The idea is simple: You can combine conditional statements when the same term appears in more than one statement. Where the sufficient terms are the same, they can be combined like this:

> If A, then B.
>
> If A, then C.
>
> Deduction: If A, then both B and C.

If the same term appears in the necessary parts of two conditional statements, you can combine them like this:

> If T, then V.
>
> If W, then V.
>
> Deduction: If either T or W (or both), then V.

Finally, by far the most useful opportunity to combine conditional statements occurs when the same term appears in the necessary part of one conditional statement and in the sufficient part of another. In that case, those two statements allow you to deduce an altogether new idea:

> If X, then Y.
>
> If Y, then Z.
>
> Deduction: If X, then Z.

(That pattern of three statements is called a syllogism, by the way. You certainly won't have to know that word on the LSAT, but the test will definitely reward your ability to accurately combine statements in this way.)

More than two premises with shared terms can produce multiple deductions:

> If D, then E.
>
> If E, then F.
>
> If F, then G.
>
> If G, then H.

Deductions:

> If D, then E and F and G and H.
>
> If E, then F and G and H.
>
> If F, then G and H.

By the way, what can you deduce if you know that you have H? Answer: Not a thing. Remember, the necessary term of an If/Then doesn't trigger any results.

Take a look at how an LSAT expert might draw deductions from a set of conditional statements:

Conditional Statements		Analysis
If Jane goes to the movies, she'll also go to the beach.	$\longrightarrow$	If movies $\rightarrow$ beach
If Jane goes to the beach, she won't go to the museum.	$\longrightarrow$	If beach $\rightarrow$ ~museum
If Jane goes to the beach, she'll go to the amusement park.	$\longrightarrow$	If beach $\rightarrow$ amusement park
If Jane goes to the amusement park, she will buy a funnel cake.	$\longrightarrow$	If amusement park $\rightarrow$ buy funnel cake

If we know that Jane...	then we also know that she...
goes to the movies	—goes to the beach —does not go to the museum —goes to the amusement park —buys a funnel cake
goes to the beach	—does not go to the museum —goes to the amusement park —buys a funnel cake We don't know whether she goes to the movies or not.
doesn't go to the museum	We can't deduce anything.
buys a funnel cake	We can't deduce anything.

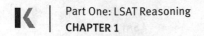

Practice

In the following exercise, first translate the given conditional statements so that you can use them to create a chain of logic. Then, answer questions about what we must know, given our new chain. The expert analysis is found on the next page.

Conditional Statements	My Analysis
52. If John doesn't bake a pie, he doesn't buy apples. If John bakes chocolate chip cookies, he does not bake a pie. If John doesn't buy apples, he doesn't have applesauce or doesn't have jelly. If John buys bananas, then he bakes chocolate chip cookies. If John goes to the store, then he buys bananas.	

If we know that John...	then we also know that John...
bought bananas	
bakes chocolate chip cookies	
does not bake a pie	
doesn't have applesauce or jelly	

Expert Analysis for the Practice exercise may be found on the following page. ▶ ▶ ▶

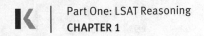
Expert Analysis

Here's how the LSAT expert translated the logic along with the valid deductions she drew from it.

Conditional Statements		Analysis
52. If John doesn't bake a pie, he doesn't buy apples.	⟶	If NOT bake pie ⟶ NOT buy apples
If John bakes chocolate chip cookies, he does not bake a pie.	⟶	If bake c/c cookies ⟶ NOT bake pie
If John doesn't buy apples, he doesn't have applesauce or doesn't have jelly.	⟶	If NOT buy apples ⟶ NOT have applesauce OR NOT have jelly
If John buys bananas, then he bakes chocolate chip cookies.	⟶	If buy bananas ⟶ bakes c/c cookies
If John goes to the store, then he buys bananas.	⟶	If goes to store ⟶ buy bananas

If we know that John...		then we also know that John...
bought bananas	⟶	baked chocolate chip cookies, did not bake a pie, didn't buy apples, and doesn't have applesauce or doesn't have jelly
bakes chocolate chip cookies	⟶	does not bake a pie, didn't buy apples, and doesn't have applesauce or doesn't have jelly
does not bake a pie	⟶	didn't buy apples and doesn't have applesauce or doesn't have jelly
doesn't have applesauce or doesn't have jelly	⟶	We can't deduce anything.

FORMAL LOGIC: CONTRAPOSITIVES

You've seen that, despite the many ways to express a conditional statement in prose, the logic underlying such statements is remarkably consistent. You're about to learn one more feature of these statements: the contrapositive. The contrapositive is simply another way to express any If/Then statement, but your ability to quickly and accurately form a statement's contrapositive is an incredibly important tool for you to have in your LSAT toolkit.

LEARNING OBJECTIVES

In this section, you'll learn to:

- · Translate a conditional statement into its contrapositive.
- · Make valid deductions from the contrapositive of a conditional statement.
- · Analyze correctly the implications of conditional statements containing *and* and *or.*
- · Analyze correctly the implications of conditional statements containing an "exclusive or."

While a conditional statement and its contrapositive express exactly the same logical premise, forming contrapositives explicitly is valuable to the LSAT test taker because the contrapositive provides another logical trigger to work with.

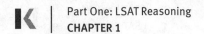

Translating If/Then Statements into Contrapositives

Let's return to our very first example to start thinking about contrapositives.

> If you're in New York, then you are in the United States.

Every single time you are in New York, then you absolutely have to be in the United States. Being in the United States is necessary for a person to be in New York. So, if someone is not in the United States, there's no way he can be in New York. Put another way, negating the necessary term means negating the sufficient term. Contrapositives are built on this insight, and forming the contrapositive is pretty straightforward:

- Reverse the terms—put the term on the left of the arrow on the right and vice versa.
- Negate the terms—where a negation word (like *not*, *no*, or *never*) appears, take it out; where such a word does not appear, put it in.

Like this:

> Original statement: If in New York → in the United States

- Reverse: If in the United States → in New York, *and*
- Negate: If NOT in the United States → NOT in New York

That's the contrapositive: If NOT in the United States → NOT in New York. If you're not in the United States, then you're not in New York.

Note: You must always reverse *and* negate simultaneously. Doing just one of those two actions distorts the meaning of the original statement:

- Reversing without negating produces "If you're in the United States, then you're in New York." Well, we know that to be wrong in real life, and it's a logical fallacy to do this to any conditional statement. The resulting sentence doesn't mean the same thing as the original. In fact, it confuses the necessary term for the sufficient one.
- Negating without reversing gives "If you're not in New York, then you're not in the United States." Again, we know that sentence is incorrect in real life as well as being a distortion of the original.

The test will include numerous wrong answers—in Logic Games and Logical Reasoning especially—that reflect both of those mistakes. Learning to avoid those wrong answers can be just as important as learning to spot correct answers that translate Formal Logic statements correctly.

It's very important to fully absorb that you can never negate without reversing or reverse without negating. This is easy to remember when you're dealing with a real-life example but easy to forget when you're in the heat of a logic game arranging abstract doo-dads, or plowing through a Logical Reasoning argument with unfamiliar scientific terms. Make sure you wrap your head around this principle now so it doesn't trip you up later.

We said earlier that a conditional statement and its contrapositive express exactly the same idea. As proof, notice that the contrapositive can be contraposed into the original statement:

> If NOT in United States → NOT in New York
> Reverse and negate: If in New York → in United States

Before you practice this, there's one more consideration for forming valid contrapositives: Along with reversing and negating, you must, whenever relevant, also change *and* to *or* and *or* to *and*. To see why, and to discern when this is the case, consider an example. Treat the following statement as a rule:

> If it doesn't rain, then we will go to the park or we will go to the beach.

In other words, a lack of rain is sufficient to know that we will go to either the park or the beach (or maybe both, if we have time). Now, translate into simple shorthand:

> If NOT rain → park OR beach

Do the first two operations needed to form the contrapositive:

- Reverse: If park OR beach → NOT rain, *and*
- Negate: If NOT park OR NOT beach → rain

But that's mistaken. What would the statement mean if we left it like that? Not going to the park would be enough to absolutely require that it rain. But that's not consistent with the original statement. According to the original statement, if it doesn't rain, we might choose to go to the beach and not to the park. Preserving the *or* in the contrapositive has warped the meaning of the original statement. But watch how the meaning of the original is preserved if we change *or* to *and* in the contrapositive:

> If NOT park AND NOT beach → rain

If we're neither at the park nor at the beach, it's raining. Now we have a statement that is logically equivalent to the original.

Our example involved an *or* in the necessary term, but you must change *and* to *or* and vice versa regardless of whether those terms appear in the sufficient or necessary term.

Another important note here: When you're dealing with multiple terms in a conditional statement, negate *each one* to avoid confusion. If we formed our contrapositive by saying "if not beach and park → rain," that could have gotten very confusing.

LSAT STRATEGY

To form the contrapositive of an If/Then statement:

- Reverse the terms.
- Negate *each* term.
- Change *and* to *or* and change *or* to *and* (whenever applicable).

Study the LSAT expert's work as she translates the following If/Then statements and forms the correct contrapositive for each. Note that, in every case, it would not matter whether the expert translated the original statement in negative or positive terms because, having formed the contrapositive, both the negative and positive equivalent statements would be clear.

Conditional Statement		Analysis
If the skies stay clear and the wind remains calm, we set sail tomorrow.	→	If skies clear AND winds calm → we sail tomorrow If NOT sail tomorrow → skies NOT clear OR winds NOT calm
There are no vacancies at the hotel unless we have a cancellation.	→	If vacancies → cancellation If NO cancellation → NO vacancies
If Joan is late for dinner, then either traffic is bad or she's lost her way.	→	If Joan is late → bad traffic OR lost If NOT bad traffic AND NOT lost → Joan is NOT late
Only the best players were invited to the tournament.	→	If invited → one of the best players If NOT one of the best players → NOT invited
If this substance is properly classified as a mineral, then it is neither animal nor vegetable.	→	If mineral → NOT animal AND NOT vegetable* If animal OR vegetable → NOT mineral

*NOTE: Remember that *neither x nor y* translates to *not x AND not y.*

Now, you're ready to pull together all of the thinking that an LSAT expert does whenever she encounters a statement indicating a sufficient-necessary relationship. She recognizes the presence of Formal Logic, translates it into If/Then format, and forms the contrapositive explicitly. When you're able to do these things accurately and quickly—in other words, when these processes become second nature—you'll be well on your way to getting a number of LSAT points that may have eluded you before (and will continue to elude your less well-trained competition).

Practice

Translate each of the following statements into simple shorthand and form the contrapositives. After each one, you can turn the page to see the work of an LSAT expert with these same statements.

Conditional Statement	My Analysis
53. Each of the boys is wearing blue and yellow.	
54. When it rains, it pours.	
55. If we have turkey for dinner, we won't have ham.	
56. Any bowl that doesn't contain goldfish contains bettas.	
57. Arianna drives to Rochester only if she visits Syracuse.	
58. If the exhibition comes to the city zoo, then it will feature elephants but not pandas.	
59. If the talent show does not have a magician, then it will have either a dance number or a comedian.	

Conditional Statement	My Analysis
60. All triathlon participants must undergo a physical and sign a waiver.	
61. All the horses in the stable are either roan or palomino.	
62. If the train is late, then Bret won't make it to Chicago today.	
63. None of the coffee in this room is decaf.	
64. All sodas in the cupboard are either diet or cherry.	
65. We visit the Colosseum today only if we also visit the Pantheon but not the Roman Forum.	

Conditional Statement	My Analysis
66. Pre-med students must take organic chemistry and biology.	
67. Unless it rains, we will go to either the beach or the park.	
68. If she injured her anterior cruciate ligament or her medial collateral ligament, then she won't be able to play for the remainder of the season.	
69. Greg can join neither the swim team nor the debate team unless he brings up his grades.	
70. If Matt wins the lottery, then he will buy a boat and sail around the world.	
71. Only faculty or staff are allowed in the lounge.	

Expert Analysis

Here's how the LSAT expert translated and contraposed each of the statements you just worked with.

Conditional Statement	Analysis
53. Each of the boys is wearing blue and yellow.	If boy → wearing blue AND wearing yellow → If NOT wearing blue OR NOT wearing yellow → NOT boy
54. When it rains, it pours.	→ If rains → pours If NOT pour → NOT rain
55. If we have turkey for dinner, we won't have ham.	→ If turkey → NOT ham If ham → NOT turkey
56. Any bowl that doesn't contain goldfish contains bettas.	→ If NOT goldfish → bettas If NOT bettas → goldfish
57. Arianna drives to Rochester only if she visits Syracuse.	If Arianna drives to Rochester → visits Syracuse → If NOT visit Syracuse → Arianna NOT drive to Rochester
58. If the exhibition comes to the city zoo, then it will feature elephants but not pandas.*	If city zoo → elephants AND NOT pandas → If NOT elephants → NOT city zoo** OR if pandas
59. If the talent show does not have a magician, then it will have either a dance number or a comedian.	If NOT magician → dance number OR comedian → If NOT dance number → magician AND NOT comedian
60. All triathlon participants must undergo a physical and sign a waiver.	If triathlon participant → undergo physical AND sign waiver → If NOT sign waiver OR NOT undergo physical → NOT triathlon participant
61. All the horses in the stable are either roan or palomino.	If horse in stable → roan OR palomino → If NOT roan AND NOT palomino → NOT horse in stable
62. If the train is late, then Bret won't make it to Chicago today.	If train late → Bret NOT make it to Chicago → If Bret makes it to Chicago → train NOT late
63. None of the coffee in this room is decaf.	→ If coffee in this room → NOT decaf If decaf → NOT coffee in this room
64. All sodas in the cupboard are either diet or cherry.	If soda in the cupboard → diet OR cherry → If NOT diet AND NOT cherry → NOT soda in the cupboard

Conditional Statement	Analysis
65. We visit the Colosseum today only if we also visit the Pantheon but not the Roman Forum.* →	If Colosseum → Pantheon AND NOT Roman Forum
	If NOT Pantheon OR if Roman Forum → NOT Colosseum
66. Pre-med students must take organic chemistry and biology. →	If pre-med student → take organic chemistry AND take biology
	If NOT take organic chemistry OR NOT take biology → NOT pre-med student
67. Unless it rains, we will go to either the beach or the park. →	If NOT beach AND NOT park → rain
	If NOT rain → beach OR park
68. If she injured her anterior cruciate ligament or her medial collateral ligament, then she won't be able to play for the remainder of the season. →	If ACL OR MCL → NOT play rest of season
	If plays (at all during the) rest of season → NOT ACL AND NOT MCL***
69. Greg can join neither the swim team nor the debate team unless he brings up his grades. →	If swim team OR debate team → brings up grades
	If NOT bring up grades → NOT swim team AND NOT debate team
70. If Matt wins the lottery, then he will buy a boat and sail around the world. →	If Matt wins lottery → buy boat AND sail around the world
	If NOT buy boat OR NOT sail around the world → Matt NOT win lottery
71. Only faculty or staff are allowed in the lounge. →	If allowed in the lounge → faculty OR staff
	If NOT faculty AND NOT staff → NOT allowed in the lounge

*The word *but*, though rhetorically different from *and*, actually functions the same as *and* in Formal Logic translations.

**Be careful with statements like this one. In the contrapositive here, the expert has jotted down "If NOT elephants or if pandas. . . ." The "if" before pandas there helps to avoid the mistaken interpretation that would result from the prose clause "If not elephants or pandas," which makes it sound as if both terms are negated. In this contrapositive, elephants are not present, but pandas *are*.

***Note that the expert has included the idea of playing at any point during the rest of the season. This makes clear, in the contrapositive, that if the athlete plays at all during the rest of the season, you can be certain she didn't injure her ACL or MCL.

Reflection

Review your practice.

- Were you careful to translate each sentence into shorthand before forming the contrapositive?
- What did you find challenging about forming the contrapositives?
- In cases involving *and* or *or*, did you convert them correctly? And did you negate each term?

In the coming days, use every opportunity you encounter to spot conditional reasoning in day-to-day life. The next time you see a sign such as "No Shirt, No Shoes, No Service," for example, translate it into If/Then terms. "If a person is not wearing shoes or is not wearing a shirt, then the person will not be served." Treat that as a rule without exceptions and practice forming the contrapositive: "If a person is being served, then he is wearing shoes and is wearing a shirt." You'll find it remarkable how often you engage in Formal Logic reasoning without even noticing it. You'll be noticing it a lot between now and Test Day.

Making Valid Deductions from the Contrapositive of a Conditional Statement

As you've seen (and practiced), a conditional statement and its contrapositive express exactly the same idea, but the contrapositive has a different trigger. Therefore, it's useful to write out the contrapositive for reference as you're thinking through how you can combine conditional statements to reveal further deductions. To start with, notice how a conditional statement and its contrapositive nicely define the field of what you do and don't know. Take a simple (and likely fictional) example:

If a creature is a cat, then that creature has nine lives.

Start by translating that into simple shorthand and then making the contrapositive:

If cat → nine lives
If NOT nine lives → NOT cat

You've already learned that you can have the result without the trigger (that is to say, the necessary term without the sufficient term), so a creature could have nine lives without being a cat. In fact, you don't know about any creature other than a cat. If someone asked you whether a unicorn has nine lives, you'd have to respond—based solely on the statement above—"I don't know." It can be useful mental shorthand on the LSAT to remember that the necessary terms of an If/Then statement and its contrapositive are not mutually exclusive. In the previous example, a creature that's not a cat may or may not have nine lives.

The contrapositive (and its implications) broadens your ability to make deductions from a set of conditional statements. Look again at the exercise about Jane and her entertainment choices and see how an expert LSAT test taker looks at the statements and their contrapositives:

Conditional Statements		Analysis
If Jane goes to the movies, she'll also go to the beach.	⟶	If movies → beach If NOT beach → NOT movies
If Jane goes to the beach, she won't go to the museum.	⟶	If beach → NOT museum If museum → NOT beach
If Jane goes to the beach, she'll go to the amusement park.	⟶	If beach → amusement park If NOT amusement park → NOT beach
If Jane goes to the amusement park, she will buy a funnel cake.	⟶	If amusement park → funnel cake If NOT funnel cake → NOT amusement park*

⟶ All the deductions made earlier are still valid, but by including the contrapositives, the following deductions are also now clear:

If Jane doesn't buy a funnel cake, then she doesn't go to the amusement park, she doesn't go to the beach, *and* she doesn't go to the movies.

It's possible for Jane to choose none of these activities: movies, beach, museum, amusement park. The negated version of each (for example, "not movies") appears in the "results" column, but none of those negated versions is a trigger that forces her to do another of the activities.

Suppose that Jane chooses none of the activities: that is, she doesn't go to the movies, beach, museum, or amusement park. In that case, does she buy a funnel cake? She may or may not.

*Notice that our expert LSAT test taker has kept all of the arrows aligned. That really makes it easier for her to run her eye down the list of triggers to search for additional deductions. You'll want to get into that habit whenever you are working with a set of related conditional statements.

Practice

It's time to get some practice using contrapositives to make all the possible deductions from a set of conditional statements. For each statement below, turn it into shorthand, form the contrapositive, and then make notes about how each one can be combined with other conditional statements in the same set to make deductions. At any time, you can turn the page to see the expert test taker's approach.

Conditional Statements	My Analysis
72. If it is Tuesday, Mary is playing tennis.	
If Mary plays tennis, she is playing with John.	
If Mary does not play tennis, then she buys golf shoes.	
If Mary does not buy golf shoes, then she is in Hawaii.	

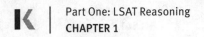

Expert Analysis

Here's the LSAT expert's thorough analysis of the example you just practiced. Compare your work to his by making sure you translated all of the rules and formed all of the contrapositives correctly. Then, compare your list of deductions to those made by the expert.

Conditional Statements		Analysis
72. If it is Tuesday, Mary is playing tennis.	→	If Tuesday → tennis If NOT tennis → NOT Tuesday
If Mary plays tennis, she is playing with John.	→	If tennis → plays with John If NOT play with John → NOT tennis
If Mary does not play tennis, then she buys golf shoes.	→	If NOT tennis → golf shoes If NOT golf shoes → tennis
If Mary does not buy golf shoes, then she is in Hawaii.	→	If NOT golf shoes → in Hawaii If NOT in Hawaii → golf shoes

If we know that...	then we also know that...
if it is Tuesday	Mary plays tennis and John plays tennis with her.
Mary plays tennis	John plays tennis with her.
John plays tennis	We can't deduce anything.
John is not playing tennis	It is not Tuesday, Mary is not playing tennis, and Mary buys golf shoes.
Mary does not play tennis	It is not Tuesday and Mary buys golf shoes.
Mary does not buy golf shoes	Mary plays tennis, John plays tennis with her, and Mary is in Hawaii.
Mary buys golf shoes	We can't deduce anything.
Mary is in Hawaii	We can't deduce anything.

Reflection

Look back over your practice.

- Did you carefully note each If/Then statement in shorthand?
- Did you carefully and correctly make all the contrapositives before trying to combine statements?
- Did you remember that a result doesn't trigger anything?
- Did you miss logical deductions that were available?

Start to pay attention to "chains" of logic that you encounter in the real world. You'll hear them in business meetings at work: "If we are able to cut shipping costs, we'll have additional capital. With additional capital, we can hire another developer. With another developer, the new product line can reach the market before our competitor's product." You might encounter something like this watching a news channel: "Without reductions in spending, programs for education will fail. Without adequate education, our nation's students won't obtain crucial skills for the global marketplace. If we lack talent for companies trying to compete globally, we will need to reform immigration laws." The more you pay attention to this kind of reasoning wherever you might see or hear it, the better you'll be at spotting mistakes and gaps in the logic. These are exactly the skills the LSAT rewards on Test Day.

Making Valid Deductions from Conditional Statements Containing "And" and "Or"

We saw previously in this chapter that the inclusion of *and* or *or* in a conditional statement adds a layer of complexity. We also saw that you have to be careful, when forming the contrapositive of a statement containing *and* or *or*, to exchange those conjunctions consistently and in the right way. This warrants additional practice. In this section, we'll look at how a test taker can make deductions by combining conditional statements that contain conjunctions and get some more practice translating these statements in the bargain.

As a reminder, to make the contrapositive of a conditional statement, do the following:

- Reverse the terms.
- Negate the terms.
- Change *and* to *or* and change *or* to *and* (whenever applicable).

Now, when we first discussed conditional statements with the word *or*, we noted that the word *or* does not express a relationship of mutual exclusivity unless the LSAT explicitly tells you otherwise. As another reminder, here's how to think about these statements in terms of Formal Logic:

Given the statement:

If *x*, then *y* or *z*

we understand it to mean:

If we have *x*, then we have to have at least *y* or *z*, and we might also have both.

Given the statement:

If *a* or *b*, then *c*

we understand it to mean:

Whenever we have *a*, then we have *c*.
Whenever we have *b*, then we have *c*.
Whenever we have both *a* and *b*, then we have *c*.

That's an important point to remember when you're employing conditional statements with *or* to draw further deductions. That's your next task: making logical deductions from sets of conditional statements in which some of the statements contain *and* or *or*.

Review the LSAT expert's thorough analysis of the following set of statements:

Conditional Statements		Analysis	
Thomas can take a road trip only if he fills up his car with gas and gets the oil changed.	→	If road trip	→ gas AND oil change
		If NOT gas OR NOT oil change	→ NOT road trip
If Thomas's friend comes to town, the two will take a road trip to Big Sur.	→	If friend in town	→ road trip
		If NOT road trip	→ NOT friend in town
If Thomas fills up his car with gas, he will also get a car wash or buy snacks.	→	If gas	→ car wash OR snacks
		If NOT car wash AND NOT snacks	→ NOT gas
Thomas cannot get an oil change unless he schedules an appointment to do so.	→	If oil change	→ appointment
		If NOT appointment	→ NOT oil change

If we know that...	then we also know that...
Thomas's friend comes to town	Thomas goes on road trip, changes oil in car, gets gas for car, makes appointment to change oil, and gets a car wash or snacks or both
Thomas does not make an appointment for an oil change	Thomas doesn't get oil change and does not go on road trip. His friend does not come to town We don't know whether he gets gas or not.
Thomas does not get an oil change OR does not fill his car up with gas or both	does not go on a road trip, and friend not in town
Thomas does not get his car washed	We can't deduce anything.
Thomas does not buy any snacks	We can't deduce anything.
Thomas does not get a car wash and also does not get snacks	doesn't get gas, doesn't go on a road trip, and his friend doesn't come to town

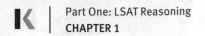

Practice

Now, get some practice translating and contraposing conditional statements containing *and* or *or*.

For each of the following statements, translate it into simple shorthand in the format: If sufficient → necessary. Then, form the contrapositives and take a moment to absorb what each one means. You can turn the page at any time to compare your work to the expert thinking.

Conditional Statements	My Analysis
73. If a white knight slays the green dragon or the purple ogre, he will save the princess.	
74. If Barry drinks his juice, he will become strong and mean.	
75. Jack will not have a lot of friends unless Jill or Jenny dates him.	
76. The flight will depart later than scheduled if the pilot and co-pilot fall asleep.	

Expert Analysis for the Practice exercise may be found on the following page. ▶ ▶ ▶

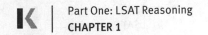
Expert Analysis

Here's how the LSAT expert interpreted the If/Then statements, formed their contrapositive, and drew valid deductions about what was certain, possible, and/or impossible given each one.

Conditional Statements		Analysis
73.	If a white knight slays the green dragon or the purple ogre, he will save the princess.	If slays green dragon OR slays purple ogre → saves the princess If NOT save the princess → NOT slays green dragon AND NOT slays the purple ogre So if he slays just one of the two, he will save the princess. If he slays both, the princess will also be saved. If he doesn't save the princess, neither the dragon nor the ogre will be slain.
74.	If Barry drinks his juice, he will become strong and mean.	If juice → strong AND mean If NOT strong OR NOT mean → NOT juice So if Barry drinks his juice, he becomes both strong and mean. We also know that if Barry becomes neither strong nor mean, he did not drink his juice.
75.	Jack will not have a lot of friends unless Jill or Jenny dates him.	If has a lot of friends → dates Jill OR dates Jenny If NOT date Jill AND NOT date Jenny → NOT a lot of friends So if Jack has a lot of friends, either Jill or Jenny dates him, and possibly both. If neither Jill nor Jenny dates Jack, Jack does not have a lot of friends.
76.	The flight will depart later than scheduled if the pilot and co-pilot fall asleep.	If pilot sleeps AND co-pilot sleeps → flight late If flight NOT late → pilot does NOT sleep OR copilot does NOT sleep So if both the pilot and co-pilot fall asleep, the flight will depart late. If the flight departs on time or even early, at least one of the pilot and copilot did not fall asleep.

Reflection

Look back over your practice.

- Did you carefully make shorthand translations of each statement and contrapositives for each?
- Did you remain clear in your mind about the meaning of *or* in each one?
- Were there logical deductions you missed?

Spot conditional statements in day-to-day life and work through their implications. If you hear someone say something along the lines of "If I forget to call my mom on her birthday, I'll have to send flowers or take her out to dinner next weekend," what does he mean? Treat the statement as a rule. If he's forgetful, could he do both? Sure. If you know this fellow didn't send flowers and didn't take his mother out for dinner, what could you validly deduce? In that case, you'd know that he didn't forget to call.

Making Valid Deductions from Conditional Statements Containing an "Exclusive Or" Provision

So far we've emphasized the fact that *or*, by itself, does not denote a relationship of mutual exclusivity. Put simply, you can have both of the things connected by an *or* unless the LSAT explicitly tells you otherwise, as in the following example from earlier in the chapter:

Conditional Statement		Analysis
If the sous chef makes the soup, she will also make either the salad or the dessert, but not both.	→	(1) The sous chef making the soup is sufficient to tell us that she must also make the salad *or* the dessert.
		(2) The sous chef making the soup also requires that she NOT make both the salad *and* the dessert.

When we first showed this example, we discussed the fact that it's most easily understood when broken into two statements, as the LSAT expert did in the previous example. But now that you've expanded your Formal Logic skills to the point that you're habitually making contrapositives for all conditional statements, it's time to get some practice with contraposing this type of "exclusive or" statement. The simplest way: Break it out into two statements, translate them both into simple shorthand, and contrapose both, like this:

Conditional Statement		Analysis	
If the sous chef makes the soup, she will also make either the salad or the dessert, but not both.	→	If soup	→ salad OR dessert
		If NOT salad AND NOT dessert	→ NOT soup
		If soup	→ NOT [salad/dessert combo]
		If [salad/dessert combo]	→ NOT soup

Notice how the expert test taker, when turning the second part of this statement into shorthand, found a way to express that the *combination* of salad and dessert (rather than salad or dessert separately) was the necessary term. If he'd noted it down like this . . .

> If soup → not salad and dessert

then his automatic contrapositive-making habits might have kicked in, and he might have been tempted to make the contrapositive like this:

> If salad or not dessert → not soup

. . . which is not at all correct. Thus, decide for yourself on a shorthand you'll use whenever a term in a conditional statement is a combination of two things so that you won't get confused and start treating them separately. That shorthand will usually only be necessary in statements like this that have an "exclusive or" clause—that is, with the phrase "but not both" appended to a clause containing *or*. You won't see many of these on the LSAT, but when you do, you'll want to know that you have the logical implications of the statement worked out perfectly.

Clear notation will be your best friend when it comes to combining conditional statements, some of which contain "exclusive or" clauses.

Consider the following demonstration of an LSAT expert's work with a set of If/Thens:

Conditional Statements		Analysis	
If today is a holiday, then Marisol does not work.	$\longrightarrow$	If holiday → NOT work	
		If work → NOT holiday	
If the post office is closed, then today is a holiday.	$\longrightarrow$	If post office closed → holiday	
		If NOT holiday → post office open	
If the post office is open, then Marisol collects her mail.	$\longrightarrow$	If post office open → collects mail	
		If NOT collect mail → post office closed	
If it is not the weekend, Marisol goes to bed early.	$\longrightarrow$	If NOT weekend → bed early	
		If NOT bed early → weekend	
		If NOT holiday → weekend OR post office open	
If today is not a holiday, then it is the weekend or the post office is open, but not both.	$\longrightarrow$	If NOT weekend AND post office closed → holiday	
		If NOT holiday → NOT [both weekend and post office open]	
		If [both weekend and post office open] → holiday	

The final statement contains an "exclusive or." When it is not a holiday, two mutually exclusive possibilities are offered: Either it is the weekend or the post office is open, but both together cannot be true. ["But not both" statements can be broken down into two separate statements, with contrapositives for each.]

Translating these statements and forming the contrapositives allows for further deductions.

For instance, if Marisol does not collect her mail, then the post office is closed. And when the post office is closed, it must be a holiday, and when it's a holiday, Marisol does not work.

What would happen if Marisol were at work? First, it is not a holiday. And when it's not a holiday, the post office is open. But "not a holiday" appears in more than one of our conditional statements. It also triggers the "exclusive or." When it's not a holiday, either it is the weekend or the post office is open, but not both. Because the post office is open, it can't be the weekend. And when it's not the weekend, Marisol collects her mail, and she goes to bed early.

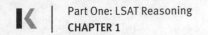
Practice

Here's an opportunity to practice forming contrapositives and making deductions with conditional statements, some of which contain "exclusive or" clauses. Record each of the following statements in If/Then shorthand and form their contrapositives. You can turn the page at any time to check your work.

Conditional Statements	My Analysis
77. When we go to the amusement park, we always ride either the teacups or the Himalayan, but we never ride both.	
78. I've noticed something about life: If you ask, you get what you asked for—but it'll be either at the right time or in the right place but never both at once!	
79. In Professor Smith's class, you'll get an A if you write an extra paper or if you do a presentation in class. Oddly enough, though, if you both write an extra paper and do a presentation, then Smith will think you're just trying to curry favor, and in that case you definitely won't get an A!	
80. If Maria is selected for the team, then Kevin or Charles will be selected but not both. Unless Vivian is selected, Kevin will not be selected. David is not selected for the team if Charles is selected. If Kevin and Charles are both selected for the team, Angela will also be selected.	

Expert Analysis for the Practice exercise may be found on the following page. ▶ ▶ ▶

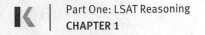

Expert Analysis

Here's how the LSAT expert looked at those two exercises. Compare your work recording the If/Then statements and forming the contrapositives. Check to see if you made all of the available deductions.

	Conditional Statements	Analysis
77.	When we go to the amusement park, we always ride either the teacups or the Himalayan, but we never ride both.	If amusement park → teacups OR Himalayan If NOT teacups AND → NOT amusement park NOT Himalayan If amusement park → NOT [teacups and Himalayan combo] → If [teacups and Himalayan combo] → NOT amusement park [So, if we are somewhere and we have just ridden both a teacups and a Himalayan, then we're somewhere other than the amusement park—the county fair, perhaps?]
78.	I've noticed something about life: If you ask, you get what you asked for—but it'll be either at the right time or in the right place but never both at once!	If ask → right time OR right place If NOT right time AND → NOT ask NOT right place → If ask → NOT [right time and right place combo] If [right time and right place combo] → NOT ask [So, if you get what you want in the right place and at the right time, you must not have asked for it (paradoxically enough).]
79.	In Professor Smith's class, you'll get an A if you write an extra paper or if you do a presentation in class. Oddly enough, though, if you both write an extra paper and do a presentation, then Smith will think you're just trying to curry favor, and in that case you definitely won't get an A!	If extra paper OR → A presentation If NOT A → NOT extra paper AND NOT presentation → If [extra paper and presentation combo] → NOT A If A → NOT [extra paper and presentation combo]

Conditional Statements		Analysis	
80. If Maria is selected for the team, then Kevin or Charles will be selected but not both.	→	If Maria	→ Kevin OR Charles
		If NOT Kevin AND NOT Charles	→ NOT Maria
		If Maria	→ NOT [Kevin and Charles combo]
		If [Kevin and Charles combo]	→ NOT Maria
Unless Vivian is selected, Kevin will not be selected.	→	If Kevin	→ Vivian
		If NOT Vivian	→ NOT Kevin
David is not selected for the team if Charles is selected.	→	If Charles	→ NOT David
		If David	→ NOT Charles
If Kevin and Charles are both selected for the team, Angela will also be selected.	→	If Kevin AND Charles	→ Angela
		If NOT Angela	→ NOT Kevin OR NOT Charles

If we know that...	then we also know that...
Kevin is selected	Vivian is selected There are no further deductions.
Charles is not selected	We can't deduce anything.
Maria is selected	Kevin or Charles is selected, and the other one is not Because we don't know which one is selected, there are no further deductions.
David is selected	Charles is not selected There are no further deductions.
Angela is selected	We can't deduce anything. Angela's being selected is never a trigger.
Kevin and Charles are selected	Maria and David are not selected, and Angela and Vivian are selected

FORMAL LOGIC: NUMERICAL DEDUCTIONS FROM CONDITIONAL STATEMENTS

> ## LEARNING OBJECTIVES
>
> In this section, you'll learn to:
>
> · Determine the valid deductions from a Conditional Statement with the "If X → ~ Y" Structure.
> · Determine the valid deductions from a Conditional Statement with the "If ~ X → Y" Structure.

You've already gotten some practice in making deductions from conditional statements. Now, we're going to devote a section of this chapter to two particular types of deductions because both are very common on the LSAT. You'll find it immensely helpful to be able to think through them quickly and accurately.

Determining the Valid Deduction from a Conditional Statement with the "If X → ~ Y" Structure

This type of conditional is very common on the LSAT:

> If Charlene acts in the play, then Daisy will not act in the play.

The trigger involves something that *does* happen, and the result is that something else *cannot* happen.

In dealing with this, let's put the statement into our standard shorthand and make the contrapositive, just as we always will when we encounter conditional statements:

> If C → ~ D
> If D → ~ C

Now, if you don't push your understanding of the rule beyond that point, you'll still be able to get through the game or Logical Reasoning stimulus . . . slowly. But you can distill the logic further, and doing so will save you from having to write it all out. Take another look at the statement and its contrapositive together. Every time you have either one of these entities acting in the play, you can't have the other one. In other words, you can't ever include both of them in the play. Be very clear, however, that it's possible for neither one to act in the play. They can't be together in the play, but they could both sit in the audience. So, there are three possible outcomes from this statement:

- C in, D out
- D in, C out
- Both C and D out

Thus, if you prefer, instead of writing out the statement and its contrapositive, you could simply note the one result that cannot happen:

> Never C and D in together

Already you've saved yourself some time. But there's another deduction to be drawn here. Before you were given this rule, it may have been possible that all actors available to be in the play are, in fact, *in* the play. This rule, however, has made that impossible. The maximum number of actors who can be in the play is now at least one less than the total pool of actors. This type of rule reduces the acceptable maximum number, which is (always in logic games, sometimes in Logical Reasoning questions) an invaluable deduction.

You'll get to practice making this type of deduction after we cover the other type of rule that commonly affects numbers on the LSAT.

Determining the Valid Deduction from a Conditional Statement with "If ~ X → Y" Structure

We just got to know a common format for a rule in which two things can't go together or can't both happen. That rule always reduces the maximum number of things that can happen. There's a sort of corollary rule that also affects numbers, and it has this structure:

> If Edith doesn't act in the play, then Frank will.

The trigger is something *not* happening, and the result is that something *does* happen.

In dealing with this, let's once again put the statement into standard shorthand and make the contrapositive, just as we always will with conditional statements:

> If ~E → F
> If ~F → E

As before, if you don't push your understanding of this rule beyond that point, you'll still be able to get through the game or Logical Reasoning stimulus. But you can become more efficient in your treatment of this type of rule by noticing something about it right now: The absence of one of the entities requires the presence of the other one—every single time. Thus, one or the other of them must always be included. If either one is left out, then the other one must be in as a consequence. And can they both be in the play? Of course, because you can have the logical results without the triggers.

So we could have . . .

- E out, F in
- F out, E in
- Both E and F in

Thus, if you find it easier, you could skip the Formal Logic translation and note the rule in shorthand with something like this:

> At least one of E or F in the play (maybe both)

Think for a moment about what this rule does to the numbers. Prior to this rule, it may have been possible that we were dealing with an avant garde play in which no one appears on stage and the audience is treated to five minutes of darkness and the sound of rain. Can that happen now? No. This rule establishes a minimum: This play has at least one actor, if not more, who appears. And knowledge of the minimum acceptable number, just like knowledge of the maximum, is priceless when reasoning through LSAT questions.

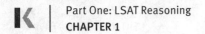
Practice

Here's an opportunity to practice working with conditional statements that affect maxima and minima, as well as everything else you've learned in this chapter.

For each of the following, translate any conditional statements into simple shorthand. You can do this by forming the If/Then and its contrapositive, or you can cut straight to one of the simpler shorthand notes described above, if appropriate. Not all of the statements will fit the two patterns discussed in this section, but part of the object here is to recognize a minimum-increaser or a maximum-reducer when you see it. If there's more than one statement, note down any logical deductions that can be made by combining them. It is possible that some of these statements might not be conditional Formal Logic statements at all. If that's the case, note that no If/Then translation is possible. Expert thinking follows on the page immediately after your practice.

Conditional Statement	My Analysis
81. If Bob gets Gouda at the store, he won't also get Emmenthaler.	
82. Wherever mosquitoes are not prevalent, rates of malaria drop significantly.	
83. If your sophomore students aren't assigned the time-consuming *War and Peace*, they will be assigned both *Anna Karenina* and *Resurrection*.	
84. If I don't get my taxes done by a professional, I will use tax-preparation software.	
85. Sheila can't go to the event if her husband doesn't stay home with the kids.	
86. If you can't say something nice, then just nod and smile.	
87. Paul won't eat anything that has mushrooms or mayonnaise.	
88. No one who really cares would ever just give to a charity without understanding how the charity operates.	

Conditional Statement	My Analysis
89. If Bob can't find Gouda at the store, then he'll get Edam instead. If he can't get Gouda and can't get Edam, then he will yell at the guy at the cheese counter.	
90. Soup that doesn't taste spicy needs a lot of salt.	
91. We can reopen the unused factory unless it's either sitting on a fault line or is contaminated with mercury.	
92. We ought to go to the memorial service.	
93. Whenever I am in Paris, I see lights reflected in the Seine and I can't get a decent taco!	
94. Mary does a great improvised barbeque, but she can cook indoors only if you give her a very specific recipe.	
95. No one who wants to be a doctor should set a bad example by smoking.	
96. Don't bother getting eggs at the store unless you also get butter in which to cook them. Don't get margarine unless they're out of butter or the butter is more than $4.	
97. The X organization won't support a bill if the Y organization is backing it. The Y organization refuses to support anything backed by the Z organization.	
98. I never believe what I read in the *Menda City Daily News*.	
99. I will make the phone call if, but only if, I can find my cell phone.	

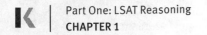

Expert Analysis

Here's how an LSAT expert would diagram each of the statements you just worked with. In some cases, the expert has added an additional comment to remind you of easily overlooked exceptions to or implications of these statements.

Conditional Statement	Analysis
81. If Bob gets Gouda at the store, he won't also get Emmenthaler.	→ If G → NOT E If E → NOT G OR Never both G and E
82. Wherever mosquitoes are not prevalent, rates of malaria drop significantly.	→ If mosquitoes NOT prevalent → malaria rates sig. drop If malaria rates NOT sig. drop → mosquitoes prevalent OR [always] either malaria rates sig. drop or mosquitoes are prevalent, or both
83. If your sophomore students aren't assigned the time-consuming *War and Peace*, they will be assigned both *Anna Karenina* and *Resurrection*.	→ If NOT WP → AK AND R If NOT AK OR NOT R → WP OR [always] Either WP or [AK and R combo] Note: Students could be assigned *War and Peace* and one of the other two books, or they could be assigned all three. The triggers in the original statement and its contrapositive are all negative statements, so there's no way to determine what happens if they *are* assigned one or more of these books. Another helpful way to translate this statement would be to break it down into smaller pieces: If ~WP → AK If ~AK → WP If ~WP → R If ~R → WP Notice how that translation covers all of the triggers and results in the statement.

Conditional Statement	**Analysis**
84. If I don't get my taxes done by a professional, I will use tax-preparation software.	If NOT pro → software If NOT software → pro OR [I will use] Either a professional or software or both
85. Sheila can't go to the event if her husband doesn't stay home with the kids.	If husband NOT home → Sheila NOT at event If Sheila at event → husband home [Remember: It is possible for Sheila's husband to stay home and for her not to go to the event.]
86. If you can't say something nice, then just nod and smile.	If NOT say something nice → nod AND smile If NOT nod OR NOT smile → say something nice [always] Either say something nice or [nod and smile combo] Note: A person could say something nice and do one of the other two gestures, or they could do all three. The triggers in the original statement and its contrapositive are all negative statements, so there's no way to determine what happens if they *do* say something nice or if they *do* nod or smile. Another helpful way to translate this statement would be to break it down into smaller pieces: If ~say something nice → nod If ~nod → say something nice If ~say something nice → smile If ~smile → say something nice Notice how that translation covers all of the triggers and results in the statement.
87. Paul won't eat anything that has mushrooms or mayonnaise.	If mushrooms OR mayo → Paul NOT eat If Paul eat → NOT mushrooms AND NOT mayo
88. No one who really cares would ever just give to a charity without understanding how the charity operates.	If really cares → does NOT give without understanding If gives without understanding → does NOT really care [Remember: You can't have "really cares" and "gives without understanding" at the same time (that is, in the same individual).]

Conditional Statement	Analysis
89. If Bob can't find Gouda at the store, then he'll get Edam instead. If he can't get Gouda and can't get Edam, then he will yell at the guy at the cheese counter.	If NOT G → E If NOT E → G [that is:] Either E or G or both at all times If NOT G AND NOT E → yell If NOT yell → G OR E [If the first rule is obeyed, the second one will never be triggered. Note that it's possible for Bob to buy Gouda or Edam or both and still yell at the guy at the cheese counter without violating these rules.]
90. Soup that doesn't taste spicy needs a lot of salt.	If NOT spicy → salt If NOT salt → spicy [Soup must always be either salty or spicy *or both* by the conditions of this rule.]
91. We can reopen the unused factory unless it's either sitting on a fault line or is contaminated with mercury.	If can NOT reopen → fault line OR mercury If NOT fault line AND → can reopen NOT mercury [Either we can reopen the factory, or it is sitting on a fault line, or it has mercury. Remember, though, that it is possible for the factory to sit on a fault line and be contaminated with mercury and still be reopened. "Can reopen" is not a trigger in this rule. Sitting on a fault line or mercury contamination are necessary to the factory's remaining closed. Their absence is not required for its reopening.]
92. We ought to go to the memorial service.	Not a conditional; no translation. This is a statement of opinion.
93. Whenever I am in Paris, I see lights reflected in the Seine and I can't get a decent taco!	If Paris → see lights AND can't-get-taco If NOT see lights OR NOT can't-get-taco (can-get-taco) → NOT Paris
94. Mary does a great improvised barbeque, but she can cook indoors only if you give her a very specific recipe.	[First clause is not a conditional. Second clause translates:] If can cook indoors → give specific recipe If NOT give specific recipe → can NOT cook indoors
95. No one who wants to be a doctor should set a bad example by smoking.	If want to be doctor → should NOT smoke If smoke → NOT want to be doctor

Conditional Statement	Analysis
96. Don't bother getting eggs at the store unless you also get butter in which to cook them. Don't get margarine unless they're out of butter or the butter is more than $4.	If eggs $\rightarrow$ butter If NOT butter $\rightarrow$ NOT eggs If margarine $\rightarrow$ NOT butter OR butter = $4+ If butter AND NOT butter = $4+ $\rightarrow$ NOT margarine That is, if the store has butter *and* it's not $4 or more, then don't get margarine. [Consider the following: —If I get eggs at the store, then I bought butter. Did I also buy margarine? If I paid $4 or less for the butter, then I did not buy margarine. If I paid more than $4 for the butter, then maybe I did buy margarine, but I don't know for sure. —If they have butter for $3, I could buy it, but I don't know that I do. I also don't know whether I buy eggs, though I do know I don't buy margarine.]
97. The X organization won't support a bill if the Y organization is backing it. The Y organization refuses to support anything backed by the Z organization.	If Y supports $\rightarrow$ X NOT support If X supports $\rightarrow$ Y NOT support That is, X and Y never support the same bill. If Z supports $\rightarrow$ Y NOT support If Y supports $\rightarrow$ Z NOT support That is, Y and Z never support the same bill. [Deductions: • If Y supports a bill, both X and Z will refuse to support it. • If Z supports a bill, Y will not support it, but we don't know about X. • If X supports a bill, Y will not also support it, but we don't know about Z. • At any time, all three could oppose the same bill.]

Conditional Statement	Analysis
98. I never believe what I read in the *Menda City Daily News*.	If read in MCDN → NOT believe If believe → NOT read in MCDN → OR An item can never be both printed in MCDN and believed by me
99. I will make the phone call if, but only if, I can find my cell phone.	If make the phone call → can find my cell phone If can NOT find my cell phone → will NOT make the phone call → If can find my cell phone → make the phone call If NOT make the phone call → can NOT find my cell phone [Deduction: Either both events will happen or neither will.]

Reflection

Look back over your practice.

- Did you take the time to understand each conditional statement before noting it down in shorthand?
- If you couldn't immediately see how to write it down in one sentence, did you make the If/Then and its contrapositive? (If so, that's great!)
- Did you tend to get confused about the side of the arrow on which *not* should appear?
- Did you remember that you can have the result without the trigger in each case?

Now, take a moment to look back over all of Chapter 1. You may not have even been thinking about it, but you've successfully employed a great many essential LSAT skills, skills you'll continue to use in law school and in the practice of law. Now that you've built this foundation, you're ready to tackle a range of LSAT material. Chapters 2–7 will take you through the Method and strategies for the Logic Games section. Chapters 8–12 cover the Method and strategies for the Logical Reasoning sections. Finally, Chapters 13–16 outline what you need to know to master Reading Comprehension. You may be tackling any of those sections in the next part of your practice. Regardless, we strongly encourage you to return to Chapter 1 whenever you feel you need a refresher about these critical thinking and Formal Logic fundamentals that form the heart of LSAT reasoning.

Logic Games

CHAPTER 2

The Kaplan Logic Games Method

Every administration of the LSAT features one scored Logic Games section. There are always four games with a total of 22–24 questions. If you've taken an LSAT, you may well have considered Logic Games to be the hardest or most confusing section on the test, as do a majority of test takers the first time they see the exam. Each game has a number of "moving parts" that can, in theory, be arranged in dozens or even hundreds of ways. While that may seem daunting, the method and strategies you'll learn in this chapter will allow you to treat games as concrete, solvable puzzles. In fact, once you have internalized the strategies introduced here, you may find yourself making a greater improvement in Logic Games than in any other section of the test. By Test Day, it's not uncommon for students to describe games and the thinking they entail as fun, or for students to identify this as their favorite LSAT section.

If you've done the work in Chapter 1, LSAT Reasoning, then much of what the Logic Games section rewards will already be familiar. Take a look at a typical LSAT Logic Games question.

---

4. Which one of the following must be true?

    (A)   Either K or else L is assigned to position 2.
    (B)   Either K or else L is assigned to position 4.
    (C)   Either M or else N is assigned to position 2.
    (D)   Either M or else N is assigned to position 5.
    (E)   Either M or else O is assigned to position 6.

PrepTest28 Sec2 Q4

We'll give you the context you need to answer this question in a moment. First, though, notice the question stem. It asks you about the level of certainty, in this case, about what "must be true." You can see that logic games target the LSAT's core reasoning skills, asking you what must, could, or cannot be true given a set of conditions, restrictions, and limitations. Many logic games questions even begin by providing an additional condition, for example, "If L is assigned to position 4, then which of the following could be false?" In other words, they're telling you that assigning L to position 4 is sufficient to know that four answer choices must be true while one answer choice could be false.

Now take a look at the game and its questions on the next page. There, you'll see question 4 in context as part of a set of questions related to the short scenario at the beginning of the game. For the LSAT expert, the questions are simply applications of the limitations, rules, and restrictions described in the opening scenario. An important and encouraging note to remember is that the opening setup—even when it seems complex and abstract—always gives you everything you need to answer all of the questions.

Analysis: This paragraph sets out the task. It defines the players or entities to account for, tells the test taker what to do with them—put the entities in order, group them, select some and reject others, or assign them certain attributes—and provides the rules and restrictions on how the entities can be arranged. This "setup" always contains all of the information needed to answer every question.

Questions 1–5

Six racehorses—K, L, M, N, O, and P—will be assigned to six positions arranged in a straight line and numbered consecutively 1 through 6. The horses are assigned to the positions, one horse per position, according to the following conditions:

K and L must be assigned to positions that are separated froin each other by exactly one position.
K and N cannot be assigned to positions that are next to each other.
N must be assigned to a higher-numbered position than M.
P must be assigned to position 3.

1. Which one of the following lists an acceptable assignment of horses to positions 1 through 6, respectively?

   (A)   K, L, P, M, N, O
   (B)   M, K, P, L, N, O
   (C)   M, N, K, P, L, O
   (D)   N, O, P, K, M, L
   (E)   O, M, P, L, N, K

2. Which one of the following is a complete and accurate list of the positions any one of which can be the position to which K is assigned?

   (A)   1, 2
   (B)   2, 3
   (C)   2, 4
   (D)   2, 4, 5
   (E)   2, 4, 6

3. Which one of the following CANNOT be true?

   (A)   K is assigned to position 2.
   (B)   L is assigned to position 2.
   (C)   M is assigned to position 1.
   (D)   M is assigned to position 5.
   (E)   O is assigned to position 2.

4. Which one of the following must be true?

   (A)   Either K or else L is assigned to position 2.
   (B)   Either K or else L is assigned to position 4.
   (C)   Either M or else N is assigned to position 2.
   (D)   Either M or else N is assigned to position 5.
   (E)   Either M or else O is assigned to position 6.

5. Which one of the following CANNOT be true?

   (A)   L and N are assigned to positions that are next to each other.
   (B)   M and K are assigned to positions that are next to each other.
   (C)   M and O are assigned to positions that are next to each other.
   (D)   L and N are assigned to positions that are separated from each other by exactly one position.
   (E)   M and P are assigned to positions that are separated from each other by exactly one position.

PrepTest 28 Sec2 Qs 1–5

Analysis: In one way or another, all of the questions reward an understanding of what is and is not possible given the game's action and restrictions—the differences between what must be true and what could be false, or between what must be false and what could be true. The first question here asks for an acceptable sequence of the game's entities. The second question asks for a list of positions that are acceptable for one of the entities. The remainder can be answered with the information in the game's "setup," the information and rules in the game's opening paragraph.

Try out this game on your own. The remainder of the chapter will use it to illustrate the Kaplan Method for Logic Games. As you work through the chapter, you'll learn how an LSAT expert uses the method to manage all logic games.

THE KAPLAN METHOD FOR LOGIC GAMES

Let's not be shy about saying that logic games are challenging and some are downright hard. On Test Day, you have about 8½ minutes to process each game's task, sketch it out and account for all of its rules and restrictions, and then answer anywhere from five to seven questions. This chapter will lay out an efficient method for approaching any game you encounter on the LSAT. Learning and practicing this method will make you efficient with your time as you manage all of the game's information and effective at applying that information to correctly answer the questions.

THE KAPLAN LOGIC GAMES METHOD

Step 1: Overview

Step 2: Sketch

Step 3: Rules

Step 4: Deductions

Step 5: Questions

In subsequent chapters, we'll go into more detail on these steps and the skills associated with them. For now, let's see how an LSAT expert would apply this method to the game about the racehorses. As we go along, you'll learn what each step of the method entails and how this will allow you to approach games of varying types and difficulty levels in the same consistent, repeatable way.

Step 1: Overview

Before you can accomplish anything in an LSAT logic game, you have to understand your task. Fortunately, the testmaker describes game scenarios as small, well-defined, real-world jobs; you may have to make a schedule of appointments, assign athletes to teams, match different costume elements to different actors in a play, or choose some items from a catering menu while rejecting others. In any event, you need to invest the first few seconds of tackling any logic game in clearly understanding your task. Doing so will allow you to make a useful, accurate sketch in which to record the specific details of the rules and restrictions set out.

LSAT Question		Analysis
Six racehorses—K, L, M, N, O, and P—will be assigned to six positions arranged in a straight line and numbered consecutively 1 through 6. The horses are assigned to the positions, one horse per position, according to the following conditions: *PrepTest28 Sec2 Qs 1–5*	$\rightarrow$	Task: Figure out which position each race horse will take. This is a Sequencing task, figuring out the order in which the horses are arranged, one horse per position.

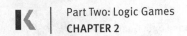

Asking four questions as you conduct your overview of the game's first paragraph will ensure that you always extract the relevant information. We'll refer to them as the SEAL questions.

STEP 1: OVERVIEW—THE SEAL QUESTIONS

Situation—What is the real-world scenario being described? What is the deliverable information—an ordered list, a calendar, a chart showing what's matched up?

Entities—Who or what are the "moving parts," the people or things I'm distributing, selecting, sequencing, or matching?

Action—What is the specific action—distribution, selection, sequencing, matching, or a combination of those—that I'm performing on the entities?

Limitations—Does the game state parameters (e.g., select four of seven, sequence the entities one per day, and so on) that restrict how I'll set up and sketch the game?

Asking those questions of the game's opening paragraph should give you a clear mental picture of your task. Notice that, in the Racehorses game, the LSAT expert even noticed that the horses are assigned one-per-position. There are no "ties" in this game, although there could be in others. In the next chapter, you'll see games representing all of the common LSAT logic games actions, and you'll refine your skill at spotting the features that help you account for what is similar and what is unique among various examples of those game types.

Step 2: Sketch

Just as important as your internal visualization of a game's task is the actual physical picture of the game you draw on the page: your sketch. Logic games are almost impossible if you try to keep all of the information in your head. By depicting the game's setup and rules, an LSAT expert is able to quickly and confidently understand a game's parameters. The ideal sketch provides a framework that captures the scenario in a clear, simple way and provides spaces in which you can record the more specific and detailed rules of the game.

LSAT Question	Analysis
Six racehorses—K, L, M, N, O, and P—will be assigned to six positions arranged in a straight line and numbered consecutively 1 through 6. The horses are assigned to the positions, one horse per position, according to the following conditions: *PrepTest28 Sec2 Qs 1–5*	K L M N O P → $\overline{}$ $\overline{}$ $\overline{}$ $\overline{}$ $\overline{}$ $\overline{}$ 1 2 3 4 5 6

Here you see how the LSAT expert has turned her understanding of the Racehorses game's Sequencing task into a simple, effective sketch. As she determines the position to which a horse is assigned, she can record that information in the appropriate slot. It is always a good idea to list out the entities above your sketch framework so that you can catalog which entities are or aren't restricted without having to go back and read the opening paragraph again and again. In the next chapter, you'll be turning your overviews of several games into effective sketches. You'll soon see that certain actions produce similar sketches time after time, resulting in some time-saving patterns. Don't ever become complacent about sketching, however. A useful sketch must reflect the game's task, and sometimes you'll need to render unique twists or variations on standard sketch patterns.

Step 3: Rules

Once you have the basic framework for your sketch, you're ready to record the game's rules. The rules are always listed under the game's opening paragraph, and they're indented in the test booklet so that they're easy to distinguish from the overall setup.

Whenever possible, build a rule directly into the framework of your sketch. When a rule is not specific enough to designate the precise spaces or boxes in which to place the entities, write the rule in shorthand just below or to the side of the sketch. Try to make your shorthand clear and comprehensible, using the same vocabulary of symbols you used to create the sketch framework.

LSAT Question	Analysis

Six racehorses—K, L, M, N, O, and P—will be assigned to six positions arranged in a straight line and numbered consecutively 1 through 6. The horses are assigned to the positions, one horse per position, according to the following conditions:
 	
    K and L must be assigned to positions that are separated from each other by exactly one position.
    K and N cannot be assigned to positions that are next to each other.
    N must be assigned to a higher-numbered position than M.
    P must be assigned to position 3.
 	
<div align="center">*PrepTest28 Sec2 Qs 1–5*</div>
	$\overset{?}{K\ L\ M\ N\ O\ P}$
	
	$\rightarrow$ $\quad$ $\overline{1}\ \ \overline{2}\ \ \overset{P}{\overline{3}}\ \ \overline{4}\ \ \overline{5}\ \ \overline{6}$
	$\quad\quad$ ~N $\quad\quad\quad\quad\quad$ ~M
	
	$\quad\quad$ $\underline{K/L}\ \underline{\ \ }\ \underline{L/K}$ $\quad\quad$ M . . . N
	
	$\quad\quad$ ~KN $\quad$ ~NK

As you depict the rules, pay careful attention to what each rule determines and what it leaves open. Note how the expert drew Rule 3 in the Racehorses game, using ellipses to show that M and N must conform to the defined sequence but leaving open the possibility that M and N may be consecutive, or may be separated by one or more spaces. The expert also depicted the negative implications of that rule: N can never be placed in position 1, and M can never take position 6. Note too that the expert was able to draw Rule 4 right into the sketch framework. Not all rules can be written right into the sketch, but when they can, do so; it makes the rule clear and easy to read. Note, too, that the expert jotted down a question mark above "O" in the list of entities. Here, O is a "floater," an entity not restricted by any rule or limitation. It is almost always valuable to label any floaters among your entities because they can take any open position.

LSAT STRATEGY

Don't make assumptions in logic games. Any restrictions must be stated.

The first two rules in the Racehorses game are perfect illustrations. While they restrict the distances between two entities, they say nothing about the order in which those entities are sequenced. You know that K and L will always have one space between them, but you don't know which comes earlier or later. Likewise, the block K-N and the block N-K are both forbidden. Take nothing for granted in logic games.

In Chapter 4, you'll have the opportunity to sketch out the rules from games representing each of the common LSAT game types. You'll also have the chance to do drills for further practice.

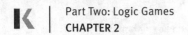
Step 4: Deductions

This is the step that the majority of untrained or poorly trained LSAT test takers miss. Even students who instinctively appreciate the value of creating a sketch and of symbolizing the rules often don't take the time to determine what must be true or must be false beyond what the rules explicitly state. In most games, however, it is possible to combine the rules with each other or to combine rules with the game's overall limitations in a way that produces a lot more certainty when you go to tackle the questions. It is always highly advantageous—in terms of both speed and accuracy—to make all of the available deductions before moving on to the questions.

In Chapter 4, you'll learn to spot the rules that produce the greatest restrictions within the game. It is not uncommon for a game's initial setup to allow for hundreds (or even thousands) of permutations. After you apply all of the rules, however, there are sometimes only a dozen (or even fewer) permutations that remain acceptable. The more of those restrictions you can see, the easier the game will be for you to work out. By starting from the most concrete rules and seeing how those interact with other rules to further limit the acceptable arrangements within the game, you can produce a final sketch that reveals everything that is determined in the game and shows just how much or how little remains to be locked down.

LSAT Question	Analysis
Six racehorses—K, L, M, N, O, and P—will be assigned to six positions arranged in a straight line and numbered consecutively 1 through 6. The horses are assigned to the positions, one horse per position, according to the following conditions:	? K L M N O P
K and L must be assigned to positions that are separated from each other by exactly one position. K and N cannot be assigned to positions that are next to each other. N must be assigned to a higher-numbered position than M. P must be assigned to position 3.	$\rightarrow$ $\dfrac{\quad}{1}$ $\dfrac{\quad}{2}$ $\dfrac{P}{3}$ $\dfrac{\quad}{4}$ $\dfrac{\quad}{5}$ $\dfrac{\quad}{6}$ ~N ~M $\underline{K/L}$ $\underline{\quad}$ $\underline{L/K}$ M . . . N ~KN ~NK
PrepTest28 Sec2 Qs 1–5	

Deductions

Rule 4 establishes P in position 3. Thus, Rule 1 can only be obeyed by placing K and L in positions 2 and 4, or in positions 4 and 6. (Neither K nor L could take positions 1 or 5 because the other would have to take position 3, which is already filled by horse P.)

(I) $\dfrac{\quad}{1}$ $\dfrac{K/L}{2}$ $\dfrac{P}{3}$ $\dfrac{L/K}{4}$ $\dfrac{\quad}{5}$ $\dfrac{\quad}{6}$
    ~N   ~M

(II) $\dfrac{\quad}{1}$ $\dfrac{\quad}{2}$ $\dfrac{P}{3}$ $\dfrac{K/L}{4}$ $\dfrac{\quad}{5}$ $\dfrac{L/K}{6}$
    ~N   ~M

Deductions (cont.)

In Option I, M, N, and O can be arranged in three ways—1) M in 1, N in 5, O in 6; 2) M in 1, O in 5, N in 6; 3) O in 1; M in 5; N in 6—too many ways to write out all of them.

In Option II, however, Rule 2 prevents N from taking position 5 (which would place N next to K), so N's only acceptable placement is position 2. Rule 3, therefore, dictates that M must take position 1 in this option. That means O (the only remaining entity) must take position 5.

$$\text{(II)} \quad \frac{M}{1} \quad \frac{N}{2} \quad \frac{P}{3} \quad \frac{K/L}{4} \quad \frac{O}{5} \quad \frac{L/K}{6}$$

Making all of the available deductions in a game without spending time chasing down dead ends or making unwarranted speculations is a subtle, but enormously important, skill to master. It takes time and practice to perfect, but once you do, you'll be well on your way to mastery of Logic Games.

Fortunately, just five kinds of restrictions produce the lion's share of available deductions in logic games. They're easy to remember with the mnemonic BLEND.

STEP 4: DEDUCTIONS

Blocks of Entities—two or more players who are always grouped together

Limited Options—rules or restrictions that limit the overall setup to one of two acceptable arrangements

Established Entities—a player locked into a specific space or group

Number Restrictions—rules or limitations that provide guidance about the number of entities assigned to a group or space

Duplications—entities that appear in two or more rules and allow the rules to be combined

You'll focus on Deductions in Chapter 4, but it's important to note that BLEND is a checklist, not a series of steps. You don't look for Blocks of Entities first necessarily, and not every game will have all of these types of rules or restrictions. Think of it as a way to make sure no available deductions slip through your fingers. The end result of Step 4 is a Master Sketch containing all of the rules, restrictions, and deductions.

Step 5: Questions

The purpose of the first four steps is to answer the game's questions quickly and accurately. You'll have about 8½ minutes per game on Test Day. To get to all of the questions in that short amount of time, the LSAT expert leverages her Master Sketch to save time. Don't be surprised if you spend three or four minutes setting up the game. You'll find that answering the questions can be a quick and confident exercise once you have an adequate Master Sketch.

Here's how the LSAT expert manages the questions from the Racehorses game.

LSAT Question	Analysis
Six racehorses—K, L, M, N, O, and P—will be assigned to six positions arranged in a straight line and numbered consecutively 1 through 6. The horses are assigned to the positions, one horse per position, according to the following conditions: K and L must be assigned to positions that are separated from each other by exactly one position. K and N cannot be assigned to positions that are next to each other. N must be assigned to a higher-numbered position than M. P must be assigned to position 3.	**?** K L M N O P (I) $\frac{}{1}$ $\frac{K/L}{2}$ $\frac{P}{3}$ $\frac{L/K}{4}$ $\frac{}{5}$ $\frac{}{6}$ ~NK ~KN ~N ~M M . . . N (II) $\frac{M}{1}$ $\frac{N}{2}$ $\frac{P}{3}$ $\frac{K/L}{4}$ $\frac{O}{5}$ $\frac{L/K}{6}$

1.	Which one of the following lists an acceptable assignment of horses to positions 1 though 6, respectively?	The correct answer is "acceptable"; each wrong answer violates a rule.
(A)	K, L, P, M, N, O	Violates Rule 1 by not having one position separating K and L from each other. Eliminate.
(B)	M, K, P, L, N, O	Correct. This one abides by all of the rules, and conforms to Option I in the Master Sketch.
(C)	M, N, K, P, L, O	Violates Rule 4 by placing P in position 4. Eliminate.
(D)	N, O, P, K, M, L	Violates Rule 3 by placing N in a lower-numbered position than M. Eliminate.
(E)	O, M, P, L, N, K	Violates Rule 2 by placing K and N in positions that are next to each other. Eliminate.

PrepTest28 Sec2 Q1

Almost every logic game has one of these Acceptability questions, asking for an answer choice that could be an accurate placement of all the entities. The LSAT expert simply checks each rule against the answer choices. This particular Acceptability question exhibits a very common pattern: Each of the four rules eliminates one of the wrong answer choices. You'll become fast and confident in dealing with Acceptability questions by using the rules to eliminate violators.

LSAT Question	Analysis

2. Which one of the following is a complete and accurate list of the positions any one of which can be the position to which K is assigned?

The correct answer will list ANY and ALL positions to which horse K may be assigned.

$$\overset{?}{K\ L\ M\ N\ O\ P}$$

→ (I)

$$\underset{\sim N}{\underset{1}{\quad}}\ \underset{2}{\overset{K/L}{\quad}}\ \underset{3}{\overset{P}{\quad}}\ \underset{4}{\overset{L/K}{\quad}}\ \underset{5}{\quad}\ \underset{\sim M}{\underset{6}{\quad}}$$

~NK   ~KN

M . . . N

(II)

$$\underset{1}{\overset{M}{\quad}}\ \underset{2}{\overset{N}{\quad}}\ \underset{3}{\overset{P}{\quad}}\ \underset{4}{\overset{K/L}{\quad}}\ \underset{5}{\overset{O}{\quad}}\ \underset{6}{\overset{L/K}{\quad}}$$

(A) 1, 2

→ Inaccurate: K cannot be assigned to position 1. Incomplete: K can be assigned positions 4 and 6. Eliminate.

(B) 2, 3

→ Inaccurate: K cannot be assigned to position 3. Incomplete: K can be assigned to positions 4 and 6. Eliminate.

(C) 2, 4

→ Incomplete: K can be assigned to position 6. Eliminate.

(D) 2, 4, 5

→ Inaccurate: K cannot be assigned to position 5. Incomplete: K can be assigned to position 6. Eliminate.

(E) 2, 4, 6

PrepTest28 Sec2 Q2

→ Correct. K can acceptably be assigned to position 2, 4, or 6.

Most games offer one or two questions that directly reward you for making the available deductions. Seeing how Rules 1 and 4 combine to restrict the placement of K and L to positions 2 and 4, or to positions 4 or 6 makes this one a snap. Always remember that rules and restrictions are your greatest allies in logic games; after all, the test wants to know what must, cannot, or could be true.

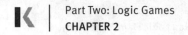

LSAT Question	Analysis
3. Which one of the following CANNOT be true?	The correct answer must be false given the game's rules and restrictions. Each of the four wrong answers could be true.

$$\overset{?}{K\ L\ M\ N\ O\ P}$$

(I)

	K/L	P	L/K			~NK ~KN
1	2	3	4	5	6	M . . . N
~N					~M	

(II)

M	N	P	K/L	O	L/K
1	2	3	4	5	6

(A) K is assigned to position 2.	→	Could be true; see Option I. Eliminate.
(B) L is assigned to position 2.	→	Could be true; see Option I. Eliminate.
(C) M is assigned to position 1.	→	This could be true in either option. Eliminate.
(D) M is assigned to position 5.	→	Could be true; see Option I. Eliminate.
(E) O is assigned to position 2. *PrepTest28 Sec2 Q3*	→	Correct. In Option I, either K or L takes position 2. In Option II, N takes position 2. O can never be assigned to position 2.

Note how the LSAT expert refers to the Master Sketch to quickly and accurately assess whether the statement in each answer choice must, could, or cannot be true. An alternate strategy that some experts employ is to refer to previous work. Because the LSAT expert knows that answer choice (B) in Question 1 lists an acceptable arrangement of horses to positions, she could quickly eliminate answer choices (A) and (C) in this question. Both contain statements that clearly "could be true" given the correct answer to Question 1.

LSAT Question	**Analysis**
4. Which one of the following must be true?	The correct answer must be true under this game's rules and restrictions. Each of the four wrong answers could be false.

$$\overset{?}{K\ L\ M\ N\ O\ P}$$

$\longrightarrow$ (I) $\dfrac{}{1}\ \dfrac{K/L}{2}\ \dfrac{P}{3}\ \dfrac{L/K}{4}\ \dfrac{}{5}\ \dfrac{}{6}$ ~NK ~KN

$\quad\quad$ ~N $\quad\quad\quad\quad\quad\quad$ ~M   M . . . N

(II) $\dfrac{M}{1}\ \dfrac{N}{2}\ \dfrac{P}{3}\ \dfrac{K/L}{4}\ \dfrac{O}{5}\ \dfrac{L/K}{6}$

(A) Either K or else L is assigned to position 2.	$\longrightarrow$ Could be false; see Option II. Eliminate.
(B) Either K or else L is assigned to position 4.	$\longrightarrow$ Correct. In either option, one of K or L must take position 4.
(C) Either M or else N is assigned to position 2.	$\longrightarrow$ Could be false; see Option I. Eliminate.
(D) Either M or else N is assigned to position 5.	$\longrightarrow$ Could be false; see Option II. Eliminate.
(E) Either M or else O is assigned to position 6.	$\longrightarrow$ Could be false; see Option II. Eliminate.

PrepTest28 Sec2 Q4

When a game breaks down into just two options as this one does, the correct answer to a "must be true" question must contain a statement that is completely and unequivocally determined in both options. Note that each of the wrong answers could be false in at least one of the options.

LSAT Question	Analysis
5. Which one of the following CANNOT be true?	The correct answer must be false given the game's rules and restrictions. Each of the four wrong answers could be true.

$$\overset{?}{K\ L\ M\ N\ O\ P}$$

(I)

	K/L	P	L/K			~NK ~KN
1	2	3	4	5	6	M . . . N
~N					~M	

(II)

M	N	P	K/L	O	L/K
1	2	3	4	5	6

(A) L and N are assigned to positions that are next to each other.	Could be true; see Option I, in which L could be in position 4 and N could be in position 5. Eliminate.
(B) M and K are assigned to positions that are next to each other.	Could be true; see Option I, in which M could be in position 1 with K in position 2, or M could be in position 5 with K in position 4. Eliminate.
(C) M and O are assigned to positions that are next to each other.	Correct. In Option II, M takes position 1 and O takes position 5. In Option I, if M is in position 1, then O takes either position 5 or position 6. If M takes position 5 in Option 1, then O must take position 1. In either option, the statement in this answer choice must be false.
(D) L and N are assigned to positions that are separated from each other by exactly one position.	Could be true; see Option I, in which L could take position 4 with N in position 6, or Option II, in which N could take position 2 with L in position 4. Eliminate.
(E) M and P are assigned to positions that are separated from each other by exactly one position.	Could be true in either option—P is always in position 3, and M can be in position 1. Eliminate.

PrepTest28 Sec2 Q5

LSAT experts always characterize the one correct and the four wrong answers before evaluating the choices. Here, the correct answer must be false ("CANNOT be true"), which means that all four wrong answers could be true. A statement that is acceptable in even one of the game's options could be true, and is, thus, a wrong answer.

REFLECTION

Now that you've seen the Logic Games Method, take a few minutes to reflect on the following questions.

- Did any part of the Logic Games Method surprise you?
- Are there specific steps in the Logic Games Method that excite you?
- Were any of the steps confusing? How will you get additional practice with those steps?
- How will you approach Logic Games differently the next time you practice them?
- What techniques did you see applied to the game in this chapter that you can immediately put to use the next time you practice Logic Games?

As you practice Logic Games further, review the explanations thoroughly. The explanations will cover each step in the Logic Games Method and help make clear how every game can be done most efficiently and effectively.

The remaining chapters of this section will delve deeper into the steps of the Logic Games Method and apply it to all of the game types that regularly appear on the LSAT.

- Chapter 3 covers Steps 1 and 2—Overview and Sketch.
- Chapter 4 takes you deeper into Steps 3 and 4—Rules and Deductions.
- Chapter 5 examines Step 5—Questions.
- Chapter 6 contains additional Logic Games for further practice.
- Chapter 7 introduces expert strategies for timing and section management in Logic Games.

Logic Games: Overviews, Sketches, and Game Types

In the last chapter, you saw a demonstration of how an expert LSAT test taker tackles an entire logic game. But before you're ready to do the same, you need to learn more about each step of the Logic Games Method. Your approach to games should be methodical, consistent, and carefully analytical. As you observed the LSAT expert doing in the last chapter, you'll tackle each piece of information in the game individually before bringing them together into a coherent picture complete with all possible deductions.

LEARNING OBJECTIVES

In this chapter, you'll learn to:

- Characterize a game's action and limitations given various game setups.
- Create a valid sketch based on a game's action and limitations.

These two learning objectives correspond to Steps 1 and 2 of the Kaplan Method for Logic Games. This chapter will define and demonstrate those two steps. But this chapter serves another function as well: Because a game can be usefully identified as being one of a certain *type* based on information you glean from the game in Step 1, and because different *types* of games are best served by different types of sketches, we'll teach you how to catalog the various types of games. (Don't worry—there are only a few!)

Thus, this chapter has four components:

First, we'll learn more about Step 1 of the Kaplan Method for Logic Games, and we'll see it applied to a real LSAT game.

Second, we'll discuss Step 2 and its application to the same logic game.

Third, we'll demonstrate the various types of logic games, discuss how to identify them, and apply Steps 1 and 2 of the Logic Games Method to all those game types using examples from real LSATs.

Fourth, you'll get some practice working through Steps 1 and 2 in several drills.

STEP 1 OF THE LOGIC GAMES METHOD: WORKING WITH GAME OVERVIEWS

You saw in the last chapter that a well-developed logic game sketch shows what must be true, must be false, and could be true in the game. You also saw that those determinations of what is true, false, and possible translate directly into points. But before you can make a useful sketch, you have to digest some crucial information in the paragraph that opens the game. Without this important step, your sketch may be incomplete or inaccurate.

We'll call that opening paragraph the "overview," and we mean just this part:

> A college dean will present seven awards for outstanding language research. The awards—one for French, one for German, one for Hebrew, one for Japanese, one for Korean, one for Latin, and one for Swahili—must be presented consecutively, one at a time, in conformity with the following constraints:

> The German award is not presented first.
> The Hebrew award is presented at some time before the Korean award is presented.
> The Latin award is presented at some time before the Japanese award is presented.
> The French award is presented either immediately before or immediately after the Hebrew award is presented.
> The Korean award is presented either immediately before or immediately after the Latin award is presented.

> *PrepTest29 Sec3 Qs 14–19*

(We'll discuss working with the indented statements, or "rules," in depth in the next chapter.)

The SEAL Questions

As you learned in the last chapter, you'll ask four questions when dealing with the overview, and those four questions can be represented with the acronym SEAL:

Situation—What is the real-world scenario being described? What is the deliverable information—an ordered list, a calendar, a chart showing what's matched up?

Entities—Who or what are the "moving parts,"—the people or things I'm distributing, selecting, sequencing, or matching?

Action—What is the specific action—distribution, selection, sequencing, matching, or a combination of those—that I'm performing with the entities?

Limitations—Are there overall limitations (e.g., select four of seven, sequence the entities one per day) that control how I'll set up the game?

Situation and Entities

Identifying the game's *situation* is important to develop a mental picture of the game and to understand the sketch you ultimately create. Imagine that a logic game asks you to arrange items in a store in order from highest priced to lowest priced. Some test takers may picture the items on a shelf, running from left to right. Other test takers may picture a list of the items with the most expensive at the top of the list. Whatever your mental picture may be, you're likely to tend to revert to it as you're working through the game, so it makes sense to set it up that way to begin with.

Identifying the game's *entities* is also an important first step. The Overview usually lists these for you. At the outset of each game, make a list composed of the first initials of each entity—like a roster of players in this logic game. Doing so will help you keep them all in mind as you're sketching and making deductions.

LSAT Question	Analysis
A college dean will present seven awards for outstanding language research. The awards—one for French, one for German, one for Hebrew, one for Japanese, one for Korean, one for Latin, and one for Swahili—must be presented consecutively, one at a time, in conformity with the following constraints:	*Situation:* Awards are presented in a certain order; they just need to be listed out in order.*
	Entities: Seven language awards—F, G, H, J, K, L, and S.

PrepTest29 Sec3 Qs 14–19

*It doesn't matter whether you picture the list of time slots going from top to bottom or left to right. Use whichever orientation is most intuitive for you—just be consistent about it throughout a given game.

Action

Now that you've developed a mental picture of the game and a roster of entities, you're ready to figure out the task. Every game asks you to *do* something, such as to put entities into a sequential order or to sort them into groups. Your task is the game's *action*. There are almost always words and phrases in the overview that signal the action; sometimes those words are verbs, and sometimes they're hints about what the worked-out game will ultimately look like.

LSAT Question	Analysis
A college dean will present seven awards for outstanding language research. The awards—one for French, one for German, one for Hebrew, one for Japanese, one for Korean, one for Latin, and one for Swahili—must be presented consecutively, one at a time, in conformity with the following constraints:	*"The awards . . . must be presented consecutively"*— this is like an event schedule or itinerary.
	Action: Determine the order in which the awards are presented, first through seventh.
PrepTest29 Sec3 Qs 14–19	

Notice how the expert zeroed in on the words describing the task. The phrase "presented consecutively" makes it clear what the game's *deliverable* is: an ordered list. We'll learn, when we come to discussing the various types of games, that each one has some characteristic markers (this, for example, is a Sequencing game, and Sequencing games often involve arranging events in chronological order). But keep an eye out for *any* clues that point you toward identifying your task.

Practice

Imagine that the following statements appeared in logic game overviews. What words or phrases help define your task—the game's action? Circle or underline them. Look both for verbs and for phrases that describe the finished product. Then go to the next page to see the expert test taker's thinking.

Overview Statement	My Analysis
1. Teams of three players each will be chosen from among nine participants in a trivia game.	
2. While shopping, Maria will select four shirts from a rack that contains seven shirts.	
3. Each of four boats docked in a harbor is painted blue, green, or red and no other color.	
4. Each of three friends shopping at a supermarket will choose exactly two of the following items: apples, bananas, carrots, donuts, éclairs, and flour.	

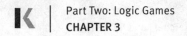

Expert Analysis

Here's how an LSAT expert might evaluate those statements.

Overview Statement		Analysis
1. Teams of three players each will be chosen from among nine participants in a trivia game.	$\longrightarrow$	Clues: "will be chosen" "Teams of three players each" Task: Sort players into groups of three each.
2. While shopping, Maria will select four shirts from a rack that contains seven shirts.	$\longrightarrow$	Clues: "will select" "four shirts from . . . seven shirts" Task: Figure out which shirts Maria buys and which she doesn't.
3. Each of four boats docked in a harbor is painted blue, green, or red and no other color.	$\longrightarrow$	Clues: "is painted blue, green, or red" Task: Match colors to boats.
4. Each of three friends shopping at a supermarket will choose exactly two of the following items: apples, bananas, carrots, donuts, éclairs, and flour.	$\longrightarrow$	Clues: "Each of three friends . . . will choose" "choose exactly two" Task: Match each person to the products they buy.

Limitations

Some less-than-well-prepared LSAT test takers may be satisfied with pulling only that much information (situation, entities, and action) out of the game's overview. However, there's usually more guidance about how the game works to be gleaned from the overview. We'll call these additional pieces of information *limitations*. Limitations are useful to formulate those point-getting statements about what's true, false, and possible in a game.

Limitations come in two kinds. On the one hand, the overview often gives you some specific instructions about working the game, as in these examples:

- Use one entity per slot (or two or three, etc.).
- Select a specific number of entities out of the original group.
- There are no ties in a ranking of entities.
- Use each entity exactly once (or twice, etc.).

On the other hand, an overview often leaves some gaps in information about how the game works. If the game overview does *not* tell you to use a specific number of the entities, it's important to realize that you don't know how many of them to use (at least until the game's rules narrow down the possibilities). If the game's overview does *not* specify that there are no ties in a ranking of entities, then it's important to remember that there might be ties in the game. If you aren't told to put an entity in every slot, then keep in mind you may have open slots. And so on.

In particular, pay attention to numerical limitations as you're examining a game's overview—and pay attention to the way numbers interact with the other instructions (or lack thereof). If you have, for example, five entities and five slots, then you *may* have a one-to-one matchup between entities and slots, but you can't take that for granted unless the overview tells you to use one entity per slot. In the absence of that specification, you may put more than one entity in some slots and leave others blank. Imagine another game in which you are given seven entities and four slots. The careless test taker might assume that some slots will take more than one entity. But you can't assume that unless and until you're told to use all the entities.

You'll get a lot more practice teasing out all varieties of logic game limitations. For starters, consider how the expert LSAT test taker thinks through the Language Awards game:

LSAT Question	Analysis
A college dean will present seven awards for outstanding language research. The awards—one for French, one for German, one for Hebrew, one for Japanese, one for Korean, one for Latin, and one for Swahili—must be presented consecutively, one at a time, in conformity with the following constraints: *PrepTest29 Sec3 Qs 14–19* →	Specific instructions: "[W]ill present seven awards": all seven must be given out, and there are no others. "The awards . . . must be presented consecutively, one at a time": no awards are given out simultaneously. Gaps in information: We don't know the order in which the awards are presented (after all, that's what the whole game is about), but that's the only unknown.

This game has clear instructions and few gaps in its information. That's a common scenario, one you're likely to see at least once per Logic Games section on the test.

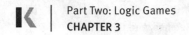

Now, compare the Racehorses game to the game you saw in Chapter 2:

LSAT Question	Analysis
Six racehorses—K, L, M, N, O, and P—will be assigned to six positions arranged in a straight line and numbered consecutively 1 through 6. The horses are assigned to the positions, one horse per position, according to the following conditions: →	Task: Figure out which position each race horse will take. This is a Sequencing task, figuring out the order in which the horses are arranged, one horse per position.

PrepTest28 Sec2 Qs 1–5

The tasks in those two games are essentially identical: The horses are being led to numbered stalls or lanes, while you're creating the order of the award presentations, but in both cases, you are placing items, one at a time, into a sequence. These tasks line up with our instinctive, "default" reaction to someone saying, "Here, put these things in order." We might just assume the person meant "one at a time, with no ties and no blank positions in the order," but on the LSAT, such limitations must be stated explicitly, and the expert test taker will never overlook such limitations, nor will she assume such limitations apply when they are not made explicit.

In summary, the very first thing you should do when you encounter an LSAT logic game is to carefully digest the overview paragraph. Identify the game's situation, entities, action, and limitations. With practice, all of that will take you only a few seconds. Once you've examined the overview, you're ready to make a sketch.

STEP 2 OF THE LOGIC GAMES METHOD: MAKING A SKETCH

You've seen that there's much more to Step 1 of the Kaplan Method for Logic Games than *reading* the overview of a game. You've learned to ask the SEAL questions before moving on from the initial paragraph. Once you're done with the overview, you're going to put those insights to use by making a sketch.

What's the value of a sketch? Keep in mind the ultimate goal of logic games: to answer questions asking for what must be true, could be true, and must be false in the game. After working through the rules of any given logic game, you'll make deductions about what is true, false, and possible. A sketch is an efficient way to record and retrieve those deductions; in fact, it's a schema of everything true, false, and possible in the game. A well-defined sketch, complete with deductions, will make the process of answering questions faster and easier.

Why make a sketch at this point, rather than after you've read the rules? After all, you'll have lots more information about how the game works after you've read all the rules. The reason is that as you work through those rules, you're going to want to interpret them in relation to an underlying framework, and that framework is your sketch. You'll often build information from the rules directly into your sketch, and when you can't, you'll note the rules in a shorthand that makes sense in light of the game's framework.

The next step is learning how to make a sketch. You'll learn that each of the different types of games works best with a particular type of sketch, and you'll develop a mental library of those sketch types. But first, note the principles of good sketches.

A sketch must be (1) easy to read, (2) quick to replicate, and (3) able to accommodate some ambiguity (for cases in which the game's framework contains uncertainties). Your sketch needs to be easy to read because you will be referring to it repeatedly as you're answering questions. Your sketch should also be built so that you can replicate it quickly because you're going to make a new sketch for questions that give you additional restrictions (you'll learn about these in Chapter 5). Finally, your sketch needs to be able to accommodate some ambiguity because you're never going to determine the placement of all the entities in your initial sketch. You may deduce, for example, that entity A will go in either slot 3 or slot 5, but not in both.

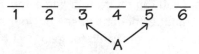

Or you may find that a certain group contains four *or* five members.

Team Red	Team Blue
— —	— —
— —	— —
(—)	

Or you may find that a group may have more than two members, but you don't know how many more.

≥ 2

Team A	Team B	Team C
—	—	—
—	—	—
—	(—)	—
—	(—)	

You'll want some way to capture those areas of uncertainty in your sketch.

LSAT STRATEGY

A Few Notes on Logic Game Sketches:

- Make sure your sketch is (1) easy to read, (2) quick to replicate, and (3) able to accommodate some ambiguity.

- Throughout this book, you'll see a library of sketch types and a standard notation for turning rules into shorthand. You don't have to use Kaplan's notation or sketches, but the explanations will use this notation, and you'll use the explanations to analyze practice problems.

- The Kaplan notation is pretty intuitive: Even if you don't use it yourself, you will likely be able to read and understand it in a logic games explanation.

- Try to keep your shorthand and your sketches clear, consistent, and easy to read—*for you*. Check to see that you can return to a game you've worked on and understand the limitations and restrictions based on your shorthand rules and sketches. Use the same type of sketch for games of the same type and similar notation for similar rules.

- Position your Master Sketch on the page so that it is large enough to be readable but not so large that you don't have any room to write down rules underneath or off to the side.

- Here's some good news: Recently, the LSAT began printing each logic game on two pages instead of one. This new format leaves much more room underneath the game overview for sketching. Because the change is so recent, though, many of the practice LSAT games you'll encounter will still be all on one page. Just be aware that you'll likely have more space on the page on Test Day.

Let's begin our study of sketches by using the same game we have been working with so far. Here, to refresh your memory, is our expert test taker's work on Step 1 of the Logic Games Method:

LSAT Question	Analysis
A college dean will present seven awards for outstanding language research. The awards—one for French, one for German, one for Hebrew, one for Japanese, one for Korean, one for Latin, and one for Swahili—must be presented consecutively, one at a time, in conformity with the following constraints: *PrepTest29 Sec3 Qs 14–19*	**Step 1:** *Situation:* Awards are presented in a certain order. *Entities:* Seven language awards—F, G, H, J, K, L, and S. *Action:* Determine the order in which the awards are presented. This is a Sequencing game. *Limitations:* No awards are presented at the same time.

The first step in making *any* sketch is to create a roster of entities. Next, consider what the framework should look like. Our mental picture is one of ordered slots into which we'll pencil the awards (once we figure out which goes where), and our limitations tell us that we have a one-to-one match-up between slots and entities. Thus, it makes perfect sense to simply draw out those slots and number them:

LSAT Question	
A college dean will present seven awards for outstanding language research. The awards—one for French, one for German, one for Hebrew, one for Japanese, one for Korean, one for Latin, and one for Swahili—must be presented consecutively, one at a time, in conformity with the following constraints: *PrepTest29 Sec3 Qs 14–19*	**Step 2:** 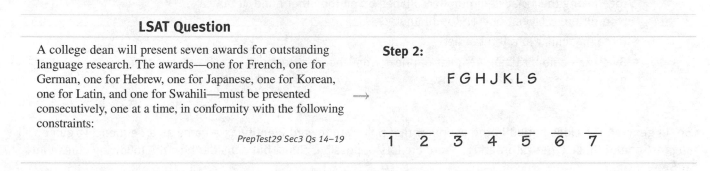

You could also draw the slots in order vertically. Whichever orientation makes the most intuitive sense to you is fine. Just be consistent about it throughout the game.

Now, measure this sketch against the criteria for good sketches. First, it's easy to read. If we determine when some or all of the language awards are presented, we can easily slot them in. Second, given its simplicity, it will be quick to replicate. Third, it can accommodate ambiguity. If we learned, for example, that either the award for German or the award for Hebrew is presented second, we could write something like "G/H" above slot 2.

You'll get to see the rest of this game worked out from start to finish, including its questions and answers, in Chapters 4 and 5. But before you tackle rules and deductions, it will be helpful for you to get familiar with the various types of games and see Steps 1 and 2 of the Logic Games Method applied to all those types of games. You'll have an opportunity for practice throughout the following sections and at the end of this chapter.

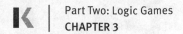
GAME TYPES

When we say there are a limited number of game types, we really mean there are a limited number of *actions* in logic games. Game types are defined by actions because once you have identified a game's action, you have a good sense of the limitations you should look out for, and you also have a pretty good idea of what your sketch will look like.

Sequencing Games

The Language Awards game, as well as the Racehorses game you saw in Chapter 2, are *Sequencing* games. Sequencing games are the most common type of LSAT game: over 50 percent of logic games on the LSAT in the last five years have been Sequencing games, and you're highly likely to see one or more on Test Day.

LSAT STRATEGY

Sequencing games ask you to put things in order

- Chronologically (either using units of time—such as years, days, weeks, or hours—or else simply using the ideas of "earlier" and "later")
- Spatially (either vertically or horizontally; imagine runners about to run a race taking their places in numbered lanes or, on the other hand, a tall cake with different layers, one on top of another)
- By rank (similar to a top ten list)
- By size or amount (imagine a list of prices from cheapest to most expensive)

So, in general, the clues buried in the overview that point you toward identifying a game as a Sequencing game will suggest one of those types of ordering. There are lots of possible clues, but consider how the following clues hint at Sequencing:

- Chronology-related hints: schedule, time, earlier, later, concurrently
- Spatial ordering–related hints: before, after, beside, adjacent, above, below
- Rank-related hints: better, higher, lower, higher-rated
- Amount-related hints: greater, less, cheaper

Your sketch for a Sequencing game will usually be slots with numbers (arranged either vertically or horizontally), just like our sketches for the Racehorses game in Chapter 2 and for the Language Awards game above.

Similarly, the limitations to look out for in Sequencing games are usually related to how many entities can go into each of the slots: Sometimes you'll have a one-to-one match-up, and sometimes the numbers will be less well defined.

A Note About Loose Sequencing

There's one type of Sequencing game in which your sketch will look different from those we've been making so far, and that's a *Loose Sequencing* game. (By the way, we'll refer to Sequencing games that aren't "loose" as *Strict Sequencing* games.) Before we address the question of how Loose Sequencing games differ from Strict Sequencing games, let's first clarify how they're similar:

- Both involve putting entities into a sequence (which could be chronological, spatial, by rank, or in any other way).
- Either could give you a limitation that there are no ties (that is, no slots with more than one entity in them), and either could allow ties (although Loose Sequencing seldom does).
- In both, it can be helpful to imagine a list of numbered slots (either vertical or horizontal).
- Both could call for one entity per slot; indeed, this is standard in Loose Sequencing games.

In other words, the ultimate task is very much the same.

However, here's the difference: in Strict Sequencing games, the rules (remember, those are the indented statements beneath the overview paragraph) will affirmatively relate the entities to the underlying framework in some way. Here are some examples of this type of rule:

- A goes in slot 3.
- Exactly one slot comes between C and D.
- E goes in either slot 4 or in slot 6.
- G comes at least two slots before H.
- J and K are in consecutive slots.

Each of those rules involves not just the order of the entities but also the number of slots between them or the specific slots they must fill or avoid. A game that gives you at least some rules of this type is a *Strict Sequencing* game.

Some rules, however, involve only entities and relate those entities only to each other. Consider these examples:

- A comes before B.
- C comes before D but after E.
- F comes later than G.
- H is earlier than both J and K.

Notice that none of these rules relate the entities to the underlying framework of numbered slots. That means it would be very hard to work them into a sketch based on numbered slots. Some LSAT logic games give you *only* rules of this type, and those games are *Loose Sequencing* games. (Note: You may, in Loose Sequencing, see a rule that relates entities to spaces negatively—for example, "W is not seventh"—but you won't see rules that affirmatively tie entities to particular spaces or that dictate a set number of spaces to appear between entities.)

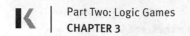
When you meet a Loose Sequencing game, you'll end up with a sketch that relates the entities to each other without relating them to numbered slots. The Loose Sequencing sketch will come out of the rules, rather than the overview. Take a look at the following example:

LSAT Question	Analysis
A movie studio is scheduling the release of six films—*Fiesta, Glaciers, Hurricanes, Jets, Kangaroos,* and *Lovebird.* No two of these films can be released on the same date. The release schedule is governed by the following conditions: *PrepTest71 Sec2 Qs 1–5*	**Step 1:** *Situation:* Movies being scheduled for release *Entities:* The six movies—F, G, H, J, K, and L *Action:* Determine the order in which the movies are released. This is a Sequencing game. *Limitations:* No films released at the same time.

So far, this is a Sequencing game quite similar to the Language Awards game. And we could make a sketch with numbered slots for it. But suppose that the expert test taker quickly runs her eye down the list of rules and notices that they're all of the Loose Sequencing variety—that is, they give only the relative order among entities, with no mention of specific spaces or the number of spaces between any two entities. In that case, she may choose to draw a sketch that simply relates the entities to each other.

Here is the game complete with rules, and here is the sketch our expert test taker draws based on them:

LSAT Question	Analysis
A movie studio is scheduling the release of six films— *Fiesta, Glaciers, Hurricanes, Jets, Kangaroos,* and *Lovebird.* No two of these films can be released on the same date. The release schedule is governed by the following conditions:	**Step 2:**
	Rule 1:

A movie studio is scheduling the release of six films—*Fiesta, Glaciers, Hurricanes, Jets, Kangaroos,* and *Lovebird.* No two of these films can be released on the same date. The release schedule is governed by the following conditions:

> *Fiesta* must be released earlier than both *Jets* and *Lovebird.*
> *Kangaroos* must be released earlier than *Jets,* and *Jets* must be released earlier than *Hurricanes.*
> *Lovebird* must be released earlier than *Glaciers.*

PrepTest71 Sec2 Qs 1–5

$\longrightarrow$

Step 2:

Rule 1:

```
    . .L
F .
    . .J
```

Rule 2: Note that J is already in the sketch.

```
    . .L
F .
    . .J . . . H
K .
```

Rule 3: Note that L is already in the sketch.

```
    . .L . . . G
F .
    . .J . . . H
K .
```

Notice how the expert test taker built each Loose Sequencing rule onto the ones that came before it. In other games, it may be best to digest each rule individually. You'll learn more about the skills of combining rules, and get some practice on it, in Chapter 4. For now, simply note that the finished sketch displays relationships among all of the entities without putting them into slots. The expert test taker has used ellipses to indicate that an entity must come after another. (Note: As always, you could make this sketch vertical or horizontal. Use the orientation that's more intuitive for you and be consistent about it throughout the game.)

Many LSAT games blend both strict and loose elements. Sometimes, you'll make an initial sketch with numbered slots, work some of the entities directly into that sketch, and also create a mini-tree relating two or three entities to each other until you can place them into the line of numbered slots.

It takes a glance at the rules to know whether a Sequencing game is Strict or Loose. As you practice additional games, it will become second nature to quickly check whether the rules mention specific slots and numbers of spaces (Strict), or whether they designate *only* the relative positions among the entities (Loose). Don't sweat it if you jot down a Strict sketch only to discover that a Loose arrangement will work better for the game you're solving. Additionally, you will find that some Loose Sequencing questions give strict "If" conditions that require you to make a new sketch with slots for that question only. You'll cover questions like that in Chapter 5. For now, just remember that the LSAT expert will distinguish between Strict and Loose Sequencing and use the appropriate sketch in each case.

Because the distinction between Strict and Loose Sequencing is driven by the nature of the rules you're given, we'll talk more about it in Chapter 4. In the meantime, assume that the games you meet in the following practice section are both Strict Sequencing and make sketches accordingly.

Practice

In each of the following examples, apply Steps 1 and 2 of the Logic Games Method. That is, identify the situation, entities, action, and limitations and make a simple sketch, complete with a roster of entities up at the top. Pay particular attention to the clues that tell you that you're dealing with a Sequencing game. You can check the next page at any time to see the expert analysis.

Overview	My Analysis
5. A newspaper editor will rank the top five college football teams (A, B, C, D, and E) from first to fifth, and there are no ties.	
6. A teacher is assigning the front row of seats in her class according to the age of six students—A, B, C, D, E, and F—from youngest to oldest. There are six seats in the front row and each student is assigned to exactly one seat. The youngest student will sit on the far left and the oldest student will sit on the far right.	

Expert Analysis

Here's how the expert test taker approaches the setups you just saw:

Overview	Analysis
5. A newspaper editor will rank the top five college football teams (A, B, C, D, and E) from first to fifth, and there are no ties.	**Step 1:** *Situation:* An editor ranking teams *Entities:* The five college football teams (A, B, C, D, E) *Action:* There are five teams, and the editor is going to "rank" them from first to fifth. Because order matters, this is a *Sequencing* game. → *Limitations:* "[T]here are no ties," so the editor will place each of the five teams in a separate spot. **Step 2:** Write out dashes for each of the five possible ranking spots; then place the entities above the sketch. <div align="center">A B C D E $\overline{1}\quad\overline{2}\quad\overline{3}\quad\overline{4}\quad\overline{5}$</div>
6. A teacher is assigning the front row of seats in her class according to the age of six students—A, B, C, D, E, and F—from youngest to oldest. There are six seats in the front row and each student is assigned to exactly one seat. The youngest student will sit on the far left and the oldest student will sit on the far right.	**Step 1:** *Situation:* A classroom with a row of seats *Entities:* The six students (A, B, C, D, E, F) *Action:* The teacher is putting students "in the front row," and some students are younger and some are older. Because the task here is to order the students according to their age, this is a *Sequencing* game. → *Limitations:* Students won't sit on top of each other, so each seat will be assigned one student. **Step 2:** In addition to setting up a standard Sequencing sketch, it will be important to signify which end of the row is the youngest and which is the oldest. <div align="center">A B C D E F (Youngest) $\overline{1}\ \overline{2}\ \overline{3}\ \overline{4}\ \overline{5}\ \overline{6}$ (Oldest)</div>

Reflection

Take a look back at your practice. Did you answer the SEAL questions for each game prior to setting up a sketch for it? Did you set up each sketch based on your knowledge of the game's central action? Were your sketches easy to read, quick to replicate, and able to accommodate ambiguity? What have you learned from this exercise?

Over the coming days, take note of real-life Sequencing tasks—scheduling, ranking, prioritizing. Try to envision how the testmaker could create logic games and the types of rules and restrictions the LSAT would need to impose.

Selection Games

We've mentioned that Sequencing games are the most common type of LSAT game. Although the frequency of Selection games pales in comparison to that of Sequencing, approximately 10 percent of games on LSATs over the last five years have been of this type. A Selection game gives you a group of entities and asks you to choose some of those entities to make a smaller group. Let's see that process in action in this example from a real LSAT by applying Step 1 of the Method to this game:

LSAT Question	Analysis
A park contains at most five of seven kinds of trees—firs, laurels, maples, oaks, pines, spruces, and yews—consistent with the following conditions: *PrepTestB Sec2 Qs 7–12*	**Step 1**: *Situation:* Different types of trees in a park *Entities*: The seven tree varieties—F, L, M, O, P, S, and Y *Action:* Determine the types of trees that are in the park. This is a Selection game. $\longrightarrow$ *Limitations:* Maximum five types of trees (no minimum) Gaps in information: No minimum number of kinds of trees is established. Unless the rules establish a minimum number of kinds of trees, we could have no trees at all, or anywhere from one to five kinds in the park.

You can spot the action in Selection games by looking for verbs that suggest it, such as *select*, *choose*, or *pick*. Those words may or may not be present, but Selection can also be signaled by any clues that suggest that some entities are *in* and some are *out*. Consider the following situations:

- A manager hiring some employees from a number of applicants
- A director deciding which actors should be on stage during a crowd scene
- A consumer shopping for items in a store full of merchandise
- A painter applying some paints, from a spectrum of tubes of paint, to a palette

In all of these situations, some entities are in and some are out. That's the hallmark of a Selection game.

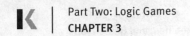
Because Selection games involve choosing a smaller group from a larger group, you can probably imagine why numbers are important in these games. A key limitation to look out for involves the number of entities to select, but keep in mind that there are often gaps in information. When you are not given a minimum or maximum number in the overview, expect the game's questions to ask about those numbers.

Selection sketches can be very simple, and, like all logic games sketches, they should be informed by your own mental picture formed when you first identified the situation. When you imagined yourself picking trees for the park in the example above, what did you see? Did you imagine creating a list of which ones you chose? Or simply writing down all the entities and circling some? Did you imagine creating two lists: one for "in" and one for "out"? Any of those approaches works. However, our recommendation is to keep it as simple as possible: write out your roster of entities, circle the ones you deduce are selected, and cross out the ones you deduce are excluded. We'll be using that type of sketch throughout our Selection games examples in this book, like this:

LSAT Question	Analysis
A park contains at most five of seven kinds of trees—firs, laurels, maples, oaks, pines, spruces, and yews—consistent with the following conditions: *PrepTestB Sec2 Qs 7–12*	**Step 2:** → F L M O P S Y (max 5)

Practice

In each of the following examples, apply Steps 1 and 2 of the Logic Games Method. Pay particular attention to the clues that tell you that these are Selection games. You can check the following page at any time to see the expert thinking.

Overview	My Analysis
7. Each of the seven members of a fraternity—A, B, C, D, E, F, and G—is deciding whether or not to go to the football game this weekend.	
8. A chef is making soup using exactly five ingredients. She chooses from among four types of spices (A, B, C, and D), three types of meat (e, f, and g), and three vegetables (H, I, and J).	

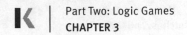

Expert Analysis

Here's how the expert test taker approaches the setups you just saw:

Overview	Analysis
7. Each of the seven members of a fraternity—A, B, C, D, E, F, and G—is deciding whether or not to go to the football game this weekend.	**Step 1:** *Situation:* A group of people deciding whether or not to attend an event
	Entities: The seven fraternity members (A, B, C, D, E, F, G)
	Action: The only action is to figure out who is going to the game and who is not, so this must be a *Selection* game.
	Limitations: Right now, anywhere from zero to seven fraternity members could go to the game. The rules will add restrictions.
	Step 2: The sketch for a Selection game is simply the list of entities.
	A B C D E F G
8. A chef is making soup using exactly five ingredients. She chooses from among four types of spices (A, B, C, and D), three types of meat (e, f, and g), and three vegetables (H, I, and J).	**Step 1:** *Situation:* A chef in a kitchen, picking ingredients for a soup
	Entities: The various ingredients—four types of spices (A, B, C, D), three types of meat (e, f, g), and three types of vegetables (H, I, J)
	Action: Selection—pick 5 out of 10 possible ingredients.
	Limitations: No limits on the number of spices, meats, or vegetables the chef must use. Expect the rules to add restrictions along these lines.
	Step 2: This is a Selection game, so the sketch can be a list of the entities. However, because the entities are sorted into groups, differentiate those groups in the sketch.

(pick 5 of 10)

spices	meats	veggies
A B C D	e f g	H I J

Reflection

Take a look back at your practice. Did you answer the SEAL questions for each game prior to setting up a sketch for it? Did you set up each sketch based on your knowledge of the game's central action? Were your sketches easy to read, quick to replicate, and able to accommodate ambiguity? What have you learned from this exercise?

Over the coming days, spot the Selection tasks you encounter in everyday life—choosing what to serve for dinner or whom to invite for a get-together, for example. How would the testmaker turn each of them into a logic game? What sort of rules or restrictions would apply?

Matching Games

So now we've seen Sequencing and Selection games, and all of the examples we've seen so far for both of those game types involved just one type of entity (e.g., languages, films, or trees). However, some LSAT games present you with two types of entities and ask you to match them to each other. *Matching* games represent about 12 percent of games on LSATs over the last five years. Take a look at the following example from a real LSAT:

LSAT Question	Analysis
There are exactly three recycling centers in Rivertown: Center 1, Center 2, and Center 3. Exactly five kinds of material are recycled at these recycling centers: glass, newsprint, plastic, tin, and wood. Each recycling center recycles at least two but no more than three of these kinds of material. The following conditions must hold: *PrepTestJune2007 Sec1 Qs 18–23*	**Step 1**: *Situation:* Types of materials being recycled at recycling centers *Entities:* The recycling centers—1, 2, and 3—and the recycled materials—G, N, P, T, and W *Action:* Determine which materials will be recycled at each center. Multiple centers can recycle the same materials, so this is a Matching game. → *Limitations:* Each center will recycle two or three materials. Each type of material will be recycled at least once (*"exactly* five kinds of materials *are* recycled"). Gaps in information: Nothing (at least until we see the rules) indicates how many centers may recycle the same material. The total number of materials recycled in the three plants may be anywhere from six to nine (because each plant recycles either two or three kinds).

Notice how the expert test taker spotted that this was a Matching game: The fact that there is more than one type of entity is one good clue, and the fact that we're linking them in some way is another. Often in Matching games, one of the types of entities will be attributes that the other type of entity takes on. Here, we see another variation: The recycled materials must be matched to the plants that recycle them. Because more than one plant may recycle a given material, this is a Matching game.

Limitations to watch out for in Matching games frequently relate to numbers—or the lack thereof. In this game, we were given both a minimum and maximum number of the kinds of materials each plant may process. Also, it was important for our expert test taker to remain aware that she may be able to use each kind of material multiple times. Pay close attention, in each Matching game you encounter, to limitations related to repeating entities and numbers.

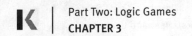

Now let's consider a sketch. What did you see in your mind while asking yourself the SEAL questions? As with most types of logic games, there's more than one way to make a workable Matching sketch. Once again, the best course is to keep your sketch as simple and flexible as possible. In this case, create three columns—one for each of the recycling plants. That allows you to list materials beneath each column header as you deduce the matches. Don't forget to begin with a roster of entities across the top of your sketch.

LSAT Question	Analysis
There are exactly three recycling centers in Rivertown: Center 1, Center 2, and Center 3. Exactly five kinds of material are recycled at these recycling centers: glass, newsprint, plastic, tin, and wood. Each recycling center recycles at least two but no more than three of these kinds of material. The following conditions must hold: *PrepTestJune2007 Sec1 Qs 18–23*	**Step 2:** G N P T W 1 2 3 — — — — — — ... ...

Notice that the sketch is easy to read and replicate, thanks to its simplicity. It's also capable of expressing ambiguity: If you were to deduce, for example, that newsprint and wood are recycled together at either one or two of the plants, this sketch gives room to express that. You may be wondering how the expert decided to put the recycling plants across the top rather than the materials. A sketch will be much easier to work with if it is anchored by the most concrete entity. This game has exactly three plants but unknown numbers of glass, plastic, tin, and so on. Hence, it makes the most sense to keep the three plants at the top of the columns in our sketch and write in deductions and uncertainties regarding the materials.

Alternatively, some students find grids intuitive for Matching games. Here's how we'd set up the same game using a grid:

LSAT Question	Analysis
There are exactly three recycling centers in Rivertown: Center 1, Center 2, and Center 3. Exactly five kinds of material are recycled at these recycling centers: glass, newsprint, plastic, tin, and wood. Each recycling center recycles at least two but no more than three of these kinds of material. The following conditions must hold: *PrepTestJune2007 Sec1 Qs 18–23*	**Step 2:** <table><tr><td></td><td>1</td><td>2</td><td>3</td></tr><tr><td>G</td><td></td><td></td><td></td></tr><tr><td>N</td><td></td><td></td><td></td></tr><tr><td>P</td><td></td><td></td><td></td></tr><tr><td>T</td><td></td><td></td><td></td></tr><tr><td>W</td><td></td><td></td><td></td></tr></table>

That sketch is also easy to read. It would take slightly longer to replicate, but that's a trade-off you may choose to make if you find it more intuitive.

Practice

Apply Steps 1 and 2 of the Logic Games Method to the following examples. Pay particular attention to the words and phrases that indicate that each game is a Matching game. You can turn the page at any time to see the expert thinking.

Overview	My Analysis
9. Four friends—A, B, C, and D—meet for dinner at a restaurant. There are five items on the menu—e, f, g, h, and i—and each person will order either 2 or 3 items.	
10. Three buildings (A, B, and C) sit next to each other on a city block, and each building has three floors. On each floor, the lights are either on or off.	

Expert Analysis

Here's how the expert test taker approaches the examples you just worked with:

Overview	Analysis
9. Four friends—A, B, C, and D—meet for dinner at a restaurant. There are five items on the menu—e, f, g, h, and i—and each person will order either 2 or 3 items.	**Step 1:** *Situation:* Friends at a restaurant, ordering items off a menu

Step 1: *Situation:* Friends at a restaurant, ordering items off a menu

Entities: The four friends (A, B, C, D) and the five menu items (e, f, g, h, i)

Action: Because we're matching menu items to the people at the restaurant and because menu items are not "used up" if they get selected, this must be a Matching game.

⟶ *Limitations:* Each person is going to select a minimum of 2 and a maximum of 3 menu items, and the items are not exhaustible (multiple friends can select the same menu item).

Step 2: Matching games can be set up either as a table or as a grid.

e f g h i

A	B	C	D
—	—	—	—
—	—	—	—
. . . . .	. . . . .	. . . . .	. . . . .

Or

(2 or 3 each)

	A	B	C	D
e				
f				
g				
h				
i				

Overview	Analysis
10. Three buildings (A, B, and C) sit next to each other on a city block, and each building has three floors. On each floor, the lights are either on or off.	**Step 1:** *Situation:* Buildings on a street, and some of the floors have their lights on. Envision standing on the opposite side of the street, looking at the building and noting which floors have lights on or off.

Entities: The three buildings (A, B, C) and the three floors of each building

Action: The positions of the buildings and floors are set—no Sequencing element. Rather, assign each floor a designation of "lights on" or "lights off"—this is a Matching game.

Limitations: Each floor will either have its lights on or off—there is no in-between designation, such as "partially on" or "mostly on."

→ **Step 2:** Set up this Matching game in a grid because each building has exactly three floors. In the box for each individual floor, write "on" or "off" (or "✓" or "✗").

	A	B	C
3			
2			
1			

Reflection

Take a look back at your practice. Did you answer the SEAL questions for each game prior to setting up a sketch for it? Did you set up each sketch based on your knowledge of the game's central action? Were your sketches easy to read, quick to replicate, and able to accommodate ambiguity? What have you learned from this exercise?

In the coming days, take note of real-life Matching tasks. What kinds of restrictions apply ("Ushers will wear black and groomsmen wear green," for example)? How would the LSAT turn these into logic games? What sorts of restrictions would the testmaker need to articulate?

Distribution Games

There are four actions the LSAT might task you with on Test Day, and we've now met three of them: Sequencing, Selection, and Matching. The only remaining single-action game type is *Distribution*. In the past five years, Distribution games have been rare, representing less than 10 percent of logic games on released LSATs. Distribution games give you a larger group of entities and ask you to sort them into two or more smaller groups. Consider the following example from a real LSAT:

LSAT Question	Analysis
On a Tuesday, an accountant has exactly seven bills—numbered 1 through 7—to pay by Thursday of the same week. The accountant will pay each bill only once according to the following rules: Either three or four of the seven bills must be paid on Wednesday, the rest on Thursday. <div align="right">*PrepTest29 Sec3 Qs 1–6*</div>	**Step 1:** *Situation:* An accountant paying bills *Entities:* The seven bills—1 through 7—and the days of the week *Action:* The game's action cannot be determined by the overview alone,* but a quick look at the first rule provides the answer: Each of the seven bills will be paid on either Wednesday or Thursday. This is a Distribution game. *Limitations:* There are exactly seven bills and each is paid only once. Gaps in information: It's unclear whether we pay three bills on Wednesday and four on Thursday, or vice versa. The sketch must account for this ambiguity.

*This will occur on the test from time to time. Don't let it throw you. If the overview paragraph doesn't clearly state your task, the rules will.

Notice how the LSAT expert discerned that this was a Distribution game: she zeroed in on the phrase "pay each bill only once" and noticed that they were to be distributed between two days. Other examples of Distribution tasks might include the following:

- Create three piles of clothes: One pile to give to the thrift store, one pile to take to the dry cleaner, and one pile to send to relatives.
- Out of a group of teenagers, each of whom is going to one of four different concerts, figure out who goes to which concert.
- Sort a group of eight runners into two relay teams.
- Assign diners to different tables in a restaurant.

The formation of groups is the key task in each of these.

This task is different from that in a Selection game, where you are given a larger group and asked to choose a single, smaller group. In Distribution games, you are asked to sort the entities into two or more smaller groups (and to use all of the entities in doing so). In Distribution games, each entity is placed only once—if Bill 2 is paid on Wednesday, then it is not paid on Thursday. Notice how this distinguishes Distribution from Matching—in the Recycling Centers game, newsprint might be recycled in two or even all three of the recycling centers.

Key limitations to watch out for in Distribution games relate to numbers: How large will the groups be? (You may or may not be told.) Is each group required to have members? (It could be that some groups are empty.) Are groups required to contain certain types of entities? (This might happen if the entities are divided to represent people of two different professions, for example, with a restriction such as "each committee will be assigned at least one physician").

Now that we have answered the SEAL questions for the Bill Paying game, it's time to make a sketch. Given that we're simply making groups, let's make short columns headed by the two days mentioned in the game. Because we know that three bills are paid each day, and a fourth bill is paid on one of the two days, we can reflect those possibilities in the sketch.

LSAT Question	Analysis
On a Tuesday, an accountant has exactly seven bills—numbered 1 through 7—to pay by Thursday of the same week. The accountant will pay each bill only once according to the following rules: $\longrightarrow$ Either three or four of the seven bills must be paid on Wednesday, the rest on Thursday. *PrepTest29 Sec3 Qs 1–6*	**Step 2:** 1 2 3 4 5 6 7 W | T — | — — | — — | — ... | ...

This is our recommended sketch for Distribution games: a set of columns headed by the name of each group or team—easy to read, quick to replicate, and able to accommodate ambiguity.

Now, you may have noticed that the sketch for our Distribution game looks very similar to our sketch for the Matching game we saw a few pages ago. That's true: The recommended sketches look the same. And you may also have noticed the similarity in the task: As you're working each game, you create a list of entities under each column heading. The key difference is conceptual: Think of a Distribution game as similar to putting individuals on teams, while a Matching game is more like assigning attributes to individuals. However, whether you mentally label a game as Matching or Distribution is relatively unimportant, provided you understand the game, your task, and the limitations you're given in the overview and provided that your sketch is clear and accurate.

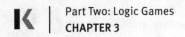
Practice

In each of the following examples, apply Steps 1 and 2 of the Logic Games Method. Pay particular attention to the clues that signal that you're looking at a Distribution game. You can check the following pages at any time to see the expert analysis.

Overview	My Analysis
11. Each of the seven members of a sorority—A, B, C, D, E, F, and G—is deciding whether to attend tonight's basketball game or tonight's volleyball game. Each member will attend exactly one of the games.	
12. Each of exactly eight movies—H, I, J, K, L, M, N, and O—will be shown in only one of three theaters. Each theater must show at least two of the movies.	

Expert Analysis for the Practice exercise may be found on the following page. ▶ ▶ ▶

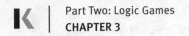

Expert Analysis

Here's how the expert test taker discerns the action in those game setups you just saw:

Overview	Analysis
11. Each of the seven members of a sorority—A, B, C, D, E, F, and G—is deciding whether to attend tonight's basketball game or tonight's volleyball game. Each member will attend exactly one of the games.	**Step 1:** *Situation:* Individual sorority members deciding which game to attend *Entities:* The seven members of the sorority (A, B, C, D, E, F, G) *Action:* Separate the members into two groups: those going to the basketball game and those going to the volleyball game; because a member cannot go to both games at the same time, this is a *Distribution* game, not a Matching game. *Limitations:* No limitations on the number of members going to either the volleyball game or the basketball game; it's possible they all go to one of the games together, or they could split up with some going to the volleyball game and others going to the basketball game. (Expect the rules to provide further restrictions here.) **Step 2:** Sketch: Columns representing the two different games; underneath each column, add the members going to that game.

$$A\ B\ C\ D\ E\ F\ G$$

Volley	Basket

Overview	Analysis

12. Each of exactly eight movies—H, I, J, K, L, M, N, and O—will be shown in only one of three theaters. Each theater must show at least two of the movies.

Step 1: *Situation:* Figuring out which movies are playing in which theaters

Entities: The eight movies (H, I, J, K, L, M, N, O)

Action: Assign the movies to the different theaters. Because each movie will be shown in only one theater, this is a *Distribution* game, not a Matching game.

Limitations: Eight movies and three theaters, with each theater showing at least two movies; that must mean at least one and possibly two theaters show more than two movies.

→

Step 2: There are three "groups" in which to place entities, with a minimum number restriction on each group.

H I J K L M N O

Theat 1	Theat 2	Theat 3
___	___	___
___	___	___
....	....	....
....	....	....

Reflection

Take a look back at your practice. Did you answer the SEAL questions for each game prior to setting up a sketch for it? Did you set up each sketch based on your knowledge of the game's central action? Were your sketches easy to read, quick to replicate, and able to accommodate ambiguity? What have you learned from this exercise?

Over the coming days, take note of real-life Distribution tasks. What sorts of restrictions do you notice (e.g., "Each team has the same number of players," "Each committee must have at least one person from the finance division and one from the marketing team")? How would the LSAT testmaker turn these into logic games? What additional rules or limitations would the testmaker have to add?

Hybrid Games

You've now seen examples of each of the actions you might see in LSAT games. There's one more way the LSAT can construct a game's central task—by combining in a single game two (or sometimes three) of the actions discussed above. There is usually one Hybrid game on any given LSAT (though some tests have had zero or two). And combining two or more actions is frequently (but not always) how the LSAT creates its most difficult game. Consider the following example:

LSAT Question	Analysis
Zeno's Unfinished Furniture sells exactly five types of furniture—footstools, hutches, sideboards, tables, and vanities. Irene buys just four items, each of a different type, and each made entirely of one kind of wood—maple, oak, pine, or rosewood. The following conditions govern Irene's purchases: *PrepTestB Sec2 Qs 19–24*	**Step 1:** *Situation:* A woman purchasing different pieces of furniture *Entities:* The types of furniture—F, H, S, T, and V—and the kinds of wood—m, o, p, and r *Action:* Determine the four of five pieces of furniture chosen and then match a wood variety to each piece. This is a Selection/Matching hybrid game. *Limitations:* Exactly four pieces of furniture are chosen, and each is a different type. There are no limitations on how many pieces of furniture are a certain type of wood. Gaps in information: We don't know whether all four types of wood are used, and cannot assume that they are unless the rules make that explicit.

The expert test taker knew that this was a Hybrid game because she kept her eyes open for clues and she spotted both Selection and Matching clues. That's how to spot Hybrid games: Watch for the kinds of clues you're already familiar with from your practice on the single-action games above. (So, from this point forward, don't stop looking for clues that point you toward an action in a logic game just because you've already identified one action in the overview. There might be another action; be on the lookout for it.)

Theoretically, the LSAT could combine any two of the four actions in a Hybrid game, and you should be prepared for that. However, in recent years some combinations have been more common than others. In particular, Sequencing-Distribution and Sequencing-Matching together represent over 60% of Hybrid games on recent exams. Every once in a while, the LSAT will combine more than two actions.

Similarly, the limitations to watch for are indicated by the actions involved. But in Hybrid games, take an extra moment to make sure you're clear about which limitations apply to which action. For example, notice that one action in this game has a tight numerical restriction (Irene selects exactly four of the five types of furniture) but the other action has looser numerical restrictions (each type of wood may be used more than once, or not at all).

It's difficult to generalize about sketches for Hybrid games because different combinations of actions call for different sketches. But we can outline a couple of principles:

- If you don't immediately see how to combine the two actions into one sketch, make two sketches along the lines that you're familiar with from your practice with single-action games.
- If you combine the two actions into one sketch, make sure that sketch adheres to the criteria you want in sketches: easy to read, quick to replicate, and able to accommodate some uncertanties.

In this case, let's assume that we don't immediately see a way to combine the two actions into one sketch. We know that we have a Selection action and a Matching action, so let's draw two initial sketches representing those two actions:

LSAT Question	Analysis
Zeno's Unfinished Furniture sells exactly five types of furniture—footstools, hutches, sideboards, tables, and vanities. Irene buys just four items, each of a different type, and each made entirely of one kind of wood—maple, oak, pine, or rosewood. The following conditions govern Irene's purchases: *PrepTestB Sec2 Qs 19–24* →	**Step 2:** F H S T V

	F	H	S	T	V
m					
o					
p					
r					

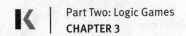

Those two sketches together would allow you to make all available deductions as you work through the rules. But in this case, it's worth consolidating the sketches. Selection-Matching Hybrid games are relatively rare on the LSAT, but the two actions combine pretty intuitively. The list of furniture pieces already anchors the sketch with columns in which you can mark the type of wood matched to each piece of furniture. You can easily circle or cross-out pieces of furniture when you deduce that they are or are not among Irene's purchases.

LSAT Overview	**Analysis**

LSAT Overview

Zeno's Unfinished Furniture sells exactly five types of furniture—footstools, hutches, sideboards, tables, and vanities. Irene buys just four items, each of a different type, and each made entirely of one kind of wood—maple, oak, pine, or rosewood. The following conditions govern Irene's purchases:

PrepTestB Sec2 Qs 19–24

Analysis

Step 2:

(Select 4)

	F	H	S	T	V
m					
o					
p					
r					

Practice

In each of the following examples, apply Steps 1 and 2 of the Logic Games Method to these Hybrid games. Take your time identifying actions and limitations and pay attention to the clues that indicate each action. You can check the following pages at any time to see the expert thinking.

Overview	My Analysis
13. Five drivers—A, B, C, D, and E—are waiting to get their cars washed. The cars are in a line, from first to last, and each car is exactly one of three different colors—f, g, or h.	
14. Six friends—A, B, C, D, E, and F—are going canoeing through a state park. The friends will rent exactly two canoes, and each canoe has a front, middle, and rear position. All six friends seat themselves in the canoes, one person per position.	

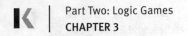

Expert Analysis

Here's how the expert test taker approaches those game overviews and sketches:

Overview	Analysis
13. Five drivers—A, B, C, D, and E—are waiting to get their cars washed. The cars are in a line, from first to last, and each car is exactly one of three different colors—f, g, or h.	**Step 1:** *Situation:* A line of cars outside a car wash *Entities:* The drivers of cars (A, B, C, D, E) and the colors (f, g, h) *Action:* Because the cars are in a line "from first to last," positional arrangement must matter; this is a *Sequencing* game. And once the cars are in order, we'll also need to *match* the car of each driver to a specific color. This must be a *Sequencing-Matching Hybrid* game. *Limitations:* The five drivers definitely have to be used up, so we'll use all of them, but we're not sure about the colors. There are no restrictions telling us how many colors we must use. Therefore, it's possible that all three colors are used; alternatively, it's possible that all five cars are the same color. **Step 2:** It is easy to envision this *Matching-Sequencing Hybrid* game as just two Sequencing games layered on top of each other. We can place the drivers on one layer and the color of their cars on the other layer.

$$\underline{\quad}\ \underline{\quad}\ \underline{\quad}\ \underline{\quad}\ \underline{\quad}\ : A\ B\ C\ D\ E$$
$$\underline{\quad}\ \underline{\quad}\ \underline{\quad}\ \underline{\quad}\ \underline{\quad}\ : f\ g\ h$$
$$\ \ 1\quad 2\quad 3\quad 4\quad 5$$

Overview	**Analysis**
14. Six friends—A, B, C, D, E, and F—are going canoeing through a state park. The friends will rent exactly two canoes, and each canoe has a front, middle, and rear position. All six friends seat themselves in the canoes, one person per position.	**Step 1:** *Situation:* Friends at a park, trying to figure out who sits where and in which canoe *Entities:* The friends (A, B, C, D, E, F) and the positions (front, middle, rear) *Action:* A pretty straightforward Distribution game—divide a group of friends into two smaller subgroups. Positioning also matters—"front, middle, and rear" signifies that friends sit *in front of* or *behind* others. This is a *Distribution-Sequencing Hybrid* game. *Limitations:* Straightforward, with no uncommon limitations. Six people and six spots in which to put them.

Step 2: Each entity is placed only once in the sketch (Distribution), and order matters (Sequencing). List the entities above the grid and add them to the sketch when you know their spot.

A B C D E F

→

	Canoe 1	Canoe 2
front		
mid		
rear		

Or

A B C D E F

	front	mid	rear
Canoe 1			
Canoe 2			

Reflection

Take a look back at your practice. Did you answer the SEAL questions for each game prior to setting up a sketch for it? Did you tease out all the actions that were present in each game? Did you make clear, simple sketches (regardless of whether you made one or two for each game)? Were you clear about which limitations applied to which action? Were there any limitations you missed?

In the coming days, take note of Hybrid tasks in real life: Do you have to select some of your employees and put them on teams? Will you choose whom to invite to a wedding and decide which table they're assigned to at the reception? How would the testmaker turn these into logic games? What restrictions and rules would you need to make the final arrangements?

Summary: Game Types and Sketches

In this chapter, you've seen Steps 1 and 2 of the Logic Games Method in action. You've learned a great deal about SEAL and about making sketches. And you've also met the full catalog of game types:

- Sequencing
- Selection
- Matching
- Distribution
- Hybrid

In the practice set that follows, you'll have the opportunity not only to apply Steps 1 and 2 to each overview, as you've been doing, but you'll also get some practice with discerning which type of game each one represents. Be careful as you answer the SEAL questions and feel free to refer to your work earlier in this chapter to review which type of sketch works best with each action you encounter.

Practice

Apply Steps 1 and 2 of the Kaplan Method for Logic Games to each of the following game overviews. Determine the situation, entities, action and limitations described. Then make a simple sketch, complete with a roster of entities. After each, you can review the expert test taker's approach.

Overview	My Analysis
15. Each of six people—A, B, C, D, E, and F—graduated from Big City High School in a different annual class, from the years 1999 to 2004.	

Overview	**My Analysis**

16. A woman goes to the library to check out some books for a long trip. She has a list of eight books she really wants to read—A, B, C, D, E, F, G, and H. She will select at least two books for her trip. The library only allows her to check out five books at a time.

17. A young boy is organizing seven baseball cards—A, B, C, D, E, F and G—into three categories, numbered 1, 2, and 3. Each card will be placed into exactly one of the three categories.

18. A four-story building houses five businesses— Shops A, B, C, D, and E—and each floor has at least one business on it. Shop B needs to be on a higher floor than Shop E.

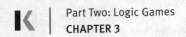
Overview	My Analysis

19. Six bicycles numbered 1 through 6 are lined up in a store window. Each bicycle is colored either A or B, is made by company c or d, and has handlebars of type *E* or *F*.

20. Eight students—A, B, C, D, E, F, G and H—hope to meet with a piano teacher this week. The piano teacher has one opening in the morning and one in the afternoon on each of Monday, Tuesday, and Wednesday. The piano teacher will schedule one lesson for each opening on her schedule, and she can only see one student at a time.

21. Two high school teachers—teacher 1 and teacher 2—will choose students to be on a debate team that will be composed of exactly five students. Each teacher will choose from among students in her own class, and each class is made up of five students—A, B, C, D, and E in teacher 1's class and F, G, H, I, and J in teacher 2's class. The final team must have at least two students from each teacher's class.

Overview	My Analysis
22. While preparing for a trip to Europe, each of three friends—A, B, and C—will research at least one and up to four countries. The friends have narrowed down the list of countries that they want to visit to five—d, e, f, g, and h.	
23. A child is going to choose five books, all with different titles, to take to her grandmother's house. She has seven books to choose from—A, B, C, D, E, F, and G—and each book is written by exactly one of four different authors—h, j, k, and m.	
24. Exactly three juniors—A, B, and C—and five seniors—d, e, f, g, and h—are working on a recycling project. In order to be more effective, they are going to create two 4-person teams. Each team needs to have at least one junior.	

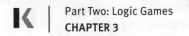

Expert Analysis

Here's how the expert test taker analyzed the overview and created the initial sketch for each of the games you just saw:

Overview	Analysis
15. Each of six people—A, B, C, D, E, and F—graduated from Big City High School in a different annual class, from the years 1999 to 2004.	**Step 1:** *Situation:* Figure out who graduated in what year. *Entities:* The graduates (A, B, C, D, E, F) and the years (1999 through 2004) *Action:* Because there are six people, and each graduated in a different class (no overlap), this is a *Sequencing* game. Each student needs to be assigned to exactly one of the six years. *Limitations:* Six people, six spots, no ties **Step 2:** A B C D E F — — — — — — 99 00 01 02 03 04
16. A woman goes to the library to check out some books for a long trip. She has a list of eight books she really wants to read—A, B, C, D, E, F, G, and H. She will select at least two books for her trip. The library only allows her to check out five books at a time.	**Step 1:** *Situation:* A woman at the library is trying to figure out which books to check out. *Entities:* The books (A, B, C, D, E, F, G, H) *Action:* Because the woman is going to "check out" or *select* only some books out of a larger total number of books, this is a *Selection* game. *Limitations:* The woman is going to check out at least two books, but she can't check out more than five. So this Selection game has minimum and maximum restrictions. **Step 2:** A Selection game sketch is no more than the list of entities. Note, however, the minimum and maximum number restrictions. (pick 2–5 out of 8) A B C D E F G H

Overview	Analysis
17. A young boy is organizing seven baseball cards—A, B, C, D, E, F and G—into three categories, numbered 1, 2, and 3. Each card will be placed into exactly one of the three categories.	**Step 1:** *Situation:* A young boy is trying to decide how to organize his baseball cards. *Entities:* Baseball cards (A, B, C, D, E, F, G) and the different groups into which the boy will place them (1, 2, 3) *Action:* Separating cards into categories—because each card can only go into one category, or group—makes this a *Distribution* game. *Limitations:* No stated minimum or maximum number of cards placed in each category. The rules will give more restrictions.

→

Step 2: Typical Distribution sketch—the groups positioned at the top of a table, with columns for the cards once we know where they go

A B C D E F G

Group 1	Group 2	Group 3

Overview	Analysis
18. A four-story building houses five businesses—Shops A, B, C, D, and E—and each floor has at least one business on it. Shop B needs to be on a higher floor than Shop E.	**Step 1:** *Situation:* A building with four floors and five businesses *Entities:* The shops (A, B, C, D, E) *Action:* Because Shop B needs to be on a higher floor than Shop E, positional arrangement matters. This is a *Sequencing* game. *Limitations:* Because there are five businesses and four floors, and because each floor must hold at least one business, exactly one floor holds two businesses and the other four floors hold one business apiece.

→

Step 2: Buildings are vertical, so it makes "real-world" sense to draw this sketch vertically.

A B C D E

4 —
3 —   (+ _ extra business)
2 —
1 —

B
.
.
.
E

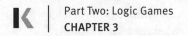
Overview	**Analysis**

19. Six bicycles numbered 1 through 6 are lined up in a store window. Each bicycle is colored either A or B, is made by company c or d, and has handlebars of type *E* or *F*.

Step 1: *Situation:* Bikes in a shop window, each one possessing a variety of features

Entities: There are the bikes (1 through 6), each bike's color (either A or B), the company that makes each bike (c or d), and the type of handlebars for each bike (*E* or *F*)

Action: The bicycles are in fixed positions, so there's no Sequencing action. The task is to match features to the bikes. Determining the attributes of fixed entities makes this a *Matching* game.

Limitations: Each bicycle is matched to exactly one of each type of attribute (color, manufacturer, and handlebar type).

⟶

Step 2: Create a grid—each of the six bikes will have exactly three characteristics. On one row of the grid, enter A or B, for color. On the next row, add c or d for brand. On the last row, place *E* or *F* for handlebar type.

1	2	3	4	5	6	
						A or B
						c or d
						E or F

Overview	Analysis

20. Eight students—A, B, C, D, E, F, G and H—hope to meet with a piano teacher this week. The piano teacher has one opening in the morning and one in the afternoon on each of Monday, Tuesday, and Wednesday. The piano teacher will schedule one lesson for each opening on her schedule, and she can only see one student at a time.

→

Step 1: *Situation:* A piano teacher is trying to schedule piano lessons for the week

Entities: The eight students (A, B, C, D, E, F, G, H), the three days of the week (Mon, Tue, Wed), and the time of day of each appointment (morning or afternoon)

Action: Eight students but only six openings—one task is to *select* the six students getting appointments. Days of the week and times of the day indicate sequential ordering—a second task is to determine the *order* in which the students are scheduled to meet with the teacher. This is a *Selection-Sequencing Hybrid* game.

Limitations: The teacher can only see one student at a time—no "double" appointments. The teacher picks six students, so two students are out. Knowing which students *are not* selected is as helpful as knowing who is selected.

Step 2: The intuitive sketch here mimics a calendar. Circle or cross-out entities to keep track of students who are definitively selected or rejected for appointment times.

A B C D E F G H

	Mon	Tues	Wed
A.M.			
P.M.			

Overview	Analysis
21. Two high school teachers—teacher 1 and teacher 2—will choose students to be on a debate team that will be composed of exactly five students. Each teacher will choose from among students in her own class, and each class is made up of five students—A, B, C, D, and E in teacher 1's class and F, G, H, I, and J in teacher 2's class. The final team must have at least two students from each teacher's class.	**Step 1:** *Situation:* Deciding whom to pick for a high school debate team

Step 1: *Situation:* Deciding whom to pick for a high school debate team

Entities: The teachers' classes (1 and 2) and the students (A, B, C, D, E, F, G, H, I, J)

Action: Five students will be chosen out of 10 students, so this is a *Selection* game.

Limitations: Five-person team with at least two from each class—either teacher 1 = two students and teacher 2 = three students or vice versa.

Step 2: Use a Selection sketch, but signify the two classes with a table.

(pick 5 out of 10)

(2 – 3)	(2 – 3)
class 1	class 2
A B C D E	f g h i j

---

22. While preparing for a trip to Europe, each of three friends—A, B, and C—will research at least one and up to four countries. The friends have narrowed down the list of countries that they want to visit to five—d, e, f, g, and h.

Step 1: *Situation:* Friends researching different countries before a trip

Entities: The friends (A, B, C) and the countries (d, e, f, g, h)

Action: The task is to determine the country or countries each friend researches—this is a *Matching* game.

Limitations: Each friend must research at least one country, but no friend can research all five. Countries can be assigned to more than one friend.

Step 2: Use a table or grid for Matching games. Set up the table to indicate that the number of countries each friend researches is unknown. Indicate number limitations above.

d e f g h

(1 – 4)	(1 – 4)	(1 – 4)
A	B	C

Overview	Analysis
23. A child is going to choose five books, all with different titles, to take to her grandmother's house. She has seven books to choose from—A, B, C, D, E, F, and G—and each book is written by exactly one of four different authors—h, j, k, and m.	**Step 1:** *Situation:* A child picking some books to take with her on a trip *Entities:* The seven books (A, B, C, D, E, F, G) and the different authors (h, j, k, m) *Action:* Choose five of seven books—a *Selection* action. Additionally, each book has an author. Because the authors are not "used up," this also has a *Matching* action. This is a *Selection-Matching Hybrid* game. *Limitations:* No mention of the number of authors that must be selected in this game. With five books and four authors, however, at least one author must be chosen twice. **Step 2:** Make a sketch linking the Selection and Matching tasks. Circle the selected books and cross out the rejected ones. Beneath each book, put a slot for the matching author.

$$A \quad B \quad C \quad D \quad E \quad F \quad G \quad (5 \text{ of } 7)$$
$$\underline{} \ \underline{} \ \underline{} \ \underline{} \ \underline{} \ \underline{} \ \underline{} \quad : h \, j \, k \, m$$

Overview	Analysis
24. Exactly three juniors—A, B, and C—and five seniors—d, e, f, g, and h—are working on a recycling project. In order to be more effective, they are going to create two 4-person teams. Each team needs to have at least one junior.	**Step 1:** *Situation:* Creating teams for a recycling project *Entities:* The juniors (A, B, C) and the seniors (d, e, f, g, h) *Action:* Eight total students divided into two groups of four. This is a *Distribution* game. *Limitations:* Each group must have exactly four students. Because each team must have at least one junior, and because there are only three juniors, one team will have one junior and three seniors, while the other has two juniors and two seniors. **Step 2:** Set up a table with the teams on top and four dashes in each column to represent the students.

jun: A B C   Team 1 | Team 2
sen: d e f g h   ———————————————

Team 1	Team 2	
——	——	jun
——	——	jun/sen
——	——	sen
——	——	sen

Reflection

Take a look back at your practice. Did you answer the SEAL questions for each game prior to setting up a sketch for it? Did you spot the textual clues that pointed you toward the appropriate game actions? Were there valuable clues you missed? Did you set up each sketch based on your knowledge of the game's central action? Were your sketches easy to read, quick to replicate, and able to accommodate ambiguity? What have you learned from this exercise?

Did you make some mistakes? You probably did, and you should be grateful for them and put them to good use! Each and every mistake you make in your practice tells you something valuable about what mistakes you'd be likely to make if you took the LSAT today. Use that information to help you understand what you most need to work on before Test Day.

Summary

All of the work you've done in this chapter involved logic games' overviews—just their opening paragraphs—and yet you've learned so much about how each game will proceed. From the overview, you're able to discern the game's situation, entities, action, and limitations, and you're able to make a sketch that will accommodate all of the game's restrictions. Now that you have some solid practice in all of those skills, you're ready to start building information into that sketch—in other words, you're ready to tackle the *rules*.

CHAPTER 4

Logic Games: Rules and Deductions

Most LSAT experts would agree that the skills you'll learn in this chapter are the most important tools you can add to your logic games repertoire. Here, you'll learn to analyze and draw a game's rules and then—and this is what sets real Logic Games masters apart from the crowd—to combine the game's rules and limitations to determine everything that can be deduced about what must, can, and cannot be true about the arrangement of entities. Gaining mastery of the skills in this chapter is your ticket to handling the questions quickly and accurately on a consistent basis.

To this point, you've seen how LSAT experts conduct the Overview and Sketch steps of the Logic Games Method. They analyze the Situation, Entities, Action, and overall Limitations to form a clear mental picture of their task. Then, they translate that mental picture into a diagram that will hold all of the relevant restrictions. In Chapter 3, we avoided displaying the rules to focus your practice on clearly analyzing a game's big picture. Now, we'll add in the rules and use the next two steps of the Logic Games Method to produce a comprehensive Master Sketch for each game we see. Along the way, you'll have plenty of opportunities to practice analyzing and sketching rules and then combining them to make all available deductions.

STEP 3 OF THE LOGIC GAMES METHOD: ANALYZE AND DRAW THE RULES

A college dean will present seven awards for outstanding language research. The awards—one for French, one for German, one for Hebrew, one for Japanese, one for Korean, one for Latin, and one for Swahili—must be presented consecutively, one at a time, in conformity with the following constraints:

The German award is not presented first.
The Hebrew award is presented at some time before the Korean award is presented.
The Latin award is presented at some time before the Japanese award is presented.
The French award is presented either immediately before or immediately after the Hebrew award is presented.
The Korean award is presented either immediately before or immediately after the Latin award is presented.

PrepTest29 Sec3 Qs 14—19

The game on the preceding page is one you saw in Chapter 3, but now we've displayed the rules below the setup paragraph, just as they would appear on the LSAT. Try drawing them into the sketch. How would you do it? Do the rules combine to create additional restrictions that you can deduce? Later in the chapter, we'll show you how an LSAT expert would handle the rules and create a Master Sketch allowing her to answer all of the game's questions quickly and accurately. (You'll learn to answer all of the Logic Games question types in Chapter 5, by the way.)

When an LSAT expert draws out a game's rules, she depicts them clearly, in a way that matches and fits into the framework of her sketch and accounts for what the rule does and does not mean. In the first part of this chapter, you'll see how the LSAT expert is able to do that within each of the common game types using the typical sketches introduced in Chapter 3.

LEARNING OBJECTIVES

In this section, you'll learn to:

- Determine accurately what a rule restricts and what it leaves undetermined.
- Determine whether to draw a rule into the Sketch framework or display it off to the side.
- Analyze and sketch rules.
- Decide whether a rule is more helpful drawn in positive or negative terms.

Because you have to apply these objectives to every rule, you can think of them as part of one overarching component of LSAT mastery: Analyze and Draw the Rules. As you practice with the following examples and drills, we'll remind you of the questions you need to ask in order to manage every rule effectively. We'll introduce the rules by game type so that you can see them within the context in which they're most likely to appear on Test Day.

Rules in Sequencing Games

From previous chapters, you know that Sequencing is by far the most common game type on recent LSATs. It's not uncommon for two of the four games in a Logic Games section to be Sequencing games or for one to be a Sequencing game and another to be a Hybrid game with a Sequencing action. It's unlikely that you need more motivation for taking Sequencing rules seriously than the knowledge that half or more of your Logic Games score will likely depend on mastering this game type. Think for a moment about what you've already learned about Sequencing games. In these games, you're always tasked with determining the order of a number of entities. That should help you anticipate the types of rules you're going to encounter here.

LSAT STRATEGY

Sequencing rules basically tell you one or more of the following things:

- The order in which two or more entities are placed
- The number of spaces between two or more entities
- The slot(s) in which a given entity can or cannot be placed

As you read through the LSAT expert's analyses of the rules in Sequencing games, think back to that list and ask in what way each rule is restricting or defining the arrangement of entities.

In Chapter 2, you saw how an LSAT expert analyzed and drew the rules for the Racehorses game, a game you'll now quickly recognize as a Strict Sequencing game. Reflect on that example with each rule broken out individually.

LSAT Question	Analysis
Six racehorses—K, L, M, N, O, and P—will be assigned to six positions arranged in a straight line and numbered consecutively 1 through 6. The horses are assigned to the positions, one horse per position, according to the following conditions:	**Steps 1 and 2:** $\quad$ K L M N O P $\overline{\ 1\ }\ \ \overline{\ 2\ }\ \ \overline{\ 3\ }\ \ \overline{\ 4\ }\ \ \overline{\ 5\ }\ \ \overline{\ 6\ }$
K and L must be assigned to positions that are separated from each other by exactly one position.	**Step 3:** $\underline{K/L}\ \ \_\_\ \ \underline{L/K}$
K and N cannot be assigned to positions that are next to each other.	~$\underline{N}\ \underline{K}$ ~$\underline{K}\ \underline{N}$
N must be assigned to a higher-numbered position than M.	M . . . N
P must be assigned to position 3. *PrepTest28 Sec2 Qs 1–5*	$\overline{\ 1\ }\ \ \overline{\ 2\ }\ \ \overset{P}{\overline{\ 3\ }}\ \ \overline{\ 4\ }\ \ \overline{\ 5\ }\ \ \overline{\ 6\ }$

Take note of how the LSAT expert drew out each rule, and see what that tells you about her thinking. **Rule 1:** This rule tells us the distance by which two entities are separated, but not their relative order. **Rule 2:** This is a negative rule telling us that two entities may not be consecutive regardless of their relative order. **Rule 3:** This rule tells us the relative order between two entities, but not the distance between them. **Rule 4:** This rule establishes precisely the position of one entity.

Notice how carefully the LSAT expert depicted each rule. She made sure that her scratchwork for Rule 1 shows the distance between K and L precisely, but does so in such a way that the entities' relative order is not determined. The expert's use of an ellipsis for Rule 3 shows the entities' relative order, but doesn't determine their distance apart. Moreover, the expert was careful to note that a "higher-numbered position" puts N to the right of M in her sketch. She built Rule 4 directly into the sketch framework because it will never be open to any other interpretation.

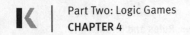

Now, take a look at the first Sequencing game you saw illustrated in Chapter 3. This time, we've added the LSAT expert's analysis and drawing for each rule. As you review the expert's thinking, take note of any ways in which he's made sure to note what the rule does and does not prescribe. (NOTE: If at any time in this chapter you have trouble remembering how the LSAT expert arrived at a particular sketch, flip back to Chapter 3 for a moment and review the Step 1 and Step 2 analysis there.)

LSAT Question	Analysis
A college dean will present seven awards for outstanding language research. The awards—one for French, one for German, one for Hebrew, one for Japanese, one for Korean, one for Latin, and one for Swahili—must be presented consecutively, one at a time, in conformity with the following constraints:	**Steps 1 and 2:** F G H J K L S $\overline{1}$ $\overline{2}$ $\overline{3}$ $\overline{4}$ $\overline{5}$ $\overline{6}$ $\overline{7}$
The German award is not presented first.	**Step 3:** Add this rule directly to the Master Sketch: $\overline{1}$ $\overline{2}$ $\overline{3}$ $\overline{4}$ $\overline{5}$ $\overline{6}$ $\overline{7}$ ~G
The Hebrew award is presented at some time before the Korean award is presented.	H . . . K
The Latin award is presented at some time before the Japanese award is presented.	L . . . J
The French award is presented either immediately before or immediately after the Hebrew award is presented.	F and H are presented consecutively, but we don't know in which order. Place F and H in a box, but note that the order is not established. (F/H)
The Korean award is presented either immediately before or immediately after the Latin award is presented. *PrepTest29 Sec3 Qs 14–19*	(K/L)

The rules in the Language Awards game break down pretty evenly. **Rule 1:** This is a negative rule preventing an entity from taking a specific position. **Rules 2 and 3:** These rules each establish the relative order between pairs of entities but tell you nothing about their distance apart. **Rules 4 and 5:** These rules each tell you that pairs of entities will appear consecutively, but tell you nothing about their relative orders.

We'll return to the Language Awards game later in the chapter to make all of the available deductions. Before you leave the game here, though, take a moment to realize what you already know from Rules 2 and 3. Because those rules dictate the order between two pairs of entities, you can be certain that neither Korean nor Japanese will be presented first. Likewise, neither Hebrew nor Latin will be presented last. Always keep in mind that the negative implications of a rule may be as strong or stronger than the rule's affirmative restrictions.

Loose Sequencing Rules

From Chapter 3, you'll remember the description and example of Loose Sequencing, the less common variant among Sequencing games. The distinguishing characteristic of Loose Sequencing games is that all of the rules are relative; they tell you only about the order among the entities and include no information about how far apart the entities are spaced. The nature of Loose Sequencing rules often allows you to combine the rules as you're interpreting them. Every time an entity is shared between two or more rules, stitching the rules together allows you to see the full impact of their restrictions.

In the following analysis, we'll show you the expert's thinking about the rules, and we'll show you how she combines the rules as she goes along. While this may not apply to every Loose Sequencing game you encounter, expect to be able to combine at least some of the rules as you analyze them.

LSAT Question	**Analysis**
A movie studio is scheduling the release of six films—Fiesta, Glaciers, Hurricanes, Jets, Kangaroos, and Lovebird. No two of these films can be released on the same date. The release schedule is governed by the following conditions:	**Steps 1 and 2:** A quick scan of the rules—they all provide for relative relationships among the entities—identifies this as a Loose Sequencing game. A roster of the entities will suffice to start with. F G H J K L
Fiesta must be released earlier than both Jets and Lovebird.	**Step 3:**
Kangaroos must be released earlier than Jets, and Jets must be released earlier than Hurricanes.	K...J...H Because Rule 1 and Rule 2 both mention J, they can be combined.
Lovebird must be released earlier than Glaciers. *PrepTest71 Sec2 Qs 1–5*	L...G Because Rule 1 and Rule 3 both mention L, this rule can be added to the overall sketch. Of course, a vertical orientation for the sketch is equally valid and useful.

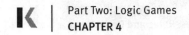

Let's be clear. There is nothing wrong with jotting down all of the rules individually and then taking a few seconds in Step 4, the Deductions step, to combine them into a comprehensive Master Sketch. The LSAT expert's analysis showed her combining as she went to illustrate how that may be done. As you practice Loose Sequencing, try both ways and use the approach that works better for you. In either case, you'll need to read the rules very carefully (did you notice that the testmaker kept changing between "before" and "after" to reward the test taker who was paying attention?) and combine the rules that share entities before tackling the questions.

One other note on Loose Sequencing sketches: Make sure you don't make unwarranted assumptions based on the picture you draw. In the final sketch on the preceding page, for example, all you know about G is that it follows F and L; you cannot assume any relationship between G and K, J, or H; G could be before all three of them, after all three of them, or it could come in between K and J, or in between J and H. F, on the other hand, is restricted by four entities (L, G, J, and H); F can only be presented first or second. We'll go even deeper in our analysis of this game in the next section of the chapter. For now, reflect for a few moments on what you know and don't know about each entity. Start learning to avoid the unwarranted visual assumptions that poor test takers make in Loose Sequencing games.

Practice

Now, you'll have the chance to practice reading, analyzing, and drawing some common Sequencing rules. In this exercise, we won't include full games, so don't worry about the overall sketch unless some indication of it is provided. Rather, focus on the kind of detail-oriented, critical analysis that an LSAT expert does with each individual rule. Here are the questions you should ask about each rule.

LSAT STRATEGY

When analyzing and drawing a rule, always ask:

- What does the rule restrict?
- What does the rule leave undetermined?
- Is the rule stated in affirmative or negative terms?
- If stated affirmatively, can I learn something concrete from its negative implications (or vice versa)?
- Can I place the rule directly into the sketch framework?
- If not, how can I best draw the rule to account for what it does and does not restrict?

Here are a couple of examples of an LSAT expert putting those questions to work.

Rule	Analysis
A and B are placed in adjacent seats.	The rule says that A and B sit next to one another.
	It does not determine whether A or B comes first.
→	The rule is in affirmative terms. The negative implication is that there are never any spaces between A and B.
	The rule doesn't assign specific seats, so this can't be placed directly into the framework.
	Sketch:
	$\underline{A/B}$ $\underline{B/A}$
	Or
	$\underline{A}$ $\underline{B}$ or $\underline{B}$ $\underline{A}$

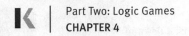

Rule	Analysis
There are at least two days after D's appointment but before C's appointment.	The rule tells us the order—D before C—and gives some restriction about the distance between the two. The rule does not say exactly how many days separate the two entities' appointments. $\longrightarrow$ The rule is stated affirmatively. The negative implication is that D and C never have appointments one or two days apart. Also, C's appointment is never earlier than the fourth day and D's appointment is never later than the fourth day from the end. The rule doesn't assign specific days, so it cannot be built into the calendar. Sketch: D ___ ___ ... C

The following is a list of other rules associated with Sequencing games (and Hybrid games with a Sequencing action).

Rule	Analysis
A appears on some day before B.	$\longrightarrow$ A . . . B
A appears on some day before B and also on some day before C.	A . . . B and A . . . C Or $\longrightarrow$ A ⋀ B C
A appears the day immediately before the day on which B appears.	$\longrightarrow$ AB
Appointments V and W have exactly one appointment separating them.	V ___ W or W ___ V $\longrightarrow$ Or V/W ___ W/V

Rule	Analysis
Appointments V and W have at least one appointment separating them.	$\underline{V}$ __ . . . $\underline{W}$ or $\underline{W}$ __ . . . $\underline{V}$ $\longrightarrow$ *Or* $\underline{V/W}$ __ . . . $\underline{W/V}$
In a game disallowing ties: R never appears before S.	$\longrightarrow$ S...R
In a game allowing ties: R never appears before S.	$\longrightarrow$ $\boxed{\dfrac{R}{S}}$ or S . . . R NOT R . . . S
C occurs on the third day after D.	$\longrightarrow$ $\underline{D}$ __ __ $\underline{C}$
In a game in which every entity is used exactly once and there are eight entities: If R is not on day 3, then R must be on day 5.	If ~R3 → R5 If ~R5 → R3 *Or* $\longrightarrow$ $\overline{1}$ $\overline{2}$ $\overline{3}$ $\overline{4}$ $\overline{5}$ $\overline{6}$ $\overline{7}$ $\overline{8}$ R (pointing to 3 and 5)
D must appear before B but after H.	$\longrightarrow$ H . . . D . . . B
B appears before (but not immediately before) C.	$\longrightarrow$ $\underline{B}$ . . . __ $\underline{C}$
In a game disallowing ties: B appears before C, or B appears before D, but not both.	$\longrightarrow$ D . . . B . . . C or C . . . B . . . D
In a game disallowing ties: B appears before C, or D appears before B, but not both.	(B . . . C and B . . . D) or (D . . . B and C . . . B) *Or* $\longrightarrow$ B (branching to) C D or D C (branching to) B
There are exactly three appointments between M and R.	$\underline{M}$ __ __ __ $\underline{R}$ or $\underline{R}$ __ __ __ $\underline{M}$ $\longrightarrow$ *Or* $\underline{M/R}$ __ __ __ $\underline{R/M}$
In a game disallowing ties: Whenever A precedes B, C is fifth.	$\longrightarrow$ If A . . . B → C5 If ~C5 → B . . . A

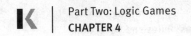
Now, try it out yourself. Examine each of the following rules. Ask the analysis questions outlined on page 169 and make your best effort at drawing the rule. You can compare your work to an LSAT expert's analysis that follows.

Rule	My Analysis
1. P is the fourth data packet received after R.	
2. P cannot be received until M, Q, and R have been received.	
3. S must be screened before L but after N.	
4. Of F, G, and H, G is the most productive.	
5. Of F, G, and H, G is the least productive.	
6. M is photographed either immediately before or immediately after N.	
7. In a game with seven train stops: The train line's second or third stop is P.	

Rule	**My Analysis**
8. In a game with seven train stops: The fifth stop is either S or T.	
9. In a game lining up six cars at a gas station: The red car is behind, but not immediately behind, the gray car.	
10. There is at most one car between the blue car and the yellow car.	
11. In a game disallowing ties: If S is served before J, then A is served before S.	
12. If R gets out at the fourth bus stop, then M does not get out at the first bus stop.	
13. In a game disallowing ties: F never precedes H unless A is third.	
14. In a game having people stand in line: G stands immediately ahead of J unless J is third in line.	

Expert Analysis

Here's how an LSAT expert would draw the rules you just saw. Don't worry if you didn't use exactly the same symbols in your pencil work, but make sure that you didn't over- or underdetermine the restriction called for by each rule.

Rule	Analysis
1. P is the fourth data packet received after R.	→ R _ _ _ P
2. P cannot be received until M, Q, and R have been received.	→ M ⋱ Q ⋯ P Or $\begin{matrix} M\ Q\ R \\ \searrow\downarrow\swarrow \\ P \end{matrix}$ R ⋰
3. S must be screened before L but after N.	→ N . . . S . . . L Or $\begin{matrix} N \\ \| \\ S \\ \| \\ L \end{matrix}$
4. Of F, G, and H, G is the most productive.	→ G ⋰ F ⋱ H Or $\begin{matrix} G \\ \diagup\diagdown \\ F\quad H \end{matrix}$
5. Of F, G, and H, G is the least productive.	→ F ⋱ G H ⋰ Or $\begin{matrix} F\quad H \\ \diagdown\diagup \\ G \end{matrix}$
6. M is photographed either immediately before or immediately after N.	→ MN *or* NM Or M/N N/M
7. In a game with seven train stops: The train line's second or third stop is P.	→ $\overline{1}\ \overline{2}\ \overline{3}\ \overline{4}\ \overline{5}\ \overline{6}\ \overline{7}$ with P pointing to 2 or 3
8. In a game with seven train stops: The fifth stop is either S or T.	→ $\overline{1}\ \overline{2}\ \overline{3}\ \overline{4}\ \overset{S/T}{\overline{5}}\ \overline{6}\ \overline{7}$
9. In a game lining up six cars at a gas station: The red car is behind, but not immediately behind, the gray car.	→ $\underline{G}$ . . . $\underline{\ \ }$ $\underline{R}$

Rule	Analysis
10. There is at most one car between the blue car and the yellow car. $\longrightarrow$	_B_ __ _Y_ or _Y_ __ _B_ or BY or YB Or B/Y __ Y/B or B/Y Y/B
11. In a game disallowing ties: If S is served before J, then A is served before S. $\longrightarrow$	If S . . . J → A . . . S (so A . . . S . . . J) If S . . . A → J . . . S (so J . . . S . . . A) There are exactly two possibilities: A . . . S . . . J or J . . . S . . . A
12. If R gets out at the fourth bus stop, then M does not get out at the first bus stop. $\longrightarrow$	If R4 → ~M1 If M1 → ~R4 Never R4 and M1 Or NOT $\left[\begin{array}{cc} M & R \\ 1 & 4 \end{array}\right]$
13. In a game disallowing ties: F never precedes H unless A is third. $\longrightarrow$	If F . . . H → A3 If ~A3 → H . . . F
14. In a game having people stand in line: G stands immediately ahead of J unless J is third in line. $\longrightarrow$	If ~J3 → GJ If ~GJ → J3

As you continue your practice with the games in Chapter 6 and with full-length LSATs, you'll have ample opportunity to analyze and sketch Sequencing rules. The wording will change slightly, but the test will use the same types of restrictions you've just seen.

Reflection

Over the coming days, pay attention to "sequencing" tasks you encounter in everyday life. Anytime you have to schedule a series of appointments or even put things in alphabetical order, you're sequencing. Notice how the real-life restrictions you face determine the way you handle your task. Alphabetizing, for example, determines the order in which you'll put two things, but not the number of spaces between them (at least not until you have a complete list of whatever you're alphabetizing). Some scheduling tasks, on the other hand, may offer different types of rules. You may need to meet with one person before you can meet with another, or you might need to take care of two different errands on the same day. The more you can demystify logic games and see that they mirror much of the same thinking and reasoning you do every day, the less intimidating and unfamiliar they'll seem on Test Day.

Rules in Selection Games

Selection games are less common than Sequencing games and do not appear on every test. Because these games always involve choosing some entities and rejecting others, almost all Selection rules involve conditional Formal Logic statements—choosing one entity may require you to reject another, for example. If you are strong at Formal Logic, you'll likely embrace Selection games and perform well on them. If not, you may want to revisit Chapter 1: LSAT Reasoning and brush up on the basics of Formal Logic before you work in depth with Selection rules.

LSAT STRATEGY

Selection rules tell you one or more of the following things:

- That at least one of two entities must be rejected
- That at least one of two entities must be selected
- That two entities must be selected or rejected as a pair (one cannot be selected or rejected without the other)
- That the selection of a specific entity requires the selection of another specific entity

---

Think back to what you learned about Selection games in Chapter 3. Do you recall that the suggested sketches for Selection games are nothing more than a list or roster of the entities? That is because, to handle the Selection task, you need do no more than circle the entities you know are chosen and cross out those you know are rejected. When you need to re-create the sketch for another question, you just write out the list of entities and start circling or crossing out again. That simple sketch combined with the conditional nature of nearly all Selection rules means that you have no need to build the rules into the sketch in Selection games. The best approach for recording Selection rules is to keep a neat list of the rules (often, but not always, in "If → then" format) right beneath your roster of entities. Whenever you jot down a Formal Logic rule in a Selection game, determine and record its contrapositive as well. Selection games will nearly always reward you for being able to see each rule in both affirmative and negative terms.

Take a look at how the LSAT expert recorded the rules associated with the Trees in the Park game you first saw in Chapter 3.

LSAT Question	Analysis
A park contains at most five of seven kinds of trees—firs, laurels, maples, oaks, pines, spruces, and yews—consistent with the following conditions:	**Steps 1 and 2:** F L M O P S Y (max 5)

If maples are in the park, yews are not.	**Step 3:**
	
	If (M) ⟶ ~Y
	If (Y) ⟶ ~M } Never MY together

If firs are in the park, pines are not.	If (F) ⟶ ~P If (P) ⟶ ~F } Never FP together

LSAT Question		**Analysis**
If yews are not in the park, then either laurels or oaks, but not both, are in the park.	$\longrightarrow$	If ~Y $\longrightarrow$ [Exactly one of (L)/(O)] If (L) and (O) $\longrightarrow$ (Y) If ~L and ~O $\longrightarrow$ (Y)
If it is not the case that the park contains both laurels and oaks, then it contains firs and spruces. *PrepTestB Sec2 Qs 7–12*	$\longrightarrow$	If ~L or ~O $\longrightarrow$ (F) and (S) If ~F or ~S $\longrightarrow$ (L) and (O)

Note, as the expert test taker did, the implications of each rule. Rules 1 and 2 both decrease the maximum number of entities available for your selection. One of M and Y must be excluded, as must one of F and P. Don't make the unwarranted assumption that one of M or Y (or one of F and P) must be included. These rules are only triggered by the inclusion of one of the named entities, not by their exclusion. Note, too, that the game's setup paragraph already stated that a maximum of five entities may be selected, so these rules, while impacting the specific pairs of entities (M and Y, F and P), do not alter that overall restriction.

Rule 3 is easy to misconstrue. Be careful. The exclusion of Y triggers a very specific outcome: Exactly one of L or O is selected. Without Y, you may never select both L and O, nor may you exclude both L and O. Without Y, you must have either L without O or O without L. To have both L and O selected, you must select Y. Likewise, to exclude both L and O, you must select Y. Notice that this establishes a minimum of at least one kind of tree that must be in the park.

Rule 4 also deserves careful scrutiny. The exclusion of any entity named in this rule triggers the selection of two other entities. If you exclude either L or O, then you must select both F and S. Likewise, if the park does not have trees of kind F or kind S, it must include trees of both kind L and kind O. The bottom line implication of Rule 4 is this: The park will have at least two kinds of trees in it, for sure.

Of course, this game doesn't include all of the variations on Formal Logic that appear in Selection games. Following, you'll see other common Selection rules and work through an exercise that will give you practice with a more exhaustive list.

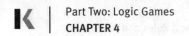

Practice

Now, you'll have the chance to practice reading, analyzing, and drawing some common Selection rules. In this exercise, we won't include full games, so don't worry about the overall sketch unless some indication of it is provided. Rather, focus on the kind of detail-oriented, critical analysis that an LSAT expert does with each individual rule in logic games. Following are the questions you should ask about each rule. Keep in mind that you're unlikely to draw Selection rules directly into the sketch because you'll just use a roster of entities, circling or crossing out to show each entity's selection status.

LSAT STRATEGY

When analyzing and drawing a rule, always ask:

- What does the rule restrict?
- What does the rule leave undetermined?
- Is the rule stated in affirmative or negative terms?
- If stated affirmatively, can I learn something concrete from its negative implications (or vice versa)?
- How can I best draw the rule to account for what it does and does not restrict?

The following is a list of other rules commonly associated with Selection games.

Rule		Analysis
R is selected only if S is selected.	→	If Ⓡ → Ⓢ If ~S → ~R
If G is selected and H is selected then J is not selected.	→	If Ⓖ and Ⓗ → ~J If Ⓙ → ~G or ~H
B is not selected unless C is selected.	→	If Ⓑ → Ⓒ If ~C → ~B
M is not selected unless Y and Z are also selected.	→	If Ⓜ → Ⓨ and Ⓩ If ~Y or ~Z → ~M *Or* If Ⓜ → Ⓨ If ~Y → ~M If Ⓜ → Ⓩ If ~Z → ~M
A and B cannot both be selected.	→	If Ⓐ → ~B If Ⓑ → ~A *Or* Never AB

Rule	Analysis
At least one of P and Q must always be selected.	→ If ~P → Ⓠ If ~Q → Ⓟ *Or* At least one of Ⓟ and Ⓠ (maybe both)
Exactly one of P and Q must be selected.	→ Ⓟ or Ⓠ (not both)
F is selected if and only if G is selected.	If Ⓕ → Ⓖ If ~G → ~F If Ⓖ → Ⓕ → If ~F → ~G *Or* FG—both or neither
Any arrangement that includes N includes neither R nor S.	IfⓃ → ~R and ~S IfⓇorⓈ → ~N *Or* IfⓃ → ~R → IfⓇ → ~N IfⓃ → ~S IfⓈ → ~N *Or* NeverⓃ Ⓡ NeverⓃ Ⓢ
T may not be included in any arrangement that includes V.	IfⓋ → ~T IfⓉ → ~V → *Or* NeverⓉⓋ
W will be included if Y is included.	→ IfⓎ → Ⓦ If ~W → ~Y
If A is selected, then either B or C is also selected but not both.	IfⒶ →Ⓑor Ⓒ IfⒶ → not [B and C combo] → If ~B and ~C → ~A If [Ⓑ andⒸ] → ~A

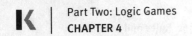

Now, try it out yourself. Examine each of the following rules. Ask the analysis questions previously outlined and make your best effort at drawing the rule. You can compare your work to an LSAT expert's analysis on the following pages.

Rule	My Analysis
15. Given that T is chosen, so is X.	
16. A is not selected if B is selected.	
17. C is included in the bag of jellybeans only if D is not.	
18. H is selected unless G is selected.	
19. In a game selecting a team of five specialists from a group of four archaeologists (A, B, C, D), four anthropologists (s, t, v, u), and four linguists (w, x, y, z): If the team includes more than two archaeologists, then it may include at most one anthropologist.	
20. If M is included, then neither O nor P is included.	

Rule	My Analysis
21. R is a member of any group of which P is a member.	
22. S is a member of any group of which Q is not a member.	
23. V is not a member of any group of which Z is a member.	
24. A is selected if, but only if, B is not selected.	
25. In a game that asks you to select an unspecified number of employees to be promoted from a group of eight: Only those employees with superb connections can be promoted.	
26. H cannot be chosen without L and K.	

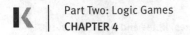
Expert Analysis

Here's how an LSAT expert would draw the rules you just saw. Don't worry if you didn't use exactly the same symbols in your pencil work, but make sure that you didn't over- or underdetermine the restriction called for by each rule.

Rule		Analysis
15.	Given that T is chosen, so is X.	→	If ⊤ → Ⓧ If ~X → ~T
16.	A is not selected if B is selected.		If Ⓑ → ~A If Ⓐ → ~B → Or Never Ⓐ Ⓑ
17.	C is included in the bag of jellybeans only if D is not.		If Ⓒ → ~D If Ⓓ → ~C → Or Never Ⓒ Ⓓ
18.	H is selected unless G is selected.		If ~G → Ⓗ If ~H → Ⓖ → Or Must have Ⓗ or Ⓖ or both.
19.	In a game selecting a team of five specialists from a group of four archaeologists (A, B, C, D), four anthropologists (s, t, v, u), and four linguists (w, x, y, z): If the team includes more than two archaeologists, then it may include at most one anthropologist.	→	If 3 or 4 of A, B, C, D → 0 or 1 of s, t, v, u If 2, 3, or 4 of s, t, v, u → 0, 1, or 2 of A, B, C, D
20.	If M is included, then neither O nor P is included.		If Ⓜ → ~O and ~P If Ⓞ or Ⓟ → ~M Or → Never Ⓜ Ⓞ Never Ⓜ Ⓟ Or If Ⓜ → ~O If Ⓞ → ~M If Ⓜ → ~P If Ⓟ → ~M
21.	R is a member of any group of which P is a member.	→	If Ⓟ → Ⓡ If ~R → ~P

Rule	Analysis
22. S is a member of any group of which Q is not a member.	→	If ~Q → Ⓢ If ~Ⓢ → Ⓠ *Or* Must have Ⓠ or Ⓢ or both.
23. V is not a member of any group of which Z is a member.	→	If Ⓩ → ~V If Ⓥ → ~Z *Or* Never Ⓥ Ⓩ
24. A is selected if, but only if, B is not selected.	→	If Ⓐ → ~B AND If ~B → Ⓐ If Ⓑ → ~A If ~A → Ⓑ Both parts of the rule must be observed, so A or B, but not both, must always be selected. Ⓐ or Ⓑ (not both)
25. In a game that asks you to select an unspecified number of employees to be promoted from a group of eight: Only those employees with superb connections can be promoted.	→	If promoted →superb connections If ~superb connections →~promoted
26. H cannot be chosen without L and K.	→	If Ⓗ → Ⓛ and Ⓚ If ~L or ~K → ~H

As you continue your practice with the games in Chapter 6 and with full-length LSATs, you'll have the opportunity to analyze and sketch additional Selection rules. More than any other game type, Selection games will test your Formal Logic skills. If you find that you need further practice, don't hesitate to return to the drills and examples in Chapter 1: LSAT Reasoning where we introduced the skills associated with identifying and translating Formal Logic statements, formulating contrapositives, and making valid deductions from multiple conditional statements.

Reflection

Over the coming days, pay attention to Selection tasks you encounter in everyday life. Anytime you have to choose certain people or items from a larger group, you're selecting. Notice how the real-life restrictions you face determine the way you handle your task. Even something as simple as a prix fixe restaurant menu may give rise to Selection rules: pick one of three appetizers and pick one of three desserts. If you choose the chicken, you may not have the prime rib. Another real-world Selection example would be a coach's task of selecting a starting lineup of 5 basketball players from a roster of 12. There, the coach faces rules along the lines of "Choose 1 center, 2 forwards, and 2 guards." The more you can demystify logic games and see that they mirror much of the same thinking and reasoning you do every day, the less intimidating and unfamiliar they'll seem on Test Day.

Rules in Matching and Distribution Games

Like Selection games, Matching and Distribution games are also less common than Sequencing and do not appear on every test. Matching and Distribution tasks are often included in Hybrid games, however, so your work on these game types is likely to be rewarded by at least one game on a typical test. Because both game types call for you to group entities under a number of headings, Matching and Distribution games often have very similar rules. The primary distinction to keep in mind is that Matching games usually allow you to "reuse" entities (e.g., matching a red jacket to one person doesn't prevent you from matching it to another), whereas Distribution typically requires you to place each entity just one time and into just one group.

In both of these game types, the Number Restrictions are central. Knowing exactly how many entities must be assigned to each group (Distribution) or how many attributes must be assigned to each entity (Matching) will be the most helpful information you can have. As you review the expert analysis and do your own practice with Matching and Distribution rules, focus on how the rules help to establish constraints on the numbers involved in the game.

LSAT STRATEGY

Distribution rules tell you one or more of the following things:

- Entities that must or cannot be assigned to the same group
- The number of entities that must, can, or cannot be assigned to a group or the relative sizes among groups (e.g., the Blue Group must have more members than the Green Group)
- Conditions triggering the assignment of an entity to a particular group (e.g., if Rachel joins the marketing team, then Gar joins the service team)

Matching rules tell you one or more of the following things:

- Attributes that must or cannot be matched to the same entity
- The number of attributes that must, can, or cannot be assigned to an entity or the relative numbers among entities (e.g., Sascha will be assigned more of the tasks than Craig will be assigned)
- Conditions triggering the assignment of an attribute to a particular entity (e.g., if Rebecca is assigned copyediting, then Jesse is assigned layout)

As you saw in Chapter 3, Matching and Distribution games use similar, if not identical, sketches. In both, columns under which you can record the assignment of an entity or attribute to a particular group or individual serve well to organize the restrictions and deductions. Whenever possible, record what you know about the number of entities you must, can, or cannot place in each column. Use slots to remind you that Group 1 will have four entities and Group 2 will have five, for example. Because the rules often include information about both the entities and the groups, drawing Matching and Distribution rules can be a little complicated at times. As you review the following expert analysis of the games and rules, pay special attention to how the LSAT expert accounts for all of the information in a rule without drawing it in a way that suggests the rule means more than it says.

Take a look at how the LSAT expert recorded the rules associated with the Recycling Centers game you first saw in Chapter 3.

LSAT Question	Analysis
There are exactly three recycling centers in Rivertown: Center 1, Center 2, and Center 3. Exactly five kinds of material are recycled at these recycling centers: glass, newsprint, plastic, tin, and wood. Each recycling center recycles at least two but no more than three of these kinds of material. The following conditions must hold:	**Steps 1 and 2:** G N P T W 1 2 3 ___ ___ ___ ___ ___ ___ ... ...
Any recycling center that recycles wood also recycles newsprint.	**Step 3:** Write this Formal Logic rule in a way that is appropriate for the sketch. If a center has wood, then it will also have newsprint, so in that situation wood and newsprint will be together in a block. If a center doesn't have newsprint, then it won't have wood. W ⟶ [W/N] ~N ⟶ ~[W/N]
Every kind of material that Center 2 recycles is also recycled at Center 1.	2 ⟶ 1 ~1 ⟶ ~2 With all Formal Logic rules, consider what it means to the sketch. This states that anything in Center 2 must be in Center 1. That does not mean that if a material is recycled in Center 1 it must be recycled in Center 2.
Only one of the recycling centers recycles plastic, and that recycling center does not recycle glass. *PrepTestJune2007 Sec1 Qs 18–23*	**Exactly one P** [G̶/P]

You'll recall this as an example of a Matching game because the materials can be recycled at more than one center (indeed, the implication of Rule 2 makes it clear that at least two materials must be recycled at more than one center—Center 2 must recycle at least two materials, and anything recycled at Center 2 must be recycled at Center 1). We'll return to the number restrictions when we reexamine this game later in the chapter to make all available deductions. There, we'll note the impact that the number restrictions have on individual materials.

Remember to be careful with Formal Logic such as we see in Rule 1. Any center recycling wood must also recycle newsprint. That does not mean that any center recycling newsprint must recycle wood. As you continue to encounter Formal Logic in Logic Games and Logical Reasoning, don't hesitate to return to Chapter 1 of this book to brush up on your skills translating conditional statements and forming their contrapositives.

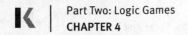
Now, take look at the Bill Paying game with its rules interpreted by an LSAT expert. Take note of similarities you see between the rules here and in the Recycling Centers game. Keep in mind, however, that the Bill Paying game is a Distribution game. Each bill is paid exactly once. No "reuse" is allowed here.

LSAT Question	Analysis
On a Tuesday, an accountant has exactly seven bills—numbered 1 through 7—to pay by Thursday of the same week. The accountant will pay each bill only once according to the following rules:	**Steps 1 and 2:** 1 2 3 4 5 6 7 → W | T
Either three or four of the seven bills must be paid on Wednesday, the rest on Thursday.	**Step 3:** W | T — | — — | — — | — ... | ...
Bill 1 cannot be paid on the same day as bill 5.	These bills must be paid on separate days. Add this directly to the sketch: W | T 1/5 | 5/1 — | — — | — ... | ...
Bill 2 must be paid on Thursday.	W | T 1/5 | 5/1 — | 2 — | — ... | ...
Bill 4 must be paid on the same day as 7.	Bills 4 and 7 must be blocked together, but it is not yet known on which day they will be paid. 4 7

LSAT Question	**Analysis**

If bill 6 is paid on Wednesday, bill 7 must be paid on Thursday.

PrepTest29 Sec3 Qs 1–6

$$\frac{W}{6} \longrightarrow \frac{T}{7}$$

Consider the contrapositive here: If bill 7 is not paid on Thursday, then bill 6 is not paid on Wednesday. Because all bills are paid on one of two days, any bill that is not paid on one day must be paid on the other. Turn the contrapositive into an affirmative deduction:

$$\frac{W}{7} \longrightarrow \frac{T}{6}$$

In Distribution games, the tradeoff for knowing that each entity is placed only once is that you may not know how many entities are placed in each group. That makes Rule 1 extremely important. When we return to this game to make its available deductions, we will set up two sketches—one with three slots on Wednesday and four on Thursday, and another with four slots on Wednesday and three on Thursday—to explore the full implications this Limited Options rule.

The other rules here are all pretty standard, providing restrictions you'll become used to seeing in Distribution games. Rule 2 keeps two entities apart. Notice how the LSAT expert built that directly into the sketch. She could not have done that if the game had three or four groups into which you were distributing the entities; in that case, she would simply have noted the restriction beneath the sketch framework. Rule 3 establishes the group for one entity, always a welcome piece of information. Rule 4—which keeps two entities together—is the converse of Rule 2. Rule 4 will take on added importance shortly when we set up the Limited Options sketches.

Rule 5 is standard Formal Logic, but in context, it deserves special comment. Because this Distribution game is binary (it has exactly two groups), knowing that an entity is not on Thursday is identical to knowing that it is on Wednesday. In situations like this, LSAT experts know that forming the contrapositive in affirmative terms can be clearer and more helpful than leaving it in negative language would be. Don't let "If-then" wording intimidate you; the practical impact of Formal Logic is often simple and always concrete.

Practice

Now, you'll have the chance to practice reading, analyzing, and drawing some common Matching and Distribution rules. In this exercise, we won't include full games, so don't worry about the overall sketch unless some indication of it is provided. Rather, focus on the kind of detail-oriented, critical analysis that an LSAT expert does with each individual rule in logic games. Here are the questions you should ask about each rule.

> ## LSAT STRATEGY
>
> When analyzing and drawing a rule, always ask:
>
> - What does the rule restrict?
> - What does the rule leave undetermined?
> - Is the rule stated in affirmative or negative terms?
> - If it's stated affirmatively, can I learn something concrete from its negative implications (or vice versa)?
> - Can I place the rule directly into the sketch framework?
> - How can I best draw the rule to account for what it does and does not restrict?

The following is a list of other rules commonly associated with Matching and Distribution games. (Remember to keep in mind that in Distribution games, all entities are used exactly once; that is, each entity is placed into exactly one subgroup.)

Rule	Analysis
In a game matching lamps to 2–3 shades each: Any lamp matched to a shade of type C may not be matched to a shade of type G.	$\rightarrow$ If C $\rightarrow$ ~G If G $\rightarrow$ ~C Never CG
In a game matching pencils to one or more colored erasers: Any pencil matched to a red eraser may not be matched to an orange eraser but must be matched to a green eraser.	If R $\rightarrow$ G and ~O If O or ~G $\rightarrow$ ~R Or $\rightarrow$ If R $\rightarrow$ ~O If O $\rightarrow$ ~R Never OR If R $\rightarrow$ G If ~G $\rightarrow$ ~R
In a game matching three flower beds to some combination of flowers (P, Q, R, S, T) planted in them: Bed #1 contains exactly three flower varieties.	$\rightarrow$ (table: columns 1 2 3, with three blank rows under column 1)
Exactly two beds must contain flower types P and R.	$\rightarrow$ $\boxed{\dfrac{P}{R}}$ 2×
At least two beds must contain flower types S and T.	$\rightarrow$ $\boxed{\dfrac{S}{T}}$ 2 – 3×

Rule	Analysis
In a game distributing eight colored marbles into bags A and B: Bag A contains either three or five marbles; the remaining marbles go into bag B.	$\rightarrow$ (see diagram)

(I) A | B   (II) A | B
— — | — —   — — | — —
— — | — —   — — | — —
         | — — | —

Rule	Analysis
In a game matching styles of ringtone to cell phones: The pink phone always plays jazz.	$\rightarrow$ If $\dfrac{\text{Pink}}{}$ → $\dfrac{\text{Pink}}{\text{J}}$ (Note, that does not mean all phones that play jazz are pink.)
In a game matching each of five students, F, G, H, J, and K, to the two or three textbooks each one purchases: Students J and K purchase exactly the same textbooks as each other.	$\rightarrow$ J = K
In a Distribution game distributing errands onto Thursday, Friday, and Saturday: Errand R and Errand S must be on different days.	Never RS *Or* $\rightarrow$ Never $\boxed{\dfrac{R}{S}}$
In a game distributing entities onto Thursday and Friday: If R is on Thursday, then S is on Friday.	If R_{Thurs} → S_{Fri} If S_{Thurs} → R_{Fri} $\rightarrow$ (Note that the contrapositive is affirmative because the entities are being distributed between exactly two days. Note, too, that R and S could both be on Friday.)
In a game distributing entities onto Thursday and Friday: If P is on Thursday, then M is on Thursday.	If P_{Thurs} → M_{Thurs} If M_{Fri} → P_{Fri} $\rightarrow$ (Note that P and M need not be on the same day. M could be on Thursday and P on Friday.)

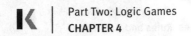

Now, try it out yourself. Examine each of the following rules. Ask the analysis questions outlined previously in the "LSAT Strategy" box and make your best effort at drawing the rule. You can compare your work to an LSAT expert's analysis on the following pages.

Rule	My Analysis
27. In a Distribution game: C is in a group with exactly two others.	
28. In a Distribution game: E and F are never in the same group.	
29. In a Distribution game: G and H are always in the same group.	
30. In a game distributing six people into two groups: Exactly twice as many people are in group 1 as in group two.	
31. In a game matching three children's birthday parties to a maximum of five games played at each one: A minimum of three and a maximum of four games are played at party #three.	
32. In a game distributing seven types of jellyfish (M, N, O, P, Q, R, S) into three tanks at a research aquarium: M is in tank two only if N is in tank 1.	

Rule	**My Analysis**
33. In a game distributing seven types of jellyfish (M, N, O, P, Q, R, S) into two tanks at a research aquarium: M is in tank 2 only if N is in tank 1.	
34. In a game distributing seven types of jellyfish (M, N, O, P, Q, R, S) into two tanks at a research aquarium: Any tank that contains O cannot contain P and cannot contain S.	
35. In a game distributing seven types of jellyfish (M, N, O, P, Q, R, S) into two tanks at a research aquarium: Any tank that contains O must also contain M.	
36. In a game matching each of five tables (P, Q, R, S, T) to the 1–3 types of wood used to manufacture them: Table P uses more types of wood than table T.	
37. In a game matching each of five tables (P, Q, R, S, T) to the 1–3 types of wood used to manufacture them: Table R must have exactly one type of wood in common with table S.	

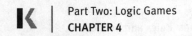

Expert Analysis

Here's how an LSAT expert would draw the rules you just saw. Don't worry if you didn't use exactly the same symbols in your pencil work, but make sure that you didn't over- or underdetermine the restriction called for by each rule.

Rule		Analysis
27.	In a Distribution game: C is in a group with exactly two others.	$\rightarrow$ $\boxed{\begin{array}{c} C \\ \hline \_ \\ \hline \_ \end{array}}$
28.	In a Distribution game: E and F are never in the same group.	$\rightarrow$ Never $\boxed{\dfrac{E}{F}}$
29.	In a Distribution game: G and H are always in the same group.	$\rightarrow$ $\boxed{\dfrac{G}{H}}$
30.	In a game distributing six people into two groups: Exactly twice as many people are in group 1 as in group 2.	$\rightarrow$ $\begin{array}{c c} 1 & 2 \\ \hline \_ \ \_ & \ \_ \ \_ \\ \_ \ \_ & \end{array}$
31.	In a game matching three children's birthday parties to a maximum of five games played at each one: A minimum of three and a maximum of four games are played at party 3.	$\rightarrow$ $\begin{array}{c c|c} 1 & 2 & 3 \\ \hline & & \_ \ \_ \\ & & \_ \ (\_) \end{array}$ *Or* (I) $\begin{array}{c|c|c} 1 & 2 & 3 \\ \hline & & \_ \ \_ \\ & & \_ \end{array}$ (II) $\begin{array}{c|c|c} 1 & 2 & 3 \\ \hline & & \_ \ \_ \\ & & \_ \ \_ \end{array}$
32.	In a game distributing seven types of jellyfish (M, N, O, P, Q, R, S) into three tanks at a research aquarium: M is in tank 2 only if N is in tank 1.	$\rightarrow$	If $M_2 \rightarrow N_1$ If $\sim N_1 \rightarrow \sim M_2$
33.	In a game distributing seven types of jellyfish (M, N, O, P, Q, R, S) into two tanks at a research aquarium: M is in tank 2 only if N is in tank 1.	$\rightarrow$	If $M_2 \rightarrow N_1$ If $N_2 \rightarrow M_1$ (M and N can both be in tank 1.)

Rule	Analysis
34. In a game distributing seven types of jellyfish (M, N, O, P, Q, R, S) into two tanks at a research aquarium: Any tank that contains O cannot contain P and cannot contain S.	If O → ~P and ~S If P or S → ~O *Or* If O → ~P If P → ~O Never OP If O → ~S If S → ~O Never OS
35. In a game distributing seven types of jellyfish (M, N, O, P, Q, R, S) into two tanks at a research aquarium: Any tank that contains O must also contain M.	If O → M If ~M → ~O
36. In a game matching each of five tables (P, Q, R, S, T) to the 1–3 types of wood used to manufacture them: Table P uses more types of wood than table T.	P > T P = 2 or 3 T = 1 or 2
37. In a game matching each of five tables (P, Q, R, S, T) to the 1–3 types of wood used to manufacture them: Table R must have exactly one type of wood in common with table S.	

Or R-S exactly 1 in common

As you continue your practice with the games in Chapter 6 and with full-length LSATs, you'll have the opportunity to analyze and sketch additional Matching and Distribution rules. In these games, you'll find the greatest emphasis on Number Restrictions. Throughout your practice, focus on how knowing the entities and attributes that must, can, or cannot be assigned together helps you to determine the acceptable arrangements within the games.

Reflection

Over the coming days, pay attention to "matching" and "distribution" tasks you encounter in everyday life. Maybe something along these lines will sound familiar: You're in charge of producing a newsletter or maintaining a website for a charity organization. You have a small team that helps you manage the tasks involved. You might assign one of your volunteers the job of taking photographs, editing articles, and bringing the donuts for the group meeting. You might need another volunteer to take photographs, too. In addition, this second person might also have the job of drafting one of the articles you'll post this month. This scenario describes a Matching game perfectly. Similarly, imagine assigning nine coworkers to three different committees for upcoming presentations. Everyone is too busy to be on more than one committee. Also, you have some coworkers whom you know cannot be assigned together (maybe their expertise is too similar, or maybe you know they'll just goof off if they are on the same team—the reason doesn't really matter). This is a Distribution game. We actually encounter little "logic games" almost every day. The more you can demystify logic games and see that they mirror much of the same thinking and reasoning you do every day, the less intimidating and unfamiliar they'll seem on Test Day.

Rules in Hybrid Games

The term *Hybrid games rules* is a bit misleading. Because Hybrid games combine two or three of the common games tasks, most of the rules you find in Hybrid games are exactly like those you see in single-action games. Usually, only one or two of the rules affect both actions. For example, in a Sequencing-Matching Hybrid game about a company's semiannual presentations, two rules might cover the relative order of pairs of entities (e.g., "Carla presents before Lionel"), two might affect attributes that can be matched to entities (e.g., "Paola does not present on marketing"), and one might combine the two actions (e.g., "If Joe is the third presenter, he presents financials").

The other thing to remember about Hybrid games is that the two actions, considered separately, are typically quite simple. Continuing with our imaginary Sequencing-Matching Hybrid game, it's likely the testmaker will ask you to sequence five or six presenters and to match each of them to a single presentation. So, don't let Hybrid games intimidate you.

LSAT STRATEGY

Hybrid rules tell you one of the following things:

- How the first of the actions is restricted
- How the second of the actions is restricted
- How the two actions are restricted simultaneously

Take a look at the Selection-Matching Hybrid game you encountered in Chapter 3, the one in which Irene buys furniture from Zeno's Unfinished Furniture. As you go over the expert's work, recall the tasks involved: You must select the four types of furniture Irene purchases, and match a kind of wood to each piece of furniture.

LSAT Question	Analysis
Zeno's Unfinished Furniture sells exactly five types of furniture—footstools, hutches, sideboards, tables, and vanities. Irene buys just four items, each of a different type, and each made entirely of one kind of wood—maple, oak, pine, or rosewood. The following conditions govern Irene's purchases:	**Steps 1 and 2:** (Select 4) <table><tr><td></td><td>F</td><td>H</td><td>S</td><td>T</td><td>V</td></tr><tr><td>m</td><td></td><td></td><td></td><td></td><td></td></tr><tr><td>o</td><td></td><td></td><td></td><td></td><td></td></tr><tr><td>p</td><td></td><td></td><td></td><td></td><td></td></tr><tr><td>r</td><td></td><td></td><td></td><td></td><td></td></tr></table>
Any vanity she buys is maple.	**Steps 3:** This can be added directly to the sketch. (See sketch on next page.)
Any rosewood item she buys is a sideboard.	If r ⟶ S / r If ~S ⟶ ~r This rule does not mean that if a sideboard is included it must be rosewood. It does mean that only a sideboard can be made of rosewood. Add this to the sketch. (See sketch on next page.)

LSAT Question	Analysis
If she buys a vanity, she does not buy a footstool.	This rule is the equivalent of saying "never V and F together." So, the one piece of furniture that is not selected is either F or V. That means the other three pieces—H, S, and T—must be selected. (See sketch below.)
If Irene buys a footstool, she also buys a table made of the same wood.	If F ⟶ T same wood If T diff't wood than F ⟶ ~F
Irene does not buy an oak table.	Add this directly to the sketch. (See sketch below.)
Exactly two of the items she buys are made of the same kind of wood as each other. *PrepTestB Sec2 Qs 19–24*	This rule can't be added directly to the sketch, so just jot it down in shorthand: **exactly 2 items same wood**

Here's how the LSAT expert added rules directly to the sketch.

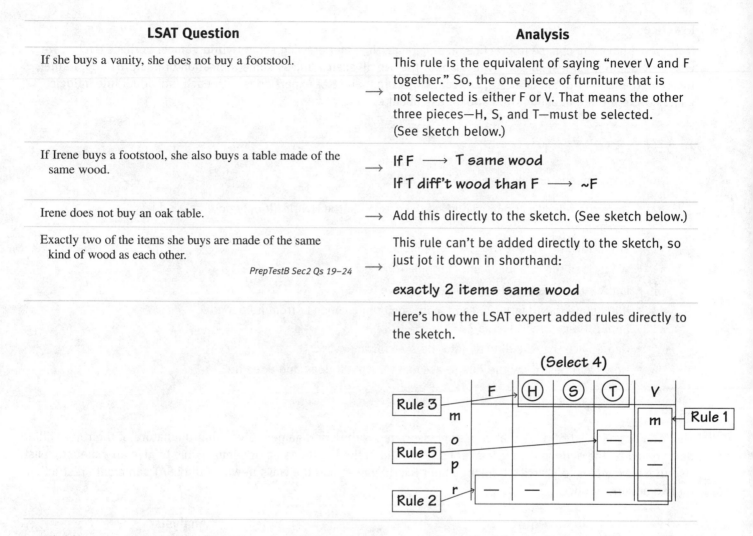

In Hybrid games, some rules will relate to one of the actions, some to the other action, and usually, one or more will impact both actions simultaneously. In this game, Rules 1 and 2 apply to the Matching action. Rule 3 applies specifically to the Selection action. Rules 4, 5, and 6 are true "hybrid rules," providing restrictions on the types of furniture and the kinds of wood Irene may purchase. With six explicit rules at the outset, this game is pretty restricted already. There won't be many additional deductions to make.

Practice

Now, you'll have the chance to practice reading, analyzing, and drawing some Hybrid games. In this exercise, we won't include full games, so don't worry about the overall sketch unless some indication of it is provided. Rather, focus on the kind of detail-oriented, critical analysis that an LSAT expert does with each individual rule in logic games. Here are the questions you should ask about each rule.

LSAT STRATEGY

When analyzing and drawing a rule, always ask:

- Does the rule affect one or both of the actions in the Hybrid? If only one, which one?
- What does the rule restrict?
- What does the rule leave undetermined?
- Is the rule stated in affirmative or negative terms?
- If it's stated affirmatively, can I learn something concrete from its negative implications (or vice versa)?
- Can I place the rule directly into the sketch framework?
- How can I best draw the rule to account for what it does and does not restrict?

The following is a list of rules that could be associated with Hybrid games. Given that the nature of the rules will be determined by the actions the testmaker has included in the Hybrid game, it's impossible to give an exhaustive list. Use these examples to practice thinking about Hybrid games and the ways in which the LSAT can create restrictions on two actions at once.

Rule	Analysis
In a Sequencing-Matching game that sequences N, O, P, Q, and R and matches each to *a*, *b*, or *c*: P is not matched to *a* unless N is first.	If $P_a \longrightarrow \dfrac{N}{1}$ If $\dfrac{\sim N}{1} \longrightarrow P_{\sim a}$
In a Distribution-Sequencing game disallowing ties that distributes music students A, B, C, D, E, and F into piano or violin classes and then orders them by age: If B plays piano, then A also plays piano, and A is older than B.	If $B_P \rightarrow A_P$ If $B_P \rightarrow A \ldots B$ Contrapositive: If $A_V \quad\; \rightarrow B_V$ If $B \ldots A \rightarrow B_V$
In a Sequencing-Matching game that sequences the towns a train passes through and also matches the towns to their respective industries: The train passes L at some time before it passes M but at some time after it passes the shoe factory.	$\dfrac{\quad\quad \ldots \quad L \quad \ldots \quad M \quad}{\text{Shoe}}$

Rule	Analysis
In a Sequencing-Matching game that sequences eight fire trucks in order of their arrival at the station and also matches them to their respective colors (red vs. chartreuse): Truck G, which arrives third, is the first red truck to arrive.	$$\begin{array}{cccccccc} & & G & & & & & \\ \hline 1 & 2 & 3 & 4 & 5 & 6 & 7 & 8 \\ C & C & R & \_ & \_ & \_ & \_ & \_ \end{array}$$
In a Selection-Sequencing game that selects six paintings from a group of nine and then arranges the chosen paintings in a straight line on a wall: P is chosen for display only if R is displayed in the second position.	If $\circled{P} \rightarrow \circled{R}_2$ If $\sim R_2 \rightarrow \sim P$
In a Selection-Matching game that selects three rubber balls from a group of seven and also matches the three balls chosen to their respective colors: L is not chosen unless it is red.	$\circled{L} \rightarrow \dfrac{L}{Red}$
In a Distribution-Selection game that selects six of eight entities and then distributes the six selected entities onto Thursday and Friday: If R is on Thursday, then S is on Friday.	If $R_T \rightarrow S_F$ If $\sim S_F \rightarrow \sim R_T$ Because we do not know whether R and S will both be selected, the opposite of "S on Friday" is "S on Thursday or S left out." It follows that we cannot write the contrapositive as "If $S_T \rightarrow R_F$" as for the similar distribution rule treated earlier.
In a Distribution-Selection game that selects six of eight entities and then distributes the six selected entities onto Thursday and Friday: If R is on Thursday, then S is on Thursday.	If $R_T \rightarrow S_T$ If $\sim S_T \rightarrow \sim R_T$ Again, the opposite of "on Thursday" is "on Friday or left out," so we cannot write the contrapositive of this rule as "If $S_F \rightarrow R_F$." Be sure to think very carefully about the opposites of the sufficient and necessary conditions when writing contrapositives.
In a Selection-Sequencing game that selects five of seven entities and then sequences the chosen entities: If A appears before B, then C is fifth.	If $A \ldots B \rightarrow C_5$ If $\sim C_5 \rightarrow \sim(A \ldots B)$ Here, the opposite of "A before B" is not necessarily "B before A" because A or B or both could be left out. So just write the opposite of "A before B" as "A not before B."
In a Selection-Matching game that selects 3–4 yarn colors for a scarf from six yarn colors (A, B, D, C, E, F) and then matches the 3–4 chosen colors to the four stripes of the scarf: Exactly one of the last two colors is color A.	$\circled{A}$ B C D E F $$\begin{array}{\|c\|c\|c\|c\|} \hline 1 & 2 & 3 & 4 \\ \hline \end{array}$$ $\nwarrow \circled{A} \nearrow$

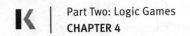

Now, try it out yourself. Examine each of the following rules. Ask the analysis questions outlined above in the "LSAT Strategy" box and make your best effort at drawing the rule. You can compare your work to an LSAT expert's in the analyses that follow.

Rule	My Analysis
38. In a Selection-Distribution game that selects an unknown number of employees who carpool together and determines which of two cars the selected employees ride in: K rides in whatever car J rides in.	
39. In the same game: Unless L is left out of the carpool, M rides in car 1.	
40. In a Selection-Sequencing game that selects five pies from a group of seven (H, J, K, L, M, P, Q) and then arranges them on a banquet table: Q is not chosen unless M is third of fifth.	
41. In a Sequencing-Distribution game that sequences the six cabs at a taxi stand by driver and matches each driver to one or more passengers: R, who drives the fourth cab, picks up exactly two passengers, one of whom is y.	
42. In a Distribution-Sequencing-Selection game that constructs a lineup for two four-person relay swim teams from a group of nine available swimmers: X is in the first position on team 1 only if W is in the third position on team 2.	

Rule	My Analysis
43. In a Sequencing-Matching game that sequences seven old airplanes arriving at a hangar in preparation for an airshow and also determines whether each plane that arrives is a monoplane or a biplane: Q, the sixth plane to arrive, is also the last monoplane to arrive.	
44. In a Sequencing-Matching game that sequences five lectures and matches them to the experts delivering them: The first and fourth lectures must be delivered by the same expert.	
45. In the same game: The second lecture is delivered by E if and only if the third lecture is delivered by H.	
46. In a Sequencing-Matching game with a no-ties limitation: A is second only if F is matched to c.	
47. In a Selection-Matching-Sequencing game that selects five of six pieces of furniture (P, Q, R, S, T, U) and matches those that are chosen to types of wood (c, d, e, f, g, h), and then sequences those pieces of furniture: Exactly two of the first three pieces of furniture are of type d wood.	

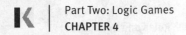

Expert Analysis

Here's how an LSAT expert would draw the rules you just saw. Don't worry if you didn't use exactly the same symbols in your pencil work but make sure that you didn't over- or underdetermine the restriction called for by each rule.

Rule		Analysis
38.	In a Selection-Distribution game that selects an unknown number of employees who carpool together and determines which of two cars the selected employees ride in: K rides in whatever car J rides in.	If Ⓙ ⟶ Ⓚ and $\boxed{\frac{J}{K}}$ If ~K or ~$\boxed{\frac{J}{K}}$ ⟶ ~J
39.	In the same game: Unless L is left out of the carpool, M rides in car 1.	If Ⓛ → Ⓜ1 If ~M1 → L out
40.	In a Selection-Sequencing game that selects five pies from a group of seven (H, J, K, L, M, P, Q) and then arranges them on a banquet table: Q is not chosen unless M is third or fifth.	If Ⓠ → Ⓜ3 or Ⓜ5 If ~M3 and ~M5 → ~Q
41.	In a Sequencing-Distribution game that sequences the six cabs at a taxi stand by driver and matches each driver to one or more passengers: R, who drives the fourth cab, picks up exactly two passengers, one of whom is y.	$\overline{1}\ \big|\ \overline{2}\ \big|\ \overline{3}\ \big|\ \begin{array}{c}R\\\overline{4}\\y\\\overline{\overline{\ \ }}\end{array}\ \big|\ \overline{5}\ \big|\ \overline{6}$
42.	In a Distribution-Sequencing-Selection game that constructs a lineup for two four-person relay swim teams from a group of nine available swimmers: X is in the first position on team 1 only if W is in the third position on team 2.	If Ⓧ1$_{first}$ → Ⓦ2$_{third}$ If ~W2$_{third}$ → ~X1$_{first}$
43.	In a Sequencing-Matching game that sequences seven old airplanes arriving at a hangar in preparation for an airshow and also determines whether each plane that arrives is a monoplane or a biplane: Q, the sixth plane to arrive, is also the last monoplane to arrive.	$\begin{array}{ccccccc}&&&&&Q\\ \overline{1}&\overline{2}&\overline{3}&\overline{4}&\overline{5}&\overline{6}&\overline{7}\\ \_\_&\_\_&\_\_&\_\_&\_\_&m&b\end{array}$
44.	In a Sequencing-Matching game that sequences five lectures and matches them to the experts delivering them: The first and fourth lectures must be delivered by the same expert.	$\overline{1}\ \overline{2}\ \overline{3}\ \overline{4}\ \overline{5}$ $\underset{\text{Same}}{\overset{\curvearrowright}{}}$ expert

Rule	Analysis
45. In the same game: The second lecture is delivered by E if and only if the third lecture is delivered by H.	If $E_2 \rightarrow H_3$ If $\sim H_3 \rightarrow \sim E_2$ If $H_3 \rightarrow E_2$ If $\sim E_2 \rightarrow \sim H_3$ Both E_2 and H_3 or neither
46. In a Sequencing-Matching game with a no-ties limitation: A is second only if F is matched to c.	If $\dfrac{A}{2} \longrightarrow F_c$ If $\sim F_c \longrightarrow \dfrac{A}{\sim 2}$
47. In a Selection-Matching-Sequencing game that selects five of six pieces of furniture (P, Q, R, S, T, U) and matches those that are chosen to types of wood (c, d, e, f, g, h), and then sequences those pieces of furniture: Exactly two of the first three pieces of furniture are of type d wood.	P,Q,R,S,T,U $\underline{\quad}_{1} \; \underline{\quad}_{2} \; \underline{\quad}_{3} \; \underline{\quad}_{4} \; \underline{\quad}_{5}$ c,d,e,f,g,h $\underline{\quad} \; \underline{\quad} \; \underline{\quad} \; \underline{\quad} \; \underline{\quad}$ $\underbrace{\qquad\qquad}$ d exactly twice

As you continue your practice with the games in Chapter 6 and with full-length LSATs, you'll have ample opportunity to analyze and sketch additional Hybrid game rules. Taken as a group, Hybrid games are the second most popular game type behind Sequencing games. Remember, though, that most Hybrid games contain a Sequencing action, so your Sequencing and Hybrid practice will reinforce many of the same skills. In any Hybrid game, identify the actions as you conduct the Overview step and try to build an integrated sketch to manage the restrictions. As you turn to the rules, ask which of the actions each rule restricts. As always, pay attention to what the rule leaves undetermined as well. Whenever possible, draw the rule within the sketch framework but, failing that, record it in shorthand beneath or to the side of the framework you've set up.

Reflection

Over the coming days, pay attention to "hybrid" tasks you encounter in everyday life. Indeed, most of the real-life logic puzzles we solve involve multiple tasks. You may have to choose bridesmaids and groomsmen for a wedding (Selection), but you're also going to determine the order in which they stand at the altar (Sequencing) and even whom they're paired with as they walk down the aisle (Matching). Or imagine you manage a clothing store. You might have to choose which outfits to put on display in a window (Selection) and, once you have the items, decide which will be placed on each of three mannequins (Matching). The varieties may seem endless, but if you focus on tasks combining the four standard LSAT logic game actions—Sequencing, Selection, Matching, and Distribution—you'll soon start to see patterns emerge. Demystify logic games by seeing how common the LSAT actions are in our lives.

STEP 4 OF THE LOGIC GAMES METHOD: COMBINE THE RULES AND RESTRICTIONS TO MAKE DEDUCTIONS

Now that you've learned to analyze and draw the rules, you're ready for Step 4 of the Logic Games Method—Deductions. In this section, you'll learn to catalog the restrictions and rules limiting the possible arrangements within a game and to combine them to establish what must and cannot be true in all cases. More than any of the other steps, this is the one that separates the LSAT expert from other test takers. Making all of the available deductions within a game will put you in control of the questions to a degree others cannot match.

LEARNING OBJECTIVES

In this section, you'll learn to:

- Identify the points of greatest restriction within a logic game.
- Use the BLEND checklist to make all available deductions with a logic game.
- Identify *Floaters* (unrestricted entities) after making all available deductions.
- Know when all available deductions have been made (and it is time to move on to answering questions).

Although making deductions stands as a distinct step within the Logic Games Method, you've actually had a bit of a head start on the thinking and analysis you'll do here. You were already making deductions when you noted, for example, that a rule such as "Jody is scheduled for an earlier day of the week than Enrique is scheduled," means that Enrique will not take the first day of appointments and Jody will not take the last day. Deductions of this sort just make explicit the implications of a rule. A similar example stems from a rule such as "Kelly and Andre will not be drafted by the same team." In a Distribution game with exactly two teams, you can deduce that each team drafts at least one player.

The work you'll do in this section takes making deductions a step further. Here, instead of making the implications of a single rule explicit, you'll learn to combine two or more rules and bring the implications of that combination to light. To see a simple example, imagine that a Sequencing game with six positions has the following rules: (1) "Barney may not occupy the first position," and (2) "Joanna will be assigned a higher-numbered position than Barney's position."

$$\overline{1} \quad \overline{2} \quad \overline{3} \quad \overline{4} \quad \overline{5} \quad \overline{6}$$
~B ~J   ~B
~J

        B...J

From Rule 1 alone, you can exclude Barney from Position 1. From the second rule alone, you know Joanna may not take Position 1 and Barney may not take Position 6. By combining these two rules, you can deduce that the earliest position Joanna may occupy is Position 3 and exclude her from Position 2 as well. Deductions such as this may not seem earth-shattering, but knowing with certainty (and noting in your Master Sketch) that an entity cannot occupy a particular position will help you answer one or more of the questions. The testmaker may reward you directly with a correct answer that mirrors the deduction or indirectly by including wrong answers suggesting that an arrangement you've determined is impossible is actually acceptable.

When they first approach Step 4, the Deductions step, some students feel that something mysterious or almost magical is happening as so much of the game takes shape. The LSAT expert, however, knows that nothing could be further from the truth. The step of making deductions is thoroughly practical and methodical. You work from what is most certain and concrete in the game and check for anything else that information allows you to determine. Moreover, the LSAT expert knows that deductions stem from combinations of five types of rules, easily memorized with the BLEND checklist you first saw in Chapter 2.

LSAT STRATEGY

Blocks of Entities—two or more players who are always grouped together

Limited Options—rules or restrictions that limit the overall setup to one of two acceptable arrangements

Established Entities—players locked into a specific space or group

Number Restrictions—rules or limitations that provide guidance about the number of entities assigned to a group or space

Duplications—entities that appear in two or more rules, thus allowing the rules to be combined

Remember, BLEND is not a series of steps, and not all games contain all five types of rules and restrictions. As you note down a game's limitations and rules, learn to ask which of the five BLEND elements they represent. That way, you'll head into Step 4 anticipating the likely deductions you'll make.

From here, we'll revisit the games you've already seen the LSAT expert working on. Once again, we'll organize these by game type so that you can begin to discern the patterns the testmaker uses. After we demonstrate the LSAT expert's analysis of the Deductions step, you'll have the chance to practice with some additional examples. Here, we'll start with Steps 1, 2, and 3 already completed. If you want to refresh your memory about how we arrived at the work in those steps, just glance back at the expert analysis earlier in this chapter. After you work through the remainder of this chapter and learn the logic games question types in Chapter 5, you can practice the complete Logic Games Method on full logic games in Chapter 6.

Deductions in Sequencing Games

Sequencing games involve putting entities in order. It stands to reason, then, that the most concrete restrictions within Sequencing games come from rules that place an entity precisely (Established Entities) or those involving the relative positions of two or more entities (Blocks of Entities). Keep in mind, though, that a rule such as "Thomas is placed exactly one position after Marianne is placed," is much more restrictive than one saying "Thomas is placed in some position after the position in which Marianne is placed." The first of those creates a Block of Entities that must occupy two consecutive positions. Given the other rules in the game, there may be only one or two places within the game's framework where you can find two open positions together.

Here, once again, is the Racehorses game first shown in Chapter 2. While we went over the Deductions step for this game there, it's worth revisiting it now that you've had so much more practice with Steps 1–3. As you review the game now, pay attention to how the LSAT expert spots the entities and positions that are most restricted, and how she uses these to determine what must or cannot be true of any acceptable arrangement.

LSAT Question	Analysis
Six racehorses—K, L, M, N, O, and P—will be assigned to six positions arranged in a straight line and numbered consecutively 1 through 6. The horses are assigned to the positions, one horse per position, according to the following conditions: K and L must be assigned to positions that are separated from each other by exactly one position. K and N cannot be assigned to positions that are next to each other. N must be assigned to a higher-numbered position than M. P must be assigned to position 3. *PrepTest28 Sec2 Qs 1–5*	**Steps 1–3:** ? K L M N O P $\underset{1}{\_\_}$ $\underset{2}{\_\_}$ $\underset{3}{\overset{P}{\_\_}}$ $\underset{4}{\_\_}$ $\underset{5}{\_\_}$ $\underset{6}{\_\_}$ ~N K K/L _ L/K ~K N M . . . N

Deductions

Step 4:

Rule 4 establishes P in position 3. Thus, Rule 1 can only be obeyed by placing K and L in positions 2 and 4, or in positions 4 and 6. (Neither K nor L could take positions 1 or 5 because the other would have to take position 3, which is already filled by horse P.)

$$\text{(I)}\quad \underset{\underset{\sim N}{1}}{\_\_}\ \ \underset{2}{\overset{K/L}{\_\_}}\ \ \underset{3}{\overset{P}{\_\_}}\ \ \underset{4}{\overset{L/K}{\_\_}}\ \ \underset{5}{\_\_}\ \ \underset{\underset{\sim M}{6}}{\_\_}$$

$$\text{(II)}\quad \underset{1}{\_\_}\ \ \underset{2}{\_\_}\ \ \underset{3}{\overset{P}{\_\_}}\ \ \underset{4}{\overset{K/L}{\_\_}}\ \ \underset{5}{\_\_}\ \ \underset{6}{\overset{L/K}{\_\_}}$$

In Option I, M, N, and O can be arranged in three ways—1) M in 1, N in 5, O in 6; 2) M in 1, O in 5, N in 6; and 3) O in 1, M in 5, N in 6—too many ways to write out all of them.

LSAT Question	**Analysis**

Deductions (cont.)

In Option II, however, Rule 2 prevents N from taking position 5 (which would place N next to K), so N's only acceptable placement is position 2. Rule 3, therefore, dictates that M must take position 1 in this option. That means O (the only remaining entity) must take position 5.

(II)
$$\frac{M}{1} \quad \frac{N}{2} \quad \frac{P}{3} \quad \frac{K/L}{4} \quad \frac{O}{5} \quad \frac{L/K}{6}$$

The final Master Sketch is simply both of those Limited Options sketches. Every arrangement in the game must conform to one or the other of those scenarios.

(I)
$$\frac{}{1} \quad \frac{K/L}{2} \quad \frac{P}{3} \quad \frac{L/K}{4} \quad \frac{}{5} \quad \frac{}{6}$$
$$\text{~N} \qquad\qquad\qquad\qquad \text{~M}$$

(II)
$$\frac{M}{1} \quad \frac{N}{2} \quad \frac{P}{3} \quad \frac{K/L}{4} \quad \frac{O}{5} \quad \frac{L/K}{6}$$

With that Master Sketch (the final sketch containing the framework, the rules, and all available deductions), the LSAT expert should have enormous confidence that she can tackle the question set.

You may be asking, "Why not go further? Why, in Option I, for example, why don't we draw out what happens when horse O is in the first position, and then how things are different when the first horse is M? Couldn't we even, with enough speculation, figure out all of the acceptable permutations?" The answer to that last question is actually "Yes, in theory we could," but the time it would take would probably make it impossible to complete the game's questions within the 8–9 minutes you have for each game. The LSAT expert chose to stop where she did for two reasons: (1) she had exhausted the BLEND checklist—there are no more Established Entities, Duplications, or Blocks of Entities to find; and (2) she is at the point where making deductions—rigorously determining what must and what cannot be true—would turn into speculation—a seemingly endless series of "Well, what if . . ." questions that would eat up her time. Knowing when to end the Deductions step and move on to the question set takes practice, but asking the questions that correspond to the criteria identified with the LSAT expert—Have I noted all rules in this game from the BLEND checklist? Have I moved beyond deduction into mere speculation?—will help you get a feel for when you've learned all that's helpful from Step 4.

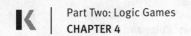

Next, take a look at the LSAT expert's deductions in the Language Awards game. Again, focus on how he focuses on Blocks to spot the entities and spaces most likely to give additional clarity within the game.

LSAT Question	Analysis
A college dean will present seven awards for outstanding language research. The awards—one for French, one for German, one for Hebrew, one for Japanese, one for Korean, one for Latin, and one for Swahili—must be presented consecutively, one at a time, in conformity with the following constraints: The German award is not presented first. The Hebrew award is presented at some time before the Korean award is presented. The Latin award is presented at some time before the Japanese award is presented. The French award is presented either immediately before or immediately after the Hebrew award is presented. The Korean award is presented either immediately before or immediately after the Latin award is presented. *PrepTest29 Sec3 Qs 14–19*	**Steps 1–3:** $\overline{1}$ $\overline{2}$ $\overline{3}$ $\overline{4}$ $\overline{5}$ $\overline{6}$ $\overline{7}$ ~G H . . . K → L . . . J ⬚ F/H ⬚ K/L

Deductions

Step 4:

Combine Duplicate entities. K is appears in Rules 2 and 5:

H . . . K/L

L appears in Rules 3 and 5:

H . . . K/L . . . J

F appears in Rules 2 and 4:

F/H . . . K/L . . . J

At this point, five of the seven entities are tied together in a large block. The F/H block can only fit into three places. Creating three Limited Option sketches will allow for further deductions:

Opt. I   F/H __ __ __ __ __

Opt. II __ F/H __ __ __ __

Opt. III __ __ F/H __ __ __
         1 2 3 4 5 6 7
         ~G

LSAT Question	Analysis

Deductions (cont.)

In Option 1, nothing else can be definitely placed on the sketch. In Option 2, however, because G can't be first, S must be the language that receives the first award. In Option 3, we can place all of the entities and blocks.

Opt. I   __(F/H)__   __   __   __   __   __

Opt. II   _S_   __(F/H)__   __   __   __   __

Opt. III   _S_   _G_   __(F/H)__   __(K/L)__   _J_

          1   2   3   4   5   6   7

     ~G

(F/H) . . . (K/L) . . . J

This game is an excellent example of the LSAT expert knowing just how far to push the Deductions step. German and Swahili are largely unrestricted, but the other five entities string together in a long chain. That chain forces French and Hebrew toward the front of the line. The expert explores what happens as French and Hebrew push deeper into the sequence, and finds that the game becomes increasingly restricted as a result. From the Limited Options sketches, it is clear that any time Swahili is not first, the F-H block must constitute the first two awards presented. That inference is certain to be rewarded in one or more questions.

Before turning to practice, take a few minutes to review the work of the LSAT expert on the Loose Sequencing example with which you've been working, the Movie Releases game. Recall that the LSAT expert demonstrated that, in Loose Sequencing, you may combine the rules even as you're analyzing and drawing them out. Indeed, that's the approach you'll likely use on Test Day. For now, though, we'll start with the rules listed individually and demonstrate one more time how to combine them. In Loose Sequencing games, almost all of the deductions will spring from Duplications, the "D" of BLEND. That's because, in most cases, at least two rules share each entity. The rules thus "snap together" to create the Master Sketch.

LSAT Question	Analysis
A movie studio is scheduling the release of six films—*Fiesta, Glaciers, Hurricanes, Jets, Kangaroos,* and *Lovebird.* No two of these films can be released on the same date. The release schedule is governed by the following conditions:	**Steps 1–3:** F *G* H J K L
Fiesta must be released earlier than both *Jets* and *Lovebird.*	(1)
Kangaroos must be released earlier than *Jets,* and *Jets* must be released earlier than *Hurricanes.*	.·L F.· ·.J
Lovebird must be released earlier than *Glaciers.*	(2)
PrepTest71 Sec2 Game1 →	K...J...H
	(3)
	L...*G*

Deductions

Step 4:

Rules 1 and 2 share J:

Rules 1 and 3 share L:

     .·L...*G*
  F.·
    ·.J...H
  K··

LSAT Question	Analysis

Deductions (cont.)

A Loose Sequencing sketch can run horizontally or vertically. Another variation would look like this:

From either sketch it is clear that:

F must be either first or second. (Only K can come earlier than F.)

G must be presented between third and sixth. (F and L must precede G. K, J, and H may precede or follow G.)

H must be presented between fourth and sixth. (F, K, and J must precede H. L and G may precede or follow H.)

J must be presented between third and fifth. (F and K must precede J. H must follow J. L and G may precede or follow J.)

K must be presented between first and fourth. (J and H must follow K. F, L, and G may precede or follow K.)

L must be presented between second and fifth. (F must precede L. G must follow L. K, J, and H may precede or follow L.)

On Test Day, the LSAT expert probably will not take the time to list out the possible positions for each entity as you see shown here, but she will be able to determine any of those possibilities in seconds. She understands that the sketch represents the sum total of restrictions and can use them to determine what must, can, and cannot be true at a glance. At the same time, she avoids unwarranted assumptions. From the sketch, it may appear that L and J are opened at roughly the same time. The restrictions in the game, however, show that L may come as early as second in the sequence, or as late as fifth. LIkewise, J could be anywhere from third through fifth.

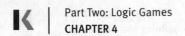
Practice

Now, try your hand at the Deductions step. Use the following brief examples to practice identifying the elements of the BLEND checklist you see represented. Look for the points of greatest restriction in the game setup. Starting from these restrictions, combine the rules and limitations to determine what else must or cannot be true.

Take five minutes for each of the following examples. Review the expert's work on Steps 1–3 of the Logic Games Method. Analyze and draw the rules if the expert has not done so. Then, use the BLEND checklist to make all available deductions. Once you're finished, check your work against the LSAT expert's analysis on the following pages.

Game	My Analysis

48. A four-story building houses five businesses— Shops A, B, C, D, and E—and each floor has at least one business on it. Shop B needs to be on a higher floor than Shop E.
  Shop A is on a higher floor than Shop B.
  Shop D is on a floor by itself.
	Step 1: *Situation:* Building with four floors and five shops
	
	Entities: The shops (A, B, C, D, E)
	
	Action: Positional arrangement matters, so this is a Sequencing game.
	
	Limitations: One floor will hold two shops, and Shop B is on a higher floor than Shop E.

$\longrightarrow$

Step 2:

A B C D E

```
4 —
3 —      (+ ___ extra business)
2 —
1 —
```

Step 3: (Transcribe the rules here.)

Deductions

Step 4: (Make your deductions and Master Sketch here)

Game	My Analysis

49. A teacher is assigning the front row of seats in her class according to the age of six students (A, B, C, D, E, and F). There are six seats in the front row. The youngest student will sit on the far left, and the oldest student will sit on the far right.

   Student B is either the fourth or sixth youngest student in class.

   Students A and D are separated by exactly one seat.

   The youngest student is either C or E.

   Students A and F cannot sit next to each other.

$\longrightarrow$

Step 1: *Situation:* A classroom with a row of seats

Entities: The six students (A, B, C, D, E, F)

Action: Sequence the students according to age.

Limitations: Each seat will be assigned one student.

Step 2:

A B C D E F

___ ___ ___ ___ ___ ___

(Youngest) 1   2   3   4   5   6 (Oldest)

Step 3: (Transcribe rules here.)

Deductions

Step 4: (Make your Deductions and Master Sketch here.)

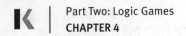
Expert Analysis

Now, compare your deductions and Master Sketch on the examples you just tried to those of the LSAT expert.

Game	Analysis

48. A four-story building houses five businesses—Shops A, B, C, D, and E—and each floor has at least one business on it. Shop B needs to be on a higher floor than Shop E.
 	
    Shop A is on a higher floor than Shop B.
    Shop D is on a floor by itself.
	Step 1: *Situation:* Building with four floors and five shops
	
	Entities: The shops (A, B, C, D, E)
	
	Action: Positional arrangement matters, so this is a Sequencing game.
	
	Limitations: One floor will hold two shops, and Shop B is on a higher floor than Shop E.

Step 2:

$$A\ B\ C\ D\ E$$

$\rightarrow$

```
4 —
3 —      (+ __ extra business)
2 —
1 —
```

Step 3: (Limitation):

```
B
⋮
E
```

Rule 1:

```
A
⋮
B
```

Rule 2:

D alone

None of these rules can, on its own, be directly added to the sketch.

Game	Analysis

Deductions

Step 4:

Both the limitation in the overview and the first rule discuss Shop B. This is a duplicate entity and, by combining both rules, we get this:

A
⋮
B
⋮
E

Combining those rules creates a larger Block of Entities. In Sequencing games, Blocks of Entities (even Blocks connected together by Loose Sequencing rules) are crucially important. In some cases, those Blocks lead to Limited Options (arrangements in which only two alternatives are acceptable). Here, three shops are connected together vertically, but there are only four floors onto which those shops can be placed. Looking at the Block of Entities, it's clear that Shop A must be on the highest floor of the three shops. Furthermore, because two floors below A are filled up with B and E, A can only go on Floor 4 or Floor 3. Placing Shop A on Floor 4 doesn't lead to any more concrete deductions, but placing Shop A on Floor 3 forces Shops B and E into specific locations on the sketch. Create a Limited Options sketch.

Opt. 1   *Opt. 2*

4 __A__   4 ____
3 ____ B   3 __A__
2 ____   2 __B__
     E
1 ____   1 __E__

The last rule says that Shop D is on a floor by itself. The Limited Option sketches show that in Option 2, Shop D must go on Floor 4 because every other floor is occupied. In Option 1, which is much more open, D can end up on any of the bottom three floors. In that case, there's no point adding that information to the sketch.

Shop C, a Floater, is not constrained to any particular floor or restricted by any other business. Because A, B, and E are all separated from each other, and because D is on a floor by itself, C *must* be one of the shops that shares a floor. Each rule has now been evaluated and combined with other rules. No more deductions can be made, so move on to the questions.

Opt. 1   *Opt. 2*

4 __A__   4 __D__
3 ____ B   3 __A__   *C shares a floor*
2 ____   2 __B__
     E
1 ____   1 __E__

Game	Analysis
49. A teacher is assigning the front row of seats in her class according to the age of six students (A, B, C, D, E, and F). There are six seats in the front row. The youngest student will sit on the far left, and the oldest student will sit on the far right.	**Step 1:** *Situation:* A classroom with a row of seats

Step 1: *Situation:* A classroom with a row of seats

Entities: The six students (A, B, C, D, E, F)

Action: Sequence the students according to age.

Limitations: Each seat will be assigned one student.

49. A teacher is assigning the front row of seats in her class according to the age of six students (A, B, C, D, E, and F). There are six seats in the front row. The youngest student will sit on the far left, and the oldest student will sit on the far right.

   Student B is either the fourth or sixth youngest student in class.

   Students A and D are separated by exactly one seat.

   The youngest student is either C or E.

   Students A and F cannot sit next to each other.

Step 2:

A B C D E F

____ ____ ____ ____ ____ ____

(Youngest) 1   2   3   4   5   6 (Oldest)

Step 3: Rule 1: (add directly to sketch)
Rule 2: A/D __ D/A
Rule 3: (add directly to sketch)
Rule 4: Never AF or FA

youngest $\dfrac{C/E}{1}$ $\dfrac{}{2}$ $\dfrac{}{3}$ $\dfrac{}{4}$ $\dfrac{}{5}$ $\dfrac{}{6}$ oldest

(B arrow from 4 to 6)

A/D __ D/A

never [AF] or [FA]

Deductions

Step 4:

   Opt. 1

youngest $\dfrac{C/E}{1}$ $\dfrac{A/D}{2}$ $\dfrac{}{3}$ $\dfrac{D/A}{4}$ $\dfrac{}{5}$ $\dfrac{}{6}$ oldest

   Opt. 2

youngest $\dfrac{C/E}{1}$ $\dfrac{}{2}$ $\dfrac{A/D}{3}$ $\dfrac{}{4}$ $\dfrac{D/A}{5}$ $\dfrac{}{6}$ oldest

In Strict Sequencing games, Blocks of Entities often lead to deductions. Here, students A and D are blocked together in either order with a mystery student in between. Where can the A-D block go? It can't start in seat 1, which takes either C or E. What about starting in seat 2? That would put entities A and D in seats 2 and 4 (in either order, with the mystery entity in seat 3). That works. What about the A-D in seats 3 and 5? That works, too. But trying to place the A-D block in seats 4 and 6 causes a problem: Student B must go in one of those two seats. Because the A-D block has only two options, create the Limited Options sketch shown.

Game	Analysis

Deductions (cont.)

Now, consider Rule 1. It says that B is either the fourth or sixth youngest. In Option 1, seat 4 is occupied by either A or D, so B must take seat 6. Add that information directly the sketch. In Option 2, both 4 and 6 are still open, so B gets drawn below the sketch, with arrows indicating it can go to either 4 or 6.

<u>Opt. 1</u>

youngest $\dfrac{C/E}{1}$ $\dfrac{A/D}{2}$ $\dfrac{}{3}$ $\dfrac{D/A}{4}$ $\dfrac{}{5}$ $\dfrac{B}{6}$ oldest

<u>Opt. 2</u>

youngest $\dfrac{C/E}{1}$ $\dfrac{}{2}$ $\dfrac{A/D}{3}$ $\dfrac{}{4}$ $\dfrac{D/A}{5}$ $\dfrac{}{6}$ oldest

4 ↖ B ↗ 6

Rule 3 has been added to the sketch, but what about Rule 4? That rule says that A and F can never sit side by side. Option 1 shows that A will sit in seat 2 or seat 4; either way, F will never be able to sit in seat 3. Because the only other open spot is seat 5, F must take seat 5. That, in turn, forces A into seat 2, which forces D into seat 4. At this point, the only open seat is seat 3, which must be filled by either C or E.

Check Option 2. Rule 4 says that A and F can never sit together. Because A will sit in either 3 or 5, student F cannot take seat 4.

<u>Opt. 1</u>

youngest $\dfrac{C/E}{1}$ $\dfrac{A}{2}$ $\dfrac{E/C}{3}$ $\dfrac{D}{4}$ $\dfrac{F}{5}$ $\dfrac{B}{6}$ oldest

<u>Opt. 2</u>

youngest $\dfrac{C/E}{1}$ $\dfrac{}{2}$ $\dfrac{A/D}{3}$ $\dfrac{}{4}$ $\dfrac{D/A}{5}$ $\dfrac{}{6}$ oldest

~F ↖ B ↗

Can more deductions be made? At this point, every rule has been combined with other rules and added directly to the sketch. The effect that each rule has on the Master Sketch, and on other rules, has been evaluated. There aren't any more deductions to be made, so it's time to move on to the questions.

Reflection

Congratulations. You've now tackled the most important steps for gaining mastery over the most important type of logic games, Sequencing games. Take a moment to summarize what you've learned about the Deductions step in Sequencing games.

> ## LSAT STRATEGY
>
> In Sequencing games, deductions are likely to stem from:
>
> - **Blocks of Entities**—two or more entities that are linked together; when one is placed, the other's movement is determined or restricted.
> - **Duplications**—entities shared by two or more rules; duplicators are almost always at the heart of Loose Sequencing games.
> - **Established Entities**—entities placed into a specific space; even if no rule directly provides for an Established Entity, you may be able to determine an entity's exact position by combining other rules.
>
> In Sequencing games, deductions may involve:
>
> - **Limited Options**—the situation that arises when a Block of Entities or a *key player* (an entity affecting the positions of other entities) can take either of two positions; when this occurs, create dual Limited Options sketches.
> - **Numbers Restrictions**—limitations or rules affecting the number of entities that can be placed in a given position; this is rare in Sequencing games—typically, the limitation is one per space.

You'll see these same deductions resurface when you turn your attention to Hybrid games because many of those involve a Sequencing action. In Chapter 5, you'll have a chance to see how the LSAT expert applied the deductions in the LSAT games covered previously when we turn to Step 5 of the Logic Games Method and answer the questions.

Deductions in Selection Games

In Selection games, your task is to choose a small number of entities out of a larger group. The test offers two standard variations on Selection games. In the first, the number of entities you are to choose is left open. In these cases, pay special attention to deductions involving the minimum or maximum number of entities you're able to select. In the second variation, the testmaker tells you how many entities must be selected (four out of seven or five out of nine, for example). In these games, the testmaker often categorizes the entities—in a game asking you to select a menu, for example, you might encounter three appetizers, two main courses, and three desserts. Numbers Restrictions are equally important in this variation of Selection, especially rules or limitations that set limits on how many entities from a specific category you can or must select.

On the following pages, review the Trees in the Park game with which you've been working.

We'll start with the expert's work on Steps 1–3 of the Logic Games Method and then show how he analyzed and combined the rules to make additional deductions.

LSAT Question	**Analysis**
A park contains at most five of seven kinds of trees—firs, laurels, maples, oaks, pines, spruces, and yews—consistent with the following conditions: 　If maples are in the park, yews are not. 　If firs are in the park, pines are not. 　If yews are not in the park, then either laurels or oaks, but not both, are in the park. 　If it is not the case that the park contains both laurels and oaks, then it contains firs and spruces. _PrepTestB Sec2 Qs 7-12_ →	**Steps 1–3:** F L M O P S Y　　(max 5) If Ⓜ ⟶ ~Y　} Never MY **together** If Ⓨ ⟶ ~M If Ⓕ ⟶ ~P　} Never FP **together** If Ⓟ ⟶ ~F If ~Y ⟶ [Exactly one of Ⓛ/Ⓞ] If Ⓛ and Ⓞ ⟶ Ⓨ If ~L and ~O ⟶ Ⓨ If ~L or ~O ⟶ Ⓕ and Ⓢ If ~F or ~S ⟶ Ⓛ and Ⓞ

Deductions

Step 4:

Multiple Formal Logic rules appear in this (and any Selection) game, so consider whether they form "chains" of logic in which the result of one statement triggers another statement.

Rule 1: Selecting M means rejecting Y. That triggers Rule 3: Rejecting Y means selecting exactly one of L or O and rejecting the other. Rejecting either L or O triggers Rule 4, thus forcing the selection of F and S. Selecting F, in turn, triggers Rule 2. P must be rejected.

The contrapositive of Rule 1—selecting Y and rejecting M—does not trigger any additional deductions.

Rule 2: Selecting F and rejecting P does not trigger any additional deductions.

The contrapositive of Rule 2, however, sets off another chain. Selecting P and, thus rejecting F, triggers Rule 4: Without F, L and O must be selected. Selecting L and O triggers the contrapositive of Rule 3, and Y must also be selected. Selecting Y triggers the contrapositive of Rule 1, and M is out.

Rule 3: Rejecting Y means selecting one of L or O and rejecting the other. Either way, that triggers Rule 4, and F and S must be selected. In turn, selecting F triggers Rule 2, and so P is out.

The contrapositive of Rule 3—not having exactly one of L and O (i.e., having either both or neither of L and O) means selecting Y. That, in turn, triggers the contrapositive of Rule 1, forcing the rejection of M.

Rule 4: Rejecting either L or O forces the selection of F and S. Selecting F then triggers Rule 2, and P must be rejected. Note that Rule 4 does not necessarily trigger Rule 3. The inclusion of just one of L or O is compatible with the rejection of Y. Only selecting or rejecting *both* L and O triggers the contrapositive of Rule 3.

LSAT Question	Analysis

Deductions (cont.)

Rule 4's contrapositive states that rejecting either F or S leads to the selection of both L and O. This triggers the contrapositive of Rule 3, and Y must be selected. That, in turn, triggers the contrapositive of Rule 1, meaning that M must be rejected.

NOTE: Some LSAT experts may write out all of the logic "chains" found among the rules. For example, they might create something like this for Rule 4:

$$\text{If} \sim\!F \text{ or} \sim\!S \longrightarrow \textcircled{L} \text{ and } \textcircled{O} \longrightarrow \textcircled{Y} \longrightarrow \sim\!M$$

$$\text{If} \sim\!L \text{ or} \sim\!O \longrightarrow \textcircled{F} \text{ and } \textcircled{S} \longrightarrow \sim\!P$$

Most experts, however, find that writing out all of the strings is unnecessary. *All* LSAT experts can quickly recognize all of the rules and contrapositives that trigger additional deductions in this way. For most experts, then, the final Master Sketch will simply be a roster of entities, and a clear, well organized list of the Formal Logic rules.

> F L M O P S Y   (max 5)
>
> If $\textcircled{M} \longrightarrow \sim\!Y$
> If $\textcircled{Y} \longrightarrow \sim\!M$
>
> If $\textcircled{F} \longrightarrow \sim\!P$
> If $\textcircled{P} \longrightarrow \sim\!F$
>
> If $\sim\!Y \longrightarrow$ [*Exactly one of* $\textcircled{L}$/$\textcircled{O}$]
> If $\textcircled{L}$ and $\textcircled{O} \longrightarrow \textcircled{Y}$
> If $\sim\!L$ and $\sim\!O \longrightarrow \textcircled{Y}$
>
> If $\sim\!L$ or $\sim\!O \longrightarrow \textcircled{F}$ and $\textcircled{S}$
> If $\sim\!F$ or $\sim\!S \longrightarrow \textcircled{L}$ and $\textcircled{O}$

In Selection games, the majority of rules are Formal Logic statements. It is very important to be able to see the impact of those rules on the number of entities you can choose, and on the combinations of entities that may be selected or rejected together. If this is an area in which you still need to gain confidence and expertise, make sure to complete (or even revisit) the relevant parts of Chapter 1.

In this game, Rule 4 is very powerful. It assures that at least two entities (either F and S, or L and O), will always be selected. Don't make unwarranted assumptions about this rule, however. F, S, L, and O may all be selected together. It is only the rejection of one of these entities that triggers Rule 4, but at a minimum, one of those pairs *must* be included in any acceptable selection.

Rules 1 and 2 both require the rejection of at least one entity: M and Y are mutually exclusive, as are F and P. Again, though, don't mistake these rules as requiring the selection of an entity. It is fine to reject both M and Y, or both F and P.

The acceptable outcomes for the Trees in the Park game will all have between two and five kinds of trees selected.

Selection Deductions Practice

Now, try your hand at the Deductions step. Use the following brief examples to practice identifying the elements of the BLEND checklist you see represented. Look for the points of greatest restriction in the game setup. Starting from these restrictions, combine the rules and limitations to determine what else must or cannot be true.

Take five minutes for each of the following examples. Review the expert's work on Steps 1–3 of the Logic Games Method. Analyze and draw the rules if the expert has not done so. Then, use the BLEND checklist to make all available deductions. Once you're finished, check your work against the LSAT expert's analysis on the following pages.

Game	My Analysis

50. Each of the seven members of a fraternity (A, B, C, D, E, F, and G) is deciding whether or not to go to the football game this weekend.
    If A goes to the game, then so does C.
    C won't go to the game unless B does.
    Either G or F will go to the game, but not both.
    If G goes to the game, then B will not go.
	Step 1: *Situation:* Members of a group each deciding whether or not to go somewhere
	
	 Entities: The fraternity members (A, B, C, D, E, F, G)
	
	 Action: Select from a larger group.
	
	 Limitations: We have no information about a minimum or maximum number to select.
	
	 Step 2:
	
	 → A B C D E F G
	
	 Step 3: (Transcribe rules here.)

Deductions

Step 4: (Make your Deductions and Master Sketch here.)

Game	My Analysis

51. A chef is going to make a soup using exactly five ingredients. She is choosing from among four types of spices (A, B, C, and D), three types of meat (e, f, and g), and three vegetables (*H*, *I*, and *J*).

    The chef will choose at least one of each type of ingredient.

    If she chooses spice A, she will also choose spice B.

    She will choose meat f only if she chooses vegetable *J*.

    Anytime the chef selects exactly two types of meat, she will also select exactly two types of vegetables, and anytime she selects exactly two types of vegetables, she will also select exactly two types of meat.

    The chef will select at most two types of spices.

→

Step 1: *Situation:* A chef picking ingredients for a soup

Entities: Four types of spices (A, B, C, D), three types of meat (e, f, g), three types of vegetables (*H, I, J*)

Action: Select five of the ten ingredients.

Limitations: We must pick five of ten, but there are no limitations within each subcategory.

Step 2:

pick 5 of 10

spices	meats	vegetables
A B C D	e f g	H I J

Step 3: (Transcribe rules here.)

Deductions

Step 4: (Make your Deductions and Master Sketch here.)

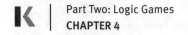
Expert Analysis

Now, compare your deductions and Master Sketch to those of the LSAT expert on the examples you just tried.

Game	Analysis
50. Each of the seven members of a fraternity (A, B, C, D, E, F, and G) is deciding whether or not to go to the football game this weekend. If A goes to the game, then so does C. C won't go to the game unless B does. Either G or F will go to the game, but not both. If G goes to the game, then B will not go.	**Step 1:** *Situation:* Members of a group each deciding whether or not to go somewhere *Entities:* The fraternity members (A, B, C, D, E, F, G) *Action:* Select from a larger group *Limitations:* We have no information about a minimum or maximum number to select.

Step 2:

A B C D E F G

Step 3: Selection game rules that are expressed in Formal Logic should be immediately transcribed, along with the contrapositive.

$\longrightarrow$

Rule 1:   If Ⓐ $\longrightarrow$ Ⓒ

        If ~C $\longrightarrow$ ~A

Rule 2:   If Ⓒ $\longrightarrow$ Ⓑ

        If ~B $\longrightarrow$ ~C

Rule 3:   If Ⓖ $\longrightarrow$ ~F

        If Ⓕ $\longrightarrow$ ~G (never GF)

        If ~G $\longrightarrow$ Ⓕ

        If ~F $\longrightarrow$ Ⓖ (at least F or G)

This rule can also be expressed without Formal Logic translation:

G/F

This indicates "exactly one of these must be chosen."

Rule 4: If Ⓖ $\rightarrow$ ~B

       If Ⓑ $\rightarrow$ ~G (never GB)

Game	**Analysis**

Deductions

Step 4:

In a Selection game, the conditional rules can rarely be built into the sketch framework. The best deductions will come from combining rules that share a common entity (Duplications, the "D" in BLEND). For example, combining Rules 1 and 2 (if A goes to the game, then C goes to the game, and if C goes, then B goes) creates the following deduction: If A goes, then B goes. Moreover, B also shows up in Rule 4. Combine Rules 1, 2, and 4: if G goes, then B doesn't go, which means C doesn't go, and then neither does A.

Minimums and Maximums: At least one member goes to the game—either F or G (per Rule 3).

Two rules—Rules 3 and 4—reduce the maximum number of members who can attend. If F attends, G is out, but everyone else could go, so the maximum with F selected is 6. If G attends, however, F is knocked out (per Rule 3) and B is knocked out (per Rule 4). Knocking out B sets off the chain involving Rules 1 and 2. With B out, C is out, too. And with C out, so is A. The maximum if G attends is 3 (D, E, and G). In this game, members D and E are Floaters, and are each marked with an asterisk.

[Some experts will note the following: Rule 3 can be depicted in a Limited Options sketch. Make one option with F selected and G out. Make another with G selected and F out. The one with G selected triggers the chain involving Rules 1, 2, and 4, as well.]

Opt. 1

A̶ B̶ C̶ D̊ E̊ F̶ Ⓖ

Opt. 2

A B C D̊ E̊ Ⓕ G̶

Game	**Analysis**
51. A chef is going to make a soup using exactly five ingredients. She is choosing from among four types of spices (A, B, C, and D), three types of meat (e, f, and g), and three vegetables (H, I, and J).	**Step 1:** *Situation:* A chef picking ingredients for a soup

51. A chef is going to make a soup using exactly five ingredients. She is choosing from among four types of spices (A, B, C, and D), three types of meat (e, f, and g), and three vegetables (H, I, and J).

> The chef will choose at least one of each type of ingredient.
>
> If she chooses spice A, she will also choose spice B.
>
> She will choose meat f only if she chooses vegetable J.
>
> Anytime the chef selects exactly two types of meat, she will also select exactly two types of vegetables, and anytime she selects exactly two types of vegetables, she will also select exactly two types of meat.
>
> The chef will select at most two types of spices.

Step 1: *Situation:* A chef picking ingredients for a soup

Entities: Four types of spices (A, B, C, D), three types of meat (e, f, g), three types of vegetables (H, I, J)

Action: Select five of the ten ingredients.

Limitations: We must pick five of ten, but there are no limitations within each subcategory.

Step 2:

pick 5 of 10

spices	meats	vegetables
A B C D	e f g	H I J

Step 3:

Rule 1: **At least one of each type** (can add directly to the sketch, with a designation above each subcategory)

Rule 2: If Ⓐ   ⟶ Ⓑ
If ~B   ⟶ ~A

Rule 3: If Ⓕ   ⟶ Ⓙ
If ~J   ⟶ ~f

Rule 4: If 2 meats   ⟶ 2 vegetables
If ~2 vegetables ⟶ ~2 meats
If 2 vegetables   ⟶ 2 meats
If ~2 meats   ⟶ ~2 vegetables

Rule 5: **At most two types of spices** (can indicate in the sketch)

pick 5 of 10

(1–2) spices	(1–3) meats	(1–3) vegetables
A B C D	e f g	H I J

Game	Analysis

Deductions

Step 4:

Most Selection games rely primarily on Duplications (the D in BLEND), but this game requires other BLEND deductions. Most readily apparent in this game are the Numbers Restrictions (the N in BLEND). These are (1) the Overview limitation—five out of ten ingredients must be selected; (2) Rule 1—at least one of each ingredient type is selected; (3) Rule 5—at most two types of spices will be selected; and (4) the complex Rule 4—if the chef selects either two types of meat or two types of vegetables, she must also select two types of vegetables and two types of meat.

Evaluate Rule 4 closely. Affirmatively, the rule says:

If 2 meat → 2 vegetable

And

If 2 vegetable → 2 meat

Either way, if the chef has two meats and two veggies, she can only have one spice (because of the Overview limitation that says choose five ingredients out of 10).

The contrapositives of the rule state:

If ~2 meat → ~2 vegetable

And

If ~2 vegetable → ~2 meat

But Rule 1 says the chef must have at least one of each ingredient type. So, if the chef doesn't have two meats, she could have 1 or 3. If she has one or three meats, she must not have two vegetables. Again, this could be 1 or 3. This limits the chef to three acceptable number arrangements for the ingredient types:

Scenario 1: 1 spice, 2 meats, 2 veggies

Scenario 2: 1 spice, 3 meats, 1 veggie (and the veggie will have to be *J* because meat *f* is selected)

Scenario 3: 1 spice, 1 meat, 3 veggies

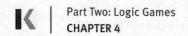
Game	Analysis

Deductions (cont.)

No scenario with two spices is acceptable, because that would require the chef to choose three ingredients from among meats and veggies. If she chooses two of either meats or veggies, she must choose two of the other ingredient types as well. That would make for a total of six (violating the Overview limitation—choose 5 of 10). Because the chef cannot select two spices, she can never select Spice A because Rule 2 would require her to select Spice B as well. Cross Spice A off the list once and for all.

Choosing three or four spices is forbidden by Rule 5.

pick 5 of 10

①	(1–3)	(1–3)
spices	meats	vegetables
ȦBCD	efg	HIJ

acceptable numbers:

1 spice, 1 meat, 3 veg
1 spice, 2 meat, 2 veg
1 spice, 3 meat, 1 veg

Reflection

Because of their focus on Formal Logic, Selection games can seem very different from other game types. Make no mistake. To master Selection games, you must sharpen your Formal Logic skill set, but don't lose sight of the crucial role that numbers play in these games as well. When the game does not specify the number of entities to be selected, at least one or two questions will usually reward you for being able to figure out the minimum or maximum number of selections that are acceptable. When the test tells you an exact number of entities to select, it will often set up a situation in which you have to choose from among different categories, and it will typically make you account for the numbers from each of those categories.

LSAT STRATEGY

In Selection games, deductions are likely to stem from:

- **Duplications**—entities shared by two or more rules; Selection games often feature "chains" of Formal Logic linked by shared entities.
- **Numbers Restrictions**—limitations on the number of entities to be selected or determinations of the minimum and maximum numbers that can be selected given the game's rules.

In Selection games, deductions may involve:

- **Limited Options**—the situation that arises when a rule specifies that only one of two selection patterns is acceptable (e.g., G is selected and F is not selected, or F is selected and G is not selected).
- **Blocks of Entities**—two or more entities that must be selected or rejected as a pair.
- **Established Entities**—entities that must be selected or rejected; this is very rare in Selection games where all or most rules are conditional; occasionally, the Numbers Restrictions will allow you to determine that a specific entity may never be selected.

You'll have additional opportunities to practice Selection deductions in Chapter 6. In Chapter 5, you'll have a chance to see how the LSAT expert applied the deductions in the Trees in the Park game when we turn to Step 5 of the Logic Games Method and answer the questions.

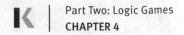

Deductions in Matching Games

To get a feel for Matching games deductions, imagine a real-world scenario. You're equipping a team of six archaeologists who will hike to a relatively remote site to do an initial excavation. If everyone's backpacks will have exactly the same thing—one laptop, one bag of food, one set of tools, etc.—you don't have much of a logic game. If you instead imagine the six people lined up on one side of a room and a big stack of supplies of various types on the other, you start to get the picture. Maybe the group needs three boxes of foodstuffs. Maybe the group only needs two sets of tools. Four people, on the other hand, will need to carry water. And so on. Now, you can start to put together the rules for your task. Food and tools are heavy, so the same person cannot carry both. Anyone taking tools will also carry maps. Some members of the team are physically capable of taking more than others can. In an LSAT Matching game, the reasons for the restrictions and rules may not be as practical or explicit, but the result will be the same. You'll have to figure out the number and types of items each entity can be matched with, so keep your eyes on rules involving Numbers Restrictions and Duplications. (Note: Order does not matter in Matching games. There will be no rules that stipulate Archaeologist A is provisioned before Archaeologist B, for example. Adding rules of that kind would transform the game into a Sequencing-Matching Hybrid game.)

With that background in mind, take another look at the Recycling Centers game. Pay special attention to what the LSAT expert discerns about the number of materials that must, can, or cannot be recycled at various recycling centers.

LSAT Question	Analysis

There are exactly three recycling centers in Rivertown: Center 1, Center 2, and Center 3. Exactly five kinds of material are recycled at these recycling centers: glass, newsprint, plastic, tin, and wood. Each recycling center recycles at least two but no more than three of these kinds of material. The following conditions must hold:

Any recycling center that recycles wood also recycles newsprint.

Every kind of material that Center 2 recycles is also recycled at Center 1.

Only one of the recycling centers recycles plastic, and that recycling center does not recycle glass.

PrepTestJune2007 Sec1 Game4

Steps 1–3:

G N P T W

1	2	3
—	—	—
—	—	—
—	—	—
...	...	...

$W \longrightarrow \boxed{\begin{array}{c}W\\N\end{array}}$

$\sim N \longrightarrow \sim \boxed{\begin{array}{c}W\\N\end{array}}$

$2 \longrightarrow 1$

$\sim 1 \longrightarrow \sim 2$

Exactly one P

$\boxed{\begin{array}{c}G\\P\end{array}}$

LSAT Question	Analysis

Deductions (cont.)

Step 4:

In a Matching game, look to Number Restrictions to make deductions. Because everything recycled at Center 2 will be recycled at Center 1, that means everything recycled at Center 2 must be recycled in at least two centers. Because P is only recycled at one center, it cannot be recycled at Center 2.

G N P T W

```
  1   2   3
  __  __  __

  __  __  __

 ...  ...  ...
     ~P
```

The final Master Sketch shows that deduction along with the other rules listed to the side or beneath the framework.

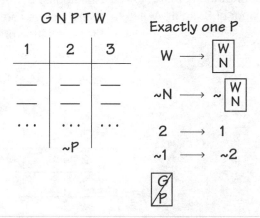

Because Matching games have two sets of entities (or a set of entities and a set of attributes to match to those entities, if you prefer to think of it that way), making them visual is key to keeping track of all the information. Here, the primary ambiguity is in how many materials overall will be recycled. Each recycling center will recycle at least two materials, and you know from the game's opening paragraph that all five kinds of material must be included ("[e]xactly five kinds of material are recycled at these recycling centers" the game says). Thus, at least two kinds of material will be recycled at more than one center (per Rule 2, any kind of material recycled at Center 2 will also be recycled at Center 1). Before tackling the questions, make sure you have a clear understanding of how the number restrictions potentially affect each entity. Plastic is the clearest, as Rule 3 says it will be recycled at exactly one center. Glass will be recycled at either one or two centers; Rule 3 also provides that glass may not be recycled at the center recycling plastic. Newsprint and wood may be recycled at one, two, or all three of the centers. Wherever wood is recycled, so is newsprint (Rule 1). But be careful. This rule does not mean that wood must be recycled wherever newsprint is, so it is possible that more centers recycle newsprint than recycle wood. Tin is a Floater, unrestricted by any rule. Tin may be recycled at one, two, or all three of the plants, and may accompany any other kind of material. The test is likely to reward you for these kinds of insights, as you'll see when we answer the questions to this game in Chapter 5.

Practice

Now, try your hand at the Deductions step. Use the following brief examples to practice identifying the elements of the BLEND checklist you see represented. Look for the points of greatest restriction in the game setup. Starting from these restrictions, combine the rules and limitations to determine what else must or cannot be true.

Take five minutes for each of the following examples. Review the expert's work on Steps 1–3 of the Logic Games Method. Analyze and draw the rules if the expert has not done so. Then, use the BLEND checklist to make all available deductions. Once you're finished, check your work against the LSAT expert's analysis on the following pages.

Game	My Analysis

52. Three buildings (A, B, and C) sit next to each other on a city block, and each building has three floors. On each floor, the lights are either on or off.

   Building B has more floors with lights on than does Building C.
   The first floor of Building C has its lights on.
   Exactly two buildings have their second-floor lights on.
   The lights on the second floor of Building B are off if the lights on the third floor of Building A are off. $\longrightarrow$

Step 1: *Situation:* Buildings on a street; different floors have lights on or off

Entities: The three buildings (A, B, C) and the three floors of each building

Action: Assign each floor a designation of "lights on" or "lights off." "On" and "off" are attributes the floors are taking on, so this is a Matching game.

Limitations: Based on the information in the Overview, we can use "on" and "off" any number of times. It's also possible, based on the Overview, for all the lights to be either on or off.

Step 2:

	A	B	C
3			
2			
1			

Step 3: (Transcribe the rules here.)

Deductions

Step 4: (Make your Deductions and Master Sketch here.)

Game

53. Four friends (A, B, C, and D) meet for dinner at a restaurant. There are five items on the menu (e, f, g, h, and i), and each person will order either 2 or 3 items.

   Exactly three friends order g.
   A orders more menu items than D.
   Each person will order either e or h, but no person orders both.
   Any menu item D orders, C also orders.
   B orders i, but A does not.

My Analysis

Step 1: *Situation:* Friends ordering items off a menu

Entities: Four friends (A, B, C, D) and five menu items (e, f, g, h, i)

Action: Matching menu items to the people at the restaurant

Limitations: There is a minimum of two and a maximum of three menu items per person. We aren't told to use all the menu items; some may remain unused.

Step 2:

→

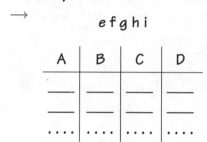

Step 3: (Transcribe the rules here.)

Deductions

Step 4: (Make your Deductions and Master Sketch here.)

Expert Analysis

Now, compare your deductions and Master Sketches for the examples you just tried to those of the LSAT expert.

Game	Analysis
52. Three buildings (A, B, and C) sit next to each other on a city block, and each building has three floors. On each floor, the lights are either on or off.	**Step 1:** *Situation:* Buildings on a street; different floors have lights on or off

52. Three buildings (A, B, and C) sit next to each other on a city block, and each building has three floors. On each floor, the lights are either on or off.

    Building B has more floors with lights on than does Building C.

    The first floor of Building C has its lights on.

    Exactly two buildings have their second-floor lights on.

    The lights on the second floor of Building B are off if the lights on the third floor of Building A are off.

Step 1: *Situation:* Buildings on a street; different floors have lights on or off

Entities: The three buildings (A, B, C) and the three floors of each building

Action: Assign each floor a designation of "lights on" or "lights off." "On" and "off" are attributes the floors are taking on, so this is a Matching game.

Limitations: Based on the information in the Overview, we can use "on" and "off" any number of times. It's also possible, based on the Overview, for all the lights to be either on or off.

→ **Step 2:**

	A	B	C
3			
2			
1			

Step 3:

Rule 1: **B > C**

Rule 2: (can add directly to the sketch)

Rule 3: **exactly 2 buildings: second floor "on"**

Rule 4: **If A3 off → B2 off**
       If B2 on → A3 on

Game	Analysis

Deductions

Step 4:

Rule 2 creates an Established Entity: C1 = on. This, in turn, triggers the Numbers Restriction in Rule 1. Building B must have at least two lighted floors. If another floor of Building C is lit, Building B must have all three floors lighted.

Rule 3 says that *exactly* two buildings have their second floors lit. If Building C has its second floor light on, then it would have two total floors lit. Based on the deduction from Rules 1 and 2, Building B would have all its floors lit in this case, and Building A would have its second floor unlit. If, on the other hand, Building C had its second floor light off, then the "exactly two buildings" with lighted second floors would be Buildings A and B. Display the two "second floor" scenarios as Limited Options:

Opt. 1

	A	B	C
3		ON	OFF
2	OFF	ON	ON
1		ON	ON

Opt. 2   (2–3) (1–2)

	A	B	C
3			
2	ON	ON	OFF
1			ON

Because Building B's second floor is always lit, the contrapositive of Rule 4 makes clear that the third story of Building A must always be lit.

In Option 1, Building C cannot have its third floor lit (Rule 1). The only question in Option 1 is whether Building A's first floor is lit or unlit.

In Option 2, Building B must have at least one more floor lit (Rule 1); if Building C has its third floor lit, Building B must have all its floors lit.

Opt. 1

	A	B	C
3	ON	ON	OFF
2	OFF	ON	ON
1		ON	ON

Opt. 2   (2–3) (1–2)

	A	B	C
3	ON		
2	ON	ON	OFF
1			ON

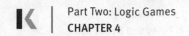

Game	Analysis

Game

53. Four friends (A, B, C, and D) meet for dinner at a restaurant. There are five items on the menu (e, f, g, h, and i), and each person will order either 2 or 3 items.

  Exactly three friends order g.

  A orders more menu items than D.

  Each person will order one of either e or h, but no person orders both.

  Any menu item D orders, C also orders.

  B orders i, but A does not.

Analysis

Step 1: *Situation:* Friends ordering items off a menu

Entities: Four friends (A, B, C, D) and five five menu items (e, f, g, h, i)

Action: Matching menu items to the people at the restaurant

Limitations: Minimum of two and a maximum of three menu items per person. We aren't told to use all the menu items; some may remain unused.

Step 2:

e f g h i

A	B	C	D
—	—	—	—
—	—	—	—
...	...	...	...

Step 3: Rule 1: **Exactly 3 order g**

Rule 2: **A will order three items and D will order two.** (Add directly to the sketch by adding/removing lines in appropriate columns or by writing "2" and "3" above the columns.)

Rule 3: (Add directly to the sketch by filling in one slot for each person with "e/h." Also note to the side "Never eh.")

Rule 4: **If D orders → C orders**
     If ~C orders → ~D orders

Game	Analysis

Rule 5: (can add directly to sketch)

(3)	(2–3)	(2–3)	(2)
A	B	C	D
e/h	*e/h*	*e/h*	*e/h*
	i		
	. . . .	. . . .	
~i			

→

Exactly 3g

Never eh

D orders ⟶ C orders

~C orders ⟶ ~D orders

Deductions

Step 4:

The sketch already has a good deal of information from the rules and their implications, but there are further deductions. Friend A is restricted directly by Rules 2 and 5 and implicitly by Rule 3, which applies to all of the friends. That means that A orders three items (more than D orders, and everyone orders two or three according to the Overview), A doesn't order item i, and A orders exactly one of items e and h. Thus, A will order both item g and item f. Place that information directly in the sketch.

Rule 1 says that three friends will order item g (and the previous deduction shows that one of these is A). This triggers the contrapositive of Rule 4. Friend C must also order item g, for if she does not, then D won't either. In that case, only Friends A and B could order item g, violating Rule 1. Match item g to Friend C. The third order of item g could go to either B or D.

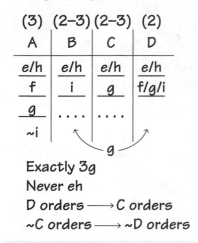

(3)	(2–3)	(2–3)	(2)
A	B	C	D
e/h	*e/h*	*e/h*	*e/h*
f	i	g	f/g/i
g	. . . .	. . . .	
~i			

g

Exactly 3g

Never eh

D orders ⟶ C orders

~C orders ⟶ ~D orders

Reflection

By asking you to match a set of attributes to a set of entities, Matching games lend themselves to sketches that resemble grids or tables. Almost always, the rules will create restrictions on both the vertical and horizontal axes. That is, some will limit the number of attributes you can assign to one or two of the entities, while others limit the number of entities to whom an attribute can be assigned. Setting out your sketch in a way that allows you to see the interactions among both types of restrictions is essential. In each of the examples above, deductions sprang from the combination of rules about the entities (any material recycled at Center 2 must also be recycled at Center 1; Building B must have more floors lit than Building C; each friend orders two or three dishes) and restrictions about the attributes (plastics are recycled at only one recycling center; two of the second floors are lit; dish g is ordered by three of the friends). Expect similar interactions on nearly every Matching game you encounter.

LSAT STRATEGY

In Matching games, deductions are likely to stem from:

- **Duplications**—entities shared by two or more rules; one rule might assign a certain attribute to entity X, and another might tell you that entity Y has more attributes matched to it than X does.

- **Numbers Restrictions**—limitations on the number of attributes that can be assigned to a given entity or limitations on the number of entities to which an attribute can be matched.

- **Established Entities**—matches between entities and attributes that must be maintained throughout the game (e.g., Entity X wears the red jacket); Established Entities are quite common in Matching games.

In Matching games, deductions may involve:

- **Blocks of Entities**—two or more entities that must both be assigned a given attribute or two or more attributes that must be assigned to the same entity or entities; Blocks are somewhat rare in Matching games.

- **Limited Options**—the situation that arises when a rule or combination of rules makes all acceptable arrangements fall into one of two patterns; Limited Options is a rare deduction to find in Matching games.

You'll have additional opportunities to practice Matching deductions in Hybrid games (Sequencing-Matching is the most common Hybrid pattern) among the Chapter 6 practice games. In Chapter 5, you'll have a chance to see how the LSAT expert applied the deductions in the Recycling Centers game when we turn to Step 5 of the Logic Games Method and answer the questions.

Deductions in Distribution Games

Distribution games are distinguished from Matching games because instead of featuring attributes that can be "reused" and assigned to multiple entities, Distribution games ask you to dole out entities among a number of groups. In Distribution games, once you've distributed an entity (assigned it to a group), the entity is "done," and you cannot assign it to a second group. This difference in task makes for a slight difference in where the LSAT expert expects to spot the game's deductions. In all Distribution games, Numbers Restrictions are paramount. If a game's Overview establishes the number of entities per group up front (e.g., three boats with three seats each), then the key deductions will involve entities that must stay together (Blocks of Entities) or must be assigned to different groups. When the game doesn't establish the number of entities per group up front, the LSAT expert focuses on rules that help establish or limit the possibilities. For example, if the game has two teams and you're told that X and Y must be assigned to different teams and that P and Q must be assigned to different teams, you now know that each team has at least two entities.

On the next page, take another look at the Bill Paying game you've seen the LSAT expert analyze up through Step 3.

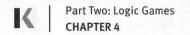
This is a game in which the number of bills per day breaks down into exactly two options. Focus on how the LSAT expert uses these limited options, along with rules about which bills must, can, or cannot be paid together, to make additional deductions.

LSAT Question	Analysis

On a Tuesday, an accountant has exactly seven bills—numbered 1 through 7—to pay by Thursday of the same week. The accountant will pay each bill only once according to the following rules:

> Either three or four of the seven bills must be paid on Wednesday, the rest on Thursday.
> Bill 1 cannot be paid on the same day as bill 5.
> Bill 2 must be paid on Thursday.
> Bill 4 must be paid on the same day as 7.
> If bill 6 is paid on Wednesday, bill 7 must be paid on Thursday.

PrepTest29 Sec3 Qs 1–6

$\longrightarrow$

Steps 1–3:

W	T
1/5	5/1
—	2
—	—
...	...

4
7

$\dfrac{W}{6} \longrightarrow \dfrac{T}{7}$

$\dfrac{W}{7} \longrightarrow \dfrac{T}{6}$

Deductions

Step 4:

In Distribution games, look to Blocks of Entities to make Limited Options. Here, placing the 4/7 block on Wednesday and on Thursday will lead to further deductions in both situations, so create Limited Options. In Option 1, place the 4/7 block on Wednesday; in Option 2, place it on Thursday:

Opt. I

W	T
1/5	5/1
4	2
7	—
...	...

Opt. II

W	T
1/5	5/1
—	2
—	4
	7

Deductions (cont.)

Now make further deductions if possible. According to the contrapositive in Rule 5, if bill 7 is paid on Wednesday, then bill 6 is paid on Thursday. Add this to Option 1. In Option 2, Thursday is completely full, and no more bills can be paid on that day. The two remaining bills, 3 and 6, must be paid on Wednesday.

Opt. I		Opt. II	
W	T	W	T
1/5	5/1	1/5	5/1
4	2	3	2
7	6	6	4
...	...		7

No more deductions can be made. Option 2 is essentially filled in (the only ambiguity is the days on which bills 1 and 5 will be paid), while in Option 1, it is not known on which day bill 3 will be paid.

Not all Distribution games allow for such far-reaching deductions as this one, but when Numbers Restrictions provide for it, this is a game type where you're likely to find Limited Options. Imagine a scenario in which you must distribute nine students between two vans, with either four in Van 1 and five in Van 2 or vice versa. Anytime you encounter a scenario such as this, build dual Limited Options sketches. They are almost guaranteed to lead to additional certainty in one or both of the sketches as you work through the rest of the rules.

Practice

Now, try your hand at the Deductions step. Use the following brief examples to practice identifying the elements of the BLEND checklist you see represented. Look for the points of greatest restriction in the game setup. Starting from these restrictions, combine the rules and limitations to determine what else must or cannot be true.

Take five minutes for each of the following examples. Review the expert's work on Steps 1–3 of the Logic Games Method. Analyze and draw the rules if the expert has not done so. Then, use the BLEND checklist to make all available deductions. Once you're finished, check your work against the LSAT expert's analysis on the following pages.

Game	**My Analysis**

54. Each of the seven members of a sorority (A, B, C, D, E, F, and G) is deciding whether to attend tonight's basketball game or to attend tonight's volleyball game. Each member will attend exactly one of the games.
  No sorority member attends either event alone.
  A attends the volleyball game if C attends the basketball game.
  B and F do not attend the same event.
  D attends the basketball game if and only if G attends the basketball game.
  D does not attend the basketball game unless E attends the volleyball game.
	Step 1: *Situation:* The individual members of a sorority are deciding which game to attend
	
	Entities: The seven members of the sorority (A, B, C, D, E, F, G) and two groups into which they will be subdivided: volleyball and basketball
	
	Action: Separate the sorority members into two groups: basketball and volleyball. Because no one can go to both games at the same time, this is a Distribution game, not a Matching game.
	
	Limitations: Each sorority member attends one and only one game. At this point, it is entirely possible that they all go to one of the games and no one goes to the other.
	
	Step 2:
	
	Basketball │ Volleyball
	
	Step 3: (Transcribe the rules here.)

Deductions

Step 4: (Make your Deductions and Master Sketch here.)

Game	My Analysis
55. A young boy is organizing seven baseball cards (A, B, C, D, E, F, and G) into three categories (1, 2, and 3). Each card will be placed into exactly one of the three categories.	**Step 1:** *Situation:* A young boy trying to decide how to organize his baseball cards

55. A young boy is organizing seven baseball cards (A, B, C, D, E, F, and G) into three categories (1, 2, and 3). Each card will be placed into exactly one of the three categories.

    The number of cards in category 3 is one greater than the number of cards in categories 1 and 2 combined.

    B and E cannot be placed into the same category.

    C and F cannot be placed into the same category.

    A is placed into the same category as D, G, and one other card.

    If there are no cards in category 1 then there must be exactly 2 cards in category 2, and if there are no cards in category 2 then there must be exactly 2 cards in category 1.

→

Step 1: *Situation:* A young boy trying to decide how to organize his baseball cards

Entities: Two sets: the baseball cards (A, B, C, D, E, F, G) and the different groups into which he'll place them (1, 2, 3)

Action: The boy is separating his cards into categories, and because each card can only go into one category, this is a Distribution game.

Limitations: The overview does not posit any minimum or maximum restrictions on the number of cards being placed into each category. So far, it is not clear whether all categories have to be used, or how many cards will wind up in each one.

Step 2:

A B C D E F G

1	2	3

Step 3: (Transcribe the rules here.)

Deductions

Step 4: (Make your Deductions and Master Sketch here.)

Expert Analysis

Now, compare your deductions and Master Sketches to those of the LSAT expert for the examples you just tried.

Game	Analysis

54. Each of the seven members of a sorority (A, B, C, D, E, F, and G) is deciding whether to attend tonight's basketball game or to attend tonight's volleyball game. Each member will attend exactly one of the games.

　No sorority member attends either event alone.

　A attends the volleyball game if C attends the basketball game.

　B and F do not attend the same event.

　D attends the basketball game if and only if G attends the basketball game.

　D does not attend the basketball game unless E attends the volleyball game.

Step 1: *Situation:* The individual members of a sorority are deciding which game to attend

Entities: The seven members of the sorority (A, B, C, D, E, F, G) and two groups into which they will be subdivided: volleyball and basketball

Action: Separate the sorority members into two groups: basketball and volleyball. Because no one can go to both games at the same time, this is a Distribution game, not a Matching game.

Limitations: Each sorority member attends one and only one game. There don't appear to be any limitations on the number of sorority members going to either the volleyball game or the basketball game, so at this point, it is entirely possible that they all go to one of the games and no one goes to the other.

Step 2:

$\longrightarrow$
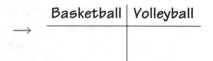

Step 3:

Rule 1: **Never 1 person at the basketball game**
Never 1 person at the volleyball game

Rule 2: **If C basketball → A volleyball**
If A basketball → C volleyball

(Note that A and C can attend the volleyball game together.)

Rule 3: **Never BF**

Rule 4: **If D basketball → G basketball**
If G volleyball → D volleyball
If G basketball → D basketball
If D volleyball → G volleyball

(In other words, DG always go together, either to volleyball or to basketball.)

Game	Analysis
$\rightarrow$	Rule 5: **If D basketball $\rightarrow$ E volleyball**
	If E basketball $\rightarrow$ D volleyball
	(Note that D and E can attend the volleyball game together.)

Deductions

Step 4:

Rule 1 states that no one attends either event alone. Rule 3, placing B and F at different events, forces at least one person to attend each event. Combining those rules, it's clear that at least two of the sorority members attend each game.

Basketball	Volleyball
B/F	F/B

This further narrows the numerical possibilities: there will be groups of 2 and 5 or else of 3 and 4. No other numerical combinations are possible, and keep in mind that D and G form a Block of Entities who see a game together (Rule 4).

According to Rule 5, it is possible to put E and D together at the volleyball game, and according to Rule 2, it is possible to put A and C together at the volleyball game. But, given the Numbers Restrictions on the game, there is not enough room for A, C, D, and E all to attend the volleyball game. D will always take Block partner G (Rule 4), and one of B or F will also attend the volleyball game. If all of these entities attended volleyball, the one of B and F attending the basketball game would be there alone (violating Rule 1). Add this deduction beside the sketch framework:

Never ACDE all in volleyball

The takeaway is that D and E must split up, or A and C must split up, or both pairs of entities must split up.

Game	Analysis

Game

55. A young boy is organizing seven baseball cards (A, B, C, D, E, F, and G) into three categories (1, 2, and 3). Each card will be placed into exactly one of the three categories.

   The number of cards in category 3 is one greater than the number of cards in categories 1 and 2 combined.

   B and E cannot be placed into the same category.

   C and F cannot be placed into the same category.

   A is placed into the same category as D, G, and one other card.

   If there are no cards in category 1, then there must be exactly 2 cards in category 2, and if there are no cards in category 2, then there must be exactly 2 cards in category 1.

Analysis

Step 1: *Situation:* A young boy trying to decide how to organize his baseball cards

Entities: Two sets: the baseball cards (A, B, C, D, E, F, G) and the different groups into which he'll place them (1, 2, 3)

Action: The boy is separating his cards into categories, and because each card can only go into one category, this is a Distribution game.

Limitations: The overview does not posit any minimum or maximum restrictions on the number of cards being placed into each category. So far, it is not clear that all categories have to be used or how many cards will wind up in each one.

Step 2:

A B C D E F G

→

Step 3: Rule 1: seven cards total, and one more in the third category than in the first two categories combined, so there must be four cards in the third category and three cards in the first two categories combined.

Rule 2: **Never BE**

Rule 3: **Never CF**

Rule 4:

Rule 5:

If 1 empty	→ exactly two cards in 2
If ~exactly two cards in 2	→ 1 not empty
If 2 empty	→ exactly two cards in 1
If ~exactly two cards in 1	→ 2 not empty

Game	Analysis

Deductions

Step 4:

Numbers Restrictions (the N in BLEND) are central in Distribution games. Rule 1 means that there are four cards in the third category and three cards in the first two categories combined. Rule 5 says that if category 1 or 2 is empty, the other of those categories must contain exactly two cards. But this is incompatible with Rule 1, which stipulates that categories 1 and 2 contain a total of three cards. It follows that neither category 1 nor category 2 can ever be empty. So there are really only two numerical possibilities: 1:2:4 or 2:1:4. A Limited Options sketch is in order:

Dealing with the numbers first makes it clear that the A-D-G block must go into category 3:

Game	Analysis

Deductions (cont.)

Now, add Rules 2 and 3—"Never BE" and "Never CF." In each sketch, there are exactly four slots left open that must be filled by B, C, E, and F. Start with Option I. B and E cannot both go into category 2, but if B and E are placed into categories 1 and 3, then C and F must go together into category 2, which is also impermissible. A similar problem arises when C and F are put into categories 1 and 3; that forces B and E together in category 2, which is impermissible. The only way to split up both pairs of entities is to place ONE of B/E and ONE of C/F into category 2:

I.

1	2	3
___	B/E	A
	C/F	D
		G
		___

The same applies in Option II:

II.

1	2	3
B/E	___	A
C/F		D
		G
		___

It is not possible to determine which of B, C, E, and F fill the remaining two slots in either Option. No more deductions can be made, so move on to the questions.

Reflection

Numbers Restrictions dominate Distribution actions. It stands to reason. If your boss or teacher asked you to form two teams from a roster of coworkers or classmates, the first questions you'd likely ask are "How many per team? Do the teams need to have equal numbers?" and the like. Only after that would you dig into other questions, such as "Are there any people you definitely want working together or that you think should be kept apart?" When the game specifies the number of entities to be assigned to each group, focus on rules that create Blocks of Entities and those that prevent entities from being placed together. When the game gives you exactly two options for the number of entities per group, draw out both possibilities in a dual Limited Options sketch and fill in the subsequent deductions under both patterns. When the game tells you nothing up front about the number of entities per group, use the Blocks of Entities and/or rules preventing entities from being placed together to establish as much certainty as possible about the number of entities per group.

LSAT STRATEGY

In Distribution games, deductions are likely to stem from:

- **Numbers Restrictions**—limitations on the number of entities per group or determinations of the minimum and maximum numbers of entities per group; in Distribution games, rules preventing entities from being assigned to the same group may act as de facto Numbers Restrictions (e.g., B and F must see different events; ergo, each event has at least one attendee).

- **Blocks of Entities**—two or more entities that must be placed in the same group.

- **Limited Options**—the situation that arises when the game specifies only two possible patterns for the number of entities per group (e.g., Group A contains four students and Group B contains five students, or Group A contains five students and Group B contains four students); in Distribution games, you can sometimes determine a Limited Options numbers scenario by applying other rules to the game's overall framework.

- **Duplications**—entities shared by two or more rules; a common occurrence in Distribution games is one rule that says A and B will be in the same group and another rule that says A and C cannot be in the same group— from this, you can deduce that B and C cannot be in the same group.

In Distribution games, deductions may involve

- **Established Entities**—entities that are assigned to one group for the entire game; this is not too common in Distribution games.

You'll have additional opportunities to practice Distribution deductions in Chapter 6 of this book. In Chapter 5, you'll have a chance to see how the LSAT expert applied the deductions in the Bill Paying game when we turn to Step 5 of the Logic Games Method and answer the questions.

Deductions in Hybrid Games

Just as we said earlier about Hybrid rules, the notion of Hybrid deductions is a bit of a misnomer. Because Hybrid games combine the actions of two (or occasionally three) of the standard logic games actions, the deductions you're likely to encounter correspond to the actions the testmaker has chosen to create the game. Thus, if you have a Selection-Sequencing Hybrid game, expect to see Numbers Restrictions informing the Selection action and Blocks of Entities driving the Sequencing action. In Sequencing-Matching Hybrids (the most common Hybrid actions), Blocks of Entities are likely to form the basis for Sequencing deductions and Duplications and/or Numbers Restrictions will give you further certainty for the Matching component. The one type of deduction unique to Hybrid games comes from rules and restrictions that cross over between the actions, providing deductions in one part of the game based on restrictions in the other.

The Zeno's Furniture game provides an example of these shared Hybrid deductions. As you'll recall from your review of the LSAT expert's previous analyses in Steps 1 through 3, this game is a Selection-Matching Hybrid.

LSAT Question	Analysis

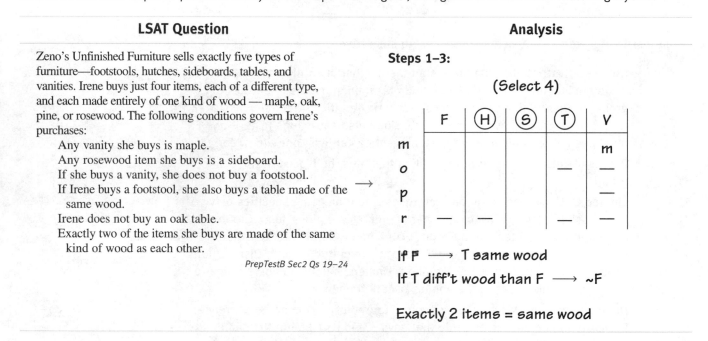

Zeno's Unfinished Furniture sells exactly five types of furniture—footstools, hutches, sideboards, tables, and vanities. Irene buys just four items, each of a different type, and each made entirely of one kind of wood — maple, oak, pine, or rosewood. The following conditions govern Irene's purchases:

Any vanity she buys is maple.
Any rosewood item she buys is a sideboard.
If she buys a vanity, she does not buy a footstool.
If Irene buys a footstool, she also buys a table made of the same wood.
Irene does not buy an oak table.
Exactly two of the items she buys are made of the same kind of wood as each other.

PrepTestB Sec2 Qs 19–24

Steps 1–3:

(Select 4)

If F ⟶ T same wood

If T diff't wood than F ⟶ ~F

Exactly 2 items = same wood

LSAT Question	Analysis

Deductions

Step 4:

The only remaining ambiguous pieces of furniture are F and V. One but not the other will be selected. If V is selected, it will be maple. If F is selected, it must have the same type of wood as T. But T cannot be made of rosewood or oak. So F also cannot be made of rosewood or oak:

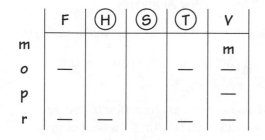

If F ⟶ T same wood

If T diff't wood than F ⟶ ~F

Exactly 2 items = same wood

Keep in mind that if Irene selects a maple F, she will also select a maple T, but she will not, in that case, select a V at all. F and T would be the two items made of the same wood (Rule 6), and H and S could not be made of maple in that case.

The Zeno's Furniture game provides another good reminder about Hybrid games: The individual actions are relatively easy. Here, the Selection action has you choosing four out of five pieces of furniture (excluding only one), and the Matching action simply matches one kind of wood to each piece of furniture. On their own, these actions would provide little challenge. Use that simplicity to your advantage by making a sketch that integrates both actions. That will allow you to see when the restrictions on one of the actions provide further certainty about what must or cannot happen in the other.

It's tough to generalize about Hybrid deductions given the various combinations of actions you may encounter. The best approach is to remember that, no matter what actions the Hybrid combines, the game's individual elements are familiar. If you practice the Logic Games section assiduously, you'll see all of the game types and the variety of rules that accompany each. Hybrid games are no exception.

Practice

Now, try your hand at the Deductions step. Use the following brief examples to practice identifying the elements of the BLEND checklist you see represented. Look for the points of greatest restriction in the game setup. Starting from these restrictions, combine the rules and limitations to determine what else must or cannot be true.

Take five minutes for each of the following examples. Review the expert's work on Steps 1–3 of the Logic Games Method. Analyze and draw the rules if the expert has not done so. Then, use the BLEND checklist to make all available deductions. Once you're finished, check your work against the LSAT expert's analysis on the following pages.

Game	My Analysis

56. Five drivers (A, B, C, D, and E) are waiting to get their cars washed. The cars are in a line, first to last, and each car is exactly one of three different colors (f, g, or h).

   C and E must be separated from one another by exactly two positions in line.
   A must be second or third in line.
   There is only one car of color g, and it is immediately behind A.
   The first car in line is not color f.

Step 1: *Situation:* A line of cars outside a car wash

Entities: The cars (A, B, C, D, E) and the colors (f, g, h)

Action: Sequence the cars from first to last and match a color to each car. This is a Sequencing-Matching Hybrid game.

Limitations: The five cars all must be used, but there is no such restriction for the colors.

Step 2: It is easy to envision this Sequencing-Matching Hybrid game as just two Sequencing games layered on top of each other. We can place the cars on one layer and match the color on the other layer.

$$\underline{\quad}\ \ \underline{\quad}\ \ \underline{\quad}\ \ \underline{\quad}\ \ \underline{\quad}\ (\text{f g h})$$
$$\overline{\underset{1}{\quad}}\ \ \overline{\underset{2}{\quad}}\ \ \overline{\underset{3}{\quad}}\ \ \overline{\underset{4}{\quad}}\ \ \overline{\underset{5}{\quad}}\ (\text{A B C D E})$$

Step 3: (Transcribe the rules here.)

Deductions

Step 4: (Make your Deductions and Master Sketch here.)

Game	My Analysis

57. Six friends (A, B, C, D, E, and F) are going canoeing through a state park. The friends rent exactly two canoes, and each canoe has a front, middle, and rear position. All six friends seat themselves in the canoes, one person per position.

 B sits in Canoe 2.

 If A sits in Canoe 1, then C will sit in a middle position.

 E sits in a position closer to the front of a canoe than does C.

 C and F sit in different canoes but in the same position.

Step 1: *Situation:* Determining who sits where in two canoes

Entities: Friends (A, B, C, D, E, F), canoes (1, 2), and positions (front, middle, rear)

Action: Divide a group of friends into two smaller subgroups; then, place them in front, middle, or rear positions. It's a Distribution-Sequencing Hybrid Game.

Limitations: Six people and six spots

Step 2:

A B C D E F

	Canoe 1	Canoe 2
front		
mid		
rear		

Step 3: (Transcribe the rules here.)

Deductions

Step 4: (Make your Deductions and Master Sketch here.)

Expert Analysis

Now, compare your deductions and Master Sketches for the examples you just tried to those of the LSAT expert.

Game	Analysis

56. Five drivers (A, B, C, D, and E) are waiting to get their cars washed. The cars are in a line, first to last, and each car is exactly one of three different colors (f, g, or h).

C and E must be separated from one another by exactly two positions in line.

A must be second or third in line.

There is only one car of color g, and it is immediately behind A.

The first car in line is not color f.

Step 1: *Situation:* A line of cars outside a car wash

Entities: The cars (A, B, C, D, E) and the colors (f, g, h)

Action: Sequence the cars from first to last and match a color to each car. This is a Sequencing-Matching Hybrid game.

Limitations: The five cars all must be used, but there is no such restriction for the colors.

Step 2: It is easy to envision this Sequencing-Matching Hybrid game as just two Sequencing games layered on top of each other. We can place the cars on one layer and match the color on the other layer.

$$— \quad — \quad — \quad — \quad — \text{(f g h)}$$

$$\overline{\underset{1}{}} \quad \overline{\underset{2}{}} \quad \overline{\underset{3}{}} \quad \overline{\underset{4}{}} \quad \overline{\underset{5}{}} \text{(A B C D E)}$$

Step 3:

Rule 1:

C/E __ __ E/C

Rule 2:

$$— \quad — \quad — \quad — \quad — \text{(f g h)}$$

$$— \quad \overset{\curvearrowleft \quad \curvearrowright}{\underset{A}{\overline{}}} \quad — \quad — \text{(A B C D E)}$$

Rule 3:

__	g
A	__

Only 1 g

Rule 4:

$$\underline{g/h} \quad — \quad — \quad — \quad — \text{(f g h)}$$

$$— \quad \overset{\curvearrowleft \quad \curvearrowright}{\underset{A}{\overline{}}} \quad — \quad — \text{(A B C D E)}$$

Game	**Analysis**

Deductions

Step 4:

The C/E _ _ E/C block (Rule 1) is a good place to start because it affects two entities and four positions. This Block can only go in positions 1 and 4 or in positions 2 and 5. Set up Limited Options, keeping in mind that A must be in position 2 or 3 (Rule 2):

I. g/h __ __ __ __
    C/E __ __ E/C __
        ↖A↗

II. g/h __ __ __ __
    __ C/E A __ E/C

Rule 3 states that the one car of color g must be immediately behind car A. That means that in Option I, car 3 or car 4 must be of color g, while in Option II, it must be car 4 that is of color g. Moreover, combine Rules 3 and 4 to deduce that because f cannot be the first car's color, and neither can g (because there is only a single g and it must be third or fourth), the only possible match for the first car is color h:

I. h __ ↗g↘ __ __
    C/E __ __ E/C __
        ↖A↗

II. h __ __ g __
    __ C/E A __ E/C

Cars A, C, and E have all been placed, so position 5 in Option I must be car B or car D. Similarly, in Option II, B and D must fill positions 1 and 4 (in either order). Because there is just one car of color g, also fill in all slots that cannot be g with "f/h":

I. h   f/h ↗g↘ __   f/h
    C/E __   __   E/C B/D
             ↖A↗

II. h   f/h f/h g   f/h
    B/D C/E A   D/B E/C

Game	Analysis

Game

57. Six friends (A, B, C, D, E, and F) are going canoeing through a state park. The friends rent exactly two canoes, and each canoe has a front, middle, and rear position. All six friends seat themselves in the canoes, one person per position.

    B sits in Canoe 2.

    If A sits in Canoe 1, then C will sit in a middle position.

    E sits in a position closer to the front of a canoe than does C.

    C and F sit in different canoes but in the same position.

Analysis

Step 1: *Situation:* Determining who sits where in two canoes

Entities: Friends (A, B, C, D, E, F), canoes (1, 2), and positions (front, middle, rear)

Action: Divide a group of friends into two smaller subgroups, then place them in front, middle, or rear positions. It's a Distribution-Sequencing Hybrid Game.

Limitations: Six people and six spots

→ **Step 2:**

A B C D E F

	Canoe 1	Canoe 2
front		
mid		
rear		

	Game		Analysis

Analysis

Step 3: Rule 1: (can add directly to the sketch)

	Canoe 1	Canoe 2
front		
mid		
rear		
		B

→ Rule 2: If A canoe 1 → C middle
If ~C middle → A canoe 2

Rule 3:

E
:
C

Rule 4: C=F or F=C; can also write this rule as

C/F	F/C

Deductions

Step 4:

This is a Sequencing-Distribution Hybrid game, so make deductions by finding an entity that is bound by both sets of game restrictions. C shows up in multiple rules, making it a good target. Rule 3 states that E sits closer to the front than C. Because there are only three positions in each canoe, E must therefore sit in a front or middle position, and C must sit in a middle or rear position.

The last rule also deals with C. It states that C and F sit in different canoes but in the same position. Combined with the previous deduction, F must also sit in a middle or rear position.

Rule 2 also deals with C. The contrapositive of this rule states that if C does not sit in the middle position in one of the canoes, A will sit in Canoe 2. Because C must sit in the rear position if he is not in the middle position, then this rule becomes: if C sits in the rear position, A sits in Canoe 2.

Game	Analysis

Deductions (cont.)

At this point, create a Limited Options sketch: the C/F block must go in either the middle or rear position. When placed in the rear, this block forces A and B (in whichever order) into the front and middle positions of Canoe 2. The only two entities remaining, D and E, must therefore occupy the front and middle positions (in whichever order) of Canoe 1.

Opt. I

	Canoe 1	Canoe 2
front	D/E	A/B
mid	E/D	B/A
rear	C/F	F/C

If the C/F block is placed instead in the middle positions, then E will be forced into one of the two front positions. Because B must go in Canoe 2, the only entities that can go in the rear position of Canoe 1 are A and D.

Opt. II

	Canoe 1	Canoe 2	
front			E
mid	C/F	F/C	
rear	A/D		
		B	

Reflection

In Hybrid games, use your knowledge of the standard game actions to anticipate the deductions you're likely to see. Remain on the lookout for cases in which restrictions in one action impact the arrangements acceptable in the other action.

LSAT STRATEGY

In Hybrid games, deductions are likely to stem from:

- **BLEND**—Because Hybrid games may involve any of the standard logic games actions, all five of the BLEND elements are on the table.
- **"Cross Over" rules**—Keep an eye out in Hybrid games for rules that present restrictions to both of the actions in the game.

You'll have additional opportunities to practice making deductions in Hybrid games in Chapter 6 of this book. In Chapter 5, you'll have a chance to see how the LSAT expert applied the deductions in the Zeno's Furniture game when we turn to Step 5 of the Logic Games Method and answer the questions.

Summary

All of the work you've done thus far in logic games has really been in preparation for the next chapter. Now, we'll get to answer the logic games questions and get the points. Steps 1–4 of the Method have covered two substantial chapters. On Test Day, those steps will take you about 3–4 minutes per game. But, you'll be glad that you've taken that time. The setup, sketch, and deductions you make will put you in a position to answer the questions much more quickly, confidently, and accurately than would have been possible without them. As you dive into Chapter 5 and the questions and then move on to logic games practice in Chapter 6, you'll be glad you spent the time to master the first four steps of the Method. Your practice will be much more valuable than if you had jumped into the questions without such a strong understanding of logic games mechanics.

Logic Games: The Questions

LOGIC GAMES QUESTION TYPES

This is where all of your work on Logic Games pays off. All that you've learned so far—how to conduct an Overview, build a Sketch, populate it with the Rules, and combine the rules to make Deductions—has prepared you for the skills you'll learn and practice here. If you've taken the preceding chapters seriously—if you've really conquered Steps 1 through 4 of the Logic Games Method—you may be surprised by how quickly and confidently you are able to answer Logic Games questions. Indeed, that's the reason that LSAT experts spend 3–4 minutes before tackling a game's questions doing the setup and critical-thinking steps that you've been practicing up to this point.

Nonetheless, there are still a few skills to learn to handle the Logic Games question sets efficiently and to avoid needless and costly mistakes. Indeed, one of the biggest components of mastery in this chapter involves identifying, quickly and accurately, what each question is calling for. Many test takers lose points in the Logic Games section because after having done strong analyses, they quite simply answer the wrong question. They might, for example, choose an answer that clearly must be true even though the question stem calls for the choice that *could be false*. Or, they pick out a scenario that could be true when the question credits only the choice that *must be true*. You first learned to assess levels of certainty and truth values back in Chapter 1: LSAT Reasoning. If you feel as if you need to brush up on these concepts or if you skipped over that section initially, now is the time to revisit that chapter.

Other mistakes that poorly trained test takers make with Logic Games questions lead to wasted time and effort even when they don't lead to wrong answers. Students who try to test every choice by drawing innumerable diagrams lose time that an LSAT expert, confident in the deductions she has made in the Master Sketch, is able to preserve. Others, who are in too much of a hurry to draw even one new sketch (to account for a new condition in a question stem, let's say), become so confused trying to hold dozens of arrangements in their heads that they can't quickly or confidently eliminate wrong answers.

In this chapter, you'll learn how best to handle every Logic Games question. We'll break the questions into a handful of question types and show you effective strategies for each one.

LSAT STRATEGY

Logic Games Question Types

- Acceptability Questions
- Must Be/Could Be Questions
- New-"If" Questions
- Other Question Types
  · Complete and Accurate List Questions
  · Completely Determine Questions
  · Numerical Questions
    » Minimum/Maximum Questions
    » Earliest/Latest Questions
    » "How Many" Questions
  · Rule Alteration Questions
    » Rule Change Questions
    » Rule Substitution Questions
  · Supply the "If" Questions

Using This Chapter Effectively

You can't practice LSAT questions without having the setup, sketch, rules, and deductions in place. So, to learn to handle LSAT questions, you'll be drawing once again on the same games you've been using in Chapters 2, 3, and 4. Where it's important, we'll present the game setup along with the Master Sketch you derived for it in Chapter 4. If you don't feel like you remember the work we did to come up with the Master Sketch, feel free to review the game in the previous chapters. For most of these games, however, taking a minute or two to review the game and study the Master Sketch will probably remind you of all the work you did in Steps 1–4, and you'll feel ready to apply the Master Sketch to the questions.

At a few key points in the chapter, you will also encounter drills to help reinforce effective analysis of Logic Games question stems.

After you've completed this chapter, there are several additional full logic games in Chapter 6. There, you can practice the Logic Games Method from start to finish and feel confident that you can handle any game you encounter on Test Day. In those games, you'll see all of the question types described here.

ACCEPTABILITY QUESTIONS

Most LSAT logic games feature one Acceptability question, and usually it is the first question in the set. On rare occasions, you'll find a game with no Acceptability question and, very rarely, a game with two. That's good news because, as you'll see, Acceptability questions can be answered in seconds if you use the LSAT expert's strategy.

LEARNING OBJECTIVES

In this section, you'll learn to:

- Answer Acceptability questions strategically.

Here's the Acceptability question from the game you first saw in Chapter 2. Try it out on your own, but don't spend too much time on it. We'll show you, step-by-step, how the LSAT expert attacks this question with ease.

Six racehorses—K, L, M, N, O, and P—will be assigned to six positions arranged in a straight line and numbered consecutively 1 through 6. The horses are assigned to the positions, one horse per position, according to the following conditions:

K and L must be assigned to positions that are separated from each other by exactly one position.

K and N cannot be assigned to positions that are next to each other.

N must be assigned to a higher-numbered position than M.

P must be assigned to position 3.

Which one of the following lists an acceptable assignment of horses to positions 1 though 6, respectively?

(A) K, L, P, M, N, O
(B) M, K, P, L, N, O
(C) M, N, K, P, L, O
(D) N, O, P, K, M, L
(E) O, M, P, L, N, K

PrepTest28 Sec2 Q1

Because the correct answer is an acceptable arrangement, each of the wrong answers is unacceptable for some reason. The LSAT expert knows that's because each of the wrong answers violates one or more rules or limitations in the game. Now, going through each choice to confirm that it's error-free can be time-consuming and confusing. It is hard to prove that nothing is wrong with a choice. There's a better way. It is easy to prove that there is something wrong with a choice. The LSAT expert checks not answer by answer but rule by rule. Observe.

LSAT Question	**Analysis**
Six racehorses—K, L, M, N, O, and P—will be assigned to six positions arranged in a straight line and numbered consecutively 1 through 6. The horses are assigned to the positions, one horse per position, according to the following conditions: K and L must be assigned to positions that are separated from each other by exactly one position. K and N cannot be assigned to positions that are next to each other. N must be assigned to a higher-numbered position than M. P must be assigned to position 3.	**Steps 1–4:** K L M N O P → (I) $\dfrac{}{1}$ $\dfrac{K/L}{2}$ $\dfrac{P}{3}$ $\dfrac{L/K}{4}$ $\dfrac{}{5}$ $\dfrac{}{6}$ $\begin{matrix}\sim K\;N\\\sim N\;K\end{matrix}$ M . . . N (II) $\dfrac{M}{1}$ $\dfrac{N}{2}$ $\dfrac{P}{3}$ $\dfrac{K/L}{4}$ $\dfrac{O}{5}$ $\dfrac{L/K}{6}$
Which one of the following lists an acceptable assignment of horses to positions 1 though 6, respectively?	→ **Step 5:** The correct answer is "acceptable"; each wrong answer violates a rule.
(A) ~~K, L, P, M, N, O~~	→ Violates Rule 1 by not having one position separating K and L from each other. Eliminate.
(B) M, K, P, L, N, O	
(C) M, N, K, P, L, O	
(D) N, O, P, K, M, L	
(E) O, M, P, L, N, K	

PrepTest28 Sec2 Q1

Notice that the LSAT expert starts with Rule 1 and crosses out any answer choice that violates it. Coincidentally, the first choice (A) violates Rule 1, so the expert crosses out choice (A) entirely. Be clear here; the LSAT expert did *not* start with choice (A) and compare it to each rule, but rather started with Rule 1 looking for any choice that violates it. The expert presses on with Rule 2.

LSAT Question	**Analysis**
Six racehorses—K, L, M, N, O, and P—will be assigned to six positions arranged in a straight line and numbered consecutively 1 through 6. The horses are assigned to the positions, one horse per position, according to the following conditions: K and L must be assigned to positions that are separated from each other by exactly one position. K and N cannot be assigned to positions that are next to each other. N must be assigned to a higher-numbered position than M. P must be assigned to position 3.	**Steps 1–4:** K L M N O P (I) $\frac{\quad}{1}$ $\frac{K/L}{2}$ $\frac{P}{3}$ $\frac{L/K}{4}$ $\frac{\quad}{5}$ $\frac{\quad}{6}$ $\sim K\,N$ $\sim N\,K$ M . . . N (II) $\frac{M}{1}$ $\frac{N}{2}$ $\frac{P}{3}$ $\frac{K/L}{4}$ $\frac{O}{5}$ $\frac{L/K}{6}$
Which one of the following lists an acceptable assignment of horses to positions 1 though 6, respectively?	**Step 5:** The correct answer is "acceptable"; each wrong answer violates a rule.
(A) ~~K, L, P, M, N, O~~	Violates Rule 1 by not having one position separating K and L from each other. Eliminate.
(B) M, K, P, L, N, O	
(C) M, N, K, P, L, O	
(D) N, O, P, K, M, L	
(E) ~~O, M, P, L, N, K~~ *PrepTest28 Sec2 Q1*	Violates Rule 2 by placing K and N In positions that are next to each other. Eliminate.

Now you get the value of this approach (and maybe see the benefit to when the testmaker includes exactly four rules).

LSAT Question	**Analysis**

Six racehorses—K, L, M, N, O, and P—will be assigned to six positions arranged in a straight line and numbered consecutively 1 through 6. The horses are assigned to the positions, one horse per position, according to the following conditions:

    K and L must be assigned to positions that are separated from each other by exactly one position.

    K and N cannot be assigned to positions that are next to each other.

    N must be assigned to a higher-numbered position than M.

    P must be assigned to position 3.

→ **Steps 1–4:**

K L M N O P

(I)

	K/L	P	L/K			~K N
1	2	3	4	5	6	~N K

M . . . N

(II)

M	N	P	K/L	O	L/K
1	2	3	4	5	6

Which one of the following lists an acceptable assignment of horses to positions 1 though 6, respectively?

→ **Step 5:** The correct answer is "acceptable"; each wrong answer violates a rule.

(A) ~~K, L, P, M, N, O~~

→ Violates Rule 1 by not having one position separating K and L from each other. Eliminate.

(B) M, K, P, L, N, O

(C) M, N, K, P, L, O

(D) ~~N, O, P, K, M, L~~

→ Violates Rule 3 by placing N in a lower-numbered position than M. Eliminate.

(E) ~~O, M, P, L, N, K~~

PrepTest28 Sec2 Q1

→ Violates Rule 2 by placing K and N in positions that are next to each other. Eliminate.

One rule left and one more wrong answer to eliminate.

LSAT Question	Analysis
Six racehorses—K, L, M, N, O, and P—will be assigned to six positions arranged in a straight line and numbered consecutively 1 through 6. The horses are assigned to the positions, one horse per position, according to the following conditions: K and L must be assigned to positions that are separated from each other by exactly one position. K and N cannot be assigned to positions that are next to each other. N must be assigned to a higher-numbered position than M. P must be assigned to position 3.	**Steps 1–4:** K L M N O P (I) $\underset{1}{\_}$ $\underset{2}{K/L}$ $\underset{3}{P}$ $\underset{4}{L/K}$ $\underset{5}{\_}$ $\underset{6}{\_}$ $\underset{\sim N K}{\sim K N}$ M . . . N (II) $\underset{1}{M}$ $\underset{2}{N}$ $\underset{3}{P}$ $\underset{4}{K/L}$ $\underset{5}{O}$ $\underset{6}{L/K}$
Which one of the following lists an acceptable assignment of horses to positions 1 though 6, respectively?	**Step 5:** The correct answer is "acceptable"; each wrong answer violates a rule.
(A) ~~K, L, P, M, N, O~~	Violates Rule 1 by not having one position separating K and L from each other. Eliminate.
(B) M, K, P, L, N, O	Correct. This one abides by all of the rules, and conforms to Option I in the Master Sketch.
(C) ~~M, N, K, P, L, O~~	Violates Rule 4 by placing P in position 4. Eliminate.
(D) ~~N, O, P, K, M, L~~	Violates Rule 3 by placing N in a lower-numbered position than M. Eliminate.
(E) ~~O, M, P, L, N, K~~	Violates Rule 2 by placing K and N in positions that are next to each other. Eliminate.

PrepTest28 Sec2 Q1

We won't reprint the questions multiple times from here on out, but you should keep this example in mind as you tackle every Acceptability question from this point forward. Use the rules to eliminate the violators. The correct answer will always be left at the end. From time to time, you'll find cases in which one rule eliminates two answer choices and cases in which a certain rule is violated by none of the answer choices. That's all right. Just remember that four of the answers are not acceptable, and work to eliminate them quickly. If you need to confirm your choice, you can check it against each of the rules and restrictions, but most of the time, the violations are so clear and demonstrable that you'll cross out four choices confidently and select the one that remains.

Take a look at the Acceptability question from the Recycling Centers game you've seen in previous chapters. As you go over it, keep in mind that the LSAT expert checked the answers rule by rule, so review it using that same pattern. Start with Rule 1. Spot the choice that violates it. Then confirm that your analysis conforms to that of the expert. Take a minute to review the setup and rules before you study the analysis. Do you remember what type of game this is? We'll tell you after you've reviewed the question.

LSAT Question	**Analysis**

There are exactly three recycling centers in Rivertown: Center 1, Center 2, and Center 3. Exactly five kinds of material are recycled at these recycling centers: glass, newsprint, plastic, tin, and wood. Each recycling center recycles at least two but no more than three of these kinds of material. The following conditions must hold:
    Any recycling center that recycles wood also recycles newsprint.
    Every kind of material that Center 2 recycles is also recycled at Center 1.
    Only one of the recycling centers recycles plastic, and that recycling center does not recycle glass.
	Steps 1–4:

Which one of the following could be an accurate account of all the kinds of material recycled at each recycling center in Rivertown?	**Step 5:** An Acceptability question. Check each rule and then eliminate any answer choice that violates that rule.
(A) Center 1: newsprint, plastic, wood; Center 2: newsprint, wood; Center 3: glass, tin, wood	This violates Rule 1. Center 3 recycles wood, but does not recycle newsprint. Eliminate.
(B) Center 1: glass, newsprint, tin; Center 2: glass, newsprint, tin; Center 3: newsprint, plastic, wood	Correct. This one abides by all of the rules, and conforms to the Master Sketch.
(C) Center 1: glass, newsprint, wood; Center 2: glass, newsprint, tin; Center 3: plastic, tin	This violates Rule 2. Here, tin is recycled at Center 2, but not at Center 1. Eliminate.
(D) Center 1: glass, plastic, tin; Center 2: glass, tin; Center 3: newsprint, wood	This violates Rule 3. Center 1 recycles both glass and plastic. Eliminate.
(E) Center 1: newsprint, plastic, wood; Center 2: newsprint, plastic, wood; Center 3: glass, newsprint, tin	This violates Rule 3. Plastic is recycled at two centers here. Eliminate.

PrepTest June 2007 Sec1 Q18

That game is a Matching game. Notice, however, that the game type made little difference in your approach to the Acceptability question. In this game, there are only three rules, so it's no surprise that one of them eliminated two wrong answer choices. Besides, Rule 3 is really two rules in one—plastic is recycled only once AND plastic and glass cannot be recycled at the same plant.

Practice

Now, try two Acceptability questions on your own. For each, take a minute to reacquaint yourself with the game's action, sketch, and rules before you tackle the questions. Once you start on the question, however, use the rule-by-rule elimination strategy and work as quickly as you can. Eliminate answer choices that violate rules and select the one choice that offers an acceptable arrangement of entities for the game. After you've selected the correct answer, check your work against that of the LSAT expert on the following pages.

LSAT Question	My Analysis

A park contains at most five of seven kinds of trees—firs, laurels, maples, oaks, pines, spruces, and yews—consistent with the following conditions:
　If maples are in the park, yews are not.
　If firs are in the park, pines are not.
　If yews are not in the park, then either laurels or oaks, but not both, are in the park.
　If it is not the case that the park contains both laurels and oaks, then it contains firs and spruces.
	Steps 1–4:
	
	F L M O P S Y　(max 5)
	
	If (M) ⟶ ~Y
	If (Y) ⟶ ~M
	
	If (F) ⟶ ~P
	→　If (P) ⟶ ~F
	
	If ~Y ⟶ [Exactly one of (L)/(O)]
	If (L) and (O) ⟶ (Y)
	If ~L and ~O ⟶ (Y)
	
	If ~L or ~O ⟶ (F) and (S)
	If ~F or ~S ⟶ (L) and (O)

1. Which one of the following could be a complete and accurate list of the kinds of trees in the park?	**Step 5:** The correct answer is an acceptable → list of trees that could be planted in the park. Check the rules one by one and eliminate answer choices that violate the rules.

(A)　firs, maples

(B)　firs, laurels, oaks

(C)　firs, laurels, pines, spruces

(D)　firs, laurels, spruces, yews

(E)　firs, maples, oaks, spruces, yews

PrepTestB Sec2 Q7

LSAT Question	**My Analysis**

LSAT Question

Zeno's Unfinished Furniture sells exactly five types of furniture—footstools, hutches, sideboards, tables, and vanities. Irene buys just four items, each of a different type, and each made entirely of one kind of wood—maple, oak, pine, or rosewood. The following conditions govern Irene's purchases:

Any vanity she buys is maple.

Any rosewood item she buys is a sideboard.

If she buys a vanity, she does not buy a footstool.

If Irene buys a footstool, she also buys a table made of the same wood.

Irene does not buy an oak table.

Exactly two of the items she buys are made of the same kind of wood as each other.

→

My Analysis

Steps 1–4:

(Select 4)

	F	(H)	(S)	(T)	V
m					m
o	—			—	
p					—
r	—	—		—	—

If F ⟶ T same wood

If T diff't wood than F ⟶ ~F

Exactly 2 items = same wood

---

2. Which one of the following could be an accurate list of the items Irene buys?

→ **Step 5:** An Acceptability question. Check each rule and then eliminate any answer choice that violates that rule.

(A) maple footstool, maple hutch, rosewood sideboard, maple table

---

(B) oak hutch, rosewood sideboard, pine table, oak vanity

(C) rosewood hutch, maple sideboard, oak table, maple vanity

(D) pine footstool, rosewood sideboard, pine table, maple vanity

---

(E) maple footstool, pine hutch, oak sideboard, maple table

PrepTestB Sec2 Q19

Expert Analysis

Here's how the LSAT expert managed each of those Acceptability questions. As you review, ask yourself if you correctly interpreted each rule and took the shortest route to the correct answer by eliminating rule violators.

LSAT Question	Analysis

A park contains at most five of seven kinds of trees—firs, laurels, maples, oaks, pines, spruces, and yews—consistent with the following conditions:
 	
If maples are in the park, yews are not.
If firs are in the park, pines are not.
If yews are not in the park, then either laurels or oaks, but not both, are in the park.
If it is not the case that the park contains both laurels and oaks, then it contains firs and spruces.
	Steps 1–4:
	
	F L M O P S Y (max 5)
	
	If (M) ⟶ ~Y
	If (Y) ⟶ ~M
	
	If (F) ⟶ ~P
	If (P) ⟶ ~F
	
	If ~Y ⟶ [Exactly one of (L)/(O)]
	If (L) and (O) ⟶ (Y)
	If ~L and ~O ⟶ (Y)
	
	If ~L or ~O ⟶ (F) and (S)
	If ~F or ~S ⟶ (L) and (O)

1. Which one of the following could be a complete and accurate list of the kinds of trees in the park?	**Step 5:** The correct answer is an acceptable list of trees that could be planted in the park. Check the rules one by one and eliminate answer choices that violate the rules.
(A) firs, maples	This violates Rule 3. Yews are not selected, yet neither laurels nor oaks are selected. Eliminate.
(B) firs, laurels, oaks	This violates Rule 3. Yews are not selected, yet both laurels and oaks are selected. Eliminate.
(C) firs, laurels, pines, spruces	This violates Rule 2. Firs and pines are both selected here. Eliminate.
(D) firs, laurels, spruces, yews	Correct. Once you've eliminated the four wrong answers, select the remaining choice and move on.
(E) firs, maples, oaks, spruces, yews PrepTestB Sec2 Q7	This violates Rule 1. Maples and yews are both selected here. Eliminate.

LSAT Question	**Analysis**

Zeno's Unfinished Furniture sells exactly five types of furniture—footstools, hutches, sideboards, tables, and vanities. Irene buys just four items, each of a different type, and each made entirely of one kind of wood—maple, oak, pine, or rosewood. The following conditions govern Irene's purchases:

  Any vanity she buys is maple.
  Any rosewood item she buys is a sideboard.
  If she buys a vanity, she does not buy a footstool.
  If Irene buys a footstool, she also buys a table made of the same wood.
  Irene does not buy an oak table.
  Exactly two of the items she buys are made of the same kind of wood as each other.

$\longrightarrow$

Steps 1–4:

(Select 4)

	F	(H)	(S)	(T)	V
m					m
o	—			—	—
p					—
r	—	—		—	—

If F $\longrightarrow$ T same wood

If T diff't wood than F $\longrightarrow$ ~F

Exactly 2 items = same wood

---

2. Which one of the following could be an accurate list of the items Irene buys?

$\longrightarrow$

Step 5: An Acceptability question. Check each rule and then eliminate any answer choice that violates that rule.

(A) maple footstool, maple hutch, rosewood sideboard, maple table

$\longrightarrow$ This violates Rule 6. Eliminate.

(B) oak hutch, rosewood sideboard, pine table, oak vanity

$\longrightarrow$ This violates Rule 1. Eliminate.

(C) rosewood hutch, maple sideboard, oak table, maple vanity

$\longrightarrow$ This violates Rule 2. Eliminate.

(D) pine footstool, rosewood sideboard, pine table, maple vanity

$\longrightarrow$ This violates Rule 3. Eliminate.

(E) maple footstool, pine hutch, oak sideboard, maple table

$\longrightarrow$ Correct. This violates none of the rules.

PrepTestB Sec2 Q19

A Note on Complete and Accurate List Questions

One of the Acceptability questions you just reviewed had the following question stem:

> Which one of the following could be a complete and
> accurate list of the kinds of trees in the park?
>
> *PrepTestB Sec 2 Q7*

That particular wording amounts to asking for an acceptable selection, and the correct answer will represent one possible "solution" to the game.

It's worth noting, however, that the testmaker will, occasionally, use the phrase "complete and accurate list" for questions that focus on a narrower part of the game. In a Sequencing game, for example, one of these questions might ask for "a complete and accurate list of the days on which Johnson's appointment may be scheduled." In a Distribution game, on the other hand, you might run across a question such as "Which of following is a complete and accurate list of all players who could play on Team B?"

For Complete and Accurate List questions such as these, the correct answer must contain *any and all* of the acceptable slots or entities called for by the question stem. In other words, each wrong answer will either be incomplete—it will not contain all of the days on which Johnson's appointment can be scheduled, or it will be missing players who are eligible for Team B—or the wrong answer will be inaccurate—it will include days on which Johnson's appointment cannot be scheduled or players ineligible for Team B. That makes sense when you think about the question. If the right answer is "complete and accurate," all four wrong answers must be incomplete or inaccurate.

You will recognize Complete and Accurate List questions from question stems like those below, but don't spend too much time trying to hunt down examples of this rare question type.

> Which one of the following is a complete and accurate
> list of the bills any one of which could be among the
> bills paid on Wednesday?
>
> *PrepTest29 Sec3 Q2*

> Which one of the following is a complete and accurate
> list of all the woods any footstool that Irene buys could
> be made of?
>
> *PrepTestB Sec2 Q21*

When you do come across Complete and Accurate List questions, don't panic or change your strategic approach to logic games. These questions are too rare to be a type that makes or breaks your score. Just distinguish them from Acceptability questions and remember that the wrong answers are always inaccurate or incomplete. Once you've characterized the answer choices, you just consult the Master Sketch to eliminate the violators and find the right answer.

While we're on the subject of completeness, let's look at another rare Logic Games question type: the Completely Determine question.

COMPLETELY DETERMINE QUESTIONS

From time to time, the LSAT will pose a question asking you for a statement that would completely determine the sequence, selection, matching, or distribution of all entities in the game. Completely Determine questions are not common—among the 60 logic games (345 questions) released from 2010 through 2014, there were only seven of these questions. It turns out, however, that one of them was in the Language Awards game.

You'll recall that this game asked you to sequence seven awards, one at a time. The expert knows that the correct answer will be a statement that determines the exact order of all seven awards, including Swahili, the unrestricted "Floater" in this game. As you review the expert's analysis of this question, pay attention to how he uses the Limited Options in the Master Sketch to eliminate answer choices that leave the exact order of two or more of the entities indeterminate. The less restrictive an option is initially, the less likely it is to be engaged by the correct answer.

LSAT Question	Analysis
A college dean will present seven awards for outstanding language research. The awards—one for French, one for German, one for Hebrew, one for Japanese, one for Korean, one for Latin, and one for Swahili—must be presented consecutively, one at a time, in conformity with the following constraints: The German award is not presented first. The Hebrew award is presented at some time before the Korean award is presented. The Latin award is presented at some time before the Japanese award is presented. The French award is presented either immediately before or immediately after the Hebrew award is presented. The Korean award is presented either immediately before or immediately after the Latin award is presented.	**Steps 1–4:** Opt. I ___ (F/H) ___ ___ ___ ___ ___ Opt. II S ___ (F/H) ___ ___ ___ ___ Opt. III S G (F/H) (K/L) J 1 2 3 4 5 6 7 ~G (F/H) . . . (K/L) . . . J
The order in which the awards are presented is completely determined if which one of the following is true?	**Step 5:** This is a Completely Determine question, so the correct answer will present an arrangement of specific entities that in turn forces all seven entities into definite positions. Any answer choice that allows for multiple permutations is incorrect.
(A) The French award is presented immediately before the German award is presented, and the Korean award is presented immediately before the Latin award is presented.	This is possible in both Option 1 and Option 2. Eliminate.
(B) The French award is presented immediately before the Hebrew award is presented, and the Hebrew award is presented immediately before the Korean award is presented.	This is possible in all three Limited Options. Eliminate.
(C) The French award is presented immediately before the Latin award is presented, and the Korean award is presented immediately before the Japanese award is presented.	This is possible in all three Limited Options. Eliminate.

LSAT Question	Analysis
(D) The German award is presented immediately before the French award is presented, and the Latin award is presented immediately before the Japanese award is presented.	Correct. This is only possible in Option 3, and it explicitly establishes relationships between all entities:

$$\frac{S}{1} \quad \frac{G}{2} \quad \frac{F}{3} \quad \frac{H}{4} \quad \frac{K}{5} \quad \frac{L}{6} \quad \frac{J}{7}$$

LSAT Question	Analysis
(E) The German award is presented immediately before the Korean award is presented, and the Hebrew award is presented immediately before the French award is presented.	This is possible in Option 1 and Option 2. Eliminate.

PrepTest29 Sec3 Q19

The correct answer to a Completely Determine question must impose restrictions sufficient to lock down all of the entities, including the Floater(s). Here, (D) becomes a likely suspect as soon as we are aware that it can only occur within the strictures of the most restrictive of our three options. Checking it with a quick sketch will confirm that (D) does, indeed, completely determine the order of all seven entities. In some Completely Determine questions, you may need to sketch out the implications of two or more of the answer choices to confirm the correct answer. Here, the Limited Options sketch saved the expert both time and effort.

Characterizing the Answer Choices in Acceptability, Complete and Accurate List, and Completely Determine Questions

Take a few minutes to study the sample question stems that follow. For each, you'll see the LSAT expert's analysis identifying the question type and characterizing the one correct and four incorrect answer choices. Remember, the analysis you see below is mental work the expert is doing. There is no need to write down any of this on Test Day. Once you feel comfortable identifying these question types, try the practice drill on the following pages to test your ability to characterize the choices on similar questions.

Question Stem		Analysis
Which of the following could be a complete and accurate list of the race cars crossing the finish line, in order from first to last?	→	This question asks for one possible, acceptable arrangement of the entities and is thus a standard Acceptability question. The correct answer could be true; the four incorrect choices must be false because they each break one or more rules. Attack Acceptability questions by going through the rules and knocking out all choices that break at least one rule. The choice that remains is the correct answer.
Which of the following could be an accurate matching of children to party hats?	→	Another Acceptability question. Correct answer could be true; incorrect choices must be false because they each break at least one rule.
Which of the following could be a complete and accurate list of each of the clients served by lawyer Z?	→	This one is a Partial Acceptability question: it doesn't ask for an acceptable arrangement of all the clients and lawyers, just a matching of lawyer Z to her clients. As in all Acceptability questions, the correct answer could be true, while incorrect choices must be false.
Which of the following is NOT an acceptable schedule of appointments, from earliest to latest?	→	Acceptability EXCEPT question: correct answer must be false; incorrect choices could be true. Because the incorrect choices all represent acceptable arrangements of the entities, go through the rules as in an ordinary Acceptability question—but the moment you find a choice that breaks a rule, stop. That's the correct answer.
Which of the following could be a complete and accurate list of the types of grass seeds selected?	→	Acceptability question. Correct answer could be true; incorrect choices must be false.
Which of the following CANNOT be a complete and accurate list of the types of grass seed selected?	→	Acceptability EXCEPT question. Correct answer must be false; incorrect choices could be true.

Question Stem	Analysis
Which of the following could be a complete and accurate list of the types of grass seed NOT selected?	Note the difference between this question and the last one. The preceding question asks for an *unacceptable* list of *selected* entities. This question, in contrast, asks for an *acceptable* list of entities that are *left out*. This is also an Acceptability question, but the line of attack will be different. For each answer choice, first deduce which entities *are* included. Then apply the rules as you would in an ordinary Acceptability question.
Which of the following is a complete and accurate list of all possible flowerbeds to which M could be assigned?	Note the word "is," as opposed to the "could be" phrasing common in Acceptability questions. This is a Complete and Accurate List question, asking for all the possible places M could go. The correct answer will list *all* the slots M could ever occupy; the incorrect choices will either give only partial lists of slots that M can occupy or will list slots M cannot occupy (or both).
Which of the following is a complete and accurate list of the flowers any one of which could be assigned to bed 3?	A Complete and Accurate List question, this time asking for all entities allowed in flowerbed 3. The correct answer will list *all* entities that could be placed into bed 3; the incorrect choices will give only partial lists of entities that could go in bed 3 or will list entities that cannot be placed into bed 3 (or both).
Which of the following is a complete and accurate list of those flowers that CANNOT be assigned to bed 2?	Complete and Accurate List question. Correct answer will list *all* entities that cannot be assigned to bed 2. Incorrect choices will give only partial lists of entities that cannot be assigned to bed 2 or will list entities that can be assigned to bed 2 (or both).
The roster for the spelling bee is completely determined if which of the following is true?	Completely Determine question. Correct answer provides a condition that pins down the position of every entity. Incorrect choices will each provide a condition that allows for more than one possible arrangement of entities.
There is only one acceptable group of five amphibians that can be selected for the school terrarium if which of the following pairs of amphibians is selected?	Completely Determine question. Correct answer provides a pair of entities that forces the selection of three additional entities so that there is only one way to select the group of five. Incorrect choices will each allow for more than one possible group of five entities.

Now, try it out on your own. The question stems on the following pages are similar, though certainly not identical, to those in the list above and the questions you've seen so far in this chapter.

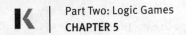
Practice

For each of the following question stems, identify the question type and characterize the one correct and four incorrect answer choices. When you're done, check your work against the LSAT expert's analysis on the following pages.

Question Stem	My Analysis
3. Which of the following could be a complete and accurate ordering of the books on shelf 2, from left to right?	
4. Which of the following is a complete and accurate list of those books that CANNOT be placed on shelf 1?	
5. Which of the following is an acceptable selection of pies and punch recipes for the office meeting?	
6. The selection of pies and punch recipes for the office meeting is completely determined if which of the following is true?	
7. Each of the following could be an accurate assignment of streets to trees planted on them EXCEPT:	
8. Which of the following is a complete and accurate list of the streets on which tree R could be planted?	

Question Stem	**My Analysis**
9. Which of the following is a complete and accurate list of trees that CANNOT be planted on Street B?	
10. All students' grades are known if which of the following is FALSE?	
11. Which of the following CANNOT be a complete and accurate ranking of brownie mixes, from most popular to least popular?	
12. Which of the following, if true, would cause the ranking of brownie mixes from most popular to least popular to be completely determined?	
13. Which of the following could be a complete and accurate matching of horses to rider W?	
14. Which of the following is NOT an acceptable matching of glasses to tableware?	

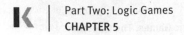
Expert Analysis

Here's how the LSAT expert analyzed each of the question stems you just practiced. Compare your work with that of the expert. You'll see more questions of these types as you practice the games in Chapter 6.

Question Stem	Analysis
3. Which of the following could be a complete and accurate ordering of the books on shelf 2, from left to right?	Partial Acceptability question because it only asks about shelf 2, not all shelves. Correct answer could be true, and the incorrect choices must be false. Attack the same way as you would a standard Acceptability question: go through the rules and knock out choices that break one or more rules. The one choice that does not break any rules will be the correct answer.
4. Which of the following is a complete and accurate list of those books that CANNOT be placed on shelf 1?	Complete and Accurate List question. Correct answer will provide a complete list of those books that cannot be on shelf 1, while the incorrect choices will each either leave out at least one book that cannot be on shelf 1 or will list at least one book that can be on shelf 1 (or both).
5. Which of the following is an acceptable selection of pies and punch recipes for the office meeting?	Acceptability question. Correct answer could be true (because it does not break any rules). Incorrect choices must be false (because they each break at least one rule).
6. The selection of pies and punch recipes for the office meeting is completely determined if which of the following is true?	Completely Determine question. Correct answer will provide a condition that allows for only one possible selection of pies and only one possible selection of punch recipes. Incorrect choices will each provide a condition that allows for multiple selections of pies, or multiple selections of punch recipes, or both.
7. Each of the following could be an accurate assignment of streets to trees planted on them EXCEPT:	Acceptability EXCEPT question. Incorrect choices each represent an acceptable arrangement and therefore could be true. Correct answer breaks at least one rule and therefore must be false.
8. Which of the following is a complete and accurate list of the streets on which tree R could be planted?	Complete and Accurate List question. Correct answer will provide *all* the streets where R can go. Incorrect choices will leave out at least one street where R can go, will list streets where R cannot go, or both.
9. Which of the following is a complete and accurate list of trees that CANNOT be planted on Street B?	Complete and Accurate List question. Correct answer will provide *all* trees that cannot go on Street B. Incorrect choices will leave out at least one tree that cannot go on Street B, will list at least one tree that can go on Street B, or both.

Question Stem		Analysis
10.	All students' grades are known if which of the following is FALSE?	Completely Determine question. Correct answer will provide a condition that, if false, forces one possible matching of students to grades. Incorrect choices will each provide a condition that, if false, allows more than one possible matching of students to grades, or that results in a conflict between rules.
11.	Which of the following CANNOT be a complete and accurate ranking of brownie mixes, from most popular to least popular?	Acceptability EXCEPT question. Incorrect choices could be true (because they do not break any rules); correct answer must be false (because it breaks at least one rule).
12.	Which of the following, if true, would cause the ranking of brownie mixes from most popular to least popular to be completely determined?	Completely Determine question. Correct answer will provide a condition that pins down the rank of every single entity. Incorrect choices will each provide a condition that allows for more than one possible ordering.
13.	Which of the following could be a complete and accurate matching of horses to rider W?	Partial Acceptability question. Correct answer could be true; incorrect choices must be false.
14.	Which of the following is NOT an acceptable matching of glasses to tableware?	Acceptability EXCEPT question. Correct answer must be false; incorrect choices could be true.

Even though those question stems weren't associated with any game setup in that exercise, were you able to imagine the entities and actions those games would include? If so, you're really getting familiar with the Logic Games section and the kinds of the games the testmaker uses over and over.

You'll see two more drills like that one later in the chapter. It's very important that you're able to understand exactly what the questions are calling for and to recognize right and wrong answers as you evaluate them. Keep that in mind as you move on in the chapter. The next two question types we'll discuss are, by far, the most important because they account for a large majority of points available in the Logic Games section.

MUST BE/COULD BE QUESTIONS

Combined, this section of the chapter and the next section (on New-"If" questions) account for the large majority of Logic Games questions you'll see on Test Day. Together, these two categories account for roughly 70 percent of all questions in the Logic Games section. Moreover, the two question types are related. Must Be/Could Be questions (about 24 percent of the section) ask you for an answer that states something that must be true, could be true, could be false, or must be false in the game. New-"If" questions ask largely the same things but add a new condition, unique to that question alone, and make you account for its implications before they pose the Must Be/Could Be question.

Because characterizing the correct and incorrect answer choices is so important to both of these question types, we'll start with the Must Be/Could Be questions without "If" conditions. Before you're done, though, you'll see and practice with plenty of examples of both question types, as there are numerous examples from all the games you've been working with up to this point.

Here's a Must Be True question from the Racehorses game. The question stem is straightforward in defining the criteria of the correct answer. Still, the LSAT expert knows that it's important to characterize the wrong answers before evaluating the choices. It may be much more efficient to eliminate choices that could be false than to spot the one that must be true.

Which one of the following must be true?

(A) Either K or else L is assigned to position 2.
(B) Either K or else L is assigned to position 4.
(C) Either M or else N is assigned to position 2.
(D) Either M or else N is assigned to position 5.
(E) Either M or else O is assigned to position 6.

PrepTest28 Sec2 Q4

You'll see the LSAT expert's analysis of that question and several others shortly. Because there are no New-"If" conditions in the stems of these questions, you can answer them by consulting your Master Sketch. Indeed, you should anticipate that one or more of these questions will reward you directly for making the game's central deduction(s).

LEARNING OBJECTIVES

In this section, you'll learn to:

- Identify and answer Must Be/Could Be Questions.
- Characterize accurately the correct and incorrect answer choices in Must Be/Could Be questions.

Even with a perfect Master Sketch, many test takers will miss points from Must Be/Could Be Questions because they don't take the time to characterize the correct answer. They'll consult their well-made Master Sketch but forget whether they're checking for what must be true or what could be false. Levels of certainty (must/could) and truth value (true/false) were discussed and drilled in Chapter 1. If you're hesitant about applying these concepts, revisit that chapter for a refresher.

Now, take a look at the LSAT expert's analysis of the question from the previous page.

LSAT Question	Analysis

Six racehorses—K, L, M, N, O, and P—will be assigned to six positions arranged in a straight line and numbered consecutively 1 through 6. The horses are assigned to the positions, one horse per position, according to the following conditions:

    K and L must be assigned to positions that are separated from each other by exactly one position.

    K and N cannot be assigned to positions that are next to each other.

    N must be assigned to a higher-numbered position than M.

    P must be assigned to position 3.

Steps 1–4:

K L M N O P

(I) $\underset{1}{\_}$ $\underset{2}{K/L}$ $\underset{3}{P}$ $\underset{4}{L/K}$ $\underset{5}{\_}$ $\underset{6}{\_}$ ~K N / ~N K

M . . . N

(II) $\underset{1}{M}$ $\underset{2}{N}$ $\underset{3}{P}$ $\underset{4}{K/L}$ $\underset{5}{O}$ $\underset{6}{L/K}$

Which one of the following must be true?

Step 5: The correct answer must be true under this game's rules and restrictions. Each of the four wrong answers could be false.

(A) Either K or else L is assigned to position 2.

→ Could be false; see Option II. Eliminate.

(B) Either K or else L is assigned to position 4.

→ Correct. In either option, one of K or L must take position 4.

(C) Either M or else N is assigned to position 2.

→ Could be false; see Option I. Eliminate.

(D) Either M or else N is assigned to position 5.

→ Could be false; see Option II. Eliminate.

(E) Either M or else O is assigned to position 6.

→ Could be false; see Option II. Eliminate.

PrepTest28 Sec2 Q4

On Test Day, the LSAT expert would have been absolutely certain of the answer as soon as she evaluated choice (B). In fact, the LSAT expert would stop right there, circle choice (B), and move on to the next question. That's a wonderful time-saver, but taking advantage of it requires confidence. Looking at the expert's analysis on choices (A), (C), (D), and (E) reveals where that confidence comes from. The expert's analysis is so certain—she knows exactly what constitutes a correct and incorrect answer—that she would fly through this question regardless of the order in which the answer choices were presented.

The Racehorses game presents a Strict Sequencing action, but open-ended Must Be/Could Be questions can be (and will be) associated with any game type. Take a look at a handful of other examples from the games you've been working with. In each case, pay attention to how the expert characterizes the one right and four wrong answers.

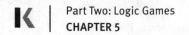

The first example is from the Movie Releases game, which is a Loose Sequencing game, but the LSAT expert doesn't approach it any differently. He establishes the criteria for the correct answer before assessing the choices, and he will not be satisfied until he finds the answer that must be true. As you review the expert's analysis, note that the question stem is identical to the question above from the Racehorses game.

LSAT Question	Analysis
A movie studio is scheduling the release of six films—*Fiesta, Glaciers, Hurricanes, Jets, Kangaroos,* and *Lovebird*. No two of these films can be released on the same date. The release schedule is governed by the following conditions: *Fiesta* must be released earlier than both *Jets* and *Lovebird*. *Kangaroos* must be released earlier than *Jets*, and *Jets* must be released earlier than *Hurricanes*. *Lovebird* must be released earlier than *Glaciers*.	**Steps 1–4:** .L...G F .. .J...H K ..
Which one of the following must be true?	**Step 5:** The correct answer must be true according to the deductions reflected in the Master Sketch above.
(A) *Fiesta* is released earlier than *Hurricanes*.	Correct. F must be released before J (Rule 1), and J must be released before H (Rule 2).
(B) *Jets* is released earlier than *Glaciers*.	The relationship between these entities is undefined. Eliminate.
(C) *Kangaroos* is released earlier than *Glaciers*.	The relationship between these entities is undefined. Eliminate.
(D) *Lovebird* is released earlier than *Hurricanes*.	The relationship between these entities is undefined. Eliminate.
(E) *Lovebird* is released earlier than *Jets*. *PrepTest71 Sec2 Q2*	The relationship between these entities is undefined. Eliminate.

So far, the questions you've seen have had simple question stems, such as, "Which one of the following must be true?" Of course, the testmaker will also ask, "Which one of the following could be true?" or "Which one of the following must be false?" In fact, the must-be-false variety is the test's favorite, constituting just over half of the Must Be/Could Be questions on recent exams. With practice, however, you won't let these changes in wording throw you. An LSAT expert always takes a couple of seconds to characterize both the right and wrong answer choices and states to himself why each choice is right or wrong as he evaluates them.

Here's an example of a Must Be False question with which you are already familiar. It is from the Racehorses game. You'll notice that the question stem asks for the answer choice that "CANNOT be true," but you know, from your work in Chapter 1, that this simply means "must be false." Thus, any answer that could be true within the strictures of this game is incorrect.

LSAT Question	Analysis
Six racehorses—K, L, M, N, O, and P—will be assigned to six positions arranged in a straight line and numbered consecutively 1 through 6. The horses are assigned to the positions, one horse per position, according to the following conditions: 　K and L must be assigned to positions that are separated from each other by exactly one position. 　K and N cannot be assigned to positions that are next to each other. 　N must be assigned to a higher-numbered position than M. 　P must be assigned to position 3.	**Steps 1–4:** K L M N O P (I) $\underset{1}{\_\_}$ $\underset{2}{K/L}$ $\underset{3}{P}$ $\underset{4}{L/K}$ $\underset{5}{\_\_}$ $\underset{6}{\_\_}$ $\quad \sim\!K\;N$ $\sim\!N\;K$ M . . . N (II) $\underset{1}{M}$ $\underset{2}{N}$ $\underset{3}{P}$ $\underset{4}{K/L}$ $\underset{5}{O}$ $\underset{6}{L/K}$
Which one of the following CANNOT be true?	**Step 5:** The correct answer must be false given the game's rules and restrictions. Each of the four wrong answers could be true.
(A)　K is assigned to position 2.	Could be true; see Option I. Eliminate.
(B)　L is assigned to position 2.	Could be true; see Option I. Eliminate.
(C)　M is assigned to position 1.	This could be true in either option. Eliminate.
(D)　M is assigned to position 5.	Could be true; see Option I. Eliminate.
(E)　O is assigned to position 2. *PrepTest28 Sec2 Q3*	Correct. In Option I, either K or L takes position 2. In Option II, N takes position 2. O can never be assigned to position 2.

Game-Specific Must Be/Could Be Questions

Many Must Be/Could Be question stems are as straightforward as those you've just reviewed. Others, however, ask questions more tailored to the specific task or arrangement of the game. They might ask what could be true of a given entity or what must be false about a certain slot in the sequence, for example. When you encounter questions such as these, use the question stem to characterize the one correct and four incorrect choices just as you would with more garden-variety Must Be/Could Be stems.

Here is an LSAT expert's analysis of one such question from the Zeno's Furniture game:

LSAT Question	Analysis
Zeno's Unfinished Furniture sells exactly five types of furniture—footstools, hutches, sideboards, tables, and vanities. Irene buys just four items, each of a different type, and each made entirely of one kind of wood—maple, oak, pine, or rosewood. The following conditions govern Irene's purchases: Any vanity she buys is maple. Any rosewood item she buys is a sideboard. If she buys a vanity, she does not buy a footstool. If Irene buys a footstool, she also buys a table made of the same wood. Irene does not buy an oak table. Exactly two of the items she buys are made of the same kind of wood as each other.	**Steps 1–4:** (Select 4) |	F	(H)	(S)	(T)	V
-----	---	---	---	---	---
m					m
o	—				—
p					—
r	—	—		—		 If F ⟶ T same wood If T diff't wood than F ⟶ ~F Exactly 2 items = same wood
Which one of the following CANNOT be the two items Irene buys that are made of the same wood as each other?	**Step 5:** The four wrong answers will present pairs of furniture types that CAN be made of the same type of wood. The correct answer will present a pair that CANNOT be made of the same wood.
(A) footstool, hutch	Correct. F and H can never share the same type of wood. If F is selected, then T must be selected, and be made of the same kind of wood as F. Were H to then also share the same wood variety, there would be three items made from the same kind of wood, breaking Rule 6 ("[e]xactly two of the items . . . are made of the same kind of wood as each other").
(B) hutch, sideboard	This is possible. H and S could share maple, oak, or pine. Eliminate.
(C) hutch, table	This is possible. H and T could share maple or pine. Eliminate.
(D) sideboard, vanity	This is possible. V and S could share maple. Eliminate.
(E) table, vanity	This is possible. T and V could share maple. Eliminate.

PrepTestB Sec2 Q23

While that question is worded in a way quite specific to this game (mentioning items of furniture and kinds of wood), the LSAT expert recognized that it was really just a Must Be False question, and handled it without hesitation.

Practice

Now, work with a handful of Must Be/Could Be questions from the games you've been analyzing. In each case, we'll supply the game's setup and Master Sketch. As always, if you want to review how we arrived at the Master Sketch, refer to the preceding chapters.

For each of the following questions, analyze the question stem and characterize the one correct and four incorrect answer choices. Then, use the Master Sketch and the deductions it contains to select the correct answer. You can compare your work to an LSAT expert's analysis on the following pages.

LSAT Question	My Analysis

A movie studio is scheduling the release of six films—*Fiesta, Glaciers, Hurricanes, Jets, Kangaroos*, and *Lovebird*. No two of these films can be released on the same date. The release schedule is governed by the following conditions:
 	
 Fiesta must be released earlier than both Jets and Lovebird.
 	
 Kangaroos must be released earlier than *Jets*, and *Jets* must be released earlier than *Hurricanes*.
 	
 Lovebird must be released earlier than *Glaciers*.
	Steps 1–4:
	
	 $\longrightarrow$ F $\cdots$ L $\cdots$ G
	          J $\cdots$ H
	    K $\cdots$

15. Which one of the following CANNOT be true?	**Step 5:** $\longrightarrow$

    (A) *Fiesta* is released second.

    (B) *Glaciers* is released third.

    (C) *Hurricanes* is released fourth.

    (D) *Kangaroos* is released fourth.

    (E) *Kangaroos* is released fifth.

PrepTest71 Sec2 Q1

LSAT Question	**My Analysis**

On a Tuesday, an accountant has exactly seven bills—numbered 1 through 7—to pay by Thursday of the same week. The accountant will pay each bill only once according to the following rules:

> Either three or four of the seven bills must be paid on Wednesday, the rest on Thursday.
> Bill 1 cannot be paid on the same day as bill 5.
> Bill 2 must be paid on Thursday.
> Bill 4 must be paid on the same day as 7.
> If bill 6 is paid on Wednesday, bill 7 must be paid on Thursday.

Steps 1–4:

1 2 3 4 5 6 7

Opt. I   Opt. II

W	T		W	T
1/5	5/1		1/5	5/1
4	2		3	2
7	6		6	4
...	...			7

16. Which one of the following statements must be true?

Step 5:

$\longrightarrow$

(A) If bill 2 is paid on Thursday, bill 3 is paid on Wednesday.

(B) If bill 4 is paid on Thursday, bill 1 is paid on Wednesday.

(C) If bill 4 is paid on Thursday, bill 3 is paid on Wednesday.

(D) If bill 6 is paid on Thursday, bill 3 is also paid on Thursday.

(E) If bill 6 is paid on Thursday, bill 4 is also paid on Thursday.

PrepTest29 Sec3 Q6

LSAT Question	My Analysis

A college dean will present seven awards for outstanding language research. The awards—one for French, one for German, one for Hebrew, one for Japanese, one for Korean, one for Latin, and one for Swahili—must be presented consecutively, one at a time, in conformity with the following constraints:

  The German award is not presented first.
  The Hebrew award is presented at some time before the Korean award is presented.
  The Latin award is presented at some time before the Japanese award is presented.
  The French award is presented either immediately before or immediately after the Hebrew award is presented.
  The Korean award is presented either immediately before or immediately after the Latin award is presented.

Steps 1–4:

Opt. I   [F/H] __ __ __ __ __ __

Opt. II   S   [F/H] __ __ __ __ __

Opt. III S   G   [F/H]   [K/L]   J
          1   2   3   4   5   6   7

~G

[F/H] . . . [K/L] . . . J

---

17. Which one of the following must be true?

Step 5:

$\longrightarrow$

(A) The French award is presented at some time before the Japanese award is presented.

(B) The French award is presented at some time before the Swahili award is presented.

(C) The German award is presented at some time before the Korean award is presented.

(D) The German award is presented at some time before the Swahili award is presented.

(E) The Swahili award is presented at some time before the Hebrew award is presented.

PrepTest29 Sec3 Q14

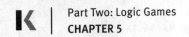

The next two questions both come from the Trees in the Park game.

LSAT Question	My Analysis
A park contains at most five of seven kinds of trees—firs, laurels, maples, oaks, pines, spruces, and yews—consistent with the following conditions:	**Steps 1–4:**

A park contains at most five of seven kinds of trees—firs, laurels, maples, oaks, pines, spruces, and yews—consistent with the following conditions:

    If maples are in the park, yews are not.

    If firs are in the park, pines are not.

    If yews are not in the park, then either laurels or oaks, but not both, are in the park.

    If it is not the case that the park contains both laurels and oaks, then it contains firs and spruces.

Steps 1–4:

F L M O P S Y   (max 5)

If Ⓜ ⟶ ~Y

If Ⓨ ⟶ ~M

If Ⓕ ⟶ ~P

⟶ If Ⓟ ⟶ ~F

If ~Y ⟶ [Exactly one of Ⓛ / Ⓞ]

If Ⓛ and Ⓞ ⟶ Ⓨ

If ~L and ~O ⟶ Ⓨ

If ~L or ~O ⟶ Ⓕ and Ⓢ

If ~F or ~S ⟶ Ⓛ and Ⓞ

---

18. Which one of the following could be true?

    Step 5:

⟶

    (A) Neither firs nor laurels are in the park.

    (B) Neither laurels, oaks, nor yews are in the park.

    (C) Neither laurels nor spruces are in the park.

    (D) Neither maples nor yews are in the park.

    (E) Neither oaks nor spruces are in the park.

PrepTestB Sec2 Q9

LSAT Question	My Analysis
19. Each of the following could be an accurate, partial list of the kinds of trees in the park EXCEPT:	**Step 5:** $\longrightarrow$
(A) oaks, spruces	
(B) oaks, yews	
(C) firs, laurels, oaks	
(D) firs, maples, oaks	
(E) laurels, maples, oaks	

PrepTestB Sec2 Q12

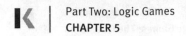
Expert Analysis

Here's how an LSAT expert analyzed and answered the questions you just saw. With practice, analyzing these question stems will become second nature, and you'll feel faster and more confident answering Must Be/Could Be questions. As you turn to the games in Chapter 6, remain diligent about characterizing the right and wrong answers before evaluating the choices. Simply by avoiding the mistake of answering the wrong question, you can improve your score and outperform other test takers.

LSAT Question	Analysis

A movie studio is scheduling the release of six films—*Fiesta, Glaciers, Hurricanes, Jets, Kangaroos,* and *Lovebird.* No two of these films can be released on the same date. The release schedule is governed by the following conditions:
    Fiesta must be released earlier than both *Jets* and *Lovebird.*
    Kangaroos must be released earlier than *Jets,* and *Jets* must be released earlier than *Hurricanes.*
    Lovebird must be released earlier than *Glaciers.*
	Steps 1–4:
	
	  ..L...G
	F..
	  .J...H
	K..

15. Which one of the following CANNOT be true?	**Step 5:** To determine if a movie can be released in a certain position, count the number of movies that must be released before and after that movie. Eliminate choices that are possible. Select the answer that must be false according to the Master Sketch.
(A) *Fiesta* is released second.	No movies need be earlier than F and four movies must be later, so it can be released first or second. Eliminate.
(B) *Glaciers* is released third.	Two movies must be earlier than G and none must be later, so it can be released anywhere from third to sixth. Eliminate.
(C) *Hurricanes* is released fourth.	Three movies must be earlier than H and none need be later, so it can be released anywhere from fourth to sixth. Eliminate.
(D) *Kangaroos* is released fourth.	No movies need be earlier than K and two must be later, so it can be released anywhere from first to fourth. Eliminate.
(E) *Kangaroos* is released fifth. *PrepTest71 Sec2 Q1*	Correct. Because two movies must always be released later than K, it cannot be scheduled fifth.

LSAT Question	**Analysis**

On a Tuesday, an accountant has exactly seven bills—numbered 1 through 7—to pay by Thursday of the same week. The accountant will pay each bill only once according to the following rules:

> Either three or four of the seven bills must be paid on Wednesday, the rest on Thursday.
> Bill 1 cannot be paid on the same day as bill 5.
> Bill 2 must be paid on Thursday.
> Bill 4 must be paid on the same day as 7.
> If bill 6 is paid on Wednesday, bill 7 must be paid on Thursday.

→

Steps 1–4:

1 2 3 4 5 6 7

Opt. I   Opt. II

W	T		W	T
1/5	5/1		1/5	5/1
4	2		3	2
7	6		6	4
...	...			7

16. Which one of the following statements must be true?

→ **Step 5:** The correct answer choice must be true in either option. Wrong answer choices do not always have to be true.

(A) If bill 2 is paid on Thursday, bill 3 is paid on Wednesday.

→ In Option 1, bill 2 is paid on Thursday but bill 3 does not have to be paid on Wednesday. Eliminate.

(B) If bill 4 is paid on Thursday, bill 1 is paid on Wednesday.

→ Bills 1 and 5 can always flip-flop days. Eliminate.

(C) If bill 4 is paid on Thursday, bill 3 is paid on Wednesday.

→ Correct. This must be true according to the Limited Option sketches.

(D) If bill 6 is paid on Thursday, bill 3 is also paid on Thursday.

→ In Option 1, bill 6 is paid on Thursday but bill 3 does not have to be paid on Thursday. Eliminate.

(E) If bill 6 is paid on Thursday, bill 4 is also paid on Thursday.

→ This is false. When bill 6 is paid on Thursday, bill 4 is paid on Wednesday. Eliminate.

PrepTest29 Sec3 Q6

LSAT Question	**Analysis**
A college dean will present seven awards for outstanding language research. The awards—one for French, one for German, one for Hebrew, one for Japanese, one for Korean, one for Latin, and one for Swahili—must be presented consecutively, one at a time, in conformity with the following constraints:	**Steps 1–4:**

Opt. I ⎡F/H⎤ ___ ___ ___ ___ ___ ___

Opt. II S ⎡F/H⎤ ___ ___ ___ ___ ___

The German award is not presented first.
The Hebrew award is presented at some time before the Korean award is presented.
The Latin award is presented at some time before the Japanese award is presented.
The French award is presented either immediately before or immediately after the Hebrew award is presented.
The Korean award is presented either immediately before or immediately after the Latin award is presented.

→ Opt. III S   G   ⎡F/H⎤   ⎡K/L⎤   J
          1   2   3   5   6   7
       ~G

⎡F/H⎤ . . . ⎡K/L⎤ . . . J

17. Which one of the following must be true?	**Step 5:** The correct answer choice must true in every situation. Any answer choice that presents something that does not have to be true is incorrect.
(A) The French award is presented at some time before the Japanese award is presented.	→ Correct. By connecting the blocks of entities, this is definitively true.
(B) The French award is presented at some time before the Swahili award is presented.	→ In Options 2 and 3, S is actually presented before F. Eliminate.
(C) The German award is presented at some time before the Korean award is presented.	→ This could be false in Options 1 and 2. Eliminate.
(D) The German award is presented at some time before the Swahili award is presented.	→ This is not true in Options 2 and 3. Eliminate.
(E) The Swahili award is presented at some time before the Hebrew award is presented.	This is not true in Option 1. Eliminate.

PrepTest29 Sec3 Q14

LSAT Question	Analysis

A park contains at most five of seven kinds of trees—firs, laurels, maples, oaks, pines, spruces, and yews—consistent with the following conditions:
    If maples are in the park, yews are not.
    If firs are in the park, pines are not.
    If yews are not in the park, then either laurels or oaks, but not both, are in the park.
    If it is not the case that the park contains both laurels and oaks, then it contains firs and spruces.
	Steps 1–4:
	
	F L M O P S Y (max 5)
	
	If Ⓜ ⟶ ~Y
	If Ⓨ ⟶ ~M
	
	If Ⓕ ⟶ ~P
	If Ⓟ ⟶ ~F
	
	If ~Y ⟶ [Exactly one of Ⓛ / Ⓞ]
	If Ⓛ and Ⓞ ⟶ Ⓨ
	If ~L and ~O ⟶ Ⓨ
	
	If ~L or ~O ⟶ Ⓕ and Ⓢ
	If ~F or ~S ⟶ Ⓛ and Ⓞ

18. Which one of the following could be true?	**Step 5:** The correct answer is something that is possible. The four wrong answers are simply not possible according to the rules.
(A) Neither firs nor laurels are in the park.	This can't be true. If laurels are out, then both firs and spruces must be in (Rule 4). Eliminate.
(B) Neither laurels, oaks, nor yews are in the park.	This can't be true. If laurels and oaks are both out, then yews must be in (Rule 3). Eliminate.
(C) Neither laurels nor spruces are in the park.	This can't be true. If laurels are out, then both firs and spruces must be in (Rule 4). Eliminate.
(D) Neither maples nor yews are in the park.	Correct. It's possible that neither variety is selected.
(E) Neither oaks nor spruces are in the park. *PrepTestB Sec2 Q9*	This can't be true. If oaks are out, then both firs and spruces must be in (Rule 4). Eliminate.

LSAT Question	Analysis
19. Each of the following could be an accurate, partial list of the kinds of trees in the park EXCEPT:	**Step 5:** The four wrong answers to this question will all include a pair or group of trees that can be together. The answer choice that presents a pair or group of trees that CANNOT be selected together will be correct.
(A) oaks, spruces	This is an acceptable pair. No rule prevents O and S from being selected together. Eliminate.
(B) oaks, yews	This is an acceptable pair. When Y is selected, exactly one of L or O must also be selected (Rule 3). Eliminate.
(C) firs, laurels, oaks	This is an acceptable group. Selecting F means rejecting P (Rule 2). Selecting L and O means rejecting Y (Rule 3). Neither of those rules prevents selecting F, L, and O. Eliminate.
(D) firs, maples, oaks	This is an acceptable group. Test it as follows.
	Select F, M, and O. Now, selecting M means rejecting Y (Rule 1), and selecting F means rejecting P (Rule 2).
	Ⓕ L Ⓜ Ⓞ P̸ S Y̸
	When Y is not selected, exactly one of L or O will be selected (Rule 3). That means L must be out.
	Ⓕ L̸ Ⓜ Ⓞ P̸ S Y̸
	Because L is out, S must be in (Rule 4).
	Ⓕ L̸ Ⓜ Ⓞ P̸ Ⓢ Y̸
	This collection of trees is possible and doesn't violate any of the rules. Eliminate.
(E) laurels, maples, oaks *PrepTestB Sec2 Q12*	Correct. When M is selected, then Y is out (Rule 1). When Y is out, then one of L or O—*but not both*—is selected (Rule 3). This choice must be false.

NEW-"IF" QUESTIONS

The next question type—the New-"If" question—is by far the most important in the Logic Games section. Nearly half of all Logic Games points come from this question type. Fortunately, once you learn to handle it strategically, the additional condition or restriction in the question stem—the distinguishing characteristic of this question type—actually makes the question easier to answer.

LEARNING OBJECTIVES

In this section, you'll learn to:

- Identify and answer New-"If" questions.
- Create new sketches to account for the "If" condition in New-"If" questions and make additional deductions applicable to the question.

Take a look at one of these questions associated with the Language Awards game, and we'll break down how these questions work.

If the Japanese award is presented at some time before the Swahili award is presented, any of the following could be true EXCEPT:

(A)   The German award is presented immediately before the French award is presented.

(B)   The German award is presented immediately before the Japanese award is presented.

(C)   The Hebrew award is presented immediately before the Latin award is presented.

(D)   The Korean award is presented immediately before the Japanese award is presented.

(E)   The Swahili award is presented immediately before the German award is presented.

PrepTest29 Sec3 Q18

Notice that you can break a question of this type into two pieces before and after the comma in the middle of the question. The first part is a condition or, if you like, an additional rule just for this question. (Don't apply the new "If" condition to any of the questions that come later in the question set.) Because rules and restrictions add certainty to logic games, the condition in a New-"If" question reduces the number of arrangements available. Shortly, you'll see how the LSAT expert draws a quick sketch, copying the essential information from the Master Sketch and adding the new "If" condition. From this, she draws any additional deductions applicable to this question. The expert will then use the completed sketch to evaluate the answer choices.

The part of the question after the comma reads almost exactly like a Must Be/Could Be question. To know what you're looking for in the correct answer, characterize the one right and four wrong answers just as you would in Must Be/Could Be questions without a New-"If" clause.

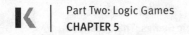
Now, take a look at how the LSAT expert handled the New-"If" question from the Language Awards game. Take note of her thinking about the question's condition and how she turns that into a quick sketch and how she uses that sketch to evaluate the answer choices.

LSAT Question	Analysis
A college dean will present seven awards for outstanding language research. The awards—one for French, one for German, one for Hebrew, one for Japanese, one for Korean, one for Latin, and one for Swahili—must be presented consecutively, one at a time, in conformity with the following constraints:	**Steps 1–4:** Opt. I __F/H__ __ __ __ __ __ Opt. II S __F/H__ __ __ __ __ Opt. III S G __F/H__ __K/L__ J
The German award is not presented first.	
The Hebrew award is presented at some time before the Korean award is presented.	~G
The Latin award is presented at some time before the Japanese award is presented.	F/H ... K/L ... J
The French award is presented either immediately before or immediately after the Hebrew award is presented.	
The Korean award is presented either immediately before or immediately after the Latin award is presented.	

If the Japanese award is presented at some time before the Swahili award is presented, any of the following could be true EXCEPT:	**Step 5:** A New-"If" Question: Add this rule to the block of rules already established: F/H ... K/L ... J ... S This can clearly only work in Option 1. So G must be presented sometime after the F/H block. Thus: F/H ... K/L ... J ... S ∴ G Now answer the question. Anything that is possible according to the sketch is incorrect; the correct answer will not be possible.

(A)	The German award is presented immediately before the French award is presented.	→	Correct. This is not possible. G must be presented after the F/H block.
(B)	The German award is presented immediately before the Japanese award is presented.	→	This is possible. The sketch for this question shows that G could be awarded right before J. Eliminate.
(C)	The Hebrew award is presented immediately before the Latin award is presented.	→	This is possible. The first four awards could be F-H-L-K here. Eliminate.
(D)	The Korean award is presented immediately before the Japanese award is presented.	→	This is possible. The sequence could begin with F/H-G-L-K-J, or with F/H-L-K-J. Eliminate.
(E)	The Swahili award is presented immediately before the German award is presented.	→	This is possible. Under the conditions of this question, nothing prevents G from being seventh. Eliminate.

PrepTest29 Sec3 Q18

In that question, the "If" condition required additional analysis. The fact that S was after J was not concrete enough to build directly into the sketch. Rather, that condition needed to be combined with information in the Master Sketch to definitively slot the newly restricted entities. Contrast that question stem with New-"If"s that unequivocally tell you what to draw into a new sketch. Questions that give more concrete conditions, such as "If J is in the 4th position" or "If A is on Team Green," tend to be easier than questions that give a vaguer New-"If," such as "If J is NOT fourth," "If J is earlier than H," or "If Team Green has more members than Team Blue." If you're struggling with a game, or just being mindful to approach easier questions before difficult questions, consider approaching questions with concrete "If" conditions before tackling those with vague "If"s. As for the Language Awards game question, once the expert combined the "If" with the information from the Master Sketch, the situation became quite restrictive, and the answer choice was apparent.

Other New-"If" questions, however, require further steps to derive all of the available deductions. On the next two pages, examine how the LSAT expert handled a New-"If" question from the Recycling Centers game. This time, the new condition is concrete and can be added immediately to a copy of the Master Sketch. Once in place, it triggers a number of the game's original rules. Follow the LSAT expert's reasoning as he applies the new "If" condition and then uses its implications to establish more certainty.

LSAT Question	**Analysis**

There are exactly three recycling centers in Rivertown: Center 1, Center 2, and Center 3. Exactly five kinds of material are recycled at these recycling centers: glass, newsprint, plastic, tin, and wood. Each recycling center recycles at least two but no more than three of these kinds of material. The following conditions must hold:

    Any recycling center that recycles wood also recycles newsprint.

    Every kind of material that Center 2 recycles is also recycled at Center 1.

    Only one of the recycling centers recycles plastic, and that recycling center does not recycle glass.

→

Steps 1–4:

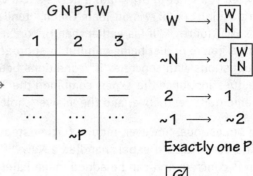

If Center 3 recycles glass, then which one of the following kinds of materials must Center 2 recycle?

Step 5: A New-"If" Question: Create a sketch for this question and add the new information:

1	2	3
—	—	G
—	—	—
...	...	...
	~P	

Look through the rules and make deductions. G and P cannot be recycled in the same center, so P cannot be recycled in Center 3. Because P cannot be recycled in Center 2 either, then P must be recycled in Center 1.

→

1	2	3
P	—	G
—	—	—
...	...	...
	~P	~P

Again, P and G cannot be recycled together. So G cannot be recycled in Center 1. And anything that is not recycled in Center 1 is not recycled in Center 2, so G is not recycled in Center 2.

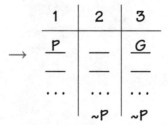

LSAT Question (cont.)	Analysis (cont.)

That leaves three possible materials to be recycled at Center 2: N, T, and W. If W is recycled there, then N must also be recycled there. If W is not recycled at Center 2, then the remaining two materials, N and T, would have to be recycled there. Therefore, no matter what happens, N will always be recycled at Center 2 in this situation.

1	2	3
P	N	G
—	—	—
...	...	...
~G	~P	~P
	~G	

Now answer the question. The material that must be recycled at Center 2 is N, newsprint.

(A)	glass	$\longrightarrow$	Eliminate.
(B)	newsprint	$\longrightarrow$	Correct.
(C)	plastic	$\longrightarrow$	Eliminate.
(D)	tin	$\longrightarrow$	Eliminate.
(E)	wood	$\longrightarrow$	Eliminate.

PrepTestJune2007 Sec1 Q22

The preceding examples give you a great baseline for thinking about New-"If" questions. On any given LSAT, a number of the Logic Games questions will work more or less as those did. Because you've been working with a variety of games, let's use them to see a few more examples of New-"If" questions and consider how they may vary slightly in different types of games.

Be patient when you work through the question stem in Loose Sequencing New-"If" questions. Remember that all of the original relationships and restrictions continue to apply. In the new, question-specific sketch, you're just adding more certainty. Don't rush so much that you inadvertently undo any of the deductions in the Master Sketch.

New-"If" Questions in Selection Games

Selection games often use New-"If" questions to test your facility with chains of Formal Logic. The "If" condition in the question stem acts as a trigger for one of the Formal Logic rules. That, in turn, may set off a long string of deductions as additional rules are triggered. Take a look at a New-"If" question from the Trees in the Park game to see this in action. As you review the expert's work, keep in mind that the sketches you see are really just steps in a single, quick new sketch the expert is creating step-by-step as she notes the question's additional deductions.

LSAT Question	Analysis

A park contains at most five of seven kinds of trees—firs, laurels, maples, oaks, pines, spruces, and yews—consistent with the following conditions:
    If maples are in the park, yews are not.
    If firs are in the park, pines are not.
    If yews are not in the park, then either laurels or oaks, but not both, are in the park.
    If it is not the case that the park contains both laurels and oaks, then it contains firs and spruces.
	Steps 1–4:
	
	F L M O P S Y (max 5)
	
	If (M) ⟶ ~Y
	If (Y) ⟶ ~M
	
	If (F) ⟶ ~P
	→ If (P) ⟶ ~F
	
	If ~Y ⟶ [Exactly one of (L)/(O)]
	If (L) and (O) ⟶ (Y)
	If ~L and ~O ⟶ (Y)
	
	If ~L or ~O ⟶ (F) and (S)
	If ~F or ~S ⟶ (L) and (O)

Question continues on the next page.

LSAT Question (cont.)	Analysis (cont.)
If pines are in the park, then which one of the following must be true?	**Step 5:** New-"If" Question: Create a new roster sketch just for this question and circle P.
	F L M O (P) S Y
	Look through the rules and make any possible deductions. When pines are selected, firs are not (Rule 2).
	F̸ L M O (P) S Y
	When firs are not selected, then both L and O must be selected (Rule 3).
	F̸ (L) M (O) (P) S Y
	When L and O are selected, Y must be selected (Rule 3).
	F̸ (L) M (O) (P) S (Y)
	When Y is selected, M cannot be selected (Rule 1).
	F̸ (L) M̸ (O) (P) S (Y)
	No more deductions can be made, so evaluate the answer choices. The correct answer is something that is definitely true. The four wrong answer choices do not have to be true.
(A) Exactly four kinds of trees are in the park.	It is possible to select S, which means it is possible to have five kinds of trees in the park. Eliminate.
(B) Exactly five finds of trees are in the park.	It is possible to not select S, which means it is possible to have four kinds of trees in the park. Eliminate.
(C) Neither firs nor maples are in the park.	Correct. This must be true.
(D) Neither firs nor oaks are in the park.	Firs are not in the park in this situation, but oaks definitely are. Eliminate.
(E) Neither laurels nor maples are in the park.	Maples are not in the park in this situation, but laurels definitely are. Eliminate.

PrepTestB Sec2 Q11

In that New-"If" question, the expert was able to make a number of additional deductions that followed from the New-"If" condition. You can expect that kind of reasoning to be tested often in Selection games. Fortunately, the sketches—mere rosters of the entities—are so quick and easy to draw that you can work out the chains of Formal Logic efficiently on the page of the test booklet.

New-"If" Questions in Games with Limited Options Sketches

Games in which you can work out a Limited Options sketch sometimes allow for shortcuts in dealing with New-"If" questions. Indeed, on some games with Limited Options, the "If" condition in the question stem amounts to no more than telling you which of the options to consider as you evaluate the answer choices for that question. Take a look at the LSAT expert's work with two questions from the Bill Paying game to see what we mean.

LSAT Question	Analysis

On a Tuesday, an accountant has exactly seven bills—numbered 1 through 7—to pay by Thursday of the same week. The accountant will pay each bill only once according to the following rules:

    Either three or four of the seven bills must be paid on Wednesday, the rest on Thursday.
    Bill 1 cannot be paid on the same day as bill 5.
    Bill 2 must be paid on Thursday.
    Bill 4 must be paid on the same day as 7.
    If bill 6 is paid on Wednesday, bill 7 must be paid on Thursday.

→

Steps 1–4:

1 2 3 4 5 6 7

Opt. I		Opt. II	
W	T	W	T
1/5	5/1	1/5	5/1
4	2	3	2
7	6	6	4
...	...		7

If exactly four bills are paid on Wednesday, then those four bills could be

→

Step 5: "If" Question: consult the Limited Options to determine which scenario will work here. Four bills on Wednesday means it's definitely Option I, and that bill 3 is paid on Wednesday:

W	T
1/5	5/1
4	2
7	6
3	

The correct answer choice will contain 3, 4, 7, and one of either 1 or 5.

(A)	1, 3, 4, and 6	→	Bill 6 is on Thursday. Eliminate.
(B)	1, 3, 5, and 6	→	Bill 6 is on Thursday. Eliminate.
(C)	2, 4, 5, and 7	→	Bill 2 is on Thursday. Eliminate.
(D)	3, 4, 5, and 7	→	Correct.
(E)	3, 4, 6, and 7	→	Bill 6 is on Thursday. Eliminate.

PrepTest29 Sec3 Q1

LSAT Question	**Analysis**

LSAT Question

On a Tuesday, an accountant has exactly seven bills—numbered 1 through 7—to pay by Thursday of the same week. The accountant will pay each bill only once according to the following rules:

> Either three or four of the seven bills must be paid on Wednesday, the rest on Thursday.
> Bill 1 cannot be paid on the same day as bill 5.
> Bill 2 must be paid on Thursday.
> Bill 4 must be paid on the same day as 7.
> If bill 6 is paid on Wednesday, bill 7 must be paid on Thursday.

Analysis

Steps 1–4:

1 2 3 4 5 6 7

Opt. I   Opt. II

W	T		W	T
1/5	5/1		1/5	5/1
4	2		3	2
7	6		6	4
. . .	. . .			7

If bill 4 is paid on Thursday, which one of the following is a pair of bills that could also be paid on Thursday?

Step 5: New-"If" Question: consider to which Limited Option sketch this condition applies. Only in Option II is bill 4 paid on Thursday.

W	T
1/5	5/1
3	2
6	4
	7

Now answer the question. The correct answer will be two other bills that can also be paid on Thursday.

(A)	1 and 5	→	1 and 5 can never be paid on the same day. Eliminate.
(B)	1 and 7	→	Correct. This is possible.
(C)	3 and 5	→	3 is paid on Wednesday in Option II. Eliminate.
(D)	3 and 6	→	3 and 6 are paid on Wednesday in Option II. Eliminate.
(E)	6 and 7	→	6 is paid on Wednesday in Option II. Eliminate.

PrepTest29 Sec3 Q5

New-"If" Conditions Involving Numbers Restrictions

Especially in Distribution and Matching games, you will encounter New-"If" questions that add Numbers Restrictions to the game. Sometimes these are very concrete rules, such as "If team 2 has exactly three members . . . ." At other times, the rules are more relative; for example, "If team 2 has more members than team 1 . . . ." In either event, treat these conditions as new rules and expect to make deductions about the placement of entities based on them. Take a look at an LSAT expert's work on a question from the Zeno's Furniture game to see New-"If" questions of this type.

LSAT Question	Analysis

Zeno's Unfinished Furniture sells exactly five types of furniture—footstools, hutches, sideboards, tables, and vanities. Irene buys just four items, each of a different type, and each made entirely of one kind of wood—maple, oak, pine, or rosewood. The following conditions govern Irene's purchases:

> Any vanity she buys is maple.
> Any rosewood item she buys is a sideboard.
> If she buys a vanity, she does not buy a footstool.
> If Irene buys a footstool, she also buys a table made of the same wood.
> Irene does not buy an oak table.
> Exactly two of the items she buys are made of the same kind of wood as each other.

$\longrightarrow$

Steps 1–4:

(Select 4)

	F	(H)	(S)	(T)	V
m					m
o	—			—	—
p					—
r	—	—		—	—

If F $\longrightarrow$ T same wood

If T diff't wood than F $\longrightarrow$ ~F

Exactly 2 items = same wood

Question continues on the next page.

LSAT Question (cont.)	Analysis (cont.)

If Irene buys one item made of rosewood and two items made of maple, then which one of the following pairs could be the items she buys?

Step 5: A New-"If" Question: Read up to the comma and consider the new information. The item made of rosewood must be S.

	F	(H)	(S)	(T)	V
2 = m				—	m
o	—		—	—	—
p			—		—
r	—	—	(r)	—	—

→   If F ⟶ T same wood

If T diff't wood than F ⟶ ~F

Exactly 2 items = same wood

As for the items made of maple, two options are possible: In one scenario V is selected, in which case either H or T will also be maple. In the other scenario, F is selected, and because F and T have the same type of wood, they must both be maple.

Find the answer choice that could be true under this question's condition. Wrong answer choices are simply not possible.

(A)	a rosewood sideboard and an oak footstool	→	An oak footstool is not possible. Eliminate.
(B)	an oak hutch and a pine sideboard	→	The rosewood item must be the sideboard. Eliminate.
(C)	an oak hutch and a maple table	→	Correct. This is possible.
(D)	a maple sideboard and a maple vanity	→	The rosewood item must be S. Eliminate.
(E)	a maple hutch and a maple table	→	Either F or V must be included, and must be made of maple. Eliminate.

PrepTestB Sec2 Q20

Take a moment to reflect on all of the New-"If" questions you've just seen demonstrated. In every case, the "If" condition required the expert to pause for a moment to consider how the new restriction affected the Master Sketch, to build the new question-specific sketch, and to characterize the correct and incorrect answer choices. But in all of the questions, that pause and the critical thinking it allowed provided a new sketch that made the expert's evaluation of the answer choices faster and more certain.

New-"If" Questions in Loose Sequencing

In most Loose Sequencing games, the Master Sketch consists of a "string" or "tree" showing the relative positions of the entities. There are no empty slots, so to speak, in Loose Sequencing sketches. However, when a New-"If" question adds restrictions to a Loose Sequencing game that definitively place an entity, draw a new sketch in Strict Sequencing format, and place the newly established entity or entities as stipulated in the New-"If" condition. Then map into the slots of the sketch the other deductions you can make. Take a look at a New-"If" question from the Movie Releases game.

LSAT Question	Analysis

A movie studio is scheduling the release of six films—*Fiesta, Glaciers, Hurricanes, Jets, Kangaroos,* and *Lovebird*. No two of these films can be released on the same date. The release schedule is governed by the following conditions:
 	
    Fiesta must be released earlier than both *Jets* and *Lovebird*.
    Kangaroos must be released earlier than *Jets*, and *Jets* must be released earlier than *Hurricanes*.
    Lovebird must be released earlier than *Glaciers*.
	Steps 1–4:
	
	$\quad$ ..L...G
	F.
	$\quad$ ..J...H
	K.

If *Lovebird* is released earlier than *Kangaroos*, which one of the following could be true?	**Step 5:** In Loose Sequencing New-"If"s, we can use a Strict Sequencing sketch if that's helpful. $\quad\quad$ ..K...J...H F$\quad$L 1$\quad$2$\quad$3$\quad$4$\quad$5$\quad$6 $\quad\quad$ ..G The new restriction locks down F and L in spaces 1 and 2. K-J-H must follow in order, but G could take any space after L. The correct answer is something that is possible according to the new sketch. Wrong answer choices must be false.
(A)$\quad$*Lovebird* is released third.	In this scenario, L must be second. Eliminate.
(B)$\quad$*Lovebird* is released fourth.	In this scenario, L must be second. Eliminate.
(C)$\quad$*Hurricanes* is released earlier than *Lovebird*.	H is released after L. Eliminate.
(D)$\quad$*Jets* is released earlier than *Glaciers*.	Correct. The only restrictions on G are that it must be shown after F and L. The relationship between G and J is undefined.
(E)$\quad$*Jets* is released earlier than *Lovebird*. $\quad\quad\quad\quad$ *PrepTest71 Sec2 Q4*	J is released later than L. Eliminate.

Practice

Because New-"If" questions are so common, there are a number of them left for you to practice from the games you've been reviewing. That's fortunate because you're now familiar with these games. So, as you practice the following questions, focus on the question stems. Analyze the new conditions and decide how to depict them in brief new sketches. Push the new sketch to certainty by making all of the available deductions. Then, characterize the right and wrong answers.

Before trying each of the following questions, take a moment to refresh your memory of the game's setup, rules, and deductions. Reacquaint yourself with the Master Sketch. Then, analyze the question stem and paraphrase the new "If" condition it contains. Draw a new sketch containing the "If" condition and make any additional deductions that it triggers. Characterize the correct and incorrect answers and evaluate the choices. When you're done, compare your work to that of the LSAT expert on the following pages.

LSAT Question	My Analysis
A movie studio is scheduling the release of six films—*Fiesta, Glaciers, Hurricanes, Jets, Kangaroos,* and *Lovebird.* No two of these films can be released on the same date. The release schedule is governed by the following conditions: *Fiesta* must be released earlier than both *Jets* and *Lovebird.* *Kangaroos* must be released earlier than *Jets,* and *Jets* must be released earlier than *Hurricanes.* *Lovebird* must be released earlier than *Glaciers.*	**Steps 1–4:** $\rightarrow$ `..L...G` `F.` `..J...H` `K..`
20. If *Glaciers* is released earlier than *Hurricanes,* then each of the following could be true EXCEPT:	**Step 5:** $\rightarrow$
(A) *Glaciers* is released fourth.	
(B) *Jets* is released third.	
(C) *Kangaroos* is released second.	
(D) *Lovebird* is released third.	
(E) *Lovebird* is released fifth. *PrepTest71 Sec2 Q3*	

The next three questions are from the Recycling Centers game.

LSAT Question	**My Analysis**

There are exactly three recycling centers in Rivertown: Center 1, Center 2, and Center 3. Exactly five kinds of material are recycled at these recycling centers: glass, newsprint, plastic, tin, and wood. Each recycling center recycles at least two but no more than three of these kinds of material. The following conditions must hold:

Any recycling center that recycles wood also recycles newsprint.

Every kind of material that Center 2 recycles is also recycled at Center 1.

Only one of the recycling centers recycles plastic, and that recycling center does not recycle glass.

Steps 1–4:

GNPTW

1	2	3
—	—	—
—	—	—
—	—	—
...	...	...
	~P	

$W \longrightarrow \boxed{\begin{array}{c} W \\ N \end{array}}$

$\sim\!N \longrightarrow \sim\!\boxed{\begin{array}{c} W \\ N \end{array}}$

$2 \longrightarrow 1$

$\sim\!1 \longrightarrow \sim\!2$

Exactly one P

$\boxed{\begin{array}{c} G \\ P \end{array}}$

21. If Center 2 recycles three kinds of material, then which one of the following kinds of material must Center 3 recycle?

Step 5:

(A) glass

(B) newsprint

(C) plastic

(D) tin

(E) wood

PrepTestJune2007 Sec1 Q20

LSAT Question	My Analysis

There are exactly three recycling centers in Rivertown: Center 1, Center 2, and Center 3. Exactly five kinds of material are recycled at these recycling centers: glass, newsprint, plastic, tin, and wood. Each recycling center recycles at least two but no more than three of these kinds of material. The following conditions must hold:

  Any recycling center that recycles wood also recycles newsprint.

  Every kind of material that Center 2 recycles is also recycled at Center 1.

  Only one of the recycling centers recycles plastic, and that recycling center does not recycle glass.

Steps 1–4:

G N P T W

22. If each recycling center in Rivertown recycles exactly three kinds of material, then which one of the following could be true?

Step 5:

(A)   Only Center 2 recycles glass.

(B)   Only Center 3 recycles newsprint.

(C)   Only Center 1 recycles plastic.

(D)   Only Center 3 recycles tin.

(E)   Only Center 1 recycles wood.

PrepTestJune2007 Sec1 Q21

LSAT Question	My Analysis

There are exactly three recycling centers in Rivertown: Center 1, Center 2, and Center 3. Exactly five kinds of material are recycled at these recycling centers: glass, newsprint, plastic, tin, and wood. Each recycling center recycles at least two but no more than three of these kinds of material. The following conditions must hold:

Any recycling center that recycles wood also recycles newsprint.

Every kind of material that Center 2 recycles is also recycled at Center 1.

Only one of the recycling centers recycles plastic, and that recycling center does not recycle glass.

Steps 1–4:

GNPTW

1	2	3
—	—	—
—	—	—
...	...	...
	~P	

W ⟶ [W N]

~N ⟶ ~[W N]

2 ⟶ 1

~1 ⟶ ~2

Exactly one P

[G/P]

⟶

23. If Center 1 is the only recycling center that recycles wood, then which one of the following could be a complete and accurate list of the kinds of material that one of the recycling centers recycles?

Step 5:

⟶

(A) plastic, tin

(B) newsprint, wood

(C) newsprint, tin

(D) glass, wood

(E) glass, tin

PrepTestJune2007 Sec1 Q23

The next two questions are from the Bill Paying game.

LSAT Question	**My Analysis**

On a Tuesday, an accountant has exactly seven bills—numbered 1 through 7—to pay by Thursday of the same week. The accountant will pay each bill only once according to the following rules:

    Either three or four of the seven bills must be paid on Wednesday, the rest on Thursday.

    Bill 1 cannot be paid on the same day as bill 5.

    Bill 2 must be paid on Thursday.

    Bill 4 must be paid on the same day as 7.

    If bill 6 is paid on Wednesday, bill 7 must be paid on Thursday.

Steps 1–4:

1 2 3 4 5 6 7

Opt. I   Opt. II

W	T	W	T
1/5	5/1	1/5	5/1
4	2	3	2
7	6	6	4
...	...		7

24. If bill 2 and bill 6 are paid on different days from each other, which one of the following must be true?

Step 5:

→

    (A) Exactly three bills are paid on Wednesday.

    (B) Exactly three bills are paid on Thursday.

    (C) Bill 1 is paid on the same day as bill 4.

    (D) Bill 2 is paid on the same day as bill 3.

    (E) Bill 5 is paid on the same day as bill 7.

PrepTest29 Sec3 Q3

LSAT Question	**My Analysis**

On a Tuesday, an accountant has exactly seven bills—numbered 1 through 7—to pay by Thursday of the same week. The accountant will pay each bill only once according to the following rules:

    Either three or four of the seven bills must be paid on Wednesday, the rest on Thursday.

    Bill 1 cannot be paid on the same day as bill 5.

    Bill 2 must be paid on Thursday.

    Bill 4 must be paid on the same day as 7.

    If bill 6 is paid on Wednesday, bill 7 must be paid on Thursday.

Steps 1–4:

$$1\ 2\ 3\ 4\ 5\ 6\ 7$$

Opt. I   Opt. II

W	T	W	T
1/5	5/1	1/5	5/1
4	2	3	2
7	6	6	4
...	...		7

25. If bill 6 is paid on Wednesday, which one of the following bills must also be paid on Wednesday?

Step 5:

(A) 1

(B) 3

(C) 4

(D) 5

(E) 7

PrepTest29 Sec3 Q4

The next two questions are from the Trees in the Park game.

LSAT Question	My Analysis
A park contains at most five of seven kinds of trees—firs, laurels, maples, oaks, pines, spruces, and yews—consistent with the following conditions:	**Steps 1–4:**

A park contains at most five of seven kinds of trees—firs, laurels, maples, oaks, pines, spruces, and yews—consistent with the following conditions:

    If maples are in the park, yews are not.

    If firs are in the park, pines are not.

    If yews are not in the park, then either laurels or oaks, but not both, are in the park.

    If it is not the case that the park contains both laurels and oaks, then it contains firs and spruces.

Steps 1–4:

F L M O P S Y   (max 5)

If ⓂM ⟶ ~Y

If ⓎY ⟶ ~M

If Ⓕ ⟶ ~P

⟶ If Ⓟ ⟶ ~F

If ~Y ⟶ [Exactly one of Ⓛ/Ⓞ]

If Ⓛ and Ⓞ ⟶ Ⓨ

If ~L and ~O ⟶ Ⓨ

If ~L or ~O ⟶ Ⓕ and Ⓢ

If ~F or ~S ⟶ Ⓛ and Ⓞ

26. If neither maples nor spruces are in the park, then which one of the following could be true?

Step 5:

⟶

(A) Exactly four kinds of trees are in the park.

(B) Exactly five kinds of trees are in the park.

(C) Laurels are not in the park.

(D) Oaks are not in the park.

(E) Yews are not in the park.

PrepTestB Sec2 Q8

LSAT Question	My Analysis

A park contains at most five of seven kinds of trees—firs, laurels, maples, oaks, pines, spruces, and yews—consistent with the following conditions:
 	
If maples are in the park, yews are not.
If firs are in the park, pines are not.
If yews are not in the park, then either laurels or oaks, but not both, are in the park.
If it is not the case that the park contains both laurels and oaks, then it contains firs and spruces.
	Steps 1–4:
	
	F L M O P S Y (max 5)
	
	If (M) ⟶ ~Y
	If (Y) ⟶ ~M
	
	If (F) ⟶ ~P
	⟶ If (P) ⟶ ~F
	
	If ~Y ⟶ [Exactly one of (L)/(O)]
	If (L) and (O) ⟶ (Y)
	If ~L and ~O ⟶ (Y)
	
	If ~L or ~O ⟶ (F) and (S)
	If ~F or ~S ⟶ (L) and (O)

27. If firs are not in the park, then which one of the following must be true?

Step 5:

⟶

(A) Maples are not in the park.

(B) Spruces are not in the park.

(C) Yews are not in the park.

(D) Pines are in the park.

(E) Spruces are in the park.

PrepTestB Sec2 Q10

The next two questions are from the Language Awards game.

LSAT Question	**My Analysis**

A college dean will present seven awards for outstanding language research. The awards—one for French, one for German, one for Hebrew, one for Japanese, one for Korean, one for Latin, and one for Swahili—must be presented consecutively, one at a time, in conformity with the following constraints:

The German award is not presented first.

The Hebrew award is presented at some time before the Korean award is presented.

The Latin award is presented at some time before the Japanese award is presented.

The French award is presented either immediately before or immediately after the Hebrew award is presented.

The Korean award is presented either immediately before or immediately after the Latin award is presented.

Steps 1–4:

Opt. I   ___ (F/H) ___ ___ ___ ___ ___

Opt. II   S   (F/H) ___ ___ ___ ___

→ Opt. III $\underset{1}{S}$ $\underset{2}{G}$ $\underset{3}{(F/H)}$ $\underset{4}{}$ $\underset{5}{(K/L)}$ $\underset{6}{}$ $\underset{7}{J}$

~G

(F/H) . . . (K/L) . . . J

28. If the Hebrew award is presented fourth, which one of the following must be true?

Step 5:

→

(A) The French award is presented fifth.

(B) The German award is presented third.

(C) The Japanese award is presented sixth.

(D) The Japanese award is presented sixth.

(E) The Swahili award is presented first.

PrepTest29 Sec3 Q15

LSAT Question	**My Analysis**

A college dean will present seven awards for outstanding language research. The awards—one for French, one for German, one for Hebrew, one for Japanese, one for Korean, one for Latin, and one for Swahili—must be presented consecutively, one at a time, in conformity with the following constraints:

The German award is not presented first.

The Hebrew award is presented at some time before the Korean award is presented.

The Latin award is presented at some time before the Japanese award is presented.

The French award is presented either immediately before or immediately after the Hebrew award is presented.

The Korean award is presented either immediately before or immediately after the Latin award is presented.

Steps 1–4:

Opt. I   ⎡F/H⎤ __ __ __ __ __

Opt. II   S   ⎡F/H⎤ __ __ __ __

$\longrightarrow$ Opt. III   S   G   ⎡F/H⎤   ⎡K/L⎤   J

      1   2   3   4   5   6   7

~G

⎡F/H⎤...⎡K/L⎤...J

---

29. If the German award is presented third, which one of the following could be true?

Step 5:

$\longrightarrow$

(A) The French award is presented fourth.

(B) The Japanese award is presented fifth.

(C) The Japanese award is presented sixth.

(D) The Korean award is presented second.

(E) The Swahili award is presented fifth.

PrepTest29 Sec3 Q16

The next two questions are from the Zeno's Furniture game.

LSAT Question	My Analysis

Zeno's Unfinished Furniture sells exactly five types of furniture—footstools, hutches, sideboards, tables, and vanities. Irene buys just four items, each of a different type, and each made entirely of one kind of wood—maple, oak, pine, or rosewood. The following conditions govern Irene's purchases:

Any vanity she buys is maple.

Any rosewood item she buys is a sideboard.

If she buys a vanity, she does not buy a footstool.

If Irene buys a footstool, she also buys a table made of the same wood.

Irene does not buy an oak table.

Exactly two of the items she buys are made of the same kind of wood as each other.

Steps 1–4:

(Select 4)

	F	(H)	(S)	(T)	V
m					m
o	—				—
p					—
r	—	—		—	—

If F ⟶ T same wood

If T diff't wood than F ⟶ ~F

Exactly 2 items = same wood

30. Suppose Irene buys a footstool. Then which one of the following is a complete and accurate list of items any one of which she could buy in maple?

Step 5:

(A) footstool, hutch, sideboard, table, vanity

(B) footstool, hutch, sideboard, table

(C) footstool, hutch, sideboard

(D) footstool, hutch

(E) footstool

PrepTestB Sec2 Q22

LSAT Question	My Analysis

Zeno's Unfinished Furniture sells exactly five types of furniture—footstools, hutches, sideboards, tables, and vanities. Irene buys just four items, each of a different type, and each made entirely of one kind of wood—maple, oak, pine, or rosewood. The following conditions govern Irene's purchases:

Any vanity she buys is maple.

Any rosewood item she buys is a sideboard.

If she buys a vanity, she does not buy a footstool.

If Irene buys a footstool, she also buys a table made of the same wood.

Irene does not buy an oak table.

Exactly two of the items she buys are made of the same kind of wood as each other.

→

Steps 1–4:

(Select 4)

	F	(H)	(S)	(T)	V
m					m
o		—			—
p					—
r		—	—		—

If F ⟶ T same wood

If T diff't wood than F ⟶ ~F

Exactly 2 items = same wood

---

31. If Irene does not buy an item made of maple, then each of the following must be true EXCEPT:

→

Step 5:

(A) Irene buys a footstool.

(B) Irene buys a pine hutch.

(C) Irene buys a rosewood sideboard.

(D) Irene buys exactly one item made of oak.

(E) Irene buys exactly two items made of pine.

PrepTestB Sec2 Q24

Expert Analysis

Here's how an LSAT expert approached each of the questions you just tried. As you review the expert's work, compare your new sketches. Did you accurately record the question stem's "If" condition? Did you make the deductions available for this question?

LSAT Question	Analysis

A movie studio is scheduling the release of six films—*Fiesta, Glaciers, Hurricanes, Jets, Kangaroos,* and *Lovebird.* No two of these films can be released on the same date. The release schedule is governed by the following conditions:
   Fiesta must be released earlier than both *Jets* and   *Lovebird.*
   Kangaroos must be released earlier than *Jets,* and *Jets*   must be released earlier than *Hurricanes.*
   Lovebird must be released earlier than *Glaciers.*
	Steps 1–4:
	
	 $\rightarrow$ F $\cdots$ .L$\ldots$G
	          J$\ldots$H
	         K $\cdots$

20. If *Glaciers* is released earlier than *Hurricanes,* then each of the following could be true EXCEPT:	**Step 5:** A New-"If" Question: sketch the new rule.
	
	 $G \ldots H$
	
	 Now build out the rest of the sketch based on this new restriction.
	
	 $\rightarrow$ F$\ldots$L$\ldots$G$\ldots$H
	        J $\cdots\cdots$
	      K $\cdots$

(A) *Glaciers* is released fourth.	$\rightarrow$ This could be true. G has two movies in front of it and one behind it, meaning it could be anywhere from third to fifth. Eliminate.
(B) *Jets* is released third.	$\rightarrow$ This could be true. J has two movies in front of it and one behind it, so its range is anywhere from third to fifth. Eliminate.
(C) *Kangaroos* is released second.	$\rightarrow$ This could be true. K has no movies definitively in front of it and two behind it, so its range is first to fourth. Eliminate.
(D) *Lovebird* is released third.	$\rightarrow$ This could be true. L must have one movie before it and two after it, so its range is second to fourth. Eliminate.
(E) *Lovebird* is released fifth. *PrepTest71 Sec2 Q3*	$\rightarrow$ Correct. This cannot work because both G and H must be shown after L.

LSAT Question	**Analysis**

There are exactly three recycling centers in Rivertown: Center 1, Center 2, and Center 3. Exactly five kinds of material are recycled at these recycling centers: glass, newsprint, plastic, tin, and wood. Each recycling center recycles at least two but no more than three of these kinds of material. The following conditions must hold:

Any recycling center that recycles wood also recycles newsprint.

Every kind of material that Center 2 recycles is also recycled at Center 1.

Only one of the recycling centers recycles plastic, and that recycling center does not recycle glass.

Steps 1–4:

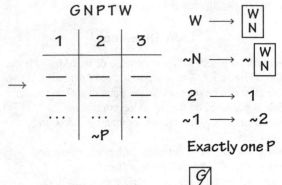

21. If Center 2 recycles three kinds of material, then which one of the following kinds of material must Center 3 recycle?

Step 5: A New-"If" Question: Consider the new information and create a new sketch. Here, we know that Center 2 recycles three kinds of materials, and that therefore Center 1 also recycles three kinds of materials.

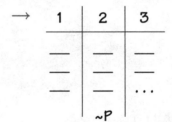

Because both Center 1 and Center 2 are recycling the same number of materials, then they must be recycling the same types of materials. That means that because Center 2 does not recycle P, Center 1 also cannot recycle P. That leaves Center 3 as the center that must recycle P.

| | LSAT Question (cont.) | | Analysis (cont.) |

1	2	3
—	—	P
—	—	—
—	—	...
~P	~P	

The question asks for a material that must be recycled at Center 3. Find P in the answer choices and select it.

(A) glass → Eliminate.

(B) newsprint → Eliminate.

(C) plastic → Correct.

(D) tin → Eliminate.

(E) wood → Eliminate.

PrepTestJune2007 Sec1 Q20

LSAT Question	Analysis

There are exactly three recycling centers in Rivertown: Center 1, Center 2, and Center 3. Exactly five kinds of material are recycled at these recycling centers: glass, newsprint, plastic, tin, and wood. Each recycling center recycles at least two but no more than three of these kinds of material. The following conditions must hold:

  Any recycling center that recycles wood also recycles newsprint.

  Every kind of material that Center 2 recycles is also recycled at Center 1.

  Only one of the recycling centers recycles plastic, and that recycling center does not recycle glass.

Steps 1–4:

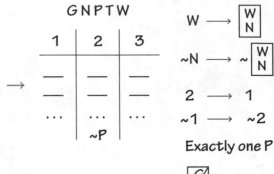

22. If each recycling center in Rivertown recycles exactly three kinds of material, then which one of the following could be true?

Step 5: A New-"If" Question: Create a new sketch and add the information in the question stem. In Question 21, it was determined that if Center 2 recycled all three materials, then that meant Centers 1 and 2 did not recycle plastic, and Center 3 did recycle plastic:

1	2	3
—	—	P
—	—	—
—	—	—
~P	~P	

Make further deductions. G and P cannot be together. That means G is not recycled in Center 3, but must be recycled in Centers 1 and 2.

1	2	3
G	G	P
—	—	—
—	—	—
~P	~P	~G

LSAT Question (cont.)	**Analysis (cont.)**
	The remaining materials are N, T, and W. Whichever center has W will also have N. That leaves T. Any center that recycles T will have to also recycle another material. In addition to either G or P, the only other material that would be able to go with T in a certain center and still satisfy the maximum limitation of three materials per center would be N. Therefore, all three centers must recycle N.

$\longrightarrow$

1	2	3
G	G	P
N	N	N
—	—	—
~P	~P	~G

Now answer the question. The correct answer is something that could be true. The wrong answers show pairings that cannot be true.

(A) Only Center 2 recycles glass.	$\longrightarrow$ Glass is recycled in both Center 2 and Center 1. Eliminate.
(B) Only Center 3 recycles newsprint.	$\longrightarrow$ All three centers recycle newsprint. Eliminate.
(C) Only Center 1 recycles plastic.	$\longrightarrow$ Plastic is recycled in Center 3. Eliminate.
(D) Only Center 3 recycles tin.	$\longrightarrow$ Correct. This could be true.
(E) Only Center 1 recycles wood. *PrepTestJune2007 Sec1 Q21*	$\longrightarrow$ Whichever material is the third type of material recycled at Center 2 will also have to be the third type recycled at Center 1 (Rule 2). Thus, it is impossible, in this question, that only Center 1 recycles wood. Eliminate.

LSAT Question	**Analysis**

LSAT Question

23. If Center 1 is the only recycling center that recycles wood, then which one of the following could be a complete and accurate list of the kinds of material that one of the recycling centers recycles?

Analysis

Step 5: A New-"If" Question: Create a sketch and add this new information: Center 1 recycles wood and Centers 2 and 3 do not.

1	2	3
W	—	—
—	—	—
...	...	...
	~P	~W
	~W	

Any center that recycles W must recycle N.

$\rightarrow$

1	2	3
W	—	—
N	—	—
...	...	...
	~P	~W
	~W	

Consult the rules and make further deductions. Because anything recycled at Center 2 must be recycled at Center 1, and because Center 2 does not recycle wood and Center 1 does, then Center 2 cannot recycle three materials. Center 2 will then recycle two materials and Center 1 will recycle three. The two materials recycled at Center 2 will match the two materials recycled at Center 1 that are not W. Therefore Center 2 does recycle N and Center 1 does not recycle P.

1	2	3
W	N	—
N	—	—
—		...
~P	~P	~W
	~W	

LSAT Question (cont.)	**Analysis (cont.)**

The remaining material recycled at Center 2 (and which is therefore also recycled at Center 1) will be either G or T. Additionally, if neither Center 1 nor Center 2 recycles P, then Center 3 must recycle P.

1	2	3
W	N	P
N	G/T	__
G/T		...
~P	~P	~W
	~W	

If Center 3 recycles P, then it cannot recycle G. That means Centers 1 and 2 definitely recycle G and not T. If they don't recycle T, then Center 3 must be the center that recycles it.

1	2	3
W	N	P
N	G	T
G		...
~P	~P	~W
	~W	~G

The question asks for a possible list of all of the materials at one of the centers. All of the answer choices list only two materials. So the correct answer will not list the materials in Center 1. In Center 2, the materials are N and G. In Center 3, the materials are P and T. Find one of those combinations in the answer choices.

(A) plastic, tin	→	Correct. This is possible in Center 3.
(B) newsprint, wood	→	This does not work in either Center 2 or Center 3. Eliminate.
(C) newsprint, tin	→	This does not work in either Center 2 or Center 3. Eliminate.
(D) glass, wood	→	This does not work in either Center 2 or Center 3. Eliminate.
(E) glass, tin	→	This does not work in either Center 2 or Center 3. Eliminate.

LSAT Question	Analysis

On a Tuesday, an accountant has exactly seven bills—numbered 1 through 7—to pay by Thursday of the same week. The accountant will pay each bill only once according to the following rules:

  Either three or four of the seven bills must be paid on Wednesday, the rest on Thursday.

  Bill 1 cannot be paid on the same day as bill 5.

  Bill 2 must be paid on Thursday.

  Bill 4 must be paid on the same day as 7.

  If bill 6 is paid on Wednesday, bill 7 must be paid on Thursday.

Steps 1–4:

$$1\ 2\ 3\ 4\ 5\ 6\ 7$$

Opt. I		Opt. II	
W	T	W	T
1/5	5/1	1/5	5/1
4	2	3	2
7	6	6	4
. . .	. . .		7

---

24. If bill 2 and bill 6 are paid on different days from each other, which one of the following must be true?

Step 5: A New-"If" Question: Consider to which Limited Option this new condition applies. This must be Option II. Use the Option II sketch to answer the question—the correct answer will be something that is definitely true.

(A) Exactly three bills are paid on Wednesday.

→ Correct. This is true.

(B) Exactly three bills are paid on Thursday.

→ Four bills are paid on Thursday. Eliminate.

(C) Bill 1 is paid on the same day as bill 4.

→ Bills 1 and 5 can be paid on either day, so while this could be true, it does not have to be true. Eliminate.

(D) Bill 2 is paid on the same day as bill 3.

→ This must be false. Eliminate.

(E) Bill 5 is paid on the same day as bill 7.

PrepTest29 Sec3 Q3

→ Bills 1 and 5 can be paid on either day, so while this could be true, it does not have to be true. Eliminate.

LSAT Question	Analysis

25. If bill 6 is paid on Wednesday, which one of the following bills must also be paid on Wednesday?

Step 5: A New-"If" Question: Consider to which Limited Option sketch this condition applies. Only in Option II is bill 6 paid on Wednesday.

Opt. II

→

W	T
1/5	5/1
3	2
6	4
	7

Now answer the question: It is clear from the Option II sketch that bill 3 is the other bill that must also be paid on Wednesday.

(A)	1	→	Eliminate.
(B)	3	→	Correct.
(C)	4	→	Eliminate.
(D)	5	→	Eliminate.
(E)	7	→	Eliminate.

PrepTest29 Sec3 Q4

LSAT Question	Analysis
A park contains at most five of seven kinds of trees—firs, laurels, maples, oaks, pines, spruces, and yews—consistent with the following conditions:	**Steps 1–4:**

A park contains at most five of seven kinds of trees—firs, laurels, maples, oaks, pines, spruces, and yews—consistent with the following conditions:

If maples are in the park, yews are not.

If firs are in the park, pines are not.

If yews are not in the park, then either laurels or oaks, but not both, are in the park.

If it is not the case that the park contains both laurels and oaks, then it contains firs and spruces.

Steps 1–4:

F L M O P S Y   (max 5)

If (M) ⟶ ~Y

If (Y) ⟶ ~M

If (F) ⟶ ~P

⟶ If (P) ⟶ ~F

If ~Y ⟶ [Exactly one of (L)/(O)]

If (L) and (O) ⟶ (Y)

If ~L and ~O ⟶ (Y)

If ~L or ~O ⟶ (F) and (S)

If ~F or ~S ⟶ (L) and (O)

---

26. If neither maples nor spruces are in the park, then which one of the following could be true?

Step 5: A New-"If" Question: Create a new roster sketch just for this question and cross off M and S.

F L M̸ O P S̸ Y

Look through the rules and make all possible deductions. "No maples" does not trigger any result, but "no spruce" means that both L and O must be selected (Rule 4).

F (L) M̸ (O) P S̸ Y

⟶ If L and O are selected, then Y must be selected (Rule 3).

F (L) M̸ (O) P S̸ (Y)

The only remaining entities are F and P. According to Rule 2, they cannot both be selected, but it is not known if one or neither is selected. No more deductions can be made.

The correct answer will be something that could be true according to the deductions made above; the four wrong answers are not possible.

LSAT Question (cont.)		**Analysis (cont.)**
(A) Exactly four kinds of trees are in the park.	→	Correct. It is possible to select one of F or P, which would bring the total to four.
(B) Exactly five kinds of trees are in the park.	→	In order to have five kinds of trees in the park, both F and P would need to be selected. This is not possible according to Rule 2. Eliminate.
(C) Laurels are not in the park.	→	Laurels are definitely in the park. Eliminate.
(D) Oaks are not in the park.	→	Oaks are definitely in the park. Eliminate.
(E) Yews are not in the park.	→	Yews are definitely in the park. Eliminate.

repTestB Sec2 Q8

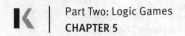
LSAT Question	**Analysis**
27. If firs are not in the park, then which one of the following must be true?	**Step 5:** A New-"If" Question: Create a new roster sketch just for this question and cross off F.

F̶ L M O P S Y

Look through the rules and make any possible deductions. "No firs" means that both L and O must be selected (Rule 4).

F̶ Ⓛ M Ⓞ P S Y

→ When both L and O are selected, Y must be selected (Rule 3).

F̶ Ⓛ M Ⓞ P S Ⓨ

When Y is selected, M cannot be selected (Rule 1).

F̶ Ⓛ M̶ Ⓞ P S Ⓨ

No more deductions can be made, so evaluate the answer choices. The correct answer is something that is definitely true. The four wrong answer choices do not have to be true.

(A) Maples are not in the park.	→ Correct. This must be true.
(B) Spruces are not in the park.	→ This may or may not be true. Eliminate.
(C) Yews are not in the park.	→ This cannot be true. Eliminate.
(D) Pines are in the park.	→ This may or may not be true. Eliminate.
(E) Spruces are in the park.	→ This may or may not be true. Eliminate.

PrepTestB Sec2 Q10

LSAT Question	Analysis

A college dean will present seven awards for outstanding language research. The awards—one for French, one for German, one for Hebrew, one for Japanese, one for Korean, one for Latin, and one for Swahili—must be presented consecutively, one at a time, in conformity with the following constraints:

> The German award is not presented first.
> The Hebrew award is presented at some time before the Korean award is presented.
> The Latin award is presented at some time before the Japanese award is presented.
> The French award is presented either immediately before or immediately after the Hebrew award is presented.
> The Korean award is presented either immediately before or immediately after the Latin award is presented.

Steps 1–4:

$\longrightarrow$

Opt. I   ___ (F/H) ___ ___ ___ ___ ___

Opt. II   S   (F/H) ___ ___ ___ ___

Opt. III   S   G   (F/H)   (K/L)   J
            1   2   3   4   5   6   7

~G

(F/H) . . . (K/L) . . . J

28. If the Hebrew award is presented fourth, which one of the following must be true?

Step 5: A New-"If" Question: Check the Limited Options sketches to see which option works with this new condition. It must be Option III. Redraw:

$\longrightarrow$

S   G   F   H   (K/L)   J
1   2   3   4   5   6   7

The correct answer will be something that must be true according to this new sketch. Wrong answer choices are either definitely false or possibly false.

(A) The French award is presented fifth.	$\longrightarrow$	F is presented third in this scenario. Eliminate.
(B) The German award is presented third.	$\longrightarrow$	G is presented second. Eliminate.
(C) The Japanese award is presented sixth.	$\longrightarrow$	J is presented seventh. Eliminate.
(D) The Korean award is presented fifth.	$\longrightarrow$	This could be true, but does not have to be true. L could also be presented fifth. Eliminate.
(E) The Swahili award is presented first.	$\longrightarrow$	Correct. S is first.

PrepTest29 Sec3 Q15

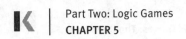

LSAT Question	**Analysis**
29. If the German award is presented third, which one of the following could be true?	**Step 5:** A New-"If" Question: Check the Limited Options sketches to see which option works with this new condition. It must be Option I. Redraw with G in the third position:

$$\underset{1}{\boxed{F/H}} \quad \underset{2}{\rule{1em}{0.4pt}} \quad \underset{3}{\overset{G}{\rule{1em}{0.4pt}}} \quad \underset{4}{\rule{1em}{0.4pt}} \quad \underset{5}{\rule{1em}{0.4pt}} \quad \underset{6}{\rule{1em}{0.4pt}} \quad \underset{7}{\rule{1em}{0.4pt}}$$

The remaining rules remain in place:

$$\boxed{K/L} \ldots J$$

The correct answer is something that might be true according to this new sketch. Any answer choice that presents something that cannot happen is incorrect.

(A) The French award is presented fourth.	F must be either first or second, so this is definitely false. Eliminate.
(B) The Japanese award is presented fifth.	This cannot be true. K and L must both go before J, so sixth is the earliest J can go in this scenario. Eliminate.
(C) The Japanese award is presented sixth.	Correct. This is possible.
(D) The Korean award is presented second.	Not possible. Either F or H will be second. Eliminate.
(E) The Swahili award is presented fifth.	If S is placed fifth, then there is no acceptable place for the K/L block to go. Eliminate.

PrepTest29 Sec3 Q16

Expert Analysis for Questions 30 and 31 begins on the next page. ▶ ▶ ▶

LSAT Question	**Analysis**

Zeno's Unfinished Furniture sells exactly five types of furniture—footstools, hutches, sideboards, tables, and vanities. Irene buys just four items, each of a different type, and each made entirely of one kind of wood—maple, oak, pine, or rosewood. The following conditions govern Irene's purchases:

    Any vanity she buys is maple.
    Any rosewood item she buys is a sideboard.
    If she buys a vanity, she does not buy a footstool.
    If Irene buys a footstool, she also buys a table made of the same wood.
    Irene does not buy an oak table.
    Exactly two of the items she buys are made of the same kind of wood as each other.

$\longrightarrow$

Steps 1–4:

(Select 4)

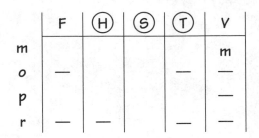

If F $\longrightarrow$ T same wood

If T diff't wood than F $\longrightarrow$ ~F

Exactly 2 items = same wood

---

30. Suppose Irene buys a footstool. Then which one of the following is a complete and accurate list of items any one of which she could buy in maple?

Step 5: This is essentially a New-"If" Question in disguise. Create a new sketch in which F is selected and V is not.

(Select 4)

$\longrightarrow$

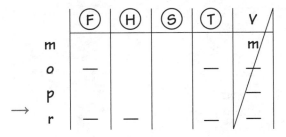

The two pieces of furniture that share the same type of wood must now be F and T. That means H and S must not be made of the same type of wood.

The correct answer choice will list all of the items that could be made in maple. V is not selected in this situation, so eliminate any answer choices that include V. And, because it is possible that both F and T are made with maple, eliminate answer choices that do not include F and T.

LSAT Question (cont.)		Analysis (cont.)
(A)	footstool, hutch, sideboard, table, vanity	$\longrightarrow$	The vanity cannot be included in this scenario. Eliminate.
(B)	footstool, hutch, sideboard, table	$\longrightarrow$	Correct. Either F and T are both made of maple, or F and T are made of pine, in which case either H or S could be made of maple.
(C)	footstool, hutch, sideboard	$\longrightarrow$	Does not include the table. Eliminate.
(D)	footstool, hutch	$\longrightarrow$	Does not include the table. Eliminate.
(E)	footstool	$\longrightarrow$	Does not include the table. Eliminate.

PrepTestB Sec2 Q22

LSAT Question	Analysis

31. If Irene does not buy an item made of maple, then each of the following must be true EXCEPT:

Step 5: A New-"If" Question: Create a new sketch and add this new information—no maples are purchased, which in turn means V is not purchased and F is purchased.

(Select 4)

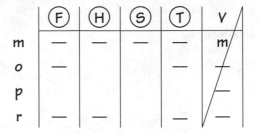

F and T must be made of pine. And, because exactly two items will be made of the same wood, H and S cannot be made of pine:

(Select 4)

$\longrightarrow$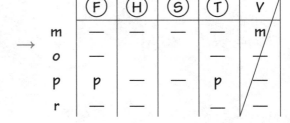

H must therefore be made of oak. Because H and S can't be made of the same type of wood (F and T are the pieces that share the same wood type here), S must be made of rosewood:

(Select 4)

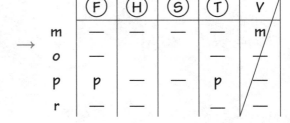

The correct answer here will be something that does not have to be the true. The four wrong answers all must be true.

LSAT Question (cont.)		Analysis (cont.)
(A) Irene buys a footstool.	$\longrightarrow$	This is true. Eliminate.
(B) Irene buys a pine hutch.	$\longrightarrow$	Correct. This is not true; Irene buys an oak hutch.
(C) Irene buys a rosewood sideboard.	$\longrightarrow$	This is true. Eliminate.
(D) Irene buys exactly one item made of oak.	$\longrightarrow$	This is true. Eliminate.
(E) Irene buys exactly two items made of pine.	$\longrightarrow$	This is true. Eliminate.

PrepTestB Sec2 Q24

Congratulations. You've completed your practice on the most important Logic Games question types. Let's pause briefly to talk about how you can use some questions to help you answer others in the same logic game more quickly. Then, you can practice analyzing and characterizing more Must Be/Could Be and New-"If" question stems in a drill.

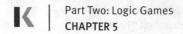

Using Previous Work to Answer Logic Games Questions

Occasionally, you'll encounter a Must Be/Could Be question that just seems too complex or confusing to handle without drawing out several sketches to test each answer choice. In those cases, LSAT experts will often put off tackling that question until they've completed the New-"If" questions associated with the game. Then, they'll use the "mini sketches" they've made for the New-"If" questions to help them evaluate the answer choices in the tough Must Be/Could Be question. This can be a very effective time-saving strategy, but you must use it carefully.

Each new sketch you make for a New-"If" question represents one acceptable arrangement for the entities in the game. So, too, does the correct answer in the Acceptability question. Thus, these sketches and the correct Acceptability answer choice represent what *could be true* in the game. If you have an open-ended Could Be True question and you see that one of the answer choices represents something you know could be true from your New-"If" sketches or Acceptability answer, you can confidently select that choice in the Could Be True question. Likewise, if you have a Must Be False question, you can eliminate any choice that *could be true* based on your other work. Be careful not to overdetermine the level of certainty: seeing that an arrangement of entities *could be true* (in the correct answer to an Acceptability question or in the sketch for a New-"If") does *not* mean that the arrangement must be true.

Remember that the correct answer to a Must Be/Could Be question is always something that you can determine from the game's Master Sketch. But when you have sketches and other previous work to draw upon, using it judiciously can be very beneficial. Chapter 7, Logic Games: Managing the Section, will provide further discussion of how to effectively use your previous work.

Characterizing the Answer Choices in Must Be/Could Be and New-"If" Questions

Take a few minutes to study the sample question stems below. For each, you'll see the LSAT expert's analysis identifying the question type and characterizing the one correct and four incorrect answer choices. Once you feel comfortable identifying these question types, try the practice drill on the following pages to test your ability to characterize the choices on similar questions.

Question Stem	Analysis
If the cat receiving the third place ribbon is the Siamese, then which one of the following must be true?	This question provides new information, so it will require a new sketch including that information. Once the new information has been added, try to make further deductions based on the preexisting rules. The correct answer will either be something drawn into this sketch or a scenario consistent across multiple sketches. The incorrect answers will include entities that have alternative possibilities.
Which of the following presenters must be scheduled for Tuesday afternoon?	This question provides no new information, so a new sketch won't be needed. The Master Sketch should have a presenter already marked in the Tuesday afternoon position, which will be the correct answer. If not, further revision to the Master Sketch may be necessary. When the upfront deductions in a game are particularly challenging, other questions may also provide the answer through their sketches, so long as the same presenter consistently appears in the Tuesday afternoon position.
If Janna is assigned to be Francis's lab partner, which of the following CANNOT be true?	This question again provides new information, requiring a new sketch and further deductions. The question asks for what cannot be true, which is logically equivalent to what must be false. The correct answer will contradict something determined in the sketch, while the incorrect answers could be true.

Question Stem		Analysis
Which of the following must be false?	→	This question provides no new information and no clue in the stem as to what kind of answer it is looking for. Characterizing the answer choices will provide some insight into what the answer should look like, and scanning the sketch will enable a prediction. The correct answer will place an entity in an impossible position or contradict one or more rules. The wrong answers will all be allowed by the sketch. As with Must Be True questions, previous work from other questions can be helpful. The big difference is that in Must Be False questions, you eliminate wrong answers that you've already seen as possible.
If Katarina plays soccer, which of the following could be true?	→	More information with which to produce a new sketch and deductions. The correct answer will include entities that haven't yet been nailed down, while each of the wrong answers will violate the rules or contradict the sketch in some way.
Which of the following could be false?	→	With no new information, this question will only reference the Master Sketch. The correct answer could be false, while each wrong answer must be true.
If the taco wagon occupies stall 4, each of the following could be true EXCEPT:	→	Use the new information to draw a new sketch. Each of the incorrect answers is something that could be true. Therefore, the correct answer must contradict the refined sketch in some way.
If Jayce is assigned to present on the day immediately after the day on which Otis is assigned to present, each of the following must be false EXCEPT:	→	The new information in this question is creating a new Block of Entities. It can be helpful to quickly sketch this new Block out before adding it into a new sketch. Because all of the incorrect answers will contradict the sketch in some way, the correct answer will be something that is still possible and may even be something that must be true.
If all of the odd numbered folders are green, then each of the following must be true EXCEPT:	→	Use the new information to draw a new sketch integrating that information with further deductions. The wrong answers will all be concretely known entities, while the correct answer will contain a statement that could be or must be false.
Each of the following could be false EXCEPT:	→	There is no new information, so the wrong answers will all be scenarios that either are undetermined or are demonstrably false in the Master Sketch. The correct answer must be true.

Practice

For each of the following, jot down the characteristics of the one correct answer and of the four incorrect answer choices.

Question Stem	My Analysis
32. If Summertide park has a fountain and a merry-go-round, then Falling Water could have each of the following EXCEPT:	
33. If Sabin is scheduled for the 3 P.M. meeting, which of the following could be true?	
34. If the west garden is planted with only begonias and cherry trees, which of the following must be true?	
35. If the last valve opened is valve H, which of the following could be false?	
36. If K is assigned to present the lecture on integration, which of the following presenters must be assigned to present the lecture on day 3?	
37. Which of the following must be false?	
38. Which of the following could be true?	
39. Which of the following items CANNOT be auctioned first?	
40. Each of the following could be true EXCEPT:	
41. Each of the following could be false EXCEPT:	

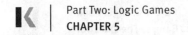

Expert Analysis

Here's how the LSAT expert analyzed each of the question stems you just practiced. Compare your work with that of the expert. You'll see more questions of these types as you practice the games in Chapter 6 and those in the full-length tests at the end of the book.

Question Stem		Analysis
32. If Summertide park has a fountain and a merry-go-round, then Falling Water could have each of the following EXCEPT:	→	This new information will need a new sketch, which allows for further deductions. The wrong answers will all be features permissible at Falling Water. The correct answer will be a feature that Falling Water cannot have.
33. If Sabin is scheduled for the 3 P.M. meeting, which of the following could be true?	→	With new information comes a new sketch. The correct answer will include an entity placed in a position that is possible, while each of the wrong answers will include entities placed in positions that are not possible.
34. If the west garden is planted with only begonias and cherry trees, which of the following must be true?	→	The new information allows for a new sketch that incorporates new deductions. The right answer will be an entity that has been concretely placed, while each of the wrong answers will have alternative possibilities.
35. If the last valve opened is valve H, which of the following could be false?	→	Place the new information in a new sketch; then, make as many deductions as possible. Each of the wrong answers will describe a placement or relationship that is now concretely determined. The correct answer will allow for an alternative possibility.
36. If K is assigned to present the lecture on integration, which of the following presenters must be assigned to present the lecture on day 3?	→	There's new information to work into the game, so a new sketch incorporating that information and new deductions is warranted. The correct answer will be the entity concretely placed on day 3, while the wrong answers will include entities that either cannot or can, but need not, be assigned to that position.
37. Which of the following must be false?	→	This question provides no new information and no clue in the stem as to what kind of answer it is looking for. Characterizing the answer choices will provide some insight into what the answer should look like, and scanning the sketch will enable a prediction. The correct answer will place an entity in an impossible position or contradict one or more rules. The wrong answers will all be allowed by the sketch.

Question Stem		Analysis
38. Which of the following could be true?	→	There's no information to add to a new sketch, so this question will rely on the Master Sketch. The correct answer will place an entity in an allowed location. Each of the wrong answers will contradict the sketch in some way. All previous work can be used to provide examples of arrangements that could be true.
39. Which of the following items CANNOT be auctioned first?	→	This question doesn't add anything new, so a new sketch isn't necessary. The correct answer will be an entity that can never be placed in the first position, while each of the incorrect answers will be possible in the first position. Remember, your previous sketches can be a great reference for eliminating wrong answers.
40. Each of the following could be true EXCEPT:	→	Without any new information, this question will rely on the original Master Sketch. Each of the wrong answers will mention an entity or scenario that the Master Sketch allows, but the correct answer will contradict the Master Sketch in some way.
41. Each of the following could be false EXCEPT:	→	There is no new information, so the wrong answers will be scenarios that are possible or that are definitely ruled out based on the Master Sketch. The correct answer will either be an entity that has been concretely placed in the sketch, or it will be a relationship that must appear in all possible sketches.

Even though those question stems weren't associated with any game setup in that exercise, were you able to imagine the entities and actions those games would include? If so, you're really getting familiar with the Logic Games section and the kinds of the games the testmaker uses over and over.

You'll see one more drill like that one near the end of this chapter. That drill will cover the handful of rare questions you're about to learn. None of these question types is likely to make or break your score, and some will not even appear on some administrations of the LSAT. Still, it's helpful to know what you might see so that you won't be caught off guard when these questions do pop up.

OTHER LOGIC GAMES QUESTION TYPES

In this section, we'll introduce a handful of other question types that have appeared in the LSAT Logic Games section. The games you've been practicing with don't contain all of these question types, and indeed, it would be hard if not impossible to find even a single Logic Games section that contains an example of all the question types we'll discuss here. Here's a list of the question types we'll discuss.

LSAT STRATEGY

Other Logic Games Question Types

- Numerical Questions
  - Minimum/Maximum Questions
  - Earliest/Latest Questions
  - "How Many" Questions
- Rule Alteration Questions
  - Rule Change Questions
  - Rule Substitution Questions
- Supply the "If" Questions

For each of these rare types, we'll define the question and give examples of how the question stem is worded. Then, we'll outline how to characterize the correct and incorrect answer choices. Where the games we've been working with contain examples of these questions, you'll have a chance to review an LSAT expert's analysis. Finally, in the drill near the end of this chapter, you can see additional examples of these unusual questions and practice identifying them.

Numerical Questions

You've already seen several ways in which Numbers Restrictions can help you set up a game, make deductions, and answer questions. Numerical questions focus directly on number limits within a game.

Minimum/Maximum Questions

The test might, for example, ask you to determine the minimum or maximum number of entities that may be selected (in a Selection game) or placed within a certain group (in a Distribution game, for instance). The question stem will be worded more-or-less like this one:

What is the maximum number of students who could be selected for the field trip?

A question like this one would, of course, be part of the question set for a Selection game. You'll use your expertise in Formal Logic to determine the maximum number of students you could choose. Any rule of the type "If A → ~B" reduces the maximum number of entities that may be selected. Rules in that pattern translate to "Never AB." Because you must exclude one of the two entities, the maximum available for selection has been reduced by one. On the flip side, rules fitting the pattern "If ~C → D" establish that at least one of C and D must be selected and so increase the minimum by one. (See Chapter 1: LSAT Reasoning if you don't remember the reasoning cited here.)

The answer choices are always listed in numerical order, either lowest to highest or the other way around. The correct answer cites the precise minimum or maximum number. The wrong answers are either too high or too low. In tests released from 2010 to 2014, there were three Minimum/Maximum questions, one of which had a New-"If" condition preceding the question.

Earliest/Latest Questions

Sequencing games (and Hybrid games with a Sequencing action) may feature a related question type: the Earliest/Latest question. In fact, one of these questions was associated with the Language Awards game. Take a look at it and review the LSAT expert's analysis.

LSAT Question	Analysis

A college dean will present seven awards for outstanding language research. The awards—one for French, one for German, one for Hebrew, one for Japanese, one for Korean, one for Latin, and one for Swahili—must be presented consecutively, one at a time, in conformity with the following constraints:
The German award is not presented first.
The Hebrew award is presented at some time before the Korean award is presented.
The Latin award is presented at some time before the Japanese award is presented.
The French award is presented either immediately before or immediately after the Hebrew award is presented.
The Korean award is presented either immediately before or immediately after the Latin award is presented.
	Steps 1–4:
	
	Opt. I ⎡F/H⎤ _ _ _ _ _ _
	
	Opt. II S ⎡F/H⎤ _ _ _ _ _
	
	→ Opt. III S G ⎡F/H⎤ ⎡K/L⎤ J
	               1 2 3 4 5 6 7
	        ~G
	
	⎡F/H⎤ . . . ⎡K/L⎤ . . . J

The earliest that the Japanese award could be presented is	**Step 5:** Find the earliest possible spot for J. In Option 1, it appears as though J could go in spot 5. Create a new sketch and try it: → ⎡F/H⎤ ⎡K/L⎤ J _ _ _ _ 1 2 3 4 5 6 7 G and S are the only languages remaining, and they could go in spots 6 and 7. This is possible. The earliest J could be presented is fifth.
(A) third	→ Eliminate.
(B) fourth	→ Eliminate.
(C) fifth	→ Correct.
(D) sixth	→ Eliminate.
(E) seventh	→ Eliminate.

PrepTest29 Sec3 Q17

From that example, you can see that Earliest/Latest questions are the Sequencing version of Minimum/Maximum questions. The correct answer gives the precise slot that represents the earliest or latest that the entity in question could appear. The incorrect answers are either too early or too late.

If you've set up the Sequencing game carefully and made all of the available deductions, Earliest/Latest questions should feel fairly straightforward. Too bad you're unlikely to see more of these on Test Day. In fact, among all the tests released between 2010 and 2014, there were no Earliest/Latest questions.

"How Many" Questions

These questions ask you about numbers that can be firmly established in the game. There's little chance you'll misinterpret one of these stems. They tend to be extremely straightforward:

How many of the auditions are there that could be the
one given on Tuesday morning?

How many of the soloists are there any one of whom could
perform third?

Exactly how many of the candidates are there any one of whom
could speak fifth?

The correct answer gives the correct number, and the four wrong answers are either too high or too low. Among the tests released between 2010 and 2014, there have been only 13 "How Many" questions. Interestingly, seven (that is, just over half) of them have been of the New-"If" variety. Here's an example:

If Dr. Shelby is hired by County General hospital, for how many
of the doctors is it known exactly which hospital hires them?

Should you encounter one of these questions in practice or on Test Day, simply make sure you've made all available deductions and count the relevant entities. You should always be able to predict the correct answer precisely before evaluating the choices.

Rule Alteration Questions

Some tests feature no questions from this subcategory, and historically, those that do have exactly one. That's good news because these questions tend to be difficult for most test takers, and they are time-consuming even for those who get them right.

Rule Substitution Questions

These questions didn't make their debut on the LSAT until PrepTest 57, so if you study with older materials, you'll never see one. Since that time, there has been exactly one on each released administration of the exam except for PrepTests 60, 67, and 68 (on which there were none), and PrepTest 71 (on which there were two). As luck would have it, there was a Rule Substitution question associated with the Movie Releases game. Take a look at the LSAT expert's analysis of it.

LSAT Question	Analysis

A movie studio is scheduling the release of six films—*Fiesta, Glaciers, Hurricanes, Jets, Kangaroos,* and *Lovebird.* No two of these films can be released on the same date. The release schedule is governed by the following conditions:
    Fiesta must be released earlier than both *Jets* and *Lovebird.*
    Kangaroos must be released earlier than *Jets,* and *Jets* must be released earlier than *Hurricanes.*
    Lovebird must be released earlier than *Glaciers.*
	Steps 1–4:
	
	  .L...G
	F.
	   .J...H
	K

Which one of the following, if substituted for the condition that *Fiesta* must be released earlier than both *Jets* and *Lovebird,* would have the same effect on the order in which the films are released?	**Step 5:** The correct answer will state a rule that impacts the game in the exact way that the first rule does. The incorrect answers will not have the same impact upon the game.
(A) Only *Kangaroos* can be released earlier than *Fiesta.*	Correct. If this is true, then this means that F must be released earlier than the other four movies. Rules 2 and 3 establish the relationships between J and H and between L and G. This recreates the sketch completely.
(B) *Kangaroos* must be released earlier than *Lovebird.*	The relationship between K and L was undefined in the original sketch. Eliminate.
(C) *Fiesta* must be released either first or second.	This doesn't go far enough. The relationships between F and J and F and L are not established. Eliminate.
(D) *Fiesta* must be released earlier than both *Kangaroos* and *Lovebird.*	The relationship between K and F was undefined in the original sketch. Eliminate.
(E) Either *Fiesta* or *Kangaroos* must be released first. *PrepTest71 Sec2 Q5*	This doesn't go far enough. The relationships between F and J and F and L are not established. Eliminate.

As you can see, the correct answer supplies a rule that would have the same impact on the game as the rule cited in the question stem. The four wrong answers will either be too weak or too strong to substitute exactly for the rule in the stem.

To answer Rule Substitution questions, review the rules and the Master Sketch. Summarize exactly what the rule cited in the question stem says and its impact on other entities within the Master Sketch. Then, imagine removing it from the Master Sketch and swapping in each answer choice. The correct answer will produce precisely the same deductions and Master Sketch you produced at the end of Step 4 of the Logic Games Method.

The placement of Rule Substitution questions within the Logic Games section suggests that the testmaker uses them to reward good time management. Rule Substitution questions have been at the end of the first game three times, at the end of the second game 4 times, and at the end of the fourth game 2 times. Because these questions can be quite time-consuming, your best strategy may be simply to guess on these questions and leave ample time to get to any remaining games and all of the points they can contribute to your LSAT score.

Rule Change Questions

In times past, Rule Change questions were more common than they have been in recent years. In fact, between 2010 and 2014, there were no Rule Change question among all 60 released logic games. There's a strong chance that you'll never encounter a question of this type on Test Day. On the off chance that you do, here's what you should know. Rule Change question stems tell you to ignore one of the rules cited in the game's setup and to use another rule (described in the stem) instead. Then, based on these altered circumstances, the stem will usually pose a Must Be/Could Be-type question.

In a sense, you can think of Rule Change questions as a cousin of the New-"If" question. The main difference is that New-"If" questions preserve the original rules, deductions, and Master Sketch and add an additional restriction, whereas the Rule Change question suspends one of the original rules. Still, if you happen across a Rule Change question, your instinct should be to create a new sketch and consult it as you evaluate the answer choices. Just make sure you actively undo the part of the Master Sketch suspended in the Rule Change question stem along with any deductions you drew using that rule.

Supply the "If" Questions

There's one more very rare question type: the Supply the "If" question. Between 2010 and 2014, there was only one of these questions among the 60 logic games released by the LSAC. As it turns out, there were none among the games selected for this chapter. You'll recognize Supply the "If" questions from question stems like these:

G must be the sixth house visited by the agent if which one of the following is true?

Team H will compete later than Team J if which one of the following is true?

These unusual questions are like New-"If" questions in reverse. The question stem gives you the necessary result and asks you to supply the sufficient condition. LSAT experts know that the best approach is to use the Master Sketch to see the possibilities for the entity or slot in question, and then use that analysis to determine the kind of additional restriction that would guarantee the desired result.

As you learned, the questions covered in this section are not common. You're best served by trying these questions when they do appear among your practice games and tests but not by spending time trying to find more examples of them in older tests. It is your facility with Acceptability, Must Be/Could Be, and New-"If" questions that will make or break your LSAT Logic Games score. In contrast, you'll likely see only a single example of one or two of these rare question types on your official LSAT. If you do, analyze their question stems patiently, consult your Master Sketch, and remember that the testmaker always includes every piece of information you need to answer every question the test asks.

Characterizing the Answer Choices in Other Logic Games Questions

Take a few minutes to study the sample question stems below. For each, you'll see the LSAT expert's analysis identifying the question type and characterizing the one correct and four incorrect answer choices. Once you feel comfortable identifying these question types, try the practice drill on the following pages to test your ability to characterize the choices on similar questions.

Question Stem	Analysis
What is the maximum number of departments that could be located on the second floor?	This question is looking for a number of entities belonging to one of several floors. Because it wants the maximum, one approach is to try assigning as many as possible, keeping on the lookout for entities that will force others into other floors. The limitations of the game will likely also dictate how spread out the entities must or cannot be. Be on the lookout for Numbers deductions from your setup of the game and what the apparent maximum is from any previously worked "If" questions.
If Printing is located on the floor immediately above Shipping, what is the minimum number of floors above Bankruptcy but below Mediation?	With new information, further deductions will be available. The question asks for the minimum number of positions between two entities, so a good strategy is to draw a sketch that forces Bankruptcy and Mediation as close together as possible. If an answer forces the new rule to be broken, it cannot be correct.
Which of the following lists the minimum number and maximum number, respectively, of breeds that could be present at the show?	Even though the question asks for both minimum and maximum, it's a better strategy to look for one or the other first and narrow options accordingly. Each Not-Both rule involving a distinct pair of entities will decrease the maximum by 1, and every At-Least-One rule will increase the minimum by 1, but there may be more subtle interactions as well.
If Margaery selects both species F and H, what is the maximum number of species she does NOT select?	Use the new information to determine what other species have been selected or deselected. Then, if a species is optional, treat it as deselected. The answer will be the largest number of species that could be simultaneously deselected.
What is the maximum number of actors who can be offstage at any given time?	This question is looking for the maximum number of entities that aren't selected. It may help to instead think of the minimum number of entities that *are* selected because the correct answer will be the total number of entities minus that minimum number who can be onstage. Every At-Least-One rule will increase the minimum by 1.

Question Stem		Analysis
Suppose the condition stating that Johnson's meeting with Tycho must occur before his meeting with Solari is replaced with a condition stating that Johnson's meeting with Solari must occur before his meeting with Tycho. If all other conditions remain the same, which of the following must be true?	→	This is a Rule Change question, which at the least will require a full rework of the Master Sketch. Because it is difficult to tell which deductions were dependent on T being before S, the best route is to rebuild the sketch from scratch, using the new rule. Given the time and work necessary, this question should therefore be tackled last, and in many cases it can be saved until all other games and questions have been dealt with. Once the revised sketch is complete, the question can be treated as a typical Must Be True question.
Suppose that the condition requiring Human Resources to be assigned to the fourth floor is replaced with a condition requiring Human Resources to be assigned to a higher-numbered floor than Mediation. If all other conditions remain unchanged, which of the following could be false?	→	Another Rule Change question, requiring a full rework of the Master Sketch. An Established Entity is being removed as a rule, and several deductions might have depended on it. The sketch will need to be completely rebuilt, with the new rule substituted for the old. It should therefore be tackled last, and in many cases it can be saved until all other games and questions have been dealt with. Once the sketch is complete, the question can be treated as a typical Could Be False question.
Suppose that the condition requiring that if Guevara is on the second team, Jedaris cannot be assigned to any team is removed. Which of the following conditions, if substituted in its place, would provide the same effect in the assignment of members to teams?	→	A Rule Substitution question. The correct answer will provide an identical effect as the original rule. Because this rule uses Formal Logic, the correct answer may be as simple as the contrapositive, but it may be more complicated and involve other entities as well. It's best to tackle this kind of question at the end of a section because it will often require testing answer choices.
Which of the following, if substituted for the condition that the Taco truck must be assigned to a higher numbered stall than the Pizza truck, would have the same effect in determining the order of the trucks?	→	A Rule Substitution question. The correct answer will provide an identical effect as the original rule. It's best to tackle this kind of question at the end of a section because it will often require testing answer choices.

Now, try it out on your own. The question stems below are similar, though certainly not identical, to those in the list above and the questions you've seen so far in this chapter.

Practice

For each of the following question stems, identify the question type and characterize the one correct and four incorrect answer choices. When you're done, check your work against the LSAT expert's analysis on the following pages.

Question Stem	My Analysis
42. Which of the following lists the minimum and maximum numbers, respectively, of groups marching in the parade this year?	
43. If the driver delivers to Sanzenin last, what is the maximum number of deliveries that could be scheduled between Takeshi and Rhea?	
44. What is the maximum number of students who do NOT speak French?	
45. If Steven visits the doctor's office on Tuesday, what is the minimum number of errands he must perform on Wednesday?	
46. What is the maximum number of days that can separate the visits to site L and site R?	
47. If Joffrey is assigned to do as many chores as possible, to which of the following chores must he be assigned?	
48. Suppose that instead of the host opening door M third, he opens it fifth. If all other conditions remain the same, which of the following could be true?	
49. Which one of the following is the latest day of the week on which Michael could be scheduled to work?	
50. Gretchen must occupy the third seat if which one of the following is true?	
51. Suppose that the condition requiring that if Jason joins the ski team, Katherine joins the tennis team is removed. Which of the following rules, if added in its place, would provide the same effect in determining the assignment of players to teams?	

Expert Analysis

Here's how the LSAT expert analyzed each of the question stems you just practiced. Compare your work with that of the expert. You'll see further examples of these question types as you practice the games in Chapter 6 and those in the full-length tests at the end of the book.

Question Stem		Analysis
42.	Which of the following lists the minimum and maximum numbers, respectively, of groups marching in the parade this year?	As this is a question asking for both minimum and maximum numbers, it's better to focus on one or the other first and narrow down the answers from there. Remember that Not-Both rules and At-Least-One rules will influence these numbers.
43.	If the driver delivers to Sanzenin last, what is the maximum number of deliveries that could be scheduled between Takeshi and Rhea?	This question is looking to place as much distance between two entities as possible. Draw a new sketch including the additional rule and any deductions it provides, then try to force the two entities to opposite ends of the sketch.
44.	What is the maximum number of students who do NOT speak French?	Looking for the maximum number of entities that *aren't* part of a group can also be determined by finding the minimum number of entities that *are* and subtracting that from the total number of entities. Use At-Least-One rule deductions to help find the right number, but be wary of potentially more subtle interactions.
45.	If Steven visits the doctor's office on Tuesday, what is the minimum number of errands he must perform on Wednesday?	Use the new information to draw a new, refined sketch. Then try to see how many entities can be forced out of Wednesday.
46.	What is the maximum number of days that can separate the visits to site L and site R?	This question is looking for the maximum distance between L and R. If the Master Sketch doesn't already place them as far apart as possible, look for rules that would prevent their placement at opposite ends of the sketch. Because the question does not dictate the order of L and R, double-check whether reversing their order opens up a greater distance.
47.	If Joffrey is assigned to do as many chores as possible, to which of the following chores must he be assigned?	This is a New-"If"/Must Be True question. The stipulation to maximize the number of chores Joffrey takes on is in the "If" clause. (Distinguish this from a question in which the correct answer represents an acceptable minimum or maximum.) The goal here is to find a way of maximizing the number of chores assigned to Joffrey. Look for rules that force the selection of several entities.

Question Stem	Analysis
48. Suppose that instead of the host opening door M third, he opens it fifth. If all other conditions remain the same, which of the following could be true?	→ This is a Rule Change question, which at the least will take a full rework of the Master Sketch. Because many of the original deductions that you made might have relied on the host opening door M third, the sketch will need to be completely rebuilt with door M being opened fifth instead. Given the amount of work and the complete restructuring of the game necessary, this question should therefore be tackled last, and in many cases it can be saved until all other games and questions have been dealt with. Once the revised sketch is complete, the question can be treated as a typical Could Be True question.
49. Which one of the following is the latest day of the week on which Michael could be scheduled to work?	→ This is an Earliest/Latest question. Look for rules (or chains of deductions) that force certain entities into days later than Michael's or that force entities other than Michael to occupy days late in the week even if those entities aren't directly related to Michael in the rules.
50. Gretchen must occupy the third seat if which one of the following is true?	→ A Supply the "If" question. The correct answer will state a condition that limits Gretchen to the third position. Look for answer choices with entities that affect Gretchen's position either directly or indirectly (through a chain of deductions, for example).
51. Suppose that the condition requiring that if Jason joins the ski team, Katherine joins the tennis team is removed. Which of the following rules, if added in its place, would provide the same effect in determining the assignment of players to teams?	→ A Rule Substitution question. The correct answer will provide an identical effect as the original rule. Because this rule uses Formal Logic, the correct answer may be as simple as the contrapositive but may be more complicated and involve other entities as well. It's best to tackle this kind of question at the end of a section because it will often require testing answer choices.

Reflection

In the coming days, take note of real-life cases in which people ask you questions similar to those you see in LSAT logic games. You'll find that people are constantly posing Must Be/Could Be– and New-"If"–type questions. "If Barbara is free this Saturday, what are you guys going to do?" "If they're out of the prawns, what will you order?" The main difference between LSAT questions and their day-to-day counterparts is that the test always provides information adequate to answer the question, whereas in everyday life, we're often merely speculating about what "must" happen or giving our opinion or preference. When you encounter these questions in everyday life, try to determine whether you are answering with adequate information and, if not, what you would need to know in order to establish a concrete answer. This reflection exercise can help make you aware of instances on the LSAT in which you are speculating rather than deducing.

If you've completed Chapters 2–5 (or at least the portions of them for which your study time allows), you're ready to practice full games. You'll find games of each type in Chapter 6, followed by complete explanations for how to set up the games and answer all of their questions.

Logic Games Practice

Now that you've mastered the steps in the Logic Games Method, it's time to apply what you've learned to full games. In the pages that follow, you'll find nine games of various types, all from recently released tests. The game types you've seen to this point are largely represented here. In fact, the games are highly representative of the frequency of the various game types that have appeared on official LSATs over the past five years. If you notice, for example, that there are more Sequencing and Hybrid games here than any other game type, that's because Sequencing has been the testmaker's favorite single-action game type, and the most common action combined with another in Hybrid games, too. It makes sense to practice what you're most likely to encounter on Test Day.

NOTES ON LOGIC GAMES PRACTICE

The games in this chapter are arranged by game type. You need not do all of the games in order, and if you haven't yet studied a particular game type, hold off on practicing a full game of that type until you're familiar with it. As you practice, keep the following pointers in mind.

Use the Logic Games Method consistently. Chapters 3 through 5 were organized around the five-step Logic Games Method first introduced in Chapter 2. That's because having a consistent, strategic approach is so important in this section of the test. So, be conscious of each step as you practice. If you practice without instilling the Method and its associated strategies, you're likely to repeat your old patterns, and that means continuing to be frustrated by the same aspects of logic games over and over again. For your convenience, here's the Logic Games Method one more time.

KAPLAN LOGIC GAMES METHOD

Step 1: Overview—Ask the SEAL questions to understand your task and get a mental picture of the actions and limitations.

Step 2: Sketch—Create a simple, helpful framework in which you can record the game's rules and restrictions.

Step 3: Rules—Analyze each rule; build it into the framework or jot it down in shorthand just to the side.

Step 4: Deductions—Combine rules and restrictions to determine what must be true or false about the arrangement of entities in the game.

Step 5: Questions—Use your understanding of the game and your Master Sketch to attack the questions efficiently and confidently.

As you practice, pay special attention to your work with Steps 1 and 4 of the Method. Many test takers underestimate the importance of these steps. If you start work on the Sketch or Rules without fully understanding the game's task and limitations, there's a good chance you'll misrepresent the game. If you launch into the questions without having taken the time to combine the rules and extract solid Deductions, you're likely to waste time by testing every answer choice against an incomplete Master Sketch.

Review your work thoroughly. Complete explanations for the games in this chapter follow right after the games. Take the time to study them even if you get all of the game's questions correct. Review how expert test takers set up the games, how they recorded the rules and made deductions. You may well discover that you could have been more efficient and knocked out the questions more quickly. Of course, when you miss a question, determine whether the problem came from a misunderstanding or oversight in the question itself or whether you missed a rule or deduction in the earlier steps.

Another way in which you can effectively use the explanations is to try Steps 1 through 4 of the game—jotting down the rules, making deductions, and producing a Master Sketch. Then, review just that much of the explanations for the game before you even try the questions. This will let you know how you're doing in recognizing game types and setting them up. After you're sure that you understand the game, try the questions and review them as well. This approach is especially helpful when you find a particular game frustrating and you feel that you're making little progress in working through the questions.

Finally, each question's difficulty is ranked in the explanations—from ★★★★ for the toughest questions to ★ for the easiest. Consulting these rankings will tell you a lot about the games and questions you're practicing. You might, for example, distinguish a very hard question in an otherwise easy game. In that case, you'll focus your review on what made that question confusing for test takers, but reassure yourself that your overall approach was on target. On the other hand, you may find a game in which, say, four out of five questions rate ★★★ or ★★★★. In that case, you'll know the game was tough for everyone and spend extra time reviewing the game's setup and deductions to discover how the testmaker made it so challenging.

Practice and Timing. On Test Day, you'll have about 8½ minutes per game. Naturally, that kind of time pressure can make even routine logic games feel stressful. As you're practicing individual games, work as quickly as you can, but make your focus the successful implementation of the Method. If you try to practice too quickly, you'll introduce time pressure at a point where you should really be working on consistency and accuracy. Speed will come with familiarity, practice, and (believe it or not) patience. When you take full tests or try 35-minute Logic Games sections, time yourself strictly. But don't be in such a rush to get faster that you don't gain the efficiencies that come from practicing the methodical application of good strategy to logic games. Chapter 7 will address timing in depth and will introduce you to strategies for effectively managing the 35-minute Logic Games section you'll be completing on Test Day. In the present chapter, practice logic games one by one and perfect your approach.

Practice logic games begin on the next page ▶ ▶ ▶

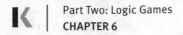
The explanations to these questions
begin on page 370.

QUESTION POOL

Sequencing

Questions 1–5

Seven singers—Jamie, Ken, Lalitha, Maya, Norton, Olive, and Patrick—will be scheduled to perform in the finals of a singing competition. During the evening of the competition, each singer, performing alone, will give exactly one performance. The schedule for the evening must conform to the following requirements:

    Jamie performs immediately after Ken.
    Patrick performs at some time after Maya.
    Lalitha performs third only if Norton performs fifth.
    If Patrick does not perform second, he performs fifth.

1.   Which one of the following is an acceptable schedule for the evening's performers, from first through seventh?

    (A)   Ken, Jamie, Maya, Lalitha, Patrick, Norton, Olive
    (B)   Lalitha, Patrick, Norton, Olive, Maya, Ken, Jamie
    (C)   Norton, Olive, Ken, Jamie, Maya, Patrick, Lalitha
    (D)   Olive, Maya, Ken, Lalitha, Patrick, Norton, Jamie
    (E)   Olive, Maya, Lalitha, Norton, Patrick, Ken, Jamie

2. If Lalitha is scheduled for the third performance, which one of the following must be scheduled for the sixth performance?

   (A) Jamie
   (B) Ken
   (C) Norton
   (D) Olive
   (E) Patrick

3. If Norton is scheduled for the fifth performance, which one of the following could be true?

   (A) Jamie is scheduled for the sixth performance.
   (B) Ken is scheduled for the second performance.
   (C) Lalitha is scheduled for the fourth performance.
   (D) Maya is scheduled for the third performance.
   (E) Olive is scheduled for the first performance.

4. If Maya is scheduled for the second performance, which one of the following could be true?

   (A) Jamie is scheduled for the sixth performance.
   (B) Ken is scheduled for the fourth performance.
   (C) Lalitha is scheduled for the third performance.
   (D) Norton is scheduled for the fifth performance.
   (E) Olive is scheduled for the fourth performance.

5. If Jamie's performance is scheduled to be immediately before Lalitha's performance, Jamie's performance CANNOT be scheduled to be

   (A) second
   (B) third
   (C) fourth
   (D) fifth
   (E) sixth

PrepTest24 Sec4 Qs6–10

Questions 6–12

A cruise line is scheduling seven week-long voyages for the ship *Freedom*. Each voyage will occur in exactly one of the first seven weeks of the season: weeks 1 through 7. Each voyage will be to exactly one of four destinations: Guadeloupe, Jamaica, Martinique, or Trinidad. Each destination will be scheduled for at least one of the weeks. The following conditions apply to *Freedom*'s schedule:

    Jamaica will not be its destination in week 4.

    Trinidad will be its destination in week 7.

    Freedom will make exactly two voyages to Martinique, and at least one voyage to Guadeloupe will occur in some week between those two voyages.

    Guadeloupe will be its destination in the week preceding any voyage it makes to Jamaica.

    No destination will be scheduled for consecutive weeks.

6. Which one of the following is an acceptable schedule of destinations for *Freedom*, in order from week 1 through week 7?

(A)   Guadeloupe, Jamaica, Martinique, Trinidad, Guadeloupe, Martinique, Trinidad

(B)   Guadeloupe, Martinique, Trinidad, Martinique, Guadeloupe, Jamaica, Trinidad

(C)   Jamaica, Martinique, Guadeloupe, Martinique, Guadeloupe, Jamaica, Trinidad

(D)   Martinique, Trinidad, Guadeloupe, Jamaica, Martinique, Guadeloupe, Trinidad

(E)   Martinique, Trinidad, Guadeloupe, Trinidad, Guadeloupe, Jamaica, Martinique

7. Which one of the following CANNOT be true about *Freedom*'s schedule of voyages?

    (A) *Freedom* makes a voyage to Trinidad in week 6.
    (B) *Freedom* makes a voyage to Martinique in week 5.
    (C) *Freedom* makes a voyage to Jamaica in week 6.
    (D) *Freedom* makes a voyage to Jamaica in week 3.
    (E) *Freedom* makes a voyage to Guadeloupe in week 3.

8. If *Freedom* makes a voyage to Trinidad in week 5, which one of the following could be true?

    (A) *Freedom* makes a voyage to Trinidad in week 1.
    (B) *Freedom* makes a voyage to Martinique in week 2.
    (C) *Freedom* makes a voyage to Guadeloupe in week 3.
    (D) *Freedom* makes a voyage to Martinique in week 4.
    (E) *Freedom* makes a voyage to Jamaica in week 6.

9. If *Freedom* makes a voyage to Guadeloupe in week 1 and a voyage to Jamaica in week 5, which one of the following must be true?

    (A) *Freedom* makes a voyage to Jamaica in week 2.
    (B) *Freedom* makes a voyage to Trinidad in week 2.
    (C) *Freedom* makes a voyage to Martinique in week 3.
    (D) *Freedom* makes a voyage to Guadeloupe in week 6.
    (E) *Freedom* makes a voyage to Martinique in week 6.

10. If *Freedom* makes a voyage to Guadeloupe in week 1 and to Trinidad in week 2, which one of the following must be true?

    (A) *Freedom* makes a voyage to Martinique in week 3.
    (B) *Freedom* makes a voyage to Martinique in week 4.
    (C) *Freedom* makes a voyage to Martinique in week 5.
    (D) *Freedom* makes a voyage to Guadeloupe in week 3.
    (E) *Freedom* makes a voyage to Guadeloupe in week 5.

11. If *Freedom* makes a voyage to Martinique in week 3, which one of the following could be an accurate list of *Freedom*'s destinations in week 4 and week 5, respectively?

    (A) Guadeloupe, Trinidad
    (B) Jamaica, Guadeloupe
    (C) Martinique, Trinidad
    (D) Trinidad, Jamaica
    (E) Trinidad, Martinique

12. Which one of the following must be true about *Freedom*'s schedule of voyages?

    (A) *Freedom* makes a voyage to Guadeloupe either in week 1 or else in week 2.
    (B) *Freedom* makes a voyage to Martinique either in week 2 or else in week 3.
    (C) *Freedom* makes at most two voyages to Guadeloupe.
    (D) *Freedom* makes at most two voyages to Jamaica.
    (E) *Freedom* makes at most two voyages to Trinidad.

PrepTestJun07 Sec1 Qs11–17

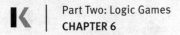

The explanations to these questions
begin on page 377.

Questions 13–17

A company employee generates a series of five-digit product codes in accordance with the following rules:

    The codes use the digits 0, 1, 2, 3, and 4, and no others.

    Each digit occurs exactly once in any code.

    The second digit has a value exactly twice that of the first digit.

    The value of the third digit is less than the value of the fifth digit.

13.   If the last digit of an acceptable product code is 1, it must be true that the

    (A)   first digit is 2

    (B)   second digit is 0

    (C)   third digit is 3

    (D)   fourth digit is 4

    (E)   fourth digit is 0

14. Which one of the following must be true about any acceptable product code?

  (A) The digit 1 appears in some position before the digit 2.
  (B) The digit 1 appears in some position before the digit 3.
  (C) The digit 2 appears in some position before the digit 3.
  (D) The digit 3 appears in some position before the digit 0.
  (E) The digit 4 appears in some position before the digit 3.

15. If the third digit of an acceptable product code is not 0, which one of the following must be true?

  (A) The second digit of the product code is 2.
  (B) The third digit of the product code is 3.
  (C) The fourth digit of the product code is 0.
  (D) The fifth digit of the product code is 3.
  (E) The fifth digit of the product code is 1.

16. Any of the following pairs could be the third and fourth digits, respectively, of an acceptable product code, EXCEPT:

  (A) 0, 1
  (B) 0, 3
  (C) 1, 0
  (D) 3, 0
  (E) 3, 4

17. Which one of the following must be true about any acceptable product code?

  (A) There is exactly one digit between the digit 0 and the digit 1.
  (B) There is exactly one digit between the digit 1 and the digit 2.
  (C) There are at most two digits between the digit 1 and the digit 3.
  (D) There are at most two digits between the digit 2 and the digit 3.
  (E) There are at most two digits between the digit 2 and the digit 4.

PrepTestJun07 Sec1 Qs1–5

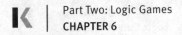
The explanations to these questions begin on page 380.

Selection

Questions 18–23

Nine different treatments are available for a certain illness: three antibiotics—F, G, and H—three dietary regimens—M, N, and O—and three physical therapies—U, V, and W. For each case of the illness, a doctor will prescribe exactly five of the treatments, in accordance with the following conditions:

> If two of the antibiotics are prescribed, the remaining antibiotic cannot be prescribed.
> There must be exactly one dietary regimen prescribed.
> If O is not prescribed, F cannot be prescribed.
> If W is prescribed, F cannot be prescribed.
> G cannot be prescribed if both N and U are prescribed.
> V cannot be prescribed unless both H and M are prescribed.

18. Which one of the following could be the five treatments prescribed for a given case?

(A) F, G, H, M, V
(B) F, G, M, O, V
(C) F, H, M, O, W
(D) G, H, N, U, W
(E) G, H, O, U, W

19. Which one of the following could be the antibiotics and physical therapies prescribed for a given case?

    (A) F, G, H, W
    (B) F, G, U, V
    (C) F, U, V, W
    (D) G, U, V, W
    (E) H, U, V, W

20. If O is prescribed for a given case, which one of the following is a pair of treatments both of which must also be prescribed for that case?

    (A) F, M
    (B) G, V
    (C) N, U
    (D) U, V
    (E) U, W

21. If G is prescribed for a given case, which one of the following is a pair of treatments both of which could also be prescribed for that case?

    (A) F, M
    (B) F, N
    (C) N, V
    (D) O, V
    (E) V, W

22. Which one of the following is a list of three treatments that could be prescribed together for a given case?

    (A) F, M, U
    (B) F, O, W
    (C) G, N, V
    (D) G, V, W
    (E) H, N, V

23. Which one of the following treatments CANNOT be prescribed for any case?

    (A) G
    (B) M
    (C) N
    (D) U
    (E) W

PrepTest24 Sec4 Qs18–23

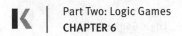
The explanations to these questions begin on page 383.

Matching/Distribution

Questions 24–30

Exactly seven film buffs—Ginnie, Ian, Lianna, Marcos, Reveka, Viktor, and Yow—attend a showing of classic films. Three films are shown, one directed by Fellini, one by Hitchcock, and one by Kurosawa. Each of the film buffs sees exactly one of the three films. The films are shown only once, one film at a time. The following restrictions must apply:

> Exactly twice as many of the film buffs see the Hitchcock film as see the Fellini film.
> Ginnie and Reveka do not see the same film as each other.
> Ian and Marcos do not see the same film as each other.
> Viktor and Yow see the same film as each other.
> Lianna sees the Hitchcock film.
> Ginnie sees either the Fellini film or the Kurosawa film.

24. Which one of the following could be an accurate matching of film buffs to films?

(A) Ginnie: the Hitchcock film; Ian: the Kurosawa film; Marcos: the Hitchcock film

(B) Ginnie: the Kurosawa film; Ian: the Fellini film; Viktor: the Fellini film

(C) Ian: the Hitchcock film; Reveka: the Kurosawa film; Viktor: the Fellini film

(D) Marcos: the Kurosawa film; Reveka: the Kurosawa film; Viktor: the Kurosawa film

(E) Marcos: the Hitchcock film; Reveka: the Hitchcock film; Yow: the Hitchcock film

25. Each of the following must be false EXCEPT:

    (A)   Reveka is the only film buff to see the Fellini film.
    (B)   Reveka is the only film buff to see the Hitchcock film.
    (C)   Yow is the only film buff to see the Kurosawa film.
    (D)   Exactly two film buffs see the Kurosawa film.
    (E)   Exactly three film buffs see the Hitchcock film.

26. Which one of the following could be a complete and accurate list of the film buffs who do NOT see the Hitchcock film?

    (A)   Ginnie, Marcos
    (B)   Ginnie Reveka
    (C)   Ginnie, Ian, Reveka
    (D)   Ginnie, Marcos, Yow
    (E)   Ginnie, Viktor, Yow

27. If exactly one film buff sees the Kurosawa film, then which one of the following must be true?

    (A)   Viktor sees the Hitchcock film.
    (B)   Ginnie sees the Fellini film.
    (C)   Marcos sees the Fellini film.
    (D)   Ian sees the Fellini film.
    (E)   Reveka sees the Hitchcock film.

28. Which one of the following must be true?

    (A)   Ginnie sees a different film than Ian does.
    (B)   Ian sees a different film than Lianna does.
    (C)   Ian sees a different film than Viktor does.
    (D)   Ian, Lianna, and Viktor do not all see the same film.
    (E)   Ginnie, Lianna, and Marcos do not all see the same film.

29. If Viktor sees the same film as Ginnie does, then which one of the following could be true?

    (A)   Ginnie sees the Fellini film.
    (B)   Ian sees the Hitchcock film.
    (C)   Reveka sees the Kurosawa film.
    (D)   Viktor sees the Hitchcock film.
    (E)   Yow sees the Fellini film.

30. Each of the following could be a complete and accurate list of the film buffs who see the Fellini film EXCEPT:

    (A)   Ginnie, Ian
    (B)   Ginnie, Marcos
    (C)   Ian, Reveka
    (D)   Marcos, Reveka
    (E)   Viktor, Yow

PrepTest27 Sec2 Qs13–19

Hybrid

Questions 31–35

Exactly three films—*Greed*, *Harvest*, and *Limelight*—are shown during a film club's festival held on Thursday, Friday, and Saturday. Each film is shown at least once during the festival but never more than once on a given day. On each day at least one film is shown. Films are shown one at a time. The following conditions apply:

    On Thursday *Harvest* is shown, and no film is shown after it on that day.

    On Friday either *Greed* or *Limelight*, but not both, is shown, and no film is shown after it on that day.

    On Saturday either *Greed* or *Harvest*, but not both, is shown, and no film is shown after it on that day.

31. Which one of the following could be a complete and accurate description of the order in which the films are shown at the festival?

(A) Thursday: *Limelight*, then *Harvest*; Friday: *Limelight*; Saturday: *Harvest*

(B) Thursday: *Harvest*; Friday: *Greed*, then *Limelight*; Saturday: *Limelight*, then *Greed*

(C) Thursday: *Harvest*; Friday: *Limelight*; Saturday: *Limelight*, then *Greed*

(D) Thursday: *Greed*, then *Harvest*, then *Limelight*; Friday: *Limelight*; Saturday: *Greed*

(E) Thursday: *Greed*, then *Harvest*; Friday: *Limelight*, then *Harvest*; Saturday: *Harvest*

32. Which one of the following CANNOT be true?

    (A)   *Harvest* is the last film shown on each day of the festival.
    (B)   *Limelight* is shown on each day of the festival.
    (C)   *Greed* is shown second on each day of the festival.
    (D)   A different film is shown first on each day of the festival.
    (E)   A different film is shown last on each day of the festival.

33. If *Limelight* is never shown again during the festival once *Greed* is shown, then which one of the following is the maximum number of film showings that could occur during the festival?

    (A)   three
    (B)   four
    (C)   five
    (D)   six
    (E)   seven

34. If *Greed* is shown exactly three times, *Harvest* is shown exactly twice, and *Limelight* is shown exactly once, then which one of the following must be true?

    (A)   All three films are shown on Thursday.
    (B)   Exactly two films are shown on Saturday.
    (C)   *Limelight* and *Harvest* are both shown on Thursday.
    (D)   *Greed* is the only film shown on Saturday.
    (E)   *Harvest* and *Greed* are both shown on Friday.

35. If *Limelight* is shown exactly three times, *Harvest* is shown exactly twice, and *Greed* is shown exactly once, then which one of the following is a complete and accurate list of the films that could be the first film shown on Thursday?

    (A)   *Harvest*
    (B)   *Limelight*
    (C)   *Greed, Harvest*
    (D)   *Greed, Limelight*
    (E)   *Greed, Harvest, Limelight*

PrepTestJun07 Sec1 Qs6–10

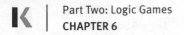

These explanations refer to questions that begin on page 358.

ANSWERS AND EXPLANATIONS

Sequencing

Singing Competition

Step 1: Overview

Situation: Singers being scheduled in a singing competition

Entities: Seven singers (Jamie, Ken, Lalitha, Maya, Norton, Olive, and Patrick)

Action: Strict Sequencing. The word *scheduled* in the overview indicates sequencing. A quick glance at the rules shows a couple of rules about specific slot numbers and a rule about an entity "immediately after" another one. That indicates Strict Sequencing.

Limitations: Each singer is singing exactly once and each slot in the schedule is occupied by only one singer. This is a classic one-to-one sequencing.

Step 2: Sketch

Begin by writing down your list of entities and creating the standard sketch for Strict Sequencing:

$$J K L M N O P$$

$$\overline{\quad 1 \quad} \ \overline{\quad 2 \quad} \ \overline{\quad 3 \quad} \ \overline{\quad 4 \quad} \ \overline{\quad 5 \quad} \ \overline{\quad 6 \quad} \ \overline{\quad 7 \quad}$$

Step 3: Rules

Rule 1 indicates a Block. Draw it next to or underneath the sketch.

$$\boxed{K\ J}$$

Because Jamie is "immediately after" Ken, draw the entities close together and put a box around them. Also, be careful and precise when interpreting rules: Although Jamie appears in the sentence before Ken, the language of the rule indicates he actually comes *after* Ken.

Rule 2 also gives another Block but it is looser because it is unknown how many other entities intervene between Maya and Patrick. When you don't

know how far apart two entities are, use an ellipsis to represent that uncertainty:

$$M \ . \ . \ . \ P$$

Rule 3 provides some Formal Logic. "Only if" is a very common construction and it always signals the necessary condition, which comes after the arrow. Lalitha performs third only if Norton performs fifth; so if Lalitha is third Norton is for sure fifth:

$$\frac{L}{3} \ \rightarrow \ \frac{N}{5}$$

Draw that along with the contrapositive (to contrapose, reverse, and negate the terms):

$$\sim\!\frac{N}{5} \ \rightarrow \ \sim\!\frac{L}{3}$$

Rule 4 tells you that if Patrick doesn't perform second, he will perform fifth. Forming the contrapositive of that rule—if Patrick does not perform fifth, then he will perform second—shows that this rule simply means that Patrick will always be either second or fifth, rather than drawing this off to the side, build it right into the sketch by putting an arrow from P to the second and fifth slots.

Step 4: Deductions

You've already made one deduction based on the last rule. In review: The rule says: "If Patrick isn't second, he's fifth . . . and if he isn't fifth, he's second, so he's always second or fifth." When you know an entity is limited to one of only two slots, build that right into the sketch.

You can also make some standard sequencing deductions from the Blocks. Rule 1's Block of KJ means that Jamie can't be first and Ken can't be last. Rule 2's Block of M . . . P means that Patrick can't be first (although you already know from Rule 4 that Patrick is always second or fifth) and that Maya can't be last. Whenever you have sequencing Blocks, consider making deductions about who can't go where on the edges or endpoints of the sketch, and if possible work your way in and add these to the sketch. You could also do this immediately after noting the rule during Step 3.

An additional deduction to observe is that Patrick is a Duplicated Entity between Rules 2 and 4. (For example, if Patrick is second, from Rule 4 you also

These explanations refer to questions that begin on page 358.

Part Two: Logic Games
Logic Games Practice

know that Maya is first, from Rule 2.) Finally, note that Olive is a Floater by marking the roster of entities with an asterisk above "O."

The final Master Sketch should look similar to this:

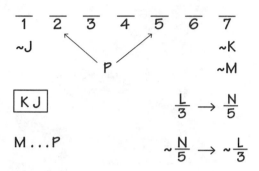

Step 5: Questions

1. (A) Acceptability ★☆☆☆

As with any other Acceptability question, go through the rules one by one and look for any choices that violate a rule. **(D)** breaks Rule 1 because Jamie is not *immediately* after Ken. **(B)** violates Rule 2 because it has Patrick performing sometime *before* Maya. **(E)** breaks Rule 3 because it has Lalitha third, but Norton is not fifth. And **(C)** breaks Rule 4 because Patrick is neither second nor fifth (he's sixth).

2. (B) "If" / Must Be True ★☆☆☆

Draw a new sketch placing Lalitha in the third position, and then consult the Master Sketch and surrounding area for information about Lalitha (or the third slot). By Rule 3, if Lalitha is third, then Norton is fifth. Include that in your sketch. Although you don't see any more info about Norton in the sketch, you do see information about the fifth position—Patrick is either in the fifth or the second position. Because you've placed Norton fifth, this must mean that Patrick is now second. Patrick is a Duplicated Entity—scanning for more information about Patrick, you see that he is involved in the M . . . P Block, which now must mean that M is first. Now the only open positions are the fourth, sixth, and seventh spots. Think about your KJ Block at this point—it must go into the sixth and seventh positions, leaving Olive in the fourth position, and making **(B)** the correct answer.

$$\frac{M}{1} \quad \frac{P}{2} \quad \frac{L}{3} \quad \frac{O}{4} \quad \frac{N}{5} \quad \frac{K}{6} \quad \frac{J}{7}$$

Here, you were able to place all the entities in this "If" question—that is fairly unusual though.

3. (C) "If" / Could Be True ★★☆☆

Because this is another "If" question, draw another sketch, placing Norton in the fifth position. Only Rule 3 discusses Norton. If Lalitha is third, then Norton is fifth. However, this does *not* mean that the reverse is true. Knowing that Norton is fifth doesn't tell you anything about where Lalitha is. However, there is information about the fifth position—Rule 4 says Patrick has to be either fifth or second. Because Norton is fifth, this must mean Patrick is second. And because Patrick duplicates in Rule 2, that means Maya is now first.

$$\frac{M}{1} \quad \frac{P}{2} \quad \frac{}{3} \quad \frac{}{4} \quad \frac{N}{5} \quad \frac{}{6} \quad \frac{}{7}$$

Because this question is asking for what "could be true" the wrong answers will all be things that *must be* false—as you evaluate each answer choice, the only question you should be asking yourself is: Could this be true or must it be false? Approaching the answer choices, **(A)** must be false because if Jamie is sixth, Ken would have to be fifth as Jamie is a member of the KJ Block. **(B)** also must be false because Patrick—not Ken—is second. **(C)** could be true and is, therefore, the correct answer. Essentially this question rewards those who do not misinterpret the Formal Logic of Rule 3. For the record, **(D)** and **(E)** must be false because Maya is definitely first.

4. (E) "If" / Could Be True ★☆☆☆

Make a new sketch and place Maya in the second position. That means Patrick must be fifth (Rule 4). If Patrick is fifth, Norton isn't, and so Lalitha can't be third (Rule 3). As for the KJ Block, it can only go third and fourth or else at the end:

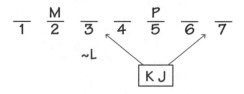

Because the question is asking for what "could be true" the wrong answers will all be things that can't

These explanations refer to questions that begin on page 359.

be true—things that must be false. **(A)** must be false because if Jamie were sixth, Ken would have to be fifth. **(B)** must be false because if Ken were fourth, Jamie would have to be fifth. **(C)** must be false because if Lalitha were third, Norton would have to be fifth. **(D)** must be false because Norton can't be fifth. **(E)** could be true because Olive—the Floater—could be fourth. Note that answer choices containing Floaters are *more likely* to be correct in questions asking for what "could be true" or "could be false."

5. (A) "If" / Must Be False (CANNOT Be True) ★★☆☆

In this "If" question, you are given a new Block. Begin by drawing it and then seeing if you can expand it using the rules in the game. Jamie is now immediately before Lalitha, and per Rule 1, Jamie is also a member of the KJ Block. Accordingly, write down the more expanded Block.

$$\boxed{\text{KJL}}$$

Examining the choices against that Block and the rest of the information: **(A)** places Jamie second. If Jamie were second, however, according to the expanded Block, Lalitha would be third . . . which means Norton would be fifth by Rule 3. However, because Patrick can only ever be second or fifth, this would leave no place at all for Patrick to go.

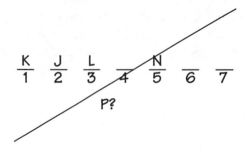

Because **(A)** *cannot* happen, it is correct, and there is no need to check the rest of the choices. **(B)**, **(C)**, **(D)**, and **(E)** all provide spots where Jamie *could* go.

These explanations refer to questions that begin on page 360.

Part Two: Logic Games
Logic Games Practice

K

Cruise Line Voyages

Step 1: Overview

Situation: A cruise line making voyages

Entities: Four destinations (Guadeloupe, Jamaica, Martinique, and Trinidad)

Action: Strict Sequencing. Determine the order in which the cruise will go to each destination. There are rules about specific weeks, so this is Strict Sequencing.

Limitations: There are seven weeklong voyages, one each week, each to only one of the destinations. Each destination will be scheduled at least once. With seven weeks and only four destinations, at least one of the destinations will be used more than once.

Step 2: Sketch

List the destinations by initial and set up a standard Strict Sequencing sketch with seven numbered spaces.

$$G\ J\ M\ T$$

$$\underline{\quad}\ \underline{\quad}\ \underline{\quad}\ \underline{\quad}\ \underline{\quad}\ \underline{\quad}\ \underline{\quad}$$
$$1\quad 2\quad 3\quad 4\quad 5\quad 6\quad 7$$

Step 3: Rules

Rule 1 eliminates a possibility: Jamaica isn't the destination in Week 4. Write "~J" under week 4.

Rule 2 establishes Trinidad at week 7. Simply draw a "T" in the last slot. Keep in mind that destinations can be duplicated, so this doesn't have to be the only week the cruise goes to Trinidad.

Rule 3 is a bit more complicated. The ship makes exactly two voyages to Martinique, and at least one voyage to Guadeloupe is made in between those voyages. There are really two parts to this rule. Start by adding a second "M" to the list of entities or putting "x2" above it (keeping track of Numbers is often crucial). Then, shorthand the sequence of having at least one voyage to Guadeloupe between those Martinique voyages:

$$\overset{\text{x2}}{G\ J\ M\ T}$$

$$\underline{\quad}\ \underline{\quad}\ \underline{\quad}\ \underline{\quad}\ \underline{\quad}\ \underline{\quad}\ \overset{T}{\underline{\quad}}$$
$$1\quad 2\quad 3\quad 4\quad 5\quad 6\quad 7$$
$$\underset{\sim J}{}$$

$$M...G...M$$

Rule 4 can easily be mistranslated. *Any* time the cruise goes to Jamaica, it must have gone to Guadeloupe the preceding week. This is Formal Logic:

$$J \rightarrow \underline{G}\ \underline{J}$$

Note that this does *not* mean that the cruise must go to Jamaica immediately after every time it goes to Guadeloupe. If it goes to Guadeloupe one week, then it *can* go to Jamaica the next week—but it doesn't have to. However, if it goes to Jamaica one week, then it *must* go to Guadeloupe the previous week.

The contrapositive is a bit complex, but consider what would trigger it: If the cruise ship does *not* go to Guadeloupe one week, then it *cannot* go to Jamaica the following week. Phrased affirmatively, if the cruise ship goes to Jamaica, Martinique, or Trinidad then it doesn't go to Jamaica the following week.

$$\overline{\sim G} \rightarrow \overline{\sim G}\ \overline{\sim J}$$
$$\text{or}$$
$$\underline{J/M/T} \rightarrow \underline{J/M/T}\ \underset{\sim J}{\underline{\quad}}$$

Rule 5 indicates that no destination can be used two weeks in a row. Simply note this in shorthand next to the sketch (e.g., "Never consecutive" or "Never GG, JJ, MM, TT").

Step 4: Deductions

Again, be careful about combining Rules 3 and 4. While the cruise *can* make a voyage to Jamaica the week after its trip to Guadeloupe, it does not have to. It could make a trip to Jamaica at another time and make a second trip to Guadeloupe the week before that. Similarly, even though Jamaica cannot be the destination during week 4 (Rule 1), Guadeloupe can still be the destination during week 3 without violating Rule 4.

K | Part Two: Logic Games
CHAPTER 6

These explanations refer to questions that begin on page 360.

However, there are two quick deductions that can be made. First, any voyage to Jamaica must have a voyage to Guadeloupe before it (Rule 4), so Jamaica cannot be the first destination. Also, with Trinidad established as the seventh voyage, it cannot also be sixth (Rule 5). Your final Master Sketch should look something like this:

x2
G J M T

| T |
| 1 | 2 | 3 | 4 | 5 | 6 | 7 |
| ~J | | | ~J | | ~T | |

M...G...M   NEVER

J → $\underline{G}$ J   GG
                         JJ
$\overline{~G}$ → $\overline{~G}$ $\overline{~J}$ MM
                         TT

Step 5: Questions

6. (A) Acceptability ★☆☆☆

The question set starts with a typical Acceptability question. Go through the rules one at a time, and eliminate answers that violate them. Rule 1 states that Jamaica cannot be fourth, which eliminates **(D)**. Rule 2 establishes Trinidad in week 7, which eliminates **(E)**. Rule 3 states that there must be a voyage to Guadeloupe in between voyages to Martinique, which eliminates **(B)**. Rule 4 states that Guadeloupe must precede *any* voyage to Jamaica. The first voyage in **(C)** is to Jamaica, with no voyage to Guadeloupe before it. That answer is eliminated, leaving **(A)** as the correct answer.

7. (A) Must Be False (CANNOT Be True) ★☆☆☆

The correct answer will be the one that must be false. The four wrong answers could be true.

Trinidad is already the seventh stop. If Trinidad were sixth, that would violate Rule 5. That immediately means **(A)** cannot be true, and is thus the correct answer. The remaining answers are all possible and can be verified like so:

(B) could be true based on this sequence:

| M | G | J | T | M | G | T |
| 1 | 2 | 3 | 4 | 5 | 6 | 7 |

(C) and **(D)** both could be true per this sketch:

| M | G | J | M | G | J | T |
| 1 | 2 | 3 | 4 | 5 | 6 | 7 |

(E) also could be true if the cruise ship makes its voyages in this order:

| G | J | G | M | G | M | T |
| 1 | 2 | 3 | 4 | 5 | 6 | 7 |

8. (D) "If" / Could Be True ★★☆☆

For this question, Trinidad will be the destination in week 5. That means Jamaica cannot be the destination in week 6 (Rule 4). Otherwise, there would be no room for Guadeloupe in the preceding week.

With weeks 5 and 7 filled, and Jamaica unable to be the destination in weeks 1, 4, or 6, that leaves two options: Jamaica in week 2 or week 3, either with Guadeloupe in the previous week.

If Jamaica was the destination for week 2, Guadeloupe would be the destination for week 1. To satisfy Rule 3, the two voyages to Martinique would have to be in weeks 3 and 6, with Guadeloupe being the destination in week 4.

| G | J | M | G | T | M | T |
| 1 | 2 | 3 | 4 | 5 | 6 | 7 |

If Jamaica was the destination for week 3, Guadeloupe would be the destination for week 2. To satisfy Rule 3, the two voyages to Martinique would have to be in weeks 1 and 4 or weeks 1 and 6. (They couldn't be weeks 4 and 6, because there wouldn't be a voyage to Guadeloupe in between.)

M	G	J		T		T
1	2	3	4	5	6	7
			~J	M	~J	
			~T		~T	

Consider both options; only **(D)** is possible (in the second option), making that the correct answer.

These explanations refer to questions that begin on page 361.

Part Two: Logic Games
Logic Games Practice K

9. (E) "If" / Must Be True ★★☆☆

For this question, Guadeloupe will be the voyage in week 1, and Jamaica will be the voyage in week 5. With Jamaica as the destination in week 5, Guadeloupe must be the destination in week 4 (Rule 4). To satisfy Rule 3, the two voyages to Martinique would have to be weeks 2 and 6 or weeks 3 and 6. Either way, one of its voyages must be the destination in week 6:

$$\frac{G}{1} \quad \frac{\ }{2} \quad \frac{\ }{3} \quad \frac{G}{4} \quad \frac{J}{5} \quad \frac{M}{6} \quad \frac{T}{7}$$
$$\overset{\nwarrow \quad \nearrow}{M}$$

The question is looking for the one answer that must be true. That makes **(E)** the correct answer. Note that **(A)** is a check to see if people mistakenly translated Rule 4 as requiring that any trip to Guadeloupe must be followed by a trip to Jamaica. That does not have to be the case, which is why **(A)** is possible, but not a *must* be true.

10. (A) "If" / Must Be True ★★☆☆

This question establishes Guadeloupe in week 1 and Trinidad in week 2. Rule 2 has already placed Trinidad in Week 7. To satisfy Rule 3, the remaining four slots need two voyages to Martinique with a trip to Guadeloupe in between. However, there also still needs to be a voyage to Jamaica (Limitations), which must be preceded immediately by a voyage to Guadeloupe. There's only one way to do both of those things and follow all the rules: The voyages to Martinique must be in weeks 3 and 6, with Jamaica in week 5 preceded by Guadeloupe in Week 4:

$$\frac{G}{1} \quad \frac{T}{2} \quad \frac{M}{3} \quad \frac{G}{4} \quad \frac{J}{5} \quad \frac{M}{6} \quad \frac{T}{7}$$

The question is asking for something that must be true. That makes **(A)** the correct answer.

11. (A) "If" / Could Be True ★★☆☆

For this question, one voyage to Martinique will be in week 3. However, it's not clear whether that's the first or second voyage to Martinique.

$$\frac{\ }{1} \quad \frac{\ }{2} \quad \frac{M}{3} \quad \frac{\ }{4} \quad \frac{\ }{5} \quad \frac{\ }{6} \quad \frac{T}{7}$$

Limited Options are not a bad idea, but there are three possible outcomes: The remaining voyage to Martinique could be in week 1, 5, or 6. That's a lot to draw.

Instead, consider the original rules and the effect of placing Martinique in week 3. The question is asking specifically about weeks 4 and 5. By Rule 1, Jamaica cannot be in week 4. That eliminates **(B)**. By Rule 3, there must a voyage to Guadeloupe in between the voyages to Martinique. That eliminates **(E)**, which would put a trip to Trinidad in between instead. By Rule 4, Jamaica must be preceded immediately by Guadeloupe. That eliminates **(D)**. By Rule 5, Martinique couldn't be the destination in week 4 here, so that eliminates **(C)**, leaving **(A)** as the correct answer.

It's worth noting that the outcome described in **(A)** was already drawn out in the first option of the third question of the set. Using previous work would have led to an immediate answer without having to test each answer individually.

12. (D) Must Be True ★★★★

If the correct answer must be true, then all of the wrong answer choices could be false.

The first two answer choices define specific days for visits to Guadalupe and Martinique. Voyages to Guadeloupe only have to be between voyages to Martinique and before trips to Jamaica. If the first two destinations were Martinique and Trinidad, there would still be plenty of room for Guadeloupe elsewhere:

$$\frac{M}{1} \quad \frac{T}{2} \quad \frac{G}{3} \quad \frac{M}{4} \quad \frac{G}{5} \quad \frac{J}{6} \quad \frac{T}{7}$$

This shows that Guadeloupe does not have to be one of the first two destinations, which eliminates **(A)**. It also shows that Martinique does not have to be in week 2 or week 3. So, it also eliminates **(B)**.

The remaining choices limit the number of voyages to three destinations. They establish a maximum of two voyages to Guadeloupe, Jamaica, and Trinidad, respectively.

Guadeloupe does not have to be limited to two voyages. It can be the destination three times, in weeks 1, 3, and 5, as so:

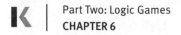

Part Two: Logic Games

CHAPTER 6

These explanations refer to questions that begin on page 361.

$$\frac{G}{1} \quad \frac{M}{2} \quad \frac{G}{3} \quad \frac{M}{4} \quad \frac{G}{5} \quad \frac{J}{6} \quad \frac{T}{7}$$

Because there can be more than two voyages to Guadeloupe, **(C)** could be false and can be eliminated.

However, the numbers of the game will certainly limit Jamaica. For each voyage to Jamaica, the cruise must also stop at Guadeloupe. If there were three voyages to Jamaica, there would also be three voyages to Guadeloupe. That would take up six of the seven weeks, and that doesn't include the two voyages to Martinique or the one to Trinidad. It's impossible to have three voyages to Jamaica. There *must* be no more than two voyages, which makes **(D)** the correct answer. For the record, there can be three trips to Trinidad, as shown here:

$$\frac{T}{1} \quad \frac{M}{2} \quad \frac{T}{3} \quad \frac{G}{4} \quad \frac{J}{5} \quad \frac{M}{6} \quad \frac{T}{7}$$

Because there can be *more* than two voyages to Trinidad, **(E)** could be false, and can be eliminated.

These explanations refer to questions that begin on page 362.

Part Two: Logic Games
Logic Games Practice

K

Product Codes

Step 1: Overview

Situation: A company at which an employee is generating product codes

Entities: The entities aren't provided until Rule 1. They are the digits in the codes: 0, 1, 2, 3, and 4.

Action: Strict Sequencing. Determine the order of the digits in each product code. There are rules about which specific slots to place the digits in, so this is Strict Sequencing rather than Loose Sequencing.

Limitations: Each code is a five-digit code. No further limitations are placed until the rules.

Step 2: Sketch

Draw a basic Strict Sequencing sketch with slots and numbers. Just be careful not to confuse the numbers of the slots with the digits going into the code! (In fact, with only five slots, it may be prudent not to number the slots to avoid such confusion.)

0 1 2 3 4

__ __ __ __ __

Step 3: Rules

Rule 1 provides the entities: 0, 1, 2, 3, and 4.

Rule 2 is typically found as a limitation in the overview: Each digit can only be used once. Because each code has five digits and there are only five digits to use, that makes this a standard one-to-one Strict Sequencing game.

Rule 3 offers a little math: The second digit must be double the first digit. A quick glance at the available digits shows only two possible outcomes: The first digit is 1 and the second digit is 2, or the first digit is 2 and the second digit is 4. Without question, this should form the basis of Limited Options:

I) __1__ __2__ __ __ __

II) __2__ __4__ __ __ __

Rule 4 offers a little more math: The third digit must be less than the fifth digit. Unlike the previous rule,

there are too many possibilities to draw them all out, so just create some shorthand for this: 3rd < 5th. (Note: You could also write out "third" and "fifth" because the entities are numbers, and this will help avoid confusion. As long as you avoid using simple digits, it should be clear.)

3rd < 5th

Step 4: Deductions

The Limited Options set up by Rule 3 are the biggest deduction to make. Otherwise, there's only one other rule to consider: Rule 4. No absolute deduction can be made, but keep track of which digits remain to be placed in each option: 0, 3, 4 in the first option, and 0, 1, 3 in the second option. Because the third digit has to be smaller than the fifth digit, the fifth digit can't be the smallest remaining digit (0) in either option. Furthermore, the third digit cannot be the largest remaining digit in either option (i.e., it can't be 4 in the first option, and it can't be 3 in the second option).

0 1 2 3 4

I) __1__ __2__ __0/3__ ___ __3/4__

II) __2__ __4__ __0/1__ ___ __1/3__

3rd < 5th

Step 5: Questions

13. (A) "If" / Must Be True ★★★★

If the last digit of the code is 1, the first two digits can only be 2 and 4, respectively (by Rule 3)—which is the second option. By Rule 4, the third digit must be less than the fifth digit, which is now 1. That makes 0 the third digit, which leaves 3 as the fourth digit:

II) __2__ __4__ __0__ __3__ __1__

In that case, only **(A)** is true, making it the correct answer.

14. (C) Must Be True ★★★★

The correct answer here must be true no matter what. The four wrong answers could all be false.

K | Part Two: Logic Games
CHAPTER 6

These explanations refer to questions that begin on page 363.

1 certainly comes before 2 in the first option, but 1 would have to come *after* 2 in the second option (as also seen in the sketch for the first question of the set). That eliminates **(A)**.

1 has to come before 3 in the first option, but could come after 3 in the second option. (Again, this is seen in the sketch for the first question of the set.) That eliminates **(B)**.

By the two options set up by Rule 3, the digit 2 is always either first or second. If it's second then the first digit must be 1. So, in either case, the digit 2 must come before the digit 3. That makes **(C)** the correct answer.

For the record:

3 could be the last digit in either option, so it doesn't have to come before anything. That eliminates **(D)**. Similarly, 4 could be the last digit in the first option, so it doesn't have to come before 3. That eliminates **(E)**. Both of these outcomes will be drawn in the sketches for the next question of the set.

It's important to note that test takers who draw out the sketches for the first and third questions of the set before tackling this question will be rewarded with enough information to eliminate all four wrong answers.

15. (C) "If" / Must Be True ★★☆☆

For this question, the third digit cannot be 0. This is possible in either option. The only rule to consider is Rule 4: The third digit is smaller than the fifth digit. The only digits left to place in the first option are 0, 3, and 4. 0 cannot be third, so the third and fifth digits must be 3 and 4, respectively, leaving 0 to be the fourth digit. The digits left to place in the second option are 0, 1, and 3. 0 cannot be third, so the third and fifth digits must be 1 and 3, respectively, leaving 0 to be the fourth digit:

$$\text{I)} \quad \underline{1} \quad \underline{2} \quad \underline{3} \quad \underline{0} \quad \underline{4}$$

$$\text{II)} \quad \underline{2} \quad \underline{4} \quad \underline{1} \quad \underline{0} \quad \underline{3}$$

In both options, the fourth digit is 0. That makes **(C)** the correct answer.

16. (E) Could Be True EXCEPT ★★★★

The correct answer to this question will be a pair of digits that cannot be third and fourth, respectively. The remaining pairs could all be third and fourth in at least one of the options.

The correct answer will violate a rule somehow. That rule will probably be Rule 4, because this question deals with the third digit of the code, and Rule 4 is the only one that affects that digit directly. If the third digit is 3, the fifth digit would have to be 4. In that case, 4 couldn't be the fourth digit, which means **(E)** is impossible, making that the correct answer.

For the record, previous sketches help out a lot. The sketch for the first question of the set shows that the third and fourth digits, respectively, could be 0 and 3, which eliminates **(B)**. The sketches for the third question of the set show that the third and fourth digits, respectively, could be 3 and 0, or 1 and 0. That eliminates **(C)** and **(D)**.

If the third digit were 0, then the fifth digit could be anything that hasn't already been placed (by Rule 4). In that case, the fourth digit could also be anything. So, the third and fourth digits could be 0 and 1, respectively, like so:

$$\text{II)} \quad \underline{2} \quad \underline{4} \quad \underline{0} \quad \underline{1} \quad \underline{3}$$

That eliminates **(A)**.

17. (E) Must Be True ★★☆☆

The correct answer to this question must be true. The remaining four answers are all false or could be false. Once again, previous sketches will help eliminate wrong answers most efficiently here.

The first sketch for the third question of the set (1 2 3 0 4) shows two digits between 0 and 1. There doesn't have to be exactly one digit in between, so that eliminates **(A)**.

The sketch for the first question of the set (2 4 0 3 1) shows three digits between 1 and 2, and the first sketch for the third question in the set has no spaces between 1 and 2. There does not have to be exactly one digit in between, so that eliminates **(B)**.

These explanations refer to questions that begin on page 363.

Part Two: Logic Games
Logic Games Practice | K

No previous work is available for **(C)**. To test whether **(C)** could be false, try to determine if there could be more than two digits between 1 and 3. The only way that can happen is if 1 and 3 are at opposite ends of the code. That could happen in the first option, which has 2 as the second digit (Rule 3). That leaves 0 and 4 for the remaining slots. By Rule 4 (the third digit is smaller than the fifth digit), the third digit would be 0, leaving 4 for the fourth digit:

I) <u>1</u> <u>2</u> <u>0</u> <u>4</u> <u>3</u>

This is acceptable, so there doesn't have to be a maximum of two digits between 1 and 3. That eliminates **(C)**.

(D), like **(A)** and **(B)**, can be eliminated using previous work. The second sketch for the third question of the set (2 4 1 0 3) shows three digits between 2 and 3. There could be more than two digits in between, so that eliminates **(D)**.

By elimination, that leaves **(E)** as the correct answer. For the record, the Limited Options show why it must be true. In the first option, 2 is the second digit. The farthest away 4 can be placed is the fifth digit, which puts only two digits in between 2 and 4. In the second option, 2 and 4 are next to each other. So, there cannot be more than two digits between 2 and 4 in any code.

EXPLANATIONS

Part Two: Logic Games
CHAPTER 6

These explanations refer to questions that begin on page 364.

Selection

Nine Treatments
Step 1: Overview

Situation: A doctor prescribing treatments

Entities: Nine different treatments divided into three subcategories (three antibiotics—F, G, and H; three diets—M, N, and O; three physical therapies—U, V, and W)

Action: Selection. Exactly five treatments will be selected from the nine available.

Limitations: It is not known which treatments must, could, or cannot be prescribed by the doctor. Also, keep an eye on which treatments must, could, or cannot be prescribed with which other treatments.

Step 2: Sketch

ANTI	diet	PHYS
FGH	mno	UVW

Step 3: Rules

Rule 1 prohibits all three antibiotics from being chosen. Of F, G, and H, only a maximum of two can be prescribed. Write "2 MAX" over the antibiotics.

Rule 2 requires that exactly one of M, N, and O be selected. Write "Exactly 1" over the diets. Pay attention to your numbers. Even if all three physical therapies and exactly one diet are selected, you still need one antibiotic to finish out the requirement of five treatments. Change the note above antibiotics to "1–2."

Rule 3 provides some Formal Logic; translate and contrapose it:

$$\sim o \rightarrow \sim F$$
$$F \rightarrow o$$

Rule 4 indicates W and F cannot both be selected. Writing down "Never WF" is a good reminder of this rule.

Rule 5 warrants some caution. Start by looking for what triggers a result, which is if N and U are

prescribed. Thus, if N and U are selected, the necessary outcome is that G cannot be selected. Similarly, if G is selected, then either N is not selected or U is not selected.

$$n \text{ AND } U \rightarrow \sim G$$
$$G \rightarrow \sim n \text{ OR } \sim U$$

Rule 6 brings in another common Formal Logic term: *unless*. V cannot be prescribed unless both H and M are prescribed, which means that if V is prescribed, then both H and M must be prescribed. The contrapositive follows that if either H or M is not prescribed, then V cannot be prescribed either.

$$V \rightarrow H \text{ AND } m$$
$$\sim H \text{ OR } \sim m \rightarrow \sim V$$

Step 4: Deductions

Examine the numbers that govern the game. One or two antibiotics (F G H) will be selected (Rule 1 and Rule 2), and exactly one diet (M N O) will be selected (Rule 2). Because five treatments will be selected overall, at least two, and maybe three, of the physical therapies (U V W) must be selected. Write "2–3" over the physical therapies column.

It may be desirable to take this further. Limited Options on whether the ratio is "1:1:3" or "2:1:2." If all three physical therapies are selected (which includes V), then the other two treatments selected must be H and M (Rule 6).

$$\text{I) } \begin{array}{c|c|c} 1 & 1 & 3 \\ \text{ANTI} & \text{diet} & \text{PHYS} \\ \hline FG\textcircled{H} & \textcircled{m}n\text{\o} & \textcircled{U}\textcircled{V}\textcircled{W} \end{array}$$

If two physical therapies are selected, then two antibiotics and one diet must be selected.

When you attempt to choose two antibiotics in Option II, you soon see that F faces strong restrictions from the rules. Selecting F as one of the antibiotics would mean selecting O as the dietary regime (Rule 3) and rejecting W as one of the physical therapies (Rule 4). Since there can be only one dietary regime (Rule 2), selecting O, means rejecting M and N. Whenever M is

These explanations refer to questions that begin on page 364.

Part Two: Logic Games
Logic Games Practice

K

not the dietary regime, V cannot be selected among the physical therapies (Rule 6). Now, the only available physical therapy available is U.

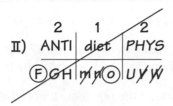

This illustrates that F cannot be among the antibiotics in Option II. Were F selected, there would be no way to select two physical therapies.

Since F cannot be the antibiotic in Option II, G and H must be.

$$\begin{array}{c|c|c} 2 & 1 & 2 \\ \text{II)} \quad \text{ANTI} & \text{diet} & \text{PHYS} \\ \hline \not{F}\,\text{G}\,\text{H} & \text{mno} & \text{UVW} \end{array}$$

Now that G is selected, either N or U (or both) must be rejected (Rule 5). Consider the implications of that deduction. If U is selected, then N must be rejected. On the other hand, if U is rejected, then the two physical therapies selected will be V and W. Selecting V requires selecting M as the one dietary regime (Rule 6), and N and O are both rejected. So, N will never be the dietary regime in Option II.

$$\begin{array}{c|c|c} 2 & 1 & 2 \\ \text{ANTI} & \text{diet} & \text{PHYS} \\ \hline \not{F}\,\text{G}\,\text{H} & \text{m}\not{n}\,\text{o} & \text{UVW} \end{array}$$

Note that you have now eliminated F and N in both options. Neither of these treatments can ever be selected in the game.

However powerful the previous deductions concerning F and N are, the questions are still manageable without them. Do not think that the game required those deductions to be approached successfully.

Step 5: Questions

18. (E) Acceptability   ★★★☆

This is an Acceptability question because the correct answer is a combination of treatments that could be selected. Apply the rules to eliminate choices. Rule

1 states that F, G, and H cannot all be selected, so cross out **(A)**. More than one diet cannot be selected (Rule 2), so cross out **(B)** and **(C)**. Rules 3 and 4 do not eliminate any further choices, but Rule 5 states that G, N, and U cannot all be selected, which allows you to cross out **(D)**. The correct answer is **(E)**. By the way, if you made the deduction that F may never be selected, you could eliminate **(A)**, **(B)**, and **(C)** for that reason alone. Likewise, you can eliminate **(D)** once you know that N may never be selected.

19. (E) Partial Acceptability   ★★☆☆

To answer this Partial Acceptability question, first eliminate choices that violate the rules. You cannot have F, G, and H all selected (Rule 1). Cross out **(A)**. Skip Rules 2 and 3 for now, as they directly involve diets. Rule 4 forbids W and F from being prescribed together, so cross out **(C)**. Rule 5 involves a diet. Rule 6 states that if V is selected, then both H and M must be selected. The remaining choices all have V selected, but **(B)** and **(D)** would require you to add two more treatments to the four shown in each choice, giving you six treatments total. Because you must select exactly five treatments, cross out **(B)** and **(D)**. That leaves **(E)** as the correct answer. If you made the deduction that F may never be selected, you can eliminate **(A)**, **(B)**, and **(C)** for that reason alone.

20. (E) "If" / Must Be True   ★★★★

This new "If" question asks which two treatments must be prescribed if O is prescribed. Use the answer to the Acceptability question to eliminate answers in a "must be true" question such as this one. The correct answer to the Acceptability question ("GHOUW") contains treatment O without F, V, M, or N, so none of those are necessary. **(A)** contains F, **(B)** and **(D)** contain V, and **(C)** lists N, so those can all be eliminated. **(E)** is correct.

If you choose to draw a mini sketch, make deductions systematically. If O is prescribed, that must be in Option II and thus a "2:1:2" ratio. Also, prescribing O means that both M and N are out (Rule 2). Because M is out, V is out (contrapositive of Rule 6). With V out, you need the other two physical therapies prescribed, U and W:

$$\begin{array}{c|c|c} 2 & 1 & 2 \\ \text{ANTI} & \text{diet} & \text{PHYS} \\ \hline \not{F}\,\text{G}\,\text{H} & \text{m}\not{n}\,\text{O} & \text{U}\,\not{V}\,\text{W} \end{array}$$

K | Part Two: Logic Games
CHAPTER 6

These explanations refer to questions that begin on page 365.

That sketch demonstrates that **(E)** is only choice in which both entities must be selected whenever O is selected.

21. (E) "If" / Could Be True ★★★★

This new "If" question asks for two treatments that can be prescribed if G is prescribed. The four wrong answer choices are all pairs of treatments that can never be prescribed with G.

Redraw the sketch. Prescribing G means that you must be in Option II because the sole antibiotic prescribed in Option I is H. Apart from that there are no immediately apparent deductions.

$$
\begin{array}{c|c|c}
2 & 1 & 2 \\
\text{ANTI} & \textit{diet} & \textit{PHYS}
\end{array}
$$

F̶ G⃝ H⃝ | m n̶ o | U V W

If you made the deductions that F and N may never be selected, you can quickly eliminate **(A)**, **(B)**, and **(C)**. Even if you didn't make those deductions, you can determine that choices **(A)** and **(B)** run afoul of Rules 2 and 3: If F were selected, then the one dietary regime would have to be O, not M or N. Similarly, **(C)** and **(D)** both break Rules 2 and 6: Whenever V is selected, the one dietary regime must be M, not N or O. That leaves **(E)** as the correct answer. Prescribing G, V, and W means that both H and M must be selected (Rule 6).

$$
\begin{array}{c|c|c}
2 & 1 & 2 \\
\text{ANTI} & \textit{diet} & \textit{PHYS}
\end{array}
$$

F̶ G⃝ H⃝ | m⃝ n̶ o̶ | U V⃝ W⃝

22. (D) Could Be True ★★★★

This question asks for three out of the five treatments that can be prescribed. Use your previous work. If you scanned the answer choices looking at your previous work, you might have noticed that the arrangement in **(E)**—G, V, and W—was an acceptable grouping in the previous question's correct answer.

You could eliminate the wrong choices one by one as well. **(A)** has F and M selected together, but were F selected, the one dietary regime would have to be O (Rule 3), not M. Cross out **(A)**. **(B)** has F and W selected together, in direct violation of Rule 4. Cross out **(B)**. **(C)** and **(E)** both have V and N selected together, but when

V is selected, the one dietary regime must be M (Rule 6), not N or O. Cross out both **(C)** nor **(E)**. That leaves only **(D)**, the correct answer.

23. (C) Must Be False (CANNOT Be True) ★★★☆

If you made the big deduction earlier that N cannot be prescribed, then that leads you directly to **(C)**.

Even if you missed the big deduction earlier, using previous work makes this question very manageable. Any treatment prescribed in an acceptable arrangement can be eliminated as a wrong answer choice. G, U, and W were selected in the correct answer to the Acceptability question. That eliminates **(A)**, **(D)**, and **(E)**. M had to be selected given that V was selected in the second question from this set. Cross out **(B)**. **(C)** must, therefore, be correct.

These explanations refer to questions that begin on page 366.

Part Two: Logic Games
Logic Games Practice

K

Matching/Distribution

Fellini, Hitchcock, and Kurosawa Films

Step 1: Overview

Situation: Film buffs attending exactly one of three films

Entities: Seven film buffs—Ginnie, Ian, Lianna, Marcos, Reveka, Viktor, and Yow

Action: Distribution. Each film buff goes to exactly one film. A game that allowed the film buffs to see more than one film would be considered Matching.

Limitations: Each film buff sees only one film. (The opening paragraph indicates that the films are shown one at a time, which may have suggested that this game has a sequencing element. However, neither the rules nor the questions explore this issue.) There are no restrictions on whether or not a film must be seen by at least one of the film buffs, so as of the overview, it's possible that only one or two films are seen, leaving the other film(s) empty.

Step 2: Sketch

List the entities and draw three columns (one for each of the films) to keep track of the action.

GILMRVY

Fel	Hit	Kur

Step 3: Rules

Rule 1 indicates the Hitchcock film gets twice as many film buffs as the Fellini film. With seven film buffs, there aren't that many ways to split them up so that exactly twice as many wind up at the Hitchcock film. Determine how many combinations there are. If one film buff attended the Fellini film, then two are needed at the Hitchcock film, and the remaining four would attend the Kurosawa film. Alternatively, you could have two at the Fellini, four at the Hitchcock, and one at the Kurosawa. That's it. It's either "1:2:4" or "2:4:1." You can't have three or more at the Fellini, because that would force six or more at the Hitchcock, and there are only seven film buffs in total. Therefore, the Master Sketch can immediately be altered to account for those Limited Options:

GILMRVY

I)
Fel	Hit	Kur
—	—	—
		—

II)
Fel	Hit	Kur
—	—	—
—	—	

Rule 2 and **Rule 3** are familiar Distribution rules creating impossible pairs. Ginnie and Reveka cannot see the same movie. Ian and Marcos cannot see the same movie.

NEVER | G R |

NEVER | I M |

Rule 4 provides a Block of Entities. Viktor and Yow see the same movie. Display them as a Block that must be placed together.

 | V Y |

Rule 5 gives an Established Entity. Build an L directly into the sketch in the Hitchcock column. Cross L off the list of entities.

Rule 6 can also be built directly into the sketch. Place G in the picture with arrows pointing to Fellini and Kurosawa or simply place a "~G" in the Hitchcock column.

Step 4: Deductions

The big deduction here was the "1:2:4" or "2:4:1" breakdown of the film buffs. This essentially comes straight out of Rule 1, but if you noticed it at this point, that's okay too. From here, see where you can place the VY Block. In Option I, it's obvious. The only film with two open seats is the Kurosawa. In Option II, it appears that VY might be able to go to either the Fellini or the Hitchcock film. Consider what would

EXPLANATIONS

K | Part Two: Logic Games
CHAPTER 6

These explanations refer to questions that begin on page 366.

happen if they saw the Fellini. That would make it impossible to separate Ginnie from Reveka and Ian from Marcos. One of those forbidden pairings would be forced together at the Hitchcock show.

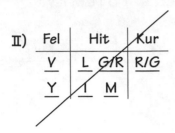

II)	Fel	Hit	Kur
	V	L G/R	R/G
	Y	I M	

Thus, in Option II, the VY block must see Hitchcock. Add V and Y to both options, and cross them off the list of entities, too.

No other deductions jump out. Ginnie is a duplicated entity (Rules 2 and 6), but for now nothing further can be determined about her placement.

GI̶L̶MR̶V̶Y̶

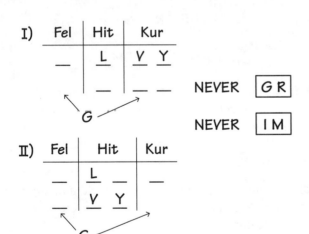

I)	Fel	Hit	Kur
	—	L	V Y
		—	— —

G →

NEVER [G R]

NEVER [I M]

II)	Fel	Hit	Kur
	—	L	—
	—	V Y	

G →

Step 5: Questions

24. (D) Partial Acceptability ★★★★

This is a Partial Acceptability question because the choices show only parts of the lineup. To eliminate some of the choices you'll need to consider what's missing.

(A) contains a straightforward violation of Rule 6. Ginnie cannot go to the Hitchcock film.

(B) can be eliminated because with Ian and Viktor at the Fellini film, Yow needs to be there, too (Rule 4), but you can't have three buffs at the Fellini film, because that would force six to attend the Hitchcock film, which

isn't possible. Also, the Limited Options from Step 4 already show that Viktor and Yow can only attend either Kurosawa or Hitchcock. If you hadn't made that deduction earlier, this question would've been an opportunity to do so.

Likewise with **(C)**, Viktor can never attend the Fellini film. That eliminates **(C)**.

In **(D)**, if Marcos, Reveka, and Viktor are at the Kurosawa film, then they are joined by Yow (Rule 4). With four buffs at the Kurosawa film (Option I), exactly one person needs to be at the Fellini film and two at the Hitchcock. Ginnie cannot go to the Hitchcock, so she must go to the Fellini film. That leaves Ian and Lianna to go to the Hitchcock.

I)	Fel	Hit	Kur
	G	I	V Y
		L	M R

This works and, thus, **(D)** is correct.

For the record, in **(E)**, if Marcos, Reveka, and Yow join Lianna at the Hitchcock film (remember, L always sees Hitchcock per Rule 5), then they're joined by Viktor (Rule 4), but that's five buffs at the Hitchcock film, which is one too many even for Option II.

25. (A) Must Be False EXCEPT ★★★☆

Each of the wrong choices must be false, so the correct answer will be the choice that could (or must) be true. From here, there's not much to do except try each choice, but the search need not be a long one. Could Reveka be the only one at the Fellini film? If she is, then you're dealing with the "1:2:4" arrangement in Option I. There, you already know that Viktor and Yow see Kurosawa, and of course Lianna sees Hitchcock. Ginnie is forbidden from seeing Hitchcock (Rule 6), so add her to the Kurosawa group. Ian and Marcos are the only buffs yet to be placed. Either could see Hitchcock or Kurosawa provided they aren't together.

I)	Fel	Hit	Kur
	R	L	V Y
		I/M	G M/I

That proves that **(A)** is possible. For the record:

These explanations refer to questions that begin on page 367.

Part Two: Logic Games
Logic Games Practice   **K**

(B) violates Rule 5. Lianna is always at the Hitchcock.
(C) violates Rule 4. Viktor and Yow are always together.
(D) and **(E)** violate Rule 1. You must have either the "1:2:4" or the "2:4:1" distribution.

26. (C) Could Be True   ★★★★

The correct answer has a possible list of all of the film buffs *not* seeing Hitchcock. So the question is really asking for an acceptable list of those film buffs seeing either Fellini or Kurosawa. This could arguably be considered a Partial Acceptability question for that reason. Regardless, first consider the number requirements from the options. A complete list of those *not* seeing Hitchcock in Option I would contain five film buffs. In Option II, such a list would need three film buffs. You could never have just two of the filmgoers outside of the Hitchcock film. Therefore, **(A)** and **(B)** are impossible. The remaining choices all include exactly three film buffs, so the question must be asking about Option II. In Option II, both Viktor and Yow *are* at the Hitchcock film, so **(D)** and **(E)** can be eliminated too.

(D) also could've been eliminated because Viktor and Yow must be together, and **(D)** has them separated. **(E)** could've also been eliminated because if Ginnie, Viktor, and Yow were the only ones not to see the Hitchcock film, then both Ian and Marcos would attend the Hitchcock film, violating Rule 3.

Regardless of how you eliminated choices, only **(C) remains**. In Option II, Lianna, Marcos, Viktor, and Yow could go together to the Hitchcock film. Ian could see Fellini along with either Ginnie or Reveka—Rule 2 keeps them apart. The other one—either Reveka or Ginnie—would be the sole attendee of Kurosawa. This choice is perfectly acceptable.

II)	Fel	Hit		Kur
	G/R	L	M	R/G
	I	V	Y	

27. (A) "If" / Must Be True   ★★★★

The question stem refers you to Option II, where only one film buff sees Kurosawa. The correct answer is something that must be true in that option. Once you're looking at Option II, it's fairly easy to see that **(A)** must be true. From the Deductions step, you determined

that Viktor and Yow must see the Hitchcock film in that scenario.

The remaining choices all refer to film buffs whose film attendance remain undetermined in Option II. Therefore, the statements in **(B)**, **(C)**, **(D)**, and **(E)** could be false.

28. (E) Must Be True   ★★★☆

This question simply rewards a careful reading and depiction of the rules. The correct answer must be true. **(E)** accurately states that Ginnie, Lianna, and Marcos cannot all be at the same film. Ginnie and Lianna can never be together, because Lianna attends the Hitchcock film (Rule 5), and Ginnie can never attend the Hitchcock film (Rule 6). Adding Marcos to the mix is just filler. For the record:

(A) could be false. Ginnie and Ian can be together at the Kurosawa in Option I or at the Fellini in Option II. **(B)** could be false. Ian and Lianna can be together at the Hitchcock film in either option. **(C)** could be false. Ian and Viktor can see Kurosawa together in Option I or Hitchcock in Option II. **(D)** could be false in Option II, where Ian, Lianna and Viktor can be together at the Hitchcock film.

29. (B) "If" / Could Be True   ★★★☆

If Viktor is with Ginnie, Yow must join them (Rule 4). That means that they must see the Kurosawa film in Option I. Ginnie never attends the Hitchcock film, so Option II doesn't warrant consideration for this question. The correct answer could be true, meaning that the four wrong answer choices must be false. Because you know that the trio created by the question stem (G, V, and Y) is at Kurosawa, you can eliminate **(A)**, **(D)**, and **(E)**.

Likewise, because Ginnie is at the Kurosawa film, Rule 2 means that Reveka won't be there. Eliminate **(C)** on that basis.

I)	Fel	Hit	Kur	
	—	L	V	Y
			G	I/M

R

EXPLANATIONS

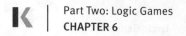

These explanations refer to questions that begin on page 367.

Only **(B)** remains. Ian could join Lianna at the Hitchcock film in this scenario, with Reveka at the Fellini and Marcos at the Kurosawa.

I)

Fel	Hit	Kur	
R	L	V	Y
	I	G	M

30. (E) Could Be True EXCEPT ★★★☆

This is another question calling for you to determine "complete and accurate" lists. This time, though, the correct answer is the one with a pair of entities that *cannot* constitute an accurate list of Fellini viewers. Note that all of the answer choices have two entities. Only in Option II could the list of Fellini viewers have two film buffs. In Option II, the Master Sketch shows Lianna, Viktor, and Yow at Hitchcock. Thus, **(E)** is impossible and correct. There's never an instance in which Viktor and Yow can see the Fellini film. Remember that if they did, one of the impossible pairings—either Ginnie and Reveka or Ian and Marcos—would be forced together at the Hitchcock show.

Any combination of one of Ginnie or Reveka along with one of Ian or Marcos is acceptable at the Fellini show in Option II. Therefore, **(A)**, **(B)**, **(C)**, and **(D)** are all wrong.

EXPLANATIONS

These explanations refer to questions that begin on page 368.

Part Two: Logic Games
Logic Games Practice **K**

Hybrid

Film Club Festival

Step 1: Overview

Situation: A film club holding a festival

Entities: Three films (*Greed*, *Harvest*, and *Limelight*) and three days (Thursday, Friday, and Saturday)

Action: Matching/Sequencing Hybrid. The game involves three days and uses ordering terms in the rules and questions (e.g., "no film shown after," "is shown first"), so there is undeniably a Sequencing component to the game. Additionally, each day can have multiple films, and each film can be shown more than once. That makes it possible to also construe this game as having a Matching aspect. So, it's a Hybrid game—matching films to the days, but also sequencing them within each day. It is also possible to perceive this as a solo action Strict Sequencing game. All of the film showings are put in sequence over the course of the three days; there's just the twist that each film can be shown on more than one day. No matter which way you choose to categorize the game, the sketch should end up centered around the sequence of the three days.

Limitations: Each film is shown at least once, but films can only be shown once on any given day. So, while some films can be shown on multiple days, they can only be shown once each day. Also, at least one film is shown each day (notice that there could be more than one). The films are shown one at a time.

Step 2: Sketch

The films will be assigned to each day. So, list the three films by initial, and then set up a table with a column for each day. Start with one slot in each day, but leave room for additional films:

G H L

Thu	Fri	Sat
—	—	—

Step 3: Rules

Rule 1 is really two rules in one: *Harvest* is shown on Thursday, and nothing is shown after *Harvest* that day. Definitely add H to Thursday. However, note that this rule allows for other movies to be shown *before* H. Close off the column below H, but be sure to leave space to add movies above it:

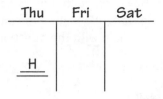

Rule 2 is a little more complex: Either *Greed* or *Limelight*, but not both, is shown on Friday. Moreover, that film is the last film shown on Friday. Similar to the previous rule, add "G/L" to Friday and close off the column below G/L, being sure to leave space to add movies above it. Also, make a note under Friday that you can never have both G and L that day.

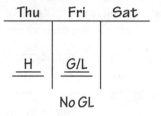

No GL

Rule 3 is basically the same thing as Rule 2, except that it deals with Saturday, and the movies involved are *Greed* and *Harvest*. So the shorthand will be substantially the same as it was for Rule 2: Add "G/H" to Saturday, close off the column leaving space above, and make a note that you cannot have G and H.

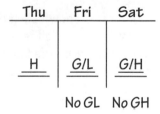

No GL No GH

Step 4: Deductions

Harvest must be shown on Thursday, but anything else could be shown that day as well. In fact, it's helpful to note that Thursday is the only day on which all three films can be shown (because pairs are restricted on the other days by Rules 2 and 3).

Greed or *Limelight*, but not both, must be show on Friday. So, if there's a second film on Friday, it would

Part Two: Logic Games
CHAPTER 6

These explanations refer to questions that begin on page 368.

have to be *Harvest* and it would be shown first. Similarly, *Greed* or *Harvest*, but not both, must be shown on Saturday. So, if there's a second film on Saturday, it would have to be *Limelight* and it would be shown first. However, neither of these films can be added for certain. Still, it's helpful to consider these outcomes as it will help with the questions.

Step 5: Questions

31. (C) Acceptability ★★★★

Treat this Acceptability question like every other, working through the rules to eliminate choices that violate them. Rule 1 requires *Harvest* to be shown last on Thursday. That eliminates **(D)**, which puts *Limelight* last. Rule 2 requires *Greed* or *Limelight* to be last on Friday. That eliminates **(E)**, which puts *Harvest* last. Rule 2 also states that *Greed* and *Limelight* cannot both be on Friday, which eliminates **(B)**. Rule 3 is not violated by either of the remaining answers.

When you run out of rules, double check the limitations in the Overview. In this case, each film must be shown at least once throughout the festival. That eliminates **(A)**, which fails to include *Greed*, leaving **(C)** as the correct answer.

32. (A) Must Be False (CANNOT Be True) ★★★★

The correct answer to this question will be the one that must be false. The four wrong answers will all be true or possibly true.

It's possible that *Harvest* is shown each day. However, the last film on Friday has to be either *Greed* or *Limelight*. So *Harvest* cannot be the last film shown on Friday. Therefore, **(A)** cannot be true, making it the correct answer. For the record:

Limelight can be shown on every day of the festival as long as *Greed* isn't shown on Friday. That eliminates **(B)**.

Greed can be second on Thursday if *Limelight* is first (and *Harvest* third); second on Friday if *Harvest* is first; and second on Saturday if *Limelight* is first again. That eliminates **(C)**.

A different film can be shown first on all three days if *Greed* is first on Thursday, *Harvest* first on Friday, and *Limelight* first on Saturday. That eliminates **(D)**.

A different film can be shown last on all three days if *Harvest* is last on Thursday, *Limelight* is last on Friday, and *Greed* is last on Saturday. That eliminates **(E)**.

Note that you could have skipped this question and drawn sketches for the remaining "If" questions first. With those sketches drawn, **(B)**, **(D)**, and **(E)** could all be eliminated as possible by looking at the sketches for the third question of the set. You would then only have to test two answers—**(A)** and **(C)**—rather than all five.

33. (D) "If" / Maximum ★★★★

This question asks for the maximum number of film showings that could occur during the festival, with the condition that *Limelight* cannot be shown once *Greed* is shown. That condition doesn't just apply on any given day; it applies for the whole festival. Once *Greed* is shown, *Limelight* cannot be shown at all, whether that happens on Thursday, Friday, or Saturday.

There are two ways to test this. First, try to show *Greed* as often as possible, getting at least one showing of *Limelight* in. Alternatively, try to show *Limelight* as much as possible, saving *Greed* until the end.

To maximize showings of *Greed*, show it on all three days. That would mean *Limelight* will be shown before it on Thursday, and that's it for *Limelight*. *Harvest* would then be last on Thursday. *Greed* would be last on Friday, but *Harvest* could be added beforehand. *Greed* would be last again on Saturday, but you can't have *Harvest* also (by Rule 3):

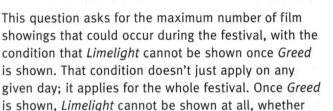

Thu	Fri	Sat
L	H	G
G	G	
H		

That's a maximum of six films so far, which eliminates **(A)**, **(B)**, and **(C)**. Check the second possibility to make sure you cannot get more films in.

To maximize showings of *Limelight*, save *Greed* for the end of the festival: the last film on Saturday, and that's it. *Harvest* then cannot be shown that day (Rule 3), but *Limelight* can be shown before *Greed*. That's two showings on Saturday. If *Greed* isn't shown on

These explanations refer to questions that begin on page 369.

Part Two: Logic Games
Logic Games Practice

K

EXPLANATIONS

Thursday or Friday, the maximum number of showings on each of those days is two (showing *Harvest* and *Limelight* each day):

Thu	Fri	Sat
L	H	L
H	L	G

Again, that's a maximum total of six films. That makes **(D)** the correct answer.

34. (E) "If" / Must Be True ★★★☆

This question indicates the number of times each of the three films is shown, but not *when* they are shown. Start with the easiest to place. If *Greed* is shown three times, it must be shown on every day of the festival. Because of that, *Limelight* can't be shown on Friday (Rule 2), and *Harvest* can't be shown on Saturday (Rule 3).

Harvest is shown twice. It can't be shown on Saturday, so it must be shown on Thursday and Friday. *Limelight* is only shown once, on either Thursday or Saturday:

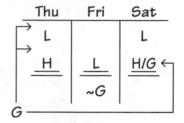

By that, **(E)** must be true, and is therefore the correct answer. The remaining answers all *could* be true, depending on when *Limelight* is shown. However, if *Limelight* is shown on Thursday, **(B)** would be false, and if *Limelight* is shown on Saturday, **(A)**, **(C)**, and **(D)** would be false.

35. (D) "If" / Complete and Accurate List ★★★★

The "If" in this question is very similar to the "If" in the previous question. Again, start with the easiest film to place. If *Limelight* is shown three times, it must be shown on all three days. This means that *Limelight* is last on Friday and that *Greed* cannot be shown on that day (Rule 2). *Limelight* must be shown earlier than

Harvest on Thursday (Rule 1) and earlier than either *Harvest* or *Greed* on Saturday (Rule 3).

Harvest is shown twice—definitely on Thursday—but the second showing could take place on Friday or Saturday. *Greed* is shown once, but it could be on either Thursday or Saturday:

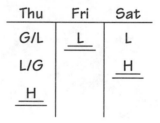

With that, the question asks for the complete and accurate list of films that could be shown *first* on Thursday. That eliminates **(A)**, **(C)**, and **(E)** immediately—*Harvest* is shown on Thursday, but it must be shown last, not first (because at least *Limelight* is also being shown that day).

The only difference between **(B)** and **(D)** is whether *Greed* can be shown first on Thursday. For this question, if *Greed* is shown on Thursday (which doesn't violate any rules), then *Harvest* would be the last film shown on Saturday. However, *Limelight* and *Greed* could be shown in either order on Thursday, as long as *Harvest* is last:

Thu	Fri	Sat
G/L	L	L
L/G		H
H		

Therefore, the first film on Thursday could be either *Greed* or *Limelight*, making **(D)** the correct answer.

CHAPTER 7

Logic Games: Managing the Section

INTRODUCTION

Of the LSAT's four scored sections, Logic Games is worth the fewest points: There are typically 22–24 questions in this section, as opposed to 24–26 questions in each of the two Logical Reasoning sections and 26–28 questions in the Reading Comprehension section. Yet Logic Games is by far the most daunting section for many students, and the anxiety produced by this section can become a distraction that impacts performance on the other sections of the exam as well. Like it or not, though, Logic Games must be dealt with; you want as big a portion of those 22–24 points as you can get, and you certainly don't want this section, the one worth the fewest points, to become a psychological obstacle to doing well on the rest of the test. Even if you like Logic Games and feel confident while doing them, don't take your performance on this section for granted. This chapter will present you with strategies to get the maximum possible points from the Logic Games section, no matter whether you love doing games or not.

LEARNING OBJECTIVES

In this chapter, you'll learn to:

- Become more efficient, and therefore faster, at attacking game setups and questions.
- Prioritize easy games and questions over difficult ones to net the maximum number of points from the Logic Games section.

As you have already learned, the Logic Games section is composed of four separate games, each of which has five to seven questions. Each question is worth one point, although some are much harder than others. Likewise, some games are harder than others to set up. Moreover, even games requiring complex deductions typically come with at least one easy question, while games that are comparatively simple to set up typically have one or more difficult questions. The chart at the top of the next page illustrates this by breaking down the Logic Games section of PrepTest 62.

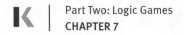
Game 1 - Strict Sequencing	
Question	Difficulty Level
1	★
2	★★
3	★★★
4	★★
5	★
6	★★★★

Game 2 - Matching	
Question	Difficulty Level
7	★
8	★★★
9	★★★
10	★★★
11	★★★★
12	★★
13	★★★★

Game 3 - Hybrid: Sequencing-Matching	
Question	Difficulty Level
14	★
15	★★★★
16	★★★★
17	★★★
18	★★★★

Game 4 - Strict Sequencing	
Question	Difficulty Level
19	★
20	★
21	★
22	★★★
23	★★

Students who did the games and questions straight through, in the order in which they appeared in this section, might well have become bogged down by Question 6 or Game 3. Spending too much time on one difficult question costs you time that can be spent getting easier points. An expert test taker is strategic, skipping or guessing on the most difficult questions when that means getting more of the straightforward ones right. In fact, notice that in PrepTest 62, you could have omitted all the 4-star questions in this section and still netted over 70 percent of the points.

Getting the greatest possible number of points out of the Logic Games section—and feeling confident while doing so—employs two basic skill sets: (1) facility and efficiency in setting up games and attacking questions and (2) the ability to discern quickly which games and questions to prioritize. We'll call these twin pillars of Logic Games competence "mastering the games" and "managing the section," respectively.

MASTERING THE GAMES

You've already learned the Logic Games Method. Now it's time to practice the Method until it becomes second nature. If you've been practicing logic games but feel frustrated, determine which of the Method's five steps are still most difficult for you and practice those steps intensively. Are you creating an appropriate sketch but failing to see the deductions? Or are you rushing past the SEAL questions and jumping into the rules before you have a workable sketch? Each step in the method builds upon the previous step: The answers to the SEAL questions tell you the game type, which in turn tells you which type of sketch you need. You build the rules into the sketch, and then combine the rules to make deductions that fill in more of the sketch. Finally, you use your completed Master Sketch to answer the questions. Mastery and consistent application of the Kaplan Method for Logic Games will make you more efficient, and thus faster, as well as more confident.

Overview and Sketch

You have four games to do in 35 minutes. That works out to an average of about 8½ minutes per game. Some games may take you more time and others less, but in all games, if you spend too much time trying to figure out the best possible (or most aesthetically pleasing) sketch, you will waste precious time that you could use to make deductions and answer questions. The answers to the SEAL questions you ask in the Overview step tell you what type of sketch to make. It doesn't need to be pretty; the lines in your sketch don't need to be perfectly parallel, and the letters don't need to be perfectly formed, just legible. If you are a visual perfectionist, try to let go of those tendencies as far as LSAT sketches are concerned. No one other than you will see your sketches; a quick, serviceable sketch (as long as you can read it!) will earn you more points than a beautiful one that takes too long to make. Once you have thoroughly practiced game overviews and sketches, it shouldn't take you more than 60–90 seconds to read the overview paragraph and set up the sketch. There's no need to write down the answers to the SEAL questions; just hold them in your head long enough to create your sketch. Time yourself as you conduct the Overview step and make a sketch for the following game scenario:

Overview	My Analysis
Five cards are dealt from a partial deck of eight cards—A, K, Q, J, 9, 8, 7, 6. Each card is exactly one of the following suits: clubs, diamonds, hearts, or spades.	

Now, take a look at the way an LSAT expert conducted the Overview step, using the SEAL questions to focus on those elements directly relevant to creating a serviceable sketch.

Overview		Analysis
Five cards are dealt from a partial deck of eight cards—A, K, Q, J, 9, 8, 7, 6. Each card is exactly one of the following suits: clubs, diamonds, hearts, or spades.	$\longrightarrow$	**Step 1:** *Situation*: Dealing out cards *Entities*: Cards (A, K, Q, J, 9, 8, 7, 6) Suits (c, d, h, s) *Action*: Select five cards of eight. Match cards to suits. This is a Selection-Matching Hybrid. *Limitations*: Choose five cards. One suit per card. **Step 2:** Draw a Selection sketch with enough room above or below the cards to note the suit of each: A K Q J 9 8 7 6 _ _ _ _ _ _ _ _ Suit (c, d, h, s)

Though this example is a Hybrid game, the overview paragraph is very short, and the sketch is uncomplicated. If it took you more than 60 seconds to come up with answers to the SEAL questions and arrive at the sketch, keep practicing these steps.

Rules

It is important to understand that the Logic Games section is testing not only your ability to make deductions, but also your attention to detail. Indeed, the way games are presented, the testmaker has stripped away any unnecessary verbiage. In this regard, the Logic Games section is different than the Reading Comprehension section, which tests your ability to assimilate the main lines of a passage and identify important details from the passage's structure without getting caught up in the minutiae. Adjust your approaches to those two different sections accordingly.

In practicing logic games, you have most likely already experienced what happens if you misinterpret a rule—or interpret it correctly in your head but write it down incorrectly. The deductions hinge on the rules, so if a rule is incorrectly recorded in your sketch, your deductions will be incorrect as well. Answer the questions based on faulty deductions and you will lose points. You could even find yourself with a question that appears to have more than one right answer (or no right answer at all). The key when going through the rules is precision and accuracy; ask yourself what the rule does and does not mean, so you don't assume something that the testmaker didn't say. In short, *get it right the first time*. Few things are as frustrating as discovering halfway through the question set that you messed up a rule that caused you to make faulty deductions.

For example, let's say that you encounter the following rule: "C is chosen if B is chosen." If you're reading too quickly, your brain registers the word *if*, and you think, *Aha, that's Formal Logic*, and immediately start scribbling it down, with the entities in the order in which they appear in the sentence: If C → B. But that's not what the rule says. The word *if* isn't in front of the C; it's in front of the B. So B is sufficient for C, and the correct translation is If B → C. Read rules carefully, and interpret them accurately. You cannot afford a single mistake here.

Deductions

You've probably noticed by now that while some games have lots of deductions for you to make, other games have very few, if any. The Logic Games Method tells you to make all possible deductions up front and then use those deductions to answer the questions. That sure sounds good, but how can you tell if you've got them all? How long do you stare at your sketch trying to fill it in before moving on to the questions? Rush to the questions, and you may miss vital deductions, but stare at the rules too long—especially in a game that doesn't allow many deductions—and you'll waste time.

Fortunately, a quick glance at the question set can settle this dilemma. Imagine a question set that consists of nothing but one Acceptability question and five New-"If" questions. You can answer the Acceptability question simply by using the rules; you don't need any deductions there. And each of the New-"If" questions will give you new information that will usually allow you to make all the deductions you need to answer the question. So in this hypothetical game, if you weren't able to make many deductions, you may still be able to answer most or all of the questions correctly. On the other hand, imagine a game that has no Acceptability question and no New-"If" questions at all. This is a rare scenario, but such a game clearly requires deductions for you to answer the questions correctly and efficiently. If you see very few New-"If" questions, and you don't have any deductions, you are probably missing something. Nevertheless, if you have been through the BLEND checklist and you simply don't see any deductions, go on to the question set. You will likely detect patterns within such a game as you work through the questions.

If you generally have trouble finding all the deductions, target this skill by splitting a logic game in half: Do Steps 1–4, then review those steps in the game's explanation. Don't worry about the questions yet. Analyze your work from Overview through Deductions, taking note of any deductions you did not make. (You might even keep track of missed deductions in a notebook; over time, you'll begin to recognize those types of deductions you previously missed.) When you have a solid understanding of the setup, return to the game and do the questions.

Questions

Imagine a question set that contains the following question: "Each of the following could be false EXCEPT." An inefficient test taker's mental process goes something like this: "Could A be false? Gosh, I don't know. What does that even mean? Well, could B be false? Hmm. How about C? Could that be false? I can't tell. Could D or E be false? Gosh, I'd better just guess and go to the next one . . ."

What is wrong with this approach? This student is mechanically moving on to the next question; he is simply doing the questions in the order in which they appear on the page. Also, note that he checks each answer choice even though he doesn't thoroughly understand what he is looking for.

It is considerably more difficult to think in terms of what could be false than to think in terms of what must be true. Asking yourself whether an answer choice could be false is asking your brain to do a task it is not particularly good at. Instead, characterize the choices: If four of them *could be false*, the correct answer *must be true*. You've just changed a daunting task into a much simpler one. Now, you are looking for the one choice that must be true. Characterizing the answer choices is absolutely essential in "must be false" and "could be false" question stems, and in EXCEPT questions.

There is no need to do the questions in order. Efficient test takers know which questions are likely to be more difficult to answer than others; they prioritize the easy points and leave the tougher ones for later, or skip them entirely in favor of saving time and getting more points from another game. They also realize that they may be able to consult work from a question they've already answered by noting what was or was not true in that case. How best to prioritize certain questions and games belongs to the topic of managing the section and will be discussed in the next section.

Putting It All Together

Given the fact that you'll need to make it through four games in 35 minutes on Test Day, you will have an average of 8–9 minutes to do each game. Many students stumble where timing is concerned and conclude that they are simply "not fast enough." But LSAT success is more a matter of efficiency than a matter of speed, and you can improve your timing incrementally. Once you know how to use the Logic Games Method, start timing yourself on individual games. If it takes you longer, on average, than 8–9 minutes to get through a game, isolate the timing problem by using a stopwatch to note how long it takes you to get as far as the Deductions step and how long it takes you to do the questions. If you spend longer than 2½ minutes setting up a game that provides for no big deductions or longer than four minutes setting up a game that allows for many deductions, keep practicing steps 1–4. On the other hand, if you are on pace making deductions but lose time on the question set, then time yourself on each individual question; you may find that you spend an inordinate amount of time on one or two questions that could be skipped. The next section of this chapter discusses the relative difficulty level of different question types and how to get the most points out of each game in the time allotted.

MANAGING THE SECTION

Certainly, if you had a bit more time to complete the Logic Games section, or if that section contained, say, only two games instead of four, you would almost surely answer a higher percentage of questions correctly. But the timing restriction is real, and it can reduce your accuracy. For this reason, your performance on a logic game given unlimited time is *not* indicative of your performance on that same logic game under timed conditions. Remember that time restrictions put pressure on everyone—you and your competition alike. By learning to manage the Logic Games section, you can outperform less well-trained test takers and turn an obstacle into an advantage.

To make the best of the exam's stringent time constraint, remember that every question counts the same; every question that you answer correctly adds one point to your raw score, no matter whether it was easy or difficult, and *no matter how much time it took you to answer.* So if you spend 3–4 minutes on a single high-difficulty question and get it right, that's one point for your raw score—but if you had used those three to four minutes to answer four low-difficulty questions instead, that would be four points for your raw score. Every question carries with it the risk that you won't be able to answer it correctly, of course—but that risk is much lower for easy questions than for hard ones. Moreover, the potential reward for attempting easy questions is greater than the reward for attempting hard questions because you can do several easy questions in the same amount of time it takes you to do a single difficult question. Prioritizing easy questions over hard ones, then, is a no-brainer. So is developing your sense of timing: You need to know how far into the section you are, how much time you have left, and how you will use that time to get the most points.

Learning solid section management skills, however, takes practice. You'll need to learn which questions and games to skip and which ones to do first. You'll need to learn to let go of questions when it becomes clear that the correct answer is not worth investing "just another minute or so," and to let go of an entire game when it becomes clear that you don't know how to set it up, or that you have set it up incorrectly. What you do on Test Day will be what you have practiced in the preceding weeks and months. If you have not practiced good section management, then you will not make good decisions about what to do and what to skip on Test Day. To maximize the effectiveness of your practice, set tangible goals for yourself every time you do a Logic Games section or take a full-length practice test. Once you set your goal, hold yourself to it by recording your actions as you move through the section. For example, if your goal on the next practice test is to spend one minute or less on any given question, then use a stopwatch to record exactly how long each question actually takes you, and once you finish the test, assess how close you came to achieving your goal.

Best Practices for Section Management: Game Triage

Managing the Logic Games section begins when you turn the page and see the first game. Because some games are more difficult to set up than others, it makes sense to start with the easiest one and to save the most difficult for last. There are a number of strategies that you can use; find a game triage strategy that works for you, and stick with it during your practice so that it becomes second nature by Test Day.

The simplest triage strategy is to do the games in the order in which they are presented but to scan each game quickly before you start setting it up and skip games that you feel will be more time-consuming than average. Your thinking might go something like this: "Okay, this first one looks like a straightforward Strict Sequencing game. I like those. I'll do this one," or "This second one is a Selection-Matching Hybrid, and those tend to give me trouble, so I'll skip it for now." You should still plan to allocate your time so that you will have time to come back to the games you skipped, but you'll have grabbed the easier points by then—and your confidence will have received a boost as a result.

If you like to know what you're up against from the beginning, you might prefer a different triage strategy: scan all four games before you actually start any of them. Make two decisions: Which game do you think will be easiest, and which do you think will be the most difficult? Start with the easiest and leave the most difficult for last. (A variation of this strategy would be to start with the first game, which is nearly always one of the two easiest games for most students, and then scan the three remaining games and order them by difficulty.)

It may also be efficient to do the games in the order in which they appear and simply skip the hardest questions in each one. Do be aware, though, that the games are not usually printed in precise order of increasing difficulty. (The two most common patterns, in order of increasing difficulty, are 1-2-4-3 and 2-1-3-4, with 1-2-3-4 just a little less common.) And if you have trouble (even sporadically) setting up games and making deductions, then it would be more advisable to use one of the other approaches just mentioned.

So what makes a game more or less difficult? There are three criteria: (1) familiarity and preference, (2) simplicity and brevity, and (3) concreteness.

Familiarity and Preference

By the time of your official LSAT Test Day, you will feel more comfortable with certain game types than with others. You may have practiced more Sequencing games than other game types, for instance, and therefore feel confident in your mastery of them. Alternatively, you may have a preference for Selection games because you enjoy Formal Logic, or you may like Distribution games because Distribution sketches make intuitive sense to you. Different test takers display different preferences, and that's fine. Whatever your favorite game type, prioritize it.

As you practice, you may develop a predilection for games that allow for many deductions or, alternatively, for games that allow for few—prioritize the kind with which you feel more comfortable. Recognize a game that likely allows many deductions by the presence of two or more non-"If" Must Be True or Must Be False questions in the question set. Recognize a game that probably doesn't allow many deductions by the presence of many New-"If" questions.

Simplicity and Brevity

Single-action games are generally easier than Hybrid games, so other factors being equal, it is logical to prioritize single-action games over Hybrids. Moreover, games that have a very long overview paragraph tend to be more complex than games with a short overview paragraph, and games with five or more rules are often more challenging than games with fewer rules. However, more rules frequently allow more deductions, so if you prefer games that allow more deductions, you may want to prioritize games with more rules over those with fewer.

Concreteness

Watch for words such as *exactly*, *only*, *just*, *precisely*, or *always*. Games that include concrete terms like this are typically easier than games that have more unknowns. For example, imagine a game that asks you to select *exactly* five entities from seven versus a game that asks you to select *at most* five entities from seven. The latter game could have zero, one, two, three, four, or five selected entities. That produces exponentially more possibilities than does the game in which you are asked to select *exactly* five.

Best Practices for Section Management: Strategic Skipping of Questions

Talking about section management presents a paradox. You are studying and practicing in order to master logic games, and the ideal outcome would be to get so fast and so confident that you can roar through the section and get the majority of points without breaking a sweat. But the reality is that time will remain an issue for most students, and you may have to skip or guess on at least a few questions. The solution is to realize that you are in control of your time and you are the one that chooses which questions to tackle and the order in which to tackle them. Skipping or guessing *strategically* is not a failure but a success.

Strategic Guessing

Many students guess only when they feel defeated by a question (and that usually means after they've spent too much time with it already). In turn, bubbling in a guess worsens their sinking confidence. But when done properly, guessing is empowering and will raise your score. We noted at the beginning of this chapter that even the most difficult games come with easy questions and that even the easiest games come with difficult questions. Now, let's say that your target on Logic Games is 18 correct. In a section that has four games, each with six questions, you could theoretically get those 18 points by doing only three games and getting every question correct—but because even easy games often come with one or more high-difficulty questions, getting every single question correct for each game is a challenge, at least within the allotted time. An alternative approach to getting those 18 points is to do all four games but to choose to skip the most difficult question or two in each game. Purposely skipping the hardest questions means that you'll have more time to answer the easier ones—and you will be more likely to get them right. Strategic skipping also puts you in the driver's seat: Instead of allowing the section to control you, you are taking control of how you attack the section. Strategic guessing helps you to get the maximum possible points from the section, and it boosts your confidence. It's a winning combination.

Strategic Ordering of Questions

So which questions should you do, and which should you skip? In what order should you approach the questions that you choose to do? This will be determined largely by what you know about the game after you complete Steps 1–4 of the Logic Games Method. If you've made strong, certain deductions, you can anticipate at least one or two Must Be True–type questions that will reward your analysis. If the game is still open-ended, you will look to the New-"If" questions to add concreteness. You cannot separate a strategic approach to the question set from a methodical approach to the game. Here are some general guidelines to manage the question set:

Acceptability Questions

Most games have one Acceptability question, and it is usually the first question in the set. Even in cases where an Acceptability question appears later in the set, get into the habit of doing the Acceptability questions first. Done the right way—that is, by using the rules to knock out the incorrect choices (Chapter 5)—an Acceptability question should take no more than 30 seconds. If you've interpreted the rules correctly, Acceptability questions yield an easy point, and doing the Acceptability question first also reaffirms your understanding of the rules and thus of the game.

New-"If" Questions

Most New-"If" questions provide a new condition that you can build into a new mini sketch supplementing the game's original rules. More restriction means more concreteness, and that will be helpful, especially in a game that gave you few solid deductions up front. Keep in mind that the second clause of a New-"If" question stem may range from "then which of the following must be true" to "then each of the following must be false EXCEPT," tasks that vary in difficulty. However, given that the "If" clause adds certainty, you'll often find these good questions to tackle right after the Acceptability question. Moreover, keep in mind that question stems with affirmative restrictions (such as "If P is placed in space 3") add more concreteness than those with negative restrictions (such as "If P is not placed in space 5"). Because you are likely to create a mini sketch illustrating one acceptable solution for the game, you can sometimes use New-"If" sketches to help answer open-ended Could Be True or Must Be False questions as well.

Must Be True/Must Be False Questions

Questions that ask for what must be true or false are usually based on a game's deductions. If you have been able to make solid deductions, then do these questions immediately after the Acceptability question; it will simply be a matter of scanning the choices for what you already know to be true. As we said a moment ago, however, if you have not been able to make deductions, then postpone these questions and prioritize New-"If" questions, as the mini sketches for this latter question type often give you a better grasp of the game. At all times, remember to characterize what a question stem calls for. An open-ended stem telling you "each of the following could be false EXCEPT" is really just a Must Be True question. Likewise, a stem that asks "Which of the following CANNOT be in space 3?" is a Must Be False question targeted to a specific slot within your framework.

Could Be True/Could Be False Questions

These questions are not always difficult, but they can be time-consuming if your approach amounts to drawing out five new sketches to test the five answer choices. In games with New-"If" questions, you are often rewarded for postponing these questions until you have some additional sketches to consult. Remember, if you've seen that a given condition could be true in one of the mini sketches, then it amounts to a correct answer for an open-ended Could Be True question (or a wrong answer for a Must Be False question, for that matter). In any event, you must characterize the one right and four wrong answer choices clearly to take full control over Could Be True/Could Be False questions. If you wind up guessing on a Could Be question, choose a Floater or largely unrestricted entity.

Complete and Accurate List Questions

These questions can be very easy in a game with a fairly complete Master Sketch, such as a Limited Options game. However, if your sketch is blank, postpone Complete and Accurate List questions until you have some previous work to help you.

Completely Determine Questions

Questions that ask you for a condition that will determine the placement of every single entity are potentially time-consuming because they may require you to check every answer choice. These questions are best postponed and are good candidates for skipping.

Rule Change and Rule Suspension Questions

These questions look like New-"If"s, but instead of adding a new rule to the ones that already exist—which does not change your original deductions—Rule Changers ask you to swap in a new rule to replace one of the original rules, while Rule Suspenders invalidate one of the original rules. Your Master Sketch is built using deductions made from the original rules, so changing or discarding one of those rules invalidates your deductions and thus your Master Sketch. Rule Changers and Rule Suspenders require a unique sketch constructed one rule at a time, just like the original Master Sketch, and are therefore time-consuming. Unless you are consistently able to get through all of the questions in the Logic Games section and to get the vast majority of them right, skip and guess on these questions.

Rule Substitution Questions

These questions ask for a rule that, if substituted for one of the original rules, would have the same effect as the original rule. They require careful analysis of the effect that the original rule has on the entire game, as well as the ability to recognize the answer choice that has precisely that same effect. These are highly challenging questions and are best skipped by all but the most expert test takers. It is worth noting that these questions almost always appear at the end of a game's question set, so they take your time precisely at the moment when you could move on to the next game and rack up its points. That makes them great reminders to never allow a single question to derail your timing for an entire Logic Games section. Fortunately, you will likely see only one question like this in a given section.

Best Practices for Section Management: Time Management

Even if you triage games brilliantly and your question-skipping strategy is perfect, you may still lose easy points if you have no sense of how much time you have used or how much remains.

If you can get through individual games in an average of 8–9 minutes and answer most of the questions correctly but still get caught short when you do an entire Logic Games section, try using a stopwatch and writing down the time at which you finish each game. Doing this will make you more aware of timing and will also present you with a record of exactly which games slowed you down.

You should also develop an appropriate bubbling strategy. Some students prefer to bubble in each answer as they arrive at it, but reaching for your grid after every question is likely to break your concentration (and thus indirectly cost you time). Moreover, if you do questions out of order (as you should!), you may make bubbling mistakes if you grid each question as you answer it. Try bubbling in the responses for each game after you finish the entire game, and talk to yourself (silently, of course) as you do so to prevent needless errors: "Question 1 is (A); 2 is (D); 3, I'm skipping for now; 4 is (B)," and so on.

Above all, be honest with yourself. If you repeatedly score 14–16 points on a Logic Games section under timed conditions, don't assume that it will be different on Test Day—and definitely don't switch to an untested strategy on Test Day in the hope that doing so will magically make you more efficient. If you want to raise your score on the section, pinpoint exactly where the problem lies: Is it less-than-perfect mastery of the Method? Is it an inability to triage games correctly? Is it a tendency to get stuck on a single question? Is it a poor sense of timing? We discuss some common problems below, but remember that everyone is different. Only you can ascertain exactly what is keeping you from achieving your dream performance in Logic Games.

COMMON FRUSTRATIONS—DIAGNOSING YOUR ISSUE AND WAYS TO IMPROVE

Here are four archetypal students: "The Anxious One," "The Rusher," "The Perfectionist," and "The Incomplete Sketch Malcontent." Chances are that none of these imaginary students will describe you perfectly, but as you read the description of each, ask yourself whether any of that student's problems apply to you—and if they do, then try out the recommended fixes.

The Anxious One

Some test takers find logic games much easier to understand and complete when there are no timing restrictions, but the moment the clock starts ticking, anxiety kicks in and overwhelms their ability to concentrate. A student who is thinking about perceived time pressure is not really focusing on the game at hand. An unfortunate negative feedback loop can result: time pressure produces anxiety, which reduces concentration, which means a reduced grasp of the games, which in turn results in more anxiety, and so on. In extreme cases, timing anxiety can bleed from the section inducing it (in this case, Logic Games) into the remainder of the exam: "Oh no, I bombed that section, I have to make it up on this next section . . . . But I'm not really concentrating well, and that's bad, because Logical Reasoning is usually my strong suit . . . (etc.)." Timing anxiety can be a grave problem that leads a test taker to score significantly lower than he or she should.

One fix for this problem uses a two-step process: (1) mastery of the Logic Games Method and (2) incremental work on timing. Once the Method is so ingrained that it has become second nature, confidence follows and anxiety decreases. Mastery of the Method brings greater efficiency and, hence, greater speed. Indeed, the only way to become faster while maintaining accuracy is to become more efficient. (See "The Rusher.") So practice at your own pace until you are tackling games in a consistent, methodical manner without having to think about it. Then start to work on timing as follows. Do individual games, not entire sections. Split each game in half. The first time, get as far as the deductions step, then write down how long it took you to finish making deductions. Now proceed to the question set and write down how long that took; also note the order in which you did the questions and if there were specific questions that took longer than one minute. Next, work incrementally to become more efficient. For instance, if a game setup takes you seven minutes at first, analyze where in the process you were inefficient (e.g., overlooking a limitation or a duplicated entity) and then try to do the next one in 6½ minutes by correcting this inefficiency. Repeat this exercise and you will become more efficient, bit by bit, in your setups. Likewise, become more efficient at the question set; look for inefficiencies in your approach, such as spending two minutes on a Could Be True question that you could have answered nearly instantly had you first completed one of the new-"If" questions. Once you can set up the game in four minutes or less and answer the questions you choose to do in five minutes or less, you're ready to start practicing complete 35-minute timing sections.

Once you start on full sections, treat each section not as one continuous period of 35 minutes but as four chunks of 8–9 minutes each. Because games will take different amounts of time, try to complete the easiest game in less than eight minutes in order to bank a little time for the most difficult game. Set a goal that you think is manageable: say, one minute for triage, 6–7 minutes for the easiest game, 8½ minutes for each of the medium difficulty games, and 10–11 minutes for the most difficult game. Use a watch to note the time when each game is completed (for example, 7:19, 16:02, etc.) Writing down the time will make you more aware of where you are in the section and will also serve as a record of where you got bogged down.

The Rusher

This is a student who confuses speed and efficiency. "I have to do four games in 35 minutes, so I'll have to go really, really fast! That means I don't have time to do all this rule transcribing. I'll just make a quick sketch framework, and I'll keep the rules in my head." Unfortunately, skipping steps of the Logic Games Method often wastes time and reduces efficiency. Trying to keep the rules in your head, or skipping the deductions step, or failing to make a separate sketch for a new-"If" question leads to confusion, which costs both time and accuracy.

The best way to fix this problem is to shift your sense of urgency: scoring well in Logic Games is not about going faster but about using the minimum possible number of steps to arrive at correct answers. Trust the Logic Games Method you learned in previous chapters; it is constructed for maximum efficiency. Err on the side of using your pencil more, rather than less: Making a separate sketch for a new-"If" question only takes a few seconds, but trying to do the question in your head may result in several false starts, as well as a higher probability of an incorrect answer.

The Perfectionist

Certain students get stuck on individual questions that they believe they should be able to answer correctly. It essentially becomes an ego battle with the question: "How can there possibly be two correct answers to this question? I can't imagine that I made a mistake somewhere. I mean, this rule is correctly transcribed, and this deduction is also right, and my previous work from this other question shows *xyz* to be true. I'm not making a mistake! The test must be making a mistake!" As discussed previously, every Logic Games section has a few questions that are intended to be difficult and time-consuming. It would be a shame to spend months studying for the LSAT but to get a low score because you were tripped up by one of these high-difficulty questions and couldn't let it go.

The fix for this problem is very simple: If you've spent longer than a minute on a given question, *move on*.

The Incomplete Sketch Malcontent

The same sort of "ego battle" can take place in the deductions step. You may feel that you cannot move on to the questions until you've made every available deduction. On the other side of the coin, you may feel that you've wasted time looking for additional deductions that aren't there. When should you stop trying to make more deductions? Quite simply, when you have looked for them in the logical places—duplicated entities, numbers limitations (in short, those elements of BLEND that apply to the game you are working on)—and you don't see any more deductions. As we discussed earlier in this chapter, the question set will give you some indication of whether or not you are likely missing deductions—but whether or not you are, *move on*. Often the question set will give you a better handle on the game. For example, imagine a Sequencing game that includes the following question: "Which of the following must be fifth?" If the fifth slot in your sketch is blank, but you have several excluded entities noted beneath it (ones that show up in the answer choices), doing this question will not only get you a quick point but will also give you a deduction that you can use while completing the remaining questions.

Even if none of these descriptions fits you perfectly, you may have gleaned some useful suggestions from them. Ultimately, whatever your personal obstacles to stellar Logic Games performance, it is up to you to ferret them out and do what is needed to overcome them. Be brutally honest in your self-assessment and attack your issues head on. Your efforts will be rewarded on Test Day.

Logical Reasoning

CHAPTER 8

The Kaplan Logical Reasoning Method

The most important skills you'll learn and master for the LSAT are those pertaining to the Logical Reasoning sections. The reason is pretty clear: With two scored sections on every test, Logical Reasoning accounts for half of your LSAT score. Recent Logical Reasoning sections have had 25 or 26 questions, but unlike Logic Games and Reading Comprehension questions, each question in the Logical Reasoning section is self-contained. The questions may ask you to identify what is missing in a short argument or ask you to identify a fact that would strengthen or weaken the argument. Other Logical Reasoning questions reward you for describing an argument's logical flaw or its author's argumentative strategy. Still others contain no argument but instead ask you to draw valid deductions from a set of statements. In Chapters 9, 10, and 11, you'll learn to identify each of the Logical Reasoning question types, and you'll practice all of the skills you need to answer them quickly and accurately. In this chapter, however, we'll focus on two features that all Logical Reasoning questions have in common: (1) their overall structure and (2) the way their incorrect answer choices are devised.

LOGICAL REASONING QUESTION FORMAT AND THE KAPLAN LOGICAL REASONING METHOD

The first and most important commonality among LSAT Logical Reasoning questions is their structure. Every Logical Reasoning question will begin with a *stimulus*, usually a paragraph-length argument or set of assertions. The stimulus is the text you need to untangle or analyze to understand the author's argument or his set of premises. Below the stimulus, the *question stem* describes the task that the LSAT asks you to perform in relation to the stimulus. Finally, there are always five *answer choices*, exactly one of which is correct, while the other four are demonstrably incorrect.

The Kaplan Logical Reasoning Method leverages the consistent structure of Logical Reasoning questions to allow you to approach each one in the most efficient and effective manner possible.

THE KAPLAN LOGICAL REASONING METHOD

Step 1: Identify the Question Type

Step 2: Untangle the Stimulus

Step 3: Predict the Correct Answer

Step 4: Evaluate the Answer Choices

There is nothing abstract about this approach. In fact, take a look at the Method mapped onto a Logical Reasoning question and you'll see just how, well, *logical* this way of attacking the questions is.

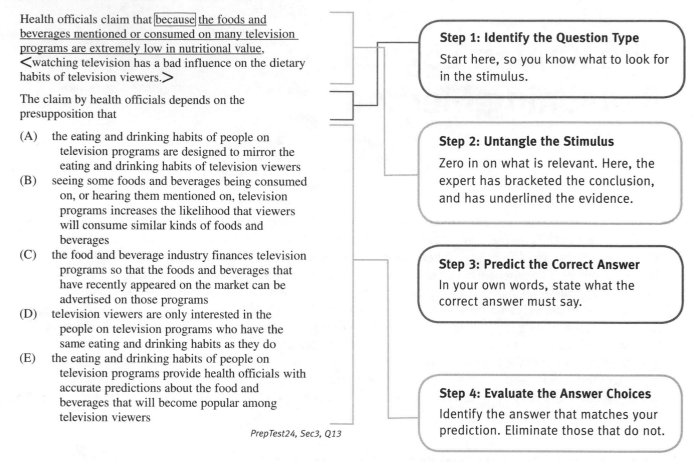

Health officials claim that |because| the foods and beverages mentioned or consumed on many television programs are extremely low in nutritional value, <watching television has a bad influence on the dietary habits of television viewers.>

The claim by health officials depends on the presupposition that

(A) the eating and drinking habits of people on television programs are designed to mirror the eating and drinking habits of television viewers
(B) seeing some foods and beverages being consumed on, or hearing them mentioned on, television programs increases the likelihood that viewers will consume similar kinds of foods and beverages
(C) the food and beverage industry finances television programs so that the foods and beverages that have recently appeared on the market can be advertised on those programs
(D) television viewers are only interested in the people on television programs who have the same eating and drinking habits as they do
(E) the eating and drinking habits of people on television programs provide health officials with accurate predictions about the food and beverages that will become popular among television viewers

PrepTest24, Sec3, Q13

Step 1: Identify the Question Type
Start here, so you know what to look for in the stimulus.

Step 2: Untangle the Stimulus
Zero in on what is relevant. Here, the expert has bracketed the conclusion, and has underlined the evidence.

Step 3: Predict the Correct Answer
In your own words, state what the correct answer must say.

Step 4: Evaluate the Answer Choices
Identify the answer that matches your prediction. Eliminate those that do not.

Notice that the LSAT expert always starts with the question stem. After all, there's no reason to read through the stimulus unless you know what you're looking for. As you learn to identify the various Logical Reasoning questions used by the testmaker, you'll start to recognize words and phrases that signal your task and, in turn, you'll be able to anticipate the relevant portions of the stimulus before you even start reading and untangling it.

Note, too, that the LSAT expert takes a moment to reflect on the information from the stimulus and to predict the correct answer before wading into the answer choices. If you've taken the LSAT before picking up this book, you know that tackling the answer choices unprepared can lead you to reread the stimulus over and over, double-checking what it said and comparing it to each choice. The Method you'll learn here avoids all of that unnecessary repetition. By predicting the meaning or content of the correct answer first, you can evaluate each choice by asking, "Does this match my prediction?" If not, eliminate that answer choice. If it matches your prediction, you've got the right answer.

Let's walk through a Logical Reasoning question step by step and see the LSAT expert's analysis as it develops using this approach.

LSAT Question	Analysis
Health officials claim that because the foods and beverages mentioned or consumed on many television programs are extremely low in nutritional value, watching television has a bad influence on the dietary habits of television viewers.	
The claim by health officials depends on the presupposition that $\rightarrow$	**Step 1:** The "presupposition" an argument "depends on" indicates a Necessary Assumption question. Determine an unstated assumption that the author believes must be true for the evidence to lead logically to the conclusion.

(A) the eating and drinking habits of people on television programs are designed to mirror the eating and drinking habits of television viewers

(B) seeing some foods and beverages being consumed on, or hearing them mentioned on, television programs increases the likelihood that viewers will consume similar kinds of foods and beverages

(C) the food and beverage industry finances television programs so that the foods and beverages that have recently appeared on the market can be advertised on those programs

(D) television viewers are only interested in the people on television programs who have the same eating and drinking habits as they do

(E) the eating and drinking habits of people on television programs provide health officials with accurate predictions about the food and beverages that will become popular among television viewers

PrepTest24 Sec3 Q13

You'll learn all about Assumption questions in Chapter 10. For now, follow the LSAT expert as he untangles the argument in the stimulus.

LSAT Question	Analysis
Health officials claim that because the foods and beverages mentioned or consumed on many television programs are extremely low in nutritional value, watching television has a bad influence on the dietary habits of television viewers. →	**Step 2:** Conclusion: Watching television negatively influences viewers' diets. *because* Evidence: Food and beverages consumed on television are low in nutrition.
The claim by health officials depends on the presupposition that →	**Step 1:** The "presupposition" an argument "depends on" indicates a Necessary Assumption question. Determine an unstated assumption that the author believes must be true for the evidence to lead logically to the conclusion.

(A) the eating and drinking habits of people on television programs are designed to mirror the eating and drinking habits of television viewers

(B) seeing some foods and beverages being consumed on, or hearing them mentioned on, television programs increases the likelihood that viewers will consume similar kinds of foods and beverages

(C) the food and beverage industry finances television programs so that the foods and beverages that have recently appeared on the market can be advertised on those programs

(D) television viewers are only interested in the people on television programs who have the same eating and drinking habits as they do

(E) the eating and drinking habits of people on television programs provide health officials with accurate predictions about the food and beverages that will become popular among television viewers

PrepTest24 Sec3 Q13

As you'll see in the upcoming chapters, your reading and untangling of the stimulus will vary, depending on the type of information relevant to the answer. Here, because the LSAT expert recognized this as a Necessary Assumption question, he focused on analyzing the health officials' argument. In particular, he zeroed in on first identifying the officials' conclusion, and then finding the evidence used to support that claim. Now he's ready to predict the correct answer for this question.

LSAT Question	Analysis
Health officials claim that because the foods and beverages mentioned or consumed on many television programs are extremely low in nutritional value, watching television has a bad influence on the dietary habits of television viewers. $\longrightarrow$	**Step 2:** Conclusion: Watching television negatively influences viewers' diets. *because* Evidence: Food and beverages consumed on television are low in nutrition.
The claim by health officials depends on the presupposition that $\longrightarrow$	**Step 1:** The "presupposition" an argument "depends on" indicates a Necessary Assumption question. Determine an unstated assumption that the author believes must be true for the evidence to lead logically to the conclusion.
	Step 3: The health officials must assume that simply *seeing* or *hearing about* foods consumed on TV will somehow *influence* the dietary choices of those watching TV.
(A) the eating and drinking habits of people on television programs are designed to mirror the eating and drinking habits of television viewers	
(B) seeing some foods and beverages being consumed on, or hearing them mentioned on, television programs increases the likelihood that viewers will consume similar kinds of foods and beverages	
(C) the food and beverage industry finances television programs so that the foods and beverages that have recently appeared on the market can be advertised on those programs	
(D) television viewers are only interested in the people on television programs who have the same eating and drinking habits as they do	
(E) the eating and drinking habits of people on television programs provide health officials with accurate predictions about the food and beverages that will become popular among television viewers	

PrepTest24 Sec3 Q13

After you read the expert's prediction in Step 3, look back at the question stem for a moment. The words "depends on the presupposition" tell you that the correct answer must be a fact that the author believes *must be true* in order for the argument's conclusion to be drawn. In a question like this, the expert knows to look for a gap between the concepts discussed in the evidence and those in the conclusion. The correct answer will tie together the idea of watching television to the idea of being influenced by television. Wrong answer choices will connect these ideas in an illogical way, discuss factors that are irrelevant to the argument, or state facts that are stronger or more extreme than what the author is assuming.

LSAT Question	Analysis
Health officials claim that because the foods and beverages mentioned or consumed on many television programs are extremely low in nutritional value, watching television has a bad influence on the dietary habits of television viewers. →	**Step 2:** Conclusion: Watching television negatively influences viewers' diets. *because* Evidence: Food and beverages consumed on television are low in nutrition.
The claim by health officials depends on the presupposition that →	**Step 1:** The "presupposition" an argument "depends on" indicates a Necessary Assumption question. Determine an unstated assumption that the author believes must be true for the evidence to lead logically to the conclusion.
	Step 3: The health officials must assume that simply *seeing* or *hearing about* foods consumed on TV will somehow *influence* the dietary choices of those watching TV.
(A) the eating and drinking habits of people on television programs are designed to mirror the eating and drinking habits of television viewers →	**Step 4:** 180. Rather than viewers copying what they see on TV, this answer suggests that TV mimics viewers' eating habits. Eliminate.
(B) seeing some foods and beverages being consumed on, or hearing them mentioned on, television programs increases the likelihood that viewers will consume similar kinds of foods and beverages →	Correct. This matches the prediction that viewers' diets are influenced by what viewers see on TV.
(C) the food and beverage industry finances television programs so that the foods and beverages that have recently appeared on the market can be advertised on those programs →	Outside the Scope. The argument is only concerned with TV's influence on viewers, not why certain foods got on TV in the first place. Eliminate.
(D) television viewers are only interested in the people on television programs who have the same eating and drinking habits as they do →	Extreme and 180. The argument states that viewers are influenced by what they see on TV. How viewers decide what to view reverses the logic of the argument. Eliminate.
(E) the eating and drinking habits of people on television programs provide health officials with accurate predictions about the food and beverages that will become popular among television viewers →	Extreme. It is necessary to the argument that foods shown on TV food influence viewers' diets, not that these foods accurately predict future trends. Eliminate.

PrepTest24 Sec3 Q13

There you see the Method in action. As you practice it on the various question types, you'll find that you'll get faster and more accurate throughout the Logical Reasoning section. For the sake of completeness, we included the analysis of all five answer choices, but, on the test, our LSAT expert would have been able to stop evaluating the answer choices as soon as he reached (B). That's the power of making a prediction in Step 3. It's a bit like making a list of features you must have in a new car before you go to the dealership. You're able to rule out any number of choices that won't fit your needs and zero in on the model that's going to make you happy. It won't happen on every Logical Reasoning question, but you'll find that a great majority of questions can be tackled effectively and efficiently by utilizing this exact approach.

Notice, too, that the expert has mentally labeled the wrong answer choices, describing why each one does not fit the task set out by the question stem. Choice (A) reverses the direction of causation in the argument; choice (C) drifts out of the scope of the argument by describing why certain foods might appear on TV; choice (D) again gets the direction of causation wrong by explaining why people might watch certain shows; and (E) is extreme—there is nothing in the original argument suggesting that health officials will begin to predict the popularity of certain foods among TV viewers. This ability to recognize wrong answers and define why they are incorrect is an invaluable skill to LSAT experts. In addition to consistently creating the same types of questions over and over again, the LSAT also repeatedly uses the same types of wrong answer choices. Quickly spotting these wrong answer types and eliminating them will help you become an even more confident test taker.

WRONG ANSWERS IN LOGICAL REASONING QUESTIONS

The LSAT is nothing if not consistent. Each test administration offers the same sections and question types, designs logic games from a small pool of actions, and even draws on much the same subject matter for passages and stimuli. It's no surprise, then, that the testmaker employs the same types of wrong answers as well. Because you get points only for selecting the correct answer on the LSAT, you may wonder why it's valuable to label the wrong answers by type. It is valuable because recognizing the common wrong answer patterns will make you more confident (and thus faster) when you eliminate choices.

Many students, when they practice, will simply check to see if they got a question right. If so, they'll move on, ignoring any analysis of the wrong answers. On Test Day, that's fine—get the right answer and go. But in practice, take the time to review the wrong answers as well. By doing so, you'll internalize the patterns—even the words and phrases—that repeatedly identify incorrect choices.

Take a look at two more Logical Reasoning questions worked out with the expert analysis. Read them through in order, from Step 1 through Step 4, so that you start to get the rhythm of the method. This time, though, pay special attention to the analysis of each wrong answer. At the end of these examples, we'll distill a list of the most common wrong answer types in Logical Reasoning. As you work through subsequent chapters, you'll see these same types of distractors appear over and over again, and in no time you'll be eliminating wrong answers without having to reread and double-check the stimulus to assuage your doubts.

LSAT Question	Analysis
The gray squirrel, introduced into local woodlands ten years ago, threatens the indigenous population of an endangered owl species, because the squirrels' habitual stripping of tree bark destroys the trees in which the owls nest. Some local officials have advocated setting out poison for the gray squirrels. The officials argue that this measure, while eliminating the squirrels, would pose no threat to the owl population, since the poison would be placed in containers accessible only to squirrels and other rodents.	**Step 2:** Conclusion: Setting out poison for the gray squirrels will pose no threat to the owl population. *because* Evidence: The poison would be accessible only to the gray squirrel and other rodents.
Which one of the following, if true, most calls into question the officials' argument?	**Step 1:** "[M]ost calls into question" signals this as a Weaken question. Find an answer choice that, if true, would cast doubt on the argument's conclusion.
	Step 3: The officials draw the extreme conclusion that the poison will pose *no threat whatsoever* to the owls. They overlook the possibility that even though the owls cannot get into the poison containers, they may still be harmed. Find an answer choice that brings up a way for the poison to negatively impact the owls.
(A) One of the species whose members are likely to eat the poison is the red squirrel, a species on which the owls do not prey.	**Step 4:** Outside the Scope. Harm to species upon which the owls do *not* prey is irrelevant to the argument. This does not raise a possible way the owls could be harmed. Eliminate.
(B) The owls whose nesting sites are currently being destroyed by the gray squirrel feed primarily on rodents.	Correct. In this scenario, the owls' primary food supply (rodents) could be decimated by the poison. It's also possible that if the rodents leave the containers, the owls could consume poisoned prey. Either way, this answer choice suggests a way in which the poison *could* negatively impact the owls.
(C) No indigenous population of any other bird species apart from the endangered owls is threatened by the gray squirrels.	Outside the Scope. What does or does not happen to any other species of birds is irrelevant to the connection between the poison and the owls. Eliminate.
(D) The owls that are threatened build their nests in the tops of trees, but the gray squirrels strip away bark from the trunks.	Outside the Scope. The evidence established that bark-stripping is harmful to the trees in which the owls live; where on the tree the squirrels strip the bark is irrelevant. Eliminate.
(E) The officials' plan entails adding the poison to food sources that are usually eaten by rodents but not by other animals. *PrepTest27 Sec1 Q8*	The fact that owls are unlikely to eat any poisoned food removed from the containers by rodents would strengthen, not weaken, this argument. Eliminate.

The LSAT expert quickly homes in on answer choice (B) as the only one that establishes a strong connection between the negative impact the poison will have on the rodents and the resulting impact on the owls. The expert quickly moves through and eliminates the other answer choices—each one just as irrelevant to the original argument as the next. As you become better at identifying why wrong answer choices are incorrect, you too will be able to move more quickly through answer choices, gaining speed and confidence along the way.

LSAT Question	Analysis
Several excellent candidates have been proposed for the presidency of United Wire, and each candidate would bring to the job different talents and experience. If the others are compared with Jones, however, it will be apparent that none of them has her unique set of qualifications. Jones, therefore, is best qualified to be the new president of United Wire.	**Step 2:** Conclusion: Jones is the best qualified candidate for the position of President. *because* Evidence: Jones has a "unique set of qualifications."
The argument is vulnerable to criticism on the ground that it	**Step 1:** The phrase "vulnerable to criticism" indicates a Flaw question. Find an answer choice that describes the reasoning error the author makes as she moves from her evidence to her conclusion.
	Step 3: The argument jumps from a discussion of *unique* qualifications in the evidence to a claim of the *best* qualifications in the conclusion. The author assumes that having a unique set of qualifications makes a candidate the best qualified. However, the author states that each candidate brings unique talents and experiences to the race. The correct answer will describe this inconsistency.
(A) uses flattery to win over those who hold an opposing position	**Step 4:** Distortion. The author does not use flattery to win anybody over. Eliminate.
(B) refutes a distorted version of an opposing position	Distortion. The author does not characterize any opposing positions in her argument. Eliminate.
(C) seeks to distinguish one member of a group on the basis of something that applies to all	Correct. The author distinguishes Jones on the basis of having unique qualifications, even though she earlier indicates that all the candidates have unique qualifications.
(D) supports a universal claim on the basis of a single example	Distortion. The author does not jump to a universal claim. Both the evidence and the conclusion are about one person: Jones. Eliminate.
(E) describes an individual in terms that appropriately refer only to the group as a whole *PrepTest24 Sec2 Q6*	Distortion. The author describes Jones' qualifications as "unique," which just as appropriately applies to the other individuals in the group. Eliminate.

Notice that the LSAT expert takes her time in Step 3 of the method and articulates the reasoning flaw in the author's argument. While her prediction isn't an exact, word-for-word match with the right answer, a clear understanding of the overlooked possibility in the argument—that the other candidates' unique talents are superior to Jones's unique talents—allows the expert to quickly move through the answer choices and find the one that most closely fits. While an untrained test taker might be tempted by wrong answer choices that evocatively describe various reasoning errors, an LSAT expert knows that her task is not simply to find a description of any old flaw in reasoning. Instead, she is focused intensely on her task: to find the answer choice that describes the *specific* flaw present in the stimulus.

The Logical Reasoning Wrong Answer Types

Not every wrong answer you see will fit neatly into one of the types you see described here. After all, sometimes when a question asks for what the author assumes, the wrong answer will just be something she doesn't assume, without clearly being a 180 or Extreme. Other wrong answers might fit more than one category. Still, it's worth your time to learn the wrong answer types in the list that follows. You'll see them referred to many times in the questions illustrated in the coming chapters.

LOGICAL REASONING: WRONG ANSWER TYPES

- **Outside the Scope**—a choice containing a statement that is too broad, too narrow, or beyond the purview of the stimulus

- **Irrelevant Comparison**—a choice that compares two items or attributes in a way not germane to the author's argument or statements

- **Extreme**—a choice containing language too emphatic to be supported by the stimulus; Extreme choices are often (though, not always) characterized by words such as *all*, *never*, *every*, or *none*

- **Distortion**—a choice that mentions details from the stimulus but mangles or misstates the relationship between them given or implied by the author

- **180**—a choice that directly contradicts what the correct answer must say (for example, a choice that strengthens the argument in a Weaken question)

- **Faulty Use of Detail**—a choice that accurately states something from the stimulus but in a manner that answers the question incorrectly; this type is rarely used in Logical Reasoning

---

Along the way, you'll see a handful of wrong answer types that apply to specific question types. In Assumption or Main Point questions, for example, it's common to see wrong answers that simply repeat the author's evidence instead of his unstated assumption or conclusion. We'll cover these wrong answers when they appear and explain why they aren't credited on the test.

It's also important to bring up Formal Logic statements here. Imagine a case in which the correct answer must say: "To vote in County Y, it is necessary to register 60 days prior to the election." A common wrong answer might say, "Anyone registered 60 days prior to the election can vote in County Y." For the purposes of our wrong answer types, that would be a Distortion. But if you think back to Chapter 1, "LSAT Reasoning," you'll recognize that the first statement, the one that matches the correct answer, holds that meeting the registration requirement is *necessary* for voting, while the wrong answer holds that the registration requirement is *sufficient* to be able to vote. Being clear with Formal Logic is just as important (arguably, *more* important) in Logical Reasoning than it is in Logic Games. Anytime you need a brush up on necessity and sufficiency, return to Chapter 1 and review the examples and drills there.

Now that you have the big picture of Logical Reasoning in order, it's time to focus on specific questions and their associated skills. The argument-based questions in Chapter 9 provide a foundation for the more numerous (and often more difficult) assumption-based questions in Chapter 10. The non-argument-based questions in Chapter 11 reward you for different skills but still conform precisely to the question format, method, and wrong answer types you've learned in this chapter.

Argument-Based Questions

In the Logical Reasoning sections of the LSAT, the majority of questions—indeed over 70 percent of Logical Reasoning questions on tests released from 2008 to 2014—reward your ability to analyze arguments. That's well over a third of all the questions on the exam. So, the skills you'll acquire in this chapter and the next have the potential to make your LSAT score skyrocket.

As we'll discuss it here, the word *argument* does not refer to a dispute between two people, though occasionally, the LSAT will present a brief dialogue in which each party presents an argument. An LSAT argument is one person's attempt to convince the reader that some assertion is true or that some action is advisable. LSAT arguments are defined by two explicit components: (1) a *conclusion*, the author's main point, and (2) one or more pieces of *evidence*, the facts or analyses he offers in support of the conclusion.

LSAT STRATEGY

Every LSAT argument contains

- a conclusion—the assertion, evaluation, or recommendation of which the author is trying to convince his readers; and
- evidence—the facts, studies, or contentions the author believes support or establish the conclusion.

The testmaker has designed several Logical Reasoning question types—Main Point, Role of a Statement, Method of Argument, Point at Issue, and Parallel Reasoning questions—to test your ability to recognize, identify, and characterize the explicit parts of arguments or to describe how the author is putting the pieces of the argument together. In this chapter, you'll learn how to strategically attack and answer each of the five question types listed above. Together, they will account for roughly 9–11 of the Logical Reasoning questions you'll see on Test Day.

But notice that we keep referring to the conclusion and evidence as the *explicit* parts of each LSAT argument. That's because almost every argument used in the stimulus of a Logical Reasoning question also contains an implicit *assumption*. Three more question types—the extremely important Assumption, Strengthen/Weaken, and Flaw questions, which are all covered in Chapter 10—reward you for identifying the unstated premise in the argument. Together, those questions account for around 24 questions per test. While it might be tempting to leap ahead to these popular question types, you should take the time to first study and practice the learning objectives outlined in Chapter 9. Without the skills to analyze the explicit parts of LSAT arguments, the all-important "Assumption family" questions are nearly impossible.

CONCLUSIONS AND MAIN POINT QUESTIONS

LEARNING OBJECTIVES

In this section, you'll learn to:

- Identify the conclusion in an LSAT argument.
- Characterize and paraphrase the conclusion.
- Identify Main Point questions and characterize their correct and incorrect answer choices.

Here's a Main Point question. Feel free to try it now. You'll see a complete analysis later in this section. By the end of this section, you will have learned how to answer questions of this type.

The authors of a recent article examined warnings of an impending wave of extinctions of animal species within the next 100 years. These authors say that no evidence exists to support the idea that the rate of extinction of animal species is now accelerating. They are wrong, however. Consider only the data on fishes: 40 species and subspecies of North American fishes have vanished in the twentieth century, 13 between 1900 and 1950, and 27 since 1950.

Which one of the following is the main point of the argument?

(A) There is evidence that the rate of extinction of animal species is accelerating.
(B) The future rate of extinction of animal species cannot be determined from available evidence.
(C) The rate of extinction of North American fishes is parallel to the rate of extinction of all animal species taken together.
(D) Forty species and subspecies of North American fishes have vanished in the twentieth century.
(E) A substantial number of fish species are in danger of imminent extinction.

PrepTest24 Sec2 Q15

Main Point questions reward you for directly locating (and sometimes for accurately paraphrasing) the author's conclusion. Because spotting the conclusion forms the basis of all argument analyses on the test, jump right in and practice this important skill.

Identify the Conclusion

Think of the conclusion as the author's point, the statement she's trying to convince you is true. In our day-to-day lives, we identify conclusions all the time, though we're seldom aware that we're doing so. When your spouse or roommate says, "I don't feel like cooking; we should order something for delivery," the second part of that sentence is his conclusion. This is because the second part of the sentence is what he's trying to convince you to do, and he offers the first part of the sentence (the evidence) as a reason why you should accept his point. Indeed, conclusions are always statements that call out for a reason; they always elicit the question "Why?"

LSAT arguments are usually (though not always) a good deal more complex than that example, but they feature multiple ways in which to identify the conclusion.

Many LSAT arguments use Keywords to introduce the conclusion.

LSAT Question	Analysis
If you know a lot about history, it will be easy for you to impress people who are intellectuals. But unfortunately, you will not know much about history if you have not, for example, read a large number of history books. Therefore, if you are not well versed in history due to a lack of reading, it will not be easy for you to impress people who are intellectuals. *PrepTest27 Sec4 Q7*	"Therefore" signals the author's conclusion here: *If you are not well versed in history, then you won't easily impress intellectuals.* Everything else is either background or evidence.

Other conclusion Keywords or phrases include *hence, thus, consequently, as a result, so,* and *it follows that*. When conclusion Keywords are present, they can be the quickest way to spot the author's point. Don't become overly reliant on conclusion Keywords, however; sometimes the author may use one or more subsidiary conclusions as part of the evidence. Look at this example.

LSAT Question	Analysis
People in the tourist industry know that excessive development of seaside areas by the industry damages the environment. Such development also hurts the tourist industry by making these areas unattractive to tourists, a fact of which people in the tourist industry are well aware. People in the tourist industry would never knowingly do anything to damage the industry. Therefore, they would never knowingly damage the seaside environment, and the people who are concerned about damage to the seaside environment thus have nothing to fear from the tourist industry. *PrepTest24 Sec3 Q12*	In the last sentence, "[t]herefore" signals a conclusion in the argument: *people in the tourist industry would never knowingly damage the seaside environment*. But the sentence continues, and another conclusion Keyword, "thus," signals the ultimate conclusion: *People concerned about damage to the seaside environment should not worry about the tourist industry.* The first part of the last sentence, then, is the argument's subsidiary conclusion, used to support the second half of the last sentence, which is the argument's ultimate conclusion.

In other LSAT arguments, Keywords may signal the evidence. The most common examples are *because*, after all, *for*, and *since*.

LSAT Question	Analysis
All actions are motivated by self-interest, since any action that is apparently altruistic can be described in terms of self-interest. For example, helping someone can be described in terms of self-interest: the motivation is hope for a reward or other personal benefit to be bestowed as a result of the helping action. *PrepTest29 Sec4 Q18* $\longrightarrow$	"[S]ince" indicates that the second half of the first sentence is evidence supporting the claim made in the first half of the sentence. "For example" simply points to an example that will be used to demonstrate the point that the author wishes to make. *All actions are motivated by self-interest* is the author's conclusion.

The toughest arguments in which to locate the conclusion are those with neither conclusion nor evidence Keywords. In these cases, you need to follow the logical flow of the argument by asking, "What is the author's point, and what is she offering to support that point?" We call this the One-Sentence Test because you're trying to strip away anything other than the one sentence or clause that constitutes the author's ultimate point.

LSAT Question	Analysis
Art Historian: Robbins cannot pass judgment on Stuart's art. While Robbins understands the art of Stuart too well to dismiss it, she does not understand it well enough to praise it. *PrepTest27 Sec4 Q20* $\longrightarrow$	The art historian begins with a very strong opinion: Robbins cannot pass judgment on Stuart's art. She then gives two reasons, or pieces of evidence, to support this subjective claim: Robbins understands Stuart's art well enough to dismiss it, but not well enough to praise it. The conclusion then is the author's subjective, opinionated claim: *Robbins cannot pass judgment on Stuart's art.*

One special case—often associated with Main Point questions, by the way—occurs when the author's conclusion is an assertion that another person's position is incorrect. Arguments with this structure will often begin with language such as "some believe" or "biologists contend" or "it has been proposed." The author's rejection of whatever these other parties are arguing for is then signaled by a Contrast Keyword, such as *but* or *however*, or a flat-out refutation, such as "This is incorrect."

LSAT Question		Analysis
The authors of a recent article examined warnings of an impending wave of extinctions of animal species within the next 100 years. These authors say that no evidence exists to support the idea that the rate of extinction of animal species is now accelerating. They are wrong, however. Consider only the data on fishes: 40 species and subspecies of North American fishes have vanished in the twentieth century, 13 between 1900 and 1950, and 27 since 1950. *PrepTest24 Sec2 Q15*	$\longrightarrow$	In this argument, we learn that "[t]he authors of a recent article … say that no evidence exists to support the idea that the rate of extinction … is now accelerating." What does the person making this argument think of the scientists' claim? "They are wrong, however." The conclusion here can thus be summed: *there is evidence to suggest that the rate of animal extinctions is increasing.*

While the author's conclusion in the argument is the sentence containing the Contrast Keyword, your understanding of the author's overall main point requires an understanding of the position held by the "authors of a recent article." Imagine an argument that begins: "Members of the other party argue that we should adopt the proposed city budget. But, they are mistaken." Here, the author's conclusion is the second sentence, but the meaning of the conclusion is "we should not adopt the proposed budget." Notice, too, that the argument would continue with the author's evidence: Here's why we should not adopt the budget. You'll practice paraphrasing conclusions shortly, and you'll look more closely at authors' evidence in the next section. First, however, get in a little practice locating the conclusion in LSAT arguments.

TEST DAY TIP

Bracket the conclusion of an argument in your test booklet. Get in the habit of doing this for all Argument-based and Assumption-family questions.

Practice

Now, practice locating the conclusion in a handful of LSAT arguments.

In each of the following arguments, locate and bracket the conclusion and, in your own words, explain how you knew that the sentence or clause you selected is the author's main point. After each, review the expert analysis on the pages following the exercise to check your work.

LSAT Question	My Analysis
1. Historian: We can learn about the medical history of individuals through chemical analysis of their hair. It is likely, for example, that Isaac Newton's psychological problems were due to mercury poisoning; traces of mercury were found in his hair. Analysis is now being done on a lock of Beethoven's hair. Although no convincing argument has shown that Beethoven ever had a venereal disease, some people hypothesize that venereal disease caused his deafness. Since mercury was commonly ingested in Beethoven's time to treat venereal disease, if researchers find a trace of mercury in his hair, we can conclude that this hypothesis is correct. *PrepTest28 Sec3 Q16*	
2. Press release: A comprehensive review evaluating the medical studies done up to the present time has found no reason to think that drinking coffee in normal amounts harms the coffee-drinker's heart. So coffee drinkers can relax and enjoy their beverage—it is safe to drink coffee. *PrepTest24 Sec2 Q1*	

| **LSAT Question** | **My Analysis** |

3. During the 1980s Japanese collectors were very active in the market for European art, especially as purchasers of nineteenth-century Impressionist paintings. This striking pattern surely reflects a specific preference on the part of many Japanese collectors for certain aesthetic attributes they found in nineteenth-century Impressionist paintings.

    PrepTest27 Sec1 Q5

4. All potatoes naturally contain solanine, which is poisonous in large quantities. Domesticated potatoes contain only very small amounts of solanine, but many wild potatoes contain poisonous levels of solanine. Since most of the solanine in potatoes is concentrated in the skin, however, peeling wild potatoes makes them at least as safe to eat as unpeeled domesticated potatoes of the same size.

    PrepTestB Sec1 Q9

Expert Analysis

Here's how an LSAT expert looks at each of the arguments you've just examined.

LSAT Question	Analysis
1. Historian: We can learn about the medical history of individuals through chemical analysis of their hair. It is likely, for example, that Isaac Newton's psychological problems were due to mercury poisoning; traces of mercury were found in his hair. Analysis is now being done on a lock of Beethoven's hair. Although no convincing argument has shown that Beethoven ever had a venereal disease, some people hypothesize that venereal disease caused his deafness. Since mercury was commonly ingested in Beethoven's time to treat venereal disease, if researchers find a trace of mercury in his hair, we can conclude that this hypothesis is correct. *PrepTest28 Sec3 Q16*	"[W]e can conclude" signals the author's conclusion: *If researchers find Mercury in Beethoven's hair, then this hypothesis is correct.* But what hypothesis? The hypothesis that "some people" have put forward. The author's conclusion can therefore be paraphrased: *If it's determined that traces of mercury were in Beethoven's hair, then his deafness was caused by a venereal disease.*
2. Press release: A comprehensive review evaluating the medical studies done up to the present time has found no reason to think that drinking coffee in normal amounts harms the coffee-drinker's heart. So coffee drinkers can relax and enjoy their beverage—it is safe to drink coffee. *PrepTest24 Sec2 Q1*	"So" signals the author's conclusion here: *Coffee drinkers can relax and enjoy their beverage—it is safe to drink coffee.*
3. During the 1980s Japanese collectors were very active in the market for European art, especially as purchasers of nineteenth-century Impressionist paintings. This striking pattern surely reflects a specific preference on the part of many Japanese collectors for certain aesthetic attributes they found in nineteenth-century Impressionist paintings. *PrepTest27 Sec1 Q5*	There are no conclusion or evidence Keywords here, so use the One Sentence Test. The first sentence is a description of a pattern of behavior that occurred in the 1980s. The second sentence then introduces the author's voice through the phrase "[T]his … surely reflects." This subjective, opinionated claim is therefore the conclusion: *Japanese art collectors preferred buying 19th century Impressionistic paintings because of their aesthetic attributes.*
4. All potatoes naturally contain solanine, which is poisonous in large quantities. Domesticated potatoes contain only very small amounts of solanine, but many wild potatoes contain poisonous levels of solanine. Since most of the solanine in potatoes is concentrated in the skin, however, peeling wild potatoes makes them at least as safe to eat as unpeeled domesticated potatoes of the same size. *PrepTestB Sec1 Q9*	The Keyword "[s]ince" directs to the argument's evidence, and "however" pivots to the author's conclusion: *Peeling wild potatoes makes them at least as safe to eat as unpeeled domesticated potatoes of the same size.*

Paraphrase and Characterize the Conclusion

Now that you can spot conclusions, you're ready to tackle the task of understanding what they actually mean. LSAT arguments don't always use the simplest or most succinct wording, and as you've seen, sometimes you'll need to combine two sentences to accurately articulate the author's main point.

Being able to put the author's conclusion into your own words is important because, in some questions, the LSAT will paraphrase the author's conclusion in the correct answer. Indeed, it will directly quote another part of the argument in a wrong answer. Being able to zero in on and accurately capture the author's meaning is a skill you'll use in the Reading Comprehension section as well.

Here's how an LSAT expert sees a complex conclusion.

LSAT Question	Analysis
On a certain day, nine scheduled flights on Swift Airlines were canceled. Ordinarily, a cancellation is due to mechanical problems with the airplane scheduled for a certain flight. However, since it is unlikely that Swift would have mechanical problems with more than one or two airplanes on a single day, some of the nine cancellations were probably due to something else. *PrepTest28 Sec3 Q19*	The first sentence establishes a fact: Nine scheduled flights were canceled on one day. "Ordinarily" indicates the normal course of events, but the Keyword "[h]owever" in the next sentence suggests an anomaly. "[S]ince" points to more evidence: It is unlikely that Swift would have mechanical problems with more than a couple of planes, and that sets up the author's conclusion: *Some of the nine canceled flights were due to something other than mechanical problems.*

As you practice paraphrasing conclusions, it's valuable to know that the conclusions to every LSAT argument fall into one of six categories.

> ## LSAT STRATEGY
>
> Conclusions of LSAT arguments almost always match one these six types:
>
> - Value Judgment (an evaluative statement; e.g., Action X is unethical or Y's recital was poorly sung)
> - If/Then (a conditional prediction, recommendation, or assertion; e.g., If X is true, then so is Y or If you are an M, you should do Y)
> - Prediction (X *will* or *will not* happen in the future)
> - Comparison (X is taller/shorter/more common/less common/etc. than Y)
> - Assertion of Fact (X is true or X is false)
> - Recommendation (we *should* or *should not* do X)

Learning to spot the category into which a conclusion falls is valuable for many Logical Reasoning question types. When the testmaker asks you to identify the conclusion in a Main Point question, the correct answer must, naturally, match the conclusion in the stimulus. In Parallel Reasoning questions, even though the arguments in the answer choices deal with different subject matter than does the stimulus argument, the conclusion type in the correct answer must match that in the stimulus. Even in the all-important Assumption-family questions, noting a particular conclusion type can help reveal the pattern in the argument, making your analysis more efficient. By the way, some conclusions fall into more than one of these categories. If an author concludes, for example, "If the city's budget is not balanced next year, the council should vote to cut funding to animal shelters," his conclusion is both an If/Then and a Recommendation.

Take a look at how an LSAT expert would recognize the conclusion types in these examples.

LSAT Question	Analysis
Alice will volunteer to work on the hospital fund-raising drive only if her brother Bruce also volunteers and a majority of the others working on the drive promise to select Bruce to manage the drive. However, although Bruce is willing to volunteer, none of the others working on the drive will promise to select Bruce to manage the drive. Thus it is certain that Alice will not volunteer. *PrepTestB Sec1 Q12*	The conclusion here—*Alice will not volunteer*—is a prediction. The author is stating that a person will not do something in the future.
Press release: A comprehensive review evaluating the medical studies done up to the present time has found no reason to think that drinking coffee in normal amounts harms the coffee-drinker's heart. So coffee drinkers can relax and enjoy their beverage—it is safe to drink coffee. *PrepTest24 Sec2 Q1*	The conclusion here—*coffee is safe to drink*—is an assertion of fact. The author is simply stating a fact that she believes to be true, based on the evidence she has provided.
Formal performance evaluations in the professional world are conducted using realistic situations. Physicians are allowed to consult medical texts freely, attorneys may refer to law books and case records, and physicists and engineers have their manuals at hand for ready reference. Students, then, should likewise have access to their textbooks whenever they take examinations. *PrepTest29 Sec4 Q25*	The conclusion here—*students should have access to textbooks whenever they take exams*—is a recommendation. The author advocates for a change in policy.

LSAT Question	Analysis
If you know a lot about history, it will be easy for you to impress people who are intellectuals. But unfortunately, you will not know much about history if you have not, for example, read a large number of history books. Therefore, if you are not well versed in history due to a lack of reading, it will not be easy for you to impress people who are intellectuals. *PrepTest27 Sec4 Q7*	The conclusion here—*if you're not well versed in history then you won't be able to impress intellectuals*—is a classic if/then conditional statement.
All potatoes naturally contain solanine, which is poisonous in large quantities. Domesticated potatoes contain only very small amounts of solanine, but many wild potatoes contain poisonous levels of solanine. Since most of the solanine in potatoes is concentrated in the skin, however, peeling wild potatoes makes them at least as safe to eat as unpeeled domesticated potatoes of the same size. *PrepTestB Sec1 Q9*	The conclusion here—*peeling wild potatoes makes them at least as safe to eat as unpeeled domesticated potatoes of the same size*—is a comparison that states that two things are equally safe.
Most people feel that they are being confused by the information from broadcast news. This could be the effect of the information's being delivered too quickly or of its being poorly organized. Analysis of the information content of a typical broadcast news story shows that news stories are far lower in information density than the maximum information density with which most people can cope at any one time. So the information in typical broadcast news stories is poorly organized. *PrepTest27 Sec4 Q19*	The conclusion here—*the information in typical broadcast news stories is poorly organized*—is a value judgment. The author is stating a personal opinion about the quality of a certain thing.

Practice

Now that you're familiar with the types of conclusions, practice locating and paraphrasing the conclusions in the following arguments. Make sure to note into which of the six conclusion categories each one falls.

In each of the following arguments, locate the conclusion, identify the conclusion type, and give a simple, accurate paraphrase of the author's meaning in your own words. After each, you can turn to the pages following the exercise to see the expert thinking and check your work.

LSAT Question	My Analysis
5. Jim will go to the party only if both Sam and Elaine also go. Sam is going to the party, but Elaine is not going. So it is certain that Jim will not go to the party. *PrepTestB Sec1 Q12*	
6. Sociologist: The intended function of news is to give us information on which to act. But in a consumer society, news becomes a product to be manufactured and dispensed to the consumer. An enormous industry for the production and consumption of news has evolved, and we ingest news with an insatiable appetite. Under such circumstances, news is primarily entertaining and cannot, therefore, serve its intended function. *PrepTestB Sec1 Q18*	
7. Barnes: The two newest employees at this company have salaries that are too high for the simple tasks normally assigned to new employees and duties that are too complex for inexperienced workers. Hence, the salaries and the complexity of the duties of these two newest employees should be reduced. *PrepTest29 Sec1 Q5*	

LSAT Question	My Analysis
8. Maude is incessantly engaging in diatribes against people who are materialistic. But her hypocrisy is evinced by the sentimental treatment of the watch her grandmother gave her. She certainly is very fond of the watch—she worries about damaging it; in fact she always sets it carefully in a special box before going to bed. *PrepTestB Sec4 Q4*	
9. Several excellent candidates have been proposed for the presidency of United Wire, and each candidate would bring to the job different talents and experience. If the others are compared with Jones, however, it will be apparent that none of them has her unique set of qualifications. Jones, therefore, is best qualified to be the new president of United Wire. *PrepTest24 Sec2 Q6*	
10. All actions are motivated by self-interest, since any action that is apparently altruistic can be described in terms of self-interest. For example, helping someone can be described in terms of self-interest: the motivation is hope for a reward or other personal benefit to be bestowed as a result of the helping action. *PrepTest29 Sec4 Q18*	

Expert Analysis

Here's how an LSAT expert looks at each of the arguments you've just examined.

LSAT Question		**Analysis**
5. Jim will go to the party only if both Sam and Elaine also go. Sam is going to the party, but Elaine is not going. So it is certain that Jim will not go to the party. *PrepTestB Sec1 Q12*	→	The Keyword "[so]" marks the conclusion: *It is certain that Jim will not go to the party.* This is a strong prediction that someone will not do something in the future.
6. Sociologist: The intended function of news is to give us information on which to act. But in a consumer society, news becomes a product to be manufactured and dispensed to the consumer. An enormous industry for the production and consumption of news has evolved, and we ingest news with an insatiable appetite. Under such circumstances, news is primarily entertaining and cannot, therefore, serve its intended function. *PrepTestB Sec1 Q18*	→	"[T]herefore" signals the conclusion, an assertion of fact: *News cannot serve its intended function.* But what is its intended function? Look back to the first sentence to fully understand the author's conclusion: *news cannot give us information on which to act.*
7. Barnes: The two newest employees at this company have salaries that are too high for the simple tasks normally assigned to new employees and duties that are too complex for inexperienced workers. Hence, the salaries and the complexity of the duties of these two newest employees should be reduced. *PrepTest29 Sec1 Q5*	→	"Hence" signals the conclusion here: *The salaries and the complexity of duties of the two newest employees should be reduced.* The Keyword "should" identifies this conclusion as a recommendation.
8. Maude is incessantly engaging in diatribes against people who are materialistic. But her hypocrisy is evinced by the sentimental treatment of the watch her grandmother gave her. She certainly is very fond of the watch—she worries about damaging it; in fact she always sets it carefully in a special box before going to bed. *PrepTestB Sec4 Q4*	→	The first sentence tells us that Maude engages in diatribes against people who are materialistic. In the second sentence, the author calls out Maude for her hypocrisy, and provides evidence to prove it. So the conclusion here is a value judgment: *Maude is a hypocrite because she is also materialistic.*
9. Several excellent candidates have been proposed for the presidency of United Wire, and each candidate would bring to the job different talents and experience. If the others are compared with Jones, however, it will be apparent that none of them has her unique set of qualifications. Jones, therefore, is best qualified to be the new president of United Wire. *PrepTest24 Sec2 Q6*	→	"[T]herefore" points us to the conclusion here: *Jones is best qualified to be the new president of United Wire.* The author is making a comparison between Jones and the other candidates.
10. All actions are motivated by self-interest, since any action that is apparently altruistic can be described in terms of self-interest. For example, helping someone can be described in terms of self-interest: the motivation is hope for a reward or other personal benefit to be bestowed as a result of the helping action. *PrepTest29 Sec4 Q18*	→	The second half of the first sentence follows the evidence Keyword "since," so the first half of the first sentence is the author's conclusion: *All actions are motivated by self-interest.* This is a conditional, or if/then statement.

Identify and Answer Main Point Questions

Once you know how to locate and paraphrase conclusions, you're ready to answer Main Point questions. On tests released from 2008 through 2014, there were an average of 2–3 Main Point questions per test with a high count of four on two exams given in 2012. While Main Point questions do not constitute a great number of questions, keep in mind how fundamental the conclusion-based skills are. You'll be analyzing the author's conclusion on dozens of questions on Test Day.

Employing the Kaplan Method for Logical Reasoning, you begin with the question stem. Although the testmaker uses different wording from time to time, Main Point questions always call for the author's final conclusion. The correct answer either restates the conclusion or paraphrases it without changing the meaning. Incorrect answers often state a piece of the author's evidence or one of his subsidiary conclusions that serve as evidence in the argument. Other incorrect answers distort or contradict the author's conclusion. If another party's position is mentioned in the argument, the testmaker may include an incorrect answer that states the other party's point.

Here are a pair of Main Point question stems seen on officially released exams.

LSAT Question		Analysis
Which one of the following is the main point of the argument? *PrepTest24 Sec2 Q15*	→	"[T]he main point of the argument": a Main Point question. The correct answer will be a paraphrase of the author's conclusion.
Which one of the following most accurately expresses the main conclusion of the essayist's argument? *PrepTest28 Sec1 Q18*	→	"[E]xpresses the main conclusion of the ... argument": a Main Point question. The correct answer will be a paraphrase of the author's conclusion.

Once you've identified a Main Point question, untangle the stimulus to locate the author's conclusion. Remember that you can use conclusion Keywords, evidence Keywords, or the One-Sentence Test. Paraphrase the conclusion and use that paraphrase as your prediction of the correct answer. Evaluate the answer choices by finding the correct answer that mirrors your prediction or by eliminating choices that restate the evidence, distort or contradict the author's conclusion, or refer to another party's point of view.

Here's how an LSAT expert might analyze a full Main Point question.

LSAT Question	Analysis
The authors of a recent article examined warnings of an impending wave of extinctions of animal species within the next 100 years. These authors say that no evidence exists to support the idea that the rate of extinction of animal species is now accelerating. They are wrong, however. Consider only the data on fishes: 40 species and subspecies of North American fishes have vanished in the twentieth century, 13 between 1900 and 1950, and 27 since 1950.	**Step 2:** Conclusion: There *is* evidence that the rate of extinctions is accelerating. The author denies the claim ("They are wrong, however") of those who say there is no such evidence.
Which one of the following is the main point of the argument?	**Step 1:** The phrasing "main point of the argument" indicates that this is a Main Point question. The correct answer will paraphrase the author's conclusion.
	Step 3: The correct answer will match the author's conclusion: *There is evidence to support the idea that the rate of animal species extinction is accelerating.*
(A) There is evidence that the rate of extinction of animal species is accelerating.	**Step 4:** Correct. This matches the prediction perfectly.
(B) The future rate of extinction of animal species cannot be determined from available evidence.	This is an extreme interpretation of what "the authors of a recent article" believe, but the person making the argument *disagrees* with those authors. Our author thinks that there *is* evidence to suggest that the rate is accelerating. Eliminate.
(C) The rate of extinction of North American fishes is parallel to the rate of extinction of all animal species taken together.	Extreme. The author does not claim that the rate of fish extinction is parallel with *all* other animal species, merely that fish provide a counterexample to her opponents' position. Eliminate.
(D) Forty species and subspecies of North American fishes have vanished in the twentieth century.	This is evidence that the author uses to support her conclusion. Eliminate.
(E) A substantial number of fish species are in danger of imminent extinction. *PrepTest24 Sec2 Q15*	Extreme and Distortion. The argument makes no claim about whether a *substantial* number of species are in *imminent* danger. Instead, the argument simply states that the rate of extinction is increasing. Eliminate.

Notice that the correct answer mirrors the meaning, if not necessarily the exact wording, of the author's main point. And, just as we suspected, the wrong answers almost always do one of the following: Restate the evidence instead of the conclusion, distort the conclusion or miss its scope, or state the view of someone other than the author.

Practice

Now, try some Main Point questions yourself. Use everything you've learned about locating, characterizing, and paraphrasing the conclusion. Take your time and record your thinking for each step in the Kaplan Method.

Apply the Kaplan Method to each Logical Reasoning question. To compare your work to the thinking of an LSAT expert, turn to the pages following this exercise.

LSAT Question	My Analysis
11. It is well known that many species adapt to their environment, but it is usually assumed that only the most highly evolved species alter their environment in ways that aid their own survival. However, this characteristic is actually quite common. Certain species of plankton for example, generate a gas that is converted in the atmosphere into particles of sulfate. These particles cause water vapor to condense, thus forming clouds. Indeed, the formation of clouds over the ocean largely depends on the presence of these particles. More cloud cover means more sunlight is reflected, and so the Earth absorbs less heat. Thus plankton cause the surface of the Earth to be cooler and this benefits the plankton.	**Step 2:**
Of the following, which one most accurately expresses the main point of the argument?	**Step 1:**
	Step 3:
(A) The Earth would be far warmer than it is now if certain species of plankton became extinct.	**Step 4:**
(B) By altering their environment in ways that improve their chances of survival, certain species of plankton benefit the Earth as a whole.	
(C) Improving their own chances of survival by altering the environment is not limited to the most highly evolved species.	
(D) The extent of the cloud cover over the oceans is largely determined by the quantity of plankton in those oceans.	
(E) Species such as plankton alter the environment in ways that are less detrimental to the well-being of other species than are the alterations to the environment made by more highly evolved species.	

PrepTest29 Sec1 Q11

LSAT Question	**My Analysis**
12. Essayist: The way science is conducted and regulated can be changed. But we need to determine whether the changes are warranted, taking into account their price. The use of animals in research could end immediately, but only at the cost of abandoning many kinds of research and making other very expensive. The use of recombinant DNA could be drastically curtailed. Many other restrictions could be imposed, complete with a system of fraud police. But such massive interventions would be costly and would change the character of science.	**Step 2:**
Which one of the following most accurately expresses the main conclusion of the essayist's argument?	**Step 1:**
	Step 3:
(A) We should not make changes that will alter the character of science.	**Step 4:**
(B) If we regulate science more closely, we will change the character of science.	
(C) The regulation of science and the conducting of science can be changed.	
(D) The imposition of restrictions on the conduct of science would be very costly.	
(E) We need to be aware of the impact of change in science before changes are made.	

PrepTest28 Sec1 Q18

Expert Analysis

Here's how an LSAT expert would look at those two questions.

LSAT Question	Analysis
11. It is well known that many species adapt to their environment, but it is usually assumed that only the most highly evolved species alter their environment in ways that aid their own survival. However, this characteristic is actually quite common. Certain species of plankton for example, generate a gas that is converted in the atmosphere into particles of sulfate. These particles cause water vapor to condense, thus forming clouds. Indeed, the formation of clouds over the ocean largely depends on the presence of these particles. More cloud cover means more sunlight is reflected, and so the Earth absorbs less heat. Thus plankton cause the surface of the Earth to be cooler and this benefits the plankton.	**Step 2:** Conclusion: [Keyword "However"] The characteristic of adapting to and altering their environment is not unique to highly evolved species; it is common to many species. The rest of the argument is an example that acts as evidence supporting the conclusion.
Of the following, which one most accurately expresses the main point of the argument?	**Step 1:** The phrasing "accurately expresses the main point" indicates that this is a Main Point question. The correct answer will paraphrase the author's conclusion.
	Step 3: The correct answer will be a close paraphrase of the author's conclusion: *Adapting to their environment is not something that only highly evolved species do.*
(A) The Earth would be far warmer than it is now if certain species of plankton became extinct.	**Step 4:** How plankton affect the temperature of the Earth is used as evidence to support the conclusion. Eliminate.
(B) By altering their environment in ways that improve their chances of survival, certain species of plankton benefit the Earth as a whole.	Distortion. Plankton alter their environment in ways that benefit plankton. Also, the example of plankton is evidence in this argument, not the conclusion. Eliminate.
(C) Improving their own chances of survival by altering the environment is not limited to the most highly evolved species.	Correct. This is a close match to the prediction.
(D) The extent of the cloud cover over the oceans is largely determined by the quantity of plankton in those oceans.	How plankton affect cloud cover is used as evidence to support the conclusion. Eliminate.
(E) Species such as plankton alter the environment in ways that are less detrimental to the well-being of other species than are the alterations to the environment made by more highly evolved species.	Irrelevant Comparison. Whether alterations to a species' environment are positive or negative to other species is not discussed. Eliminate.

PrepTest29 Sec1 Q11

LSAT Question	Analysis
12. Essayist: The way science is conducted and regulated can be changed. But we need to determine whether the changes are warranted, taking into account their price. The use of animals in research could end immediately, but only at the cost of abandoning many kinds of research and making other very expensive. The use of recombinant DNA could be drastically curtailed. Many other restrictions could be imposed, complete with a system of fraud police. But such massive interventions would be costly and would change the character of science.	**Step 2:** Conclusion: [Keyword "But"] In order to determine whether changes to the way science is conducted and regulated are warranted, we need to take into account the cost of such changes.
Which one of the following most accurately expresses the main conclusion of the essayist's argument?	**Step 1:** The phrasing "accurately expresses the main conclusion" indicates that this is a Main Point question. The correct answer will paraphrase the author's conclusion.
	Step 3: The correct answer will be a close paraphrase of the author's conclusion: *While changes in science are possible, we must take into account the costs of such changes before we determine whether those changes are warranted.*
(A) We should not make changes that will alter the character of science.	**Step 4:** Extreme. The author does not make a recommendation for or against the adoption of changes in science. Eliminate.
(B) If we regulate science more closely, we will change the character of science.	The author concedes that *massive* interventions would change the character of science, but this is evidence used to support the author's conclusion. Eliminate.
(C) The regulation of science and the conducting of science can be changed.	This is Sentence 1, and is background information that the author considers to be a fact. The conclusion does not come until the next sentence. Eliminate.
(D) The imposition of restrictions on the conduct of science would be very costly.	The fact that some restrictions may be costly is used as evidence. Eliminate.
(E) We need to be aware of the impact of change in science before changes are made.	Correct. This matches the prediction.

PrepTest28 Sec1 Q18

FOR FURTHER PRACTICE

You'll find more Main Point questions in the Question Pool at the end of this chapter.

Keep in mind that you'll practice locating, characterizing, and paraphrasing conclusions in all of the upcoming Assumption, Strengthen/Weaken, Flaw, Parallel Reasoning, and Method of Argument questions—and many Principle, Role of a Statement, and Point at Issue questions as well.

These are skills you'll reuse and reinforce throughout your Logical Reasoning practice.

Reflection

Congratulations on developing a core set of Logical Reasoning skills and on mastering your first Logical Reasoning question type. Over the next few days, reflect on this session.

Take note of how often you or someone you're talking to makes an argument. What was his or her conclusion? What type was it? Even statements as simple and everyday as "We should go get some ice cream," or "The singing on this song is really weak," can help reinforce your mastery of LSAT conclusion types.

When you're watching TV or reading the news, keep an eye out for arguments. When you spot them, locate and characterize their conclusions. You'll be shocked by how many arguments you encounter on a daily basis.

EVIDENCE AND ARGUMENTS: ROLE OF A STATEMENT, METHOD OF ARGUMENT, AND POINT AT ISSUE QUESTIONS

Several question types besides Main Point questions reward your ability to understand argument structures and parts, and we're about to learn the skills necessary for grabbing those points. Taken together, the question types we'll cover in this chapter are worth 8–10 questions on an average LSAT. In addition, the more you know about working with arguments, the better prepared you'll be to start tackling Assumptions and other key question types in Chapter 10. Remember, argument-based questions make up over 70 percent of the LR section and over one-third of the LSAT. Also, keep in mind that a strong understanding of arguments will serve you well in the Reading Comprehension section, too—not to mention in law school.

So far in this chapter, you've learned how to identify conclusions. Take a moment to look back at the questions you just practiced earlier in this chapter and notice how many different ways the authors tried to establish their main points. You're about to work in greater depth with these different ways of supporting a conclusion. In other words, you're ready to tackle *evidence*.

Evidence and Role of a Statement Questions

LEARNING OBJECTIVES

In this section, you'll learn to:

- Distinguish evidence from background information.
- Identify Role of a Statement questions and characterize the correct and incorrect answers.

You learned in the previous section that evidence is the set of facts, analyses, or other considerations that an author uses to try to persuade her reader that her conclusion is correct. Evidence can be long or short, convincing or questionable, and accurate or wildly fictitious. Don't get hung up on comparing the claims you read on the LSAT with what you know about real life. You'll never be asked whether an author's evidence, by itself, is true or believable, but you will frequently be asked about how an author's evidence interacts with her conclusion: whether her evidence does a good job supporting her conclusion, how that support could be made stronger or weaker, or what additional evidence is needed to establish the conclusion. The first step in being able to answer those questions is to identify and paraphrase an author's evidence.

(By the way, evidence is sometimes referred to on the LSAT as the author's "premises." The premises of an argument are that argument's complete set of evidence, and "a premise" is a piece of evidence.)

Just as conclusions are sometimes marked with Keywords, evidence also is sometimes marked with a Keyword. Similarly, just as conclusions can come anywhere in an argument (first sentence, last sentence, in the middle), so too can evidence. Authors use evidence Keywords to say, "Here's why I think the conclusion is true."

Chicago is a great city. After all, there's so much fun stuff to do there.

Notice that there's no conclusion Keyword, but "after all" signals that the second sentence exists to support the first one. That second sentence is the author's evidence.

We could write that same argument a different way:

Because there's so much fun stuff to do there, Chicago is a great city.

Here the conclusion and evidence appear in the same sentence. The first clause of that sentence is evidence, and the second clause is the author's overall conclusion. Don't be thrown off when wording changes on the LSAT. Stay focused on the role played by each clause in the argument and take advantage of evidence Keywords like "because." Other common Keywords indicating evidence are *since* and *for*. Remember, too, that phrases like *this shows* and *from this one can conclude* indicate a conclusion and tell you that the main evidence comes just prior to this in the argument.

Restate the argument about Chicago using each of those Keywords. (Of course, you can substitute the city of your choice if you like.) How would you construct that same argument using the various evidence Keywords in this list? Which evidence Keywords work best *after* a conclusion, and which work best *before* a conclusion?

Practice using evidence Keywords to spot an author's evidence. Take a look at this example from a real LSAT question:

LSAT Question	Analysis
Historian: We can learn about the medical history of individuals through chemical analysis of their hair. It is likely, for example, that Isaac Newton's psychological problems were due to mercury poisoning; traces of mercury were found in his hair. Analysis is now being done on a lock of Beethoven's hair. Although no convincing argument has shown that Beethoven ever had a venereal disease, some people hypothesize that venereal disease caused his deafness. Since mercury was commonly ingested in Beethoven's time to treat venereal disease, if researchers find a trace of mercury in his hair, we can conclude that this hypothesis is correct. *PrepTest28 Sec3 Q16*	The conclusion here is indicated by the Keywords "we can conclude": *The hypothesis that Beethoven's deafness was caused by a venereal disease is correct.* This claim, however, is dependent on some lab results: *if researchers find a trace of mercury in his hair.* The evidence is signaled by the evidence Keyword "[s]ince": *mercury was commonly ingested in Beethoven's time to treat venereal disease.* Earlier in the argument we had more evidence, indicated by the common phrasing "for example": *it's likely Newton's psychological problems were due to mercury poisoning, since mercury was found in this hair.*

(By the way, did you have trouble buying the author's reasoning here? If so, good for you! Many LSAT arguments are flawed, and the LSAT frequently rewards you for spotting argumentative flaws. We'll discuss flaws thoroughly in Chapter 10.)

Sometimes evidence isn't marked with a Keyword. In those cases, you need to ask yourself which parts of the argument answer the question "What supports this?" That is, identify the author's conclusion using conclusion Keywords or the One-Sentence Test. Then imagine yourself saying to the author, "Here's your claim. Why so? What makes you believe that?" The parts of the argument that answer that question are the author's evidence. To see this, turn to the next page and revisit an argument you saw in the last section.

LSAT Question	Analysis
The authors of a recent article examined warnings of an impending wave of extinctions of animal species within the next 100 years. These authors say that no evidence exists to support the idea that the rate of extinction of animal species is now accelerating. They are wrong, however. Consider only the data on fishes: 40 species and subspecies of North American fishes have vanished in the twentieth century, 13 between 1900 and 1950, and 27 since 1950. *PrepTest24 Sec2 Q15* →	The conclusion here is a rebuttal: *The authors of the article are wrong.* But what are they wrong about? Always articulate a full, clear understanding of an argument's conclusion: *There* is *evidence to support the idea that the rate of animal extinctions is increasing.* In the absence of clear evidence Keywords, look for the data and facts that the author presents in order to support her conclusion. "Consider only the data on fishes…" Aha! That's the evidence: *13 fish species vanished in the first half of the century, while 27 species vanished in the second half of the century.*

Did anything strike you about the nature of the evidence in that argument? The author used scientific data to back up her claim. (In fact, phrases such as "research has shown" and "consider the data" are subtle clues that you're looking at evidence.) It's frequently helpful on the LSAT to note what kind of evidence an author is using: Is it made up of examples? Research studies? General principles about how the universe works? Expert opinion? Something else? We'll practice characterizing an author's argumentative strategy later in this chapter. For now, get in the habit of making a mental note of the kind of evidence you're looking at.

LSAT Question	Analysis
The play *Mankind* must have been written between 1431 and 1471. It cannot have been written before 1431, for in that year the rose noble, a coin mentioned in the play, was first circulated. The play cannot have been written after 1471, since in that year King Henry VI died, and he is mentioned as a living monarch in the play's dedication. *PrepTest24 Sec3 Q9* →	The first sentence, a strong assertion of fact, is the conclusion: Mankind *must have been written between 1431 and 1471.* The evidence here is the rest of the argument, but notice what the author does. In the second sentence she uses evidence pertaining to the year a coin was first circulated to support a subsidiary conclusion that the play could not have been written before 1431. In the third sentence, she uses evidence regarding the year King Henry VI died to support another subsidiary conclusion that the play could not have been written after 1471. So two distinct pieces of evidence support two subsidiary conclusions, both of which are then used to draw the main conclusion.

TEST DAY TIP

Underline (or use a checkmark to denote) the evidence in your test booklet. This will highlight the evidence and keep it distinct from the bracketed conclusion. Get in the habit of doing this for all Argument-based and Assumption-family questions.

Practice

Now, practice identifying the evidence in a handful of LSAT arguments.

In each of the following arguments, locate the evidence the author or speaker in question uses to support her conclusion. In your own words, explain how you knew that the sentence or clause you selected is evidence for the author's conclusion. After each, you can turn to the expert thinking and check your work.

LSAT Question	My Analysis
13. Recent research shows that sound change (pronunciation shift) in a language is not gradual. New sounds often emerge suddenly. This confounds the classical account of sound change, whose central tenet is gradualness. Since this classical account must be discarded, sound-change theory in general must also be. *PrepTest27 Sec1 Q16*	
14. The widespread staff reductions in a certain region's economy are said to be causing people who still have their jobs to cut back on new purchases as though they, too, had become economically distressed. Clearly, however, actual spending by such people is undiminished, because there has been no unusual increase in the amount of money held by those people in savings account. *PrepTest24 Sec3 Q17*	
15. Research indicates that 90 percent of extreme insomniacs consume large amount of coffee. Since Tom drinks a lot of coffee, it is quite likely that he is an extreme insomniac. *PrepTest27 Sec1 Q23*	

Expert Analysis

Here's how an LSAT expert looks at each of the arguments you've just examined.

LSAT Question	Analysis
13. Recent research shows that sound change (pronunciation shift) in a language is not gradual. New sounds often emerge suddenly. This confounds the classical account of sound change, whose central tenet is gradualness. Since this classical account must be discarded, sound-change theory in general must also be. *PrepTest27 Sec1 Q16*	Conclusion: Sound-change theory in general must be discarded. *because* Evidence: The classical account of sound change must be discarded.

Notice that in the argument, the first sentence starts with the evidence Keywords "[r]ecent research shows." An untrained test taker might imagine that that is the only—or at least the most significant—piece of evidence in the argument. But keep reading. What role does the research play in the argument? It is used by the author to show that the classical account of sound change may be incorrect. The argument continues: because the classical account should be discarded, sound-change theory in general must be discarded. A well-trained LSAT expert separates the many different possible pieces of an argument—background information, evidence, subsidiary conclusions, main conclusions—by constantly asking: What role does this statement play? Why is it here? Is it supporting something else?

LSAT Question	Analysis
14. The widespread staff reductions in a certain region's economy are said to be causing people who still have their jobs to cut back on new purchases as though they, too, had become economically distressed. Clearly, however, actual spending by such people is undiminished, because there has been no unusual increase in the amount of money held by those people in savings account. *PrepTest24 Sec3 Q17*	Conclusion: people who still have jobs are still spending on new purchases *because* Evidence: there has been no unusual increase in the savings accounts of people who still have jobs

What purpose does the first sentence serve in this example? It's the opposing claim that we need in order to understand the author's argument, but does not, by itself, advance the author's conclusion.

LSAT Question	**Analysis**
15. Research indicates that 90 percent of extreme insomniacs consume large amount of coffee. Since Tom drinks a lot of coffee, it is quite likely that he is an extreme insomniac. *PrepTest27 Sec1 Q23* →	Conclusion: Tom is an extreme insomniac. *because* Evidence: [1] 90 percent of extreme insomniacs consume large amounts of coffee; and [2] Tom drinks a lot of coffee.

Did you notice what the author did in this argument? He provided evidence showing that overwhelmingly, insomniacs are people who drink a lot of coffee. He then drew a conclusion suggesting that a person who drinks a lot of coffee is likely an insomniac. Does that argument structure seem familiar to you? The author is confusing the sufficient and necessary terms of a conditional statement. Determining that a person is an insomniac is sufficient to know that that person likely drinks a lot of coffee, but being an insomniac is not necessarily an attribute of a person who drinks a lot of coffee. The stronger your grasp of the principles of Formal Logic (covered in Chapter 1), the more easily and quickly you'll be able to spot this common reasoning flaw.

Reflection

Review the practice you just did: How efficiently were you able to identify the author's evidence? Did you paraphrase the evidence in your own words? Did you make a mental note of what kind of evidence the author was using? What, if anything, distracted you from homing in on the relevant evidence?

Did you make some mistakes? That's great! Mistakes are a tremendously valuable source of information for you: Every error tells you something about what you need to work on before Test Day. How did you misidentify the evidence in this practice? Do you see any patterns in your mistakes?

Identify and Answer Role of a Statement Questions

You've gotten some practice with identifying conclusions and evidence. Ready to put it to use? One LSAT question type, called Role of a Statement, rewards your ability to simply identify the various pieces of an argument—such as evidence, conclusion, opponent's argument, or background information. You know you're dealing with a Role of a Statement question if you see a question stem like this:

LSAT Question	Analysis
That consumers are buying more durable goods than before figures in the economist's argument in which one of the following ways? *PrepTest24 Sec2 Q10*	The question stem quotes a statement from the stimulus (here, "consumers are buying more durable goods than before") and then asks us to determine *how* the statement figures into the argument. This is a Role of a Statement question. Our task is to identify the statement as the argument's conclusion, evidence, background information, or something else.

As always when working with arguments on the LSAT, start with identifying and paraphrasing evidence and conclusion. Then formulate a prediction to use when looking at the answer choices. Your prediction on a Role of a Statement question will sound something like this: "the statement is evidence," "the statement is the author's conclusion," or "the statement is evidence cited by the author's opponents." Wrong answer choices on a Role of a Statement question will likely describe *other* parts of the author's argument or distort the argument in some way.

Let's look at an LSAT expert's analysis of a full LSAT Role of a Statement question.

LSAT Question	**Analysis**
The stable functioning of a society depends upon the relatively long-term stability of the goals of its citizens. This is clear from the fact that unless the majority of individuals have a predictable and enduring set of aspirations, it will be impossible for a legislature to craft laws that will augment the satisfaction of the citizenry, and it should be obvious that a society is stable only if its laws tend to increase the happiness of its citizens.	**Step 2:** Conclusion: A society will not remain stable without the long-term stability of its citizens' goals. *because* Evidence: [Key phrase "This is clear from the fact"] [1] A legislature cannot make laws that satisfy citizens without most people having predictable aspirations; and [2] A society will remain stable only if its laws tend to make its citizens happier. [This is the statement in the question stem.]
The claim that a society is stable only if its laws tend to increase the happiness of its citizens plays which one of the following roles in the argument?	**Step 1:** The phrasing "the claim … plays which one of the following roles" indicates that this is a Role of a Statement question. The correct answer choice will describe how the statement functions in the overall argument.
	Step 3: The claim in the question stem is one of two pieces of evidence used to support the argument's conclusion.
(A) It is the conclusion of the argument.	**Step 4:** The conclusion is the first sentence in the argument. Eliminate.
(B) It helps to support the conclusion of the argument.	Correct. This matches the prediction.
(C) It is a claim that must be refuted if the conclusion is to be established.	180. The conclusion is supported by the claim. Eliminate.
(D) It is a consequence of the argument.	Distortion. The statement is simply evidence for the conclusion. A consequence is something that would *follow from* the argument. Eliminate.
(E) It is used to illustrate the general principle that the argument presupposes.	The claim itself is a general rule, not a specific example. Eliminate.

PrepTest27 Sec1 Q17

On Test Day, you could stop with (B) once you've seen that it matches your prediction perfectly. As you're practicing for the LSAT, however, it's always valuable to review all four wrong answers and make sure you see why each is incorrect.

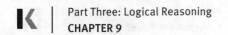
Practice

Practice solving Role of a Statement questions using the approach just illustrated.

Apply the Kaplan Logical Reasoning Method to answer each of the following questions. Here, note clues in the question stem to determine that these are Role of a Statement questions. Then, untangle the stimulus by identifying the author's conclusion and evidence. Find and underline the statement cited in the question stem and describe the role it plays in the argument. Use that as your prediction of the correct answer and evaluate the answer choices. After each question, you can turn to the expert thinking and check your work.

LSAT Question	My Analysis
16. Economist: The economy seems to be heading out of recession. Recent figures show that consumers are buying more durable goods than before, indicating that they expect economic growth in the near future.	Step 2:
That consumers are buying more durable goods than before figures in the economist's argument in which one of the following ways?	Step 1:
	Step 3:
(A) It is the phenomenon that the argument seeks to explain.	Step 4:
(B) Its truth is required in order for the argument's conclusion to be true.	
(C) It is an inference drawn from the premise that the recession seems to be ending.	
(D) It is an inference drawn from the premise that consumers expect economic growth in the near future.	
(E) It is the primary evidence from which the argument's conclusion is drawn.	

PrepTest24 Sec2 Q10

LSAT Question	My Analysis
17. Ambiguity inspires interpretation. The saying, "We are the measure of all things," for instance, has been interpreted by some people to imply that humans are centrally important in the universe, while others have interpreted it to mean simply that, since all knowledge is human knowledge, humans must rely on themselves to find the truth.	**Step 2:**
That claim that ambiguity inspires interpretation figures in the argument in which one of the following ways?	**Step 1:**
	Step 3:
(A) It is used to support the argument's conclusion.	**Step 4:**
(B) It is an illustration of the claim that we are the measure of all things.	
(C) It is compatible with either accepting or rejecting the argument's conclusion.	
(D) It is a view that other statements in the argument are intended to support.	
(E) It sets out a difficulty the argument is intended to solve.	

PrepTest29 Sec4 Q15

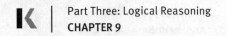
Expert Analysis

Here's how an LSAT expert looks at each of the arguments you've just examined.

LSAT Question	Analysis
16. Economist: The economy seems to be heading out of recession. Recent figures show that consumers are buying more durable goods than before, indicating that they expect economic growth in the near future.	**Step 2:** Conclusion: The economy seems to be heading out of recession. *because* Evidence: [Key phrase "Recent figures show"] [1] Consumers are buying more durable goods [this is the statement in the question stem], which indicates that [2] they expect economic growth in the near future.
That consumers are buying more durable goods than before figures in the economist's argument in which one of the following ways?	**Step 1:** The phrasing "figures in the … argument in which one of the following ways" indicates that this is a Role of a Statement question. The correct answer choice will describe how the statement functions in the overall argument.
	Step 3: The statement is used as evidence to support the economist's conclusion.
(A) It is the phenomenon that the argument seeks to explain.	**Step 4:** Distortion. While the relevant statement is a phenomenon that has occurred, the author does not seek to explain what caused that phenomenon; instead, he uses it to make a prediction. Eliminate.
(B) Its truth is required in order for the argument's conclusion to be true.	Extreme. While the statement is evidence for the conclusion, the argument does not claim that it must be true for the conclusion to be drawn. Eliminate.
(C) It is an inference drawn from the premise that the recession seems to be ending.	180. The fact that consumers are buying more durable goods is a premise used to support the claim that the recession seems to be ending. Eliminate.
(D) It is an inference drawn from the premise that consumers expect economic growth in the near future.	180. Again, the statement in the question stem is itself a premise and not an inference. Eliminate.
(E) It is the primary evidence from which the argument's conclusion is drawn. *PrepTest24 Sec2 Q10*	Correct. The first part of sentence 2 is a piece of evidence from which the author draws an inference; that inference is then used to reach the argument's conclusion.

LSAT Question	Analysis
17. Ambiguity inspires interpretation. The saying, "We are the measure of all things," for instance, has been interpreted by some people to imply that humans are centrally important in the universe, while others have interpreted it to mean simply that, since all knowledge is human knowledge, humans must rely on themselves to find the truth. →	**Step 2:** Conclusion: Ambiguity inspires interpretation. [This is the statement in the question stem.] *because* Evidence: [Key phrase "for instance"] A certain saying has been interpreted in different ways.
That claim that ambiguity inspires interpretation figures in the argument in which one of the following ways? →	**Step 1:** The phrasing "figures in the ... argument in which one of the following ways" indicates that this is a Role of a Statement question. The correct answer choice will describe how the statement functions in the overall argument.
	Step 3: The statement referenced in the question stem is the argument's conclusion.
(A) It is used to support the argument's conclusion. →	**Step 4:** This describes evidence, not the conclusion. Eliminate.
(B) It is an illustration of the claim that we are the measure of all things. →	The claim, "we are the measure of all things" is used by the author as an example to show how statements can be interpreted differently. Eliminate.
(C) It is compatible with either accepting or rejecting the argument's conclusion. →	Because the statement *is* the conclusion, this can't be right. Eliminate.
(D) It is a view that other statements in the argument are intended to support. →	Correct. The conclusion of an argument is the view or claim that the other statements in the argument are intended to support.
(E) It sets out a difficulty the argument is intended to solve. →	The argument does not intend to solve anything. Eliminate.

PrepTest29 Sec4 Q15

Look back over your practice. Did you identify and paraphrase the author's conclusion and evidence before making a prediction about the statement quoted in the question stem? Did you keep your prediction in mind as you evaluated answer choices?

If these questions didn't go well, treat that as a blessing in disguise by using your mistakes as powerful sources of information about what you need to work on. What led you to misidentify the role played by the statement you were asked about?

Outlining Complete Arguments and Point at Issue Questions

> ### LEARNING OBJECTIVES
>
> In this section, you'll learn to:
>
> - Outline complete arguments.
> - Identify Point at Issue questions and characterize the correct and incorrect answers.

Here you see a Point at Issue question. You'll review it piece by piece shortly. These questions reward you for zeroing in on the particular point about which two speakers disagree. Preparing to tackle this question type provides the perfect opportunity to learn another valuable LSAT Logical Reasoning skill: outlining complete arguments.

P: Complying with the new safety regulations is useless. Even if the new regulations had been in effect before last year's laboratory fire, they would not have prevented the fire or the injuries resulting from it because they do not address its underlying causes.

Q: But any regulations that can potentially prevent money from being wasted are useful. If obeyed, the new safety regulations will prevent some accidents, and whenever there is an accident here at the laboratory, money is wasted even if no one is injured.

A point at issue between P and Q is whether

(A) last year's fire resulted in costly damage to the laboratory

(B) accidents at the laboratory inevitably result in personal injuries

(C) the new safety regulations address the underlying cause of last year's fire

(D) it is useful to comply with the new safety regulations

(E) the new safety regulations are likely to be obeyed in the laboratory

PrepTest 27 Sec4 Q11

Outline Complete Arguments

Expert LSAT test takers are able to sum up and paraphrase the arguments in Logical Reasoning questions logically and accurately. They sort out the complex prose and sometimes indirect sentence structure in a way that makes every argument as simple as saying, "The author believes y (his conclusion) because of x (his evidence)."

Recall some of the arguments you've seen already in this chapter. At times, the evidence appeared before the conclusion, and at other times, after it. You've even seen arguments that had two pieces of evidence, one before and one after the conclusion. Those can all be effective ways of expressing an argument, but when you're outlining the argument—summarizing and paraphrasing it for your own understanding—you'll want to arrange the premises and conclusion logically:

[Conclusion] because [Evidence]

or

[Evidence]. Thus, [Conclusion]

Take a look at how an LSAT expert would outline this LSAT Logical Reasoning argument.

LSAT Question	Analysis
Historian: We can learn about the medical history of individuals through chemical analysis of their hair. It is likely, for example, that Isaac Newton's psychological problems were due to mercury poisoning; traces of mercury were found in his hair. Analysis is now being done on a lock of Beethoven's hair. Although no convincing argument has shown that Beethoven ever had a venereal disease, some people hypothesize that venereal disease caused his deafness. Since mercury was commonly ingested in Beethoven's time to treat venereal disease, if researchers find a trace of mercury in his hair, we can conclude that this hypothesis is correct. *PrepTest28 Sec3 Q16*	Conclusion: If researchers find traces of mercury in Beethoven's hair, then a venereal disease caused his deafness. *because* → Evidence: During his time, mercury was commonly ingested to treat venereal disease.

Like many of the arguments you'll see on the LSAT, the argument given here is, at its heart, quite simple. The author states that if it is determined that Beethoven had traces of mercury in his hair, then one can conclude that his deafness was caused by a certain type of disease. What's the evidence for this argument? Simply that during Beethoven's time, mercury was commonly used to treat that type of disease.

While the argument itself is relatively simple, the way it was presented on the LSAT is not. The author begins the argument by providing background information. The first sentence sets the stage by defining the scope of the argument to come. The next sentence, signaled by "for example," gives us historical information that provides support for the idea that chemical analysis of hair can be useful in determining the medical history of certain people. How necessary is all of that to the author's central argument? Not necessary at all. While untrained test-takers might stumble over or get confused by such a lengthy preamble, a well-trained test taker cuts through the fluff and seeks out the conclusion and the direct evidence used to support that conclusion.

The argument is further complicated by the fact that the author does not explicitly state the argument's conclusion. Instead, the author describes the hypothesis of "some people," and then later confirms that hypothesis to be correct if a certain condition is met.

Don't be confused or frustrated by lengthy arguments. Instead, do what the LSAT expert above did: Seek out the conclusion and put it into your own words. Then find the evidence that most directly supports that conclusion.

Here are some more examples. Notice that the following arguments aren't constructed in exactly the same way as the preceding argument. No matter; focus on identifying the conclusion and the evidence and then reconstruct the argument with those pieces.

LSAT Question		Analysis
Plant Manager: We could greatly reduce the amount of sulfur dioxide our copper-smelting plant releases into the atmosphere by using a new process. The new process requires replacing our open furnaces with closed ones and moving the copper from one furnace to the next in solid, not molten, form. However, not only is the new equipment expensive to buy and install, but the new process also costs more to run than the current process, because the copper must be reheated after it has cooled. So overall, adopting the new process will cost much but bring the company no profit. *PrepTest29 Sec4 Q14*	→	Conclusion: Even though it would reduce sulfur dioxide, the new process (closed furnaces and moving copper in solid form) will cost a lot and not be profitable. *because* Evidence: The equipment for the new process is expensive to buy and install, and it costs more to run.
A recent study concludes that prehistoric birds, unlike modern birds, were cold-blooded. This challenges a widely held view that modern birds descended from warm-blooded birds. The conclusion is based on the existence of growth rings in prehistoric birds' bodily structures, which are thought to be found only in cold-blooded animals. Another study, however, disputes this view. It concludes that prehistoric birds had dense blood vessels in their bones, which suggests that they were active creatures and therefore had to be warm-blooded. *PrepTest28 Sec3 Q13*	→	Position #1: Conclusion: Prehistoric birds were cold-blooded. *because* Evidence: Presence of growth rings in prehistoric birds' bodily structures (thought to be only in cold-blooded animals). Position #2: Conclusion: Prehistoric birds were warm-blooded. *because* Evidence: Prehistoric birds had dense blood vessels in their bones, which suggests they were active.

Notice how, in the second stimulus, the test expert untangles and keeps separate two distinctly different arguments. The author of that stimulus never steps in and provides a judgment as to which of the two arguments is preferable, or more accurate. The test expert is unperturbed: She simply identifies both conclusions and the evidence for each, and will then approach the rest of the question accordingly.

In all three of the preceding examples, our LSAT expert maintains a singular focus: identifying, separating, and paraphrasing an argument's evidence and conclusion. You'll find that having the ability to summarize and outline LSAT arguments in this way is enormously helpful in many Logical Reasoning question types—Assumption, Strengthen/Weaken, and Flaw, as well as three question types still to come in this chapter, Point at Issue, Method of Argument, and Parallel Reasoning.

Practice

Now, try untangling and outlining a handful of LSAT arguments on your own. Strive to make your summaries as clear and simple as the expert thinking you saw above.

For each of the following arguments, locate the conclusion and the relevant evidence. Then, outline the complete argument in the following format: [Conclusion] because [Evidence]. When the argument has more than one piece of evidence, make sure you can outline the logical progression of the author's reasoning. When you're done, you can check your work and review the expert thinking on the next page.

LSAT Question	My Analysis
18. Unplugging a peripheral component such as a "mouse" from a personal computer renders all of the software programs that require that component unusable on that computer. On Fred's personal computer, a software program that requires a mouse has become unusable. So it must be that the mouse for Fred's computer became unplugged. *PrepTest27 Sec4 Q10*	
19. Combustion of gasoline in automobile engines produces benzene, a known carcinogen. Environmentalists propose replacing gasoline with methanol, which does not produce significant quantities of benzene when burned. However, combustion of methanol produces formaldehyde, also a known carcinogen. Therefore the environmentalists' proposal has little merit. *PrepTest29 Sec4 Q1*	
20. The miscarriage of justice in the Barker case was due to the mistaken views held by some of the forensic scientists involved in the case, who believed that they owed allegiance only to the prosecuting lawyers. Justice was thwarted because these forensic scientists failed to provide evidence impartially to both the defense and the prosecution. Hence it is not forensic evidence in general that should be condemned for this injustice. *PrepTestB Sec4 Q16*	

Expert Analysis

Here's how an LSAT expert would untangle the arguments you just looked at.

LSAT Question	Analysis
18. Unplugging a peripheral component such as a "mouse" from a personal computer renders all of the software programs that require that component unusable on that computer. On Fred's personal computer, a software program that requires a mouse has become unusable. So it must be that the mouse for Fred's computer became unplugged. *PrepTest27 Sec4 Q10*	Conclusion: The mouse on Fred's computer is unplugged. *because* Evidence: A mouse must be plugged in for a certain software program to work. *and* Evidence: One of the programs on Fred's computer that requires a mouse doesn't work.
19. Combustion of gasoline in automobile engines produces benzene, a known carcinogen. Environmentalists propose replacing gasoline with methanol, which does not produce significant quantities of benzene when burned. However, combustion of methanol produces formaldehyde, also a known carcinogen. Therefore the environmentalists' proposal has little merit. *PrepTest29 Sec4 Q1*	Conclusion: We shouldn't replace gasoline with methanol. *because* Evidence: Combustion of methanol produces formaldehyde, a carcinogen. *even though* Evidence: Combustion of gasoline produces benzene, a carcinogen.
20. The miscarriage of justice in the Barker case was due to the mistaken views held by some of the forensic scientists involved in the case, who believed that they owed allegiance only to the prosecuting lawyers. Justice was thwarted because these forensic scientists failed to provide evidence impartially to both the defense and the prosecution. Hence it is not forensic evidence in general that should be condemned for this injustice. *PrepTestB Sec4 Q16*	Conclusion: Forensic evidence in general should not be condemned for this miscarriage of justice. *because* Evidence: Justice was miscarried in this case because the forensic scientists, believing they owed allegiance only to the prosecution, were not impartial.

Identify and Answer Point at Issue Questions

As you master the skill of untangling and outlining complete arguments, you're ready to tackle another LSAT Logical Reasoning question type: Point at Issue questions. Point at Issue questions are relatively rare—a typical test will likely have 1–3 of them. Point at Issue questions always have a dialogue in the stimulus. Both speakers make arguments, and they always disagree about one particular aspect of their arguments. The correct answer states or paraphrases this point of disagreement. The wrong answers to these questions come in three flavors: (1) a point about which only one of the speakers has an opinion, (2) a point outside the scope of both speakers' arguments, or (3) a point over which the two speakers *agree*. That last wrong answer type can be tempting because it is something about which both speakers have expressed an opinion.

Take a look at a couple of typical Point at Issue question stems.

LSAT Question	Analysis
Steven and Miguel's statements provide the most support for holding that they would disagree about the truth of which one of the following statements? $\longrightarrow$ *PrepTest 24 Sec2 Q14*	"[D]isagree about"—a Point at Issue question. The correct answer is a statement about which one speaker would say "yes, I agree," and the other "no, I disagree."
A point at issue between P and Q is whether *PrepTest27 Sec4 Q11* $\longrightarrow$	"[P]oint at issue"—a Point at Issue question. The correct answer will be a statement about which the speakers have opposite opinions.

On very rare occasions, the testmaker will ask a Point of Agreement question, in which case the correct answer will be the one containing a statement on which the two speakers have the same point of view. Make sure that you always respond to the task the test has set out for you.

Once you've identified a Point at Issue question, untangle both speakers' arguments to make sure you understand their conclusions and how they're supporting them. The two parties in the dialogue won't always disagree with each other's conclusions. Here's a simple example:

Tom: Our football team will win this game because our quarterback is great.

Jenny: You're wrong. Our quarterback is pretty average. We're going to win because our defense is so strong.

Here, Tom and Jenny share the same conclusion: Their team is going to win. They disagree about why that will be the case. In particular, they are directly at odds in their assessment of the quarterback.

In other cases, the two speakers may share the same evidence but reach different conclusions.

Michelle: The expansion of Superior Corporation's factory will bring workers into the area. That means a lot of new houses will be built in our town.

Sundeep: But these aren't the kind of jobs that lead to housing starts. The workers coming for jobs at Superior will be seasonal, so they'll likely seek apartments or other rental options.

Michelle and Sundeep see eye to eye on the fact that the factory expansion will bring workers into the area, but from that information, they draw opposed inferences about what this means for the town's housing market.

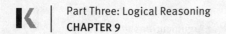

When you're able to spot the issue over which the two speakers are at odds, you have predicted the correct answer and can evaluate the answer choices.

TEST DAY TIP

A great way to evaluate the answer choices in Point at Issue questions is to apply the questions in Kaplan's Point at Issue Decision Tree.

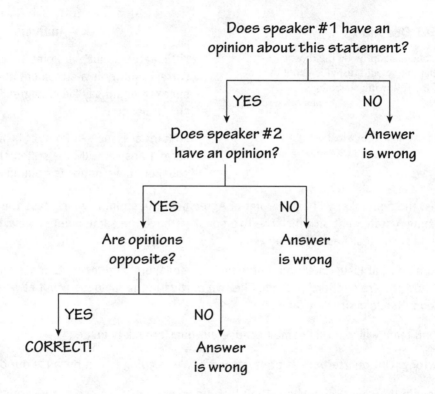

Because the correct answer must be the one statement over which the two speakers are committed to disagreeing, it will be the only choice that produces a "yes" to all three questions in the Decision Tree. In other words, if the speaker doesn't have an opinion about an answer choice you can immediately eliminate it.

Take a look at how an LSAT expert approaches a Point at Issue question.

LSAT Question	Analysis
P: Complying with the new safety regulations is useless. Even if the new regulations had been in effect before last year's laboratory fire, they would not have prevented the fire or the injuries resulting from it because they do not address its underlying causes.	**Step 2:** P's argument: [conclusion] Complying with the new safety regulations is useless, because [evidence] the regulations do not address the underlying causes of accidents like last year's lab fire.
Q: But any regulations that can potentially prevent money from being wasted are useful. If obeyed, the new safety regulations will prevent some accidents, and whenever there is an accident here at the laboratory, money is wasted even if no one is injured.	Q's response: [conclusion] The regulations will be useful if they save the company money, because [evidence] anything that saves money is useful, and these new regulations will prevent costly accidents.
A point at issue between P and Q is whether	**Step 1:** The phrasing "point at issue between P and Q" indicates that this is a Point at Issue question. The correct answer choice will represent a point on which P and Q disagree. Wrong answer choices will represent statements that P and Q agree on, or statements upon which one of them has no opinion.
	Step 3: Q's response indicates that she disagrees with P's conclusion. While P believes that the new safety regulations are useless, Q believes they can be useful.
(A) last year's fire resulted in costly damage to the laboratory	**Step 4:** Q does not state her opinion of last year's fire. Eliminate.
(B) accidents at the laboratory inevitably result in personal injuries	Neither P nor Q hold this extreme position. Eliminate.
(C) the new safety regulations address the underlying cause of last year's fire	Q does not state whether she believes the regulations would have addressed the underlying cause of last year's fire. Eliminate.
(D) it is useful to comply with the new safety regulations	Correct. P believes compliance is useless, while Q believes compliance can be useful.
(E) the new safety regulations are likely to be obeyed in the laboratory	Neither P nor Q offers an opinion on whether the regulations will be obeyed. Eliminate.

PrepTest27 Sec4 Q11

Notice how, once again, a strong prediction allows the test expert to quickly move through and eliminate wrong answer choices, and to quickly and confidently select the right answer choice once it is found.

Practice

Now, try a couple of Point at Issue questions on your own. Remember to outline each side's argument before you evaluate the answer choices. Use the Decision Tree to help you eliminate wrong answers and zero in on the one credited response.

Apply the Kaplan Logical Reasoning Method to answer the following questions. When you're done, check your work and review the expert thinking on the pages that follow these questions.

LSAT Question	My Analysis
21. Hospital auditor: The Rodriguez family stipulated that the funds they donated to the neurological clinic all be used to minimize patients' suffering. The clinic administration is clearly violating those terms, since it has allocated nearly one fifth of those funds for research into diagnostic technologies, instead of letting that money flow directly to its patients.	**Step 2:**
Clinic administrator: But the successful development of new technologies will allow early diagnosis of many neurological disorders. In most cases, patients who are treated in the early stages of neurological disorders suffer far less than do patients who are not treated until their neurological disorders reach advanced stages.	
Which one of the following is the main point at issue between the hospital auditor and the clinic administrator?	**Step 1:**
	Step 3:
(A) whether early treatment of many neurological disorders lessens the suffering associated with those disorders rather than completely eliminating such suffering	**Step 4:**
(B) whether the patients being treated at the neurological clinic are currently receiving adequate treatment for the neurological disorders from which they suffer	
(C) whether the Rodriguez family clearly stipulated that the funds they donated to the neurological clinic be used to minimize patients' suffering	
(D) whether the neurological clinic is adhering strictly to the conditions the Rodriguez family placed on the allocation of the funds they donated to the clinic	
(E) whether the Rodriguez family anticipated that some of the funds they donated to the neurological clinic would be used to pay for research into new diagnostic technologies	

PrepTest28 Sec1 Q6

LSAT Question	My Analysis
22. Steven: The allowable blood alcohol level for drivers should be cut in half. With this reduced limit, social drinkers will be deterred from drinking and driving, resulting in significantly increased highway safety.	**Step 2:**
Miguel: No, lowering the current allowable blood alcohol level would have little effect on highway safety, because it would not address the most important aspect of the drunken driving problem, which is the danger to the public posed by heavy drinkers, who often drive with a blood alcohol level of twice the current limit.	
Steven and Miguel's statements provide the most support for holding that they would disagree about the truth of which one of the following statements?	**Step 1:**
	Step 3:
(A) Social drinkers who drink and drive pose a substantial threat to the public.	**Step 4:**
(B) There is a direct correlation between a driver's blood alcohol level and the driver's ability to drive safely.	
(C) A driver with a blood alcohol level above the current legal limit poses a substantial danger to the public.	
(D) Some drivers whose blood alcohol level is lower than the current legal limit pose a danger to the public.	
(E) A driver with a blood alcohol level slightly greater than half the current legal limit poses no danger to the public.	

PrepTest24 Sec2 Q14

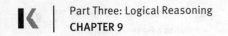

Expert Analysis

Here's how LSAT experts would answer the problems you just tried.

LSAT Question	Analysis
21. Hospital auditor: The Rodriguez family stipulated that the funds they donated to the neurological clinic all be used to minimize patients' suffering. The clinic administration is clearly violating those terms, since it has allocated nearly one fifth of those funds for research into diagnostic technologies, instead of letting that money flow directly to its patients.	**Step 2:** Hospital auditor's argument: [Conclusion] The clinic is not using the Rodriguez family funds as the family intended ("to minimize patients' suffering"), because [evidence] it is allocating a lot of money to technology research instead of directly to patients.
Clinic administrator: But the successful development of new technologies will allow early diagnosis of many neurological disorders. In most cases, patients who are treated in the early stages of neurological disorders suffer far less than do patients who are not treated until their neurological disorders reach advanced stages.	Clinic Administrator's response: [Conclusion] Using the money for technology research *will* reduce suffering, because [evidence] that technology will lead to early diagnoses, and patients treated in early stages of a neurological disorder will suffer far less than those treated later.
Which one of the following is the main point at issue between the hospital auditor and the clinic administrator?	**Step 1:** The phrasing "the main point at issue" indicates that this is a Point at Issue question.
	Step 3: The auditor and the administrator disagree over whether or not all of the donated money is being used to reduce suffering in patients at the neurological clinic. The auditor does not believe that the money set aside for research reduces suffering, while the administrator believes it does.
(A) whether early treatment of many neurological disorders lessens the suffering associated with those disorders rather than completely eliminating such suffering	**Step 4:** Irrelevant Comparison. The distinction between lessening suffering and eliminating suffering is not at issue in either argument. Eliminate.
(B) whether the patients being treated at the neurological clinic are currently receiving adequate treatment for the neurological disorders from which they suffer	Outside the Scope. The focus in each argument is the reduction of patients' suffering. Adequate treatment is not at issue in either argument. Eliminate.
(C) whether the Rodriguez family clearly stipulated that the funds they donated to the neurological clinic be used to minimize patients' suffering	While not explicitly mentioned by the administrator, it can be inferred that, if anything, she would agree with this statement. This is a point of agreement, not a point of disagreement. Eliminate.
(D) whether the neurological clinic is adhering strictly to the conditions the Rodriguez family placed on the allocation of the funds they donated to the clinic	Correct. The auditor believes that *no*, the clinic is not adhering to the conditions set forth by the Rodriguez family (i.e., to reduce patients' suffering); the administrator believes that *yes*, the clinic is adhering to those conditions.

LSAT Question	Analysis
(E) whether the Rodriguez family anticipated that some of the funds they donated to the neurological clinic would be used to pay for research into new diagnostic technologies *PrepTest28 Sec1 Q6*	Outside the Scope. What the Rodriguez family expected would happen with the money is not the point of disagreement here; instead, the issue is whether the clinic followed the family's instructions. Eliminate.

LSAT Question	Analysis
22. Steven: The allowable blood alcohol level for drivers should be cut in half. With this reduced limit, social drinkers will be deterred from drinking and driving, resulting in significantly increased highway safety.	**Step 2:** Steven's argument: [Conclusion] Lowering the allowable blood alcohol level for drivers will increase highway safety, because [evidence] social drinkers won't drink and drive as much.
Miguel: No, lowering the current allowable blood alcohol level would have little effect on highway safety, because it would not address the most important aspect of the drunken driving problem, which is the danger to the public posed by heavy drinkers, who often drive with a blood alcohol level of twice the current limit.	Miguel's response: [Conclusion] Lowering the allowable blood alcohol level for drivers won't increase highway safety, because [evidence] it won't do anything to deter heavy drinkers from drinking past the legal limit.
Steven and Miguel's statements provide the most support for holding that they would disagree about the truth of which one of the following statements?	**Step 1:** The phrasing "they would disagree about" indicates that this is a Point at Issue question.
	Step 3: Steven and Miguel disagree over whether or not lowering the allowable blood alcohol level will result in safer highways. While Steven believes that deterring social drinkers will result in safer highways, Miguel doesn't consider the behavior of social drinkers to be a significant factor in the drunk driving problem.
(A) Social drinkers who drink and drive pose a substantial threat to the public.	**Step 4:** Correct. Steven believes that they do pose a substantial threat; Miguel believes that they do not.
(B) There is a direct correlation between a driver's blood alcohol level and the driver's ability to drive safely.	Both would presumably agree with this. Eliminate.
(C) A driver with a blood alcohol level above the current legal limit poses a substantial danger to the public.	Both would presumably agree with this. Eliminate.
(D) Some drivers whose blood alcohol level is lower than the current legal limit pose a danger to the public.	Outside the Scope. The danger posed by drivers who are below the legal limit is not at issue here. Eliminate.
(E) A driver with a blood alcohol level slightly greater than half the current legal limit poses no danger to the public. *PrepTest24 Sec2 Q14*	Both Steven and Miguel believe drunk driving is a problem, so presumably both would disagree with this statement, and thus, agree with one another. Eliminate.

Reflection

Pay attention to some of the arguments, disputes, and disagreements you see or hear. Are the parties actually talking about the same thing? Try to pinpoint the actual issue(s) over which they disagree.

When you're listening to disagreements, try to determine whether the two speakers accept the same facts but draw different conclusions from them or see the same result but attribute it to different causes. These are like LSAT dialogues, which almost always feature a disagreement involving the reasoning, that is, a dispute about what the facts mean. Distinguish these from day-to-day arguments in which the parties simply disagree about the facts. The LSAT almost never features a dispute of that kind.

Describing Argumentative Strategy and Method of Argument Questions

---

LEARNING OBJECTIVES

In this section, you'll learn to:

- Describe an author's argumentative strategy.
- Identify Method of Argument questions and characterize the correct and incorrect answers.

Now that you've gotten some practice with describing arguments and their structures, you're ready to learn to characterize an author's argumentative strategy.

You saw as you were working with different kinds of evidence in the previous section that authors make choices about how to support their conclusions. One author might think that citing studies is really compelling, while another tries to persuade her readers by applying commonsense principles to the subject at hand. Another makes a generalization and backs it up with a handful of examples. Another author might claim that a statement must be true because Professor Thingummy, who's an expert, said so. Yet another might simply attack her opponent's position and figure that doing so will make her own position seem more compelling.

All those choices can be thought of as argumentative strategies, a phrase we'll use a great deal in this section. You've already gotten some good practice identifying *what* an author says and putting it into your own words. Now you'll learn how to describe in your own words *how* the author tries to convince the reader. Then, in a few pages, you'll meet a question type that rewards you for doing just that.

Always start by identifying and paraphrasing the author's conclusion, then the author's evidence. Then describe how the author has chosen to back up her conclusion.

LSAT Question	Analysis
It is well known that many species adapt to their environment, but it is usually assumed that only the most highly evolved species alter their environment in ways that aid their own survival. However, this characteristic is actually quite common. Certain species of plankton for example, generate a gas that is converted in the atmosphere into particles of sulfate. These particles cause water vapor to condense, thus forming clouds. Indeed, the formation of clouds over the ocean largely depends on the presence of these particles. More cloud cover means more sunlight is reflected, and so the Earth absorbs less heat. Thus plankton cause the surface of the Earth to be cooler and this benefits the plankton. *PrepTest29 Sec1 Q11*	Conclusion: While it is "usually assumed" that only the most highly evolved species alter their environment, the author disputes this interpretation. The Keyword "[h]owever" points us to the author's claim: *It is quite common for species to alter their environment.* Evidence: "Certain species of plankton, for example ..." The rest of the argument provides evidence by describing the behavior of types of plankton. Argumentative strategy: The author uses the specific example of plankton to counter a previously held belief.

LSAT Question	Analysis
The play Mankind must have been written between 1431 and 1471. It cannot have been written before 1431, for in that year the rose noble, a coin mentioned in the play, was first circulated. The play cannot have been written after 1471, since in that year King Henry VI died, and he is mentioned as a living monarch in the play's dedication. *PrepTest24 Sec3 Q9*	Conclusion: The first sentence gives a strong assertion of fact: *The play Mankind must have been written between 1431 and 1471.* Evidence: There are two pieces of evidence, each leading to two subsidiary conclusions. The first piece of evidence is that *1431 was the year the rose noble, a coin mentioned in the play, was first circulated.* From that the author concludes that the play could not have been written before 1431. The other piece of evidence, that *King Henry VI died in 1471 and yet the play mentions him as alive*, is used to draw the conclusion that the play could not have been written after 1471. Argumentative strategy: The author uses two separate pieces of evidence to draw two distinct subsidiary conclusions about the time range in which a play could have been written.

Again, stay focused on what the author *does*—not what the author says. This strategy could be applied in any number of arguments about any number of subjects.

LSAT STRATEGY

Common methods of argument on the LSAT include:

- Argument by analogy, in which an author draws parallels between two unrelated (but purportedly similar) situations
- Use of examples, in which an author cites specific cases to justify a generalization
- Use of counterexamples, in which an author seeks to discredit an opponent's argument by citing a specific case in which an opponent's conclusion appears to be invalid
- Appeal to authority, in which an author cites an expert or other authority figure as support for her conclusion
- Eliminating alternatives, in which an author lists possibilities and discredits all but one
- *Ad hominem* attack, in which an author attacks not her opponent's argument but rather her opponent's personal credibility
- Means/Requirement, in which the author argues that something is needed to achieve a desired result

Practice

Practice describing argumentative strategies using the following LSAT questions.

In each of the following arguments, identify the author's conclusion and the relevant evidence. Once you've done so, describe in your own words *how* the author goes about supporting her conclusion. After each question, use the expert thinking on the next page to check your work.

LSAT Question	My Analysis
23. The miscarriage of justice in the Barker case was due to the mistaken views held by some of the forensic scientists involved in the case, who believed that they owed allegiance only to the prosecuting lawyers. Justice was thwarted because these forensic scientists failed to provide evidence impartially to both the defense and the prosecution. Hence it is not forensic evidence in general that should be condemned for this injustice. *PrepTestB Sec4 Q16*	
24. Formal performance evaluations in the professional world are conducted using realistic situations. Physicians are allowed to consult medical texts freely, attorneys may refer to law books and case records, and physicists and engineers have their manuals at hand for ready reference. Students, then, should likewise have access to their textbooks whenever they take examinations. *PrepTest29 Sec4 Q25*	

Expert Analysis

Here's how an LSAT expert looks at each of the arguments you've just examined.

LSAT Question	Analysis
23. The miscarriage of justice in the Barker case was due to the mistaken views held by some of the forensic scientists involved in the case, who believed that they owed allegiance only to the prosecuting lawyers. Justice was thwarted because these forensic scientists failed to provide evidence impartially to both the defense and the prosecution. Hence it is not forensic evidence in general that should be condemned for this injustice. *PrepTestB Sec4 Q16* →	Conclusion: Following the Keyword "Hence": *forensic evidence in general should not be condemned for this miscarriage of justice.* Evidence: The Keyword "because" helps us identify the evidence: *The forensic scientists in this case were partial to the prosecution over the defense.* Additionally, the miscarriage of justice was "due to" *the mistaken views of the forensic scientists.* Argumentative strategy: The author discredits a specific group of forensic scientists and attempts to demonstrate that they are not representative of their profession.
24. Formal performance evaluations in the professional world are conducted using realistic situations. Physicians are allowed to consult medical texts freely, attorneys may refer to law books and case records, and physicists and engineers have their manuals at hand for ready reference. Students, then, should likewise have access to their textbooks whenever they take examinations. *PrepTest29 Sec4 Q25* →	Conclusion: A classic recommendation conclusion signified by the Keyword "should": *Students should be able to use textbooks during their exams, just like certain professionals.* Evidence: There aren't any strong evidence Keywords here, but the three examples provided in the second sentence provide the basis for the author's conclusion: *Physicians, lawyers, and scientists all get to consult texts during formal performance evaluations.* Argumentative strategy: The author uses an analogy to demonstrate why one group of people should be allowed to do the same thing as another group of people.

Reflection

Look back over your practice. Did you identify and paraphrase the author's conclusion and evidence before describing the entire argument? Did you describe the argumentative strategy in your own words? Did you stay focused on what the author *does* instead of what the author *says*?

Did you make some mistakes? Good! Use those mistakes as sources of insight about what you need to work on. How did you mischaracterize the author's evidence? Do you see any patterns in your mistakes?

Identify and Answer Method of Argument Questions

Your ability to break down and analyze arguments will be rewarded with points throughout the LR and RC sections. One question type that rewards those skills in a very direct way is the Method of Argument question. There are typically 1–2 of these on an average LSAT. As you described argumentative strategies in the last section, you were (without knowing it perhaps) already applying the Kaplan method for Method of Argument questions.

Method of Argument questions on the LSAT reward you for describing an author's argumentative strategy. The following are examples of question stems that tell you you're looking at a Method of Argument question:

LSAT Question	Analysis
The argument in the passage proceeds by doing which one of the following? *PrepTest24 Sec3 Q17* $\longrightarrow$	"The argument ... proceeds by" tells you to focus on the argument's rhetorical moves rather than on the argument's content—to describe *how* the argument is constructed, not *what* the argument is about.
Which of the following accurately describes the argumentative strategy employed? *PrepTest29 Sec1 Q12* $\longrightarrow$	"[D]escribes the argumentative strategy employed" directs you to identify and characterize the author's method of argumentation.

It's important to be able to predict what you're looking for in the correct answer choice. The right choice will match your description of the author's argumentative strategy. The wrong answers may describe argumentative strategies not used by the author, or they might distort the argument in some way.

Look at how an expert LSAT taker attacks a Method of Argument question:

LSAT Question	Analysis
It is well known that many species adapt to their environment, but it is usually assumed that only the most highly evolved species alter their environment in ways that aid their own survival. However, this characteristic is actually quite common. Certain species of plankton for example, generate a gas that is converted in the atmosphere into particles of sulfate. These particles cause water vapor to condense, thus forming clouds. Indeed, the formation of clouds over the ocean largely depends on the presence of these particles. More cloud cover means more sunlight is reflected, and so the Earth absorbs less heat. Thus plankton cause the surface of the Earth to be cooler and this benefits the plankton.	**Step 2:** Conclusion: [Keyword "However"] The characteristic of adapting to and altering their environment is not unique to highly evolved species; it is common to many species. The rest of the argument is an example that acts as evidence supporting the conclusion.
Which of the following accurately describes the argumentative strategy employed?	**Step 1:** The phrasing "describes the argumentative strategy" indicates that this is a Method of Argument question.
	Step 3: The author uses a detailed example of the characteristics of plankton to refute a commonly held belief.
(A) A general principle is used to justify a claim made about a particular case to which that principle has been shown to apply.	**Step 4:** This gets the author's strategy a bit backward; the author is using an example of a particular situation to refute a general understanding. Eliminate.
(B) An explanation of how a controversial phenomenon could have come about is given in order to support the claim that this phenomenon did in fact come about.	The author is challenging a conventional belief, not supporting a claim about a phenomenon. Eliminate.
(C) A generalization about the conditions under which a certain process can occur is advanced on the basis of an examination of certain cases in which that process did occur.	The author is not presenting an example to advance a generalization about species; instead, she is challenging that generalization. Eliminate.
(D) A counterexample to a position being challenged is presented in order to show that this position is incorrect.	Correct. This closely matches our prediction.
(E) A detailed example is used to illustrate the advantage of one strategy over another. *PrepTest29 Sec1 Q12*	Out of Scope. The author is concerned about determining how common a certain strategy is; whether it's more or less optimal to other strategies is not at issue here. Eliminate.

Sometimes the LSAT will give us two speakers in dialogue, and ask how one speaker responds to the other. Here's an example:

LSAT Question	Analysis
P: Complying with the new safety regulations is useless. Even if the new regulations had been in effect before last year's laboratory fire, they would not have prevented the fire or the injuries resulting from it because they do not address its underlying causes. Q: But any regulations that can potentially prevent money from being wasted are useful. If obeyed, the new safety regulations will prevent some accidents, and whenever there is an accident here at the laboratory, money is wasted even if no one is injured.	**Step 2:** P's argument: [conclusion] Complying with the new safety regulations is useless, because [evidence] the regulations do not address the underlying causes of accidents like last year's lab fire. Q's response: [conclusion] The regulations will be useful if they save the company money, because [evidence] anything that saves money is useful, and these new regulations will prevent costly accidents.
Q responds to P's position by	**Step 1:** The phrasing "responds ... by" indicates that this is a Method of Argument question. The correct answer will describe how Q constructs her response to P.
	Step 3: Q responds by changing the definition of "useful" to include things that will save the company money. This more inclusive definition allows Q to conclude that the regulations will be useful.
(A) extending the basis for assessing the utility of complying with the new regulations	**Step 4:** Correct. "Extending the basis for assessing" is another way of saying that Q is broadening the scope of what is considered "useful."
(B) citing additional evidence that undermines P's assessment of the extent to which the new regulations would have prevented injuries in last year's laboratory fire	Out of Scope. Q neither cites additional evidence nor discusses whether the regulations would have prevented injuries. Eliminate.
(C) giving examples to show that the uselessness of all regulations cannot validly be inferred from the uselessness of one particular set of regulations	Q uses broad rules to demonstrate her point; she does not give examples. Eliminate.
(D) showing that P's argument depends on the false assumption that compliance with any regulations that would have prevented last year's fire would be useful	Extreme. While Q might believe this, this is not her approach to responding to P. Instead, Q simply broadens the definition of a term to include more situations. Eliminate.
(E) pointing out a crucial distinction, overlooked by P, between potential benefits and actual benefits *PrepTest 27 Sec4 Q12*	Distortion. While Q believes saving money is a real benefit, she does not infer that P overlooks the difference between potential and actual benefits. Eliminate.

Practice

Let's get some practice applying this method to Method of Argument questions.

In each of the following arguments, identify the author's conclusion and the relevant evidence. Once you've done so, describe in your own words *how* the author goes about supporting her conclusion. That description is the prediction you'll use to evaluate each answer choice. Find the answer choice that matches your prediction. Keep in mind the wrong answers will describe *other* argumentative strategies or somehow distort the argument. When you're done, check your work by reviewing the expert analysis that follows.

LSAT Question	My Analysis
25. Laura: Harold is obviously lonely. He should sell his cabin in the woods and move into town. In town he will be near other people all the time, so he will not be lonely anymore.	**Step 2:**
Ralph: Many very lonely people live in towns. What is needed to avoid loneliness is not only the proximity of other people but also genuine interaction with them.	
Ralph responds to Laura by pointing out that	**Step 1:**
	Step 3:
(A) something needed for a certain result does not necessarily guarantee that result.	**Step 4:**
(B) what is appropriate in one case is not necessarily appropriate in all cases.	
(C) what is logically certain is not always intuitively obvious.	
(D) various alternative solutions are possible for a single problem.	
(E) a proposed solution for a problem could actually worsen that problem.	

PrepTest28 Sec3 Q10

LSAT Question	**My Analysis**
26. The widespread staff reductions in a certain region's economy are said to be causing people who still have their jobs to cut back on new purchases as though they, too, had become economically distressed. Clearly, however, actual spending by such people is undiminished, because there has been no unusual increase in the amount of money held by those people in savings account.	**Step 2:**
The argument in the passage proceeds by doing which one of the following?	**Step 1:**
	Step 3:
(A) concluding that since an expected consequence of a supposed development did not occur, that development itself did not take place	**Step 4:**
(B) concluding that since only one of the two predictable consequences of a certain kind of behavior is observed to occur, this observed occurrence cannot, in the current situation, be a consequence of such behavior	
(C) arguing that since people's economic behavior is guided by economic self-interest, only misinformation or error will cause people to engage in economic behavior that harms them economically	
(D) arguing that since two alternative developments exhaust all the plausible possibilities, one of those developments occurred and the other did not	
(E) concluding that since the evidence concerning a supposed change is ambiguous, it is most likely that no change is actually taking place	

PrepTest24 Sec3 Q17

Expert Analysis

Here's how an expert test taker works through the problems you just saw:

LSAT Question	Analysis
25. Laura: Harold is obviously lonely. He should sell his cabin in the woods and move into town. In town he will be near other people all the time, so he will not be lonely anymore. Ralph: Many very lonely people live in towns. What is needed to avoid loneliness is not only the proximity of other people but also genuine interaction with them.	**Step 2:** Laura: [Conclusion] Harold won't be lonely if he sells his cabin and moves into town, because [evidence] in town he'll be around people. Ralph: [Conclusion] Just being near people isn't enough to avoid loneliness, because [evidence] to avoid loneliness, genuine interaction is also required.
Ralph responds to Laura by pointing out that	**Step 1:** "X responds to Y by" indicates that this is a Method of Argument question. The rest of the question, "by pointing out that," indicates that the correct answer will be something that Ralph feels Laura has overlooked or failed to consider.
	Step 3: Ralph points out that Laura is incorrect in thinking that proximity to others is sufficient to avoid loneliness; instead, Ralph believes it is a requirement. Look for an answer choice that describes a confusion of necessary and sufficient terms.
(A) something needed for a certain result does not necessarily guarantee that result.	**Step 4:** Correct. Ralph points out that something needed for a certain result [proximity to others] does not necessarily guarantee that result [avoiding loneliness].
(B) what is appropriate in one case is not necessarily appropriate in all cases.	Distortion. Ralph does not point to Harold as an exception to a rule. Eliminate.
(C) what is logically certain is not always intuitively obvious.	Outside the Scope. What is logically certain and intuitively obvious is not at issue here. Eliminate.
(D) various alternative solutions are possible for a single problem.	Distortion. Ralph states that more than one requirement is necessary to prevent loneliness, but that is far from offering alternative solutions. Eliminate.
(E) a proposed solution for a problem could actually worsen that problem.	Distortion. Ralph never suggests that proximity to others will make Harold *more* lonely. Eliminate.

PrepTest28 Sec3 Q10

LSAT Question	**Analysis**
26. The widespread staff reductions in a certain region's economy are said to be causing people who still have their jobs to cut back on new purchases as though they, too, had become economically distressed. Clearly, however, actual spending by such people is undiminished, because there has been no unusual increase in the amount of money held by those people in savings account. $\longrightarrow$	**Step 2:** Conclusion: [Keyword "Clearly"] People who still have jobs are not cutting back on spending due to concern over widespread staff reductions. Evidence: [Keyword "because"] There has been no "unusual" increase in the amount of money added to the savings accounts of the still-employed.
The argument in the passage proceeds by doing which one of the following? $\longrightarrow$	**Step 1:** The phrase "argument in the passage proceeds by" identifies this as a Method of Argument question. The correct answer will describe *how* the author makes her point.
	Step 3: The author claims that the employed are spending just as much as before because they are not putting more money into their savings accounts. The author must assume that those worried about losing their jobs will increase their savings. The correct answer will say: "If we are not seeing x (the behavior of distressed people), then y (distress) isn't happening."
(A) concluding that since an expected consequence of a supposed development did not occur, that development itself did not take place $\longrightarrow$	**Step 4:** Correct. This answer choice describes the author's argumentative strategy in generic terms: The "expected consequence" being an increase in savings, and the "development" being a reduction in spending.
(B) concluding that since only one of the two predictable consequences of a certain kind of behavior is observed to occur, this observed occurrence cannot, in the current situation, be a consequence of such behavior $\longrightarrow$	Distortion. The author does not make any claims about the result of an action; instead, the author claims that an action is not occurring. Eliminate.
(C) arguing that since people's economic behavior is guided by economic self-interest, only misinformation or error will cause people to engage in economic behavior that harms them economically $\longrightarrow$	Economic self-interest, misinformation, and error are all Outside the Scope of the argument. Eliminate.
(D) arguing that since two alternative developments exhaust all the plausible possibilities, one of those developments occurred and the other did not $\longrightarrow$	Distortion. The author doesn't claim that something else happened *as a result of* people not adding money to their savings accounts. Eliminate.
(E) concluding that since the evidence concerning a supposed change is ambiguous, it is most likely that no change is actually taking place $\longrightarrow$	The author never claims that the evidence is ambiguous. Eliminate.

PrepTest24 Sec3 Q17

By the way, did you notice in that last question a gap between the author's evidence and conclusion? You may have paused and said to yourself, "Wait a minute, spending money on new purchases and putting that money into a savings account aren't the only two things people can do with their income." If so, you're starting to think like an LSAT expert. Most LSAT arguments have gaps of this kind. In Chapter 10, we're going to start working in depth with those gaps, otherwise known as assumptions, and we're going to pick up a lot of points in doing so. But your work so far in this chapter—analyzing evidence and conclusions—has been necessary groundwork for getting those points. You should congratulate yourself for building a good foundation to tackle assumptions!

Reflection

Look back over your practice in this section. Did you describe the argumentative strategy in your own words? Did you formulate a prediction regarding the author's argumentative strategy before looking at answer choices? Did you efficiently eliminate answer choices that didn't match your prediction?

If you made some mistakes in this practice section, good! You now have some valuable information about where you need to work on your skills before Test Day. How did you mischaracterize the arguments? Do you see any commonalities among the wrong answer choices you were drawn to?

PARALLEL REASONING QUESTIONS

Another way in which you will be tested on your ability to recognize argument structures on the LSAT is to identify two different arguments that use the same pattern to reach a similar conclusion. Questions that ask you to spot two identically structured arguments are called Parallel Reasoning questions.

LEARNING OBJECTIVES

In this section, you'll learn to:

- Rule out incorrect answer choices in Parallel Reasoning questions based on conclusion type.
- Identify similar argument structures in Parallel Reasoning questions.

You won't see many Parallel Reasoning questions on Test Day. There has been an average of three to four per test over the past five years. For many students, however, their length and complexity can make these questions some of the most time-consuming questions they encounter. Parallel Reasoning questions are, on average, the longest questions in the Logical Reasoning section. While the length of these questions is off-putting to many students, LSAT experts know that there is a way to tackle these questions quickly and efficiently. Because the correct answer choice in these questions will be an argument that is parallel to the argument in the stimulus, both arguments must have similar conclusions. More on that in a second. First, let's figure out how to identify Parallel Reasoning question stems.

The question stem for Parallel Reasoning questions will ask you to find the answer choice whose reasoning is "most parallel to," "most similar to," or "most like" the reasoning in the stimulus.

First, take a look at some typical Parallel Reasoning question stems as they appear on the LSAT.

LSAT Question Stem		Analysis
In which one of the following arguments is the pattern of reasoning most similar to the pattern of reasoning in the argument above? *PrepTestB, Sec1, Q12*	→	The phrase "reasoning most similar to" indicates this is a Parallel Reasoning question.
The reasoning in the passage is most similar to that in which one of the following? *PrepTest28 Sec1 Q13*	→	The phrase "reasoning in the passage is most similar to" indicates this is a Parallel Reasoning question.

Parallel Reasoning questions require you to find an answer choice that uses the same *kind* of evidence to reach the same kind of conclusion as in the stimulus. The *content* of the stimulus will likely be different from that in the correct answer; in fact, each answer choice will probably discuss material unrelated to the information in the stimulus. Additionally, the order in which the evidence and the conclusion are presented in the stimulus may be different from the order in which the evidence and conclusion appear in the correct answer. In other words, if the conclusion in the stimulus is the first sentence, the conclusion in the correct answer does not necessarily need to be the first sentence. In short, the correct answer will be similar in *structure* (though perhaps not in sequence of evidence and conclusion) to the stimulus—the only difference is that the answer will discuss different ideas and concepts.

The ability to correctly identify and characterize conclusions will help you tackle Parallel Reasoning questions. Remember the six different conclusion types discussed earlier in this chapter: value judgment, if/then, prediction, comparison, assertion of fact, and recommendation. Because the correct answer must have the same type of evidence leading to the same type of conclusion, any answer choice that has a different type of conclusion than does the stimulus is automatically incorrect and can be eliminated. And because checking the conclusion in each answer choice is faster than reading (and characterizing the structure of) the entire stimulus and of each answer choice, your first line of attack when faced with a Parallel Reasoning question should be to identify and characterize the conclusion in the stimulus, then eliminate any answer choices that do not contain the same conclusion type. This process will occasionally allow you to arrive at the correct answer even without breaking down the evidence. While other test takers spend minutes wading through six separate arguments (the stimulus and five answer choices), experts are able to quickly evaluate just the conclusions. Even if this strategy doesn't always lead directly to the right answer, it will often, at the very least, eliminate a few wrong answer choices.

In addition to characterizing a conclusion's *type*, pay attention to two other things: whether the conclusion is positive or negative (does the author state that something is or will be true, or that something is not or won't become true) and the level of certainty that exists (whether the conclusion is forceful or uses qualified language). For example, a conclusion stating that something will definitely occur is very different from a conclusion stating that something might not occur. The former is a strong prediction that something will happen, while the latter is a qualified prediction that something might not happen.

Practice

To sharpen your ability to characterize conclusions, try the following drill. You've seen some of these conclusions earlier in this chapter, so they may look familiar. Characterize each by type, level of certainty, positive or negative language, and any other unique qualities it may have. The more specific you can be in your description of the conclusion in a Parallel Reasoning stimulus, the more useful the conclusion-typing method will be when you attack the answer choices. Examine the conclusions in this drill closely, then turn the page and compare your thinking to the expert analysis that follows.

LSAT Conclusion	My Analysis
27. [W]atching television has a bad influence on the dietary habits of television viewers. *PrepTest24 Sec3 Q13*	
28. [H]owever, peeling wild potatoes makes them at least as safe to eat as unpeeled domesticated potatoes of the same size. *PrepTestB Sec1 Q9*	
29. Hence, the salaries and the complexity of the duties of these two newest employees should be reduced. *PrepTest29 Sec1 Q5*	
30. Therefore, if you are not well versed in history due to a lack of reading, it will not be easy for you to impress people who are intellectuals. *PrepTest27 Sec4 Q7*	
31. [I]t is quite likely that he is an extreme insomniac. *PrepTest27 Sec1 Q23*	
32. Thus it is certain that Alice will not volunteer. *PrepTestB Sec1 Q12*	

LSAT Conclusion	**My Analysis**
33. Thus, supertasters experience sharp cheddar as tasting more bitter than mild cheddar, but nontasters experience sharp cheddar as tasting no more bitter than mild cheddar. *PrepTestB Sec4 Q22*	
34. Thus, the size of the interstitial nucleus determines whether or not male cats can contract disease X. *PrepTest28 Sec3 Q25*	
35. Hence, depictions of violence among teenagers should be prohibited from movies and television programs, if only in those programs and movies promoted to young audiences. *PrepTest28 Sec3 Q5*	
36. [I]t is likely that Steve will work alone at the sale. *PrepTestB Sec1 Q12*	
37. So if Paula does not work, Arthur will work with both Jane and Elise. *PrepTestB Sec1 Q12*	
38. [F]loors made out of narrow floorboards were probably once a status symbol, designed to proclaim the owner's wealth. *PrepTest24 Sec3 Q23*	
39. So the information in typical broadcast news stories is poorly organized. *PrepTest27 Sec4 Q19*	

Expert Analysis

Here's how an LSAT expert analyzed the conclusions you just characterized.

LSAT Conclusion		Analysis
27. [W]atching television has a bad influence on the dietary habits of television viewers. *PrepTest24 Sec3 Q13*	→	This is a Value Judgment ("bad").
28. [H]owever, peeling wild potatoes makes them at least as safe to eat as unpeeled domesticated potatoes of the same size. *PrepTestB Sec1 Q9*	→	The phrasing "as safe … as" indicates a Comparison, with the qualifier "at least."
29. Hence, the salaries and the complexity of the duties of these two newest employees should be reduced. *PrepTest29 Sec1 Q5*	→	The word "should" makes this a Recommendation. This counts as a definite recommendation since there is no qualifier, such as "probably."
30. Therefore, if you are not well versed in history due to a lack of reading, it will not be easy for you to impress people who are intellectuals. *PrepTest27 Sec4 Q7*	→	This conclusion has clear If/Then phrasing.
31. [I]t is quite likely that he is an extreme insomniac. *PrepTest27 Sec1 Q23*	→	This is an Assertion of Fact, qualified by the phrase "quite likely." An "extreme insomniac" is merely a medical condition, not a value judgment.
32. Thus it is certain that Alice will not volunteer. *PrepTestB Sec1 Q12*	→	The word "will" indicates a negative Prediction. More specifically, it is a definite prediction that something will *not* happen.

LSAT Conclusion	Analysis
33. Thus, supertasters experience sharp cheddar as tasting more bitter than mild cheddar, but nontasters experience sharp cheddar as tasting no more bitter than mild cheddar. *PrepTestB Sec4 Q22*	The word "than" indicates a Comparison. Note that this conclusion makes two separate comparisons.
34. Thus, the size of the interstitial nucleus determines whether or not male cats can contract disease X. *PrepTest28 Sec3 Q25*	This is an Assertion of Fact claiming a causal relationship between two things.
35. Hence, depictions of violence among teenagers should be prohibited from movies and television programs, if only in those programs and movies promoted to young audiences. *PrepTest28 Sec3 Q5*	This conclusion contains If/Then phrasing, while the word "should" indicates a Recommendation. This is a conditional recommendation.
36. [I]t is likely that Steve will work alone at the sale. *PrepTestB Sec1 Q12*	The word "will" indicates a Prediction, which is qualified by "likely."
37. So if Paula does not work, Arthur will work with both Jane and Elise. *PrepTestB Sec1 Q12*	This conclusion contains If/Then phrasing, while the word "will" indicates a Prediction. This is a conditional prediction.
38. [F]loors made out of narrow floorboards were probably once a status symbol, designed to proclaim the owner's wealth. *PrepTest24 Sec3 Q23*	This is an Assertion of Fact qualified by the word "probably."
39. So the information in typical broadcast news stories is poorly organized. *PrepTest27 Sec4 Q19*	The word "poorly" indicates a Value Judgment.

LSAT STRATEGY

When approaching Parallel Reasoning questions:

- First, characterize the conclusion in the stimulus.
- Characterize the conclusion in each answer choice, and eliminate any answer choice that has a conclusion of a type different than that of the conclusion in the stimulus.
- If more than one answer choice remains, analyze the evidence in the stimulus; find the answer choice that presents an argument structurally identical to the stimulus.

Take a look at an LSAT expert's analysis of a full Parallel Reasoning question.

LSAT Argument	Analysis
The amount of electricity consumed in Millville on any day in August is directly proportional to peak humidity on that day. Since the average peak humidity this August was three points higher than the average peak humidity last August, it follows that more energy was consumed in Millville this August than last August.	**Step 2:** Conclusion: [A strong comparison of one quantity over two different time periods] Millville consumed more energy this August than last August. *because* Evidence: 1) [A proportionality rule] Energy consumption is proportional to humidity. *and* 2) [A comparison of the relevant condition] Humidity in Millville was higher this August than last August.
Which one of the following arguments has a pattern of reasoning most similar to the one in the argument above?	**Step 1:** "[M]ost similar to"—this is a Parallel Reasoning question.
	Step 3: The correct answer must contain a conclusion that makes a strong comparison of the same quantity over two different time periods. The evidence must also be of the same type as that in the stimulus.
(A) The amount of art supplies used in any of the Aesthetic Institute's 25 classes is directly proportional to the number of students in that class. Since in these classes the institute enrolled 20 percent more students overall last year than in the previous year, more art supplies were used in the institute's classes last year than in the previous year.	**Step 4:** Correct. The conclusion is a strong comparison of the same quantity over two different time periods. The evidence is a proportionality rule and a comparison of the relevant condition.
(B) The number of courses in painting offered by the Aesthetic Institute in any term is directly proportional to the number of students enrolled in the institute in that term. But the institute offers the same number of courses in sculpture each term. Hence, the institute usually offers more courses in painting than in sculpture.	Here, the conclusion is weak ("usually") and compares two different quantities ("courses in painting" versus "courses in sculpture"), rather than the same quantity at two different times. Eliminate.
(C) The number of new students enrolled at the Aesthetic Institute in any given year is directly proportional to the amount of advertising the institute has done in the previous year. Hence, if the institute seeks to increase its student body it must increase the amount it spends on advertising.	Here, the conclusion is conditional ("if"), and offers a recommendation for how to increase a number, rather than comparing a quantity at two different times. Eliminate.

LSAT Argument (cont.)	Analysis (cont.)
(D) The fees paid by a student at the Aesthetic Institute are directly proportional to the number of classes in which that student enrolls. Since the number of students at the Aesthetic Institute is increasing, it follows that the institute is collecting a greater amount if fees paid by students that it used to. $\longrightarrow$	Here, the conclusion is the comparison of a quantity at present to that same quantity "in the past." This is not as clear cut as the comparison between "this August" and "last August." Moreover, the evidence does not align to that in the stimulus. Here, the proportionality rule is triggered by the "number of classes in which [a] student enrolls," but the next piece of evidence tells us that the overall number of students is increasing. Eliminate.
(E) The number of instructors employed by the Aesthetic Institute in any term is directly proportional to the number of classes offered in that term and also directly proportional to the number of students enrolled at the institute. Thus, the number of classes offered by the institute in any term is directly proportional to the number of students enrolled in that term. $\longrightarrow$	Here, the conclusion is a proportionality rule, not a comparison. The proportionality rule is part of the *evidence* in the stimulus. Eliminate.

PrepTest24 Sec3 Q21

Practice

Now that we have covered the basics of Parallel Reasoning questions, try your hand at a couple of examples of this question type. Characterize the conclusion in the stimulus; then eliminate any choices that do not share the same conclusion type. Be sure to check each answer choice, as there may be more than one choice that has the same type of conclusion as the stimulus. If you are unable to rule out all incorrect choices based upon your characterization of the conclusion, then move back to the stimulus and examine the evidence. The correct answer will use the same type of evidence to support the same type of conclusion as the stimulus. If you need to, simplify the original argument by replacing the various terms and concepts with letters (such as "All X are Y, and no Y is Z ..."). Then match that same structure to one of the answer choices.

When you're finished, compare your analyses to those of an LSAT expert.

	LSAT Question	My Analysis
40.	People who say that Dooney County is flat are clearly wrong. On flat land, soil erosion by water is not a problem. Consequently, farmers whose land is flat do not build terraces to prevent erosion. Yet I hear that the farms in Dooney County are dotted with terraces.	Step 2:
	The reasoning in the passage is most similar to that in which one of the following?	Step 1:
		Step 3:
(A)	If we paint the room white, it will get smudged, and we will have to paint it again soon. Therefore, we should paint it dark blue.	Step 4:
(B)	People with children need more space than those without children. Yet people with no children can usually afford bigger houses.	
(C)	People who get a lot of exercise have no trouble falling asleep; hence, people who get a lot of exercise do not use medication to help them fall asleep. Jack is taking many kinds of medication, so he must not be getting a lot of exercise.	
(D)	If I go grocery shopping when I am hungry, I buy snack foods and cannot resist eating them. Therefore, I cannot lose weight.	
(E)	People who have many friends tend to go out often, so they need cars. Therefore, if Joe wants to have many friends, he must buy a car.	

PrepTest28 Sec1 Q13

LSAT Question	My Analysis
41. Carl's Coffee Emporium stocks only two decaffeinated coffees: French Roast and Mocha Java. Yusef only serves decaffeinated coffee, and the coffee he served after dinner last night was far too smooth and mellow to have been French Roast. So, if Yusef still gets all his coffee from Carl's, what he served last night was Mocha Java.	**Step 2:**
The argument above is most similar in its logical structure to which one of the following?	**Step 1:**
	Step 3:
(A) Samuel wants to take three friends to the beach. His mother owns both a sedan and a convertible. The convertible holds four people so, although the sedan has a more powerful engine, if Samuel borrows a vehicle from his mother, he will borrow the convertible.	**Step 4:**
(B) If Anna wants to walk from her house to the office where she works, she must either go through the park or take the overpass across the railroad tracks. The park paths are muddy, and Anna does not like using the overpass, so she never walks to work.	
(C) Rose can either take a two-week vacation in July or wait until October and take a three-week vacation. The trail she had planned to hike requires three weeks to complete but is closed by October, so if Rose takes a vacation, it will not be the one she had planned.	
(D) Werdix, Inc., has offered Arno a choice between a job in sales and a job in research. Arno would like to work at Werdix but he would never take a job in sales when another job is available, so if he accepts one of these jobs, it will be the one in research.	
(E) If Teresa does not fire her assistant, her staff will rebel and her department's efficiency will decline. Losing her assistant would also reduce its efficiency, so, if no alternative solution can be found, Teresa's department will become less efficient.	

PrepTest24 Sec2 Q13

Expert Analysis

Here's how an LSAT expert worked through the questions you just completed.

LSAT Question	Analysis
40. People who say that Dooney County is flat are clearly wrong. On flat land, soil erosion by water is not a problem. Consequently, farmers whose land is flat do not build terraces to prevent erosion. Yet I hear that the farms in Dooney County are dotted with terraces.	**Step 2:** Conclusion: The *assertion of fact* that should be paraphrased as: Dooney County is definitely not flat. *Because* Evidence: 1) Dooney County is dotted with terraces; 2) farmers only use erosion control terraces on land that is not flat.
The reasoning in the passage is most similar to that in which one of the following?	**Step 1:** The phrase "reasoning ... most similar" indicates a Parallel Reasoning question.
	Step 3: Eliminate any answers with a conclusion that is not a definite assertion of fact.
(A) If we paint the room white, it will get smudged, and we will have to paint it again soon. Therefore, we should paint it dark blue.	**Step 4:** The conclusion here is a *recommendation*. Eliminate.
(B) People with children need more space than those without children. Yet people with no children can usually afford bigger houses.	This answer does not even contain an argument, so much as it states a paradox. Also, the qualifier "usually" has no correlate in the argument in the stimulus. Eliminate.
(C) People who get a lot of exercise have no trouble falling asleep; hence, people who get a lot of exercise do not use medication to help them fall asleep. Jack is taking many kinds of medication, so he must not be getting a lot of exercise.	Correct. This is the only answer that has the right type of conclusion. As in the stimulus, the evidence indicates the presence of something (the medication) and uses its presence to make an assertion about a present-tense condition.
(D) If I go grocery shopping when I am hungry, I buy snack foods and cannot resist eating them. Therefore, I cannot lose weight.	This conclusion is actually a statement of impossibility that extends into the future, rather than a mere assertion of a current state. The conclusion in the stimulus does not assert that Dooney County cannot be made flat, merely that it currently is not flat. Additionally, the evidence provides a chain of causation not present in the stimulus. Eliminate.
(E) People who have many friends tend to go out often, so they need cars. Therefore, if Joe wants to have many friends, he must buy a car.	The conclusion here is a *conditional recommendation*. Eliminate.

PrepTest28 Sec1 Q13

LSAT Question	Analysis
41. Carl's Coffee Emporium stocks only two decaffeinated coffees: French Roast and Mocha Java. Yusef only serves decaffeinated coffee, and the coffee he served after dinner last night was far too smooth and mellow to have been French Roast. So, if Yusef still gets all his coffee from Carl's, what he served last night was Mocha Java.	**Step 2:** Conclusion: A *conditional* identification of a single specific result: "*If* Yusef still gets *all* his coffee from Carl's," it was Mocha Java. *because* Evidence: 1) Carl's only supplies two decaf varieties; 2) Yusef only serves decaf; and 3) reasons to eliminate one of the two varieties.
The argument above is most similar in its logical structure to which one of the following?	**Step 1:** The phrase "similar in its logical structure" indicates a Parallel Reasoning question.
	Step 3: Eliminate choices that do not have a conclusion that conditionally results in the specific choice of a single option. If choices remain, the evidence should match the identification of only two possible options, and a reason that one of the options is impossible.
(A) Samuel wants to take three friends to the beach. His mother owns both a sedan and a convertible. The convertible holds four people so, although the sedan has a more powerful engine, if Samuel borrows a vehicle from his mother, he will borrow the convertible.	**Step 4:** While the conclusion appropriately is the conditional selection of a specific one of two options, the evidence is not a match. There is no evidence that one of the options has to be eliminated from consideration. Eliminate.
(B) If Anna wants to walk from her house to the office where she works, she must either go through the park or take the overpass across the railroad tracks. The park paths are muddy, and Anna does not like using the overpass, so she never walks to work.	The conclusion in this choice is not overtly conditional. Eliminate. One could reasonably argue that the conclusion is conditional—*if work, then not walk*—but choice (B) would still be wrong because, as with (C), the conclusion in choice (B) merely eliminates a possibility (rather than resulting in the selection of a specific option).
(C) Rose can either take a two-week vacation in July or wait until October and take a three-week vacation. The trail she had planned to hike requires three weeks to complete but is closed by October, so if Rose takes a vacation, it will not be the one she had planned.	The conclusion, while conditional, does not result in the identification of a specific chosen option. Instead, this conclusion merely indicates that the choice, whatever it may be, will *not* be the one planned. Eliminate.

LSAT Question (cont.)		Analysis (cont.)
(D)	Werdix, Inc., has offered Arno a choice between a job in sales and a job in research. Arno would like to work at Werdix but he would never take a job in sales when another job is available, so if he accepts one of these jobs, it will be the one in research.	Correct. The evidence identifies two options and provides a reason that one will definitely not occur, with a conditional conclusion that specifically identifies the remaining option.
(E)	If Teresa does not fire her assistant, her staff will rebel and her department's efficiency will decline. Losing her assistant would also reduce its efficiency, so, if no alternative solution can be found, Teresa's department will become less efficient. *PrepTest24 Sec2 Q13*	While this conclusion is conditional, the result, rather than indicating a specific choice of an option, has the relative relationship "become *less* efficient." Eliminate.

QUESTION POOL

Mixed Practice: Argument-Based Questions

Assess your skills on some further examples of the question types introduced in this chapter—Main Point, Role of a Statement, Point At Issue, Method of Argument, and Parallel Reasoning.

1. Economist: Every business strives to increase its productivity, for this increases profits for the owners and the likelihood that the business will survive. But not all efforts to increase productivity are beneficial to the business as a whole. Often, attempts to increase productivity decrease the number of employees, which clearly harms the dismissed employees as well as the sense of security of the retained employees.

    Which one of the following most accurately expresses the main conclusion of the economist's argument?

    (A) If an action taken to secure the survival of a business fails to enhance the welfare of the business's employees, that action cannot be good for the business as a whole.
    (B) Some measures taken by a business to increase productivity fail to be beneficial to the business as a whole.
    (C) Only if the employees of a business are also its owners will the interests of the employees and owners coincide, enabling measures that will be beneficial to the business as a whole.
    (D) There is no business that does not make efforts to increase its productivity.
    (E) Decreasing the number of employees in a business undermines the sense of security of retained employees.

    PrepTestJun07 Sec2 Q1

2. Antonio: One can live a life of moderation by never deviating from the middle course. But then one loses the joy of spontaneity and misses the opportunities that come to those who are occasionally willing to take great chances, or to go too far.

    Marla: But one who, in the interests of moderation, never risks going too far is actually failing to live a life of moderation: one must be moderate even in one's moderation.

    Antonio and Marla disagree over

    (A) whether it is desirable for people occasionally to take great chances in life
    (B) what a life of moderation requires of a person
    (C) whether it is possible for a person to embrace other virtues along with moderation
    (D) how often a person ought to deviate from the middle course in life
    (E) whether it is desirable for people to be moderately spontaneous

    PrepTestJun07 Sec3 Q7

3. A group of unusual meteorites was found in Shergotty, India. Their structure indicates that they originated on one of the geologically active planets, Mercury, Venus, or Mars. Because of Mercury's proximity to the Sun, any material dislodged from that planet's surface would have been captured by the Sun, rather than falling to Earth as meteorites. Nor could Venus be the source of the meteorites, because its gravity would have prevented dislodged material from escaping into space. The meteorites, therefore, probably fell to Earth after being dislodged from Mars, perhaps as the result of a collision with a large object.

    The argument derives its conclusion by

    (A) offering a counterexample to a theory
    (B) eliminating competing alternative explanations
    (C) contrasting present circumstances with past circumstances
    (D) questioning an assumption
    (E) abstracting a general principle from specific data

    PrepTest24 Sec2 Q3

The explanations to these questions begin on page 492.

4. Suppose I have promised to keep a confidence and someone asks me a question that I cannot answer truthfully without thereby breaking the promise. Obviously, I cannot both keep and break the same promise. Therefore, one cannot be obliged both to answer all questions truthfully and to keep all promises.

Which one of the following arguments is most similar in its reasoning to the argument above?

(A) It is claimed that we have the unencumbered right to say whatever we want. It is also claimed that we have the obligation to be civil to others. But civility requires that we not always say what we want. So, it cannot be true both that we have the unencumbered right to say whatever we want and that we have the duty to be civil.

(B) Some politicians could attain popularity with voters only by making extravagant promises; this, however, would deceive the people. So, since the only way for some politicians to be popular is to deceive, and any politician needs to be popular, it follows that some politicians must deceive.

(C) If we put a lot of effort into making this report look good, the client might think we did so because we believed our proposal would not stand on its own merits. On the other hand, if we do not try to make the report look good, the client might think we are not serious about her business. So, whatever we do, we risk her criticism.

(D) If creditors have legitimate claims against a business and the business has the resources to pay those debts, then the business is obliged to pay them. Also, if a business has obligations to pay debts, then a court will force it to pay them. But the courts did not force this business to pay its debts, so either the creditors did not have legitimate claims or the business did not have sufficient resources.

(E) If we extend our business hours, we will either have to hire new employees or have existing employees work overtime. But both new employees and additional overtime would dramatically increase our labor costs. We cannot afford to increase labor costs, so we will have to keep our business hours as they stand.

PrepTestJun07 Sec2 Q12

5. Although the concept of free will is essential to that of moral responsibility, its role in determining responsibility is not the same in all situations. We hold criminals morally responsible for the damage they cause, assuming that they freely chose their activities. But we do not hold someone who has a heart attack while driving morally responsible for the damage caused, if any, even when we have good reason to believe that the heart attack could have been prevented by eating different foods and that one's choice of diet is made freely.

The claim that a choice of diet can affect whether or not one has a heart attack plays which one of the following roles in the argument?

(A) It is a subsidiary conclusion of the argument.
(B) It is used to show that we should hold someone morally responsible for damages caused by having a heart attack while driving.
(C) It is cited as evidence that our concept of moral responsibility should be the same in all situations.
(D) It is used to disprove the claim that we should not hold criminals morally responsible for damages.
(E) It is used in support of the conclusion of the argument.

PrepTestB Sec1 Q11

6. Novel X and Novel Y are both semiautobiographical novels and contain many very similar themes and situations, which might lead one to suspect plagiarism on the part of one of the authors. However, it is more likely that the similarity of themes and situations in the two novels is merely coincidental, since both authors are from very similar backgrounds and have led similar lives.

Which one of the following most accurately expresses the conclusion drawn in the argument?

(A) Novel X and Novel Y are both semiautobiographical novels, and the two novels contain many very similar themes and situations.

(B) The fact that Novel X and Novel Y are both semiautobiographical novels and contain many very similar themes and situations might lead one to suspect plagiarism on the part of one of the authors.

(C) The author of Novel X and the author of Novel Y are from very similar backgrounds and have led very similar lives.

(D) It is less likely that one of the authors of Novel X or Novel Y is guilty of plagiarism than that the similarity of themes and situations in the two novels is merely coincidental.

(E) If the authors of Novel X and Novel Y are from very similar backgrounds and have led similar lives, suspicions that either of the authors plagiarized are very likely to be unwarranted.

PrepTestJun07 Sec3 Q12

7. Carolyn: The artist Marc Quinn has displayed, behind a glass plate, biologically replicated fragments of Sir John Sulston's DNA, calling it a "conceptual portrait" of Sulston. But to be a portrait, something must bear a recognizable resemblance to its subject.

Arnold: I disagree. Quinn's conceptual portrait is a maximally realistic portrait, for it holds actual instructions according to which Sulston was created.

The dialogue provides most support for the claim that Carolyn and Arnold disagree over whether the object described by Quinn as a conceptual portrait of Sir John Sulston

(A) should be considered to be art
(B) should be considered to be Quinn's work
(C) bears a recognizable resemblance to Sulston
(D) contains instructions according to which Sulston was created
(E) is actually a portrait of Sulston

PrepTestJun07 Sec3 Q3

8. Sam: In a recent survey, over 95 percent of people who purchased a Starlight automobile last year said they were highly satisfied with their purchase. Since people who have purchased a new car in the last year are not highly satisfied if that car has a manufacturing defect, Starlight automobiles are remarkably free from such defects.

Tiya: But some manufacturing defects in automobiles become apparent only after several years of use.

Which one of the following most accurately describes how Tiya's response is related to Sam's argument?

(A) It argues that Sam's conclusion is correct, though not for the reasons Sam gives.

(B) It provides evidence indicating that the survey results Sam relies on in his argument do not accurately characterize the attitudes of those surveyed.

(C) It offers a consideration that undermines the support Sam offers for his conclusion.

(D) It points out that Sam's argument presupposes the truth of the conclusion Sam is defending.

(E) It presents new information that implies that Sam's conclusion is false.

PrepTest28 Sec3 Q7

9. It is now a common complaint that the electronic media have corroded the intellectual skills required and fostered by the literary media. But several centuries ago the complaint was that certain intellectual skills, such as the powerful memory and extemporaneous eloquence that were intrinsic to oral culture, were being destroyed by the spread of literacy. So, what awaits us is probably a mere alteration of the human mind rather than its devolution.

The reference to the complaint of several centuries ago that powerful memory and extemporaneous eloquence were being destroyed plays which one of the following roles in the argument?

(A) evidence supporting the claim that the intellectual skills fostered by the literary media are being destroyed by the electronic media

(B) an illustration of the general hypothesis being advanced that intellectual abilities are inseparable from the means by which people communicate

(C) an example of a cultural change that did not necessarily have a detrimental effect on the human mind overall

(D) evidence that the claim that the intellectual skills required and fostered by the literary media are being lost is unwarranted

(E) possible evidence, mentioned and then dismissed, that might be cited by supporters of the hypothesis being criticized

PrepTestJun07 Sec2 Q11

10. Gamba: Muñoz claims that the Southwest Hopeville
Neighbors Association overwhelmingly opposes
the new water system, citing this as evidence of
citywide opposition. The association did pass a
resolution opposing the new water system, but
only 25 of 350 members voted, with 10 in favor
of the system. Furthermore, the 15 opposing
votes represent far less than 1 percent of
Hopeville's population. One should not assume
that so few votes represent the view of the
majority of Hopeville's residents.

Of the following, which one most accurately describes
Gamba's strategy of argumentation?

(A) questioning a conclusion based on the results of
a vote, on the grounds that people with certain
views are more likely to vote

(B) questioning a claim supported by statistical data
by arguing that statistical data can be
manipulated to support whatever view the
interpreter wants to support

(C) attempting to refute an argument by showing
that, contrary to what has been claimed, the
truth of the premises does not guarantee the
truth of the conclusion

(D) criticizing a view on the grounds that the view
is based on evidence that is in principle
impossible to disconfirm

(E) attempting to cast doubt on a conclusion by
claiming that the statistical sample on which
the conclusion is based is too small to be
dependable

PrepTestJun07 Sec2 Q20

11. Double-blind techniques should be used whenever
possible in scientific experiments. They help prevent
the misinterpretations that often arise due to
expectations and opinions that scientists already hold,
and clearly scientists should be extremely diligent in
trying to avoid such misinterpretations.

Which one of the following most accurately expresses
the main conclusion of the argument?

(A) Scientists' objectivity may be impeded by
interpreting experimental evidence on the basis
of expectations and opinions that they already
hold.

(B) It is advisable for scientists to use double-blind
techniques in as high a proportion of their
experiments as they can.

(C) Scientists sometimes neglect to adequately
consider the risk of misinterpreting evidence on
the basis of prior expectations and opinions.

(D) Whenever possible, scientists should refrain
from interpreting evidence on the basis of
previously formed expectations and
convictions.

(E) Double-blind experimental techniques are often
an effective way of ensuring scientific
objectivity.

PrepTestJun07 Sec2 Q10

12. Taylor: Researchers at a local university claim that
61 percent of the information transferred during a
conversation is communicated through nonverbal
signals. But this claim, like all such
mathematically precise claims, is suspect, because
claims of such exactitude could never be
established by science.

Sandra: While precision is unobtainable in many areas
of life, it is commonplace in others. Many
scientific disciplines obtain extremely precise
results, which should not be doubted merely
because of their precision.

The statements above provide the most support for
holding that Sandra would disagree with Taylor about
which one of the following statements?

(A) Research might reveal that 61 percent of the
information taken in during a conversation is
communicated through nonverbal signals.

(B) It is possible to determine whether 61 percent of
the information taken in during a conversation
is communicated through nonverbal signals.

(C) The study of verbal and nonverbal
communication is an area where one cannot
expect great precision in one's research results.

(D) Some sciences can yield mathematically precise
results that are not inherently suspect.

(E) If inherently suspect claims are usually false,
then the majority of claims made by scientists
are false as well.

PrepTestJun07 Sec2 Q16

These explanations refer to questions that begin on page 487.

Part Three: Logical Reasoning
Argument-Based Questions

K

ANSWERS AND EXPLANATIONS

1. (B) Main Point ★☆☆☆

Step 1: Identify the Question Type

The question stem directly asks for the main conclusion of the economist's argument.

Step 2: Untangle the Stimulus

A contrast Keyword, in this case *but*, will often highlight the author's transition to her conclusion. In this argument, [b]*ut* precedes the conclusion that "not all efforts to increase productivity are beneficial to the business as a whole." The subsequent sentence provides a supporting example for this assertion.

Step 3: Make a Prediction

There is no need to analyze the evidence or formulate the assumption; the correct answer to a Main Point question should match what you identify as the conclusion of the argument.

Step 4: Evaluate the Answer Choices

(B) is correct. With minor rephrasing ("not all are beneficial" is equivalent in meaning to "some fail to be beneficial"), this choice is a match for the conclusion.

(A) works as the argument's sufficient assumption, linking the evidence of harm to employees with the conclusion's concern for the good of the business as a whole. This answer goes beyond simply identifying the argument's conclusion.

(C) discusses employees who are also owners, which goes well beyond the scope of the argument.

(D) rephrases the first phrase in the stimulus. Admittedly, this first idea that "every business strives to increase its productivity" is supported by the premise that "this increases profits for the owners and the likelihood that the business will survive." However, it is very common on the LSAT for the author to begin an argument with an alternative viewpoint or common belief before using a contrast Keyword to segue to her main point.

(E) is a deduction implicit in the evidence at the end of the passage, which is support for the preceding conclusion.

2. (B) Point at Issue ★☆☆☆

Step 1: Identify the Question Type

Because the correct answer will describe what Antonio and Marla "disagree over," this is a Point at Issue question.

Step 2: Untangle the Stimulus

Paraphrase each speaker's statements. Antonio suggests that you can achieve a moderate life by sticking to the middle course. The downside of this is that you would lose the benefits that come from taking great chances and going too far. Marla suggests that people who are always moderate are actually not moderate because they are extreme in their moderation.

Step 3: Make a Prediction

While you can always use the Point at Issue Decision Tree to work through the answer choices to a Point at Issue question, you may be able to predict the point of disagreement based on the content of the stimulus. Here, the disagreement seems to be about how one could actually achieve a life of moderation. Antonio thinks that always sticking to the middle course would lead to a life of moderation. Marla thinks that always sticking to the middle course would not lead to a life of moderation. The correct answer will reflect this point of disagreement.

Step 4: Evaluate the Answer Choices

(B) matches the prediction. Antonio and Marla disagree about how one could actually achieve a life of moderation.

(A) is Out of Scope because Marla voices no opinion on the desirability of taking chances.

(C) is Out of Scope because neither Antonio nor Marla discuss virtues other than moderation.

(D) is 180 because both speakers seem to agree that people should sometimes stray from the middle course, although neither states precisely how often they should do so.

K | Part Three: Logical Reasoning
CHAPTER 9

These explanations refer to questions that begin on page 487.

(E) is a Distortion because neither really discusses "moderate spontaneity," which is essentially just a mixture of terms from the stimulus. Regardless, Marla states no opinion on the desirability of any sort of spontaneity.

3. (B) Method of Argument ★★★★

Step 1: Identify the Question Type

The phrase "derives its conclusion by" is a clear sign that this is a Method of Argument question. Keep your focus on *how* the author structures the evidence and conclusion rather than on *what* the argument specifically claims.

Step 2: Untangle the Stimulus

The Keyword *therefore* indicates the conclusion: The meteorites discovered in Shergotty, India, probably fell to Earth after being dislodged from Mars. The author reaches this conclusion in a linear fashion. First, the author says that the meteorites must have come from Mercury, Venus, or Mars. Then, she says the meteorites could not have come from Mercury (it is too close to the Sun) or Venus (its gravity would not have allowed the meteorites to reach space). So, Mars is their likely source.

Step 3: Make a Prediction

The argument concludes that Mars is the source of the meteorites by eliminating the other two possible sources.

Step 4: Evaluate the Answer Choices

(B) is correct. The argument claims that Mars is the source of the meteorites by eliminating Mercury and Venus as possible sources.

(A) is incorrect because no particular examples are cited and the author never offers a counterexample to anything.

(C) is Outside the Scope. The argument describes what must have been the case based on what is known about the planets. No contrast between past and present circumstances is ever made.

(D) is incorrect because the author never critiques an argument by questioning an assumption; the only view presented is her own.

(E) is Outside the Scope. There is no general principle in the argument; the author's conclusion is limited to the source of these specific meteorites in Shergotty, India.

4. (A) Parallel Reasoning ★★☆☆

Step 1: Identify the Question Type

The phrase "similar in its reasoning" indicates a Parallel Reasoning question. Characterize the conclusion and knock out any answer in which the conclusion doesn't match.

Step 2: Untangle the Stimulus

The author concludes that "one cannot be obliged both to answer all questions truthfully and to keep all promises" because there could be situations in which those obligations would conflict.

Step 3: Make a Prediction

Always start Parallel Reasoning questions by eliminating any answers that do not have the proper type of conclusion. The correct answer should have an Assertion of Fact conclusion that similarly indicates that two broad obligations or claims cannot always both be met on the grounds that circumstances can exist in which they would conflict.

Step 4: Evaluate the Answer Choices

(A) is correct. It concludes that two obligations or rights—free speech and the duty to be civil—contradict each other. That is the same type of conclusion as in the stimulus, while all the other choices contain deviations as described below.

(B) cannot be correct because the conclusion is different. This conclusion asserts that some politicians must deceive. To be the same type of conclusion, it would have to state something along the lines of, "it cannot be true that a politician is always popular and never deceives." Additionally, the conclusion wouldn't be true universally, since the evidence is only about *some* politicians.

(C) also cannot be correct because the conclusion doesn't match. This answer choice presents a lose-lose situation; it does not state the general impossibility of always complying with two different claims or dictates. Additionally, the evidence—about what "might" occur—is too uncertain.

These explanations refer to questions that begin on page 488.

Part Three: Logical Reasoning
Argument-Based Questions

K

(D) also does not match the stimulus. The answer presents two Formal Logic statements and then uses the contrapositives to draw a conclusion. This conclusion states that one of two things must have occurred, whereas the conclusion in the stimulus says two things cannot always occur together. The difference is subtle, but important.

(E) also presents Formal Logic: If hours are extended, then employees must be hired or current employees must work overtime. The conclusion says the necessary condition is unacceptable, so the sufficient condition cannot happen. It doesn't argue that two broad rules can't always occur at the same time.

5. (E) Role of a Statement ★★★☆

Step 1: Identify the Question Type

This question stem presents a claim from this stimulus and asks for its "role in the argument," making this a Role of a Statement question.

Step 2: Untangle the Stimulus

Start by browsing the stimulus for the claim in question (about how diet choices affect heart attacks). Mark that claim, then break the argument into evidence and conclusion, determining how the marked claim functions within that argument. This argument investigates the concept of free will by looking at two examples. In the first, a criminal is morally responsible for his actions because of free will. In the second, someone who has an accident while having a heart attack is not, even if that person's choice of diet (free will) directly contributed to the heart attack. These examples support the author's point that free will's role in assigning responsibility changes from situation to situation.

Step 3: Make a Prediction

The claim in question is part of the second example at the bottom. That example is merely used to back up the author's conclusion. The correct answer will identify the claim in question as part of this supporting evidence.

Step 4: Evaluate the Answer Choices

(E) accurately identifies the claim as part of the supporting evidence.

(A) is incorrect because the claim is not a conclusion of any kind; it's part of a hypothetical example. There is no supporting evidence for the claim in question.

(B) is a 180. The author claims that we do *not* hold such people morally responsible. No recommendation is made by the author otherwise.

(C) is also a 180. The author claims that responsibility is *not* determined the same way in all situations and never suggests it should be otherwise.

(D) is a Distortion. Criminal activity is part of the first example. The claim in question is part of the second example and does not address, let alone *disprove*, the first example in any way.

6. (D) Main Point ★★☆☆

Step 1: Identify the Question Type

Because the correct answer "accurately expresses the conclusion" of the argument, this is a Main Point question.

Step 2: Untangle the Stimulus

Paraphrase the stimulus. First, the author says that because two novels are similar, some people might suspect one of them is plagiarized. Next, the author suggests it is more likely that the similarities are coincidental, rather than a result of plagiarism. The reason for this is that there are many similarities between the lives of the two authors.

Step 3: Make a Prediction

The first sentence of the stimulus introduces the topic and puts forward a view that some people might have. The second sentence starts with the contrast Keyword *however*, which introduces the author's point of view. This view, not surprisingly, goes against the view that some people might have. Finally, the author finishes by providing a reason why this new view is correct. Thus, the first clause of the second sentence is the author's conclusion. The main point is that the similarities between the two novels are more likely due to mere coincidence than to plagiarism.

K | Part Three: Logical Reasoning
CHAPTER 9

These explanations refer to questions that begin on page 489.

Step 4: Evaluate the Answer Choices

(D) matches the prediction.

(A) is the evidence for why some people might think that the one of the authors plagiarized the other.

(B) is the view that some people might hold regarding the two authors as well as the reason why they might hold that view.

(C) is the author's evidence.

(E) distorts the argument by making the evidence a condition ("If the authors . . ."), and the conclusion a result. Moreover, it adds the Extreme word *very*. The author says it is "more likely" that the similarities are coincidental, which is not as strong as saying plagiarism is "very likely" not to be the case. Regardless, the correct answer to a Main Point question needs to be a paraphrase of just the author's conclusion, not of the evidence as well.

7. (E) Point at Issue

Step 1: Identify the Question Type

This is a Point at Issue question because the correct answer is the claim about which the two speakers *disagree*. Additionally, this stem directs you to the disagreement; it will have something to do with Sir John Sulston's *portrait*.

Step 2: Untangle the Stimulus

Paraphrase the argument made by each speaker. Carolyn's basic point is that the conceptual portrait is no portrait at all, because it does not look like Sir John Sulston. Arnold thinks that the conceptual portrait is a "maximally realistic" portrait, because it contains the genetic instructions for making Sulston.

Step 3: Make a Prediction

The two speakers disagree about their conclusions. Carolyn thinks the artwork is not a portrait. Arnold thinks it is. Additionally, they have differing ideas on what a portrait must entail. Carolyn thinks it has to resemble the subject, whereas Arnold does not.

Step 4: Evaluate the Answer Choices

(E) matches the prediction.

(A) is Out of Scope. Neither Carolyn nor Arnold mentions art.

(B) is Out of Scope. Neither speaker contests Quinn's authorship of the "conceptual portrait."

(C) is Out of Scope because even though Carolyn implies that the portrait fails to resemble Sulston, Arnold never contradicts her. Instead, Arnold disputes that the proper criteria for a portrait is that it resembles its subject.

(D) is Out of Scope because only Arnold addresses whether or not the portrait contains instructions for Sulston's creation.

8. (C) Method of Argument

Step 1: Identify the Question Type

This question stem asks you to determine *how* Tiya's response is related to Sam's argument, which makes this a Method of Argument question.

Step 2: Untangle the Stimulus

Before you assess anything about Tiya's response, read and dissect Sam's argument. *Since* at the beginning of Sam's last sentence indicates evidence, so the second clause of that sentence is Sam's conclusion: The Starlight is quite free of manufacturing defects. Sam's evidence is that nearly all of last year's Starlight purchasers said they were satisfied, and no one would claim to be satisfied with a car if that car had a manufacturing defect. In response, Tiya points out that some defects can only be detected after several years.

Step 3: Make a Prediction

Tiya is implicitly disagreeing with Sam's assumption that if the cars had defects, the owners would know about them. What she's implying is that the cars may in fact have defects, contrary to Sam's optimistic conclusion, but those defects didn't affect the survey because they hadn't yet been discovered. Tiya is accusing Sam of committing the classic flaw of failing to consider alternative possibilities.

These explanations refer to questions that begin on page 489.

Part Three: Logical Reasoning
Argument-Based Questions

Step 4: Evaluate the Answer Choices

(C) matches the prediction. By undermining Sam's evidence, Tiya has cast doubt on his certainty that these cars are trouble-free. Knowledge of classic flaws will help with Method of Argument questions.

(A) is incorrect because nothing in Tiya's response indicates that she agrees with Sam's conclusion.

(B) is Out of Scope. Tiya never mentions either the survey results or the attitudes of others, so there's no way that **(B)** could describe her response to Sam. She doesn't contest the 95-percent satisfaction figure from the survey; her opposition lies in the fact that the satisfaction could be misguided.

(D) has Tiya accusing Sam of circular logic, of assuming his conclusion to be true to prove it. However, his evidence and conclusion are different from each other, and all she does is attack an assumption he's making.

(E) may be tempting in that it picks up on the Tiya/Sam disagreement. It begins in a promising way, considering that Tiya does indeed bring up a new point. Contrary to **(E)**, however, Tiya stops short of saying, "No, Sam, you're wrong, those cars *do* have problems." She simply casts doubt on his *certainty* about the cars. Tiya would concede that Sam *could* be right and the cars *could* be defect-free, but she would argue that the survey results don't prove it.

9. (C) Role of a Statement ★★☆☆

Step 1: Identify the Question Type

A question stem that takes a portion of the stimulus and asks you what role it plays in the argument is a Role of a Statement question. Start by finding the referenced statement in the stimulus and underlining it. Then read the argument in full, breaking it down into the evidence and conclusion. Focus on the structure of the argument and how the underlined statement fits into that structure.

Step 2: Untangle the Stimulus

The question stem focuses on the "complaint of several centuries ago that powerful memory and extemporaneous eloquence were being destroyed," which is found in the second sentence. Underline it and then go back to the top and parse the argument's structure.

In the first sentence, the author identifies a common present-day complaint that electronic media has corroded intellectual skills fostered by literature. Then the author presents a similar complaint from centuries ago: The spread of the written word was destroying intellectual skills fostered by oral culture. The author then concludes that the human mind will merely change, not degrade.

Step 3: Make a Prediction

The referenced statement is an old complaint that the author uses to put into perspective the current complaint. The author uses both to support the conclusion that the human mind is evolving and adapting, not deteriorating. Therefore, the statement in question is evidence and being used as an analogy to dismiss the alleged coming harm to the human mind. As you move to the answer choices, make sure you understand the conclusion of the stimulus as well. Many Role of a Statement answer choices will indicate that the statement is "evidence in support of the claim that . . . " To be correct, the answer must *accurately* describe the conclusion that the evidence supports.

Step 4: Evaluate the Answer Choices

(C) correctly matches the role of the statement. The complaint from centuries ago did revolve around a cultural change, and the author uses it to downplay concerns that such changes are harmful to the human mind.

(A) incorrectly describes the conclusion of the argument. This answer choice actually describes the current complaint, which the author then proceeds to downplay.

(B) is Out of Scope. This choice makes up a conclusion that is found nowhere in the argument.

(D) is a tempting answer yet subtly distorts the conclusion. The author may actually accept that intellectual skills fostered by literary media *are* being lost in the shift to electronic media. But the author's point is that this loss of some skills (and likely replacement by others) should not be considered a degradation of the human mind, just a change.

(E) is incorrect because the author uses this example in support of her argument. The author does not dismiss it, nor is there any suggestion that the statement would be used by those the author counters.

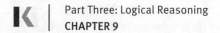
These explanations refer to questions
that begin on page 490.

10. (E) Method of Argument

Step 1: Identify the Question Type

A question that asks you to identify the method, strategy, or technique employed by the author is a Method of Argument question. Focus on the structure, or *how* the author constructs the argument.

Step 2: Untangle the Stimulus

Gamba first points out someone else's claim: Muñoz believes that there is citywide opposition to a new water system, based on an *overwhelming* vote by a neighborhood association. Gamba then attacks Muñoz's evidence. Gamba points out that only 25 of 350 members voted, and only 15 of those opposed the new water system. Finally, Gamba asserts that "the 15 opposing votes represent far less than 1 percent of Hopeville's population." Gamba then concludes that "so few votes" should not be taken as representative of the majority of residents.

Step 3: Make a Prediction

With enough Flaw question practice, you should recognize the classic LSAT flaw of representativeness that Gamba highlights. Gamba attacks the assumption that a subset or survey group represents the broader population. Notice, however, that Gamba's conclusion is that Muñoz's claim is not *necessarily* correct; Gamba does *not* go so far as to say the claim is incorrect or, further, that the city *supports* the water system.

Step 4: Evaluate the Answer Choices

(E) is correct. This describes exactly what the author does. Gamba tries to cast doubt on Muñoz's conclusion by claiming that 15 opposing votes is too small a percentage of all voters to be representative.

(A) is a Distortion. The first part is accurate, but Gamba questions the vote by saying the number of voters is too *small* to be representative. Gamba does not suggest that the representativeness flaw is because people with certain views are more likely to vote.

(B) is a Distortion. Gamba argues that the statistical data is insufficient, not that it can be manipulated to support any view.

(C) is not an accurate description of what the author does. At a very general level, in LSAT arguments, the truth of the premises usually does not guarantee the truth of the conclusion. Gamba points out something more specific. Indeed, in this case, the author does not necessarily accept the truth of Muñoz's premise, which is that the neighborhood association *overwhelmingly* opposes the new water system. Muñoz uses the association's opposition to claim that there is citywide opposition. Gamba, however, points out that the vote was not *overwhelming*. Also, Gamba is not trying to *refute* Muñoz's conclusion; Gamba merely points out that it does not necessarily follow.

(D) is incorrect because Gamba accepts the accuracy of the numbers in the vote. Gamba merely says those numbers don't necessarily mean what Muñoz says they do. The possibility of confirming or disconfirming the evidence is Out of Scope.

11. (B) Main Point

Step 1: Identify the Question Type

The question stem explicitly asks you for the main conclusion of the argument.

Step 2: Untangle the Stimulus

The first sentence is the author's conclusion: a recommendation. Identifying the conclusion may be somewhat difficult here because the last phrase in the argument is both a recommendation and emphasized by the word *clearly*. However, the entire last sentence provides reasons for using the double-blind techniques recommended in the first sentence. If unsure, ask yourself which piece supports the other. Which makes sense: (1) Scientists should use double-blind techniques because scientists should try to avoid misinterpretations, or (2) scientists should try to avoid misinterpretations because scientists should use double-blind techniques? The former does and the latter does not.

Step 3: Make a Prediction

Find the answer that matches the recommendation to use double-blind techniques whenever possible. Avoid answers that stray into the evidence, formulate the assumption, or speculate beyond the stated conclusion.

These explanations refer to questions that begin on page 490.

Part Three: Logical Reasoning
Argument-Based Questions

Step 4: Evaluate the Answer Choices

(B) is correct. It matches the recommendation to use double-blind techniques as much as possible.

(A) incorrectly focuses on the evidence describing what double-blind techniques help to prevent.

(C) incorrectly focuses on the evidence, and speculates beyond that evidence as well. The author doesn't mention what scientists *do*, just what they *should* do.

(D) fails to mention double-blind techniques, which are integral to the author's conclusion. **(D)** rephrases the final sentence, which is merely a piece of evidence.

(E) is Extreme and a Distortion. The author says double-blind techniques help *mitigate* subjectivity, but does not say that those techniques *ensure* objectivity.

12. (D) Point at Issue ★★★☆

Step 1: Identify the Question Type

A question asking what two people "disagree" about is a Point at Issue question. Identify what both speakers address and where their opinions differ.

Step 2: Untangle the Stimulus

Taylor concludes that a specific claim, like all mathematically precise claims, is suspect because science cannot establish such exact claims.

Sandra, on the other hand, doesn't address the specific claim Taylor discusses. Instead, she asserts that precise claims need not always be doubted because some scientific disciplines can yield extremely precise results.

Step 3: Make a Prediction

The point of disagreement is about whether to doubt all precise scientific claims. If you do not recognize a point of disagreement, dive right into the answers, asking in turn whether each speaker has an opinion on the answer choice and whether those opinions conflict. Watch out for answers that mention topics that only one person addresses or on which they might actually agree.

Step 4: Evaluate the Answer Choices

(D) is correct. Taylor believes that *all* mathematically precise results are inherently suspect while Sandra believes that *some* sciences can yield precise results.

(A) is incorrect. While you know Taylor would be suspect of such results, Sandra doesn't mention this specific finding. You can't know whether Sandra would think this is one of those scientific disciplines for which she thinks precise results *can* be obtained.

(B) says the same thing as **(A)**, only slightly stronger. Again, you do not know Sandra's beliefs regarding the possibility of precision in this particular scientific discipline.

(C) is wrong for the same reason the first two answer choices are. It is unknown whether the study of verbal and nonverbal communication is one of the fields of scientific study within which Sandra believes precise results are possible.

(E) is Out of Scope. While Taylor mentions inherently suspect claims, Sandra doesn't. Moreover, neither speaker addresses the falsity of scientific claims in general.

Assumption Family Questions

As you learned in Chapter 9, the ability to analyze arguments is a valuable skill for LSAT mastery. A student who is able to separate evidence from conclusion in an LSAT argument will dominate Main Point, Role of a Statement, and Method of Argument questions. But this skill is useful for other, even more important question types. In this chapter, you'll face Assumption, Flaw, Strengthen, Weaken, and select Principle questions—together known as the Assumption Family questions—that also require you to quickly and effectively analyze arguments into their constituent parts. There is one big difference, though, between the types of questions you saw in Chapter 9 and the types of questions you'll see in this chapter: here, the untangling of arguments into their explicit parts (evidence and conclusion) is an important but insufficient task. That's because Assumption Family questions also depend on your ability to determine the implicit assumption, or unstated premise, of an argument. They reward test takers who are constantly skeptical of the arguments presented and, more precisely, skeptical of the shift from the author's evidence to the author's conclusion.

One thing that is consistently true about arguments on the LSAT is that too little evidence is provided in support of a conclusion that the author reaches too hastily. This jump to the conclusion means that there is an informational gap between the evidence and the conclusion. Because of this gap in the argument's reasoning, the testmaker is able to generate questions that test your ability to do a number of things: to find the assumption in an argument, to point out the error in an author's reasoning, or to strengthen or weaken an argument.

LSAT STRATEGY

Every Assumption Family argument contains:

- A conclusion—the author's main point: an assertion, evaluation, or recommendation
- Evidence—the facts and information the author presents in support of the conclusion
- An assumption—the *unstated* premise that logically connects the evidence to the conclusion

Knowing the structure of these arguments is crucial to test takers. By learning and understanding the common ways in which an LSAT argument can move from evidence to conclusion and by developing strategies to identify an author's assumption (the unstated evidence in an argument), you are able to anticipate, or predict, the correct answer choice before you even begin evaluating the answer choices. For the vast majority of the questions discussed in this section, predicting the correct answer will help you earn more points, and earn them more quickly, than will a process of elimination or guesswork.

This chapter will focus on two big ideas: In the first half of the chapter, you'll learn to identify the common ways in which arguments on the LSAT move from evidence to conclusion. In the second half of the chapter, you'll learn to approach strategically the question types that reward the ability to analyze arguments. Understanding the structure of arguments and identifying authors' assumptions are the most valuable skills you can develop for the LSAT. In fact, more than a quarter of all questions on the LSAT test your ability to do just these things.

LEARNING OBJECTIVES

In this chapter, you'll learn to:

- Identify Mismatched Concepts in an argument.
- Identify Overlooked Possibilities in an argument.
- Identify the assumption in both types of arguments.
- Use an argument's assumption to predict a correct answer for each Assumption Family question type.

The first thing we'll do is discuss the ways in which arguments on the LSAT tend to be constructed. The jump from the evidence to the conclusion takes two basic forms: either (1) the author moves from a discussion of particular terms and concepts in the evidence to a conclusion that introduces a new, seemingly unrelated term or concept (what we will refer to as a "Mismatched Concepts" argument), or (2) the author uses relevant evidence to jump to a conclusion that is too extreme, without considering potential objections or alternatives to that conclusion (an "Overlooked Possibilities" argument).

MISMATCHED CONCEPTS

Consider this argument:

Chemical X is harmful because poison is harmful.

Does this argument seem completely sound to you? It probably doesn't. That's because, just like the arguments you will see on Test Day, this argument is incomplete. There is a gap between what the evidence states and what the author concludes. Assumption Family arguments always follow this pattern—the evidence presented is never enough to completely support the argument's conclusion. Your job, then, will be to determine *why* a particular argument's evidence isn't enough to establish its conclusion. Take a moment now and describe to yourself what's wrong with the Chemical X argument. Here's the catch, though: You have to do it without using any of the following words (or synonyms): chemical X, poison, harmful, or assumes.

Having a hard time? There's a good chance you already know what's missing in this argument: The piece of evidence that should be there but isn't. But how can you know what it is? And more importantly, how will you know what the missing piece is in more complicated LSAT arguments? To learn how to spot the problem in an argument, you first need to learn what those problems are.

Take a look at this argument from a different angle. Imagine a game in which a person is given a piece of evidence, and his task is to predict a conclusion based on that evidence. If he guesses correctly, he is awarded a million-dollar prize. Now, imagine that the person is given this piece of evidence: "poison is harmful." How long would it take him to guess that the conclusion is "Chemical X is harmful"? Frankly, that contestant is probably never going to see that million-dollar prize. The reason is simple: The concept *Chemical X* is, for all we know, completely unrelated to the concept *poison*. That's the problem with this argument: The author is using evidence that, without an additional, unstated assumption, may be unrelated to the conclusion.

Mismatched Concepts: The Basics

LSAT STRATEGY

How can you tell an argument contains mismatched concepts?

- The terms or concepts in the evidence appear unrelated to the conclusion.
- A new term or concept—not related to the evidence—appears in the conclusion.

In Assumption Family questions, the LSAT consistently tests your ability to determine when an author is using evidence that is not inherently relevant (i.e., that may be unrelated) to the conclusion. Think of these as Apples and Oranges arguments: the author is concluding something about apples, while the evidence deals with oranges. Just because the author *assumes* that a relationship between the terms or concepts is apparent does not mean that the relationship is true. Our job then is to learn how to spot when the author is making this leap, then build a bridge that logically connects the mismatched concepts. If properly constructed, this bridge—the author's assumption—completes the argument by "filling in" the gap between the evidence and the conclusion. The good news is that there is a straightforward, repeatable process you can go through to derive the assumption when you're dealing with Mismatched Concepts arguments.

Let's go back to Chemical X to illustrate the process. First, one of the most common signs of a Mismatched Concepts argument is a conclusion that brings up a new concept that did not appear in the evidence. Taking a look at our argument, it's clear that the new, out-of-nowhere term in the conclusion is *Chemical X*.

Conclusion	Evidence
Chemical X is harmful	because poison is harmful

Next, take a look at the evidence and check for any mismatched concepts there—a concept that is in the evidence but never showed up in the conclusion. In this case, that would be *poison*.

Conclusion	Evidence
Chemical X is harmful	because **poison** is harmful

Now that you have your mismatched concepts, ask whether these two things are inherently related to each other. Usually the concepts *could* be related, but they don't *have to be* related—this is what creates the gap between the evidence and the conclusion. In this instance, given that we have no idea what Chemical X is, it's safe to say that it isn't by definition related to poison. It's possible, but without more evidence, there's no way to know for sure.

If you have mismatched concepts, then relate them to each other in a way that fixes the argument. Ask what the author must believe to be true about *Chemical X* and *poison* to fix this argument. The answer is that the author needs Chemical X *to be* a poison. If that's true, then the argument is complete! If Chemical X is a poison, and poisons are harmful, then it must be true that Chemical X is harmful:

Chemical X is harmful because

Chemical X is a poison and **poison is harmful.**

Mismatched Concepts arguments won't always use such straightforward terminology. In fact, many arguments on the LSAT contain academic, legal, or philosophical jargon that might make it difficult to understand the argument in full. Don't get flustered. Sometimes, the abstract nature of the concepts presented in arguments makes it easier for you to spot the mismatched concepts in the evidence and conclusion. Take this argument as an example:

Dweezil is a zulzey alien. Therefore, Dweezil can perform the amazing *yeerchta* move.

These are all made-up terms, of course—we have no real-world understanding of these things. Start by looking for any mismatched concepts in the conclusion. In both the evidence and conclusion, we have Dweezil; because there is no gap between Dweezil in the evidence and Dweezil in the conclusion, we don't have to "build a bridge" between them. The conclusion mentions the amazing *yeerchta* move, which never showed up in the evidence. From there, search the evidence for signs of a mismatch—zulzey aliens are discussed there, though such things are never mentioned in the conclusion. Because these concepts are made up, there is no inherent (i.e., "by definition") relationship between them. However, based on the structure of the argument, we can relate the two concepts in a way that makes sense of the argument. In this case, the author's assumption must be that all zulzey aliens are able to do the amazing *yeerchta* move. If the author had simply bothered to mention that in the evidence, then there would be no problem with this argument. With the assumption filled in, the argument becomes whole, and the conclusion makes sense; it follows logically from the evidence.

Mismatched Concepts arguments don't always use abstract or unfamiliar terms, though. In fact, the more realistic or understandable an argument is, the more cognizant you need to be of your *own* assumptions. There are times on the LSAT when it can be all too easy for you to mentally fill in an argument's assumption without even realizing it— you read the argument and think, "Oh, right, that makes sense." Take this argument as an example:

Kim is a nice person. Therefore, it's easy for Kim to make friends.

A quick look at the conclusion shows us that it's about making friends, but the evidence is about being a nice person. The next step is to ask ourselves if these things are necessarily related to each other. It's easy to think, "Okay, sure. Kim is a nice person. People tend to like other people who are nice, so Kim should be able to make friends easily. Makes sense to me!" The problem is that the relevance of being nice to the ease of making friends is not explicitly stated; it has not, *within this argument*, been established. Maybe being nice does affect your ability to make friends, but then again, maybe not. The argument's assumption, then, is that people who are nice make friends easily. Indeed, if this assumption were *not* true, then the evidence would not support the conclusion.

Even when an argument seems to make all the sense in the world, evaluate the evidence and conclusion with an eye toward spotting mismatched concepts. Are the terms and concepts presented in the evidence *inherently* relevant to those in the conclusion? When you are a lawyer, part of your job will be to expose the weaknesses in the other side's arguments. Looking at every argument and saying, "Sure, that argument makes all the sense in the world to me!" is, to put it mildly, an ineffective legal skill. Finding the gap in an argument, on the other hand, will expose its weakness. Starting today, train yourself to become a skeptical thinker.

LSAT STRATEGY

When tackling an argument containing Mismatched Concepts:

- Separate concepts in evidence from concepts in conclusion.
- Identify the mismatched concepts that the author assumes are somehow related.
- Find the assumption by making a sentence that logically relates the mismatched concepts—this sentence serves as a bridge to make the evidence relevant to the conclusion.

Mismatched Concepts: Sample Arguments

Here are some brief Mismatched Concepts arguments and the assumption of each. After reviewing these examples, you'll have a chance to try some others on your own.

Argument		Analysis
Cady attended North High School. Therefore, Cady is good at sculpture.	→	The author assumes North High School students are good at sculpture.
Spending time with pets relieves stress. Therefore, spending time with pets makes people happy.	→	The author assumes relieving stress makes people happy.
Ivan is an astronaut. Therefore, Ivan doesn't like jazz.	→	The author assumes astronauts don't like jazz.
You haven't done your homework. Therefore, you can't go to the concert.	→	The author assumes you need to do your homework before going to the concert.
People who play ping pong are also good at skiing. Therefore, the wealthy are good at skiing.	→	The author assumes that the wealthy play ping pong.
The city council members are all vegan. Therefore, Grace is a vegan.	→	The author assumes Grace is a member of the city council.

Practice

Practice your ability to spot the gap between concepts in the evidence and the conclusion by analyzing the following simple arguments. In each one of these arguments, follow this simple approach:

· Separate the evidence from the conclusion.
· Identify a new term or concept in the conclusion that was not present in the evidence.
· Look in the evidence for an important term or concept not in the conclusion.
· Determine the relationship the author assumes exists between those terms.
· Put the mismatched terms or concepts into a sentence to form the author's assumption.

After each argument, feel free to look at the expert analysis on the next two pages. If you're feeling confident, try all four and then read the expert's thinking.

Argument	My Analysis
1. Brand D teddy bears are fluffy; therefore, children like Brand D teddy bears.	
2. Because Ariel likes to have fun, he enjoys amusement parks.	
3. Gopher tortoises burrow in the desert. Therefore, gopher tortoises don't eat grubs.	
4. People who text while driving are not safe drivers because one needs to be attentive in order to be a safe driver.	

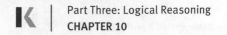
Expert Analysis

Now take a look at how an LSAT expert would analyze these arguments you've just evaluated.

Argument	Analysis
1. Brand D teddy bears are fluffy; therefore, children like Brand D teddy bears.	Conclusion: Children like Brand D teddy bears. Evidence: Brand D teddy bears are fluffy. Analyze: "[C]hildren like" is in the conclusion but not evidence. "[F]luffy" is in the evidence but not conclusion. The author assumes some sort of relationship exists between these distinct concepts. Connect the terms in a sentence to form the piece of evidence that the author assumes is true: "Children like things that are fluffy."
2. Because Ariel likes to have fun, he enjoys amusement parks.	Conclusion: Ariel enjoys amusement parks. Evidence: Ariel likes to have fun. Analyze: The conclusion is about "amusement parks," but there's nothing about them in the evidence. The evidence is about "having fun," but there's nothing in the conclusion about fun. The author assumes a relationship exists between these distinct concepts. Connect the terms in a sentence to form the piece of evidence that the author assumes is true: "Anyone who likes to have fun enjoys amusement parks."
3. Gopher tortoises burrow in the desert. Therefore, gopher tortoises don't eat grubs.	Conclusion: Gopher tortoises don't eat grubs. Evidence: Gopher tortoises burrow in the desert. Analyze: The conclusion is about "not eating grubs," but the evidence isn't about that at all. The evidence is about "burrowing in the desert," but that isn't in the conclusion. The author assumes some sort of relationship exists between these otherwise unrelated concepts. Connect the terms in a sentence to form the piece of evidence that the author assumes is true: "Creatures that burrow in the desert don't eat grubs."

Argument	Analysis
4. People who text while driving are not safe drivers because one needs to be attentive in order to be a safe driver.	Conclusion: Drivers who are texting aren't safe.

Evidence: Safe drivers must be attentive.

→ Analyze: The conclusion is about "drivers who text," but the evidence never mentions that. The evidence is about "being attentive," but that isn't in the conclusion. The author assumes some sort of relationship exists between these two concepts. Connect the terms in a sentence to form the piece of evidence that the author assumes is true:

"Drivers who text aren't attentive." |

The LSAT, of course, will present more difficult arguments than the ones you just saw, but the fundamental *structure* of arguments with mismatched concepts will remain the same. Regardless of the topic being discussed in the argument—whether it be on matters philosophical, legal, or scientific—your method and objective will always remain the same. First, separate evidence from conclusion. Then, analyze the concepts discussed in both. If the author introduces a distinct or unrelated term or idea in the conclusion, find the assumption by connecting a mismatched concept in the evidence to the mismatched concept in the conclusion.

Practice

Try that now with an actual LSAT argument.

LSAT Argument	My Analysis
Press release: A comprehensive review evaluating the medical studies done up to the present time has found no reason to think that drinking coffee in normal amounts harms the coffee-drinker's heart. So coffee drinkers can relax and enjoy their beverage—it is safe to drink coffee.

PrepTest24 Sec2 Q1 | |

Did you see a new term or concept in the conclusion that seemed to come out of the blue? Did the evidence contain terms that are not inherently relevant (i.e., might be unrelated) to those in the conclusion drawn by the author?

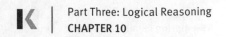
Expert Analysis

Take a look at how an LSAT expert would break down this argument.

LSAT Argument	Analysis
Press release: A comprehensive review evaluating the medical studies done up to the present time has found no reason to think that drinking coffee in normal amounts harms the coffee-drinker's heart. So coffee drinkers can relax and enjoy their beverage—it is safe to drink coffee. *PrepTest24 Sec2 Q1* ⟶	Keywords "studies" and "So" indicate evidence and conclusion, respectively. Conclusion: Drinking coffee is safe. *because* Evidence: Drinking coffee in normal amounts does not harm a coffee drinker's heart. The mismatched terms are *not harms the coffee-drinker's heart* and *safe to drink coffee.* So the author's assumption connects these terms: What does not harm the heart is, overall, safe.

Even though this argument comes from an actual LSAT question, it is really no more complicated than the examples you saw earlier in this chapter. Once the expert has identified the evidence and conclusion, she simplifies the argument to herself: "okay, so the press release is saying that because drinking normal amounts of coffee doesn't harm the heart, coffee is safe to drink." Phrased that way—that *simply*—the gap in the argument becomes much easier to spot. By equating "doesn't harm the heart" with "overall safe," the press release overlooks any number of possible objections: What about consuming more than normal amounts of coffee? What about the possibility that coffee harms some other part of the body? Note again the steps the expert works through to arrive at this point: logically separating and paraphrasing the evidence and conclusion, looking for a gap between terms discussed in each, then connecting those mismatched terms to formulate the argument's assumption.

Hopefully you're starting to get the hang of evaluating arguments that introduce a new, unrelated concept in the conclusion. Let's dive in even deeper and discuss some of the most common relationships you'll see between mismatched concepts in LSAT arguments.

Going Deeper: Common Relationships Between Mismatched Concepts

By now, you've seen the benefit of skeptically looking at the relationship between the concepts in an argument's evidence and its conclusion. If the author introduces, seemingly out of nowhere, a new term or concept in an argument's conclusion, suspect a Mismatched Concepts argument. Connect those mismatched concepts in a sentence to identify the argument's assumption. Fortunately, a few relationships between the mismatched concepts will make up the bulk of the arguments you will see. Knowing what they are can make you faster and more efficient at tackling Assumption Family questions.

LSAT STRATEGY

The most commonly assumed relationships between mismatched concepts:

- The terms or concepts are alike/equivalent.
- The terms or concepts are mutually exclusive.
- One term or concept is needed for the other.
- One term or concept represents another.

For many questions, merely finding the mismatched concepts is enough to get you to the correct answer, as the correct answer will be the only choice to mention both of them. But for more challenging questions, you may be asked to choose between two or more answer choices, each one of which contains the same mismatched concepts. The difference between the answer choices will be the specific relationships between the mismatched concepts. One answer choice may say that the two concepts are mutually exclusive, while another may say that they are alike. As you go deeper into Assumption Family questions, the ability to determine the difference between an argument that assumes two things are equivalent and an argument that assumes one thing is representative of another, for example, will become increasingly important. Fortunately, the fact that most arguments make use of one of just a few relationships makes this easier than it may sound.

Consider the following statement:

I like games because I am serious.

The conclusion is about liking games, but the evidence is about being serious. These two concepts are not inherently (i.e., "by definition") related to each other, so the author is making an assumption. In this case, the author assumes that liking games and being serious are equivalent to each other—that one leads to the other. But what if we change the wording slightly:

I don't like games because I am serious.

The statement uses all the same terms as the previous one; it's still about liking games and being serious. Now, however, there's a very different relationship between liking games and being serious. The author in this example assumes that liking games and being serious are incompatible or mutually exclusive—you can't like games and be serious at the same time.

Now let's change the wording one last time:

> I don't like games because I am not serious.

This last example again has the same mismatched concepts as do the previous examples, but here, the terms have a different relationship: The author assumes that being serious is a necessary condition to liking games. It's worth noting that a Mismatched Concepts argument in the form of *Not X because Not Y* will always mean that the evidence concept (Y) is necessary for the conclusion concept (X). Expect answer choices in these arguments to test you on which concept is necessary!

While the three relationships just discussed are the most common, there is a fourth relationship that you will probably also see on the LSAT. In these arguments, the author assumes that one thing represents another. Representation arguments on the LSAT usually involve a mismatch between one group in the evidence and a different group in the conclusion. Consider the following argument:

> The oranges at my local store are all rotten. I know this because the three I just bought from that store are rotten.

Notice that the author uses information about the three oranges he bought to draw a conclusion about *all* of the oranges in the local store. The author assumes that the three oranges purchased must represent all of the oranges at the store. Be on the lookout for arguments in which the author uses a particular sample in the evidence and tries to draw an overly general conclusion from it. Though this kind of argument is most common in Flaw questions, it can show up in any of the Assumption Family questions.

The reality is that most Mismatched Concepts arguments on the LSAT are just more elaborate versions of the four arguments above. Your job isn't to find a new and unique relationship between mismatched concepts every time you see an Assumption Family argument—that would be frustrating and far too difficult. Instead, your goal is to spot the mismatched concepts, then connect the concepts in a way that matches up with other arguments like these.

Take a look at the following LSAT argument and try to match it up with one of the four relationships you just learned about:

Barnes: The two newest employees at this company have salaries that are too high for the simple tasks normally assigned to new employees and duties that are too complex for inexperienced workers. Hence, the salaries and the complexity of the duties of these two newest employees should be reduced.

PrepTest29 Sec1 Q5

The keyword "[h]ence" indicates the argument's conclusion. Notice that before *hence,* in the evidence, the author refers to the subjects of the argument as "inexperienced workers." After *hence,* those same people are referred to as the two "newest employees." These are the argument's mismatched concepts. The next question is this: Which stock relationship does the author need these two concepts to have? If you said alike/equivalent, then you are correct. Much like the author of the very first example (liking games and being serious), this author is assuming that the mismatched concepts are equivalent in some way—that being new entails being inexperienced. Now, you might have re-phrased this a bit and thought the author assumes that being new is incompatible with having experience. That also would be a correct way of dealing with the negative phrasing in the argument.

Practice

Now try some LSAT Mismatched Concepts arguments on your own. Your job is to match the following two arguments to one of these four examples:

- I like games because I am serious. (alike/equivalent)
- I don't like games because I am serious. (mutually exclusive)
- I don't like games because I am not serious. (need evidence for conclusion)
- The store's oranges are all rotten because the ones I bought from them are rotten. (representation)

LSAT Argument	My Analysis

5. Sociologist: The intended function of news is to give us information on which to act. But in a consumer society, news becomes a product to be manufactured and dispensed to the consumer. An enormous industry for the production and consumption of news has evolved, and we ingest news with an insatiable appetite. Under such circumstances, news is primarily entertaining and cannot, therefore, serve its intended function.

    PrepTestB Sec1 Q18

6. Art Historian: Robbins cannot pass judgment on Stuart's art. While Robbins understands the art of Stuart too well to dismiss it, she does not understand it well enough to praise it.

    PrepTest27 Sec4 Q20

Expert Analysis

Having an understanding of the specific relationship between mismatched terms will help you form the correct assumption. Do the terms have a positive relationship? Are they mutually exclusive? Check out how an LSAT expert evaluated the same arguments.

LSAT Argument	Analysis
5. Sociologist: The intended function of news is to give us information on which to act. But in a consumer society, news becomes a product to be manufactured and dispensed to the consumer. An enormous industry for the production and consumption of news has evolved, and we ingest news with an insatiable appetite. Under such circumstances, news is primarily entertaining and cannot, therefore, serve its intended function. *PrepTestB Sec1 Q18* $\longrightarrow$	Conclusion: Under the described circumstances, news cannot serve its intended function to give us information to act on. *because* Evidence: Under the described circumstances, news is primarily entertaining. The author in the evidence refers to news as "primarily entertaining." The conclusion indicates that the news "cannot, therefore, serve its intended function." If the conclusion contains a vague term (*intended function*) that is defined elsewhere, it is important to build that definition into your paraphrase of the conclusion. So the author shifts from indicating that news is *primarily entertaining* to concluding that it **cannot** give us *information to act upon*, which assumes those concepts are mutually exclusive. This is just a more elaborate version of "I don't like games because I am serious."
6. Art Historian: Robbins cannot pass judgment on Stuart's art. While Robbins understands the art of Stuart too well to dismiss it, she does not understand it well enough to praise it. *PrepTest27 Sec4 Q20* $\longrightarrow$	Conclusion: Robbins can't judge Stuart's art. *because* Evidence: 1) Robbins understands Stuart's art too well to dismiss it; 2) Robbins doesn't understand it well enough to praise it. The author jumps from evidence that Robbins can neither dismiss nor praise the art to a conclusion that he can't judge the art. This assumes that judging art requires being able at least to either dismiss or praise it, and is a match for: "I don't like games because I am not serious."

Whenever you are trying to link mismatched concepts for your prediction, keep the four common relationships in mind. The LSAT has a limited menu of relationships, and your job is to simply learn to recognize them in slightly different clothing.

Yet another tool for analyzing Mismatched Concepts arguments is in the toolbox of every LSAT expert: understanding Formal Logic.

Formal Logic in Mismatched Concepts

As you've seen in earlier chapters in this book, a fundamental understanding of Formal Logic is an enormously useful skill in mastering Logic Games. Deconstructing rules and making deductions based on conditional rules is the key to simplifying and demystifying some of that section's most difficult games. But having a firm grasp of the machinery of Formal Logic isn't helpful only in the Logic Games section of the LSAT. In fact, arguments that are composed of sufficient and necessary terms litter the Logical Reasoning section of the exam as well. Sometimes the Formal Logic relationship between terms is explicit; other times it is more subtle. In this section, we'll lay out for you some of the most basic patterns of Formal Logic found in Mismatched Concepts arguments.

A quick word of warning before we begin: Though a mastery of Formal Logic is a valuable tool that will help you in this section, most Assumption Family questions don't have conditional statements at all. The most important skill you can develop in evaluating Mismatched Concepts arguments is the ability to recognize the gap between evidence and conclusion and then connect the mismatched terms or concepts. Looking at every argument as a Formal Logic puzzle that needs to be decoded will lead to frustration. Instead, think of tackling Mismatched Concepts arguments as a two-step process: Start by identifying the relationships between the mismatched terms or concepts and then, if needed, use Formal Logic to determine the directionality of the concepts in the assumption.

LEARNING OBJECTIVES

In this section, you'll learn to:

· Recognize common Formal Logic patterns in arguments containing Mismatched Concepts.
· Use knowledge of Formal Logic and contrapositives to determine an argument's assumption.
· Understand when directionality of terms is important.

When Mismatched Concepts arguments on the LSAT contain Formal Logic, the most basic structural pattern is as follows: "If A then B. Therefore, if A then C," where the letters A, B, and C represent unique terms.

	Sample Argument	My Analysis
evidence	If A → B	
assumption		
conclusion	If A → C	

First of all, how would you know that this argument contains mismatched concepts? The evidence discusses A and B, while the conclusion jumps to a discussion of A and C. This is about as straightforward as a Mismatched Concepts argument gets. The author must assume that B and C are in some way connected. Give it a shot: How would you fill in the assumption in this argument?

	Sample Argument	My Analysis
evidence	If A → B	If A → **B**
assumption		
conclusion	If A → C	If A → **C**

If you said that the assumption must be "If B then C" (or drew If B → C), then good work.

	Sample Argument	Analysis
evidence	If A → B	If A → **B**
assumption		**If B → C**
conclusion	If A → C	If A → **C**

This assumption, combined with the evidence, produces a chain of logic: If A → B → C. It is then clear that the author can deduce that If A → C, the argument's conclusion. To see how this plays out in an argument that uses less abstract terms, consider this argument:

> Dolphins are social animals that live in groups. Therefore, dolphins are intelligent.

Both the evidence and the conclusion discuss dolphins, but only the evidence mentions "social animals," while the conclusion moves to a discussion of "intelligence." Therefore, it's easy to see that this is a Mismatched Concepts argument. But how would you know that the evidence and conclusion also use Formal Logic? Words like *are*, *every*, and *any* allow the statements to be turned into conditional statements:

	Sample Argument	My Analysis
evidence	If dolphins → social animals	
assumption		
conclusion	If dolphins → intelligent	

To make this argument work, we need to make a connection between "social animals" and "intelligent." But which direction? Is it that animals that are intelligent live in groups? Or that social animals are intelligent? The missing piece, the assumption, will not just connect the mismatched terms but connect them in the right direction:

	Sample Argument	Analysis	
evidence	If dolphins → social animals	If dolphins	→ **social animals**
assumption		**If social animals → intelligent**	
conclusion	If dolphins → intelligent	If dolphins	→ **intelligent**

As you can see, the argument fits the original pattern of If "A → B; therefore, If A → C." That means the assumption must be If B → C for the conclusion to be logically inferred. Now, based on the previous example, which of these would be an assumption that would allow the conclusion to be logically drawn?

(1) Social animals that live in groups are intelligent.

(2) All intelligent animals are social and live in groups.

In this case, the correct choice is (1), not (2). The assumption is that social animals living in groups must be intelligent, not that all animals that are intelligent are social animals living in groups. Although the testmaker won't always include answer choices with the same terms relating to each other in different ways, it does happen occasionally. By offering two answer choices that, to the unprepared test taker, appear nearly identical—and particularly by offering two distinct choices in which the relationship between concepts is alike/equivalent—the testmaker is able to increase the difficulty of a question. This shows up most often in Sufficient Assumption questions, which we will discuss later in the chapter. For now, just remember this: When you analyze an argument that contains Formal Logic, pay attention to which terms are sufficient and which are necessary.

To see why distinguishing mismatched concepts in the necessary terms from those in the sufficient terms is so valuable, consider another Formal Logic pattern often found in LSAT arguments: "If A, then B. Therefore, if C, then B."

	Sample Argument	My Analysis
evidence	If A → B	
assumption		
conclusion	If C → B	

This time, the mismatched terms or concepts are in the sufficient terms of the evidence and of the conclusion. Identify them.

	Sample Argument	My Analysis
evidence	If A → B	If **A** → B
assumption		
conclusion	If C → B	If **C** → B

In this case, the author assumes that if something is a C (or has the characteristic C), then that thing is an A (or has the characteristic A).

	Sample Argument	Analysis
evidence	If A → B	If **A** → B
assumption		If **C** → **A**
conclusion	If C → B	If **C** → B

You may recognize this pattern as fitting argument we used earlier in the chapter: "Chemical X is harmful because poison is harmful." To match the diagrams above, rewrite the argument as "If poison (A), then harmful (B). Therefore, if Chemical X (C), then harmful (B)." As we clearly saw, the author assumes that Chemical X (C) is a poison (A).

Here's another argument fleshed out in "real world" terms that illustrates this pattern:

All first-year associates at the firm will be mentored by a partner. Thus, Mark will be mentored by a partner.

Lay out this argument to match the diagrams above and determine the author's unstated assumption.

	Sample Argument	My Analysis
evidence	If 1st year assoc → partner mentors	
assumption		
conclusion	If Mark → partner mentors	

Here, the mismatched terms/concepts are in the sufficient terms of both the evidence and the conclusion.

	Sample Argument	Analysis
evidence	If 1st year assoc → partner mentors	If **1st year assoc** → partner mentors
assumption		If **Mark** → **1st year assoc**
conclusion	If Mark → partner mentors	If **Mark** → partner mentors

The author must assume that Mark is a first-year associate at the firm.

A quick note about the direction of connection between the mismatched terms in these formal logic diagrams. If the mismatched concepts are on the right side of the arrows (the necessary side) then the direction of connection goes downward from evidence to conclusion. This is the most common configuration. If the mismatched concepts are on the left side of the arrow (the sufficient side) then the direction of connection goes upward from conclusion to evidence. This could also be visualized and remembered by using clockwise arrows going around the diagram connecting the four terms (note: the clockwise rule only works when evidence is placed above the conclusion). This always shows you the proper direction of connection. Here are the two arguments you just analyzed with arrows to illustrate this approach:

Making It More Difficult: Adding an Extra Concept in the Evidence

Though the most basic Formal Logic Mismatched Concepts argument structure includes three terms (two terms in the evidence and two terms in the conclusion, with one term in the evidence identical to one term in the conclusion), many arguments contain more than just three concepts. A common pattern is for the testmaker to construct arguments with one or more extra terms in the evidence. If the terms are necessary for each other, combine them and remove the redundant term. This makes the evidence simpler and, in turn, easier to compare to the conclusion. Here is the most common pattern for this type of argument on the LSAT:

	Sample Argument	My Analysis
evidence	If A → B If B → C	
assumption		
conclusion	If A → D	

Since the two statements in the evidence share term B—and note that B is the necessary term in one statement and the sufficient term in the other—they can be combined to simplify the evidence. Doing this reveals the terms that are unique to the evidence and to the conclusion.

	Sample Argument	My Analysis
evidence	If A → B If B → C	If A → **C**
assumption		
conclusion	If A → D	If A → **D**

That step reveals that we are back to the simple pattern illustrated by the argument about intelligent, socials dolphins you saw above. The author assumes that all things C (or things with the attribute C) are things D (or things with the attribute D).

	Sample Argument	Analysis
evidence	If A → B If B → C	If A → **C**
assumption		If C → **D**
conclusion	If A → D	If A → **D**

Let's use another "real world" argument to illustrate this pattern as you will analyze it on the LSAT.

All students in Dr. Peterson's class are juniors. Every junior has taken a public speaking class. Therefore, all students in Dr. Peterson's class have given a speech to a large crowd.

Start by laying out the argument in the diagram we've been using.

	Sample Argument	My Analysis
evidence	If Dr. P's student → junior If junior → speech class	
assumption		
conclusion	If Dr. P's student → speech to crowd	

Make sure that the two statements in the evidence can be combined. Once again, because the necessary term in the first statement is the same as the sufficient term in the second statement, they can. (Note that the order of the statements does not matter. The statements could still be combined if the original argument began "Every junior has taken a public speaking class. All students in Dr. Peterson's class are juniors.") Once the evidentiary statements are combined, identify the terms or concepts that are different between the evidence and the conclusion.

	Sample Argument	My Analysis
evidence	If Dr. P's student → junior If junior → speech class	If Dr. P's student → **speech class**
assumption		
conclusion	If Dr. P's student → speech to crowd	If Dr. P's student → **speech to crowd**

Finally, formulate the statement that logically links the author's evidence to his conclusion. That's the author's assumption.

	Sample Argument	Analysis
evidence	If Dr. P's student → junior If junior → speech class	If Dr. P's student → **speech class**
assumption		**If speech class → speech to crowd**
conclusion	If Dr. P's student → speech to crowd	If Dr. P's student → **speech to crowd**

Now, when you read through the argument, you can see that it is complete. If all of Dr. Peterson's students has had a speech class, and if everyone who has had a speech class has given a speech to a large crowd, then it is certain that anyone who is Dr. Peterson's student has given a speech to a large crowd. The additional term in the original argument ("junior") was just there to link up Dr. Peterson's students with the speech class attribute, but it plays no role in the author's unstated assumption. Recognizing this pattern will help you efficiently tackle Assumption Family questions in which the evidence contains two linked statements.

Mismatched Concepts in the Evidence

Mismatched Concepts arguments typically move from one concept in the evidence to a new concept in the conclusion, but it's also possible for an author to present two mismatched concepts in the evidence. Though this is rare, it does occasionally show up, so don't be surprised if you see such an argument on the exam. Here's the algebraic diagram for an argument of this type:

	Sample Argument	**My Analysis**
evidence	If A → B If C → D	
assumption		
conclusion	If A → D	

Notice two things. First, both of the terms in the conclusion are also present in the evidence; there is no mismatch there. Second, there is no way to link up the two evidentiary terms; they share no common terms. In such a case, the author's assumption (her missing, unstated "bridge") lies between the two pieces of evidence. Rewriting the diagram like this makes this clear.

	Sample Argument	**My Analysis**
evidence	If A → B	If A → **B**
assumption		
evidence	If B → C	If **C** → D
conclusion	If A → D	If A → D

Now you can see what the author has left out of the argument.

	Sample Argument	**Analysis**
evidence	If A → B	If A → **B**
assumption		**If B → C**
evidence	If B → C	If **C** → D
conclusion	If A → D	If A → D

Reading through this argument, you can see that it is complete and logical. If As are Bs, and Bs are Cs, and Cs are Ds, then it is valid to conclude that As are Ds.

For good measure, do the same analysis with a "real world" example.

> Whenever people watch a good movie, they get a happy feeling. And people always do the right thing when they feel the urge to help others. Therefore, watching a good movie makes people do the right thing.

Plug that argument into the diagram.

	Sample Argument	My Analysis
evidence	If good movie → happy feeling If urge to help → do the right thing	
assumption		
conclusion	If good movie → do the right thing	

Once again, both terms in the conclusion are found in the evidence, and there is no term shared between the two pieces of evidence. The author needs to bridge the two pieces of evidence; she is assuming they are linked.

	Sample Argument	My Analysis
evidence	If good movie → happy feeling	If good movie → **happy feeling**
assumption		
evidence	If urge to help → do the right thing	If **urge to help** → do the right thing
conclusion	If good movie → do the right thing	If good movie → do the right thing

Finally, determining the assumption, and reading it into the argument, reveals a complete, logical argument.

	Sample Argument	Analysis
evidence	If good movie → happy feeling	If good movie → **happy feeling**
assumption		**If happy feeling → urge to help**
evidence	If urge to help → do the right thing	If **urge to help** → do the right thing
conclusion	If good movie → do the right thing	If good movie → do the right thing

Again, an argument with mismatched concepts in the evidence is rare—in fact, you might not even see it on the LSAT you take. Just know that the testmaker *can* present an argument this way; to find the assumption, find the mismatched concepts in the evidence and connect them.

Strict Formal Logic statements tend to show up most often in Sufficient Assumption questions, which we will discuss in depth later in this chapter. In other Assumption Family questions, strict Formal Logic is less common. The thing to keep in mind is that the underlying Formal Logic structure of "If A → B (evidence); therefore, If A → C (conclusion)" *is* common. Knowing that this pattern underlies many of the Mismatched Concepts arguments you'll see on the LSAT will help you achieve mastery in Assumption Family questions. Remember to approach Mismatched Concepts arguments in two steps: Start by identifying the relationships between the mismatched terms or concepts and then, if needed, use Formal Logic to determine the directionality of the concepts in the assumption.

LSAT STRATEGY

Formal Logic in arguments containing Mismatched Concepts:

- The most common structure is: "If A → B; therefore, If A → C."
- When possible, connect multiple terms in the evidence and simplify.
- Difficult wrong answer choices may confuse necessary and sufficient terms.

You now have a more solid understanding of the common relationships and patterns you'll see in Mismatched Concepts arguments. Later in this chapter, you'll get much more practice identifying and analyzing these types of arguments in Assumption Family questions. Now, though, let's turn our attention to the other type of argument structure you'll see in Assumption Family arguments: Overlooked Possibilities.

OVERLOOKED POSSIBILITIES

Consider this argument

> Last night Maria parked her car in an area of town where many car thefts occur. This morning, Maria woke up and discovered that her car was no longer in its parking spot. Therefore, _____.

Remember the million-dollar prize game we described earlier? Just like before, your job is to figure out what the conclusion is by filling in the blank. Take a moment and think about it.

Unlike in the argument you saw earlier about poison and Chemical X, you probably *would* be able to come up with the conclusion fairly quickly: "I bet the author's going to say that Maria's car was stolen." And if you guessed something along those lines, you're making a reasonable conjecture as to the author's conclusion. Remember, though, that the LSAT doesn't present complete, reasonable arguments—it presents incomplete arguments. Here's what an LSAT argument would likely say:

> Last night Maria parked her car in an area of town where many car thefts occur. This morning, Maria woke up and discovered that her car was no longer in its parking spot. Therefore, Maria's car *must* have been stolen.

Take a moment now and try to describe to yourself what is wrong with the LSAT version of this argument without using any of the words from the stimulus.

To understand what is wrong with the argument, begin by envisioning the author's argument as a road: The author is driving from the evidence to the conclusion. As far as she's concerned, it's a clear path, but an LSAT expert is trained to see all of the roadblocks along the way that the author can't. That's exactly what went wrong with the argument above: The author starts the trip with evidence that introduces the *possibility* of the car having been stolen, and from there she tries to reach a conclusion that it *must* be the explanation for the disappearance. Unfortunately for the author, there are many possible explanations for the car's disappearance, and if even one of them is possible, the author's entire conclusion falls apart. These are the roadblocks (in other words, the possible objections) to the argument. The only way the author's argument will work is if they're all removed.

Overlooked Possibilities: The Basics

Not all LSAT arguments have a problem of relevance. The reason why you could reasonably predict the conclusion in this argument is that it does use the right *kind* of evidence: The information given helps us figure out whether or not Maria's car was stolen. Contrast that with the Chemical X example from earlier in the chapter. In that argument, the evidence about poison didn't help us figure out whether or not Chemical X was harmful. In fact, on roughly half of the LSAT arguments you'll see on Test Day, the author is using pieces of evidence that *are* in some way related and relevant to the terms and concepts in the conclusion, but the author's conclusion will be too extreme for its evidence. Instead of a jump or shift in the *types* of concepts discussed, the author's shift will be one of *degree*.

LSAT STRATEGY

How can you identify an argument containing Overlooked Possibilities?

- The terms or concepts in the evidence *are* related to the conclusion.
- The conclusion reached is too strong or extreme based on the evidence.
- The author has failed to consider possible objections to the conclusion.

Finding the assumption in these arguments is fundamentally different from our approach to Mismatched Concepts problems. Instead of linking two concepts from within the stimulus, our job is to consider the potential objections to the author's conclusion: Any unconsidered information that would prove the conclusion false. Going back to Maria's vanishing car, for example, couldn't it also be true that Maria's car was towed? Or that she gave her keys to a friend, who took the car? Or that the car was impounded due to Maria's failure to make her loan payments in a timely manner? We could actually spend all day thinking of all of the various fates that could have befallen her poor car aside from being stolen, and there's often no way to know which one will be brought up in the correct answer. Overlooked Possibilities assumptions are thus best thought of as negative assumptions—they are about all of the things that the author *didn't* consider, or at least didn't mention considering or ruling out as possibilities. In this case, the author is assuming that there are *no* other reasons for the car's disappearance—if that's true, then all potential objections have been removed from the argument. Most of the time, the questions will specifically test you on these unconsidered objections.

LSAT STRATEGY

When tackling an argument containing Overlooked Possibilities:

· Focus on the conclusion.
· Determine the possible objections to that conclusion.
· Understand the assumption in negative terms: The author assumes that the possible objections are not present, or did not happen.

Overlooked Possibilities: Sample Arguments

Here are some brief Overlooked Possibilities arguments and the assumption of each. After reviewing these examples, you'll have a chance to try some others on your own.

Argument		Analysis
These berries taste delicious. Therefore, we should eat them!	→	The author assumes that there are no other considerations when determining whether or not to eat the berries.
When I wore a tracksuit to the party, I was ignored. Therefore, the tracksuit caused people to ignore me.	→	The author assumes that nothing else, besides the tracksuit, caused people to ignore him at the party.
Sad movies make my friend cry. She's crying now. Therefore, she must have watched a sad movie.	→	The author assumes that there is no other possible explanation for why her friend is crying.
There's no cash in William's wallet. Therefore, he won't be able to buy any gum.	→	The author assumes that there is no other possible way for William to pay for gum besides cash from William's wallet.
Our team has the best player in the game. Therefore, we will win the game.	→	The author assumes that there are no other considerations to take into account when determining the winner besides which team has the best player.

Practice

Practice your ability to evaluate Overlooked Possibilities arguments by analyzing the following arguments. In each one of these arguments, follow this approach:

· Separate the evidence from the conclusion.
· Describe to yourself why the evidence is relevant.
· Ask yourself what the possible objections to the conclusion are.
· Phrase the assumption in negative terms (i.e., what didn't happen).

After each argument, feel free to turn to the next page to see the expert analysis.

Argument	My Analysis
7. Medication B has more side effects than Medication A. Therefore, we should use Medication A.	
8. The pet store down the street has only cats and dogs for sale. I'm definitely going to get a pet, but my parents won't let me get a cat. Clearly, then, I'm going to get a dog.	
9. Sally suggests driving to work on the highway, but the highway tends to have much more traffic than the side streets. So I am going to ignore Sally's advice and take the side streets instead.	

Expert Analysis for this exercise is on the next page. ▶ ▶ ▶

Expert Analysis

Now take a look at how an LSAT expert would look at the arguments you've just evaluated.

Argument	Analysis
7. Medication B has more side effects than Medication A. Therefore, we should use Medication A.	Conclusion: We should use Med. A (instead of Med. B). Evidence: Med. B has more side effects than Med. A. → The author considers only the side effects of the two medications in making a decision; therefore, the author is *not* considering any other reasons why Med. B might be preferable to Med. A. What if Med. A simply isn't effective? Or if Med. A is astronomically expensive? Phrase the assumption negatively: "There are no unconsidered benefits of Med. B and no unconsidered drawbacks of Med. A."
8. The pet store down the street has only cats and dogs for sale. I'm definitely going to get a pet, but my parents won't let me get a cat. Clearly, then, I'm going to get a dog.	Conclusion: I am going to get a dog. Evidence: The store down the street only has cats and dogs, and I can't get a cat. → There's nothing new in the conclusion, but the conclusion goes too far. The unconsidered objections to this argument would be anything that says the author *doesn't* have to get a dog. Specifically, there may be other pet stores in the area that sell more than just cats and dogs. Phrase the assumption negatively: "There is no other place to get a pet aside from the pet store down the street."
9. Sally suggests driving to work on the highway, but the highway tends to have much more traffic than the side streets. So I am going to ignore Sally's advice and take the side streets instead.	Conclusion: I'm going to take the side streets to work. Evidence: The highway tends to have more traffic than side streets. → There's nothing new in this conclusion either, but much as in the first argument, the author is not considering potential objections to the conclusion. Specifically, the author fails to rule out any additional reasons why the highway may be a good idea or additional information about potential cons of the side streets. Phrase the assumption negatively: "There are no unconsidered pros of the highway or cons of the side streets that would make the highway the better choice."

The LSAT, of course, will present more difficult arguments than the ones just shown, but the fundamental *structure* of Overlooked Possibilities arguments will remain the same. Regardless of the topic being discussed in the argument—whether it be on matters philosophical, legal, or scientific—your method and objective will always remain the same. First, separate evidence from conclusion. Then, evaluate the concepts discussed in both—if the author uses relevant information to draw a conclusion that is too strong or extreme, find the assumption by identifying the factors the author is not considering.

Practice

Try that now with an actual LSAT argument.

LSAT Argument	My Analysis
10. Economist: In the interaction between producers and consumers, the only obligation that all parties have is to act in the best interests of their own side. And distribution of information about product defects is in the best interests of the consumer. So consumers are always obligated to report product defects they discover, while producers are never obligated to reveal them. *PrepTestB Sec1 Q8*	

Did the terms and concepts in the evidence relate to the conclusion drawn? Did the author then overlook potential objections to the conclusion?

Expert Analysis

Take a look at how an LSAT expert would break down this argument.

LSAT Argument	Analysis
10. Economist: In the interaction between producers and consumers, the only obligation that all parties have is to act in the best interests of their own side. And distribution of information about product defects is in the best interests of the consumer. So consumers are always obligated to report product defects they discover, while producers are never obligated to reveal them. *PrepTestB Sec1 Q8* $\longrightarrow$	Conclusion: Consumers are always obligated to report product defects, but producers are never obligated to reveal them. *because* Evidence: 1) Producers must act in the best interest of producers and consumers must act in the best interest of consumers; 2) reporting defects is in the best interest of consumers. Though the evidence does relate to reporting defects, the author jumps to a very extreme conclusion that ignores the fact that the evidence, while indicating what is in the best interest of consumers, fails to indicate what is in the best interest of producers. The author assumes that it is in the best interest of producers to *not* have defects disclosed.

Hopefully you're starting to get the hang of evaluating these types of arguments. Let's dive in even deeper and discuss some of the most common types of Overlooked Possibilities arguments you'll see on the LSAT.

Going Deeper: Common Patterns and Relationships in Arguments with Overlooked Possibilities

By now, you've seen the benefit of skeptically looking at an argument in which the author uses relevant evidence to support a conclusion that goes too far. In doing so, the author chooses to overlook alternate possibilities that would hurt his conclusion. Indeed, the author's assumption is that no potential objections to the conclusion exist. Now we'll take a look at several of the most common patterns that show up in Overlooked Possibilities arguments.

No Other Explanation, Reason, or Outcome

One of the most common patterns within the Overlooked Possibilities argument class consists of a conclusion that posits only one explanation or reason for something or only one likely outcome. Invariably, the assumption will then be that there is no other possible explanation, reason, or outcome. For example, consider the following simple argument:

> Chlorophyll A is a type of green-pigmented chlorophyll abundant in plants. Clearly, the presence of chlorophyll A must be what gives plants their green coloration.

Notice that the conclusion provides only one explanation for the green color of plants: It must be due to the presence of chlorophyll A. Yet the evidence alludes to the fact that chlorophyll A might not be the only type of chlorophyll in existence. The author is overlooking the possibility that there are other kinds of chlorophyll—or other pigments unrelated to chlorophyll—that also contribute to the green color of plants. In other words, the possible objections to this argument are other explanations for the green color of plants.

Practice

Now take a look at an LSAT stimulus built on this same pattern. You've seen this argument before, in Chapter 9. Here, see if you can spot the overlooked explanation or outcome; then compare your thinking to the expert analysis on the next page.

LSAT Argument	My Analysis
11. During the 1980s Japanese collectors were very active in the market for European art, especially as purchasers of nineteenth-century Impressionist paintings. This striking pattern surely reflects a specific preference on the part of many Japanese collectors for certain aesthetic attributes they found in nineteenth-century Impressionist paintings.	

PrepTest27 Sec1 Q5

Does this conclusion strike you as particularly strong? "This striking pattern *surely* reflects a specific preference . . . for certain aesthetic attributes . . .." Such a confident-sounding conclusion indicates that this is likely an Overlooked Possibilities argument.

Expert Analysis

Here's how an LSAT expert might analyze that argument.

LSAT Argument	Analysis
11. During the 1980s Japanese collectors were very active in the market for European art, especially as purchasers of nineteenth-century Impressionist paintings. This striking pattern surely reflects a specific preference on the part of many Japanese collectors for certain aesthetic attributes they found in nineteenth-century Impressionist paintings. *PrepTest27 Sec1 Q5*	**Step 2:** Conclusion: Japanese art collectors were enticed by the aesthetic attributes of 19th-century Impressionist paintings during the 1980s. *because* Evidence: Japanese collectors purchased much 19th-century Impressionist art during the 1980s. The evidence is merely that a certain phenomenon occurred and the author's conclusion attributes a specific causal explanation, which is entirely reasonable but stated with far too much certainty. Overlooked possibilities include any other reasons that Japanese collectors might have purchased this specific type of art. The author assumes that no other explanations could apply.

Here, the author is overlooking the possibility that the Japanese collectors of the 1980s purchased significant amounts of this particular art for reasons other than aesthetic attributes. For example, perhaps the investors believed the artwork had strong investment potential. Or maybe a strong Japanese economy in the 1980s allowed the collectors to purchase significant amounts of many types of art. Indeed, there might be many alternative explanations for why the investors were purchasing such art.

Although the failure to consider alternative explanations is one of the most common overlooked possibilities, this argument class includes a number of other variants as well. The ability to recognize the following five patterns will give you an advantage over other test takers who have to reinvent the wheel each time they see an argument type they do not recognize. Try out the examples for each pattern and watch for them while you practice.

Necessity versus Sufficiency: Assuming that What Is Sufficient Is Actually Necessary

You've seen how Formal Logic statements can be tested in Mismatched Concepts arguments. Occasionally, though, an author will commit a Formal Logic error in an Overlooked Possibilities argument. This happens when an argument either confuses sufficient and necessary terms or incorrectly negates the terms. The result of both of these errors is that the author overlooks other potential causes for a given event. For instance, take a look at the following simple argument:

> Every time my cat jumps onto the coffee table, she knocks over the lamp. I just got home and found the lamp on the coffee table knocked over. Obviously my cat has been at it again.

This author concludes that there is only one possible cause for the lamp having been knocked over: the cat. But is that necessarily true? Just because the cat *can* cause the lamp to fall over doesn't mean that there are no other ways it could happen. Perhaps the dog is at fault, for example, or perhaps a human living in the house is responsible, or perhaps there was an earthquake. Think of it in terms of sufficiency and necessity: The fact that the cat is sufficient to cause the lamp to fall down does not mean that the cat is necessary for the lamp to fall down—there could be lots of other sufficient conditions as well.

Looking at this argument in clear Formal Logic terminology helps illuminate the error:

> Evidence: If cat on table → lamp down

> Conclusion: If lamp down → cat on table

As you remember from Chapter 1, you can't read the conditional statement "If the cat is on the table then the lamp gets knocked down" backward as "If lamp got knocked down then cat was on the table." Whenever an author switches the necessary and sufficient sides of a conditional statement without negating the terms, she automatically overlooks the fact that there could be other triggers for an event, just as the author of the cat-and-lamp argument assumes that no other factor besides the cat could have caused the lamp to be knocked over.

Practice

Try out the following LSAT argument that confuses necessary and sufficient conditions:

LSAT Argument	My Analysis
12. If you know a lot about history, it will be easy for you to impress people who are intellectuals. But unfortunately, you will not know much about history if you have not, for example, read a large number of history books. Therefore, if you are not well versed in history due to a lack of reading, it will not be easy for you to impress people who are intellectuals. *PrepTest27 Sec4 Q7*	

The repeated use of the term *if* indicates that this argument uses Formal Logic. In such arguments, suspect either a Mismatched Concepts argument or an Overlooked Possibilities argument that confuses sufficient and necessary.

Expert Analysis

Here's how an LSAT expert might analyze that argument.

LSAT Argument	Analysis
12. If you know a lot about history, it will be easy for you to impress people who are intellectuals. But unfortunately, you will not know much about history if you have not, for example, read a large number of history books. Therefore, if you are not well versed in history due to a lack of reading, it will not be easy for you to impress people who are intellectuals. *PrepTest27 Sec4 Q7*	**Conclusion:** One who is not knowledgeable about history cannot easily impress intellectuals. *because* **Evidence:** Those who are knowledgeable about history can easily impress intellectuals. → The evidence indicates that knowledge of history is sufficient to easily impress intellectuals. The author then concludes that a lack of knowledge about history will preclude easily impressing intellectuals. This is another way of stating that knowledge of history is necessary to impress intellectuals.

Assuming that There Are No Overlooked Advantages or Disadvantages that Impact a Recommendation

Consider the following:

> The deli down the street is currently offering a lunch special, so we should eat lunch there today.

Okay, so the deli's running a special. But what if it's still more expensive than the pizza place across the street? Or what if the deli's been cited for food safety violations repeatedly during the past month and, in fact, your friend just got sick from eating there yesterday? Or what if the deli's food doesn't taste good? If the deli has any of these disadvantages, should you still eat there? Perhaps not.

Whenever the author of an LSAT argument cites an advantage (or disadvantage) and makes a recommendation based upon it, the possible objections to the argument are any disadvantages (or advantages) that could outweigh it. In the argument above, the author assumes that the deli offers no disadvantages that could tilt the scale in favor of eating elsewhere.

Practice

Now try to spot the author's assumption in an LSAT argument that involves a recommendation based upon advantages or disadvantages:

LSAT Argument	My Analysis
13. Formal performance evaluations in the professional world are conducted using realistic situations. Physicians are allowed to consult medical texts freely, attorneys may refer to law books and case records, and physicists and engineers have their manuals at hand for ready reference. Students, then, should likewise have access to their textbooks whenever they take examinations. *PrepTest29 Sec4 Q25*	

Notice that the conclusion of this argument is a recommendation. If the author of the argument bases the recommendation on citing advantages or disadvantages to the proposal, suspect an Overlooked Possibilities argument.

Expert Analysis

Take a look at how an LSAT expert evaluates the argument.

LSAT Argument	Analysis
13. Formal performance evaluations in the professional world are conducted using realistic situations. Physicians are allowed to consult medical texts freely, attorneys may refer to law books and case records, and physicists and engineers have their manuals at hand for ready reference. Students, then, should likewise have access to their textbooks whenever they take examinations. *PrepTest29 Sec4 Q25*	Conclusion: Students should have access to their textbooks during their exams. *because* Evidence: Professionals are allowed to consult texts and manuals during performance evaluations. → The author cites an analogy (to professional performance evaluations) that identifies a possible advantage of the recommendation to allow students to use textbooks during their examinations. The unconsidered objections here are any reasons why students should not be allowed to use textbooks, including any differences between the goals of professional evaluations and student examinations. As is typical with an argument with a recommendation conclusion, the author assumes that there are no disadvantages that outweigh the benefits.

Assuming that Something that Could Occur, Will Occur

The fact that something might happen doesn't necessarily mean that it actually will happen. Yet, authors of LSAT arguments sometimes wrongly assume the opposite—that is, they assume that something merely possible is definitely true. Here's a simplified example to illustrate:

> Skateboarding can cause all sorts of injuries. It follows that Aaron, who just went skateboarding, must be injured.

The fact that skateboarding *can* cause injuries does not mean that it *always* causes injuries. But that's exactly what this author assumes in concluding that Aaron must be injured just because he went skateboarding. Stated differently, the author overlooks the possibility that Aaron might have managed to go skateboarding without incurring an injury.

Practice

See if you can recognize the shift from language of *possibility* in the evidence to language of *certainty* in the conclusion in this LSAT argument:

LSAT Argument	My Analysis
14. All actions are motivated by self-interest, since any action that is apparently altruistic can be described in terms of self-interest. For example, helping someone can be described in terms of self-interest: the motivation is hope for a reward or other personal benefit to be bestowed as a result of the helping action.	

PrepTest29 Sec4 Q18

Expert Analysis

Now take a look at the same argument, through the lens of an LSAT expert:

LSAT Argument	Analysis
14. All actions are motivated by self-interest, since any action that is apparently altruistic can be described in terms of self-interest. For example, helping someone can be described in terms of self-interest: the motivation is hope for a reward or other personal benefit to be bestowed as a result of the helping action. *PrepTest29 Sec4 Q18*	Conclusion: *All* actions *are* motivated by self-interest. *because* Evidence: Any action *can be* described in terms of self-interest. → The evidence is provisional: Actions *"can be* described in terms of self-interest." But the conclusion uses much stronger language: *"All* actions *are* motivated by self-interest." This overlooks the fact that just because something can be described a certain way doesn't mean that there isn't another (and maybe better or more accurate) way to describe it.

Causal Arguments: Assuming that Correlation Proves Causation

Thing A happens. At the same time (or soon after), Thing B happens. So A caused B. This is the classic argument of causation based on evidence of a correlation. Because they come with such a wealth of overlooked possibilities, causal arguments show up most frequently in Flaw, Strengthen, and Weaken questions. Here's a basic causal argument:

> Over the past half century, worldwide sugar consumption has nearly tripled. During the same time period, there has been a marked increase in the rate of global technological advancement. It follows that the increase in global sugar consumption has caused the acceleration in technological advancement.

The author concludes that increased sugar consumption caused the acceleration in technological advancement. In doing so, the author assumes that there are *no other possible relationships* between sugar consumption and technological advancement. Specifically, the three possible objections to any causal argument are:

1. There is an **alternate cause**. Perhaps something else caused the accelerated technological advancement.

2. The causation is **reversed**. Perhaps it's the other way around: Technological advances allow for easier sugar refinement, which leads to higher sugar consumption.

3. The correlation is purely **coincidental**. Perhaps the fact that increased sugar consumption and technological innovation occurred at the same time is merely a coincidence.

The author of a causal argument assumes, then, that (1) there is no alternate cause, (2) the causation is not reversed, and (3) the correlation is not coincidental. In the future, remind yourself of these overlooked objections by using the acronym **ARC**. And, because the author isn't considering them, we can say that the flaw in these arguments is that the author improperly assumes that there is **"No ARC."**

Practice

Try out an LSAT argument that includes a claim of causation based on evidence of a correlation and ask yourself which of these overlooked possibilities are most likely:

LSAT Argument	My Analysis
15. Unplugging a peripheral component such as a "mouse" from a personal computer renders all of the software programs that require that component unusable on that computer. On Fred's personal computer, a software program that requires a mouse has become unusable. So it must be that the mouse for Fred's computer became unplugged.	

PrepTest27 Sec4 Q10

While this argument's conclusion does not explicitly assert a claim of causation, the author must believe that an unplugged mouse caused the program to stop working. If the author explicitly concludes or implicitly assumes that one thing is making another thing happen, you're dealing with a causal argument.

Expert Analysis

Take a look at one LSAT expert's analysis of the argument about Fred's computer and mouse.

LSAT Argument	Analysis
15. Unplugging a peripheral component such as a "mouse" from a personal computer renders all of the software programs that require that component unusable on that computer. On Fred's personal computer, a software program that requires a mouse has become unusable. So it must be that the mouse for Fred's computer became unplugged. *PrepTest27 Sec4 Q10*	Conclusion: The mouse on Fred's computer became unplugged. *because* Evidence: A program on Fred's computer that requires a mouse has stopped working. By concluding so definitively that the mouse on Fred's computer must have become unplugged, the author assumes that it is the only possible cause of the problem with the program.

Predictions: Assumptions about Circumstances

As you learned in Chapter 9, a conclusion stating that something is likely to happen in the future is called a "prediction." To illustrate the classic assumption underlying predictions, consider the following weather prediction:

> Due to the current prevailing northwesterly breeze, the weather in Flooville will remain clear and cold tomorrow.

The problem with this prediction is that if the northwesterly breeze unexpectedly shifts to, say, southeasterly, the weather in Flooville might not "remain clear and cold." The author assumes that the circumstances under which the prediction was made *will not change*.

Now consider this prediction:

> Despite the prevailing northwesterly breeze that is currently bringing clear and cold weather to Flooville, the weather in Flooville will shift tomorrow to overcast and warm.

This time, the author assumes that the northwesterly breeze will have changed direction by tomorrow—in other words, the assumption is that there *will be* a change in circumstances.

Anyone making a prediction is making an assumption about circumstances. Keep this in mind whenever you see that an argument's conclusion is a prediction.

Practice

Analyze the following LSAT argument:

LSAT Argument	**My Analysis**
16. Plant Manager: We could greatly reduce the amount of sulfur dioxide our copper-smelting plant releases into the atmosphere by using a new process. The new process requires replacing our open furnaces with closed ones and moving the copper from one furnace to the next in solid, not molten, form. However, not only is the new equipment expensive to buy and install, but the new process also costs more to run than the current process, because the copper must be reheated after it has cooled. So overall, adopting the new process will cost much but bring the company no profit.	
PrepTest29 Sec4 Q14	

Notice how this conclusion is phrased: a confident prediction that something will definitely happen. Take a look at how an LSAT expert evaluates this argument:

Expert Analysis

Review an LSAT expert's analysis of that argument.

LSAT Argument	Analysis
16. Plant Manager: We could greatly reduce the amount of sulfur dioxide our copper-smelting plant releases into the atmosphere by using a new process. The new process requires replacing our open furnaces with closed ones and moving the copper from one furnace to the next in solid, not molten, form. However, not only is the new equipment expensive to buy and install, but the new process also costs more to run than the current process, because the copper must be reheated after it has cooled. So overall, adopting the new process will cost much but bring the company no profit. *PrepTest29 Sec4 Q14* $\longrightarrow$	Conclusion: Even though adopting closed furnaces will greatly reduce the amount of sulfur dioxide it releases, doing so will cost much without earning a profit. *because* Evidence: 1) The new equipment is expensive to buy and install, and 2) the new process costs more to run because of an extra reheating step. The author assumes that no other circumstances or change of circumstances will affect the results of adopting the new process. This particular argument also reflects the assumption inherent in any recommendation conclusion that no other factors will figure into the equation.

As with Mismatched Concepts arguments, the better you can become at spotting these various Overlooked Possibilities argument patterns, the more efficient you will become at analyzing arguments. You'll be ahead of the game when you encounter Assumption, Strengthen, Weaken, and Flaw questions—which, taken together, constitute about one-fourth of the LSAT.

LSAT STRATEGY

Overlooked Possibilities tend to fit one of the following patterns:

- Fails to consider other explanations, reasons, or outcomes based on the evidence
- Confuses sufficient and necessary terms
- Does not consider potential advantages or disadvantages when making a recommendation
- Assumes that something *will* occur just because it *could* occur
- Author arrives at a claim of causation based on evidence that is only correlated
- Prediction is based on an assumption that circumstances will or will not change

On the next page, you get a chance to put all of this knowledge into practice and analyze some arguments.

UNTANGLING AND ANALYZING LSAT ARGUMENTS

At this point, you should have more confidence in your ability to identify the assumption in LSAT arguments. If an argument contains a new concept in the conclusion that is not inherently relevant or related to the concept in the evidence, the author's assumption is that a logical relationship exists between mismatched concepts in the evidence and conclusion. On the other hand, if an argument uses clearly applicable or relevant evidence, but jumps to a conclusion that overlooks other potentially relevant factors, explanations, or criteria, then the author's assumption is that there are no possible objections to the conclusion. Understanding the common ways an LSAT argument moves from its evidence to its conclusion will help you tackle Assumption Family questions. Use this new knowledge to analyze a few LSAT arguments.

Practice

In each of the following arguments, separate the evidence from the conclusion. Simplify each, and then compare them. Is the author assuming that two mismatched concepts are somehow related? Or is the author using relevant evidence to jump to an extreme conclusion without considering potential objections?

	LSAT Argument	My Analysis
17.	All potatoes naturally contain solanine, which is poisonous in large quantities. Domesticated potatoes contain only very small amounts of solanine, but many wild potatoes contain poisonous levels of solanine. Since most of the solanine in potatoes is concentrated in the skin, however, peeling wild potatoes makes them at least as safe to eat as unpeeled domesticated potatoes of the same size. *PrepTestB Sec1 Q9*	
18.	Recent research shows that sound change (pronunciation shift) in a language is not gradual. New sounds often emerge suddenly. This confounds the classical account of sound change, whose central tenet is gradualness. Since this classical account must be discarded, sound-change theory in general must also be. *PrepTest27 Sec1 Q16*	
19.	On a certain day, nine scheduled flights on Swift Airlines were canceled. Ordinarily, a cancellation is due to mechanical problems with the airplane scheduled for a certain flight. However, since it is unlikely that Swift would have mechanical problems with more than one or two airplanes on a single day, some of the nine cancellations were probably due to something else. *PrepTest28, Sec3, Q19*	
20.	The miscarriage of justice in the Barker case was due to the mistaken views held by some of the forensic scientists involved in the case, who believed that they owed allegiance only to the prosecuting lawyers. Justice was thwarted because these forensic scientists failed to provide evidence impartially to both the defense and the prosecution. Hence it is not forensic evidence in general that should be condemned for this injustice. *PrepTestB Sec4 Q16*	

Expert Analysis

Now, take a look at how an LSAT expert would untangle and evaluate the arguments you've just examined.

LSAT Argument	Analysis
17. All potatoes naturally contain solanine, which is poisonous in large quantities. Domesticated potatoes contain only very small amounts of solanine, but many wild potatoes contain poisonous levels of solanine. Since most of the solanine in potatoes is concentrated in the skin, however, peeling wild potatoes makes them at least as safe to eat as unpeeled domesticated potatoes of the same size. *PrepTestB Sec1 Q9* →	**Step 2:** Conclusion: Peeled wild potatoes are as safe to eat as unpeeled domesticated potatoes. *because* Evidence: 1) Solanine is poisonous in large quantities; 2) domesticated potatoes have small amounts; and 3) wild potatoes have poisonous levels, with most concentrated in the skin. The argument assumes that once "most" of the solanine in wild potatoes is removed by peeling, the solanine levels in wild potatoes will drop to the same or lower levels than in entire domesticated potatoes. This overlooks the possibility that the amount of solanine in the core of wild potatoes could still be higher than the overall amount in domesticated potatoes.
18. Recent research shows that sound change (pronunciation shift) in a language is not gradual. New sounds often emerge suddenly. This confounds the classical account of sound change, whose central tenet is gradualness. Since this classical account must be discarded, sound-change theory in general must also be. *PrepTest27 Sec1 Q16* →	**Step 2:** Conclusion: Sound theory generally must be discarded. *because* Evidence: The classical account of sound theory must be discarded. This is a classic Mismatched Concepts argument: While the evidence is about the classical account of sound theory, the conclusion is about sound theory generally. More specifically, the argument assumes that sound theory in general is dependent upon the classical account.

LSAT Argument	**Analysis**
19. On a certain day, nine scheduled flights on Swift Airlines were canceled. Ordinarily, a cancellation is due to mechanical problems with the airplane scheduled for a certain flight. However, since it is unlikely that Swift would have mechanical problems with more than one or two airplanes on a single day, some of the nine cancellations were probably due to something else. *PrepTest28 Sec3 Q19*	Conclusion: Some of the nine cancellations were due to something other than mechanical problems. *because* Evidence: It is unlikely that more than one or two airplanes on a single day would have mechanical problems. → The Mismatched Concepts in this argument are the number of *planes* that have mechanical problems and the number of canceled *flights* that are due to mechanical problems. The argument assumes that there is no way that one or two planes being grounded could lead to nine canceled flights; this overlooks the possibility that all nine of the cancelled flights could have been scheduled to use only one or two planes (such as in short commuter hops between nearby cities).
20. The miscarriage of justice in the Barker case was due to the mistaken views held by some of the forensic scientists involved in the case, who believed that they owed allegiance only to the prosecuting lawyers. Justice was thwarted because these forensic scientists failed to provide evidence impartially to both the defense and the prosecution. Hence it is not forensic evidence in general that should be condemned for this injustice. *PrepTestB Sec4 Q16*	Conclusion: Forensic evidence in general is not to blame for the injustice in the Barker case. *because* → Evidence: The forensic scientists on the case failed to be impartial. The Mismatched Concepts in the argument are individual forensic scientists and forensic science generally, with the author assuming that the failings of individual forensic scientists should not be attributed broadly as failings of forensic science generally.

You've now had a lot of practice breaking down LSAT arguments and identifying the author's central assumption. But just evaluating and analyzing arguments alone won't get you to your target score; to do that, you'll have to correctly answer the Assumption Family questions you'll face on Test Day. The good news is that the fundamental understanding you now have of the common ways LSAT arguments move from their evidence to their conclusion puts you light-years ahead of your competition. You'll soon see that Assumption, Strengthen, Weaken, and Flaw questions—which taken together constitute about 25 percent of the LSAT—will seem much easier to analyze, evaluate, and correctly answer.

Let's take a look now at the first of these question types.

ASSUMPTION QUESTIONS

> ## LEARNING OBJECTIVES
>
> In this section, you'll learn to:
>
> · Identify Assumption questions.
> · Recognize Sufficient Assumption questions.
> · Recognize Necessary Assumption questions.
> · Phrase a prediction of the correct answer choice.

On Test Day, you will be asked to correctly answer roughly eight Assumption questions. Put plainly, these questions will ask you to determine an argument's assumption. This seems straightforward and easy enough; after all, you are now already in the habit of determining the unstated premise of each Assumption Family question argument you see. To identify an Assumption question, look for the words *assumption*, *assumes*, or *presupposes* in the question stem. The correct answer to these questions will always present a new piece of information that the author has not included in his argument. In fact, if an answer choice restates evidence that has already been explicitly stated in the argument, then it will never be correct in an Assumption question. The LSAT will phrase an Assumption question in one of two distinct ways. Take a look at these two LSAT question stems:

> Which one of the following, if assumed, allows the argument's conclusion to be properly drawn?
>
> *PrepTest24 Sec2 Q21*

> Which one of the following is an assumption on which the argument depends?
>
> *PrepTest27 Sec4 Q9*

Although both question stems include references to the assumption—the terms *assumed* and *assumption*—they actually ask for two distinctly different things. Notice that the first question stem asks you to determine an assumption that, if true, would allow for the conclusion to be properly drawn. This means that the correct answer will be an assumption that, when added to the evidence, will *guarantee* the conclusion. We will refer to these as Sufficient Assumption questions.

Now take a look at the second question stem. Here, the testmaker asks you to determine an assumption that the argument requires, or depends on. For this question stem, a correct answer doesn't need to guarantee the conclusion; instead, the correct answer choice to such a Necessary Assumption question will be an assumption that is *necessary* for the conclusion to make logical sense.

To understand the basic difference between Sufficient and Necessary Assumption questions, let's revisit the argument about Dweezil:

> Dweezil is a zulzey alien. Therefore, Dweezil can perform the amazing *yeerchta* move.

Previously, we said that the assumption of this argument is that zulzey aliens are able to perform the amazing *yeerchta* move. So what if an answer choice to an Assumption question said something like this: "Every type of alien is capable of performing the *yeerchta* move." Would that be correct? Actually, we don't know—it all depends on whether or not the question we're evaluating is a Sufficient Assumption or Necessary Assumption question. First, let's look at this assumption in the context of a Sufficient Assumption question:

> Which one of the following, if assumed, allows the
> argument's conclusion to be properly drawn?
>
> *PrepTest24 Sec2 Q21*

Here, "Every type of alien is capable of performing the *yeerchta* move" *would* be correct. Because we know that Dweezil is an alien (the type of alien doesn't really matter), we could add this assumption to the evidence and draw the conclusion that, yes, Dweezil can definitely perform the *yeerchta* move. But what about this next question? Will the assumption "Every type of alien is capable of performing the *yeerchta* move" be correct here, as well?

> Which one of the following is an assumption on which
> the argument depends?
>
> *PrepTest27 Sec4 Q9*

For this Necessary Assumption question, we don't need to find an assumption that guarantees the conclusion; instead, we need to find an assumption that is *necessary* or *required* for the conclusion to follow. The statement "Every type of alien is capable of performing the *yeerchta* move" doesn't satisfy this question because the author's argument doesn't *need* every alien to be able to do the *yeerchta* move, only zulzey aliens. So long as at least one zulzey alien is capable of doing it—and, particularly, so long as Dweezil herself is able to do it—the author's conclusion could still stand.

It is worth noting that a statement can be both necessary and sufficient to establish a conclusion. For example, in this fictional argument, the premise "Zulzey aliens named Dweezil can perform the amazing *yeertcha* move" is both necessary (the argument could not be completed if it were not true) and sufficient (it is enough to establish the conclusion beyond doubt on the basis of the evidence). Similarly, the premise "Nothing prevents a zulzey alien from performing the amazing *yeertcha* move" is necessary, but not sufficient, to establish the conclusion in that argument.

Though the two Assumption question sub-types are similar in some ways, you'll see that recognizing the distinction between the two will help you determine the right answer choice more efficiently and confidently.

Sufficient Assumption Questions

As you just saw, Sufficient Assumption questions will ask you to consider an assumption that, "if assumed," allows the conclusion to be drawn logically. In these questions, which make up about 40 percent of all Assumption questions, you are asked to find an assumption that would be *sufficient* to establish the conclusion from the evidence. In other words, when added to the evidence, the assumption will *guarantee* that the conclusion is true. The language of Sufficient Assumption question stems will include phrases like "if assumed," "conclusion follows logically," or "allows the conclusion to be drawn." You can also spot these questions by the words and terms they *don't* include; unlike Necessary Assumption questions, Sufficient Assumption questions won't use language like "needs," "requires," or "depends."

Take a look at some actual LSAT Sufficient Assumption question stems:

LSAT Question Stem		Analysis
Which one of the following, if assumed, enables the conclusion above to be properly inferred? *PrepTestB Sec4 Q22*	$\longrightarrow$	Sufficient Assumption question. Find an answer choice that, when connected to the evidence, would guarantee the conclusion is true.
The conclusion of the argument follows logically if which one of the following is assumed? *PrepTest24 Sec3 Q19*	$\longrightarrow$	Sufficient Assumption question. Find an answer choice that, when combined with the evidence, will guarantee that the conclusion is true.

In Sufficient Assumption questions, the argument pattern is overwhelmingly Mismatched Concepts arguments that contain Formal Logic. Your goal for most of these questions, then, will be to find the mismatched terms between the evidence and the conclusion, connect those terms strongly, and eliminate any answer choices that bring in outside information. If you do come across the rare Sufficient Assumption question that uses an Overlooked Possibilities argument, be sure to find an answer choice that rules out *all* potential objections to the author's conclusion. Because the correct answer choice to a Sufficient Assumption question will, when added to the argument's evidence, definitely lead to the author's conclusion, it is acceptable for these assumptions to be broader than the argument itself.

LSAT STRATEGY

Some facts to remember about Sufficient Assumption Questions:

- Recognize these questions by the phrasing "if assumed" or "conclusion follows logically."
- The correct answer, when combined with the evidence, will guarantee the conclusion.
- Mismatched Concepts arguments with Formal Logic dominate Sufficient Assumption questions.

To demonstrate how Sufficient Assumption questions operate, review an LSAT expert's work on the following LSAT question.

LSAT Question	Analysis
All material bodies are divisible into parts, and everything divisible is imperfect. It follows that all material bodies are imperfect. It likewise follows that the spirit is not a material body. →	**Step 2:** Conclusion: "spirit is not a material body." *because* Evidence: 1) "All material bodies are divisible"; and 2) "everything divisible is imperfect" (which are combined by the author to: material → not perfect).
The final conclusion above follows logically if which one of the following is assumed? →	**Step 1:** The formulation "conclusion . . . follows logically if . . . assumed" indicates a Sufficient Assumption question.
	Step 3: Contrapose the combined evidence deduction provided in the second sentence to yield: Evid: Perfect → Not Material Body Conc: Spirit → Not Material Body With the mismatched terms on the left of the arrows, the direction of connection is up, so the correct answer will indicate: Spirit → Perfect (or) Not Perfect → Not Spirit.
(A) Everything divisible is a material body. →	**Step 4:** The correct answer must at a minimum provide a connection to "spirit," which is the unique term in the conclusion. This is merely an incomplete contrapositive of one of the pieces of evidence. Eliminate.
(B) Nothing imperfect is indivisible. →	As with (A), there is no connection to "spirit" and this is merely a Distortion of one of the pieces of evidence. Eliminate.
(C) The spirit is divisible. →	180. In addition to the prediction above, which used the endpoints of the combined evidence, the conclusion could also be proved true by a rule that the "spirit is *in*divisible." If the spirit were indivisible, the contrapositive of the first piece of evidence would dictate that it also would be not material. Eliminate.
(D) The spirit is perfect. →	Correct. Precise match of the prediction.
(E) The spirit is either indivisible or imperfect. *PrepTest24 Sec3 Q10* →	180. As discussed in (C), the spirit is indivisible proves the conclusion, or, as discussed in (D), the spirit is *perfect* proves the conclusion. Eliminate.

Later, in the Practice at the end of this section and in the Question Pool at the end of the chapter, you'll have an opportunity to work on even more Sufficient Assumption questions. Now, though, let's discuss Necessary Assumption questions.

Necessary Assumption Questions

Necessary Assumption questions are different from Sufficient Assumption questions in that they ask for an assumption that is *necessary* for the argument's conclusion to make sense. Necessary Assumption questions are a bit more common than Sufficient Assumption questions and tend to make up about 60 percent of all Assumption questions. You can identify these questions because they will use the terms *depends*, *require*, or *is necessary* in the question stems.

Take a look at some actual LSAT Necessary Assumption question stems:

LSAT Question Stem		Analysis
Which one of the following is an assumption that the argument requires in order for its conclusion to be properly drawn? *PrepTest27 Sec4 Q19*	$\longrightarrow$	Necessary Assumption question. Find an assumption required for the conclusion to make logical sense.
The argument depends on which one of the following assumptions? *PrepTest28 Sec3 Q19*	$\longrightarrow$	Necessary Assumption question. Find an assumption required for the conclusion to make logical sense.
Which one of the following is an assumption required by the economist's argument? *PrepTestB Sec1 Q8*	$\longrightarrow$	Necessary Assumption question. Find an assumption required for the conclusion to make logical sense.

In Necessary Assumption questions, the argument pattern is as likely to be Mismatched Concepts as Overlooked Possibilities. If it's a Mismatched Concepts argument, look for an assumption that establishes some sort of relationship between the mismatched concepts. If it's an Overlooked Possibilities argument, look for an assumption that removes at least one possible objection to the conclusion that the author has not considered. In both argument types, look for an assumption that is required or essential to the argument. Additionally, because you are looking for an assumption that is necessary for the argument, you can test the validity of answer choices by "denying" them. We'll talk about that strategy more later. Now, though, let's discuss Mismatched Concepts arguments in Necessary Assumption questions.

LSAT STRATEGY

Some facts to remember about Necessary Assumption Questions:

- Recognize these questions by the phrasing "an assumption required by the argument" or "the argument depends on the assumption that."
- The correct answer doesn't have to be sufficient for the conclusion to be drawn, just necessary.
- Both Mismatched Concepts and Overlooked Possibilities arguments will be tested.
- Use the Denial Test to distinguish the correct answer.

Mismatched Concepts in Necessary Assumption Questions

To see the difference between necessary and sufficient assumptions in a Mismatched Concepts argument, evaluate the following test-like question and the two answer choices that follow:

> Bill: A recent book reviewer called Mary's novel "boring and prosaic." But the reviewer is clearly wrong because not only is the entire first half of Mary's novel all about pirates, but part of the second half is, as well.

The argument depends on the assumption that

(A)   any novel that mentions pirates cannot be boring and prosaic

(B)   a novel that is mostly about pirates cannot be boring and prosaic

Start by untangling the argument. Bill's conclusion is that Mary's novel is not boring and prosaic. Why? Because more than half of Mary's novel is all about pirates. There is a disconnect here between the concepts "boring and prosaic" and "a novel mostly about pirates": Bill assumes that they are mutually exclusive. The correct answer will tie these two concepts together.

Both answer choices present assumptions formed from these mismatched concepts, and neither one brings in outside information. But are they both *necessary* assumptions? Answer choice (A) does give us a sufficient connection between the evidence and conclusion. After all, Mary's book mentions pirates, so if (A) is established, then it follows that her novel is not boring and prosaic. However, (A) is not a necessary assumption required for the conclusion to hold up. Bill's evidence is explicit: most of the novel is about pirates, and *that's* why it shouldn't be considered boring and prosaic. In fact, we have no idea what Bill thinks about novels that *only mention* pirates. It's possible that Bill would find a novel that discusses pirates once, in passing, to be boring and prosaic.

Now evaluate answer choice (B). Here, we see an assumption that *is* required by the argument. Bill's evidence directly states that a majority of Mary's novel is about pirates. It's not just because Mary's novel *mentions* pirates that Bill believes the reviewer to be wrong; it's because Mary's novel is *mostly* about pirates. To prove that this answer is correct, deny it and see what happens to the argument: "novels that are mostly about pirates *can* be boring and prosaic." If that's true, then Bill's entire argument falls apart, and his conclusion can no longer stand. We'll revisit this idea of "denying" the right answer choice to prove if it is correct later in the section.

Now, though, take a look an LSAT expert's analysis of a full Necessary Assumption question based on an argument that you've seen earlier in the chapter.

LSAT Question	Analysis
Sociologist: The intended function of news is to give us information on which to act. But in a consumer society, news becomes a product to be manufactured and dispensed to the consumer. An enormous industry for the production and consumption of news has evolved, and we ingest news with an insatiable appetite. Under such circumstances, news is primarily entertaining and cannot, therefore, serve its intended function.	**Step 2:** Conclusion: Under the described circumstances, news cannot give us information to act on. *because* Evidence: Under the described circumstances, news is primarily entertaining.
Which one of the following is an assumption on which the sociologist's argument depends?	**Step 1:** The phrase "assumption on which . . . argument depends" indicates a Necessary Assumption question.
	Step 3: Both the evidence and conclusion relate to the news under the described circumstances, so the Mismatched Concepts unique to the evidence and conclusion respectively are: *primarily entertaining* and *cannot give information to act on*. The correct answer will indicate that news that is primarily entertaining will not provide information on which to act.
(A) News that serves its intended function should not be entertaining.	**Step 4:** Distortion. The argument assumes that news cannot be *primarily* entertaining—not that it shouldn't be entertaining at all—and still serve its intended function. Eliminate.
(B) Most viewers prefer that news be entertaining.	Outside the Scope. The argument is not concerned with viewer preferences; only whether news serves its intended function of providing information on which to act. Eliminate.
(C) News has only one important function.	This answer merely paraphrases—and arguably distorts—a stated premise, so it cannot be the unstated assumption. Eliminate.
(D) News that primarily entertains does not give us information on which to act.	Correct. This choice matches the prediction in linking the Mismatched Concepts of *primarily entertain* and *not give information on which to act*.
(E) A news industry that aims to make a profit inevitably presents news as entertainment. *PrepTestB Sec1 Q18*	Outside the Scope. The argument does not make the causal claim that the news industry's profit motive inevitably leads to the presentation of news as entertainment. Eliminate.

The assumption of this argument as articulated in choice (D) is necessary for the argument's conclusion to be drawn. If you were to deny that answer choice—if you were to state that news that primarily entertains *does* give us information on which to act—then the argument falls apart, and the conclusion can no longer stand.

You'll get more practice with Mismatched Concepts arguments in Necessary Assumption questions later in this section, as well as at the end of the chapter. Now, though, let's take a look at how Overlooked Possibilities arguments show up in Necessary Assumption questions.

Overlooked Possibilities in Necessary Assumption Questions

Not all Necessary Assumption questions contain mismatched concepts. In an Overlooked Possibilities argument that asks for a necessary assumption, your approach will change slightly. In these arguments, seek an answer choice that removes at least one possible objection to the author's conclusion. This is one of the reasons why learning to phrase the assumption of an Overlooked Possibilities argument in negative terms is so valuable.

To demonstrate, let's revisit this argument:

> Last night Maria parked her car in an area of town where lots of car thefts occur. This morning Maria woke up and discovered that her car was no longer in its parking spot. Therefore, Maria's car must have been stolen.

We said earlier that the possible objections to this argument include any other explanation for the vanishing car: Maria's friend Patty moving the car, her car being towed, that she moved the car to a different parking spot and forgot, and so on. The author's *sufficient* assumption is that none of the potential objections happened. In other words, the answer to a Sufficient Assumption question would say something like this:

- There are no other ways Maria's car could have vanished aside from theft.
- Theft is the only possible explanation for the disappearance of Maria's car.

Sufficient Assumption questions require you to rule out *all* other possible explanations to guarantee that the car was stolen. The correct answer to a Necessary Assumption question, on the other hand, only needs to rule out *one* possible objection. Consider the following answer choices:

- Maria's friend Patty didn't move the car.
- Maria's car was not towed.
- Maria didn't forget that she moved the car to a different parking spot in the middle of the night.

In a Necessary Assumption question, any one of the above answer choices would be correct because each one of them *needs* to be ruled out for this conclusion to be true. Unlike Mismatched Concepts arguments, the answers to Overlooked Possibilities arguments can and do routinely mention new, but relevant, information. But such answers should not be considered Outside the Scope of the argument because rather than bring in that new concept the answer identifies it as what the author is *not* considering. Because you can't always predict the exact objection that the answer choice will rule out, it's important to make a prediction that is broad enough that you can spot whichever one they choose.

The Denial Test

To test whether an answer choice in a Necessary Assumption question is actually necessary, you can use a strategy we call the "Denial Test." *Deny* in this context means to negate the assumption, or to say that it is not true. After all, if the assumption is *required* by the conclusion, then saying that the assumption is *not true* should directly undermine that conclusion. In the preceding example, let's deny the second answer choice and see what happens. As it is written, it reads, "Maria's car was not towed." Denied, that answer choice would say, "Maria's car *was* towed." If this newly denied assumption were true, then the author's conclusion could not stand. Therefore, it must be an assumption required by the argument and would be confirmed as the correct answer.

The Denial Test works only in Necessary Assumption questions and is not meant to be your initial approach to these questions. Tackling every Necessary Assumption question by denying each answer choice is ultimately a time-consuming and potentially confusing approach. Instead, use the Denial Test as a final strategy to "prove" the correct answer. If you are able to deny the assumption in an answer choice and still draw the conclusion, then that is not the right answer. Once you deny the assumption in the right answer, however, and add that newly denied assumption to the argument's evidence, you'll find that the argument crumbles and the conclusion no longer stands. Additionally, you can use the Denial Test on your prediction from Step 3 to determine whether you have predicted a valid Necessary Assumption.

To see how Overlooked Possibilities arguments are tested in Necessary Assumption questions, review an LSAT expert's work on the following question. Its stimulus contains an argument you saw earlier.

LSAT Question	Analysis
Economist: In the interaction between producers and consumers, the only obligation that all parties have is to act in the best interests of their own side. And distribution of information about product defects is in the best interests of the consumer. So consumers are always obligated to report product defects they discover, while producers are never obligated to reveal them.	**Step 2:** Conclusion: Consumers are always obligated to report product defects, but producers are never obligated to reveal them. *because* Evidence: 1) Producers must act in the best interest of all producers and consumers must act in the best interest of all consumers; and 2) reporting defects is in the best interest of consumers.
Which one of the following is an assumption required by the economist's argument?	**Step 1:** The phrase "assumption required by the . . . argument" indicates a Necessary Assumption question.
	Step 3: Combining the evidence about consumers (that exposure of defects is in their best interests and that consumers must do what is in the best interest of all consumers) logically leads to the portion of the conclusion that asserts consumers must report defects. In contrast, the evidence is silent as to what is in the best interest of producers. Thus, the author must assume that not exposing defects is in the best interest of the producers.

LSAT Question (cont.)	**Analysis (cont.)**
(A) It is never in the best interests of producers for a producer to reveal a product defect. →	**Step 4:** Correct. This matches the prediction. For the author to conclude that producers are not obligated to reveal defects requires that he assume that such exposure is *not* in the interest of producers.
(B) No one expects producers to act in a manner counter to their own best interests. →	Outside the Scope. The argument concerns what *should* be done, not what is *expected*. Also, the argument does not explicitly establish that hiding defects is in the producers' best interest. Eliminate.
(C) Any product defect is likely to be discovered by consumers. →	Outside the Scope. The argument concerns what should be done regarding defects that *are* discovered, not the likelihood of discovery. Eliminate.
(D) A product defect is more likely to be discovered by a consumer than by a producer. →	Irrelevant Comparison. As with (C), the relative likelihood of discovery is irrelevant. Eliminate.
(E) The best interests of consumers never coincide with the best interests of producers. *PrepTestB Sec1 Q8* →	Extreme. The argument only presumes that consumers and producers have divergent interests in regards to exposure of defects, not universally. Eliminate.

By Identifying the structure of this argument as Overlooked Possibilities, the expert is able to predict the correct answer choice. Apply the Denial Test to answer choice (A): *It is at least sometimes in the best interests of producers for a producer to reveal a product defect.* If that were true, is it possible to conclude that producers are never obligated to reveal a defect, knowing that producers must act in the interest of all producers? No! Thus answer choice (A) is necessary to the argument.

Good work. Now it's time to put into practice what you've learned about Sufficient and Necessary Assumption questions.

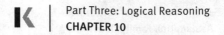

Practice

Try some Assumption questions on your own. Remember to follow the Logical Reasoning Method. In Step 1, identify the stem as a Sufficient or Necessary Assumption question. In Step 2, identify the evidence and the conclusion. In Step 3, ask: Does the author move from certain terms or concepts in the evidence to different terms or concepts in the conclusion? Or does the author use relevant evidence to draw a conclusion that is too strong? Determine the argument's assumption and then, in Step 4, match it to the correct answer. When you're finished, check the expert analyses on the pages that follow the exercise.

LSAT Question	My Analysis
21. Health officials claim that because the foods and beverages mentioned or consumed on many television programs are extremely low in nutritional value, watching television has a bad influence on the dietary habits of television viewers.	**Step 2:**
The claim by health officials depends on the presupposition that	**Step 1:**
	Step 3:
(A) the eating and drinking habits of people on television programs are designed to mirror the eating and drinking habits of television viewers	**Step 4:**
(B) seeing some foods and beverages being consumed on, or hearing them mentioned on, television programs increases the likelihood that viewers will consume similar kinds of foods and beverages	
(C) the food and beverage industry finances television programs so that the foods and beverages that have recently appeared on the market can be advertised on those programs	
(D) television viewers are only interested in the people on television programs who have the same eating and drinking habits as they do	
(E) the eating and drinking habits of people on television programs provide health officials with accurate predictions about the food and beverages that will become popular among television viewers	

PrepTest24 Sec3 Q13

LSAT Question	My Analysis
22. The only physical factor preventing a human journey to Mars has been weight. Carrying enough fuel to propel a conventional spacecraft to Mars and back would make even the lightest craft too heavy to be launched from Earth. A device has recently been invented, however, that allows an otherwise conventional spacecraft to refill the craft's fuel tanks with fuel manufactured from the Martian atmosphere for the return trip. Therefore, it is possible for people to go to Mars in a spacecraft that carries this device and then return.	**Step 2:**
Which one of the following is an assumption on which the argument depends?	**Step 1:**
	Step 3:
(A) The amount of fuel needed for a spacecraft to return from Mars is the same as the amount of fuel needed to travel from Earth to Mars.	**Step 4:**
(B) The fuel manufactured from the Martian atmosphere would not differ in composition from the fuel used to travel to Mars.	
(C) The device for manufacturing fuel from the Martian atmosphere would not take up any of the spaceship crew's living space.	
(D) A conventional spacecraft equipped with the device would not be appreciably more expensive to construct than current spacecraft typically are.	
(E) The device for manufacturing fuel for the return to Earth weighs less than the tanks of fuel that a conventional spacecraft would otherwise need to carry from Earth for the return trip.
PrepTest27 Sec4 Q9	

LSAT Question	My Analysis
23. Most people feel that they are being confused by the information from broadcast news. This could be the effect of the information's being delivered too quickly or of its being poorly organized. Analysis of the information content of a typical broadcast news story shows that news stories are far lower in information density than the maximum information density with which most people can cope at any one time. So the information in typical broadcast news stories is poorly organized.	**Step 2:**
Which one of the following is an assumption that the argument requires in order for its conclusion to be properly drawn?	**Step 1:**
	Step 3:
(A) It is not the number of broadcast news stories to which a person is exposed that is the source of the feeling of confusion.	**Step 4:**
(B) Poor organization of information in a news story makes it impossible to understand the information.	
(C) Being exposed to more broadcast news stories within a given day would help a person to better understand the news.	
(D) Most people can cope with a very high information density.	
(E) Some people are being overwhelmed by too much information.	

PrepTest27 Sec4 Q19

	LSAT Question	**My Analysis**

24. Children fall into three groups—nontasters, regular tasters, and supertasters—depending on how strongly they experience tastes. Supertasters strongly prefer mild cheddar cheese to sharp, regular tasters weakly prefer mild to sharp, and nontasters show no preference. Also, the more bitter a food tastes, the less children like it. Thus, supertasters experience sharp cheddar as tasting more bitter than mild cheddar, but nontasters experience sharp cheddar as tasting no more bitter than mild cheddar.

Step 2:

Which one of the following, if assumed, enables the conclusion above to be properly inferred?

Step 1:

Step 3:

(A) Supertasters like mild cheddar cheese more than do regular tasters.

Step 4:

(B) The age of the child is the most important factor in determining whether that child is a nontaster, a regular taster, or a supertaster.

(C) The sweeter a food tastes, the more children like it.

(D) Bitterness is the only factor relevant to how strongly children prefer sharp cheddar cheese to mild cheddar cheese.

(E) Nontasters tend to like a wider variety of foods than do regular tasters, who in turn like a wider variety of foods than do supertasters.

PrepTestB Sec4 Q22

LSAT Question	My Analysis
25. We ought to pay attention only to the intrinsic properties of a work of art. Its other, extrinsic properties are irrelevant to our aesthetic interactions with it. For example, when we look at a painting we should consider only what is directly presented in our experience of it. What is really aesthetically relevant, therefore, is not what a painting symbolizes, but what it directly presents to experience.	**Step 2:**
The conclusion follows logically if which one of the following is added to the premises?	**Step 1:**
	Step 3:
(A) What an artwork symbolizes involves only extrinsic properties of that work.	**Step 4:**
(B) There are certain properties of our experiences of artworks that can be distinguished as symbolic properties.	
(C) Only an artwork's intrinsic properties are relevant to our aesthetic interactions with it.	
(D) It is possible in theory for an artwork to symbolize nothing.	
(E) An intrinsic property of an artwork is one that relates the work to itself.	

PrepTest28 Sec1 Q24

LSAT Question	My Analysis
26. Maude is incessantly engaging in diatribes against people who are materialistic. But her hypocrisy is evinced by the sentimental treatment of the watch her grandmother gave her. She certainly is very fond of the watch—she worries about damaging it; in fact she always sets it carefully in a special box before going to bed.	**Step 2:**
Which one of the following is an assumption on which the argument depends?	**Step 1:**
	Step 3:
(A) Possessions that come from relatives are treated with better care than those that do not.	**Step 4:**
(B) Sentimental attachment to a single possession indicates being materialistic.	
(C) People who care about material things in general tend to take special care of all their possessions.	
(D) Maude's watch is not the only material thing she especially cares for.	
(E) People who are not materialistic tend to have merely sentimental attachments to things.	

PrepTestB Sec4 Q4

LSAT Question	My Analysis
27. Historian: We can learn about the medical history of individuals through chemical analysis of their hair. It is likely, for example, that Isaac Newton's psychological problems were due to mercury poisoning; traces of mercury were found in his hair. Analysis is now being done on a lock of Beethoven's hair. Although no convincing argument has shown that Beethoven ever had a venereal disease, some people hypothesize that venereal disease caused his deafness. Since mercury was commonly ingested in Beethoven's time to treat venereal disease, if researchers find a trace of mercury in his hair, we can conclude that this hypothesis is correct.	**Step 2:**
Which one of the following is an assumption on which the historian's argument depends?	**Step 1:**
	Step 3:
(A) None of the mercury introduced into the body can be eliminated.	**Step 4:**
(B) Some people in Beethoven's time did not ingest mercury.	
(C) Mercury is an effective treatment for venereal disease.	
(D) Mercury poisoning can cause deafness in people with venereal disease.	
(E) Beethoven suffered from psychological problems of the same severity as Newton's.	

PrepTest28 Sec3 Q16

Expert Analysis

Take a look at how an LSAT expert evaluates these arguments.

LSAT Question	Analysis
21. Health officials claim that because the foods and beverages mentioned or consumed on many television programs are extremely low in nutritional value, watching television has a bad influence on the dietary habits of television viewers. →	**Step 2:** Conclusion: Watching television negatively influences viewers' diets. *because* Evidence: Food and beverages seen on television are low in nutrition.
The claim by health officials depends on the presupposition that →	**Step 1:** The "presupposition" an argument "depends" on indicates a Necessary Assumption question.
	Step 3: The author jumps from *seeing* foods on TV to being *influenced* in dietary choices. The assumption here is that simply watching TV is enough to influence TV watchers' behavior.
(A) the eating and drinking habits of people on television programs are designed to mirror the eating and drinking habits of television viewers →	**Step 4:** 180. Rather than viewers copying TV, this indicates TV mimics viewers' eating habits. Eliminate.
(B) seeing some foods and beverages being consumed on, or hearing them mentioned on, television programs increases the likelihood that viewers will consume similar kinds of foods and beverages →	Correct. This matches the prediction that viewers are influenced by TV in their food choices.
(C) the food and beverage industry finances television programs so that the foods and beverages that have recently appeared on the market can be advertised on those programs →	Outside the Scope. The argument is only concerned with TV's influence on viewers, not why certain foods got on TV in the first place. Eliminate.
(D) television viewers are only interested in the people on television programs who have the same eating and drinking habits as they do →	Extreme ("only") and 180. This answer suggests that viewers are drawn to TV characters who dine as they do, while the argument assumes that seeing TV characters eat particular foods will lead viewers to dine on the same foods. Eliminate.
(E) the eating and drinking habits of people on television programs provide health officials with accurate predictions about the food and beverages that will become popular among television viewers →	Extreme. It is merely necessary that foods shown on TV have some negative influence on viewers' diets, not that they are accurate predictors of future trends. Eliminate.

PrepTest24 Sec3 Q13

LSAT Question	Analysis
22. The only physical factor preventing a human journey to Mars has been weight. Carrying enough fuel to propel a conventional spacecraft to Mars and back would make even the lightest craft too heavy to be launched from Earth. A device has recently been invented, however, that allows an otherwise conventional spacecraft to refill the craft's fuel tanks with fuel manufactured from the Martian atmosphere for the return trip. Therefore, it is possible for people to go to Mars in a spacecraft that carries this device and then return.	**Step 2:** Conclusion: The new device will allow for a return trip to and from Mars. *because* Evidence: 1) weight is the only factor precluding such a trip; 2) fuel for round-trip travel is too heavy for the craft to launch; 3) a new device allows spacecraft to re-fuel with fuel manufactured on Mars.
Which one of the following is an assumption on which the argument depends?	**Step 1:** The "assumption on which the argument depends" indicates a Necessary Assumption question.
	Step 3: The argument assumes that eliminating fuel previously needed for a return trip will reduce weight enough to allow the spacecraft to launch. It further assumes that the positives of the device (fuel weight reduction) will not be outweighed by the negatives of the device (presumably it weighs something itself, but not as much as the fuel).
(A) The amount of fuel needed for a spacecraft to return from Mars is the same as the amount of fuel needed to travel from Earth to Mars.	**Step 4:** Irrelevant comparison. A balance between fuel use for outbound and inbound trips is not necessary to the argument. In fact, if the outbound trip uses less fuel, then an imbalance would make it easier to launch from Earth. Eliminate.
(B) The fuel manufactured from the Martian atmosphere would not differ in composition from the fuel used to travel to Mars.	As with (A), such precision is not required. All that matters about the composition of the Martian fuel is that it suitably powers the craft. Eliminate.
(C) The device for manufacturing fuel from the Martian atmosphere would not take up any of the spaceship crew's living space.	Outside the Scope. The issue in the argument is weight, not living space. Eliminate.
(D) A conventional spacecraft equipped with the device would not be appreciably more expensive to construct than current spacecraft typically are.	Outside the Scope. Costs are irrelevant to the conclusion regarding the physical possibility of making the trip. Eliminate.
(E) The device for manufacturing fuel for the return to Earth weighs less than the tanks of fuel that a conventional spacecraft would otherwise need to carry from Earth for the return trip. *PrepTest27 Sec4 Q9*	Correct. This matches the prediction. If the device weighs as much, or more, than the fuel it replaces, then a spacecraft would be too heavy to launch.

LSAT Question	Analysis
23. Most people feel that they are being confused by the information from broadcast news. This could be the effect of the information's being delivered too quickly or of its being poorly organized. Analysis of the information content of a typical broadcast news story shows that news stories are far lower in information density than the maximum information density with which most people can cope at any one time. So the information in typical broadcast news stories is poorly organized.	**Step 2:** Conclusion: Information in typical news broadcasts is poorly organized. *because* Evidence: 1) There are two potential sources of people's confusion from information in broadcast news: i) news is delivered too quickly or ii) news is poorly organized; and 2) there is a reason to believe the news is not delivered too quickly.
Which one of the following is an assumption that the argument requires in order for its conclusion to be properly drawn?	**Step 1:** The phrase "assumption that the argument requires" indicates a Necessary Assumption question.
	Step 3: This argument identifies two explanations, discounts one, and concludes it must be the other. The assumption is that there can be no other explanation besides the two presented in the evidence. The correct answer may also eliminate a specific alternative explanation for the confusion.
(A) It is not the number of broadcast news stories to which a person is exposed that is the source of the feeling of confusion.	**Step 4:** Correct. This matches the prediction that a correct answer will eliminate an alternative explanation for the confusion. If it were the number of stories that causes the confusion, then it no longer makes sense to conclude that the poor organization is the cause.
(B) Poor organization of information in a news story makes it impossible to understand the information.	Extreme. It is necessary to the argument that poor organization *can cause* confusion, not that it *makes it impossible* to understand the information. Eliminate.
(C) Being exposed to more broadcast news stories within a given day would help a person to better understand the news.	This is consistent with poor organization being the cause of the confusion, but even if more exposure would not help understanding the news, poor organization could still be the cause of the confusion. Also, this potentially suggests (rather than excludes) an alternative cause of the confusion (too little exposure). Eliminate.
(D) Most people can cope with a very high information density.	At most, this supports the premise that the news is not delivered too quickly. But since that premise should be accepted as true, this support is not necessary to the argument. Eliminate.
(E) Some people are being overwhelmed by too much information. *PrepTest27 Sec4 Q19*	180. While not contradictory, this runs counter to the argument's assertion that most people are *not* exposed to too much information too quickly. Eliminate.

LSAT Question	Analysis
24. Children fall into three groups—nontasters, regular tasters, and supertasters—depending on how strongly they experience tastes. Supertasters strongly prefer mild cheddar cheese to sharp, regular tasters weakly prefer mild to sharp, and nontasters show no preference. Also, the more bitter a food tastes, the less children like it. Thus, supertasters experience sharp cheddar as tasting more bitter than mild cheddar, but nontasters experience sharp cheddar as tasting no more bitter than mild cheddar.	**Step 2: Conclusion:** To a child supertaster, sharp cheddar tastes more bitter than mild cheddar; to nontasters, sharp cheddar tastes no more bitter than mild cheddar. *because* **Evidence:** 1) There are three types of child tasters (non, regular, and super); 2) the more bitter a food tastes, the less children like it; and 3) child supertasters strongly prefer mild cheddar, regular tasters weakly prefer mild, and non-tasters have no preference.
Which one of the following, if assumed, enables the conclusion above to be properly inferred?	**Step 1:** The formulation "if assumed . . . conclusion . . . properly inferred" indicates a Sufficient Assumption question.
	Step 3: Based on the preferences of child supertasters and the rule that the more bitter a food tastes the less children like it, it is reasonable to conclude that child supertasters find sharp cheddar more bitter than mild, while non-tasters do not. This assumes that there is no distinguishing factor in the taste of cheese other than its bitterness.
(A) Supertasters like mild cheddar cheese more than do regular tasters.	**Step 4:** While this is consistent with the information provided, it does not prove that bitterness is the factor explaining the relative preferences among the three types of tastes. Eliminate.
(B) The age of the child is the most important factor in determining whether that child is a nontaster, a regular taster, or a supertaster.	Outside the Scope. The argument is not concerned with what makes one a super, regular, or non-taster in the first place; it merely describes how those in the different groups experience tastes. Eliminate.
(C) The sweeter a food tastes, the more children like it.	If one assumes that sweet is the opposite of bitter, then this is merely redundant with the rule stated in the evidence. If one considers sweetness a separate factor from bitterness that could alternatively explain the preferences, then this is a 180. Either way: eliminate.
(D) Bitterness is the only factor relevant to how strongly children prefer sharp cheddar cheese to mild cheddar cheese.	Correct. This matches the prediction and proves the conclusion by eliminating any other potential factor explaining the preferences among the groups.

LSAT Question (cont.)	**Analysis (cont.)**
(E) Nontasters tend to like a wider variety of foods than do regular tasters, who in turn like a wider variety of foods than do supertasters. *PrepTestB Sec4 Q22*	Irrelevant Comparison/Outside the Scope. The argument is concerned with what accounts for the cheddar cheese type preferences among the groups and not which group likes a wider variety of foods. Eliminate.

LSAT Question	**Analysis**
25. We ought to pay attention only to the intrinsic properties of a work of art. Its other, extrinsic properties are irrelevant to our aesthetic interactions with it. For example, when we look at a painting we should consider only what is directly presented in our experience of it. What is really aesthetically relevant, therefore, is not what a painting symbolizes, but what it directly presents to experience.	**Step 2:** Conclusion: One's direct experience of a painting is aesthetically relevant; a painting's symbolism is not aesthetically relevant. *because* Evidence: 1) Intrinsic properties are aesthetically relevant; 2) extrinsic properties are aesthetically irrelevant; 3) direct experience should be considered (i.e., is relevant).
The conclusion follows logically if which one of the following is added to the premises?	**Step 1:** The formulation "conclusion follows logically . . . if which one of the following is added" indicates a Sufficient Assumption question.
	Step 3: The new, unique concept appearing in the conclusion is *what a painting symbolizes*. Because the evidence states that *extrinsic properties* are irrelevant, and because the author concludes that *symbolism* is irrelevant, then the author must believe that extrinsic properties and symbolism are alike/equivalent.
(A) What an artwork symbolizes involves only extrinsic properties of that work.	**Step 4:** Correct. This matches the prediction.
(B) There are certain properties of our experiences of artworks that can be distinguished as symbolic properties.	Distortion. This conflates one's experience of an artwork with its symbolic properties, contrary to the argument, which distinguishes them. This in no way shows that symbolic properties are irrelevant. Eliminate.
(C) Only an artwork's intrinsic properties are relevant to our aesthetic interactions with it.	This merely reiterates one of the premises explicit in the argument. Eliminate.
(D) It is possible in theory for an artwork to symbolize nothing.	Outside the Scope. The argument pertains to the symbolism in paintings, so an artwork that symbolizes nothing is irrelevant. Eliminate.
(E) An intrinsic property of an artwork is one that relates the work to itself. *PrepTest28 Sec1 Q24*	At most, this relates to the evidence, providing a definition of intrinsic, but it neither connects evidence to conclusion nor proves that symbolism is aesthetically irrelevant. Eliminate.

LSAT Question	**Analysis**
26. Maude is incessantly engaging in diatribes against people who are materialistic. But her hypocrisy is evinced by the sentimental treatment of the watch her grandmother gave her. She certainly is very fond of the watch—she worries about damaging it; in fact she always sets it carefully in a special box before going to bed.	**Step 2:** Conclusion: Maude, herself, is materialistic. → *because* Evidence: Maude gives sentimental treatment to a watch.
Which one of the following is an assumption on which the argument depends?	**Step 1:** The phrase "assumption on which the argument depends" indicates a Necessary Assumption question.
	Step 3: The Mismatched Concepts in this argument are *sentimental treatment* of a possession and being *materialistic*. The assumption is that such sentimental treatment is equivalent to materialistic behavior.
(A) Possessions that come from relatives are treated with better care than those that do not.	**Step 4:** Irrelevant Comparison. This is consistent with the background details regarding the watch, but does nothing to connect such sentimentality to materialism. Eliminate.
(B) Sentimental attachment to a single possession indicates being materialistic.	Correct. Matches the prediction by linking sentimental attachment to materialism.
(C) People who care about material things in general tend to take special care of all their possessions.	Extreme. This argument involves a claim based on the treatment of a single possession and doesn't extend to people's treatment of all their possessions. Eliminate.
(D) Maude's watch is not the only material thing she especially cares for.	This supports the claim that Maude is materialistic, but it is not necessary to the argument. The author's claim that Maude is materialistic would not fall apart if Maude was only materialistic regarding the watch. Eliminate.
(E) People who are not materialistic tend to have merely sentimental attachments to things. *PrepTestB Sec4 Q4*	180. This argument bases its claim of materialism on a sentimental attachment. Eliminate.

LSAT Question	**Analysis**
27. Historian: We can learn about the medical history of individuals through chemical analysis of their hair. It is likely, for example, that Isaac Newton's psychological problems were due to mercury poisoning; traces of mercury were found in his hair. Analysis is now being done on a lock of Beethoven's hair. Although no convincing argument has shown that Beethoven ever had a venereal disease, some people hypothesize that venereal disease caused his deafness. Since mercury was commonly ingested in Beethoven's time to treat venereal disease, if researchers find a trace of mercury in his hair, we can conclude that this hypothesis is correct.	**Step 2:** Conclusion: If researchers find traces of mercury in Beethoven's hair, then he had venereal disease. *because* Evidence: In Beethoven's time, mercury was commonly ingested to treat venereal disease.
Which one of the following is an assumption on which the historian's argument depends?	**Step 1:** The phrase "assumption on which the . . . argument depends" indicates a Necessary Assumption question.
	Step 3: The evidence identifies the treatment of venereal disease as a possible explanation for the presence of any mercury found in Beethoven's hair, while the conclusion treats it as the only reason for the presence of mercury. The correct answer will either indicate that the presence of mercury is not universal among people of that time, or it will eliminate an alternative explanation for the presence of any mercury.
(A) None of the mercury introduced into the body can be eliminated.	**Step 4:** Extreme. The argument does not rely on the claim that no mercury, once ingested, can ever leave the body. Indeed, the conclusion is conditioned on finding even "a trace of mercury" in the hair. Eliminate.
(B) Some people in Beethoven's time did not ingest mercury.	Correct. The Denial Test proves that this assumption is necessary to the argument. If "everybody in Beethoven's time ingested mercury," then finding a trace of mercury in Beethoven's hair would not distinguish Beethoven from any of his contemporaries. It would not be more likely that he had venereal disease, or that venereal disease caused his deafness.
(C) Mercury is an effective treatment for venereal disease.	Outside the Scope. Whether mercury was actually effective in treating venereal disease is irrelevant to explaining the presence of mercury in Beethoven's hair. Eliminate.

LSAT Question (cont.)	Analysis (cont.)
(D) Mercury poisoning can cause deafness in people with venereal disease.	Outside the Scope. The argument concludes that a trace of mercury is evidence of venereal disease, not that Beethoven had mercury poisoning, or that mercury poisoning caused his deafness. Eliminate.
(E) Beethoven suffered from psychological problems of the same severity as Newton's. *PrepTest28 Sec3 Q16*	Outside the Scope. Newton's psychological problems merely provide context and are irrelevant to the argument regarding mercury and venereal disease in Beethoven. Eliminate.

OTHER ASSUMPTION FAMILY QUESTION TYPES

By now, you should have a good grasp of the two main argument structures you'll see on the LSAT: Mismatched Concepts and Overlooked Possibilities. You've also seen the ways in which the testmaker can evaluate your understanding of these argument types by asking you to identify an argument's sufficient or necessary assumption. But the LSAT can test you on more than just your ability to discern an argument's assumption. From the same argument, the testmaker can ask you a number of different questions: you may be asked to identify the flaw in an author's reasoning, to strengthen or weaken an argument, or even to determine an underlying principle of the argument. One thing to keep in mind is that even though different question types may change the format of the answers, the argument itself and the assumption of the argument will not change. Each of the arguments you see on the LSAT will be constructed in a similar way: an author fails to provide evidence sufficient to establish his conclusion. As such, the way in which you approach these questions will be the same as the way in which you approach Assumption questions. The only difference is in Step 3; here, you will use your knowledge of the different question types to create an appropriate and question-specific prediction.

As an example, let's take a look at an argument we've seen before.

The miscarriage of justice in the Barker case was due to the mistaken views held by some of the forensic scientists involved in the case, who believed that they owed allegiance only to the prosecuting lawyers. Justice was thwarted because these forensic scientists failed to provide evidence impartially to both the defense and the prosecution. Hence it is not forensic evidence in general that should be condemned for this injustice.

PrepTestB Sec4 Q16

Previously, we used this argument to provide you practice in breaking down an argument and recognizing an author's assumption: that the Barker case is representative of forensic science generally. Indeed, this argument could have been used for an Assumption question on the LSAT. However, it actually appeared on the LSAT as a Strengthen question: "Which one of the following, if true, most strengthens the argument?" It also would have been right at home as the argument in a Weaken or Flaw question, as well.

Take a look at how an LSAT expert characterizes each question stem, and how she relates each to the stimulus about the Barker case.

LSAT Question Stem	Analysis
The reasoning in the argument is most vulnerable to criticism on the grounds that the argument $\longrightarrow$	The correct answer to this **Flaw** question will describe the way in which the author's reasoning is flawed. For the argument about the Barker case, you might see an answer choice such as "Overlooks the possibility that the forensic scientists in the Barker case are representative of the practices of the vast majority of forensic scientists across the nation."
Which of the following, if true, most seriously weakens the argument? $\longrightarrow$	The correct answer to this **Weaken** question will present a new piece of information that, if true, will make the author's conclusion less likely. For the argument about the Barker case, you might see an answer choice such as "In confidential surveys, a majority of forensic scientists acknowledge that they believe their primary obligations are to the prosecution in criminal cases."
Which of the following, if true, provides the most support for the argument? $\longrightarrow$	The correct answer to this **Strengthen** question will present a new piece of information that, if true, will make the author's conclusion more likely. For the argument about the Barker case, you might see an answer choice such as "Most forensic scientists acknowledge a professional obligation to provide evidence impartially to both the defense and the prosecution." As the actual correct answer to this question stated.

In the next part of the chapter, we'll take a look at each one of these unique question types. By the end, you'll be able to (1) identify each question type based on the phrasing in the question stem and (2) turn any argument's assumption into a prediction that is appropriate for the specific question type.

FLAW QUESTIONS

> ## LEARNING OBJECTIVES
>
> In this section, you'll learn to:
>
> · Identify Flaw questions.
> · Recognize and characterize the most common flawed argument patterns.
> · Recognize an abstractly worded but correct answer choice in a Flaw question.

One of the ways the LSAT can test your ability to analyze arguments is by asking you to determine the error in the author's reasoning. These Flaw questions, as we call them, might be thought of as *describe the flaw* questions because that's what you are being asked to do. On Test Day, you'll face roughly eight of these questions. With a few notable exceptions discussed later in this section, the arguments you'll find in Flaw questions are identical to the ones you see in other Assumption Family questions.

As always in the Logical Reasoning section, your first step is to identify the question type from the stem. To recognize a Flaw question, look for language that uses words or phrases like "point out a flaw," "identify the error in reasoning," or "vulnerable to criticism." Take a look at the following to see some common Flaw question stems:

LSAT Question Stem		Analysis
The reasoning in the argument is questionable because the argument *PrepTest29 Sec4 Q25*	$\longrightarrow$	The correct answer to this Flaw question will describe the way in which the evidence fails to properly support the conclusion.
The argument's reasoning is flawed because the argument overlooks the possibility that *PrepTest27 Sec4 Q7*	$\longrightarrow$	The correct answer to this Flaw question will describe an overlooked possibility that the author did not take into account.
The plant manager's argument is most vulnerable to criticism on which one of the following grounds? *PrepTest29 Sec4 Q14*	$\longrightarrow$	The correct answer to this Flaw question will describe the way in which the evidence fails to properly support the conclusion.

Your approach to Flaw questions starts in the same way as your approach to other Assumption Family questions: Untangle the stimulus into evidence and conclusion, then identify the author's assumption. The types of arguments you'll see In Flaw questions are generally the same as those discussed earlier in the chapter—either the author uses evidence that is not necessarily related to the conclusion (Mismatched Concepts) or the author uses relevant evidence to draw an extreme conclusion (Overlooked Possibilities). Indeed, in Flaw questions, you're likely to run into the specific types of Mismatched Concepts and Overlooked Possibilities discussed earlier in the chapter. The good news is that the bulk of Flaw questions will ask you about just a handful of common argument types, which are listed on the next page. Being able to anticipate the likelihood of certain argument patterns based on the question type will help you untangle arguments and form predictions more quickly and efficiently.

Common Flaw Types

> ### LSAT STRATEGY
>
> Flaw questions are dominated by these common argument types:
>
> · Overlooked Possibilities: Failure to consider alternative explanations
> · Overlooked Possibilities: A conclusion of causation based on evidence of correlation
> · Overlooked Possibilities: Confusing necessary and sufficient terms
> · Mismatched Concepts (including alike/equivalent, mutually exclusive, and representation)

For many test takers, finding the assumption or determining the pattern of an argument in a Flaw question is not hugely challenging. Instead, the difficult part of correctly answering a Flaw question is matching a prediction to the correct answer choice. This is because the LSAT words the correct answers to Flaw questions differently than it does the correct answers to other Assumption Family questions. Consider, for example, the following argument:

> Joe started feeling sick a short while after eating at the restaurant around the corner. Clearly, he got food poisoning from the food he ate there!

This is a classic causal argument. The author takes two things that happened around the same time, eating at the restaurant and getting sick, and concludes that one of them must have caused the other. As you learned earlier in this chapter, the assumption of the argument is *No ARC*: There is no *alternative cause* for the illness; the illness isn't the reason why the author went out to eat (*reversal*); and, the fact that the author went out to eat right before getting ill isn't just a *coincidence*. The correct answer to a Necessary Assumption question would rule out *A*, *R*, or *C*. Consider:

> Joe did not catch a stomach virus from his neighbor.

This rules out an *alternative cause*. But a Flaw question's answer might say something like . . .

> Overlooks the possibility that Joe caught a stomach virus from his neighbor.

or even . . .

> Mistakes a correlation between two events for one event causing the other.

The difference between the first two of these answer choices is not very great. The only distinction is that the Flaw answer choice is descriptive—it tells us that the author is overlooking something rather than ruling out a specific possibility. The difference between the Necessary Assumption answer and the second Flaw answer, however, is much bigger. The second Flaw answer is also describing the problem, but it is doing so in much more abstract terms. One key to success in Flaw questions is learning how to spot your prediction stated in different language.

Take a look at how an LSAT expert might analyze a Flaw question.

LSAT Question	Analysis
People in the tourist industry know that excessive development of seaside areas by the industry damages the environment. Such development also hurts the tourist industry by making these areas unattractive to tourists, a fact of which people in the tourist industry are well aware. People in the tourist industry would never knowingly do anything to damage the industry. Therefore, they would never knowingly damage the seaside environment, and the people who are concerned about damage to the seaside environment thus have nothing to fear from the tourist industry.	**Step 2:** Conclusion: The tourist industry will not damage the seaside environment. *because* Evidence: People in the tourist industry wouldn't knowingly damage the tourist industry, and so. Subsidiary Conclusion: People in the tourist industry wouldn't knowingly damage the seaside environment.
The reasoning in the argument is most vulnerable to criticism on which one of the following grounds?	**Step 1:** The phrase "vulnerable to criticism" indicates a Flaw question.
	Step 3: The author concludes that the tourist industry will cause no harm to the seaside environment from evidence that people in the tourist industry would not *knowingly* do something that would harm their industry. This overlooks the possibility those in the industry might *unintentionally* harm the seaside environment.
(A) No support is provided for the claim that excessive development hurts the tourist industry.	**Step 4:** Outside the Scope. The author is not obligated to provide support for something he claims that people in the tourist industry already know. Eliminate.
(B) That something is not the cause of a problem is used as evidence that it never coexists with that problem.	Extreme. The argument does not conclude that excessive development *never coexists* with damage to the seaside environment, but simply that the tourist industry will not knowingly cause excessive development in this case. Eliminate.
(C) The argument shifts from applying a characteristic to a few members of a group to applying the characteristic to all members of that group.	Distortion. There is no shift from some members of the tourist industry to all. The evidence is about the tourist industry writ large. Eliminate.
(D) The possibility that the tourist industry would unintentionally harm the environment is ignored.	Correct. This matches the prediction perfectly. The only difference is that this answer choice is written in the passive voice.
(E) The argument establishes that a certain state of affairs is likely and then treats that as evidence that the state of affairs is inevitable.	180. The argument does not shift from *likely* to definite; the author is quite definite throughout. Eliminate.

PrepTest24 Sec3 Q12

The correct answer choice (D) points out that the author ignores the possibility of *unintentional* harm to the seaside environment, which, if true, would undermine his argument. This is simply a twist on how the answer to an Assumption question would have been worded. The heart of prediction in Assumption Family questions is learning to say the same few things in a variety of different ways.

LSAT STRATEGY

Some facts to remember about Flaw questions:

- The correct answer will *describe* the error in the author's reasoning.
- You will be tested on your ability to identify flaws in both Mismatched Concepts arguments and Overlooked Possibilities arguments.
- Correct answer choices are often written in abstract language; form a prediction and match it to the closest answer choice.

Less Common Flaw Types

In addition to the common flaws previously listed (as well as the argument types you read about earlier in the chapter), the testmaker may ask you to identify a few rarer types of arguments. These are not included on the test often, but it's important to know them when you see them. The following are short descriptions of the most important ones:

Mismatched Concepts—Equivocation: On the LSAT, an error of equivocation means using the same word or phrase twice in an argument but with two different meanings. For example: "Jason says that when Alex is around, it drives him crazy; therefore I have decided to have him evaluated by a psychologist who specializes in crazy people." Notice that the argument uses the word *crazy* in the evidence to mean "annoyed," but it uses the word *crazy* in the conclusion to mean "mentally disturbed." This pattern is quite rare in LSAT stimuli. However, wrong answer choices in Flaw questions frequently refer to equivocation, so it's important to understand the flaw this term describes.

Mismatched Concepts—Parts to Whole: A parts-to-whole argument is very similar to a representation argument. The author of an argument looks at one piece of something—say a chapter in a book—and uses that to make a conclusion about the entirety of that thing—say the book itself. Or the author of an argument will look at many pieces individually and then make a deduction regarding the pieces together: "Each of these seven energy drinks is safe to drink, and so I'll be fine if I drink them all at once." This argument is rare, but when it shows up on the LSAT, it is almost always in a Flaw question.

Circular Reasoning: Circular reasoning describes an argument in which the author uses equivalent statements for both the evidence and the conclusion, for example, "Chris must be in debt, for if Chris says he is not in debt, he is surely lying." Much like equivocation, circular reasoning almost never shows up on the LSAT as the correct answer describing the author's flaw in the stimulus argument, but it is a common wrong answer choice in Flaw questions.

Evidence Contradicts Conclusion: There have been very few instances of this particular argument on the LSAT. Here is a simple example: "This book didn't sell well at all; nearly all copies printed were returned to the publisher. It follows that the publisher should print more copies as soon as possible." If the book didn't sell, the logical inference is that more copies should *not* be printed. Again, this pattern is rare; though the evidence in any Assumption Family question will never fully prove the conclusion, it almost never happens that the evidence actually contradicts the conclusion. Despite the fact that this pattern has shown up only a handful of times, it is a common wrong answer choice in Flaw questions. Be wary of choosing such an answer if you didn't initially predict it.

That list is not exhaustive. Through the decades, LSAT Flaw questions have included rare instances of arguments flawed in the following ways.

LSAT STRATEGY

Some extremely rare flaw arguments you might see on the LSAT:

- Conflating numerical values with percent values
- Using evidence of belief to draw a conclusion of fact
- Attacking the person making the argument instead of the argument (ad hominem)
- Stating that absence of evidence is evidence of absence
- Making an inappropriate appeal to authority
- Failing to address the other speaker's point

Of course, the odds of running into any of the flaws listed above are extremely low. At the end of the day, if you know the common argument patterns discussed earlier in the chapter, you should be able to tackle everything you will see on Test Day.

Drill: Identifying Argument Types in Flaw Question Answer Choices

Understanding the different ways in which the LSAT can describe familiar argument patterns requires a careful study of the answer choices in Flaw questions. When you study, be sure to spend time looking at answer choices and asking yourself which argument patterns they are referencing. Doing so will help you quickly eliminate tempting choices on Test Day. Let's start that process now with a short exercise. A list of sample answer choices follows. Your job is to match those answer choices to the flawed argument type they are describing.

Answer Choices	My Analysis
28. Overlooks the possibility that there are some red cars that do not take unleaded gas.	
29. Two events that merely occur together are taken as though one is the cause of the other.	
30. Bases a general claim on a few exceptional instances.	
31. Treats as similar two cases that may be different in a fundamental way.	
32. Allows a key term to shift in meaning during the course of the argument.	
33. Presupposes what it seeks to establish.	
34. Mistakes something that is necessary to bring about a situation for something that merely can bring about that situation.	

Expert Analysis for this exercise is on the next page. ▶ ▶ ▶

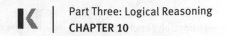
Expert Analysis

Now take a look at the expert analysis to see how you did:

Answer Choices		Analysis
28. Overlooks the possibility that there are some red cars that do not take unleaded gas.	→	"Overlooks the possibility that" is a classic phrase that is most often a reference to Overlooked Possibilities arguments. In this case, it would mean the author assumes that all red cars take unleaded gas, overlooking the possibility that some do not.
29. Two events that merely occur together are taken as though one is the cause of the other.	→	Describes the flaw of confusing correlation for causation.
30. Bases a general claim on a few exceptional instances.	→	Making a general claim about a group using evidence about a smaller group is the definition of Mismatched Concepts—Representation.
31. Treats as similar two cases that may be different in a fundamental way.	→	This is just another way of describing Mismatched Concepts–Alike/Equivalent. The author assumes that two different things are the same.
32. Allows a key term to shift in meaning during the course of the argument.	→	Any answer choice that says that a term is given more than one meaning in an argument is a reference to equivocation (and is probably wrong).
33. Presupposes what it seeks to establish.	→	This is the definition of circular reasoning.
34. Mistakes something that is necessary to bring about a situation for something that merely can bring about that situation.	→	The word "necessary" indicates that this is an Overlooked Possibilities—Necessary versus Sufficient problem.

Here's an LSAT expert's analysis of another full Flaw question. Review it to see how the expert uses the tactics and tools you've been learning.

LSAT Question	Analysis
Unplugging a peripheral component such as a "mouse" from a personal computer renders all of the software programs that require that component unusable on that computer. On Fred's personal computer, a software program that requires a mouse has become unusable. So it must be that the mouse for Fred's computer became unplugged.	**Step 2:** Conclusion: The mouse on Fred's computer became unplugged. *because* Evidence: A program on Fred's computer that requires a mouse has stopped working.
The argument is most vulnerable to which one of the following criticisms?	**Step 1:** The phrase "vulnerable to . . . criticism" indicates a Flaw question.
	Step 3: The evidence indicates that an unplugged mouse would cause the program to stop working, but that does not mean nothing else can be the cause. The correct answer could offer an overlooked possibility, but will more likely describe how the argument treats a condition *sufficient* to cause the program to crash as though it were *necessary* for the program to crash.
(A) It contains a shift in the meaning of "unusable" from "permanently unusable" to "temporarily unusable."	**Step 4:** Distortion. The argument simply does not do this. Eliminate.
(B) It treats an event that can cause a certain result as though that event is necessary to bring about that result.	Correct. The evidence indicates that an unplugged mouse *can* cause the program to stop working (i.e., sufficient), but the conclusion treats an unplugged mouse as the *only* potential cause of the problem (i.e., necessary).
(C) It introduces information unrelated to its conclusion as evidence in support of that conclusion.	Distortion. The evidence *is* related to the conclusion; the conclusion merely goes too far with that evidence. Eliminate.
(D) It attempts to support its conclusion by citing a generalization that is too broad.	Distortion. The evidence is not overly broad. Rather, the conclusion interprets it more broadly than is warranted. Eliminate.
(E) It overlooks the possibility that some programs do not require a peripheral component such as a mouse.	Outside the Scope. The argument is only concerned with a program that *does* require a mouse. Eliminate.

PrepTest27 Sec4 Q10

Common Wording of Flaw Types in Answer Choices

Take a moment now to look over some of the most common argument patterns and answer types in Flaw questions in the LSAT Strategy box. Feel free to return to this list from time to time to hone your ability to get through Flaw answer choices quickly and efficiently.

LSAT STRATEGY

Common Flaw Question Answer Choices by Argument Pattern

Overlooked Possibilities— General	"overlooks the possibility that"/"ignores the possibility that"/"fails to consider"
	"assumes only one possibility when more exist"
	"treats one explanation of many as though it were the only one"
Overlooked Possibilities— Causation	"mistakes a correlation for causation"
	"presumes that because one event was followed by another, the first event caused the second"
	"ignores the possibility that two things that occur together may be only coincidentally related"
Overlooked Possibilities— Nec vs Suff	"confuses a result with a condition that is required to bring about that result"
	"mistakes something that is necessary for a particular outcome for something that is merely sufficient for that outcome"
	"ignores the possibility that a particular outcome may be sufficient but not necessary for another"
Mismatched Concepts— General	"facts that are not directly related to the case are used to support a conclusion about it"
	"draws an analogy between two things that are not alike enough in the ways they would need to be in order for the conclusion to be properly drawn"
Mismatched Concepts— Representation	"draws a general conclusion from a few isolated instances"
	"generalizes from an unrepresentative sample"
	"treats the children living in County X as though they were representative of all children that age living in State Y"
Mismatched Concepts— Equivocation	"relies on an ambiguity in the term *plant*"
	"allows a key phrase to shift in meaning from one use to the next"
	"fails to provide a sufficient definition of a key term"
Circular Reasoning	"the conclusion is no more than a restatement of the evidence used to support it"
	"restates its conclusion without providing sufficient justification for accepting it"
	"presupposes the truth of what it seeks to establish"
Evidence Contradicts the Conclusion	"the evidence given actually undermines the argument's conclusion"
	"some of the evidence given is inconsistent with other evidence presented"
	"draws a recommendation that is inconsistent with the evidence given to support it"

Practice

Now that you've had a chance to learn the basics of Flaw questions, take some time to practice a few on your own. As always, follow the Kaplan Method and work to make a prediction in Step 3. After you've tried these on your own, check out the expert analyses on the following pages.

LSAT Question	My Analysis
35. Television allows us to transmit images of ourselves that propagate into space. The earliest of these transmissions have by now reached all of our neighboring star systems. None of these transmissions, so far as we know, has been recognized; we have yet to receive any messages of extraterrestrial origin. We must conclude that there is no extraterrestrial intelligence in any of our neighboring star systems.	**Step 2:**
The reasoning in the argument is questionable because the argument	**Step 1:**
	Step 3:
(A) fails to provide an adequate definition of the word "messages"	**Step 4:**
(B) infers that there is no extraterrestrial intelligence in neighboring star systems from the lack of proof that there is	
(C) assigns too little importance to the possibility that there is extraterrestrial intelligence beyond our neighboring star systems	
(D) neglects to mention that some governments have sent meticulously prepared messages and recordings on spacecraft	
(E) overlooks the immense probability that most star systems are uninhabited	

PrepTestB Sec4 Q13

LSAT Question	My Analysis
36. Several excellent candidates have been proposed for the presidency of United Wire, and each candidate would bring to the job different talents and experience. If the others are compared with Jones, however, it will be apparent that none of them has her unique set of qualifications. Jones, therefore, is best qualified to be the new president of United Wire.	**Step 2:**
The argument is vulnerable to criticism on the ground that it	**Step 1:**
	Step 3:
(A) uses flattery to win over those who hold an opposing position	**Step 4:**
(B) refutes a distorted version of an opposing position	
(C) seeks to distinguish one member of a group on the basis of something that applies to all	
(D) supports a universal claim on the basis of a single example	
(E) describes an individual in terms that appropriately refer only to the group as a whole	

PrepTest24 Sec2 Q6

LSAT Question	My Analysis
37. Research indicates that 90 percent of extreme insomniacs consume large amount of coffee. Since Tom drinks a lot of coffee, it is quite likely that he is an extreme insomniac.	**Step 2:**
Which one of the following most accurately describes a flaw in the argument's reasoning?	**Step 1:**
	Step 3:
(A) It fails to acknowledge the possibility that Tom is among the 10 percent of people who drink large amounts of coffee who are not extreme insomniacs.	**Step 4:**
(B) It fails to consider the possible contribution to extreme insomnia of other causes of insomnia besides coffee.	
(C) It relies on evidence that does not indicate the frequency of extreme insomnia among people who drink large amounts of coffee.	
(D) It draws an inference about one specific individual from evidence that describes only the characteristics of a class of individuals	
(E) It presumes without warrant that drinking coffee always causes insomnia.	

PrepTest27 Sec1 Q23

LSAT Question	My Analysis
38. A number of Grandville's wealthiest citizens have been criminals. So, since it is of utmost importance that the Grandville Planning Committee be composed solely of individuals whose personal standards of ethics are beyond reproach, no wealthy person should be appointed to that committee.	**Step 2:**
The argument is most vulnerable to the criticism that it	**Step 1:**
	Step 3:
(A) confuses a result with something that is sufficient for bringing about that result	**Step 4:**
(B) mistakes a temporal relationship for a causal relationship	
(C) assumes that because a certain action has a certain result the person taking that action intended that result	
(D) judges only by subjective standards something that can be readily evaluated according to objective standards	
(E) generalizes on the basis of what could be exceptional cases	

PrepTest28 Sec3 Q2

LSAT Question	My Analysis
39. Jane: Television programs and movies that depict violence among teenagers are extremely popular. Given how influential these media are, we have good reason to believe that these depictions cause young people to engage in violent behavior. Hence, depictions of violence among teenagers should be prohibited from movies and television programs, if only in those programs and movies promoted to young audiences.	**Step 2:**
Maurice: But you are recommending nothing short of censorship! Besides which, your claim that television and movie depictions of violence cause violence is mistaken: violence among young people predates movies and television by centuries.	
Maurice's attempted refutation of Jane's argument is vulnerable to criticism on which one of the following grounds?	**Step 1:**
	Step 3:
(A) It presupposes that an unpopular policy cannot possibly achieve its intended purpose.	**Step 4:**
(B) It confuses a subjective judgment of private moral permissibility with an objective description of social fact.	
(C) It rules out something as a cause of a current phenomenon solely on the ground that the phenomenon used to occur without that thing.	
(D) It cites purported historical facts that cannot possibly be verified.	
(E) It relies on an ambiguity in the term "violence" to justify a claim.	

PrepTest28 Sec3 Q5

Expert Analysis

Now that you've had a chance to do these on your own, check your reasoning against the expert analyses below.

LSAT Question	Analysis
35. Television allows us to transmit images of ourselves that propagate into space. The earliest of these transmissions have by now reached all of our neighboring star systems. None of these transmissions, so far as we know, has been recognized; we have yet to receive any messages of extraterrestrial origin. We must conclude that there is no extraterrestrial intelligence in any of our neighboring star systems.	**Step 2:** Conclusion: There is not intelligent extraterrestrial life in neighboring star systems. *because* Evidence: No extraterrestrials have responded to our televised messages.
The reasoning in the argument is questionable because the argument	**Step 1:** The phrase "argument is questionable" indicates a Flaw question.
	Step 3: The author here uses the absence of any evidence demonstrating alien intelligence to prove that alien intelligence does not exist. The argument also assumes that any "intelligent" extraterrestrial life would have the capability or desire to respond to our calls.
(A) fails to provide an adequate definition of the word "messages"	**Step 4:** The LSAT does not generally consider it a logic flaw to fail to provide a definition for a word, and "messages" is not even an inherently ambiguous term. Eliminate.
(B) infers that there is no extraterrestrial intelligence in neighboring star systems from the lack of proof that there is	Correct. Matches the prediction and describes how the argument commits the classic flaw of using "an absence of evidence as evidence of absence."
(C) assigns too little importance to the possibility that there is extraterrestrial intelligence beyond our neighboring star systems	Outside the Scope. The argument is limited to whether intelligent life exists in neighboring star systems. Eliminate.
(D) neglects to mention that some governments have sent meticulously prepared messages and recordings on spacecraft	180. This fact would strengthen the conclusion that there is no life in neighboring systems. So it is not a logic flaw to fail to consider this information. Eliminate.
(E) overlooks the immense probability that most star systems are uninhabited *PrepTestB Sec4 Q13*	180. This possibility supports the author's conclusion and it is not a logic flaw to fail to consider a possibility that supports one's argument. Eliminate.

LSAT Question	Analysis
36. Several excellent candidates have been proposed for the presidency of United Wire, and each candidate would bring to the job different talents and experience. If the others are compared with Jones, however, it will be apparent that none of them has her unique set of qualifications. Jones, therefore, is best qualified to be the new president of United Wire.	**Step 2:** Conclusion: Jones is the best qualified candidate for president. *because* Evidence: Jones has a unique set of qualifications to be president.
The argument is vulnerable to criticism on the ground that it	**Step 1:** The phrase "vulnerable to criticism" indicates a Flaw question.
	Step 3: The argument contains a mismatch between *unique qualifications* in the evidence and *best qualifications* in the conclusion. The assumption here is that a unique set of qualifications makes for the best qualified candidate. Additionally, the first sentence tells us that all of the candidates have their own unique qualifications, so it's not clear why Jones is being singled out.
(A) uses flattery to win over those who hold an opposing position	**Step 4:** Distortion. The author simply does not use flattery to win anybody over. Eliminate.
(B) refutes a distorted version of an opposing position	Distortion. This classic rhetorical strategy, known as a "straw man" argument, is not something the author does. Eliminate.
(C) seeks to distinguish one member of a group on the basis of something that applies to all	Correct. The author distinguishes Jones on the basis of having *unique* qualifications, even though all of the candidates are themselves unique in their set of qualifications.
(D) supports a universal claim on the basis of a single example	Distortion. The author does not jump to a universal claim. The evidence is about Jones and the conclusion is about Jones. Eliminate.
(E) describes an individual in terms that appropriately refer only to the group as a whole *PrepTest24 Sec2 Q6*	Distortion. The author describes Jones' qualifications as "unique," which just as appropriately applies to her, and the others, individually as to the group. Eliminate.

LSAT Question	Analysis
37. Research indicates that 90 percent of extreme insomniacs consume large amount of coffee. Since Tom drinks a lot of coffee, it is quite likely that he is an extreme insomniac.	**Step 2:** Conclusion: Tom is likely an extreme insomniac. → *because* Evidence: 1) Tom drinks lots of coffee; and 2) the vast majority of extreme insomniacs consume lots of coffee.
Which one of the following most accurately describes a flaw in the argument's reasoning?	→ **Step 1:** The phrase "flaw in . . . reasoning" indicates a Flaw question.
	Step 3: In the evidence, knowing that someone is an extreme insomniac is *sufficient* to know that that person is likely a heavy coffee drinker. In the conclusion, though, the author states that a heavy coffee drinker (Tom) is likely an insomniac. This argument confuses necessary and sufficient terms, and overlooks the possibility that there could be a vastly larger number of heavy coffee drinkers than extreme insomniacs.
(A) It fails to acknowledge the possibility that Tom is among the 10 percent of people who drink large amounts of coffee who are not extreme insomniacs.	→ **Step 4:** Distortion. The argument implies that 10 percent of extreme insomniacs don't drink coffee, not that 10 percent of people who drink a lot of coffee are not insomniacs. Eliminate.
(B) It fails to consider the possible contribution to extreme insomnia of other causes of insomnia besides coffee.	→ Outside the Scope. This possibility, even if true, is irrelevant to the conclusion regarding the likelihood that Tom is an extreme insomniac. Eliminate.
(C) It relies on evidence that does not indicate the frequency of extreme insomnia among people who drink large amounts of coffee.	→ Correct. This choice relates to the possibility that there could be many more heavy coffee drinkers than extreme insomniacs. If there were, say, only 10 extreme insomniacs but 100,000 heavy coffee drinkers, the fact that 9 of 10 extreme insomniacs were heavy coffee drinkers would only dictate that at least 9 of 100,000 heavy coffee drinkers were extreme insomniacs.

LSAT Question (cont.)	Analysis (cont.)
(D) It draws an inference about one specific individual from evidence that describes only the characteristics of a class of individuals	This answer passes the baseline test of something the author does. However, this is not necessarily a logical flaw. The evidence that 90% of extreme insomniacs are heavy coffee drinkers could well be used to reach a conclusion that an individual extreme insomniac is "likely" a heavy coffee drinker. Eliminate.
(E) It presumes without warrant that drinking coffee always causes insomnia. *PrepTest27 Sec1 Q23*	Extreme and Outside the Scope. The argument does not assume any particular causal relationship, let alone that any level of coffee drinking always causes some level of insomnia. Eliminate.

LSAT Question	Analysis
38. A number of Grandville's wealthiest citizens have been criminals. So, since it is of utmost importance that the Grandville Planning Committee be composed solely of individuals whose personal standards of ethics are beyond reproach, no wealthy person should be appointed to that committee.	**Step 2:** Conclusion: Not a single wealthy person should be appointed to the Grandville Planning Committee. *because* Evidence: 1) Everybody on the GPC must have ethics beyond reproach; and 2) some of Grandville's wealthy have been criminals.
The argument is most vulnerable to the criticism that it	**Step 1:** The phrase "vulnerable to . . . criticism" indicates a Flaw question.
	Step 3: The argument makes a number of assumptions, including the assumption that members of the GPC must be from Grandville. However, the most dramatic scope shift is from evidence about an unspecified number of wealthy people from Grandville to a conclusion encompassing all wealthy people. In other words, the author generalizes from a sample that may be too small.
(A) confuses a result with something that is sufficient for bringing about that result	**Step 4:** Distortion. This answer is another way of saying the argument confuses cause and effect, but the argument is not about causation. Eliminate.
(B) mistakes a temporal relationship for a causal relationship	Distortion. The argument deals with neither temporal nor causal relationships. Eliminate.
(C) assumes that because a certain action has a certain result the person taking that action intended that result	Distortion. As with (A) and (B), cause and effect (actions and results) are not involved in this argument. Eliminate.
(D) judges only by subjective standards something that can be readily evaluated according to objective standards	Outside the Scope. The author claims that some wealthy citizens have been criminals, but there is no indication that such a claim is subjective. The author's problem is that he wants all wealthy citizens banned when only some have been criminals. Eliminate.
(E) generalizes on the basis of what could be exceptional cases *PrepTest28 Sec3 Q2*	Correct. Matches the prediction by describing how the argument uses evidence that some wealthy people are criminals to reach a conclusion about all wealthy people.

LSAT Question	Analysis
39. Jane: Television programs and movies that depict violence among teenagers are extremely popular. Given how influential these media are, we have good reason to believe that these depictions cause young people to engage in violent behavior. Hence, depictions of violence among teenagers should be prohibited from movies and television programs, if only in those programs and movies promoted to young audiences. Maurice: But you are recommending nothing short of censorship! Besides which, your claim that television and movie depictions of violence cause violence is mistaken: violence among young people predates movies and television by centuries.	**Step 2:** Jane's Conclusion: Movies and television programs promoted to young audiences shouldn't be allowed to depict violence among teenagers. *because* → Evidence: There is "good reason to believe" that depictions of violence among teenagers "cause young people to engage in violent behavior." Maurice's Conclusion: Depictions of violence in movies does not cause violence. *because* Evidence: Violence among young people occurred for centuries before there were movies and television.
Maurice's attempted refutation of Jane's argument is vulnerable to criticism on which one of the following grounds?	**Step 1:** The phrase "vulnerable to criticism" indicates a Flaw question. Note that you are directed to identify the flaw in *Maurice's* argument.
	Step 3: Maurice's argument fails to consider that a new factor could contribute to or exacerbate the continuation of violence that has occurred for centuries.
(A) It presupposes that an unpopular policy cannot possibly achieve its intended purpose.	**Step 4:** Outside the Scope. Although he describes Jane's proposal as censorship, Maurice makes no comment about the proposal's popularity. Eliminate.
(B) It confuses a subjective judgment of private moral permissibility with an objective description of social fact.	This profound sounding answer really does not directly relate to Maurice's argument. Eliminate.
(C) It rules out something as a cause of a current phenomenon solely on the ground that the phenomenon used to occur without that thing.	Correct. This matches the prediction and is an accurate description of the argument.
(D) It cites purported historical facts that cannot possibly be verified.	Outside the Scope. Presumably, Maurice's claim could be verified. The problem is that, even if his claim is verified, Maurice's response doesn't damage Jane's argument. His response treats Jane's claim that video game violence is sufficient to cause violence among the young as though it were a claim that video game violence is necessary to cause such violence. Eliminate.
(E) It relies on an ambiguity in the term "violence" to justify a claim. *PrepTest28 Sec3 Q5*	The argument is consistent in its use of the term "violence." Eliminate.

WEAKEN QUESTIONS

Another way in which the LSAT will test your ability to evaluate an argument is to ask you to identify a piece of information that, if true, would weaken the author's argument. Here, "weaken an argument" doesn't mean that you have to conclusively disprove the conclusion. All you need to do is find the answer choice containing a fact that makes the author's conclusion less likely to be true based on the evidence.

First, let's take a look at some typical Weaken question stems as they appear on the LSAT:

LSAT Question Stem		Analysis
Which one of the following, if true, most seriously weakens the argument? *PrepTest29 Sec1 Q16*	→	The correct answer will be a new piece of information that will weaken the author's argument.
The argument would be most seriously weakened if which one of the following were discovered? *PrepTest24 Sec3 Q9*	→	The correct answer will a new piece of information that will weaken the author's argument.

Weaken questions tend to use the words *weakens, call into question,* or *undermines* in the question stem. Though most students are able to identify Weaken questions easily, some students occasionally confuse Weaken and Flaw questions. To keep the two question types straight, remember that in a Flaw question, you are being asked to *describe* that argument's error in reasoning. In a Weaken question, the testmaker wants you to identify a *new piece of information* that, if true, will undermine the author's assumption and thus weaken the conclusion. Accept the answer choices as true in a Weaken question and evaluate them by saying, "Okay, if this piece of information were true, would the author's conclusion be less likely to follow from her evidence?"

Your approach to Weaken questions begins in the same way as your approach to other Assumption Family questions: Start by untangling the stimulus into evidence and conclusion; then find the author's central assumption. Only occasionally will you see a Mismatched Concepts argument in a Weaken question. Instead, the nature of Weaken questions is such that you will largely be asked to evaluate Overlooked Possibilities arguments. By now, you are already in the habit of phrasing the assumption of these types of arguments in negative terms: "the author is assuming that *no other* explanation or potential objections to this conclusion exists." To weaken an Overlooked Possibilities argument, then, identify one of these possible objections in the answer choices. Review how the LSAT expert does that in the following Weaken question.

Here is an LSAT expert's analysis of a Weaken question. Take note of how the expert uses the argument type to predict the correct answer.

LSAT Question	Analysis
In a study in which secondary school students were asked to identify the teachers they liked the best, the teachers most often identified possessed a personality that constitutes 20 percent of the general public but only 5 percent of teachers. Thus something must discourage the people who would be the best-liked teachers from entering the profession.	**Step 2:** Conclusion: Something is discouraging the potentially best-liked teachers from pursuing teaching. *because* Evidence: The personality type most correlated with being liked by students is found in 20 percent of the general public but only 5 percent of teachers.
Which of the following, if true, most weakens the argument?	**Step 1:** The phrase "most weakens the argument" indicates a Weaken question.
	Step 3: The conclusion seems to directly follow from the evidence, thus the correct answer will provide an overlooked possibility; it will cite a reason why those with the personality type are underrepresented in the teaching profession *other than* the argument's explanation that they are discouraged from *entering* the profession.
(A) People with the personality type constitute 5 percent of the medical profession.	**Step 4:** Outside the Scope. Potential underrepresentation in the medical profession does nothing to explain their underrepresentation among teachers. Eliminate.
(B) People with the personality type constitute 5 percent of college students pursuing a degree in education.	180. Underrepresentation in education degree programs supports the claim that something is discouraging these people from going into teaching. Eliminate.
(C) Students of teachers with the personality type are intensely recruited for noneducational professions.	180. This answer identifies what is discouraging them from going into teaching. Eliminate.
(D) Students with the personality type are more likely to be liked by teachers than those with other personality types.	Irrelevant Comparison. How well liked *by teachers* those with personality type are has no clear effect on the likelihood of the conclusion. Eliminate.
(E) Teachers with the personality type are more likely to quit teaching than those with other personality types. *PrepTestB Sec4 Q18*	Correct. This choice provides an alternative explanation for the underrepresentation of this personality type among teachers. It is not that they are discouraged from entering the teaching profession; it's that they don't remain in the teaching profession.

LSAT STRATEGY

Some facts to remember about Weaken questions:

- A correct answer doesn't have to disprove the conclusion, just weaken it.
- The most common argument type in Weaken questions is Overlooked Possibilities.
- Correct answer choices nearly always introduce a possible objection to the conclusion that the author has not considered.

If you find yourself getting lost or frustrated in a specific Weaken question, take a step back from the argument and focus solely on the argument's conclusion. While many Weaken questions require you to understand how the evidence relates to the conclusion, some Weaken questions do not. In these, simply understanding the conclusion will be enough to identify a correct answer choice.

Here's an LSAT expert's analysis of another Weaken question. Review it with an eye to the skills and strategies you've been learning.

LSAT Question	Analysis
The interstitial nucleus, a subregion of the brain's hypothalamus, is typically smaller for male cats than for female cats. A neurobiologist performed autopsies on male cats who died from disease X, a disease affecting no more than .05 percent of male cats, and found that these male cats had interstitial nuclei that were as large as those generally found in female cats. Thus, the size of the interstitial nucleus determines whether or not male cats can contract disease X.	**Step 2:** Conclusion: The size of the interstitial nucleus dictates the potential for male cats to contract disease X. *because* Evidence: In a sample of male cats that died from the extremely rare disease X, all had enlarged interstitial nuclei.
Which of the following statements, if true, most seriously weakens the argument?	**Step 1:** The phrase "most . . . weakens the argument" indicates a Weaken question.
	Step 3: This argument jumps from evidence of correlation to a conclusion of some causal connection between the size of the interstitial nuclei and the occurrence of disease X in male cats. The Weaken answer will break the causal connection by suggesting one of three things: 1) an alternative cause; 2) reverse causation; or 3) coincidence (a lack of connection).
(A) No female cats have been known to contract disease X, which is a subtype of disease Y.	**Step 4:** Outside the Scope. The argument is not concerned with occurrences of disease X in female cats. Eliminate.
(B) Many male cats who contract disease X also contract disease Z, the cause of which is unknown.	Outside the Scope. This unspecified level of correlation of disease X and Z does not affect the likelihood of a causal connection between the size of the interstitial nucleus and disease X. Eliminate.
(C) The interstitial nuclei of female cats who contract disease X are larger than those of female cats who do not contract disease X.	180. The argument is not concerned with female cats, but this evidence would, if anything, *strengthen* the author's claim. Eliminate.
(D) Of 1,000 autopsies on male cats who did not contract disease X, 5 revealed interstitial nuclei larger than those of the average male cat.	Finding a low correlation between enlarged interstitial nuclei and the *absence* of disease X does not damage the author's argument. If anything, it strengthens it. Eliminate.
(E) The hypothalamus is known not to be causally linked to disease Y, and disease X is a subtype of disease Y. *PrepTest28 Sec3 Q25*	Correct. Breaking the causal connection between the hypothalamus and disease Y breaks (or at least undermines) any causal connection between their relative subparts and subtypes.

Later, you'll get an opportunity to try some Weaken questions on your own and to compare your thinking to that of an LSAT expert. For now, though, take a look at a question type that is intimately related to Weaken questions: Strengthen questions.

STRENGTHEN QUESTIONS

LEARNING OBJECTIVES

In this section, you'll learn to:

· Identify and answer Strengthen questions.
· Turn assumptions into accurate predictions.
· Recognize answer choices that strengthen the author's assumption.

At this point, you've learned how to evaluate an LSAT argument, find its assumption, describe its flaw, and identify an answer choice that would weaken the argument. Here's yet another task: Identify a piece of information that, if true, would strengthen the argument. Strengthen, in this context, doesn't mean "prove" the argument or "confirm" the conclusion—that's too strong. Instead, Strengthen questions ask you to identify an answer choice that makes the conclusion more likely to be true. Combined, you will see about eight Strengthen and Weaken questions on Test Day.

First, let's take a look at some typical Strengthen question stems as they appear on the LSAT:

LSAT Question Stem		Analysis
Which one of the following, if true, most helps to strengthen the historians' argument? *PrepTest24 Sec3 Q23*	$\longrightarrow$	Since we're looking for something that, "if true," would most help to "strengthen" an argument, this is a Strengthen question.
Which one of the following, if true, most strongly supports the explanation above? *PrepTest27 Sec1 Q5*	$\longrightarrow$	The correct answer choice, "if true, most strongly supports" the stimulus above indicates that this is a Strengthen question.
Which one of the following, if true, provides the strongest additional support for the hypothesis above? *PrepTest27 Sec1 Q18*	$\longrightarrow$	"[I]f true, provides the strongest . . . support," marks this as a Strengthen question.

Your approach to Strengthen questions starts in the same way as your approach to other Assumption Family questions. Begin by untangling the author's argument into evidence and conclusion. Next, note the argument pattern and identify the assumption. Then predict an answer choice that would strengthen the argument's conclusion. For a Strengthen question that uses a Mismatched Concepts argument, that means looking for an answer choice that affirms the relationship the author assumes exists between mismatched terms. In a Strengthen question that uses an Overlooked Possibilities argument, seek an answer choice that removes a potential objection that the author is overlooking. And in both types of arguments, you may actually find that the correct answer choice simply provides information that directly strengthens the author's conclusion.

Take a look at an LSAT expert's analysis of a Strengthen question.

LSAT Question	Analysis
Combustion of gasoline in automobile engines produces benzene, a known carcinogen. Environmentalists propose replacing gasoline with methanol, which does not produce significant quantities of benzene when burned. However, combustion of methanol produces formaldehyde, also a known carcinogen. Therefore the environmentalists' proposal has little merit.	**Step 2:** Environmentalists' Conclusion: Replace gasoline with methanol. *because* Evidence: Methanol combustion does not produce significant quantities of benzene. Author's Conclusion: Don't listen to the environmentalists (stick with gasoline). *because* Author's Evidence: Methanol combustion does produce another known carcinogen, formaldehyde.
Which one of the following, if true, most supports the environmentalists' proposal?	**Step 1:** The phrase "most supports the . . . proposal" indicates a Strengthen question. The question stem further specifies that the task is to strengthen the environmentalists' claim.
	Step 3: Based on the author's evidence and the environmentalists' evidence, the choice between methanol and gasoline comes down to a choice between the formaldehyde and benzene found in each, respectively. Thus, a reason to favor formaldehyde over benzene would strengthen the environmentalists' proposal to use methanol.
(A) The engines of some automobiles now on the road burn diesel fuel rather than gasoline.	**Step 4:** Outside the Scope. The argument is between gasoline and methanol, not diesel. Eliminate.
(B) Several large research efforts are underway to formulate cleaner-burning types of gasoline.	180. This potentially minimizes the benefits of switching to methane, as the environmentalists propose. Eliminate.
(C) In some regions, the local economy is largely dependent on industries devoted to the production and distribution of automobile fuel.	Outside the Scope. The environmentalists' proposal is based on health concerns. Eliminate.
(D) Formaldehyde is a less potent carcinogen than benzene.	Correct. Matches the prediction by indicating a reason to prefer formaldehyde over benzene, and, thus, methanol over gasoline.
(E) Since methanol is water soluble, methanol spills are more damaging to the environment than gasoline spills. *PrepTest29 Sec4 Q1*	180. Supports the author's rejection of the environmentalists' proposal to replace gasoline with methanol. Eliminate.

LSAT STRATEGY

Some facts to remember about Strengthen Questions:

· The correct answer, when added to the evidence, doesn't have to prove the conclusion—just make it more likely.

· Both Mismatched Concepts and Overlooked Possibilities arguments show up in Strengthen questions, although overlooked possibilities are more common.

· In a Mismatched Concepts argument, look for an answer choice that either affirms the author's assumption or directly supports the conclusion.

· In an Overlooked Possibilities argument, look for an answer choice that removes a potential objection that the author is not considering.

As in some Weaken questions, it's possible in some Strengthen questions to find the right answer by focusing solely on an argument's conclusion. If you get lost or frustrated by a Strengthen question, return to the conclusion and try to find an answer choice that most strengthens that conclusion.

Here's an LSAT expert's analysis of another Strengthen question. Review it to see the strategies and tactics in action.

LSAT Question	Analysis
Astronauts who experience weightlessness frequently get motion sickness. The astronauts see their own motion relative to passing objects, but while the astronauts are weightless their inner ears indicate that their bodies are not moving. The astronauts' experience is best explained by the hypothesis that conflicting information received by the brain about the body's motion causes motion sickness.	**Step 2:** Conclusion: The explanation for motion sickness in astronauts is the conflicting information received by the brain about the body's motion. *because* Evidence: Astronauts see their motion, but, due to weightlessness, their inner ears indicate they are not moving.
Which one of the following, if true, provides the strongest additional support for the hypothesis above?	**Step 1:** The phrase "support for the hypotheses" indicates a Strengthen question.
	Step 3: The conclusion provides a causal explanation for the phenomenon of motion sickness in astronauts. The correct answer will eliminate an alternative explanation or provide further support for the hypothesis that conflicting signals to the brain cause the motion sickness.
(A) During rough voyages ship passengers in cabins providing a view of the water are less likely to get motion sickness than are passengers in cabins providing no view.	**Step 4:** Correct. This answer provides an analogous situation in which motion sickness occurs in conjunction with conflicting signals to the brain.
(B) Many people who are experienced airplane passengers occasionally get motion sickness.	Outside the Scope. This is an irrelevant situation that does not involve conflicting signals, so it cannot strengthen the conclusion. Eliminate.
(C) Some automobile passengers whose inner ears indicate that they are moving and who have a clear view of the objects they are passing get motion sickness.	180. A small number of contrary examples would not technically weaken the argument, but generally this runs counter to the argument as it involves motion sickness in the absence of conflicting signals. Eliminate.
(D) People who have aisle seats in trains or airplanes are as likely to get motion sickness as are people who have window seats.	Irrelevant Comparison. Both people in window and aisle seats can see the motion of the background. Eliminate.
(E) Some astronauts do not get motion sickness even after being in orbit for several days. *PrepTest27 Sec1 Q18*	Outside the Scope. The mere existence of some astronauts who do not experience motion sickness provides no information relevant to the cause of motion sickness in those who do. Eliminate.

Rare Strengthen and Weaken Questions

Weaken and Strengthen EXCEPT Questions

In addition to asking straightforward Weaken and Strengthen questions, the LSAT may ask you to identify an answer choice that *does not* weaken or *does not* strengthen the author's conclusion. Though these Strengthen/Weaken EXCEPT questions are rare (constituting fewer than 5 percent of all Strengthen/Weaken questions), it's important to know how to tackle them when you see them. The first thing you need to be able to do is identify these question types. Take a look at the following typical Strengthen/Weaken EXCEPT question stems:

Question Stem		Analysis
Each of the following, if true, weakens the argument EXCEPT	→	The four wrong answer choices will weaken the conclusion. The right answer will strengthen the conclusion or have no impact.
Each of the following, if true, supports the claim above EXCEPT	→	The four wrong answer choices will strengthen the conclusion. The right answer will weaken the conclusion or have no impact.

In these Weaken and Strengthen EXCEPT questions, understand that the correct answer does not need to strengthen or weaken an argument. In fact, the correct answer to these EXCEPT questions may have no impact on the argument at all. The only thing you can be sure of in these questions is that the four incorrect answer choices will *definitely* weaken the argument in a Weaken EXCEPT question and *definitely* strengthen the argument in a Strengthen EXCEPT question.

For this reason, you need to be able to characterize what the correct answer choice requires in Strengthen/Weaken EXCEPT questions. In a Weaken EXCEPT question, the correct answer will either strengthen the argument or have no impact. Similarly, the correct answer to a Strengthen EXCEPT question will either weaken the argument or have no impact.

> ## LSAT STRATEGY
>
> Some facts to remember about Strengthen and Weaken EXCEPT questions:
>
> - Always slow down and characterize what the right and wrong answer choices will look like.
> - The correct answer in a Strengthen EXCEPT question will either weaken the argument or have no impact.
> - The correct answer in a Weaken EXCEPT question will either strengthen the argument or have no impact.

Evaluate Questions

Evaluate Questions are an even rarer subspecies of Strengthen and Weaken questions. In fact, it's likely you won't see one on the LSAT. On the last 21 released LSATs (seven years' worth), only seven questions have fallen into this category. However, because they do show up on occasion, it's good to know about them and to have a plan, just in case. The first thing you need to be able to do is identify Evaluate questions. Take a look at the following typical Evaluate question stems:

Question Stem	Analysis
Which one of the following would be most useful to know in order to evaluate the legitimacy of the philosopher's argument?	The correct answer will provide a piece of information that, if true, would make the argument either stronger or weaker and, if false, would have the opposite effect. In other words, the correct answer is *relevant* to the argument's validity.
Information about which one of the following would be LEAST useful in evaluating the doctor's hypothesis?	Four of the answer choices will be useful in evaluating the hypothesis, while the correct answer choice won't be useful. That means it will be irrelevant or have no impact on the hypothesis.

As with other Assumption Family questions, start by breaking down the argument in an Evaluate question into evidence and conclusion. Determine the assumption and use that information to identify an answer choice that will help you evaluate the argument. Answer choices in Evaluate questions are not straightforward strengtheners or weakeners—instead, they are typically phrased as questions, whose answers may or may not help you evaluate the validity of the argument. Select the answer choice that allows you to say that the argument is strong or weak. In an Evaluate EXCEPT or Evaluate LEAST question, your goal is to find the answer choice that has *no impact* on the argument.

LSAT STRATEGY

Some facts to remember about Evaluate questions:

· These questions are similar to Strengthen and Weaken questions.

· Untangle the stimulus, and then determine the author's assumption.

· The correct answer will often present a question the answer to which has either a positive or negative impact on the argument.

Practice

Now it's time to try some Strengthen and Weaken questions on your own. Use your knowledge of argument patterns to determine the author's assumption. In Weaken questions, the assumption is often that the author is overlooking potential objections to the conclusion, so be on the lookout for an answer choice that introduces one of these objections. In Strengthen questions, the correct answer affirms the assumption or removes a possible objection.

LSAT Question	My Analysis
40. Historians of North American architecture who have studied early nineteenth-century houses with wooden floors have observed that the boards used on the floors of bigger houses were generally much narrower than those used on the floors of smaller houses. These historians have argued that, since the people for whom the bigger houses were built were generally richer than the people for whom the smaller houses were built, floors made out of narrow floorboards were probably once a status symbol, designed to proclaim the owner's wealth.	Step 2:
Which one of the following, if true, most helps to strengthen the historians' argument?	Step 1:
	Step 3:
(A) More original floorboards have survived from big early nineteenth-century houses than from small early nineteenth-century houses.	Step 4:
(B) In the early nineteenth century, a piece of narrow floorboard was not significantly less expensive than a piece of wide floorboard of the same length.	
(C) In the early nineteenth century, smaller houses generally had fewer rooms than did bigger houses.	
(D) Some early nineteenth-century houses had wide floorboards near the walls of each room and narrower floorboards in the center, where the floors were usually carpeted.	
(E) Many of the biggest early nineteenth-century houses but very few small houses from that period had some floors that were made of materials that were considerably more expensive.	

PrepTest24 Sec3 Q23

LSAT Question	**My Analysis**
41. The play *Mankind* must have been written between 1431 and 1471. It cannot have been written before 1431, for in that year the rose noble, a coin mentioned in the play, was first circulated. The play cannot have been written after 1471, since in that year King Henry VI died, and he is mentioned as a living monarch in the play's dedication.	**Step 2:**
The argument would be most seriously weakened if which one of the following were discovered?	**Step 1:**
	Step 3:
(A) The Royal Theatre Company includes the play on a list of those performed in 1480.	**Step 4:**
(B) Another coin mentioned in the play was first minted in 1422.	
(C) The rose noble was neither minted nor circulated after 1468.	
(D) Although Henry VI was deposed in 1461, he was briefly restored to the throne in 1470.	
(E) In a letter written in early 1428, a merchant told of having seen the design for a much-discussed new coin called the "rose noble."	

PrepTest24 Sec3 Q9

LSAT Question	**My Analysis**
42. The most reliable way to detect the presence of life on a planet would be by determining whether or not its atmosphere contains methane. This is because methane completely disappears from a planet's atmosphere through various chemical reactions unless it is constantly replenished by the biological processes of living beings.	**Step 2:**
Which one of the following statements, if true, most seriously weakens the argument?	**Step 1:**
	Step 3:
(A) There are other ways of detecting the presence of life on a planet.	**Step 4:**
(B) Not all living beings have the ability to biologically produce methane.	
(C) We are incapable at present of analyzing a planet's atmosphere for the presence of methane.	
(D) Some living beings biologically produce only very small amounts of methane.	
(E) Earth is the only planet whose atmosphere is known to contain methane.	

PrepTestB Sec4 Q5

LSAT Question	My Analysis
43. To allay public concern about chemicals that are leaking into a river from a chemical company's long-established dump, a company representative said, "Federal law requires that every new chemical be tested for safety before it is put onto the market. This is analogous to the federal law mandating testing of every pharmaceutical substance for safety."	**Step 2:**
Which one of the following, if true, most seriously weakens the representative's implied argument that the public need not be concerned about the leak?	**Step 1:**
	Step 3:
(A) When pharmaceutical substances are tested for safety pursuant to federal requirements, a delay is imposed on the entry of potentially lifesaving substances onto the market.	**Step 4:**
(B) Leakage from the dump has occurred in noticeable amounts only in the last few months.	
(C) Before the federal law requiring testing of nonpharmaceutical chemicals went into effect recently, there were 40,000 such chemicals being manufactured, many of them dangerous.	
(D) The concentration of chemicals leaking into the river is diluted, first by rainwater and then by the water in the river.	
(E) The water in the river is murky because of the runoff of silt from a number of nearby construction projects.	

PrepTestB Sec4 Q9

LSAT Question	My Analysis
44. Surviving seventeenth-century Dutch landscapes attributed to major artists now equal in number those attributed to minor ones. But since in the seventeenth century many prolific minor artists made a living supplying the voracious market for Dutch landscapes, while only a handful of major artists painted in the genre, many attributions of seventeenth-century Dutch landscape paintings to major artists are undoubtedly erroneous.	**Step 2:**
Which one of the following, if true, most strengthens the argument?	**Step 1:**
	Step 3:
(A) Technically gifted seventeenth-century Dutch landscape artists developed recognizable styles that were difficult to imitate.	**Step 4:**
(B) In the workshops of major seventeenth-century artists, assistants were employed to prepare the paints, brushes, and other materials that the major artists then used.	
(C) In the eighteenth century, landscapes by minor seventeenth-century artists were often simply thrown away or else destroyed through improper storage.	
(D) Seventeenth-century art dealers paid minor artists extra money to leave their landscapes unsigned so that the dealers could add phony signatures and pass such works off as valuable paintings.	
(E) More seventeenth-century Dutch landscapes were painted than have actually survived, and that is true of those executed by minor artists as well as of those executed by major artists.	

PrepTest28 Sec3 Q24

LSAT Question	My Analysis
45. A recent study concludes that prehistoric birds, unlike modern birds, were cold-blooded. This challenges a widely held view that modern birds descended from warm-blooded birds. The conclusion is based on the existence of growth rings in prehistoric birds' bodily structures, which are thought to be found only in cold-blooded animals. Another study, however, disputes this view. It concludes that prehistoric birds had dense blood vessels in their bones, which suggests that they were active creatures and therefore had to be warm-blooded.	Step 2:
Which one of the following, if true, would most help to resolve the dispute described above in favor of one party to it?	Step 1:
	Step 3:
(A) Some modern warm-blooded species other than birds have been shown to have descended from cold-blooded species.	Step 4:
(B) Having growth rings is not the only physical trait of cold-blooded species.	
(C) Modern birds did not evolve from prehistoric species of birds.	
(D) Dense blood vessels are not found in all warm-blooded species.	
(E) In some cold-blooded species the gene that is responsible for growth rings is also responsible for dense blood vessels.

PrepTest28 Sec3 Q13 | |

Expert Analysis

Now take a look at how an LSAT expert would approach and analyze these Strengthen and Weaken questions.

LSAT Question	Analysis
40. Historians of North American architecture who have studied early nineteenth-century houses with wooden floors have observed that the boards used on the floors of bigger houses were generally much narrower than those used on the floors of smaller houses. These historians have argued that, since the people for whom the bigger houses were built were generally richer than the people for whom the smaller houses were built, floors made out of narrow floorboards were probably once a status symbol, designed to proclaim the owner's wealth.	**Step 2:** Conclusion: The purpose of narrow floorboards was to show status and wealth. *because* Evidence: Bigger houses, which were generally built for wealthy people, contained more narrow floorboards than did smaller houses.
Which one of the following, if true, most helps to strengthen the historians' argument?	**Step 1:** The phrase "most helps to strengthen" indicates a Strengthen question.
	Step 3: Since the conclusion provides a causal explanation for the observation that bigger houses correlate with narrow floorboards, find an answer that either eliminates an alternative explanation (e.g., no structural reason for using narrow floorboards in big houses) or firms up the connection between narrow floorboards and wealth (e.g., narrow floorboards are costly).
(A) More original floorboards have survived from big early nineteenth-century houses than from small early nineteenth-century houses.	**Step 4:** Irrelevant Comparison. The age of the surviving houses has no relevance to why narrow floorboards were used in big houses. Eliminate.
(B) In the early nineteenth century, a piece of narrow floorboard was not significantly less expensive than a piece of wide floorboard of the same length.	Correct. This strengthens the argument by eliminating a possibility (narrow floorboards were cheaper) that would have weakened the argument.
(C) In the early nineteenth century, smaller houses generally had fewer rooms than did bigger houses.	Irrelevant Comparison. The number of rooms in a house, as with (A), has no relevance to why narrow floorboards were used in big houses. Eliminate.
(D) Some early nineteenth-century houses had wide floorboards near the walls of each room and narrower floorboards in the center, where the floors were usually carpeted.	180. If narrow floorboards were hidden from view, then the assertion that narrow floorboards were a status symbol would be undermined. Eliminate.
(E) Many of the biggest early nineteenth-century houses but very few small houses from that period had some floors that were made of materials that were considerably more expensive. *PrepTest24 Sec3 Q23*	Outside the Scope. At most, this would be marginally relevant as a weakener by indicating that the real status symbol flooring was made of other materials. Eliminate.

LSAT Question	Analysis
41. The play *Mankind* must have been written between 1431 and 1471. It cannot have been written before 1431, for in that year the rose noble, a coin mentioned in the play, was first circulated. The play cannot have been written after 1471, since in that year King Henry VI died, and he is mentioned as a living monarch in the play's dedication.	**Step 2:** Conclusion: The play *Mankind* was definitely written between 1431 and 1471. *because* Evidence: 1) A coin mentioned in the play was first circulated in 1431; and 2) the play's dedication indicates King Henry VI, who died in 1471, was living at that time.
The argument would be most seriously weakened if which one of the following were discovered?	**Step 1:** The phrase "most seriously weakened" indicates a Weaken question.
	Step 3: The argument assumes that the two pieces of evidence preclude the possibility of the play being written before 1431 or after 1471. The correct answer to this Weaken question will provide new information that allows for the possibility that the play could have been written earlier or later. Perhaps the dedication to King Henry was written before the play itself, or the coin was known to exist before its circulation.
(A) The Royal Theatre Company includes the play on a list of those performed in 1480.	**Step 4:** Outside the Scope. A performance in 1480 does not call into question the author's claim that the play was written between 1431 and 1471. Eliminate.
(B) Another coin mentioned in the play was first minted in 1422.	Outside the Scope. Similar to (A), this merely indicates the play was written any time from 1422 on. Eliminate.
(C) The rose noble was neither minted nor circulated after 1468.	Similar to (A) and (B), this fact, if true, allows the play to have been written before, during or after the time frame purported by the author. Eliminate.
(D) Although Henry VI was deposed in 1461, he was briefly restored to the throne in 1470.	This information provides a distinction that would potentially eliminate nine of the years within the author's time frame for dating the play, but in no way undermines the conclusion that the play was written between 1431 and 1471. Eliminate.
(E) In a letter written in early 1428, a merchant told of having seen the design for a much-discussed new coin called the "rose noble." *PrepTest24 Sec3 Q9*	Correct. If people knew about the coin before it was first circulated, then the earliest circulation date is not a valid cut-off for dating the play.

609

LSAT Question	Analysis
42. The most reliable way to detect the presence of life on a planet would be by determining whether or not its atmosphere contains methane. This is because methane completely disappears from a planet's atmosphere through various chemical reactions unless it is constantly replenished by the biological processes of living beings.	**Step 2:** Conclusion: Checking the atmosphere for methane would be the most reliable way to detect life on a planet. *because* Evidence: The continuing presence of methane in the atmosphere requires living beings to constantly replenish it.
Which one of the following statements, if true, most seriously weakens the argument?	**Step 1:** The phrase "most seriously weakens" indicates a Weaken question.
	Step 3: The author provides evidence that the production of methane by living creatures is *necessary* to sustain methane in a planet's atmosphere. He concludes, however, that the presence of methane in the atmosphere is *sufficient* to prove the existence of life on a planet. The correct answer will present a fact suggesting that there could be life on a planet that does not have methane in its atmosphere.
(A) There are other ways of detecting the presence of life on a planet.	**Step 4:** By asserting that checking for methane is the *most* reliable method, the argument does not dismiss the possibility of using other methods. Eliminate.
(B) Not all living beings have the ability to biologically produce methane.	Correct. Checking for methane would not be a reliable method of detecting these forms of life, which would undercut the reliability of the method to at least some degree.
(C) We are incapable at present of analyzing a planet's atmosphere for the presence of methane.	Outside the Scope. The conclusion is conditioned on an ability to detect methane (using the hypothetical *would be*, rather than asserting it *is* the most reliable method), thus an actual inability to detect methane is outside the scope of the argument. Eliminate.
(D) Some living beings biologically produce only very small amounts of methane.	Similar to (C), this possibility only increases the technical difficulty of detecting methane, and the author's argument is conditioned on being able to do so. Eliminate.
(E) Earth is the only planet whose atmosphere is known to contain methane. *PrepTestB Sec4 Q5*	This is consistent with the argument, since currently Earth is also the only planet known to contain life. Eliminate.

LSAT Question	Analysis
43. To allay public concern about chemicals that are leaking into a river from a chemical company's long-established dump, a company representative said, "Federal law requires that every new chemical be tested for safety before it is put onto the market. This is analogous to the federal law mandating testing of every pharmaceutical substance for safety." →	**Step 2:** Conclusion: The public doesn't need to be concerned about chemicals leaking into a river from a dump. *because* Evidence: There is a program that requires the testing of new chemicals similar to the testing of pharmaceuticals.
Which one of the following, if true, most seriously weakens the representative's implied argument that the public need not be concerned about the leak? →	**Step 1:** The phrase "most seriously weakens" indicates a Weaken question. The question stem further clarifies the conclusion to weaken: "the public need not be concerned about the leak."
	Step 3: The argument assumes that the testing program for new chemicals, similar to the testing of pharmaceuticals, does not overlook any potential cause for concern. The correct answer will either distinguish these chemicals from pharmaceuticals or indicate an Overlooked Possibility of inadequacy in the testing program. Note that the testing only applies to *new* chemicals, so if older chemicals are at the *long established* dump, that would be a reason for concern.
(A) When pharmaceutical substances are tested for safety pursuant to federal requirements, a delay is imposed on the entry of potentially lifesaving substances onto the market. →	**Step 4:** Outside the Scope. This is a potential downside to the testing of pharmaceuticals, but in no way indicates a cause for concern regarding the leaking chemicals. Eliminate.
(B) Leakage from the dump has occurred in noticeable amounts only in the last few months. →	Outside the Scope. This may alleviate concerns of people who previously lived in the area, but the conclusion is focused on any present need for concern from the leak among the current public. Eliminate.
(C) Before the federal law requiring testing of nonpharmaceutical chemicals went into effect recently, there were 40,000 such chemicals being manufactured, many of them dangerous. →	Correct. Matches the prediction by pointing out an inadequacy in the testing program focused solely on *new* chemicals, especially for a *long established* dump.
(D) The concentration of chemicals leaking into the river is diluted, first by rainwater and then by the water in the river. →	180. This provides an additional reason, along with the testing, to *not* be concerned. Eliminate.
(E) The water in the river is murky because of the runoff of silt from a number of nearby construction projects. *PrepTestB Sec4 Q9* →	The effect of this information on the argument is unclear; while it could be a reason to not be concerned about further pollution, the combined effects of pollution on the river might be a cause for heightened concern. Eliminate.

LSAT Question	Analysis
44. Surviving seventeenth-century Dutch landscapes attributed to major artists now equal in number those attributed to minor ones. But since in the seventeenth century many prolific minor artists made a living supplying the voracious market for Dutch landscapes, while only a handful of major artists painted in the genre, many attributions of seventeenth-century Dutch landscape paintings to major artists are undoubtedly erroneous.	**Step 2:** Conclusion: Many 17th century Dutch landscapes were not painted by the major artists attributed to them. *because* Evidence: 1) there are an equal number of such paintings attributed to major artists as to minor artists, while 2) there were many prolific minor artists in the genre but only a handful of major artists.
Which one of the following, if true, most strengthens the argument?	**Step 1:** The phrase "most strengthens the argument" indicates a Strengthen question.
	Step 3: The numbers set out in the evidence do seem to support the conclusion, so the author is overlooking the possibility that while there were fewer major artists making these paintings, they still nonetheless created as many paintings as the minor artists. A correct answer to this Strengthen question, then, will eliminate an overlooked possibility, or provide further evidence supporting false attributions.
(A) Technically gifted seventeenth-century Dutch landscape artists developed recognizable styles that were difficult to imitate.	**Step 4:** 180. This reduces the potential for false attributions. Eliminate.
(B) In the workshops of major seventeenth-century artists, assistants were employed to prepare the paints, brushes, and other materials that the major artists then used.	Distortion. The author argues that many landscapes attributed to major artists are actually the work of minor artists, not merely that minor artists assisted by doing prep work. Eliminate.
(C) In the eighteenth century, landscapes by minor seventeenth-century artists were often simply thrown away or else destroyed through improper storage.	180. This provides an alternative explanation for why there are currently an equal number of paintings attributed to major and minor artists, despite the greater number and productivity of minor artists of the genre. Eliminate.
(D) Seventeenth-century art dealers paid minor artists extra money to leave their landscapes unsigned so that the dealers could add phony signatures and pass such works off as valuable paintings.	Correct. This provides clear motive and opportunity for a scheme that plausibly could avoid detection and result in a large number of excess paintings attributable to major artists.
(E) More seventeenth-century Dutch landscapes were painted than have actually survived, and that is true of those executed by minor artists as well as of those executed by major artists. *PrepTest28 Sec3 Q24*	Distortion. The loss of paintings by both major and minor artists does nothing to make the author's explanation for the apparent discrepancy any more or less likely. Eliminate.

LSAT Question	Analysis
45. A recent study concludes that prehistoric birds, unlike modern birds, were cold-blooded. This challenges a widely held view that modern birds descended from warm-blooded birds. The conclusion is based on the existence of growth rings in prehistoric birds' bodily structures, which are thought to be found only in cold-blooded animals. Another study, however, disputes this view. It concludes that prehistoric birds had dense blood vessels in their bones, which suggests that they were active creatures and therefore had to be warm-blooded.	**Step 2:** 1st Study's Conclusion: Prehistoric birds were cold-blooded. *because* Evidence: Prehistoric birds had growth rings believed to only occur in cold-blooded animals. 2nd Study's Conclusion: Prehistoric birds were warm-blooded. *because* Evidence: Prehistoric birds had dense blood vessels in their bones, which suggests they were active creatures.
Which one of the following, if true, would most help to resolve the dispute described above in favor of one party to it?	**Step 1:** The question stem directs us to find an answer that would support one party in a dispute over another; this indicates a Strengthen/Weaken question (strengthen one argument while weakening the other).
	Step 3: The two studies use different pieces of evidence to reach opposite conclusions. The correct answer will suggest that one of the pieces of evidence is consistent with either cold-bloodedness or warm-bloodedness, or will raise a reason why in prehistoric birds one of those features would not be indicative of that study's conclusion.
(A) Some modern warm-blooded species other than birds have been shown to have descended from cold-blooded species.	**Step 4:** Outside the Scope. The dispute referenced in the question stem is between the opposing conclusions of warm-blooded versus cold-blooded. The reference in the second sentence to the descent of modern birds is mere contextual information. Eliminate.
(B) Having growth rings is not the only physical trait of cold-blooded species.	Distortion. A relevant question would be whether growth rings really are *only* found in cold-blooded species, as thought, not whether cold-blooded species lack any other physical trait besides growth rings, as this answer suggests. Eliminate.
(C) Modern birds did not evolve from prehistoric species of birds.	Outside the Scope. As with (A), the evolution of modern birds is not relevant to the specific dispute referenced in the question stem regarding whether prehistoric birds were warm or cold-blooded. Eliminate.

LSAT Question (cont.)		Analysis (cont.)
(D)	Dense blood vessels are not found in all warm-blooded species.	$\longrightarrow$	Distortion. This certainly does not support the conclusion of warm-blooded, but neither does it provide any support for the conclusion of cold-blooded; provides no reason to believe that the presence of dense blood vessels is consistent with cold-bloodedness. Eliminate.
(E)	In some cold-blooded species the gene that is responsible for growth rings is also responsible for dense blood vessels. *PrepTest28 Sec3 Q13*	$\longrightarrow$	Correct. This shows that the traits described in each of the studies' evidence are consistent with a single conclusion: cold-bloodedness.

ASSUMPTION FAMILY PRINCIPLE QUESTIONS

> ## LEARNING OBJECTIVES
>
> In this section, you'll learn to:
>
> · Recognize Principle question stems.
> · Distinguish Identify the Principle questions from other Principle question types.
> · Use your knowledge of Assumption-based questions to attack Principle Assumption and Principle Strengthen questions.

Now that you've worked with several question types in the Assumption Family, let's turn our attention to Principle questions—a question type that often mimics Assumption Family questions. There has been an average of about five Principle questions per exam in recent years. Principle questions come in three main varieties: Identify the Principle, Apply the Principle, and Parallel Principle. In this section, you will learn to distinguish these three types, as well as how to attack argument-based Identify the Principle questions. You'll learn about Parallel Principle questions later in this chapter, and the remaining types of Principle questions will be covered in Chapter 11.

Recognizing Principle Question Stems

The common thread that appears throughout these three main Principle question types is the presence of a "principle." On the LSAT, a "principle" is a law-like general rule that can be applied not only to the particular situation in an argument but also to other, comparable situations. The question stem for a Principle question will often simply include the word *principle*. The words *proposition* or *policy*, as well as variations on the phrases "most closely conforms to" and "best illustrates," are all strong indicators of a Principle question. In general, any question that asks you to identify or apply a general rule is a Principle question.

Take a look at a few typical Principle question stems:

LSAT Question Stem		Analysis
Which one of the following principles, if established, most helps to justify the conclusion in the passage? *PrepTestB Sec1 Q14*	→	"The following principles" indicates this is a Principle question stem.
Which one of the following principles underlies the arbitrator's argument? *PrepTest29 Sec1 Q19*	→	"The following principles" is a clear indication that this is a Principle question.
The information above conforms most closely to which one of the following principles? *PrepTestB Sec4 Q12*	→	"Conforms most closely to" and "following principles" both indicate that this is a Principle question.

Distinguishing Types of Principle Questions

Identify the Principle questions, a subset of which we will be examining in this chapter, present a specific argument or set of events in the stimulus, then ask you to identify an applicable, more generalized principle in the answer choices. Because Identify the Principle questions move from specific in the stimulus to general in the conclusion, using a ∧ can be a great shorthand note to yourself while tackling Step 1 in these questions.

Apply the Principle questions do just the opposite: They will present a general principle in the stimulus (often expressed as a Formal Logic statement), then ask you to identify a more specific, nonconflicting situation in the correct answer choice. Similarly to ID the Principle questions, using a ∨ is a great way to shorthand that you are moving from a general statement in your stimulus to a specific situation in your answer choices.

Parallel Principle questions combine the actions used in Identify and Apply the Principle questions. First, identify the underlying principle in the specific situation in the stimulus. Then, apply that general principle to a new specific situation located in one of the answer choices. Your shorthand for this question type looks like this ◊ and represents moving from a specific stimulus to general and back to specific in the answer choices.

Practice

Take a look at the following question stems. Can you identify your specific task in each one?

LSAT Question Stem	My Analysis
46. Which one of the following principles, if established, most helps to justify the conclusion in the passage? *PrepTestB Sec1 Q14*	
47. Which one of the following principles underlies the arbitrator's argument? *PrepTest29 Sec1 Q19*	
48. The information above conforms most closely to which one of the following principles? *PrepTestB Sec4 Q12*	
49. This argument most closely conforms to which one of the following principles? *PrepTest24 Sec2 Q22*	
50. Which one of the following judgments most closely conforms to the principle described above? *PrepTest24 Sec3 Q24*	

Expert Analysis

Now take a look at how an LSAT Expert would break apart these question stems.

LSAT Question Stem	Analysis
46. Which one of the following principles, if established, most helps to justify the conclusion in the passage? *PrepTestB Sec1 Q14* →	"[W]hich of the following principles" indicates that the "following" answer choices are principles "justify[ing]" the "conclusion" in the stimulus. This is an Identify the Principle question. ^
47. Which one of the following principles underlies the arbitrator's argument? *PrepTest29 Sec1 Q19* →	This is an Identify the Principle question. But since the principle in the answer "underlies" the argument in the stimulus, it will be a broad statement of the argument's assumption. ^
48. The information above conforms most closely to which one of the following principles? *PrepTestB Sec4 Q12* →	"[W]hich one of the following principles" indicates that the "following" answer choices are principles that conform to the "information" in the stimulus. This is an Identify the Principle question. ^
49. This argument most closely conforms to which one of the following principles? *PrepTest24 Sec2 Q22* →	This is an Identify the Principle question. ^ But note that the stimulus here contains an "argument," which you should break down to evidence and conclusion.
50. Which one of the following judgments most closely conforms to the principle described above? *PrepTest24 Sec3 Q24* →	"[T]he principle described above" indicates that there is a general statement in the stimulus to which one of the "following" more specific judgments will conform. This question moves from general to specific, so it is an Apply the Principle question. ∨

Principle–Assumption and Principle–Strengthen Questions

As we mentioned earlier, Identify the Principle questions often mimic familiar Assumption Family question types. Specifically, you are likely to see Identify the Principle questions that mimic Assumption and Strengthen questions. For example, consider the following question stem:

Which one of the following is a principle underlying the advice given to police officers?

PrepTest29 Sec4 Q17

This question stems states that there is a principle "underlying" the advice in the stimulus. As a foundation underlies a house (it is unseen, but it holds the house together), so does an assumption underlie an argument (it is unstated, but holds the argument together). Thus, the correct answer will be a necessary assumption, and the stimulus should be attacked as you would attack a Necessary Assumption question stimulus: Find the conclusion and evidence and identify the disconnect. The only difference in approach will come in Step 3, when the scope of your prediction will be broadened. We'll discuss that difference in a moment. First, though, take a look at another example of a Principle question stem that mimics a different question type:

Which one of the following principles, if valid, most strongly supports the reasoning above?

PrepTest24 Sec2 Q25

The phrase "if valid, most strongly supports" sounds very much like phrasing from a Strengthen question stem. In this question, you can expect to see an argument with both a conclusion and evidence. Approach this question in the same way you would approach a Strengthen question, but expect the correct answer choice to be broader in scope and perhaps stronger in wording.

In fact, anticipating the broad wording of the correct answer is the only difference between tackling Assumption and Principle–Assumption questions, and between tackling Strengthen and Principle–Strengthen questions. Because Principle–Assumption questions and Principle–Strengthen questions move from specific situations in the stimulus to broadly worded answer choices (the choices describe principles, after all), once you have broken down the argument into evidence and conclusion and identified the assumption, take a moment to strip that assumption of words specific to the particular situation described in the stimulus. For example, if the stimulus in a Principle–Strengthen question discusses "bank managers," expect the correct answer to be written in terms applicable to any manager, or even any person. Or if the stimulus discusses "fertilization methods of tulips," anticipate a correct answer that discusses the fertilization of all bulbous plants, or even all plants.

Here's how an LSAT expert might analyze a Principle question that mimics a Strengthen question task.

LSAT Question	Analysis
The publisher of a best-selling self-help book had, in some promotional material, claimed that it showed readers how to become exceptionally successful. Of course, everyone knows that no book can deliver to the many what, by definition, must remain limited to the few: exceptional success. Thus, although it is clear that the publisher knowingly made a false claim, doing so should not be considered unethical in this case.	**Step 2:** Conclusion: The publisher's false claim was not unethical. *because* Evidence: Everyone should know that the publisher's claim was, by definition, impossible.
Which one of the following principles, if valid, most strongly supports the reasoning above?	**Step 1:** The phrase "principle[] . . . supports the reasoning" indicates a Principle-Strengthen question.
	Step 3: The prediction for a Principle-Strengthen question can simply rephrase the argument with the formulation: "If [this type of evidence], then [this conclusion]." In this case: If a false claim is something everyone knows to be impossible, then making such a claim is not unethical. Said more simply, making a false claim is unethical only when some people might think it could be true.
(A) Knowingly making a false claim is unethical only if it is reasonable for people to accept the claim as true.	**Step 4:** Correct. This choice matches the contrapositive of the prediction: If claim unethical, then possibly true.
(B) Knowingly making a false claim is unethical if those making it derive a gain at the expense of those acting as if the claim were true.	The argument does not identify or assume what conditions do make a claim unethical. Eliminate.
(C) Knowingly making a false claim is unethical in only those cases in which those who accept the claim as true suffer a hardship greater than the gain they were anticipating.	Outside the Scope. The argument does not refer to or depend on any such balancing of hardships. Eliminate.
(D) Knowingly making a false claim is unethical only if there is a possibility that someone will act as if the claim might be true.	Distortion. A similar structure as the correct answer but goes astray in focusing on whether it is possible someone might act as if the claim were true, rather than it being actually possible for the claim to be true. Eliminate.
(E) Knowingly making a false claim is unethical in at least those cases in which for someone else to discover that the claim is false, that person must have acted as if the claim were true.	Outside the Scope. The argument concerns the possibility of the claim actually being true, not the possibility of discovering it to be false. Eliminate.

PrepTest24 Sec2 Q25

Practice

Now that we have covered the basics of Principle-Assumption and Principle-Strengthen questions, try your hand at a few examples. Remember to approach them exactly the same way you would approach ordinary Assumption and Strengthen questions in Steps 1 and 2, while broadening your scope in Step 3. The expert analyses follow.

LSAT Question	My Analysis
51. If an artist receives a public subsidy to support work on a specific project—e.g., making a film—and if this project then proves successful enough to allow the artist to repay the subsidy, is the artist morally obliged to do so? The answer is clearly yes, since the money returned to the agency distributing the subsidies will be welcome as a source of support for other artists deserving of public subsidies.	Step 2:
Which one of the following principles, if established, most helps to justify the conclusion in the passage?	Step 1:
	Step 3:
(A) An artist has a moral duty to urge deserving fellow artists to try to obtain public subsidies, especially if those artists' projects promise to be financially successful.	Step 4:
(B) A financially successful artist should acknowledge that financial success is not solely a function of artistic merit.	
(C) A subsidy should be understood as creating a debt that, though routinely forgiven, is rightly forgiven only if either the debtor is unable to repay it or the creditor is not interested in repayment.	
(D) The provider of a subsidy should judge as most deserving of subsidies those whose projects are most likely to turn into financial successes.	
(E) An artist requesting a subsidy for a potentially profitable project should be required to make a reasonable effort to obtain a bank loan first.	

PrepTestB Sec1 Q14

621

LSAT Question	My Analysis
52. Editorial: Our society has a vested interest in maintaining a political system in which candidates are free to adhere to their principles. Yet campaigning for elected office is extremely costly, and because only the wealthiest individuals are able to finance their own political campaigns, most candidates must seek funding from private sources. In so doing, the candidates are almost invariably obliged to compromise their principles. Thus, government itself should assume the cost of candidates' campaigns.	**Step 2:**
Which one of the following principles, if valid, most helps to justify the conclusion as it is drawn in the argument?	**Step 1:**
	Step 3:
(A) Candidates should not run for elected office if doing so would compel the candidates to compromise their principles.	**Step 4:**
(B) Candidates wealthy enough to finance their own political campaigns should not be permitted to raise additional funds from private sources.	
(C) Voters should not support a candidate if that candidate is known to have accepted funding from private sources.	
(D) The government should finance a given activity if doing so will further a vested interest of society.	
(E) Private funding for political campaigns should be encouraged only if it redresses an imbalance among candidates' financial means.	

PrepTestB Sec1 Q24

LSAT Question	My Analysis
53. Arbitrator: The shipping manager admits that he decided to close the old facility on October 14 and to schedule the new facility's opening for October 17, the following Monday. But he also claims that he is not responsible for the business that was lost due to the new facility's failing to open as scheduled. He blames the contractor for not finishing on time, but he too, is to blame, for he was aware of the contractor's typical delays and should have planned for this contingency.	**Step 2:**
Which one of the following principles underlies the arbitrator's argument?	**Step 1:**
	Step 3:
(A) A manager should take foreseeable problems into account when making decisions.	**Step 4:**
(B) A manager should be able to depend on contractors to do their jobs promptly.	
(C) A manager should see to it that contractors do their jobs promptly.	
(D) A manager should be held responsible for mistakes made by those whom the manager directly supervises.	
(E) A manager, and only a manager, should be held responsible for a project's failure.	

PrepTest29 Sec1 Q19

Expert Analysis

Now look at the approach an LSAT expert took.

LSAT Question	Analysis
51. If an artist receives a public subsidy to support work on a specific project—e.g., making a film—and if this project then proves successful enough to allow the artist to repay the subsidy, is the artist morally obliged to do so? The answer is clearly yes, since the money returned to the agency distributing the subsidies will be welcome as a source of support for other artists deserving of public subsidies.	**Step 2:** Conclusion: An artist is morally obliged to repay a public subsidy if the artist's project is successful. *because* Evidence: The public agency would welcome the money for use in supporting other artists deserving of public subsidies.
Which one of the following principles, if established, most helps to justify the conclusion in the passage?	**Step 1:** The question stem directs you to identify a principle to help "justify the conclusion," which indicates a Principle–Strengthen question.

	Step 3: The argument assumes that these circumstances result in a moral obligation to repay:
	    If 1) able to repay and 2) repayment would be welcome, then morally obligated to repay.
	
	And, in the contrapositive:
	    If no moral obligation to repay, then 1) not able to repay or 2) repayment not welcome.
	
	The correct answer choice will broadly take one of these two forms.

(A) An artist has a moral duty to urge deserving fellow artists to try to obtain public subsidies, especially if those artists' projects promise to be financially successful.	**Step 4:** Distortion. The argument concerns a moral duty to repay, not to urge fellow artists to seek subsidies. Eliminate.
(B) A financially successful artist should acknowledge that financial success is not solely a function of artistic merit.	Distortion. The argument concerns a moral duty to repay, not to acknowledge financial success. Eliminate.
(C) A subsidy should be understood as creating a debt that, though routinely forgiven, is rightly forgiven only if either the debtor is unable to repay it or the creditor is not interested in repayment.	Correct. This choice matches the contrapositive form of the prediction: For debt to be forgiven (no obligation to repay), then not able to repay or repayment not welcome.
(D) The provider of a subsidy should judge as most deserving of subsidies those whose projects are most likely to turn into financial successes.	Outside the Scope. The argument is not concerned with which projects are most deserving of subsidies. Eliminate.
(E) An artist requesting a subsidy for a potentially profitable project should be required to make a reasonable effort to obtain a bank loan first. *PrepTestB Sec1 Q14*	Outside the Scope. Any eligibility conditions for obtaining the subsidy in the first place are irrelevant to this argument regarding repayment. Eliminate.

LSAT Question	Analysis
52. Editorial: Our society has a vested interest in maintaining a political system in which candidates are free to adhere to their principles. Yet campaigning for elected office is extremely costly, and because only the wealthiest individuals are able to finance their own political campaigns, most candidates must seek funding from private sources. In so doing, the candidates are almost invariably obliged to compromise their principles. Thus, government itself should assume the cost of candidates' campaigns.	**Step 2:** Conclusion: The government should finance election campaigns. *because* Evidence: Most candidates have to compromise their principles in seeking financing from wealthy private individuals.
Which one of the following principles, if valid, most helps to justify the conclusion as it is drawn in the argument?	**Step 1:** The phrasing "principles, if valid, most helps to justify" indicates a Principle-Strengthen question.
	Step 3: The correct answer should set out a rule that states that the government should finance election campaigns in situations where candidates would have to compromise their principles otherwise. The correct choice could be phrased more broadly than the terms of the argument.
(A) Candidates should not run for elected office if doing so would compel the candidates to compromise their principles.	**Step 4:** Distortion. This choice fails to set out a rule that results in government financing election campaigns. Eliminate.
(B) Candidates wealthy enough to finance their own political campaigns should not be permitted to raise additional funds from private sources.	Distortion. This choice fails to set out a rule that results in government financing election campaigns. Eliminate.
(C) Voters should not support a candidate if that candidate is known to have accepted funding from private sources.	Distortion. This choice fails to set out a rule that results in government financing election campaigns. Eliminate.
(D) The government should finance a given activity if doing so will further a vested interest of society.	Correct. This choice is stated far more broadly than the terms of the argument, but financing elections falls under the category of financing a "given activity" and avoiding candidates compromising their principles falls under the category of "further[ing] a vested interest of society."
(E) Private funding for political campaigns should be encouraged only if it redresses an imbalance among candidates' financial means. *PrepTestB Sec1 Q24*	Distortion. The author argues that campaigns should be funded by the public. He doesn't offer criteria for when private funding should be used. Eliminate.

	LSAT Question		Analysis
53.	Arbitrator: The shipping manager admits that he decided to close the old facility on October 14 and to schedule the new facility's opening for October 17, the following Monday. But he also claims that he is not responsible for the business that was lost due to the new facility's failing to open as scheduled. He blames the contractor for not finishing on time, but he too, is to blame, for he was aware of the contractor's typical delays and should have planned for this contingency.	→	**Step 2:** Conclusion: The manager shares at least some blame for the lost business. *because* Evidence: The manager was aware of the typical delays and failed to plan for them.
	Which one of the following principles underlies the arbitrator's argument?	→	**Step 1:** The phrase "principle[] underl[ying] the . . . argument" indicates a Principle-Assumption question.
			Step 3: The arbitrator assumes that managers who are aware of and then fail to plan for a problem are then responsible for the consequences of that problem. The correct answer in this Principle Assumption question may use broader language.
(A)	A manager should take foreseeable problems into account when making decisions.	→	**Step 4:** Correct. The contractor's typical delays fall under the category of "foreseeable problems" and planning for contingencies falls under the category of "making decisions."
(B)	A manager should be able to depend on contractors to do their jobs promptly.	→	180. The arbitrator ruled that the manager should not depend on the contractor, but instead plan for likely delays. Eliminate.
(C)	A manager should see to it that contractors do their jobs promptly.	→	Distortion. The arbitrator ruled that the manager should plan for a delay, not necessarily prevent any such delay. This choice changes the terms of the argument, not just broadens them. Eliminate.
(D)	A manager should be held responsible for mistakes made by those whom the manager directly supervises.	→	Distortion. First, it is unclear whether the manager "directly supervises" the contractor. Second, the problem is contractor delays, not "mistakes." A "delay" does not fall neatly under the category of a "mistake." Eliminate.
(E)	A manager, and only a manager, should be held responsible for a project's failure. *PrepTest29 Sec1 Q19*	→	Distortion. The arbitrator actually rules that the manager *shares* at least some of the blame, and not that he is solely to blame. Eliminate.

PARALLEL FLAW QUESTIONS

LEARNING OBJECTIVE

In this section, you'll learn to:

· Identify and answer Parallel Flaw questions.

Your initial approach to Parallel Flaw questions should be the same as your approach to Flaw questions. Identify the author's conclusion and evidence, and determine why her assumption is flawed. The correct answer will contain an argument that is flawed in precisely the same way. You are likely to see one of the common reasoning errors in Parallel Flaw questions—Causation versus Correlation; Necessity versus Sufficiency; Unrepresentative Sample; and so on. Just as you learned to do in Parallel Reasoning questions (Chapter 9), you can also approach Parallel Flaw questions by identifying the type of conclusion used in the stimulus argument. The correct answer's conclusion type will match.

Be aware that many Parallel Flaw questions will contain Formal Logic. When you see Formal Logic in a Parallel Flaw stimulus, jot the terms down in some sort of shorthand—you'll see in our explanations that we use letters to represent the various terms in Formal Logic statements. Doing this will help you identify more easily how the argument is flawed and find an answer choice that commits the same reasoning error in the same way. For example, imagine a stimulus that says: "John plays catch whenever he goes to the beach. John said he played catch yesterday, so he must have been at the beach." This argument confuses necessary and sufficient terms. Let (A) replace "John plays catch" and let (B) replace "beach." The argument's structure is now revealed: whenever (B) → (A). Therefore, because (A) → (B). You would then seek an answer choice that messes up Formal Logic terms in the same way.

LSAT STRATEGY

When approaching Parallel Flaw questions:

· Characterize the flaw in the stimulus argument; the correct answer will be flawed in precisely the same way.

· You may compare the conclusion in stimulus argument to those in the answer choice arguments.

· Be on the lookout for flawed Formal Logic.

Here's an example of an LSAT expert's analysis of a Parallel Flaw argument.

LSAT Question	Analysis
A local chemical plant produces pesticides that can cause sterility in small mammals such as otters. Soon after the plant began operating, the incidence of sterility among the otters that swim in a nearby river increased dramatically. Therefore, pesticides are definitely contaminating the river. →	**Step 2:** Conclusion: It is certain that pesticides are contaminating the river. *because* Evidence: Pesticides produced at the plant could cause sterility in otters living in the river, and recently more otters in the river have become sterile.
Which one of the following arguments contains a flaw in reasoning that is similar to one in the argument above? →	**Step 1:** The phrase "flaw . . . similar to" indicates a Parallel Flaw question.
	Step 3: The conclusion is a definite assertion of causation based on evidence of a potential cause. The correct answer will contain a causal argument that contains that same shift from a potential cause to definite cause.
(A) The bacteria that cause tetanus live in the digestive tract of horses. Tetanus is a highly infectious disease. Consequently it must be that horses contract tetanus more frequently than do most other animals. →	**Step 4:** This choice can be eliminated based on the conclusion type: a comparison ("horses . . . more frequently than . . . other animals"). Eliminate.
(B) A diet low in calcium can cause a drop in egg production in poultry. When chickens on a local farm were let out in the spring to forage for food, their egg production dropped noticeably. So the food found and eaten by the chickens is undeniably low in calcium. →	Correct. This choice contains a shift from a potential cause of the drop in egg production (diet low in calcium) to a claim that the diet must be the cause of the drop in egg production.
(C) Animals that are undernourished are very susceptible to infection. Animals in the largest metropolitan zoos are not undernourished, so they surely must not be very susceptible to disease. →	Rather than jumping from a possible cause to a definite cause, this choice commits a Formal Logic flaw; the conclusion is an incomplete contrapositive of the evidence (negates both terms without reversing the sides). Eliminate.
(D) Apes are defined by having, among other characteristics, opposable thumbs and no external tail. Recently, fossil remains of a previously unknown animal were found. Because this animal had opposable thumbs, it must have been an ape. →	This argument assumes that meeting one necessary condition (out of the two mentioned) for being an ape is sufficient to guarantee it is an ape. Not a match. Eliminate.
(E) The only animal that could have produced a track similar to this one is a bear. But there are no bears in this area of the country, so this animal track is a fake. *PrepTest27 Sec1 Q11* →	This argument proceeds by eliminating the sole plausible explanation to conclude something is a fake. Not a match. Eliminate.

Practice

Now, try a Parallel Flaw question on your own. Work through it using the strategies you've just learned; then check the following page to see how an LSAT expert would approach the same question.

LSAT Question	My Analysis
54. Linda says that, as a scientist, she knows that no scientist appreciates poetry. And, since most scientists are logical, at least some of the people who appreciate poetry are illogical.	**Step 2:**
Which one of the following is most parallel in its reasoning to the flawed reasoning above?	**Step 1:**
	Step 3:
(A) Ralph says that, as an expert in biology, he knows that no marsupial lays eggs. And, since most marsupials are native to Australia, at least some of the animals native to Australia do not lay eggs.	**Step 4:**
(B) Franz says that, as a father of four children, he knows that no father wants children to eat candy at bedtime. And, since most fathers are adults, at least some of the people who want children to eat candy at bedtime are children.	
(C) Yuri says that, as a wine connoisseur, he knows that no wine aged in metal containers is equal in quality to the best wine aged in oak. And, since most California wine is aged in metal containers, California wine is inferior to at least the best French wine aged in oak.	
(D) Xi says that, as an experienced photographer, she knows that no color film produces images as sharp as the best black-and-white film. And, since most instant film is color film, at least some instant film produces images less sharp than the best black-and-white film.	
(E) Betty says that, as a corporate executive, she knows that no corporate executives like to pay taxes. And, since most corporate executives are honest people, at least some people who like to pay taxes are honest people.	

PrepTest29 Sec1 Q23

Expert Analysis

Here's how an LSAT expert applied the Logical Reasoning Method to the question you just tried.

LSAT Question	Analysis
54. Linda says that, as a scientist, she knows that no scientist appreciates poetry. And, since most scientists are logical, at least some of the people who appreciate poetry are illogical.	**Step 2:** Conclusion: Some of the people who appreciate poetry are illogical. *because* Evidence: 1) Most scientists are logical, and 2) no scientists appreciate poetry.
Which one of the following is most parallel in its reasoning to the flawed reasoning above?	**Step 1:** The phrase "most parallel . . . to the flawed reasoning" indicates a Parallel Flaw question.
	Step 3: The evidence supports the deduction that at least *some logical* people do *not appreciate* poetry. The author instead concludes that *some illogical* people *do appreciate* poetry. The conclusion, then, simply negates both terms from the evidence. Look for an answer choice that does the same.
(A) Ralph says that, as an expert in biology, he knows that no marsupial lays eggs. And, since most marsupials are native to Australia, at least some of the animals native to Australia do not lay eggs.	**Step 4:** 180. This argument is not flawed. The evidence does support a conclusion that at least some of the animals native to Australia do not lay eggs. Eliminate.
(B) Franz says that, as a father of four children, he knows that no father wants children to eat candy at bedtime. And, since most fathers are adults, at least some of the people who want children to eat candy at bedtime are children.	Correct. This matches the structure of the stimulus. The evidence supports the deduction that at least *some adults* do *not want* children to eat candy at bedtime, but the conclusion states that *some non-adults* do *want* children to eat candy at bedtime
(C) Yuri says that, as a wine connoisseur, he knows that no wine aged in metal containers is equal in quality to the best wine aged in oak. And, since most California wine is aged in metal containers, California wine is inferior to at least the best French wine aged in oak.	Distortion. This argument does not contain a blatant flaw, as does the stimulus. It does assume that the "best French wine aged in oak" is equivalent to the "best wine aged in oak". The stimulus does not make a similar assumption. Eliminate.
(D) Xi says that, as an experienced photographer, she knows that no color film produces images as sharp as the best black-and-white film. And, since most instant film is color film, at least some instant film produces images less sharp than the best black-and-white film.	180. This argument is not flawed. The evidence does support a conclusion that at least some instant film produces images less sharp than the best black-and-white film. Eliminate.
(E) Betty says that, as a corporate executive, she knows that no corporate executives like to pay taxes. And, since most corporate executives are honest people, at least some people who like to pay taxes are honest people. *PrepTest29 Sec1 Q23*	Distortion. The evidence in this argument supports the deduction that at least some honest people do not like to pay taxes. The conclusion instead asserts that at least some honest people do like to pay taxes. To match the stimulus, the argument would have to conclude that at least some dishonest people do like to pay taxes. Eliminate.

PARALLEL PRINCIPLE QUESTIONS

The final question type we'll discuss in this chapter asks you to identify the principle underlying the argument in the stimulus and then apply the principle to a similar argument in the correct answer. These Parallel Principle questions appear rarely on the LSAT. One has been included on only about half of all recently administered LSATs. Fortunately, Parallel Principle questions are very similar to Parallel Reasoning and Parallel Flaw questions, so if you feel comfortable with those other question types, you should feel comfortable with Parallel Principle questions as well.

In the same way that the stimulus and correct answer in Parallel Flaw questions both contain the same faulty pattern of reasoning, the stimulus and correct answer in Parallel Principle questions both follow the same principle. Parallel Principle questions are similar to Parallel Reasoning and Parallel Flaw questions in that the correct answer will likely discuss a different topic than the stimulus; the only requirement is that the correct answer must be founded on the same principle as the stimulus. To attack Parallel Principle questions efficiently, identify the principle—the broad, general rule—at work in the stimulus and then go through the choices to find the one that applies the identical principle.

Practice

Now, try a Parallel Principle question on your own. When you finish, compare your work with the expert's analysis on the next page.

LSAT Question	My Analysis
55. Parents should not necessarily raise their children in the ways experts recommend, even if some of those experts are themselves parents. After all, parents are the ones who directly experience which methods are successful in raising their own children.	**Step 2:**
Which one of the following most closely conforms to the principle that the passage above illustrates?	**Step 1:**
	Step 3:
(A) Although music theory is intrinsically interesting and may be helpful to certain musicians, it does not distinguish good music from bad: that is a matter of taste and not of theory.	**Step 4:**
(B) One need not pay much attention to the advice of automotive experts when buying a car if those experts are not interested in the mundane factors that concern the average consumer.	
(C) In deciding the best way to proceed, a climber familiar with a mountain might do well to ignore the advice of mountain climbing experts unfamiliar with that mountain.	
(D) A typical farmer is less likely to know what types of soil are most productive than is someone with an advanced degree in agricultural science.	
(E) Unlike society, one's own conscience speaks with a single voice; it is better to follow the advice of one's own conscience than the advice of society.	

PrepTest29 Sec4 Q10

Expert Analysis

Here's how an LSAT expert applied the Logical Reasoning Method to the question you just tried.

LSAT Question	Analysis
55. Parents should not necessarily raise their children in the ways experts recommend, even if some of those experts are themselves parents. After all, parents are the ones who directly experience which methods are successful in raising their own children. →	**Step 2:** Conclusion: Parents don't need listen to experts when raising children. Evidence: Parents have the direct experience in seeing what is successful in raising their own children.
Which one of the following most closely conforms to the principle that the passage above illustrates? →	**Step 1:** This question stem asks for a situation that "conforms to" the principle "illustrated" above. So the principle is never explicitly stated in the stimulus, but the specific situation in the stimulus and the correct answer choice will each share the same principle—this is a Parallel Principle question.
	Step 3: Paraphrase the argument in the stimulus in a broad, general form: "If [this evidence], then [this conclusion]": If somebody has direct experience in a matter, then they don't need to listen to experts. The correct answer will contain a specific situation that matches that general rule.
(A) Although music theory is intrinsically interesting and may be helpful to certain musicians, it does not distinguish good music from bad: that is a matter of taste and not of theory. →	**Step 4:** There is nothing in this answer choice about direct experience, so it's not a match. Eliminate.
(B) One need not pay much attention to the advice of automotive experts when buying a car if those experts are not interested in the mundane factors that concern the average consumer. →	While the conclusion here matches the claim that one doesn't need to listen to experts, the evidence provided is not about consumers' direct experiences. Eliminate.
(C) In deciding the best way to proceed, a climber familiar with a mountain might do well to ignore the advice of mountain climbing experts unfamiliar with that mountain. →	Correct. The conclusion that one doesn't need to heed experts is backed up by evidence regarding a climber's direct experience.
(D) A typical farmer is less likely to know what types of soil are most productive than is someone with an advanced degree in agricultural science. →	180. This implies that a typical farmer should listen to experts. Eliminate.
(E) Unlike society, one's own conscience speaks with a single voice; it is better to follow the advice of one's own conscience than the advice of society. *PrepTest29 Sec4 Q10* →	There is nothing in this choice about having direct experience; additionally, it says not to heed *society*, instead of saying not to heed *experts*. Eliminate.

IDENTIFYING QUESTION STEMS

You've seen how the LSAT can test your ability to analyze and evaluate argument-based questions in a number of different ways. On Test Day, it will be essential for you to be able to differentiate among question types. If you struggle to understand what a question is asking or how to get to the right answer, you'll lose valuable time and energy. Experts know that the path to success in the Logical Reasoning section is to become familiar with each question type and to know immediately how to attack each question.

Practice

For each of the following question stems, identify the question type and mentally characterize the correct answer. Then compare your thinking to the expert analysis that follows.

Question Stem	My Analysis
56. Which of the following, if added to the premises, allows the argument's conclusion to be properly drawn?	
57. Which of the following best characterizes the argument's error of reasoning?	
58. Each of the following, if true, casts doubt on the argument EXCEPT:	
59. In evaluating the argument's conclusion, it would be most valuable to know whether	
60. Which of the following is an assumption required by the argument?	
61. Which of the following, if true, would do most to justify the conclusion drawn above?	
62. Which of the following, if true, most calls into question the argument above?	
63. The reasoning in the argument above is questionable because	

Question Stem	**My Analysis**
64. Which of the following is an assumption upon which the argument depends?	
65. The argument is vulnerable to criticism on which of the following grounds?	
66. Which of the following lends most support to the argument above?	
67. The conclusion drawn above is unwarranted because	
68. Which of the following principles most helps to justify the reasoning above?	
69. The conclusion of the argument follows logically if which one of the following is presupposed?	
70. Which of the following, if true, most undermines the argument above?	
71. The author makes which one of the following assumptions?	
72. The flawed reasoning in which one of the following is most similar to that in the argument above?	

Expert Analysis

Here's how an LSAT expert would characterize the question stems in that exercise.

Question Stem		Analysis
56. Which of the following, if added to the premises, allows the argument's conclusion to be properly drawn?	$\longrightarrow$	Sufficient Assumption question. The correct answer will guarantee the conclusion.
57. Which of the following best characterizes the argument's error of reasoning?	$\longrightarrow$	Flaw question. The correct answer will describe the argument's flawed assumption.
58. Each of the following, if true, casts doubt on the argument EXCEPT:	$\longrightarrow$	Weaken EXCEPT question. Incorrect choices will each weaken the argument's conclusion. The correct answer will be a strengthener or will have no impact on the conclusion.
59. In evaluating the argument's conclusion, it would be most valuable to know whether	$\longrightarrow$	Evaluate question. The correct answer will provide information that, if true, will either strengthen or weaken the conclusion and, if false, will have the opposite effect. Incorrect choices will be irrelevant, having no effect on the conclusion's likelihood.
60. Which of the following is an assumption required by the argument?	$\longrightarrow$	Necessary Assumption question. The correct answer will state an assumption that is necessary for the conclusion to stand. Confirm the correct answer using the Denial Test: when a necessary assumption is negated, the conclusion falls apart.
61. Which of the following, if true, would do most to justify the conclusion drawn above?	$\longrightarrow$	Strengthen question. The correct answer will strengthen conclusion by supporting the argument's assumption.
62. Which of the following, if true, most calls into question the argument above?	$\longrightarrow$	Weaken question. The correct answer will weaken conclusion by attacking the argument's assumption.
63. The reasoning in the argument above is questionable because	$\longrightarrow$	Flaw question. The correct answer will describe the argument's flawed assumption.

Question Stem	Analysis
64. Which of the following is an assumption upon which the argument depends?	Necessary Assumption question. The correct answer will state an assumption that is necessary for the conclusion to stand. Confirm the correct answer using the Denial Test: when correct answer is negated, the conclusion falls apart.
65. The argument is vulnerable to criticism on which of the following grounds?	Flaw question. The correct answer will describe the argument's flawed assumption.
66. Which of the following lends most support to the argument above?	Strengthen question. The correct answer will strengthen the conclusion by supporting the argument's assumption.
67. The conclusion drawn above is unwarranted because	Flaw question. The correct answer will describe the argument's flawed assumption.
68. Which of the following principles most helps to justify the reasoning above?	Principle-Strengthen question. The correct answer will strengthen the conclusion in broadly worded terms.
69. The conclusion of the argument follows logically if which one of the following is presupposed?	Sufficient Assumption question. The correct answer will guarantee the conclusion.
70. Which of the following, if true, most undermines the argument above?	Weaken question. Correct answer will weaken the conclusion by attacking the argument's assumption.
71. The author makes which one of the following assumptions?	Necessary Assumption question. The correct answer will state an assumption that is necessary for the conclusion to stand. Confirm the correct answer using the Denial Test: when a necessary assumption is negated, the conclusion falls apart.
72. The flawed reasoning in which one of the following is most similar to that in the argument above?	Parallel Flaw question. The correct answer will contain an argument that is flawed in the same way as the argument in the stimulus is flawed.

Reflection

You may find that as you work through more and more argument-based questions, you start to notice the weak points in the arguments that you confront in everyday life—in advertisements, on the news, in written articles, in conversations. That's a good thing! If you are noticing that a television news anchor has just made an assumption, or thinking about how an article in a popular science journal could strengthen its main point, or thinking about how you could knock down a friend's argument against going to see your favorite jazz band with you, or noticing that a subway advertisement leaps to a conclusion without considering alternate possibilities, then you are learning to think like a lawyer. The more you can engage with the arguments you encounter on a daily basis in a skeptical, thoughtful way, the better prepared you will be for the LSAT and for what lies ahead in law school.

QUESTION POOL

Assumption

Assess your skills on some further examples of Assumption questions.

1. Naturalist: The recent claims that the Tasmanian tiger is not extinct are false. The Tasmanian tiger's natural habitat was taken over by sheep farming decades ago, resulting in the animal's systematic elimination from the area. Since then naturalists working in the region have discovered no hard evidence of its survival, such as carcasses or tracks. In spite of alleged sightings of the animal, the Tasmanian tiger no longer exists.

Which one of the following is an assumption on which the naturalist's argument depends?

(A) Sheep farming drove the last Tasmanian tigers to starvation by chasing them from their natural habitat.
(B) Some scavengers in Tasmania are capable of destroying tiger carcasses without a trace.
(C) Every naturalist working in the Tasmanian tiger's natural habitat has looked systematically for evidence of the tiger's survival.
(D) The Tasmanian tiger did not move and adapt to a different region in response to the loss of habitat.
(E) Those who have reported sightings of the Tasmanian tiger are not experienced naturalists.

PrepTestJun07 Sec3 Q9

2. Feathers recently taken from seabirds stuffed and preserved in the 1880s have been found to contain only half as much mercury as feathers recently taken from living birds of the same species. Since mercury that accumulates in a seabird's feathers as the feathers grow is derived from fish eaten by the bird, these results indicate that mercury levels in saltwater fish are higher now than they were 100 years ago.

The argument depends on assuming that

(A) the proportion of a seabird's diet consisting of fish was not as high, on average, in the 1880s as it is today
(B) the amount of mercury in a saltwater fish depends on the amount of pollution in the ocean habitat of the fish
(C) mercury derived from fish is essential for the normal growth of a seabird's feathers
(D) the stuffed seabirds whose feathers were tested for mercury were not fully grown
(E) the process used to preserve birds in the 1880s did not substantially decrease the amount of mercury in the birds' feathers

PrepTestJun07 Sec3 Q11

The explanations to these questions begin on page 649.

3. A new government policy has been developed to avoid many serious cases of influenza. This goal will be accomplished by the annual vaccination of high-risk individuals: everyone 65 and older as well as anyone with a chronic disease that might cause them to experience complications from the influenza virus. Each year's vaccination will protect only against the strain of the influenza virus deemed most likely to be prevalent that year, so every year it will be necessary for all high-risk individuals to receive a vaccine for a different strain of the virus.

Which one of the following is an assumption that would allow the conclusion above to be properly drawn?

(A) The number of individuals in the high-risk group for influenza will not significantly change from year to year.
(B) The likelihood that a serious influenza epidemic will occur varies from year to year.
(C) No vaccine for the influenza virus protects against more than one strain of that virus.
(D) Each year the strain of influenza virus deemed most likely to be prevalent will be one that had not previously been deemed most likely to be prevalent.
(E) Each year's vaccine will have fewer side effects than the vaccine of the previous year since the technology for making vaccines will constantly improve.

PrepTestJun07 Sec2 Q15

4. An undergraduate degree is necessary for appointment to the executive board. Further, no one with a felony conviction can be appointed to the board. Thus, Murray, an accountant with both a bachelor's and a master's degree, cannot be accepted for the position of Executive Administrator, since he has a felony conviction.

The argument's conclusion follows logically if which one of the following is assumed?

(A) Anyone with a master's degree and without a felony conviction is eligible for appointment to the executive board.
(B) Only candidates eligible for appointment to the executive board can be accepted for the position of Executive Administrator.
(C) An undergraduate degree is not necessary for acceptance for the position of Executive Administrator.
(D) If Murray did not have a felony conviction, he would be accepted for the position of Executive Administrator.
(E) The felony charge on which Murray was convicted is relevant to the duties of the position of Executive Administrator.

PrepTestJun07 Sec2 Q6

Flaw

Assess your skills on some further examples of Flaw questions.

5. Advertisement: Fabric-Soft leaves clothes soft and fluffy, and its fresh scent is a delight. We conducted a test using over 100 consumers to prove Fabric-Soft is best. Each consumer was given one towel washed with Fabric-Soft and one towel washed without it. Ninety-nine percent of the consumers preferred the Fabric-Soft towel. So Fabric-Soft is the most effective fabric softener available.

    The advertisement's reasoning is most vulnerable to criticism on the grounds that it fails to consider whether

    (A) any of the consumers tested are allergic to fabric softeners
    (B) Fabric-Soft is more or less harmful to the environment than other fabric softeners
    (C) Fabric-Soft is much cheaper or more expensive than other fabric softeners
    (D) the consumers tested find the benefits of using fabric softeners worth the expense
    (E) the consumers tested had the opportunity to evaluate fabric softeners other than Fabric-Soft

    PrepTestJun07 Sec3 Q8

6. Editorialist: In all cultures, it is almost universally accepted that one has a moral duty to prevent members of one's family from being harmed. Thus, few would deny that if a person is known by the person's parents to be falsely accused of a crime, it would be morally right for the parents to hide the accused from the police. Hence, it is also likely to be widely accepted that it is sometimes morally right to obstruct the police in their work.

    The reasoning in the editorialist's argument is most vulnerable to criticism on the grounds that this argument

    (A) utilizes a single type of example for the purpose of justifying a broad generalization
    (B) fails to consider the possibility that other moral principles would be widely recognized as overriding any obligation to protect a family member from harm
    (C) presumes, without providing justification, that allowing the police to arrest an innocent person assists rather than obstructs justice
    (D) takes for granted that there is no moral obligation to obey the law
    (E) takes for granted that the parents mentioned in the example are not mistaken about their child's innocence

    PrepTestJun07 Sec3 Q18

7. Some anthropologists argue that the human species could not have survived prehistoric times if the species had not evolved the ability to cope with diverse natural environments. However, there is considerable evidence that *Australopithecus afarensis*, a prehistoric species related to early humans, also thrived in a diverse array of environments, but became extinct. Hence, the anthropologists' claim is false.

    The reasoning in the argument is most vulnerable to criticism on the grounds that the argument

    (A) confuses a condition's being required for a given result to occur in one case with the condition's being sufficient for such a result to occur in a similar case
    (B) takes for granted that if one species had a characteristic that happened to enable it to survive certain conditions, at least one related extinct species must have had the same characteristic
    (C) generalizes, from the fact that one species with a certain characteristic survived certain conditions, that all related species with the same characteristic must have survived exactly the same conditions
    (D) fails to consider the possibility that *Australopithecus afarensis* had one or more characteristics that lessened its chances of surviving prehistoric times
    (E) fails to consider the possibility that, even if a condition caused a result to occur in one case, it was not necessary to cause the result to occur in a similar case

    PrepTestJun07 Sec3 Q25

Strengthen/Weaken

Assess your skills on some further examples of Strengthen/Weaken questions.

8. Although video game sales have increased steadily over the past 3 years, we can expect a reversal of this trend in the very near future. Historically, over three quarters of video games sold have been purchased by people from 13 to 16 years of age, and the number of people in this age group is expected to decline steadily over the next 10 years.

Which one of the following, if true, would most seriously weaken the argument?

(A)   Most people 17 years old or older have never purchased a video game.

(B)   Video game rentals have declined over the past 3 years.

(C)   New technology will undoubtedly make entirely new entertainment options available over the next 10 years.

(D)   The number of different types of video games available is unlikely to decrease in the near future.

(E)   Most of the people who have purchased video games over the past 3 years are over the age of 16.

PrepTestJun07 Sec2 Q9

9. A cup of raw milk, after being heated in a microwave oven to 50 degrees Celsius, contains half its initial concentration of a particular enzyme, lysozyme. If, however, the milk reaches that temperature through exposure to a conventional heat source of 50 degrees Celsius, it will contain nearly all of its initial concentration of the enzyme. Therefore, what destroys the enzyme is not heat but microwaves, which generate heat.

Which one of the following, if true, most seriously weakens the argument?

(A)   Heating raw milk in a microwave oven to a temperature of 100 degrees Celsius destroys nearly all of the lysozyme initially present in that milk.

(B)   Enzymes in raw milk that are destroyed through excessive heating can be replaced by adding enzymes that have been extracted from other sources.

(C)   A liquid exposed to a conventional heat source of exactly 50 degrees Celsius will reach that temperature more slowly than it would if it were exposed to a conventional heat source hotter than 50 degrees Celsius.

(D)   Milk that has been heated in a microwave oven does not taste noticeably different from milk that has been briefly heated by exposure to a conventional heat source.

(E)   Heating any liquid by microwave creates small zones within it that are much hotter than the overall temperature that the liquid will ultimately reach.

PrepTestJun07 Sec2 Q14

10. A consumer magazine surveyed people who had sought a psychologist's help with a personal problem. Of those responding who had received treatment for 6 months or less, 20 percent claimed that treatment "made things a lot better." Of those responding who had received longer treatment, 36 percent claimed that treatment "made things a lot better." Therefore, psychological treatment lasting more than 6 months is more effective than shorter-term treatment.

Which one of the following, if true, most seriously weakens the argument?

(A) Of the respondents who had received treatment for longer than 6 months, 10 percent said that treatment made things worse.

(B) Patients who had received treatment for longer than 6 months were more likely to respond to the survey than were those who had received treatment for a shorter time.

(C) Patients who feel they are doing well in treatment tend to remain in treatment, while those who are doing poorly tend to quit earlier.

(D) Patients who were dissatisfied with their treatment were more likely to feel a need to express their feelings about it and thus to return the survey.

(E) Many psychologists encourage their patients to receive treatment for longer than 6 months.

PrepTestJun07 Sec3 Q15

11. Editor: Many candidates say that if elected they will reduce governmental intrusion into voters' lives. But voters actually elect politicians who instead promise that the government will provide assistance to solve their most pressing problems. Governmental assistance, however, costs money, and money can come only from taxes, which can be considered a form of governmental intrusion. Thus, governmental intrusion into the lives of voters will rarely be substantially reduced over time in a democracy.

Which one of the following, if true, would most strengthen the editor's argument?

(A) Politicians who win their elections usually keep their campaign promises.

(B) Politicians never promise what they really intend to do once in office.

(C) The most common problems people have are financial problems.

(D) Governmental intrusion into the lives of voters is no more burdensome in nondemocratic countries than it is in democracies.

(E) Politicians who promise to do what they actually believe ought to be done are rarely elected.

PrepTestJun07 Sec3 Q19

12. Ethicist: On average, animals raised on grain must be fed sixteen pounds of grain to produce one pound of meat. A pound of meat is more nutritious for humans than a pound of grain, but sixteen pounds of grain could feed many more people than could a pound of meat. With grain yields leveling off, large areas of farmland going out of production each year, and the population rapidly expanding, we must accept the fact that consumption of meat will soon be morally unacceptable.

Which one of the following, if true, would most weaken the ethicist's argument?

(A) Even though it has been established that a vegetarian diet can be healthy, many people prefer to eat meat and are willing to pay for it.

(B) Often, cattle or sheep can be raised to maturity on grass from pastureland that is unsuitable for any other kind of farming.

(C) If a grain diet is supplemented with protein derived from non-animal sources, it can have nutritional value equivalent to that of a diet containing meat.

(D) Although prime farmland near metropolitan areas is being lost rapidly to suburban development, we could reverse this trend by choosing to live in areas that are already urban.

(E) Nutritionists agree that a diet composed solely of grain products is not adequate for human health.

PrepTestJun07 Sec3 Q21

Assumption-Family Principle

Assess your skills with some further examples of Assumption-Family Principle questions.

13. Sociologist: Romantics who claim that people are not
    born evil but may be made evil by the imperfect
    institutions that they form cannot be right, for
    they misunderstand the causal relationship
    between people and their institutions. After all,
    institutions are merely collections of people.

    Which one of the following principles, if valid, would
    most help to justify the sociologist's argument?

    (A)   People acting together in institutions can do
          more good or evil than can people acting
          individually.
    (B)   Institutions formed by people are inevitably
          imperfect.
    (C)   People should not be overly optimistic in their
          view of individual human beings.
    (D)   A society's institutions are the surest gauge of
          that society's values.
    (E)   The whole does not determine the properties of
          the things that compose it.

    PrepTestJun07 Sec3 Q24

Parallel Flaw

Assess your skills with some further examples of Parallel Flaw questions.

14. All Labrador retrievers bark a great deal. All Saint Bernards bark infrequently. Each of Rosa's dogs is a cross between a Labrador retriever and a Saint Bernard. Therefore, Rosa's dogs are moderate barkers.

Which one of the following uses flawed reasoning that most closely resembles the flawed reasoning used in the argument above?

(A) All students who study diligently make good grades. But some students who do not study diligently also make good grades. Jane studies somewhat diligently. Therefore, Jane makes somewhat good grades.

(B) All type A chemicals are extremely toxic to human beings. All type B chemicals are nontoxic to human beings. This household cleaner is a mixture of a type A chemical and a type B chemical. Therefore, this household cleaner is moderately toxic.

(C) All students at Hanson School live in Green County. All students at Edwards School live in Winn County. Members of the Perry family attend both Hanson and Edwards. Therefore, some members of the Perry family live in Green County and some live in Winn County.

(D) All transcriptionists know shorthand. All engineers know calculus. Bob has worked both as a transcriptionist and as an engineer. Therefore, Bob knows both shorthand and calculus.

(E) All of Kenisha's dresses are very well made. All of Connie's dresses are very badly made. Half of the dresses in this closet are very well made, and half of them are very badly made. Therefore, half of the dresses in this closet are Kenisha's and half of them are Connie's.

PrepTestJun07 Sec2 Q2

15. We should accept the proposal to demolish the old train station, because the local historical society, which vehemently opposes this, is dominated by people who have no commitment to long-term economic well-being. Preserving old buildings creates an impediment to new development, which is critical to economic health.

The flawed reasoning exhibited by the argument above is most similar to that exhibited by which one of the following arguments?

(A) Our country should attempt to safeguard works of art that it deems to possess national cultural significance. These works might not be recognized as such by all taxpayers, or even all critics. Nevertheless, our country ought to expend whatever money is needed to procure all such works as they become available.

(B) Documents of importance to local heritage should be properly preserved and archived for the sake of future generations. For, if even one of these documents is damaged or lost, the integrity of the historical record as a whole will be damaged.

(C) You should have your hair cut no more than once a month. After all, beauticians suggest that their customers have their hair cut twice a month, and they do this as a way of generating more business for themselves.

(D) The committee should endorse the plan to postpone construction of the new expressway. Many residents of the neighborhoods that would be affected are fervently opposed to that construction, and the committee is obligated to avoid alienating those residents.

(E) One should not borrow even small amounts of money unless it is absolutely necessary. Once one borrows a few dollars, the interest starts to accumulate. The longer one takes to repay, the more one ends up owing, and eventually a small debt has become a large one.

PrepTestJun07 Sec3 Q20

Mixed Practice: Assumption-Family Questions

Assess your skills with some further examples of the most important question types introduced in this chapter—Assumption, Flaw, and Strengthen/Weaken.

16. Atrens: An early entomologist observed ants carrying particles to neighboring ant colonies and inferred that the ants were bringing food to their neighbors. Further research, however, revealed that the ants were emptying their own colony's dumping site. Thus, the early entomologist was wrong.

Atrens's conclusion follows logically if which one of the following is assumed?

(A) Ant societies do not interact in all the same ways that human societies interact.

(B) There is only weak evidence for the view that ants have the capacity to make use of objects as gifts.

(C) Ant dumping sites do not contain particles that could be used as food.

(D) The ants to whom the particles were brought never carried the particles into their own colonies.

(E) The entomologist cited retracted his conclusion when it was determined that the particles the ants carried came from their dumping site.

PrepTestJun07 Sec3 Q5

17. Many corporations have begun decorating their halls with motivational posters in hopes of boosting their employees' motivation to work productively. However, almost all employees at these corporations are already motivated to work productively. So these corporations' use of motivational posters is unlikely to achieve its intended purpose.

The reasoning in the argument is most vulnerable to criticism on the grounds that the argument

(A) fails to consider whether corporations that do not currently use motivational posters would increase their employees' motivation to work productively if they began using the posters

(B) takes for granted that, with respect to their employees' motivation to work productively, corporations that decorate their halls with motivational posters are representative of corporations in general

(C) fails to consider that even if motivational posters do not have one particular beneficial effect for corporations, they may have similar effects that are equally beneficial

(D) does not adequately address the possibility that employee productivity is strongly affected by factors other than employees' motivation to work productively

(E) fails to consider that even if employees are already motivated to work productively, motivational posters may increase that motivation

PrepTestJun07 Sec3 Q4

18. Standard aluminum soft-drink cans do not vary in the amount of aluminum that they contain. Fifty percent of the aluminum contained in a certain group (M) of standard aluminum soft-drink cans was recycled from another group (L) of used, standard aluminum soft-drink cans. Since all the cans in L were recycled into cans in M and since the amount of material other than aluminum in an aluminum can is negligible, it follows that M contains twice as many cans as L.

The conclusion of the argument follows logically if which one of the following is assumed?

(A) The aluminum in the cans of M cannot be recycled further.
(B) Recycled aluminum is of poorer quality than unrecycled aluminum.
(C) All of the aluminum in an aluminum can is recovered when the can is recycled.
(D) None of the soft-drink cans in group L had been made from recycled aluminum.
(E) Aluminum soft-drink cans are more easily recycled than are soft-drink cans made from other materials.

PrepTestJun07 Sec2 Q13

19. Consumer: The latest *Connorly Report* suggests that Ocksenfrey prepackaged meals are virtually devoid of nutritional value. But the *Connorly Report* is commissioned by Danto Foods, Ocksenfrey's largest corporate rival, and early drafts of the report are submitted for approval to Danto Foods' public relations department. Because of the obvious bias of this report, it is clear that Ocksenfrey's prepackaged meals really are nutritious.

The reasoning in the consumer's argument is most vulnerable to criticism on the grounds that the argument

(A) treats evidence that there is an apparent bias as evidence that the *Connorly Report*'s claims are false
(B) draws a conclusion based solely on an unrepresentative sample of Ocksenfrey's products
(C) fails to take into account the possibility that Ocksenfrey has just as much motivation to create negative publicity for Danto as Danto has to create negative publicity for Ocksenfrey
(D) fails to provide evidence that Danto Foods' prepackaged meals are not more nutritious than Ocksenfrey's are
(E) presumes, without providing justification, that Danto Foods' public relations department would not approve a draft of a report that was hostile to Danto Foods' products

PrepTestJun07 Sec2 Q4

20. Scientist: Earth's average annual temperature has increased by about 0.5 degrees Celsius over the last century. This warming is primarily the result of the buildup of minor gases in the atmosphere, blocking the outward flow of heat from the planet.

Which one of the following, if true, would count as evidence against the scientist's explanation of Earth's warming?

(A) Only some of the minor gases whose presence in the atmosphere allegedly resulted in the phenomenon described by the scientist were produced by industrial pollution.
(B) Most of the warming occurred before 1940, while most of the buildup of minor gases in the atmosphere occurred after 1940.
(C) Over the last century, Earth received slightly more solar radiation in certain years than it did in others.
(D) Volcanic dust and other particles in the atmosphere reflect much of the Sun's radiation back into space before it can reach Earth's surface.
(E) The accumulation of minor gases in the atmosphere has been greater over the last century than at any other time in Earth's history.

PrepTestJun07 Sec2 Q5

21. Philosopher: An action is morally right if it would be reasonably expected to increase the aggregate well-being of the people affected by it. An action is morally wrong if and only if it would be reasonably expected to reduce the aggregate well-being of the people affected by it. Thus, actions that would be reasonably expected to leave unchanged the aggregate well-being of the people affected by them are also right.

The philosopher's conclusion follows logically if which one of the following is assumed?

(A) Only wrong actions would be reasonably expected to reduce the aggregate well-being of the people affected by them.
(B) No action is both right and wrong.
(C) Any action that is not morally wrong is morally right.
(D) There are actions that would be reasonably expected to leave unchanged the aggregate well-being of the people affected by them.
(E) Only right actions have good consequences.

PrepTestJun07 Sec2 Q23

22. Political candidates' speeches are loaded with promises and with expressions of good intention, but one must not forget that the politicians' purpose in giving these speeches is to get themselves elected. Clearly, then, these speeches are selfishly motivated and the promises made in them are unreliable.

Which one of the following most accurately describes a flaw in the argument above?

(A) The argument presumes, without providing justification, that if a person's promise is not selfishly motivated then that promise is reliable.

(B) The argument presumes, without providing justification, that promises made for selfish reasons are never kept.

(C) The argument confuses the effect of an action with its cause.

(D) The argument overlooks the fact that a promise need not be unreliable just because the person who made it had an ulterior motive for doing so.

(E) The argument overlooks the fact that a candidate who makes promises for selfish reasons may nonetheless be worthy of the office for which he or she is running.

PrepTestJun07 Sec3 Q23

23. Hospital executive: At a recent conference on nonprofit management, several computer experts maintained that the most significant threat faced by large institutions such as universities and hospitals is unauthorized access to confidential data. In light of this testimony, we should make the protection of our clients' confidentiality our highest priority.

The hospital executive's argument is most vulnerable to which one of the following objections?

(A) The argument confuses the causes of a problem with the appropriate solutions to that problem.

(B) The argument relies on the testimony of experts whose expertise is not shown to be sufficiently broad to support their general claim.

(C) The argument assumes that a correlation between two phenomena is evidence that one is the cause of the other.

(D) The argument draws a general conclusion about a group based on data about an unrepresentative sample of that group.

(E) The argument infers that a property belonging to large institutions belongs to all institutions.

PrepTestJun07 Sec2 Q17

24. Historian: The Land Party achieved its only national victory in Banestria in 1935. It received most of its support that year in rural and semirural areas, where the bulk of Banestria's population lived at the time. The economic woes of the years surrounding that election hit agricultural and small business interests the hardest, and the Land Party specifically targeted those groups in 1935. I conclude that the success of the Land Party that year was due to the combination of the Land Party's specifically addressing the concerns of these groups and the depth of the economic problems people in these groups were facing.

Each of the following, if true, strengthens the historian's argument EXCEPT:

(A) In preceding elections the Land Party made no attempt to address the interests of economically distressed urban groups.

(B) Voters are more likely to vote for a political party that focuses on their problems.

(C) The Land Party had most of its successes when there was economic distress in the agricultural sector.

(D) No other major party in Banestria specifically addressed the issues of people who lived in semirural areas in 1935.

(E) The greater the degree of economic distress someone is in, the more likely that person is to vote.

PrepTestJun07 Sec2 Q19

25. When exercising the muscles in one's back, it is important, in order to maintain a healthy back, to exercise the muscles on opposite sides of the spine equally. After all, balanced muscle development is needed to maintain a healthy back, since the muscles on opposite sides of the spine must pull equally in opposing directions to keep the back in proper alignment and protect the spine.

Which one of the following is an assumption required by the argument?

(A) Muscles on opposite sides of the spine that are equally well developed will be enough to keep the back in proper alignment.

(B) Exercising the muscles on opposite sides of the spine unequally tends to lead to unbalanced muscle development.

(C) Provided that one exercises the muscles on opposite sides of the spine equally, one will have a generally healthy back.

(D) If the muscles on opposite sides of the spine are exercised unequally, one's back will be irreparably damaged.

(E) One should exercise daily to ensure that the muscles on opposite sides of the spine keep the back in proper alignment.

PrepTestJun07 Sec3 Q17

26. Therapist: Cognitive psychotherapy focuses on changing a patient's conscious beliefs. Thus, cognitive psychotherapy is likely to be more effective at helping patients overcome psychological problems than are forms of psychotherapy that focus on changing unconscious beliefs and desires, since only conscious beliefs are under the patient's direct conscious control.

Which one of the following, if true, would most strengthen the therapist's argument?

(A) Psychological problems are frequently caused by unconscious beliefs that could be changed with the aid of psychotherapy.

(B) It is difficult for any form of psychotherapy to be effective without focusing on mental states that are under the patient's direct conscious control.

(C) Cognitive psychotherapy is the only form of psychotherapy that focuses primarily on changing the patient's conscious beliefs.

(D) No form of psychotherapy that focuses on changing the patient's unconscious beliefs and desires can be effective unless it also helps change beliefs that are under the patient's direct conscious control.

(E) All of a patient's conscious beliefs are under the patient's conscious control, but other psychological states cannot be controlled effectively without the aid of psychotherapy.

PrepTestJun07 Sec3 Q13

27. Driver: My friends say I will one day have an accident because I drive my sports car recklessly. But I have done some research, and apparently minivans and larger sedans have very low accident rates compared to sports cars. So trading my sports car in for a minivan would lower my risk of having an accident.

The reasoning in the driver's argument is most vulnerable to criticism on the grounds that this argument

(A) infers a cause from a mere correlation
(B) relies on a sample that is too narrow
(C) misinterprets evidence that a result is likely as evidence that the result is certain
(D) mistakes a condition sufficient for bringing about a result for a condition necessary for doing so
(E) relies on a source that is probably not well-informed

PrepTestJun07 Sec2 Q21

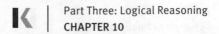
These explanations refer to questions that begin on page 637.

ANSWERS AND EXPLANATIONS

Assumption

1. (D) Assumption (Necessary)   ★ ★ ★ ★

Step 1: Identify the Question Type

Because the correct answer is the "assumption on which the . . . argument depends," this is a Necessary Assumption question.

Step 2: Untangle the Stimulus

Break the argument into evidence and conclusion. The conclusion actually comes at two places: the beginning and end of the stimulus. Whichever place you identify it, the naturalist's main point is that the Tasmanian tiger is extinct. There are two pieces of evidence. First, the tiger was eliminated from its native habitat decades ago, and second, naturalists have found no physical traces of the tiger in this area since its elimination.

Step 3: Make a Prediction

This argument relies on a classic pattern of reasoning. The conclusion is possible, and there's no evidence to contradict it. In other words, absence of evidence is taken to be evidence of absence. Moreover, notice how the argument shifts in scope. The conclusion is broad: The tiger "no longer exists." But the evidence says only that it hasn't been found where it traditionally existed. The author assumes that if you don't find the tiger here, it doesn't exist anywhere. That, in turn, overlooks the possibility that the tigers have survived in a region other than their natural range.

Step 4: Evaluate the Answer Choices

(D) rules out the possibility that the tigers are still alive in some new habitat. It can be confirmed as the correct answer by applying the Denial Test. The denied version would state that the Tasmanian tiger *did* move to a different region. If that were true, then it would make perfect sense why naturalists searching in the tiger's old region found no evidence of it. More importantly, if the Tasmanian tiger moved somewhere else, that would directly contradict the conclusion that the tiger is altogether extinct. Because the denied version directly contradicts the conclusion, that proves that **(D)** is a necessary assumption for the argument.

(A) goes Outside the Scope by introducing starvation. It is not necessary for the argument that any one particular cause, in this case starvation, is what caused the tigers to become extinct. It could also be that the tigers were shot, captured, etc.

(B) is a 180. It weakens the argument by providing an explanation for why naturalists have not found tiger carcasses. Thus, it makes it more likely to be true that the Tasmanian tiger still survives.

(C) is Extreme. The argument relies on the fact that no evidence has been found. The argument doesn't depend on whether all or most or some of the naturalists looked systematically. Even if they have not *all* looked systematically, the tiger could still be extinct. **(C)** does not survive the Denial Test.

(E) While this information supports the naturalist's dismissal of the alleged sightings, it is not necessary to her argument. Using the Denial Test, even if the alleged sightings were from experienced naturalists, they could be wrong and the author could still be correct in concluding that the tiger is extinct based on her reasons.

2. (E) Assumption (Necessary)   ★ ★ ★ ★

Step 1: Identify the Question Type

Because the correct answer is the assumption that the argument "depends on," this is a Necessary Assumption question.

Step 2: Untangle the Stimulus

Start by identifying evidence and conclusion. The conclusion ends the stimulus: there is more mercury in saltwater fish than there was 100 years ago. The evidence comes in two pieces. Following the Keyword *since*, we learn that mercury in seabirds' feathers comes from the fish that they eat. From the beginning of the stimulus, we learn feathers from living birds were compared to feathers taken from stuffed birds that lived in the 1880s and the feathers from living birds had twice as much mercury.

Step 3: Make a Prediction

In any argument that depends upon a comparison, examine the items being compared to ensure they are the same things. In this case, if there is no difference between the feathers of living birds and those of stuffed birds, the comparison may be useful. However, if there is something about the preservation process that would affect mercury levels in the stuffed birds, this comparison would be questionable. To draw her conclusion, the author is assuming that the mercury level in the stuffed birds' feathers was not affected by the preservation process.

Step 4: Evaluate the Answer Choices

(E) matches the prediction by ruling out the possibility that the preservation process could have changed the amount of mercury in the stuffed seabird feathers.

(A) is a 180 because it weakens the argument. If seabirds in the 1880s ate fewer fish, then we should expect the level of mercury in their feathers to be lower than the seabird feathers of today, regardless of how much mercury is in the fish. Thus, **(A)** makes it less likely that today's fish have twice as much mercury.

These explanations refer to questions that begin on page 637.

Part Three: Logical Reasoning
Assumption Family Questions

(B) goes Out of Scope by providing an explanation for why the mercury level in fish might change. The argument is about whether or not fish have twice as much mercury now as they did in the 1880s, not about what causes them to have more mercury now. The idea of *pollution* is not in the stimulus.

(C) goes Out of Scope by suggesting a benefit seabirds get from mercury. Whether or not mercury helps seabirds is irrelevant to determining how much mercury is in fish.

(D) is another 180. It weakens the argument because it provides a reason that the feathers from stuffed birds were different from the feathers from live birds. In contrast to **(D)**, the correct answer needs to show that the feathers from the stuffed birds were similar to the feathers recently taken from live birds.

3. (D) Assumption (Sufficient) ★★☆☆

Step 1: Identify the Question Type

An assumption that would allow the conclusion to be properly drawn is a Sufficient Assumption.

Step 2: Untangle the Stimulus

The author concludes that it will be necessary to vaccinate high-risk individuals every year for a different strain of the flu virus because the vaccination will only protect against the strain anticipated to be most prevalent that year.

Step 3: Make a Prediction

The author jumps from the evidence—that a vaccine for any particular year only protects against the most prevalent strain predicted for that year—to a conclusion that every single year a new vaccination for a different strain will be required. The author ignores the possibility that the same strain might dominate in multiple years and that a previous vaccination will continue to work when that strain shows up again. In order for the author's conclusion to make logical sense, that possibility can't happen. So the correct answer will indicate that repetition of a prevalent strain will not occur.

If you did not recognize that, then for each answer ask if this would guarantee that every year high-risk individuals will need a new vaccine for a new strain. A Sufficient Assumption answer, when added to the evidence, should guarantee that the conclusion is true.

Step 4: Evaluate the Answer Choices

(D) is correct. If every year there will be a new dominant strain of influenza, then the conclusion that every year a different vaccine will be required must be true.

(A) does not guarantee that a vaccine for a different strain of the virus will be needed every year. The *number* of high-risk individuals is irrelevant, because the conclusion says all of them (regardless of count) need an annual vaccine.

(B) is Out of Scope. The issue is whether the prevalent strain of the virus will vary year to year, not whether the seriousness of the epidemic will vary from year to year. Additionally, the stimulus doesn't mention anything about *epidemics* at all; it just says the government is trying to limit serious *cases*.

(C) is a Faulty Use of Detail. It restates the evidence, which already indicates that each year's vaccine will protect *only* against the one strain most likely to be prevalent. So, adding this choice to the evidence wouldn't affect anything at all.

(E) is Out of Scope. The number of the vaccinations' side effects does not have any effect on whether a different vaccination will be needed every year.

4. (B) Assumption (Sufficient) ★★☆☆

Step 1: Identify the Question Type

The "conclusion follows logically if . . . assumed" wording indicates a Sufficient Assumption question, which requires you to select the answer that, in combination with the evidence, would prove the conclusion true. Sufficient Assumption stimuli often contain Formal Logic statements that should be diagrammed.

Step 2: Untangle the Stimulus

Evidence:

> *If appointment to executive board → undergrad degree*
>
> *If felony conviction → ~ appointment to executive board*

Murray has an undergraduate degree but also a felony conviction.

Conclusion:

> *Murray cannot be accepted to position of Executive Administrator.*

Step 3: Make a Prediction

First, combine the Formal Logic statements of the evidence. The contrapositive of the second statement says:

> *If appointment to executive board → ~ felony connection.*

Therefore, the combination of both statements says that any person appointed to the executive board must have an undergraduate degree and can't have a felony conviction. The contrapositive would be:

> *If ~ undergraduate degree → ~ appointed to*
> *OR felony conviction   executive board*

You know that Murray has a felony conviction. Based on the Formal Logic in the evidence, that means he can't be appointed to the *executive board*. However, the conclusion says he can't become the *Executive Administrator*. The "executive board" and the "Executive Administrator" are not necessarily the same thing. The author assumes either that

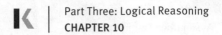

These explanations refer to questions that begin on page 638.

EXPLANATIONS

the requirements are the same for the Executive Administrator position or that the two are somehow connected in another manner.

Step 4: Evaluate the Answer Choices

(B) is correct because it indicates that eligibility requirements are the same for both the board and the Executive Administrator position.

(A) is incorrect because it does not connect the executive board to the Executive Administrator position. Additionally, the argument discusses a *necessary* condition for acceptance to the board while this choice provides a *sufficient* condition.

(C) also is incorrect because it does not connect the executive board to the Executive Administrator position. Additionally, while the argument assumes necessary conditions for the position of Executive Administrator (undergraduate degree and no felony conviction), this choice indicates the absence of a necessary condition.

(D) may be true but, again, it does not connect the executive board to the Executive Administrator position. Also, again, while the argument assumes *necessary* conditions for the position of Executive Administrator, this choice indicates a *sufficient* condition (no felony conviction) for acceptance as the Executive Administrator.

(E) is Out of Scope. Regardless of its relevance to the duties of the position, a felony conviction disqualified Murray. The question is why it disqualified him. This choice, like the other incorrect answers, does not connect the requirements of the board to the requirements of the position.

Flaw

5. (E) Flaw ★☆☆☆

Step 1: Identify the Question Type

Because the correct answer will describe what the argument in the stimulus "fails to consider," this is a Flaw question. Keep an eye out for the advertisement's overlooked alternative.

Step 2: Untangle the Stimulus

Break down the argument into evidence and conclusion. The conclusion is at the end of the stimulus, marked by the conclusion keyword *so*. The advertisement's main point is that Fabric-Soft is the most effective fabric softener. The evidence summarizes a test that was performed using Fabric-Soft. Basically, consumers said they preferred towels washed with Fabric-Soft over towels washed without any fabric softener.

Step 3: Make a Prediction

The question stem has already warned you what the flaw in the argument is—an overlooked possibility. The stimulus introduces a survey, which are always questionable on the LSAT. Look for where the survey goes wrong. The conclusion

compares Fabric-Soft to all other fabric softeners. But, the survey compares Fabric-Soft to *no* fabric softener, let alone *all* the other fabric softeners. Thus, the advertisement overlooks the fact that no information is actually provided about how Fabric-Soft compares to other fabric softeners.

Step 4: Evaluate the Answer Choices

(E) matches the prediction. To determine whether Fabric-Soft really is the best fabric softener, it would have to be compared against other fabric softeners.

(A) is Out of Scope because it introduces the idea of allergies.

(B) goes Out of Scope by introducing the idea of harm to the environment.

(C) veers Out of Scope with the introduction of cost.

(D) is Out of Scope because it asks about a cost/benefit analysis. The scope of the argument is simply whether or not Fabric-Soft is the most effective, regardless of whether or not consumers want to use fabric softeners in general.

6. (B) Flaw ★★★☆

Step 1: Identify the Question Type

Because the correct answer describes how the argument in the stimulus is "vulnerable to criticism," this is a Flaw question.

Step 2: Untangle the Stimulus

Analyze the argument's evidence and conclusion. The conclusion ends the stimulus, indicated by the Keyword *hence*. The author concludes that sometimes getting in the way of police work is morally right. The evidence comes in two pieces. First, it is generally believed that one has the duty to prevent a family member from being harmed. Second, if parents know their child has been falsely accused of a crime, then it would be morally right for them to hide their child from the police.

Step 3: Make a Prediction

The argument shifts scope from evidence about preventing a family member from being harmed to a conclusion about obstructing police work. The author assumes that just because it is morally right to protect family members from harm, and because the police might occasionally pose harm to a family member, it can be morally right to obstruct the police. This assumption overlooks the possibility that there are other moral obligations related to the police. For example, there might be a moral obligation to follow the law or to contest false accusations within the legal system.

Step 4: Evaluate the Answer Choices

(B) matches the prediction. There could be other moral principles related to the police that would outweigh the obligation to protect family members.

These explanations refer to questions that begin on page 639.

Part Three: Logical Reasoning
Assumption Family Questions

K

(A) is a Distortion. The conclusion is not truly a broad generalization. The editorialist states only that *sometimes* (under the circumstances described in the evidence) it is okay to get in the way of police. The scope of the conclusion is no broader than that of the evidence.

(C) goes Out of Scope by introducing the idea of justice. This stimulus is merely about police work. The argument only assumes that the police arresting an innocent man would result in that person being harmed; not that it would assist justice.

(D) is Extreme. The author never suggests there is *no* moral obligation to obey the law. The argument is merely that there might be times when another moral obligation (to protect family members from harm) outweighs any potential obligation to obey the law.

(E) questions the evidence given, rather than the argument's assumption. In any LSAT question, you must take the evidence for granted. Here, the stimulus clearly states that the parents know their child has been falsely accused. The flaw is that even if the parents know their child has been falsely accused, it is still possible that they have a moral obligation to cooperate with the police.

7. (A) Flaw ★★★★

Step 1: Identify the Question Type

Because the correct answer describes the grounds on which the argument in the stimulus is "most vulnerable to criticism," this is a Flaw question.

Step 2: Untangle the Stimulus

The conclusion is the last sentence, marked by the Keyword *hence*. The anthropologists are wrong. In other words, the human species did not need the ability to cope with many different natural environments to survive prehistoric times. The evidence is that a species related to early humans also had the ability to cope with many different natural environments, but did not survive prehistoric times. The Formal Logic would look like this:

Some anthropologists' view:

If species ~ cope with diverse environments → ~ survive

If survive → species can cope with diverse environments

The author treats the anthropologists' evidence as this:

If species can cope with diverse environments → survive

So, when the *Australopithecus afarensis* had the ability to cope and did not survive, the author concluded the anthropologists were wrong.

Step 3: Make a Prediction

The conclusion is that the ability to cope with different environments was not necessary for humans to survive. The evidence is that another species with that ability did not survive. However, this evidence has little to do with whether or not coping with different environments is *necessary* for survival. In contrast, the evidence merely shows that coping with different environments is not *sufficient* for survival. If coping with different environments were sufficient for survival then the other species would have survived. Thus, the author assumes that just because coping with different environments is not sufficient for survival, that it is also not necessary. The classic flaw made by this author is confusing necessity and sufficiency.

Step 4: Evaluate the Answer Choices

(A) matches the prediction.

(B) is a Distortion. The author doesn't "take for granted" that an extinct species must share a characteristic with a surviving species. In fact, the author explicitly presents evidence that the other species and humans shared the ability to cope with different environments.

(C) mischaracterizes the argument and is Extreme. First, the author only discusses humans and *Australopithecus afarensis*, not *all* related species. Second, the author never says the two species survived "*exactly* the same" conditions, just that they both had the same characteristic: the ability to thrive in diverse environments.

(D) is probably an accurate claim about the author, but it is not the argument's flaw. The conclusion concerns what is true about humans, not what is true about the other species. For an overlooked possibility to be the correct answer to a Flaw question, it must weaken the argument if true. Whether or not the extinct species at issue had characteristics that lessened its chances of survival would not weaken the argument about the human species.

(E) is a tempting wrong answer, because it includes words such as *condition*, *result*, and *necessary*. However, **(E)** distorts the argument. Our author treated the other anthropologists' claim of necessity (humans had to adapt to diverse environments) as though it was a claim of sufficiency (adapting to diverse environments ensures survival). This choice suggests that the author failed to consider that a condition sufficient in one case could be necessary in another. That's simply misstates what the author did in the argument.

Strengthen/Weaken

8. (E) Weaken ★☆☆☆

Step 1: Identify the Question Type

The question stem explicitly directs you to weaken the argument. Identify the assumption and attack it.

K | Part Three: Logical Reasoning
CHAPTER 10

These explanations refer to questions that begin on page 640.

EXPLANATIONS

Step 2: Untangle the Stimulus

Highlighted by the contrast Keyword *although*, the author's conclusion is the prediction that "we can expect a reversal of this trend in the very near future." Never leave a vague term (i.e., "this trend") in your paraphrase of the conclusion. Therefore, the author predicts that video game sales will decline in the near future, despite a recent three-year surge. The author's evidence is that the number of 13- to 16-year-olds, historically the prime purchasers of video games, is expected to decline steadily over the next 10 years.

Step 3: Make a Prediction

This argument presents a twist on a classic LSAT argument pattern. A prediction conclusion typically predicts that the future will be like the past, with the built-in assumption that past trends will continue. In this argument, however, the author's conclusion predicts a *divergence* from past trends because the author foresees a changing demographic, a reduction in the number of young teens. Thus, to weaken this argument, you want a choice that indicates the recent three-year trend of increased video game sales will continue, despite the decline in 13- to 16-year-olds.

Step 4: Evaluate the Answer Choices

(E) correctly provides a reason to believe the recent three-year trend of increased video game sales will continue despite the projected decline in 13- to 16-year-olds. While *historically* those young teens bought most of the video games, this choice indicates that the *recent* three-year surge in sales was driven by those older than 16. Therefore, this generation of video game fans is continuing to purchase video games into adulthood.

(A) is a 180, strengthening the argument that video game sales will decline along with the decline in the 13- to 16-year-old age cohort.

(B) is largely irrelevant. It could arguably strengthen or weaken the argument depending on its actual implications. Perhaps a decline in rentals indicates a decline in video game popularity overall, or maybe it indicates that people are choosing to buy instead of rent. Because this answer requires you to make further inferences, and could either weaken or strengthen potentially, it cannot be correct.

(C) is another 180, adding another reason why video game purchases will likely decline.

(D) has no significant effect on the likelihood that video game sales will decline over the next 10 years. All this choice indicates is that the number of video game *types* (not the number of games themselves) will likely *not* decline. While this answer indicates one past condition will continue into the future, there is an extremely tenuous connection, if any, between this fact and the author's conclusion.

9. (E) Weaken

Step 1: Identify the Question Type

The question stem directly asks you to weaken the argument.

Step 2: Untangle the Stimulus

The author concludes that when milk is heated in a microwave oven, the microwaves themselves, not the heat, destroy the lysozyme enzymes in the milk. The evidence is that heating milk in a microwave kills half the enzymes in the milk, but heating milk in a conventional way to the same temperature kills very few of the enzymes.

Step 3: Make a Prediction

This is a causal argument. The author chooses between two potential causes of the destruction of the milk enzymes: heat or microwaves. Because the author concludes the microwaves are at fault, the correct weaken answer choice will provide a reason to believe heat is actually the culprit. The choice will have to explain why heat was a factor when the microwave (but not the conventional heat source) heated the milk. Without specialized technical knowledge, which you do not need, it is impossible to predict more specifically what the correct answer will state.

Step 4: Evaluate the Answer Choices

(E) provides the requisite explanation for how the same overall temperature can kill a larger proportion of enzymes in a microwave than when a conventional heat source is used. Enzymes are caught in hotter zones in the microwaved milk and so experience higher than 50 degree temperatures. In comparison, those isolated higher temperatures don't occur in conventionally heated milk. Thus, it could be the heat itself and not the microwaves directly that kill the enzymes.

(A) shows that increasing the temperature in a microwave is more detrimental to the lysozyme enzyme, but this choice fails in two ways. There is a good deal of similarity between this question and a Paradox question. To correctly weaken this argument, an answer choice must both assert that the heat is the killer and then answer the subsequent paradox of why 50 degrees produces different results in the two heat sources. First, this choice doesn't indicate that something specific about the heat kills the enzymes. Second, this choice does not explain why milk reacts differently when heated by a microwave versus by a conventional heat source.

(B) is irrelevant. Whether enzymes can be replaced has no bearing on what is killing them.

(C) is Out of Scope because it only discusses conventional heating. It does not provide the necessary comparison or distinction between liquid heated to the same overall temperature by a conventional heat source versus by a microwave oven. This choice would be correct if it indicated that a liquid exposed to a *conventional* heat source of 50

These explanations refer to questions that begin on page 640.

Part Three: Logical Reasoning
Assignment Family Questions

degrees will reach that temperature more slowly than a liquid exposed to a *microwave* heat source of 50 degrees. That would bring in the issue of speed between the two heat sources, which could be a reason—other than microwaves themselves—for the difference in enzyme destruction.

(D) is Out of Scope. Taste has nothing to do with discerning what is killing the enzymes.

10. (C) Weaken ★★★☆

Step 1: Identify the Question Type

Because the correct answer is the one that "most seriously weakens the argument," this is a Weaken question.

Step 2: Untangle the Stimulus

Break down the argument into evidence and conclusion. The conclusion is the last sentence, marked by the Keyword *therefore*. The author believes that psychological treatments lasting longer than six months work better than those that last less than six months. The evidence is based on a survey in which a slightly larger percentage of people who had received treatment for more than six months claimed that their treatment helped a lot.

Step 3: Make a Prediction

There are two problems with this argument. First, the conclusion is based on a survey, which means you should automatically ask yourself if the survey was representative. The survey shows more people who had longer treatments said they really work. Maybe there is something about that group of people that distorts the results. Additionally, the author assumes that because people *report* that their longer treatment is better, the longer treatment actually is more effective. The weakener will likely suggest an alternative reason why people with longer treatments report better results.

Step 4: Evaluate the Answer Choices

(C) matches the prediction because it suggests that people who like their treatment stay in it longer. Therefore, it is not necessarily the length of treatment that causes better results. Rather, it is the feeling of better results that leads people to stay in treatment longer. This choice actually indicates reverse causality.

(A) is Out of Scope. It introduces the percentage of people in lengthier treatments who said their treatment made things worse. For this statistic to be relevant, we would also need to know the percentage of people in shorter treatments who said their treatments made things worse.

(B) is an Irrelevant Comparison. The results of the survey are reported as percentages, rather than as raw numbers, so it doesn't matter that more people from the group with longer treatments responded.

(D) fails to distinguish between survey respondents in longer versus shorter treatments. If dissatisfied patients from both groups were more likely to respond to the survey, it would help to explain why the percentages of very satisfied patients are relatively low. Nevertheless, it wouldn't explain why more people from the group with longer treatment thought treatment "made things a lot better."

(E) goes Out of Scope by focusing on what psychologists recommend, rather than on what is actually effective.

11. (A) Strengthen ★★★☆

Step 1: Identify the Question Type

Because the correct answer strengthens the argument in the stimulus, this is a Strengthen question.

Step 2: Untangle the Stimulus

Break down the argument into the evidence and conclusion. The conclusion follows *thus*, in the last sentence: it is very difficult to reduce governmental intrusion into the lives of voters in a democracy. The evidence is a three-part chain. Voters elect politicians who promise government assistance. Government assistance requires taxes. Taxes are a governmental intrusion.

Step 3: Make a Prediction

Find the assumption. The conclusion is about the inevitability of governmental intrusion, but the evidence is about what politicians promise before they get elected. Thus, the assumption is that once they are elected, politicians keep their promises to solve problems with governmental assistance. If there is governmental assistance, then there are taxes and governmental intrusion. The correct answer will reinforce this assumption.

Step 4: Evaluate the Answer Choices

(A) matches the prediction. If the elected politicians keep their promises of solving problems with government assistance, then it would lead to taxes and governmental intrusion.

(B) is a 180, because it weakens the argument. If politicians do not do what they promise, then there is no reason to believe that the government will provide assistance and that therefore, governmental intrusion is inevitable.

(C) goes Out of Scope by focusing on what *types* of problems are most common, rather than on whether or not governmental assistance will be used to fix them, resulting in inevitable intrusion.

(D) is an Irrelevant Comparison. The stimulus is only about whether or not governmental intrusion is inevitable in democracies. Other types of governments are immaterial.

(E) is Out of Scope. It focuses on what politicians *believe* and whether it lines up with what they promise, rather than what

K | Part Three: Logical Reasoning
CHAPTER 10

These explanations refer to questions
that begin on page 641.

they actually do once in office. This choice suggests that those politicians who get elected usually don't believe in what they promise, but that doesn't indicate whether or not they keep those promises once in office.

12. (B) Weaken ★★★☆

Step 1: Identify the Question Type

Because the correct answer weakens the argument in the stimulus, this is a Weaken question.

Step 2: Untangle the Stimulus

Analyze the argument's evidence and conclusion. The conclusion ends the stimulus, after the phrase "we must accept the fact that." Basically, the ethicist believes eating meat will soon be considered immoral. The evidence is based on equivalence between meat and grain. When animals are raised on grain, it takes 16 pounds of grain to make one pound of meat. More people could be fed with 16 pounds of grain than with one pound of meat. Further, the population is growing and the supply of grain is limited.

Step 3: Make a Prediction

The conclusion is about *all* meat, but the evidence is only about meat from animals raised on grain. Thus, the author overlooks the possibility that not all meat comes from animals raised on grain. If some meat comes from animals not raised on grain, then eating that meat would not reduce the amount of grain used to feed people. The correct answer will point out that some meat is not raised on grain that could otherwise be used to feed humans.

Step 4: Evaluate the Answer Choices

(B) matches the prediction by pointing out that sheep and cattle can be fed grass instead of grain.

(A) goes Out of Scope by introducing people's preferences. The argument is about whether or not eating meat will be immoral, not about whether or not people will still like it.

(C) focuses on a minor piece of evidence that says a pound of meat is more nutritious than a pound of grain. This answer choice indicates that it's possible to have a nutritious diet without meat, but doesn't address the ethicist's conclusion that a meat diet will soon be immoral.

(D) is initially tempting because it introduces a way people could avoid contributing to the decrease of farmland, which was part of the chain of evidence for why eating meat would become immoral. However, halting suburban development would only affect farmland near metropolitan areas; it could be true that the total amount of farmland would still decrease for other reasons, and the ethicist's conclusion could still follow. Also, **(D)** doesn't provide a reason why using grain to raise meat is acceptable given that the grain could be used to feed humans directly. Even if farmland is maintained,

there are still the issues of grain yields leveling off and an expanding population, so **(D)** does not weaken the author's moral argument against eating meat.

(E) goes Out of Scope like **(C)** does by focusing on health, rather than on morality. This choice suggests you shouldn't eat grain alone, but that doesn't mean meat is necessary. There are other types of food beyond grain and meat. Both the nutritionists and the ethicist could be correct.

Assumption-Family Principle

13. (E) Principle (Identify/Strengthen) ★★★☆

Step 1: Identify the Question Type

Because the correct answer is the principle that would "help to justify" the argument in the stimulus, this is an Identify the Principle question that resembles a Strengthen question. The correct answer will restate the argument in more general terms, which if true, would make the argument more likely.

Step 2: Untangle the Stimulus

Follow the strategy for approaching a Strengthen question. Analyze the argument's evidence and conclusion. The conclusion is the first sentence. The sociologist believes that romantics are wrong to think people are made evil by institutions. In other words, institutions do not make people evil. The sociologist's reason for believing this comes after the evidence Keywords *after all*: Institutions are just groups of people.

Step 3: Make a Prediction

Boiled down, the argument says collections of people can't make people evil. The assumption is simply that that connection between the evidence and conclusion is accurate. In other words, the author assumes that a collective group (institutions) cannot determine the characteristics of the individuals of which it is made (people). That is, institutions must be shaped by the people in them, and not vice versa. The correct answer will reinforce this assumption in general terms.

Step 4: Evaluate the Answer Choices

(E) matches the prediction. The *whole* would be institutions and the "things that compose it" would be the individual people.

(A) is an Irrelevant Comparison. The stimulus doesn't indicate that institutions are more effective than individuals. Additionally, the argument focuses on whether or not institutions *make* people evil (an attribute), not on how people can *do* the most good or evil (an action).

(B) is Outside the Scope. Even if all institutions are imperfect, **(B)** still doesn't address whether those imperfect institutions can or cannot make people evil.

These explanations refer to questions that begin on page 642.

Part Three: Logical Reasoning
Assumption Family Questions

K

(C) fails to address whether there is a connection between institutions and people's character. Additionally, the way people should view others is Out of Scope.

(D) veers Out of Scope by introducing the idea of gauging society's values. Additionally, like **(B)** and **(C)**, **(D)** fails to include anything about whether institutions can make people evil.

Parallel Flaw

14. (B) Parallel Flaw ★★★★

Step 1: Identify the Question Type

A question stem that asks you to find the flawed reasoning that resembles the flawed reasoning in the stimulus is a Parallel Flaw question.

Step 2: Untangle the Stimulus

The author concludes that Rosa's dogs are moderate barkers. The evidence is that each dog is a cross of a Lab and a Saint Bernard. Also, the Formal Logic statements at the beginning of the stimulus indicate that all Labs bark a lot and all Saint Bernards bark a little.

Step 3: Make a Prediction

The author assumes without evidence that the mixed dogs will blend the characteristics of each breed. He's overlooking the possibility that one of the traits may be dominant or that some of the mixed dogs might have the barking tendencies of Labs and others those of Saint Bernards. Your task is to find an answer choice that commits that same flaw (i.e., a conclusion that a middle ground between two potential extremes will be the result). **(C)**, **(D)**, and **(E)** all can be eliminated just based on the conclusions, because only **(A)** and **(B)** have conclusions that result in a middle ground.

Step 4: Evaluate the Answer Choices

(B) is correct because just like with Rosa's dogs, the author here assumes that if the cleaner is a mix of the two types of chemicals, then the properties of those chemicals mix. Once again, the author is overlooking the possibility that one of the chemicals might be much stronger than the other: The mixed cleaner could still be very toxic or completely nontoxic (if type B neutralizes the effects of type A, for example).

(A) contains a scope shift that is not present in the stimulus' argument. The evidence tells us about the grades of diligent students and non-diligent students, but Jane is not a part of either of these groups. Unlike the arguments in the stimulus and choice **(B)**, there's no claim that Jane mixes the attributes of diligent and non-diligent students. More importantly, the stimulus says all members of one group were one way and all members of the other group were their opposites. In this argument, the evidence didn't mention all non-diligent

students and their bad grades, only some of them and their good grades.

(C) can be eliminated because there is no flaw in its logic.

(D) also can be eliminated because it is essentially not flawed, except to the extent that it ignores the possibility that Bob has forgotten one or both of his skills since he held those jobs. Nevertheless, that flaw is unrelated to the flaw identified in the stimulus assuming a middle ground between two extremes.

(E) describes a necessity-versus-sufficiency flaw, which isn't at play here. Just because all of Kenisha's dresses are well made doesn't mean that all well-made dresses are Kenisha's. The same is true of Connie's poorly made dresses. There may be dresses in the closet belonging to someone else, for example.

15. (C) Parallel Flaw ★★★★

Step 1: Identify the Question Type

Because the correct answer is the argument that demonstrates the same flawed reasoning as the argument in the stimulus, this is a Parallel Flaw question.

Step 2: Untangle the Stimulus

Attack the stimulus as you would a Flaw question. Break down the argument into evidence and conclusion. The conclusion opens the stimulus. The author believes that we should demolish the old train station. The author's evidence is that the historical society does not want to demolish the old train station and the members of the historical society are generally opposed to long-term economic health. Abstractly, the author concludes that we should take an action because the people who oppose it have what he considers a bad characteristic.

Step 3: Make a Prediction

The flaw is a variation on the *ad hominem* attack flaw; that is, the author justifies his recommendation by attacking those who oppose it. Specifically, the author questions the motives of the opposition. The correct answer will model this flawed method of reasoning. Even if you did not see the flaw in this argument, you can still get the point by comparing the answer choice arguments piece by piece against the stimulus. The conclusion recommends a course of action that goes against an opposition group that the author distrusts for a particular reason. This alone will likely be enough to distinguish the right answer. The author fails to consider any reasons for *not* demolishing the train station and relies solely on his belief that preserving old buildings will impede economic health.

Step 4: Evaluate the Correct Answer

(C) matches the prediction. The only reason the author of **(C)** suggests that you have your hair cut no more than once a month is because of the self-interested motives of beauticians, who suggest you have your hair cut more than once a month.

K | Part Three: Logical Reasoning
CHAPTER 10

These explanations refer to questions that begin on page 643.

(A) is incorrect because it doesn't refer to an opposition group. This argument mentions groups that might not *recognize* art as significant, but concludes that we shouldn't let that deter us in our preservation efforts. This argument might not have very strong evidence, but it doesn't commit any *reasoning* errors.

(B) fails like **(A)** by failing to mention an opposition group. The author of **(B)** does not oppose anyone else, and although the argument may not be terribly convincing, it commits no *reasoning* error.

(D) fails to match the stimulus because the author's recommendation is based on complying with the point of view of the residents. In other words, both of the points of view in **(D)** want the same thing.

(E) goes awry for two reasons. First, it has the same problem as **(A)** and **(B)**—there is only one point of view in the stimulus. Second, the conclusion here is qualified by a condition, signaled by the word *unless*. The stimulus's conclusion didn't mention any exceptions to the recommendation (not even absolute necessity), so the conclusion types do not match.

Mixed Practice: Assumption-Family Questions

16. (C) Assumption (Sufficient) ★☆☆☆

Step 1: Identify the Question Type

The correct answer is the assumption that makes the conclusion follow logically. In other words, if the assumption is true, then the conclusion is true. Thus, this is a Sufficient Assumption question.

Step 2: Untangle the Stimulus

Atrens puts the conclusion at the very end of the stimulus, after the conclusion Keyword *thus*. It says the entomologist was wrong, but you can't let your summary of the conclusion be that vague. Added to the first sentence, the conclusion essentially says ants were not bringing food to their neighbors. The evidence is that research showed the ants were emptying their dumping site.

Step 3: Make a Prediction

Find the mismatched concepts. The conclusion says that whatever the ants were doing, it was not food delivery. The evidence says the ants were emptying their dumping site. The assumption must create a connection between these two ideas. The author assumes that the two actions are mutually exclusive or, in other words, that stuff from one ant's dumping site cannot be food for another ant.

Step 4: Evaluate the Answer Choices

(C) matches the prediction.

(A) veers Out of Scope by contrasting ants to humans.

(B) is also Out of Scope, introducing a new term: gifts. Another assumption would be required to connect bringing food to bringing gifts. Additionally, the new study merely casts doubt on the idea that the ants were bringing food in that situation, but it has nothing to do with their *capacity* to give gifts.

(D) goes Out of Scope by focusing on what the receiving ants did with the particles, rather than on what the particles were. The receiving ants' actions don't indicate whether or not the particles were food.

(E) is Out of Scope, focusing on what the entomologist did after learning about the additional research. Even if the entomologist retracted his claims, it doesn't necessarily follow that Atrens's conclusion is correct.

17. (E) Flaw ★☆☆☆

Step 1: Identify the Question Type

This is a Flaw question because the correct answer describes how the argument in the stimulus is "vulnerable to criticism." Identify what's wrong about the gap between the evidence and conclusion, and keep common flaws in mind.

Step 2: Untangle the Stimulus

Break down the argument into evidence and conclusion. The conclusion comes at the end of the stimulus, marked by the conclusion Keyword *so*. Basically, the conclusion is that corporations that hang motivational posters are not likely to boost the motivation of their workers. The evidence is that almost all workers at those companies are already motivated.

Step 3: Make a Prediction

Start by finding the author's assumption. Here, the conclusion is that the posters will not *boost* workers' motivation. The evidence is that workers are already motivated. The author must be assuming that there aren't degrees of motivation. This overlooks the possibility that workers who are already motivated could become even more motivated. Additionally, the conclusion is about all workers, while the evidence is about "almost all." It's possible that the posters could work on that small group of workers who are not yet motivated. The correct answer will point out one of these overlooked alternatives.

Step 4: Evaluate the Answer Choices

(E) matches the prediction. It could be true that motivational posters lead already motivated workers to become even more motivated.

(A) is Out of Scope because it introduces corporations that do not use motivational posters. The argument focuses only on those corporations that *do* use motivational posters. Ignoring those others is not a flaw.

These explanations refer to questions that begin on page 644.

Part Three: Logical Reasoning
Assumption Family Questions

K

(B) describes a representativeness flaw, which is not at play here. Both the author's evidence and conclusion are limited to the same corporations.

(C) is not a flaw. While the author does ignore other possible benefits, that oversight doesn't affect the conclusion, which is solely about the posters' influence on motivation.

(D) is Out of Scope. The argument is focused only on whether posters will increase motivation to work productively, not whether they'll affect productivity itself. Whether or not productivity may be affected by other factors is irrelevant.

18. (C) Assumption (Sufficient)   ★★★★

Step 1: Identify the Question Type

The "conclusion . . . follows logically if . . . assumed" formulation indicates a Sufficient Assumption question.

Step 2: Untangle the Stimulus

The stimulus presents two groups of aluminum cans: group M and group L. The conclusion states that group M contains twice as many cans as group L. The evidence for this is rather convoluted, so break it down piece by piece.

First, standard aluminum cans contain the same amount of aluminum. Both groups M and L contain standard aluminum cans (therefore, the amount of aluminum in each can in each group is the same). Second, half of the aluminum used to make the cans in group M came from the recycled cans of group L. Third, *all* the cans in group L were recycled and turned into cans in group M. Finally, materials other than aluminum in cans are insignificant.

Step 3: Make a Prediction

If half of the aluminum in group M came from the entirety of group L, then half came from elsewhere. In other words, group M must contain twice as much aluminum as group L did. The author thinks this means group M contains twice as many cans at group L did. Indeed, the logic seems sound. So, there must be something very basic to this calculation that is being assumed because the numbers seem to add up correctly. The author must be making a subtle scope shift between double the *aluminum* and double the *cans*. Look for an answer choice that, if added, proves that these two are actually equivalent. The correct answer may do this by eliminating an overlooked reason why they would not be comparable.

Step 4: Evaluate the Answer Choices

(C) is correct. Sure, the numbers add up correctly, but only if it is as straightforward as it seems. The ignored possibility is that some aluminum is lost during the recycling process. In that case, the number of cans in group M would not be exactly twice as many as in group L. However, once this choice confirms that that possibility is not occurring, it proves group M has twice as many cans. The hint at this assumption in the

stimulus was the evidence that a negligible amount of other materials is added. That could have led you to ponder whether any aluminum was lost.

(A) is Out of Scope. Whether the group M cans could be recycled further does not at all affect the comparison between the number of cans in each group.

(B) also is Out of Scope. The aluminum's *quality* is irrelevant to the numbers comparison. The evidence says cans do not vary in the amount of aluminum they contain, regardless of what grade it is.

(D) is Out of Scope in the same way that (A) is. The stimulus is restricted to group L's transformation into group M. The future of group M—in answer choice (A)—and the past of group L—in this answer choice—are both irrelevant.

(E) is an Irrelevant Comparison to cans of other materials. The ease of recycling does not affect whether the math adds up nicely.

19. (A) Flaw   ★★★★

Step 1: Identify the Question Type

The phrase "vulnerable to criticism" is one of the most common phrases indicating a Flaw question. Be on the lookout for a disconnect between the evidence and conclusion, and keep classic LSAT flaws in mind.

Step 2: Untangle the Stimulus

The consumer concludes that Ocksenfrey's meals are nutritious. A report indicates that the meals are *not* nutritious, but the consumer asserts that the source of the report makes it biased.

Step 3: Make a Prediction

Two classic LSAT flaws intersect in this argument.

First, there is no actual evidence supporting the claim that Ocksenfrey meals are nutritious. All the consumer has done is cast doubt on a negative report. Assuming the consumer is correct, the report's dismissal leaves us with a complete lack of evidence. The absence, or disproving, of evidence does not support or prove the opposite, yet on the LSAT, authors often assume it does.

Additionally, even though in real life it may be relevant to point out a bias, the LSAT considers it a flaw to make an *ad hominem* attack against the source of an argument rather than address the substance of that argument. The consumer does that here, jumping from an assertion of bias in those producing the report to a complete refutation of its claims.

Step 4: Evaluate the Answer Choices

(A) is correct. It is in line with the prediction and is an accurate description of the argument. Many correct answers to Flaw questions are simply accurate descriptions of the argument. A

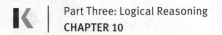

Part Three: Logical Reasoning
CHAPTER 10

These explanations refer to questions that begin on page 645.

good test for Flaw answer choices is to ask: "Does the author do this?"

(B) describes a representativeness flaw and does not pass the basic test just described: "Does the author do this?" There is no indication that a nonrepresentative sample of the meals was used in the report. Both the evidence and the conclusion stick to the same scope: prepackaged meals. Even though you could speculate that bias led to the improper selection of unhealthy examples of meals, this will not be the correct answer unless there is some concrete indication of that in the stimulus.

(C) may be true, but isn't correct. To be correct, an "ignored possibility" answer to a Flaw question must, if true, weaken the argument. The author may indeed have failed to consider this possibility, but even if it were true it would not impact the consumer's claim that the meals are nutritious.

(D) is similarly not a flaw. Even if such evidence were submitted, the level of nutrition as compared to Danto's meals does not impact an absolute claim that Ocksenfrey's meals are, or are not, qualitatively nutritious. The conclusion does not make a comparative claim, so comparisons are irrelevant.

(E) is Out of Scope. This answer choice discusses reports that are hostile to *Danto's* meals, while the stimulus deals with a report that is hostile to *Ocksenfrey's* meals. The consumer doesn't mention or assume anything about how Danto's public relations department would react to a report on that company's own products.

20. (B) Weaken ★★☆☆

Step 1: Identify the Question Type

A question stem that asks you to identify evidence against an argument is a Weaken question. This stem asks you to weaken the scientist's explanation. The classic way to weaken an argument with an explanatory conclusion is to provide an alternative explanation.

Step 2: Untangle the Stimulus

As is often the case for a Strengthen or Weaken question, the question stem directs you to the conclusion, i.e., the "explanation of Earth's warming." The first sentence simply states that the Earth has warmed by 0.5 degrees Celsius. The second sentence contains the scientist's explanation: The warming is caused by the accumulation of gases in the atmosphere, which blocks the planet from releasing heat.

Step 3: Make a Prediction

This is a classic LSAT argument pattern in which an author points out an interesting phenomenon and then provides a causal explanation for that phenomenon. The built-in assumption is that no other explanation exists. The typical way to weaken such an argument is to look for any of the classic alternatives to causation: The causation is reversed, a third

factor causes both, or the correlation is merely coincidence. You don't need to predict the specific cause; just keep in mind that you need an answer that indicates one of those three situations is at play.

Step 4: Evaluate the Answer Choices

(B) is correct. A great way to weaken a claim of causality is to show the result preceded the purported cause. If the bulk of the warming occurred *before* the greatest buildup of the gases, then it is less likely that the buildup caused the warming.

(A) is Out of Scope. The argument is concerned only with the cause of the global warming, not the cause of the gas buildup. Additionally, it never mentions industrial pollution, so the amount of gases that arose from pollution (whether it's "some" or "most" or "all") is irrelevant.

(C) is appealing as it might initially seem to provide an alternative explanation for the warming: increased solar radiation. However, all this choice really indicates is that solar radiation was not constant year over year. To provide an alternative explanation for the *average* increase in Earth's temperature over the past century, there would need to be a trend of an *average* increase in solar radiation over the past century, not just yearly fluctuations.

(D) is irrelevant because it includes no reference to time or change. There is no indication that the amount of volcanic dust increased or decreased over the past century, so this choice can't explain the changing temperature.

(E) is a 180 because it strengthens the argument. If the buildup of minor gases was uncharacteristically greater in the past century, then it is more likely that the built up gases may be responsible for the trapping of heat and, therefore, also responsible for higher temperatures.

21. (C) Assumption (Sufficient) ★★★☆

Step 1: Identify the Question Type

The "conclusion follows logically if . . . assumed" phrasing indicates a Sufficient Assumption question. Choose the answer that, if combined with the evidence, proves the conclusion to be true. Sufficient Assumption questions often contain Formal Logic that needs to be mapped out, especially when the question falls in the danger zone, as this one does.

Step 2: Untangle the Stimulus

The philosopher concludes that actions that can reasonably be expected to not affect the general well-being of those affected by them are right. The philosopher supports this conclusion by several Formal Logic statements.

Evidence:

> *If increase aggregate well-being* → *morally right*
>
> *If reduce aggregate well-being* → *morally wrong*

These explanations refer to questions that begin on page 645.

Part Three: Logical Reasoning
Assumption Family Questions

If morally wrong   →   **reduce aggregate well-being**

(Note: The first sentence just has a single word indicating Formal Logic, *if*, but the second sentence has the "if but only if" form, which means you must diagram it twice. First translate the statement using the *if* and ignoring the "only if," then translate it using the "only if" and ignoring the *if*.)

Step 3: Make a Prediction

Look at the second sentence of the stimulus. It includes the rare but informative "if and only if." In addition to saying that actions that reduce aggregate well-being are morally wrong, the statement indicates that *only* actions that reduce aggregate well-being can be called morally wrong. In other words, any other actions must be something other than morally wrong. The conclusion, for example, mentions actions that don't change the aggregate well-being. Based on the Formal Logic, those actions must therefore be something other than morally wrong. But does that necessarily mean that they are, as the conclusion asserts, morally right? Or is there another possibility? Arguably, actions could be morally neutral. If that's possible, then the philosopher's conclusion doesn't logically have to follow. For the philosopher's logic to be correct, then morality must be binary (right or wrong), and there cannot be a "neutral" possibility. The correct answer will state that assumption.

Step 4: Evaluate the Answer Choices

(C) matches the prediction that if something is not morally wrong, then it has to be morally right. This eliminates the possibility of moral neutrality, which guarantees the philosopher's conclusion that an unchanged aggregate well-being (which cannot be morally bad) must be morally right.

(A) is a Faulty Use of Detail. Assuming that "morally wrong" and "wrong" actions are synonymous, this answer merely restates existing evidence. Restated evidence cannot provide the missing link between the evidence and conclusion.

(B) says actions can't be wrong *and* right, but it doesn't say actions have to be wrong *or* right. It does not eliminate the possibility of moral neutrality and thus does not guarantee the conclusion.

(D) is incorrect because philosophizing about actions that would leave the aggregate well-being unchanged does not require that such actions exist. And, even if that were the case, that would be a necessary assumption of the argument, rather than a sufficient assumption that would prove the conclusion true. The mere existence of such actions would not guarantee that they are morally right.

(E) is Out of Scope. It mentions "good consequences," a term that doesn't appear in the stimulus. Even if you assume that "good consequences" is synonymous with "increase the aggregate well-being," then this choice merely restates the

first Formal Logic statement. Furthermore, this choice doesn't remove the possibility of moral neutrality.

22. (D) Flaw   ★★☆☆

Step 1: Identify the Question Type

Because the correct answer "accurately describes a flaw in the argument," this is a Flaw question.

Step 2: Untangle the Stimulus

Break down the argument into the evidence and conclusion. Following the conclusion Keyword *clearly*, at the end of the stimulus, the conclusion is that political candidates' speeches are selfish and the promises contained therein are unreliable. The evidence is that political candidates give speeches to get elected.

Step 3: Make a Prediction

The author suggests that just because politicians have selfish motives for making promises that those promises may be unreliable. This overlooks the possibility that politicians might reliably keep their promises after they are elected. After all, there could be some additional reason that motivates politicians to keep their campaign promises.

Step 4: Evaluate the Answer Choices

(D) matches the prediction. Just because politicians make promises to get elected does not necessarily mean they will not keep those promises.

(A) distorts the logic of the argument. The argument says if promises are selfishly motivated, then they are unreliable. This answer choice negates that logic without reversing it. Even if you didn't see the Formal Logic, the conclusion is only about unreliable promises. The author doesn't conclude anything about reliable promises and what would make them so.

(B) is Extreme. The author says such promises are *unreliable*, not that they are *never* kept.

(C) is Out of Scope. The argument in the stimulus is not a causal argument. Even if the author's argument was phrased as, "selfish motivations cause promises to be unreliable," this answer still would not be correct. The author never confuses that causal relationship with the reverse: Unreliable promises cause motivations to be selfish.

(E) goes Outside the Scope by introducing the idea of "worthy for office." The stimulus focuses on whether the promises politicians make in speeches are unreliable, not on how well suited for office the politicians are.

23. (B) Flaw   ★★★★

Step 1: Identify the Question Type

This question stem contains a slight modification of the very common Flaw question phrase "vulnerable to criticism."

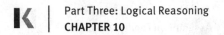

Part Three: Logical Reasoning
CHAPTER 10

These explanations refer to questions that begin on page 646.

Step 2: Untangle the Stimulus

The hospital executive concludes with the recommendation to make protection of client confidentiality the hospital's highest priority. The evidence is the assertion by several computer experts that unauthorized access to computer data is the most significant threat faced by large institutions, including universities and hospitals.

Step 3: Make a Prediction

It might strike you as odd that a hospital is prioritizing computer security over, say, saving lives, merely on the advice of computer experts. The computer experts' analysis of the threat of unauthorized access might be real, but their overall understanding of other threats facing hospital management is likely little to none. Otherwise, the basic test for Flaw question answers is to ask if the author actually does what the answer describes.

Step 4: Evaluate the Answer Choices

(B) is correct because it accurately describes the argument and its inadequacy. The argument relies on the guidance of experts whose expertise is in computers, not in overall hospital management. To accurately pinpoint the most significant threat faced by a hospital, an expert should have some experience in medicine and hospital administration.

(A) does not relate to the argument, which is focused on identifying the highest priority. The *cause* of unauthorized access to confidential data is not discussed, nor is a possible *solution*. Therefore, the executive can't possibly mix up those two.

(C) describes a classic causal flaw, which is not at play here. There is simply no evidence of two things being correlated nor a conclusion that one thing causes another within the argument.

(D) refers to a representativeness flaw, which is unrelated to this argument. According to this choice, the argument draws a *general* conclusion about a group; however, the hospital executive's conclusion is specific to his one hospital.

(E) also fails to describe the argument. The stimulus discusses large institutions only, not institutions in general. The computer experts' advice was for large institutions, such as hospitals, so the hospital executive was right to consider his hospital a proper target of the advice, but he was flawed in assessing the validity of the advice.

24. (A) Strengthen (EXCEPT) ★★★☆

Step 1: Identify the Question Type

The question stem directly indicates that this is a Strengthen EXCEPT question, for which you need to identify the one answer choice that does *not* strengthen the argument.

The correct answer could weaken or have no effect on the argument.

Step 2: Untangle the Stimulus

The historian explicitly indicates in the last sentence that her conclusion is that Land Party success in 1935 was due to addressing the concerns of farmers and small business owners, and the depth of the economic problems those groups faced. Notice this paraphrase defines the vague terms in the conclusion, such as "that year" and "these groups." The historian's evidence is relatively extensive. First, 1935 was the only year the Land Party was successful. Second, the majority of support came from rural and semirural areas, where the majority of Banestria's population lived. Third, the economic woes of farmers and small businesses were particularly acute that year. Finally, the Land Party specifically targeted farmers and small businesses.

Step 3: Make a Prediction

This is a classic LSAT argument pattern. The author observes an interesting phenomenon, i.e., Land Party's only victory was in 1935, and then concludes with an explanation for that event. In other words, the author makes a causal argument. The built-in assumption is that there is no other explanation. The classic weakener will suggest an alternative explanation, while strengtheners will bolster the proffered explanation or *eliminate* alternative explanations. Remember the correct EXCEPT answer could also be irrelevant.

Step 4: Evaluate the Answer Choices

(A) is correct. What the Land Party did in preceding elections is largely irrelevant to determining whether the specific factors the author identified in the 1935 election were responsible for that year's victory. The correct answer to an EXCEPT question is often the odd one out. Notice that this choice is the only one focused on urban groups, which were not part of the author's explanation for the Land Party victory in 1935.

(B) strengthens the author's assumption that focusing on the economic problems of farmers and small business owners caused those groups to vote for the Land Party in 1935.

(C) also strengthens the author's explanation that the Land Party's success in the national election in 1935 was due to economic conditions. This choice indicates that Land Party successes at other levels (not national) also occurred during periods of economic distress. This choice reinforces the correlation.

(D) strengthens the assumption that addressing the economic concerns of the rural areas garnered their votes for the Land Party, because no other party bothered.

(E) strengthens the idea that economic distress produced the rare Land Party victory in 1935 by increasing the likelihood that the constituents the party targeted would actually vote.

These explanations refer to questions that begin on page 646.

Part Three: Logical Reasoning
Assumption Family Questions

K

25. (B) Assumption (Necessary)

Step 1: Identify the Question Type

Because the correct answer is the assumption "required by the argument," this is a Necessary Assumption question.

Step 2: Untangle the Stimulus

Break down the argument into evidence and conclusion. There is no conclusion Keyword to help you here, but context tells you that the first sentence, a recommendation, is the argument's conclusion. The author's main point is that you need to exercise muscles on both sides of the spine equally in order to have a healthy back. Signaled by the Keywords "after all," the author's evidence is that balanced muscle development is needed for a healthy back. The rest of the sentence justifies the need for balanced muscle development. In Formal Logic terms, the argument looks like this:

Evidence:

   If healthy back → balanced muscle development

Conclusion:

   If healthy back → exercise sides equally

Step 3: Make a Prediction

Find the matched and mismatched concepts. The idea of a healthy back is mentioned in both the evidence and conclusion, so that is the matched concept. In the conclusion, the mismatched concept is exercising muscles on opposite sides of the spine equally. In the evidence, the mismatched concept is balanced muscle development. Therefore, the assumption is that balanced muscle development requires exercising muscles on opposite sides of the spine equally. Contraposed, the assumption would be if you don't exercise the opposite sides equally, you won't have balanced muscle development.

Step 4: Evaluate the Answer Choices

(B) matches the prediction. Because the author assumes equal exercise is necessary to balanced development, she must also assume that unequal exercise will lead to unbalanced development. Be prepared for the testmaker to sometimes phrase the correct answer as the contrapositive.

(A) is a Distortion. You can't conclude from the argument that equal development is enough—i.e., sufficient—for proper alignment. **(A)** confuses a necessary term of the evidence for a sufficient one. It also fails to link the mismatched concepts of exercising both sides equally and balanced development.

(C) is a Distortion just like **(A)**. This time, though, it confuses necessity and sufficiency in the conclusion. Although a healthy back *requires* equal exercise on opposite sides, you cannot say that equal exercise guarantees (is *sufficient* for) a healthy back. Also, once again, it fails to link the mismatched concepts of exercising both sides equally and balanced development.

(D) is Extreme. The contrapositive of the conclusion indicates that if exercise is not done equally, then one can't maintain a healthy back. However, the idea of *irreparable* back damage goes beyond that statement. Also, **(D)** fails to connect balanced muscle development to equal exercise.

(E) goes Out of Scope by introducing the idea of daily exercise. The argument doesn't mention or rely on prescribed frequency of exercise. As with the other wrong answers, **(E)** fails to connect the mismatched concepts.

26. (B) Strengthen

Step 1: Identify the Question Type

Because the correct answer "would most strengthen" the argument in the stimulus, this is a Strengthen question.

Step 2: Untangle the Stimulus

The conclusion is at the beginning of the second sentence, marked by the Keyword *thus*. Basically, the therapist's main point is that cognitive psychotherapy, which changes conscious beliefs, is more effective than other forms of therapy, which change unconscious beliefs. After *since*, the evidence is that only conscious beliefs are under a patient's direct conscious control.

Step 3: Make a Prediction

The conclusion is all about the effectiveness of a type of therapy. The evidence, however, deals with the patient's ability to control his beliefs. The author is assuming that the effectiveness of a therapy is related to the patient's ability to control his beliefs. To strengthen the argument, a fact is needed to confirm this connection or to rule out the ability to improve by changing unconscious beliefs.

Step 4: Evaluate the Answer Choices

(B) matches the prediction.

(A) is a 180. If changing unconscious beliefs can *frequently* solve some psychological problems, the assumption that effectiveness depends on conscious control of beliefs is undermined.

(C) is Out of Scope because the argument is about whether or not cognitive therapy is more effective than therapies which do not focus on changing conscious beliefs. Whether or not there are other forms of therapy that also focus on changing conscious beliefs is irrelevant.

(D) is Extreme. The therapist's argument is comparative, i.e., cognitive therapy is more likely to be effective than therapies focused on the unconscious. **(D)** says that no therapy focused on the unconscious will be effective unless it also changes conscious beliefs under the patient's control. The author could acknowledge that at times some therapies focused exclusively on the unconscious may have success, while maintaining his argument that cognitive therapy is *likely* to be more effective.

EXPLANATIONS

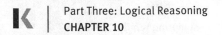

These explanations refer to questions that begin on page 647.

(E) goes Out of Scope by failing to distinguish between psychotherapies that focus on changing conscious beliefs and psychotherapies that focus on changing unconscious beliefs. Nothing in (E) suggests which of those types of therapy would be most useful for controlling those psychological states that "cannot be controlled effectively without the aid of psychotherapy."

27. (A) Flaw ★★★★

Step 1: Identify the Question Type

"Vulnerable to criticism" indicates a Flaw question. Notice how the conclusion goes beyond or deviates from the evidence. Keep in mind the common LSAT flaws.

Step 2: Untangle the Stimulus

The author concludes that trading in his sports car will lower his risk of having an accident. The evidence is that minivans and sedans have low accident rates compared to sports cars.

Step 3: Make a Prediction

This is a variation on a causal argument. The issue is whether the type of car causes accidents or whether the type of driver who chooses that type of car causes accidents.

Step 4: Evaluate the Answer Choices

(A) is correct. Only (A) and (D) relate to causation. This choice accurately describes the argument. There is evidence of a correlation between the type of car and the number of accidents in which it is involved. The author jumps from that correlation to a conclusion that the car type is responsible for the likelihood of accidents. However, it could just as easily be that the type of driver who selects that type of car is responsible for the accident rate.

(B) describes a representativeness flaw. However, there is no indication of the size or range of the sample, so this flaw is not at play here. This could be correct only if the stimulus actually indicates an inadequate sample size; *no* mention of sample size is not sufficient.

(C) indicates that the driver's conclusion is extreme, but that is not an accurate description of the argument. The driver is consistent, using evidence regarding the likelihood of an accident to reach a conclusion that also involves the likelihood of an accident. The driver does not conclude that he is certain to have *no* accidents in a minivan or sedan.

(D) also does not match the argument. The driver does not conclude that trading in the sports car for a minivan or sedan is the *only* way to reduce the risk of an accident, which is what this choice suggests. To assert something is a necessary condition is to assert that it is the only way to accomplish a goal. Additionally, from the evidence, it's not even clear if switching to a minivan or sedan would be *sufficient* to accomplish the driver's goal.

(E) is incorrect because there is no indication of this in the stimulus. The driver never mentions his research sources. Unlike in a Weaken question, in which the correct answer choice adds evidence that hurts an argument, the correct answer in a Flaw question must reference a problem *already* existing within the stimulus.

CHAPTER 11

Non-Argument Questions

Not all questions in the Logical Reasoning section involve analyzing or evaluating arguments. A significant number of questions test your ability to make deductions; we will call these Inference questions, an inference—in LSAT terms—being a valid deduction from a set of statements or assertions. Inference questions give you a set of facts or assertions and ask for what must be true based on the facts or what follows logically from them. Other questions give you a general principle and ask for a specific case that correctly applies the principle, or they supply a case and ask you to infer the principle upon which it was decided. A small number of questions give you two paradoxical or seemingly inconsistent statements and ask for a fact that would help explain or reconcile the apparent inconsistency.

Let's break it down by the numbers. Inference questions account for just over 13 percent of the Logical Reasoning section, around six or seven questions per test. Add to that one or two Principle questions calling for inferences and typically three or four Paradox questions per test, and the material in this chapter constitutes a healthy chunk of the Logical Reasoning section.

These questions are not based on arguments; there's no need for you to determine conclusion and evidence here or to try to figure out what an author is assuming. Rather, these questions all reward you for seeing the implications of facts and assertions. In non-argument questions, you're interested in what *follows from* the statements in the stimulus, not in what you could add to the stimulus to make it stronger, weaker, or more complete.

MAKING DEDUCTIONS AND INFERENCE QUESTIONS

Here's an example of a typical LSAT Inference question. Feel free to try it now or just read through it to get a sense of what these questions require. You'll see this question explained in detail a little later in the chapter. In this section, you will learn how to handle questions such as this one; you'll learn what the testmaker is asking for and how to untangle the stimulus effectively.

> The axis of Earth's daily rotation is tilted with respect to the plane of its orbit at an angle of roughly 23 degrees. That angle can be kept fairly stable only by the gravitational influence of Earth's large, nearby Moon. Without such a stable and moderate axis tilt, a planet's climate is too extreme and unstable to support life. Mars, for example, has only very small moons, tilts at wildly fluctuating angles, and cannot support life.
>
> If the statements above are true, which one of the following must also be true on the basis of them?
>
> (A)   If Mars had a sufficiently large nearby moon, Mars would be able to support life.
> (B)   If Earth's Moon were to leave Earth's orbit, Earth's climate would be unable to support life.
> (C)   Any planet with a stable, moderate axis tilt can support life.
> (D)   Gravitational influences other than moons have little or no effect on the magnitude of the tilt angle of either Earth's or Mars's axis.
> (E)   No planet that has more than one moon can support life.
>
> *PrepTest28 Sec1 Q14*

By asking for an answer that must be true based on the statements in the stimulus, the LSAT is asking you to make a valid deduction from those statements. Now, you make deductions every day. You might wake up to find the ground wet and water dripping from the trees and deduce that it rained during the night. You might find a piece of pie you left in the refrigerator gone, and given that the only person in the house was your roommate, deduce that she ate your pie. But many of the deductions we make in real life are based on partial information and hunches. In most cases, they're very likely, but they may or may not be true.

A deduction, as defined on the LSAT, applies logic more rigorously than most real-life deductions. To illustrate the difference between the kind of deduction rewarded by an LSAT question and the kind we make in everyday life, suppose a house guest told you, "I don't eat ice cream." Given this fact about your guest, you might speculate, "She must be on a diet," or "I wonder if she's lactose intolerant." Either is possible. However, neither of your reasonable speculations would be a valid deduction on the LSAT because neither *must be true* and neither follows unequivocally from the statement itself. On the LSAT, a valid inference, were it negated, would contradict the given information. So, if the LSAT asked you for an inference based on your guest's statement, the correct answer would be something like "If the only dessert I serve after dinner tonight is ice cream, she won't eat any dessert." This fact is conditional, a little convoluted, and may even seem obvious, but it must be true given that your guest does not eat ice cream.

While all of the questions covered in this chapter deal with what follows from the statements in the stimulus, let's begin with Inference questions. They're the most numerous of the questions covered here, and more importantly, they're the ones that most directly reward you for assessing statements and making valid deductions based on them.

LEARNING OBJECTIVES

In this section, you'll learn to:

· Make valid inferences from a single statement of fact.
· Combine two or more statements to make valid inferences.
· Recognize and use Keywords to make valid inferences.
· Recognize and use Formal Logic to make valid inferences.
· Recognize and use uncertain statements to make valid inferences.
· Identify and answer Inference questions.

What Inference Question Stems Ask For

An *inference* on the LSAT is a deduction made from facts given in the question. For LSAT purposes, treat *inference* and *deduction* as synonyms. With a few exceptions, the stimulus of an Inference question serves the same role as the rules of a logic game. Like a deduction in a logic game, the correct answer to an Inference question is a fact that *must be true* given the statements that the testmaker provides.

The question stem in the previous sample question was very direct: If the stimulus is true, the right answer must be true also. Here are a few other representative Inference question stems along with the LSAT expert's analysis.

LSAT Argument		Analysis
Which one of the following is most strongly supported by the information above? *PrepTest27 Sec1 Q12*	→	The "information above" (statements in the stimulus) supports the correct answer (the valid inference). Remember that Strengthen questions could also use the word *support* in the question stem. Strengthen questions ask you to support the conclusion or argument above, while Inference questions ask you to support one of the following answers.
Which one of the following can be properly inferred from the passage? *PrepTest28 Sec3 Q1*	→	The correct answer is a valid deduction ("properly inferred") from the statements in the stimulus.
Which one of the following is a conclusion that can be properly drawn from the information above? *PrepTest27 Sec4 Q17*	→	This stimulus will be composed of assertions that act as evidence without a conclusion. The correct answer, then, will be a valid conclusion (deduction) drawn from those statements.

All of these stems ask for essentially the same thing: the answer choice that *must be true* if the facts in the stimulus are true. (Note that from time to time, the test will ask for the choice that *must be false* or *could be true* based on the statements. We'll cover those relatively rare question stems before the end of the section.) A precise understanding of what the testmaker is asking for leads to a handful of important observations about Inference questions that make learning how to make deductions more meaningful.

LSAT STRATEGY

Some facts to remember about LSAT inferences:

· An inference follows only from the facts given. No outside knowledge is required.

· An inference need not be mind-blowing. Sometimes it will be simple, even obvious.

· An inference may come from a single fact, or it may require combining multiple facts. It may not be necessary to take into account all the facts given in the stimulus.

Every Inference question stem contains a strong reminder of these strategy points: The correct answer must be based entirely and exclusively on the statements in the stimulus. Thus, it makes a lot of sense to untangle the stimulus by looking for the strongest statements (those that lead to the strongest deductions) and by looking for statements that can be combined (those that share the same terms, for example).

Cataloging and Paraphrasing Statements in the Stimulus

Without an argument to analyze—that is, without an explicit conclusion and evidence to identify—untrained test takers may find themselves at a loss when approaching Inference stimuli. Added to this confusion is the fact that Inference stimuli often use wordy, complicated, or confusing language. The LSAT expert, however, untangles the Inference stimulus efficiently by asking, "What do I *know* to be true?" Asking this question focuses the expert's attention on two criteria: (1) She notes statements that are the most concrete, and (2) she spots statements that can be combined. As always, the LSAT expert actively paraphrases convoluted statements to be sure she understands precisely what the statement does *and does not* assert.

Note the Most Concrete Statements

Think back for a moment to the example we used earlier, your guest's statement: "I don't eat ice cream." You were able to draw a valid inference from that statement because it was so strong. Had she said, "I don't know—maybe I'll have some ice cream," you could not draw a conclusion about what she might have for dessert. When untangling an Inference stimulus, the LSAT expert is always on the lookout for the most concrete statements.

LSAT Question	Analysis
Sharks have a higher ratio of cartilage mass to body mass than any other organism. They also have a greater resistance to cancer than any other organism. Shark cartilage contains a substance that inhibits tumor growth by stopping the development of a new blood network. In the past 20 years, none of the responses among terminal cancer patients to various therapeutic measures has been more positive than the response among those who consumed shark cartilage.	The strongest statements here are the superlatives regarding sharks in the first two sentences. Since the rest of the passage is focused on cancer as well, the second sentence stands out: "[sharks] have a greater resistance to cancer than *any* other organism."

PrepTest28 Sec1 Q11

Identifying the strongest statements can have immediate benefits. On the next page, take a look at the full question from which that stimulus came, and notice how an LSAT expert approached it. Make sure to first note that the question asks for what must be *false*, rather than what must be true.

LSAT Question	Analysis
Sharks have a higher ratio of cartilage mass to body mass than any other organism. They also have a greater resistance to cancer than any other organism. Shark cartilage contains a substance that inhibits tumor growth by stopping the development of a new blood network. In the past 20 years, none of the responses among terminal cancer patients to various therapeutic measures has been more positive than the response among those who consumed shark cartilage.	**Step 2:** The strongest statement is in the second sentence: "[sharks] have a great resistance to cancer than any other organism." The final sentence is also a forceful statement regarding the unmatched cancer resistance of sharks, in this case as a therapeutic measure.
If the claims made above are true, then each of the following could be true EXCEPT:	**Step 1:** The phrasing "could be true EXCEPT" indicates an Inference question that asks for what *must be false*.
	Step 3: The wrong answers here all could be true, while the correct answer will contradict something in stimulus. Look first for an answer that contradicts the most concrete statement that sharks are the animals most resistant to cancer. Eliminate Outside the Scope answer choices, since they could be true.
(A) No organism resists cancer better than sharks do, but some resist cancer as well as sharks.	**Step 4:** Correct. The first clause of this answer is consistent with the concrete statement regarding shark supremacy in resisting cancer, but the second clause contradicts that supremacy by indicating that some species are just as good at resisting cancer as sharks.
(B) The organism most susceptible to cancer has a higher percentage of cartilage than some organisms that are less susceptible to cancer.	Outside the Scope. There is no information about the most susceptible species. Also, it cannot be deduced from the information that the ratio of cartilage to body mass is the reason for the shark's resistance to cancer. Eliminate.
(C) The substance in shark cartilage that inhibits tumor growth is found in most organisms.	It is possible that most organisms also contain the tumor inhibiting substance, even if they do not match sharks in levels of effectiveness. Eliminate.
(D) In the past 20 years many terminal cancer patients have improved dramatically following many sorts of therapy.	Such patients using other therapies could have improved dramatically, even if not as dramatically as those on shark therapy. Eliminate.
(E) Some organisms have immune systems more efficient than a shark's immune system. *PrepTest28 Sec1 Q11*	Outside the Scope. The stimulus focuses only on cancer resistance, not entire immune systems. Eliminate.

In this case, the correct answer is supported because it contradicts a single, strong statement in the stimulus. From time to time, the testmaker will reward you for making simple, straightforward inferences. Note, too, that the stimulus provides some basis for speculation that answer choices (B), (C), (D), and (E) also would be false statements. But for a *must be false* question such as this one, ask yourself: "even if this answer choice seems to go *somewhat* against the grain of the information, could it still *possibly* be true?" If it *could be true* then you have to get rid of it.

Practice

First, use the question stem to characterize the one correct and four incorrect answers. Then, catalog the statements in this Inference stimulus. Identify the strongest, most concrete assertion(s) you find. As a hint, the most concrete statement in this stimulus is also highlighted by a contrast Keyword phrase, which we will focus on shortly.

LSAT Question	My Analysis
1. Letter to the Editor: Your article on effective cockroach control states that vexone is effective against only one of the more than 4,000 cockroach species that infest North America: the German cockroach. In actuality, vexone has been utilized effectively for almost a decade against all of the species that infest North America. In testing our product, Roach Ender, which contains vexone, we have conducted many well-documented studies that prove this fact.	Step 2:
Each of the following statements conflicts with the letter writer's view EXCEPT: *PrepTest28 Sec3 Q12*	Step 1:

Expert analysis of the entire question is on the next page. ▶ ▶ ▶

Expert Analysis

Here's how an LSAT expert might analyze the question stem and stimulus you just saw. You can also see her analysis of the answer choices accompanying this question.

LSAT Question	Analysis
1. Letter to the Editor: Your article on effective cockroach control states that vexone is effective against only one of the more than 4,000 cockroach species that infest North America: the German cockroach. In actuality, vexone has been utilized effectively for almost a decade against all of the species that infest North America. In testing our product, Roach Ender, which contains vexone, we have conducted many well-documented studies that prove this fact. $\longrightarrow$	**Step 2:** The first sentence has a concrete statement, but recognize it as the view of another voice; it is not the author's. The contrast phrase "[i]n actuality" leads into the author's statements and her most concrete statement: Vexone has been effective against *all* North American cockroach species. The third sentence is merely an assertion that studies exist that document vexone's effectiveness.
Each of the following statements conflicts with the letter writer's view EXCEPT: $\longrightarrow$	**Step 1:** The phrase "conflicts with . . . EXCEPT" indicates an Inference question asking for what does *not* contradict information in the stimulus.
	Step 3: The most concrete statement in the stimulus holds that vexone is effective against *all* species of cockroach. The correct answer could simply agree with that statement, and it is likely that at least some of the wrong answers will contradict that concrete statement.
(A) Vexone is effective against only two species of cockroach that infest North America. $\longrightarrow$	**Step 4:** This answer contradicts the concrete statement that vexone is effective against *all* such species. Eliminate.
(B) Not all of the major species of cockroach that infest North America can be controlled by Roach Ender. $\longrightarrow$	This answer also contradicts the concrete statement that vexone is effective against *all* such species. Eliminate.
(C) Every species of cockroach that infests North America can be controlled by vexone. $\longrightarrow$	Correct. This answer comports with the concrete statement that vexone is effective against *all* such species.
(D) The cockroach infestations that have been combated with vexone have not included all of the cockroach species that infest North America. $\longrightarrow$	This answer also contradicts the concrete statement that vexone is effective against *all* such species. Eliminate.
(E) Roach Ender was tested against exactly 4,000 cockroach species that infest North America. *PrepTest28 Sec3 Q12* $\longrightarrow$	This answer contradicts the letter, which states that studies have demonstrated Vexone to be effective against all of the *more than* 4,000 cockroach species found in North America. Eliminate.

Combine Statements to Make Valid Inferences

In most cases, you won't be able to get the correct answer to an Inference question by rephrasing a single statement; when this happens, you'll need to combine two or more statements (much as you combine the rules in logic games) in order to predict the correct answer. Even so, it is still crucial to pay attention to the strength or concreteness of the statements in the stimulus. Imagine you learn two facts: (1) All practicing attorneys are eligible for the state bar's insurance plan, and (2) Joe graduated from a law school in the state. From those statements, the best you can say is that Joe may be eligible for the bar's insurance plan. After all, he may or may not be a practicing attorney. But, make the second statement more concrete as it applies to the first statement—Joe is a practicing attorney in the state—and you can easily conclude that Joe is eligible for the plan.

Take a look at an LSAT expert's analysis of an example stimulus from a real LSAT Inference question.

LSAT Question	Analysis
These days, drug companies and health professionals alike are focusing their attention on cholesterol in the blood. The more cholesterol we have in our blood, the higher the risk that we shall die of a heart attack. The issue is pertinent since heart disease kills more North Americans every year than any other single cause. At least three factors—smoking, drinking, and exercise— can each influence levels of cholesterol in the blood. $\longrightarrow$	The stimulus provides two causal relationships: 1) Increased cholesterol results in increased risk of death from heart attack, and, 2) smoking, drinking and exercise can each affect cholesterol levels. Combining these statements yields: smoking, drinking, and exercise can each influence the risk of death from heart attack.

PrepTest29 Sec1 Q6

The final sentence in the stimulus can be combined with the second because the two sentences both discuss how *levels of cholesterol* factor into two separate causal relationships. You can combine those statements to yield a chain of causation. Does this process feel familiar? It should if you've tackled the chapters on Logic Games. There, you always looked to combine rules that share common entities as a way to produce valid deductions (the "D" in BLEND—Duplications). The principle is much the same with statements in Inference questions.

Take a look at the full question from which we drew that stimulus. You'll see that the correct answer directly rewards making the logical combination of statements the expert noted.

LSAT Question		Analysis
These days, drug companies and health professionals alike are focusing their attention on cholesterol in the blood. The more cholesterol we have in our blood, the higher the risk that we shall die of a heart attack. The issue is pertinent since heart disease kills more North Americans every year than any other single cause. At least three factors—smoking, drinking, and exercise—can each influence levels of cholesterol in the blood.	→	**Step 2:** The stimulus provides two causal relationships: 1) Increased cholesterol results in increased risk of death from heart attack, and, 2) smoking, drinking, and exercise can each affect cholesterol levels.
Which one of the following can be properly concluded from the passage?	→	**Step 1:** Rather than asking for what the author *did conclude*, this question asks for what "*can be properly concluded*," indicating an Inference question.
		Step 3: Combining the two causal relationships yields a chain of causation: Smoking, drinking, and exercise can each influence cholesterol levels, which, in turn, affects the risk of death from heart attack. The typical Inference answer will focus on the endpoints (three factors influence risk of fatal heart attack), rather than the connecting term (level of cholesterol).
(A) If a person has low blood cholesterol, then that person's risk of fatal heart disease is low.	→	**Step 4:** Distortion. The LSAT demands distinguishing an absolute value ("low" risk) from a relative value ("lower" risk). The stimulus only deals with relative or comparable risk levels. This answer could also be viewed as an incomplete contrapositive of the first causal relationship in the stimulus (negates both terms without reversing the sides). Eliminate.
(B) Smoking in moderation can entail as great a risk of fatal heart disease as does heavy smoking.	→	Irrelevant Comparison. While smoking is cited as a factor affecting cholesterol levels in the blood, nothing in the passage distinguishes the effects of moderate versus heavy smoking. Eliminate.
(C) A high-cholesterol diet is the principal cause of death in North America.	→	Extreme. It cannot be deduced that high-cholesterol is the "*principal* cause of death in North America." Indeed, the stimulus says nothing about a high-cholesterol *diet*, just levels in the blood, wherever it comes from. Eliminate.
(D) The only way that smoking increases one's risk of fatal heart disease is by influencing the levels of cholesterol in the blood.	→	Extreme. The stimulus does not preclude the possibility that smoking may increase the risk of fatal heart disease in other ways. Eliminate.
(E) The risk of fatal heart disease can be altered by certain changes in lifestyle. *PrepTest29 Sec1 Q6*	→	Correct. This answer matches the prediction by linking "changes in lifestyle" (which would encompass changes in smoking, drinking, and exercise habits) to the risk of fatal heart disease.

Practice

Try another example. First, use the question stem to characterize the one correct and four incorrect answers. Then, catalog the statements in stimulus and note which two statements can be combined.

LSAT Question	My Analysis
2. Poppy petals function to attract pollinating insects. The pollination of a poppy flower triggers the release into that flower of a substance that causes its petals to wilt within one or two days. If the flower is not pollinated, the substance will not be released and the petals will remain fresh for a week or longer, as long as the plant can nourish them. Cutting an unpollinated poppy flower from the plant triggers the release into the flower of the same substance whose release is triggered by pollination.	Step 2:
The statements above, if true, most strongly support which one of the following? *PrepTest28 Sec1 Q16*	Step 1:

Expert Analysis

Here's how an LSAT expert might analyze the question stem and stimulus you just saw. You can also see his analysis of the answer choices accompanying this question.

LSAT Question	Analysis
2. Poppy petals function to attract pollinating insects. The pollination of a poppy flower triggers the release into that flower of a substance that causes its petals to wilt within one or two days. If the flower is not pollinated, the substance will not be released and the petals will remain fresh for a week or longer, as long as the plant can nourish them. Cutting an unpollinated poppy flower from the plant triggers the release into the flower of the same substance whose release is triggered by pollination.	**Step 2:** Catalog the statements: (1) Poppy petals attract pollinating insects, (2) pollination triggers a substance causing petals to wilt within two days, (3) if not pollinated then petals can remain fresh for a week or more, and (4) cutting an unpollinated flower releases the same substance as pollination.
The statements above, if true, most strongly support which one of the following?	**Step 1:** A question stem that asks you to use the "statements above" to "support" an answer indicates an Inference question.
	Step 3: Since cutting an unpollinated flower releases the same substance as pollination does, one can deduced that cutting an unpollinated flower will also cause the petals to wilt.
(A) Pollinating insects are not attracted to wilted poppy flowers.	**Step 4:** Distortion. The information indicates that pollination causes wilting, but does not say anything about the effect of wilting on the attractiveness of flowers to pollinating insects. Eliminate.
(B) Even if cut poppies are given all necessary nutrients, their petals will tend to wilt within a few days.	Correct. This follows from the prediction (in other words, the deduction made in Step 3).
(C) Flowers of all plants release the substance that causes wilting when they are cut, although the amount released may vary	Outside the Scope. There is no information about plants other than poppies. Eliminate.
(D) The pollen on pollinated poppy flowers prevents their petals from absorbing the nutrients carried to them by their stems.	Distortion. It is the substance released following pollination, and not the pollen itself, that is responsible for the wilting. There is no other information regarding the effect of pollen. Eliminate.
(E) Poppy plants are unable to draw nutrients from soil or water after the substance that causes wilting has been released.	Distortion. The stimulus does not indicate how the substance causes the poppy flowers to wilt. The reference to nutrients did not apply to the effects on pollinated plants. Eliminate.

PrepTest28 Sec1 Q16

In the examples we just looked at, two or more statements shared common terms and thus combined to produce valid inferences that must be true based on the statements in the stimulus. Just like in Logic Games, always look to combine statements when possible in Inference questions.

Using Keywords to Make Valid Inferences

Interestingly, the skills required to dominate Logical Reasoning Inference questions are many of the same skills needed to do well in Logic Games and Reading Comprehension. You've already seen the parallels in analyzing and combining concrete statements to the Logic Games section. In Reading Comprehension, as you will learn in future chapters, we rely heavily on Keywords to ascertain the structure of a passage and to recognize what will be important in answering questions. You will see a preview of that in this segment as we apply those Reading Comprehension style skills to Logical Reasoning Inference questions. As you saw when we discussed concrete statements, the answer to an Inference question can derive from a single statement. Now we will see how the testmaker often highlights that vital statement using an Emphasis Keyword, such as *importantly* or *unfortunately*. Even more important are Contrast Keywords—words like *but, yet,* or *despite* or phrases such as *on the other hand*. These Keywords tell you that the author considers two terms or concepts to be at odds, and they allow you to see how to potentially connect such statements. Take a look at an LSAT expert's analysis of the following LSAT Inference stimulus.

LSAT Question	Analysis
Ideally, scientific laws should display the virtues of precision and generality, as do the laws of physics. However, because of the nature of their subject matter, laws of social science often have to use terms that are imprecise: for example, one knows only vaguely what is meant by "republicanism" or "class." As for generality, laws that apply only in certain social systems are typically the only ones possible for the social sciences. $\longrightarrow$ *PrepTestB Sec4 Q15*	"Ideally" and "should" emphasize the first sentence as the author's assertion of the scientific ideals of precision and generality. "However," highlights the contrast in the following two sentences, which respectively indicate the limits on precision and generality.

The Keywords very explicitly set out the structure of the passage. First, the author forcefully asserts the scientific ideals of precision and generality. Next, "however" highlights the contrasting limitations on achieving precision and generality that follow. These statements do not combine neatly to form a clear deduction, so the answer may derive from a single statement. Which statement is both emphasized and the most concrete?

Here's how the LSAT expert might analyze the entire question.

LSAT Question	Analysis
Ideally, scientific laws should display the virtues of precision and generality, as do the laws of physics. However, because of the nature of their subject matter, laws of social science often have to use terms that are imprecise: for example, one knows only vaguely what is meant by "republicanism" or "class." As for generality, laws that apply only in certain social systems are typically the only ones possible for the social sciences.	**Step 2:** "Ideally" and "should" emphasize the first sentence as the author's assertion of the scientific ideals of precision and generality. "However," highlights the contrast in the following two sentences, which respectively indicate the limits on precision and generality.
Which one of the following statements is most strongly supported by the information above?	**Step 1:** A question stem that directs using "information above" to "support" an answer indicates an Inference question.
	Step 3: The statements do not neatly combine to yield a deduction. The first sentence is both emphasized ("ideally") and the most concrete. Scan for a match to the first sentence; if necessary, assess each answer by attempting to find direct support in the stimulus.
(A) All else being equal, a precise, general scientific law is to be preferred over one that is not general.	**Step 4:** Correct. This is a re-statement of the first sentence, and, thus, directly supported by the passage.
(B) The social sciences would benefit if they redirected their focus to the subject matter of the physical sciences.	Distortion. This suggests that the social sciences essentially should cease to exist, which is not indicated in the stimulus. Eliminate.
(C) Terms such as "class" should be more precisely formulated by social scientists.	Distortion. While the author acknowledges the imprecision of social science terms, he makes no recommendation for increasing the precision of their definitions. According to the passage, social science will just be stuck with some vague terms. Eliminate.
(D) Social scientists should make an effort to construct more laws that apply to all societies.	Distortion. The author does not make any suggestions about the types of laws social scientists should or should not formulate. Eliminate.
(E) The laws of social science are invariably not truly scientific. *PrepTestB Sec4 Q15*	Extreme. The information supports a deduction that laws of social science do not meet the scientific *ideal*, but this choice goes too far in stating they are "invariably not *truly* scientific." Eliminate.

The correct answer is clearly supported by the author's most concrete statement, while three of the wrong answers (B, C, and D) are distortions or contradictions of the less concrete statements in the stimulus. Answer choice (E) attempts to combine the statements in a way suggested by the contrast word "however," but it states the deduction too forcefully.

Practice

First, use the question stem to characterize the one correct and four incorrect answers. Then, catalog the statements in the stimulus, using Keywords to combine statements where possible.

LSAT Question	My Analysis
3. Physical education should teach people to pursue healthy, active lifestyles as they grow older. But the focus on competitive sports in most schools causes most of the less competitive students to turn away from sports. Having learned to think of themselves as unathletic, they do not exercise enough to stay healthy.	**Step 2:**
Which one of the following is most strongly supported by the statements above, if they are true? *PrepTest29 Sec4 Q3*	**Step 1:**

Expert Analysis

Here's how an LSAT expert might analyze the question stem and stimulus you just saw. You can also see her analysis of the answer choices accompanying this question.

LSAT Question	Analysis
3. Physical education should teach people to pursue healthy, active lifestyles as they grow older. But the focus on competitive sports in most schools causes most of the less competitive students to turn away from sports. Having learned to think of themselves as unathletic, they do not exercise enough to stay healthy.	**Step 2:** "But" contrasts the laudable goal of physical education with the unfortunate result of physical education's focus on competitive sports. The third sentence provides the reason: In a competitive environment, less competitive students see themselves as unathletic and in turn stop exercising.
Which one of the following is most strongly supported by the statements above, if they are true?	**Step 1:** A question that asks you to use the "statements above" to "support" an answer indicates an Inference question.
	Step 3: The contrast Keyword, "[b]ut," points out a dilemma: Physical education should promote healthy, active lifestyles, but its focus on competitive sports has the opposite effect on less competitive students. The correct answer will follow from this dilemma. It could either summarize the problem or offer a solution.
(A) Physical education should include noncompetitive activities.	**Step 4:** Correct. Because a focus on competitive sports prevents P.E. from doing what it should for some students, it follows that P.E. should include noncompetitive activities as well.
(B) Competition causes most students to turn away from sports.	Extreme. The stimulus only states that competition causes "most *of the less competitive* students to turn away from sports." There is no information about the population of students as a whole. Eliminate.
(C) People who are talented at competitive physical endeavors exercise regularly.	Distortion. The stimulus states that the unathletic "do not exercise enough to stay healthy," but it is silent as to the exercise habits of the talented competitors. Eliminate.
(D) The mental aspects of exercise are as important as the physical ones.	Irrelevant Comparison. The stimulus does not make this comparison. Eliminate.
(E) Children should be taught the dangers of a sedentary lifestyle. *PrepTest29 Sec4 Q3*	Outside the Scope. The passage does not imply that teaching students about the *dangers* of too little exercise is effective or recommended. Eliminate.

Using Formal Logic to Make Valid Inferences

Think back to the work you did on Formal Logic in Chapter 1 and again in the Logic Games part of this book, and it will be clear why the testmaker often uses Formal Logic in Inference stimuli. While challenging to read and interpret, conditional Formal Logic statements are easy to combine in ways that reveal their implications. From "If A, then B," and "If B, then C," you can deduce "If A, then C," with absolute confidence. Sometimes, Logical Reasoning inferences are just that straightforward, although you can expect to encounter some pretty convoluted language in these stimuli. Your familiarity with Formal Logic will be an enormous benefit on many Inference questions. Once you recognize that a stimulus contains Formal Logic, its statements are easy to catalog and assess. You can, of course, even jot them down in Formal Logic shorthand in your test booklet.

With that in mind, take a look at how an LSAT expert would analyze the stimulus from the first Inference question you saw in this chapter.

LSAT Question	Analysis
The axis of Earth's daily rotation is tilted with respect to the plane of its orbit at an angle of roughly 23 degrees. That angle can be kept fairly stable only by the gravitational influence of Earth's large, nearby Moon. Without such a stable and moderate axis tilt, a planet's climate is too extreme and unstable to support life. Mars, for example, has only very small moons, tilts at wildly fluctuating angles, and cannot support life. *PrepTest28 Sec1 Q14*	Two Formal Logic Statements: (1) stable angle $\rightarrow$ moon has gravitational influence (2) no stable angle $\rightarrow$ climate not support life

At this point, the LSAT expert seeks to combine the two Formal Logic statements, but recognizes that they do not link up neatly as written. However, taking the contrapositive of the second statement would allow them to link up through the *stable angle* term, yielding:

Climate support life $\rightarrow$ stable angle $\rightarrow$ moon has gravitational influence

This means that for the Earth's climate to support life, the moon must be exerting a gravitational influence; equally true, we know that without the moon's gravitational influence, the Earth's climate would not support life. Rather than testing each answer choice, the LSAT expert seeks out the answer choice containing that formal logic deduction.

LSAT Question	Analysis
The axis of Earth's daily rotation is tilted with respect to the plane of its orbit at an angle of roughly 23 degrees. That angle can be kept fairly stable only by the gravitational influence of Earth's large, nearby Moon. Without such a stable and moderate axis tilt, a planet's climate is too extreme and unstable to support life. Mars, for example, has only very small moons, tilts at wildly fluctuating angles, and cannot support life.	**Step 2:** Two Formal Logic Statements: (1) Earth's stable angle → moon has gravitational influence (2) no stable angle → climate not support life
If the statements above are true, which one of the following must also be true on the basis of them?	**Step 1:** The phrases "If the statements above are true," and "must also be true," indicate an Inference question.
	Step 3: Contraposing the second statement and then combining the statements yields the deduction: If Earth's climate supports life → moon has gravitational influence Or Without moon's influence → Earth's climate cannot support life
(A) If Mars had a sufficiently large nearby moon, Mars would be able to support life.	**Step 4:** It cannot be known what would result if Mars *did* have a large moon. This answer treats the necessary condition of having a large moon as a sufficient condition, but there may be other prerequisites for supporting life. Eliminate.
(B) If Earth's Moon were to leave Earth's orbit, Earth's climate would be unable to support life.	Correct. This matches the deduction from combining the formal logic statements: No moon → Earth not support life.
(C) Any planet with a stable, moderate axis tilt can support life.	As with answer choice (A), this answer confuses the necessity of a stable angle with being sufficient to support life. Eliminate.
(D) Gravitational influences other than moons have little or no effect on the magnitude of the tilt angle of either Earth's or Mars's axis.	Beyond knowing that a moon's influence is necessary for a stable tilt, there is no information as to what degree other gravitational influences play a role. Eliminate.
(E) No planet that has more than one moon can support life. *PrepTest28 Sec1 Q14*	While a moon is necessary, the stimulus does not specify that there must be *exactly one* moon in order to support life. Two moons, or more, might be better than one, or at least as good, for stability.

In that example, two Formal Logic statements linked neatly together in A → B → C form; at least once the contrapositive of the second statement was taken. Sometimes there are additional variables, or there might be a factual statement to combine with the Formal Logic.

Practice

First, use the question stem to characterize the one correct and four incorrect answers. Then, catalog the statements in the stimulus. Translate any Formal Logic statements you find and determine whether and how they can be combined. Also, note if there is a factual statement that *triggers* a Formal Logic rule.

LSAT Question	My Analysis
4. Editorialist: Drivers with a large number of demerit points who additionally have been convicted of a serious driving-related offense should either be sentenced to jail or be forced to receive driver re-education, since to do otherwise would be to allow a crime to go unpunished. Only if such drivers are likely to be made more responsible drivers should driver re-education be recommended for them. Unfortunately, it is always almost impossible to make drivers with a large number of demerit points more responsible drivers.	**Step 2:**
If the editorialist's statements are true, they provide the most support for which one of the following? *PrepTest29 Sec4 Q12*	**Step 1:**

Expert Analysis

Here's how an LSAT expert might analyze the question stem and stimulus you just saw. You can also see his analysis of the answer choices accompanying this question.

LSAT Question	Analysis
4. Editorialist: Drivers with a large number of demerit points who additionally have been convicted of a serious driving-related offense should either be sentenced to jail or be forced to receive driver re-education, since to do otherwise would be to allow a crime to go unpunished. Only if such drivers are likely to be made more responsible drivers should driver re-education be recommended for them. Unfortunately, it is always almost impossible to make drivers with a large number of demerit points more responsible drivers.	**Step 2:** Two Formal Logic Statements about drivers with many demerits: another conviction → i) jail or ii) driver re-education re-education → likelihood of increased responsibility Factual Statement: Increased responsibility is nearly impossible for such drivers.
If the editorialist's statements are true, they provide the most support for which one of the following?	**Step 1:** A question that asks you to use the "statements above" to "support" an answer indicates an Inference question.
	Step 3: The fact that it is nearly impossible to increase the level of responsibility of repeat offenders dictates that only one of the two possible results can occur: jail.
(A) Drivers with a large number of demerit points who have been convicted of a serious driving-related offense should be sent to jail.	**Step 4:** Correct. Two options were identified: re-education or jail. However, re-education depends on the possibility of increasing a driver's responsibility. Since that is nearly impossible, the only option left is jail.
(B) Driver re-education offers the best chance of making drivers with a large number of demerit points responsible drivers.	While technically it is possible that driver education is the *best chance*, there is no support for this assertion; only that increasing the responsibility level of such drivers is nearly impossible. Eliminate.
(C) Driver re-education is not harsh enough punishment for anyone convicted of a serious driving-related offense who has also accumulated a large number of demerit points.	Distortion. The concern is the effectiveness of re-education in increasing driver responsibility levels, not whether it is *harsh* enough. Eliminate.
(D) Driver re-education should not be recommended for those who have committed no serious driving-related offenses.	Outside the Scope. The stimulus does not discuss drivers who have no serious driving-related offenses. Eliminate.
(E) Drivers with a large number of demerit points but no conviction for a serious driving-related offense should receive driver re-education rather than jail.	Outside the Scope. As with choice (D), the stimulus does not discuss drivers who have no serious driving-related offenses. Eliminate.

PrepTest29 Sec4 Q12

Practice

First, use the question stem to characterize the one correct and four incorrect answers. Then, catalog the statements in the stimulus. Paraphrase the statements, translating any conditional Formal Logic. Look for clues as to how the author considers the statements to relate to one another.

LSAT Question	My Analysis
5. A poem is any work of art that exploits some of the musical characteristics of language, such as meter, rhythm, euphony, and rhyme. A novel, though it may be a work of art in language, does not usually exploit the musical characteristics of language. A symphony, though it may be a work of art that exploits the musical characteristics of sounds, rarely involves language. A limerick, though it may exploit some musical characteristics of language, is not, strictly speaking, art.	**Step 2:**
The statements above, if true, most strongly support which one of the following? *PrepTest27 Sec1 Q20*	**Step 1:**

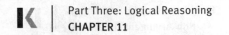

Expert Analysis

Here's how an LSAT expert might analyze the question stem and stimulus you just saw. You can also see her analysis of the answer choices accompanying this question.

LSAT Question	Analysis
5. A poem is any work of art that exploits some of the musical characteristics of language, such as meter, rhythm, euphony, and rhyme. A novel, though it may be a work of art in language, does not usually exploit the musical characteristics of language. A symphony, though it may be a work of art that exploits the musical characteristics of sounds, rarely involves language. A limerick, though it may exploit some musical characteristics of language, is not, strictly speaking, art.	**Step 2:** Formal Logic statement: Exploit musical aspect of language → Poem Characteristics of three items: Novel: possible work of art in language; does not usually exploit musical aspects Symphony: possible work of art that exploits musical aspects of sound, but rarely of language Limerick: not art
The statements above, if true, most strongly support which one of the following?	**Step 1:** A question that asks you to use the "statements above" to "support" an answer indicates an Inference question.
	Step 3: The most concrete information from among the three examples is that a limerick is not art; thus, limericks do not meet the sufficient conditions set out in the stimulus. As to novels and symphonies, while they do not typically meet the sufficient conditions set out to establish what is a poem, there does exist the possibility that each of them could meet those conditions. Anticipate an answer that allows you to know that either a novel or a symphony meets the sufficient conditions for being designated a poem.
(A) If a creation is neither a poem, nor a novel, nor a symphony, then it is not a work of art.	**Step 4:** Distortion. The stimulus does not dictate that nothing beyond a poem, novel, or symphony could be a work of art. Eliminate.
(B) An example of so-called blank verse, which does not rhyme, is not really a poem.	The stimulus does not discuss *blank verse* and rhyming is not a singular necessary condition to qualify as poem. Thus, this answer is not supported. Eliminate.
(C) If a novel exploits meter and rhyme while standing as a work of art, then it is both a novel and a poem.	Correct. If a novel, in addition to being based in language is a work of art that exploits meter and rhyme, then it meets the sufficient conditions set out in the stimulus and, thus, must be a poem.
(D) Limericks constitute a nonartistic type of poetry.	The stimulus defines poems as works of art, without any discussion of *nonartistic* types of poetry. Eliminate.
(E) If a symphony does not exploit the musical characteristics of sound, then it is not a work of art. <div align="center">*PrepTest27 Sec1 Q20*</div>	The stimulus does not indicate that exploiting musical characteristics of sound is a necessary condition for a symphony to be a work of art, as this choice suggests. Eliminate.

Using Uncertain Statements to Make Valid Inferences

The process of making inferences from Formal Logic statements probably felt a lot like the deduction step in Logic Games. You used conditional assertions to assess the truth of other statements or combined if/then statements to reveal unstated certainties. For you, as a well-trained test taker, words like *any, all,* and *none* signal clear Formal Logic relationships of necessity and sufficiency. In many Inference questions, however, you will also have to deal with statements that are less absolute, statements that use words like *most, many, several,* and *some.*

The good news is that the LSAT follows reliable conventions that can help to create inferences out of statements containing these indeterminate terms. The word *most,* for example, means any amount greater than 50 percent. The word *some,* on the other hand, signifies one or more (i.e., *some* = not none). Note that both of these words—*most* and *some*—have the possibility of also meaning *all.* Although this runs counter to our normal usage and our instincts, it is important to understand how the LSAT uses these words, especially because they can be used to create inferences in some predictable ways. Other indeterminate words—*several, many,* and *few*—should be treated in the same way. Don't try to give them any special meaning; they're inclusive of every possibility between *two* and *all.*

LSAT STRATEGY

Levels of Certainty

Here are the types of statements you'll encounter in Inference stimuli, arranged from most concrete to least:

- **Unqualified Assertions** (e.g., *Bob is an attorney* or *Monday will be a rainy day*)
- **Conditional Statements/Formal Logic** (e.g., *If the company hopes to meet its budget, then it must cut travel costs* or *McLaren will lose the election unless the county sees record voter turnout*)
- **Statements with "most"**—this means *more than half* but could include *all* (e.g., *Most of Company Y's employees are college graduates* or *A majority of the respondents preferred the new logo*)
- **Statements with "some" or "few"**—this means anywhere from one to all, just not zero (e.g., *Some architects are painters*)

It's rare for a stimulus to be comprised exclusively of uncertain statements. You might, on occasion, see something along the lines of "Most pizza restaurants in town are family run businesses, and most pizza restaurants in town employ more than 10 people." Do you see what that allows you to infer? Right, at least one family run business in town employs more than 10 people. Most of the time, however, the testmaker will include stronger statements— assertions of fact or conditional Formal Logic statements—along with statements containing less certain terms like *many* or *most.*

Here's an LSAT expert's analysis of a stimulus containing statements with varying degrees of certainty.

LSAT Question	**Analysis**
Critic: Most chorale preludes were written for the organ, and most great chorale preludes written for the organ were written by J. S. Bach. One of Bach's chorale preludes dramatizes one hymn's perspective on the year's end. This prelude is agonizing and fixed on the passing of the old year, with its dashed hopes and lost opportunities. It does not necessarily reveal Bach's own attitude toward the change of the year, but does reflect the tone of the hymn's text. People often think that artists create in order to express their own feelings. Some artists do. Master artists never do, and Bach was a master artist. *PrepTest29 Sec4 Q22*	Cataloging the statements: Two uncertain statements: i) *most* preludes written for organ ii) *most* great preludes for organ by Bach → An example regarding one Bach prelude A statement about what other people *often* think Two concrete statements: i) master artists never create to express their own feelings ii) Bach was a master artist

This stimulus contains examples of all the levels of certainty—some ("often"), most, Formal Logic (If an artist is a master artist, then he never creates in order to express his own feelings), as well as an unqualified assertion ("Bach was a master artist"). Which statements do you think are most likely to yield a deduction about what *must be true* (or false)? Take a look at the LSAT expert's analysis on the following page.

Here's the LSAT expert's analysis of the full question associated with that stimulus.

LSAT Question	Analysis
Critic: Most chorale preludes were written for the organ, and most great chorale preludes written for the organ were written by J. S. Bach. One of Bach's chorale preludes dramatizes one hymn's perspective on the year's end. This prelude is agonizing and fixed on the passing of the old year, with its dashed hopes and lost opportunities. It does not necessarily reveal Bach's own attitude toward the change of the year, but does reflect the tone of the hymn's text. People often think that artists create in order to express their own feelings. Some artists do. Master artists never do, and Bach was a master artist.	**Step 2:** Cataloging the statements: Two uncertain statements: i) most preludes written for organ ii) most great preludes for organ by Bach An example regarding one Bach prelude A statement about what other people often think Two concrete statements: i) master artists never create to express their own feelings ii) Bach was a master artist
If the critic's statements are true, then on the basis of them which one of the following CANNOT be true?	**Step 1:** The phrase "CANNOT be true" indicates an Inference question asking for what *must be false*.
	Step 3: The last two statements yield a deduction: Bach never created art to express his own feelings. Check for an answer that contradicts that deduction before considering the less certain information that makes up the bulk of the stimulus.
(A) Bach believed that the close of the year was not a time for optimism and joyous celebration.	**Step 4:** The stimulus indicates that we do not know "Bach's own attitude toward the change of the year." This could be true. Eliminate.
(B) In composing music about a particular subject, Bach did not write the music in order to express his own attitude toward the subject.	180. Based on the deduction at the end of the stimulus, this choice qualifies as a *must be true*. Eliminate.
(C) In compositions other than chorale preludes, Bach wrote music in order to express his feelings toward various subjects.	Correct. This answer contradicts the deduction that can be derived from the concrete statements at the end of the stimulus: Bach never wrote music to express his feelings.
(D) Most of Bach's chorale preludes were written for instruments other than the organ.	While it is true that Bach wrote most of the *great* choral preludes for the organ, it is still possible that Bach wrote an even larger number of preludes for other instruments. Eliminate.
(E) Most of the great chorale preludes were written for instruments other than the organ. *PrepTest29 Sec4 Q22*	While it is true that most chorale preludes were written for the organ, it is still possible that most *great* choral preludes were written for other instruments. Eliminate.

Answer choice (C) is correct because it directly contradicts the deduction that can be made from the last sentence and its two concrete statements. The other answers either are in agreement with the stimulus or are statements that could be true. Answering this question efficiently and confidently is a result of prioritizing the more certain statements, especially any that can be combined to yield a deduction. On the next page, take a look at an example in which you are required to use less definite information to answer an Inference question.

Practice

First, use the question stem to characterize the one correct and four incorrect answers. Then, catalog the statements in the stimulus. Look for statements of greater and lesser certainty. Catalog the statements from most certain to least and determine what can be logically inferred.

LSAT Question	My Analysis
6. Dr. Z: Many of the characterizations of my work offered by Dr. Q are imprecise, and such characterizations do not provide an adequate basis for sound criticism of my work.	**Step 2:**
Which one of the following can be properly inferred from Dr. Z's statement? *PrepTest24 Sec3 Q15*	**Step 1:**

The word "many" on the LSAT is an uncertain term which, along with words such as *some* and *few*, should be interpreted as *at least one*. All of these words tell us very little about numbers and quantities, and should be distinguished from the more concrete term "most," which means more than half. The second clause—"such characterizations"—is unqualified and should be interpreted as *all such characterizations*.

Expert analysis of the entire question is on the next page. ▶ ▶ ▶

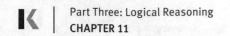

Expert Analysis

Here's how an LSAT expert might analyze the question stem and stimulus you just saw. You can also see her analysis of the answer choices accompanying this question.

LSAT Question	Analysis
6. Dr. Z: Many of the characterizations of my work offered by Dr. Q are imprecise, and such characterizations do not provide an adequate basis for sound criticism of my work.	**Step 2:** Cataloging the statements: One Formal Logic statement: → Imprecise characterization → not adequate basis for sound criticism One uncertain statement: *Many* of Dr. Q's characterizations are imprecise.
Which one of the following can be properly inferred from Dr. Z's statement?	→ **Step 1:** The phrase "properly inferred" indicates an Inference question. The correct answer must be true based on the statements in the stimulus.
	Step 3: Since many of Dr. Q's characterizations are imprecise, the formal logic rule dictates that those characterizations are not an adequate basis for sound criticism.
(A) Some of Dr. Q's characterizations of Dr. Z's work provide an adequate basis for sound criticism of Dr. Z's work.	→ **Step 4:** At least some of Dr. Q's characterizations are *not* an adequate basis, and it is possible that all of them are inadequate. Eliminate.
(B) All of Dr. Q's characterizations of Dr. Z's work that are not imprecise provide an adequate basis for sound criticism of Dr. Z's work.	→ Distortion. It can be deduced that precision is necessary for providing an adequate basis, not that it is sufficient, as this choice indicates. Eliminate.
(C) All of the characterizations of Dr. Z's work by Dr. Q that do not provide an adequate basis for sound criticism of Dr. Z's work are imprecise.	→ The formal logic in this choice reverses the direction of the arrow of the statement in the stimulus. Eliminate.
(D) If the characterization of someone's work is precise, then it provides a sound basis for criticizing that work.	→ Distortion. It can be deduced that precision is necessary for providing an adequate basis, not that it is sufficient, as this choice indicates. Eliminate.
(E) At least one of Dr. Q's characterizations of Dr. Z's work fails to provide an adequate basis for sound criticism of that work.	→ Correct. This choice matches the prediction.

PrepTest24 Sec3 Q15

Reflection

In day-to-day life, we make inferences all the time, but we are seldom as rigorous as the LSAT requires us to be. Over the coming days, pay attention to the unstated implications of statements you hear and read, anything from television news analysis to your friends' conversations. Try to assess what can be inferred or deduced from them. Are the inferences logical and supported by the statements themselves, or are you bringing in outside information? Are the deductions within the scope of the statements, or are they actually too extreme to be supported?

Inference Questions

You are just about ready to tackle some full Inference questions in practice, but first, do a quick review of what the question stems ask for. Throughout the previous examples, you saw the LSAT expert characterize the one right and four wrong answer choices before diving into his evaluation. While most LSAT Inference questions ask for a deduction that must be true, some questions create a twist by asking instead for a fact that could be true or must be false. Take a moment to drill on this important step with a handful of different Inference question stems.

Practice

Consider the following question stems and characterize the one correct and four incorrect answer choices for each. When you're done, turn the page and check your analysis against that of the LSAT expert.

LSAT Question	My Analysis
7. If the statements above are true, which one of the following must also be true? *PrepTest29 Sec1 Q18*	
8. Each of the following is supported by the information above EXCEPT: *PrepTest28 Sec3 Q4*	
9. Which one of the following is most strongly supported by the nutritionist's statements? *PrepTest29 Sec1 Q8*	
10. Which one of the following is strictly implied by the above? *PrepTestB Sec4 Q17*	

Expert Analysis

Here's how an LSAT expert would characterize the answer choices for each of those question stems.

LSAT Question	Analysis
7. If the statements above are true, which one of the following must also be true? *PrepTest29 Sec1 Q18* ⟶	Correct answer choice: Must be true based on the stimulus. Wrong answer choices: Could be false based on the stimulus.
8. Each of the following is supported by the information above EXCEPT: *PrepTest28 Sec3 Q4* ⟶	Correct answer choice: Unsupported by the stimulus. Wrong answer choices: Supported by information in the stimulus.
9. Which one of the following is most strongly supported by the nutritionist's statements? *PrepTest29 Sec1 Q8* ⟶	Correct answer choice: Strongly supported by the statements in the stimulus. Wrong answer choices: Unsupported by the stimulus.
10. Which one of the following is strictly implied by the above? *PrepTestB Sec4 Q17* ⟶	Correct answer choice: Must be true based on the stimulus. Wrong answer choices: Could be false based on the stimulus.

In every section of the test, the LSAT expert makes a habit of characterizing right and wrong answers before untangling the stimulus. This is especially important to avoid confusion in EXCEPT questions. Many test takers find it helpful to jot down a shorthand note (such as "MBT" for *must be true*) in their test booklets to remind them of the correct answer's characteristic. Don't be overly concerned with the EXCEPT variations, though; over the past five years, they've represented just over 3 percent of the Inference questions in released exams.

Frequently (especially in high-difficulty questions), it is not immediately obvious that an answer choice must be true. In that case, testing whether each answer could be false helps to eliminate wrong choices. An answer choice that must be false can often be found by eliminating any answer choice that is possible in light of the facts.

Practice

Now it's time to practice your skills on some more Inference questions. For each question, work on recognizing and (when possible) combining concrete statements. Note how Keywords indicate an author's perspective on facts in the stimulus. If there is Formal Logic, combine statements and form contrapositives. When there are uncertain statements, slow down and understand what could be true, but does not have to be true. Use the corresponding blanks to record your thinking for each step and then, after each question, compare your work to the thinking of an LSAT expert on the following pages.

LSAT Question	My Analysis
11. Nutritionist: Many people claim that simple carbohydrates are a reasonable caloric replacement for the fatty foods forbidden to those on law-fat diets. This is now in doubt. New studies show that, for many people, a high intake of simple carbohydrates stimulates an overproduction of insulin, a hormone that is involved in processing sugars and starches to create energy when the body requires energy, or, when energy is not required, to store the resulting by-products as fat.	**Step 2:**
Which one of the following is most strongly supported by the nutritionist's statements?	**Step 1:**
	Step 3:
(A) People on low-fat diets should avoid consumption of simple carbohydrates if they wish to maintain the energy that their bodies require.	**Step 4:**
(B) People who produce enough insulin to process their intake of simple carbohydrates should not feel compelled to adopt low-fat diets.	
(C) People who consume simple carbohydrates should limit their intake of foods high in fat.	
(D) People who wish to avoid gaining body fat should limit their intake of foods high in simple carbohydrates.	
(E) People who do not produce an excessive amount of insulin when they consume foods high in simple carbohydrates will not lose weight if they restrict only their intake of these foods.	

PrepTest29 Sec1 Q8

LSAT Question	My Analysis
12. Everyone who is excessively generous is not levelheaded, and no one who is levelheaded is bold.	**Step 2:**
Which one of the following is strictly implied by the above?	**Step 1:**
	Step 3:
(A) Everyone who is excessively generous is not bold.	**Step 4:**
(B) Everyone who is not bold is excessively generous.	
(C) No one who is not bold lacks excessive generosity.	
(D) If someone is levelheaded, then that person is neither bold nor excessively generous.	
(E) If someone is not levelheaded, then that person is either bold or excessively generous.	

PrepTestB Sec4 Q17

LSAT Question	My Analysis
13. Some planning committee members—those representing the construction industry—have significant financial interests in the committee's decisions. No one who is on the planning committee lives in the suburbs, although many of them work there.	**Step 2:**
If the statements above are true, which one of the following must also be true?	**Step 1:**
	Step 3:
(A) No persons with significant financial interests in the planning committee's decisions are not in the construction industry.	**Step 4:**
(B) No person who has significant financial interest in the planning committee's decisions lives in the suburbs.	
(C) Some persons with significant financial interests in the planning committee's decisions work in the suburbs.	
(D) Some planning committee members who represent the construction industry do not work in the suburbs.	
(E) Some persons with significant financial interests in the planning committee's decisions do not live in the suburbs.	

PrepTest29 Sec1 Q18

LSAT Question	**My Analysis**
14. Editorial: The government claims that the country's nuclear power plants are entirely safe and hence that the public's fear of nuclear accidents at these plants is groundless. The government also contends that its recent action to limit the nuclear industry's financial liability in the case of nuclear accidents at power plants is justified by the need to protect the nuclear industry from the threat of bankruptcy. But even the government says that unlimited liability poses such a threat only if injury claims can be sustained against the industry; and the government admits that for such claims to be sustained, injury must result from a nuclear accident. The public's fear, therefore, is well founded.	**Step 2:**
If all of the statements offered in support of the editorial's conclusion correctly describe the government's position, which one of the following must also be true on the basis of those statements?	**Step 1:**
	Step 3:
(A) The government's claim about the safety of the country's nuclear power plants is false.	**Step 4:**
(B) The government's position on nuclear power plants is inconsistent.	
(C) The government misrepresented its reasons for acting to limit the nuclear industry's liability.	
(D) Unlimited financial liability in the case of nuclear accidents poses no threat to the financial security of the country's nuclear industry.	
(E) The only serious threat posed by a nuclear accident would be to the financial security of the nuclear industry. *PrepTest29 Sec1 Q21*	

LSAT Question	My Analysis
15. Raising the humidity of a room protects furniture, draperies, and computers from damage caused by excessively dry air. Further, it can make people feel warmer, helps the body's defenses against viruses, and alleviates some skin rashes.	**Step 2:**
Each of the following is supported by the information above EXCEPT:	**Step 1:**
	Step 3:
(A) Humidity can be bad for computers.	**Step 4:**
(B) A room can be too dry for the optimal maintenance of its furnishings.	
(C) Dry air can feel cooler than humid air of the same temperature.	
(D) Increased humidity can be beneficial to the skin.	
(E) The human immune system can benefit from humidity.	

PrepTest28 Sec3 Q4

Expert Analysis

Here's how an LSAT expert looked at the questions you just tried.

LSAT Question	Analysis
11. Nutritionist: Many people claim that simple carbohydrates are a reasonable caloric replacement for the fatty foods forbidden to those on law-fat diets. This is now in doubt. New studies show that, for many people, a high intake of simple carbohydrates stimulates an overproduction of insulin, a hormone that is involved in processing sugars and starches to create energy when the body requires energy, or, when energy is not required, to store the resulting by-products as fat.	**Step 2:** Other people claim carbs are a reasonable replacement for fatty foods, but the nutritionist casts doubt on that claim. The evidence indicates two causal relationships: i) high intake of simple carbohydrates results in excess insulin ii) insulin is involved in production of energy or storage of excess as fat
Which one of the following is most strongly supported by the nutritionist's statements?	**Step 1:** A question stem directing the use of statements above to support an answer indicates an Inference question.
	Step 3: Though the stimulus is in the form of an argument, focus on the factual evidence in this Inference question. Combined, the statements produce a chain of causation: High intake of simple carbohydrates can lead to the storage of excess body fat.
(A) People on low-fat diets should avoid consumption of simple carbohydrates if they wish to maintain the energy that their bodies require.	**Step 4:** 180. The stimulus indicates that a diet of simple carbohydrates can provide the energy the body requires. Eliminate.
(B) People who produce enough insulin to process their intake of simple carbohydrates should not feel compelled to adopt low-fat diets.	Distortion. The reasons some people need to be on low-fat diets are not indicated, and are not related to the concerns regarding simple carbohydrates and insulin. Eliminate.
(C) People who consume simple carbohydrates should limit their intake of foods high in fat.	Outside the Scope. The only question in the stimulus is whether those who already limit their intake of fat should replace it with simple carbohydrates. Eliminate.
(D) People who wish to avoid gaining body fat should limit their intake of foods high in simple carbohydrates.	Correct. The information establishes a causal chain from the intake of simple carbohydrates to the storage of excess body fat.
(E) People who do not produce an excessive amount of insulin when they consume foods high in simple carbohydrates will not lose weight if they restrict only their intake of these foods. *PrepTest29 Sec1 Q8*	The stimulus provides no information to support speculation regarding what happens to people who do not produce excess insulin. Eliminate.

LSAT Question	Analysis
12. Everyone who is excessively generous is not levelheaded, and no one who is levelheaded is bold.	**Step 2:** Two Formal Logic statements: i) excessively generous → not levelheaded ii) levelheaded → not bold
Which one of the following is strictly implied by the above?	**Step 1:** The phrase "implied by" indicates an Inference question.
	Step 3: The two Formal Logic statements do not link in a chain. However, take the contrapositive of the first statement and combine it with the second sentence to deduce the following: Anyone who is levelheaded is both not bold and not excessively generous.
(A) Everyone who is excessively generous is not bold.	**Step 4:** This answer incorrectly links the two statements in a chain as though "not levelheaded" equaled "levelheaded." Eliminate.
(B) Everyone who is not bold is excessively generous.	This answer commits the same error as choice (A); it also erroneously changes the direction of the connection. Eliminate.
(C) No one who is not bold lacks excessive generosity.	This answer is identical in meaning to choice (B). Eliminate.
(D) If someone is levelheaded, then that person is neither bold nor excessively generous.	Correct. Taking the contrapositive of the first statement shows that levelheadedness triggers not excessively generous and in the second statement levelheadedness triggers not bold, so both must be true.
(E) If someone is not levelheaded, then that person is either bold or excessively generous. *PrepTestB Sec4 Q17*	None of the statements or their contrapositives has the term "not levelheaded" as a trigger, so this does not have to be true. Eliminate.

LSAT Question	Analysis
13. Some planning committee members—those representing the construction industry—have significant financial interests in the committee's decisions. No one who is on the planning committee lives in the suburbs, although many of them work there.	**Step 2:** Catalog the statements: Formal Logic statement: Planning committee → Not live in suburbs Uncertain Statements: *Some* on planning committee have financial interest in committee decisions. *Some* on planning committee work in the suburbs.
If the statements above are true, which one of the following must also be true?	**Step 1:** The phrase "must also be true" indicates an Inference question.
	Step 3: The two uncertain statements cannot be combined together to make a deduction. However, either uncertain statement could be combined with the Formal Logic statement to yield two deductions: i) *some* who work in the suburbs do not live in the suburbs, and, ii) *some* with financial interest in committee decisions do not live in the suburbs.
(A) No persons with significant financial interests in the planning committee's decisions are not in the construction industry.	**Step 4:** Extreme. It's not supported that *every* person with a significant financial interest in committee decisions is in the construction industry. The information does not preclude others outside the construction industry from having such interests in committee decisions. Eliminate.
(B) No person who has significant financial interest in the planning committee's decisions lives in the suburbs.	Extreme. It's not supported that *every* person with significant financial interest in committee decisions does not live in the suburbs. Eliminate.
(C) Some persons with significant financial interests in the planning committee's decisions work in the suburbs.	This answer improperly purports to combine the two uncertain statements. Eliminate.
(D) Some planning committee members who represent the construction industry do not work in the suburbs.	This cannot be deduced for certain because it is possible that all planning committee members work in the suburbs. Eliminate.
(E) Some persons with significant financial interests in the planning committee's decisions do not live in the suburbs. *PrepTest29 Sec1 Q18*	Correct. If some people on the planning committee have significant financial interests in their decisions and all people on the planning committee do not live in the suburbs, then it must be true that some people with significant financial interests in committee decisions do not live in the suburbs.

LSAT Question	Analysis
14. Editorial: The government claims that the country's nuclear power plants are entirely safe and hence that the public's fear of nuclear accidents at these plants is groundless. The government also contends that its recent action to limit the nuclear industry's financial liability in the case of nuclear accidents at power plants is justified by the need to protect the nuclear industry from the threat of bankruptcy. But even the government says that unlimited liability poses such a threat only if injury claims can be sustained against the industry; and the government admits that for such claims to be sustained, injury must result from a nuclear accident. The public's fear, therefore, is well founded.	**Step 2:** The Keyword "also" helps focus on the two separate claims about nuclear power: i) It is entirely safe; and ii) limiting the nuclear industry's financial liability is justified. The Keyword "but" highlights the paradoxical nature of needing to grant liability limitations to something that is completely safe.
If all of the statements offered in support of the editorial's conclusion correctly describe the government's position, which one of the following must also be true on the basis of those statements?	**Step 1:** The phrase "must also be true" indicates an Inference question. The question stem further directs you to only accept the Editorial's evidence as true, not its conclusion. Catalogue the editorial's evidence, and use it to decide which answer also must be true.
	Step 3: An important LSAT concept, such as a paradox, in an Inference stimulus will likely be the focus of the correct answer. Here the government is making contradictory claims regarding nuclear power.
(A) The government's claim about the safety of the country's nuclear power plants is false.	**Step 4:** One of the claims must be false, but it is not known which one based on the evidence. Even though the author concludes that the claim about safety must be false, the question stem dictates that the answer should not be based on that conclusion but rather on the "statements offered in support the . . . conclusion." Eliminate.
(B) The government's position on nuclear power plants is inconsistent.	Correct. This merely restates the idea that the government's claims are contradictory.
(C) The government misrepresented its reasons for acting to limit the nuclear industry's liability.	As with choice (A), you cannot know which of the two claims by the government is false.
(D) Unlimited financial liability in the case of nuclear accidents poses no threat to the financial security of the country's nuclear industry.	180. The information suggests that unlimited liability at least could pose a threat to the financial security of the nuclear industry.
(E) The only serious threat posed by a nuclear accident would be to the financial security of the nuclear industry. *PrepTest29 Sec1 Q21*	180. The information suggests that at least one of the government's claims, potentially the claim regarding the safety of nuclear power, is false.

LSAT Question	Analysis
15. Raising the humidity of a room protects furniture, draperies, and computers from damage caused by excessively dry air. Further, it can make people feel warmer, helps the body's defenses against viruses, and alleviates some skin rashes.	**Step 2:** Cataloging the statements reveals that the stimulus is a list of benefits derived from raising the humidity.
Each of the following is supported by the information above EXCEPT:	**Step 1:** A question directing the use of "information above" to "support" an answer indicates an Inference question; in this case, select the choice that is *not* supported by the stimulus.
	Step 3: Since the stimulus consists entirely of a list of *benefits* of raising the humidity, what would *not* be supported by the information is something negative about a rise in humidity.
(A) Humidity can be bad for computers.	**Step 4:** Correct. The stimulus in no way suggests that humidity can be bad.
(B) A room can be too dry for the optimal maintenance of its furnishings.	The indication that raising the humidity can help protect furnishings supports this. Eliminate.
(C) Dry air can feel cooler than humid air of the same temperature.	The indication that raising humidity can make people feel warmer supports this. Eliminate.
(D) Increased humidity can be beneficial to the skin.	The stimulus indicates increased humidity can alleviate skin rashes. Eliminate.
(E) The human immune system can benefit from humidity.	The stimulus indicates increased humidity can help defend against viruses. Eliminate.

PrepTest28 Sec3 Q4

Reflection

For some students, Inference questions can be among some of the most challenging types of questions on the LSAT. Some students find it difficult to avoid bringing in outside information and knowledge. Others are tempted by answer choices that make overly strong deductions. Practice your Inference question skills whenever you read magazine articles or newspaper editorials. Catalog facts and paraphrase the author's statements. Ask yourself whether the author has drawn valid deductions from the facts she cites. Or maybe she exaggerated certain statements. Or maybe she even relied on assumptions and outside knowledge to make inferences that were not directly supported. No matter how strong your analytical skills are now, you'll likely become a much more rigorous and critical reader in law school. Consider your practice with Inference questions as a head start in your legal education (and as an added bonus, you'll also be improving your LSAT score).

PRINCIPLE QUESTIONS ASKING FOR INFERENCES

In Chapter 10, you learned about Principle questions that reward the same skills tested in Assumption and Strengthen questions—the ability to identify the assumption that underlies the argument. Other Principle questions, however, mimic Inference questions. The stimulus in these Principle questions may state a principle and ask you to identify a specific case that appropriately applies the principle, or the stimulus may present a specific case and ask you to infer the principle from which that case follows. Either way, you'll be rewarded for approaching these questions with the same skills you learned and practiced for standard Inference questions.

Most recent tests have featured one Apply the Principle—Inference question and one or two Identify the Principle—Inference questions.

Here's a typical question asking you to infer the principle illustrated by the specific case described in the stimulus.

Nearly everyone has complained of a mistaken utility bill that cannot easily be corrected or of computer files that cannot readily be retrieved. Yet few people today would tolerate waiting in long lines while clerks search for information that can now be found in seconds, and almost no one who has used a word processor would return to a typewriter.

The information above conforms most closely to which one of the following principles?

(A) The fact that people complain about some consequences of technology cannot be taken as a reliable indication that they would choose to live without it.

(B) If people do not complain about some technology, then it is probably not a significant factor in their daily lives.

(C) The degree to which technologies elicit complaints from people is always an accurate measure of the extent to which people have become dependent on them.

(D) The complaints people make about technological innovations are more reliable evidence of the importance of those innovations than the choices people actually make.

(E) The less willing people are to do without technology the more likely they are to complain about the effects of the technology.

PreptTestB Sec4 Q12

Note that the question stem asks for an answer containing a principle that *conforms to* the scenario or individual case described in the stimulus. That tells you that the correct answer will represent a broad rule that can be applied to the specific situation in the stimulus. Apply the Principle questions swap the places of the narrow case and the broad rule. These questions state a broad rule in the stimulus and ask you to identify the answer choice containing a narrow case that correctly applies the principle. In both formats, you can think of your job as identifying the one answer choice that provides a perfect one-to-one matchup with the stimulus.

LEARNING OBJECTIVES

In this section, you'll learn to:

· Infer a principle (general rule) from a specific case that illustrates it.
· Identify a specific case that appropriately applies a principle (general rule).
· Identify and answer Identify the Principle–Inference questions.
· Identify and answer Apply the Principle questions.

Infer a Principle (General Rule) from a Specific Case That Illustrates It

The stimuli for Principle questions that ask you to identify the principle illustrated by a specific case tend to fall into two broad categories: (1) cases that describe a set of actions and outcomes, and (2) cases that make recommendations. Take a look at an example of each.

Cases That Describe Actions and Outcomes

Let's use the introductory question to illustrate how to attack Infer a Principle questions for stimuli that describe a specific situation, action or outcome. You want to try to generalize the case into a rule covering other, similar cases. In discussing the relative merits of computers, in very broad terms, what is the author pointing out? Can you paraphrase the outcome generally without using the specific subject matters (utility bills, computer files, waiting in line, typewriters) mentioned in the stimulus?

Take a look at an LSAT expert's thinking as it relates to this stimulus.

LSAT Question	Analysis
Nearly everyone has complained of a mistaken utility bill that cannot easily be corrected or of computer files that cannot readily be retrieved. Yet few people today would tolerate waiting in long lines while clerks search for information that can now be found in seconds, and almost no one who has used a word processor would return to a typewriter.	**Step 2:** The contrast word "yet" highlights a paradox: While people are often frustrated with certain inconveniences of modern technologies, they don't want to return to older modes of technology. Generalization: People may complain about the *new way* despite not wanting to return to the *old way*.
The information above conforms most closely to which one of the following principles? *PreptTestB Sec4 Q12*	**Step 1:** The Keywords "conforms closely to . . . principles" indicate that this is a Principle question.

The LSAT expert first recognizes all the helpful hints that can be gleaned from Principle question stems. The question stem tells her that the answer choices contain the principle or broad generalization, while the stimulus merely contains "information," which will often be referred to as a "situation." Because the question stem here did not ask us to analyze the "reasoning" or "argument," there is no need to untangle the stimulus into evidence and conclusion. Instead, our prediction here will consist of putting the specific situation into very broad terms. The correct answer might be in somewhat more specific language and possibly use some terminology from the stimulus, but it could well be as generalized as the LSAT expert's prediction.

(A)	The fact that people complain about some consequences of technology cannot be taken as a reliable indication that they would choose to live without it.
(B)	If people do not complain about some technology, then it is probably not a significant factor in their daily lives.
(C)	The degree to which technologies elicit complaints from people is always an accurate measure of the extent to which people have become dependent on them.
(D)	The complaints people make about technological innovations are more reliable evidence of the importance of those innovations than the choices people actually make.
(E)	The less willing people are to do without technology the more likely they are to complain about the effects of the technology.

PrepTestB Sec4 Q12

Answer choice (A) neatly matches the prediction. Principle questions can be very intuitive. Don't overthink them and don't be intimidated by all the variations in the question stems (principle in stimulus, principle in answers, argument based, or non-argument based). In each case, you are just matching a situation to a generalization, and the question stems almost always will provide you clear guidance on what you will find in the stimulus and the answer choices.

Cases That Make Recommendations

Sometimes, a Principle question may ask you to infer a general rule from a specific case in which the author advances a recommendation, prediction, or value judgment—in other words, when the author makes an argument. Your task then becomes to paraphrase that argument in general terms. Rather than complicating, this simplifies your task because there is a routine way to paraphrase any argument: If [this type of Evidence], then [this Conclusion].

Take a look at the following example.

LSAT Question	Analysis
Commentator: In academic scholarship, sources are always cited, and methodology and theoretical assumptions are set out, so as to allow critical study, replication, and expansion of scholarship. In open-source software, the code in which the program is written can be viewed and modified by individual users for their purposes without getting permission from the producer or paying a fee. In contrast, the code of proprietary software is kept secret, and modifications can be made only by the producer, for a fee. This shows that open-source software better matches the values embodied in academic scholarship, and since scholarship is central to the mission of universities, universities should use only open-source software.	**Step 2:** Conclusion: Universities should use only open-source software. *because* Evidence: i) Open-source software better embodies values of scholarship; ii) scholarship is central to mission of universities. Paraphrase of Principle: If some tool or resource better embodies values central to mission of a university (or some organization) then it should be used.
The commentator's reasoning most closely conforms to which one of the following principles? *PreptTestJune07 Sec3 Q14*	**Step 1:** The Keywords "reasoning most closely conforms to . . . principles" tells us this is a Principle question. Because it mentions the commentator's "reasoning," we know that the stimulus will be in *conclusion, because evidence* form.

What a relief that you only need to paraphrase the *reasoning* in this stimulus! The LSAT expert used the evidence Keywords and phrases ("this shows that" and "since") and the conclusion-indicating opinion word "should" to home in on the last sentence. Do you see the match for the prediction?

(A) Whatever software tools are most advanced and can achieve the goals of academic scholarship are the ones that should alone be used in universities.

(B) Universities should use the type of software technology that is least expensive, as long as that type of software technology is adequate for the purposes of academic scholarship.

(C) Universities should choose the type of software technology that best matches the values embodied in the activities that are central to the mission of universities.

(D) The form of software technology that best matches the values embodied in the activities that are central to the mission of universities is the form of software technology that is most efficient for universities to use.

(E) A university should not pursue any activity that would block the achievement of the goals of academic scholarship at that university.

PrepTestJune07 Sec3 Q14

Answer choice (C) is right on point! The argument is all about choosing what best matches the values central to the mission of the university. The author's reason is not what is *most advanced* (choice (A)), or what is *least expensive* (choice (B)). And answer choice (D) misses the argument's recommendation to actually *use* the technology, rather than simply judging something as the *most efficient* to use. Finally, answer choice (E) states what universities should not do, which is outside the scope of the argument in the stimulus, which was all about what universities *should* do.

Now, let's look at Apply the Principle questions, in which the stimuli contain broad rules, and the answer choices present specific situations.

Identify a Specific Case That Applies a Principle (General Rule)

Apply the Principle questions, more than most LSAT questions, mirror the kind of deductions a student makes on a law school exam. For example, as a first-year law student, you will learn the elements of the tort of battery: the intentional offensive touching of a person without consent. The exam question will present you with some facts. Your task will be to match the facts to the elements of battery to determine if the defendant described in the exam's fact pattern is liable for the offense. Was the victim touched? Was the touch intentional? Was the intentional touch offensive? Did the victim give consent to be touched? If you determine that the given facts correctly match each of the elements of the rule, you can conclude that the defendant is liable. But, if even one of those elements is missing, the defendant will prevail.

In the same way, Apply the Principle questions will present you with one or more rules, very often in the form of conditional, Formal Logic statements. Your task is to examine five cases (the five answer choices) and select the one that perfectly matches or applies the rule(s) articulated in the stimulus.

Take a look at how an LSAT expert analyzes an Apply the Principle question. Focus on how he identifies the principles or general rules found in the stimulus.

LSAT Question	Analysis
Politician: Governments should tax any harmful substance that is available to the general public at a level that the tax would discourage continued use of the substance.	**Step 2:** The stimulus contains a single statement in conditional Formal Logic: If harmful substance and available to the public → should tax at levels to discourage use If don't tax at levels to discourage use → either not harmful or not available to public
Which one of the following is an application of the politician's principle of taxation?	**Step 1:** The Keywords "application of the . . . principle" indicate that this is an Apply the Principle question.
	Step 3: In Apply the Principle questions, it is common for the principle to be a Formal Logic rule. The correct answer will match the statement in the stimulus: *If a substance is harmful and available to the public, it should be taxed at a level that discourages its use.*
(A) The tax on products containing sugar is raised in an effort to raise revenue to be applied to the health costs resulting from the long-term use of these products.	**Step 4:** Distortion. Here, the tax is used to *raise revenue*, not to *discourage the use* of the harmful substance. Eliminate.
(B) The tax on certain pain relievers that, even though harmful, are available over the counter is raised, since studies have shown that the demand for these products will not be affected.	Distortion. This choice fails to apply the politician's principle because the tax will *not* discourage use. Eliminate.
(C) The tax on a pesticide that contains an organic compound harmful to human beings is raised to give people an incentive to purchase pesticides not containing the compound.	Correct. The product mentioned here is harmful, and apparently, available to the public. The politician's principle holds that such a product should be taxed to discourage its use.
(D) The tax on domestically produced alcoholic beverages is not raised, since recent studies show that the tax would have a negative impact on the tourist industry.	Distortion. This answer choice doesn't state if alcohol is harmful, or if it is available to the general public. If it is, the politician would hold that it should be taxed at a rate that discourages use. The politician makes no exception for *other* negative impacts. Eliminate.
(E) The tax on products that emit fluorocarbons, substances that have proven to be harmful to the earth's ozone layer, is lowered to stimulate the development of new, less environmentally harmful ways of using these substances.	Distortion. Nothing in the politician's principle tells us when taxes on a product should be lowered. Eliminate.

PrepTest27 Sec4 Q1

Identify the Principle—Inference and Apply the Principle Questions

When an LSAT expert confronts a question stem identifying a Principle question calling for an inference, the first thing she's likely to note is whether the broad, general rule is in the stimulus or in the correct answer. Take a look at the thinking that helps a well-trained test taker distinguish between "Identify the Principle—Inference" questions and their "Apply the Principle" cousins.

LSAT Question	Analysis
Which one of the following is an application of the politician's principle of taxation? *PrepTest27 Sec4 Q1*	→ The correct answer will be a specific case that applies the principle (broad rule) of taxation stated in the stimulus. This is an Apply the Principle question. ∨
The commentator's reasoning most closely conforms to which one of the following principles? *PrepTestJune07 Sec3 Q14*	→ The correct answer will rephrase the specific argument ("reasoning") above into a more broad and generalized principle. This is an Identify the Principle question. ∧

Practice

Practice identifying your task in the following question stems. For each, make sure you can accurately say whether the stimulus contains the broad principle and the answer choices contain specific cases, or vice versa.

LSAT Question	My Analysis
16. The reasoning above conforms most closely to which one of the following principles? *PrepTestB Sec4 Q24*	
17. Which one of the following judgments most closely conforms to the principle cited above? *PrepTest27 Sec4 Q3*	
18. Which one of the following is an application of the economic principle above? *PrepTest28 Sec1 Q10*	
19. Which one of the following most closely conforms to the principle the ethicist endorses? *PrepTest28 Sec3 Q23*	

Expert Analysis

Here's how the LSAT expert would examine each of those question stems and what she would anticipate about the rest of the question.

LSAT Question		Analysis
16. The reasoning above conforms most closely to which one of the following principles? *PrepTestB Sec4 Q24*	→	The correct answer is a broad principle that summarizes the argument ("reasoning") above. This is an Identify the Principle question.
17. Which one of the following judgments most closely conforms to the principle cited above? *PrepTest27 Sec4 Q3*	→	The correct answer will be a decision ("judgment") about a specific case that matches the broad principles set forth in the stimulus. This is an Apply the Principle question.
18. Which one of the following is an application of the economic principle above? *PrepTest28 Sec1 Q10*	→	The correct answer will be a specific application of the broad economic principle described in the stimulus. This is an Apply the Principle question.
19. Which one of the following most closely conforms to the principle the ethicist endorses? *PrepTest28 Sec3 Q23*	→	The correct answer will conform to the broad ethical principle described in the stimulus. This is an Apply the Principle question.

Practice

Apply the Kaplan Method to the following questions. After each, compare your work to the thinking of an LSAT expert on the following pages.

LSAT Question	My Analysis
20. It is a principle of economics that a nation can experience economic growth only when consumer confidence is balanced with a small amount of consumer skepticism.	**Step 2:**
Which one of the following is an application of the economic principle above?	**Step 1:**
	Step 3:
(A) Any nation in which consumer confidence is balanced with a small amount of consumer skepticism will experience economic growth.	**Step 4:**
(B) Any nation in which the prevailing attitude of consumers is not skepticism will experience economic growth.	
(C) Any nation in which the prevailing attitude of consumers is either exclusively confidence or exclusively skepticism will experience economic growth.	
(D) Any nation in which the prevailing attitude of consumers is exclusively confidence will not experience economic growth.	
(E) Any nation in which consumer skepticism is balanced with a small amount of consumer confidence will experience economic growth.	

PrepTest28 Sec1 Q10

LSAT Question	**My Analysis**

21. A just government never restricts the right of its citizens to act upon their desires except when their acting upon their desires is a direct threat to the health or property of other of its citizens.

Step 2:

Which one of the following judgments most closely conforms to the principle cited above?

Step 1:

Step 3:

(A) A just government would not ban the sale of sports cars, but it could prohibit unrestricted racing of them on public highways.

Step 4:

(B) An unjust government would abolish many public services if these services did not require compulsory labor.

(C) A just government would provide emergency funds to survivors of unavoidable accidents but not to survivors of avoidable ones.

(D) A just government would not censor writings of Shakespeare, but it could censor magazines and movies that criticize the government.

(E) An unjust government would incarcerate one of its citizens even though it had been several years since that citizen harmed someone.

PrepTest27 Sec4 Q3

LSAT Question	**My Analysis**
22. If an external force intervenes to give members of a community political self-determination, then that political community will almost surely fail to be truly free, since it is during the people's struggle to become free by their own efforts that the political virtues necessary for maintaining freedom have the best chance of arising.	**Step 2:**
The reasoning above conforms most closely to which one of the following principles?	**Step 1:**
	Step 3:
(A) Political freedom is a virtue that a community can attain through an external force.	**Step 4:**
(B) Self-determination is not the first political virtue that the members of a community achieve in their struggle to become free.	
(C) A community cannot remain free without first having developed certain political virtues.	
(D) Political self-determination is required if a community is to remain truly free.	
(E) Real freedom should not be imposed on a community by external forces.	

PrepTestB Sec4 Q24

LSAT Question	**My Analysis**
23. Ethicist: It is widely believed that it is always wrong to tell lies, but this is a rule almost no one fully complies with. In fact, lying is often the morally appropriate thing to do. It is morally correct to lie when telling the truth carries the reasonable expectation of producing considerable physical or psychological harm to others.	**Step 2:**
Which one of the following most closely conforms to the principle the ethicist endorses?	**Step 1:**
	Step 3:
(A) When Juan asked Judy if the movie they were going to was *North by Northwest*, Judy said yes, though she knew that *Persona* was playing instead. This was the only way Juan would see the film and avoid losing an opportunity for an aesthetically pleasing experience.	**Step 4:**
(B) A daughter asked her father which candidate he supported, McBride or Chang. Though in fact he preferred Chang, the father responded by saying he preferred McBride, in order to avoid discussion.	
(C) A husband told his wife he felt ready to go on a canoe trip, though he had recently had severe chest pains; his wife had determined a year ago that they would go on this trip, so to ask to cancel now would be inconvenient.	
(D) A young boy asked his mother if she loved his older sister more than she loved him. The mother said she loved them both to the same degree, even though it was not true.	
(E) A friend invited Jamal to a party, but Jamal was afraid that he might see his ex-wife and her new husband there. To spare himself emotional pain, as well as the embarrassment of telling his friend why he did not want to go, Jamal falsely claimed he had to work.	

PrepTest28 Sec3 Q23

Here's how an LSAT expert tackled the questions you just saw. Review her analysis step-by-step, following the Logical Reasoning Method. The more consistently you approach both your practice and review, the faster and more confident you'll be on Test Day.

LSAT Question	Analysis
20. It is a principle of economics that a nation can experience economic growth only when consumer confidence is balanced with a small amount of consumer skepticism. →	**Step 2:** The stimulus contains a single statement in conditional Formal Logic: If economic growth → confidence and skepticism in balance If confidence and skepticism NOT in balance → NO economic growth
Which one of the following is an application of the economic principle above? →	**Step 1:** A principle question with the broad rule in the stimulus and an application of the rule in the choices. Apply the Principle.
→	**Step 3:** The principle in the stimulus was in Formal Logic form, so the correct answer should match the conditional rule or its contrapositive.
(A) Any nation in which consumer confidence is balanced with a small amount of consumer skepticism will experience economic growth. →	**Step 4:** Balance → Growth. This choice changes the direction of arrow. Eliminate.
(B) Any nation in which the prevailing attitude of consumers is not skepticism will experience economic growth. →	Not mostly skeptical → Growth. This choice also changes the direction of the arrow. Eliminate.
(C) Any nation in which the prevailing attitude of consumers is either exclusively confidence or exclusively skepticism will experience economic growth. →	All confidence or all skepticism (not balanced) → Growth. Distorts the contrapositive. A lack of balance should result in *no* growth. Eliminate.
(D) Any nation in which the prevailing attitude of consumers is exclusively confidence will not experience economic growth. →	Correct. All confidence (not balanced) → No growth. This matches the contrapositive.
(E) Any nation in which consumer skepticism is balanced with a small amount of consumer confidence will experience economic growth. *PrepTest28 Sec1 Q10* →	As with choice (A), this choice reverses the direction of the arrow, and, further, distorts the desired balance of confidence with a small amount of skepticism. Eliminate.

LSAT Question	**Analysis**
21. A just government never restricts the right of its citizens to act upon their desires except when their acting upon their desires is a direct threat to the health or property of other of its citizens. →	**Step 2:** A rule: a just government never restricts the right of its citizens to act on desires. And an exception: when acting upon desires threatens other citizens' health or property.
Which one of the following judgments most closely conforms to the principle cited above? →	**Step 1:** "[M]ost closely conforms to the principle cited above" indicates that in this Principle question, there will be a principle (broad rule) above, and the correct answer will follow that rule. This is an Apply the Principle question.
→	**Step 3:** The exception to the rule doesn't tell us that the government will definitely restrict rights when citizens threaten others' health or property. It's simply a possibility. The firm and hard rule here is that if a citizen does not threaten others' health or property, then a just government will not restrict that person's rights.
(A) A just government would not ban the sale of sports cars, but it could prohibit unrestricted racing of them on public highways. →	**Step 4:** Correct. This follows the rule (and its potential exception) to the letter.
(B) An unjust government would abolish many public services if these services did not require compulsory labor. →	Outside the Scope. The stimulus doesn't define the behavior of unjust governments. Eliminate.
(C) A just government would provide emergency funds to survivors of unavoidable accidents but not to survivors of avoidable ones. →	Outside the Scope. The stimulus discusses citizens' desires, not what should be done in the event of an accident. Eliminate.
(D) A just government would not censor writings of Shakespeare, but it could censor magazines and movies that criticize the government. →	Movies that criticize the government hardly fall under the category of "direct threat to the health or property of other . . . citizens." Eliminate.
(E) An unjust government would incarcerate one of its citizens even though it had been several years since that citizen harmed someone. →	Outside the Scope. The stimulus doesn't define the behavior of unjust governments. Eliminate.

PrepTest27 Sec4 Q3

LSAT Question	Analysis
22. If an external force intervenes to give members of a community political self-determination, then that political community will almost surely fail to be truly free, since it is during the people's struggle to become free by their own efforts that the political virtues necessary for maintaining freedom have the best chance of arising.	**Step 2:** Conclusion: If external forces intervene, then a political community is not truly free. *because* Evidence: One's own struggle to be free develops virtues necessary for maintaining freedom.
The reasoning above conforms most closely to which one of the following principles?	**Step 1:** A Principle question in which the stimulus contains *reasoning* and the answers contain *broad principles* is an Identify the Principle question. The correct answer should match the form: If [this Evidence], then [this Conclusion].
	Step 3: The correct answer should indicate: If NOT develop certain → NOT truly free political virtues or the contrapositive: If truly free → developed certain political virtues
(A) Political freedom is a virtue that a community can attain through an external force.	**Step 4:** This is a 180. The author believes the intervention of external forces interferes with developing the virtues necessary for freedom. Eliminate.
(B) Self-determination is not the first political virtue that the members of a community achieve in their struggle to become free.	The argument is not concerned with the sequence of achieving different virtues. Eliminate.
(C) A community cannot remain free without first having developed certain political virtues.	Correct. Translating "without" to "if not," this sentence conforms to "if don't develop certain political virtues → won't be truly free."
(D) Political self-determination is required if a community is to remain truly free.	This is a Distortion. The author indicates that political self-determination, if given by an external force, is not sufficient to be free and that other virtues are necessary. Eliminate.
(E) Real freedom should not be imposed on a community by external forces. *PrepTestB Sec4 Q24*	The argument is not concerned with freedom being *imposed*, but with whether an external force *giving* freedom is effective in the long run.

LSAT Question	**Analysis**
23. Ethicist: It is widely believed that it is always wrong to tell lies, but this is a rule almost no one fully complies with. In fact, lying is often the morally appropriate thing to do. It is morally correct to lie when telling the truth carries the reasonable expectation of producing considerable physical or psychological harm to others.	**Step 2:** Broad rule: If telling the truth would cause considerable physical or psychological harm to others, then it's morally correct to lie.
Which one of the following most closely conforms to the principle the ethicist endorses?	**Step 1:** "[M]ost closely conforms to the principle" indicates that this is an Apply the Principle question. There will be a principle (broad rule) above, and the correct answer will follow that rule.
	Step 3: Find an answer choice in which someone lies in order to avoid causing physical or psychological harm to others.
(A) When Juan asked Judy if the movie they were going to was *North by Northwest*, Judy said yes, though she knew that *Persona* was playing instead. This was the only way Juan would see the film and avoid losing an opportunity for an aesthetically pleasing experience.	**Step 4:** Judy does not lie to prevent physical or psychological harm to Juan. Eliminate.
(B) A daughter asked her father which candidate he supported, McBride or Chang. Though in fact he preferred Chang, the father responded by saying he preferred McBride, in order to avoid discussion.	The father does not lie to prevent physical or psychological harm to his daughter. Eliminate.
(C) A husband told his wife he felt ready to go on a canoe trip, though he had recently had severe chest pains; his wife had determined a year ago that they would go on this trip, so to ask to cancel now would be inconvenient.	The husband does not lie to prevent physical or psychological harm to his wife. Eliminate.
(D) A young boy asked his mother if she loved his older sister more than she loved him. The mother said she loved them both to the same degree, even though it was not true.	Correct. The mother lies to prevent psychological harm to her son.
(E) A friend invited Jamal to a party, but Jamal was afraid that he might see his ex-wife and her new husband there. To spare himself emotional pain, as well as the embarrassment of telling his friend why he did not want to go, Jamal falsely claimed he had to work.	Jamal lies to prevent physical or psychological harm to *himself*, but not to others. Eliminate.
PrepTest28 Sec3 Q23	

Reflection

Congratulations on acquiring another valuable LSAT (and law school) skill. In the coming days, pay attention to conversations you have in which people apply or infer principles from specific events and situations. Even simple statements can provide practice for these Principle/Inference question types. For example, if you hear a father tell a child, "You should clean up your room because I told you to," he's implying the principle that children should obey their parents. On the other hand, if you hear a mom say, "You need to clean up your room because everyone in this family has responsibilities," she's implying a different principle. What is it?

We generalize rules from specific cases all the time, and we often expect people to act in a certain way or have a particular response because of general rules we follow. As you encounter situations of this type, take the time to make the implied rules explicit to yourself and to note the principles upon which people are acting even when they haven't articulated those principles.

RESOLVING DISCREPANCIES AND PARADOX QUESTIONS

One more non-argument-based Logical Reasoning question type, the Paradox question, features a stimulus that contains two seemingly contradictory statements. That's the essence of a paradox, a situation that seems impossible, inconsistent, or contradictory but actually isn't. The correct answer to an LSAT Paradox question will always be a fact that, if true, will help explain how the apparent discrepancy can be resolved, that is, how the two problematic facts can be shown to be consistent. Over the past five years, most LSATs have included three or four Paradox questions.

Take a look at a typical LSAT Paradox question. Go ahead and try it now. You'll see this question explained in full a little later in the chapter.

Because of the recent recession in Country A, most magazines published there have experienced decreases in advertising revenue, so much so that the survival of the most widely read magazines is in grave doubt. At the same time, however, more people in Country A are reading more magazines than ever before, and the number of financially successful magazines in Country A is greater than ever.

Which one the following, if true, most helps to resolve the apparent discrepancy in the information above?

(A) Most magazines reduce the amount they charge for advertisements during a recession.

(B) The audience for a successful television show far exceeds the readership of even the most widely read magazine.

(C) Advertising is the main source of revenue only for the most widely read magazines; other magazines rely on circulation for their revenue.

(D) Because of the recession, people in Country A have cut back on magazine subscriptions and are reading borrowed magazines.

(E) More of the new general interest magazines that were launched this year in Country A have survived than survived in previous years.

PrepTest27 Sec1 Q7

Notice that the question stem asks you to resolve the apparent discrepancy in the stimulus. Two terms should really stand out: "resolve" and "apparent discrepancy." Virtually every Paradox question will ask you to explain, resolve, or reconcile two statements. The fact that these statements merely *appear* contradictory or inconsistent tells you that they can actually be compatible.

LEARNING OBJECTIVES

In this section, you'll learn to:

· Identify and paraphrase an apparent contradiction.

· Infer what must be true to resolve an apparent contradiction.

· Identify and answer Paradox questions.

· Identify and answer Paradox EXCEPT questions.

Identify and Paraphrase an Apparent Contradiction and Infer What Must Be True to Resolve It

Before you can spot the answer choice that will explain or resolve the paradox in the stimulus, you must be sure you've correctly understood the seeming discrepancy. To make sure you are clear on the scope and terms of the situation, always paraphrase the paradox in your own words. Once you've got a clear picture of the situation, you can predict the kind of fact that will help explain that the facts or statements are actually compatible.

Take a look at how an LSAT expert identifies and paraphrases the paradoxes found in a couple of Paradox question stimuli. You'll see that there is almost always a Contrast Keyword signaling the facts or assertions apparently in conflict. Let's start with the stimulus from the example at the beginning of this section.

LSAT Question	**Analysis**
Because of the recent recession in Country A, most magazines published there have experienced decreases in advertising revenue, so much so that the survival of the most widely read magazines is in grave doubt. At the same time, however, more people in Country A are reading more magazines than ever before, and the number of financially successful magazines in Country A is greater than ever. *PrepTest27 Sec1 Q7*	Fact 1: Most magazines, including those that are most widely read, are suffering critical losses in ad revenue. *Yet* Fact 2: The number of financially successful magazines is greater than ever. Paradox: How can it be that most magazines are losing ad revenue but the number of successful magazines is growing?

Can you anticipate the kind of fact that might help resolve the apparent discrepancy here? Note that the LSAT expert was precise when forming her paraphrase of the paradox. It would distort the stimulus to say that the magazines are losing "money" or becoming "less profitable." Instead, she notes that most magazines are losing ad revenue. But is that the only way magazines can generate income? What if we learned that more magazines were being sold at newsstands? Or what if we discovered that magazine subscriptions were on the rise? And do magazines have to increase revenue to be successful? What if they've lost ad revenue but have found a way to cut production costs so significantly that their profits have actually increased? The LSAT expert recognizes that there are many different ways the paradox could be resolved, but she doesn't spend a great amount of time thinking through them. Instead, her prediction is much simpler: The correct answer will be anything that explains the central paradox outlined in the stimulus.

Here's another example. Read the stimulus and review the expert's analysis of it.

LSAT Question	Analysis
When a community opens a large shopping mall, it often expects a boost to the local economy, and in fact a large amount of economic activity goes on in these malls. Yet the increase in the local economy is typically much smaller than the total amount of economic activity that goes on in the mall. *PrepTest28 Sec1 Q17* $\longrightarrow$	Fact 1: Communities expect a boost in the local economy after opening a shopping mall. *Yet* Fact 2: The increase in the local economy is smaller than the amount of economic activity occurring in the mall. Paradox: Why does the local economy not receive an economic boost equal to or larger than the amount of economic activity in the new mall?

If you find yourself scratching your head after reading a Paradox stimulus, good for you. That means you've really spotted the apparent contradiction. But remember that there is *always* a way to reconcile or resolve the discrepancy in these LSAT questions. What fact might explain why the local economy doesn't receive a boost, if the mall is a hub of economic activity? Again, you'll find the answer by sticking close to the terms of the stimulus. The two facts aren't really talking about the same thing. In Fact 1, we learn that local economies expect to see a *boost*, or increase in their economy. In Fact 2, the scope of the stimulus shifts to the *total amount of economic activity* at the shopping malls. But do we know if the economic activity, as large as it might be, is providing a boost to the local economy? What if the stores in the mall are all running a deficit? What if the mall only has economic activity because of investment from the local economy? Stay focused on the big difference between the two facts when you evaluate the answer choices to this paradox later in the chapter.

Now, try doing the same kind of analysis on your own.

Practice

Untangle the following stimuli. Identify the two facts that the author believes are in conflict. Paraphrase the paradox or apparent discrepancy the facts raise. Then, anticipate the kind of fact(s) that would explain, resolve, or reconcile the seeming contradiction.

LSAT Question	My Analysis
24. The symptoms of hepatitis A appear no earlier than 60 days after a person has been infected. In a test of a hepatitis A vaccine, 50 people received the vaccine and 50 people received a harmless placebo. Although some people from each group eventually exhibited symptoms of hepatitis A, the vaccine as used in the test is completely effective in preventing infection with the hepatitis A virus. *PrepTest29 Sec1 Q10*	
25. The indigenous people of Tasmania are clearly related to the indigenous people of Australia, but were separated from them when the land bridge between Australia and Tasmania disappeared approximately 10,000 years ago. Two thousand years after the disappearance of the land bridge, however, there were major differences between the culture and technology of the indigenous Tasmanians and those of the indigenous Australians. The indigenous Tasmanians, unlike their Australian relatives, had no domesticated dogs, fishing nets, polished stone tools, or hunting implements like the boomerang and the spear-thrower. *PrepTest29 Sec1 Q25*	
26. Generally speaking, if the same crop is sown in a field for several successive years, growth in the later years is poorer than growth in the earlier years, since nitrogen in the soil becomes depleted. Even though alfalfa is a nitrogen-fixing plant and thus increases the amount of nitrogen in the soil, surprisingly, it too, if planted in the same field year after year, grows less well in the later years than it does in the earlier years. *PrepTest28 Sec1 Q8*	

Did you take advantage of the Contrast Keywords in each example? If so, you likely spotted the apparent contradiction. Having done that, were you able to see how the paradox might be resolved? Compare your analysis to that of the LSAT expert on the next page.

Expert Analysis

Here's how an LSAT expert untangled the stimuli you just saw. Take note of the expert's paraphrasing of the paradox in each example and how she anticipates the apparent discrepancies may be resolved.

LSAT Question	Analysis
24. The symptoms of hepatitis A appear no earlier than 60 days after a person has been infected. In a test of a hepatitis A vaccine, 50 people received the vaccine and 50 people received a harmless placebo. Although some people from each group eventually exhibited symptoms of hepatitis A, the vaccine as used in the test is completely effective in preventing infection with the hepatitis A virus. *PrepTest29 Sec1 Q10* →	Fact 1: A vaccine is completely effective in preventing hepatitis A infection. *Yet* Fact 2: Some people who received the vaccine eventually exhibited symptoms of hepatitis A. Paradox: If the vaccine is completely effective in preventing hepatitis A infection, how could people who received the vaccine later show symptoms of hepatitis A?
25. The indigenous people of Tasmania are clearly related to the indigenous people of Australia, but were separated from them when the land bridge between Australia and Tasmania disappeared approximately 10,000 years ago. Two thousand years after the disappearance of the land bridge, however, there were major differences between the culture and technology of the indigenous Tasmanians and those of the indigenous Australians. The indigenous Tasmanians, unlike their Australian relatives, had no domesticated dogs, fishing nets, polished stone tools, or hunting implements like the boomerang and the spear-thrower. *PrepTest29 Sec1 Q25* →	Fact 1: Indigenous peoples of Tasmania and Australia are clearly related and are only separated by the disappearance of a land bridge. *Yet* Fact 2: Two thousand years after the disappearance of the land bridge, Australians had a number of impressive cultural and technological inventions that the Tasmanians did not. Paradox: Why would there be such great differences between two groups of people, despite their being related and only separated two thousand years ago?
26. Generally speaking, if the same crop is sown in a field for several successive years, growth in the later years is poorer than growth in the earlier years, since nitrogen in the soil becomes depleted. Even though alfalfa is a nitrogen-fixing plant and thus increases the amount of nitrogen in the soil, surprisingly, it too, if planted in the same field year after year, grows less well in the later years than it does in the earlier years. *PrepTest28 Sec1 Q8* →	Fact 1: Alfalfa doesn't deplete the soil of nitrogen. *Yet* Fact 2: Alfalfa shows the same reduction in crop yield after years in the same field as do crops that deplete nitrogen. Paradox: Why does alfalfa production decline over the years (just like other plants), even though it has solved the problem from the loss of nitrogen?

You will see the complete questions accompanying the stimuli for these questions a little later in this section.

As you reflect on the stimuli you just untangled, take a moment to consider a key distinction. In an Inference question, the stimulus provides facts that are mutually consistent and can be combined to create a new deduction. By contrast, a Paradox question provides facts that appear to be incompatible but actually are not. Allow your paraphrase of the apparent discrepancy or paradox to guide your prediction of the correct answer. Ask what is in need of explanation. Indeed, you should be able to say, "The fact that *x* and *y* are both true is confusing." Then, when you select the correct answer, you can say, "Okay. This clears it up."

Paradox Questions and Paradox EXCEPT Questions

Paradox question stems overwhelmingly use one of three verbs: *resolve*, *reconcile*, or *explain*. Sometimes, there will be an extra word in the question stem indicating that it is a discrepancy, anomaly, or paradox. Other times, the content of the paradox will even be mentioned in the question stem. Rarely, the test will ask a Paradox EXCEPT question, asking for the only answer that doesn't help to reconcile the seeming contradiction. Take a look at how an LSAT expert analyzes Paradox question stems.

LSAT Question		Analysis
Which one of the following, if true, most helps to explain the discrepancy described above? *PrepTest28 Sec1 Q17*	→	The correct answer will be a fact that reconciles the apparent discrepancy—a Paradox question.
Each of the following, if true, contributes to reconciling the apparent discrepancy indicated above EXCEPT: *PrepTest24 Sec3 Q14*	→	The four wrong answers will provide facts that help explain the apparent discrepancy. The correct answer will not explain it (either by deepening the paradox or by being Outside the Scope)—a Paradox EXCEPT question.

Practice

Practice Step 1 of the Logical Reasoning Method on a handful of Paradox question stems. Take note of the verbs signaling a Paradox question. Is there any additional guidance in the stem helping you see what to look for as you untangle the stimulus? How would you characterize the correct and incorrect answer choices?

LSAT Question	My Analysis
27. Which one of the following, if true, most helps resolve the apparent discrepancy in the information above? *PrepTest29 Sec1 Q10*	
28. Which one of the following, if true, most helps to explain the similarity described above between alfalfa and non-nitrogen-fixing plants? *PrepTest28 Sec1 Q8*	
29. Each of the following, if true, would contribute to an explanation of differences described above EXCEPT: *PrepTest29 Sec1 Q25*	

Expert Analysis

Here's how the LSAT expert viewed each of those question stems.

LSAT Question	Analysis
27. Which one of the following, if true, most helps resolve the apparent discrepancy in the information above? *PrepTest29 Sec1 Q10* →	The correct answer will be a fact that reconciles the apparent discrepancy in the stimulus above—a Paradox question.
28. Which one of the following, if true, most helps to explain the similarity described above between alfalfa and non-nitrogen-fixing plants? *PrepTest28 Sec1 Q8* →	The correct answer will be a fact that explains why alfalfa acts in a way similar to non-nitrogen-fixing plants—a Paradox question.
29. Each of the following, if true, would contribute to an explanation of differences described above EXCEPT: *PrepTest29 Sec1 Q25* →	The four incorrect answers will explain the differences described in the stimulus. The correct answer will deepen the mystery or discuss something beyond the scope of the stimulus—a Paradox EXCEPT question.

Notice that the LSAT expert used the question stem not only to identify the question type but also to anticipate how she would need to approach the stimulus. Paradox EXCEPT questions ask for an answer choice that does *not* resolve the contradiction. Wrong answer choices provide four possible explanations, and the correct answer will likely be Outside the Scope of the facts or will only talk about one of the facts.

> # LSAT STRATEGY
>
> Remember this about Paradox questions:
>
> · The statements in a Paradox question stimulus appear to be contradictory only because a fact is missing that explains how everything can be true.
>
> · The correct answer to a Paradox question must account for both of the apparently contradictory facts and not merely state that the situation described is common or that one of the facts in the paradox is easy to understand.

Paradox questions run the gamut of difficulty levels. Don't become complacent if you find that some of the Paradox questions you practice seem obvious or easy. That's true of all question types. The best test takers are rigorous and vigilant against sloppy reading or taking something for granted. Taking time to understand the nature of the paradoxical facts in the stimulus is essential to recognizing what is needed to explain them.

Before you practice full Paradox questions, take a look at the LSAT expert's analysis of the questions associated with the stimuli you've seen in this section. Pay close attention to how the expert predicts the kind of fact she will find in the correct answer and to why she eliminated each of the wrong answers in these questions.

LSAT Question	Analysis
The symptoms of hepatitis A appear no earlier than 60 days after a person has been infected. In a test of a hepatitis A vaccine, 50 people received the vaccine and 50 people received a harmless placebo. Although some people from each group eventually exhibited symptoms of hepatitis A, the vaccine as used in the test is completely effective in preventing infection with the hepatitis A virus.	**Step 2:** Fact 1: A vaccine is completely effective in preventing hepatitis A infection. Yet Fact 2: Some people who received the vaccine eventually exhibited symptoms of hepatitis A.
Which one of the following, if true, most helps resolve the apparent discrepancy in the information above? *PrepTest29 Sec1 Q10*	**Step 1:** The Keywords "most helps to resolve the apparent discrepancy" indicate that this is a Paradox question.
	Step 3: The correct choice will answer this question: If the vaccine is completely effective in preventing hepatitis A infection, how could people who received the vaccine later show symptoms of hepatitis A?
(A) The placebo did not produce any side effects that resembled any of the symptoms of hepatitis A.	**Step 4:** What the placebo did or didn't do won't explain why people getting the vaccine showed symptoms. Eliminate.
(B) More members of the group that had received the placebo recognized their symptoms as symptoms of hepatitis A than did members of the group that had received the vaccine.	What happened to the placebo group won't solve the mystery. Eliminate.
(C) The people who received the placebo were in better overall physical condition than were the people who received the vaccine.	What happened to the placebo group won't solve the mystery. Eliminate.
(D) The vaccinated people who exhibited symptoms of hepatitis A were infected with the hepatitis A virus before being vaccinated.	Correct. This solves the mystery. The vaccine prevents hepatitis A, but nowhere in the stimulus does it say it cures it.
(E) Of the people who developed symptoms of hepatitis A, those who received the vaccine recovered more quickly, on average, than those who did not. *PrepTest29 Sec1 Q10*	Recovering more or less quickly doesn't explain why some who received the vaccine still showed symptoms. Eliminate.

LSAT Question	Analysis
Generally speaking, if the same crop is sown in a field for several successive years, growth in the later years is poorer than growth in the earlier years, since nitrogen in the soil becomes depleted. Even though alfalfa is a nitrogen-fixing plant and thus increases the amount of nitrogen in the soil, surprisingly, it too, if planted in the same field year after year, grows less well in the later years than it does in the earlier years.	**Step 2:** Fact 1: Alfalfa doesn't deplete the soil of nitrogen. → *Yet* Fact 2: Alfalfa shows the same reduction in crop yield after years in the same field as do crops that deplete nitrogen.
Which one of the following, if true, most helps to explain the similarity described above between alfalfa and non-nitrogen-fixing plants?	**Step 1:** The Keywords "most helps to explain" indicates that this is a Paradox question.
→	**Step 3:** The correct choice will answer this question: Why does alfalfa production decline over the years (just like other plants), even though it has solved the problem from the loss of nitrogen?
(A) Some kinds of plants grow more rapidly and are more productive when they are grown among other kinds of plants rather than being grown only among plants of their own kind.	**Step 4:** This information might not even pertain to alfalfa, and so can't explain the mystery. Eliminate.
(B) Alfalfa increases the amount of nitrogen in the soil by taking nitrogen from the air and releasing it in a form that is usable by most kinds of plants.	This explains how alfalfa increases nitrogen levels in the soil, but not why yields decrease. Eliminate.
(C) Certain types of plants, including alfalfa, produce substances that accumulate in the soil and that are toxic to the plants that produce those substances.	Correct. An "accumulation of toxins" explains why alfalfa yields decrease over time if planted in the same field despite alfalfa's ability to decrease nitrogen in the soil.
(D) Alfalfa increases nitrogen in the soil in which it grows only if a certain type of soil bacteria is present in the soil.	Without knowing whether the bacteria is beneficial or harmful, it's impossible to determine if this explains alfalfa's decreased yields. Eliminate.
(E) Alfalfa is very sensitive to juglone, a compound that is exuded from the leaves of black walnut trees. *PrepTest28 Sec1 Q8*	This fact does nothing to explain why alfalfa (despite its being a nitrogen-fixing plant) grows less well when planted in the same field year after year. Eliminate.

LSAT Question	Analysis
The indigenous people of Tasmania are clearly related to the indigenous people of Australia, but were separated from them when the land bridge between Australia and Tasmania disappeared approximately 10,000 years ago. Two thousand years after the disappearance of the land bridge, however, there were major differences between the culture and technology of the indigenous Tasmanians and those of the indigenous Australians. The indigenous Tasmanians, unlike their Australian relatives, had no domesticated dogs, fishing nets, polished stone tools, or hunting implements like the boomerang and the spear-thrower.	**Step 2:** Fact 1: Indigenous peoples of Tasmania and Australia are clearly related and are only separated by the disappearance of a land bridge. *Yet* Fact 2: Two thousand years after the disappearance of the land bridge, Australians had a number of impressive cultural and technological inventions that the Tasmanians did not.
Each of the following, if true, would contribute to an explanation of differences described above EXCEPT:	**Step 1:** The Keywords "contribute to an explanation" indicate that this is a Paradox question. "EXCEPT" alerts us to the fact that the four wrong answers will help resolve the apparent discrepancy, while the correct answer will either have no impact or deepen the mystery.
	Step 3: The four wrong choices will answer this question: Why would there be such great differences between two groups of people, despite their being related and only separated two thousand years ago? The correct answer will either deepen the mystery or have no impact.
(A) After the disappearance of the land bridge the indigenous Tasmanians simply abandoned certain practices and technologies that they had originally shared with their Australian relatives.	**Step 4:** This would explain the difference. Eliminate.
(B) Devices such as the spear-thrower and the boomerang were developed by the indigenous Tasmanians more than 10,000 years ago.	Correct. This does nothing to explain why later, after the groups were separated, only one group would continue to use these tools.
(C) Technological innovations such as fishing nets, polished stone tools, and so on, were imported to Australia by Polynesian explorers more recently than 10,000 years ago.	This would explain the difference. Eliminate.
(D) Indigenous people of Australia developed hunting implements like the boomerang and the spear-thrower after the disappearance of the land bridge.	This would explain the difference. Eliminate.
(E) Although the technological and cultural innovations were developed in Australia more than 10,000 years ago, they were developed by groups in northern Australia with whom the indigenous Tasmanians had no contact prior to the disappearance of the land bridge.	This would explain the difference. Eliminate.

PrepTest28 Sec1 Q8

Now, try some full Paradox questions. As you untangle each stimulus, paraphrase the apparent discrepancy in your own words. While you may not be able to predict the exact fact that the correct answer will contain, make sure you're preparing yourself to evaluate the choices by predicting the kind of fact that the right answer needs to have.

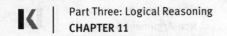

Practice

For each of the following, apply the Logical Reasoning Method to a Paradox question. Use the corresponding blanks to record your thinking for each step. After each, compare your work to the thinking of an LSAT expert on the following pages.

LSAT Question	My Analysis
30. Because of the recent recession in Country A, most magazines published there have experienced decreases in advertising revenue, so much so that the survival of the most widely read magazines is in grave doubt. At the same time, however, more people in Country A are reading more magazines than ever before, and the number of financially successful magazines in Country A is greater than ever.	Step 2:
Which one the following, if true, most helps to resolve the apparent discrepancy in the information above?	Step 1:
	Step 3:
(A) Most magazines reduce the amount they charge for advertisements during a recession.	Step 4:
(B) The audience for a successful television show far exceeds the readership of even the most widely read magazine.	
(C) Advertising is the main source of revenue only for the most widely read magazines; other magazines rely on circulation for their revenue.	
(D) Because of the recession, people in Country A have cut back on magazine subscriptions and are reading borrowed magazines.	
(E) More of the new general interest magazines that were launched this year in Country A have survived than survived in previous years.	

PrepTest27 Sec1 Q7

LSAT Question	My Analysis
31. When a community opens a large shopping mall, it often expects a boost to the local economy, and in fact a large amount of economic activity goes on in these malls. Yet the increase in the local economy is typically much smaller than the total amount of economic activity that goes on in the mall.	**Step 2:**
Which one of the following, if true, most helps to explain the discrepancy described above?	**Step 1:**
	Step 3:
(A) When large shopping malls are new they attract a lot of shoppers but once the novelty has worn off they usually attract fewer shoppers than does the traditional downtown shopping district.	**Step 4:**
(B) Most of the money spent in a large shopping mall is spent by tourists who are drawn specifically by the mall and who would not have visited the community had that mall not been built.	
(C) Most of the jobs created by large shopping malls are filled by people who recently moved to the community and who would not have moved had there been no job offer in the community.	
(D) Most of the money spent in a large shopping mall is money that would have been spent elsewhere in the same community had that mall not been built.	
(E) Most of the jobs created by the construction of a large shopping mall are temporary, and most of the permanent jobs created are low paying.	

PrepTest28 Sec1 Q17

LSAT Question	My Analysis
32. Birds startled by potential predators generally try to take cover in nearby vegetation. Yet many birds that feed at bird feeders placed in suburban gardens are killed when, thus startled, they fly away from the vegetation in the gardens and into the windowpanes of nearby houses.	**Step 2:**
Which one of the following, if true, most helps to explain the anomalous behavior of the birds that fly into windowpanes?	**Step 1:**
	Step 3:
(A) Predator attacks are as likely to occur at bird feeders surrounded by dense vegetation as they are at feeders surrounded by little or no vegetation.	**Step 4:**
(B) The bird feeders in some suburban gardens are placed at a considerable distance from the houses.	
(C) Large birds are as likely as small birds to fly into windowpanes.	
(D) Most of the birds startled while feeding at bird feeders placed in suburban gardens are startled by loud noises rather than by predators.	
(E) The windowpanes of many houses clearly reflect surrounding vegetation.	

PrepTest28 Sec3 Q3

LSAT Question	My Analysis
33. People always seem to associate high prices of products with high quality. But price is not necessarily an indicator of quality. The best teas are often no more expensive than the lower-quality teas.	**Step 2:**
Which one of the following, if true, does most to explain the apparent counterexample described above?	**Step 1:**
	Step 3:
(A) Packing and advertising triple the price of all teas.	**Step 4:**
(B) Most people buy low-quality tea, thus keeping its price up.	
(C) All types of tea are subject to high import tariffs.	
(D) Low-quality teas are generally easier to obtain than high quality teas.	
(E) The price of tea generally does not vary from region to region.	

PrepTest27 Sec4 Q8

LSAT Question	**My Analysis**
34. In an effort to boost sales during the summer months, which are typically the best for soft-drink sales, Foamy Soda lowered its prices. In spite of this, however, the sales of Foamy Soda dropped during the summer months.	**Step 2:**
Each of the following, if true, contributes to reconciling the apparent discrepancy indicated above EXCEPT:	**Step 1:**
	Step 3:
(A) The soft-drink industry as a whole experienced depressed sales during the summer months.	**Step 4:**
(B) Foamy Soda's competitors lowered their prices even more drastically during the summer months.	
(C) Because of an increase in the price of sweeteners, the production costs of Foamy Soda rose during the summer months.	
(D) A strike at Foamy Soda's main plant forced production cutbacks that resulted in many stores not receiving their normal shipments during the summer months.	
(E) The weather during the summer months was unseasonably cool, decreasing the demand for soft drinks.	

PrepTest24 Sec3 Q14

Expert Analysis

Check your work by studying the LSAT expert's analysis of the questions you just practiced. Review the analysis by following the steps of the Logical Reasoning Method and pay attention to why the expert eliminated each wrong answer (even if you got the question correct).

LSAT Question	Analysis
30. Because of the recent recession in Country A, most magazines published there have experienced decreases in advertising revenue, so much so that the survival of the most widely read magazines is in grave doubt. At the same time, however, more people in Country A are reading more magazines than ever before, and the number of financially successful magazines in Country A is greater than ever.	**Step 2:** Fact 1: Most magazines, including those most widely read, are suffering critical losses in ad revenue. *Yet* Fact 2: The number of financially successful magazines is greater than ever.
Which one the following, if true, most helps to resolve the apparent discrepancy in the information above?	**Step 1:** The phrase "resolve the apparent discrepancy" indicates a Paradox question.
	Step 3: The correct choice will answer this question: How can it be that most magazines are losing ad revenue but the number of successful magazines is growing?
(A) Most magazines reduce the amount they charge for advertisements during a recession.	**Step 4:** This helps explain the decrease in ad revenue but does nothing to explain the mystery of the financial success of certain magazines. Eliminate.
(B) The audience for a successful television show far exceeds the readership of even the most widely read magazine.	Irrelevant Comparison. This helps explain the bad financial straits of some magazines, but does nothing to explain the mystery of the financial success of certain magazines. Eliminate.
(C) Advertising is the main source of revenue only for the most widely read magazines; other magazines rely on circulation for their revenue.	Correct. This choice describes an alternative factor that explains the financial success of certain magazines, despite the loss of ad revenue.
(D) Because of the recession, people in Country A have cut back on magazine subscriptions and are reading borrowed magazines.	180. This makes it even more unfathomable that some magazines are enjoying financial success in the face of declining ad revenues. Eliminate.
(E) More of the new general interest magazines that were launched this year in Country A have survived than survived in previous years. *PrepTest27 Sec1 Q7*	This fact does nothing to explain *why* more magazines are financially successful despite the loss in advertising revenue. Eliminate.

LSAT Question	Analysis
31. When a community opens a large shopping mall, it often expects a boost to the local economy, and in fact a large amount of economic activity goes on in these malls. Yet the increase in the local economy is typically much smaller than the total amount of economic activity that goes on in the mall.	**Step 2:** Fact 1: Communities expect a boost in the local economy after opening a shopping mall. *Yet* Fact 2: The increase in the local economy is smaller than the amount of economic activity occurring in the mall.
Which one of the following, if true, most helps to explain the discrepancy described above?	**Step 1:** The phrase "explain the discrepancy" indicates a Paradox question.
	Step 3: The correct choice will answer this question: Why does the local economy not receive an economic boost equal to or larger than the amount of economic activity in the new mall?
(A) When large shopping malls are new they attract a lot of shoppers but once the novelty has worn off they usually attract fewer shoppers than does the traditional downtown shopping district.	**Step 4:** This explains why the economic benefits of a new mall would not be long lasting, but does not explain the discrepancy between the amount of financial activity in the mall and the lesser level of benefits to the local economy. Eliminate.
(B) Most of the money spent in a large shopping mall is spent by tourists who are drawn specifically by the mall and who would not have visited the community had that mall not been built.	180. This suggests that the economic activity at the new mall should be purely additive to the local economy. Eliminate.
(C) Most of the jobs created by large shopping malls are filled by people who recently moved to the community and who would not have moved had there been no job offer in the community.	Another 180. As with choice (B), this suggests that the economic activity at the new mall should be purely additive to the local economy. Eliminate.
(D) Most of the money spent in a large shopping mall is money that would have been spent elsewhere in the same community had that mall not been built.	Correct. This is the flip side of choices (B) and (C). Rather than adding economic activity to the local economy, the new mall is simply displacing previously existing economic activity.
(E) Most of the jobs created by the construction of a large shopping mall are temporary, and most of the permanent jobs created are low paying. *PrepTest28 Sec1 Q17*	As with choice (A), this explains why the economic benefits of a new mall would not be long lasting, but does not explain the discrepancy between the amount of financial activity in the mall and the lesser level of benefits to the local economy. Eliminate.

LSAT Question	Analysis
32. Birds startled by potential predators generally try to take cover in nearby vegetation. Yet many birds that feed at bird feeders placed in suburban gardens are killed when, thus startled, they fly away from the vegetation in the gardens and into the windowpanes of nearby houses.	**Step 2:** Fact 1: When startled, birds want to fly to vegetation. *Yet* Fact 2: When startled, birds in suburbs often instead fly into windowpanes.
Which one of the following, if true, most helps to explain the anomalous behavior of the birds that fly into windowpanes?	**Step 1:** The phrase "helps to explain" indicates a Paradox question.
	Step 3: The correct choice will answer this question: Why do birds, when startled, fly into windowpanes despite wanting to fly to vegetation?
(A) Predator attacks are as likely to occur at bird feeders surrounded by dense vegetation as they are at feeders surrounded by little or no vegetation.	**Step 4:** This does nothing to explain *why* the birds fly into windowpanes. Eliminate.
(B) The bird feeders in some suburban gardens are placed at a considerable distance from the houses.	180. This just makes it more mysterious *why* birds would fly such a distance to strike a windowpane. Eliminate.
(C) Large birds are as likely as small birds to fly into windowpanes.	Irrelevant Comparison. Such a distinction doesn't explain *why* any birds would fly into windowpanes. Eliminate.
(D) Most of the birds startled while feeding at bird feeders placed in suburban gardens are startled by loud noises rather than by predators.	This choice also does not explain *why* birds would fly into windowpanes regardless of what startles them. Eliminate.
(E) The windowpanes of many houses clearly reflect surrounding vegetation. *PrepTest28 Sec3 Q3*	Correct. This choice provides *a reason why* birds seeking vegetation would strike a windowpane.

LSAT Question	Analysis
33. People always seem to associate high prices of products with high quality. But price is not necessarily an indicator of quality. The best teas are often no more expensive than the lower-quality teas. →	**Step 2:** Fact 1: Higher quality usually means higher price. *Yet* Fact 2: Higher quality teas are often no more expensive than lower quality teas.
Which one of the following, if true, does most to explain the apparent counterexample described above? →	**Step 1:** The phrase "explain the apparent counterexample" indicates a Paradox question.
→	**Step 3:** The correct choice will answer this question: Why do low quality teas costs as much as high quality teas?
(A) Packing and advertising triple the price of all teas. →	**Step 4:** Something that applies to all teas cannot explain what is raising the price of low quality teas relative to high quality. Eliminate.
(B) Most people buy low-quality tea, thus keeping its price up. →	Correct. This provides a distinction between the different quality teas that explains why the low quality varieties cost as much as the high quality varieties.
(C) All types of tea are subject to high import tariffs. →	As with (A), this cannot explain the discrepancy because it applies to all teas. Eliminate.
(D) Low-quality teas are generally easier to obtain than high quality teas. →	180. This deepens the mystery because this is a further reason why low quality teas should be cheaper. Eliminate.
(E) The price of tea generally does not vary from region to region. *PrepTest27 Sec4 Q8* →	Irrelevant Comparison. The cost of teas generally across different regions does not address the discrepancy between the price of low and high quality teas. Eliminate.

LSAT Question	Analysis
34. In an effort to boost sales during the summer months, which are typically the best for soft-drink sales, Foamy Soda lowered its prices. In spite of this, however, the sales of Foamy Soda dropped during the summer months.	**Step 2:** Fact 1: Foamy Soda lowered its prices during the prime soda season, summer. *Yet* Fact 2: Sales of Foamy Soda dropped.
Each of the following, if true, contributes to reconciling the apparent discrepancy indicated above EXCEPT:	**Step 1:** The phrase "reconcil[e] the apparent discrepancy" indicates a Paradox question. In this case, a Paradox EXCEPT.
	Step 3: The four wrong choices will each provide an answer to this question: Why would Foamy Soda's sales drop despite the fact that it is summer and the fact that Foamy has lowered its prices? The correct answer will deepen the mystery, or have no impact.
(A) The soft-drink industry as a whole experienced depressed sales during the summer months.	**Step 4:** This is a reason for lower soda sales. Eliminate.
(B) Foamy Soda's competitors lowered their prices even more drastically during the summer months.	Steeper price cuts by competitors could explain Foamy Soda's sales losses. Eliminate.
(C) Because of an increase in the price of sweeteners, the production costs of Foamy Soda rose during the summer months.	Correct. This could hurt Foamy Soda's profit margins, but does nothing to explain why its *sales* would decline.
(D) A strike at Foamy Soda's main plant forced production cutbacks that resulted in many stores not receiving their normal shipments during the summer months.	Foamy Soda can't sell what doesn't get to the stores. Eliminate.
(E) The weather during the summer months was unseasonably cool, decreasing the demand for soft drinks.	This is a reason for lower soda sales across the board. Eliminate.

PrepTest24 Sec3 Q14

739

Reflection

Keep an eye out for apparent discrepancies, seeming contradictions, and paradoxes in your day-to-day life. The next time a friend sees something that puzzles him and asks you, "How can that be?" take the opportunity to practice your Paradox question skills. Find facts that show how the situation can be resolved, reconciled, or explained. You may be surprised to discover how often we fail to explain paradoxes but instead respond by saying things like, "Oh, that happens all the time; don't be surprised," or how often we explain only one side of the discrepancy (just as wrong answers do on the LSAT) and fail to clear up the paradox at all.

Summary

Congratulations. Over the last three chapters, you've learned how to answer all of the Logical Reasoning question types on the LSAT. Continue to improve your performance on non-argument-based questions with the items in the Question Pool following this section. When you're ready to move on, Chapter 12 covers Logical Reasoning section management; it will give you the best strategies for being efficient and effective with your time, not getting bogged down, and using the 35 minutes in each Logical Reasoning section to get the most points possible.

QUESTION POOL

Inference

Assess your skills on some further examples of Inference questions.

1. Flavonoids are a common component of almost all plants, but a specific variety of flavonoid in apples has been found to be an antioxidant. Antioxidants are known to be a factor in the prevention of heart disease.

   Which one of the following can be properly inferred from the passage?

   (A) A diet composed largely of fruits and vegetables will help to prevent heart disease.
   (B) Flavonoids are essential to preventing heart disease.
   (C) Eating at least one apple each day will prevent heart disease.
   (D) At least one type of flavonoid helps to prevent heart disease.
   (E) A diet deficient in antioxidants is a common cause of heart disease.

   PrepTest28 Sec3 Q1

2. In response to requests made by the dairy industry, the government is considering whether to approve the synthetic hormone BST for use in dairy cows. BST increases milk production but also leads to recurring udder inflammation, decreased fertility, and symptoms of stress in cows who receive the hormone. All of these problems can be kept under control with constant veterinary care, but such levels of veterinary help would cost big farms far less per cow than they would small farms.

   If the statements above are true, which one of the following claims is most strongly supported by them?

   (A) The government is unlikely to approve the synthetic hormone BST for use in cows.
   (B) The proportion of cows that suffer from udder inflammation, decreased fertility, and symptoms of stress is currently greater on big dairy farms than on small ones.
   (C) At the present time milk from cows raised on small farms is safer to drink than milk from cows raised on big farms.
   (D) The milk from cows who receive BST will not be safe for people to drink.
   (E) Owners of big farms stand to gain more from government approval of BST than do owners of small farms.

   PrepTest24 Sec3 Q7

3. A century in certain ways is like a life, and as the end of a century approaches, people behave toward that century much as someone who is nearing the end of life does toward that life. So just as people in their last years spend much time looking back on the events of their life, people at a century's end _____.

   Which one of the following most logically completes the argument?

   (A) reminisce about their own lives
   (B) fear that their own lives are about to end
   (C) focus on what the next century will bring
   (D) become very interested in the history of the century just ending
   (E) reflect on how certain unfortunate events of the century could have been avoided

   PrepTestJun07 Sec2 Q3

4. Advertisers have learned that people are more easily encouraged to develop positive attitudes about things toward which they originally have neutral or even negative attitudes if those things are linked, with pictorial help rather than exclusively through prose, to things about which they already have positive attitudes. Therefore, advertisers are likely to _____.

   Which one of the following most logically completes the argument?

   (A) use little if any written prose in their advertisements
   (B) try to encourage people to develop positive attitudes about products that can be better represented pictorially than in prose
   (C) place their advertisements on television rather than in magazines
   (D) highlight the desirable features of the advertised product by contrasting them pictorially with undesirable features of a competing product
   (E) create advertisements containing pictures of things most members of the target audience like

   PrepTestJun07 Sec3 Q10

5. Proponents of the electric car maintain that when the technical problems associated with its battery design are solved, such cars will be widely used and, because they are emission-free, will result in an abatement of the environmental degradation caused by auto emissions. But unless we dam more rivers, the electricity to charge these batteries will come from nuclear or coal-fired power plants. Each of these three power sources produces considerable environmental damage. Thus, the electric car _____.

Which one of the following most logically completes the argument?

(A) will have worse environmental consequences than its proponents may believe

(B) will probably remain less popular than other types of cars

(C) requires that purely technical problems be solved before it can succeed

(D) will increase the total level of emissions rather than reduce it

(E) will not produce a net reduction in environmental degradation

PrepTestJun07 Sec2 Q8

6. If the economy is weak, then prices remain constant although unemployment rises. But unemployment rises only if investment decreases. Fortunately, investment is not decreasing.

If the statements above are true, then which one of the following must be false?

(A) Either the economy is weak or investment is decreasing.

(B) If unemployment rises, the prices remain constant.

(C) The economy is weak only if investment decreases.

(D) Either the economy is weak or prices are remaining constant.

(E) Either unemployment is rising or the economy is not weak.

PrepTest28 Sec1 Q20

7. If the price it pays for coffee beans continues to increase, the Coffee Shoppe will have to increase its prices. In that case, either the Coffee Shoppe will begin selling noncoffee products or its coffee sales will decrease. But selling noncoffee products will decrease the Coffee Shoppe's overall profitability. Moreover, the Coffee Shoppe can avoid a decrease in overall profitability only if its coffee sales do not decrease.

Which one of the following statements follows logically from the statements above?

(A) If the Coffee Shoppe's overall profitability decreases, the price it pays for coffee beans will have continued to increase.

(B) If the Coffee Shoppe's overall profitability decreases, either it will have begun selling noncoffee products or its coffee sales will have decreased.

(C) The Coffee Shoppe's overall profitability will decrease if the price it pays for coffee beans continues to increase.

(D) The price it pays for coffee beans cannot decrease without the Coffee Shoppe's overall profitability also decreasing.

(E) Either the price it pays for coffee beans will continue to increase or the Coffee Shoppe's coffee sales will increase.

PrepTestJun07 Sec3 Q22

8. Philosopher: Nations are not literally persons; they have no thoughts or feelings, and, literally speaking, they perform no actions. Thus they have no moral rights or responsibilities. But no nation can survive unless many of its citizens attribute such rights and responsibilities to it, for nothing else could prompt people to make the sacrifices national citizenship demands. Obviously, then, a nation _____.

Which one of the following most logically completes the philosopher's argument?

(A) cannot continue to exist unless something other than the false belief that the nation has moral rights motivates its citizens to make sacrifices

(B) cannot survive unless many of its citizens have some beliefs that are literally false

(C) can never be a target of moral praise or blame

(D) is not worth the sacrifices that its citizens make on its behalf

(E) should always be thought of in metaphorical rather than literal terms

PrepTestJun07 Sec3 Q16

9. Editorialist: News media rarely cover local politics thoroughly, and local political business is usually conducted secretively. These factors each tend to isolate local politicians from their electorates. This has the effect of reducing the chance that any particular act of resident participation will elicit a positive official response, which in turn discourages resident participation in local politics.

Which one of the following is most strongly supported by the editorialist's statements?

(A) Particular acts of resident participation would be likely to elicit a positive response from local politicians if those politicians were less isolated from their electorate.

(B) Local political business should be conducted less secretively because this would avoid discouraging resident participation in local politics.

(C) The most important factor influencing a resident's decision as to whether to participate in local politics is the chance that the participation will elicit a positive official response.

(D) More-frequent thorough coverage of local politics would reduce at least one source of discouragement from resident participation in local politics.

(E) If resident participation in local politics were not discouraged, this would cause local politicians to be less isolated from their electorate.

PrepTestJun07 Sec2 Q22

10. Modern science is built on the process of posing hypotheses and testing them against observations—in essence, attempting to show that the hypotheses are incorrect. Nothing brings more recognition than overthrowing conventional wisdom. It is accordingly unsurprising that some scientists are skeptical of the widely accepted predictions of global warming. What is instead remarkable is that with hundreds of researchers striving to make breakthroughs in climatology, very few find evidence that global warming is unlikely.

The information above provides the most support for which one of the following statements?

(A) Most scientists who are reluctant to accept the global warming hypothesis are not acting in accordance with the accepted standards of scientific debate.

(B) Most researchers in climatology have substantial motive to find evidence that would discredit the global warming hypothesis.

(C) There is evidence that conclusively shows that the global warming hypothesis is true.

(D) Scientists who are skeptical about global warming have not offered any alternative hypotheses to explain climatological data.

(E) Research in global warming is primarily driven by a desire for recognition in the scientific community.

PrepTestJun07 Sec2 Q18

The explanations to these questions begin on page 752.

Principle (Inference)

Assess your skills on some further examples of Principle questions that reward you for making valid Inferences.

11. Jablonski, who owns a car dealership, has donated cars to driver education programs at area schools for over five years. She found the statistics on car accidents to be disturbing, and she wanted to do something to encourage better driving in young drivers. Some members of the community have shown their support for this action by purchasing cars from Jablonski's dealership.

    Which one of the following propositions is best illustrated by the passage?

    (A) The only way to reduce traffic accidents is through driver education programs.
    (B) Altruistic actions sometimes have positive consequences for those who perform them.
    (C) Young drivers are the group most likely to benefit from driver education programs.
    (D) It is usually in one's best interest to perform actions that benefit others.
    (E) An action must have broad community support if it is to be successful.

    PrepTestJun07 Sec3 Q6

12. Situation: Someone living in a cold climate buys a winter coat that is stylish but not warm in order to appear sophisticated.

    Analysis: People are sometimes willing to sacrifice sensual comfort or pleasure for the sake of appearances.

    The analysis provided for the situation above is most appropriate for which one of the following situations?

    (A) A person buys an automobile to commute to work even though public transportation is quick and reliable.
    (B) A parent buys a car seat for a young child because it is more colorful and more comfortable for the child than the other car seats on the market, though no safer.
    (C) A couple buys a particular wine even though their favorite wine is less expensive and better tasting because they think it will impress their dinner guests.
    (D) A person sets her thermostat at a low temperature during the winter because she is concerned about the environmental damage caused by using fossil fuels to heat her home.
    (E) An acrobat convinces the circus that employs him to purchase an expensive outfit for him so that he can wear it during his act to impress the audience.

    PrepTestJun07 Sec3 Q1

13. Ethicist: The most advanced kind of moral motivation is based solely on abstract principles. This form of motivation is in contrast with calculated self-interest or the desire to adhere to societal norms and conventions.

    The actions of which one of the following individuals exhibit the most advanced kind of moral motivation, as described by the ethicist?

    (A) Bobby contributed money to a local charity during a charity drive at work because he worried that not doing so would make him look stingy.
    (B) Wes contributed money to a local charity during a charity drive at work because he believed that doing so would improve his employer's opinion of him.
    (C) Donna's employers engaged in an illegal but profitable practice that caused serious damage to the environment. Donna did not report this practice to the authorities, out of fear that her employers would retaliate against her.
    (D) Jadine's employers engaged in an illegal but profitable practice that caused serious damage to the environment. Jadine reported this practice to the authorities out of a belief that protecting the environment is always more important than monetary profit.
    (E) Leigh's employers engaged in an illegal but profitable practice that caused serious damage to the environment. Leigh reported this practice to the authorities only because several colleagues had been pressuring her to do so.

    PrepTestJun07 Sec2 Q7

14. Car companies solicit consumer information on such human factors as whether a seat is comfortable or whether a set of controls is easy to use. However, designer interaction with consumers is superior to survey data; the data may tell the designer why a feature on last year's model was given a low rating, but data will not explain how that feature needs to be changed in order to receive a higher rating.

The reasoning above conforms most closely to which one of the following propositions?

(A) Getting consumer input for design modifications can contribute to successful product design.

(B) Car companies traditionally conduct extensive postmarket surveys.

(C) Designers aim to create features that will appeal to specific market niches.

(D) A car will have unappealing features if consumers are not consulted during its design stage.

(E) Consumer input affects external rather than internal design components of cars.

PrepTestJun07 Sec2 Q24

Paradox

Assess your skills on some further examples of Paradox questions.

15. Cats spend much of their time sleeping; they seem to awaken only to stretch and yawn. Yet they have a strong, agile musculature that most animals would have to exercise strenuously to acquire.

Which one of the following, if true, most helps to resolve the apparent paradox described above?

(A) Cats have a greater physiological need for sleep than other animals.

(B) Many other animals also spend much of their time sleeping yet have a strong, agile musculature.

(C) Cats are able to sleep in apparently uncomfortable positions.

(D) Cats derive ample exercise from frequent stretching.

(E) Cats require strength and agility in order to be effective predators.

PrepTest29 Sec1 Q4

16. After replacing his old gas water heater with a new, pilotless, gas water heater that is rated as highly efficient, Jimmy's gas bills increased.

Each of the following, if true, contributes to an explanation of the increase mentioned above EXCEPT:

(A) The new water heater uses a smaller percentage of the gas used by Jimmy's household than did the old one.

(B) Shortly after the new water heater was installed, Jimmy's uncle came to live with him, doubling the size of the household.

(C) After having done his laundry at a laundromat, Jimmy bought and started using a gas dryer when he replaced his water heater.

(D) Jimmy's utility company raised the rates for gas consumption following installation of the new water heater.

(E) Unusually cold weather following installation of the new water heater resulted in heavy gas usage.

PrepTestJun07 Sec3 Q2

17. During the nineteenth century, the French academy of art was a major financial sponsor of painting and sculpture in France; sponsorship by private individuals had decreased dramatically by this time. Because the academy discouraged innovation in the arts, there was little innovation in nineteenth century French sculpture. Yet nineteenth century French painting showed a remarkable degree of innovation.

Which one of the following, if true, most helps to explain the difference between the amount of innovation in French painting and the amount of innovation in French sculpture during the nineteenth century?

(A) In France in the nineteenth century, the French academy gave more of its financial support to painting than it did to sculpture.

(B) The French academy in the nineteenth century financially supported a greater number of sculptors than painters, but individual painters received more support, on average, than individual sculptors.

(C) Because stone was so much more expensive than paint and canvas, far more unsponsored paintings were produced than were unsponsored sculptures in France during the nineteenth century.

(D) Very few of the artists in France in the nineteenth century who produced sculptures also produced paintings.

(E) Although the academy was the primary sponsor of sculpture and painting, the total amount of financial support that French sculptors and painters received from sponsors declined during the nineteenth century.

PrepTestJun07 Sec2 Q25

These explanations refer to questions that begin on page 741.

Part Three: Logical Reasoning
Non-Argument Questions

ANSWERS AND EXPLANATIONS

Inference

1. (D) Inference ★☆☆☆

Step 1: Identify the Question Type

This question asks what can be "properly inferred," indicating an Inference question. The correct answer must be true based on the information given in the stimulus.

Step 2: Untangle the Stimulus

This brief paragraph contains three facts: First, that almost all plants contain flavonoids; second, that there is a specific flavonoid in apples that's an antioxidant; and third, that antioxidants can help prevent heart disease.

Step 3: Make a Prediction

With Inference stimuli, be on the lookout for words or terms that connect statements. Here, you learn that the flavonoid in apples is an antioxidant and that antioxidants can be a factor that helps prevent heart disease. Anticipate that the correct answer will link apples or flavonoids with the prevention of heart disease. Be prepared, however, to eliminate answers with extreme language. From this stimulus, you can infer that the flavonoid in apples *may help* prevent heart problems, not that they'll cure them or that someone eating apples will never have a heart attack.

Step 4: Evaluate the Answer Choices

(D) fits all of the information in the passage. If apples contain a flavonoid that is an antioxidant, and antioxidants help prevent heart disease, then there is at least one type of flavonoid that helps prevent heart disease.

(A) is too broad. The stimulus contains nothing about diets rich in fruits and vegetables in general. You learn about only one flavonoid in apples. Be careful of statements like this one that sound reasonable based on the "real world," but aren't supported by the stimulus.

(B) is Extreme. Only one type of flavonoid is mentioned in the stimulus as an antioxidant—flavonoids, in general, are not cited as beneficial. Also, **(B)**'s phrase "are essential to" is much stronger than the cautious language of the stimulus.

(C) is Extreme. An apple a day may keep the doctor away, but **(C)**'s prescription is more extreme than the stimulus warrants. "Known to be a factor in prevention" does not translate into "will prevent." Moreover, there's nothing here to support the specific "at least one apple per day" recommendation. Although apples contain the beneficial flavonoid, it is unknown what quantity of apples would need to be consumed to get the antioxidant benefit.

(E) is Outside the Scope. The stimulus deals with the *prevention* of heart disease, not at all with its *cause*.

2. (E) Inference ★★★☆

Step 1: Identify the Question Type

When a question stem asks for an answer choice that *supports* the argument, you have a Strengthen question. Here, however, you are asked to find the answer choice that is "*supported by*" the stimulus, so this is an Inference question.

Step 2: Untangle the Stimulus

The dairy industry wants the government to approve the use of BST to increase milk production, but BST causes several side effects. "[C]onstant veterinary care" can control all of these side effects. However, such care would cost small farms more per cow than it would cost big farms.

Step 3: Make a Prediction

With Inference questions, it is not always possible to predict the correct answer exactly, but often you can string some thoughts together and anticipate where the testmaker is going. Because the big farms will have to spend less money per cow than small farms on veterinary care, they won't incur as much relative expense as the small farms will if the government approves BST. The big farms should make out better because they're going to get increased milk production with BST's use and pay less per cow to ward off the side effects.

Step 4: Evaluate the Answer Choices

(E) is correct and must be true based on the last sentence in the stimulus.

(A) is incorrect because nothing in the stimulus mentions the actual likelihood that the government will approve BST. The stimulus simply states that the government "is considering whether to approve" BST.

(B) is an Irrelevant Comparison. This laundry list of ailments represents the side effects of the proposed hormone BST, but you do not know whether any cows—on farms of whatever size—are *currently* suffering from them. Even if they are, there is no evidence that a greater percentage of ailing cows live on big farms rather than on little farms.

(C) is an Irrelevant Comparison. The safety of milk at the present time is not discussed; the stimulus simply mentions the negative health effects of BST on cows and how those effects might be controlled.

(D) is Outside the Scope. The stimulus never mentions anything about whether milk from cows treated with BST will be safe to drink.

These explanations refer to questions that begin on page 741.

EXPLANATIONS

3. (D) Inference ★★★★

Step 1: Identify the Question Type

Treat a question that asks you to fill in the blank for a conclusion of an argument as an Inference question. The correct answer should act as a logical conclusion, falling neatly within the scope of what has already been stated without extrapolation.

Step 2: Untangle the Stimulus

The argument begins by analogizing a century to a life, equating how people act as the end of a century approaches with how they act near the end of their life. Then the author states that people at the end of their life start looking back at the events of their life.

Step 3: Make a Prediction

You need to complete the analogy that the author has set up, resisting any urge to extrapolate or get creative. The author equates people's actions at the end of a century with those at the end of their lives; thus, if they look back on their life events, they should also look back on the events of an ending century.

Step 4: Evaluate the Answer Choices

(D) matches the prediction that people will contemplate events of the past century.

(A) repeats what people do at the end of their lives and does not complete the analogy to the end of a century.

(B) might have made sense in 1999 when Y2K was a rampant worry, but it does not logically complete the analogy. *Fear* is Out of Scope.

(C) is a 180. Completing the analogy requires looking back on the century just as one looks back on one's own life. This answer would only work if the stimulus said people at the end of their lives focus on what will happen after they die.

(E) is a Distortion. While the answer choice correctly incorporates reminiscing on past events, the stimulus doesn't mention anything about focusing on unfortunate events or second-guessing any events.

4. (E) Inference ★★★★

Step 1: Identify the Question Type

Because the correct answer "logically completes the argument," it is the statement that must be true based on information in the stimulus. Thus, this is an Inference question.

Step 2: Untangle the Stimulus

Paraphrase the information in the stimulus. Advertisers know that people are more likely to develop positive feelings about things, if those things are linked to something else people already like. This is true even if people start out with neutral or even negative feelings. Pictures forge this link better than words do.

Step 3: Make a Prediction

Given that pictures effectively create positive links, it would make sense that advertisers would create advertisements that use pictures of things toward which people already have positive feelings.

Step 4: Evaluate the Answer Choices

(E) matches the prediction.

(A) is a Distortion. Just because pictures work *better* than prose for linking products to things people already like does not mean advertisers would use *little* or *no* prose. After all, advertisers might use pictures to make the link and prose for some other purpose.

(B) is another Distortion. The stimulus is about linking products to positive images, not whether the products themselves are easily represented pictorially.

(C) is an Irrelevant Comparison. The stimulus doesn't discuss where ads are placed, just that they should include images. Both television and magazines would therefore be appropriate media, though you have no way to know which is used more.

(D) goes Out of Scope by introducing the idea of contrasting advertisers' products with things that people do not like. The stimulus focuses exclusively on linking advertisers' products to things people like.

5. (A) Inference ★★★★

Step 1: Identify the Question Type

Treat a question that asks you to fill in the blank at the end of an argument with a conclusion as an Inference question. The correct answer, when tagged onto the argument, should fall neatly within the scope of what has already been stated.

Step 2: Untangle the Stimulus

Proponents of the electric car believe that because the cars are emission-free, their wide use will result in less environmental degradation from auto emissions. In contrast (indicated by the Keyword "but"), the author points out that the electricity to charge electric car batteries will come from hydroelectric dams, nuclear energy, or coal power plants, all of which produce considerable environmental damage. Then, the author makes a conclusion regarding the electric car that you must complete.

Step 3: Make a Prediction

Do not get too creative when adding a conclusion at the end of an argument. Typically, the answer should be consistent with what has already been stated or flow from a logical deduction. In this case, complete the contrast that the author is setting up. Proponents of the electric car believe that they will reduce environmental damage from car emissions, but the author points out an indirect way electric cars will continue causing environmental damage. When assessing answers, remember to treat this like an Inference question and be very wary of answers that are Out of Scope or Extreme.

These explanations refer to questions that begin on page 742.

Part Three: Logical Reasoning
Non-Argument Questions

K

Step 4: Evaluate the Answer Choices

(A) is correct. It completes the disagreement the author has with the proponents of electric cars. This type of modest, safe answer is exactly what you want in an Inference question. The author must believe this is true because the proponents don't consider a negative result that he sees.

(B) is an Irrelevant Comparison. It speculates about the future popularity of electric cars versus other cars, which you cannot determine. This argument is merely about the environmental effects of electric cars.

(C) is a Faulty Use of Detail. This refers to the first sentence, which details the proponents' view, not the author's. Additionally, success and its requirements are Out of Scope.

(D) is Extreme. While the author does not believe that electric cars are *emission-free*, due to their indirect effect on emissions, the author does not go so far as to claim that electric cars *will* increase the *total* emissions currently being released.

(E), while slightly more modest than **(D)**, is also Extreme. It must be true that the author believes the electric car will not produce as great a reduction in environmental degradation as the proponents of electric cars believe. Nevertheless, the author's statements leave open the possibility that the electric car could, on balance, be at least a little better for the environment than gasoline-powered cars.

6. (A) Inference   ★★★★

Step 1: Identify the Question Type

This is an unusual twist on an Inference question. As with any Inference question, the correct answer choice will be logically based on what the stimulus provides, which here consists merely of statements rather than a complete argument. However, the correct answer here "must be false" (i.e., impossible). That means the wrong answers will all be possible, if not definitely true.

Step 2: Untangle the Stimulus

The first two claims are pure Formal Logic and should be interpreted properly. According to the first, if the economy is weak, two effects would follow: Prices would be constant and unemployment would rise. By the contrapositive, if the prices *don't* stay constant *or* unemployment does *not* rise, then the economy is *not* weak:

If economy weak → prices constant AND unemployment rises

If ~ prices constant OR ~ unemployment rises → ~ economy weak

In the second claim, "only if" signals a necessary condition. That means for unemployment to rise, investment *must* decrease. By contrapositive, if investment does *not* decrease, then unemployment will *not* rise:

If unemployment rises → investment decreases
If ~ investment decrease → ~ unemployment rise

The final claim is a given: Investment is *not* decreasing.

Step 3: Make a Prediction

That final claim sets off a string of deductions using the earlier Formal Logic. Fact 1: Investment is not decreasing. The second claim's contrapositive leads to Fact 2: Unemployment is not rising. The first claim's contrapositive leads to Fact 3: The economy is not weak. The only factor not accounted for is prices, which may or may not be constant. That cannot be determined. Remember that the correct answer *must* be false. Most likely, it will directly conflict with the three given, or deduced, facts.

Step 4: Evaluate the Answer Choices

(A) is impossible, making it the correct answer. It's a given that investment is *not* decreasing, and that leads to the deduction that the economy is *not* weak. Neither option in this answer is true, which means it must be false.

(B) is possible because unemployment has no stated effect on prices.

(C) is a 180. By the first two claims, a weak economy requires a rise in unemployment, which in turn, requires a decrease in investment. This answer must be *true*, which makes it a wrong answer for this question.

(D) is possible. While it's true that the economy is *not* weak, which denies the first option of this answer, it's still possible the prices are constant. That leaves the possibility of truth, meaning **(D)** cannot be guaranteed false.

(E) is another 180. Because unemployment is *not* rising, the contrapositive of the first sentence allows for the deduction that the economy is indeed not weak. That means the second option is definitely true, making the entire statement valid.

7. (C) Inference   ★★★☆

Step 1: Identify the Question Type

Because the correct answer is the statement that "follows logically" from the statements in the stimulus, this is an Inference question. The correct answer must be true based on the information in the stimulus.

Step 2: Untangle the Stimulus

Notice that the first sentence begins with *[i]f*, as do the first two answer choices. Expect this stimulus to be built of Formal Logic statements. Translate them as you read the stimulus.

If coffee beans cost increases → increase prices

If increase prices → add noncoffee products OR coffee sales decrease

If add noncoffee products → overall profits decrease

If ~ overall profits decrease → ~ coffee sales decrease

K | Part Three: Logical Reasoning
CHAPTER 11

These explanations refer to questions that begin on page 742.

Step 3: Make a Prediction

Start by looking for connections between the Formal Logic statements. Notice that the first two statements can be combined into one chain:

If coffee beans → *increase prices* → *add noncoffee*
cost increases *products OR coffee*
sales decrease

Based on the third sentence and the contrapositive of the fourth sentence, both adding noncoffee products and decreasing coffee sales would result in decreased overall profits. Therefore, if the cost of coffee beans increases, then no matter what the Coffee Shoppe does, the shop's profitability will decline.

Step 4: Evaluate the Answer Choices

(C) matches the prediction.

(A) reverses the Formal Logic of the deduction without negating. In the stimulus, a decrease in overall profitability is a *necessary* result, not a sufficient condition.

(B) reverses the Formal Logic of the last two sentences without negating. In the stimulus, losing profitability is a necessary result in both the third and fourth sentences, never a sufficient condition.

(D) is a 180. The stimulus says that if the price of coffee beans *increases*, then profitability decreases. This says that if the price of coffee beans *decreases*, then profitability decreases. The stimulus doesn't provide any information about what would happen if the cost of coffee beans goes down. Presumably though, even without consulting the Formal Logic, it would be unlikely that a decrease in overhead costs would cause a decrease in overall profitability.

(E) goes Out of Scope by introducing the idea of the Coffee Shoppe *increasing* its coffee sales. That idea simply is not in the stimulus. The stimulus only discusses a decrease in coffee sales. Even a negation of *decrease* would only be "not decrease." There's no way to know about an increase.

8. (B) Inference ★★★★

Step 1: Identify the Question Type

Because the correct answer is the one that "logically completes the . . . argument," this is an Inference question. The correct answer must be true based on the information in the stimulus.

Step 2: Untangle the Stimulus

Paraphrase the information in the stimulus. First, the philosopher suggests that because nations do not think, feel, or act, they are not persons. Because they are not persons, they have no moral rights or responsibilities. However, the philosopher says a nation needs many citizens to think the nation *does* have moral rights and responsibilities, because only that would lead people to make sacrifices for their nation.

Step 3: Make a Prediction

Connect the ideas in the stimulus together. Nations do not literally have moral rights and responsibilities. But, if nations are going to survive, then citizens need to think that they do. Thus, it appears that a nation needs its citizens to believe something that is not literally true.

Step 4: Evaluate the Answer Choices

(B) matches the prediction. Translated into Formal Logic, it reads:

If a nation survives → *many citizens have literally*
false beliefs

(A) is Out of Scope. It suggests that something else would need to motivate citizens to make sacrifices. But based on the stimulus, it could be true that the false belief that a nation has moral rights is adequate to motivate citizens.

(C) mentions moral praise and blame, both of which are Out of Scope. Neither appears in the stimulus.

(D) goes Out of Scope by introducing the value judgment that nations are not worth the sacrifices citizens make for them. While the philosopher argues that the sacrifices citizens make for nations might be based on a false belief, it still could be true that nations are worth those sacrifices.

(E) is Extreme. While the stimulus does suggest that in the case of moral rights and responsibilities, it makes sense for citizens to think of the nation metaphorically, the stimulus only covers this one scenario. It could be true that in plenty of other cases, it makes better sense to think of the nation in literal terms.

9. (D) Inference ★★★★

Step 1: Identify the Question Type

A question stem that asks you to use the statements above to support one of the answers (direction of support flowing downward) is an Inference question. Look for Formal Logic deductions or try to combine pieces of information.

Step 2: Untangle the Stimulus

While not in Formal Logic form, the statements create a chain of causality. The media doesn't thoroughly cover local politics, and political business is conducted secretively. That leads to isolating local politicians from the electorate. That leads to a reduced chance that public participation will get a positive response from officials. Finally, that discourages resident participation in local politics.

Step 3: Make a Prediction

Typically, when presented with a chain of events, line them up sequentially (as these conveniently already are) and focus on the endpoints. So, the editorialist believes that the lack of media coverage and secret nature of local politics eventually

These explanations refer to questions that begin on page 743.

Part Three: Logical Reasoning
Non-Argument Questions

results in discouraging resident participation in local politics. The correct answer will likely relate to that connection. Otherwise, check each answer choice against the stimulus to see if it *must* be true.

Step 4: Evaluate the Answer Choices

(D) is correct. Because infrequent media coverage of local politics triggers a chain of results that tend to discourage resident involvement in local politics, increasing such coverage would reduce "at least" that one cause.

(A) is subtly Extreme. The stimulus only indicates that some level of isolation has the effect of reducing the chance of a positive official response. From that, it cannot be deduced that less isolation would be *likely* to produce a positive response. If this choice said "more likely" (comparative) it would be correct. But *likely* (absolute) goes too far.

(B) is incorrect. The opinionated recommendation language (*should*) is a red flag. The editorialist merely presents a causal chain; she doesn't present her own opinion about preserving or changing that chain. Additionally, the phrase "this *would avoid* discouraging resident participation" is Extreme. Compare that language to the correct answer **(D)**: "reduce at least one source of discouragement."

(C) is Extreme. The phrase "most important factor" is a large red flag here. Beware of Inference question answer choices that mention the "most important" or "primary" factor. You can know that the possibility of positive official response is *a* factor in resident participation, but not that it is the *most important* factor.

(E) is incorrect. It superficially appears to be the contrapositive of the causal chain, but because the statements in the stimulus are not stated absolutely, it is inappropriate to indicate that the absence of a result *causes* the absence of a trigger. For example, a brick thrown through a window always causes the glass to break. However, while the contrapositive says the absence of broken glass is sufficient to know that a brick has not been thrown through the window, you cannot assert that the absence of broken glass *caused* the brick to not be thrown.

10. (B) Inference

Step 1: Identify the Question Type

A question that directs you to use information from the stimulus to *support* an answer choice (the direction of support flowing down) is an Inference question.

Step 2: Untangle the Stimulus

The first couple of sentences focus on the importance in science of testing hypotheses and gaining recognition from

overthrowing conventional wisdom. Subsequently, the author indicates that though predictions of global warming are widely accepted, some scientists remain skeptical. Finally, though hundreds of researchers are striving to make breakthroughs in that area, very few have found evidence against the likelihood of global warming.

Step 3: Make a Prediction

The correct answer to an Inference question is not always readily predictable. In the absence of Formal Logic or a clear deduction resulting from combining two pieces of information, inventory the facts and note any emphasized information. In this stimulus, the second and fourth sentences are the most emphasized and absolute: "*Nothing brings more recognition* than overthrowing conventional wisdom" and it's *remarkable* that hundreds of scientists are focusing on climatology yet few find evidence against global warming. Combined, those statements suggest that a scientist could make her mark by being the one to disprove global warming. In the absence of that choice, approach each answer by asking, "Does the stimulus support this statement?"

Step 4: Evaluate the Answer Choices

(B) is correct. The author indicates that global warming is "widely accepted" with only a few finding evidence against it, and that "[n]othing brings more recognition than overthrowing conventional wisdom." Thus, recognition would act as a motive for scientists to discredit the conventional wisdom that global warming is likely. The use of the qualifier *most* is acceptable here, because, based on the stimulus, all scientists in climatology have this motive to some degree.

(A) is a 180. The author states that science is built on attempting to show that hypotheses are incorrect, and then says it is "accordingly unsurprising" that some scientists are skeptical of global warming predictions.

(C) is Extreme. The author says global warming predictions are widely accepted, but also acknowledges that a few have found counter evidence. This answer goes too far in asserting that global warming has been *conclusively* proven true.

(D) is Out of Scope. The stimulus does not indicate whether or not skeptics have offered any alternative hypotheses.

(E) is Extreme. The word *primarily* is a red flag in Inference answers. While the author believes that recognition is a motivator of scientists—and indeed recognition is the only motivation the author mentions—the author never compares the importance of this motivator to other motivations. You cannot assume that because an LSAT author mentions only one factor, it is the primary or most important factor.

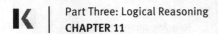
 These explanations refer to questions that begin on page 744.

Principle (Inference)

11. (B) Principle (Identify/Inference) ★☆☆☆
Step 1: Identify the Question Type

Because the correct answer is the *proposition* "best illustrated by the passage," this is a Principle question. You have to determine the principle illustrated by the stimulus and then find it in the answer choices, which means this is an Identify the Principle question.

Step 2: Untangle the Stimulus

The question stem describes the stimulus as a *passage*, so don't necessarily expect to find an argument in the stimulus. Read it like you would an Inference question, paraphrasing the information as you go. First, Jablonski has a longstanding practice of donating cars to the local schools' drivers ed programs. Second, Jablonski donated the cars in order to encourage better driving in hopes of decreasing car accidents. Third, some people have bought cars from Jablonksi because they support her donations of cars to the schools.

Step 3: Make a Prediction

The correct answer will summarize the information from the stimulus in more general terms. So, someone (Jablonski) who did a good deed (donating cars to the schools) with a good intention (stopping car accidents) also profited from the good deed (because locals bought cars from Jablonski).

Step 4: Evaluate the Answer Choices

(B) matches the prediction. Because *altruistic* means "helping others," Jablonski's action certainly qualifies. Not only did her good deed help local students, she also profited from it when locals bought cars from her.

(A) is not supported by the stimulus. There may be many ways to reduce accidents. Jablonski just happens to support driver education.

(C) makes a claim that is not supported by the stimulus. It may be that older drivers, too, could benefit from driver education.

(D) is Extreme because it says altruistic actions are *usually* in one's best interest. The stimulus describes one situation where altruistic actions benefited the person performing them; you cannot infer from a single situation that altruistic actions usually work out in one's best interest.

(E) goes Out of Scope by introducing the idea of what makes an action successful. The stimulus does not include information about whether or not Jablonski's action actually accomplished its intention of preventing car accidents. Additionally, while the stimulus says *some* members of the community showed their support for her actions, that doesn't necessarily mean there was *broad* support.

12. (C) Principle (Apply/Inference) ★★★☆
Step 1: Identify the Question Type

Despite a lack of usual terms, this is a Principle question. However, it's interesting in that the stimulus provides both a specific situation and an "analysis." So, you'll need to treat the analysis as a broad principle and find a specific situation in the answers that conforms to that rule, which is what makes it an Apply the Principle question. However, it could also be construed as an Identify and Apply the Principle question. The situation paragraph in the stimulus can be used to identify the principle, which is confirmed in the analysis paragraph. Then another situation that matches that same principle can be found in the answer choices. Under either categorization, the correct answer will contain a specific situation that would also be covered by the principle.

Step 2: Untangle the Stimulus

The principle presented in the analysis is that people sometimes choose appearances over comfort or pleasure. The situation of someone living in a cold climate that buys a coat that is stylish but not warm is an example of that principle.

Step 3: Make a Prediction

The correct answer will present someone else who chooses appearances over comfort or pleasure.

Step 4: Evaluate the Answer Choices

(C) matches the prediction. The couple chooses a wine to appear more impressive, rather than selecting their favorite wine, which is more pleasurable (better tasting) and more comfortable (cheaper).

(A) is Out of Scope. The person in this answer choice does not choose based on appearances. In fact, **(A)** does not indicate why the person chooses the automobile over public transportation. Nor does it indicate that public transportation would be more comfortable or pleasurable than driving to work.

(B) is Out of Scope because the parent chooses based on color and comfort, not safety. The stimulus does not include the idea of safety. Additionally, comfort is sought, not sacrificed as it is in the stimulus.

(D) is Out of Scope because the person chooses based on environmental concerns, not appearances, over comfort (warmth). The stimulus does not include the idea of environmental concerns.

(E) is Out of Scope because even though the acrobat acquires something for its appearance (the impressive outfit), there is no information suggesting that any comfort or pleasure was sacrificed.

These explanations refer to questions that begin on page 744.

Part Three: Logical Reasoning
Non-Argument Questions

K

13. (D) Principle (Apply/Inference) ★★★★

Step 1: Identify the Question Type

The stimulus asks for an individual whose actions exemplify the ethicist's criteria for "the most advanced kind of moral motivation." Taking the ethicist's criteria as a rule or principle, apply it to the actions described in each answer choice. Only the correct answer will feature a person acting in accordance with the ethicist's description of the "most advanced" morality.

Step 2: Untangle the Stimulus

The stimulus defines the "most advanced kind of moral motivation" straightaway: It is "based solely on abstract principles." The second sentence defines what is not "most advanced": "calculated self-interest" and conformity to social norms.

Step 3: Make a Prediction

The correct answer will describe someone behaving in a way that is motivated solely by abstract principles and that is not motivated by self-interest, a desire to conform, or both.

Step 4: Evaluate the Answer Choices

(D) is an example of a person who behaves according to a belief that protecting the environment is more important than money. The individual here is motivated by an abstract ideal and shuns self-interest, so this answer meets the ethicist's definition of advanced moral motivation.

(A) has a person who acts because he fears he will look stingy. This self-interested adherence to social norms is the opposite of what the ethicist would consider to be advanced moral motivation.

(B) is incorrect because it has a person who acts to improve his employer's opinion of him. This is an example of acting from self-interest, the opposite of the ethicist's advanced moral motivation.

(C) is also incorrect because Donna is acting in self-interest. She fears retaliation from her employers, so according to the ethicist's criteria, she is not acting in accordance with advanced moral motivation.

(E) is incorrect because Leigh is acting to conform to her colleague's expectations while avoiding the abstract ideal. Desiring to adhere to social norms and conventions goes against the ethicist's definition of advanced moral motivation.

14. (A) Principle (Identify/Inference) ★★★★

Step 1: Identify the Question Type

The word *proposition*, like policy, rule, or generalization, indicates a Principle question. Because the question stem indicates the general principle is located in the answer choices, the stimulus will contain a specific situation. Your job is to broaden that specific situation into a rule. Oftentimes, the correct answer will merely summarize the reasoning in general terms.

Step 2: Untangle the Stimulus

The author's conclusion, indicated by the contrast Keyword *[h]owever*, is that "designer interaction with consumers is superior to survey data." Contrast Keywords also often highlight the most important piece of evidence; in this case, *but* emphasizes that survey data can't explain to designers how to change a feature to improve customer satisfaction.

Step 3: Make a Prediction

The author says survey data can't help designers understand how to improve features and then argues that interaction with consumers is *superior*. The author's reasoning indicates that interaction with consumers *can* help designers understand how to improve features. The correct answer should focus on consumer interaction helping designers improve a product.

Step 4: Evaluate the Answer Choices

(A) matches the prediction. It incorporates the argument's conclusion regarding "interaction with consumers" and the evidence regarding changes to a product to "receive a higher rating."

(B) avoids the main point of the argument: that consumer interaction is beneficial.

(C) is Out of Scope. There is no reference to "specific market niches."

(D) is Extreme. The author prefers one type of consumer feedback over another, but he does not indicate that failure to consult consumers will guarantee that a product has unappealing features.

(E) is an Irrelevant Comparison. The argument does not distinguish between external and internal design components.

EXPLANATIONS

753

K | Part Three: Logical Reasoning
CHAPTER 11

These explanations refer to questions that begin on page 746.

Paradox

15. (D) Paradox

Step 1: Identify the Question Type

The question stem calls for the answer choice that will resolve or explain an apparent paradox. Remember that Paradox questions rarely have a conclusion or evidence. Rather, they consist of a set of seemingly contradictory facts. Find the answer choice that makes those facts make sense together.

Step 2: Untangle the Stimulus

The stimulus says that cats mostly just stretch and yawn. The Keyword [y]et signals the unexpected, paradoxical fact. Cats, the stimulus continues, have a strong musculature that most animals would need lots of exercise to acquire.

Step 3: Make a Prediction

You don't need to have a specifically worded prediction, just articulate what the correct answer must do. Here, it will explain how cats do nothing but sleep, stretch, and yawn all the time yet have a strong, agile musculature.

Step 4: Evaluate the Answer Choices

(D) is correct. It shows how both parts of this stimulus could be true. If cats get ample exercise from frequent stretching, that helps to explain how they get the exercise necessary to maintain their agile musculature.

(A) is incorrect because it tells you only why cats sleep; it doesn't tell you how such a somnolent lifestyle manages to provide them with an agile musculature.

(B) is a 180. It deepens the mystery because it indicates that other animals are similar to cats in this respect. It doesn't help explain the main puzzle: *how* cats get adequate exercise from sleeping. **(B)** just asserts that cats aren't unique.

(C) cites yet another fact about cats, but it doesn't explain how it would contribute to their strong, agile musculature. Be careful not to add several additional assumptions to an answer choice to try to make it more relevant than it is.

(E) is Out of Scope. It says *why* cats need a strong, agile, musculature, but it doesn't say *how* they get it.

16. (A) Paradox (EXCEPT)

Step 1: Identify the Question Type

Because the correct answer will not explain the increase mentioned in the stimulus, this is a Paradox EXCEPT question. The correct answer will deepen the paradox or go outside the scope of the stimulus. The four incorrect answers will resolve the paradox.

Step 2: Untangle the Stimulus

Start by identifying the paradox. After Jimmy bought an efficient gas heater, his gas bill went up.

Step 3: Make a Prediction

Because they are more concrete than the correct answer, predict the four incorrect answers in Logical Reasoning EXCEPT questions. Here, each incorrect answer will resolve the paradox by explaining why Jimmy's gas bill increased. Here, likely something about the gas heater, the gas, or Jimmy's lifestyle would explain the increase. When you find an answer that explains why Jimmy's gas bill went up, eliminate it. If you find an answer that does not explain why Jimmy's gas bill went up, choose it.

Step 4: Evaluate the Answer Choices

(A) deepens the paradox. This choice confirms that the gas heater uses a smaller percentage of gas, and so an increased bill makes even less sense. Thus, this is the correct choice because it does not explain the paradox.

(B) resolves the paradox by providing a reason why Jimmy's gas use would go up: More people may be using hot water, so more gas is likely consumed.

(C) resolves the paradox. Jimmy's laundry would increase the amount of water that needs to be heated every month, not to mention the additional gas cost from the dryer.

(D) resolves the paradox. If gas itself costs more, then Jimmy's gas bill would reasonably increase, possibly even if the water heater uses less gas than before.

(E) resolves the paradox. It confirms that gas usage was particularly heavy in general after installation, whether from the gas water heater or perhaps his home's gas furnace.

17. (C) Paradox

Step 1: Identify the Question Type

A question stem that asks you to *explain* a difference is a Paradox question. This question stem points out the two seemingly contradictory facts to be reconciled.

Step 2: Untangle the Stimulus

In the nineteenth century, much of the funding for the arts came from the French Academy of Art, which discouraged innovation. Accordingly, French sculpture of that time showed little innovation. However, French painting showed lots of innovation.

Step 3: Make a Prediction

The stimulus provides a reason for the limited innovation in French sculpture. You need an answer choice that explains the large amount of innovation in French painting that arose despite the discouragement of the French academy, which funded both sculpture and painting. Your prediction doesn't need to identify a specific explanation; a general prediction is usually best and sufficient for a Paradox question.

These explanations refer to questions that begin on page 746.

Part Three: Logical Reasoning
Non-Argument Questions

K

Step 4: Evaluate the Answer Choices

(C) provides a factor that accounts for innovation in French painting despite the disapproval of the French academy of art. Painters, unlike sculptors, did not need funding to afford the inexpensive tools of their trade and were thus free to be creative.

(A) is a 180. The academy discouraged innovation, so those who were most beholden to the academy would have been most likely to see their creativity stifled.

(B) is a 180 similar to **(A)**. If individual painters received more support from the academy than sculptors did, then it would seem painters would be more likely to have their creativity stifled.

(D) is Out of Scope. The lack of overlap doesn't explain why the innovation levels between the groups varied.

(E) does not provide a distinction between painters and sculptors. The fact that overall funding decreased for both types of artists doesn't explain why painters were more innovative.

CHAPTER 12

Logical Reasoning: Managing the Section

INTRODUCTION

As you've learned, every LSAT has two scored Logical Reasoning sections, typically containing 25 or 26 questions each. Those questions are spread out over eight pages, with anywhere from two to four questions on each page. That's a lot of content to get through in 35 minutes. In terms of word count, in fact, each Logical Reasoning section presents you with approximately as much reading as does a Reading Comprehension section.

This isn't by accident, of course. Getting through these sections in the time provided is *supposed* to be difficult. Although a handful of test takers in each test administration will confidently get through all of the questions in a section in 35 minutes, many more will not be able to do so or will be forced to rush and cut corners. That's because the LSAT is testing not only how well you can complete a variety of tasks, but also your ability to perform as well as possible within time constraints. Law schools are interested in this facet of the test. They realize that good lawyers (and law students) don't spend all of their resources fighting losing battles. Instead, effective lawyers successfully prioritize the most important elements of their cases.

LEARNING OBJECTIVES

In this chapter, you'll learn to:

- Move through individual Logical Reasoning questions efficiently.
- Recognize and approach strategically the difficult questions in the Logical Reasoning section.

LOGICAL REASONING SECTION MANAGEMENT—WHY IT MATTERS

When it comes to the Logical Reasoning section of the test, here's what LSAT experts know: Successful time management is more than moving from the first question to the last, answering *x* number of questions in *y* amount of time. The distribution of questions in the Logical Reasoning section is patterned so that typically one or two difficult problems show up early in the section, while a handful of less difficult questions show up at the end. In this way, the LSAT is able to evaluate a test taker's time management ability: Do you sink your finite time and energy into a few difficult questions, or do you move on with the knowledge that easier questions await? Take a look at the graph on the following page. It shows question difficulty on a typical Logical Reasoning section.

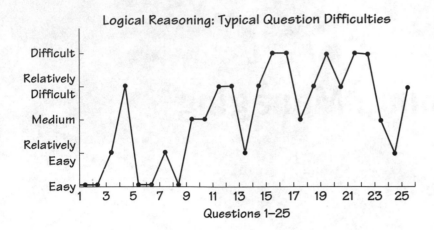

Logical Reasoning: Typical Question Difficulties

Notice that, in general, the difficulty level of questions in the Logical Reasoning section moves from relatively easy to relatively difficult. However, there are a few surprises along the way. The first speed bump comes in one of the first 10 questions—usually somewhere between questions 4 and 9. At this point in the section, a difficult question could rattle an insecure or unprepared test taker. But LSAT experts know not to get rattled. They know that a methodical approach will help them answer even the most difficult questions; additionally, they realize that if they face a troublesome question on one of the first two pages, they can simply skip that question and move on to the easier questions among the following pages.

LSAT experts are also cognizant of the fact that the most difficult questions in the Logical Reasoning section are clustered together somewhere among questions 14 to 22. Because of the distribution of difficult questions in this part of the section, we call this area the "Danger Zone." Knowing about the "Danger Zone" is an important tool in the LSAT expert's toolbox: Not only is the LSAT expert mentally prepared for some difficult questions in this part of the section, but she also knows that one or two less difficult questions likely await her at the end of the section, if she can get to them.

Understanding how the Logical Reasoning section is structured helps LSAT experts move through this section effectively and confidently, but even this knowledge is not a cure-all for the challenge of getting to and correctly answering as many questions as possible. After all, even if you are skipping questions and coming back to them later, you may find that you are still unable to get to a significant number of questions in a section because you are spending too long on individual questions. So, how can good section management help you avoid this situation? How do you deal with the section's timing restriction in a way that allows you to both answer individual questions in an appropriate amount of time *and* avoid the most difficult of the bunch until the end?

The answer has two parts. First, success in the Logical Reasoning section does not require you to evaluate and correctly answer every question. LSAT experts know that a test taker can miss four or five questions per section and still receive a 90th percentile score. Letting go of the need to read and evaluate every single question is a powerful way to take control of the test. If you forgo the questions you find most difficult and time-consuming, you will be light-years ahead of your competition.

But section management is not simply a matter of improving your ability to efficiently navigate each section as a whole by recognizing and avoiding difficult questions. The second, and arguably more important way to improve your efficiency in this section is to improve your timing on individual problems by reading question stems and stimuli strategically, using that reading to predict the correct answer, and using that prediction to evaluate answer choices efficiently and purposefully. In short, use the Logical Reasoning Method to make you more efficient on individual questions and thus faster throughout the section as a whole.

To use those two strategies, you'll need a thorough understanding of the structure of the Logical Reasoning section as well as the construction of individual Logical Reasoning questions. And don't ignore your personal performance. Expert section management relies on the test taker knowing her individual strengths and weaknesses. As you read through this chapter, keep in mind that developing specific time management goals is an important step in conquering the LSAT—especially if you're one of those students who struggles to get through each section in 35 minutes. Don't make the mistake of just reading through this chapter passively. Find the strategies that work for you and put them into practice.

HONING YOUR APPROACH TO EACH QUESTION—GETTING FASTER BY GETTING BETTER

The first and best way to improve your timing efficiency in the Logical Reasoning section is simple: Just get better and faster at tackling individual questions. Easily said, right? It would be great to snap your fingers and say, "Now go—be faster!"

If only it were that easy to do. If you struggle with timing in Logical Reasoning, then telling yourself to "read faster" isn't going to cut it on the LSAT. In fact, the mantra of "read faster" often makes a bad situation worse. Ask yourself if this has ever happened to you: After reading a question stem too quickly, you read the stimulus without a clear goal or objective. As a result, you're not sure what the argument is saying, so you reread it, this time even faster than before. Still lacking a full understanding of either the question or the statements in the stimulus (but now with a heightened concern that you need to speed up even more), you skip the prediction step and move directly to the answer choices. There, once again, you find yourself rereading as you search through answer choices without ever really knowing what you're looking for. Reflect on that (perhaps familiar) scenario. Even if you did "read faster," the underlying dilemma remains unresolved. It's not a pacing issue—it's a comprehension issue. This negative feedback loop of confusion and frustration is a time killer. Though you may feel like you're moving through the test at a brisk pace, the constant re-evaluation of question stems, stimuli, and answer choices is actually slowing you down and preventing you from maximizing your performance. You aren't reading too slowly; you're reading the same sentences too many times. All of that unfocused reading and rereading leads to a predictable result: You end up spending longer on individual questions, which in turn leads to increased anxiety, which in turn leads to—you guessed it—an even greater perceived need to "read faster" on other problems.

If the preceding paragraph describes you, good news: While it may be difficult to read *faster*, it's definitely possible to read *better*. Reading efficiently and effectively is a vital LSAT skill that you *can* improve. And that improvement will lead to points on Test Day because reading more strategically will allow you to work through problems in less time. LSAT experts know this, and they utilize four positive habits to keep them focused and engaged in the Logical Reasoning section. These can be distilled down to four words: *Plan*, *Pause*, *Paraphrase*, and *Predict*. By focusing on these steps, LSAT experts are able to move through individual questions in this section in a confident, controlled, and efficient manner. And while some of these skills have been discussed in previous chapters, it's good to see them again in a way that demonstrates how they tie into Logical Reasoning section management.

Plan: Knowing What to Do for Each Question

Your approach to questions in the Logical Reasoning section of the LSAT shouldn't be left to chance. Would you walk into court and present an argument without knowing whether you were working for the prosecution or the defense? Of course you wouldn't. Yet in the Logical Reasoning section of the test, many students try to tackle questions without knowing exactly what the question is asking or what the statements in the stimulus are saying. Without an understanding of the specific task required by each question, Logical Reasoning can be difficult and time-consuming.

In previous chapters, you've seen the various types of questions you'll face in the Logical Reasoning section and how each rewards you for untangling the stimulus differently. Knowing, for example, that a Sufficient Assumption question will present an argument with Mismatched Concepts will help you attack that question type with maximum effectiveness. The LSAT expert has internalized the various Logical Reasoning question types and knows instantly how to approach each one. This is the first building block to Logical Reasoning mastery: For each question, you must have a plan.

Having a plan gives the LSAT expert confidence in the Logical Reasoning section, confidence that leads to speed and accuracy. If Step 1 of the Kaplan Method for Logical Reasoning is not yet second nature to you, you're squandering time and leaving points on the table. Ask yourself a question: Am I able to read and then *immediately* know how to attack each question type? Take a look at the following question stems and answer the questions that follow:

"The statements above, if true, most strongly support which of the following?"

"Which of the following, if true, most strongly supports the argument above?"

What question type is each of these? What will your task be as you evaluate each question's stimulus? In each question, how will the statements in the stimulus relate to each other?

Even though these question types may look similar (the first question stem includes the phrase "strongly support," while the second includes "strongly supports"), your task for each question differs significantly. The first stem is an Inference question that asks you to determine an answer choice that must be true based on the statements in the stimulus, while the second is a Strengthen question that asks you to bolster an argument that is composed of evidence and a conclusion (and therefore contains an assumption). Approaching one type of question as though it were the other will invariably lead to confusion and frustration.

Of course, all of this confusion and frustration comes at a cost. Students who misread question types are often unable to correctly deconstruct stimuli; in turn, they struggle to make accurate predictions. This fog of misunderstanding leads to a predictable result: As students feel themselves getting off track, they start over and attempt to do the question again. As they do so, the clock ticks away, and precious time is lost.

If you were able to immediately and confidently (and correctly) identify the question stems that we just discussed, excellent work. If instead you struggled to type the questions, or if you were in any way a bit unsure how to attack those different question types, then you've just identified an opportunity to improve your timing and efficiency in this section.

SUGGESTED EXERCISE

Find a Logical Reasoning section that you've already completed. Next to each question stem, write the type of question it is (Flaw, Necessary Assumption, Inference, etc.) and the strategy that best fits that question type. Do this without looking at the stimuli or reworking the problems. Once you have identified the question types and written a strategy next to each question, go back through and evaluate your original performance. Compare your approach the first time you did the question to the approach you now have written down next to each stimulus. Then, check the explanations and make sure that you were identifying question types correctly and that the strategies and approaches you outlined for each question type matched up with those outlined in the explanations. Finally, ask yourself a few questions: Did you simply not have an approach the first time? Did you confuse Inference questions with Strengthen questions or Weaken questions with Flaw questions? Were there specific question types that consistently gave you trouble? Use this knowledge to help you quickly and correctly identify future Logical Reasoning question types.

Think back to the question stems you identified on the preceding page. Although confusing Inference questions with Strengthen questions is a common mistake, it's certainly not the only problem students have when it comes to recognizing and tackling question types. In addition to knowing how to type a question stem quickly, it's also important to know how to tackle each corresponding question. Understanding that you're facing a Paradox question, for example, is only part of the battle. The next step requires you to analyze and evaluate the stimulus. The LSAT expert knows that in a Paradox question, her task is to identify the two seemingly contradictory facts in the stimulus, then find an answer choice that explains the relationship between them.

Becoming more efficient and effective in the Logical Reasoning section requires a plan. First, recognize and identify each question, then analyze the stimulus and break down its different parts in the way or ways appropriate to that question type. As you untangle the stimulus, though, remember to do two things: Pause and Paraphrase.

Pause and Paraphrase: Reading the Stimulus for Maximum Clarity

So you've mastered Step 1 of the Kaplan Method. But what about Step 2? What exactly does "untangle" the stimulus mean? For untrained test takers, their handling of the stimulus amounts to reading it through quickly and superficially. LSAT experts, on the other hand, "untangle" the stimulus by slowing down, seeking out key information, and putting the concepts expressed in the stimulus into their own words. We'll call this process "pausing and paraphrasing." Logical Reasoning questions are often wordy and indirect, so being able to whittle away excess verbiage in a stimulus and home in on just those parts of the stimulus that are useful for answering the question will increase your efficiency and proficiency. One of the problems with tackling an entire Logical Reasoning question without this strategy is that short-term memory allows us to hold only a certain amount of information in our heads at one time. By reducing the amount of text to remember and the number of concepts to evaluate, you are able to more easily pick out the statements in the stimulus relevant to answering the question.

Take a look at the following question:

Reducing stress lessens a person's sensitivity to pain. This is the conclusion reached by researchers who played extended audiotapes to patients before they underwent surgery and afterward while they were recovering. One tape consisted of conversation; the other consisted of music. Those who listened only to the latter tape required less anesthesia during surgery and fewer painkillers afterward than those who listened only to the former tape.

Which one of the following is an assumption on which the researchers' reasoning depends?

PrepTest52 Sec3 Q9

In Step 1, the LSAT expert recognizes this as a Necessary Assumption question. She then pauses to ask, "What am I looking for in the statements above?" This pause between Step 1 and Step 2 is important. Knowing that this is a Necessary Assumption question, the expert knows that her first task is to look for language that indicates the conclusion. Now, the expert's eye is drawn to the start of the second sentence: "This is the conclusion reached by . . . ." She has found the conclusion—it must be the first sentence.

The expert also knows it will be easier to digest this argument by putting that conclusion into her own words. Thus, she paraphrases: "So, researchers believe that less stress means less pain." With that clear paraphrase of the conclusion in hand, the expert next asks, "Why do the researchers think this is true?" This question helps the expert zero in on the author's primary piece of evidence. After all, the LSAT expert knows that not every single piece of the stimulus is equally important. Instead of taking note of each individual word, she is going to evaluate the evidence by pausing after each sentence and paraphrasing. This simple process clarifies the concepts present in the stimulus, which helps the expert better comprehend the argument being made.

Sentence 2 (evidence): Researchers played audiotapes for patients during and after surgery.

Sentence 3 (evidence): One tape was conversation; the other was music.

Sentence 4 (evidence): Patients who listened to music needed less anesthesia and fewer painkillers than those who listened to conversations.

The LSAT expert knows to combine these three statements, if possible. Concepts that are repeated, or redundant, within a stimulus often link two other ideas together. Here, the second sentence provides background for the argument but does not provide the evidence that the researchers use to draw their conclusion. The third sentence provides information regarding what is on each tape, important only in that it allows us to replace "former" and "latter" with "conversation" and "music," respectively, in our paraphrase of the fourth sentence. Finally, the fourth sentence discusses patients who need "less anesthesia during surgery and fewer painkillers afterward," which is a long-winded way of saying those patients felt less pain. When all three sentences are combined, the expert is able to paraphrase the entirety of the evidence: "Listening to music instead of listening to conversations reduces the amount of pain a person feels."

With a clear plan, the LSAT expert was able to slow down, pause, and ultimately paraphrase the conclusion and evidence. One good habit that allows experts to understand how the evidence relates to the conclusion is to read the argument back using the following template: "Conclusion because evidence." Though this may take an additional few seconds, the clearer understanding of the argument's structure and logic it provides will save time by allowing the LSAT expert to quickly home in on the right answer. The argument now looks like this: "Reducing stress reduces the amount of pain a person feels; researchers believe this because listening to music instead of listening to conversations reduced the amount of pain a person feels."

Does this rewrite of the argument make more sense to you? It's the same argument as above; it's just been shortened and "demystified" by the process of pausing and paraphrasing. Here, we wrote out the entire thought process, but with practice, untangling a stimulus in this way takes only a few seconds. By the way, are you now easily able to determine the researchers' assumption? They assume that listening to music reduces stress. This approach will help you understand Logical Reasoning arguments more clearly, and that understanding will in turn help you answer questions more confidently and more quickly.

Predict: Looking for Patterns

Reading questions strategically and with purpose is a hugely important skill that LSAT experts utilize as they approach the Logical Reasoning section. But another significant tool in the LSAT expert's toolbox is the ability to recognize common argument patterns and to predict correct answer choices. This skill can be developed by recognizing that the LSAT, by virtue of the fact that it is a standardized test, asks the same types of questions over and over again.

So how do you improve your ability to recognize patterns in Logical Reasoning questions? It requires a two-step process. The first step is to use a resource (like this book, for example) to identify the patterns that the testmaker uses when constructing this test. In earlier chapters you saw, for example, how the LSAT structures Assumption-family arguments in a number of recognizable, repeated configurations. You've also practiced questions with familiar Logical Reasoning flaws that show up on test after test. Know the patterns and then move on to the second step: practice, practice, practice. As you become more familiar with the material, you will begin to recognize more and more of the test's patterns.

SUGGESTED EXERCISE

If you're having trouble identifying patterns in Logical Reasoning questions, perform an exercise we call "Post-phrasing." Here's what you do: Before you attempt the problems in a Logical Reasoning section, turn to the explanations and note the correct answer choice for each question in the section. Go through and mark the right answers before you ever read the questions. Now that you've done that, go through the question set and explain to yourself why each marked correct answer is correct. There is no guessing or searching for the right answer on your part here. Because you already know the correct answers, your goal instead is to link the right answer to the relevant part or parts of the stimulus. In an Assumption question, how does the correct answer link with the evidence to lead to the conclusion? In a Strengthen/Weaken question, how does the correct answer either negatively or positively affect the argument? In an Inference question, why is the right answer supported by the statements in the stimulus, and why are the wrong answer choices not supported? Continue in this manner for each question in the section.

APPROACHING THE SECTION EFFICIENTLY

LSAT experts Plan, Pause and Paraphrase, and Predict to efficiently and strategically tackle individual questions. But improving accuracy and timing on individual questions is only part of Logical Reasoning section management. Effective time management also involves knowing which questions to tackle and which to avoid.

Think of it this way. Imagine you're participating in a scavenger hunt at a friend's house and your goal is to find as many items as possible in, say, five minutes. The list contains some familiar items: keys, a remote control, a spoon, a pillow, a mug. But in addition, there are some odd items, like an old postcard and a pocket watch. You've been to your friend's house enough times to know where the keys, the remote, and the silverware can be found. But old postcards and pocket watches? Those might be anywhere—the attic, garage, or bedroom closet. Now, here's the real kicker: The list isn't in order of familiarity—"old postcard" might be dropped in among several more familiar items. Your friend yells, "Go!" and the hunt is on. What do you do? Do you immediately rush to a far corner of the house in search of the mysterious objects? Of course you don't, because the reward isn't worth the trouble. And you don't necessarily tackle the list in order, either. Instead, you're going to gather as many items as possible from the familiar landscape in front of you: the spoon and the mug from the kitchen, the pillow and remote control from the living room. Only *after* the easily accessible items are found and gathered will you think about possibly searching for the obscure items.

The type of person who starts the hunt by searching for the pocket watch and the postcard is an ineffective time manager. On the LSAT, this is the person who spends nearly all of her time on a few of the most difficult questions in each section. Now, it may be satisfying to be the only person to come up with the most unusual item on the scavenger hunt list, but the objective of the game was to get the *most* items. Likewise, while it feels good to get the most difficult Logical Reasoning questions right, the LSAT does not award bonus points or extra credit for harder questions. A test taker who manages time well and answers 20 questions correctly while missing the five most difficult questions will have performed—by the only measure that matters, the LSAT score—better than a test taker who answers the five most difficult questions but runs out of time and is not able to answer the section's final seven questions. Every right answer is worth exactly the same, so make it a priority to answer the easier and faster questions first.

Where Are the Difficult Questions?

As the question difficulty graph from earlier in the chapter showed, the difficulty level of questions in the Logical Reasoning section moves from relatively easy to relatively difficult. Question difficulty doesn't increase linearly, though. Most of the section's difficult questions are clustered in the "Danger Zone," stretching roughly from question 14 to question 22. Here, you'll find a high frequency of three- and four-star questions. A couple of things to note, though: First of all, not every question in this range is extremely difficult. Within the Danger Zone, there will be a couple of questions that most students find to be pretty manageable. That means it's not a good idea to completely skip this part of the section and leave those easy points behind. The other thing to be cognizant of is the difficulty level of questions *after* the Danger Zone. LSAT experts know that a couple of manageable questions typically wait at or near the end of the section.

Because the Logical Reasoning section is structured in this way, many students find that an effective strategy for dealing with the Danger Zone is to work from question 1 to question 15, then jump to the end of the section and work backward. This strategy guarantees that the Danger Zone questions—those most likely to be harder, more time-consuming, and often the most frustrating—will be the last questions a test taker faces. This simple strategy, however, is often not enough to maximize time management in this section. Even though difficult questions may show up in predictable areas of the test, no one can predict exactly the questions in a section that are considered high difficulty. Thus, experts are able to recognize when a question is difficult, no matter where it appears in the section.

Recognizing Difficult Questions

Given that all test takers have individual strengths and weaknesses, questions can be difficult on a personal and subjective level. The difference between an average student and an LSAT expert is that the expert is self-aware enough to realize where she is strong and where she is weak. There is no substitute for self-evaluation.

But the best test takers know that the test will present questions that, at least at first, are hard to figure out. That's why it's good to give yourself the option of moving on from a question that you feel is difficult or confusing. Regardless of whether it is question 2 or question 22, your best strategy for a question on which you are making no progress is to move on and, if time allows, return to the question later. As a general rule, if after 30 seconds you're confused and frustrated by the stimulus, move on to the next question. If you're approaching the section and utilizing good time management techniques, then you know that you will most likely have an opportunity to return to this question later and see it again with fresh eyes. If it turns out that you don't have the chance to come back, you've strategically skipped a question you were unlikely to get right anyway.

In addition to subjective factors, difficult questions generally contain one or more of the following attributes:

It is difficult to know what the question is asking. Even though LSAT experts are able to read a question stem and quickly recognize the question type, a few question stems have the potential to be confusing and ambiguous. If you're not able to determine precisely what a question is asking, it's probably a good candidate to skip and return to later.

It is difficult to break the stimulus into its parts. As you are now aware, the ability to untangle the stimulus into its various parts is crucial. If you are having difficulty finding the evidence and conclusion in an argument-based question, for example, skip the question and return to it later.

The answer choices are difficult to evaluate. Rarely, a question and stimulus are straightforward enough, but the language in the answer choices is difficult to understand. You may have noticed this in some of the more difficult Flaw, Method of Argument, and Role of a Statement questions. The answer choices to these questions are often presented in abstract and convoluted terms. When dealing with these problems, your best strategy is to make a prediction and then work to match it as best you can to one of the answer choices. However, if you're too confused or frustrated by the wording in the answer choices, strike through those you are certain are incorrect, then move on and return when your mind is clearer.

The stimulus includes Formal Logic. Although some test takers naturally pick up the concepts of Formal Logic and master the art of piecing together sufficient and necessary statements, many students struggle with these concepts. Additionally, when the test maker uses Formal Logic, the answer choices often rearrange the sufficient and necessary terms. This leads to confusion among test takers who are not able to distinguish among answer choices containing the same terms but presenting different logical relationships. Tackling or skipping questions with Formal Logic is a subjective measure. Know yourself—your strengths and weaknesses. If you determine that Formal Logic statements in Logical Reasoning questions give you trouble, then these are good questions to skip and return to later.

Every test taker is different. Evaluate your performance after every timed Logical Reasoning section to determine your strengths and weaknesses. Did you get bogged down by one of the difficult questions and spend an impractical amount of time on it? Did you get mired in the Danger Zone without finding time to evaluate the questions at the end of the section? Did you struggle with a particular question type? Did you find yourself making predictions and then second-guessing yourself once you started reading the answers?

Your Test Day goal for the Logical Reasoning section is to be able to recognize when a question is difficult, to be comfortable skipping it and returning to it later, and to have a methodical approach and plan to tackle that question when you get to it.

Putting the Pencil to Paper

Now that you know that skipping questions and returning to them later is an important strategy for managing time in the Logical Reasoning section, you'll want to develop a written system that allows "present you" to make things as easy and straightforward as possible for "future you."

Marking your test booklet clearly and gridding answer choices strategically can have an immediate impact on your timing proficiency in the Logical Reasoning section. If you skip a question, how can you signal that to "future you"? A good strategy is to circle questions that you've skipped and to cross out or draw a line through questions that you've answered. Additionally, it's often helpful to "future you" to write down the letters when "present you" is between two choices. For example, if you're between answer choices (A) and (D), write "A/D" next to the stimulus and return later. Making clear and understandable marks in your test booklet will clarify the task that "present you" has assigned to "future you."

Another way to improve your efficiency in this section is to strategically grid in answer choices on the bubble sheet. This is especially important for test takers at a testing facility where the desks have small surface areas. Determining an answer choice in your test booklet and transferring that information to your answer grid can be a multistep process for these students. If you find that you're losing precious seconds every time you grab your answer grid, fill in a bubble, and then return to your test booklet, utilize this strategy: Wait until you have finished answering questions on two facing pages, then grab your answer grid and bubble in the six to eight answer choices at that time (making sure to leave the bubbles for any questions you've skipped blank, of course).

SUGGESTED EXERCISE

In addition to bubbling in answer choices strategically, making specific notations in your test booklet is an excellent way to practice great test-taking habits. By tying a physical process (the movement of your pencil) to a psychological process, you'll be able to figure out not only where some of your issues are coming from, but also how to overcome them. Here are some notations you can start making today that will help you think like an expert. First, write down an "R" whenever you find yourself excessively rereading. These are questions on which it would be beneficial to slow down—remember the mantra of "pause and paraphrase." Another notation you can make is a "P" next to any question where you find yourself skipping the prediction stage. Additionally, when a question seems as if it will be especially time-consuming after 30 seconds of evaluation, put a star next to it. When you go back and review your performance, check to see how your markings lined up with your performance. How could you have performed better on the questions you marked with a "P" or "R"? For the questions you starred, did you end up skipping them and, if so, was that a wise move? Or did a question simply seem harder than it really was? Use your notations to continue to evaluate and hone your performance.

COMMON FRUSTRATIONS—DIAGNOSING YOUR ISSUE AND WAYS TO IMPROVE

Becoming an LSAT expert doesn't happen by accident. Great test takers recognize the areas in which they need improvement, then work to improve and hone their approach in those areas. Here, we've written descriptions of four archetypical LSAT students, each of whom is not reaching his or her maximum LSAT scores because of one or more bad habits. Now, chances are that none of these imaginary students describes you perfectly, but ask yourself if any of their issues sound familiar. If so, check out and implement the recommended exercises.

The Real World Applicator

Some students get so frustrated with the abstract nature of some LSAT questions that they lose sight of the fact that the LSAT exists as its own self-contained evaluative test. If you are always thinking about how scenarios relate to the real world, then you are unnecessarily making the test more difficult for yourself. For example, consider this simple, LSAT-like argument: "The basketball player who distributes the most assists should be considered the most valuable player in the league because in hockey, players who accumulate the most assists are often deemed to be the most valuable." What is the assumption that underlies this argument?

Maybe you were tempted to make a prediction like "We should give the most valuable player award to the basketball player with the most assists because she deserves it the most." Whether that is the right standard for evaluating basketball players (it might or might not be) in the real world is beside the point. More importantly for the LSAT test taker, that is not what the argument assumes. On the LSAT, all we care about is the argument presented to us and the ideas and concepts it contains. If you keep this in mind, the test should instantly become much easier for you. In this argument, the assumption must connect hockey and basketball and state that their players should be evaluated by similar standards. We don't even need to look to the answer choices to help us out. This is the power of predicting correct answer choices. The right answer must bridge the gap between the evidence and the conclusion. Though it may be reasonable (in the real world) to discuss whether or not a player deserves to win the most valuable player award, the concept of what is or is not "deserved" is not addressed in the argument, so it won't be a part of the right answer choice.

To overcome this tendency to be a "Real World Applicator," keep a few things in mind. First of all, go back to the basics and read with purpose (pausing and paraphrasing). By breaking stimuli into pieces that can be compared (Assumption Family) or combined (Inference questions), you keep yourself from bringing in ideas that are out of scope. If you focus on predicting the correct answer by using only the terms in the stimulus, then you will be less tempted by wrong answer choices involving concepts Outside the Scope of the argument, making Irrelevant Comparisons, or making Extreme claims.

SUGGESTED EXERCISE

Go through several Logical Reasoning questions, untimed, and write down the different pieces of the stimulus (using your paraphrasing skills). Without looking at any of the answer choices, use the pieces to predict, as clearly as possible, what the right answer will contain. In argument-based questions, rewrite each stimulus in this form: "Conclusion *because* evidence." In non-argument-based questions, jot down the paraphrased pieces of the stimulus with an eye toward spotting the most concrete claims and combining statements if possible. Once you have the pieces written down, check the explanations. Did your prediction match the correct answer choice as described by the explanation? If you didn't make a prediction, does the explanation describe how to connect the pieces of the stimulus to arrive at the right answer?

If you are a "Real World Applicator," it is incredibly important for you to slow down and focus on Steps 2 and 3 of the Logical Reasoning Method. The preceding exercise will help you see the value of those two steps.

The Rusher

Some test takers don't have a clear understanding of question types and approaches. In fact, some test takers even forget to read the question stem first, rushing headlong into every problem as though tackling the LSAT with the appropriate level of enthusiasm will be sufficient to do well. But as we've seen before, attacking the Logical Reasoning section without a plan and a purpose can negatively affect both timing and accuracy.

Impatient test takers often get tripped up by the learning curve involved in mastering Logical Reasoning questions. That's understandable given all that must be learned at the outset—the Logical Reasoning Method, the many different question types, and a variety of reading and reasoning skills. In their rush to use newfound strategies and tactics, overeager test takers allow themselves to get sloppy, skipping steps in the Method, or failing to identify the question type before jumping into the stimulus paragraph. For anxious test takers, it can even feel as if the Logical Reasoning Method is slowing them down or making them miss questions. That is because they haven't practiced enough to make the Method second nature. It's comparable to learning to drive a car with a stick shift and manual transmission. At the beginning, each step—depressing the clutch, engaging the gear, pressing the gas while releasing the clutch—seems awkward and frustrating. But you cannot skip one of those steps. So, you practice, maybe failing more often than you succeed at first. Then, one day it all comes together and you begin doing all of the steps automatically, without thinking. The Logical Reasoning Method will be much like that. Just keep at it, reminding yourself consciously of each step. Before you know it, you'll be using the Method effortlessly, and your timing and accuracy will both improve.

A person who is having difficulty categorizing questions will often struggle with timing in the Logical Reasoning section. After adequate practice, that tendency will turn around because identifying question types allows you to slow down, approach each question with a plan, and predict the correct answer before evaluating answer choices. And LSAT experts know that there is a direct, positive correlation between predicting the correct answer and time management.

> ## SUGGESTED EXERCISE
>
> Flip to a Logical Reasoning section and identify each question's type before actually tackling any questions. If you are really struggling, note the question type *and* jot down your strategy for it. After you do this, go back through the section and actually answer the questions. Note that this is an exercise, not a Test Day strategy. The point of this exercise is to show you that knowing the type of question, the pattern it will present, and the best strategy to use will allow for greater control and mastery, which ultimately leads to effective time management.

The Anxious One

Mastery of Steps 1–3 of the Logical Reasoning Method is an integral part of conquering the Logical Reasoning section. But correctly identifying question stem types and analyzing stimuli isn't enough for complete mastery. At the end of the day, you still have to find the correct answer choice.

Imagine this scenario: You've read a question stem, you've analyzed the question's stimulus, and you've predicted the correct answer. So far, so good. Then you look down and evaluate the answer choices and you notice that choice (A) seems somewhat convincing. It doesn't quite fit your prediction, but what if that's the right answer and you just overlooked something important in the stimulus? You keep reading, and you notice that (C) and (D) are also convincing. Did you possibly misread the question stem? You go back and reread, only to confirm that you identified the question type correctly. Now, you reread the stimulus and again find you analyzed it well. Your prediction also remains the same, and as you reread the answer choices, you see that answer choice (D) matches your prediction the best. Earlier, you had been thrown off by answer choices (A) and (C), but now you see that they introduce Extreme language that pushes them into wrong answer territory. You select (D) and move on.

Sound familiar? Notice that the Anxious One actually gets this question correct, but he does so by essentially doing the problem twice. The tendency to rework problems is a time killer on the LSAT. To improve your ability to get through the Logical Reasoning section in time, you need to be able to make good predictions, have the confidence to match those predictions to correct answer choices, and be comfortable moving on from answer choices that do not match your prediction.

SUGGESTED EXERCISE

If the Anxious One description fits you, then it's hard for you to believe, "I should be more confident in my initial reading of the question." So, to overcome the doubts that impair your performance, try this: In the next Logical Reasoning section you do, time yourself for each question. Start the timer when you start a question, then work through it as you normally would, making a prediction and matching it as best you can. Stop the timer when you've spotted the answer choice that most closely matches your answer. Write down that time on your page next to the question. Now, start the timer again and continue with the same problem, evaluating answer choices more thoroughly. Reread the question stem or the stimulus if you need more clarity. If you'd like, change your answer based on this second pass. Stop the timer once you're reasonably comfortable that you have the right answer. Now ask yourself a few questions. How much time did the second pass of the question cost you? Did you change your answer? If you did change your answer, did you change it to the *correct* answer? Look at this extra time in terms of a cost/benefit analysis: How many more questions are you answering correctly because of this constant questioning versus how much time are you losing? If you notice that you are losing a lot of time and that you are not answering more questions correctly, then you will finally be able to convince yourself that an initial, thorough, strategic reading of the stimulus is the best strategy to manage time effectively in this section.

The Perfectionist

If you're taking the LSAT, then you're probably planning to go to law school, and if you're planning to attend law school, then chances are good that you're interested in being a lawyer. And boy, do lawyers enjoy being right. "Perfectionist" is a common personality type among budding lawyers, and while that trait has its positive aspects, it can also be a drawback on the LSAT. Students who get into a battle with the test by silently arguing with answer choices or by refusing to skip questions will see their score suffer. The desire to confront and conquer every single question leads the Perfectionist to a familiar but unfortunate destination: the proctor announcing "time" before she is able to finish the section.

The first thing the Perfectionist needs to do is let go. Change your focus from *perfection* (achieving a perfect score, getting every difficult question correct, or hitting each timing benchmark to the second) to *ideal performance* (maximizing your results, remaining strategic, and managing time effectively). Remember, just like the scavenger hunter who is trying to collect as many items as possible, you don't care where you find your points; it only matters that you get as many of them as possible.

One thing the Perfectionist needs to determine as soon as possible is just how long, exactly, it takes to do a question. Ask yourself: Am I cognizant of how long it takes me to read a stimulus? To make a prediction? To evaluate answer choices? If you are a person who can easily get lost in a problem and has no idea how long it takes to do individual questions, then it would be instructive to time yourself on individual questions. Keep track of how and where you get bogged down—is it in the stimulus-reading stage (rereading), the prediction stage (trying too hard to come up with an exact prediction), the evaluating answer choices stage (thoroughly reading each answer choice), or all three?

SUGGESTED EXERCISE

To break the habit of reading straight through from beginning to end, set yourself the challenge of taking 15 minutes to answer as many questions correct out of the last 15 questions in a Logical Reasoning section. What will you do? You know there's no way you will be able to answer all 15 questions—that approach is immediately out the door. But your goal is to answer correctly as many as possible, so you start by tackling the easiest or shortest questions. This "game" is the same game the LSAT presents in a full section. To break the habit of reading every answer choice, evaluate how often your prediction is correct by drawing a line under the first answer choice you think is correct. If you changed your answer, was it correct? If you didn't change your answer, do you know how long it took you to evaluate the other answer choices?

Individual Problems Require Individual Solutions

In this chapter, we've discussed the good habits that LSAT experts utilize to get through the Logical Reasoning section in a timely manner. Planning for each question type, pausing and paraphrasing as you read, and predicting answer choices will help you manage each question effectively and efficiently. In addition, knowing where the difficult questions are can help you manage your time well by answering the easier questions first, then tackling difficult questions later.

The important thing to keep in mind is that if you're having difficulty getting through this section in time, it could be because of a number of different issues. Evaluate yourself and figure out what is preventing you from moving through the section efficiently. Ultimately, you will need to find the approach that allows you to answer as many questions correctly as possible.

Reading Comprehension

CHAPTER 13

The Kaplan Reading Comprehension Method

Every administration of the LSAT features one scored Reading Comprehension section. There are always four passages, each around 450–500 words long and with typically a set of 6–8 questions, for a total of 26–28 questions in the section. For many first-time LSAT test takers, Reading Comprehension is the section that feels most familiar, so it should be no surprise if it is your strongest section initially. Reading Comprehension is the section most similar to other tests you've probably taken, such as the SAT or ACT. Given that the Reading Comprehension section tasks you with reading academic material and answering questions about it, the section may even remind you a bit of standard college class tests.

This superficial similarity to other kinds of testing, however, masks some very unique features of LSAT Reading Comprehension. Moreover, LSAT test takers' initial comfort with Reading Comprehension often leads them to ignore this section to the detriment of their overall LSAT score. From over 40 years of experience working with LSAT test takers, we at Kaplan know that Reading Comprehension is the section in which many test takers have the hardest time improving their performance. After all, having been good readers throughout their academic careers, LSAT test takers are reluctant to change the way in which they read to suit the types of questions the LSAT testmaker asks.

We also know, however, that LSAT Reading Comprehension tests reading and reasoning skills that can be learned and mastered. Mastering them requires that you understand what is being tested and adopt a strategic reading approach that will distinguish the text relevant to LSAT questions from the details and general background information the test questions will largely ignore. And once you understand what the test is asking for, learning to read and answer Reading Comprehension questions quickly and accurately will take practice—a lot of practice.

A STRATEGIC APPROACH TO LSAT READING COMPREHENSION

Notice that we referred to the kind of reading that the expert test taker does as *strategic*. This is an important concept for all that follows. Rather than *deep* or *critical* reading, the kind you might do for a difficult seminar course in college, your job on the LSAT is to get the big picture of a passage—the author's Purpose and Main Idea—and to zero in on how the author makes key points and illustrates ideas or concepts. You're not preparing to have an in-depth conversation about the passage; you're preparing to answer LSAT questions. Take a look at one, and we'll discuss what it reveals about this important LSAT section.

According to the passage, the statements of Picasso and Braque indicate that

(A)   they had a long-standing interest in politics
(B)   they worked actively to bring about social change
(C)   their formal innovations were actually the result of chance
(D)   their work was a deliberate attempt to transcend visual reality
(E)   the formal aspects of their work were of little interest to them

PrepTest29 Sec2 Q3

In a moment, you'll see the passage from which this question came. For now, start your analysis by looking at the question stem. First off, it begins with "[a]ccording to the passage." LSAT Reading Comprehension questions can always be answered from the text you're given; outside knowledge of the subject matter is neither expected nor rewarded. How many future law students are likely to have any expertise in the subject of early modernist painters, anyway? Even more important, the question references statements made in the passage and asks what they "indicate." *How* the author uses a detail or *why* she has included it is far more relevant to LSAT questions than what might be true about the detail.

Now, let's put that question into its context on the test. On the next page, you'll see the passage and three of the questions from its question set. Try it out on your own. Read the passage and take down whatever notes seem relevant and helpful. Try to answer the questions that accompany it. Don't take too much time, though—no more than 5–6 minutes. We'll spend the rest of this chapter using this passage and its questions to illustrate how an LSAT expert reads and analyzes a Reading Comprehension passage and subsequently answers its questions efficiently and effectively. Along the way, you'll learn the Kaplan Reading Comprehension Method, the approach you'll use to tackle many more passages in the two chapters that follow this one.

For some years before the outbreak of World War I, a number of painters in different European countries developed works of art that some have described as prophetic: paintings that by challenging
(5) viewers' habitual ways of perceiving the world of the present are thus said to anticipate a future world that would be very different. The artistic styles that they brought into being varied widely, but all these styles had in common a very important break with traditions
(10) of representational art that stretched back to the Renaissance.

So fundamental is this break with tradition that it is not surprising to discover that these artists—among them Picasso and Braque in France, Kandinsky in
(15) Germany, and Malevich in Russia—are often credited with having anticipated not just subsequent developments in the arts, but also the political and social disruptions and upheavals of the modern world that came into being during and after the war. One art
(20) critic even goes so far as to claim that it is the very prophetic power of these artworks, and not their break with traditional artistic techniques, that constitutes their chief interest and value.

No one will deny that an artist may, just as much as
(25) a writer or a politician, speculate about the future and then try to express a vision of that future through making use of a particular style or choice of imagery; speculation about the possibility of war in Europe was certainly widespread during the early years of the
(30) twentieth century. But the forward-looking quality attributed to these artists should instead be credited to their exceptional aesthetic innovations rather than to any power to make clever guesses about political or social trends. For example, the clear impression we get
(35) of Picasso and Braque, the joint founders of cubism, from their contemporaries as well as from later statements made by the artists themselves, is that they were primarily concerned with problems of representation and form and with efforts to create a far
(40) more "real" reality than the one that was accessible only to the eye. The reformation of society was of no interest to them as artists.

It is also important to remember that not all decisive changes in art are quickly followed by
(45) dramatic events in the world outside art. The case of Delacroix, the nineteenth-century French painter, is revealing. His stylistic innovations startled his contemporaries—and still retain that power over modern viewers—but most art historians have decided
(50) that Delacroix adjusted himself to new social conditions that were already coming into being as a result of political upheavals that had occurred in 1830, as opposed to other artists who supposedly told of changes still to come.

1. According to the passage, the statements of Picasso and Braque indicate that

(A) they had a long-standing interest in politics
(B) they worked actively to bring about social change
(C) their formal innovations were actually the result of chance
(D) their work was a deliberate attempt to transcend visual reality
(E) the formal aspects of their work were of little interest to them

2. The art critic mentioned in lines 19–20 would be most likely to agree with which one of the following statements?

(A) The supposed innovations of Picasso, Braque, Kandinsky, and Malevich were based on stylistic discoveries that had been made in the Renaissance but went unexplored for centuries.
(B) The work of Picasso, Braque, Kandinsky, and Malevich possessed prophetic power because these artists employed the traditional techniques of representational art with unusual skill.
(C) The importance of the work of Picasso, Braque, Kandinsky, and Malevich is due largely to the fact that the work was stylistically ahead of its time.
(D) The prophecies embodied in the work of Picasso, Braque, Kandinsky, and Malevich were shrewd predictions based on insights into the European political situation.
(E) The artistic styles brought into being by Picasso, Braque, Kandinsky, and Malevich, while stylistically innovative, were of little significance to the history of post-World War I art.

3. Which one of the following characteristics of the painters discussed in the second paragraph does the author of the passage appear to value most highly?

(A) their insights into pre–World War I politics
(B) the visionary nature of their social views
(C) their mastery of the techniques of representational art
(D) their ability to adjust to changing social conditions
(E) their stylistic and aesthetic accomplishments

PrepTest29 Sec2 Qs 2, 3, and 7

Using a Roadmap to Answer Reading Comprehension Questions

Reflect a moment on your performance. How long did you spend reading the passage? Did you distinguish certain parts of the passage as more important or more likely to be asked about in the questions? When you turned to the questions, were you surprised by what they asked? Did you have a good idea where in the passage the relevant text could be found?

By the time you've learned and mastered the Reading Comprehension Method, you'll find that you can create a helpful Roadmap as you read the passage. To Roadmap passages effectively, LSAT experts circle Keywords within the passage and jot down brief notes in the margins that help them focus on the relevant parts of the passage and quickly research the answers to questions. In fact, if you learn to read as strategically as the best experts, you'll find that you can anticipate many, if not most, of the questions before you even read them.

To learn how to read Reading Comprehension passages strategically and to make good, useful Roadmaps of the passage, it's important to see how LSAT experts use Roadmaps to answer questions. Take a look at how an LSAT expert approached the questions from the passage you just tried. Don't worry if you're not sure why the expert circled certain words in the passage at this point. You'll learn to read and analyze as she did when we introduce the Reading Comprehension Method in full, and you'll practice it extensively in the next two chapters.

First up is the question you saw at the beginning of this chapter.

LSAT Question	Analysis
(30) . . . But the forward-looking quality attributed to these artists should instead be credited to their exceptional aesthetic innovations rather than to any power to make clever guesses about political or social trends. For example, the clear impression we get of (35) Picasso and Braque, the joint founders of cubism, from their contemporaries as well as from later statements made by the artists themselves, is that they were primarily concerned with problems of representation and form and with efforts to create a far more "real" (40) reality than the one that was accessible only to the eye. The reformation of society was of no interest to them as artists. *Au.—painters int'd in future of art, not pol/soc* *Ex. Pic/Brq*	The author makes a clear argument starting at line 30: The painters were "forward-looking" in terms of art, not politics and society. The author supports this assertion with an example: the statements of Picasso, Braque, and their peers. These statements reveal an emphasis ("they were *primarily* concerned with") on the technical problems of art (how does one create "a far more 'real' reality"?), and not on societal reformation.
1. According to the passage, the statements of Picasso and Braque indicate that $\longrightarrow$	The statements of Picasso and Braque are found in the third paragraph. The author emphasizes their interest in the form and technique of art, and their attempt to "create a far more 'real' reality." The author says they weren't much interested in predicting or fomenting societal change.
(A) they had a long-standing interest in politics $\longrightarrow$	180. This runs counter to the author's point in the passage. Eliminate.
(B) they worked actively to bring about social change $\longrightarrow$	180. This is contradicted by the paragraph's final sentence. Eliminate.
(C) their formal innovations were actually the result of chance $\longrightarrow$	Outside the Scope. If anything, the passage implies that they thought about art and worked actively to change it. Eliminate.
(D) their work was a deliberate attempt to transcend visual reality $\longrightarrow$	Correct. This is supported by lines 37–40, precisely where the author added the emphatic "primarily concerned with" language.
(E) the formal aspects of their work were of little interest to them *PrepTest29 Sec2 Q3* $\longrightarrow$	180. According to the passage, these artists were "primarily concerned with . . . representation and form." Eliminate.

Notice how the LSAT expert uses his "map" of the passage to research the text and predict the correct answer. The detail cited in the question stem ("the statements of Picasso and Braque") is evidence for the author's main point. So, the correct answer will have to illustrate that point (and wrong answers—such as (A) and (B) in this case—may contradict that main point). Moreover, the expert has taken note of the author's emphasis (by circling the Keyword "primarily") on the painters' interest in artistic form, and their attempts to transcend reality. LSAT experts become so strategic at reading LSAT passages that they will often spot language in the passage that will be asked about in the question set even before they have read the question stems.

The second question you answered asked about a different part of the passage and, more importantly, about the opinion of someone other than the author of the passage.

LSAT Question	Analysis
So fundamental is this break with tradition that it is not surprising to discover that these artist—among them Picasso and Braque in France, Kandinsky in (15) Germany, and Malevich in Russia—are often credited with having anticipated not just subsequent developments in the arts, but also the political and social disruptions and upheavals of the modern world that came into being during and after the war. One art (20) critic even goes so far as to claim that it is the very prophetic power of these artworks, and not their break with traditional artistic techniques, that constitutes their chief interest and value. *critics said prophets of soc/pol* *Au.—this view extreme*	In the second paragraph, the author says that the Pre-WWI painters' break with tradition was "so fundamental" that it led some critics (again, not the author) to think that the painters were actually predicting political and societal changes. The author, however, thinks that the painters' "chief interest and value" was in their artistic and technical breakthroughs.
2. The art critic mentioned in lines 19–20 would be most likely to agree with which one of the following statements? →	Lines 19–20 are in Paragraph 2. There, the author characterized the views of critics (with whom he disagrees) who thought that the Pre-WWI painters were most interesting because of their works' "prophetic power" in areas such as politics and society.
(A) The supposed innovations of Picasso, Braque, Kandinsky, and Malevich were based on stylistic discoveries that had been made in the Renaissance but went unexplored for centuries. →	Outside the Scope. It is the author, not the critics, who is interested in the painters' stylistic breakthroughs. What's more, the author says that these painters broke with the styles that had begun during the Renaissance.
(B) The work of Picasso, Braque, Kandinsky, and Malevich possessed prophetic power because these artists employed the traditional techniques of representational art with unusual skill. →	Outside the Scope. We don't know if the critics attributed the painters' prophetic power to particular techniques. Even if they did, it would not be the representational techniques that the Pre-WWI painters rejected.
(C) The importance of the work of Picasso, Braque, Kandinsky, and Malevich is due largely to the fact that the work was stylistically ahead of its time. →	180. This view is closer to that of the author, who finds the painters' break with traditional techniques to constitute their "chief interest and value." The critics were more interested in the paintings' "prophetic power."
(D) The prophecies embodied in the work of Picasso, Braque, Kandinsky, and Malevich were shrewd predictions based on insights into the European political situation. →	Correct. This matches the view of the critics (and opposes that of the author).
(E) The artistic styles brought into being by Picasso, Braque, Kandinsky, and Malevich, while stylistically innovative, were of little significance to the history of post-World War I art. →	180. The statement in this answer contradicts both the critics *and* the author, both of whom find the painters' work significant.

PrepTest29 Sec2 Q2

It is very common to find multiple opinions and points of view expressed in LSAT Reading Comprehension passages. The author may agree or disagree in whole or in part with the other positions he cites or describes. LSAT experts always keep track of who thinks what. The preceding question was about a view the author seeks to discredit, but sure enough, one of the wrong answers—(C)—accurately reflected the author's argument. Pay attention to multiple voices in the text of the passage, and make sure you know whose viewpoint is being called for in the question stem.

The next question also rewarded your ability to keep track of the points of view, and to accurately summarize them. This time, it's the author's position about which the question asks.

LSAT Question	Analysis
(15) So fundamental is this break with tradition that it is not surprising to discover that these artists—among them Picasso and Braque in France, Kandinsky in Germany, and Malevich in Russia—are often credited with having anticipated not just subsequent developments in the arts, but also the political and social disruptions and upheavals of the modern world that came into being during and after the war. One art (20) critic even goes so far as to claim that it is the very prophetic power of these artworks, and not their break with traditional artistic techniques, that constitutes their chief interest and value. *[critics said prophets of soc/pol]* *[Au.–this view extreme]*	In the second paragraph, the author says that the Pre-WWI painters' break with tradition was "so fundamental" that it led some critics (again, not the author) to think that the painters were actually predicting political and societal changes. The author, however, thinks that the painters' "chief interest and value" was in their artistic and technical breakthroughs.
(30) . . . But the forward-looking quality attributed to these artists should instead be credited to their exceptional aesthetic innovations rather than to any power to make clever guesses about political or social trends. *[Au.–painters int'd in future of art, not pol/soc]*	The author makes a clear argument starting at line 30: The painters were "forward-looking" in terms of art, not politics and society.
3. Which one of the following characteristics of the painters discussed in the second paragraph does the author of the passage appear to value most highly? →	While the painters are first discussed in Paragraph 2, the author continues to explain his appreciation of them in Paragraph 3. The author thinks the stylistic and technical break with tradition is what is most valuable about their work. He puts little stock in the view that they were "prophets" of politics or society.
(A) their insights into pre–World War I politics →	180. This contradicts the author's position. This is what the critics find so intriguing. Eliminate.
(B) the visionary nature of their social views →	180. This contradicts the author's position. This is more of what the critics find so intriguing. Eliminate.
(C) their mastery of the techniques of representational art →	Distortion. The author values the painters' break with representational art. We don't know if he thinks they mastered it first. Eliminate.
(D) their ability to adjust to changing social conditions →	Faulty Use of Detail. The author seems to appreciate Delacroix's response to societal change, but Delacroix is discussed in Paragraph 4, and this question asks about the Pre-WWI artists discussed in Paragraph 2. Eliminate.
(E) their stylistic and aesthetic accomplishments →	Correct. This agrees with the author's position as it is presented in Paragraphs 2 and 3.

PrepTest29 Sec2 Q7

It is not uncommon for your research on one Reading Comprehension question to help you predict the correct answer to another. Here, your work on Questions 2 and 3 are just two sides of the same coin. LSAT experts know that the testmaker often presents questions that reward your ability to characterize multiple points of view. The notes that the expert jotted down in the margins of the passage helped him research and predict both of those questions efficiently and effectively.

The LSAT expert never considered the possibility that two or more answers were technically correct and then tried to choose the one that was more correct. He stuck to the principle of "one right; four demonstrably wrong" in all cases. It may be hard to accept that the correct and incorrect answers are just as clear-cut in Reading Comprehension as they are in Logic Games and Logical Reasoning, but they are.

Now that you've seen how the LSAT expert uses the Roadmap to research the passage and predict the correct answer, let's examine the entire process from start to finish.

THE KAPLAN READING COMPREHENSION METHOD

To handle four passages in 35 minutes and to get as many right answers as possible from this section, you need to have an approach that you can use consistently. There are five steps to the Kaplan Reading Comprehension Method. The first is all about reading and Roadmapping the passage. The next four steps provide the fastest and surest way to answer the questions correctly.

THE KAPLAN READING COMPREHENSION METHOD

Step 1: Read the Passage Strategically—circle Keywords and jot down margin notes to summarize the portions of the passage relevant to LSAT questions; summarize the author's Topic/Scope/Purpose/Main Idea.

Step 2: Read the Question Stem—identify the question type, characterize the correct and incorrect answers, and look for clues to guide your research.

Step 3: Research the Relevant Text—based on the clues in the question stem, consult your Roadmap; for open-ended questions, refer to your Topic/Scope/Purpose/Main Idea summaries.

Step 4: Predict the Correct Answer—based on research (or, for open-ended questions, your Topic/Scope/Purpose/Main Idea summaries) predict the meaning of the correct answer.

Step 5: Evaluate the Answer Choices—select the choice that matches your prediction of the correct answer or eliminate the four wrong answer choices.

As you practice, make it your goal to complete Step 1 in about 3–4 minutes, leaving 4–5 minutes for the question set. If you've completed the chapters on Logical Reasoning, Steps 2–5 of the Reading Comprehension Method should look pretty familiar. They're identical to the steps for handling a Logical Reasoning question with the exception of Step 3. In Reading Comprehension, you will already have read and Roadmapped the passage before you analyze the question stem. Discipline yourself to *research* targeted parts of the passage (that is, to consult the Roadmap you've already made) based on the clues in the stem. Test takers who *reread* the passage (or big chunks of it) for each question run out of time; it's clear that these test takers do not trust their original reading of the passage and aren't reading strategically from the start.

Step 1—Read the Passage Strategically

Reading strategically means reading not to memorize factual details but to get LSAT questions correct. As you've already seen, the LSAT is far more interested in *how* the author uses a detail than in *what* the facts about the detail are. Similarly, the LSAT is interested in your ability to discern *why* the author is writing the passage (or some portion of it)—his Purpose in writing, if you will. The first step of the Reading Comprehension Method targets the parts of the passage the test is likely to ask about and, when mastered, allows you to read the passage one time and be ready to research and answer every question.

There are two aspects to Strategic Reading, one physical and one mental.

The Physical Roadmap—Keywords and Margin Notes

As an LSAT expert reads a Reading Comprehension passage, she reads with pencil in hand. This allows her to circle or underline Keywords, words that indicate the structure of the passage. As you learn to identify Keywords, your reading will become much more strategic because Keywords prompt you to read actively, asking why the author is emphasizing a certain point or contrasting one idea with another. There are six categories of Keywords you should look for. You'll see them highlighted in every Roadmap you review in Chapter 14, in the Sample Roadmaps accompanying the explanations for the passages in Chapter 15, and in the online explanations for full-length tests at the end of the book.

> ### LSAT STRATEGY
>
> Strategic Reading Keywords
>
> - **Emphasis/Opinion**—words that signal that the author finds a detail noteworthy or has a positive or negative opinion about it or, indeed, any subjective or evaluative language on the author's part (e.g., *especially, crucial, unfortunately, disappointing, I suggest, it seems likely*)
> - **Contrast**—words indicating that the author thinks two details or ideas are incompatible or illustrate conflicting points (e.g., *but, yet, despite, on the other hand*)
> - **Logic**—words that indicate an argument, either the author's or someone else's (e.g., *thus, therefore, because*)
> - **Illustration**—words indicating an example offered to clarify or support another point (e.g., *for example, this shows, to illustrate*)
> - **Sequence/Chronology**—words showing an order to certain steps in a process or to developments over time (e.g., *traditionally, in the past, recently, today, first, second, finally, earlier, since*)
> - **Continuation**—words indicating that a subsequent example or detail supports the same point or illustrates the same idea (e.g., *moreover, in addition, and, also, further*)

As you review sample Roadmaps, you'll see that the LSAT experts seldom circle the sorts of factual information you would likely pinpoint in a conventional textbook for a subject-matter course in school. Instead, their focus on Keywords helps them discern the structure of the passage and thus the author's point of view and purpose in writing.

The other thing the LSAT expert does with her pencil is to jot down brief, abbreviated margin notes wherever she encounters an important point in the text. As you review the LSAT experts' Roadmaps, don't make too much of the specific wording in these margin notes. They may be as simple as "Ex" for an example or as thorough as a short description. Everyone will have slightly different notes next to a passage. The important thing is that your margin notes are simple, accurate, and legible and that they target the author's key points in the passage and are not just a list of facts that repeats the passage.

Some test takers wonder why they should take notes at all. The answer is simple: Your job in strategic reading is to highlight the parts of the passage that will help you answer LSAT questions. If you leave a passage entirely blank, you haven't distinguished the parts you're likely to need when researching the questions. Likewise, if you have circled or underlined almost everything in the passage, you haven't distinguished what's relevant in that case either. The LSAT expert leaves the passage marked up in a way that is extremely helpful when it comes to answering the questions.

The Mental Roadmap—Summarizing Topic/Scope/Purpose/Main Idea

While the LSAT expert's pencil is occupied circling Keywords and jotting down margin notes, her mind is also keeping track of the author's "big picture" in the passage. The most helpful way to grasp the big picture is to build a summary as you read. Pay attention to the four concepts outlined below. You'll usually encounter them in the text in the order they're presented in the strategy box.

LSAT STRATEGY

Reading Comprehension—the "big picture"

- **Topic**—the overall subject of the passage
- **Scope**—the particular aspect of the Topic that the author is focusing on
- **Purpose**—the author's reason for writing the passage (express this as a verb—e.g., *to refute*, *to outline*, *to evaluate*, *to critique*)
- **Main Idea**—the author's conclusion or overall takeaway; if you combine the author's Purpose and Scope, you'll usually have a good sense of the Main Idea.

On Test Day, there is no need for you to write down these summaries. Just make sure you can clearly articulate the author's Purpose and Main Idea within the scope of the passage so that you can predict the correct answers to Global questions and Inference questions that ask you for the author's overall point of view or opinion. In practice, it is a good idea to jot down your summaries of the author's Purpose and Main Idea so that you can compare them to the summaries outlined in the explanations. You'll quickly start to see when and why your summaries were too broad or too narrow or missed the scope of the passage.

Take a look now at an LSAT expert's strategic reading and Roadmap for the passage on the Pre-WWI European Painters. We'll take Step 1 paragraph by paragraph. In the left-hand column you'll see the physical Roadmap of Keywords and margin notes. In the right-hand "Analysis" column, you get some idea of what the LSAT expert was thinking as he read the passage.

LSAT Passage		Analysis
For some years before the outbreak of World War I, a number of painters in different European countries developed works of art that some have described as prophetic: paintings that by challenging (5) viewers' habitual ways of perceiving the world of the present are thus said to anticipate a future world that would be very different. The artistic styles that they brought into being varied widely, but all these styles had in common a very important break with traditions of (10) representational art that stretched back to the Renaissance.	*Pre WW I Eu. painters* *some—prophetic* *Au.—broke with art trad.*	**Step 1:** The passage's **Topic** is a group of Pre-World War I European painters. "Some" art historians or critics (but not necessarily the author) consider their paintings "prophetic." The author, however, emphasizes ("very important") their break with traditional, representational art. That break, and the author's assessment of it, is likely to be the passage's **Scope**.

Take note of how the LSAT expert zeros in on Keywords in order to ask what the author is trying to present and why. You'll usually, as the LSAT expert did here, find the Topic and Scope in the first paragraph. Don't force these summaries, however. If the Scope doesn't emerge until the second paragraph, that's okay.

By the end of the first paragraph, the LSAT expert is fairly confident that the "very important" break with tradition constitutes the passage's Scope. This is confirmed at the beginning of the second paragraph, where the author calls the break "[s]o fundamental."

LSAT Passage	Analysis
(15) So fundamental is this break with tradition that it is not surprising to discover that these artists—among them Picasso and Braque in France, Kandinsky in Germany, and Malevich in Russia—are often credited with having anticipated not just subsequent developments in the arts, but also the political and social disruptions and upheavals of the modern world that came into being during and after the war. One art (20) critic even goes so far as to claim that it is the very prophetic power of these artworks, and not their break with traditional artistic techniques, that constitutes their chief interest and value. *critics said prophets of soc/pol* *Au.—this view extreme*	**Step 1 (cont.):** The author underlines the Scope of the passage: The Pre-WWI painters' break with tradition was "so fundamental" that it led some critics (again, not the author) to think that the painters were actually predicting political and societal changes. The author, however, thinks that the painters' "chief interest and value" was in their artistic and technical breakthroughs.

LSAT experts always read actively. They anticipate where the author will go in the subsequent paragraph. They note which points need further clarity or support. By the end of the second paragraph, the expert knows the author's position, and how it differs from that of the critics, so he may be a little surprised by the first sentence of the third paragraph.

LSAT Passage	Analysis
(25) No one will deny that an artist may, just as much as a writer or a politician, speculate about the future and then try to express a vision of that future through making use of a particular style or choice of imagery; speculation about the possibility of war in Europe was certainly widespread during the early years of the (30) twentieth century. But the forward-looking quality attributed to these artists should instead be credited to their exceptional aesthetic innovations rather than to any power to make clever guesses about political or social trends. For example, the clear impression we get of (35) Picasso and Braque, the joint founders of cubism, from their contemporaries as well as from later statements made by the artists themselves, is that they were primarily concerned with problems of representation and form and with efforts to create a far more "real" (40) reality than the one that was accessible only to the eye. The reformation of society was of no interest to them as artists. *Au.—painters int'd in future of art, not pol/soc* *Ex. Pic/Brq*	**Step 1 (cont.):** Paragraph 3 begins with a concession by the author: Of course the painters, just like everyone else, were interested in political and social developments. The author resumes his argument at line 30. The author's **Purpose** and **Main Idea** are signaled by the keyword "[b]ut": The painters were predictive ("forward-looking") in terms of artistic style and technique, not in the realms of politics and society. The author supports this conclusion with an example: the statements of Picasso, Braque, and their peers. These statements reveal an emphasis ("they were *primarily* concerned with") on the technical problems of art (how does one create "a far more 'real' reality"?), and not on societal reformation.

The author began the third paragraph with a small concession (of course, everyone was thinking about war), but then he resumes his argument in earnest. For the LSAT expert, the structure of the third paragraph is pure gold: The keyword "[b]ut" at line 30 is a good indication that the author's Main Point will follow, and the keyword phrase "[f]or example" at line 34 signals his primary evidence. You even saw, in the expert's handling of Question 3, how the emphasis keyword "primarily" (line 38) helped the expert predict the correct answer and zero in on the correct choice.

In a passage like this one, where the Main Point is made and supported before the final paragraph, it may be harder to predict what the end of the passage will cover. It might provide additional support for the author's position, or discuss the implications of his findings. Here, the LSAT expert notes "also important to remember" in the fourth paragraph's first line.

LSAT Passage	Analysis
It is also important to remember that not all decisive changes in art are quickly followed by dramatic events (45) in the world outside art. The case of Delacroix, the nineteenth-century French painter, is revealing. His stylistic innovations startled his contemporaries—and still retain that power over modern viewers—but most art historians have decided that Delacroix adjusted (50) himself to new social conditions that were already coming into being as a result of political upheavals that had occurred in 1830, as opposed to other artists who supposedly told of changes still to come. *Author— art/soc change Indep'ly* *Ex Delacroix*	**Step 1 (cont.):** The passage's final paragraph offers further evidence ("also important") in the form of a parallel example. The author considers Delacroix's work "revealing" in that it shows that changes in art aren't always followed by changes in society. Delacroix was artistically novel, but his work was a reflection of social changes already occurring, not an attempt to predict or trigger future changes.

PrepTest29 Sec2 Qs 1-7

As you learn to emulate the LSAT expert's approach in Step 1, you'll find yourself summarizing the Purpose and Main Idea without even having to stop and remind yourself to do so.

You'll see more examples of LSAT experts' strategic reading and Roadmapping in the next chapter. But keep Step 1 in perspective. You don't get LSAT points directly from the Roadmap, and there's no such thing as an objectively right or wrong Roadmap as there are credited and incorrect answer choices. The Roadmap is a tool to help you answer questions correctly, quickly, and confidently. If, upon completing Step 1, you find yourself ready for the question set and able to move through it efficiently, you're Roadmapping well.

Steps 2–5—Answering Reading Comprehension Questions

Several standard question types accompany Reading Comprehension passages—Global, Inference, Detail, Logic Reasoning, and Logic Function. You'll learn the characteristics of each of these in the next chapter along with strategies specific to each.

Earlier in this chapter, you saw how the LSAT expert consulted his Roadmap to answer three of the questions associated with the passage on Pre-WWI European Painters. Now, take a look at how the expert answered the remaining questions with this passage. This time, though, we'll be explicit about the expert's thinking during Steps 2 through 5 of the Reading Comprehension Method. Whenever you need to refer to the passage, turn to the preceding pages and refresh your memory of the expert's Roadmap.

The first question associated with this passage is much broader than any you've seen up to this point. It's a Global question that illustrates how the LSAT expert's summaries of the passage's Big Picture turn directly into points.

LSAT Question	Analysis
Which one of the following most accurately states the main idea of the passage?	**Step 2:** A Global question calling for the author's "main idea."
	Step 3: While Roadmapping, we summarized the author's Main Point.
→	**Step 4:** The Main Point summary will serve as a prediction for the correct answer: The painters, through their break with representational art, were predictive ("forward-looking") in terms of artistic style and technique, not in the realms of politics and society.
(A) Although they flourished independently, the pre–World War I European painters who developed new ways of looking at the world shared a common desire to break with the traditions of representational art.	**Step 5:** This choice is too narrow to reflect the Main Point. It doesn't address the critics' view ("prophetic power") or the author's position that the break with tradition led to the future of art. Eliminate.
(B) The work of the pre–World War I European painters who developed new ways of looking at the world cannot be said to have intentionally predicted social changes but only to have anticipated new directions in artistic perception and expression.	Correct. This reflects the author's position accurately vis-à-vis the artists and the other critics. It matches the prediction perfectly.
(C) The work of the pre–World War I European painters who developed new ways of looking at the world was important for its ability to predict social changes and its anticipation of new directions in artistic expression.	Distortion. This choice blends the views of the critics ("predict social changes") and the author ("anticipation of new directions in [art]"). Eliminate.
(D) Art critics who believe that the work of some pre–World War I European painters foretold imminent social changes are mistaken because art is incapable of expressing a vision of the future.	Outside the Scope. The passage never gets into whether art can express the future. The author calls the Pre-WWI painters' predictions "clever guesses about political and social trends" but that doesn't mean he thinks all art is *incapable* of such a vision. Eliminate.

LSAT Question	Analysis
(E) Art critics who believe that the work of some pre–World War I European painters foretold imminent social changes are mistaken because the social upheavals that followed World War I were impossible to predict. *PrepTest29 Sec2 Q1*	Distortion. The author thinks the critics are wrong because they find the Pre-WWI painters' work more interesting for its "predictive power" than for its artistic innovation. He never says that World War I could not have been predicted.

Note that the LSAT expert could comfortably have stopped and moved on once he read answer choice (B). Having summarized the passage's Big Picture in Step 1, he was prepared for a Global question, and could be confident that this answer was correct.

Not surprisingly, since the fourth and final paragraph of the passage offered only a further example to support the author's main point, there was just one question here that addressed that paragraph. Take a look at how the LSAT expert attacked it.

LSAT Question	Analysis
The author presents the example of Delacroix in order to illustrate which one of the following claims?	**Step 2:** A Logic Function question asking why ("in order to") the author mentions an example. **Step 3:** Delacroix was discussed in the fourth paragraph, and served as a distinct, but parallel example of an artist dealing with social change. **Step 4:** The author says that it is "important to remember that not all . . . changes in art are . . . followed by dramatic events in the world outside art." He then cites Delacroix as an artist who adjusted his style to changes already happening in the outside world.
(A) Social or political changes usually lead to important artistic innovations.	**Step 5:** Extreme. The author does not claim that societal changes lead to artistic innovation more often than not ("usually"). Eliminate.
(B) Artistic innovations do not necessarily anticipate social or political upheavals.	Correct. Sometimes artistic innovations *follow* social changes. Delacroix is an example.
(C) Some European painters have used art to predict social or political changes.	Outside the Scope. Some artists may have done this, but the author doesn't use Delacroix as an example of such artists. Eliminate.
(D) Important stylistic innovations are best achieved by abandoning past traditions.	Outside the Scope. The author never attempts to argue about the *best* way to achieve artistic innovation. Eliminate.
(E) Innovative artists can adapt themselves to social or political changes. *PrepTest29 Sec2 Q4*	Distortion. The case of Delacroix may show that this statement is true, but that is not *why* the author discusses Delacroix. He's interested in showing that artistic innovation isn't always about trying to predict the future. Eliminate.

There, again, the physical Roadmap (the Keywords circled by the LSAT expert, and the margin notes he jotted down) allowed the expert to research the passage quickly, and to predict the correct answer before evaluating the choices. The expert knew that the testmaker would likely ask one question about this peripheral example.

The next question is another Global question, but this time, instead of asking about the author's Purpose or Main Idea, it rewards the test taker who can sum up the passage's structure. As you review the expert's analysis, go back and compare the answers to the Keywords and margin notes on the original Roadmap.

LSAT Question	Analysis
Which one of the following most accurately describes the contents of the passage?	**Step 2:** A Global question looking for an accurate outline of the passage.
	Step 3: The Roadmap serves as an outline of the passage.
	→ **Step 4:** Here, the author introduced the Pre-WWI European painters, presented why some critics find them important, contradicts those critics with his own idea of why the painters are important, and then supports his position with examples.
(A) The author describes an artistic phenomenon; introduces one interpretation of this phenomenon; proposes an alternative interpretation and then supports this alternative by criticizing the original interpretation.	→ **Step 5:** Correct. This outline follows the passage accurately step-by-step, paragraph-by-paragraph.
(B) The author describes an artistic phenomenon; identifies the causes of that phenomenon; illustrates some of the consequences of the phenomenon and then speculates about the significance of these consequences.	→ Distortion. The author does not discuss the "consequences" of the break with tradition, nor does he speculate about their "significance." Eliminate.
(C) The author describes an artistic phenomenon; articulates the traditional interpretation of this phenomenon; identifies two common criticisms of this view and then dismisses each of these criticisms by appeal to an example.	→ Distortion. The author does not provide two criticisms of the critics' position (or "traditional interpretation," as it is called here), and he certainly does not dismiss such criticism. His main point is about why the critics are wrong. Eliminate.
(D) The author describes an artistic phenomenon; presents two competing interpretations of the phenomenon; dismisses both interpretations by appeal to an example and then introduces an alternative interpretation.	→ Distortion. This overcomplicates things. The author gives one opposing view, and counters it with his own. There's no third "alternative" in the passage. Eliminate.
(E) The author describes an artistic phenomenon; identifies the causes of the phenomenon; presents an argument for the importance of the phenomenon and then advocates an attempt to recreate the phenomenon.	→ Distortion. This answer is wrong in everything except its first statement, most noticeably when it says that the author "advocates an attempt to recreate" the Pre-WWI painters' work. Eliminate.

PrepTest29 Sec2 Q5

Note how each answer choice begins identically. An LSAT expert knows that this pattern makes a focus on the end of each answer choice the more strategic approach.

There was one more short question associated with this passage. Like many LSAT Reading Comprehension questions, it begins with "[a]ccording to the author." But pay attention to what it is actually asking. The lessons you learned back in Chapter 1 about the Levels of Truth and characterizing right and wrong answer choices will pay dividends once again here in the Reading Comprehension section.

LSAT Question	Analysis
According to the author, the work of the pre–World War I painters described in the passage contains an example of each of the following EXCEPT:	**Step 2:** A Detail question, but one in which the four wrong answers are details that the author associated with the Pre-WWI painters; the correct answer, on the other hand, is *not* something that the author claims these artists included in their work.
	Step 3: The details about the Pre-WWI painters are found primarily in Paragraphs 2 and 3.
	Step 4: It is impossible to predict what the author did not say was an example of something the Pre-WWI painters did. However, if an answer choice is something that the critics would say, it will be correct in this case.
(A) an interest in issues of representation and form	**Step 5:** The author does mention this (lines 38–39). Eliminate.
(B) a stylistic break with traditional art	The author does mention this (lines 9–10, 12, and 20–21). Eliminate.
(C) the introduction of new artistic techniques	The author does mention this (lines 21–22). Eliminate.
(D) the ability to anticipate later artists	The author does mention this (lines 16–17). Eliminate.
(E) the power to predict social changes *PrepTest29 Sec2 Q6*	Correct. This is in the passage (lines 17–19), but it is a claim made by the critics, not by the author.

The majority of Reading Comprehension questions start with something like "[a]ccording to the passage" or "[b]ased on the passage," and support for the correct answer is present in the text. Take your cue from the LSAT expert: Note the clues in the stem, research the passage, and predict the correct answer. Never answer based on what you think you remember from the passage or what "sounds right" to you. Learn to make a helpful Roadmap and then use it to identify precisely what the correct answer must say.

Reading Comprehension Wrong Answer Types

As you were reviewing the LSAT expert's work on the Pre-WWI European Painters passage, you may have noticed certain wrong answer types popping up over and over again. This is not by chance. Just as you saw in Logical Reasoning, the testmaker uses certain patterns of distracters test after test, question after question. Take a few minutes to learn about the wrong answer types most common in Reading Comprehension before you move on to the next chapter.

Not every wrong answer you see will fit neatly into one of the types you see described here. After all, sometimes when a question asks for what the passage suggests, the wrong answer will just be something the author does *not* suggest, without clearly being a 180 or Extreme. Other wrong answers might fit more than one category. Still, it's worth your time to learn the wrong answer types in the list that follows. You'll see them referred to many times in the questions illustrated in the coming chapters.

LSAT STRATEGY

Reading Comprehension—Wrong Answer Types

- **Outside the Scope**—a choice containing a statement that is too broad, too narrow, or beyond the purview of the passage
- **Extreme**—a choice containing language too emphatic (*all*, *never*, *every*, *none*) to be supported by the passage
- **Distortion**—a choice that mentions details or ideas from the passage but mangles or misstates the relationship between them given or implied by the author
- **180**—a choice that directly contradicts what the correct answer must say
- **Faulty Use of Detail**—a choice that accurately states something from the stimulus but in a matter that incorrectly answers the question
- **Half-Right/Half-Wrong**—a choice in which one clause follows from the passage but has another clause that contradicts or distorts the passage

---

Along the way, you'll see a handful of wrong answers that appear to defy categorization. When that happens, we'll still explain clearly how the LSAT expert can recognize them as demonstrably incorrect. Whenever a wrong answer does fit clearly into one of the types outlined above, however, we'll note that too.

Now that you see the value of approaching each Reading Comprehension passage and question set with a deliberate and repeatable method, we'll practice applying it to more passages and question sets in the next chapter. We'll build on what you've learned here by diving deeper into each step of the Reading Comprehension Method. Additionally, you'll see examples of passages that fit a handful of rhetorical or structural patterns the testmaker uses over and over. As you become more familiar with these passage structures, your strategic reading will become even more targeted. In some passages, for example, you will focus on the author's disagreement with a critic. In others, you'll see that the author has no personal opinion to express but rather is simply interested in explaining other experts' ideas on a subject. In any case, remember that the LSAT questions will focus on the author's Purpose and Main Idea and will reward you for paying attention to *why* the author has included a detail or *how* he's using it within the text. We'll outline the common Reading Comprehension question types in Chapter 14 as well.

Reading Comprehension: Passage Types and Question Types

In this chapter, you'll learn the specific skills involved in applying the Reading Comprehension Method to passages and their question sets. Along the way, you'll discover that the LSAT uses certain patterns over and over, both in the way passages are structured and in the types of questions the test asks.

If you have already worked in or completed the sections on Logic Games and Logical Reasoning, this chapter will feel different. That's because it's difficult to practice Reading Comprehension skills outside the context of full passages. We won't be able to atomize the skills as neatly in this chapter as we have in others. That makes it very important for you to study the Learning Objectives at the beginning of each section and keep them in mind as you're reviewing the expert analysis of the LSAT material. Don't hesitate to mark the pages where Learning Objectives are introduced and refer to them often to keep the goals of the lessons at the front of your mind.

Because LSAT Reading Comprehension passages are often densely written and because the questions shift their focus from the passage as a whole to details scattered throughout the text, it's easy to miss the forest for the trees in this section. To remain strategic and effective in Reading Comprehension, you must proactively engage the material. Don't sit back and read passively, waiting for the author's point to come to you. LSAT experts constantly question and challenge the author as they read. They anticipate where the passage will go and even the questions that the testmaker will ask. That's not easy, but it will make a huge difference in law school where you have to do a similar kind of targeted, interrogative, and skeptical reading. Start disciplining yourself as a strategic reader now, and you'll be well ahead of the game on Test Day and in your first year as a law student.

Job one in gaining this expertise is to internalize the Reading Comprehension Method. Use it unfailingly until it becomes second nature.

THE KAPLAN READING COMPREHENSION METHOD

Step 1: Read the Passage Strategically—circle Keywords and jot down margin notes to summarize the portions of the passage relevant to LSAT questions; summarize the author's Topic/Scope/Purpose/Main Idea.

Step 2: Read the Question Stem—identify the question type, characterize the correct and incorrect answers, and look for clues to guide your research.

Step 3: Research the Relevant Text—based on the clues in the question stem, consult your Roadmap; for open-ended questions, refer to your Topic/Scope/Purpose/Main Idea summaries.

Step 4: Predict the Correct Answer—based on research, (or, for open-ended questions, your Topic/Scope/Purpose/Main Idea summaries) predict the meaning of the correct answer.

Step 5: Evaluate the Answer Choices—select the choice that matches your prediction of the correct answer or eliminate the four wrong answer choices.

The first big section of this chapter will concentrate on Step 1, on the active reading and note taking you'll need to do in order to answer all of the passage's questions efficiently. As you learn and practice Step 1, we'll also introduce common passage structures you'll see in LSAT passages.

The second section of the chapter will cover Steps 2–5. You'll learn and practice the most effective ways to answer Reading Comprehension questions. As you do so, you'll learn the characteristics of the question types the testmaker uses for this section.

At the end of the chapter, you'll have a chance to practice a complete passage and question set and compare your work to that of an LSAT expert step-by-step. Chapter 15 contains 11 more full passages, so you'll have ample opportunity to put all that you learn here to work.

STRATEGIC READING AND READING COMPREHENSION PASSAGE TYPES

With four passages in the 35-minute Reading Comprehension section, you have about 8½ minutes per passage. Of that, you'll spend between three and four minutes on Step 1 of the Reading Comprehension Method, reading the passage strategically and creating a Roadmap. In Chapter 13, you saw an example of how this targeted reading and note taking sets you up to answer the questions quickly and confidently. Let's quickly outline and explain the skills associated with Step 1.

Strategic Reading and Roadmapping Skills

If you ask most untrained test takers how they start out in Reading Comprehension, they would probably say something like, "I read the passage, I guess." That's accurate, as far as it goes. If you ask LSAT experts, however, their answer would be more nuanced: "I prepare myself to answer all of the passage's questions." Step 1 is not just reading; it's reading strategically, and that's a complex task. You'll be taking note of Keywords that reveal the author's opinion and the passage structure, you'll make margin notes to correspond with the most important points in the passage, and you'll summarize the author's Purpose and Main Idea. Here's the good news: Each of those tasks has a handful of manageable, learnable skills associated with it.

LEARNING OBJECTIVES

In this portion of the chapter, you'll learn to use:

Keywords

- Identify Keywords from six categories (Emphasis/Opinion, Contrast, Logic, Illustration, Sequence/Chronology, Continuation).
- Use Keywords to accurately paraphrase the text (author's purpose, passage structure etc.).
- Use Keywords to accurately predict where the passage will go (scope and purpose of remaining paragraphs, for example).
- Use Keywords to predict points in the passage to which LSAT questions will refer.

Margin Notes

- Identify text that warrants a margin note.
- Capture key content in a brief, accurate margin note.

"Big-Picture" Summaries—Topic/Scope/Purpose/Main Idea

- Read a passage and identify the author's Topic and Scope.
- Read a passage and identify the author's Purpose.
- Read a passage and identify the author's Main Idea.

On the following pages, you'll learn what each of these skill sets involves and why they're vital to the strategic reading of LSAT Reading Comprehension passages.

Why Use Keywords?

The short, but very compelling, answer is that Keywords indicate points of view and important spots in the passage's structure, and knowing where those are is often the key to distinguishing between right and wrong answers on the test. Here's why. Take two simple statements:

> Jessica earned an outstanding LSAT score. Jessica is going to attend Gilligan University Law School next fall.

If that was all you knew, you could not answer this typical LSAT question: "With which one of the following statements about Gilligan University Law School would the author most likely agree?" You know two facts about Jessica but nothing about the author's point of view toward her future alma mater. Add a Contrast Keyword, however, and the answer to the LSAT question is clear:

> Jessica earned an outstanding LSAT score; despite this fact, she will attend Gilligan University Law School next fall.

Now, you know that the correct answer to the LSAT question would be something along the lines of "It's unexpected that someone with an outstanding LSAT score would choose Gilligan." On the other hand, what if the two facts were connected by a Logic Keyword?

> Because Jessica earned an outstanding LSAT score, she will attend Gilligan University Law School next fall.

This signals a profound difference in the author's point of view. The correct answer now would be something like, "Gilligan University Law School generally requires high LSAT scores for admission." Consider the implications of this example: In both cases, the facts were absolutely identical, yet the correct answers to the LSAT question were polar opposites. Keywords signal an author's purpose or position, they highlight what she wants to emphasize, and they reveal how she is making her argument. These are the aspects of the text that LSAT questions focus upon.

LSAT Reading Comprehension questions never ask for factual details that a test taker might just happen to know from the outside world. Take the following assertion, for example.

> During the Civil War, President Lincoln deliberately sought out the advice of cabinet members whose opinions were at odds with his own.

The LSAT will not ask, "Which of the following is true of Lincoln's cabinet?" and expect you to report on the multiplicity of opinions. After all, you may be able to answer a question like that without reading the passage at all. Indeed, it would not even matter if you were a history major who could write an essay on the subject and challenge the statement about Lincoln with facts of your own. LSAT Reading Comprehension is not a test of expertise; like the rest of the LSAT, it's a test of skill.

Now, put the statement about Lincoln into the context of an LSAT passage.

> Effective leaders allow for open dialogue. For example, during the Civil War, President Lincoln deliberately sought out the advice of cabinet members whose opinions were at odds with his own.

From this, the LSAT might draw a question such as "The author most likely refers to Lincoln and his cabinet in order to . . . ." The correct answer, you'll notice, must start with a verb. Because the sentence on Lincoln is prefaced with the Illustration Keywords "[f]or example," the correct answer here would say something like "to illustrate one characteristic of effective leaders." Regardless of how much (or how little) you know about leadership or the Lincoln administration, strategic reading will get you the LSAT point.

As you learned in Chapter 13, there are six types of Keywords you'll want to identify and use as you are reading LSAT passages. In the chart that follows, the categories are listed roughly in order of importance.

LSAT STRATEGY

Strategic Reading Keywords

· **Emphasis/Opinion**—words that signal that the author finds a detail noteworthy or has a positive or negative opinion about it or, indeed, any subjective or evaluative language on the author's part (e.g., *especially, crucial, unfortunately, disappointing, I suggest, it seems likely*)

· **Contrast**—words indicating that the author thinks two details or ideas are incompatible or illustrate conflicting points (e.g., *but, yet, despite, on the other hand*)

· **Logic**—words that indicate an argument, either the author's or someone else's (e.g., *thus, therefore, because*)

· **Illustration**—words indicating an example offered to clarify or support another point (e.g., *for example, this shows, to illustrate*)

· **Sequence/Chronology**—words showing an order to certain steps in a process or to developments over time (e.g., *traditionally, in the past, recently, today, first, second, finally, earlier, since*)

· **Continuation**—words indicating that a subsequent example or detail supports the same point or illustrates the same idea (e.g., *moreover, in addition, and, also, further*)

As you start to recognize Keywords as a part of your strategic reading approach, concentrate first on Emphasis/ Opinion and Contrast signals. You'll see that they are most often associated with LSAT questions because they most directly reveal the author's point of view and purpose in including a detail in the passage. Once you're comfortable recognizing those categories, move on to Logic (these should be familiar to you from working with Logical Reasoning questions) and Illustration. Finally, add the Sequence/Chronology and Continuation signals to your repertoire. You'll find that you understand LSAT passages more quickly and are able to stay focused on the most important aspects of the passages as you read.

As you review the LSAT experts' analyses on the passages that follow, pay attention to where the experts noted Keywords and used them to understand the passages.

Why Take Margin Notes?

LSAT passages are around 450–500 words long, and while they stay focused on a single Topic and Scope, they abound in details and often reflect two or more points of view. Labeling the key points in the margin next to the passage makes it much easier for you to target your research for individual questions. Unlike some pre-college tests, the order of LSAT Reading Comprehension questions doesn't necessarily correspond to the order of the passage. Question 2 might take you to the third paragraph, question 3 might point back to the first paragraph, and question 4 might ask for an answer about the passage as a whole. Margin notes help you navigate the passage quickly to find the text relevant to a specific question.

No two test takers' margin notes will be identical. Even two high-scoring LSAT experts who routinely ace the Reading Comprehension section will not jot down exactly the same words or phrases. So, don't construct the unrealistic idea of a "perfect Roadmap" in your mind. The experts' notes will have some things in common, however.

Take another look at the work of one expert on the opening paragraph of the passage about pre-World War I European painters.

       For some years before the outbreak of World War I, a number of painters in different European countries developed works of art that some have described as prophetic: paintings that by challenging
(5) viewers' habitual ways of perceiving the world of the present are thus said to anticipate a future world that would be very different. The artistic styles that they brought into being varied widely, but all these styles had in common a very important break with traditions
(10) of representational art that stretched back to the Renaissance.

Pre WW I Eu. painters

some—prophetic

Au.—broke with art trad.

PrepTest29 Sec2 Qs 1–7

Notice that the expert has accounted for both points of view here: those of the critics—just referred to as "some" at this point in the passage—and of the author. LSAT experts are always cognizant of multiple points of view within a passage, and they know that the testmaker will reward them for keeping track of who thinks what.

At times, you may have as little as one note per paragraph. Something like "Prof. Brown's hypothesis" or "steps in the process" may suffice if the scope of a paragraph is limited and its organization clear. When the author uses a single paragraph to portray two or more ideas, examples, or theories, however, multiple notes are in order. Take a look at how an LSAT expert Roadmapped a paragraph in which the author evaluates a scientific hypothesis:

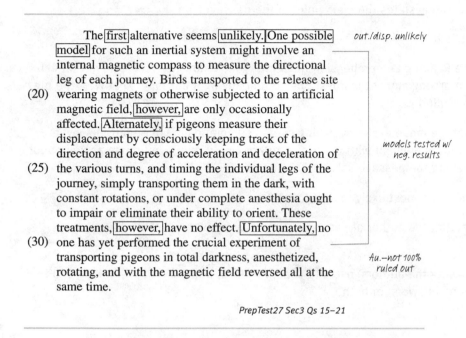

PrepTest27 Sec3 Qs 15–21

That's a dense paragraph outlining the reasons the author is skeptical about a proposed scientific explanation. It presents two possible models along with details about experiments performed to test them. And, for most LSAT test takers, none of this subject matter is at all familiar. Still, the LSAT expert has left herself a very navigable map. She has clearly noted the author's opinions, and in conjunction with the keywords circled in the passage, jotted down notes sufficient to locate the two models and their experiments should a question ask about them. You'll see this passage later in the chapter. As you examine more expert Roadmaps, take the time to study their margin notes and reflect on why successful test takers note certain details.

Why Summarize the Author's Topic, Scope, Purpose, and Main Idea?

The answer here isn't much different than it has been for the other features of the Roadmap. We summarize the big picture of the passage because the LSAT asks questions that reward you for having these summaries in mind. Global questions ask for the Purpose or Main Idea directly:

> Which one of the following most accurately states the main point of the passage?

> The primary purpose of the passage is to

In fact, as you'll see when we discuss the Reading Comprehension question types below, we recommend that you answer a passage's Global questions first among any of the questions accompanying a passage. That way, the big picture of the passage is still fresh in your mind.

Global questions aren't the only ones that are made easier by having overall summaries in your mind, however. Open-ended Inference questions asking for a statement with which the author would agree and those asking about the author's attitude also benefit from having the passage succinctly summarized:

> It can be inferred that the author would be most likely to agree that

> The passages most strongly suggest that the author of Passage B would agree with which of the following statements in Passage A?

Both of those are questions in which knowing the authors' overall Scope, Purpose, and Main Idea will help you to identify the correct answer, eliminate wrong answers, or both.

Whenever you see an LSAT expert's physical Roadmap (circled Keywords and margin notes), you'll also have a chance to consider his "mental Roadmap" (the big-picture summaries) as you review his analysis of the passage. Don't gloss over the way in which the LSAT expert paraphrases and condenses the author's points and perspective. Strong paraphrasing is perhaps the most important indicator of active, strategic reading.

LSAT STRATEGY

Reading Comprehension—the "big picture"

- **Topic**—the overall subject of the passage
- **Scope**—the particular aspect of the Topic that the author is focusing on
- **Purpose**—the author's reason for writing the passage (express this as a verb—e.g., *to refute, to outline, to evaluate, to critique*)
- **Main Idea**—the author's conclusion or overall takeaway; if you combine the author's Purpose and Scope, you'll usually have a good sense of the Main Idea.

Summary: Step 1—Read the Passage Strategically

Now, think back to the LSAT expert's answer to the question about how she starts out in Reading Comprehension: "I prepare myself to answer all of the passage's questions." Step 1 is a complex process, but each of its elements has a clear objective: Highlight the parts of the passage that will help get correct answers. The Roadmap an expert produces (both on the test booklet page and in her mind) is a tool for answering the questions. Keep that as your primary objective, and you'll improve your strategic reading skills and your Reading Comprehension score.

LSAT Reading Comprehension Passage Types

Before turning to examples and practice with passages, take a few minutes to learn about the common passage structures you'll see in LSAT Reading Comprehension. There are two ways to categorize LSAT Reading Comprehension passages: by subject matter and by passage structure.

Subject Matter

Every LSAT Reading Comprehension section contains four passages, and it's true that nearly every section has one passage each in the areas of natural science, social science, humanities, and law. Most future law students come from undergraduate backgrounds in the social sciences or the humanities, so there may be an instinctive preference for passages on topics from these areas and a concomitant distrust of one's ability in natural science passages dealing with physics, chemistry, or biology. However, empirical data show that there is little, if any, correlation between subject matter areas and difficulty levels. So, if you encounter a passage and have a subjective preference for the topic, that's fine, but don't make subject matter more important than it is. Learn to read all Reading Comprehension passages strategically, and you'll be at a decided advantage over much of your competition on the exam.

Passage Structures

For you as a test taker, organizing Reading Comprehension passages by their structures may be a much more meaningful taxonomy. The passage structure offers you a clue to the author's purpose in writing the passage, and that in turn gives you a start in creating a helpful Roadmap. There are four structures you should recognize, listed here from most common to least.

READING COMPREHENSION PASSAGE TYPES

- **Theory/Perspective**—The passage focuses on a thinker's theory or perspective on some part of the Topic; typically (though not always), the author disagrees and critiques the opponent's perspective or defends his own.

- **Event/Phenomenon**—The passage focuses on an event, a breakthrough development, or a problem that has arisen; when a solution to the problem is proposed, the author most often agrees with the solution (and that represents the passage's Main Idea).

- **Biography**—The passage discusses something about a notable person; the aspect of the person's life emphasized by the author reflects the Scope of the passage.

- **Debate**—The passage outlines two opposing positions (neither of which is the author's) on some aspect of the Topic; the author may side with one of the positions, may remain neutral, or may critique both. (This structure has been rare on recent LSATs.)

In this chapter, you'll see examples of each of the first three structures. The passages you work on in Chapter 15 and in the full-length tests offer additional examples. Many years ago, Debate passages were much more common than they have been on tests since around 2008. This may be because it was in 2007 that the testmaker introduced the paired Comparative Reading passages that now accompany one of the four question sets on LSAT exams. At any rate, if you use older materials and tests during your LSAT preparation, be aware that you may overestimate the likelihood of encountering this passage structure.

Step 1 in Action: Strategic Reading Examples and Practice

In this section, you'll see three Reading Comprehension passages. In each one, you'll have a chance to practice Step 1 of the Reading Comprehension Method; that is, you'll read the passage strategically and create a Roadmap. On the test, you'll take 3–4 minutes for this step, but don't worry if you take a little longer at this point. It's more important to practice the strategic reading skills and to get comfortable with this new and different way of approaching a piece of text. Along the way, we'll give you clues about how to approach passages with different structures. Additionally, you'll see a note about Comparative Reading when you have the opportunity to try out a set of paired passages (something you'll do just once in a full Reading Comprehension section).

Theory/Perspective Passages

Passages with this structure account for over half of all passages on recent LSATs, and that means they account for over half of the points you can get from the Reading Comprehension section. As previously noted, Theory/ Perspective passages outline an opinion of someone other than the author on some aspect of the passage's Topic. Once you identify the presence of another opinion, pay attention to the author's response. Does he agree or disagree? Why? What arguments and evidence does the author or his opponent offer? Use margin notes to keep track of where you hear the differing opinions in the passage. Summarize the author's Purpose (most likely, to critique his opponents' position or defend his own) and Main Idea ("the opposing view is faulty because . . . " or "my view prevails because . . . ").

Perhaps, as you were reading that, it occurred to you that the passage from Chapter 13 on the pre-World War I European painters is a Theory/Perspective passage. There, the author told you about the opinion of certain critics, those who believe that the painters were interesting because they seemed to predict the political and social future of Europe. The author of the passage disagreed with that perspective, and argued that the painters were noteworthy for their interest in aesthetic and technical innovations, and should not be considered "prophets" of politics and society.

Keep that passage in mind as you practice a new Theory/Perspective passage on the following pages.

Practice

Read and Roadmap the following passage. As you read, circle or underline Keywords within the passage, and record margin notes highlighting the key opinions or main points of each paragraph. We've also left space for you to add additional analysis, or to record your thoughts paragraph by paragraph. The LSAT expert's Roadmap and analysis begins on the following pages.

LSAT Passage	My Analysis
Personal names are generally regarded by European thinkers in two major ways, both of which deny that names have any significant semantic content. In philosophy and linguistics, John Stuart Mill's (5) formulation that "proper names are meaningless marks set upon…persons to distinguish them from one another" retains currency; in anthropology, Claude Lévi-Strauss's characterization of names as being primarily instruments of social classification has been (10) very influential. Consequently, interpretation of personal names in societies were names have other functions and meanings has been neglected. Among the Hopi of the southwestern United States, names often refer to historical or ritual events in order both to place (15) individuals within society and to confer an identity upon them. Furthermore, the images used to evoke these events suggest that Hopi names can be seen as a type of poetic composition.	**Step 1:**
Throughout life, Hopis receive several names in a (20) sequence of ritual initiations. Birth, entry into one of the ritual societies during childhood, and puberty are among the name-giving occasions. Names are conferred by an adult member of a clan other than the child's clan, and names refer to that name giver's clan, (25) sometimes combining characteristics of the clan's totem animal with the child's characteristics. Thus, a name might translate to something as simple as "little rabbit," which reflects both the child's size and the representative animal.	

LSAT Passage	My Analysis

(30)   More often, though, the name giver has in mind a specific event that is not apparent in a name's literal translation. One Lizard clan member from the village of Oraibi is named Lomayayva, "beautifully ascended." This translation, however, tells nothing

(35)   about either the event referred to—who or what ascended—or the name giver's clan. The name giver in this case is from Badger clan. Badger clan is responsible for an annual ceremony featuring a procession in which masked representations of spirits

(40)   climb the mesa on which Oraibi sits. Combining the name giver's clan association with the receiver's home village, "beautifully ascended" refers to the splendid colors and movements of the procession up the mesa. The condensed image this name evokes—a typical

(45)   feature of Hopi personal names—displays the same quality of Western Apache place names that led one commentator to call them "tiny imagist poems."

    Hopi personal names do several things simultaneously. They indicate social relationships—but

(50)   only indirectly—and they individuate persons. Equally important, though, is their poetic quality; in a sense they can be understood as oral texts that produce aesthetic delight. This view of Hopi names is thus opposed not only to Mill's claim that personal names

(55)   are without inherent meaning but also to Lévi-Strauss's purely functional characterization. Interpreters must understand Hopi clan structures and linguistic practices in order to discern the beauty and significance of Hopi names.

PrepTest27 Sec 3 Qs 8–14

Expert Analysis

Now, compare your Roadmap to that of an LSAT expert. Look for places in which you missed an important Keyword or mischaracterized a point in the passage. Determine whether your big-picture summaries were similar to those of the LSAT expert as well.

LSAT Passage		Analysis
Personal names are generally regarded by European thinkers in two major ways, both of which deny that names have any significant semantic content. In philosophy and linguistics, John Stuart Mill's (5) formulation that "proper names are meaningless marks set upon…persons to distinguish them from one another" retains currency; in anthropology, Claude Lévi-Strauss's characterization of names as being primarily instruments of social classification has been (10) very influential. Consequently, interpretation of personal names in societies were names have other functions and meanings has been neglected. Among the Hopi of the southwestern United States, names often refer to historical or ritual events in order both to place (15) individuals within society and to confer an identity upon them. Furthermore, the images used to evoke these events suggest that Hopi names can be seen as a type of poetic composition.	*Euro view of names* *phil/ling–marks* *anth–soc classif'n* *West overlooks other function*	**Step 1:** The first paragraph lays out the entire Big Picture for this passage. The **Topic** is the scholarship of personal names. The **Scope** will focus on Hopi names. The author's **Purpose/Main Idea** is to show that Hopi names illustrate the shortcomings of the two major European theories about personal names. The paragraph starts with the two theories. Mill (philosophy/linguistics) says names are arbitrary; we just use them to keep people separate. Lévi-Strauss (anthropology) says names are used for social classification. The author says Hopi names are different in two ways: 1) They go beyond mere individual identity by being associated with rituals or events, and 2) they use images and so, are poetic. We can anticipate seeing those differences explained in the next two paragraphs.
Throughout life, <Hopis receive several names in a (20) sequence of ritual initiations.> Birth, entry into one of the ritual societies during childhood, and puberty are among the name-giving occasions. Names are conferred by an adult member of a clan other than the child's clan, and names refer to that name giver's clan, (25) sometimes combining characteristics of the clan's totem animal with the child's characteristics. Thus, a name might translate to something as simple as "little rabbit," which reflects both the child's size and the representative animal.	*How Hopi get names Rites* *represents name given* *clan and child's char.*	As expected, this paragraph outlines how the Hopi confer names through rituals. Their names refer to both a person's clan, and to his or her individual characteristics or events from the person's life. Thus, Hopi names contain "meaning" beyond merely identifying a person.

LSAT Passage		Analysis
(30)	[More often, though,] the name giver has in mind a specific event that is not apparent in a name's literal translation. One Lizard clan member from the village of Oraibi is named Lomayayva, "beautifully ascended." This translation, [however,] tells nothing	*more common– nonspecific*	This paragraph goes into more detail about what the author considers Hopi names' second distinguishing characteristic: They are poetic. The Hopi often give names that are not literal. The author cites a detailed example to illustrate this, and concludes that (like Apache place names) Hopi names may be considered "tiny imagist poems."
(35)	about either the event referred to—who or what ascended—or the name giver's clan. The name giver in this case is from Badger clan. Badger clan is responsible for an annual ceremony featuring a procession in which masked representations of spirits		
(40)	climb the mesa on which Oraibi sits. Combining the name giver's clan association with the receiver's home village, "beautifully ascended" refers to the splendid colors and movements of the procession up the mesa. The condensed image this name evokes—a [typical]	*Ex*	
(45)	[feature] of Hopi personal names—displays the same quality of Western Apache place names that led one commentator to call them "tiny imagist poems."	*makes names poetic* *Hopi name funtions*	

	Hopi personal names do several things simultaneously. They indicate social relationships—[but]		Here, the author reiterates his thesis (or Main Idea) and his evidence for it. Because they 1) indirectly indicate social relationships and 2) have poetical qualities, Hopi names do not fit into Mill's "names are just arbitrary" theory or into Lévi-Strauss's functional "social classification" theory.
(50)	only indirectly—and they individuate persons. [Equally] important, though, is their poetic quality; in a sense they can be understood as oral texts that produce aesthetic delight. This view of Hopi names is [thus] opposed [not only] to Mill's claim that personal names	*uses counter to Euro views*	
(55)	are without inherent meaning [but also] to Lévi-Strauss's purely functional characterization. Interpreters must understand Hopi clan structures and linguistic practices in order to discern the beauty and significance of Hopi names.		

PrepTest27 Sec 3 Qs 8–14

The next time you see a Theory/Perspective structure, the subject matter may be drawn from natural science or law rather than social science (as it was here), or humanities (as it was with the pre-World War I painters). You could also find that the author's response to the theory or perspective surfaces later in the passage. That said, you'll encounter similar patterns that will help you stay focused on the two points of view and highlight the pieces of the passage that will be tested in the question set.

You'll see the questions associated with this passage a little later in the chapter. For now, continue to practice Roadmapping, this time on a passage with a different structure.

Event/Phenomenon Passages

On recent tests, the Event/Phenomenon structure has appeared in a little over 25 percent of the passages. While not as common as the Theory/Perspective structure, this is still significant. Here, the author will inform you about a recent event, a change that has occurred over time, or a problem or dilemma. Always ask whether the author presents an interpretation of the event or change or presents a solution to the problem (identified as her own solution or someone else's proposal). These passages are often neutral and detail heavy—note names, dates, or places as you see them, but don't lose sight of the big picture by getting too caught up in the small stuff.

Before practicing the next passage (or more properly, passages), it's important that we take a moment to discuss Comparative Reading because that's the format you're about to see.

LSAT STRATEGY

A Note on Comparative Reading

One time per section, the LSAT presents a Comparative Reading selection. Instead of seeing a single 450- to 500-word passage, you'll see two shorter passages labeled Passage A and Passage B. The two passages always share a common Topic and sometimes a common Scope. The passages almost always differ, however, in terms of Purpose and Main Idea. That doesn't mean that the two authors must oppose each other. Indeed, it's often not clear that either passage was written in response to (or even with knowledge of) the other. It may be that Passage A presents an argument against a theory while Passage B presents a model for testing the validity of such theories. It could be that Passage A identifies a problem confronting biologists and Passage B offers a solution to the problem. Of course, a good, old-fashioned debate could take place as well, with Passage A arguing that a proposed law will be good for the country and Passage B contending that it will be bad.

Regardless of how the passages are related, your approach to Comparative Reading should differ little from your approach to Reading Comprehension passages in general. You'll still begin by reading strategically and Roadmapping the passages. The primary difference in preparing yourself to answer the questions comes right after you finish your Roadmaps but before you tackle the question set. Because almost all of the questions associated with these paired passages ask you to compare the passages in some way, you need to take a moment to briefly catalog the similarities and differences between Passage A and Passage B. Here are a handful of questions to ask and answer before diving into the questions:

- Are the passages different in Scope, Purpose, or Main Idea? The answer will generally be yes; make sure to characterize the differences.
- Do the passages share common details, examples, or evidence? The answer is often yes, but beware, the two authors may reach very different conclusions or make different recommendations based on the same underlying facts.
- If either author makes a contention or recommendation, how would the other author respond to it? The test is fond of Inference questions that ask whether one author would agree or disagree with something the other said.
- Do the two passages share a common principle? If yes, paraphrase the principle. If no, characterize how the authors approach the Topic differently.

Comparing and contrasting the two passages should only take a few seconds, but it will leave you much better prepared to research and answer the questions that follow.

Practice

With that in mind, read and Roadmap the following Comparative Reading passages. We've left space for you to add additional analysis or record your thoughts paragraph by paragraph, but make sure you are marking Keywords within the passage itself and recording margin notes that would fit into the limited space next to the passage in the test booklet. After you finish reading and Roadmapping the passages individually, take a minute or two to record what you find similar and different about the two passages. Then check your work against the LSAT expert's analysis that follows.

LSAT Passage	My Analysis
Passage A is from a source published in 2004 and passage B is from a source published in 2007.	**Step 1:**

Passage A

Millions of people worldwide play multiplayer online games. They each pick, say, a medieval character to play, such as a warrior. Then they might band together in quests to slay magical beasts; their
(5) avatars appear as tiny characters striding across a Tolkienesque land.

The economist Edward Castronova noticed something curious about the game he played: it had its own economy, a bustling trade in virtual goods.
(10) Players generate goods as they play, often by killing creatures for their treasure and trading it. The longer they play, the wealthier they get.

Things got even more interesting when Castronova learned about the "player auctions." Players would
(15) sometimes tire of the game and decide to sell off their virtual possessions at online auction sites.

As Castronova stared at the auction listings, he recognized with a shock what he was looking at. It was a form of currency trading! Each item had a value
(20) in the virtual currency traded in the game; when it was sold on the auction site, someone was paying cold hard cash for it. That meant that the virtual currency was worth something in real currency. Moreover, since players were killing monsters or skinning animals to
(25) sell their pelts, they were, in effect, creating wealth.

Passage B

Most multiplayer online games prohibit real-world trade in virtual items, but some actually encourage it, for example, by granting participants intellectual property rights in their creations.

(30) Although it seems intuitively the case that someone who accepts real money for the transfer of a virtual item should be taxed, what about the player who only accumulates items or virtual currency within a virtual world? Is "loot" acquired in a game taxable,
(35) as a prize or award is? And is the profit in a purely in-game trade or sale for virtual currency taxable? These are important questions, given the tax revenues at stake, and there is pressure on governments to answer them, given that the economies of some virtual
(40) worlds are comparable to those of small countries.

LSAT Passage	My Analysis
Most people's intuition probably would be that accumulation of assets within a game should not be taxed even though income tax applies even to noncash accessions to wealth. This article will argue that (45) income tax law and policy support that result. Loot acquisitions in game worlds should not be treated as taxable prizes and awards, but rather should be treated like other property that requires effort to obtain, such as fish pulled from the ocean, which is taxed only (50) upon sale. Moreover, in-game trades of virtual items should not be treated as taxable barter.	
By contrast, tax doctrine and policy counsel taxation of the sale of virtual items for real currency, and, in games that are intentionally commodified, (55) even of in-world sales for virtual currency, regardless of whether the participant cashes out. This approach would leave entertainment value untaxed without creating a tax shelter for virtual commerce.	

PrepTest71 Sec4 Qs 7–13

Compare/Contrast the Passages

Expert Analysis

Now, compare your Roadmap to that of an LSAT expert. Look for places in which you missed an important Keyword or mischaracterized a point in the passage. Compare your big-picture summaries to those of the LSAT expert and review her notes on how these paired passages were similar and how they were different.

LSAT Passage		Analysis
Passage A is from a source published in 2004 and passage B is from a source published in 2007.		
Passage A Millions of people worldwide play multiplayer online games. They each pick, say, a medieval character to play, such as a warrior. Then they might band together in quests to slay magical beasts; their (5) avatars appear as tiny characters striding across a Tolkienesque land.	*Multiplayer online games popular*	**Step 1:** The short first paragraph appears to be background information: multiplayer role-playing games are popular.
The economist Edward Castronova noticed something curious about the game he played: it had its own economy, a bustling trade in virtual goods. (10) Players generate goods as they play, often by killing creatures for their treasure and trading it. The longer they play, the wealthier they get.	*Castronova discovers economy within game*	Here, the **Topic** starts to take shape: An economist noticed that players in these games collect virtual goods.
Things got even more interesting when Castronova learned about the "player auctions." Players would (15) sometimes tire of the game and decide to sell off their virtual possessions at online auction sites.	*Further discovery: auctions*	This paragraph narrows the **Scope** of the passage: Virtual goods are auctioned/sold online.
As Castronova stared at the auction listings, he recognized with a shock what he was looking at. It was a form of currency trading! Each item had a value (20) in the virtual currency traded in the game; when it was sold on the auction site, someone was paying cold hard cash for it. That meant that the virtual currency was worth something in real currency. Moreover, since players were killing monsters or skinning animals to (25) sell their pelts, they were, in effect, creating wealth.	*Auctions = currency trading* *Virtual converted to real*	And, here in the final paragraph, we get the **Purpose** and **Main Idea**—to reveal an economist's startling discovery: Virtual items have value in "real world" currency; thus, the "work" players are doing in the game creates wealth.
Passage B Most multiplayer online games prohibit real-world trade in virtual items, but some actually encourage it, for example, by granting participants intellectual property rights in their creations.	*Some games encourage real trade*	From the outset, this passage addresses the same **Topic** and **Scope** as Passage A: the trade/sale of virtual items from online games. It adds a fact not contained in Passage A: some games forbid, while others encourage, these sales.
(30) Although it seems intuitively the case that someone who accepts real money for the transfer of a virtual item should be taxed, what about the player who only accumulates items or virtual currency within a virtual world? Is "loot" acquired in a game taxable, (35) as a prize or award is? And is the profit in a purely in-game trade or sale for virtual currency taxable? These are important questions, given the tax revenues at stake, and there is pressure on governments to answer them, given that the economies of some virtual (40) worlds are comparable to those of small countries.	*Should virtual items be taxed? Qs raised* *Govts pressed to answer*	The author of Passage B has a distinct **Purpose**: to raise "important questions" about the taxability of commerce in virtual items. Note the three distinct questions here.

LSAT Passage		Analysis
Most people's intuition probably would be that accumulation of assets within a game should not be taxed even though income tax applies even to noncash accessions to wealth. This article will argue that (45) income tax law and policy support that result. Loot acquisitions in game worlds should not be treated as taxable prizes and awards, but rather should be treated like other property that requires effort to obtain, such as fish pulled from the ocean, which is taxed only (50) upon sale. Moreover, in-game trades of virtual items should not be treated as taxable barter.	*Auth: don't tax items that stay in virtual world*	The author starts to formulate his **Main Idea** (almost in the style of a thesis statement): In-game trade of virtual items should not be taxable. The author draws an analogy: Acquiring virtual items in a game is like catching fish; we don't tax fish until they are sold.
By contrast, tax doctrine and policy counsel taxation of the sale of virtual items for real currency, and, in games that are intentionally commodified, (55) even of in-world sales for virtual currency, regardless of whether the participant cashes out. This approach would leave entertainment value untaxed without creating a tax shelter for virtual commerce. *PrepTest71 Sec4 Qs 7–13*	*Auth: tax when virtual items sold for real $*	In the final paragraph, however, the author of Passage B expands on his **Main Idea**: When virtual items are sold for "real world" currency, or when they are commodified within a game, they should be taxable. The author's main support for his argument is that having this system allows the games to remain fun but not to become virtual "tax shelters."

Compare/Contrast the Passages

The relationship between the two passages is pretty simple: Passage A announces the discovery of a new economic phenomenon, while Passage B explores practical legal questions raised by that phenomenon.

Passage A is neutral; its author describes the economist's "shock" at discovering virtual goods with real-world value, but neither the author nor the economist offers any judgment on the discovery. Passage B's author, on the other hand, makes an argument. The argument's conclusion is a recommendation about when trade in virtual items should and should not be taxed.

Passage A contains facts (e.g., how virtual items are auctioned and traded) not found in Passage B. Passage B reveals differences among games (some encourage trading while others forbid it) not discussed in Passage A. The economist in Passage A takes note of in-game activities ("skinning animals to sell their pelts" (lines 24–25)), while the author of Passage B compares such activities to "real-world" work ("[pulling] fish . . . from the ocean" (lines 48–49)).

Taken together, these passages illustrate Event/Phenomenon passages very well. Even in a regular, single passage, this would be a common Event/Phenomenon structure: A discovery is noted, a problem arises from it, and the author proposes a solution.

You'll see the questions for these paired passages a little later in the chapter. Look forward to applying your analysis of the similarities and differences between the two short passages on several questions. Now, let's return to a standard-length LSAT passage to look at the third and last of the passage structures we'll practice with.

Debate Passages

This passage structure is less common than the previous two, constituting somewhere around 10 percent of recent passages. You're unlikely to see more than one of these in a Reading Comprehension section, and on some tests, they may be absent altogether. Make sure to distinguish Debate passages from Theory/Perspective passages that may focus on the point of view of a particular individual. In Debate passages, there will be two (or more) views distinct from that of the author. The author may remain neutral, simply explaining the debate. He may clearly choose one side or the other. Or, perhaps most often, he will declare one side more promising or more likely, but conclude that the debate is not yet settled.

Practice

With that in mind, read and Roadmap the following passage. We've left space for you to add additional analysis or record your thoughts paragraph by paragraph, but make sure you are marking Keywords within the passage itself and recording margin notes that would fit into the limited space next to the passage in the test booklet. When you're finished, compare your work to that of the LSAT expert on the following pages.

LSAT Passage	My Analysis
Homing pigeons can be taken from their lofts and transported hundreds of kilometers in covered cages to unfamiliar sites and yet, when released, be able to choose fairly accurate homeward bearings within a (5) minute and fly home. Aside from reading the minds of the experimenters (a possibility that has not escaped investigation), there are two basic explanations for the remarkable ability of pigeons to "home": the birds might keep track of their outward displacement (the (10) system of many short-range species such as honeybees); or they might have some sense, known as a "map sense," that would permit them to construct an internal image of their environment and then "place" themselves with respect to home on some internalized (15) coordinate system.	Step 1:
The first alternative seems unlikely. One possible model for such an inertial system might involve an internal magnetic compass to measure the directional leg of each journey. Birds transported to the release site (20) wearing magnets or otherwise subjected to an artificial magnetic field, however, are only occasionally affected. Alternately, if pigeons measure their displacement by consciously keeping track of the direction and degree of acceleration and deceleration of (25) the various turns, and timing the individual legs of the journey, simply transporting them in the dark, with constant rotations, or under complete anesthesia ought to impair or eliminate their ability to orient. These treatments, however, have no effect. Unfortunately, no (30) one has yet performed the crucial experiment of transporting pigeons in total darkness, anesthetized, rotating, and with the magnetic field reversed all at the same time.	

LSAT Passage	**My Analysis**

(35)   The other alternative, that pigeons have a "map sense," seems more promising, yet the nature of this sense remains mysterious. Papi has posited that the map sense is olfactory: that birds come to associate odors borne on the wind with the direction in which the wind is blowing, and so slowly build up an olfactory

(40) map of their surroundings. When transported to the release site, then, they only have to sniff the air en route and/or at the site to know the direction of home. Papi conducted a series of experiments showing that pigeons whose nostrils have been plugged are poorly

(45) oriented at release and home slowly.

     One problem with the hypothesis is that Schmidt-Koenig and Phillips failed to detect any ability in pigeons to distinguish natural air (presumably laden with olfactory map information) from pure, filtered air.

(50) Papi's experimental results, moreover, admit of simpler, nonolfactory explanations. It seems likely that the behavior of nostril-plugged birds results from the distracting and traumatic nature of the experiment. When nasal tubes are used to bypass the olfactory

(55) chamber but allow for comfortable breathing, no disorientation is evident. Likewise, when the olfactory epithelium is sprayed with anesthetic to block smell-detection but not breathing, orientation is normal.

PrepTest27 Sec3 Qs 15–21

Expert Analysis

Now, compare your Roadmap to that of an LSAT expert. Look for places in which you missed an important Keyword or mischaracterized a point in the passage. Determine whether your big-picture summaries were similar to those of the LSAT expert as well.

LSAT Passage	Analysis
Homing pigeons can be taken from their lofts and transported hundreds of kilometers in covered cages to unfamiliar sites and yet, when released, be able to choose fairly accurate homeward bearings within a (5) minute and fly home. Aside from reading the minds of the experimenters (a possibility that has not escaped investigation), there are two basic explanations for the remarkable ability of pigeons to "home": the birds might keep track of their outward displacement (the (10) system of many short-range species such as honeybees); or they might have some sense, known as a "map sense," that would permit them to construct an internal image of their environment and then "place" themselves with respect to home on some internalized (15) coordinate system. *Homing pigeons How do they "home"?* *Two expl's: out./disp.* *map sense*	**Step 1:** The **Topic**—homing pigeons—and the **Scope**—the question of how they home—are clear from the first paragraph. After dismissing a rather hare-brained suggestion (maybe they read human minds!), the author presents two reasonable hypotheses: 1) outward displacement (which other species, e.g., honeybees, use), and 2) "map sense." We can anticipate that the next two paragraphs will evaluate these hypotheses in more detail.
The first alternative seems unlikely. One possible model for such an inertial system might involve an internal magnetic compass to measure the directional leg of each journey. Birds transported to the release site (20) wearing magnets or otherwise subjected to an artificial magnetic field, however, are only occasionally affected. Alternately, if pigeons measure their displacement by consciously keeping track of the direction and degree of acceleration and deceleration of (25) the various turns, and timing the individual legs of the journey, simply transporting them in the dark, with constant rotations, or under complete anesthesia ought to impair or eliminate their ability to orient. These treatments, however, have no effect. Unfortunately, no (30) one has yet performed the crucial experiment of transporting pigeons in total darkness, anesthetized, rotating, and with the magnetic field reversed all at the same time. *out./disp. unlikely* *models tested w/ neg. results* *Au.–not 100% ruled out*	The author finds outward displacement "unlikely," but not 100 percent ruled out. She cites two possible models for outward displacement: Homing pigeons may have "an internal magnetic compass" (lines 16–19), or they may keep track of turns and acceleration (lines 22–28). When tested, neither model was supported by the findings. "Unfortunately," says the author, no one has done the complete rule-out experiment of impairing, simultaneously, all of the pigeons' potential modes for tracking outward displacement. That's why the author won't say the hypothesis is completely disproven. Because the author thinks outward displacement "unlikely," she will give her evaluation of the "map sense" in the next paragraph.

LSAT Passage	**Analysis**

<table>
<tr>
<td>

(35)   The other alternative, that pigeons have a "map sense," seems more promising, yet the nature of this sense remains mysterious. Papi has posited that the map sense is olfactory: that birds come to associate odors borne on the wind with the direction in which the wind is blowing, and so slowly build up an olfactory

(40) map of their surroundings. When transported to the release site, then, they only have to sniff the air en route and/or at the site to know the direction of home. Papi conducted a series of experiments showing that pigeons whose nostrils have been plugged are poorly

(45) oriented at release and home slowly.

map sense—promising but still questions

Papi hypo: smell map

</td>
<td>

As expected, here's the author's evaluation of pigeons' "map sense." This hypothesis she finds "promising." Nonetheless, "map sense" "remains mysterious." So, our author doesn't think the map sense has been completely explained.

The rest of the paragraph details how a scientist named Papi tested an olfactory model for the map sense with some success.

</td>
</tr>
<tr>
<td>

(50)   One problem with the hypothesis is that Schmidt-Koenig and Phillips failed to detect any ability in pigeons to distinguish natural air (presumably laden with olfactory map information) from pure, filtered air. Papi's experimental results, moreover, admit of simpler, nonolfactory explanations. It seems likely that the behavior of nostril-plugged birds results from the distracting and traumatic nature of the experiment. When nasal tubes are used to bypass the olfactory

(55) chamber but allow for comfortable breathing, no disorientation is evident. Likewise, when the olfactory epithelium is sprayed with anesthetic to block smell-detection but not breathing, orientation is normal.

PrepTest27 Sec3 Qs 15-21

Problems with Papi

</td>
<td>

This paragraph outlines three criticisms of Papi's experiments (signaled by the keywords "[o]ne problem," "moreover," and "[l]ikewise"). The criticisms come from a pair of scientists: Schmidt-Koenig and Phillips. They tested pigeons using filtered air (no smells, in other words) and found no difference in their ability to home. They also suggested that Papi's experiments had traumatized the birds, and so performed two tests that blocked the pigeons' olfactory senses without injuring them. The results, again, undermined Papi's model.

There is no explicit thesis statement or conclusion sentence in this passage. The author's **Purpose**, as shown by Paragraphs 2–4 is to *evaluate* the two main hypotheses. Her **Main Point** is that pigeons probably home using a map sense (outward displacement is unlikely), but that we don't yet know what kind of map they use.

</td>
</tr>
</table>

Instead of viewing this as a natural science passage (and thus focusing on how much he doesn't know about the complex models and experiments), the LSAT expert identifies this as a classic Debate passage. Doing so demystifies the subject matter and makes it easier to understand the author's Purpose and the overall organization of the passage.

Keep the expert's summaries and margin notes in mind when we turn to the questions associated with this passage, which we'll do in the next section of this chapter.

Reflection

In all three of the examples you just looked at, the LSAT expert:

- Used Keywords to discern the structure of the passage and note the author's purpose for offering certain details and examples.
- Took down brief, accurate margin notes highlighting the points in the passage most likely to surface in the questions.
- Summarized the author's Topic, Scope, Purpose, and Main Idea while reading the passage.

Keep those examples in mind as you practice additional Reading Comprehension passages. For all of the passages included in this book, you'll find sample Roadmaps and complete discussions of the passages in addition to explanations of individual questions. In practice, don't hesitate to spend 3–4 minutes reading and Roadmapping a passage and then compare your work in Step 1 to that of the LSAT expert reflected in the explanations. After you review the strategic reading step, you'll feel much more confident going into the question set.

It is possible to practice the kind of strategic reading you'll do on the LSAT with almost anything you read, at least anything academic or nonfiction. Next time you're perusing a newspaper editorial, a well-written commentary piece, or an article in a science magazine, roadmap it. Try to imagine, or even write, the kinds of questions the LSAT would ask about the piece you've just finished. Look for places in which the author has used Contrast, Illustration, or Opinion Keywords in ways that would allow for the testmaker to ask an Inference or Logic Function question. Learning to read in a new way will not happen overnight, but if you start to read this way consistently, by Test Day, you'll be far ahead of the average test taker.

READING COMPREHENSION QUESTION STRATEGIES

The universal characteristic of LSAT Reading Comprehension questions is this: *they reward you for having read and understood the passage*. That may sound almost tautological—Reading Comprehension questions are obviously about whether I comprehended the reading?! Well, yes. But that obvious truth masks a subtler, more important one: Reading Comprehension questions do *not* reward what you (or anyone else) knew before reading the passage. The questions are always worded such that they must be answered from the text. We'll keep coming back to that truth, and we'll build the strategies for answering the questions based on the text throughout this section.

Reading Comprehension Question Types

The LSAT testmaker uses five main types of questions in the Reading Comprehension section. You'll learn to recognize them shortly. Moreover, depending on the wording of the question stem, many of those question types may contain clues that will allow you to target your research to specific portions of the text.

LEARNING OBJECTIVES

In this portion of the chapter, you'll learn to:

- Recognize Global questions.
- Recognize Inference questions.
- Recognize Detail questions.
- Recognize Logic Function questions.
- Recognize Logic Reasoning questions.
- Determine whether the question stem contains research clues.

Let's define and see examples of each Reading Comprehension question type. As we go through the question types, pay attention to the analysis that the LSAT expert does for Step 2—read the question stem and look for clues—of the Reading Comprehension Method.

Global Questions

Global questions ask about the passage as a whole. They are designed to test your comprehension of the author's Main Idea or Purpose. These questions lack research clues, naturally, as they take the entire passage into account. To predict the correct answer, use your summary of the Purpose or Main Idea. Nearly all passages contain one Global question, and it is usually (but not always) the first question in the set. Occasionally, you'll encounter a passage with two Global questions. In such cases, one is likely to be the first question in the set and the other at (or near) the end of the question set. Very rarely, you'll find a passage with no Global question accompanying it.

LSAT Question Stem		Analysis
Which one of the following most accurately expresses the main point of the passage?	→	**Step 2:** "[M]ain point"—a Global question. Use the Main Idea summary to predict the correct answer and evaluate the choices.
The primary purpose of the passage is to	→	**Step 2:** "[P]rimary purpose"—a Global question. Use the Purpose summary to predict the correct answer and evaluate the choices.

The language of Global question stems is fairly standardized. You may find small variations, but expect to see "main point" or "primary purpose" most often.

One rare variation on the Global question asks you to describe the organization of the passage. You actually saw an example of this type among the questions accompanying the pre-World War I European painters passage in Chapter 13.

LSAT Question Stem		Analysis
Which one of the following most accurately describes the organization of the passage?	→	**Step 2:** "[D]escribes the organization of the passage"—a Global question variant. Consult the Roadmap to outline the overall structure and use that to evaluate the choices.

This is the one type of Global question that benefits from research. Whereas the standard "main point" and "primary purpose" Global questions can be answered with your big-picture summaries, "organization" Global questions need you to match the correct answer to the flow of the passage. It's helpful with "organization" Global questions to consult the Roadmap before you evaluate the choices.

Inference Questions

Inference questions account for a little less than half of the points in Reading Comprehension. In a typical 27-question section, there will usually be anywhere from 10 to 12 Inference questions, although one recent test had 14. Inference questions are characterized by language in the stem telling you that the correct answer *is based on* or *follows from* the passage without necessarily being stated in the passage.

LSAT Question Stem		Analysis
Based on the passage, the author would be most likely to agree with which one of the following statements about unified field theory?	→	**Step 2:** "Based on the passage" and "most likely to agree"—an Inference question. "[U]nified field theory" is the research clue.
The passage suggests which one of the following about the behavior of migratory water fowl?	→	**Step 2:** "The passage suggests"—an Inference question. "[M]igratory water fowl" is the research clue.
Given the information in the passage, to which one of the following would radiocarbon dating techniques likely be most applicable?	→	**Step 2:** "Given the information in the passage" and "likely be . . . applicable"*—an Inference question. The correct answer follows from the passage. "[R]adiocarbon dating techniques" is the research clue.

*When a question stem asks you to apply something from the passage, treat it as an Inference question. The correct answer still follows from the information in the passage; it's just applied to a new or hypothetical context in the correct answer.

In each of those cases, the expert noted research clues in the question stem. She will be able to quickly check her Roadmap at those points and use the text to predict the correct answer. Other Inference questions are open-ended, and call for a different approach to evaluating the choices.

LSAT Question Stem		Analysis
It can be inferred that the author would be most likely to agree that	→	**Step 2:** "[I]nferred"—an Inference question. No research clues. Evaluate the choices using the Scope, Purpose, and Main Idea summaries *or* use the answer choices as research clues and check them against the text.
Which one of the following statements is most strongly supported by the passage?	→	**Step 2:** "[S]upported by the passage"—an Inference question. No research clues. Evaluate the choices using the Scope, Purpose, and Main Idea summaries *or* use the answer choices as research clues and check them against the text.

In those questions, no targeted research clue is present. When you see an Inference question of this type, quickly check the answer choices. If they all relate to the same portion of the passage, you can simply use them as research clues and test each one against the text. If they seem vague, broad, or scattered, start by checking the choices against your Scope, Purpose, and Main Idea summaries. Eliminate all those with which the author would not agree. That will either leave you with the one correct choice or will narrow down the number of choices you need to research.

One other variant on the Inference question is fairly common: the Author's Attitude question. A strong strategic reader, who has identified Emphasis/Opinion Keywords in the passage, can research these questions quickly.

LSAT Question Stem		Analysis
The author's attitude toward the use of DNA evidence in the appeals by convicted felons is most accurately described as	→	**Step 2:** "[A]uthor's attitude"—an Inference question about the author's attitude. "[T]he use of DNA evidence in the appeals by convicted felons" is the research clue. Look for Opinion Keywords that indicate the author's view.
The author's stance regarding monetarist economic theories can most accurately be described as one of	→	**Step 2:** "[A]uthor's stance"—an Inference question about the author's attitude. "[M]onetarist economic theories" is the research clue. Look for Opinion Keywords that indicate the author's view.

You may see other slight variations in the wording of Inference question stems, but don't let that throw you. The feature they all have in common is that the correct answer follows from the passage without being directly stated in it.

Detail Questions

Detail questions are less common than Inference questions. You'll typically see 4–5 per test, though not every passage will necessarily be accompanied by a Detail question. The identifying characteristic of the Detail question stem is that, in some way, it tells you that the correct answer will closely paraphrase something stated explicitly in the passage: "according to the passage" and "the passage states" are common phrasings of these questions.

LSAT Question Stem		Analysis
According to the passage, some critics have criticized Gilliam's films on the ground that	→	**Step 2:** "According to the passage"—a Detail question. "[C]ritics have criticized Gilliam's films on the ground that" is the research clue.
The passage states that a role of a municipality's comptroller in budget decisions by the city council is to	→	**Step 2:** "The passage states"—a Detail question. "[A] municipality's comptroller in budget decisions by the city council" is the research clue.
The author identifies which one of the following as a commonly held but false preconception?	→	**Step 2:** "[I]dentifies which one"—a Detail question. "[C]ommonly held but false preconception" is the research clue.

Almost all Detail questions contain research clues; after all, you're looking for a detail. Do not, however, think that questions containing line references are Detail questions. When the question stem points you to a particular line in the passage, it is usually asking for an Inference that can be drawn from what is said there, or it is a Logic Function question asking you *why* the author has included that particular detail.

Be ready to encounter 1–2 Detail EXCEPT questions. Not every test includes one of these, but if you should see one, treat it as the LSAT expert does in these examples.

LSAT Question Stem		Analysis
The passage does NOT provide evidence that Mead utilizes which one of the following techniques in one or more of her ethnographies?	→	**Step 2:** "NOT provide evidence"—a Detail EXCEPT question. Use the answer choices as research clues and eliminate the four stated in the passage.
The author attributes each of the following to the Federalists EXCEPT:	→	**Step 2:** "The author attributes each . . . EXCEPT"—a Detail EXCEPT question. Use the answer choices as research clues and eliminate the four stated in the passage.

Because all four wrong answers are included in the text, you can use the answer choices as research clues. Eliminate any answers that are stated. If, as you're checking the choices, you find a choice with which the author would clearly disagree or that falls completely outside the scope of the passage, you can choose it with confidence as the correct answer.

Logic Function Questions

Logic Function questions are less common than Detail questions. You'll usually see around three of these in a Reading Comprehension section. These questions will always include a research clue, and it's easy to see why. The question stem points you to a portion of the passage—a detail, a reference, or a paragraph—and asks you *why* the author included it or *how* it functions within the passage.

LSAT Question Stem	Analysis
The author of the passage mentions declining inner-city populations in the first paragraph most likely in order to →	**Step 2:** "[I]n order to"—a Logic Function question. The correct answer states *why* the author mentions declining inner-city populations. "[F]irst paragraph" is the research clue.
The author's discussion of Rimbaud's travels in the Mediterranean (lines 23–28) functions primarily to →	**Step 2:** "[F]unctions primarily to"—a Logic Function question. The correct answer states why the author discusses Rimbaud's Mediterranean travels. The line reference is the research clue.
Which one of the following best states the function of the third paragraph of the passage? →	**Step 2:** "[S]tates the function"—a Logic Function question. "[T]hird paragraph" is the research clue. This is almost like a mini Global question asking for the purpose of Paragraph 3 instead of the "primary purpose" of the entire passage.

Be careful on Logic Function questions to avoid answer choices that accurately reflect what the passage said about the detail or reference but do not explain *why* the author included it.

Logic Reasoning Questions

These questions are slightly more common than Logic Function questions. You'll likely see 3–4 per section. It's very unlikely that every passage will have a Logic Reasoning question in its question set. The distinguishing characteristic of Logic Reasoning questions in Reading Comprehension is that they mirror the task of a question type typically found in the Logical Reasoning section. Take a look at the LSAT expert's analyses of a couple of questions to see this illustrated.

LSAT Question Stem	Analysis
Which one of the following would, if true, most strengthen the claim made by the author in the last sentence of the passage (lines 51–55)? →	**Step 2:** "[I]f true, most strengthen"—a Logic Reasoning question mirroring a Strengthen question from the LR section. Research the passage around the line reference.
Which one of the following pairs of proposals is most closely analogous to the pair of studies discussed in the passage? →	**Step 2:** "[M]ost closely analogous"—a Logic Reasoning question mirroring a Parallel Reasoning question from the LR section. "[T]he pair of studies" is the research clue.

The most common Logical Reasoning question types mirrored by Reading Comprehension Logic Reasoning questions are Strengthen/Weaken, Parallel Reasoning, Method of Argument, and Principle (with the first two types in the list being far more common than the others). When you encounter one of these questions in the Reading Comprehension section, use the same approach you would in the Logical Reasoning section, treating the referenced portion of the passage as the question's stimulus.

A note about research clues. In her analyses of the question stems, the LSAT expert identified research clues whenever they were present. Knowing where to look in the passage for the text relevant to the correct answer will make you faster and more accurate throughout the question set. As you prepare to do more practice with Reading Comprehension question stems, learn to spot these five types of research clues.

LSAT STRATEGY

Reading Comprehension Research Clues

- **Line References**—research around the referenced detail; look for Keywords indicating why the referenced text has been included or how it's used.
- **Paragraph References**—consult your Roadmap to see the paragraph's scope and function.
- **Quoted Text** (often accompanied by a line reference)—check the context of the quoted term or phrase; ask what the author meant by it in the passage.
- **Proper Nouns**—check the context of the person, place, or thing; ask whether the author had a positive, negative, or neutral evaluation of it; ask why it was included in the passage.
- **Content Clues**—terms, concepts, or ideas highlighted in the passage, but not included as direct quotes in the question stem; these will almost always refer you to something the author emphasized or stated an opinion on.

You'll see those research clues in action when we turn to Steps 3 and 4 of the Reading Comprehension Method. For now, get a little practice with Step 2 using the questions that accompany the Hopi Personal Names passage.

Practice

For each of the following, identify the question type and state whether the question stem includes a research clue. You can check your work against the expert analysis on the following pages.

LSAT Question	My Analysis
1. Which one of the following statements most accurately summarizes the passage's main point?	**Step 2:**
2. The author most likely refers to Western Apache place names (line 46) in order to	**Step 2:**
3. Which one of the following statements describes an example of the function accorded to personal names under Lévi-Strauss's view?	**Step 2:**
4. The primary function of the second paragraph is to	**Step 2:**
5. Based on the passage, with which one of the following statements about Mill's view would the author of the passage be most likely to agree?	**Step 2:**
6. It can be inferred from the passage that each of the following features of Hopi personal names contributes to their poetic quality EXCEPT:	**Step 2:**
7. The author's primary purpose in writing the passage is to	**Step 2:**

PrepTest27 Sec3 Qs 8–14

Expert Analysis

Here's how an LSAT expert would analyze each of those question stems.

LSAT Question	Analysis
1. Which one of the following statements most accurately summarizes the passage's main point? →	**Step 2:** "[M]ain point"—A Global question asking for the author's Main Idea. Consult the Big Picture summaries.
2. The author most likely refers to Western Apache place names (line 46) in order to →	**Step 2:** "[I]n order to"—This is a Logic Function question asking how or why the author cited a particular detail. The line reference provides the research clue.
3. Which one of the following statements describes an example of the function accorded to personal names under Lévi-Strauss's view? →	**Step 2:** An Inference question asking us to apply what the passage says about Lévi-Strauss's theory of names. "Lévi-Strauss's view" is the research clue.
4. The primary function of the second paragraph is to →	**Step 2:** "[P]rimary function . . . is to"—A Logic Function question asking for the purpose of a full paragraph. The paragraph reference is the research clue.
5. Based on the passage, with which one of the following statements about Mill's view would the author of the passage be most likely to agree? →	**Step 2:** "Based on the passage . . . with which . . . would the author . . . agree?"—An Inference question rewarding an understanding of the author's opinion about Mill's theory. "Mill's view" is the research clue.
6. It can be inferred from the passage that each of the following features of Hopi personal names contributes to their poetic quality EXCEPT: →	**Step 2:** "[C]an be inferred . . . EXCEPT"—This is an Inference EXCEPT question. The four wrong answers will follow from the passage. The correct answer will not. The Hopi names' "poetic quality" is the research clue.
7. The author's primary purpose in writing the passage is to *PrepTest27 Sec3 Qs 8–14* →	**Step 2:** "[P]rimary purpose"—A Global question calling for the author's purpose in writing the passage. Consult the Big Picture summaries.

How did you do? You'll have more opportunities to perform Step 2, interpreting the question stems and looking for research clues, as you work through the questions from the passages on Online Gaming and Homing Pigeons later in the chapter. For now, though, let's take the questions from the Hopi Personal Names passage and work through the next two steps of the Reading Comprehension Method: Step 3—Research the Relevant Text and Step 4—Predict the Correct Answer.

Researching Reading Comprehension Questions and Predicting the Correct Answer

In Reading Comprehension, poorly trained test takers often lose a lot of points (and, just as importantly, a lot of time) because they essentially answer questions by re-reading the passage. They aren't sure quite where to find the correct answer and wind up looking all over the passage in response to each answer choice. You *should* answer the questions based on the passage, of course, but there is a big difference between researching the relevant text and simply re-reading the passage.

LEARNING OBJECTIVES

In this part of the chapter, you'll learn to:

· Identify and employ five kinds of research clues (line reference, paragraph reference, quoted text, proper names, and content clues) in question stems to research the relevant text in a passage.

· Research the relevant text and accurately predict the correct answer to Inference questions featuring referent reading clues.

· Use Topic, Scope, Purpose, and Main Idea summaries to predict the correct answer to Global questions.

· Use Topic, Scope, Purpose, and Main Idea summaries to predict broadly the correct answer to Inference questions lacking referent reading clues.

Step 3 is where you earn the payoff for the time you spend reading the passage strategically and creating a helpful Roadmap. Take a look at how an LSAT expert handles Steps 3 and 4 in the Hopi Personal Names passage. For reference, we've reprinted the expert's Roadmap and Step 1 analysis. Consult it along with the expert to see how he's working through the Research and Prediction steps.

LSAT Passage		Analysis
Personal names are generally regarded by European thinkers in two major ways, both of which deny that names have any significant semantic content. In philosophy and linguistics, John Stuart Mill's (5) formulation that "proper names are meaningless marks set upon…persons to distinguish them from one another" retains currency; in anthropology, Claude Lévi-Strauss's characterization of names as being primarily instruments of social classification has been (10) very influential. Consequently, interpretation of personal names in societies were names have other functions and meanings has been neglected. Among the Hopi of the southwestern United States, names often refer to historical or ritual events in order both to place (15) individuals within society and to confer an identity upon them. Furthermore, the images used to evoke these events suggest that Hopi names can be seen as a type of poetic composition.	*Euro view of names* *phil/ling– marks* *anth–soc classif'n* *West overlooks other function*	**Step 1:** The first paragraph lays out the entire Big Picture for this passage. The **Topic** is the scholarship of personal names. The **Scope** will focus on Hopi names. The author's **Purpose/ Main Idea** is to show that Hopi names illustrate the shortcomings of the two major European theories about personal names. The paragraph starts with the two theories. Mill (philosophy/linguistics) says names are arbitrary; we just use them to keep people separate. Lévi-Strauss (anthropology) says names are used for social classification. The author says Hopi names are different in two ways: 1) They go beyond mere individual identity by being associated with rituals or events, and 2) they use images and so, are poetic. We can anticipate seeing those differences explained in the next two paragraphs.

LSAT Passage		Analysis
(20) Throughout life, Hopis receive several names in a sequence of ritual initiations. Birth, entry into one of the ritual societies during childhood, and puberty are among the name-giving occasions. Names are conferred by an adult member of a clan other than the (25) child's clan, and names refer to that name giver's clan, sometimes combining characteristics of the clan's totem animal with the child's characteristics. Thus, a name might translate to something as simple as "little rabbit," which reflects both the child's size and the representative animal.	*How Hopi get names Rites* *represents name given* *clan and child's char.*	As expected, this paragraph outlines how the Hopi confer names through rituals. Their names refer to both a person's clan, and to his or her individual characteristics or events from the person's life. Thus, Hopi names contain "meaning" beyond merely identifying a person.
(30) More often, though, the name giver has in mind a specific event that is not apparent in a name's literal translation. One Lizard clan member from the village of Oraibi is named Lomayayva, "beautifully ascended." This translation, however, tells nothing (35) about either the event referred to—who or what ascended—or the name giver's clan. The name giver in this case is from Badger clan. Badger clan is responsible for an annual ceremony featuring a procession in which masked representations of spirits (40) climb the mesa on which Oraibi sits. Combining the name giver's clan association with the receiver's home village, "beautifully ascended" refers to the splendid colors and movements of the procession up the mesa. The condensed image this name evokes—a typical (45) feature of Hopi personal names—displays the same quality of Western Apache place names that led one commentator to call them "tiny imagist poems."	*more common-nonspecific* — Ex *makes names poetic* *Hopi name funtions*	This paragraph goes into more detail about what the author considers Hopi names' second distinguishing characteristic: They are poetic. The Hopi often give names that are not literal. The author cites a detailed example to illustrate this, and concludes that (like Apache place names) Hopi names may be considered "tiny imagist poems."
Hopi personal names do several things simultaneously. They indicate social relationships—but (50) only indirectly—and they individuate persons. Equally important, though, is their poetic quality; in a sense they can be understood as oral texts that produce aesthetic delight. This view of Hopi names is thus opposed not only to Mill's claim that personal names (55) are without inherent meaning but also to Lévi-Strauss's purely functional characterization. Interpreters must understand Hopi clan structures and linguistic practices in order to discern the beauty and significance of Hopi names.	*uses counter to Euro views*	Here, the author reiterates his thesis (or Main Idea) and his evidence for it. Because they 1) indirectly indicate social relationships and 2) have poetical qualities, Hopi names do not fit into Mill's "names are just arbitrary" theory or into Lévi-Strauss's functional "social classification" theory.

PrepTest27 Sec 3 Qs 8–14

LSAT Question	Analysis
Which one of the following statements most accurately summarizes the passage's main point?	**Step 2:** A Global question asking for the author's Main Idea.
	Step 3: Consult the Big Picture summaries.
	Step 4: The author's Main Idea is that Hopi names, because of their ritual and poetic qualities, illustrate the shortcomings of the two major European theories about personal names.
The author most likely refers to Western Apache place names (line 46) in order to	**Step 2:** This is a Logic Function question asking how or why the author cited a particular detail.
	Step 3: The author refers to Apache place names at the end of Paragraph 3. He tells us that another scholar described Apache place names as "tiny imagist poems," and our author thinks that description is also applicable to Hopi personal names.
	Step 4: The function of the detail is to *apply* a scholar's description of Apache place names to Hopi personal names.
Which one of the following statements describes an example of the function accorded to personal names under Lévi-Strauss's view?	**Step 2:** An Inference question asking us to apply what the passage says about Lévi-Strauss's theory of names.
	Step 3: Lévi-Strauss's theory is described in the first paragraph: Names are "instruments of social classification" (line 9).
	Step 4: The correct answer will provide an example of a name revealing something about a person's place in society.

LSAT Question	Analysis
The primary function of the second paragraph is to	**Step 2:** A Logic Function question asking for the purpose of a full paragraph. **Step 3:** The second paragraph outlined ways in which Hopi names refer to events in a person's life, and so, go beyond simply identifying the person. **Step 4:** The correct answer will say something along the lines of: provide evidence/examples of Hopi names having meaning beyond that of a simple identity "tag."
Based on the passage, with which one of the following statements about Mill's view would the author of the passage be most likely to agree?	**Step 2:** An Inference question rewarding an understanding of the author's opinion about Mill's theory. **Step 3:** The author describes Mill's theory in Paragraph 1 (lines 4–7) and Paragraph 4 (lines 54–55): Names are arbitrary, meaningless beyond the fact that they identify individuals. **Step 4:** The author finds Mill's individual identity theory unacceptable because it is too narrow to cover the types of meaning and poetic value found in Hopi names.

LSAT Question	Analysis
It can be inferred from the passage that each of the following features of Hopi personal names contributes to their poetic quality EXCEPT	**Step 2:** This is an Inference EXCEPT question. The four wrong answers will follow from the passage. The correct answer will not.
	Step 3: The author discussed Hopi names' poetic qualities in Paragraph 1 (lines 16–18), throughout Paragraph 3, and Paragraph 4 (lines 50–53).
	Step 4: We cannot predict an answer NOT found in the passage. We will test each answer choice and eliminate those that follow from the passage's comments on poetic quality.
The author's primary purpose in writing the passage is to *PrepTest27 Sec 3 Qs 8–14*	**Step 2:** A Global question calling for the author's purpose in writing the passage.
	Step 3: Consult the Big Picture summaries.
	Step 4: The author's purpose is to illustrate how Hopi names reveal the shortcomings of the two major European theories of personal names.

You'll see the answer choices for those questions shortly, when we discuss Step 5 of the Reading Comprehension Method. It is actually very good for you to practice predicting the correct answers without seeing the answer choices. As you work through additional passages in Chapter 15, you may find it very helpful to cover up the answer choices until you've predicted the correct answer, especially if you find it difficult to fully invest in Step 4 of the Method.

Step-by-step, you're building the Reading Comprehension skills. By the end of the chapter, you'll be able to tackle full passages, from reading and Roadmapping all the way through answering the questions.

Practice

Before moving on to the answer choices, try Steps 2–4 on the passages discussing Online Gaming. For your convenience, we'll reprint the paired Comparative Reading passages and the expert's Roadmap and analysis. Review those briefly before you dive into the question stems. When you've completed Steps 2–4, check your work against that of the LSAT expert on the following pages.

LSAT Passage		Analysis
Passage A is from a source published in 2004 and passage B is from a source published in 2007.		
Passage A Millions of people worldwide play multiplayer online games. They each pick, say, a medieval character to play, such as a warrior. Then they might band together in quests to slay magical beasts; their (5) avatars appear as tiny characters striding across a Tolkienesque land.	*Multiplayer online games popular*	**Step 1:** The short first paragraph appears to be background information: Multiplayer role-playing games are popular.
The economist Edward Castronova noticed something curious about the game he played: it had its own economy, a bustling trade in virtual goods. (10) Players generate goods as they play, often by killing creatures for their treasure and trading it. The longer they play, the wealthier they get.	*Castronova discovers economy within game*	Here, the **Topic** starts to take shape: An economist noticed that players in these games collect virtual goods.
Things got even more interesting when Castronova learned about the "player auctions." Players would (15) sometimes tire of the game and decide to sell off their virtual possessions at online auction sites.	*Further discovery: auctions*	This paragraph narrows the **Scope** of the passage: Virtual goods are auctioned/sold online.
As Castronova stared at the auction listings, he recognized with a shock what he was looking at. It was a form of currency trading! Each item had a value (20) in the virtual currency traded in the game; when it was sold on the auction site, someone was paying cold hard cash for it. That meant that the virtual currency was worth something in real currency. Moreover, since players were killing monsters or skinning animals to (25) sell their pelts, they were, in effect, creating wealth.	*Auctions = currency trading* *Virtual converted to real*	And, here in the final paragraph, we get the **Purpose** and **Main Idea**–to reveal an economist's startling discovery: Virtual items have value in "real world" currency; thus, the "work" players are doing in the game creates wealth.
Passage B Most multiplayer online games prohibit real-world trade in virtual items, but some actually encourage it, for example, by granting participants intellectual property rights in their creations.	*Some games encourage real trade*	From the outset, this passage addresses the same **Topic** and **Scope** as Passage A: the trade/sale of virtual items from online games. It adds a fact not contained in Passage A: Some games forbid, while others encourage, these sales.

LSAT Passage		Analysis
(30) Although it seems intuitively the case that someone who accepts real money for the transfer of a virtual item should be taxed, what about the player who only accumulates items or virtual currency within a virtual world? Is "loot" acquired in a game taxable, (35) as a prize or award is? And is the profit in a purely in-game trade or sale for virtual currency taxable? These are important questions, given the tax revenues at stake, and there is pressure on governments to answer them, given that the economies of some virtual (40) worlds are comparable to those of small countries.	*Should virtual items be taxed? Qs raised* *Govts pressed to answer*	The author of Passage B has a distinct **Purpose**: to raise "important questions" about the taxability of commerce in virtual items. Note the three distinct questions here.
(45) Most people's intuition probably would be that accumulation of assets within a game should not be taxed even though income tax applies even to noncash accessions to wealth. This article will argue that income tax law and policy support that result. Loot acquisitions in game worlds should not be treated as taxable prizes and awards, but rather should be treated like other property that requires effort to obtain, such as fish pulled from the ocean, which is taxed only (50) upon sale. Moreover, in-game trades of virtual items should not be treated as taxable barter.	*Auth: don't tax items that stay in virtual world*	The author starts to formulate his **Main Idea** (almost in the style of a thesis statement): In-game trade of virtual items should not be taxable. The author draws an analogy: Acquiring virtual items in a game is like catching fish; we don't tax fish until they are sold.
(55) By contrast, tax doctrine and policy counsel taxation of the sale of virtual items for real currency, and, in games that are intentionally commodified, even of in-world sales for virtual currency, regardless of whether the participant cashes out. This approach would leave entertainment value untaxed without creating a tax shelter for virtual commerce. *PrepTest71 Sec4 Qs 7–13*	*Auth: tax when virtual items sold ( ) for real $*	In the final paragraph, however, the author of Passage B expands on his **Main Idea**: When virtual items are sold for "real world" currency, or when they are commodified within a game, they should be taxable. The author's main support for his argument is that having this system allows the games to remain fun but not to become virtual "tax shelters."

Compare/Contrast the Passages

The relationship between the two passages is pretty simple: Passage A announces the discovery of a new economic phenomenon, while Passage B explores practical legal questions raised by that phenomenon.

Passage A is neutral; its author describes the economist's "shock" at discovering virtual goods with real-world value, but neither the author nor the economist offers any judgment on the discovery. Passage B's author, on the other hand, makes an argument. The argument's conclusion is a recommendation about when trade in virtual items should and should not be taxed.

Passage A contains facts (e.g., how virtual items are auctioned and traded) not found in Passage B. Passage B reveals differences among games (some encourage trading, while others forbid it), not discussed in Passage A. The economist in Passage A takes note of in-game activities ("skinning animals to sell their pelts" (lines 24–25)), while the author of Passage B compares such activities to "real-world" work ("[pulling] fish . . . from the ocean" (lines 48–49)).

LSAT Question	My Analysis
8. Which one of the following pairs of titles would be most appropriate for passage A and passage B, respectively?	**Step 2:**
	Step 3:
	Step 4:
9. Which one of the following most accurately expresses how the use of the phrase "skinning animals" in passage A (line 24) relates to the use of the phrase "fish pulled from the ocean" in passage B (line 49)?	**Step 2:**
	Step 3:
	Step 4:
10. With regard to their respective attitudes toward commerce in virtual items, passage A differs from passage B in that passage A is more	**Step 2:**
	Step 3:
	Step 4:

LSAT Question	My Analysis
11. Based on what can be inferred from their titles, the relationship between which one of the following pairs of documents is most analogous to the relationship between passage A and passage B?	**Step 2:** **Step 3:** **Step 4:**
12. The passages were most likely taken from which one of the following pairs of sources?	**Step 2:** **Step 3:** **Step 4:**
13. Which one of the following most accurately describes the relationship between the two passages?	**Step 2:** **Step 3:** **Step 4:**
14. Based on passage B, which one of the following is a characteristic of some "games that are intentionally commodified" (line 54)? *PrepTest71 Sec4 Qs 7–13*	**Step 2:** **Step 3:** **Step 4:**

Expert Analysis

Here's how the LSAT expert analyzed each of those question stems. Compare your work to his. Did your identification of the question types match? Did you know where in the passage to find the relevant text for those questions containing research clues?

LSAT Question	Analysis
8. Which one of the following pairs of titles would be most appropriate for passage A and passage B, respectively?	**Step 2:** The passages' "titles" would reflect their Main Ideas, so this is a Global question. **Step 3:** Consult the Big Picture summaries to predict the correct answer. **Step 4:** Passage A is about an economist making the shocking discovery of a new form of wealth. Passage B presents a model for how to tax trade in virtual items.
9. Which one of the following most accurately expresses how the use of the phrase "skinning animals" in passage A (line 24) relates to the use of the phrase "fish pulled from the ocean" in passage B (line 49)?	**Step 2:** This question asks you to determine how a phrase was used, and to apply it to another phrase. Thus, it is an Inference question. **Step 3:** Passage A cited "skinning animals" as a type of in-game "work," while Passage B used catching fish as a real-world analogy to in-game work. **Step 4:** The correct answer will describe the relationship noted in Step 3's research.
10. With regard to their respective attitudes toward commerce in virtual items, passage A differs from passage B in that passage A is more	**Step 2:** An Inference question about both authors' attitudes. **Step 3:** Passage A describes the economist's "shock" (line 18). Passage B addresses the subject by raising "important questions" (line 37). **Step 4:** The correct answer will say something along the lines of "startled and excited."
11. Based on what can be inferred from their titles, the relationship between which one of the following pairs of documents is most analogous to the relationship between passage A and passage B?	**Step 2:** The correct answer will apply the relationship between the two passages to that between two distinct documents. This is a Logic Reasoning question that rewards Parallel Reasoning skills. **Step 3:** Consult the Big Picture summaries of both passages, and compare them. **Step 4:** The correct answer will describe a document that announces a new discovery, and then one that asks practical, legal questions raised by the discovery.

LSAT Question	Analysis
12. The passages were most likely taken from which one of the following pairs of sources?	**Step 2:** This is an Inference question. It asks you to use the passages' content and style to infer the type of literature from which each was culled.

Step 3: Passage A is informal and narrative; it feels like it comes from a popular newspaper or magazine. Passage B's author states that this text is from the beginning of an "article" (line 44) that is going to go into more detail about law and policy, as would be the case in a law journal.

Step 4: The correct answer will likely say: Passage A—a popular magazine; Passage B—an academic law journal. |
| 13. Which one of the following most accurately describes the relationship between the two passages? | **Step 2:** A Global question rewarding accurate summaries of the two passages, and a valid comparison of them.

Step 3: Consult the Big Picture summaries (the mental Roadmap, if you will).

Step 4: The correct answer will be something along these lines: Passage A announces a shocking discovery; Passage B identifies important questions raised by the discovery, and recommends an answer. |
| 14. Based on passage B, which one of the following is a characteristic of some "games that are intentionally commodified" (line 54)?

PrepTest71 Sec4 Qs 7–13 | **Step 2:** The correct answer will be found in the passage ("Based on the passage, which one . . . is a characteristic . . ."), making this a Detail question.

Step 3: The author of Passage B describes "intentionally commodified" games at lines 28–29. These games grant intellectual property rights to players who create virtual goods in the game. The author also argues that virtual goods in these games should be taxed when sold for real-world currency, or in-game virtual currency.

Step 4: The correct answer will restate or closely paraphrase something the author of Passage B said about intentionally commodified games. |

With all of that work done, evaluating the answer choices will be much easier and much faster. That's what you'll do in the next part of this chapter.

Evaluating Reading Comprehension Answer Choices

This is what the entire Reading Comprehension Method is set up to do: answer the questions correctly. Pay close attention to how the LSAT expert uses his prediction to make bold, accurate assessments of whether each choice is correct or incorrect.

LEARNING OBJECTIVES

In this portion of the chapter, you'll learn to:

- Use a prediction of the correct answer to evaluate the answer choices.
- Use the Topic, Scope, Purpose, and Main Idea summaries to evaluate the answer choices.
- Evaluate answer choices by efficiently checking them against the passage text.

It is not uncommon for test takers to get bogged down in the Reading Comprehension section, especially as they evaluate the answer choices. Do you find yourself reading through answer choices multiple times, unsure which of two or three tempting choices is correct? The way to overcome that hesitation, and thus to increase your speed and accuracy, is to practice the Reading Comprehension Method. The more comfortable you get researching the passage and making accurate, pointed predictions, the quicker you'll find, and the more confidently you'll select, the correct answer. As you review the LSAT expert's evaluations below, keep all of the work you've done through Steps 1–4 in mind.

Let's start by taking one more look at the Hopi Personal Names passage. We'll reprint the passage, Roadmap, and Step 1 analysis for reference. Along with each question, we'll repeat the expert's Step 2–4 analyses as well. This time, though, we'll add the answer choices and show you how the expert zeros in on the correct choice.

LSAT Passage		Analysis
Personal names are generally regarded by European thinkers in two major ways, both of which deny that names have any significant semantic content. In philosophy and linguistics, John Stuart Mill's (5) formulation that "proper names are meaningless marks set upon…persons to distinguish them from one another" retains currency; in anthropology, Claude Lévi-Strauss's characterization of names as being primarily instruments of social classification has been (10) very influential. Consequently, interpretation of personal names in societies were names have other functions and meanings has been neglected. Among the Hopi of the southwestern United States, names often refer to historical or ritual events in order both to place (15) individuals within society and to confer an identity upon them. Furthermore, the images used to evoke these events suggest that Hopi names can be seen as a type of poetic composition.	*Euro view of names* *phil/ling- marks* *anth–soc classif'n* *West overlooks other function*	**Step 1:** The first paragraph lays out the entire Big Picture for this passage. The **Topic** is the scholarship of personal names. The **Scope** will focus on Hopi names. The author's **Purpose/Main Idea** is to show that Hopi names illustrate the shortcomings of the two major European theories about personal names. The paragraph starts with the two theories. Mill (philosophy/linguistics) says names are arbitrary; we just use them to keep people separate. Lévi-Strauss (anthropology) says names are used for social classification. The author says Hopi names are different in two ways: 1) They go beyond mere individual identity by being associated with rituals or events, and 2) they use images and so, are poetic. We can anticipate seeing those differences explained in the next two paragraphs.

LSAT Passage		Analysis

(20) Throughout life, Hopis receive several names in a sequence of ritual initiations. Birth, entry into one of the ritual societies during childhood, and puberty are among the name-giving occasions. Names are conferred by an adult member of a clan other than the child's clan, and names refer to that name giver's clan, (25) sometimes combining characteristics of the clan's totem animal with the child's characteristics. Thus, a name might translate to something as simple as "little rabbit," which reflects both the child's size and the representative animal.	*How Hopi get names Rites* *represents name given* *clan and child's char.*	As expected, this paragraph outlines how the Hopi confer names through rituals. Their names refer to both a person's clan, and to his or her individual characteristics or events from the person's life. Thus, Hopi names contain "meaning" beyond merely identifying a person.
(30) More often, though, the name giver has in mind a specific event that is not apparent in a name's literal translation. One Lizard clan member from the village of Oraibi is named Lomayayva, "beautifully ascended." This translation, however, tells nothing (35) about either the event referred to—who or what ascended—or the name giver's clan. The name giver in this case is from Badger clan. Badger clan is responsible for an annual ceremony featuring a procession in which masked representations of spirits (40) climb the mesa on which Oraibi sits. Combining the name giver's clan association with the receiver's home village, "beautifully ascended" refers to the splendid colors and movements of the procession up the mesa. The condensed image this name evokes—a typical (45) feature of Hopi personal names—displays the same quality of Western Apache place names that led one commentator to call them "tiny imagist poems."	*more common– nonspecific* —*Ex* *makes names poetic*	This paragraph goes into more detail about what the author considers Hopi names' second distinguishing characteristic: They are poetic. The Hopi often give names that are not literal. The author cites a detailed example to illustrate this, and concludes that (like Apache place names) Hopi names may be considered "tiny imagist poems."
Hopi personal names do several things simultaneously. They indicate social relationships—but (50) only indirectly—and they individuate persons. Equally important, though, is their poetic quality; in a sense they can be understood as oral texts that produce aesthetic delight. This view of Hopi names is thus opposed not only to Mill's claim that personal names (55) are without inherent meaning but also to Lévi-Strauss's purely functional characterization. Interpreters must understand Hopi clan structures and linguistic practices in order to discern the beauty and significance of Hopi names.	*Hopi name funtions* *uses counter to Euro views*	Here, the author reiterates his thesis (or Main Idea) and his evidence for it. Because they 1) indirectly indicate social relationships and 2) have poetical qualities, Hopi names do not fit into Mill's "names are just arbitrary" theory or into Lévi-Strauss's functional "social classification" theory.

PrepTest27 Sec 3 Qs 8–14

LSAT Question	Analysis
Which one of the following statements most accurately summarizes the passage's main point?	**Step 2:** A Global question asking for the author's Main Idea.
	Step 3: Consult the Big Picture summaries.
	Step 4: The author's Main Idea is that Hopi names, because of their ritual and poetic qualities, illustrate the shortcomings of the two major European theories about personal names.
(A) Unlike European names, which are used exclusively for identification or exclusively for social classification, Hopi names perform both these functions simultaneously.	**Step 5:** Distortion. The passage is not about what European names do, but what scholars say all names do. Additionally, this choice doesn't touch on the ritual or poetic features that the author thinks make Hopi names illustrative. Eliminate.
(B) Unlike European names, Hopi names tend to neglect the functions of identification and social classification in favor of a concentration on compression and poetic effects.	Distortion. The author does not say that Hopi names don't identify individuals. Indeed, he says the opposite (line 30). Moreover, this answer choice says nothing about the European theories about names. Eliminate.
(C) Lacking knowledge of the intricacies of Hopi linguistic and tribal structures, European thinkers have so far been unable to discern the deeper significance of Hopi names.	Distortion. This choice mirrors the author's recommendation at the very end of the passage (lines 56–58), but it doesn't capture the passage's Main Idea, that Hopi names illustrate the shortcomings of the major European theories. Eliminate.
(D) Although some Hopi names may seem difficult to interpret, they all conform to a formula whereby a reference to the name giver's clan is combined with a reference to the person named.	This choice is far too narrow in Scope. It focuses on only one of the two distinguishing features of Hopi names, and says nothing about the European theories. Eliminate.
(E) While performing the functions ascribed to names by European thinkers, Hopi names also possess a significant aesthetic quality that these thinkers have not adequately recognized. *PrepTest27 Sec 3 Q8*	Correct. This choice briefly summarizes the author's argument that Hopi names' ritual and poetic qualities reveal the shortcomings of the major European theories about names.

LSAT Question	Analysis
The author most likely refers to Western Apache place names (line 46) in order to	**Step 2:** This is a Logic Function question asking how or why the author cited a particular detail. **Step 3:** The author refers to Apache place names at the end of Paragraph 3. He tells us that another scholar described Apache place names as "tiny imagist poems," and our author thinks that description is also applicable to Hopi personal names. **Step 4:** The function of the detail is to *apply* a scholar's description of Apache place names to Hopi personal names.
(A) offer an example of how names can contain references not evident in their literal translations	**Step 5:** Faulty Use of Detail. The author's example is found earlier in the paragraph (lines 32–43). The detail in question here is another scholar's description of an analogous naming practice. Eliminate.
(B) apply a commentator's characterization of Western Apache place names to Hopi personal names	Correct. This choice matches the prediction perfectly.
(C) contrast Western Apache naming practices with Hopi naming practices	180. The author thinks the naming practices are similar, not opposed. Eliminate.
(D) demonstrate that other names besides Hopi names may have some semantic content	Distortion. The author's purpose is not to provide further evidence, but simply to apply what he considers an apt description to his evidence. Eliminate.
(E) explain how a specific Hopi name refers subtly to a particular Western Apache site *PrepTest27 Sec 3 Q9*	Outside the Scope. The author neither states nor implies that Hopi personal names refer to places named by the Apache. Eliminate.

LSAT Question	Analysis
Which one of the following statements describes an example of the function accorded to personal names under Lévi-Strauss's view?	**Step 2:** An Inference question asking us to apply what the passage says about Lévi-Strauss's theory of names.
	Step 3: Lévi-Strauss's theory is described in the first paragraph: Names are "instruments of social classification" (line 9).
	Step 4: The correct answer will provide an example of a name revealing something about a person's place in society.
(A) Some parents select their children's names from impersonal sources such as books.	**Step 5:** Outside the Scope. Lévi-Strauss says nothing about giving people names from books. Eliminate.
(B) Some parents wait to give a child a name in order to choose one that reflects the child's looks or personality.	Outside the Scope. Lévi-Strauss is not said to consider looks or personalities in the meaning of names. Eliminate.
(C) Some parents name their children in honor of friends or famous people.	Distortion. This type of naming may well happen, but it doesn't fit into Lévi-Strauss's social classification theory. Eliminate.
(D) Some family members have no parts of their names in common.	Outside the Scope. This phenomenon is not mentioned in the passage at all. Eliminate.
(E) Some family names originated as identifications of their bearers' occupations.	Correct. Identifying a person by his or her occupation fits Lévi-Strauss's social classification theory perfectly.

PrepTest27 Sec 3 Q10

LSAT Question	Analysis
The primary function of the second paragraph is to	**Step 2:** A Logic Function question asking for the purpose of a full paragraph. **Step 3:** The second paragraph outlined ways in which Hopi names refer to events in a person's life, and so, go beyond simply identifying the person. **Step 4:** The correct answer will say something along the lines of: provide evidence/examples of Hopi names having meaning beyond that of a simple identity "tag."
(A) present reasons why Hopi personal names can be treated as poetic compositions	**Step 5:** Faulty Use of Detail. This choice describes the purpose of Paragraph 3. Eliminate.
(B) support the claim that Hopi personal names make reference to events in the recipient's life	This choice is too narrow. It doesn't get at the purpose of Paragraph 2, which is to show how Hopi names confer additional meaning. Eliminate.
(C) argue that the fact that Hopis receive many names throughout life refutes European theories about naming	Distortion. The author does not argue that multiple naming events are what distinguishes Hopi names; it is, rather, the meaning conferred through the names given. Eliminate.
(D) illustrate ways in which Hopi personal names may have semantic content	Correct. "[S]emantic content" is a fancy way of saying "meaning."
(E) demonstrate that the literal translation of Hopi personal names often obscures their true meaning *PrepTest27 Sec 3 Q11*	Distortion. Someone unaware of Hopi culture and language might well be confused by a literal translation, but the author did not write Paragraph 2 *in order to* demonstrate this rather obvious fact. Eliminate.

LSAT Question	**Analysis**
Based on the passage, with which one of the following statements about Mill's view would the author of the passage be most likely to agree?	**Step 2:** An Inference question rewarding an understanding of the author's opinion about Mill's theory.
	Step 3: The author describes Mill's theory in Paragraph 1 (lines 4–7) and Paragraph 4 (lines 54–55): Names are arbitrary, meaningless beyond the fact that they identify individuals.
	Step 4: The author finds Mill's individual identity theory unacceptable because it is too narrow to cover the types of meaning and poetic value found in Hopi names.
(A) Its characterization of the function of names is too narrow to be universally applicable.	**Step 5:** Correct. This matches the Step 4 prediction, and perfectly captures the author's primary purpose in writing the passage.
(B) It would be correct if it recognized the use of names as instruments of social classification.	This choice is too narrow. Adding Lévi-Strauss's theory would not be enough to account for the additional meaning and poetic qualities found in Hopi names. Eliminate.
(C) Its influence single-handedly led scholars to neglect how names are used outside Europe.	Extreme. Mill's theory hasn't *single-handedly* influenced scholars; at a minimum, Lévi-Strauss's has also played a role. Eliminate.
(D) It is more accurate than Lévi-Strauss's characterization of the purpose of names.	Distortion. The author considers both theories inadequate. He doesn't compare their relative accuracy. Eliminate.
(E) It is less relevant than Lévi-Strauss's characterization in understanding Hopi naming practices.	Distortion. The author considers both theories inadequate. He doesn't compare their relative relevance to Hopi names. Eliminate.

PrepTest27 Sec 3 Q12

LSAT Question	Analysis
It can be inferred from the passage that each of the following features of Hopi personal names contributes to their poetic quality EXCEPT:	**Step 2:** This is an Inference EXCEPT question. The four wrong answers will follow from the passage. The correct answer will not.
	Step 3: The author discussed Hopi names' poetic qualities in Paragraph 1 (lines 16–18), throughout Paragraph 3, and Paragraph 4 (lines 50–53).
	Step 4: We cannot predict an answer NOT found in the passage. We will test each answer choice and eliminate those that follow from the passage's comments on poetic quality.
(A) their ability to be understood as oral texts	**Step 5:** This is supported by lines 51–53. Eliminate.
(B) their use of condensed imagery to evoke events	This is supported by line 44. Eliminate.
(C) their capacity to produce aesthetic delight	This is supported by lines 51–53. Eliminate.
(D) their ability to confer identity upon individuals	Correct. The author associates the identity conferring qualities of Hopi names with the naming rituals described in Paragraph 2, not with their poetic qualities.
(E) their ability to subtly convey meaning *PrepTest27 Sec 3 Q13*	This is supported by lines 30–32, in which the author says that Hopi names refer to events "not apparent in a name's literal meaning." Eliminate.

LSAT Question	Analysis
The author's primary purpose in writing the passage is to	**Step 2:** A Global question calling for the author's purpose in writing the passage.
	Step 3: Consult the Big Picture summaries.
	Step 4: The author's purpose is to illustrate how Hopi names reveal the shortcomings of the two major European theories of personal names.
(A) present an anthropological study of Hopi names	**Step 5:** Distortion. The passage contains a lot of anthropological data, but its purpose is to critique the predominant theories, not merely to present an ethnographic study. Eliminate.
(B) propose a new theory about the origin of names	Distortion. The author doesn't get this far in the passage. He shows how the major theories are inadequate, but doesn't propose a new one. Eliminate.
(C) describe several competing theories of names	Distortion. The author describes two theories, not several, and his purpose is to demonstrate the inadequacy of the two he presents. Eliminate.
(D) criticize two influential views of names	Correct. All of the details offered in the passage are given to show that the two major European theories cannot account for certain features of Hopi names.
(E) explain the cultural origins of names	Outside the Scope. This goal is never addressed in the passage. Eliminate.

PrepTest27 Sec 3 Q14

Notice that the expert never compares the answers to one another. She never thinks, "Which is more correct, choice (A) or choice (C)?" Knowing what the correct answer must contain, and having predicted its meaning accurately, she can assess the choices with confidence. Naturally, she may confirm a choice by referring to the text. Likewise, she may do a quick research check to be certain that a wrong answer distorts or contradicts the passage. Never, though, will she engage in multiple re-reads as she makes her way through a set of questions.

The chapter continues with a practice exercise on the next page. ▶ ▶ ▶

Practice

Now, try Step 5 on your own. Use the work you've already done with the Comparative Reading passages on Online Gaming. Take a few moments to refresh your memory of the passages, Roadmap, and strategic reading analysis. Then, turn to the questions one at a time. You've already completed Steps 2–4 here, so review the research you did and predictions you made. Use them to evaluate the answer choices. Avoid comparing answers to one another and keep in mind that the one correct answer will be justified by the passage, while all four wrong answers will not. When you're finished, check your answers and compare your analysis to that of an LSAT expert on the following pages.

LSAT Passage		Analysis
Passage A is from a source published in 2004 and passage B is from a source published in 2007.		
Passage A		
Millions of people worldwide play multiplayer online games. They each pick, say, a medieval character to play, such as a warrior. Then they might band together in quests to slay magical beasts; their (5) avatars appear as tiny characters striding across a Tolkienesque land.	*Multiplayer online games popular*	**Step 1:** The short first paragraph appears to be background information: Multiplayer role-playing games are popular.
The economist Edward Castronova noticed something curious about the game he played: it had its own economy, a bustling trade in virtual goods. (10) Players generate goods as they play, often by killing creatures for their treasure and trading it. The longer they play, the wealthier they get.	*Castronova discovers economy within game*	Here, the **Topic** starts to take shape: An economist noticed that players in these games collect virtual goods.
Things got even more interesting when Castronova learned about the "player auctions." Players would (15) sometimes tire of the game and decide to sell off their virtual possessions at online auction sites.	*Further discovery: auctions*	This paragraph narrows the **Scope** of the passage: Virtual goods are auctioned/sold online.
As Castronova stared at the auction listings, he recognized with a shock what he was looking at. It was a form of currency trading! Each item had a value (20) in the virtual currency traded in the game; when it was sold on the auction site, someone was paying cold hard cash for it. That meant that the virtual currency was worth something in real currency. Moreover, since players were killing monsters or skinning animals to (25) sell their pelts, they were, in effect, creating wealth.	*Auctions = currency trading* *Virtual converted to real*	And, here in the final paragraph, we get the **Purpose** and **Main Idea**—to reveal an economist's startling discovery: Virtual items have value in "real world" currency; thus, the "work" players are doing in the game creates wealth.
Passage B		
Most multiplayer online games prohibit real-world trade in virtual items, but some actually encourage it, for example, by granting participants intellectual property rights in their creations.	*Some games encourage real trade*	From the outset, this passage addresses the same **Topic** and **Scope** as Passage A: the trade/sale of virtual items from online games. It adds a fact not contained in Passage A: Some games forbid, while others encourage, these sales.

LSAT Passage		Analysis
(30) Although it seems intuitively the case that someone who accepts real money for the transfer of a virtual item should be taxed, what about the player who only accumulates items or virtual currency within a virtual world? Is "loot" acquired in a game taxable, (35) as a prize or award is? And is the profit in a purely in-game trade or sale for virtual currency taxable? These are important questions, given the tax revenues at stake, and there is pressure on governments to answer them, given that the economies of some virtual (40) worlds are comparable to those of small countries.	*Should virtual items be taxed? Qs raised* *Govts pressed to answer*	The author of Passage B has a distinct **Purpose**: to raise "important questions" about the taxability of commerce in virtual items. Note the three distinct questions here.
Most people's intuition probably would be that accumulation of assets within a game should not be taxed even though income tax applies even to noncash accessions to wealth. This article will argue that (45) income tax law and policy support that result. Loot acquisitions in game worlds should not be treated as taxable prizes and awards, but rather should be treated like other property that requires effort to obtain, such as fish pulled from the ocean, which is taxed only (50) upon sale. Moreover, in-game trades of virtual items should not be treated as taxable barter.	*Auth: don't tax items that stay in virtual world*	The author starts to formulate his **Main Idea** (almost in the style of a thesis statement): In-game trade of virtual items should not be taxable. The author draws an analogy: Acquiring virtual items in a game is like catching fish; we don't tax fish until they are sold.
By contrast, tax doctrine and policy counsel taxation of the sale of virtual items for real currency, and, in games that are intentionally commodified, (55) even of in-world sales for virtual currency, regardless of whether the participant cashes out. This approach would leave entertainment value untaxed without creating a tax shelter for virtual commerce. *PrepTest71 Sec4 Qs 7–13*	*Auth: tax when virtual items sold for real $*	In the final paragraph, however, the author of Passage B expands on his **Main Idea**: When virtual items are sold for "real world" currency, or when they are commodified within a game, they should be taxable. The author's main support for his argument is that having this system allows the games to remain fun but not to become virtual "tax shelters."

Compare/Contrast the Passages

The relationship between the two passages is pretty simple: Passage A announces the discovery of a new economic phenomenon, while Passage B explores practical legal questions raised by that phenomenon.

Passage A is neutral; its author describes the economist's "shock" at discovering virtual goods with real-world value, but neither the author nor the economist offers any judgment on the discovery. Passage B's author, on the other hand, makes an argument. The argument's conclusion is a recommendation about when trade in virtual items should and should not be taxed.

Passage A contains facts (e.g., how virtual items are auctioned and traded) not found in Passage B. Passage B reveals differences among games (some encourage trading, while others forbid it), not discussed in Passage A. The economist in Passage A takes note of in-game activities ("skinning animals to sell their pelts" (lines 24–25)), while the author of Passage B compares such activities to "real-world" work ("[pulling] fish . . . from the ocean" (lines 48–49)).

LSAT Question	My Analysis
15. Which one of the following pairs of titles would be most appropriate for passage A and passage B, respectively?	**Step 2:** The passages' "titles" would reflect their Main Ideas, so this is a Global question. **Step 3:** Consult the Big Picture summaries to predict the correct answer. **Step 4:** Passage A is about an economist making the shocking discovery of a new form of wealth. Passage B presents a model for how to tax trade in virtual items.
(A) "The Economic Theories of Edward Castronova" "Intellectual Property Rights in Virtual Worlds"	**Step 5:**
(B) "An Economist Discovers New Economic Territory" "Taxing Virtual Property"	
(C) "The Surprising Growth of Multiplayer Online Games" "Virtual Reality and the Law"	
(D) "How to Make Money Playing Games" "Closing Virtual Tax Shelters"	
(E) "A New Economic Paradigm" "An Untapped Source of Revenue"	

PrepTest71 Sec4 Q7

LSAT Question	**My Analysis**
16. Which one of the following most accurately expresses how the use of the phrase "skinning animals" in passage A (line 24) relates to the use of the phrase "fish pulled from the ocean" in passage B (line 49)?	**Step 2:** This question asks you to determine how a phrase was used, and to apply it to another phrase. Thus, it is an Inference question. → **Step 3:** Passage A cited "skinning animals" as a type of in-game "work," while Passage B used catching fish as a real-world analogy to in-game work. **Step 4:** The correct answer will describe the relationship noted in Step 3's research.
(A) The former refers to an activity that generates wealth, whereas the latter refers to an activity that does not generate wealth.	**Step 5:**
(B) The former refers to an activity in an online game, whereas the latter refers to an analogous activity in the real world.	
(C) The former, unlike the latter, refers to the production of a commodity that the author of passage B thinks should be taxed.	
(D) The latter, unlike the former, refers to the production of a commodity that the author of passage B thinks should be taxed.	
(E) Both are used as examples of activities by which game players generate wealth.	

PrepTest71 Sec4 Q8

LSAT Question	**My Analysis**
17. With regard to their respective attitudes toward commerce in virtual items, passage A differs from passage B in that passage A is more	**Step 2:** An Inference question about both authors' attitudes.
	Step 3: Passage A describes the economist's "shock" (line 18). Passage B addresses the subject by raising "important questions" (line 37).
	Step 4: The correct answer will say something along the lines of "startled and excited."
(A) critical and apprehensive	**Step 5:**
(B) academic and dismissive	
(C) intrigued and excited	
(D) undecided but curious	
(E) enthusiastic but skeptical	

PrepTest71 Sec4 Q9

LSAT Question	**My Analysis**
18. Based on what can be inferred from their titles, the relationship between which one of the following pairs of documents is most analogous to the relationship between passage A and passage B?	**Step 2:** The correct answer will apply the relationship between the two passages to that between two distinct documents. This is a Logic Reasoning question that rewards Parallel Reasoning skills.
	→ **Step 3:** Consult the Big Picture summaries of both passages, and compare them.
	Step 4: The correct answer will describe a document that announces a new discovery, and then one that asks practical, legal questions raised by the discovery.
(A) "Advances in Artificial Intelligence" "Human Psychology Applied to Robots"	**Step 5:**
(B) "Internet Retailers Post Good Year" "Lawmakers Move to Tax Internet Commerce"	
(C) "New Planet Discovered in Solar System" "Planet or Asteroid: Scientists Debate"	
(D) "Biologists Create New Species in Lab" "Artificially Created Life: How Patent Law Applies"	
(E) "A Renegade Economist's Views on Taxation" "Candidate Runs on Unorthodox Tax Plan"	

PrepTest71 Sec4 Q10

LSAT Question	My Analysis
19. The passages were most likely taken from which one of the following pairs of sources?	**Step 2:** This is an Inference question. It asks you to use the passages' content and style to infer the type of literature from which each was culled. **Step 3:** Passage A is informal and narrative; it feels like it comes from a popular newspaper or magazine. Passage B's author states that this text is from the beginning of an "article" (line 44) that is going to go into more detail about law and policy, as would be the case in a law journal. **Step 4:** The correct answer will likely say: Passage A—a popular magazine; Passage B—an academic law journal.
(A) passage A: a magazine article addressed to a general audience passage B: a law journal article	**Step 5:**
(B) passage A: a technical journal for economists passage B: a magazine article addressed to a general audience	
(C) passage A: a science-fiction novel passage B: a technical journal for economists	
(D) passage A: a law journal article passage B: a speech delivered before a legislative body	
(E) passage A: a speech delivered before a legislative body passage B: a science-fiction novel	

PrepTest71 Sec4 Q11

LSAT Question	My Analysis
20. Which one of the following most accurately describes the relationship between the two passages?	**Step 2:** A Global question rewarding accurate summaries of the two passages, and a valid comparison of them.
	Step 3: Consult the Big Picture summaries (the mental Roadmap, if you will).
	Step 4: The correct answer will be something along these lines: Passage A announces a shocking discovery; Passage B identifies important questions raised by the discovery, and recommends an answer.
(A) Passage A summarizes a scholar's unanticipated discovery, while passage B proposes solutions to a problem raised by the phenomenon discovered.	**Step 5:**
(B) Passage A explains an economic theory, while passage B identifies a practical problem resulting from that theory.	
(C) Passage A reports on a subculture, while passage B discusses the difficulty of policing that subculture.	
(D) Passage A challenges the common interpretation of a phenomenon, while passage B reaffirms that interpretation.	
(E) Passage A states a set of facts, while passage B draws theoretical consequences from those facts.	

PrepTest71 Sec4 Q12

LSAT Question	My Analysis
21. Based on passage B, which one of the following is a characteristic of some "games that are intentionally commodified" (line 54)?	**Step 2:** The correct answer will be found in the passage ("Based on the passage, which one . . . is a characteristic . . ."), making this a Detail question. **Step 3:** The author of Passage B describes "intentionally commodified" games at lines 28–29. These games grant intellectual property rights to players who create virtual goods in the game. The author also argues that virtual goods in these games should be taxed when sold for real-world currency, or in-game virtual currency. **Step 4:** The correct answer will restate or closely paraphrase something the author of Passage B said about intentionally commodified games.
(A) The game allows selling real items for virtual currency.	**Step 5:**
(B) The game allows players to trade avatars with other players.	
(C) Players of the game grow wealthier the longer they play.	
(D) Players of the game own intellectual property rights in their creations.	
(E) Players of the game can exchange one virtual currency for another virtual currency. *PrepTest71 Sec4 Q13*	

Expert Analysis

Here's how an LSAT expert answered the questions from the Online Gaming passage. Compare your analysis of the correct and incorrect answers to his.

LSAT Question	Analysis
15. Which one of the following pairs of titles would be most appropriate for passage A and passage B, respectively?	**Step 2:** The passages' "titles" would reflect their Main Ideas, so this is a Global question. **Step 3:** Consult the Big Picture summaries to predict the correct answer. **Step 4:** Passage A is about an economist making the shocking discovery of a new form of wealth. Passage B presents a model for how to tax trade in virtual items.
(A) "The Economic Theories of Edward Castronova" "Intellectual Property Rights in Virtual Worlds"	**Step 5:** The description of Passage A is Extreme: We learn only about Castronova's discovery, not his theories. This choice also distorts Passage B, which is about taxation, not IP law. Eliminate.
(B) "An Economist Discovers New Economic Territory" "Taxing Virtual Property"	Correct. This answer matches the predictions and accurately summarizes the two articles.
(C) "The Surprising Growth of Multiplayer Online Games" "Virtual Reality and the Law"	Distortion. Passage A is about the economist's surprise over the trade of virtual items, not the popularity of the games from which they come. Passage B is about tax law specifically. Eliminate.
(D) "How to Make Money Playing Games" "Closing Virtual Tax Shelters"	Distortion. Passage A doesn't provide any tips for exploiting trade in virtual items. Passage B wants to *prevent*, not close, one potential tax shelter. Eliminate.
(E) "A New Economic Paradigm" "An Untapped Source of Revenue" *PrepTest71 Sec4 Q7*	Extreme/Distortion. The term "[p]aradigm" is too broad to fit Passage A. Passage B is about taxing an already "tapped" source of revenue. Eliminate.

LSAT Question	Analysis
16. Which one of the following most accurately expresses how the use of the phrase "skinning animals" in passage A (line 24) relates to the use of the phrase "fish pulled from the ocean" in passage B (line 49)?	**Step 2:** This question asks you to determine how a phrase was used, and to apply it to another phrase. Thus, it is an Inference question.
	→ **Step 3:** Passage A cited "skinning animals" as a type of in-game "work," while Passage B used catching fish as a real-world analogy to in-game work.
	Step 4: The correct answer will describe the relationship noted in Step 3's research.
(A) The former refers to an activity that generates wealth, whereas the latter refers to an activity that does not generate wealth.	→ **Step 5:** Half-Right/Half-Wrong. In both passages, the referenced activities are said to generate wealth. Eliminate.
(B) The former refers to an activity in an online game, whereas the latter refers to an analogous activity in the real world.	→ Correct. This choice correctly describes the in-game activity from Passage A, and the real-world analogy applied in Passage B.
(C) The former, unlike the latter, refers to the production of a commodity that the author of passage B thinks should be taxed.	→ Distortion. The author of Passage B thinks real-world fish should only be taxed *when sold*, and thus, would say the same thing about the in-game pelts. Eliminate.
(D) The latter, unlike the former, refers to the production of a commodity that the author of passage B thinks should be taxed.	→ Distortion. The author of Passage B thinks real-world fish should only be taxed *when sold*, and thus, would say the same thing about the in-game pelts. Eliminate.
(E) Both are used as examples of activities by which game players generate wealth. *PrepTest71 Sec4 Q8*	→ Half-Right/Half-Wrong. In Passage B, catching fish is offered as a real-world analogy to in-game activities. Eliminate.

LSAT Question	Analysis
17. With regard to their respective attitudes toward commerce in virtual items, passage A differs from passage B in that passage A is more	**Step 2:** An Inference question about both authors' attitudes.
	Step 3: Passage A describes the economist's "shock" (line 18). Passage B addresses the subject by raising "important questions" (line 37).
	Step 4: The correct answer will say something along the lines of "startled and excited."
(A) critical and apprehensive	**Step 5:** 180. The economist in Passage A seems neither critical nor apprehensive about the trade in virtual items. Eliminate.
(B) academic and dismissive	180. The economist may have academic interest in the phenomenon, but the passage describes his excitement, and contains no dismissive tone. Eliminate.
(C) intrigued and excited	Correct. This captures the economist's wonder and curiosity at his discovery.
(D) undecided but curious	Distortion. The economist notices something "curious" (line 8), in the sense of unusual or intriguing, but his response is not undecided; it is enthusiastic. Eliminate.
(E) enthusiastic but skeptical *PrepTest71 Sec4 Q9*	Half-Right/Half-Wrong. The economist does appear enthusiastic, but not skeptical. Indeed, the passage describes wonder at his discovery. Eliminate.

LSAT Question	Analysis
18. Based on what can be inferred from their titles, the relationship between which one of the following pairs of documents is most analogous to the relationship between passage A and passage B?	**Step 2:** The correct answer will apply the relationship between the two passages to that between two distinct documents. This is a Logic Reasoning question that rewards Parallel Reasoning skills.
	→ **Step 3:** Consult the Big Picture summaries of both passages, and compare them.
	Step 4: The correct answer will describe a document that announces a new discovery, and then one that asks practical, legal questions raised by the discovery.
(A) "Advances in Artificial Intelligence" "Human Psychology Applied to Robots"	**Step 5:** This choice mischaracterizes both passages. Passage A isn't about advances in understanding a phenomenon; it is about discovering one. And Passage B is about *legal* questions a new phenomenon raises. Eliminate.
(B) "Internet Retailers Post Good Year" "Lawmakers Move to Tax Internet Commerce"	This choice mischaracterizes both passages. Passage A isn't an announcement of economic boon, and Passage B isn't about a legislative response. Eliminate.
(C) "New Planet Discovered in Solar System" "Planet or Asteroid: Scientists Debate"	Half-Right/Half-Wrong. The first document here might be parallel to Passage A, but Passage B doesn't describe a debate about the new phenomenon. Eliminate.
(D) "Biologists Create New Species in Lab" "Artificially Created Life: How Patent Law Applies"	Correct. The first document announces a new phenomenon. The second raises legal questions that apply to the phenomenon.
(E) "A Renegade Economist's Views on Taxation" "Candidate Runs on Unorthodox Tax Plan" *PrepTest71 Sec4 Q10*	Distortion. Passage A in no way states nor implies that the economist is a renegade. And Passage B doesn't apply the discovery to a political campaign. Eliminate.

LSAT Question	Analysis
19. The passages were most likely taken from which one of the following pairs of sources?	**Step 2:** This is an Inference question. It asks you to use the passages' content and style to infer the type of literature from which each was culled.
	Step 3: Passage A is informal and narrative; it feels like it comes from a popular newspaper or magazine. Passage B's author states that this text is from the beginning of an "article" (line 44) that is going to go into more detail about law and policy, as would be the case in a law journal.
	Step 4: The correct answer will likely say: Passage A—a popular magazine; Passage B—an academic law journal.
(A) passage A: a magazine article addressed to a general audience passage B: a law journal article	**Step 5:** Correct. This matches the prediction perfectly.
(B) passage A: a technical journal for economists passage B: a magazine article addressed to a general audience	180. Passage A is noteworthy for its lack of technical jargon. Passage B promises to go much deeper than would a general audience magazine. Eliminate.
(C) passage A: a science-fiction novel passage B: a technical journal for economists	180/Distortion. Passage A is decidedly nonfiction. Passage B is addressed more to lawyers than it is to economists. Eliminate.
(D) passage A: a law journal article passage B: a speech delivered before a legislative body	Outside the Scope/Distortion. Passage A doesn't touch on any legal topics. Passage B is explicitly an article, not a speech. Eliminate.
(E) passage A: a speech delivered before a legislative body passage B: a science-fiction novel *PrepTest71 Sec4 Q11*	Outside the Scope. Nothing in Passage A implies that legislative recommendations are to follow. Passage B is clearly nonfiction. Eliminate.

859

LSAT Question	Analysis
20. Which one of the following most accurately describes the relationship between the two passages?	**Step 2:** A Global question rewarding accurate summaries of the two passages, and a valid comparison of them. **Step 3:** Consult the Big Picture summaries (the mental Roadmap, if you will). **Step 4:** The correct answer will be something along these lines: Passage A announces a shocking discovery; Passage B identifies important questions raised by the discovery, and recommends an answer.
(A) Passage A summarizes a scholar's unanticipated discovery, while passage B proposes solutions to a problem raised by the phenomenon discovered.	**Step 5:** Correct. This matches the Step 4 prediction.
(B) Passage A explains an economic theory, while passage B identifies a practical problem resulting from that theory.	Outside the Scope. We learn nothing of the economist's theories, and the questions in Passage B are the result of a discovery, not of a theory. Eliminate.
(C) Passage A reports on a subculture, while passage B discusses the difficulty of policing that subculture.	Distortion. Online gaming communities might be considered a subculture, but Passage A isn't a report on them. Passage B proposes a model for taxation, not difficulties in enforcement. Eliminate.
(D) Passage A challenges the common interpretation of a phenomenon, while passage B reaffirms that interpretation.	Outside the Scope. Passage A does not challenge anyone's interpretation, nor does Passage B reaffirm Passage A in any way. Eliminate.
(E) Passage A states a set of facts, while passage B draws theoretical consequences from those facts. *PrepTest71 Sec4 Q12*	Distortion. Passage A does communicate facts, although "states" seems too dry a description of its tone. Passage B does not outline consequences; it raises questions and provides an answer. Eliminate.

LSAT Question	Analysis
21. Based on passage B, which one of the following is a characteristic of some "games that are intentionally commodified" (line 54)?	**Step 2:** The correct answer will be found in the passage ("Based on the passage, which one . . . is a characteristic . . ."), making this a Detail question. **Step 3:** The author of Passage B describes "intentionally commodified" games at lines 28–29. These games grant intellectual property rights to players who create virtual goods in the game. The author also argues that virtual goods in these games should be taxed when sold for real-world currency, or in-game virtual currency. **Step 4:** The correct answer will restate or closely paraphrase something the author of Passage B said about intentionally commodified games.
(A) The game allows selling real items for virtual currency.	**Step 5:** Distortion. The issue is the sale of virtual items for real currency. This choice gets that backwards. Eliminate.
(B) The game allows players to trade avatars with other players.	Outside the Scope. There is nothing about avatars in either passage. Eliminate.
(C) Players of the game grow wealthier the longer they play.	Faulty Use of Detail. This is a fact mentioned in Passage A (lines 11–12).
(D) Players of the game own intellectual property rights in their creations.	Correct. This is stated explicitly in lines 28–29.
(E) Players of the game can exchange one virtual currency for another virtual currency. *PrepTest71 Sec4 Q13*	Distortion. The passages address the sale of virtual items for either virtual or real currency. Virtual-to-virtual *currency exchanges* are not mentioned. Eliminate.

It's good to build up your practice step-by-step as you're learning the Method. If you continue to practice these steps diligently, by Test Day you'll do them as if they were second nature.

Practice: Steps 2–5

Now you're ready to try Steps 2–5 on a question set. Here, you see the Debate passage on Homing Pigeons, complete with the Roadmap and strategic reading analysis. This time, all of the questions associated with that passage are included. Take a few minutes to refresh your memory of the passage and then work through the entire question set. Don't time yourself. Record your analysis for each Step of the Reading Comprehension Method involved in handling the question set. When you're done, compare your work to the expert analysis that follows.

LSAT Passage	Analysis
Homing pigeons can be taken from their lofts and transported hundreds of kilometers in covered cages to unfamiliar sites and yet, when released, be able to choose fairly accurate homeward bearings within a (5) minute and fly home. Aside from reading the minds of the experimenters (a possibility that has not escaped investigation), there are two basic explanations for the remarkable ability of pigeons to "home": the birds might keep track of their outward displacement (the (10) system of many short-range species such as honeybees); or they might have some sense, known as a "map sense," that would permit them to construct an internal image of their environment and then "place" themselves with respect to home on some internalized (15) coordinate system. *[margin notes: Homing pigeons How do they "home"? / Two expl's: out./disp. / map sense]*	**Step 1:** The **Topic**—homing pigeons—and the **Scope**—the question of how they home—are clear from the first paragraph. After dismissing a rather hare-brained suggestion (maybe they read human minds!), the author presents two reasonable hypotheses: 1) outward displacement (which other species, e.g., honeybees use), and 2) "map sense." We can anticipate that the next two paragraphs will evaluate these hypotheses in more detail.
The first alternative seems unlikely. One possible model for such an inertial system might involve an internal magnetic compass to measure the directional leg of each journey. Birds transported to the release site (20) wearing magnets or otherwise subjected to an artificial magnetic field, however, are only occasionally affected. Alternately, if pigeons measure their displacement by consciously keeping track of the direction and degree of acceleration and deceleration of (25) the various turns, and timing the individual legs of the journey, simply transporting them in the dark, with constant rotations, or under complete anesthesia ought to impair or eliminate their ability to orient. These treatments, however, have no effect. Unfortunately, no (30) one has yet performed the crucial experiment of transporting pigeons in total darkness, anesthetized, rotating, and with the magnetic field reversed all at the same time. *[margin notes: out./disp. unlikely / models tested w/ neg. results / Au.—not 100% ruled out]*	The author finds outward displacement "unlikely," but not 100 percent ruled out. She cites two possible models for outward displacement: Homing pigeons may have "an internal magnetic compass" (lines 16–19), or they may keep track of turns and acceleration (lines 22–28). When tested, neither model was supported by the findings. "Unfortunately," says the author, no one has done the complete rule-out experiment of impairing, simultaneously, all of the pigeons' potential modes for tracking outward displacement. That's why the author won't say the hypothesis is completely disproven. Because the author thinks outward displacement "unlikely," she will give her evaluation of the "map sense" in the next paragraph.

LSAT Passage		Analysis

(35)   The other alternative, that pigeons have a "map sense," seems more promising, yet the nature of this sense remains mysterious. Papi has posited that the map sense is olfactory: that birds come to associate odors borne on the wind with the direction in which the

(40) wind is blowing, and so slowly build up an olfactory map of their surroundings. When transported to the release site, then, they only have to sniff the air en route and/or at the site to know the direction of home. Papi conducted a series of experiments showing that pigeons whose nostrils have been plugged are poorly

(45) oriented at release and home slowly.

map sense—promising but still questions

Papi hypo: smell map

As expected, here's the author's evaluation of pigeons' "map sense." This hypothesis she finds "promising." Nonetheless, "map sense" "remains mysterious." So, our author doesn't think the map sense has been completely explained.

The rest of the paragraph details how a scientist named Papi tested an olfactory model for the map sense with some success.

(45)   One problem with the hypothesis is that Schmidt-Koenig and Phillips failed to detect any ability in pigeons to distinguish natural air (presumably laden with olfactory map information) from pure, filtered air.

(50) Papi's experimental results, moreover, admit of simpler, nonolfactory explanations. It seems likely that the behavior of nostril-plugged birds results from the distracting and traumatic nature of the experiment. When nasal tubes are used to bypass the olfactory

(55) chamber but allow for comfortable breathing, no disorientation is evident. Likewise, when the olfactory epithelium is sprayed with anesthetic to block smell-detection but not breathing, orientation is normal.

PrepTest27 Sec3 Qs 15–21

Problems with Papi

This paragraph outlines three criticisms of Papi's experiments (signaled by the keywords "[o]ne problem," "moreover," and "[l]ikewise"). The criticisms come from a pair of scientists: Schmidt-Koenig and Phillips. They tested pigeons using filtered air (no smells, in other words) and found no difference in their ability to home. They also suggested that Papi's experiments had traumatized the birds, and so performed two tests that blocked the pigeons' olfactory senses without injuring them. The results, again, undermined Papi's model.

There is no explicit thesis statement or conclusion sentence in this passage. The author's **Purpose**, as shown by Paragraphs 2–4 is to *evaluate* the two main hypotheses. Her **Main Point** is that pigeons probably home using a map sense (outward displacement is unlikely), but that we don't yet know what kind of map they use.

LSAT Question	My Analysis
22. Which one of the following best states the main idea of the passage?	**Step 2:**
	Step 3:
	→
	Step 4:
(A) The ability of pigeons to locate and return to their homes from distant points is unlike that of any other species.	**Step 5:**
	→
(B) It is likely that some map sense accounts for the homing ability of pigeons, but the nature of that sense has not been satisfactorily identified.	
(C) The majority of experiments on the homing ability of pigeons have been marked by design flaws.	
(D) The mechanisms underlying the homing ability of pigeons can best be identified through a combination of laboratory research and field experimentation.	
(E) The homing ability of pigeons is most likely based on a system similar to that used by many short-range species.	

PrepTest27 Sec3 Q15

LSAT Question	My Analysis
23. According to the passage, which one of the following is ordinarily true regarding how homing pigeons "home"?	**Step 2:**
	Step 3: →
	Step 4:
(A) Each time they are released at a specific site they fly home by the same route.	**Step 5:** →
(B) When they are released they take only a short time to orient themselves before selecting their route home.	
(C) Each time they are released at a specific site they take a shorter amount of time to orient themselves before flying home.	
(D) They travel fairly long distances in seemingly random patterns before finally deciding on a route home.	
(E) Upon release they travel briefly in the direction opposite to the one they eventually choose.	

PrepTest27 Sec3 Q16

LSAT Question	My Analysis
24. Which one of the following experiments would best test the "possibility" referred to in line 6?	**Step 2:**
	Step 3: $\longrightarrow$
	Step 4:
(A) an experiment in which the handlers who transported, released, and otherwise came into contact with homing pigeons released at an unfamiliar site were unaware of the location of the pigeons' home	**Step 5:** $\longrightarrow$
(B) an experiment in which the handlers who transported, released, and otherwise came into contact with homing pigeons released at an unfamiliar site were asked not to display any affection toward the pigeons	
(C) an experiment in which the handlers who transported, released, and otherwise came into contact with homing pigeons released at an unfamiliar site were asked not to speak to each other throughout the release process	
(D) an experiment in which all the homing pigeons released at an unfamiliar site had been raised and fed by individual researchers rather than by teams of handlers	
(E) an experiment in which all the homing pigeons released at an unfamiliar site were exposed to a wide variety of unfamiliar sights and sounds	

PrepTest27 Sec3 Q17

LSAT Question	**My Analysis**
25. Information in the passage supports which one of the following statements regarding the "first alternative" (line 16) for explaining the ability of pigeons to "home"?	**Step 2:**
	Step 3:
	$\longrightarrow$
	Step 4:
(A) It has been conclusively ruled out by the results of numerous experiments.	**Step 5:**
	$\longrightarrow$
(B) It seems unlikely because there are no theoretical models that could explain how pigeons track displacement.	
(C) It has not, to date, been supported by experimental data, but neither has it been definitively ruled out.	
(D) It seems unlikely in theory, but recent experimental results show that it may in fact be correct.	
(E) It is not a useful theory because of the difficulty in designing experiments by which it might be tested.	

PrepTest27 Sec3 Q18

LSAT Question	My Analysis
26. The author refers to "the system of many short-range species such as honeybees" (lines 9–11) most probably in order to	**Step 2:**
	Step 3: →
	Step 4:
(A) emphasize the universality of the ability to home	**Step 5:** →
(B) suggest that a particular explanation of pigeons' homing ability is worthy of consideration	
(C) discredit one of the less convincing theories regarding the homing ability of pigeons	
(D) criticize the techniques utilized by scientists investigating the nature of pigeons' homing ability	
(E) illustrate why a proposed explanation of pigeons' homing ability is correct	

PrepTest27 Sec3 Q19

LSAT Question	My Analysis
27. Which one of the following, if true, would most weaken Papi's theory regarding homing pigeons' homing ability?	**Step 2:**
	Step 3: $\rightarrow$
	Step 4:
(A) Even pigeons that have been raised in several different lofts in a variety of territories can find their way to their current home when released in unfamiliar territory.	**Step 5:** $\rightarrow$
(B) Pigeons whose sense of smell has been partially blocked find their way home more slowly than do pigeons whose sense of smell has not been affected.	
(C) Even pigeons that have been raised in the same loft frequently take different routes home when released in unfamiliar territory.	
(D) Even pigeons that have been transported well beyond the range of the odors detectable in their home territories can find their way home.	
(E) Pigeons' sense of smell is no more acute than that of other birds who do not have the ability to "home."	

PrepTest27 Sec3 Q20

LSAT Question	My Analysis
28. Given the information in the passage, it is most likely that Papi and the author of the passage would both agree with which one of the following statements regarding the homing ability of pigeons?	**Step 2:**
	Step 3:
	→
	Step 4:
(A) The map sense of pigeons is most probably related to their olfactory sense.	**Step 5:**
	→
(B) The mechanism regulating the homing ability of pigeons is most probably similar to that utilized by honeybees.	
(C) The homing ability of pigeons is most probably based on a map sense.	
(D) The experiments conducted by Papi himself have provided the most valuable evidence yet collected regarding the homing ability of pigeons.	
(E) The experiments conducted by Schmidt-Koenig and Phillips have not substantially lessened the probability that Papi's own theory is correct.	

PrepTest27 Sec3 Q21

Expert Analysis

Here's how the LSAT expert performed Steps 2–5 on the passage about Homing Pigeons. Compare your work to that of the expert. Don't check merely to see whether you got the correct answers. Ask questions that help you dig into your mastery of these important steps in the Reading Comprehension Method. Did you recognize each question type? Where there were research clues, did you use them to research the passage? Did you predict the correct answer whenever possible?

LSAT Question	Analysis
22. Which one of the following best states the main idea of the passage?	**Step 2:** A Global question calling for the author's main idea.
	Step 3: Consult the Big Picture summaries.
	Step 4: The author's Main Point is that pigeons probably home using a map sense (outward displacement is unlikely), but that we don't yet know what kind of map they use.
(A) The ability of pigeons to locate and return to their homes from distant points is unlike that of any other species.	**Step 5:** Outside the Scope. Not only is this far too narrow to represent the passage's Main Idea, it is also something the author never said. Eliminate.
(B) It is likely that some map sense accounts for the homing ability of pigeons, but the nature of that sense has not been satisfactorily identified.	Correct. This matches the Big Picture summary of the passage, and thus, our Step 4 prediction.
(C) The majority of experiments on the homing ability of pigeons have been marked by design flaws.	Extreme/180. First, we have no idea whether the experiments described in the passage represent a *majority* of the experiments on homing by pigeons. Second, the experiments described in Paragraph 2 were, apparently, well designed; their results make outward displacement less likely to explain pigeons' homing abilities. Eliminate.
(D) The mechanisms underlying the homing ability of pigeons can best be identified through a combination of laboratory research and field experimentation.	Outside the Scope. The author does not opine on the *best* way to identify pigeons' homing mechanisms. More importantly, this is not the point of the passage. Eliminate.
(E) The homing ability of pigeons is most likely based on a system similar to that used by many short-range species. *PrepTest27 Sec3 Q15*	180. The system used by short-range species (lines 9–11) is outward displacement, the explanation the author finds *un*likely (line 16).

LSAT Question	Analysis
23. According to the passage, which one of the following is ordinarily true regarding how homing pigeons "home"?	**Step 2:** "According to the passage . . ." signals a Detail question. The correct answer will come directly from the text.
	Step 3: The author states facts known about pigeons' homing ability only at the beginning of Paragraph 1. After that, she discusses only possible explanations for *how* they home.
	Step 4: The correct answer will say something akin to lines 1–5: Pigeons can home from many kilometers away; when released, they take under a minute to orient themselves, and then fly home.
(A) Each time they are released at a specific site they fly home by the same route.	**Step 5:** Outside the Scope. The author never tells us if pigeons use the same route home. Eliminate.
(B) When they are released they take only a short time to orient themselves before selecting their route home.	Correct. This matches the passage at lines 1–5 perfectly.
(C) Each time they are released at a specific site they take a shorter amount of time to orient themselves before flying home.	Outside the Scope. The author does not discuss this issue one way or the other. Eliminate.
(D) They travel fairly long distances in seemingly random patterns before finally deciding on a route home.	180. This statement contradicts the opening lines of the passage, which say that the pigeons orient within one minute. Eliminate.
(E) Upon release they travel briefly in the direction opposite to the one they eventually choose. *PrepTest27 Sec3 Q16*	Outside the Scope. The author makes no mention of pigeons flying in the direction opposite to their home. Eliminate.

LSAT Question	Analysis
24. Which one of the following experiments would best test the "possibility" referred to in line 6?	**Step 2:** This question asks you to identify an experiment that would test the hypothesis from line 6. This makes it an Inference question.
	Step 3: The hypothesis at line 6 was that pigeons read the minds of their handlers.
	Step 4: The correct answer will describe an experiment that could disprove the mind-reading hypothesis.
(A) an experiment in which the handlers who transported, released, and otherwise came into contact with homing pigeons released at an unfamiliar site were unaware of the location of the pigeons' home	**Step 5:** Correct. If the pigeons' handlers do not know where the pigeons' home is, and if the pigeons are still able to home, we could disprove the mind-reading hypothesis.
(B) an experiment in which the handlers who transported, released, and otherwise came into contact with homing pigeons released at an unfamiliar site were asked not to display any affection toward the pigeons	Distortion. This would help disprove the hypothesis that pigeons are able to home because humans are affectionate toward them. Eliminate.
(C) an experiment in which the handlers who transported, released, and otherwise came into contact with homing pigeons released at an unfamiliar site were asked not to speak to each other throughout the release process	Distortion. This would help disprove the hypothesis that pigeons are able to home because they can understand human language or verbal cues. Eliminate.
(D) an experiment in which all the homing pigeons released at an unfamiliar site had been raised and fed by individual researchers rather than by teams of handlers	Distortion. This would help disprove the hypothesis that pigeons are able to home because of their relationship with a specific individual. Eliminate.
(E) an experiment in which all the homing pigeons released at an unfamiliar site were exposed to a wide variety of unfamiliar sights and sounds *PrepTest27 Sec3 Q17*	Distortion. This would help disprove the hypothesis that pigeons are able to home because they recognize familiar sights and sounds. Eliminate.

LSAT Question	Analysis
25. Information in the passage supports which one of the following statements regarding the "first alternative" (line 16) for explaining the ability of pigeons to "home"?	**Step 2:** This is an Inference question. The correct answer follows from information in the passage.
	Step 3: The "first alternative" is outward displacement, discussed throughout Paragraph 2.
	Step 4: The author thinks outward displacement is unlikely the mechanism by which pigeons home (line 16), but she admits that it has not been 100 percent ruled out (lines 29–33).
(A) It has been conclusively ruled out by the results of numerous experiments.	**Step 5:** 180. No one has yet performed the "crucial experiment" (line 30) that would definitely disprove outward displacement. Eliminate.
(B) It seems unlikely because there are no theoretical models that could explain how pigeons track displacement.	180. The author presents two theoretical models in Paragraph 2: an internal magnetic compass and the measurement of acceleration and turns. Eliminate.
(C) It has not, to date, been supported by experimental data, but neither has it been definitively ruled out.	Correct. This follows from the author's opinion that outward displacement is "unlikely" (line 16) but has not been ruled out by the "crucial experiment" (lines 29–30).
(D) It seems unlikely in theory, but recent experimental results show that it may in fact be correct.	180. The experimental results in Paragraph 2 all weaken the likelihood that pigeons use outward displacement. Eliminate.
(E) It is not a useful theory because of the difficulty in designing experiments by which it might be tested.	180. Given the results discussed in Paragraph 2, it appears that experimenters have had no trouble testing outward displacement. Eliminate.

PrepTest27 Sec3 Q18

LSAT Question	Analysis
26. The author refers to "the system of many short-range species such as honeybees" (lines 9–11) most probably in order to	**Step 2:** This is a Logic Function question asking *how* or *why* the author cited a particular detail.
	Step 3: The reference from the question stem is associated with outward displacement. When the author first cites outward displacement as one of the two "basic explanations," he notes that outward displacement is the system used by honeybees and other short-range homing species.
	Step 4: By bringing up the fact that other species are able to home through outward displacement, the author suggests a reason why scientists may want to investigate whether this could also explain homing pigeons' homing abilities.
(A) emphasize the universality of the ability to home	**Step 5:** Extreme. The author never claims that all animals can home, and certainly doesn't cite honeybees, a single species, to try to emphasize that point. Eliminate.
(B) suggest that a particular explanation of pigeons' homing ability is worthy of consideration	Correct. This is precisely how the reference to honeybees and other short-range species is used in the first paragraph.
(C) discredit one of the less convincing theories regarding the homing ability of pigeons	180. While the author considers outward displacement "unlikely," her evaluation of the hypothesis doesn't come up until Paragraph 2. At the point in the passage where she mentions honeybees, she is trying to show that outward displacement is one of two "basic explanations" that deserve testing. Eliminate.
(D) criticize the techniques utilized by scientists investigating the nature of pigeons' homing ability	Faulty Use of Detail. The author's critiques of scientists' experiments are found at the end of Paragraph 2 and in Paragraph 4. Eliminate.
(E) illustrate why a proposed explanation of pigeons' homing ability is correct *PrepTest27 Sec3 Q19*	180. Outward displacement is the explanation the author considers "unlikely" to be valid. Eliminate.

LSAT Question	Analysis
27. Which one of the following, if true, would most weaken Papi's theory regarding homing pigeons' homing ability?	**Step 2:** This is a Logic Reasoning question, worded like a Weaken question would be in the Logical Reasoning section.
	Step 3: Papi's model is found in Paragraph 3. He thinks that pigeons home through an olfactory map sense. They smell their way home, if you will.
	Step 4: The correct answer will provide a set of facts that makes it unlikely that pigeons use a "smell map" to find their way home.
(A) Even pigeons that have been raised in several different lofts in a variety of territories can find their way to their current home when released in unfamiliar territory.	**Step 5:** Outside the Scope. This doesn't address smell as a factor in the pigeons' homing ability. Eliminate.
(B) Pigeons whose sense of smell has been partially blocked find their way home more slowly than do pigeons whose sense of smell has not been affected.	180. This supports Papi's model. Eliminate.
(C) Even pigeons that have been raised in the same loft frequently take different routes home when released in unfamiliar territory.	Outside the Scope. This doesn't address smell as a factor in the pigeons' homing ability. Eliminate.
(D) Even pigeons that have been transported well beyond the range of the odors detectable in their home territories can find their way home.	Correct. If pigeons are taken to places with wholly unfamiliar smells, and yet are still able to home, Papi's model is less likely to explain their "map sense."
(E) Pigeons' sense of smell is no more acute than that of other birds who do not have the ability to "home." *PrepTest27 Sec3 Q20*	Irrelevant Comparison. Papi's hypothesis does not require that pigeons have a better developed sense of smell than other birds have. A bird of prey, for example, might have an extremely acute sense of smell, but would use it to hunt rather than to home. Eliminate.

LSAT Question	Analysis
28. Given the information in the passage, it is most likely that Papi and the author of the passage would both agree with which one of the following statements regarding the homing ability of pigeons?	**Step 2:** This is an Inference question; the correct answer follows from the passage. Note that this question is similar to a Point at Issue question from Logical Reasoning, but asks for a point of *agreement* between two people rather than a point of disagreement.
	→ **Step 3:** Papi's position is found in Paragraph 3. The author's point of view is best expressed through our Big Picture summaries.
	Step 4: The author and Papi would agree that pigeons probably home through the use of a "map sense." Only Papi, however, would claim that the map was olfactory in nature.
(A) The map sense of pigeons is most probably related to their olfactory sense.	→ **Step 5:** Half-Right/Half-Wrong. Papi would agree with this statement; the author would not (see lines 35–36). Eliminate.
(B) The mechanism regulating the homing ability of pigeons is most probably similar to that utilized by honeybees.	→ 180. The system used by honeybees is outward displacement, an explanation that both the author and Papi would find unlikely. Eliminate.
(C) The homing ability of pigeons is most probably based on a map sense.	→ Correct. Both the author and Papi consider map sense the most promising explanation for pigeons' homing ability.
(D) The experiments conducted by Papi himself have provided the most valuable evidence yet collected regarding the homing ability of pigeons.	→ Distortion. Presumably Papi would think his own experiments pretty valuable, but the author is unconvinced (see lines 35–36, and all of Paragraph 4). Eliminate.
(E) The experiments conducted by Schmidt-Koenig and Phillips have not substantially lessened the probability that Papi's own theory is correct. *PrepTest27 Sec3 Q21*	→ Distortion. We have no idea whether Papi thinks Schmidt-Koenig and Phillips's experiments have damaged his model. Presumably, the author thinks so, since she cites their work to demonstrate why the precise nature of the map sense "remains mysterious." Eliminate.

Reflection

Take a moment to reflect on how you built your skills to the point where you could more efficiently tackle that last question set. You're certainly not yet as fast and confident as you will be after more practice, but already, by concentrating on the steps of the Reading Comprehension Method, you're almost certainly taking a straighter, more effective line to the correct answer.

Reading Comprehension Practice

Now that you've mastered the steps in the Reading Comprehension Method, it's time to apply what you've learned to passages and question sets you haven't seen. In the pages that follow, you'll find four additional passages. Among these passages, you'll find both standard and Comparative Reading passages, you'll see further examples of the common structural patterns found on the LSAT, and you'll get more practice with all of the Reading Comprehension question types. This set of practice passages is representative of the various passage patterns and subject matter that has appeared on official LSATs over the past five years.

NOTES ON READING COMPREHENSION PRACTICE

The passages in this chapter are arranged by difficulty (from easiest to hardest). To assess passage difficulty, we calculated the average difficulty of all questions from each passage's question set. That said, don't place undue emphasis on the difficulty assessment of entire passages. Even the easiest passages may have one or more very difficult questions, and the hardest may have a couple of "gimmes." As you review, check the difficulty level of each question and read the explanations to see what may have made it easier or harder for the majority of test takers. Because the passages are organized by difficulty, if you practice them straight through the chapter, you will encounter different patterns and subject matter at random, just as you will on the exam. That is a good reminder that subject matter alone does not determine the difficulty of Reading Comprehension questions and that different subject areas are easier or harder for different individuals. You need not do all of the passages in order. If you have limited time, you may decide to do some easy and some difficult passages to balance your practice.

As you tackle the Reading Comprehension passages and questions in this chapter, keep the following pointers in mind.

Use the Reading Comprehension Method consistently. Chapter 14 was organized around the Reading Comprehension Method introduced in Chapter 13. That's because having a consistent, strategic approach is essential in this section of the test. Be conscious of each step as you practice. If you practice without instilling the Method and its associated strategies, you're likely to repeat your old patterns, and that means continuing to be frustrated by the same Reading Comprehension pitfalls over and over again.

THE KAPLAN READING COMPREHENSION METHOD

Step 1: Read the Passage Strategically—circle Keywords and jot down margin notes to summarize the portions of the passage relevant to LSAT questions; summarize the author's Topic/Scope/Purpose/Main Idea.

Step 2: Read the Question Stem—identify the question type, characterize the correct and incorrect answers, and look for clues to guide your research.

Step 3: Research the Relevant Text—based on the clues in the question stem, consult your Roadmap; for open-ended questions, refer to your Topic/Scope/ Purpose/Main Idea summaries.

Step 4: Predict the Correct Answer—based on research (or, for open-ended questions, your Topic/Scope/Purpose/Main Idea summaries), predict the meaning of the correct answer.

Step 5: Evaluate the Answer Choices—select the choice that matches your prediction of the correct answer or eliminate the four wrong answer choices.

As you practice, pay special attention to your work in Step 1 of the Method. Many test takers underestimate the importance of strategic reading. If you find that you are encountering questions that surprise you or for which you have little idea of where in the passage the relevant information would be, it's likely that you needed a stronger Roadmap or better big-picture summaries back in Step 1.

Review your work thoroughly. Complete explanations for the passages and questions in this chapter follow right after the question pool. Take the time to study them even if you get all of a passage's questions correct. Review how expert test takers Roadmapped the passage, the Keywords they circled, the margin notes they jotted down, and how they summarized the author's overall Purpose and Main Idea. You may well discover that with more effective strategic reading, your work on the questions could have been both faster and more accurate. Of course, when you miss a question, determine whether the problem came from a misunderstanding or an oversight in the question itself, or whether you misread or overlooked a key piece of the passage.

Another way in which you can effectively use the explanations is to first complete Step 1—create a Roadmap and summarize the author's Purpose and Main Idea. Then, review just that much of the explanations for the passage before you even try the questions. This will let you focus on how you're doing in Step 1, laying the crucial groundwork for effective management of the question set. After you're sure that you understand the passage, try the questions and review them as well. This approach is especially helpful when you find a particular passage frustrating and you feel that you're making little progress working through the questions.

Finally, each question's difficulty is ranked in the explanations—from ★★★★ for the toughest questions to ★ for the easiest. Consulting these rankings will tell you a lot about the passages and questions you're practicing. You might, for example, distinguish a very hard question in an otherwise easy passage. In that case, you'll focus your review on what made that question confusing for test takers while reassuring yourself that your overall approach was on target. Conversely, you may find a passage in which, say, four out of six questions rate ★★★ or ★★★★. In that case, you'll know the passage was tough for everyone, which means you should spend extra time reviewing the Roadmap and big-picture summaries to discover how the testmaker made a passage so challenging.

Practice and Timing. On Test Day, you'll have about 8½ minutes per passage. Naturally, that kind of time pressure can make even routine reading feel stressful. As you practice individual passages, work quickly, but make your focus the successful implementation of the Method. Practicing too quickly could introduce time pressure at a point where you should really be working on consistency and accuracy. Speed will come with familiarity, practice, and (believe it or not) patience. When you take full tests or try 35-minute Reading Comprehension sections, time yourself strictly. But don't be in such a rush to get faster that you fail to gain the efficiencies that come from practicing the methodical application of good Reading Comprehension strategy. Chapter 16 will address timing in depth and will introduce you to strategies to effectively manage the 35-minute Reading Comprehension section that you'll complete on Test Day. In the present chapter, practice *and review* passages one by one to perfect your approach.

QUESTION POOL

For decades, there has been a deep rift between poetry and fiction in the United States, especially in academic settings; graduate writing programs in universities, for example, train students as poets or as
(5) writers of fiction, but almost never as both. Both poets and writers of fiction have tended to support this separation, in large part because the current conventional wisdom holds that poetry should be elliptical and lyrical, reflecting inner states and
(10) processes of thought or feeling, whereas character and narrative events are the stock-in-trade of fiction.

Certainly it is true that poetry and fiction are distinct genres, but why have specialized education and literary territoriality resulted from this distinction?
(15) The answer lies perhaps in a widespread attitude in U.S. culture, which often casts a suspicious eye on the generalist. Those with knowledge and expertise in multiple areas risk charges of dilettantism, as if ability in one field is diluted or compromised by
(20) accomplishment in another.

Fortunately, there are signs that the bias against writers who cross generic boundaries is diminishing; several recent writers are known and respected for their work in both genres. One important example of
(25) this trend is Rita Dove, an African American writer highly acclaimed for both her poetry and her fiction. A few years ago, speaking at a conference entitled "Poets Who Write Fiction," Dove expressed gentle incredulity about the habit of segregating the genres.
(30) She had grown up reading and loving both fiction and poetry, she said, unaware of any purported danger lurking in attempts to mix the two. She also studied for some time in Germany, where, she observes, "Poets write plays, novelists compose libretti, playwrights
(35) write novels—they would not understand our restrictiveness."

It makes little sense, Dove believes, to persist in the restrictive approach to poetry and fiction prevalent in the U.S., because each genre shares in the nature of
(40) the other. Indeed, her poetry offers example after example of what can only be properly regarded as lyric narrative. Her use of language in these poems is undeniably lyrical—that is, it evokes emotion and inner states without requiring the reader to organize
(45) ideas or events in a particular linear structure. Yet this lyric expression simultaneously presents the elements of a plot in such a way that the reader is led repeatedly to take account of clusters of narrative details within the lyric flow. Thus while the language is lyrical, it
(50) often comes to constitute, cumulatively, a work of narrative fiction. Similarly, many passages in her fiction, though undeniably prose, achieve the status of lyric narrative through the use of poetic rhythms and elliptical expression. In short, Dove bridges the gap
(55) between poetry and fiction not only by writing in both genres, but also by fusing the two genres within individual works.

1. Which one of the following most accurately expresses the main point of the passage?

   (A) Rita Dove's work has been widely acclaimed primarily because of the lyrical elements she has introduced into her fiction.

   (B) Rita Dove's lyric narratives present clusters of narrative detail in order to create a cumulative narrative without requiring the reader to interpret it in a linear manner.

   (C) Working against a bias that has long been dominant in the U.S., recent writers like Rita Dove have shown that the lyrical use of language can effectively enhance narrative fiction.

   (D) Unlike many of her U.S. contemporaries, Rita Dove writes without relying on the traditional techniques associated with poetry and fiction.

   (E) Rita Dove's successful blending of poetry and fiction exemplifies the recent trend away from the rigid separation of the two genres that has long been prevalent in the U.S.

2. Which one of the following is most analogous to the literary achievements that the author attributes to Dove?

   (A) A chef combines nontraditional cooking methods and traditional ingredients from disparate world cuisines to devise new recipes.

   (B) A professor of film studies becomes a film director and succeeds, partly due to a wealth of theoretical knowledge of filmmaking.

   (C) An actor who is also a theatrical director teams up with a public health agency to use street theater to inform the public about health matters.

   (D) A choreographer defies convention and choreographs dances that combine elements of both ballet and jazz dance.

   (E) A rock musician records several songs from previous decades but introduces extended guitar solos into each one.

GO ON TO THE NEXT PAGE.

3. According to the passage, in the U.S. there is a widely held view that

    (A) poetry should not involve characters or narratives
    (B) unlike the writing of poetry, the writing of fiction is rarely an academically serious endeavor
    (C) graduate writing programs focus on poetry to the exclusion of fiction
    (D) fiction is most aesthetically effective when it incorporates lyrical elements
    (E) European literary cultures are suspicious of generalists

4. The author's attitude toward the deep rift between poetry and fiction in the U.S. can be most accurately described as one of

    (A) perplexity as to what could have led to the development of such a rift
    (B) astonishment that academics have overlooked the existence of the rift
    (C) ambivalence toward the effect the rift has had on U.S. literature
    (D) pessimism regarding the possibility that the rift can be overcome
    (E) disapproval of attitudes and presuppositions underlying the rift

5. In the passage the author conjectures that a cause of the deep rift between fiction and poetry in the United States may be that

    (A) poets and fiction writers each tend to see their craft as superior to the others' craft
    (B) the methods used in training graduate students in poetry are different from those used in training graduate students in other literary fields
    (C) publishers often pressure writers to concentrate on what they do best
    (D) a suspicion of generalism deters writers from dividing their energies between the two genres
    (E) fiction is more widely read and respected than poetry

6. In the context of the passage, the author's primary purpose in mentioning Dove's experience in Germany (lines 32–36) is to

    (A) suggest that the habit of treating poetry and fiction as nonoverlapping domains is characteristic of English-speaking societies but not others
    (B) point to an experience that reinforced Dove's conviction that poetry and fiction should not be rigidly separated
    (C) indicate that Dove's strengths as a writer derive in large part from the international character of her academic background
    (D) present an illuminating biographical detail about Dove in an effort to enhance the human interest appeal of the passage
    (E) indicate what Dove believes to be the origin of her opposition to the separation of fiction and poetry in the U.S.

7. It can be inferred from the passage that the author would be most likely to believe which one of the following?

    (A) Each of Dove's works can be classified as either primarily poetry or primarily fiction, even though it may contain elements of both.
    (B) The aesthetic value of lyric narrative resides in its representation of a sequence of events, rather than in its ability to evoke inner states.
    (C) The way in which Dove blends genres in her writing is without precedent in U.S. writing.
    (D) Narrative that uses lyrical language is generally aesthetically superior to pure lyric poetry.
    (E) Writers who successfully cross the generic boundary between poetry and fiction often try their hand at genres such as drama as well.

8. If this passage had been excerpted from a longer text, which one of the following predictions about the near future of U.S. literature would be most likely to appear in that text?

    (A) The number of writers who write both poetry and fiction will probably continue to grow.
    (B) Because of the increased interest in mixed genres, the small market for pure lyric poetry will likely shrink even further.
    (C) Narrative poetry will probably come to be regarded as a sub-genre of fiction.
    (D) There will probably be a rise in specialization among writers in university writing programs.
    (E) Writers who continue to work exclusively in poetry or fiction will likely lose their audiences.

PrepTestJun07 Sec4 Qs1-8

The two passages discuss recent scientific research on music. They are adapted from two different papers presented at a scholarly conference.

Passage A

Did music and human language originate separately or together? Both systems use intonation and rhythm to communicate emotions. Both can be produced vocally or with tools, and people can produce
(5) both music and language silently to themselves.

Brain imaging studies suggest that music and language are part of one large, vastly complicated, neurological system for processing sound. In fact, fewer differences than similarities exist between the
(10) neurological processing of the two. One could think of the two activities as different radio programs that can be broadcast over the same hardware. One noteworthy difference, though, is that, generally speaking, people are better at language than music. In music, anyone
(15) can listen easily enough, but most people do not perform well, and in many cultures composition is left to specialists. In language, by contrast, nearly everyone actively performs and composes.

Given their shared neurological basis, it appears
(20) that music and language evolved together as brain size increased over the course of hominid evolution. But the primacy of language over music that we can observe today suggests that language, not music, was the primary function natural selection operated on.
(25) Music, it would seem, had little adaptive value of its own, and most likely developed on the coattails of language.

Passage B

Darwin claimed that since "neither the enjoyment nor the capacity of producing musical notes are
(30) faculties of the least [practical] use to man…they must be ranked amongst the most mysterious with which he is endowed." I suggest that the enjoyment of and the capacity to produce musical notes are faculties of indispensable use to mothers and their infants and
(35) that it is in the emotional bonds created by the interaction of mother and child that we can discover the evolutionary origins of human music.

Even excluding lullabies, which parents sing to infants, human mothers and infants under six months
(40) of age engage in ritualized, sequential behaviors, involving vocal, facial, and bodily interactions. Using face-to-face mother-infant interactions filmed at 24 frames per second, researchers have shown that mothers and infants jointly construct mutually
(45) improvised interactions in which each partner tracks the actions of the other. Such episodes last from one-half second to three seconds and are composed of musical elements—variations in pitch, rhythm, timbre, volume, and tempo.
(50) What evolutionary advantage would such behavior have? In the course of hominid evolution, brain size increased rapidly. Contemporaneously, the increase in bipedality caused the birth canal to narrow. This resulted in hominid infants being born ever-more
(55) prematurely, leaving them much more helpless at birth. This helplessness necessitated longer, better maternal care. Under such conditions, the emotional bonds created in the premusical mother-infant interactions we observe in *Homo sapiens* today—behavior whose
(60) neurological basis essentially constitutes the capacity to make and enjoy music—would have conferred considerable evolutionary advantage.

9. Both passages were written primarily in order to answer which one of the following questions?

(A) What evolutionary advantage did larger brain size confer on early hominids?

(B) Why do human mothers and infants engage in bonding behavior that is composed of musical elements?

(C) What are the evolutionary origins of the human ability to make music?

(D) Do the human abilities to make music and to use language depend on the same neurological systems?

(E) Why are most people more adept at using language than they are at making music?

10. Each of the two passages mentions the relation of music to

(A) bonding between humans
(B) human emotion
(C) neurological research
(D) the increasing helplessness of hominid infants
(E) the use of tools to produce sounds

GO ON TO THE NEXT PAGE.

11. It can be inferred that the authors of the two passages would be most likely to disagree over whether

(A) the increase in hominid brain size necessitated earlier births
(B) fewer differences than similarities exist between the neurological processing of music and human language
(C) brain size increased rapidly over the course of human evolution
(D) the capacity to produce music has great adaptive value to humans
(E) mother-infant bonding involves temporally patterned vocal interactions

12. The authors would be most likely to agree on the answer to which one of the following questions regarding musical capacity in humans?

(A) Does it manifest itself in some form in early infancy?
(B) Does it affect the strength of mother-infant bonds?
(C) Is it at least partly a result of evolutionary increases in brain size?
(D) Did its evolution spur the development of new neurological systems?
(E) Why does it vary so greatly among different individuals?

13. Which one of the following principles underlies the arguments in both passages?

(A) Investigations of the evolutionary origins of human behaviors must take into account the behavior of nonhuman animals.
(B) All human capacities can be explained in terms of the evolutionary advantages they offer.
(C) The fact that a single neurological system underlies two different capacities is evidence that those capacities evolved concurrently.
(D) The discovery of the neurological basis of a human behavior constitutes the discovery of the essence of that behavior.
(E) The behavior of modern-day humans can provide legitimate evidence concerning the evolutionary origins of human abilities.

14. Which one of the following most accurately characterizes a relationship between the two passages?

(A) Passage A and passage B use different evidence to draw divergent conclusions.
(B) Passage A poses the question that passage B attempts to answer.
(C) Passage A proposes a hypothesis that passage B attempts to substantiate with new evidence.
(D) Passage A expresses a stronger commitment to its hypothesis than does passage B.
(E) Passage A and passage B use different evidence to support the same conclusion.

PrepTestJun07 Sec4 Qs9-14

The World Wide Web, a network of electronically
produced and interconnected (or "linked") sites, called
pages, that are accessible via personal computer, raises
legal issues about the rights of owners of intellectual
(5) property, notably those who create documents for
inclusion on Web pages. Some of these owners of
intellectual property claim that unless copyright law is
strengthened, intellectual property on the Web will not
be protected from copyright infringement. Web users,
(10) however, claim that if their ability to access
information on Web pages is reduced, the Web cannot
live up to its potential as an open, interactive medium
of communication.

The debate arises from the Web's ability to link
(15) one document to another. Links between sites are
analogous to the inclusion in a printed text of
references to other works, but with one difference: the
cited document is instantly retrievable by a user who
activates the link. This immediate accessibility creates
(20) a problem, since current copyright laws give owners of
intellectual property the right to sue a distributor of
unauthorized copies of their material even if that
distributor did not personally make the copies. If
person A, the author of a document, puts the document
(25) on a Web page, and person B, the creator of another
Web page, creates a link to A's document, is B
committing copyright infringement?

To answer this question, it must first be
determined who controls distribution of a document on
(30) the Web. When A places a document on a Web page,
this is comparable to recording an outgoing message
on one's telephone answering machine for others to
hear. When B creates a link to A's document, this is
akin to B's giving out A's telephone number, thereby
(35) allowing third parties to hear the outgoing message for
themselves. Anyone who calls can listen to the
message; that is its purpose. While B's link may
indeed facilitate access to A's document, the crucial
point is that A, simply by placing that document on the
(40) Web, is thereby offering it for distribution. Therefore,
even if B leads others to the document, it is A who
actually controls access to it. Hence creating a link to a
document is not the same as making or distributing a
copy of that document. Moreover, techniques are
(45) already available by which A can restrict access to a
document. For example, A may require a password to
gain entry to A's Web page, just as a telephone owner
can request an unlisted number and disclose it only to
selected parties. Such a solution would compromise
(50) the openness of the Web somewhat, but not as much as
the threat of copyright infringement litigation.
Changing copyright law to benefit owners of
intellectual property is thus ill-advised because it
would impede the development of the Web as a public
(55) forum dedicated to the free exchange of ideas.

15. Which one of the following most accurately expresses
the main point of the passage?

(A) Since distribution of a document placed on a
Web page is controlled by the author of that
page rather than by the person who creates a
link to the page, creating such a link should
not be considered copyright infringement.

(B) Changes in copyright law in response to the
development of Web pages and links are
ill-advised unless such changes amplify rather
than restrict the free exchange of ideas
necessary in a democracy.

(C) People who are concerned about the access
others may have to the Web documents they
create can easily prevent such access without
inhibiting the rights of others to exchange
ideas freely.

(D) Problems concerning intellectual property rights
created by new forms of electronic media are
not insuperably difficult to resolve if one
applies basic commonsense principles to these
problems.

(E) Maintaining a free exchange of ideas on the
Web offers benefits that far outweigh those
that might be gained by a small number of
individuals if a radical alteration of copyright
laws aimed at restricting the Web's growth
were allowed.

16. Which one of the following is closest in meaning to the
term "strengthened" as that term is used in line 8 of the
passage?

(A) made more restrictive
(B) made uniform worldwide
(C) made to impose harsher penalties
(D) dutifully enforced
(E) more fully recognized as legitimate

GO ON TO THE NEXT PAGE.

17. With which one of the following claims about documents placed on Web pages would the author be most likely to agree?

    (A) Such documents cannot receive adequate protection unless current copyright laws are strengthened.

    (B) Such documents cannot be protected from unauthorized distribution without significantly diminishing the potential of the Web to be a widely used form of communication.

    (C) The nearly instantaneous access afforded by the Web makes it impossible in practice to limit access to such documents.

    (D) Such documents can be protected from copyright infringement with the least damage to the public interest only by altering existing legal codes.

    (E) Such documents cannot fully contribute to the Web's free exchange of ideas unless their authors allow them to be freely accessed by those who wish to do so.

18. Based on the passage, the relationship between strengthening current copyright laws and relying on passwords to restrict access to a Web document is most analogous to the relationship between

    (A) allowing everyone use of a public facility and restricting its use to members of the community

    (B) outlawing the use of a drug and outlawing its sale

    (C) prohibiting a sport and relying on participants to employ proper safety gear

    (D) passing a new law and enforcing that law

    (E) allowing unrestricted entry to a building and restricting entry to those who have been issued a badge

19. The passage most strongly implies which one of the following?

    (A) There are no creators of links to Web pages who are also owners of intellectual property on Web pages.

    (B) The person who controls access to a Web page document should be considered the distributor of that document.

    (C) Rights of privacy should not be extended to owners of intellectual property placed on the Web.

    (D) Those who create links to Web pages have primary control over who reads the documents on those pages.

    (E) A document on a Web page must be converted to a physical document via printing before copyright infringement takes place.

20. According to the passage, which one of the following features of outgoing messages left on telephone answering machines is most relevant to the debate concerning copyright infringement?

    (A) Such messages are carried by an electronic medium of communication.

    (B) Such messages are not legally protected against unauthorized distribution.

    (C) Transmission of such messages is virtually instantaneous.

    (D) People do not usually care whether or not others might record such messages.

    (E) Such messages have purposely been made available to anyone who calls that telephone number.

21. The author's discussion of telephone answering machines serves primarily to

    (A) compare and contrast the legal problems created by two different sorts of electronic media

    (B) provide an analogy to illustrate the positions taken by each of the two sides in the copyright debate

    (C) show that the legal problems produced by new communication technology are not themselves new

    (D) illustrate the basic principle the author believes should help determine the outcome of the copyright debate

    (E) show that telephone use also raises concerns about copyright infringement

22. According to the passage, present copyright laws

    (A) allow completely unrestricted use of any document placed by its author on a Web page

    (B) allow those who establish links to a document on a Web page to control its distribution to others

    (C) prohibit anyone but the author of a document from making a profit from the document's distribution

    (D) allow the author of a document to sue anyone who distributes the document without permission

    (E) should be altered to allow more complete freedom in the exchange of ideas

PrepTestJun07 Sec4 Qs15-22

The explanations to these questions begin on page 903.

In tracing the changing face of the Irish landscape, scholars have traditionally relied primarily on evidence from historical documents. However, such documentary sources provide a fragmentary record at
(5) best. Reliable accounts are very scarce for many parts of Ireland prior to the seventeenth century, and many of the relevant documents from the sixteenth and seventeenth centuries focus selectively on matters relating to military or commercial interests.

(10)   Studies of fossilized pollen grains preserved in peats and lake muds provide an additional means of investigating vegetative landscape change. Details of changes in vegetation resulting from both human activities and natural events are reflected in the kinds
(15) and quantities of minute pollen grains that become trapped in sediments. Analysis of samples can identify which kinds of plants produced the preserved pollen grains and when they were deposited, and in many cases the findings can serve to supplement or correct
(20) the documentary record.

For example, analyses of samples from Long Lough in County Down have revealed significant patterns of cereal-grain pollen beginning by about 400 A.D. The substantial clay content of the soil in this part
(25) of Down makes cultivation by primitive tools difficult. Historians thought that such soils were not tilled to any significant extent until the introduction of the moldboard plough to Ireland in the seventh century A.D. Because cereal cultivation would have required
(30) tilling of the soil, the pollen evidence indicates that these soils must indeed have been successfully tilled before the introduction of the new plough.

Another example concerns flax cultivation in County Down, one of the great linen-producing areas
(35) of Ireland during the eighteenth century. Some aspects of linen production in Down are well documented, but the documentary record tells little about the cultivation of flax, the plant from which linen is made, in that area. The record of eighteenth-century linen
(40) production in Down, together with the knowledge that flax cultivation had been established in Ireland centuries before that time, led some historians to surmise that this plant was being cultivated in Down before the eighteenth century. But pollen analyses
(45) indicate that this is not the case; flax pollen was found only in deposits laid down since the eighteenth century.

It must be stressed, though, that there are limits to the ability of the pollen record to reflect the vegetative
(50) history of the landscape. For example, pollen analyses cannot identify the species, but only the genus or family, of some plants. Among these is madder, a cultivated dye plant of historical importance in Ireland. Madder belongs to a plant family that also comprises
(55) various native weeds, including goosegrass. If madder pollen were present in a deposit it would be indistinguishable from that of uncultivated native species.

23. Which one of the following most accurately expresses the main point of the passage?

(A) Analysis of fossilized pollen is a useful means of supplementing and in some cases correcting other sources of information regarding changes in the Irish landscape.

(B) Analyses of historical documents, together with pollen evidence, have led to the revision of some previously accepted hypotheses regarding changes in the Irish landscape.

(C) Analysis of fossilized pollen has proven to be a valuable tool in the identification of ancient plant species.

(D) Analysis of fossilized pollen has provided new evidence that the cultivation of such crops as cereal grains, flax, and madder had a significant impact on the landscape of Ireland.

(E) While pollen evidence can sometimes supplement other sources of historical information, its applicability is severely limited, since it cannot be used to identify plant species.

24. The passage indicates that pollen analyses have provided evidence against which one of the following views?

(A) The moldboard plough was introduced into Ireland in the seventh century.

(B) In certain parts of County Down, cereal grains were not cultivated to any significant extent before the seventh century.

(C) In certain parts of Ireland, cereal grains have been cultivated continuously since the introduction of the moldboard plough.

(D) Cereal grain cultivation requires successful tilling of the soil.

(E) Cereal grain cultivation began in County Down around 400 A.D.

25. The phrase "documentary record" (lines 20 and 37) primarily refers to

(A) documented results of analyses of fossilized pollen

(B) the kinds and quantities of fossilized pollen grains preserved in peats and lake muds

(C) written and pictorial descriptions by current historians of the events and landscapes of past centuries

(D) government and commercial records, maps, and similar documents produced in the past that recorded conditions and events of that time

(E) articles, books, and other documents by current historians listing and analyzing all the available evidence regarding a particular historical period

GO ON TO THE NEXT PAGE.

26. The passage indicates that prior to the use of pollen
analysis in the study of the history of the Irish
landscape, at least some historians believed which one
of the following?

(A) The Irish landscape had experienced significant
flooding during the seventeenth century.

(B) Cereal grain was not cultivated anywhere in
Ireland until at least the seventh century.

(C) The history of the Irish landscape during the
sixteenth and seventeenth centuries was well
documented.

(D) Madder was not used as a dye plant in Ireland
until after the eighteenth century.

(E) The beginning of flax cultivation in County
Down may well have occurred before the
eighteenth century.

27. Which one of the following most accurately describes
the relationship between the second paragraph and the
final paragraph?

(A) The second paragraph proposes a hypothesis for
which the final paragraph offers a supporting
example.

(B) The final paragraph describes a problem that
must be solved before the method advocated in
the second paragraph can be considered viable.

(C) The final paragraph qualifies the claim made in
the second paragraph.

(D) The second paragraph describes a view against
which the author intends to argue, and the final
paragraph states the author's argument against
that view.

(E) The final paragraph offers procedures to
supplement the method described in the second
paragraph.

PrepTestJun07 Sec4 Qs23-27

K Part Four: Reading Comprehension
CHAPTER 15

These explanations refer to questions
that begin on page 882.

ANSWERS AND EXPLANATIONS

Passage 1—Poetry and Fiction

Step 1: Read the Passage Strategically

Sample Roadmap

For decades, there has been a deep rift between poetry and fiction in the United States, especially in academic settings; graduate writing programs in universities, for example, train students as poets or as
(5) writers of fiction, but almost never as both. Both poets and writers of fiction have tended to support this separation, in large part because the current conventional wisdom holds that poetry should be elliptical and lyrical, reflecting inner states and
(10) processes of thought or feeling, whereas character and narrative events are the stock-in-trade of fiction.

Rift between poetry/fiction in US

Rift supported by writers b/c of different qualities

Certainly it is true that poetry and fiction are distinct genres, but why have specialized education and literary territoriality resulted from this distinction?
(15) The answer lies perhaps in a widespread attitude in U.S. culture, which often casts a suspicious eye on the generalist. Those with knowledge and expertise in multiple areas risk charges of dilettantism, as if ability in one field is diluted or compromised by
(20) accomplishment in another.

Reason for rift: US suspicion of generalists

Fortunately, there are signs that the bias against writers who cross generic boundaries is diminishing; several recent writers are known and respected for their work in both genres. One important example of
(25) this trend is Rita Dove, an African American writer highly acclaimed for both her poetry and her fiction. A few years ago, speaking at a conference entitled "Poets Who Write Fiction," Dove expressed gentle incredulity about the habit of segregating the genres.
(30) She had grown up reading and loving both fiction and poetry, she said, unaware of any purported danger lurking in attempts to mix the two. She also studied for some time in Germany, where, she observes, "Poets write plays, novelists compose libretti, playwrights
(35) write novels—they would not understand our restrictiveness."

Genre crossing becoming OK

Ex: Rita Dove

Dove's POV on mixing genres

It makes little sense, Dove believes, to persist in the restrictive approach to poetry and fiction prevalent in the U.S., because each genre shares in the nature of
(40) the other. Indeed, her poetry offers example after example of what can only be properly regarded as lyric narrative. Her use of language in these poems is undeniably lyrical—that is, it evokes emotion and inner states without requiring the reader to organize
(45) ideas or events in a particular linear structure. Yet this lyric expression simultaneously presents the elements of a plot in such a way that the reader is led repeatedly to take account of clusters of narrative details within the lyric flow. Thus while the language is lyrical, it

Dove: poetry/fiction share traits

Ex: her poetry

Dove's poems = narr. fiction

(50) often comes to constitute, cumulatively, a work of narrative fiction. Similarly, many passages in her fiction, though undeniably prose, achieve the status of lyric narrative through the use of poetic rhythms and elliptical expression. In short, Dove bridges the gap
(55) between poetry and fiction not only by writing in both genres, but also by fusing the two genres within individual works.

Dove's fiction = lyric narr.

Dove bridges fiction/poetry gap

These explanations refer to questions that begin on page 882.

Part Four: Reading Comprehension
Reading Comprehension Practice

Discussion

Paragraph 1 jumps right into the **Topic**: the division between poetry and fiction in the United States. The Scope and Purpose won't become clear until later in the passage, but the first paragraph does narrow the Topic a bit by focusing on how writers have perpetuated the division between fiction and poetry.

Paragraph 2 suggests a possible reason for the division: U.S. culture doesn't think much of generalists. You also get a taste of the author's perspective in the last sentence, ". . . as if ability in one field is diluted or compromised by accomplishment in another." This suggests that the author thinks ability is not diminished by involvement in multiple fields, and starts to suggest the Scope of the passage.

Paragraph 3 starts with another strong indication of the author's view, the Keyword *[f]ortunately*. The author thinks it's a good thing that the boundaries are starting to break down. The rest of the paragraph (and, indeed, the rest of the passage) is devoted to the example of Rita Dove, an author whose work blends elements traditionally associated with poetry and those traditionally associated with fiction. Here, the Scope and Purpose should become clearer. The **Scope**, or specific aspect of the Topic explored by the author, is the move toward the breakdown of the barrier between poetry and fiction, as represented by Rita Dove. The author's **Purpose** is simply to illustrate the trend toward breaking down the poetry/fiction divide. The **Main Idea** is that Rita Dove is an example of a trend in which the rigid boundaries between poetry and fiction in America are starting to erode.

The author's attitude suggests that she advocates for further breakdown of the barrier, but the rest of the passage doesn't quite go that far. Rather than advocating anything, paragraph 4 simply explains how Dove not only writes in both genres, but also melds elements of poetry and fiction in some of her work.

1. (E) Global ★★★★

Step 2: Identify the Question Type

This is a Global question because it asks you to identify the passage's "main point."

Step 3: Research the Relevant Text

The entire text is relevant when answering a Global question. Use your understanding of the passage's big picture from Step 1 to predict your answer.

Step 4: Make a Prediction

Use the author's statements of opinion to confirm the Main Idea, which is that Rita Dove's work is evidence that the rift between fiction and poetry is diminishing.

Step 5: Evaluate the Answer Choices

(E) is a match for this prediction. It even uses the word *exemplifies*, which perfectly captures the author's use of Rita Dove as an example (line 24).

(A) is a Distortion. The author makes no claim that the blending of elements is the reason Dove's work has been well received.

(B) is too narrow. The particular elements of Dove's writing described in lines 45–49 are just details. A list of subsidiary details will never be correct when a question asks you for the main point of the entire passage.

(C) is also a Distortion. The bias in the United States is against writers who cross genres, not against writers who use lyrical language in fiction.

(D) is too narrow. There's no mention of the poetry/fiction rift that forms the foundation for the passage. Furthermore, Rita Dove's techniques aren't necessarily nontraditional; she just uses them across genres.

2. (D) Logic Reasoning (Parallel Reasoning) ★★★★

Step 2: Identify the Question Type

The phrase "most analogous to" also appears in Parallel Reasoning questions in the Logical Reasoning section, so this is the same type of question.

Step 3: Research the Relevant Text

Rita Dove is mentioned in both paragraphs 3 and 4, but paragraph 4 is probably more relevant because paragraph 3 mainly discusses Dove's background and her views on segregating poetry and fiction.

Step 4: Make a Prediction

In paragraph 4, the author tells us that Dove uses techniques typically associated with poetry in her narrative fiction and vice versa. Our correct answer, then, will be about an artist or practitioner who crosses genres or disciplines in the creation of individual works.

Step 5: Evaluate the Answer Choices

(D), in which a choreographer combines elements of two different types of dance, is parallel to Dove's attempts to write works that combine elements of poetry and fiction. **(D)** is therefore correct.

(A)'s combination element might be tempting, but this ultimately distorts the author's point—Dove's writing doesn't combine "traditional and nontraditional" methods.

(B)'s "theoretical knowledge" is Outside the Scope of the passage. The rift the author discusses isn't between academics and practitioners, but between practitioners of two different literary genres.

(C) has no true blending of genres; instead, one medium is consciously used to promote another.

EXPLANATIONS

K | Part Four: Reading Comprehension
CHAPTER 15

These explanations refer to questions
that begin on page 882.

(E) doesn't discuss two genres; guitar solos aren't exactly a departure from rock. **(E)** also introduces the element of work that's not original, something that doesn't come into play at all in the passage.

3. (A) Detail ★☆☆☆

Step 2: Identify the Question Type

This is a Detail question because it begins with the phrase "[a]ccording to the passage." The focus is simply on what the author states directly.

Step 3: Research the Relevant Text

The author talked about widely held views regarding poetry and fiction in the United States in both of the first two paragraphs.

Step 4: Make a Prediction

The author directly mentions two prevailing views: From lines 7–11, that poetry should be lyrical and elliptical while fiction should be rooted in character and narrative; and from lines 15–20, that American culture is suspicious of generalists.

Step 5: Evaluate the Answer Choices

(A) is a match for lines 7–11.

(B) is a Distortion. The author discusses the differences between the genres, but never makes a value judgment. Also, no evidence is given that university writing programs favor one genre over another.

(C) is another Distortion; the first paragraph says that fiction programs and poetry programs tend to be operated independently, but says nothing about the balance between the two.

(D)'s use of the phrase "most aesthetically effective" is too strong; the author does speak favorably of the outcome when fiction (at least, Dove's fiction) incorporates lyrical elements, but makes no comparison to fiction that doesn't employ lyrical language.

(E) is Outside the Scope. The views of Europeans are never mentioned; it's U.S. culture that the author says is suspicious of generalists.

4. (E) Inference ★☆☆☆

Step 2: Identify the Question Type

Any question that asks about the author's attitude toward a particular part of the passage is an Inference question.

Step 3: Research the Relevant Text

The "deep rift" between poetry and fiction in the United States is discussed mainly in the first two paragraphs and briefly at the beginning of paragraph 3.

Step 4: Make a Prediction

Fortunately in line 21 tells you that the author's not a fan of the rift between poetry and fiction, and that she's glad to see it diminishing. Also, the end of paragraph 2 suggests skepticism from the author toward the idea that crossing genres dilutes a writer's competence in either genre.

Step 5: Evaluate the Answer Choices

(E) correctly characterizes the author's negative position toward the "attitudes and presuppositions underlying the rift."

(A) is unsupported. The author isn't perplexed about what caused the rift; she tells us explicitly in paragraph 2.

(B) is Extreme and Outside the Scope of the passage. *Astonishment* is too strong a word, and there's no reason to believe that the author thinks academics are unaware of the rift.

(C) suggests that the author is conflicted about her position on the rift, but there's no sign of ambivalence; the author makes her position on the division crystal clear.

(D) is unsupported. The final sentence of the passage announces that one writer, at least, bridges the gap. If the author were truly pessimistic, then the hopeful example of Rita Dove would be left out of the passage entirely.

5. (D) Detail ★☆☆☆

Step 2: Identify the Question Type

This is a Detail question because it asks about what the author conjectures, and not about what the author implies or suggests.

Step 3: Research the Relevant Text

Your Roadmap quickly tells you that the cause of the deep rift between poetry and fiction is discussed in paragraph 2.

Step 4: Make a Prediction

Lines 15–17 say that the poetry-fiction rift is likely due to a widespread attitude in American culture that is skeptical of the generalist; in the case of literature, that would be a writer who works in and blends elements of multiple genres.

Step 5: Evaluate the Answer Choices

(D) matches this prediction perfectly.

(A) is Outside the Scope. The author never discusses how poets and fiction writers see each other's work.

(B) is a Distortion. The author does tell us that the programs for poetry and fiction are usually segregated, but she doesn't discuss teaching methods, nor does she imply that the methods are the cause of the rift. Furthermore, she does not discuss "other literary fields" beyond poetry and fiction.

(C) is also Outside the Scope. The author doesn't blame publishers and doesn't mention the pressure they may or may not exert on writers.

These explanations refer to questions that begin on page 883.

Part Four: Reading Comprehension
Reading Comprehension Practice

(E) might be a view held by someone, somewhere, but the author doesn't advance that view.

6. (B) Logic Function ★☆☆☆

Step 2: Identify the Question Type

The phrase "primary purpose" might have led you to label this a Global question, but this is a Logic Function question because it asks about the author's purpose for including a particular detail, not for writing the passage as a whole.

Step 3: Research the Relevant Text

Lines 32–36 are of course relevant, but in order to understand the author's purpose in mentioning a particular experience, we have to understand the purpose of the passage as a whole and of the paragraph in which the reference occurs—in this case, paragraph 3.

Step 4: Make a Prediction

The mention of Rita Dove's experience in Germany comes on the heels of a description of her disbelief at the aversion to blending genres. The Germany reference simply builds on that, providing some background and context for her different perspective on crossing genre lines.

Step 5: Evaluate the Answer Choices

(B) is therefore correct.

(A) is a Distortion. The author does locate the rift between poetry and fiction in specific American attitudes, but the author never broadens those attitudes to all English-speaking cultures.

(C) is a Distortion. Any praise the author reserves for Dove and her work is given in the context of her blending of poetry and fiction, not of her studies abroad.

(D) might be correct if the author were writing a profile on Rita Dove. However, Dove is being used as an example in the passage, so the author gains nothing by drumming up "human interest" in Dove or her life.

(E) ignores lines 30–32, which mention that Dove grew up reading both poetry and fiction and was unaware of any problems with mixing elements of the two. It's hard to make the case, therefore, that her experience in Germany was the origin of her position on the poetry-fiction rift.

7. (A) Inference ★★★☆

Step 2: Identify the Question Type

Two clues indicate that this is an Inference question: the word *inferred* and the phrase "author would be most likely to believe."

Step 3: Research the Relevant Text

The question stem doesn't help much in guiding your research, other than to point you to places where the author gives her point of view (that is, primarily paragraphs 2 through 4).

Step 4: Make a Prediction

When an Inference stem doesn't give you any clues to help you research the passage, don't work from memory or hunch. Use the content clues in the answer choices to guide your research. Don't stop until you find the answer choice that *must* be true based on the author's statements.

Step 5: Evaluate the Answer Choices

(A) is a valid inference. In paragraph 4, the author refers to each of the works she mentions as either poetry or fiction, even while describing how it incorporates elements of the other genre. **(A)** is therefore correct.

(B) is a Distortion. The author talks about these two effects of lyric narrative in paragraph 4, but she's focused on the value of the blend, not on a comparison of one effect to the other.

(C) is Extreme. "Without precedent" is a tip-off; such strong language is rarely warranted in an Inference question. Although the author doesn't specifically reference another writer who blends elements of the two genres, she says that Dove is merely one example of a trend.

(D) is an Irrelevant Comparison; the author doesn't set up any value comparisons among the various types of writing she discusses.

(E) seems reasonable, but doesn't have to be true. The only place the author talked about other forms like drama was in the reference to Dove's experience in Germany, and it's being mentioned as an example of boundary crossing.

8. (A) Inference ★☆☆☆

Step 2: Identify the Question Type

This is an Inference question because it asks you to determine how the author might continue the passage beyond the last paragraph. Use the author's stated opinion to predict how she might view the future of U.S. literature.

Step 3: Research the Relevant Text

The author's viewpoint toward the future of U.S. literature is clearest in lines 21–22.

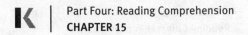

These explanations refer to questions that begin on page 883.

Step 4: Make a Prediction

Lines 21–22 say that the divisions between poetry and fiction are eroding. In fact, the author uses the extended example of Rita Dove to prove that point. The correct answer will be consistent with this idea.

Step 5: Evaluate the Answer Choices

(A) is entirely consistent with the beginning of paragraph 3. If the author says that "the bias against writers who cross generic boundaries is diminishing" (line 22), she must expect that the trend is likely to continue.

(B) is Outside the Scope. The market for poetry has no bearing on the author's predictions concerning whether writers will continue to cross genres.

(C) goes too far; the author doesn't talk about the relationship between narrative poetry and the fiction genre as a whole; you only know that she thinks the boundaries are coming down.

(D) is a 180. It contradicts the passage because this is precisely the trend the author says we're finally breaking free of.

(E) is Extreme and Outside the Scope; the focus throughout the passage is on the writers, not on the audiences.

EXPLANATIONS

These explanations refer to questions that begin on page 884.

Part Four: Reading Comprehension
Reading Comprehension Practice

K

Passage 2—Evolutionary Value of Music

Step 1: Read the Passage Strategically

Sample Roadmap

Passage A

Did music and human language originate separately or together? Both systems use intonation and rhythm to communicate emotions. Both can be produced vocally or with tools, and people can produce
(5) both music and language silently to themselves.

Music/lang origins: separate or together?

Brain imaging studies suggest that music and language are part of one large, vastly complicated, neurological system for processing sound. In fact, fewer differences than similarities exist between the
(10) neurological processing of the two. One could think of the two activities as different radio programs that can be broadcast over the same hardware. One noteworthy difference, though, is that, generally speaking, people are better at language than music. In music, anyone
(15) can listen easily enough, but most people do not perform well, and in many cultures composition is left to specialists. In language, by contrast, nearly everyone actively performs and composes.

Similarities

Neur. evidence: music/lang same system

Similarities > Differences

Big difference: people better at lang

Given their shared neurological basis, it appears
(20) that music and language evolved together as brain size increased over the course of hominid evolution. But the primacy of language over music that we can observe today suggests that language, not music, was the primary function natural selection operated on.
(25) Music, it would seem, had little adaptive value of its own, and most likely developed on the coattails of language.

Auth: music/ lang evolved together

Lang took primacy

Music on coattails of lang

Passage B

Darwin claimed that since "neither the enjoyment nor the capacity of producing musical notes are
(30) faculties of the least [practical] use to man...they must be ranked amongst the most mysterious with which he is endowed." I suggest that the enjoyment of and the capacity to produce musical notes are faculties of indispensable use to mothers and their infants and
(35) that it is in the emotional bonds created by the interaction of mother and child that we can discover the evolutionary origins of human music.

Darwin: music mysterious

Auth: music evolved to create mother/ child bonds

Even excluding lullabies, which parents sing to infants, human mothers and infants under six months
(40) of age engage in ritualized, sequential behaviors, involving vocal, facial, and bodily interactions. Using face-to-face mother-infant interactions filmed at 24 frames per second, researchers have shown that mothers and infants jointly construct mutually
(45) improvised interactions in which each partner tracks the actions of the other. Such episodes last from one-half second to three seconds and are composed of musical elements—variations in pitch, rhythm, timbre, volume, and tempo.

Evid: ritual interactions between mothers/infants

Interactions have mus. elem.

(50) What evolutionary advantage would such behavior have? In the course of hominid evolution, brain size increased rapidly. Contemporaneously, the increase in bipedality caused the birth canal to narrow. This resulted in hominid infants being born ever-more
(55) prematurely, leaving them much more helpless at birth. This helplessness necessitated longer, better maternal care. Under such conditions, the emotional bonds created in the premusical mother-infant interactions we observe in *Homo sapiens* today—behavior whose
(60) neurological basis essentially constitutes the capacity to make and enjoy music—would have conferred considerable evolutionary advantage.

Evol. advantage of behavior:

Bigger brain → earlier birth → need more care

Musical behavior creates emotional bonds

K | Part Four: Reading Comprehension
CHAPTER 15

These explanations refer to questions that begin on page 884.

Discussion

In Comparative Reading, your work has an added element: After determining **Purpose** and **Main Idea** for each passage, you need to understand the relationship between the two passages. Most, if not all, of the questions will focus in some way on this relationship.

Passage A begins with a question that reveals the **Scope** of the passage: the question of whether music and language developed together. The paragraph structure is straightforward: The author poses the question in paragraph 1; introduces research indicating the similarities (and one difference) in paragraph 2; and concludes in paragraph 3 that music and language likely evolved together, but that language is the primary driver of natural selection. Passage A's **Purpose**: To set forth evidence that music and language likely developed in tandem. Its **Main Idea**: Given the common neurological basis for music and language, it seems likely that they developed together as brain size increased, but music developed "on the coattails of language."

Passage B starts out with a quote from Darwin, but you get a strong statement of the author's belief before the end of paragraph 1: Music has evolutionary benefits in the bonding of mothers and infants. Paragraph 2 is devoted to research on mother-infant interactions and paragraph 3 to the possible evolutionary benefits. Passage B's **Purpose**: to argue that the ability to produce music has evolutionary benefits related to emotional bonding between mother and child. Its **Main Idea**: Music is likely a bonding mechanism that has conferred evolutionary advantage.

Remember that your work isn't done—you must define the relationship between the passages before moving on. The author of passage A believes that music developed in tandem with language, but regards music as almost an unnecessary side effect of language with no evolutionary benefit. The author of passage B believes that music represents a useful ability that confers an evolutionary benefit by solidifying the mother/infant relationship. The authors thus disagree regarding the evolutionary significance and advantages of musical ability in humans.

Both passages have the same **Topic** (music) and both are concerned with the development of musical ability in humans, but the data presented differs greatly: Passage A focuses on neurological data, while passage B concerns itself primarily with observed human behavior.

9. (C) Global ★☆☆☆

Step 2: Identify the Question Type

The word *primarily* indicates that the question is asking about the passages as a whole, which is the scope of a Global question.

Step 3: Research the Relevant Text

Although the question refers to both passages, it's only asking you to use the work you've already done in Step 1, just like every other Global question in the RC section.

Step 4: Make a Prediction

You should have already determined that both passages are concerned with how and why our musical abilities evolved.

Step 5: Evaluate the Answer Choices

(C) matches this prediction.

(A) is too broad. The passages are concerned specifically with the development of music; there are presumably many advantages of larger brain size outside the scope of these passages.

(B) introduces an issue addressed only in passage B. In Comparative Reading questions concerned with both passages, many wrong answers will focus only on one of the two passages.

(D) poses a question that is answered in passage A, but not passage B. Furthermore, passage A only answers this question in the interest of answering the larger question posed in the first paragraph.

(E) can be eliminated because it's discussed only in passage A, but even there the question isn't answered.

10. (B) Detail ★★★☆

Step 2: Identify the Question Type

This is a Detail question because it asks about what the passages mention explicitly.

Step 3: Research the Relevant Text

Anything mentioned in either passage concerning music is relevant to answering this question. That doesn't narrow your research very much, so save your research for the answer choices.

Step 4: Make a Prediction

Predicting this answer could be incredibly time-consuming because the question stem doesn't give enough content clues to focus your research. When this happens, save your research for the answer choices. Don't select an answer until you can find a reference to it in each passage, as the question stem demands.

Step 5: Evaluate the Answer Choices

(B) is correct, although it's easy to overlook. Passage A doesn't delve deeply into the emotional ramifications of music as passage B does (lines 35–37), and it's easy to gloss right over the reference in lines 2–3.

(A) is wrong because bonding between humans is mentioned only in passage B (lines 35–37, 57–59).

These explanations refer to questions that begin on page 884.

Part Four: Reading Comprehension
Reading Comprehension Practice

K

(C) is wrong because only passage A discusses neurological research (lines 6–8).

(D) is wrong because only passage B addresses the helplessness of hominid infants (lines 54–57).

(E) is mentioned in passage A only (lines 3–4).

11. (D) Inference ★★☆☆

Step 2: Identify the Question Type

Any question asking what the passages would be "most likely" to agree or disagree over is an Inference question. The passages weren't necessarily written in direct response to each other, so you'll have to infer points of agreement and disagreement.

Step 3: Research the Relevant Text

Whenever you're reading Comparative Reading passages, remember to take some time during Step 1 of the Reading Comprehension Method to predict larger points of agreement and disagreement between the passages; they're almost guaranteed to come up in the questions.

Step 4: Make a Prediction

You can't always predict the answer to Inference questions, but based on your global understanding of the passages, this one should be pretty straightforward. The authors disagree about the reason for the development of musical ability: Author A sees it as a tag-along to language which doesn't serve much purpose of its own, while author B thinks it confers an important evolutionary benefit.

Step 5: Evaluate the Answer Choices

(D) paraphrases this well.

(A) raises an issue only discussed in passage B. You have no idea what the author of passage A thinks about this.

(B) only focuses on something from passage A. Passage B doesn't tackle the neurological data, nor does it discuss the relationship between music and language.

(C) is a Distortion. Passage B says directly that brain size increased rapidly (lines 51–52); passage A says only that it increased (lines 20–21). That's a difference, but not a disagreement; you don't know what author A thinks about the rate of increase. It's possible this is a point of agreement between the authors.

(E) introduces mother-infant bonding, which isn't mentioned at all in passage A.

12. (C) Inference ★★☆☆

Step 2: Identify the Question Type

Like the previous question, this one focuses on agreement or disagreement between the two authors, so this is also an Inference question.

Step 3: Research the Relevant Text

The content clue "musical capacity in humans" isn't terribly helpful for research because that's the scope of both passages. However, your global understanding of the passages could come in handy here.

Step 4: Make a Prediction

The area of overlap between the two passages is relatively small, so even if you can't predict the right answer, you know that it needs to deal with subject matter covered by both passages.

Step 5: Evaluate the Answer Choices

(C) is correct. Although the authors interpret the role of brain size differently, each points to a role that hominid brain development had in the evolution of musical ability; passage A does so in lines 19–21, and passage B does so in lines 51–57.

(A) is an area covered only by passage B. Passage A doesn't take a position on this.

(B) also covers territory only discussed in passage B. Mothers and infants aren't mentioned at all in passage A.

(D) is not touched upon in either passage.

(E) is only touched upon in passage A, and even there, the author doesn't say *why* musical ability varies among individuals.

13. (E) Logic Reasoning (Principle) ★★★★

Step 2: Identify the Question Type

Like its analogous question type in Logical Reasoning, this question asks for a principle underlying both passages.

Step 3: Research the Relevant Text

This question stem provides no content clues to help you research, so any part of the passage could form the basis of the correct answer. The correct answer will likely come from your broader assessment of the passages.

Step 4: Make a Prediction

Because the question stem focuses on a principle underlying both passages, look for points of agreement or common methods of argument. Both passages come to conclusions about the evolutionary significance of music, and the likelihood that music conferred evolutionary advantages. You might predict something like "modern traits can be explained on the basis of the evolutionary advantages they might confer."

Step 5: Evaluate the Answer Choices

(E) is the closest to that prediction, and has the additional advantage of referring to modern-day humans, another overlap between the passages.

EXPLANATIONS

These explanations refer to questions that begin on page 885.

(A) would be correct if the authors cited the behavior of nonhuman animals as part of their data. That's not happening, so you have no evidence that either author believes this.

(B) is Extreme ("all human capacities"). **(B)** need not be true in order for either author to make his/her argument.

(C) is a principle underlying passage A, but not of passage B, which does not allude to the concurrent development of language.

(D), like **(C)**, introduces neurological foundations of behavior. Neither passage, however, claims that discovering the neurological basis of a behavior constitutes discovery of the behavior's "essence."

14. (A) Logic Reasoning (Method of Argument) ★★☆☆

Step 2: Identify the Question Type

Don't be thrown by the wording in the question type. Even if you identified this as a Global question, the task is still the same: determine in general terms what each passage does in relation to the other. The *relationship* question is very common in Comparative Reading, so learning to attack it effectively will earn you points on Test Day.

Step 3: Research the Relevant Text

There's no specific place to research this answer; instead, use the relationship between the passages that you determined during Step 1 to answer this question.

Step 4: Make a Prediction

The data presented by the two authors was very different in nature; their conclusions differed as well. The key difference is their view of the evolutionary significance of musical ability; even though the answer choices are general, knowing that they fundamentally disagree on their main point should help you eliminate choices.

Step 5: Evaluate the Answer Choices

(A) sums up the passages' relationship neatly and is therefore correct.

(B) is a Distortion. Not only does passage A actually answer the question it poses, but passage B also sets out to answer a slightly different question—the question of whether music has evolutionary benefit.

(C) is nearly a 180. Passage B doesn't support passage A—it reaches an entirely different conclusion.

(D) is unsupported. Both authors are clear and consistent in the presentation of their cases; if anything, passage B is more strongly worded because passage A uses tentative language like "it would seem" (line 25).

(E) is a 180 because the passages' conclusions differ.

These explanations refer to questions that begin on page 886.

Part Four: Reading Comprehension
Reading Comprehension Practice | **K**

Passage 3—Copyright Law and the World Wide Web

Step 1: Read the Passage Strategically

Sample Roadmap

The World Wide Web, a network of electronically and interconnected (or "linked") sites, called pages, that are accessible via personal computer, raises legal issues about the rights of owners of intellectual
(5) property, notably those who create documents for inclusion on Web pages. Some of these owners of intellectual property claim that unless copyright law is strengthened, intellectual property on the Web will not be protected from copyright infringement. Web users,
(10) however, claim that if their ability to access information on Web pages is reduced, the Web cannot live up to its potential as an open, interactive medium of communication.

Web creates IP issues for creators of docs

IP owners: must tighten copyright law

Web users: tighter laws keep Web from being open/free

The debate arises from the Web's ability to link
(15) one document to another. Links between sites are analogous to the inclusion in a printed text of references to other works, but with one difference: the cited document is instantly retrievable by a user who activates the link. This immediate accessibility creates
(20) a problem, since current copyright laws give owners of intellectual property the right to sue a distributor of unauthorized copies of their material even if that distributor did not personally make the copies. If person A, the author of a document, puts the document
(25) on a Web page, and person B, the creator of another Web page, creates a link to A's document, is B committing copyright infringement?

Reason for debate: ability to link

Links immed. access. → problem for laws

Does linking = infringement?

To answer this question, it must first be determined who controls distribution of a document on
(30) the Web. When A places a document on a Web page, this is comparable to recording an outgoing message on one's telephone answering machine for others to hear. When B creates a link to A's document, this is akin to B's giving out A's telephone number, thereby
(35) allowing third parties to hear the outgoing message for themselves. Anyone who calls can listen to the message; that is its purpose. While B's link may indeed facilitate access to A's document, the crucial point is that A, simply by placing that document on the
(40) Web, is thereby offering it for distribution. Therefore, even if B leads others to the document, it is A who actually controls access to it. Hence creating a link to a document is not the same as making or distributing a copy of that document. Moreover, techniques are
(45) already available by which A can restrict access to a document. For example, A may require a password to gain entry to A's Web page, just as a telephone owner can request an unlisted number and disclose it only to selected parties. Such a solution would compromise
(50) the openness of the Web somewhat, but not as much as the threat of copyright infringement litigation.

Who controls distrib on the Web?

Analogy: outgoing phone message

Owners = distributors

Linking ≠ distribution

Owner can restrict access

Ex: password

Owner restrictions preferable to tougher laws

Changing copyright law to benefit owners of intellectual property is thus ill-advised because it would impede the development of the Web as a public
(55) forum dedicated to the free exchange of ideas.

Changing laws a bad idea

These explanations refer to questions that begin on page 886.

Discussion

Beware of familiar topics! Intellectual property on the Web, the **Topic** of this Law passage, is a well-known topic and nearly everyone has an opinion; remember to stay focused on what's presented in the passage, not your own opinions.

Paragraph 1 sets forth the conflict. Some owners of intellectual property rights feel stronger protection is required, but Web users fear this will limit the potential of the Web. The paragraph ends with a strong sense of the **Scope** (the conflict over strengthening copyright law). The author's Purpose doesn't emerge right away, but you can guess that she'll probably take a side.

Paragraph 2 explains the root of the issue: Web page links, and the problems created by the instant accessibility these links afford. The author also poses what she sees as the underlying question in the debate over increased protection—does linking to someone else's Web page constitute copyright infringement?

Paragraph 3 provides an analysis, by analogy, that demonstrates the author's view. According to the author, linking to a Web page is not copyright infringement. This statement reveals the author's **Purpose**: to analyze the need for increased copyright protection and advise against it. The **Main Idea** is therefore that changing copyright law to further protect owners would impede development of the Web and is thus ill-advised.

15. (A) Global ★★★★

Step 2: Identify the Question Type

This is a Global question because it asks you for the "main point" of the passage.

Step 3: Research the Relevant Text

The entire passage is relevant in a Global question. Instead of rereading a specific part, base your prediction on the Main Idea you determined during Step 1.

Step 4: Make a Prediction

From Step 1, you can see that the passage sets up a critical question in the debate over the need for increased copyright protection: are an owner's rights infringed by someone linking to his Web page? The author's answer is that those rights are not infringed and that thus there is no reason to increase protection.

Step 5: Evaluate the Answer Choices

(A) is a match for this idea.

(B) goes further than the passage does by distorting lines 52–55—the author never provides a condition that, if satisfied, would make changes to copyright law anything but ill-advised. Furthermore, the introduction of the term *democracy* is Outside the Scope.

(C) both overemphasizes and misrepresents a detail from lines 44–50. The author only mentions the ability to restrict access

to Web documents as an alternative to strengthening copyright law. Furthermore, the author says that if an owner did restrict access, that the openness of the Web would be compromised.

(D) is too broad. The passage isn't about resolution of problems concerning intellectual property rights in the electronic age generally. Rather, the passage concerns only one such problem. Also, the author never points to basic commonsense principles as a cure-all.

(E) has its focus in the wrong place. The author does argue against changing the law, but not because such changes would benefit only a small number of individuals. You don't know from the passage how many people create Web documents.

16. (A) Inference ★☆☆☆

Step 2: Identify the Question Type

This is an Inference question because it asks for the meaning of a word as it's used in the passage. The author doesn't state the word's meaning directly, so you'll need to infer its meaning from context.

Step 3: Research the Relevant Text

Line 8 is of course relevant text, but you'll need to read around that line to predict what the author means by *strengthened*.

Step 4: Make a Prediction

Lines 6–9 lay out the position that unless copyright law is *strengthened*, some owners of content will not be protected. The immediate counterpoint is that Web users don't want their access reduced. Therefore, *strengthened* means "made to create additional limitations on access."

Step 5: Evaluate the Answer Choices

(A) is a match.

(B) is Outside the Scope. The passage doesn't discuss the geographic uniformity of copyright laws.

(C) is also Outside the Scope. The passage doesn't discuss penalties for violating copyright laws.

(D) concerns enforcement of laws, which is Outside the Scope.

(E) touches on the legitimacy of current intellectual property law, but the passage focuses on the desire for *additional* restrictions in the law and the arguments against such restrictions.

17. (E) Inference ★★★☆

Step 2: Identify the Question Type

Any question that asks what the author would be "most likely to agree with" is an Inference question.

Step 3: Research the Relevant Text

Documents placed on Web pages are discussed briefly in paragraphs 1 and 2, but the author discusses them primarily in paragraph 3.

These explanations refer to questions that begin on page 887.

Part Four: Reading Comprehension
Reading Comprehension Practice | **K**

Step 4: Make a Prediction

The author says a few things in paragraph 3 about documents placed on the Web: They're still controlled by their owners (lines 41–42); linking to them isn't copyright infringement (lines 42–44); and restrictions on access to those documents "would compromise the openness of the Web," as would copyright infringement litigation (lines 49–51). Even if you can't predict the correct answer, you know that it will be a statement that *must* be true based on these claims made by the author.

Step 5: Evaluate the Answer Choices

(E) is correct because it must be true based on the author's statements in lines 49–55.

(A) is a 180. Lines 52–53 explicitly state that copyright laws should not be strengthened. Furthermore, the author offers passwords as a possible safeguard for authors who want to better protect their documents.

(B) is a subtle Distortion: The passage says that password protection would compromise the openness of the Web *somewhat* (line 50), not that it would *significantly* threaten to reduce the number of people using the Web for communication.

(C) is Extreme. The author has provided a suggested means of limiting access (a required password), so she wouldn't agree that limiting access is impossible.

(D) contradicts the author's view. The last sentence of the passage clearly indicates that the author considers changes to copyright law potentially harmful to public interest.

18. (C) Logic Reasoning (Parallel Reasoning)   ★★★★

Step 2: Identify the Question Type

This resembles a Parallel Reasoning question from the Logical Reasoning section because it asks you to find the answer choice providing a relationship "most analogous to" one put forth in the passage.

Step 3: Research the Relevant Text

"Relying on passwords to restrict access to a Web document" is a content clue leading you to paragraph 3, lines 44–51 specifically.

Step 4: Make a Prediction

The author sees tightening the laws as far more damaging to the potential of the Web than password protection is; password protection restricts access and creates some limitations on free exchange and development, but it's better than changing the law and creating even greater limitations. The correct answer will deal with the relationship between a legal solution and a non-legal, self-help solution to unrestricted access.

Step 5: Evaluate the Answer Choices

(C) is analogous to the passage and therefore correct. Prohibiting a sport is a restrictive legal remedy, and relying on par-

ticipants to play safe is a self-help remedy that allows greater access while protecting those playing the game.

(A) only addresses the password issue (the self-help remedy), not the relationship to strengthening current copyright laws (the legal remedy). Allowing everyone use of a facility would have the opposite effect of tightening restrictions in copyright law.

(B) might be tempting at first because it describes two different plans of attack on restricting the same activity, but both courses of action offered by **(B)** are laws. In the passage's scenario, it's tougher laws versus protections created by the owners themselves.

(D) involves legislation and enforcement of a law, but offers nothing analogous to the self-devised passwords from the passage.

(E) is like **(A)** in that it only offers an analogue to the Web passwords. Allowing unrestricted access to a building is analogous to repealing copyright laws, not strengthening them.

19. (B) Inference   ★★★★

Step 2: Identify the Question Type

This is an Inference question because it asks you to determine what the passage *implies*.

Step 3: Research the Relevant Text

This question stem doesn't have any content clues to guide your research. Therefore, be prepared to save your research for Step 5 as you evaluate the answer choices.

Step 4: Make a Prediction

The passage implies plenty of things, so prediction might be tough here. However, keep in mind that a valid inference is a statement that *must* be true based on the passage. Make sure you can find direct textual support for an answer choice before you select it.

Step 5: Evaluate the Answer Choices

(B) is a valid inference and therefore correct. Copyright infringement is unlawful distribution, and the author's analogy in paragraph 3 establishes that linking is not copyright infringement, presumably because control over a document's distribution remains in the hands of its owner.

(A) is unsupported. "Creators of links to Web pages" and "owners of intellectual property" are discussed as two different groups in paragraph 3, but the passage gives no reason why there couldn't be people who are members of both groups.

(C) is Outside the Scope of the passage. Privacy rights aren't mentioned at all; this passage is about copyright infringement.

(D) is a 180. It contradicts the author's view, illustrated by the analogy in paragraph 3. The author believes that control rests in the hands of the documents' creators, not those who link to the pages containing those documents.

![K] Part Four: Reading Comprehension
CHAPTER 15

These explanations refer to questions
that begin on page 887.

(E) is Outside the Scope; no evidence is given that the format of the document in question affects the issue of who controls the rights to distribute it.

20. (E) Detail ★☆☆☆

Step 2: Identify the Question Type

The phrase "according to the passage" indicates a Detail question.

Step 3: Research the Relevant Text

This question stem offers a clear content clue ("features of outgoing messages left on telephone answering machines") leading you to lines 31–37.

Step 4: Make a Prediction

The question asks for the feature of outgoing phone messages that makes them relevant to the copyright debate. The phrase "this is akin to" in lines 33–34 points to that feature. The person who possesses the telephone number leaves the outgoing message available to anyone who calls the number, just as the owner of a document leaves that document available to anyone who visits the Web page.

Step 5: Evaluate the Answer Choices

(E) matches this prediction.

(A) is merely coincidental. That both telephones and Web pages are electronic means of communication doesn't figure into the author's argument.

(B) is unsupported. Not only does the author not address legal protections for phone messages, but she also states that no unauthorized distribution takes place.

(C)'s reference to instantaneous distribution is in the discussion of Web pages in paragraph 2. It's not related to the phone message analogy.

(D) is Outside the Scope. Recording isn't at issue; the issue that makes outgoing phone messages relevant to Web copyright issues is access and distribution.

21. (D) Logic Function ★★☆☆

Step 2: Identify the Question Type

The phrase "serves primarily to" indicates a Logic Function question. The correct answer won't detail what the author says about telephone answering machines, but why the author included them in the passage in the first place.

Step 3: Research the Relevant Text

The author discusses telephone answering machines in lines 31–37.

Step 4: Make a Prediction

Line 31 contains the phrase "this is comparable to" before launching into the answering machine discussion. This means

that answering machines are being used as an analogy. The author offers the telephone analogy to illustrate the point that no unauthorized distribution occurs when one provides a link to an existing Web page.

Step 5: Evaluate the Answer Choices

(D) is a match, even though it is phrased in more general terms.

(A) is a Distortion. Remember the context; the whole passage is about whether increased copyright protections are required for Web pages. Telephones are relevant only as an analogy.

(B) is wrong because the answering machine analogy is offered in support of the author's position, not the other side.

(C) misstates the author's purpose. He does not use the telephone analogy to demonstrate that similar copyright issues predate the internet.

(E) also misstates the author's purpose. He doesn't use the analogy to prove a point about copyright as it relates to telephone usage, but rather to illustrate his point about copyright on websites.

22. (D) Detail ★★★★

Step 2: Identify the Question Type

The words "according to the passage" indicate that this is a Detail question.

Step 3: Research the Relevant Text

"Present copyright laws" is a content clue that means the same as "current copyright laws," which are mentioned in line 20.

Step 4: Make a Prediction

Line 20 gives you only one piece of direct information: Copyright holders can sue for unauthorized distribution.

Step 5: Evaluate the Answer Choices

(D) correctly paraphrases this idea.

(A) is a Distortion. There are some new issues with content on the Web, but current law clearly prohibits unauthorized distribution (lines 20–23).

(B) contradicts the author's view that the owner or publisher of a document controls access to it.

(C) is Outside the Scope. It is a trap for those prone to bringing in outside knowledge; the profit issue is batted around a lot in the debate over copyright issues, but it's not mentioned in this passage.

(E) is a 180. The author advocates leaving copyright law as it is, not loosening (or tightening) its restrictions further.

These explanations refer to questions that begin on page 888.

Part Four: Reading Comprehension
Reading Comprehension Practice | K

Passage 4—Pollen Analysis and the Irish Landscape

Step 1: Read the Passage Strategically

Sample Roadmap

In tracing the changing face of the Irish landscape, scholars have traditionally relied primarily on evidence from historical documents. However, such documentary sources provide a fragmentary record at
(5) best. Reliable accounts are very scarce for many parts of Ireland prior to the seventeenth century, and many of the relevant documents from the sixteenth and seventeenth centuries focus selectively on matters relating to military or commercial interests.

Scholars rely on hist. docs to trace hist. of land

Hist. docs not so reliable

(10) Studies of fossilized pollen grains preserved in peats and lake muds provide an additional means of investigating vegetative landscape change. Details of changes in vegetation resulting from both human activities and natural events are reflected in the kinds
(15) and quantities of minute pollen grains that become trapped in sediments. Analysis of samples can identify which kinds of plants produced the preserved pollen grains and when they were deposited, and in many cases the findings can serve to supplement or correct
(20) the documentary record.

Pollen fossils an add'l way to track changes

What pollen grains can show

For example, analyses of samples from Long Lough in County Down have revealed significant patterns of cereal-grain pollen beginning by about 400 A.D. The substantial clay content of the soil in this part
(25) of Down makes cultivation by primitive tools difficult. Historians thought that such soils were not tilled to any significant extent until the introduction of the moldboard plough to Ireland in the seventh century A.D. Because cereal cultivation would have required
(30) tilling of the soil, the pollen evidence indicates that these soils must indeed have been successfully tilled before the introduction of the new plough.

Ex: cereal pollen in Co. Down

Historians: soils not tilled before 7th C.

Cereal pollen = soil was tilled before 7th C.

Another example concerns flax cultivation in County Down, one of the great linen-producing areas
(35) of Ireland during the eighteenth century. Some aspects of linen production in Down are well documented, but the documentary record tells little about the cultivation of flax, the plant from which linen is made, in that area. The record of eighteenth-century linen
(40) production in Down, together with the knowledge that flax cultivation had been established in Ireland centuries before that time, led some historians to surmise that this plant was being cultivated in Down before the eighteenth century. But pollen analyses
(45) indicate that this is not the case; flax pollen was found only in deposits laid down since the eighteenth century.

Ex: flax pollen in Co. Down

Doc. record scarce on flax

Historians: flax grown pre–18th C.

Pollen: flax grown only since 18th C.

It must be stressed, though, that there are limits to the ability of the pollen record to reflect the vegetative
(50) history of the landscape. For example, pollen analyses cannot identify the species, but only the genus or family, of some plants. Among these is madder, a

Limits on pollen's ability to show hist.

Ex: madder

cultivated dye plant of historical importance in Ireland.
(55) Madder belongs to a plant family that also comprises various native weeds, including goosegrass. If madder pollen were present in a deposit it would be indistinguishable from that of uncultivated native species.

Pollen can't disting. madder from other species

K | Part Four: Reading Comprehension
CHAPTER 15

These explanations refer to questions that begin on page 888.

Discussion

Paragraph 1 of this Natural Science passage introduces limitations on the traditional study of Ireland's landscape: accounts of the landscape are scarce, and where they do exist, they are incomplete. That provides our **Topic** (the historical Irish landscape), but Scope and Purpose are still wide open.

Paragraph 2 introduces a supplemental source of information that will eventually become the **Scope** of the passage: studies of fossilized pollen grains, and what they can tell us about changes in the landscape. The paragraph outlines the information pollen grains can provide about the vegetative history of a region, and then relates that information to the historical record. The author seems to value the pollen evidence for its ability to "supplement or correct" the historical record (line 19).

Paragraphs 3 and 4 provide examples of how pollen grain information has changed beliefs about some aspects of historical land development. Don't worry too much about the details of these paragraphs—you can come back to them if a question asks you to.

Finally, paragraph 5 notes that pollen analysis isn't without its own limitations and gives an example. It's not until the end that we can be sure of the author's **Purpose**, which is largely informative: to explain the impact of a new information source on our understanding of the evolution of the Irish landscape. The **Main Idea** reflects this: The author believes that studies of fossilized pollen can be useful for supplementing or correcting the historical record when studying changes in Ireland's landscape.

23. (A) Global ★★★☆

Step 2: Identify the Question Type

Any question asking for the "main point" of the passage is a Global question.

Step 3: Research the Relevant Text

The entire passage is relevant in a Global question. Use your knowledge of the passage's big picture (Topic, Scope, Purpose, Main Idea) to predict your answer.

Step 4: Make a Prediction

As you know from Step 1, the Main Idea of the passage is that fossilized pollen records can sometimes help make more accurate determinations than can the historical record when it comes to the development of the Irish landscape.

Step 5: Evaluate the Answer Choices

(A) is a match for this prediction.

(B) is a Distortion. The analysis of historical documents is what led historians to their mistaken hypotheses in the first place.

(C) incorrectly shifts the passage's focus from the historical development of Ireland's landscape to the identification of

plant species. Furthermore, lines 50–51 tell you that pollen analysis can't identify the species of some plants.

(D) misuses some of the passage's details. The idea that cultivation of cereal, flax, and madder had a significant impact on the Irish landscape was never in question.

(E)'s phrase "severely limited" is Extreme, and its tone is all wrong. The author presents the pollen analysis as a valuable additional tool, even though it has some limitations.

24. (B) Detail ★★★☆

Step 2: Identify the Question Type

The phrase "the passage indicates" signals a Detail question.

Step 3: Research the Relevant Text

The words "provided evidence against which one of the following views" is a content clue. Research wherever the author has described a claim that was challenged by any of the pollen evidence. Your Roadmap tells you that lines 26–29 and lines 39–44 describe those claims.

Step 4: Make a Prediction

Pollen evidence from paragraph 3 refutes the view that soils weren't successfully tilled and cereals cultivated in County Down before the seventh century (lines 25–29), and the pollen evidence in paragraph 4 refutes the view that flax was cultivated in Down before the eighteenth century (lines 39–44).

Step 5: Evaluate the Answer Choices

(B) is a match for the historians' view from lines 25–29.

(A) is a Distortion. The moldboard plough is referenced in paragraph 3, but isn't part of what the pollen evidence contradicted.

(C) is also a Distortion. The evidence presented relates to the period predating the plough, not after. Also, no one in the passage espouses the view that cereal cultivation continued unabated since the moldboard plough was introduced.

(D) is mentioned in paragraph 3, but it's mentioned not as a view of the historians, but as a pure fact.

(E) is a tempting 180, because this is the information provided *by* the pollen fossils, but that's not what you were asked for. You were asked for the view the pollen fossil evidence argued *against*, not what it argued *for*.

25. (D) Inference ★★★☆

Step 2: Identify the Question Type

This is an Inference question because it asks you to infer the meaning of a word or phrase as it's used by the author in context.

Step 3: Research the Relevant Text

Questions with line references often require context. Don't limit yourself to just the line mentioned, but delve into the

EXPLANATIONS

These explanations refer to questions that begin on page 888.

Part Four: Reading Comprehension
Reading Comprehension Practice | K

rest of the passage as needed. There are two references to the "documentary record" cited in the question stem, but they both refer back to an earlier part of the passage: the "fragmentary record" provided by "documentary sources" (line 4).

Step 4: Make a Prediction

The historical record referred to by the author is the record that the fossilized pollen data is supplementing and, in some cases, correcting; it's the history that was recorded at the time, much of it military and commercial (line 9).

Step 5: Evaluate the Answer Choices

(D) is a perfect match.

(A) mentions pollen, which isn't part of the documentary record. The author discusses pollen because the documentary record is incomplete.

(B) also refers to the pollen evidence, but such evidence isn't part of the documentary record. Rather, it supplements and/or corrects the documentary record (lines 19–20).

(C) fails when it brings up "current historians." The documentary record was created during the relevant time period, not reconstructed later.

(E) again mentions "current historians"; the documentary record consists of documents from the actual time. These documents are studied by current historians, not created by them.

26. (E) Detail ★★★☆

Step 2: Identify the Question Type

The question stem begins with the phrase "the passage indicates"; this categorical wording indicates a Detail question.

Step 3: Research the Relevant Text

This question focuses on the beliefs of some historians. Look for where you identified these historians' views in your Roadmap. Lines 26–29 and 39–44 will provide the basis for your prediction.

Step 4: Make a Prediction

Lines 26–29 say that historians believed that soils in County Down weren't tilled until the seventh century A.D., when the moldboard plough was introduced to Ireland. Lines 39–44 say that historians believed that flax was being cultivated in County Down before the eighteenth century.

Step 5: Evaluate the Answer Choices

(E) perfectly paraphrases the historians' belief about flax cultivation.

(A) is Outside the Scope. Flooding isn't mentioned anywhere in the passage. Also, the seventeenth century is mentioned only in connection with recordkeeping, in the first paragraph.

(B) is too broad. The historians believed cereal wasn't cultivated in one part of Ireland before the seventh century because the soil in this location was hard to till.

(C) is directly contradicted by lines 5–9, which say that sixteenth- and seventeenth-century records of the Irish landscape focus "selectively on matters relating to military or commercial interests."

(D) misuses the details concerning madder. Madder is mentioned, but in the context of the limitations of the pollen evidence; there's nothing in the passage concerning views about when it was first used as a dye plant.

27. (C) Logic Reasoning (Method of Argument) ★★★★

Step 2: Identify the Question Type

Like questions that concern the relationship between the passages in Comparative Reading, this question asks about the relationship between two paragraphs. That makes this a Method of Argument question.

Step 3: Research the Relevant Text

Use your Roadmap to determine the purpose of the second paragraph and the final paragraph, and then predict how those relate to each other.

Step 4: Make a Prediction

The final paragraph, which talks about the limitations of pollen fossil data, is intended to qualify the second paragraph, which introduces pollen fossil data as a valuable new addition to the analysis of the development of the Irish landscape.

Step 5: Evaluate the Answer Choices

(C) is a match.

(A) is a Distortion. The final paragraph doesn't support the idea set forth in paragraph 2, but explains its limitations.

(B) might be tempting because it uses the word *problem*, but the problem in the final paragraph isn't going to be solved; it's simply a limitation on the information that's available through this method.

(D) is a 180. The author never argues against the view that the pollen fossil is a valuable addition to the record. In fact, the whole passage is set up to argue for that view.

(E) is Outside the Scope. The final paragraph doesn't offer any procedures, just some limitations.

CHAPTER 16

Reading Comprehension: Managing the Section

INTRODUCTION

The layout of the Reading Comprehension section is very similar to the layout of the Logic Games section. In Reading Comprehension, there are four passages and you have 35 minutes to complete the section. Superficially, the only difference is that while the Logic Games section has 22–24 questions, with 5–7 per game, the Reading Comprehension section has 26–28 questions and 5–8 questions per passage. This means that you are required to do even more work in the same amount of time, which is no small feat. The time crunch leaves most test takers feeling out of control, as though the test is in charge and they are along for the ride.

This is why the highest scorers on the LSAT are not simply the folks who understand the content the best. Generally, the difference between a good score and a great one is the difference between a good test taker and a great test taker. A great test taker understands how to look at a section both as a collection of individual questions and as a whole section of 26–28 questions. You may or may not have been a great test taker in the past. Up until now, odds are no one has had any particular interest in making you great at it. Usually the people who talk to you about tests are the ones who wrote them, and your high school social studies teacher was not about to give you tips on which questions she wrote that were worth answering and which ones you should skip. Things have changed now, however, because you're learning the methods and strategies in this book. Today, you are on your way to being the test taker that everyone wishes they could be. To control the Reading Comprehension section, you need to understand how it's constructed.

LEARNING OBJECTIVES

In this chapter, you'll learn to:

· Prioritize passages and questions to maximize the number of questions you get right.
· Allocate your time efficiently to reading the passage and reading and researching each question.
· Recognize when you should spend more time on a passage or question, as well as when you should skip a question altogether.

MASTERING READING COMPREHENSION

First, it is worth noting that the difficulty levels of Reading Comprehension passages are fairly consistent across tests. Each section will tend to have one easier passage, one challenging passage, and two passages that are somewhere in between. What changes, test to test, is the order in which these passages are presented. Test takers more often than not find that the easiest of the passages will be one of the first two and that the most challenging passage will be one of the last two. Beyond that, the specific ordering of the passages varies from test to test. Muddying the waters further is the fact that the individual questions themselves do not line up neatly with the difficulty of the passage. In the Reading Comprehension section (just as in the Logic Games section), the testmaker distributes easy and challenging questions among each of the passages, which means that no passage can be counted on as a slam dunk, and no passage should be entirely written off.

Scoring in Reading Comprehension is the same as on the rest of the exam: Each question is worth one point, and there is no penalty for guessing. Do not be fooled by the simplicity of that statement, however. When it comes to the scoring on the LSAT, keep in mind that you can miss a question for one of two reasons: issues with content or issues with section management. Most students understand the content side of things: If you don't know how to answer a particular question type or how to recognize a common wrong answer pattern, then you are likely to miss questions. Great test takers, however, also understand that the way you manage a question can affect not only that question but also those later in the section.

SUGGESTED EXERCISE

Whenever you review a timed RC exercise, make a list with two columns. The first column is for the "silly mistakes"—the questions you feel you missed for reasons other than content—such as rushing, misreading, and so on. The second column is for the questions you missed because there was something you just didn't know at the time—that is, for content reasons such as failing to spot something as Outside the Scope or not being certain of the Method. Put each question you missed into one of the columns. This is a great way to get an idea of how many of the questions you missed due to missteps in section management and of how many you missed due to content issues. If there are a lot in the first column, then you need a heavy focus on section management. If they are mostly in the second column, then you have some content work to do first!

Managing the Questions

When dealing with an individual question, you can either get it right or wrong, and you can do so quickly or slowly. You understand intuitively that the best possible outcome for a question is to get it right quickly and the worst possible outcome is to get it wrong slowly. But what about getting a question right slowly or wrong quickly? Which one do you think is better? The correct answer is that, generally, it is better to get a question wrong quickly than it is to get it right slowly.

If this surprises you, imagine that you are working on question 10 in a section and you take so long doing it that it keeps you from getting to question 24, which you would have answered correctly. *If* you answer question 10 correctly, you will get that point, but you will lose the point from question 24. At the end of the day, it is a wash: you sacrificed a later point for an earlier one. Your score would have been the same either way.

But now imagine that you answer question 10 incorrectly. There is no penalty for answering a question incorrectly, so you simply do not get a point. But remember that you spent so much time on question 10 that you could not grab the point from question 24. You have traded in a question you would have answered correctly for a question you answered incorrectly. By spending so much time on question 10, you have effectively *lowered* your LSAT score. Now imagine you spend so much time on question 10 that it keeps you from getting to *two* later questions you would have answered correctly: You just lost two points! This only has to happen a few times in a section to put a serious dent in your score.

If that same test taker instead recognizes that question 10 is going to take him longer than it should and decides to skip out of it quickly, he will have plenty of time to pick up the points from those later questions. Even though he is probably going to get question 10 wrong (but never forget that, statistically, 20 percent of even completely random guesses turn out to be right), he has lost nothing and may very well gain more points because of it. Making these smart decisions over the course of a section can make a dramatic difference in your score.

A great test taker understands that the risk-versus-reward ratio for an individual question is highly skewed on the LSAT. No one question on the LSAT is ever worth more than one point, but taking too long on a single question on the LSAT can cost you several points. So, while no one question can ever make your LSAT score, it can definitely break it.

For this reason, the fundamental rule of all section management is simple: never prioritize a harder, more time-consuming question over an easier, faster one. There are enough easy- to medium-level questions to get you into the high 150s–low 160s on any given exam. The reason why the majority of test takers will never achieve these scores, let alone score above them, is that they get so bogged down in harder questions that they never get to the easier ones, or they rush through the easiest ones and make careless mistakes just so they can get to harder questions they end up missing. Everything you read in the rest of this chapter, as well as the other section management chapters, is based on this one, simple philosophy.

Triaging the Passages and the One-Minute Rule

In the Reading Comprehension section, making these smart decisions about time investment begins with putting the order of the section in your control. As mentioned previously, you have only 35 minutes to tackle four passages of variable difficulty. Because the passages are not always printed in order of difficulty, however, harder passages may come before easier passages. Tackling the passages in an order based purely on where they fall in the section is risky. If you do not end up getting to all of your passages, the one you skip might have yielded more points than one of the passages you did get to. Likewise, starting off with a passage that you find particularly challenging can trigger anxiety that can be hard to recover from. Being in control means doing things in the order that is best for *you*, not the order predetermined by the testmaker.

Learning to *triage* your passages will help you avoid these problems. In its most basic form, triaging a passage means quickly determining whether the passage is likely to be easier or harder. The quick and dirty way of figuring this out is to *very* briefly skim the introductory paragraph of a passage and then to glance at the first sentences of the other paragraphs. If you have some sense of what the passage is about and how it is organized, then it is probably a good passage to do up front. If you have only a vague sense of what is going on in the passage, then it is probably worth skipping the passage for now to see if any of the later passages in the section feel more manageable. This tactic works best when the passage has at least three paragraphs.

When you scan the passage, you are assessing three things:

- Language
- Structure
- Opinions

If the language of the passage is dense and abstract, then you will more than likely struggle with the passage. On the flip side, if the language is clear and concrete, then you will likely get through the passage efficiently. The number of paragraphs and obvious Keywords are another indication as to the difficulty of the passage. Because paragraphs make it visually clear when an author has started and finished a point, passages with more paragraphs tend to be easier to follow than passages with fewer paragraphs. The same goes for Keywords. Passages with more structural Keywords are easier to follow, and those with fewer of those words are harder to summarize accurately. Finally, because the LSAT tests opinions more heavily than anything else, it will be easier to predict where the questions will come from when reading a passage with clearly marked opinions than when reading a neutral passage with few or no opinions.

In general, don't focus on the number of questions attached to a passage. Most passages have six to eight questions. On any two passages—even one with five questions and another with eight—your goal is to get as many correct answers as possible. Keep in mind that a very difficult passage with eight questions might produce no more points (and could take much more of your time) than a very easy passage with only five or six questions in its set.

There are a few ways to triage the passages in a section. The simplest method is to take the passages in order but to scan each passage as you get to it to figure out whether it is to be done now or later. Another method is to do the first passage first—assuming a quick scan confirms that it does not appear too challenging—and then, upon completing it, to scan each of the remaining three passages to figure out the best order to do them in. This often works well because the first passage *tends* to be one of the easier ones and the last passage *tends* to be one of the harder ones. Finally, some students prefer to spend the first minute of each section looking over each of the four passages briefly and ordering them up front. There are pros and cons to each of these strategies. Practice each of these methods a few times and use the one that is most effective for you. Note, however, that triaging the section should never take longer than one minute. Spending more time than that defeats the purpose of the exercise by taking up more time than you are saving.

You are not psychic, and nobody expects you to be. Even those most adept at triage are sometimes wrong. As a fail-safe, if you are one minute into a passage and you are struggling, *get out*! Tackle another passage and come back to the one you're struggling with when you've finished the rest. Triage is your best guess at the difficulty level of the passages, but it is not set in stone. Your job on the LSAT is to keep moving. If one passage is harder than you thought it would be, there is a chance that another is easier than you expected. Go find it.

SUGGESTED EXERCISE

Whenever you triage a Reading Comprehension section, make sure you record the order in which you do the passages. While you review the section, spend some time considering your triage order. If you could do it all again, would you have stuck to the same order? If not, what order would you have done the passages in, and using the checklist from above, how could you have known that was the best order up front?

The 8- to 9-Minute Rule

While you will generally have an easier time answering questions from easier passages than you will those from harder ones, remember that each of the passages is accompanied by a mix of easier questions and harder questions. It is to most test takers' advantage to get to those easier questions on each of the four passages, which means learning not to spend so much time on one passage that you are unable to get to another.

Here's why the 8- to 9-Minute Rule was invented. Subtracting approximately a minute for passage triage, you have about 34 minutes left to tackle your four passages. Divided evenly, this means you have 8–9 minutes for each of those passages. The 8- to 9-Minute Rule is simple: *Never spend more than eight or nine minutes on a passage if there are still passages you have not yet started.* Following the 8- to 9-Minute Rule ensures that you have an adequate amount of time to tackle the lion's share of questions in any given passage without sacrificing your ability to get the easier points from the other passages. Just as spending too much time on any one question can cost you more points down the line, spending too much time on any one passage can cost you. Your harder passages should generally be allotted more time than your easier passages. Start by giving yourself eight minutes for your two earlier/easier passages and nine minutes for your two later/harder passages. As you get better at managing your section, you may find that you need less time for the easier passages and can then spend more time on the later passages. Many test takers, however, find the 8/8/9/9 division to be their sweet spot. At first, following the 8- to 9-Minute Rule is likely to be challenging. But rest assured, mastering it is vital to your success on Test Day, and setting these time limits in advance will help you to become more efficient both in Roadmapping and answering questions.

Prioritizing Questions Over the Passage

To make the most of the 8- to 9-Minute Rule, it is crucial to keep in mind that the Reading Comprehension section requires a delicate balancing act between time spent reading a passage and time spent answering questions. The first instinct of most test takers is to spend as much time as they feel they need on the passage and then, with whatever time remains, to dive into the questions. As you have learned from previous chapters, you should spend about three to four minutes reading and Roadmapping a passage, leaving at least four minutes to tackle the question set. Unfortunately, many students spend significantly more time reading the passage, which means they are spending significantly less time answering the questions. In short, many test takers are prioritizing the *passage* over the *questions*. Years of reading for high school and college classes makes it feel as though this type of reading will make answering the questions easier, but this strategy tends to backfire for two reasons.

First, the human brain can only hold so much information at once in short-term memory. Picture your memory as an empty glass. What happens when someone pours more water into it than it can hold? Either the excess water has to spill over out of the glass, or the glass has to be emptied to make room for the new water. The same thing happens with your brain as you read. Reading a passage too carefully means filling your memory up quickly. This is why many students who spend too long reading only remember the first half of the passage: They fill up so fast that they cannot absorb the new information in the second half. Alternately, others can only remember the second half because they were forced to dump what they learned in the first half to make room for the rest of the passage. Either way, that student is in trouble when it comes to answering the questions.

The second reason is that the LSAT does not award points for memorizing the passage. The LSAT awards you points for answering the questions correctly. Even if you were able to read the passage carefully and retain all of the information, being the person who retains the details of the passage best does not make you the person who scores best. The LSAT does not test the majority of the passage. In fact, on average, the LSAT only tests a few sentences. Most test takers read each sentence as though it has a good chance of being tested, but the opposite is true. Reading the whole passage carefully up front not only makes it harder to understand and remember what you are reading, but it also means less time to turn your reading into points. Additionally, by not trying to retain all of the information in a passage up front, you will be less likely to trick yourself into thinking you know the answer to a question without researching it.

SUGGESTED EXERCISE

If you are struggling to differentiate between trash and treasure, try out this RC post-phrasing exercise: Take a passage you haven't tried before, consult the explanations, and circle the correct answer to every non-Global question. Do a quick Roadmap as you normally would and tackle the Global questions. Then, do the following with the remaining questions, one by one: For each question, read the correct answer and search the passage to find out where that answer comes from. When you find it, read the explanation to be sure you are correct and then ask yourself why that piece of the passage was tested. The most common reasons are that the tested portion is someone's opinion, that it's part of a contrast, or that it's an important detail. Look for any clues, such as Keywords, that would have told you this was important enough to be tested, and write a Roadmap note that would have been helpful. When you are finished, put a big star next to each piece of the passage for each question that it yielded just to get a strong visual of which pieces of the passage mattered and which ones did not. Do this on occasion to help you build a sense of what matters and what doesn't.

For most test takers, the 8- to 9-Minute Rule's first benefit is the realization that they are spending too much time reading the passage and not enough time earning points in the questions. Do not be alarmed if the first few times you follow the 8- to 9-Minute Rule, you end up feeling like the section is even harder: That's part of the point. Never confuse being *uncomfortable* with being *incapable*. You will not start learning to read and Roadmap more efficiently or to manage your questions better until you force yourself to deal with the timing constraints of the exam. By holding fast to the 8- to 9-Minute Rule, you will be building the foundation necessary to put you in control of your section.

Building Time Awareness

Most test takers have a hard time finishing their section, yet very few of them track their time carefully enough to figure out why. This lack of time awareness is responsible for many of the section management mistakes students make, as well as the anxiety that many students feel at the mere thought of being timed. Worse still, it is also what keeps many of these students from improving.

The simplest and most effective way to build time awareness is to incorporate timing notation into your timed Reading Comprehension work. Regardless of whether you are working on one passage or a section of four, you should always record your time at the following intervals:

· Start of Roadmap
· End of Roadmap
· When you leave the question set

This will allow you to track how much time you are spending reading the passage versus answering the questions. You should also check your time after two or three questions to figure out how much of your eight or nine minutes you have left before you have to move on.

Following the 8- to 9-Minute Rule makes this kind of time awareness a necessity. After all, you won't know when it's time to move on until you know how much time has passed. But these notations also give you the ability to review a section afterward to get a complete picture of why you are scoring what you are scoring. Remember that you can miss questions for content or section management reasons. Looking back over a section to see where you spent your time can help you determine which section management issues are affecting your overall score. Are you spending so much time reading that you do not have enough time to answer more than one or two questions? Are you reading the passage in a reasonable amount of time but getting so bogged down in one or two questions that you cannot get to the rest? Recording your timing intervals will take the guesswork out of determining your individual section management hurdles.

SUGGESTED EXERCISE

If you are spending too much time reading, time yourself reading a passage under normal conditions. Subtract 15–30 seconds from that time to come up with your Goal Time. Using a new passage, divide your Goal Time among the paragraphs, giving longer paragraphs more time and shorter ones less time. Now, read and Roadmap the passage one paragraph at a time using a timer to let you know when the time is up for that paragraph. After time is up for each paragraph and before you read the next one, review the paragraph without time constraints and make a note of which parts of the passage you wish you had spent less time on and which parts you wish you had spent more time on. Repeat for every paragraph, trying to meet the timing goal you set for that paragraph. Repeat this regularly with new passages until you are able to hit your Goal Time comfortably. As soon as you can hit that Goal Time, reduce it by another 15–30 seconds and create a new Goal Time. Keep doing this from now until Test Day to slowly but surely reduce the time it takes you to Roadmap a passage.

QUESTIONS ARE CHOICES

Imagine that you have four minutes to answer four questions. Question 1 will take two minutes to answer, question 2 will take four minutes, and questions 3 and 4 will each take one minute.

If you add that up, answering all four questions would take eight minutes, which is far more time than you actually have. So, no matter how you tackle this question set, you are not going to be able to get to every question. But the order in which you do the questions will have a huge impact on your score. Say, for example, that you ended up doing the questions in the order in which they are printed. Answering question 1 and question 2 will take a total of six minutes—two more than you have—so you will be forced to stop before you have finished answering the second question. This would leave you with only one point to show for your four minutes.

But, say you recognize that question 2 is going to be more time-consuming and decide to skip over it and answer question 3 instead. That will give you two points with a minute to spare. If you go to question 4 next, then you will answer it and get a total of three points. So, the same person tackling the same question set with the same amount of time to do it suddenly gets a very different score.

You read earlier that one of the differences between good test takers and great test takers is the ability to see a full section and not just individual questions. Up to this point, you have been learning how to adopt a big-picture approach to your RC section. Now it is time to use that perspective to delve deeper into managing individual questions, and that begins by understanding that every question is a choice.

Earlier in the chapter, you learned that no question is worth more than any other but that one question can cost you more than another. Because of this, there are two choices you must make for each question set: Which of the questions will you attempt? And, in what order will you attempt them? The test taker who does the questions in the order they are printed is assuming that these decisions have already been made for her. This test taker is not in control. Great test takers, on the other hand, know that these decisions are theirs to make. In the next section, you will learn how to make those decisions.

SUGGESTED EXERCISE

If you are getting bogged down in individual questions, try adding the following to your timing notations: Place a star next to a question number if, within 30 seconds, you feel the question is going to be time-consuming. This will help train you to ask yourself whether or not a question feels worth your time. Also, circle a question the second you realize you are bogged down. This will help train you to skip out of questions more quickly. You can also use these notations when you review the section to help you figure out the characteristics of questions that tend to bog you down and those of questions that don't.

Question Triage

Learning to quickly spot low-hanging fruit and likely time sinks is a vital skill for determining the order in which you tackle a section, but how you go about triaging the questions depends on the section. In Reading Comprehension, your first priority should always be Global questions. This is the reason why you should read passages primarily for the Big Picture: You are reading to predict the answers to these questions. Everything else in the passage can be researched, and during your initial read, you'll be highlighting the details likely to be tested as you note Keywords along the way.

Afterward, your job is to assess the remaining question stems to find the easier points. The most important factor here is ease of research. Take for example, the following two question stems:

The author and the critics would most likely disagree over
which one of the following statements?

Which of the following can be properly inferred from the passage?

Take a look at the first question stem. It has three clear clues as to where in the passage the answer will come from. First, it mentions two speakers: the critics and the author. But, it also mentions disagreeing. That should narrow things down enough for you to quickly research the passage and predict the correct answer to the question, which in turn means being able to spot the correct answer quickly while evaluating the answer choices. Contrast that with the second stem. There are no clues in that stem to indicate where in the passage the answer will come from. You cannot do any research up front or make more than a basic prediction about the Big Picture, meaning you may spend a significant amount of time in the answer choices reading them and comparing them against the passage. If there is a question you are not going to get to, then hedge your bets and skip the second one in favor of the first.

Beyond that, you may also find it easier to answer the second question after having researched the first one. Remember that the LSAT only tests a handful of the sentences in a passage, but it uses five to eight questions to test them. That means that the LSAT routinely assigns multiple questions to the same part of a passage. After you have answered all of the more easily researched questions, you have a good chance of having already researched the area of the passage to which the second question stem refers.

Ease of research is the most important factor in deciding whether or not to do a question, but it is definitely not the only one. Other factors to consider are question type (if some are easier for you than others) and length of answer choices. Question order, however, only goes so far if you are not dealing with the questions properly.

Rushing Never Helps

Earlier in the chapter, you learned that you can miss a question for either content reasons or management reasons. In many cases, however, the root of content errors is actually poor section management. When a test taker mismanages the section, anxiety begins to kick in. And when anxiety kicks in, the rushing begins. If you have ever had the feeling that you weren't taking the test so much as the test was taking you, you were probably in the middle of just such a cycle. Consider the following common scenario:

You spent a lot of time reading the passage for the question set and you now have less time than you had hoped to tackle the questions. After getting bogged down in a question, you guess and move on to the next one. You glance at the question stem in front of you and notice that it mentions a speaker you remember from the passage. To save time, you skip researching and predicting and dive right into the answer choices because you hate the idea of skipping a question. Because you don't have a strong prediction, you end up reading all of the answer choices just to be certain. Unfortunately, a few of the answer choices look good—you remember seeing some of the phrases used in the choices. You stare at the answer choices for a minute or two, trying to figure out which of them is more correct than the others. The longer you stare at them, though, the better they all look. Panicking, you realize you have spent far too long on this question, and you finally pick an answer and move to the next question feeling even more stressed out and behind on time as the cycle continues.

Sound familiar? This is a classic example of cutting all the wrong corners to save time and losing time instead. At the end of the day, the order in which you do your questions doesn't matter if you are not going to do them well. When timing-related anxiety takes over, it becomes very hard to stick to the Method, but sticking to the Method is the only way to stay in control. Rushing *never* helps. When you review a section you have rushed through, you will find that many of the questions you struggled with are actually quite manageable. It's a very frustrating experience to look back at a question and wonder, *Why on earth did I choose this answer*? Having such reactions when you review questions is the classic red flag that you are rushing and that it is hurting your score. When it comes to answering questions on the LSAT, you have to slow down to speed up.

The first mistake in the scenario we described was taking too much time to read the passage. For many test takers, this is the beginning of the cycle in Reading Comprehension. Starting a question set stressed about timing is a recipe for disaster. From there, the mistakes predictably followed one after another.

Now, perceiving that time was short, the test taker failed to read the question stem carefully. It may sound basic, but it is shocking how often test takers rush through question stems and try to answer a question they don't understand. When the anxiety/rushing cycle starts, it is easy to focus on a question stem's reference to something you vaguely remember from the passage but to ignore the specific task the stem is setting for you. Always paraphrase the question stem *before* you research the passage. If you find yourself reading question stems simply to look for a name or a line reference, then you are needlessly costing yourself time and points. If you don't understand what the question is asking, it is impossible to research efficiently, and inefficient research costs you time in the long run.

From there, it is just as easy to make the mistake of skipping research entirely. Even if the answer to the question comes from the part of the passage you think it does, and even if you remember that part well, you probably don't understand it in the way the question needs you to. While you can predict which pieces of a passage will be tested, you cannot predict how the LSAT will test them. If the LSAT tests you on a specific example in a passage, it could ask you a Detail question that merely expects you to spot a paraphrase of the text, but it could instead ask you about someone's opinion on that detail. Alternately, it could ask you for the role that example played, or it might expect you to identify an argument parallel to the one that the example is used in. Each of these questions requires a different prediction for the correct answer. This is why it is important to research the relevant pieces of the passage *after* reading the question. Understanding the need for research also allows you to Roadmap a passage more quickly up front: You know you will be able to come back to any piece you actually need.

Without proper research, it is impossible to make a good prediction. Even when you understand the question stem, forgoing research makes any prediction barely better than a guess. A poor prediction will have you jumping into the answer choices with no reliable way to assess them. At that point, the best anyone can do is to look for word matches between the answer choices and the passage. The problem is that there are usually several answer choices with phrasing from the passage; furthermore, the correct answers in the Reading Comprehension section are more likely to paraphrase the text than to repeat it directly, which makes looking for word matches counterproductive. There is a good chance that none of the answers that someone in this situation is choosing among are actually correct. And even if one of them is, there is no way to separate it from the others without going back to the passage. This is what leads to the inevitable "sit and stare" approach before finally doing what should have been done in the first place: guess and move on. Unfortunately, a test taker caught in this cycle is probably going to feel even more anxious at this point and is likely on the way to doing it all over again on the next question. So, how do you prevent this cycle from starting? How do you stop it once it starts? The answer is simple: skip questions.

Proactive Skipping

On the LSAT, *strategically* skipping some questions can enhance your score. Though many test takers struggle initially with the idea of skipping questions, the choice between skipping and not skipping is clear. Take the four questions in four minutes example from earlier. If the test taker had been reluctant to skip and stuck with question 2, then he would have ended up skipping questions 3 and 4. But if that same person decided to strategically skip question 2, then he would end up getting to more questions. If your refusal to skip questions means spending so much time on a handful of them that you are not able to get to even more at the end, then you are already skipping. You're just not skipping strategically. As you probably guessed, for most test takers, the 8- to 9-Minute Rule will not leave enough time to correctly answer every question in the passage. Proactive skipping means strategically cutting out questions from the outset to buy you enough time to invest in the questions that are more likely to pay off. If the idea of skipping questions outright makes you anxious, take a look at the following calculations and then read the explanation:

LSAT STRATEGY

Skipping Strategically

Questions/Passage × 4 Passages + "Skip Points" = Total Score (out of 27)

3 × 4 passages + 3 = 15

4 × 4 passages + 2 = 18

5 × 4 passages + (1 or 2) = 21 or 22

6 × 4 passages + (0 or 1) = 24 or 25

Imagine that you only did three questions per passage in a 27-question Reading Comprehension section. The 8- to 9-Minute Rule gives you 8–9 minutes to Roadmap the passage and tackle those questions. Now imagine that you pick the three easiest questions for you—the ones you feel the most certain you can answer quickly and correctly. You have plenty of time to research the answer to the question, to make a strong prediction, and to read and analyze the answer choices against your prediction. Any question you see that seems time-consuming or that begins to bog you down, you skip out of quickly and confidently, knowing you have plenty of time to find another question that seems more likely to reward you. Then you guess on the remaining 15 questions in the section. For most test takers, this is a terrifying prospect that feels like a worst-case scenario. After all, guessing on 15 questions means guessing on over half of the section.

But take a moment and do the math. Assuming you selected the easiest questions and got them correct, that would give you 12 points total. And given that guessing on a question has a 1-in-5 chance of yielding a point, skipping 15 questions should give you (on average) 3 more points. The total score would be around a 15. For many test takers, this would be a solid improvement in score—or at least not much of a change from what they are getting now. If you bump that up to 4 questions per passage, you would still be skipping a total of 11 questions, but you would be getting around 18 correct answers—a correct response rate better than the majority of test takers will achieve on the test as a whole. And that scenario has you skipping from two to four questions per passage!

There are two main benefits to this kind of proactive skipping. First, it frees you from getting bogged down on time-consuming questions and allows you to instead focus on the questions that are more likely to pay off. If done well, it forces you to ask yourself whether a question is worth your time. After all, if you are only getting to four, you have to be choosy about which four you get to. Second, strategic skipping buys you enough time to do your questions well. On the LSAT, it is nearly always better to do a few questions well than to do more questions poorly. Your approach doesn't need to be as regimented as that in the chart, but you should look for a way to incorporate the basic idea into your management goals.

If you find yourself getting bogged down on individual questions, not getting to entire passages, or making a lot of "careless" mistakes, then you can use the sample calculations shown to help you set goals. If you are currently scoring around a 19, for example, then try doing only five questions per passage to improve your score. As you get more comfortable doing a certain number of questions per passage, you can set new goals to gradually improve.

SUGGESTED EXERCISE

If you are having a hard time convincing yourself to skip questions proactively, then try doing a full Reading Comprehension section under timed conditions, but use a digital timer to time yourself on how long each individual question takes you. When you are finished, find the four questions you spent the longest on and add up the total time you spent on them and how many points they yielded. It's not uncommon to find that you are spending 7–11 minutes on four questions for only 1 or 2 points. What would your score have been like if you had used the time you spent on the more time-consuming questions to slow down on some of the other questions you did or to get to questions you couldn't get to at the end?

Reactive Skipping

No matter how careful you are about question selection, research, and prediction, sometimes a question doesn't go your way. For each question you try, quickly decide whether or not the question is worth your time. If you are unsure of what the question is asking, if you are not sure where in the passage to research, or if you are struggling to make a prediction, then odds are the question is not going to turn into a point. Even if it does, it may cost you more time than it is worth. Keep moving and find yourself a question that is more likely to reward you quickly. This sort of reactive skipping is the bread and butter of any great test taker.

Sometimes, you will not realize that you are in trouble until you get to the answer choices. In an ideal situation, you will have a strong enough prediction that you can spot the correct answer easily, stop reading, and move on to the next question. Other times you may find yourself stuck between choices. The longer you look at the right answer, the more you tend to poke holes in it. The longer you look at the wrong answers, the more you talk yourself into them. Avoid the "stare and compare" approach at all costs and instead keep in mind that the correct answer isn't perfect, it's flawless. If you are looking for the "best" answer, you are in for a world of trouble. All of the answers may have good things in them, and a wrong answer may seem to have more of what you are looking for in it than the right one does. The one thing that separates the right answer from the wrong ones, however, is that the right answer has *nothing wrong* with it. There is nothing to argue with in the correct answer. When stuck between answer choices, stop looking for what is right and start looking for what is wrong!

If looking for what is wrong does not immediately give you a clear answer, *get out*! Your best bet is to circle the answer your first instinct said is correct and to move on to another question. From there you have two options: you can return to the question or leave it alone. If you get out fast enough and have some time to spare, then you can come back to the question with a fresh perspective after you have done another question or two. You have probably had the experience of reviewing an answer choice and realizing that you grossly misread it. It is easy to rush your reading during timed sections and to make reading mistakes. Unfortunately, when you reread something you have just read, your brain has a tendency to read from memory and not from the page. This is why it can be so hard to spot a mistake in the moment. After you have moved on to another question or two, however, your brain replaces the information in your short-term memory with the new questions. When you return to the original question, you are forced to read from the page again, which gives you a better chance of catching your mistake.

Alternately, you can opt to let the question go. Never get into an ego battle with the test. If you feel that coming back to the question isn't likely to change anything, then don't bother. You will be far better off for the rest of the section if you avoid sinking time into a question you end up getting wrong. It is worth pointing out that you should put an answer down for every question—even the ones you guess on. We recommend gridding by visiting your answer sheet between each of the passages and bubbling in your answers as a group. If there are any questions you have guessed on, you can either bubble in a guess letter for them now (and change the answer later if you end up coming back to the question) or leave them blank and return at the end of the section to fill them in. Practice both approaches to find out what works best for you. This means you are going to the answer sheet only four times during the section, and gridding the questions in groups makes it easier to avoid accidentally skipping a line.

SUGGESTED EXERCISE

Whenever you complete timing work and get to an answer that you feel is correct, draw a line under it. Note to yourself whether you kept reading or moved on. When you are reviewing the section, ask yourself how often you continued to read and changed your answer. Many students spend a lot of time reading answer choices when it is clear they have already found the right answer. Others may struggle with impulsively selecting wrong answers and moving on before they have analyzed the answer carefully enough. Get an idea of how much time you are investing in your answers. Is continuing to read helping you or hurting you?

COMMON FRUSTRATIONS—DIAGNOSING YOUR ISSUE AND WAYS TO IMPROVE

Up to this point, you have been learning about how the Reading Comprehension section is structured. Great test takers, however, not only understand the test's sections, but they also understand themselves. Though everyone is unique, a few common archetypal student experiences are worth discussing: the anxious one, the rusher, and the perfectionist. You may relate exceedingly well to one of these, or you may relate in small part to more than one.

Take a look at each to help you figure out what you need to work on and, more importantly, how to address your challenges. No matter what those challenges are, the first step is to recognize that there is *always* a solution!

The Anxious One

Test taking and anxiety go hand in hand for most. For some test takers, though, it is the biggest mountain to climb. Test anxiety is a very real phenomenon that has potentially serious consequences. Fortunately, like all problems, it can be dealt with. When you are first learning the Reading Comprehension Method, don't put time pressure on yourself. Practice methodically, and internalize the steps you need to take. As those steps become second nature, integrate timing practice into your regimen. If you find yourself repeatedly thinking, "I'm not ready for timing. I'll deal with it when I have my method completely down," then you are probably in an anxiety/avoidance cycle. While it is important to begin with Mastery work in order to learn the Reading Comprehension Method, it is equally important to remember that, with Reading Comprehension in particular, following the Method involves being able to go through the process in a certain amount of time. You don't need to make everything timed, but aside from the early stages of prep, you should never leave timing out entirely.

The good news is that once you begin timing, you don't need to jump right into full 35-minute sections or full-length tests. In fact, it's to your benefit to start with micro timing exercises. Begin your timed work with one passage and question set to help ease you into the process and to minimize your anxiety. If the mere thought of being timed sends you into an anxiety spiral, then give yourself a chance to adjust to having a timing device around while you work. Don't be prohibitive about your time at this point—you don't have to stop yourself for taking a long time. Just get used to the idea of having a timer around. As you become more comfortable, you can start setting time limits on yourself to read and answer questions. Start off with a generous amount of time and incrementally reduce the time by small amounts—challenge yourself just a little bit. Gradually, you can start adding more passages to your timed work until you are ready for a full section of four.

The more you suffer from anxiety, the more crucial the section management strategies mentioned in this chapter will become. Nothing kicks anxiety into gear like a lack of control. Pay special attention to the exercises that deal with time awareness and notation. Making these a regular part of what you do will help to keep you in control and keep your anxiety in check.

The Rusher

Rushing is a perennial problem on the LSAT, and it is very often related to anxiety. If your problem is rushing, be sure to read about the Anxious One above to make sure that's not your core issue. Looking at the problem of rushing, it is important to start by getting an idea of where the rushing begins. Everyone is different in this regard. Some people start by racing through reading the question stems. Others tend to forsake research and prediction but spend a lot of time on the answer choices, thinking over them carefully. Often, rushing starts with one step and then spreads to others as a consequence. As previously discussed, rushing through reading the question stem, for example, can lead to a series of "downstream" mistakes in research and prediction. If you don't understand the question stem well enough, then you can't efficiently research. If that happens often enough, you will find yourself increasingly eager to skip research entirely in order to save time, which will cost you time as you try to evaluate the answer choices. Ultimately, the steps you rush through and the ones you don't tell you a lot about how to tame this bad habit.

To figure out what triggers your rushing instinct, try a passage and its question set under timed conditions and make sure you record how long you spend reading. This will tell you if your rushing is a product of anxiety that comes from spending too much time in the passage. Then, as you tackle the questions, every time you find yourself racing through a question stem, make a note next to that stem. Every time you decide not to research a question that could have been researched, put a big "R" next to the question. If you end up jumping into the answer choices without making a prediction, put a big "P" next to the question. If you find yourself stuck between answer choices, put a big "A/B" (or whichever choices you were caught between) next to the question. Finally, if you get bogged down, circle the question the moment you realize you're spending too much time in it. When you are finished, figure out what your triggers are for rushing. If you are rushing through a series of steps, try to find the earliest step you are rushing through; in many cases, that is the important point.

Next, retrain yourself to stop rushing through these steps. While doing another passage/question set under timed conditions, stop the timer at the beginning of each of the steps you identified in the previous exercise. Now record your work on each step on another sheet of paper. If you are rushing through the stem, write down your paraphrase of it; if you are skipping research, write down where you are going to go research. When you finish, start the timer again and continue. The key here is consistency. You are always either ingraining good habits or bad ones. The only way to ensure you don't rush through the Kaplan Method in the future is to force yourself to do each step properly every single time. By tying that to a physical process—writing it down on another sheet of paper—you will achieve that consistency.

When dealing with full sections, you should also use the goal-setting exercise mentioned in the last paragraph of the "Proactive Skipping" section of this chapter to buy yourself enough time to relax. As you become more comfortable, you can slowly increase the number of questions you complete per passage.

The Perfectionist

The Perfectionist is someone who generally has a hard time letting go. Perfectionism is typically a product of anxiety, and it often leads to rushing to make up for lost time (see both the profiles above). Having said that, there are two particular areas that perfectionists tend to struggle with in Reading Comprehension.

The first area is the initial read of the passage. Perfectionists often have a difficult time coming to terms with having a limited understanding of the passage when jumping into the question set. The best defense against this is to face your fears head-on. Take a passage you have never done before and get out your timer. Give yourself two minutes to read the introductory paragraph and the first sentence of every paragraph after that, making a brief Roadmap as you go. Now, take a moment to go through each of the question stems for all of the non-Global questions. How many of these could you research at this point? Of those you couldn't quickly and easily research, is it because the question stem is too vague or because you genuinely don't recall the reference? What you will likely find is that the vast majority of the questions can be easily researched even when you haven't read a majority of the text. You will also find that most of the questions you can't easily research are hard to research because the stem is devoid of research clues, *not* because you didn't read carefully enough. On Test Day, you will read the entire passage, of course, but this exercise will stand as a strong reminder to read *strategically* and Roadmap the passage rather than to concentrate on comprehending every nuance and detail of the subject matter.

The other area that perfectionists tend to struggle with is question skipping. Once again, facing your fears is the solution. Complete the exercise in the gray box in the "Proactive Skipping" part of the chapter. If you want to simplify it, you can always use an individual passage instead of a full section. Perfectionists often struggle with the concept of leaving a question behind that they could have answered correctly when the real emphasis should be on how much time it will take to answer it correctly. When you have finished the exercise, ask yourself which questions you could have skipped to maximize the number of questions you could have answered. How long did it take you to realize that the questions that took you the longest weren't worth your time? Now, try another section under timed conditions. This time, whenever you feel you are getting bogged down, circle the question and move on immediately. When you finish the section, compare it to the original section. Which one went better? Which one felt more controlled?

You Are On Your Way

Clearly, a lot goes into becoming a great test taker, but you have a good idea of how to start the process. The easiest way to grab points quickly and to keep your score consistent is to build these skills from now until Test Day. There is no single skill on the LSAT that is worth more points than section management, so be sure to incorporate it as a regular part of your prep. Every time you sit down to do timed work, you should have one or more section management goals in mind. Are you going to work on building time awareness? Do you need to work on spending less time reading the passage? Maybe this time you are going to work on proactively skipping questions or triaging questions. Whatever you choose to work on, make sure that you focus on the *process* that leads you to points, not on the points themselves. Building a good process now means you'll be using it on Test Day to get the best possible score.

Reading Comprehension Passage Acknowledgments

Acknowledgment is made to the following sources from which material has been adapted for use in this book:

Valerie A. Hall, "The Development of the Landscape of Ireland over the Last Two Thousand Years; Fresh Evidence from Historical and Pollen Analytical Studies." ©1997 by Chronicon, UCC.

Francis Haskell, "Art & the Apocalypse." ©1993 by NYREV, Inc.

Leandra Lederman, "'Stranger than Fiction': Taxing Virtual Worlds." ©2007 by New York University Law Review.

Timothy Miller, *How to Want What You Have.* ©1995 by Timothy Miller.

Carol Muske, "Breaking Out of the Genre Ghetto." ©1995 by Poetry in Review Foundation.

Clive Thompson, "Game Theories." ©2004 by The Walrus Magazine.

Peter Whiteley, "Hopuutungwni: 'Hopi Names' as Literature." ©1992 by the Smithsonian Institution.

PART FIVE

Countdown to Test Day

CHAPTER 17

Test Day

Is it starting to feel like your whole life is a buildup to the LSAT? You've known about it for years, worried about it for months, and now spent weeks in solid preparation for it. As the test gets closer, you may find your anxiety is on the rise. You shouldn't worry. After the preparation you've done, you're in good shape. To calm any pre-test jitters you may have, though, here are a few strategies for the days before the test.

THE WEEK BEFORE THE TEST

Your goal during the week before the LSAT is to set yourself up for success on Test Day. Up until this point, you have been working to build your LSAT potential, but Test Day is about achievement. That process begins with taking care of your basic needs: food, sleep, and exercise. It's easy to get caught up in the stress of balancing your life with your studying, but if taking an extra hour to study every night leaves you sleep deprived and exhausted on Test Day, it's hurting you more than helping. Figure out what time you need to go to sleep the night before the exam and make sure you're in bed at that time every night the week before the exam. This is particularly important if you're a night owl who tends to get a second wind later in the evening. If at all possible, start doing some LSAT work—even if it's only a few problems— each morning at the same time as the test. Finally, if you are someone who regularly goes to the gym or engages in other physical activity, this is *not* the week to stop. Physical activity helps lower stress and increases production of dopamine and norepinephrine, two neurotransmitters that play a crucial role in memory, attention, and mood!

You should also take at least one trip to your test center sometime before the actual exam to figure out the logistics: how long it takes to get there, where to park, how to get to your room, and where the bathrooms and drinking fountains are. The last thing you want to end up doing the morning of the test is running into unexpected construction on your route or not being able to find your room when you arrive! If the test center is a classroom or public building, try to take a practice test or timed section in the room to get a feel for it. Pay close attention to things like noise levels and temperature while you're there. The more you can mentally prepare for these conditions, the less they will distract you on Test Day.

Early in the week, make sure to print out your admissions ticket from the LSAC website and check it against your government-issued ID. Be sure that the names match and that the ID isn't expired! (As of the time this book went to press, LSAC accepts photo IDs that expired *within 90 days* of the test date, but check the LSAC website for the latest information.) If the names don't match, contact LSAC *immediately* so you can remedy the situation. If that isn't fixed by Test Day, you will be denied admission to the exam. You will also need a passport photo taken within the last six months to affix to your admissions ticket. LSAC is strict about the photo requirements, so Kaplan recommends that you have your photos taken professionally at a place that specializes in passport photos, such as the post office, a chain drug store, or a photocopy shop.

For a complete list of the LSAC photo requirements, visit LSAC's website, www.lsac.org.

The kind of practice that you do the week before the exam is important. Resist the temptation to focus on your weaknesses and instead focus primarily on shoring up your strengths. It's all fine and good to grab two more points in games, for example, but if you start losing points in the other sections from neglect, you may very well end up worse off than you started. The reality is that you are more likely to grab a few points in your strengths at the last minute than you are in the areas you struggle with the most. Of course, be sure to work on all three areas during this time: no one section should be fully ignored. Also keep in mind that the actual LSAT is a test of timing and endurance. A majority of your work should be under timed conditions, and you should try to fit in a complete test or two if you have the time in your schedule. Having said that, do not fall into the trap of doing nothing but tests right before the LSAT. As always, there is a balancing act between test taking and review: taking a test every day can make it difficult to find time to review them, which means you aren't learning from them. You also need to watch your stress levels carefully: Taking too many exams can lead to a stress spiral that is hard to climb out of.

Finally, the week before the exam is the time to decide whether or not you are ready to take your test. As of the time of writing, LSAC's policy allows you to withdraw your registration all the way up until 11:59 P.M. Eastern time the night before the exam without it showing up on your record. There is no right or wrong answer to the question of whether or not you are ready to take your exam, but if you are having any doubts, ask yourself two questions:

- What is the lowest score I would be okay with an admissions officer seeing?
- Am I scoring at least that high now?

You can choose your goals in life, but you can't always choose your timelines. If the answer to the second question was a resounding no, then it may be in your best interest to change your test date. Though there is a modest benefit to applying early, submitting a score that is well below a school's median early is more likely to result in a faster rejection than a surprise admission. Don't expect any miracles on Test Day. It's possible that your score will suddenly jump up to an all-time high on the day of the exam, but it isn't likely. More importantly, it's risky. This is especially important if you already have one score or cancellation within the last five years: Admissions officers can be understanding about one blemish on your record, but two starts to become a pattern.

LSAT STRATEGY

In the last week before the test:

- Print out your admission ticket.
- Get your body on schedule for the time of your test (either 8:30 A.M. or 12:30 P.M.).
- Visit the testing center.
- Don't take any practice tests within 48 hours of the test.
- Decide whether you want to take the test or withdraw.

THE DAY BEFORE THE TEST

The day before the test is as important as the six days before it. The first instinct of most test takers is to cram as much as possible in hopes of grabbing a few last-second points. But the LSAT isn't an AP exam or your history final: You cannot "cram" for the LSAT. You should think of Test Day as Game Day. An athlete doesn't try to run 10 miles the day before a big race: She rests up to make sure that she can hit her potential when it counts. Though this advice is hard to follow, trust Kaplan's decades of experience with tens of thousands of students. You should make the day before the test a wonderful, relaxing day. There's a good chance that during the last few weeks or months, the stress of balancing prep with the rest of your life has meant you've had less time to yourself or with your family and loved ones. Spend a day with your significant other or kids. Go to the spa or spend the day in a movie marathon. Whatever you do, make sure that today is as restful and relaxing as possible. Put your LSAT materials away and leave them there because, while you aren't going to cram your way to a good score, you may cram your way into a bad one. Think of how you normally feel when you get a score on something that is less than you hoped for. Now imagine how it would feel the day before the exam and what that kind of anxiety could do to you on Test Day. The benefits to studying the day before are almost nonexistent, but the risks are sky-high.

Don't forget to cap off the day with a full meal for dinner and a good night of sleep. It's not going to be easy to fall asleep the night before the test, so make sure you are in bed on time. Resist the urge to stare at a television or computer screen: they tend to make it even harder to sleep. For what it's worth, however, the most important night of sleep isn't the night before the test; it's two nights before the test. For various reasons, the effects of sleep deprivation tend to skip a day, so getting a great night of sleep two nights before the exam will help make sure that you are well rested the day of the test!

LSAT STRATEGY

On the day before the test:

- Relax! Read a book, watch a movie, go shopping, etc.
- Get all of your materials together—your admission ticket, passport photo, watch, snack, plastic bag, etc.
- Eat a full meal for dinner and get plenty of sleep.

You also want to make sure that everything you need for tomorrow is packed up and ready. Don't put yourself in the position of fumbling around the next morning trying to find everything you need. Everything you bring into the test center **must** be in a clear, one-gallon zip-top bag.

LSAT FACTS

The following items are required for admission on Test Day:

- Admissions ticket
- Government-issued ID
- A passport photo affixed to your admissions ticket
- Regular No. 2 pencils (no mechanical pencils)

In addition to those required items, there are a few other things you should bring with you as well:

LSAT STRATEGY

Kaplan recommends you bring the following items with you on Test Day:

- A snack for the break (things like granola bars are best; avoid sugary snacks that might make you crash)
- Bottled water or juice box (metal cans are not permitted)
- Erasers
- Pain reliever
- Tissues (even if they end up being for someone else in the room with the sniffles)
- A nondigital timing device (i.e., an analog watch!)
- A positive, upbeat attitude

On occasion, the LSAC will change its admissions requirements. Because of this, it's important that you consult its website (www.lsac.org) to get updated information on what is and is not acceptable to bring on Test Day!

THE MORNING OF THE TEST

On the morning of the exam, you should obviously get up early to give yourself some time to wake up and to leave for the test center early. A relaxed morning is a much better start than a frantic, stressful one. After you wake up, make sure you have a great breakfast that is both high in protein and high in carbohydrates. You'll need the energy later! Also, make sure you pack an appropriate snack. While it's important to have a protein-rich breakfast, you want to *avoid* a protein-rich snack. You will have a chance to eat your snack during the 15-minute break after the third section, and you'll want the energy it provides as quickly as possible. Because carbohydrates digest much faster than protein, foods like fruit and granola are much more practical than peanut butter and jelly sandwiches. Try to avoid any processed sugars or caffeine (a notorious diuretic), as they could lead to a crash. Finally, you are allowed a drink, but it must be contained in either a juice box or in a plastic bottle of no more than 20 ounces. Avoid energy drinks (as they are mostly sugar and caffeine) and instead opt for water or 100 percent juice.

When choosing what to wear, go for layers. It's hard to tell what the temperature will be in the room, and heating and cooling systems tend to kick in erratically. You want to be sure you can adjust your clothing as needed to stay as comfortable as possible. It's important to note, however, that you may not wear hats or hoods during the exam unless LSAC has given you a religious exemption.

Before you head to the test center, be sure to read LSAC's website one more time to see a complete and official list of what is and is not allowed into the room beforehand.

LSAT FACTS

The following items are prohibited:

- Cell phones (leave it at home or in the car)
- Electronic devices of any kind, including tablets, MP3 players, or digital watches
- Ear plugs
- Backpacks or purses
- Mechanical pencils
- Papers or books
- Hats and hooded sweatshirts

This is not a complete list, so be sure to check the LSAC website to get the most updated information. But do know that once you check in, you may not have any of these items on your person. If you bring any of them into the testing center, you risk having your score immediately cancelled and a misconduct letter placed in your file. So, as hard as it may be for you to part with it, leave the cell phone in the car—it's not worth the risk.

LSAT STRATEGY

On the morning of the test:

- Get up early and plan accordingly for traffic and parking.
- Eat an appropriate breakfast.
- Dress in layers (but do not wear a hooded sweatshirt).
- Don't forget your one-gallon plastic bag with permissible items for the testing center.

AT THE LSAC FACILITY AND DURING THE TEST

Aim to arrive at your testing facility at least 30 minutes before the test is scheduled to begin. Traffic, parking, and other unforeseen circumstances may delay you, so don't risk arriving late to the facility. The LSAC is strict about when the test begins—if you are even a minute late, the proctors have the right to deny you entry. Arriving early also allows you to familiarize yourself with your surroundings and to scope out where the bathrooms and drinking fountains are (though, as mentioned before, this is something you were hopefully able to do in the week leading up to the test).

There are also a number of things you'll want to do once you arrive at the testing facility. After all, if the only point of arriving 30 minutes early is to sit around and twiddle your thumbs, any anxiety you might feel would get worse, not better. That's why it's so important to have a game plan for what to do at the testing facility on Test Day. First of all, make sure you get a drink of water and go to the bathroom. Though that advice might seem like common sense, you'd be surprised by how many students get so nervous that they actually skip this important step. But going to the bathroom before the test is really important. After all, having to leave the testing room during Section 3 to go to the bathroom will cost you time and, in the process, undo the months of effort and practice you put into this test.

The other thing you'll want to do at the testing facility in the minutes before the test begins is get your brain in "LSAT mode." Bring with you a quick warm-up exercise to do while you wait to check in. Find a game, passage, or set of Logical Reasoning questions that you've done before and that you know well. Reviewing LSAT material and walking through the various steps you took to get to the right answer will get your brain prepared for the test to come. Many students find that if they don't do this, they start the test "cold." Don't wait until the second section to get your brain "warmed up." A word of caution: Be sure that your warm-up exercise is something you've already done. There's enough stress on Test Day without adding the anxiety of getting stumped by one of your warm-up questions right before the exam!

Because paper materials are not allowed in the testing room, do your warm-up exercise in a hallway or other room at the testing facility in the minutes leading up to the test start. While other students rush into the testing room 30 minutes before the test starts, take your time and review your material outside the testing room. Then, when there are 5–7 minutes to go, get in line and officially check in. Once you enter the testing room, you'll have little to do besides sit with your thoughts and wait for the proctors to begin the test. Remember, of course, to discard any practice materials prior to check-in.

Checking in on Test Day will involve showing your identification and having the proctors examine the materials you're bringing into the facility. Don't get flustered when they check your identification and belongings as you enter the testing room—this is standard operating procedure. The test administrators do this because (1) they want to make sure that everyone is who they say they are and (2) the materials used by each test taker should never distract others. That's one of the reasons why items like mechanical pencils (which can click) and cell phones (which can ring) are prohibited. To avoid any uncertainty or stress over what to bring, again, check the LSAC website for a list of acceptable and prohibited items. Additionally, make sure to follow the most up-to-date requirements for identification, lest all of your preparation be squandered when you are not allowed into the facility.

Once you enter the testing room and find your seat, you'll have to wait for the proctors to let everyone else in the room, pass out the test booklets, and recite a long list of rules. For some students, this time before the test can be nerve-racking. What thoughts will go through your head when this moment comes? Some students, no doubt, will think, "Gee, I hope I do well," or "I better not bomb this, or my life is over!" This time before the test begins is an opportunity for you to take control of your thoughts for the next four hours. Visualize yourself doing well. Walk through a logic game in your head. Identify the assumption from an old Strengthen question you've done. Tell yourself you will be successful. "I am going to do really well on this test. I'm well prepared and have seen thousands of LSAT problems. I know exactly how to tackle every question they throw at me. If they give me an Inference question, I'm going to read the stimulus and make deductions . . . ." While the heads of the test takers around you fill with nervous thoughts, game-plan for the test and build your mental confidence.

After the test booklets have been handed out and once you've filled out the required information, the test will begin. Your proctor may or may not write the starting and ending time of each section in the front of the room, but the proctor should *always* announce a "five minutes remaining" warning. Even though this is one of the proctors' duties, don't rely solely on them for timing cues. Your watch is there to accurately measure time, so the only thing you need to hear from the proctor is "you may begin."

During the break, be sure to eat your snack, drink your beverage, and go to the bathroom. Stretch and move around a bit. Use the time during the break to recharge for the second half of the test. One thing you'll probably notice during the break is that people will talk—they'll talk about a section that was particularly hard, or particularly easy, or they may even talk about a section that you haven't even taken yet! That's because LSAT sections are organized differently in different test booklets. Your booklet may go LR, LG, LR in the first three sections, while the person next to you may have a booklet that goes RC, LR, LG. Additionally, you are never sure which section will end up being the experimental section until after the test is over. That's why the LSAC and the proctors will expressly prohibit discussion of the test during the break. Moral of the story? Don't worry about what people are talking about during the break; in fact, actively avoid anyone who seems to be discussing the test because it can lead to a misconduct letter or expulsion from the test. Focus only on yourself and your own progress. Forget about what happened during the first part of the test and turn your attention to the next three sections.

After the fifth section of the test, take a moment to relax and breathe. Congratulations. You have finished the scored sections of the LSAT. The only section that now remains is the Writing Sample. Though this section is not unimportant, it's nowhere near as important as the previous sections. Between the fifth and sixth sections, feel free to decompress before gathering yourself and moving forward to the Writing Sample.

LSAT STRATEGY

At the testing facility on Test Day:

- Arrive 30 minutes early.
- Find and use the drinking fountains and bathroom.
- Get into "LSAT mode" by reviewing previous work.
- Enter the testing room a few minutes before the test is set to begin.
- Use the time before the test begins to mentally prepare yourself for the test.
- Don't look backward—always keep moving through the test and stay focused on the section you're currently in, not sections you've already done or will do in the future.

AFTER THE TEST

If it turns out that Test Day doesn't go *exactly* as planned, that's alright—it rarely, if ever, does, and the LSAT does not require perfection! All of your fellow test takers will likely experience some level of self-doubt as well; that's fairly typical.

If it turns out you feel like you did well on Test Day, then skip this section and head to the Post-LSAT Festivities section later in this chapter. If, however, you end up having a particularly unusual Test Day, you may think about canceling your score. Canceling your score means that neither you nor the law schools will have access to whatever your score would have been. But here's the rub: Law schools will still know that you took the test at that administration, and it will count against your limit of three tests in a two-year period. For many law schools, a cancellation can raise a red flag. If you do cancel, you may want to consider attaching an addendum to your application explaining why you canceled.

You have two opportunities to cancel your score. The first opportunity is immediately after you finish the test on Test Day. In fact, there is a part of the scoring grid where you can indicate your wish to cancel. The second, less impetuous way, is to send in a written cancellation request to the LSAC within six calendar days after the exam. If you're considering canceling, check the LSAC's website to verify the most recent means and deadlines for canceling your score.

Should You Cancel Your Score?

If you're wondering whether canceling is the right decision, the information on the next page should be helpful. If you feel confident in your Test Day abilities and are not considering canceling your score, feel free to skip this section entirely.

First, let's examine the *benefits* of not canceling your LSAT score.

No matter how you "feel" about how things went, you *don't know for sure*. You may have actually done much better than you think. According to LSAC, many test takers who cancel their score and then retest would've been better off sticking with the first score. (While the examinee never finds out the cancelled score, the LSAC still computes it internally and can compare the cancelled and subsequent results.)

Additionally, if you cancel your score, you will never have access to the answers you selected during Test Day. If you keep your score, you will receive an official score report and a PDF copy of the test you took (except for February administrations, for which the exam is not released). This information can be extremely helpful if you do choose to take the test again, as you will be able to review and evaluate the decisions you made during an official LSAT, when everything was on the line. Allowing your score to stay in place gives you access not only to the right answers but also to the answers *you* picked. Even weeks later, you'll be amazed as you go question by question through the sections of the exam and say, "Hmmm, now why did I find wrong answer (A) so alluring?" or "Shoot, I should've stuck with my first answer there!" By canceling your score, you forfeit access to this information.

Another reason why it may not be in your best interest to cancel a score is that in recent years, more and more law schools are *not* averaging scores. In fact, law schools have been given careful guidelines from LSAC *against* averaging. That doesn't mean that every school follows this policy, though, and our recommendation from above still stands: The most preferable scenario is to take the test once and ace it. However, if your decision is between canceling and taking it again and *not* canceling and taking it again, it's likely that the latter option will be preferable. (Again, schools can see when you cancel.) Even a so-so score followed by a much better score won't hurt you as it might have in the past, when averaging was the common practice. As a rule, law schools want to assess you fairly, and most agree that the fairest thing is to take the better of two scores, irrespective of the order in which tests were taken. So, even if you decide you want to retest at the next administration, there will be less pressure next time if you don't cancel *this time*. By having a score already on record, you won't have the anxiety of thinking that you absolutely must use the retest score.

So, based on the benefits of not canceling, the following situations **would NOT warrant a score cancellation:**

- There were some minor distractions in the testing facility. Yes, it's hard to define exactly what counts as "minor" versus "major." Pencil tapping, coughing, and the humming of an air conditioner may all have been distractions, but that's also part of the test environment, and you'd likely experience the same things next time. It's highly unlikely you'll ever have a perfectly distraction-free atmosphere!

- You didn't get to finish or forgot to bubble in the last few questions of a section (or two), even though you usually finish those sections when you practice. Although these time-management issues are not ideal, they do not warrant a cancellation. Yes, a few questions here or there can affect your overall score, but the material at the end of a section can be of a higher level of difficulty, so even if you had completed those questions, there is no guarantee they would have markedly affected your score. Also, there is always the possibility that a section you struggled with was the Experimental section.

Now, let's talk about **when you should cancel your LSAT score:**

- If you have already taken the real test two or three (or more) times, you probably have a much better "feel" for whether or not a particular exam has truly gone well. Also, with two or three scores already on the record, one more cancellation isn't going to significantly damage your profile. However, remember that you can't take the LSAT more than three times in any two-year period. Those three times include any times you've opted to cancel your score.

- If you had been consistently scoring in a certain range but became physically ill with flu or nausea on Test Day, or had some other serious difficulty during the test that prevented you from staying focused to the point that you were unable to complete large sections of the exam, then you should consider cancellation. This may have been due to test anxiety, lack of sleep the night before, personal stress not related to the LSAT, severe illness, etc. To be clear, the situations described would have affected *every* section; they wouldn't cause just a moment of panic during a single section.

- If you realized that you made significant gridding mistakes for entire sections, thereby putting many questions in jeopardy of being incorrect, you should consider cancellation (e.g., #8 was gridded in spot #7, #9 in spot #8, etc.).

- Large-scale time issues, such as a proctor who mistakenly shorted time in a section (without having it immediately brought to his or her attention), can significantly change test performance. Minor issues related to the location of clocks, times written on the board, or the exact precision of a five-minute warning are all things that can be prevented by using one's own watch and only relying on the proctor for the words, "You may begin." So, a significant loss of time covering multiple sections could warrant a cancellation, but small, single-section timing issues will usually not.

- Remember that you can (and should) explain valid reasons for a score cancellation in an addendum to your law school application.

Post-LSAT Festivities

So, you've just taken the LSAT. After months of preparation and hard work, it's finally over. What to do now? First, give yourself a great big pat on the back. You've just completed (and hopefully rocked) the most important factor in law school admissions. Go celebrate and enjoy the moment—but of course, don't celebrate *too* hard. Law schools are in the business of recruiting future lawyers, which means they're typically not interested in applicants with criminal records. Don't be the person who destroys the LSAT in the morning, then acts inappropriately in the evening.

Instead, take a moment to reach out to anyone who has helped you prepare for the test—teachers, tutors, study buddies, friends, and family members who have invested in your decision to go to law school and become a lawyer. Let them know how you did and share your success with them.

After you've celebrated, and after you've taken a couple of days off from thinking about the LSAT and law school, it's time to once again start thinking about putting together the other pieces of your application. Be sure to get a good head start on your letters of recommendation, personal statement, and transcripts.

Congratulations on your journey!

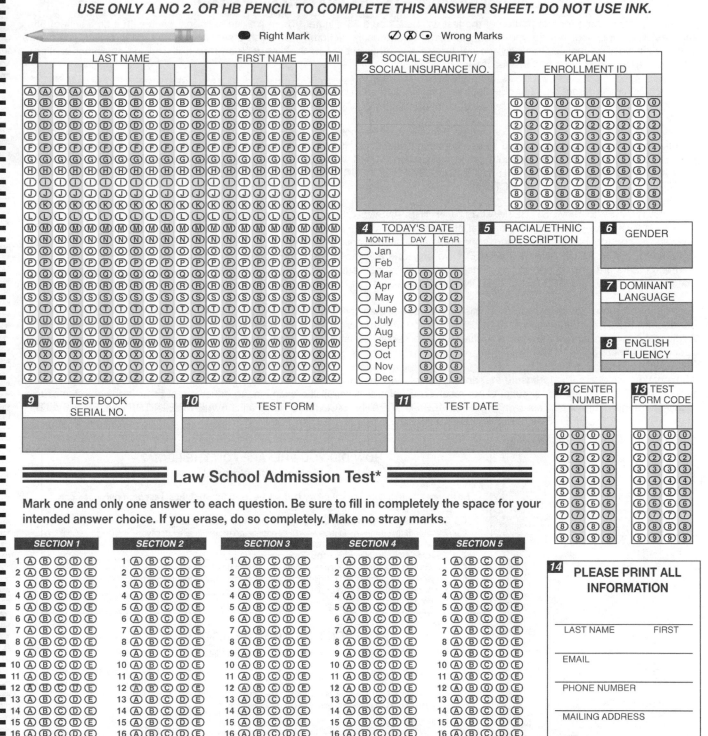

USE ONLY A NO 2. OR HB PENCIL TO COMPLETE THIS ANSWER SHEET. DO NOT USE INK.

● Right Mark   ⊘ ⊗ ⊙ Wrong Marks

1 LAST NAME / FIRST NAME / MI

2 SOCIAL SECURITY/ SOCIAL INSURANCE NO.

3 KAPLAN ENROLLMENT ID

4 TODAY'S DATE

MONTH / DAY / YEAR

○ Jan
○ Feb
○ Mar
○ Apr
○ May
○ June
○ July
○ Aug
○ Sept
○ Oct
○ Nov
○ Dec

5 RACIAL/ETHNIC DESCRIPTION

6 GENDER

7 DOMINANT LANGUAGE

8 ENGLISH FLUENCY

9 TEST BOOK SERIAL NO.

10 TEST FORM

11 TEST DATE

12 CENTER NUMBER

13 TEST FORM CODE

Law School Admission Test*

Mark one and only one answer to each question. Be sure to fill in completely the space for your intended answer choice. If you erase, do so completely. Make no stray marks.

SECTION 1 | **SECTION 2** | **SECTION 3** | **SECTION 4** | **SECTION 5**

(Questions 1–30, each with answer bubbles A B C D E)

14 PLEASE PRINT ALL INFORMATION

LAST NAME   FIRST

EMAIL

PHONE NUMBER

MAILING ADDRESS

CLASS CODE

KAPLAN TEST PREP

www.kaptest.com/lsat
1-800-KAP-TEST

LSAT is a registered trademark of the Law School Admissions Council, Inc.

SCANTRON   Mark Reflex® EM-284925-2:654321   LL3225A

General Directions for the LSAT* Answer Sheet

The actual testing time for this portion of the test will be 2 hours 55 minutes. There are five sections, each with a time limit of 35 minutes. The supervisor will tell you when to begin and end each section. If you finish a section before time is called, you may check your work on that section <u>only</u>; do not turn to any other section of the test book and do not work on any other section either in the test book or on the answer sheet.

There are several different types of questions on the test, and each question type has its own directions. <u>Be sure you understand the directions for each question type before attempting to answer any questions in that section.</u>

Not everyone will finish all the questions in the time allowed. Do not hurry, but work steadily and as quickly as you can without sacrificing accuracy. You are advised to use your time effectively. If a question seems too difficult, go on to the next one and return to the difficult question after completing the section. MARK THE BEST ANSWER YOU CAN FOR EVERY QUESTION. NO DEDUCTIONS WILL BE MADE FOR WRONG ANSWERS. YOUR SCORE WILL BE BASED ONLY ON THE NUMBER OF QUESTIONS YOU ANSWER CORRECTLY.

ALL YOUR ANSWERS MUST BE MARKED ON THE ANSWER SHEET. Answer spaces for each question are lettered to correspond with the letters of the potential answers to each question in the test book. After you have decided which of the answers is correct, blacken the corresponding space on the answer sheet. BE SURE THAT EACH MARK IS BLACK AND COMPLETELY FILLS THE ANSWER SPACE. Give only one answer to each question. If you change an answer, be sure that all previous marks are <u>erased completely</u>. Since the answer sheet is machine scored, incomplete erasures may be interpreted as intended answers. ANSWERS RECORDED IN THE TEST BOOK WILL NOT BE SCORED.

There may be more questions noted on this answer sheet than there are questions in a section. Do not be concerned but be certain that the section and number of the question you are answering matches the answer sheet section and question number. Additional answer spaces in any answer sheet section should be left blank. Begin your next section in the number one answer space for that section.

Kaplan takes various steps to ensure that answer sheets are returned from test centers in a timely manner for processing. In the unlikely event that an answer sheet(s) is not received, Kaplan will permit the examinee to either retest at no additional fee or to receive a refund of his or her test fee. THESE REMEDIES ARE THE EXCLUSIVE REMEDIES AVAILABLE IN THE UNLIKELY EVENT THAT AN ANSWER SHEET IS NOT RECEIVED BY KAPLAN.

Score Cancellation

Complete this section only if you are absolutely certain you want to cancel your score. A CANCELLATION REQUEST CANNOT BE RESCINDED. IF YOU ARE AT ALL UNCERTAIN, YOU SHOULD <u>NOT</u> COMPLETE THIS SECTION.

To cancel your score from this administration, you <u>must</u>:

A. fill in both ovals here..... ◯◯

B. read the following statement. Then sign your name and enter the date.
YOUR SIGNATURE ALONE IS NOT SUFFICIENT FOR SCORE CANCELLATION. BOTH OVALS MUST BE FILLED IN FOR SCANNING EQUIPMENT TO RECOGNIZE YOUR REQUEST FOR SCORE CANCELLATION.

I certify that I wish to cancel my test score from this administration. I understand that my request is irreversible and that my score will not be sent to me or to the law schools to which I apply.

_____
Sign your name in full

_____
Date

HOW DID YOU PREPARE FOR THE LSAT*?
(Select all that apply.)

Responses to this item are voluntary and will be used for statistical research purposes only.

◯ By attending a Kaplan LSAT* prep course or tutoring program
◯ By attending a non-Kaplan prep course or tutoring program (Please specify:_____)
◯ By using a Kaplan LSAT* prep book
◯ By using a non-Kaplan prep book (Please specify: _____)
◯ By working through the sample questions and free sample tests provided by the LSAC
◯ By working through official LSAT* PrepTests and/or other LSAC test prep products
◯ Other preparation (Please specify: _____)
◯ No preparation

CERTIFYING STATEMENT

Please write (DO NOT PRINT) the following statement. Sign and date.

I certify that I am the examinee whose name appears on this answer sheet and that I am here to take the LSAT for the sole purpose of being considered for application to law school. I further certify that I will neither assist nor receive assistance from any other candidate, and I agree not to copy or retain examination questions or to transmit them to or discuss them with any other person in any form.

_____
_____
_____
_____
_____
_____
_____
_____
_____
_____

SIGNATURE: _____ TODAY'S DATE: _____/_____/_____
                                                      MONTH   DAY   YEAR

*LSAT is a registered trademark of the Law School Admissions Council, Inc.